W9-CFH-766

COSTA RICA
HANDBOOK

COSTA RICA HANDBOOK

THIRD EDITION

CHRISTOPHER P. BAKER

MOON
TRAVEL
HANDBOOKS

COSTA RICA HANDBOOK
THIRD EDITION

Published by
Moon Publications, Inc.
P.O. Box 3040
Chico, California 95927-3040, USA

Printed by
Colorcraft Ltd.

© Text and photographs copyright Christopher P. Baker, 1999.
All rights reserved.

© Illustrations and maps copyright Moon Publications, Inc., 1999.
All rights reserved.

Some photos and illustrations are used by permission
and are the property of the original copyright owners.

ISBN: 1-56691-124-9
ISSN: 1082-4847

Please send all comments,
corrections, additions,
amendments, and critiques to:

**COSTA RICA HANDBOOK
MOON TRAVEL HANDBOOKS
P.O. BOX 3040
CHICO, CA 95927-3040, USA
e-mail: travel@moon.com
www.moon.com**

Printing History
1st edition—1994
3rd edition—January 1999

Editor: Gregor Johnson Krause
Map Editor: Gina Wilson Birtcil
Copy Editors: Emily Kendrick, Asha Johnson
Production & Design: Rob Warner, Carey Wilson
Illustration: Bob Race
Cartography: Chris Folks, Mike Morgenfeld
Index: Sondra Nation, Asha Johnson

Front cover photo: *Heliconiid Butterfly* (Dryas iulia: Heliconidae), by Thomas Boyden

All photos by Christopher P. Baker unless otherwise noted.

Distributed in the United States and Canada by Publishers Group West

Printed in the USA

All rights reserved. No part of this book may be translated or reproduced in any form, except brief extracts by a reviewer for the purpose of a review, without written permission of the copyright owner.

Although the author and publisher have made every effort to ensure that the information was correct at the time of going to press, the author and publisher do not assume and hereby disclaim any liability to any party for any loss or damage caused by errors, omissions, or any potential travel disruption due to labor or financial difficulty, whether such errors or omissions result from negligence, accident, or any other cause.

CONTENTS

*This book is dedicated with love
to my parents.*

CONTENTS

MAPS

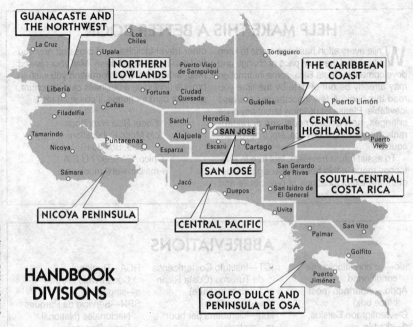

HANDBOOK DIVISIONS

GUANACASTE AND THE NORTHWEST

NORTHERN LOWLANDS

THE CARIBBEAN COAST

CENTRAL HIGHLANDS

SAN JOSÉ

SAN JOSÉ

SOUTH-CENTRAL COSTA RICA

NICOYA PENINSULA

CENTRAL PACIFIC

GOLFO DULCE AND PENINSULA DE OSA

La Cruz
Los Chiles
Upala
Tortuguero
Liberia
Fortuna
Ciudad Quesada
Puerto Viejo de Sarapiquí
Guápiles
Puerto Limón
Filadelfia
Cañas
Sarchí
Heredia
Alajuela
Turrialba
Puerto Viejo
Tamarindo
Puntarenas
Escazú
Cartago
Nicoya
Esparza
San Gerardo de Rivas
Sámara
Jacó
San Isidro de El General
Quepos
Uvita
San Vito
Palmar
Golfito
Puerto Jiménez

© MOON PUBLICATIONS, INC.

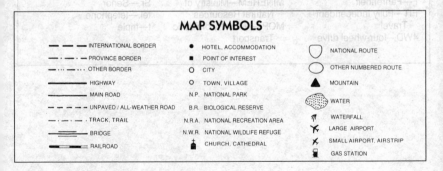

MAP SYMBOLS

— — — INTERNATIONAL BORDER	● HOTEL, ACCOMMODATION	⬭ NATIONAL ROUTE
— · — · PROVINCE BORDER	■ POINT OF INTEREST	⬭ OTHER NUMBERED ROUTE
— ··· — ··· OTHER BORDER	⊙ CITY	▲ MOUNTAIN
——— HIGHWAY	○ TOWN, VILLAGE	WATER
——— MAIN ROAD	N.P. NATIONAL PARK	
– – – UNPAVED / ALL-WEATHER ROAD	B.R. BIOLOGICAL RESERVE	𝅘 WATERFALL
— · — · TRACK, TRAIL	N.R.A. NATIONAL RECREATION AREA	✈ LARGE AIRPORT
BRIDGE	N.W.R. NATIONAL WILDLIFE REFUGE	✕ SMALL AIRPORT, AIRSTRIP
RAILROAD	✝ CHURCH, CATHEDRAL	⛽ GAS STATION

HELP MAKE THIS A BETTER BOOK

While every effort has been made to keep abreast of the rapid pace of change and development in Costa Rica, some information may already be out of date by the time you read this book. A few inaccuracies are also inevitable. Please let us know about any price changes, new accommodations or restaurants, map errors, travel tips, etc. that you encounter.

To assist future travelers, feel free to photocopy maps in this book: while sightseeing, mark the exact locations of new hotels and other travel facilities, and cross off any you find that have closed down. Mail your revised map, along with any information you wish to provide (including a business card, brochure, and rate card for hotels, if possible) to:

Costa Rica Handbook
c/o Moon Publications
P.O. Box 3040
Chico, CA 95927 U.S.A.
e-mail: travel@moon.com

ABBREVIATIONS

a/c—air conditioning/air-conditioned
Apdo.—Apartado (post office box)
C—centigrade/Celsius
d—double
F—Fahrenheit
FIT—Fully Independent Travel
4WD—four-wheel drive

ICT—Instituto Costarricense de Turismo (Costa Rican Tourism Institute)
km—kilometer(s)
kph—kilometers per hour
m—meter(s)
MINEREM—Ministry of Natural Resources
MOPT—Ministry of Public Transport

RCA—Regional Conservation Area
s—single
SPN—Servicio de Parques Nacionales (National Parks Service)
Sr.—Señor
tel.—telephone
t—triple

ACKNOWLEDGMENTS

I could not have sustained the third edition of this book without the support—sometimes minor, often colossal—of a coterie of friends and others to whom thanks are due.

First, no number of words can sufficiently express the thanks due to Eldon and Lori Cooke, who flung open the doors of the finest hotel in San José—Hotel Grano de Oro—on numerous occasions. Their fathomless hospitality and that of their staff added immense pleasure to my capital experience.

Thanks, too, go to Natalie Ewing and Michael Kaye of Costa Rica Expeditions for providing efficient assistance in tour arrangements, and hospitality at Tortuga Lodge and Monteverde Lodge. I also wish to thank Xinia Novoa Espinoza of Prego Rent-a-Car for facilitating transportation to research this edition.

The following also offered miscellaneous assistance, and credit is due to one and all: Peter Aspinall, of Tiskita Lodge; Amos Bien, of Rara Avis; Jocelyne Boucher, of Villa del Sol Bed and Breakfast; Sherrill Broudy, of Xandari; Gabriella Corazo, of Villa Blanca; Patricia Costa Padilla, of Hotel Alta; Jeff Crandall, of Villa Decary; Haydeé Cuadrado Ramírez and Gail Hewson, of Wilson Botanical Garden; Darlys and Fred, of Orquideas Inn; Ms. Dee, of Cabañas Río Blanco; Loic Dervieu, of Fleur de Lys; Thomas Douglas, of Hotel Santo Tomás; Etienne, of Jardín del Eden; Marlene and Julian Grae, of La Perla Negra; Jim Hamilton, of Tilajari; Amba Henderson and Don Stapelton, of Nosara Retreat; Christopher Howard, of *Costa Rica Books;* Glenn Jampol of Finca Rosa Blanca; Timothy Johnson, of Hotel Del Rey; Scott Miller, of Avalon; Eileen Mitchell, of Hotel Palma Real; Patricia Murillo, of Inocentes Lodge; Mark Nelson, of Tambor Tropical; Elizabeth Newton, of Magellan Inn; Adrienne Pellizzari, of Café Milagro; Ruedi, of Capitán Suizo; Denise Richards and Michael Holm, of Villas Escaleras; Luis Rodriguez, of Hotel Villablanca; Romy and Lee Rodríguez, of El Cafetal; Denis Roi, of Villa Caletas; Michele de Rojas, of Casa Turire; William Rojas, of Fiesta Village; Laura Salazar, of Tricolor Rent-a-Car; Javier Slein Sandi, of Ecoplaya Beach Resort; Mariamalia Sotela, of El Gavilán; Matt Sport, of Escondido Trex; Karin Stein, of Selva Bananito; Mike Terzano, of Gringo Mike's Pizza Café; Klaus Thomsen, of Hotel Sugar Beach; Loriana Vargas, of Hotel Jade y Oro; Kim West, of Toad Hall; Louis Wilson, of Hotel Tortuga; and Jim Wolfe, of Jardín de Mariposa.

Thanks also to Marlene Alvarez, of JGR Associates, and Lillian Martinez, of Martinez Associates, and to my dear friend Ginny Craven, of Progressive Public Relations, for her support, encouragement, and fun-filled times aboard the *Temptress Explorer.* I am also indebted to Tomás Posuelo, owner of Temptress Adventure Cruises, for acting as congenial host.

To friends Shirley Miller and Randy Case (in spring 1998 they stopped publishing their splendid newsletter, *Costa Rica Outlook.* Shirley and Randy, you and your wonderful newsletter are deeply admired and will be greatly missed), and Federico Grant Esquivel (naturalist guide)—thanks for being such fun to be with. Andrzej Nowacki, of Hotel Tres Banderas, helped me in time of need and also introduced me to elements of life unsuspected. Lastly, I send a lifelong hug to Karla Taylor, whose affection and gaiety added sunlight to the tropical warmth.

To all others who lent their support but who through my senility or thoughtlessness have not been acknowledged, a sincere apology and a heartfelt thank you.

A Special Note on Photography

I am indebted for the gracious support of Jean Mercier and John Anderson, whose photography graces this book. Those with a commercial interest in Jean's photography should contact him at Apdo. 1798, Alajuela 4050, Costa Rica, tel. (506) 441-2897 or (506) 441-2282.

WHY COSTA RICA?

If San Salvador were hosed down, all the shacks cleared and the people re-housed in tidy bungalows, the buildings painted, the stray dogs collared and fed, the children given shoes, the trash picked up in the parks, the soldiers pensioned off—there is no army in Costa Rica—and all the political prisoners released, those cities would, I think, begin to look a little like San José. In El Salvador I had chewed the end of my pipestem to pieces in frustration. In San José I was able to have a new pipestem fitted . . . [Costa Rica] was that sort of place.

—PAUL THEROUX, *THE OLD PATAGONIAN EXPRESS*

I N HIS HIGHLY ENTERTAINING and incisive book *The Old Patagonian Express,* describing his journey south by rail from Massachusetts to Tierra del Fuego, Paul Theroux portrays a litany of places one might want to avoid. But Costa Rica is different. One of his characters sums it up. Freshly arrived in San José, the capital city, Theroux finds himself talking to a Chinese man in a bar. The Asian—a Costa Rican citizen—had left his homeland in 1954 and traveled widely throughout the Americas. He disliked every country he had seen except one. "What about the United States?" Theroux asked. "I went all around it," replied the Chinese man, "Maybe it is a good country, but I don't think so. I could not live there. I was still traveling, and I thought to myself, 'What is the best country?' It was Costa Rica—I liked it very much here. So I stayed."

At first sight, Costa Rica appears almost too good to be true. The temptations and appeals of this tiny nation are so abundant that an estimated 30,000 North American citizens and an equal number of other nationals (constituting more than two percent of Costa Rica's population) have moved here in recent years and now call Costa Rica home, attracted by financial incentives and a quality of life among the highest in the Western Hemisphere. *Pensionados* and other foreigners in residence seem to have known for quite some time what travelers only a decade ago began wising up to: Costa Rica isn't simply one of the world's best-kept travel secrets but also a great place to live.

For years travelers had neglected this exciting yet peaceful nation—primarily because of a muddled grasp of Central American geopolitics. While its neighbors have been racked by turmoil, Costa Rica has been blessed with a remarkable normalcy—few extremes of wealth and poverty, no standing army, and a proud history as Central America's most stable democracy (elections are so trouble-free that crowd control at polling stations is handled in part by schoolchildren). Of the 53 presidents who have reigned since the nation won independence from Spain, in 1821, only three have been military men and only six could be considered dictators.

Ticos—as the friendly, warmhearted Costa Ricans are known—pride themselves on having more teachers than policemen, a higher male life expectancy than does the United States, an egalitarianism and strong commitment to peace and prosperity, and an education and social-welfare system that should be the envy of many developed nations. Even the smallest town is electrified, water most everywhere is potable, and the telecommunications system is the best in Latin America. In 1990, the United Nations declared Costa Rica the country with the best human-development index among underdeveloped nations—and in 1992, it was taken off the list of underdeveloped nations altogether. No wonder *National Geographic* called it the "land of the happy medium."

This idyllic vision, however, doesn't take into account the country's problems. The political system is mired in cronyism and corruption that Ticos are only now beginning to acknowledge. One-third of Costa Rica's 520,000 families live in poverty. Traffic fatality statistics are frightening. Theft and petty fraud are endemic. Deforestation outside the national parks is occurring at a rate faster than in the Amazon. And the state of the roads would be a joke if it weren't such a deplorable embarrassment.

Despite its diminutive size (the country is about as big as Nova Scotia or West Virginia), Costa Rica proffers more beauty and adventure per acre than any other country on earth. It is in fact a kind of microcontinent unto itself. The diversity of terrain—most of it supremely beautiful—is remarkable. Costa Rica is sculpted to show off the full potential of the tropics. You can journey, as it were, from the Amazon to a Swiss alpine forest simply by starting in a Costa Rican valley and walking uphill. Within a one-hour journey from San José, the capital city, the tableau metamorphoses from dense rainforest to airy deciduous forest, montane cloud forest swathing the slopes of towering volcanoes, dry open savanna, lush sugarcane fields, banana plantations, rich cattle ranches set in deep valleys, rain-soaked jungle, lagoons, estuaries, and swamps teeming with wildlife in the northern lowlands. The lush rainforest spills down the steep mountains to greet the Pacific and Atlantic Oceans, where dozens of inviting beaches remain unspoilt by footprints, and in places offshore coral reefs open up a world more beautiful than a casket of gems.

Costa Rica's varied ecosystems—particularly its tropical rainforests—are a naturalist's dream. Unlike many destinations, where man has driven the animals into the deepest seclusion, Costa Rica's wildlife seems to love to put on a song and dance. Animals and birds are prolific and in many cases relatively easy to spot—sleek jaguars on the prowl, tattered moth-ridden sloths moving languidly among the high branches, scarlet macaws that fall from their perches and go squalling away, coatimundis, toucans, brightly colored tree frogs, and other exotic species in abundance. That sudden flutter of blue is a giant morpho butterfly. That mournful two-note whistle is the quetzal, the tropical birder's Holy Grail. The pristine forests and jungles are full of arboreal sounds that are, according to one writer, "music to a weary ecotraveler's ears." You can almost feel the vegetation growing around you. There is a sense of life at flood tide.

The nation's 12 distinct ecological zones are home to an astonishing array of flora and fauna—approximately five percent of all known species on earth in a country that occupies less than three ten-thousandths of its land area—including more butterflies than in the whole of Africa, and more than twice the number of bird species than the whole of the United States—in colors so brilliant that their North American cousins seem drab by comparison. Stay here long enough and you'll begin to think that with luck you might, like Noah, see examples of all the creatures on earth.

Scuba divers, fishermen, golfers, spa addicts, kayakers and whitewater rafters, hikers, surfers, honeymoon romantics, and every other breed of escape artist can find his or her nirvana in Costa Rica. The adventure travel industry here has matured into one of the world's finest.

For better or worse, Costa Rica has also burst into blossom as a contender on the international beach-resort scene. The nation boasts a number of supremely attractive resorts, civilized hotels, and rustic lodges and *cabinas* where, lazing in a hammock dramatically overlooking the beach, you might seriously contemplate giving up everything back home and settling down to while away the rest of your days enjoying the never-winter climate.

Fortunately, as yet, Costa Rica has no Acapulcos or Cancúns scarring the coast with endless discos, concrete beachfronts, and vast high-rise condominiums: Costa Rica's progressive conservationist tradition and dedication to development with a genteel face have helped keep rapacious developers at bay. (This seems to be changing, unfortunately. Although Luis Manuel Chacón, the country's first minister of tourism, vowed to allow no buildings "taller than a palm tree" to blight the beaches, megaresort complexes are sprouting along the jungled shoreline like mushrooms on a damp log.)

The country is finally having to face a paradoxical problem—that of being loved to death. As the word spreads, more people come, and more big developers are drawn. I hope it will be many years before Costa Rica is spoiled, and I urge you to go now.

BOB RACE

INTRODUCTION
THE LAND

A traveler moving south overland through Central America gradually has his choice of routes whittled away until he finally reaches the end of the road in the swamps and forests of Darien, in Panamá, where the tenuous land bridge separating the two great American continents is almost pinched out and the Pacific Ocean and the Caribbean Sea almost meet. Costa Rica lies at the northern point of this apex—a pivotal region separating two oceans and two continents vastly different in character.

The region is a crucible. There are few places in the world where the forces of nature so actively interplay. Distinct climatic patterns clash and merge; the great landmasses and their offshore cousins, the Cocos and Caribbean plates, jostle and shove one another, triggering earthquakes and spawning sometimes cataclysmic volcanic eruptions; and the flora and fauna of the North and South American realms—as well as those of the Caribbean and the Pacific—come together and play Russian roulette with the forces of evolution. The result is an incredible diversity of terrain, biota, and weather concentrated in a country barely bigger than the state of New Hampshire.

At 50,895 square kilometers, Costa Rica is the second-smallest Central American nation after El Salvador. At its narrowest point, in the south, only 119 km separate the Caribbean from the Pacific. Even in the north one can savor a leisurely breakfast on the Caribbean and take an ambling five-hour drive to the Pacific for dinner. At its broadest point, Costa Rica is a mere 280 km wide. On the ruler-straight eastern seaboard, barely 160 km separate the Nicaraguan and Panamanian borders. And while the Pacific coast is longer, it is still only 480 km from the northernmost tip to the Panamanian border as the crow flies.

Lying between 8 and 11 degrees north of the equator, Costa Rica sits wholly within the tropics, a fact quickly confirmed in the middle of a rainy afternoon in the middle of the rainy season in the middle of the sodden Caribbean lowlands or the Talamanca mountains. Elevation and extremes of relief, however, temper the stereotypical tropical climate. In fact, the nation boasts

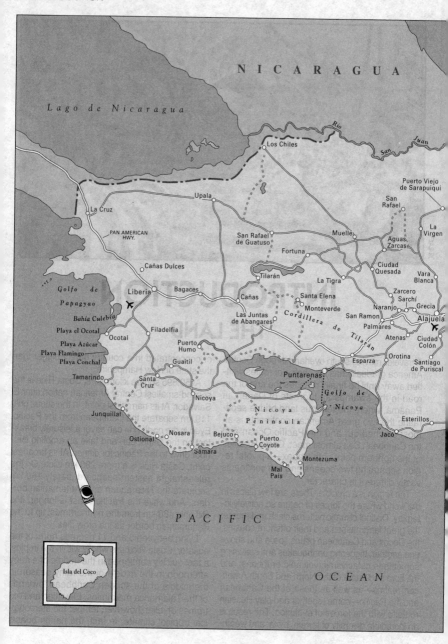

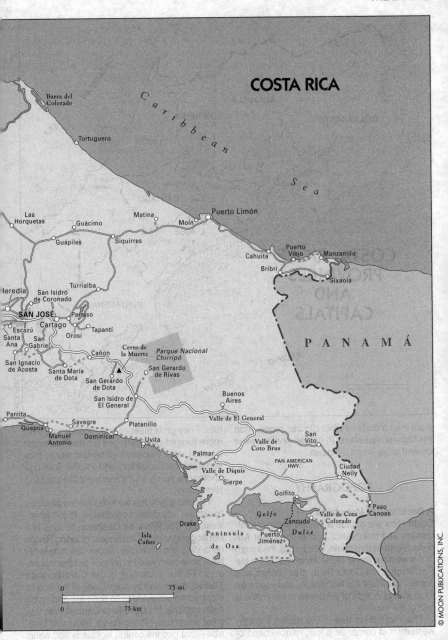

COSTA RICA

Caribbean Sea

Barra del Colorado

Tortuguero

Las Horquetas

Guácimo

Matina

Moín

Puerto Limón

Guápiles

Siquirres

Puerto Viejo

Manzanillo

Cahuita

Heredia

San Isidro de Coronado

Turrialba

Bribrí

Sixaola

San José

Paraíso

Cartago

Escazú

Orosí

Tapantí

Santa Ana

San Gabriel

San Ignacio de Acosta

Cañón

Cerro de la Muerte

Parque Nacional Chirripó

San Gerardo de Rivas

PANAMÁ

Santa María de Dota

San Gerardo de Dota

San Isidro de El General

Buenos Aires

Parrita

Valle de El General

Quepos

Savegre

Platanillo

San Vito

Manuel Antonio

Dominical

Uvita

Valle de Coto Brus

Palmar

PAN AMERICAN HWY.

Ciudad Neily

Valle de Diquis

Sierpe

Golfito

Paso Canoas

Drake

Golfo Dulce

Zancudo

Valle de Cota Colorado

Isla Caños

Península de Osa

Puerto Jiménez

0   75 mi

0   75 km

© MOON PUBLICATIONS, INC.

COSTA RICA'S
PROVINCES
AND
CAPITALS

© MOON PUBLICATIONS, INC.

more than a dozen distinct climatic zones. Atop the highest mountains in cooler months, even ice and snow aren't unknown.

TOPOGRAPHY

A Backbone of Mountains

Costa Rica sits astride a jagged series of volcanoes and mountains, part of the great Andean-Sierra Madre chain, which runs the length of the western littoral of the Americas. From the Pacific coast of Costa Rica, great cones and domes dominate the landscape, and you're almost always in sight of volcanoes in the northern part of the country.

The mountains rise in the nation's northwesternmost corner as a low, narrow band of hills. They grow steeper and broader and ever more rugged until they gird Costa Rica coast to coast at the Panamanian border, where they separate the Caribbean and Pacific from one another as surely as if these were the towering Himalayas.

Volcanic activity has fractured this mountainous backbone into distinct cordilleras. In the northwest, the **Cordillera de Guanacaste** rises in a leapfrogging series of volcanoes, including Rincón de la Vieja and Miravalles, whose steaming vents have been harnessed to provide geothermal energy. To the southeast is the **Cordillera de Tilarán,** dominated by Arenal, one of the world's most active volcanoes. To the east and rising even higher is the **Cordillera Central,** with four great volcanoes—Poás, Barva, Irazú and Turrialba—that gird the central highlands and within whose cusp lies the Meseta Central, an elevated plateau ranging in height from 900 to 1,787 meters. To the south of the valley rises the **Cordillera Talamanca,** an uplifted mountain region that tops out at the summit of Cerro Chirripó (3,819 meters), Costa Rica's highest peak.

Meseta Central

In Costa Rica, all roads radiate from the Meseta Central, the heart and heartbeat of the nation. This rich agricultural valley is cradled by the flanks of the Cordillera Talamanca to the south, and by the fickle volcanoes of the Cordillera Central to the north and east. San José, the capital, lies at its center. At an elevation of 1,150 meters, San José enjoys year-round temperatures above 21° C (70° F), reliable rainfall, and rich volcanic soils—major reasons why almost two-thirds of the nation's population of 3,087,000 lives in the valley.

The Meseta Central—which measures about 40 km north to south and 80 km east to west—is divided into two separate valleys by the low-lying crests of the **Cerros de la Carpintera,** which rise a few miles east of San José. Beyond lies the somewhat smaller Cartago Valley, at a slightly higher elevation. The Carpinteras mark the Continental Divide. To the east the turbulent Reventazón—a favorite of whitewater enthusiasts—slices through the truncated eastern extreme of the Cordillera Central and tumbles helter-skelter to the Caribbean lowlands. The Río Virilla exits more leisurely, draining the San José Valley to the west.

Northern Lowlands and Caribbean Coast

The broad, pancake-flat, wedge-shaped northern lowlands are cut off from the more densely populated highlands by a languorous drape of virtually impenetrable hardwood forest that only the most accomplished outdoor types can penetrate without local guides. The low-lying plains or *llanuras,* which make up one-fifth of the nation's land area, extend along the entire length of the Río San Juan, whose course demarcates the Nicaraguan border. Farther south the plains narrow to a funnel along the Caribbean coast.

Westward, banana and citrus plantations give way to pleats of green velveteen jungle ascending the steep eastern slopes of the central mountains, which run along a northwest-southeast axis, forming the third side of the wedge. Numerous rivers drop quickly from the mountains to the plains, where they snake along sluggishly. Beautiful beaches, many of gray or black sand, line the Caribbean coast, which sidles gently south.

Pacific Coast

Beaches are a major calling card of Costa Rica's Pacific coast, which is deeply indented with bays and inlets and two large gulfs—the Golfo de Nicoya (in the north) and Golfo Dulce (in the south), enfolded by the hilly, hook-nosed peninsulas of Nicoya and Osa, respectively. Mountains tilt precipitously toward the Pacific, coming closer to the ocean here than on the Caribbean side, and the slender coastal plain is nowhere more than a few kilometers wide. North of the

PLATE TECTONICS: A WORLD IN UPHEAVAL

Until the 1960s, when the theory of plate tectonics revolutionized the earth sciences, geologists trying to explain the distribution of earthquakes and volcanoes were at a loss. When earthquakes and volcanoes were plotted on a map, geologists realized that the planet is a puzzle—literally. The pieces of the terrestrial jigsaw are some 25 tectonic plates, interconnected pieces of the earth's crust (the lithosphere), 40-95 miles thick. Seven major plates carry the continents and ocean basins on their backs.

These plates are in continual motion, ponderously inching along on endless journeys across the surface of the earth, powered by forces originating deep within the earth. They ride on a viscous layer called the aesthenosphere, whose molten component wells up to the earth's surface on great convection currents fueled by heat from the core of our planet.

As the plates move, they pull apart or collide, unleashing titanic geological forces. When two plates slide past each other or converge—as off the Pacific coast of Central America—the geological forces generally drive one plate beneath the other, causing earthquakes. The friction created by one plate grinding beneath another melts part of both crusts, forming magma—molten rock—which wells up under pressure, erupting to form a chain of volcanoes.

© MOON PUBLICATIONS, INC.

COSTA RICA—PHYSICAL

Caribbean

Sea

Río Parismina

Río Pacuare

Puerto Limón

Isla Uvita

Río Estrella

Punta Cahuita

Punta Uva

Río Sixaola

Cerro Chirripó

Cerro Durika

de

Cerro Kamúk

Talamanca

Chirripó

Valle de El General

Río Grande de Terraba

Río General

Valle de Coto Brus

Valle de Diquís

P A N A M Á

Río Sierpe

Coto Colorado

Golfo

Golfito

PLAYA PLATANARES

PLAYA ZANCUDO

Valle de Coto Colorado

Dulce

Cabo Matapalo

Península de Burica

Punta Burica

Golfo de Nicoya, the coastal strip widens to form a broad lowland belt of savanna—the Tempisque Basin. The basin is drained, appropriately, by the Río Tempisque, and narrowing northward until hemmed in near the Nicaraguan border by the juncture of the Cordillera de Guanacaste and rolling, often steep coastal hills that follow the arc of the Nicoya Peninsula.

Of growing importance to the national economy is the narrow, 64-km-long intermontane basin known as the Valle de El General, which runs parallel to and nestles comfortably between the Cordillera Talamanca and the coastal mountains—*Fila Costeña*—of the Pacific southwest. The Ríos General and Coto Brus and their many tributaries have carved a deep, steep-sided trough, long isolated from the rest of the nation, although the construction of the Pan-American Highway through the valley in the 1950s brought thousands of migrant farmers and their families in its wake.

GEOLOGY

Costa Rica lies at the boundary where the Pacific's Cocos Plate—a piece of the earth's crust some 510 km wide—meets the crustal plate underlying the Caribbean. The two are converging as the Cocos Plate moves east at a rate of about 10 cm a year. It is a classic subduction zone in which the Caribbean Plate is forced under the Cocos—one of the most dynamic junctures on earth. Central America has been an isthmus, a peninsula, and even an archipelago in the not-so-distant geological past. It has therefore been both a corridor for and a barrier to landward movements, and it has been an area in which migrants have flourished, new life forms have emerged, and new ways of life have evolved. Yet a semblance of the Central America we know today became recognizable only in recent geological history. In fact, Costa Rica has one of the youngest surface areas in the Americas—only three million years old—for the volatile region has only recently been thrust from beneath the sea.

Earthquakes
In its travels eastward, the Cocos Plate gradually broke into seven fragments, which today move forward at varying depths and angles. This fracturing and competitive movement causes the fre-

HOW EARTHQUAKES ARE TRIGGERED

The downward pressure of the subducting plate strains the elasticity of the lithospere, creating pent-up energy.

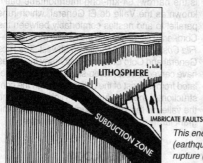

IMBRICATE FAULTS

This energy is suddenly released as seismic waves (earthquakes) that radiate outward from the point of rupture (the epicenter). Associated ruptures along the imbricate faults cause other, lower-matgnitude tremors.

BRIAN BARDWELL

quent earthquakes with which Costa Ricans contend. The forces that thrust the Cocos and Caribbean Plates together continue to build inexorably.

From insignificant tremors to catastrophic blockbusters, most earthquakes are caused by the same phenomenon: the slippage of masses of rock along earth fractures or faults. Rocks possess elastic properties, and in time this elasticity allows rocks to accumulate strain energy as tectonic plates or their component sections jostle each other. Friction can contain the strain and hold the rocks in place for years. But eventually, as with a rubber band stretched beyond its breaking point, strain overcomes frictional lock and the fault ruptures at its weakest point.

Suddenly, the pent-up energy is released in the form of an earthquake—seismic waves that radiate in all directions from the point of rupture, the epicenter. This seismic activity can last for a fraction of a second to, for a major earthquake, several minutes. Pressure waves traveling at five miles per second race from the quake's epicenter through the bedrock, compressing and extending the ground like an accordion. Following in their wake come waves that thrust the

earth up and down, whipping along at three miles per second.

For Costa Ricans, the bad news is that the most devastating earthquakes generally occur in subduction zones, when one tectonic plate plunges beneath another. Ocean trench quakes off the coast of Costa Rica have been recorded at 8.9 on the Richter scale and are among history's most awesome, heaving the sea floor sometimes scores of feet. These ruptures often propagate upward, touching off other, lower-magnitude tremors in a system of overlapping cracks in rock called imbricate faults. This is what happened when the powerful 7.4 quake struck Costa Rica on 22 April 1991.That massive quake, which originated near the Caribbean town of Pandora (112 km southeast of San José), was stronger than the San Francisco, California earthquake of 17 October 1989—and the strongest earthquake to rattle Costa Rica since 1910. The quake left at least 27 people dead, more than 400 injured, 13,000 homeless, and more than 3,260 buildings destroyed in Limón Province.

Though economically the country quickly got over the shakes, the physical legacy endures.

The temblor provides a magnificent example of the processes that continue to thrust the Central America landmass from the sea. The earthquake caused the Atlantic coastline to rise permanently—in parts by as much as 1.5 meters. In consequence, many of the beaches are deeper, and coral reefs have been thrust above the ocean surface and reduced to bleached calcareous skeletons. Also uplifted was the bedrock underlying the natural waterways that connect Puerto Limón with Tortuguero on the northern Caribbean coast. Although formerly level with the Atlantic, many of the canals inland from the ocean have also been left high and dry.

Volcanoes

Costa Rica lies at the heart of one of the most active volcanic regions on earth. The beauty of the Costa Rican landscape has been enhanced by volcanic cones—part of the Pacific Rim of Fire—that march the length of Central America. Costa Rica is home to seven of the isthmus' 42 active volcanoes, plus 60 dormant or extinct ones. Some have the look classically associated with volcanoes—a graceful, symmetrical cone rising to a single crater. Others are sprawling, weathered mountains whose once-noble summits have collapsed into huge depressions called calderas (from the Portuguese word for "cauldron"). Still

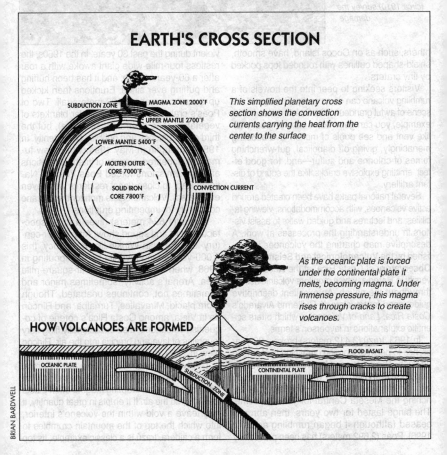

EARTH'S CROSS SECTION

This simplified planetary cross section shows the convection currents carrying the heat from the center to the surface

SUBDUCTION ZONE
MAGMA ZONE 2000°F
UPPER MANTLE 2700°F
LOWER MANTLE 5400°F
MOLTEN OUTER CORE 7000°F
SOLID IRON CORE 7800°F
CONVECTION CURRENT

HOW VOLCANOES ARE FORMED

As the oceanic plate is forced under the continental plate it melts, becoming magma. Under immense pressure, this magma rises through cracks to create volcanoes.

FLOOD BASALT
OCEANIC PLATE
SUBDUCTION ZONE
CONTINENTAL PLATE

BRIAN BARDWELL

Four survivors of the Cartago earthquake (circa 1910) survey the damage.

others, such as on Cocos Island, have smooth, shield-shaped outlines with rounded tops pocked by tiny craters.

Visitors seeking to peer into the bowels of a rumbling volcano can do so easily. The reward is a scene of awful grandeur. Atop Poás's crater rim, for example, you can gape down into the great well-like vent and see pools of molten lava bubbling menacingly, giving off diabolical, gut-wrenching fumes of chlorine and sulfur—and, for good effect, emitting explosive cracks, like the sound of distant artillery.

Several national parks have been created around active volcanoes, with accommodations, viewing facilities, and lectures and guided walks to assist visitors in understanding the processes at work. A descriptive map charting the volcanoes is published by the **Vulcanological and Seismological Observatory** of Costa Rica, at the National University in Heredia, which monitors volcanic activity throughout the nation. An excellent descriptive guide, good for travelers, is Guillermo Alvarado's *Costa Rica; Land of Volcanoes,* which offers scientific explanations in layperson's terms.

In 1963, Irazú (3,412 meters) broke a 20-year silence to begin disgorging great clouds of smoke and ash. The eruptions triggered a bizarre storm that showered San José with 13 cm of muddy ash, snuffing out the 1964 coffee crop but enriching the Meseta Central for years to come. The binge lasted for two years, then abruptly ceased (although it began rumbling again in 1996). Poás (2,692 meters) has been particularly

violent during the past 30 years. In the 1950s, the restless four-mile-wide giant awoke with a roar after a 60-year snooze, and it has been huffing and puffing ever since. Eruptions then kicked up a new cone about 100 meters tall. Two of Poás's craters now slumber under blankets of vegetation (one even cradles a lake), but the third crater belches and bubbles persistently. In 1989 and again in May 1994, when new fumaroles appeared, a spate of intense eruptions and gas emissions forced Poás Volcano National Park to close (local residents were even evacuated). Volcanologists monitor the volcano constantly for impending eruptions.

Arenal (1,624 meters) gives a more spectacular light and sound show. After a four-century-long Rip van Winkle-like dormancy, this 4,000-year-young juvenile began spouting in 1968, when it laid waste to a four-square-mile area. Arenal's activity, sometimes minor and sometimes not, continues unabated. Though more placid, Miravalles, Turrialba, and Rincón de la Vieja, among Costa Rica's coterie of coquettish volcanoes, also occasionally fling fiery fountains of lava and breccia into the air. Rincón blew in 1995, doing damage in Upala.

The type of magma that fuels most Central American volcanoes is thick, viscous, and so filled with gases that the erupting magma often blasts violently into the air. If it erupts in great quantity, it may leave a void within the volcano's interior, into which the top of the mountain crumbles to form a caldera. Irazú is a classic example. Its top fell in eons ago. Since then, however, small eruptions have built up three new volcanic cones—"like a set of nesting cups," says one writer—within the ancient caldera.

CLIMATE

When talk turns to Costa Rica's climate, hyperbole flows as thick and as fast as the waterfalls that cascade in ribbons of quicksilver down through the forest-clad mountains. English 19th-century novelist Anthony Trollope was among the first to wax lyrical: "No climate can, I imagine, be more favorable to fertility and to man's comfort at the same time than that of the interior of Costa Rica." Merlin the wizard couldn't have conjured the elements into a more blissful climate.

The country lies wholly within the tropics yet boasts at least a dozen climatic zones and is markedly diverse in local microclimates, which make generalizations on temperature and rainfall misleading.

Most regions have a rainy season (May-Nov.) and a dry season (Dec.-April). And the rainfall almost everywhere follows a predictable schedule. In general, highland ridges are wet—and windward sides always the wettest.

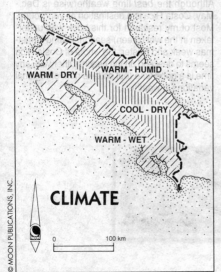

When planning your trip, don't be misled by the terms "summer" and "winter," which Ticans use to designate their dry and wet seasons. Since the Tican "summer"—which in broad terms lasts December through April—occurs in what are winter months elsewhere in the Northern Hemisphere (and vice versa) it can be confusing. Don't be put off by the term "rainy season." Costa Rica promotes it as the "green season"—and it's a splendid time to travel, generally.

Temperatures

Temperatures, dictated more by elevation and location than by season, range from tropical on the coastal plains to temperate in the interior highlands. Mean temperatures hover near 22° C (72° F) on the central plateau, average 27° C (82° F) at sea level on the Caribbean coast and 32° C (89° F) on the Pacific lowlands. Balmy San José and the Meseta Central have an average year-round temperature of 23° C (74° F). Temperatures fall steadily with elevation (about one degree for every 100-meter gain). They rarely exceed a mean of 10° C (48° F) atop Chirripó, where frost is frequent and enveloping clouds drift dark and ominous among the mountain passes. You'll definitely need a warm sweater or jacket for the mountains, where the difference between daytime highs and nighttime lows is greatest.

The length of daylight varies only slightly throughout the year. Sunrise is around 6 a.m. and sunset about 6 p.m., and the sun's path is never far from overhead, so seasonal variations in temperatures rarely exceed five degrees in any given location.

Everywhere, March to May are the hottest months, with September and October not far behind. Cool winds bearing down from northern latitudes lower temperatures during December, January, and February, particularly on the northern Pacific coast, where certain days during summer (dry season) months can be surprisingly cool. The most extreme daily fluctuations occur during the dry season, when clear skies at night allow maximum heat loss through radiation. In the wet season, nights are generally warmer, as the heat built up during the day is trapped by clouds.

Rainfall

Rain is a fact of life in Costa Rica. The winds and weather of two great oceans meet above

Costa Rica's jungles and mountains. Oceans—especially in tropical latitudes—spell moisture, and mountains spell condensation. Annual precipitation averages 250 cm (100 inches) nationwide. Depending on the region, the majority of this may fall in relatively few days—sometimes fewer than 15 per year. In drier years, the Tempisque Basin in Guanacaste, for example, receives as little as 48 cm (18 inches), mostly in a few torrential downpours. The mountains, by contrast, often exceed 385 cm (150 inches) per year, sometimes as much as 7.6 meters (25 feet) on the more exposed easterly facing slopes. And don't expect to stay dry in the montane rainforests; even on the sunniest days, the humid forests produce their own internal rain as water vapor condenses on the cool leaves and falls.

Generally, rains occur in the early afternoons in the highlands, midafternoons in the Pacific lowlands, and late afternoons (and commonly during the night) in the Atlantic lowlands. Sometimes it falls in sudden torrents called *aguaceros,* sometimes it falls hard and steady, and sometimes it sheets down without letup for several days and nights.

Dry season on the Meseta Central and throughout the western regions is December through April. In Guanacaste, the dry season usually lingers slightly longer; the northwest coast (the driest part of the country) often has few rainy days even during wet season. On the Atlantic coast, the so-called dry season occurs January-April.

Even in the rainy season, days often start out warm and sunny, although *temporales* (morning rainfall) are not uncommon. As in many tropical destinations worldwide, only newly arrived gringos go out without an umbrella after noon during the wet season. In the highlands, rainy season usually brings an hour or two of rain midafternoon. Still, be prepared: 23 hours of a given day may be dry and pleasant; during the 24th, the rain can come down with the force of a waterfall. The sudden onset of a relatively dry period, called *veranillo* (little summer), sometimes occurs July-Aug. or Aug.-Sept., particularly along the Pacific coast.

Be aware, though, that seasonal patterns can vary, especially in years when the occasional weather phenomenon known as El Niño may set in, as it did with devastating force in 1997. The freak weather it produces is caused by an abnormal warming of ocean waters off the Pacific coast, most often when warm currents from the Western Pacific shift, resulting in volatile changes in air masses.

Rarely do **hurricanes** strike Costa Rica, although Hurricane Cesár came ashore on 27 July 1996, killing 41 people and trashing the Pacific southwest in the nation's worst national disaster in a decade. Large-scale deforestation in the region contributed to massive flooding.

When to Go

Although the *best* time weatherwise is Dec.-May, Costa Rica is a destination all year round. Most of my research for this book was undertaken in the wet (green) season. During Christmas week and Easter, the whole of Costa Rica seems to descend on the beach. Otherwise, any time is a good time (but do take note of regional variations in weather).

ECOSYSTEMS

In 1947, biologist L.H. Holdridge introduced a system of classifying vegetation types or "zones" according to a matrix based on combinations of temperature, rainfall, and seasonality. Each zone has a distinct natural vegetation and ecosystem. Costa Rica has 12 such zones, ranging from tidal mangrove swamps to subalpine *paramó,* with stunted dwarf plants above the timberline atop the high mountains.

Costa Rican Natural History, edited by Daniel Janzen, provides a description of the vegetation types associated with each life zone. You can also obtain a life-zone map from the **Tropical Science Center,** Calle 1, Avenidas 4/6, San José, a private nonprofit organization that operates the Monteverde Cloud Forest Preserve.

Costa Rica's tropical situation, in combination with both a remarkable diversity of local relief and climates—plus generous infusions since Miocene times of plants and animals from the adjoining continents—has resulted in the evolution of a stupendously rich biota. Some habitats, such as the mangrove swamps, are relatively simple. Others, particularly the ecosystem of the

TROPICAL
Dry Forest
Humid Forest

SUB TROPICAL
Humid Forest
Very Humid Forest

LOW MOUNTAIN
Humid Forest
Very Humid Forest
Rainforest

MOUNTAIN
Very Humid Forest

SUB-ALPINE
Humid Paramó

NICARAGUA

ECOSYSTEMS

Caribbean

Sea

PACIFIC

OCEAN

PANAMÁ

0   30 mi
0   30 km

© MOON PUBLICATIONS, INC.

RECYCLING NUTRIENTS IN THE RAINFOREST

One of the most important differences between tropical and temperate environments is what biologists call "species richness." A natural forest patch of a few hundred acres in Michigan, for example, might contain 25-30 species of trees; an equivalent tract of Costa Rican rainforest might contain more than 400. The U.S. state of Ohio has only about 10 species of bats; Costa Rica has more than 100, although Ohio is twice the size.

Why such complexity, such stupefying abundance of *species* in the neotropics—the tropics of the New World? It all has to do with the rapid pace of nutrient recycling and the way the natural world competes most effectively for nourishment.

In the temperate world, with the warm days and sunlight of spring, plants burst forth with protein-rich buds, shoots, and young leaves, which appear simultaneously in a protein "pulse." Animals bring forth their young during this period of protein abundance: birds return from the south to lay eggs and raise their broods, insect eggs hatch, frogs and toads crawl out of hibernation to reproduce. Come autumn, the same plants produce a second protein glut as tender berries, seeds, and nuts, which critters pack in to sustain themselves through the hardships of impending winter. The synchronized budding and fruiting of foliage is so great that all the hungry mouths gobbling protein hardly threaten a plant species's survival.

In the tropics, by contrast, the seasonal cycle is far less pronounced: sunlight, rain, and warm temper-

DECAYING PLANTS AND ANIMALS

NUTRIENTS LOST BY SEEPAGE

NUTRIENTS DISSOLVED FROM ROCKS

BOB RACE

tropical rainforests of the Caribbean lowlands and the Osa Peninsula (the only rainforest still extant on the Pacific side of Central America), are among the most complex on the planet.

There is no barrier in Costa Rica to the entry of South American species of flora; as a result, the lowland rainforests have strong affinities with the *selva* (jungle) of South America and form a distinctive assemblage of species in which the large number of palms, tree ferns, lianas, and epiphytes attest to the constant heat and humidity of the region. The impressive tropical rainforest of eastern Costa Rica and the Osa Peninsula gives way on the central Pacific to a dry evergreen forest at lower elevations and dry deciduous forest farther north. These, too, are of essentially South

American composition. Above about 1,000 meters, the species are fewer and the affinities with North America are stronger. In the Cordillera Talamanca, conifers of South American provenance are joined by North American oaks. Above the treeline (approximately 3,000 meters), hikers familiar with the midelevation flora of the high Andes of Peru and Ecuador will find many affinities in the shrubby open landscape of Costa Rica's cordillera.

FLORA: AN OVERVIEW

Costa Rica offers an extraordinary abundance of flora, including more than 9,000 species of "high-

atures are constant, and plants germinate, grow, flower, and seed year-round. Hence, there is no distinct protein surplus. Leaf fall, too, occurs continuously and slowly in the tropical rainforest, unlike the autumnal drops of temperate deciduous forests, and the same tropical conditions of heat and moisture that fuel year-round growth also sponsor fast decomposition of dead leaves. The humus that enriches the soils of more temperate latitudes doesn't have a chance to accumulate in the tropics. Thus, soils are thin and, after millions of years of daily rainfall and constant heat, leached of their nutrient content.

Result? The ecosystem of a tropical rainforest is upside down when compared to forests in the temperate zone, where nutrients are stored in the soil. In the tropics they're stored overhead: in the densely leafed canopy. Leaves and young shoots represent a major investment of scarce nutrients, which plants cannot afford to have gobbled up by hungry multitudes of animals, insects, and birds. Hence, says one biologist, "It might be said that the plants 'want' to be different from one another in order to avoid being devoured." Intense competition has pressured tropical plants to diversify greatly, to disperse, and to develop defense mechanisms, such as thorns or sickening toxins. Other species stagger their production of shoots and new leaves throughout the year so that they never expose too much new growth to predation at any one time.

Because plant protein is scarce at any given time, and because plants have evolved stratagems to guard it, animals have been forced to compete fiercely. They've diversified like the plants, and competition has resulted in notable examples of specialization, with individual species staking claims to a narrow ecological niche in which other creatures can't compete. One bird species eats only insects driven up from the ground by army ants, while its droppings provide food for a certain species of butterfly.

Through these intricate associations, specific plants and predators become totally dependent on one another. A perfect example is the ant acacia, a tree common along the Pacific coast. The plant is weak and defenseless, a poor competitor in the upward race for sunlight, and easily overshadowed by faster-growing neighbors. Its tiny nectaries (glands that exude sugar) and leaf-tip swellings filled with proteins and vitamins are tempting morsels for hungry insects and birds. None, however, dares steal a nibble, for a species of tiny yet aggressive ants acts as the acacia's praetorian guard. In exchange for the honeylike food that they love, the ants defend their plant fiercely. Any predator foolish enough to touch the acacia is attacked; if a vine threatens to envelop the tree, the ants cut the vine down. If the branches of a neighboring plant threaten to steal the acacia's sunlight, the ants will prune the interloper; if a neighbor's seeds fall to the ground beneath the acacia, the insects will cart them off before they can germinate. If the ants were to become extinct, the plant would never survive. If the plant disappeared, the ants would starve. Each is inextricably in the debt of the other.

er plants." It has many more species of ferns—about 800—than the whole of North America, including Mexico. Of heliconias (members of the banana family more familiarly known as "birds of paradise"), there are some 30 species. It is a nation of green upon green upon green.

The forests and grasslands flare with color—some flamboyantly so, as plants advertise the delights and rewards they offer, including the ultimate bribe, nectar. Begonias, anthuriums, and blood of Christ, named for the red splotches on the underside of its leaves, are common. My favorite plant is the "hot lips" *(labios ardientes),* sometimes called "hooker's lips" *(labios de puta),* whose bright red bracts remind me of Mick Jagger's famous pout or, perhaps more appropriately, Madonna's smile. The vermilion *poró* tree (the bright flame-of-the-forest), pink-and-white meadow oak,

purple jacaranda, and the almost fluorescent yellow *corteza amarilla* all add their seasonal bouquets to the landscape. And the morning glory spreads its thick lavender carpets across lowland pastures, joined by carnal red (but unromantically foulsmelling—a crafty device to enlist the help of flies in pollination) passionflowers.

Many plants play out the game of love and reproduction in the heat of the tropical night, when they emit fragrances designed to attract specific insect species. Other flowering species employ markings on their petals to indicate the exact placing of the rewards insects seek. Many orchid species, for example, are marked with lines and spots like an airfield, to show the insect where to land and in which direction to taxi. Others display colors invisible to the human eye yet clearly perceptible by insects whose eyesight spans the ultraviolet spectrum. And a remarkable holly species *(Ocotea tenera)* occasionally changes sex, being male one year and female the next, to increase its chance of pollination. What makes them change sex isn't known, though it seems they respond to the previous year's reproductive success, or lack of it.

The most abundant flora in rainforest environments are ferns, light-gap pioneers found from sea level to the highest elevations. The ancient terrestrial ferns once served as food for many a prehistoric beast. The big tree ferns—sometimes called *rabo de mico* (monkey-tail) ferns, an allusion to the uncurling young fronds—are relics from the age of the dinosaurs, sometimes four meters tall, with fiddleheads large enough to grace a cello. Others are epiphytic, arboreal "nesters," or climbers whose long leaves can grapple upward for 20 meters or more.

The epiphytic environment is extremely poor in mineral nutrients. The bromeliads—brilliantly flowering, spiky-leafed "air" plants up to 120 cm across—have developed tanks or cisterns that hold great quantities of rainwater and decaying detritus in the whorled bases of their tightly overlapping stiff leaves. The plants gain nourishment from dissolved nutrients in the cisterns (it's a symbiotic relationship: often the host tree will put roots down into the epiphyte to absorb its nutrients). Known as tank epiphytes, they provide trysting places and homes for tiny aquatic animals high above the ground. Costa Rica has more than 2,000 species of bromeliads (including the pineapple)—the richest deposit of such flora on the isthmus.

All plants depend on light to power the chemical process by which they synthesize their body substances from simple elements. Height is therefore of utmost importance. When an old tree falls, the strong, unaccustomed light triggers seeds that have lain dormant, and banana palms and ginger plants, heliconias and cecropias—all plants that live in the sunshine on riverbanks or in forest clearings—burst into life and put out big broad leaves to soak up the sun, to flower and to fruit. Another prominent plant is the poor man's umbrella *(sombrilla de pobre),* whose name you'll remember if you get caught in a downpour while in the rainforest; its giant leaves make excellent impromptu shelters.

Orchids

It's appropriate that the orchid is the national flower of Costa Rica: the country has more than 1,400 identified species, the richest orchid flora in Central America. And countless others probably await discovery. At any time of year you're sure to find dozens of species in bloom, from sea level to the highest, subfreezing reaches of Chirripó. There is no best time for viewing orchids, although the beginning of both the dry season (especially in the wettest rainforest regions) and the wet season are said to be particularly favorable.

Orchids are not only the largest family of flowering plants, they're also the most diverse—poke around with magnifying glass in hand and you'll come across species with flowers less than one millimeter across. Others, like the native *Phragmipedium caudatum,* have pendulant petals that can reach more than half a meter. Some flower for only one day, others last several weeks. Orchid lovers should head for the cloud forests; there, the greatest diversity exists in humid—not wet—midelevation environments where they are abundant as tropical epiphytes (constituting 88% of orchid species). One biologist found 47 different orchid species growing on a single tree.

While not all orchids lead epiphytic lives—the Spanish called them *parasitos*—those that do are the most exotic of epiphytes, classics of their kind, so heartachingly beautiful that collectors can't resist their siren call and threaten their existence.

Orchids have evolved a remarkable array of ingenious pollination techniques. Some species self-pollinate. Others attract insects by sexual impersonation. One species, for example, produces a flower that closely resembles the form of a female wasp—complete with eyes, antennae, and wings. It even gives off the odor of a female wasp in mating condition. Male wasps, deceived, attempt to copulate with it. In their vigor, they deposit pollen within the orchid flower and immediately afterward receive a fresh batch to carry to the next false female. Then there's the orchid called *La Putita de Noche* ("Little Prostitute of the Night") because by day it smells of nothing but at night no decent person will let it into the house.

Guile seems to be the forte of orchids. Another species drugs its visitors. Bees clamber into its throat and sip a nectar so intoxicating that after the merest taste they become so inebriated they lose their footing and slip into a small bucket of liquid. Escape is offered up a spout—the proverbial light at the end of the tunnel. As the drunken insect totters up, it has to wriggle beneath an overhanging rod, which showers its back with pollen. Pollination techniques have become so species-specific that hybridization of different orchid species is avoided by each having developed its own morphological configuration to attach its pollen, and receive it in return, to a specific part of the insect's body.

Lankester Gardens, part of the University of Costa Rica, features more than 800 orchid species, including the collection of Charles Lankester, who once ran Lankester as a private garden. It's about seven km east of Cartago on the road to Paraíso. The **Orquídeas de Monteverde** is an exquisite orchid garden in Monteverde, in Guanacaste. **Orchid Alley,** at La Garita in the central highlands, of-fers a stunning array of orchids for sale, suitably packed for export. Nearby, at Palmares, is **Jardín de Las Guarias,** the largest private orchid collection in the country, all raised by farmer Javier Solorzano Murillo. Orchidologist Eugenio Esquivel has a nursery open to visitors in Puriscal. See the Central Highlands chapter for more information.

An annual orchid show is held each March in San José. **Costa Rica Connections,** 975 Osos St., San Luis Obispo, CA 93401, tel. (805) 543-8823 or (800) 345-7422, fax (805) 543-3626, offers a weeklong "Costa Rica National Orchid Show and Tour."

If you're serious in your study, check out the *Field Guide to the Orchids of Costa Rica and Panama,* by Robert L. Dressler (Ithaca, NY: Comstock Publishing, 1993).

TROPICAL RAINFOREST

Once upon a time, about 140 million years ago, near the beginning of the Cretaceous period in the

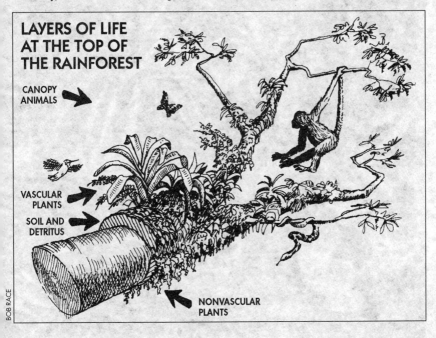

LAYERS OF LIFE AT THE TOP OF THE RAINFOREST

CANOPY ANIMALS

VASCULAR PLANTS

SOIL AND DETRITUS

NONVASCULAR PLANTS

BOB RACE

TROPICAL HUMID FOREST

SCARLET MACAW

TAMANDUA ANTEATER

OCELOT

PALM VIPER

OTTER

JAGUAR

BOB RACE

age of dinosaurs, before the freezing embraces of the Ice Ages, thick evergreen forests blanketed much of the world's warm, humid surface. Today's tropical rainforests—the densest and richest proliferation of plants ever known—are the survivors of these primeval jungles of ages past.

These forests, the largest of which is Brazil's Amazonian jungle, are found in a narrow belt that girdles the earth at the equator. In the tropics, constant sunlight, endless rains and high temperatures year-round spell life. The steamy atmosphere and fast nutrient turnover have promoted favorable growth conditions and intense competition that have allowed the forest flora to evolve into an extraordinary multitude of different species, exploiting to the full every conceivable niche. Nowhere else on earth is biological productivity and diversity so evident: tropical rainforests contain more than half of all living things known to man (the number of insect species in a hectare of rainforest is so great that no successful count has been made). Entomologists have collected from just one species of tree more than 950 different species of beetles.

Only superficially does the rainforest resemble the fictional jungles of Tarzan. Yes, the foliage can indeed be so dense that you cannot move without a machete. But since only about 10% of the total sunlight manages to penetrate through the forest canopy, the undergrowth is generally correspondingly sparse, and the forest floor surprisingly open and relatively easy to move about in. Within the shadowed jungle the dark subaqueous greens are lit here and there by beams of sunlight pouring down from above. (The plants array their leaves to avoid leaf shade; others are shaded purple underneath to help reflect back the light passing through the leaf; and the "walking palm" literally walks across the forest floor on its stilt-like roots.)

The stagnant air, however, is loaded with moisture. Even the briefest trail walk leaves clothing saturated with sweat, and molds and fungus seem to appear virtually overnight. There is supposedly even a fungus that flourishes inside binoculars and cameras and eats away the protective coating of lenses. To a visitor, the tropical rainforest seems always the same: uniform heat and stifling 90% humidity which scarcely varies. But this is true only near the ground. High in the tops of the trees, where the

sun comes and goes, breezes blow, and moisture has a chance to be carried away, the swings in temperature between day and night are as much as 15 degrees, whereas the humidity may drop from 95%, its fairly constant nighttime level, to as low as 60% as the sun rises and warms the forest. Thus, within 30 vertical meters, two distinctly different climates prevail.

In 1898 the German botanist A.F.W. Schimper coined the phrase "tropical rainforest." Since then botanists have distinguished among 30 or so different types of rainforest, whose species content is determined by temperature and rainfall. Tropical evergreen rainforest exists in areas of high rainfall (at least 200 cm) and regular high temperatures averaging no less than 25° C (77° F). In Costa Rica, the lush tropical evergreen rainforest of the Caribbean lowlands gives way on the Pacific side to a seasonally dry evergreen forest in the well-watered south, and tropical deciduous forest—dry forest—in the northwest.

Costa Rica's tropical rainforests are places of peace and renewal, like a vast vaulted cathedral, mysterious, strangely silent, and of majestic proportions. As one writer says: "a fourteenth century stonemason would have felt at home [in the rainforest], with its buttressed, moss-columned, towering trees and dark recesses."

Plunging deep into the forest, you are soon struck by how much variety there is. While in temperate forests distinct species of flora congregate neatly into distinctive plant "neighborhoods" with few other species interspersed, in the rainforest you may pass one example of a particular tree species, then not see another for half a mile. In between, however, are hundreds of other species. In the rainforest, too, you'll notice that life is piled upon life—literally. The firm and unyielding forest floor is a "dark factory of decomposition," where bacteria, mold, and insects work unceasingly, degrading the constant rain of leaf litter and dislodged fruits into nutrient molecules.

Strange-shaped umbrellas, curtains, and globes of fungi proliferate, too. They are a key to providing the nourishment vital to the jungle's life cycle. While a fallen leaf from a North American oak may take a year to decompose, a leaf in the tropical rainforest will fully decay within a month. If these precious nutrients and minerals thus released are not to be washed away by the daily drenching of rain, they must be reclaimed quickly and returned to the canopy to restart the cycle of life. The trees suck up the minerals and nutrients through a thick mat of rootlets that grow close to the surface of the inordinately thin soil. To counteract their inherent instability, many species grow side buttresses: wafer-thin flanges that radiate in a ring around the base of the tree like the tail fins of rockets.

The dark nave of the rainforest cathedral is rich with ferns, saplings, and herbaceous plants, seeping in moisture. For every tree in the jungle, there is a clinging vine fighting for a glimpse of the sun. Instead of using up valuable time and energy in building their own supports, these clutching vines and lianas rely on the straight, limbless trunks typical of rainforest tree species to provide a support in their quest for sunlight. They ride piggyback to the canopy, where they continue to snake through the treetops, sometimes reaching lengths of 300 meters. One species spirals around its host like a corkscrew; another cements itself to a tree with three-pronged tendrils.

The bully of the forest, however, is the strangler fig, which isn't content to merely coexist. While most lianas and vines take root in the ground and grow upward, the strangler figs do the opposite. After sprouting in the forest canopy from seeds dropped by birds and bats, the strangler fig sends roots to the ground, where they dig into the soil and provide a boost of sustenance. Slowly but surely—it may take a full century—the roots grow and envelop the host tree, choking it till it dies and rots away, leaving a hollow, trellised, freestanding cylinder.

The vigorous competition for light and space has promoted the evolution of long, slender, branchless trunks, many well over 35 meters tall, and flat-topped crowns with foliage so dense that rainwater from driving tropical downpours often may not reach the ground for 10 minutes. Above this dense carpet of greenery rise a few scattered giants towering to heights of 70 meters or more. This great vaulted canopy—the clerestory of the rainforest cathedral—is the jungle's powerhouse, where more than 90% of photosynthesis takes place.

The scaffolding of massive boughs is colonized at all levels by a riot of bromeliads, ferns, and other epiphytes (plants that take root on plants but that are not parasitic). Tiny spores sprout on the bark, gain a foothold, and spread like luxuriant carpets. As they die and decay, they form a compost on the branch capable of supporting larger plants that feed on the leaf mold and draw moisture by dangling their roots into the humid air. Soon every available surface is a great hanging gallery of giant elkhorns and ferns, often reaching such weights that whole tree limbs are torn away and crash down to join the decaying litter on the forest floor.

The Babylonian gardens of the jungle ceiling—naturalist William Beebe called it an "undiscovered continent"—also, of course, host a staggeringly complex, unseen world of wildlife. The rich rainforest green backdrops the jewel colors of its many inhabitants. Sit still awhile and the unseen beasts and birds will get used to your presence and emerge from the shadows. Enormous morpho butterflies float by, flashing like bright neon signs. Is that vine really moving? More likely it's a brilliantly costumed tree python, so green it is almost iridescent, draped in sensuous coils on a branch.

Scarlet macaws and lesser parrots plunge and sway in the high branches, announcing their playacting with an outburst of shrieks. Arboreal rodents leap and run along the branches, searching for nectar and insects, while insectivorous birds watch from their vantage points for any movement that will betray a stick insect or leaf-green tree frog to scoop up for lunch. Legions of monkeys, sloths, and fruit- and leaf-eating mammals also live in the green world of the canopy, browsing and hunting, thieving and scavenging, breeding and dying.

Larger hunters live up there, too. In addition to the great eagles plunging through the canopy to grab monkeys, there are also tree-dwelling cats. These superbly athletic climbers are quite capable of catching monkeys and squirrels as they leap from branch to branch and race up trunks. There are also snakes here. Not the great monsters so common in romantic fiction, which dangle, says David Attenborough, "optimistically from a branch, waiting to pick up a human passer-by," but much smaller creatures, some twig-thin, such as the chunk-headed snake with catlike eyes, which feasts on frogs and lizards and nestling birds.

Come twilight, the forest soaks in a brief moment of silence. Slowly, the lisping of insects begins. There is a faint rustle as nocturnal rodents come out to forage in the ground litter. And the squabbling of fruit bats replaces that of the birds. All around, myriad beetles and moths take wing in the moist velvet blanket of the tropical night.

The **Organization of Tropical Studies** offers 10-day "Rainforest Ecology Workshops" at field stations in Costa Rica ($1,995). In addition, many locations throughout Costa Rica offer "canopy tours," making it possible for you to get a monkey's eye view of life in the canopy. With an expert guide, you travel from tree to tree and platform to platform using pulleys on horizontal traverse cables before rappeling back to the jungle floor.

TROPICAL DRY FOREST

Unlike Costa Rica's rainforests, the rare tropical dry forest is relatively sparsely vegetated, with far fewer tree species and only two strata. Canopy trees have short, stout trunks with large, flat-topped crowns, rarely more than 15 meters above the ground. Beneath is an understory with small, open-top crowns, and a layer of shrubs with vicious spines and thorns. Missing are the great profusion of epiphytes and the year-round lush evergreens of the rainforest.

November through March, no rain relieves the parching heat. Then, the deciduous dry forests undergo a dramatic seasonal transformation, the purple jacaranda, pink-and-white meadow oak, yellow *corteza amarilla*, scarlet *poró*, and the bright orange flame-of-the-forest exploding in Monet colors in the midst of drought.

Before the arrival of the Spanish in the early 16th century, dry forests blanketed the Pacific coastal lowlands from Panamá to Mexico. Today, they cling precariously to some two percent of their former range—a mere 520 square kilometers of Costa Rica in scattered patches centered on the lower Río Tempisque of Guanacaste. Far rarer than rainforests, they are significantly more endangered, especially by fires, which eviscerate whole forest patches, opening holes in which ecological opportunists—weeds and grasses such as African jaragua—rush in. Eventually savanna comes to replace the forest.

Fires set by the Spanish and by generations of farmers and ranchers thereafter spread savan-nas across the province, whose flat alluvial plains and rich volcanic soils are perfect for crops and cattle ranchland. The fate of even the preserved dry-forest parcels hinges on the success of two ambitious conservation projects (see the special topic **Restoring the Dry Forest** in the Guanacaste and the Northwest chapter).

MANGROVE ESTUARIES

Costa Rica's shorelines are home to five species of mangroves that form unique ecosystems. These pioneer land builders thrive at the interface of land and sea, forming a stabilizing tangle that fights tidal erosion and reclaims land from the water. The irrepressible, reddish-barked, shrubby mangroves rise from the dark water on interlocking stilt roots. Small brackish streams and labyrinthine creeks wind among them like snakes, sometimes interconnecting, sometimes petering out in narrow culs-de-sac, sometimes opening suddenly into broad lagoons. A few clear channels may run through the rich and redolent world of the mangroves, but the trees grow so thickly over much of it that you cannot force even a small boat between them.

Mangroves are what botanists call halophytes, plants that thrive in salty conditions. Although they do not require salt (they in fact grow better

red mangrove

BOB RACE

in fresh water), they thrive where no other tree can. Costa Rica's young rivers have short and violent courses that keep silt and volcanic ash churned up and suspended, so that a great deal of it is carried out of the mountains onto the coastal alluvial plains. The nutrient-rich mud generates algae and other small organisms that form the base of the marine food chain. Food is delivered to the estuaries every day from both the sea and the land so those few plants—and creatures—that can survive here flourish in immense numbers. And their sustained health is vital to the health of other marine ecosystems.

The nutrients the mangrove seeks lie not deep in the acid mud but on its surface, where they have been deposited by the tides. There is no oxygen to be had in the mud either: estuarine mud is so fine-grained that air cannot diffuse through it, and the gases produced by the decomposition of the organic debris within it stay trapped until your footsteps release them, producing a strong whiff of rotten eggs. Hence, there is no point in the mangroves sending down deep roots. Instead, the mangroves send out peculiar aerial roots, like a spider's legs, to form a horizontal platform that sits like a raft, maintaining a hold on the glutinous mud and giving the mangroves the appearance of walking on water. The mangroves draw oxygen from the air through small patches of spongy tissue on their bark.

Mangrove swamps are esteemed as nurseries of marinelife and as havens for water birds—cormorants, frigate birds, pelicans, herons, and egrets—which feed and nest here by the thousands, producing guano that makes the mangroves grow faster. The big birds roost on the top canopy, while smaller ones settle for the underbrush. Frigate birds are particularly fond of mangrove bushes and congregate in vast numbers along the swampy shorelines of the Golfo de Nicoya. The bushes in which they build their nests rise some two to three meters above the mudflats—just right to serve as launching pads.

A look down into the water reveals luxuriant life: oysters and sponges attached to the roots, small stingrays flapping slowly over the bottom, and tiny fish in schools of tens of thousands. Baby black-tipped sharks and other juvenile fish, too, spend much of their early lives among mangrove roots, out of the heavy surf, shielded by the root maze that keeps out large predators.

High tide brings larger diners—big mangrove snappers and young barracudas hang motionless in the water. Raccoons, snakes, and, as everywhere, insects and other arboreal creatures also inhabit the mangroves. There is even an arboreal mangrove tree crab (Aratus pisonii), which eats mangrove leaves and is restricted to the very crowns of the trees by the predatory activities of another arboreal crab, Goniopsis pulcra.

Mangroves are aggressive colonizers, thanks to one of nature's most remarkable seedlings. The heavy, fleshy mangrove seeds, shaped like plumb bobs, germinate while still on the tree. The flowers bloom for a few weeks in the spring and then fall off, making way for a fruit. A seedling shoot soon sprouts from each fruit and grows to a length of 15-30 cm before dropping from the tree. Falling like darts, at low tide they will land in the mud and put down roots immediately. Otherwise, the seedlings—great travelers—become floating scouts and outriders ahead of the advancing roots.

The seaborne seedling can remain alive for as long as a year, during which time it may drift for hundreds of miles. Eventually, it touches the muddy floor and anchors itself, growing as much as 60 cm in its first year. By its third year a young tree starts to sprout its own forest of arching prop roots; in about 10 years it has fostered a thriving colony of mangroves, which edge ever out to sea, forming a great swampy forest. As silt builds up among the roots, land is gradually reclaimed from the sea. Mangroves build up the soil until they strand themselves high and dry. In the end they die on the land they have created.

CONSERVATION

Deforestation
In the time it takes you to read this page, some 32 hectares of the world's tropical rainforests will be destroyed. The statistics defy comprehension. One hundred years ago, rainforests covered two billion hectares, 14% of the earth's land surface. Now only half remains, and the rate of destruction is increasing: an area larger than the U.S. state of Florida is lost every year. If the destruction continues apace, the world's rainforests will vanish within 40 years.

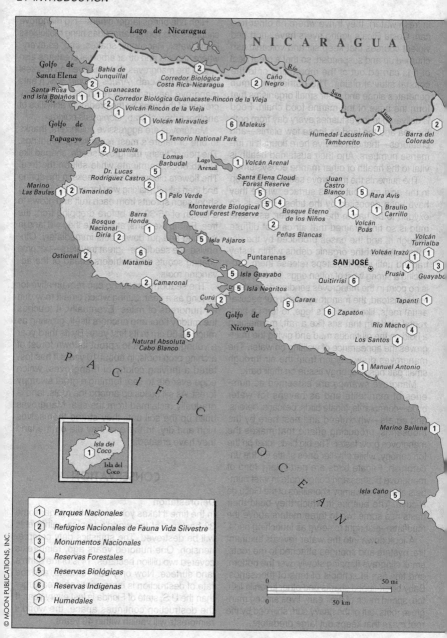

NICARAGUA

Lago de Nicaragua

Golfo de Santa Elena

Bahía de Junquillal

Corredor Biológica Costa Rica-Nicaragua

Caño Negro

Río San Juan

Barra del Colorado

Santa Rosa and Isla Bolaños

Guanacaste

Corredor Biológica Guanacaste-Rincón de la Vieja

Volcán Rincón de la Vieja

Golfo de Papagayo

Volcán Miravalles

Malekus

Humedal Lacustrino Tamborcito

Iguanita

Tenorio National Park

Lomas Barbudal

Lago Arenal

Volcán Arenal

Dr. Lucas Rodríguez Castro

Juan Castro Blanco

Rara Avis

Marino Las Baulas

Tamarindo

Palo Verde

Santa Elena Cloud Forest Reserve

Braulio Carrillo

Barra Honda

Monteverde Biological Cloud Forest Preserve

Bosque Eterno de los Niños

Volcán Poás

Bosque Nacional Diría

Peñas Blancas

Volcán Turrialba

Volcán Irazú

Ostional

Matambú

Isla Pájaros

Puntarenas

SAN JOSÉ

Prusia

Guayabo

Camaronal

Isla Guayabo

Quitirrísi

Curú

Isla Negritos

Carara

Tapantí

Golfo de Nicoya

Zapatón

Río Macho

Natural Absoluta Cabo Blanco

Los Santos

PACIFIC

Manuel Antonio

Marino Ballena

OCEAN

Isla del Coco

Isla Caño

Isla del Coco

1. Parques Nacionales
2. Refugios Nacionales de Fauna Vida Silvestre
3. Monumentos Nacionales
4. Reservas Forestales
5. Reservas Biológicas
6. Reservas Indígenas
7. Humedales

0   50 mi

0   50 km

© MOON PUBLICATIONS, INC.

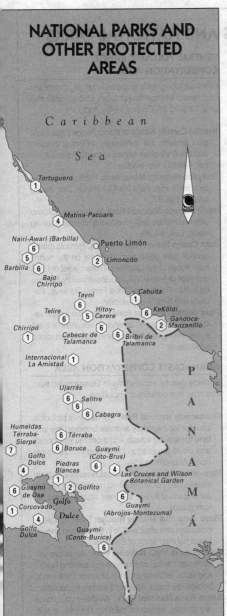

NATIONAL PARKS AND OTHER PROTECTED AREAS

Caribbean

Sea

Tortuguero 1

Matina-Pacuare 4

Nairi-Awari (Barbilla) 6
5
Puerto Limón
Barbilla 6
Bajo
Chirripó
2 Limoncito

Tayni 6
Telire 6
Hitoy-
Cerere 5
Cahuita 1
KeKôldi 6
Chirripó 1
Cabecar de
Talamanca 6
Gandoca-
Manzanillo 2
Bribrí de
Talamanca

Internacional 1
La Amistad

Ujarrás
Salitre 6
6
Cabagra 6

Humeldas
Térraba-
Sierpe
Térraba 6
Boruca 6
Guaymí
(Coto-Brus)
7
Golfo
Dulce 4
Piedras
Blancas 4
1
Las Cruces and Wilson
Botanical Garden
Guaymí
de Osa 6
1
Corcovado
2 Golfito
6
Guaymí
(Abrojos-Montezuma)
Golfo
Dulce
Golfo
Dulce
Guaymí
(Conte-Burica) 6

P
A
N
A
M
Á

By anyone's standards, Costa Rica leads the way in moving Central America away from the soil-leaching deforestation that plagues the isthmus. The country has one of the world's best conservation records: about one-quarter of the country is under some form of official protection. Despite Costa Rica's achievements in conservation, however, deforestation continues at an alarming rate.

The Evidence: Along the Río San Juan, in the heart of the *llanuras* of the Atlantic lowlands, along the border with Nicaragua, is some of the wildest, wettest, most densely canopied rainforest in Costa Rica. It is a crown jewel of Central American jungle, as shining and sweet-smelling and innocent as it must have been in the first light of Creation.

The humid *llanura* is the biggest piece of primeval rainforest left on the Caribbean rim, a tiny enclave of the original carpet that once covered most of lowland Central America. Caimans, manatees, peccaries, and sloths move amid the small sloughs, and deep in the cobalt shadows jaguars and tapirs move unseen. Very wet and isolated, these mist-enshrouded waves of green have been relatively untouched by man until recently. Today, the lowland rainforests resound with the carnivorous buzz of chain saws; in the "dry" season, in isolated patches, they are on fire.

It is a story that's been repeated again and again during the past 400 years. Logging, ranching, and the development of large-scale commercial agriculture have transformed much of Costa Rica's wildest terrain. This is particularly true in the highlands, where the temperate and moist environment is ideal for the production of coffee and tea, and the Pacific lowlands, where beef and cotton have become major export products. Cattle ranching has been particularly wasteful. Large tracts of virgin forest were felled in the 1960s to make way for cattle, stimulated by millions of dollars of loans provided by U.S. banks and businesses promoting the beef industry to feed the North American market. Author Beatrice Blake claims that "Costa Rica loses 2.5 tons of topsoil to erosion for every kilo of meat exported" and that although a "farmer can make 86 times as much money per acre with coffee, and 284 times as much with bananas," cattle ranching takes up more than 20 times the amount of land devoted to bananas and coffee.

CONSERVATION AREAS AND NATIONAL PARKS

At press time, Costa Rica had 13 conservation areas. The most important touristically include those listed below.

AMISTAD CONSERVATION AREA

The country's largest and least accessible protected area encompasses rugged, mountainous terrain in southern Costa Rica plus parks of the southern Caribbean littoral. It incorporates several **indigenous reserves**, plus **Las Cruces Biological Station** as well as the following:

Cahuita National Park: Coral reefs and beautiful beaches backed by lowland rainforest replete with wildlife.

Chirripó National Park: Costa Rica's highest peak, spanning diverse ecosystems including cloud forest and tundra *(paramó)*.

Gandoca-Manzanillo National Wildlife Refuge: Beautiful, lonesome shoreline favored for nesting by marine turtles; estuaries protect rare ecosystems plus manatees and a species of freshwater dolphin.

Hitoy-Cerere Biological Reserve: Rugged and remote; mountain slopes and deep valleys smothered with rainforest. Large wildlife population.

La Amistad International Peace Park Encompasses Chirripó, Hitoy-Cerere and other mountainous parks of the Talamanca mountains. Much of the park is unexplored. Large population of big cats and other endangered wildlife.

Tapantí National Park: Two life zones—lower montane and premontane rainforest—replete with endangered wildlife and copious birdlife, on northeast side of Talamancas.

ARENAL CONSERVATION AREA

This conservation area encompasses wildlife-rich environments of the Cordillera de Tilarán, including three private cloud-forest reserves: **Monteverde Cloud Forest Biological Reserve**, the **Children's Eternal Forest**, and the **Santa Elena Cloud Forest Reserve**, plus:

Arenal National Park: Protects the watershed draining into Lake Arenal and includes Arenal Volcano.

Caño Negro National Wildlife Refuge: Vast wetland region replete with birdlife, crocodiles, and other wildlife. A prime sportfishing locale.

CENTRAL VOLCANIC RANGE CONSERVATION AREA

Dramatic topography and a wide range of montane and humid tropical forest types characterize this area flanking the Central Valley. Includes:

Braulio Carrillo National Park: Rugged mountain park protects the rainforests on Barva volcano and the Caribbean slopes of the Cordillera Central. Replete with wildlife.

Guayabo National Monument: Protects Costa Rica's most important pre-Columbian site, dating back to 500 B.C.

Irazú Volcano National Park: A drive-up volcano with two craters and good hiking offering stunning views. Little wildlife.

Juan Castro Blanco National Park: Remote mountainous park protecting rainforest on the northeast slopes of the Cordillera Tilarán, west of Poás and east of Arenal Volcano. Bordered by Bosque de la Paz Rainforest/Cloud Forest Reserve. Replete with birdlife and wildlife.

Poás Volcano National Park: Costa Rica's most visited park, centered on an drive-up volcano that is still active. Hiking trails lead to three craters and varied ecosystems.

GUANACASTE CONSERVATION AREA

Protects diverse ecosystems in Guanacaste, from shoreline to mountaintop, including:

Guanacaste National Park: Forms a vital biological corridor for migratory animals between the lowland tropical dry forests and montane wet forests and cloud forest atop Orosí and Cacao volcanoes. Abundant wildlife.

Miravalles Volcano and Forest Reserve Another steep-sided volcano flanked by montane rainforest and cloud forest. Includes several prime hot spring sites.

Playa Junquillal Wildlife Refuge: Small refuge for crocodiles and other wildlife in the wetland and dry forest habitats north of Santa Rosa.

Rincón de la Vieja National Park: An active volcano with several craters (good for spotting tapirs), and varied ecosystems, from montane rainforest to tropical dry forest. Abundant mammal population.

Santa Rosa National Park: Wildlife-rich tropical dry forests, important nesting sites for green, leatherback, and ridley turtles, plus La Casona, an important national monument

Tenorio Volcano National Park: Similar to Miravalles.

OSA CONSERVATION AREA

This humid region, in the Pacific southwest, comprises some of the largest stands of rainforest in Central America, and includes:

Ballena National Marine Park: A protected coastal strip sheltering mangrove and wetland systems, and including offshore waters used by whales and other marine mammals

Caño Island Biological Reserve: A remote island covered with rainforest; an important pre-Columbian site. Marine life offshore.

Corcovado National Park: Protects the last significant stand of virgin rainforest in Central America. Boasts one of the most diverse and healthy wildlife populations, including tapirs, jaguars, crocodiles, and scarlet macaws.

Golfito National Wildlife Refuge: Contiguous with Corcovado, protects the watershed of the coastal mountains surrounding Golfito.

TEMPISQUE CONSERVATION AREA

This RCA (Regional Conservation Area) unites varied ecosystems protected in:

Barra Honda National Park: A diverse and large cave network with stalagmites and stalactites; deciduous forest up top protects a large wildlife population.

Las Baulas Marine National Park: Protects the preeminent nesting site of the leatherback turtle in Costa Rica.

Lomas Barbudal Biological Reserve: Borders Palo Verde and likewise abounds with waterfowl and other bird species, as well as mammals. Predominantly tropical dry forest. Often called the "insect park" because of the diversity and profusion of its bee, moth, and other insect populations.

Ostional National Wildlife Refuge: A shoreline and offshore refuge for ridley turtles, which nest here en masse several times a year.

Palo Verde National Park: Wetlands and rare tropical dry forest predominate in this park encompassing the estuarine ecosystems of the Río Tempisque and its tributaries. Large population of crocodiles and waterfowl.

Tamarindo Wildlife Refuge: Small but vitally important estuarine system behind Las Baulas harbors crocodiles, waterfowl, and a large mammal population.

TORTUGUERO CONSERVATION AREA

Combines vast wetland and forest regions of the northeast Caribbean, most significantly:

Barra del Colorado National Wildlife Refuge: Protecting important tropical humid and wet forests, swamplands, and mangroves bisected by the Ríos Colorado and San Juan and their tributaries. Large populations of crocodiles, birds, and game fish—notably tarpon and snook.

Tortuguero National Park: One of Costa Rica's most important lowland watersheds—with 11 distinct ecosystems—harboring large wildlife populations, including caimans, manatees, green macaws, river otters. The shoreline is the major nesting site for green turtles in the Caribbean.

NICOYA CONSERVATION AREA

A recently created RCA in southern Nicoya, where the following parks are being linked by creation of new wildlife refuges and national parks:

Cabo Blanco Absolute Nature Reserve: The first national park in the country protects moist tropical forests and a large population of wildlife, including several endangered species.

Curú Biological Reserve: A private reserve boasting a diversity of habitats and wildlife that belies their size. Whales are often seen offshore. Turtles nest on the beaches.

OTHER AREAS

On the Central Pacific coast are **Carara Biological Reserve,** a vital preserve at the juncture of the dry and wet zones, and protecting species from both habitats; the **Tácoles** estuary, famous for copious waterfowl and a large crocodile population; and tiny **Manuel Antonio National Park,** famous for its beaches, coral reef, and humid forest, where endangered bird and animal species—including spider monkeys and scarlet macaws—are easily seen.

Cocos Island UNESCO World Heritage Site, about 300 miles southwest of Costa Rica, has rare birds closely related to those of the Galápagos Islands, to which it is geologically related. Most famous for its large pelagic populations, including sharks.

The Defense: The nation has attempted to protect large areas of natural habitat and to preserve most of its singularly rich biota. But it is a policy marked by the paradox of good intent and seemingly poor application. Many reserves and refuges are accused of being poorly managed, and the Forestry Directorate, the government office in charge of managing the country's forest resources, has reportedly never functioned efficiently in more than 20 years of existence. While the administration of Oscar Arias Sánchez (1986-90) consolidated conservation efforts by creating a Ministry of Natural Resources, and President Rafael Angel Calderón (1990-94) called for a "New Ecological Order," the country continues to suffer the kind of environmental degradation and deforestation that plague most tropical countries. Environmentalists, with some justification, claimed that the Calderón administration abandoned the ecological principles of preceding administrations. Sadly, the Rafael Calderón administration proved more a friend of agricultural expansionists than environmentalists. In July 1992, for example, the legislature eliminated a key clause in the Forestry Law designed to protect the remaining forests. The 1994 elections were fought with that issue at the forefront; Calderón lost to José María Figueres, who campaigned on a platform of fostering "sustainable development." The jury of conservationists is still debating the legacy of the Figueres administration, with some notable battles won, and others lost. Alas, a new Forestry Law passed in 1996 favors the loggers (and the number of complaints against loggers has since doubled). In 1997, a 90-day moratorium on all logging in the Osa Peninsula was announced while an independent commission investigated reports of illegal logging and formulated a management policy for the Osa; satellite photographs showed that logging continued during the ban.

It's a daunting battle. Every year Costa Rica's population grows by 2.5%, exacerbating the land-pressure problem and forcing squatters onto virgin land, where they continue to deplete the forests that once covered 80% of Costa Rica. Fires set by ranchers today lap at the borders of Santa Rosa National Park. And oil-palm plantations squeeze Manuel Antonio against the Pacific. In the lowlands, fires from slash-and-burn agriculture burn uncontrolled for weeks; in the highlands, forests are logged for timber, roof shingles, and charcoal, while farmers and plantation owners continue to clear mountain slopes.

In the 1970s, the Costa Rican government banned export of more than 60 diminishing tree species, and national law proscribes cutting timber without proper permits. It happens anyway, much of it illegally, with logs reportedly trucked into San José and the coastal ports at night. Wherever new roads are built, the first vehicles in are usually logging trucks, which rumble along the highways loaded high with thick tree trunks. In Costa Rica the remaining tropical forest is disappearing at a rate of at least 520 square kilometers a year, and less than 1.5 million hectares of primal forest remain (about 20% of its original habitat). Despite the seemingly sincere efforts of the Costa Rican government, the nation's forests are falling faster than anywhere else in the Western Hemisphere and, as a percentage of national land area, reportedly nine times faster than the rainforests of Brazil.

The Cost: Many animal and plant species can survive only in large areas of wilderness. Most rainforest species are so highly specialized that they are quickly driven to extinction by the disturbance of their forest homes. Isolation of patches of forest is followed by an exponential decline. The decline of a single species has a domino effect on many dependent species, particularly plants, since tropical plants are far more dependent on individual animal and bird species for seed dispersal than are plants in temperate climates. Eventually these biological islands become depauperate. The reduction of original habitat to one-tenth of its original area means an eventual loss of half its species.

At the current rate of world deforestation, plant and animal species may well be disappearing at the rate of 50,000 a year; by the end of the 20th century, an estimated one million species will have vanished without ever having been identified. Among them will be many species whose chemical compounds might hold the secrets to cures for a host of debilitating and deadly diseases. The bark of the cinchona tree, for example, has long been the prime source of quinine, an important antimalarial drug. Curare, the vine extract used by South American Indians to poison their arrows and darts, is used as a muscle relaxant in modern surgery. And scientists recently discovered a peptide secreted by an Amazonian frog called *Phyllomedusa bicolor* that may lead to medicines for strokes, seizure, depression, and Alzheimer's disease. In fact, some 40% of all drugs manufactured in the United States are to some degree dependent on natural sources; more than 2,000 tropical rainforest plants have been identified as having some potential to combat cancer.

Nonrenewable Resources: Once the rainforests have been felled, they are gone forever. Despite the rainforests' abundant fecundity, the soils on which they grow are generally very poor, thin, and acidic.

When humans cut the forest down, the organic-poor soils are exposed to the elements and are rapidly washed away by the intense rains, and the ground is baked by the blazing sun to leave an infertile wasteland. At lower elevations, humans find their natural water sources diminishing and floods increasing after removal of the protective cover, for intact the montane rainforest acts as a giant sponge. Thus, indigenous groups such as the Bribrí and Cábecar Indians who inhabit remote regions close to the Panamanian border are finding their tenuous traditional livelihoods threatened.

Reforestation and Protection
Part of the government's answer to deforestation has been to promote reforestation, mostly through a series of tax breaks, which have led to a series of tree farms predominantly planted in nonnative species such as teak. The government, for example, has extended legal residency status to anyone participating in reforestation programs, with a required minimum nontaxable investment of US$50,000. These efforts, however, do little to replace the precious native hardwoods or to restore the complex natural ecosystems, which take generations to reestablish. Such efforts are being taken up by a handful of dedicated individuals and organizations determined to preserve and even replenish core habitats, such as attempts spearheaded by Daniel Janzen and the Friends of Lomas Barbudal to reestablish the tropical dry forests of Guanacaste.

International Efforts: Private and foreign agencies are becoming increasingly active in the battle to preserve Costa Rica's natural heritage. The country is now home to a plethora of con-

servation groups and projects, ranging from private nature reserves and children's reforestation projects to a $22.5 million forest-management project for the Central Volcanic Mountain Range funded by the U.S. Agency for International Development. Many of these organizations are attempting to bridge the gap between conservation funding and the nation's massive foreign-debt problems by developing "debt for nature" swaps. Swapping land for debt, for example, the U.S.-based Nature Conservancy has helped swell conservation coffers while curbing the outflow of foreign currency from Costa Rica. Using Conservancy money, the National Parks Foundation bought a share of the nation's debt from a U.S. bank, paying in dollars after the debt was discounted to only 17 cents on the dollar. Costa Rica then paid off the National Parks Foundation with bonds in the local currency, with the agreement that the money would be used on conservation projects.

And Barbilla National Park was created in late 1997 as the first park officially designated to trap greenhouse gases in an effort to promote the sale of "Carbon Bonds" to industrialized nations. The bonds will finance the park. Norway offered to purchase 200,000 tons of carbon "captured" in forests and timber plantations for $2 million. The bonds are to be traded on the Chicago stock exchange.

Private Efforts: Privately owned forests constitute the majority of unprotected primary forest remaining in Costa Rica outside the national parks. "While national programs have attempted to force compliance with Costa Rica's forestry law, little effort has been directed toward encouraging private landowners to willingly conserve and rationally manage their forests," says **COMBOS,** Conservación y Manejo de Bosques Tropicales, or Conservation and Management of Tropical Forests, Apdo. 1456, San Pedro 2050, tel. 253-0889, fax 253-4750, a nonprofit association that promotes the conservation and management of tropical forests through private action.

Many private reserves have been conceived to prove that rainforests can produce more income from such schemes as ecotourism, harvesting ornamental plants, and raising iguanas, pacas, and *tepezcuintles* (the giant and endangered forest-dwelling rodents that Ticos, sadly, consider popular snacks) for food than if cleared for cattle.

CONSERVATION ORGANIZATIONS

The following organizations are active in conservation efforts in Costa Rica and need volunteers and/or contributions to help implement their programs. Most accept volunteers.

Amigos de las Aves
Friends of the Birds, Apdo. 32-4001 Río Segundo de Alajuela, tel. 441-2658, breeds scarlet and green macaws for eventual release into the wild. Volunteers are needed to assist with raising the birds.

Amigos de Lomas Barbudal
Friends of Lomas Barbudal, 691 Colusa Ave., Berkeley, CA 94707, tel. (510) 526-4115, fax 528-0346, works to protect and restore the deciduous tropical dry forest of Guanacaste.

ARBOFILIA
The Association for Tree Protection, Apdo. 512-1100 Tibas, tel. 236-7145, fax 240-8832, is a grassroots organization that helps Costa Rican farmers reforest environmentally degraded areas with native tree species.

**Asociación Preservacionista
de Flora y Fauna Silvestre**
The Assocation for Protection of Wildlife, APREFLORAS, Apdo. 917-2150 Moravia, San José, tel. 240-6987, fax 222-5977, organizes volunteers to patrol wilderness areas to report illegal activities such as logging and hunting. Can be risky work.

**Asociación Costarricense para la
Conservación de la Naturaleza**
This watchdog organization, ASCONA, Apdo. 8-3790, San José 1000, tel. 297-1711, specializes in investigation of and legal action against environmental infringements. Volunteers with appropriate backgrounds are needed.

Caribbean Conservation Corps
CCC, P.O. Box 2866, Gainesville, FL 32602, tel. (352) 373-6441 or (800) 678-7853, fax (352) 375-2449; in Costa Rica, P.O. Box 246-2050, San Pedro, San José, tel. (506) 224-9215, fax 225-7516, e-mail: ccc@cccturtle.org, works to protect turtle populations and accepts donations and volunteers to assist in research and patrols.

CEDARENA
The Legal Center for the Environment and Natural Resources, Apdo. 134-2050 San Pedro, San José, tel. 224-8239, fax 253-4750, e-mail: cedarena@nicarao.apc.org, is a legal support group that researches and maintains a database on environmental laws and infringements. Volunteers with appropriate backgrounds are needed.

Conservation International
This group, 1015 18th St. N.W., Suite 1000, Washington, D.C. 20036, tel. (202) 429-5660, fax 887-5188, supports conservation projects worldwide; in Costa Rica it has been active in supporting La Amistad International Biosphere Reserve.

**Federación Costarricense para la
Conservación del Ambiente**
The Costa Rican Federation for Environmental Conservation, FECON, Apdo. 1948-1002, San José,

Several organizations sponsor private voluntary action on the part of landowners. For example, COMBOS, working with CEDARENA and the Nature Conservancy, has inscribed "conservation easements," legal agreements whereby property owners guarantee to restrict the type and amount of development that may take place on the property. Any subsequent owners are bound by the agreement.

Working against these valiant philanthropists is a legal system that grants significant inalienable rights to squatters: if they "improve" the land, they are entitled to just compensation; if they are not ejected in good time, the land becomes theirs. The law has given rise to professional squatters acting on behalf of businesspeople; once the former gains legal title it is signed over to the sponsor and then the squatter moves to another plot. Author Tom Huth, in *Condé Nast Traveler*, writes, "If the gringo wants his land back, he has to pay the squatters for having destroyed his forests." The temptation is for foreigners who buy land to *build* right away or hire a caretaker *(cuidador)* to hold squatters at bay (even the *cuidador,* if allowed to live on the property, can legally claim it as his own after six months' tenure).

New Approaches: The Costa Rican government's own conservation efforts have been undermined by the International Monetary Fund's structural-adjustment program, which requires government departments to cut their budgets and staffs. Particularly worrisome is the fact that

tel. 283-6046, fax 283-6128, e-mail: fecon@nicarao
.apc.org is an umbrella organization representing
several conservation organizations.

Fundación Neotrópica

The Neotropic Foundation, Apdo. 236-1002, San José,
tel. 253-2130, fax 253-4210, helps promote sustainable
development and conservation among local communities. Also sells a wide range of T-shirts, books, maps,
postcards, and souvenirs to promote environmental
education. Also arranges "debt-for-nature" swaps.

Monteverde Conservation League

The league, Apdo. 10165-1000, San José, tel. 645-
5003, fax 645-5053, e-mail: acmmcl@sol.racsa.co.cr,
promotes reforestation projects and works to assist
farmers of the Monteverde region to increase productivity in a sustainable manner. Administers the
Children's Eternal Cloud Forest Reserve.

Nature Conservancy

A leading North American organization, 1815 N.
Lynn St., Arlington, VA 22209, tel. (703) 841-5300 or
(800) 628-6860, fax (703) 841-1283, that identifies
species in need of protection and acquires land to
protect them; the largest "private sanctuary" in the
world. Its Latin America division works closely with
Fundación Neotrópica and other organizations.

Rainforest Alliance

This environmental group, 270 Lafayette St., Suite
512, New York, NY 10012, tel. (212) 941-1900, fax
941-4986, works to save rainforests worldwide.

SEJETKO

The Cultural Association of Costa Rica, Apdo. 1293-
2150, Moravia, San José, tel. 234-7115, works with
indigenous communities to help preserve their cultural integrity and achieve sustainable development.
It accepts volunteers for year-long assignments.

World Wildlife Fund

This world-renowned organization, 1250 24th St.
N.W., Washington, D.C. 20037, tel. (202) 293-4800,
fax 293-9211, works to protect endangered wildlife
around the world. You can make donations earmarked to specific Costa Rica conservation projects.

VOLUNTEER ORGANIZATIONS

The following organizations also accept volunteers
for community service in Costa Rica.

Amigos de las Américas, 5616 Star Lane, Houston, TX 77057, tel. (800) 231-7796

Global Services Corps, 300 Broadway #28, San
Francisco, CA 94133-3312, tel. (415) 788-
3666, e-mail: gsc@igc.apc.org

University Research Expeditions, University of
California Berkeley, Berkeley, CA 94720-7050,
tel. (510) 642-6586

Volunteers for Peace, 43 Tiffany Rd., Belmont,
VT 05730, tel. (802) 259-2759

much of the land incorporated into the national
park system has not yet been paid for and,
hence, could revert to private use.

Partly in response to this pressure, but also in
an attempt to improve the efficiency of its conservation programs, Costa Rica has reorganized
management of its protected areas. Costa Rica's
National Biodiversity Institute recently signed an
avant-garde contract with the world's largest pharmaceutical company, the New Jersey-based
Merck Co., which calls for the Institute to provide
Merck with samples of plant and insect species in
exchange for royalties from any marketable products. The objective is to finance the conservation of biodiversity and to ensure that Costa Rica
receives a small percentage of the massive profits derived from pharmaceutical extracts. (U.S.-
based Lilly, for example, earns some $100 million
a year from periwinkle extract used in treating

leukemia—but Madagascar, where the plant was
first collected, receives none of the profits.)

Another concept of land protection evolving in
Costa Rica places the needs of local communities in the equation by attempting to integrate
local livelihoods into the philosophy and day-
to-day operation of the national park system.
The intent is to give local inhabitants a vested interest by teaching them that they can earn a
living by preserving natural resources rather
than by destroying them. Governmental agencies have recently placed an emphasis on such
efforts along the Nicaraguan border, where the
Si-a-Paz cross-border preserve poses a new
challenge, and in so-called buffer zones surrounding existing parks and reserves.

In recent years, a campaign has also been
launched to protect the vitally important wetlands and waterways.

National Parks

Although contradictions abound, Costa Rica is blessed with a conscientious leadership that appreciates the value of the nation's natural heritage.

While much of Costa Rica has been stripped of its forests, the country has managed to protect a larger proportion of its land than any other country in the world. In 1970 there came a growing acknowledgment that something unique and lovely was vanishing, and a systematic effort was begun to save what was left of the wilderness. In that year, the progressive Costa Ricans formed a national park system that has won worldwide admiration. Costa Rican law declared inviolate 10.27% of a land once compared to Eden; an additional 17% is legally set aside as forest reserves, "buffer zones," wildlife refuges, and Indian reserves. Throughout the country representative sections of all the major habitats and ecosystems are protected for tomorrow's generations. The National Conservation Areas System (SINAC) protects more than 125 protected wildlife areas, including—at press time—24 national parks, 10 biological reserves, 12 forest reserves, and 34 wildlife refuges.

Besides providing Costa Ricans and foreign travelers with the privilege of admiring and studying the wonders of nature, the national parks and reserves protect the soil and watersheds and harbor an estimated 75% of all Costa Rica's species of flora and fauna, including species that have all but disappeared in neighboring countries. They contain active volcanoes and hot springs, high-reaching mountains and mysterious caves, historic battlefields, inviting beaches, and pre-Columbian settlements, and provide last, vital reservoirs of rainforests whose chemical secrets may one day reveal the cures for AIDS and other diseases.

The Yellowstones and Yosemites of Costa Rica—the lure for 90% of all visitors to the park system—are Manuel Antonio, with its beautiful beaches; Braulio Carrillo, with its rainforest beside a highway; Irazú, where on a clear day you can see both the Caribbean and the Pacific; and Poás, where you can peer into a steaming crater and see the earth's crust being rearranged.

While deforestation continues throughout the country, wildlife preservation in Costa Rica—at least in theory—is only a matter of due process and cash. Money is still needed to buy private landholdings within the parks (accounting for ap-

WORKING AS A PARK VOLUNTEER

The **Association of National Park Volunteers** (ASVO) recruits foreign volunteers with appropriate skills to work alongside rangers on a temporary basis. If you can handle basic living for a while and would enjoy applying your skills and energies in a noble cause, give it a try. Work might include digging at an archaeological site, life-guard duty at a park beach, or protecting nesting marine turtles. Volunteers receive free transportation and lodging. However, you may need to provide your own food, living conditions are rustic, and the work is often hard, long, and lonely. You must be at least 18 years old and provide two references from relevant organizations or individuals in Costa Rica. Contact the Asociación de Voluntarias de Parques Nacionales, Apdo. 10104, San José 1000, tel. 224-1331.

Arborea Project Foundation, Apdo. 65-8150 Palmar Norte, tel. 786-6565, fax 786-6358, in the UK, tel. 1631-770214, also recruits volunteers to assist rangers in establishing and maintaining trails, camps, and archaeological sites in Corcovado National Park and Caño Island. It also has a "Week for Wilderness" fieldwork program for volunteers, with activities such as seed collection, bird counts, and surveillance for illegal hunting and logging in the Osa Peninsula ($30 daily).

proximately 20% of park areas). And the government's budgetary constraints prohibit the severely understaffed Parks Service from hiring more people. It's a problem that is forcing Costa Rica to rely more heavily on foreign donations—the Scandinavians and Germans have been particularly supportive—to bolster local conservation efforts.

Much of the praise heaped on the National Parks Service more rightly belongs to individuals (preponderantly foreigners), private groups, and local communities whose efforts—often in the face of bureaucratic opposition—have resulted in creation of many of the wildlife refuges and parks for which the NPS takes credit. (The creation of the National Parks Service itself was the product of lobbying on behalf of a foreigner, as related in David Rains Wallace's *The Quetzal and the Macaw*.) Poaching continues inside national parks, often with the connivance of rangers and corrupt NPS officials, many of whom receive shares of the booty.

Facing the Challenge: The parks are in the midst of an important series of changes in which the focus is on increasing the degree of protection—turning poorly managed forest reserves and wildlife refuges into national parks, for example, and integrating adjacent national parks, reserves, and national forests into Regional Conservation Areas (RCAs) to create corridors in which wildlife might be able to move with greater freedom over much larger areas. Since farming, logging, and other activities are allowed within buffer zones on the edges of the parks, the intent is to more carefully manage this land. Responsibility for management is being shifted from central offices in San José to regional offices and, in some cases, to nongovernmental organizations.

To accomplish this, in 1989 the country began reorganizing its parks system. Following the model of the Guanacaste Regional Conservation Area, parks are being amalgamated to form eight more RCAs based on the premise that larger parks—being more complete ecosystems—are more easily preserved than smaller ones. Each unit is characterized by its unique ecology: Amistad, Arenal, Cordillera Volcánica Central, Isla del Coco, Osa, Pacífico Central, Tempisque, and Tortuguero. The **Sistema Nacional de Area de Conservació,** tel. 283-7343, which administers the units, is responsible to the Ministry of the Environment and Energy (MINAE), tel. 233-4533, formerly the Ministry of Natural Resources, Energy, and Mines (MINEREM). There were 11 RCAs at press time.

Costa Rican tourism has boomed so quickly that some parks are beginning to show wear and tear from too much visitation. In 1994, a visitor management policy was introduced to control the adverse effects on all the parks. Limits have been set on the numbers of visitors allowed in each park at any one time.

Until 1994, the Costa Rican Legislative Assembly had refused to revise its fee system upward despite the fact that the park system has been so short of funds that it could not afford uniforms or vehicles for many park rangers *(guardaparques)*, who are hard-pressed. Revenues generated by park visits were not available for park use; they were usurped by the Instituto Costarricense de Turismo (ICT). The **Ecotourism Society,** an organization of travel professionals and conservationists, began a campaign to raise park fees so that the country could afford to maintain the parks.

Unfortunately, in September 1994, the bureaucrats overreacted, and MIRENEM raised the park entrance fees more than 1,000% for tourists—to $15. Not surprisingly, the National Chamber of Tourism reported a 59% drop in visits. Tour operators complained that the whopping rise was killing off some of their business. A review body was established and revisions were made in spring 1995.

Information: The **Servicio de Parques Nacionales,** SPN (National Parks Service), tel. 257-0922, has a special toll-free telephone line for tourist information: tel. 192; from abroad, the same information is offered by fax at (506) 223-6963 and via a worldwide toll-free number c/o ICT, tel. (800) 343-6332.

Alternately, you can call or write the **public information office,** tel. 257-0922 or 256-9120, at the SPN headquarters in the Ministerio de Ambiente y Energia, Apdo. 10094, San José 1000, tel. 233-4533, or go in person to the office at Calle 25, Avenidas 8/10, open Mon.-Fri. 8 a.m.-4 p.m., or visit the **Fundación de Parques Nacionales,** Calle 23 and Avenida 15, tel. 257-2239.

The SPN maintains radio contact with each park through the radio communications office, tel. 233-4160, and can arrange accommodations and meals at many ranger stations on your behalf.

If you need specialized information on scientific aspects of the parks, contact the Conservation Data Center, **Instituto Nacional de Biodiversidad,** Apdo. 22-3310 Santo Domingo de Heredia, tel. 244-0690. Detailed topographical maps of the parks and reserves are available at **Librería Lehmann,** Calle 3, Avenida Central, and the **Instituto Geográfico Nacional,** Avenida 20, Calle 5/7; tel. 257-7798, ext. 2625, both in San José.

Fees and Facilities: No permits are required at most national parks, though you will need permits for a few of the biological reserves. These can be obtained in advance from the public information office, or write the Servicio de Parques Nacionales, Ministerio de Ambiente y Energia, Apdo. 10094, San José 1000.

Tickets for walk-in visitors are $6 and are valid for 24 hours only ($2 extra for overnight stays). Many ranger booths sell maps and pamphlets.

Most national parks and reserves have camping sites ($1-2 per night), although a few of the more remote wildlife refuges lack even the most rudimentary accommodations. You may be able to stay in park ranger housing or at biological research stations if space permits. Don't expect hotel service. You'll usually need to provide your own towels and bedding; there are no restaurants or snack bars, so bring enough food and drink for your anticipated stay.

Megaparks
Wildlife doesn't observe political borders. Birds migrate. Plants grow on each side. "It's not enough to draw lines on a map and call it a park," says Alvaro Ugalde, the former National Parks director. "These days, park management is tied into eco-

nomic issues, war and peace, agriculture, forestry, and helping people find a way to live." With peace breaking out all over Central America, park management increasingly requires international cooperation through the creation of a transnational park network. In this rare interlude of calm and fresh governments, there is an opportunity for neighboring countries to forget ancient border disagreements and see the rivers and rainforests along their borders not as dividing lines but as rich tropical ecosystems that they share.

The idea is fruiting as the **Paseo Pantera,** a five-year, $4 million project dedicated to preserving biodiversity through the creation of a

COSTA RICA AND NICARAGUA'S BINATIONAL PARK

The idea for a transboundary park along the northern border with Nicaragua germinated in 1974. Little progress was made, however, until 1985, when Nicaraguan President Daniel Ortega seized on the idea as a way to demilitarize the area, which was then being used by anti-Sandinista rebels. Ortega proposed the region be declared an international park for peace and gave it the name Si-a-Paz—Yes to Peace. Efforts by the Arias administration to kick the rebels out of Costa Rica's northern zone led to demilitarization of the area, but lack of funding and political difficulties prevented the two countries from making much progress on the Si-a-Paz project. Since 1990, improved relations between the countries and the end of the Nicaraguan war have allowed the governments to dedicate more money to Si-a-Paz.

Si-a-Paz represents a last chance to save Central America's largest and wettest tract of rainforest. Natural resources once made inaccessible by guerrilla warfare are now being plundered by loggers. In the wake of peace in Nicaragua, thousands of people displaced by the war are drifting back to the area, chasing dreams of a better life through the rainforest of the Río San Juan, one of Costa Rica's last seductive frontiers and the boundary between the two countries.

The idea is to enable people to make a living in one place, to involve them in conservation efforts and provide them with ecologically sustainable livelihoods so that they won't have to keep eating away at the forest's receding edge. The park design requires a full evaluation of existing human and natural

resources; social and cultural considerations, demographics, and development potential. Si-a-Paz planners want to wrap buffer zones of low-impact agriculture and agroforestry around core habitats, with whole communities integrated into the park design.

The goal is to establish a wildlife refuge along the southern shore of Lake Nicaragua, whose Solentiname Islands would be reforested and designated a cultural preserve. Other areas along the Río San Juan would be included in the park, making it a paradigm of ecosystem protection. The Costa Ricans plan to expand Tortuguero National Park to include the eastern part of Barra del Colorado Wildlife Refuge, which would connect the park with Nicaragua's Indio Maíz Biological Reserve.

There are also plans to create a corridor between the Caño Negro Wildlife Refuge and Nicaragua's Los Guatusos Wildlife Refuge and to create a new protected area west of where the Sarapiquí River pours into the San Juan, in Tambor. Also, the two-km-wide protected border zone will be expanded to a width of 10 km on the southern side of the San Juan.

The Nicaraguan part of the project is centered on Indio Maíz, which protects nearly half a million hectares of rainforest—one of the largest areas of undisturbed wilderness in Central America—in the southeast corner of the country. The Si-a-Paz region is such an El Dorado of biodiversity that conservation groups from around the world already have projects pending, from butterfly farms to sophisticated horticulture systems of intercropping.

chain of conservation areas from Belize to Panamá. This cooperative effort between Wildlife Conservation International and the Caribbean Conservation Corps takes its name from the Path of the Panther, a historical forested corridor that once spanned from Tierra del Fuego to Alaska. The ultimate dream is a Central American "biogeographic corridor," a contiguous chain of protected areas from Mexico to Colombia. Then the isthmus could once again be a bridge between continents for migrating species.

The most advanced of the transfrontier parks is the **La Amistad International Peace Park,** created in 1982 when Costa Rica and Panamá signed a pact to join two adjacent protected areas—one in each country—to create one of the richest ecological biospheres in Central America. UNESCO cemented the union by recognizing the binational zone as a biosphere reserve. La Amistad (the Friendship Park) covers 622,000 hectares and includes six Indian reserves and nine protected areas.

FAUNA

Anyone who has traveled in the tropics in search of wildlife can tell you that disappointment comes easy (and often at considerable expense). But Costa Rica is one place that lives up to its word. Costa Rica is nature's live theater—and the actors aren't shy.

My friend Lynn Ferrin wrote, "The birds are like jewels, the animals like creatures in a Rousseau painting." Noisy flocks of oropendolas, with long tails "the color of daffodils," sweep from tree to tree. The scarlet macaws are like rainbows, the toucans and hummingbirds like the green flash of sunset. The tiny poison-dart frogs, red and evil, are bright enough to scare away even the most dimwitted predator. And the electric-blue morphos, the neon narcissi of the butterfly world, make even the most unmoved of viewers gape in awe.

Then there are all the creatures that mimic other things and are harder to spot: insects that look like rotting leaves, moths that look like wasps, the giant *Caligo memnon* (cream owl) butterfly whose huge open wings resemble the wide-eyed face of an owl, and the mottled, bark-colored *machaca* (lantern fly), which is partly to blame for Costa Rica's soaring birthrate. According to local folklore, if a girl is stung by a *machaca* she must go to bed with her boyfriend within 24 hours or she will die.

Much of the wildlife is glimpsed only as shadows. (Some, like the dreaded fer-de-lance, for example, uncurling in the rotten leaves, you *hope* you don't meet.) Well-known animals that you are *not* likely to see are the cats—pumas, jaguars, margays, and ocelots—and tapirs and white-lipped peccaries. With patience, however, you can usually spot monkeys galore, as well as iguanas, quetzals, and three-toed sloths (looking,

as someone has said, like "long-armed tree-dwelling Muppets"), that get most of their aerobic exercise by scratching their bellies.

The **Instituto Nacional de Biodiversidad** (INBIO, National Institute of Biodiversity), a private, nonprofit organization formed in 1989, has been charged with the formidable task of collecting, identifying, and labeling every plant and animal species in Costa Rica. The task is expected to take at least 10 years to complete. "After 100 years of work by the National Museum we still only know 10-20% of what we have in the country," says Rodrigo Gómez, director of the NIBR. Over the course of the last 110 years, the National Museum collected some 70,000 specimens. In their first 18 months, the NIBR's hundreds of "parataxonomists" (ordinary citizens trained to gather and preserve specimens) gathered almost two million.

Identifying the species is a prodigious task, which every day turns up something new. Insects, for example, make up about half of the estimated 500,000 to one million plant and animal species in Costa Rica. The country is home seasonally to more than 850 bird species—10% of all known bird species (the U.S. and Canada combined have less than half that number). One source reports there are 5,000 different species of grasshoppers, 160 known amphibians, 220 reptiles, and 10% of all known butterflies (Corcovado National Park alone has at least 220 different species). It's like being caught up in a kind of zoological rush hour.

INBIO publishes the *Biodiversity of Costa Rica* newsletter. Look, too, for David Norman's excellent *Educational Pamphlet Series,* pocket booklets on individual species, Apdo. 387-3000 Heredia; $1.50 apiece.

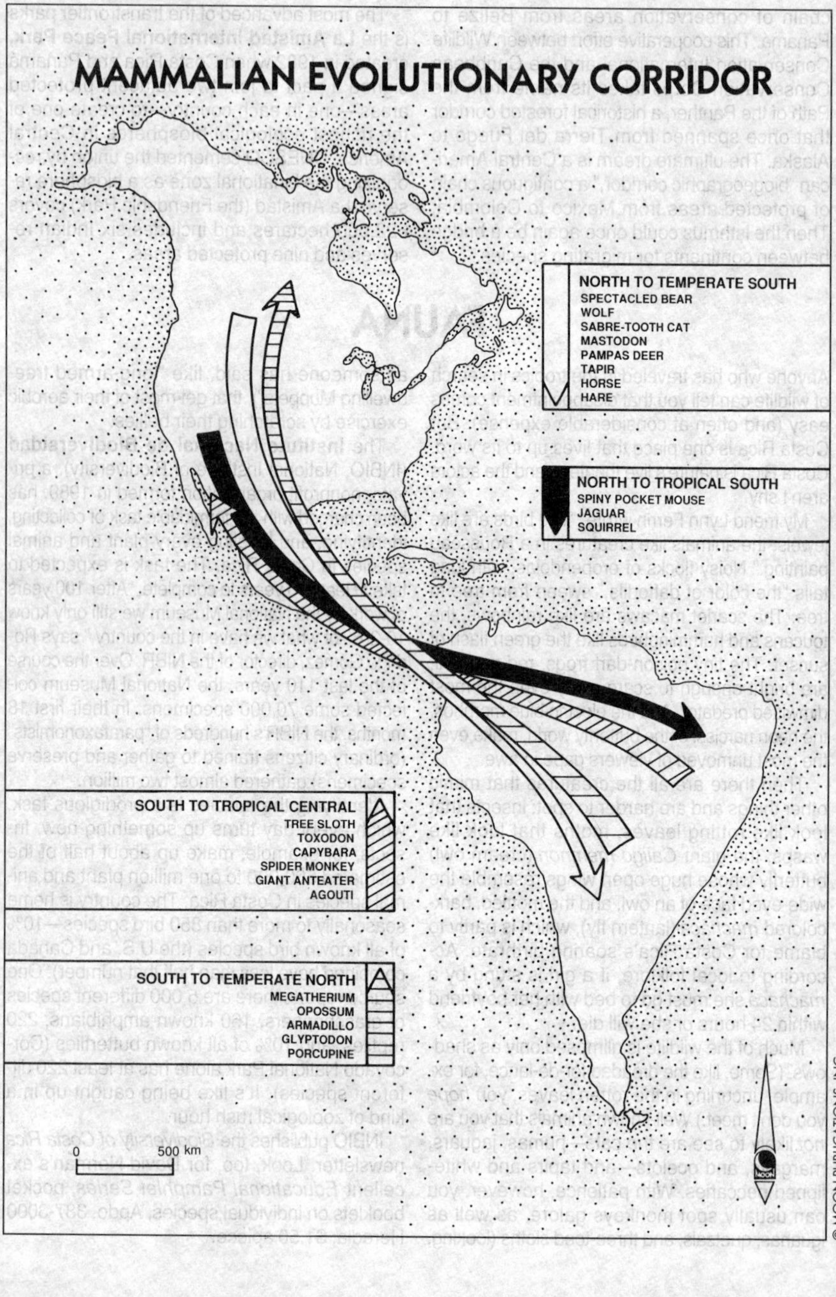

MAMMALIAN EVOLUTIONARY CORRIDOR

NORTH TO TEMPERATE SOUTH
SPECTACLED BEAR
WOLF
SABRE-TOOTH CAT
MASTODON
PAMPAS DEER
TAPIR
HORSE
HARE

NORTH TO TROPICAL SOUTH
SPINY POCKET MOUSE
JAGUAR
SQUIRREL

SOUTH TO TROPICAL CENTRAL
TREE SLOTH
TOXODON
CAPYBARA
SPIDER MONKEY
GIANT ANTEATER
AGOUTI

SOUTH TO TEMPERATE NORTH
MEGATHERIUM
OPOSSUM
ARMADILLO
GLYPTODON
PORCUPINE

0   500 km

© MOON PUBLICATIONS, INC.

Early Migrations

About three million years ago, the Central American isthmus began to rise from the sea to form the first tentative link between the two Americas. Going from island to island, birds, insects, reptiles, and the first mammals began to move back and forth between the continents. During this period, rodents of North America reached the southern continent, and so did the monkeys, which found the tropical climate to their liking.

In due course, South America connected with North America. Down this corridor came the placental mammals to dispute the possession of South America with the marsupial residents. Creatures poured across the bridge in both directions. The equids used it to enter South America, the opossums to invade North America. A ground sloth the size of an elephant headed north, too, reaching all the way to what is now Texas before it died out. Only a few South American mammals, notably armadillos, ground sloths, and porcupines, managed to establish themselves successfully in the north. The greatest migration was in the other direction.

A procession of North American mammals swarmed south, with disastrous effects on native populations. The mammals soon came to dominate the environment, diversifying into forms more appropriate to the tropics. In the course of this rivalry, many marsupial species disappeared, leaving only the tough, opportunistic opossums.

The isthmus has thus served as a "filter bridge" for the intermingling of species and the evolution of modern distinctive Costa Rican biota, a fairly recent amalgam as the isthmus has been in existence for only some three million years. Costa Rica's unique location and tropical setting, along with a great variety of local relief and microclimates, have meant that refuge areas for ancient species endangered by changes in environmental conditions have been widely available, and species that have died out elsewhere can still be found here. This, together with generous infusions of plants and animals from both continents, has resulted in a proliferation of species that in many important respects is vastly richer than the biota of either North or South America. Costa Rica's biota shares much with both.

MAMMALS

Given the rich diversity of Costa Rica's ecosystems, it may come as a surprise that only 200 mammal species—half of which are bats—live here. And Costa Rica, like most neotropical countries, is depauperate in marine mammal flora. Several species of dolphins and seven species of whales are common in Costa Rican waters, but there are no seals. And the only endemic species of any significance is the endangered manatee.

Before man hunted them to extinction, there were many more mammal species. Even today all large- and many small-mammal populations are subject to extreme pressure from hunting or habitat destruction, and it is only recently that large-mammal populations in the national parks are beginning to recover. Like most large mammals, jaguars and tapirs are shy and stay well clear of people. Sighting one would be cause for great celebration! Still, most visitors can expect to see representatives of one or more species of monkeys, one of Costa Rica's four ecologically unique tropical mammals; the others are sloths, anteaters, and noninsectivorous bats. And luck, patience, and the aid of a professional guide can lead to thrilling encounters with other species.

Early morning and late afternoon are the best times for wildlife viewing, particularly around waterholes (the dry regions of Guanacaste offer prime locations). I recommend joining a natural-history tour or guided day tours through one of the many tour companies specializing in wildlife programs.

The *Costa Rica Mammal Flip Chart,* by Anthony Schmitz, provides a handy, simple guide to 44 mammals—$6 plus $2 shipping; Rebecca Thompson, P.O. Box 1221, Centralia, WA 98531, tel. (206) 748-8731. No technical verbiage here; it's an informative little pocket-scale wonder replete with drawings of each mammal, plus range map, drawings of tracks, and other data for laypeople.

Anteaters

Anteaters are common in lowland and middle-elevation habitats throughout Costa Rica. Anteaters are purists and subsist solely on a diet of ants and termites, plus a few unavoidable bits of dirt. There is no doubt about what the best tool is for the job—a long tongue with zillions of microscopic spines. The anteater's toothless jaw is one long tube. When it feeds using its powerful forearms and claws to rip open ant and termite nests, its thong of a tongue flicks in and out of its tiny mouth, running deep into the galleries. Each time it withdraws, it brings with it a load of ants, which are scraped off inside the tunnel of its mouth and swallowed, to be ground down by small quantities of sand and gravel in its stomach.

The most commonly seen of Costa Rica's three anteater species is the tree-dwelling **lesser anteater** (or *tamandua* locally), a beautiful creature with a prehensile tail and the gold-and-black coloration of a panda bear. It can grow to 1.5 meters and weigh up to eight kilograms. One of my fondest memories is of seeing a *tamandua* climbing down a tree in Santa Rosa National Park. When it saw me, it climbed back up again!

The **giant anteater,** with its huge, bushy tail and astonishingly long proboscis, is now restricted to the less sparsely forested areas of the Osa Peninsula. It can grow to two meters long and when threatened rears itself on its hind legs and slashes wildly with its claws. It also raises its tail over its head. Even machetes cannot cut through the tough bristles; thus the fearsome critter is revered among *campesinos* for its magical abilities.

At night you may with luck see the strictly arboreal, cat-sized **silky anteater,** which can hang from its strong prehensile tail.

Bats

The most numerous mammals by far are the bats, found throughout Costa Rica. You may easily come across them slumbering by day halfway up a tree or roosting in a shed. In true Dracula fashion, most bats are lunarphobic: they avoid the bright light. On nights one week before and after the full moon, they suspend foraging completely and stay in their roosts while the moon is at its peak, probably for fear of owls.

Many bat species—like the giant **Jamaican fruit bat** *(murciélago frútero),* with a wingspan of more than 50 cm—are frugivores (fruit eaters) or insectivores, and quite harmless. The Jamaican bat favors figs, taken on the wing.

The **vampire bats** (Ticos call them *vampiros*)—which belong to the Neotropics, not Transylvania—are a different matter: they inflict an estimated $100 million of damage on domestic farm animals throughout Central and South America by transmitting rabies and other diseases. The vampire bat's modus operandi is almost as frightening as the stuff of Bram Stoker's *Dracula*. It lands on or close to a sleeping mammal, such as a cow. Using its two razor-sharp incisors, it then punctures the unsuspecting beast and, with the aid of an anticoagulant saliva, merrily squats beside the wound and laps up the blood while it flows. They're pretty much harmless to humans.

The most interesting of bats, however, and one easily seen in Tortuguero, is the **fishing bulldog bat** *(murciélago pescador),* with its huge wingspan (up to 60 cm across) and great gaff-shaped claws with which it hooks fish. It fishes by sonar. Skimming the water surface it is able to detect slight ripples ahead. The bat then drops its hooked feet at just the right moment and—presto!—supper.

Cats

Costa Rica boasts six members of the cat family. All are active by day and night, but being endangered, are rarely seen. Although they are legally protected and spotted cat trophies cannot be imported into the U.S., hunting of cats still occurs in Costa Rica. However, the main threat to the remaining jaguar population is deforestation.

One of the rarest of the wildcats is the **jaguarundi** (called *león breñero* locally), a dark-brown or tawny critter about the size of a large house cat. It has a long, slender body, short stocky legs, and a venal face with yellow eyes suggesting a nasty temperament. **Pumas** *(león)* also inhabit a wide variety of terrains, though they are rarely seen. This large cat—also called the "mountain lion"—is generally dun-colored, though its coloration varies markedly among individuals and from region to region.

jaguar

BOB RACE

The spotted cats include the cute-looking, house-cat-sized **margay** *(caucel),* which has a special joint that permits it to rotate its foot backwards, and its smaller cousin, the **oncilla.** Both wear an ocher coat spotted with black and brown spots, like tiny leopards. Their chests are white. The most commonly seen cat is the exquisitely spotted **ocelot** *(manigordo),* their larger cousin, which is well-distributed throughout the country and among various habitats; it grows to the size of a large dog.

Jaguars: Worshiped as a god in pre-Columbian civilizations, the jaguar is the symbol of the Central American jungle. *Panthera onca* (or *tigre* to locals) was once especially abundant in the dense forests, coastal mangroves, and lowland savannas of Central America. Today this magnificent and noble beast is an endangered species, rare except in parts of the larger reserves: Santa Rosa, Tortuguero, and Corcovado National Parks, the Río Macho Forest Reserve, and lower levels of the Cordillera Talamanca. In recent years, fortunately, jaguar sightings have been more common, suggesting that better preservation of their habitat is paying dividends.

While a few of the famous black "panther" variety exist, most Central American jaguars are a rich yellow, spotted with large black rosettes. Jaguars are the largest and most powerful of the American members of the cat family—a mature jaguar measures over two meters, stands 60 cm at the shoulders, and weighs up to 90 kg. The animal's head and shoulders are massive, the legs relatively short and thick. An adept climber and swimmer, the beast is a versatile hunter, at home in trees, on ground, and even in water. Not surprisingly, it feeds on a wide range of arboreal, terrestrial, and aquatic animals and is powerful enough to kill a full-grown cow.

Don't be surprised if you come across a jaguar's footprints alongside a mangrove islet or streambed in the gallery forest. Don't get your hopes up, however. You're not likely to see one prowling its territory or lying lazily by the riverbank (a favorite pastime), one paw dangling in the water, as it waits to flip out a passing fish or turtle.

Like all wild cats, jaguars are extremely shy, not particularly dangerous, and attack humans very rarely. When roads penetrate the primeval forest, the jaguar is among the first large mammals to disappear.

These splendid beasts are easily seen at the **Las Pumas Zoo** outside Cañas, where injured and orphaned cats are nursed back to health and/or prepared for a second life in the wild. Similarly, the **Profelis Wildcat Center,** near Dominical, welcomes tourists.

Deer

Yes, Costa Rica has two species of deer: the **red brocket deer** (called *cabro de monte*), which favors the rainforests, and the larger, more commonly seen **white-tailed deer** (*venado*), widely dispersed in habitats throughout the country, but especially Guanacaste. The former is slightly hump-backed and bronze. Males have single-prong horns. The latter—a smaller variant of its North American counterpart—varies from gray to red, normally with a white belly and a white dappled throat and face. Males have branched antlers.

Manatees

Anyone venturing to Tortuguero National Park or Gandoca-Manzanillo National Park will no doubt be hopeful of seeing a West Indian manatee. This herbivorous marine mammal has long been hunted for its flesh, which is supposedly tender and delicious, and for its very tough hide, once used for machine belts and high-pressure hoses. The heavily wrinkled beast looks like a tuskless walrus, with small round eyes, fleshy lips that hang over the sides of its mouth, and no hind limbs, just a large, flat, spatulate tail. Now endangered throughout their former range, these creatures once inhabited brackish rivers and lagoons along the whole coast of Central America's Caribbean shoreline. Today, only a few remain in the most southerly waters of the U.S. and isolated pockets of Central America. Tortuguero, where the animals are legally protected, has one of the few significant populations.

They are not easy to spot, for they lie submerged with only nostrils showing. Watch for rising bubbles in the water: manatees suffer from flatulence, a result of eating up to 45 kg of water hyacinths and other aquatic flora daily. The animals, sometimes called sea cows, can be huge, growing to four meters long and weighing as much as a ton. Good fortune may even provide an encounter with groups of manatees engaged in courtship ritual. Interestingly, the manatee is one of very few species in which males engage in homosexual activity. Affectionate animals, they kiss each other, sometimes swim with linked flippers, and always make solicitous parents.

Monkeys

Costa Rica has four species of monkeys: the cebus (or capuchin), howler, spider, and squirrel. Along with approximately 50 other species, they belong to a group called New World monkeys, which evolved from a single simian group that appeared about 40 million years ago in Africa and Asia. Some of these early primates migrated to North America and then down the land bridge to Central and South America.

Though the North American monkeys gradually died out, their southern cousins flourished and evolved along lines that differ markedly from those of their ancestors in the Old World. While African and Asian monkeys have narrow noses with nostrils that point down (much like human noses), New World monkeys evolved broad, widely spaced nostrils. New World females, too, evolved a singular ability to bear twins. And, perhaps most important, some New World species—notably the cebus, howler, and spider monkeys—developed long prehensile tails for added purchase and balance in the high treetops.

They inhabit a wide range of habitats, from the rainforest canopy to the scrubby undergrowth of the dry forests, though each species occupies its own niche and the species seldom meet. Together, they are the liveliest and most vocal jungle

tenants. Beyond the reach of most predators, they have little inhibition about announcing their presence with their roughhousing and howls, chatterings, and screeches. The sudden explosive roar of the howler monkey—a sound guaranteed to make your hair stand on end—is said to be the loudest sound in the animal kingdom.

The distinctive-looking **capuchin** is the smartest and most inquisitive of Central American simians. It derives its name from its black body and monklike white cowl. You've probably seen them dancing at the end of a tether at street fairs in Europe or South America—they're the little guys favored by organ-grinders worldwide. Capuchins range widely throughout the wet lowland forests of the Caribbean coast and the deciduous dry forests of the Pacific northwest below 1,500 meters. Two excellent places to see them are Santa Rosa and Manuel Antonio National Parks, where family troops are constantly on the prowl, foraging widely through the treetops and over the forest floor.

These opportunistic feeders are fun to watch as they search under logs and leaves or tear off bark as they seek out insects and small lizards soon after dawn and again in late afternoon. Capuchins also steal birds' eggs and nestlings. Some crafty coastal residents, not content with grubs and insect larvae, have developed a taste for oysters and other mollusks, which they break open on rocks. The frugal capuchin sometimes hoards his food for "rainy days." While their taste is eclec-

white-faced capuchin monkey

JEAN MERCIER

tic, they *are* fussy eaters: they'll meticulously pick out grubs from fruit, which they test for ripeness by smelling and squeezing. And capuchins are not averse to crop-raiding, especially corn, as the farmers of Guanacaste will attest.

The **howler** is the most abundant as well as the largest of Central American monkeys (it can weigh up to five kg). It inhabits both lowland and montane forests throughout Costa Rica. Fortunately, it is less sensitive to habitat destruction than the spider monkey and can be found clinging precariously to existence in many relic patches of forest.

While howlers are not particularly aggressive, they sure *sound* it! The stentorian males greet each new day with reveille calls that seem more like the explosive roars of lions than those of small arboreal leaf-eaters. The hair-raising vocalizations can carry for almost a mile in even the densest of jungle. The males sing in chorus again at dusk (or whenever trespassers get too close) as a spacing mechanism to keep rivals at a safe distance. Their Pavarotti-like vocal abilities are due to unusually large larynxes and throats that inflate into resonating balloons. Females generally content themselves with loud wails and groans—usually to signal distress or call a straying infant. This noisy yet sedentary canopy browser feeds on leaves (64% of its diet) and fruit. Although capable of eating anything that grows, howlers are extremely selective feeders.

The smallest Costa Rican primate, the **squirrel monkey**, or titi, grows to 25-35 cm, plus a tail up to 45 cm. It is restricted to the rainforests of the southern Pacific lowlands. Always on the go, day and night, they scurry about in the jungle understory and forest floor on all fours, where they are safe from raptor predators. Squirrels are more gregarious than most other monkeys; bands of 40 individuals or more are not uncommon. Like the larger capuchins, the golden-orange titi (with its face of white and black) is the arboreal goat of the forest. It will eat almost anything: fruits, insects, small lizards. In times of abundance (May-Oct.), the two species have been known to forage together. When food is scarce they become rivals; the heftier capuchin invariably is the victor. The titi is an endangered species well on its way to extinction.

The large, loose-limbed **spider monkey**—the supreme acrobat of the forest—was once the most widespread of the Central American monkeys. Unfortunately, they are very sensitive to human intrusion and are among the first primate species to decline with disturbance. The last few decades have brought significant destruction of spider monkey habitats, and land clearance and hunting (their flesh is said to be very tasty) have greatly reduced spider monkey populations throughout much of their former range. If you inadvertently come across them you'll soon know it: they often rattle the branches and bark and screech loudly to demonstrate their fearlessness.

These copper-colored acrobats can attain a length of a meter and a half. They have evolved extreme specialization for a highly mobile arboreal lifestyle. Long slender limbs allow spider monkeys to make spectacular leaps. But the spider's greatest secret is its extraordinary prehensile tail, which is longer than the combined length of its head and body. The underside is ridged like a human fingertip for added grip at the end of treetop leaps (it is even sensitive enough for probing and picking). You might even see individuals hanging like ripe fruit by their tails.

Gregarious by night (they often bed down in heaps), by day they are among the most solitary of primates. The males stay aloof from the females. While the latter tend to their young, which they carry on their backs, the males are busy marking their territory with secretions from their chest glands.

Peccaries

With luck you may come upon peccaries, but preferably at a distance. These wild pigs are notoriously fickle and potentially aggressive creatures whose presence in the rainforest may be betrayed by their pungent, musky odor and by the churned-up ground from their grubbing. Gregarious beasts, they forage in herds and make a fearsome noise if frightened or disturbed. Like most animals, they prefer to flee from human presence. Occasionally, however, an aggressive male may show his bravado by threatening to have a go at you, usually in a bluff charge. Rangers advise that you should climb a tree if threatened. The more common **collared peccary** *(saíno)* is marked by an ocher-colored band of hair running from its shoulders down to its nose; the rest of its body is dark brown. The larger **white-lipped peccary** *(cariblanco),* which can grow to one meter long, is all black, or brown, with a white mustache or "beard."

Raccoons

Raccoons, familiar to North Americans, are present throughout Costa Rica, where they are frequently seen begging tidbits from diners at hotel restaurants. The **northern raccoon** *(mapache* to Ticos) is a smaller but otherwise identical cousin of the North American raccoon, and can be found widely in Costa Rica's lowlands, predominantly in moist areas. The white-faced animal is unmistakable with its bandit-like black mask, and its tail of alternating black and white hoops. Don't mistake this animal with its cousin, the darker-colored **crab-eating raccoon,** found only along the Pacific coast,

Another endearing and commonly seen mammal is the long-nosed **coatimundi** (called *pizote* locally), the most diurnal member of the raccoon family, found throughout the country. Coatis wear many coats, from yellow to deepest brown, though all are distinguished by their faintly ringed tail, white-tipped black snout, and pandalike eye-rings. The animal is at home both on the ground and in the treetops, where it can sometimes be spotted moving from tree to tree. (The name coatimundi refers specifically to lone coatis; the animals are usually gregarious critters and are often seen in packs.) The animal has a fascinating defense technique against predators. When attacked, it raises itself on its hind leg, thrusts its tail between its legs, and waves its tail in front of its face. The attacker goes for the tail, giving the coati a chance to rake the predator in the eyes with its sharp claws. *Yow!* I've had several coatimundis walk past me without blinking an eye on wilderness trails.

Another charming member of the raccoon family is the small and totally nocturnal **kinkajou** (known to Ticos as the *martilla*) with its large limpid eyes and velvet-soft coat of golden brown. It's a superb climber (it can hang by its prehensile tail) and spends most of its life feeding on fruit, honey, and insects in the treetops. By day it is very drowsy; if picked up, its first instinct is to cuddle against your chest, bury its head to avoid the light, and drop back off to sleep. It's smaller cousins are the much rarer, grayish, bug-eyed **olingo** and the ring-tailed **cacomistle.**

Rodents

The **agouti** *(guatusa* to Ticos) is a large brown rodent related to the guinea pig and the size of a large house cat. It inhabits the forests up to 6,500 feet elevation, and is often seen by day feeding on the forest floor on fruits and nuts (the wet-forest agoutis are darker than their chestnut colored dry-forest cousins). It looks like a giant tailless squirrel with the thin legs and tip-toeing gait of a deer, but it sounds like a small dog. They are solitary critters that mark their turf with musk. They form monogamous pairs and produce two or three litters a year.

Agoutis have long been favored for their meat and they are voraciously hunted by humans. Their nocturnal cousin, the **paca** (called *tepezcuintle* by locals) also makes good eating—and can grow to a meter long and weigh 10 kg, three times larger than the agouti—and is favored by a wide variety of predators. It is brown with rows of white spots along its side. Both are easily captured because of the strong anal musks they use to scent their territories and because of their habit of running in circles but never leaving their home turf (pacas, at least, are intelligent enough to leap into water and stay submerged for a considerable time). If you disturb one in the forest, you may hear its high-pitched alarm bark before you see it.

Costa Rica also has five squirrel species, including the ubiquitous **variegated squirrel** *(chiza* or *ardilla tricolor* to locals), whose black, white, and red coloration varies in form. The brown and chestnut **red-tailed squirrel** *(ardilla roja)* is also common.

Costa Rica has about 40 species of rats, mice, and gophers.

Sloths

Ask anyone to compile a list of the world's strangest creatures and the sloth would be right up there with the duck-billed platypus. And while the creature moves with the grace and deliberation of a tai chi master, few would argue about the beast's ugly looks. The sloth, which grows to about the size of a medium-size dog, has a small head and flat face with snub nose, beady eyes, and rudimentary ears (its hearing is reputedly so poor that one can fire a gun within centimeters and its only response will be a slow turn of the head). Its long, bony arms are well-developed, however, with curving claws, which hook over and grasp the branches from which it spends almost its entire life suspended upside down.

The arboreal beast pays no attention to personal hygiene. Its shaggy fur harbors algae and mold that make the sloth greenly inconspicuous—wonderful camouflage from prowling jaguars and keen-eyed eagles, its chief predators. Hordes of mites and grubs graze on its moldy hair. And the sloth even has communities of moths that live in the depths of its fur and feed on the algae.

three-toed sloth

Lulled by its relative treetop security, the sloth, says naturalist David Attenborough, "has sunken into an existence just short of complete torpor." The creature spends up to 18 hours daily sleeping curled up with its feet drawn close together and its head tucked between the forelimbs. Actually, Costa Rica has two species of sloths: the **three-toed sloth** *(persozo de tres dedos)* and the nocturnal **Hoffman's two-toed sloth** *(perozoso de dos dedos)*. You're more likely to see the three-toed sloth, which is active by day.

At top speed a sloth can barely cover a mile in four hours. On the ground, it is even more awkward and crawls with great difficulty or simply falls on the ground. In fact, there's a very good reason sloths move at a rate barely distinguishable from rigor mortis.

A sloth's digestion works as slowly as its other bodily functions. Its metabolic rate is half that of other animals of similar size, and food remains in its stomach for up to a week. Hence, it has evolved a large ruminant-like stomach and intestinal tract to process large quantities of relatively indigestible food. To compensate, it has sacrificed heavy muscle mass—and, hence, mobility—to maximize body size in proportion to weight. Thus, the sloth has evolved as a compromise between a creature large enough to store and process large quantities of food and one light enough to move about in trees without breaking the branches.

When nature calls (about once a week), the animal descends to ground level, where it digs a small hole with its hind limbs. It then defecates into the depression, urinates, covers the broth with

leaves, and returns much relieved to its arboreal life. During this 30-minute period, the female "sloth moths" have been busy laying their eggs on the sloth dung. When hatched, the larvae feed and pulpate on the feces. The newly emerged adults then fly off to seek a new sloth.

Sloths, which may live up to 20 years or longer, reach sexual maturity at three years, a relatively old age for mammals of their size. Females give birth once a year (the gestation period is about six months) and spend half their adult lives pregnant. Although female sloths are never separated by choice from their offspring, they are peculiarly unsentimental about their young: if a baby tumbles, its plaintive distress calls go unheeded. And when the juvenile reaches six months old, the mother simply turns tail on her youngster, which inherits her "home range" of trees.

An easy way to find sloths is to look up into the green foliage of cecropia trees, which form one of the sloth's favorite food staples. More adventurous individuals might even be basking in the sunlight, feigning death halfway up a tree. The sloth's heavy fur coat provides excellent insulation against heat loss. Still, its body temperature drops almost to the temperature of its surroundings at night and, much like cold-blooded reptiles, the sloth needs to take in the sun's rays to bring its temperature to normal mammalian levels. The sight of a sloth languishing in open cecropia crowns is a heavenly vision to harpy eagles, which swoop in to snatch the torpid creature much like plucking ripe fruit.

Tapirs

Another symbol of the New World tropics is the strange-looking **Baird's tapir** *(danta* locally), a solitary, ground-living, plant-eating, forest-dwelling, ungainly mixture of elephant, rhinoceros, pig, and horse. The tapir uses its short, highly mobile proboscis—an evolutionary forerunner to the trunk of the elephant—for plucking leaves and shoveling them into its mouth. This endangered species is the largest indigenous terrestrial land mammal in Central America. Like its natural predator the jaguar, the tapir has suffered severely at the hands

ERIN DWYER

of man. The animal was common in Costa Rica and ranged far and wide in the lowland swamps and forests. It was even present in the bamboo thickets up to 3,000 meters elevation in the Talamanca mountains. Hunters have brought it to the edge of extinction.

Today, tapirs are found only in national parks and reserves where hunting is restricted, with the greatest density in Corcovado National Park, which has a population of fewer than 300. They have learned to be wary of man, and few travelers have the privilege of sighting them in the wild. Tapirs live in dense forests and swamps and rely on concealment for defense. They are generally found wallowing up to their knees in swampy waters. In fact, tapirs are rarely seen far from water, to which they rush precipitously at the first sign of danger. The animals make conspicuous trails in the forest, and because tapirs maintain territories which they mark with dung or scent, they are easily tracked by dogs.

Weasels

Costa Rica boasts seven members of the weasel family. The most ubiquitous is the skunk (*zorro* in local parlance), one of the most commonly seen—and smelled—mammal species, of which Costa Rica has three species. The black **striped hog-nosed skunk,** with its bushy white tail and white stripe along its rump, will be familiar to North Americans. The smaller **spotted skunk** and **hooded skunk** are more rarely seen. Their defense is a disgusting scent sprayed at predators from an anal gland.

Costa Rica is also home to a badger-like animal called the **grison,** another skunk-like member of the weasel family that can weigh three kg (seven pounds) and is often seen hunting alone or in groups in lowland rainforest during the day. The grison is gray, with a white stripe running across its forehead and ears, white eye patches, and a black nose, chest, and legs. It looks like a cross between a badger and an otter. Meter-long **otters**

manatee

(*perro de agua,* or water-dog, to locals) are most commonly seen in lowland rivers, especially in Tortuguero.

Its cousin, the sleek, long-haired, chocolate-brown **tayra** (locals call it *tolumuco*)—a meter-long giant of the weasel family—resembles a mix of grison and otter. It is often seen in highland habitats throughout Costa Rica. Weighing up to five kg, the tayra habitually preys on rodents but can make quick work of small deer. Keep an eye off the ground, too, particularly in Santa Rosa National Park, where tayras can sometimes be seen stalking squirrels in the crowns of deciduous trees with a motion so fluid they seem to move like snakes.

Other Mammals

The mostly nocturnal and near-blind **nine-banded armadillo** *(cusuco),* an armor-plated oddity, and one of only two of the 20 or so species of *edentates* found in Costa Rica, will be familiar to anyone from Texas. The animal can grow to almost one meter long. They are terrestrial dwellers that grub about on the forest floor, feeding on insects and fungi. The female lays a single egg that, remarkably, divides to produce identical triplets. Its smaller cousin, the **naked-tailed armadillo** is far less frequently seen.

The dog family is represented by the brown-gray **coyote** and nocturnal **gray fox,** both found mostly in the dry northwestern regions.

The marsupials—mammals whose embryonic offspring crawl from the birth canal and are reared in an external pouch—are represented by nine species of opossums, including the black-and-gray banded, long-legged **water opossum** and the two-toned, short-legged **common opossum** *(zorro pelón),* a large rat-like critter with a dark brown body and tan underside, and a more lively disposition than normal—this opossum defends itself rather than feigning death.

ERIN DWYER

The blunt-nosed, short-spined, **prehensile-tailed porcupine** *(puerco espín)* is also present, though being nocturnal and arboreal is rarely seen. There are also two species of **rabbits** *(conejos)*.

REPTILES AND AMPHIBIANS

Costa Rica is home to approximately 160 species of amphibians and more than 200 species of reptiles, half of them snakes.

Crocodiles and Caimans

Many travelers visit Costa Rica in the hope of seeing American crocodiles and caimans, the croc's diminutive cousins. In fact, both species are easily seen in the wet lowlands, especially in small creeks, *playas,* and brackish mangrove swamps, or basking on the banks of streams and ponds. They are superbly adapted for water. Their eyes and nostrils are atop their heads for easy breathing and vision (and smell) while otherwise entirely submerged, and their thick, muscular tails provide tremendous propulsion.

To this reptile, home is a "gator hole" or pond, a system of trails, and a cavelike den linked by a tunnel to the hole. As it moves between its nest and its pond and along its trails through the aquatic vegetation, it helps keep the water open and clear. Enriched by the crocs' droppings and by the remains of its meals, the waters around the holes supports a rich growth of algae and higher plants, which in turn support a profusion of animal life. The croc also helps maintain the health of aquatic watersystems by weaning out weak and large predatory fish.

Mating season begins in December, when males are overcome with a desire to find a female. The polygamous males (males form harems) will defend their breeding turf from rival suitors with bare-toothed gusto. When estrous females approach, the ardent male gets very excited and goes through a nuptial dance, roaring intensely and even kicking up clouds of spray with his lashing tail. A curtsey by the damsel and the male clasps her ardently with his jaws, their tails intertwine, and the mating is over before you can wipe the steam from your camera.

A female crocodile selects a spot above the high-water mark and exposed to both sunlight and shade, then makes a large nest mound out of sticks, soft vegetation and mud, which she hollows to make room for her eggs (usually between 30 and 70). Eggs are laid March-May, during dry season. The creature is an exceptional guardian. She will guard the nest and keep it moist for several months after laying. The rotting vegetation creates heat, which incubates the eggs. When they are ready to hatch, the hatchlings pipe squeakily and she uncovers the eggs and takes the babies into a special pouch inside her mouth. She then swims away with the youngsters peering out between a palisade of teeth. The male assists, and soon the young crocs are feeding and playing in a special nursery, guarded by the two watchful parents (only 10% of newborn hatchlings survive; 90% survive in captive breeding programs). For all their beastly behavior, crocodiles are devoted parents.

Despite being relics from the age of the dinosaurs, croc brains are far more complex than those of other reptiles. They are sharp learners (in the Tempisque basin, crocs have been seen whacking tree trunks with their tails to dislodge chicks from their nests) They also have an amazing immunology system that can even defeat gangrene. Cuba is looking at the commercial potential, including extraction and development of potential medicines and, purportedly, aphrodisiacs. **Granja de Cocodrilos,** in Jacó, is a crocodile-breeding farm open to visitors.

American crocodiles (not to be confused with the American alligator that inhabits the Florida Everglades) have been heavily hunted for their skins until their numbers were so reduced that by the 1960s they were almost extinct. Perhaps because crocodiles (called *lagartos* or *cocodrilos* locally) have ugly toothy leers and a stigma of primeval wickedness, there hasn't been the same love of crocs that has brought international support for the turtles. As biologist David Janzen says: "We may never again see the huge four-meter animals that used to terrify the *campesinos* and eat their dogs." Fortunately, since the 1970s, the American crocodile has been protected under the Convention on International Trade in Endangered Species and making a strong comeback, repopulating many rivers from which it has been absent for years. It can easily be seen in dozens of rivers throughout the lowlands and estuaries along the Pacific coastline. A study in 1992 found as many as 240 crocodiles per mile in sections of the Tárcoles River, far higher than anywhere else in Costa Rica.

The creatures, which can live 80 years or more and reach 15 feet (4.5 meters) in length, spend much of their days basking on mudbanks, maintaining an even body temperature, which they regulate by opening their gaping mouths. At night, they sink down into the warm waters of the river for the hunt. The American crocodile—one of four species of New World crocodiles—is generally a fish-eater, but older adults are known to vary their diet with meat . . . so watch out! Although they are commonly thought to be sluggish, crocodiles, who prefer stealth, can run very fast in short bursts. Crocs cannot chew. They simply snap, tear, and swallow. Powerful stomach acids dissolve everything, including bones. A horrible way to go!

One of the smallest of western crocodilians—no more than six feet (two meters) long—and possibly the most abundant in existence today, the speckled **caiman** (called *guajipal* locally) is still relatively common in parts of wet lowland Costa Rica on both the Atlantic and Pacific coasts. Palo Verde and Tortuguero are both good places to spot them in small creeks, *playas,* and brackish mangrove swamps, or basking on the banks of streams and ponds.

The scales of the caiman take on the blue-green color of the water it slithers through. Such camouflage and even the ability to breathe underwater, through nostrils raised just above the surface, have not protected the caiman. Their nests are heavily disturbed by dogs, foxes, tegu lizards, and humans. And increasingly they are being sought for their skins, which are tragically turned into trivia. Ironically, this is easing the pressure on the crocodiles, which are fast disappearing as humanity takes their hides and habitats.

Caiman or croc? It's easy to tell. Besides being smaller, the former is dark brown with darker bands around its tail, and holds its head high when sunning. The crocodile is an olive color with black spots on its tail.

Iguanas and Lizards

The most common reptile you'll see is the dragonlike, tree-dwelling iguana, which seems to have little fear of man and can grow to a meter in length. You'll spot them in all kinds of forest habitats, crawling through the forest leaf litter or basking for long hours on branches that hang over water, its preferred route of escape when threatened. They are most common in drier areas below 2,500 feet elevation.

There's no mistaking this reptilian nightmare for any other lizard. Its head—the size of a man's fist—is crested with a frightening wig of leathery spines, its heavy body encased in a scaly hide, deeply wrinkled around the sockets of its muscular legs. Despite its menacing *One Million Years B.C.* appearance, it is quite harmless, a nonbelligerent vegetarian with a fondness for leaves and fruit.

There are two species in Costa Rica: the **green** and the **spiny-tailed** iguana. The green iguana *(Iguana iguana),* which is a dull to bright green, with a black-banded tail, can grow to two meters long. The males turn a bright orange when they get ready to mate in November/December and choose a lofty perch from which to advertise their showy dewlap, sexual flush, and erect crest of spines (they revert to darker green by night). The horny male will forego food for six weeks to win over the love of his life. Females nest in holes in the ground, then abandon their eggs (fewer than five percent of hatchlings will survive to adulthood).

The smaller, gray or tan-colored spiny iguana, also called the **ctenosaur** *(Iguana negra)*—known locally as the *garrobo*—has a tail banded with rings of hard spines that it uses to guard against predators by blocking the entrance to holes in trees or the ground.

Campesinos and local gourmands, for reasons you may not wish to know, call the green iguana the "tree chicken." (The iguana population of neighboring countries has been decimated for meat, spurring a cross-border commerce of iguanas; fortunately, Costa Ricans are not avid consumers of iguana meat.) The ctenosaur is considered even more edible, and you may see them on sale in *mercados* of major cities. The KekoLdi Indian Reserve and Iguana Park, near Orotina, both have projects to raise iguanas for meat.

Iguanas are territorial. They defend their turf aggressively against competitors. The first warning sign is a head bobbing. Often, the defending iguana will become lighter in color, like a chameleon.

Another miniature dinosaur is *Basilicus basilicus,* or **Jesus Christ lizard,** a Pacific lowland dweller common in Santa Rosa, Palo Verde, and Corcovado National Parks. These, too, have large crests atop their heads, backs, and tails, and use water as their means of escape, running across it on hind legs (hence, their name).

Snakes
Although rarely seen by the casual tourist in Costa Rica, the 138 species of snakes make up more than half of all reptile species in the nation. Wherever you are in the country snakes are sure to be about. They are reclusive, however, and it is a fortunate traveler indeed who gets to see in the wild the fantastically elongated **chunk-headed snake,** with its catlike elliptical eyes, or the slender, beak-nosed, bright green vinelike **vine snake.**

Among the more common snake species you are likely to see are the wide-ranging and relatively benign **boas,** which, with luck, you might spot crawling across a cultivated field or waiting patiently in the bough of a tree in wet or dry tropical forest, savanna, or dry thorn scrub. Boas are aggressive when confronted: though not poisonous, they are quite capable of inflicting serious damage with their large teeth and will not hesitate to bite. Heaven forbid a full-grown adult (three meters or more) should sink its teeth in sufficiently to get its constricting coils around you!

Here are two fascinating tidbits to sink your teeth into. The **coffee palm viper** is a heat-seeking missile that can detect 1/3,000° C per meter! And *Clelia clelia* eats only other snakes and likes its salsa *muy caliente*—it prefers the fearsome fer-de-lance.

Venomous Snakes: Only 18 species of snakes in Costa Rica are venomous (nine are *very* venomous), including a species of tropical **rattlesnake** found in Guanacaste and a few relic areas of the Meseta Central. It produces a venom considerably more toxic than its North American cousin—blindness and suffocation are typical effects on humans—and it rarely uses its well-developed rattle to warn off the unwary. All Costa Rica's poisonous snakes produce the same venom except the coral snake. Hence there are two anti-venoms: one for the coral snake and a second for all others.

The most talked-about snake in Central America is the **fer-de-lance,** much feared for its aggressiveness—it accounts for 80% of all snake bites in Costa Rica—and lethal venom. One of several Central American pit vipers—another is the **bushmaster**—the fer-de-lance can grow to a length of three meters and is abundant throughout the country, particularly in overgrown fields and river courses in drier lowland regions. Costa Ricans call this lethal creature *terciopelo,* Spanish for "velvet." As juveniles, fer-de-lance are arboreal critters that feed on lizards and frogs, which they attract with a yellow-tipped tail. As adults, they come down to earth, where they move about at night and, by daylight, rest in loose coils of burnished brown on the forest floor.

Give the fer-de-lance a wide berth! Unlike other vipers, which usually slither away at the approach of humans and will not strike unless provoked, the fer-de-lance stands its ground and will bite with little provocation. The snake's powerful venom dissolves nerve tissue and destroys blood cells and artery walls; those fortunate enough to survive may suffer paralysis or tissue damage so massive as to require amputation of the bitten limb. The fer-de-lance frequently disgorges venom, which is said to smell like dog shit—a good warning sign when hiking.

Among the more colorful snakes are the four species of **coral snakes,** with small heads, blunt tails, and bright bands of red, black, and yellow or white. These *highly* venomous snakes (often fatal to humans) exhibit a spectacular defensive display: they flatten their bodies and snap back and forth while swinging their heads side to side and coiling and waving their tails.

Along the Pacific beaches, you may sometimes encounter venomous pelagic **sea snakes,** yellow-bellied and black-backed serpents closely related to terrestrial cobras and coral snakes. This gregarious snake has developed an oarlike tail to paddle its way through the ocean. It tends to drift passively with its buddies among drift-lines of flotsam, where it feeds on small fish.

The Serpentario in San José, Parque Viborona near Pochotel, and El Mundo de los Serpientes (World of Snakes) near Grecia, are good places to learn to identify snakes and their habits and habitats. There is also a snake laboratory at the Clodomiro Picando Institute in Coronado, where you can watch snakes being milked for venom.

Turtles

Six of the world's eight species of marine turtles nest on Costa Rica's beaches, and you can see turtles laying eggs somewhere in Costa Rica virtually anytime of year.

Tortuguero National Park, in northeastern Costa Rica, is one of fewer than 30 places in the world that the **green turtle** considers clean and safe enough to lay its eggs. Although green turtles were once abundant throughout the Caribbean, *green sea turtle* today there are only three important sites in the region where they nest: one on Aves Island, 62 km west of Montserrat, a second at Gandoca-Manzanillo (and occasionally on beaches north toward Cahuita), and another at Tortuguero, the only major nesting site in the western Caribbean. June through November, peaking Aug.-Sept., more than 5,000 greens swim from their feeding grounds as far away as the Gulf of Mexico and Venezuela to lay their eggs at the eons-old nesting site on the oceanside 21-km stretch of beach on Tortuguero's barrier island.

On the Pacific coast, the most spectacular nestings are at Playa Nancite, in Santa Rosa National Park, and Ostional Wildlife Refuge, where tens of thousands of **olive ridley turtles** come ashore July-Dec. in synchronized mass nestings known as *arribadas* (see special topic, **Respite for the Ridley,** in the Nicoya Peninsula chapter). Giant **leatherback turtles,** which can weigh as much as a ton and reach a length of three meters, nest at Playa Grande, near Tamarindo, Oct.-April (see special topic, **The Leatherback Turtle,** in the Nicoya Peninsula chapter). Hawksbills, ridleys, leatherbacks, Pacific greens and occasionally loggerheads (primarily Caribbean nesters) appear in lesser numbers at other beaches along the Pacific coast.

Terrestrial turtles are also common in Costa Rica, particularly in the Caribbean lowlands, where you can see them going about their business in the midmorning hours and after heavy rains. One species—the red turtle, found in northern Pacific lowlands—is particularly easy to spot: its high-domed carapace is gaudily patterned in oranges, reds, yellows, and blacks.

Several species of aquatic turtles also frequent the swamps and creeks. Look for them squatting on partially submerged logs.

Turtle Turmoils: One hundred years ago, green turtles were as numerous as the bison on the North American plains. They were highly prized for their meat by Central American and Carib Indians, who netted and harpooned them. And British and Spanish fleets, buccaneers, and merchantmen counted on turtle meat to feed their crews while cruising in New World waters. An average adult green turtle weighs 115 kg.

They're easy to catch and easy to keep alive for weeks on their backs in a space no bigger than the turtle itself. ("Turtle turners" patrolled nesting beaches, where they wrestled female turtles on to their backs to be picked up the next day.)

The end of colonialism offered no respite. Large-scale green turtle export from Tortuguero, for example, began in 1912 when turtle soup became a delicacy in Europe. And the recurrent massing of olive ridley turtles at a few accessible beaches fostered intensive human exploitation. Despite legislation outlawing the taking of turtle eggs or disturbance of nesting turtles, nest sites continue to be raided by humans (encouraged by an ancient Mayan legend that says the eggs are aphrodisiacs).

When not nesting in Costa Rica, Pacific ridleys congregate in Mexican and Ecuadorian waters, where commercial exploitation continues in earnest. Turtle oil is used in the manufacture of cosmetics and perfumes, the shells used in jewelry and ornaments, and the offal dried and processed as fertilizer. Hawksbills, which rarely exceed 55 kg, are hunted illegally for the tourist trade: one occasionally still sees stuffed turtle specimens for sale.

Mother Nature, too, poses her own challenges. Coatis, dogs, raccoons, and peccaries dig up nest sites to get at the tasty eggs. Gulls, vultures, and hungry frigate birds, with their piercing eyes and sharp beaks, pace the beach hungrily awaiting the hatchlings; crabs lie in wait for the tardy; and hungry jacks, barracudas, and sharks come close to shore for the feast. Ridley hatchlings have even been found in the stomachs of leatherback turtles. Of the hundreds of eggs laid by a female in one season, only a handful will survive to reach maturity. (As many as 70% of the hatchlings are eaten before they reach the water.)

Most of the important nesting sites in Costa Rica are now protected, and access to some is restricted. Still, there is a shortage of undisturbed beaches where turtles can safely nest. Most turtle populations continue to decline because of illegal harvesting and environmental pressures, despite the best efforts of conservationists inspired by Dr. Archie Carr, of the University of Florida, who has written and lectured indefatigably on behalf of turtle protection (see **Tortuguero National Park** in the Caribbean Coast chapter).

Turtle Ecology: Turtles have hit on a formula for outwitting their predators, or at least for surviving despite them. Each female normally comes ashore 2-6 times each season and lays an average of 100 eggs on each occasion. Some marvelous internal clock arranges for most eggs to hatch at night when hatchlings can make their frantic rush for the sea concealed by darkness. Often, baby turtles will emerge from the eggs during the day and wait beneath the surface of the beach until nightfall. The young hatch together and dig their way up and out through up to a meter of sand as a kind of "simple-minded, cooperative brotherhood," says Archie Carr, "working mindlessly together to lower the penalties of being succulent on a hostile shore." They are programmed to travel fast across the beach to escape the hungry mouths. Even after reaching the sea they continue to swim frantically for several days—flippers paddling furiously—like clockwork toys.

No one knows where baby turtles go. They swim off and generally are not seen again until they appear years later as adults. Turtles are very slow growing; most immature turtles of all

---

WHERE THE TURTLES NEST

CARIBBEAN

Tortuguero: Loggerheads and hawksbills come ashore year-round, but especially in August. The major attraction is green turtles, which nest here June-Nov. in vast numbers.

Barra de Matina Beach: Leatherbacks, greens, and hawksbills come ashore at this private sanctuary north of Puerto Limón.

Gandoca-Manzanillo Wildlife Refuge: Four species of turtles lay their eggs, Jan.-April, on this beautiful beach south of Punta Uva. April and May are the best months to spot leatherbacks. By July, they are gone, replaced by greens, which can be seen in large numbers through September. Hawksbills also come ashore year-round, mostly March-August.

PACIFIC

Curú Wildlife Refuge: Three species of turtles come ashore at this private refuge, on the eastern coast of the Nicoya Peninsula.

Las Baulas Marine National Park: Playa Grande is Costa Rica's preeminent nesting site for leatherback turtles. It has evolved into perhaps the nation's best-managed site. Leatherbacks come ashore Oct.-April; up to 100 on any one night. Olive ridley and green turtles can be seen here in small numbers May-August. There's a splendid turtle museum.

Ostional National Wildlife Refuge: This 248-hectare refuge, north of Playa Nosara, protects the major nesting site of olive ridleys (locally called *lora*). It is one of two sites in Costa Rica where synchronized mass nestings (*arribadas*) of the olive ridley occur, at two- to four-week intervals (generally between the third quarter and full moon) April-Dec., with a peak in July-September. During each *arribada* (which may last 4-8 days), up to 120,000 turtles may nest at Ostional. Solitary nesters can be seen on most nights. Leatherbacks and Pacific greens also nest here.

Playa Nancite: Located in Santa Rosa National Park, Nancite—which is off-limits to anyone but scientists—is the second major site for *arribadas*. Some 200,000 ridleys choose Nancite. Leatherbacks and Pacific greens also nest here. Peak arrival for ridleys (called *carpentaria* locally) is midsummer, with a peak in October.

Turtles come ashore at many other beaches along the Pacific coast, notably beaches south of Playa Sámara in Nicoya, and along the southern Pacific coast.

VOLUNTEER PROGRAMS TO SAVE THE TURTLES

If you're interested in helping save turtles, consider volunteering services to the following organizations.

The **Caribbean Conservation Corps**, P.O. Box 2866, Gainesville, FL 32602, tel. (352) 373-6441 or (800) 678-7853, fax (352) 375-2449; in Costa Rica, P.O. Box 246-2050, San Pedro, tel. (506) 224-9215, fax 225-7516, e-mail: ccc@cccturtle.org, enlists volunteers to patrol Tortuguero during nesting season to protect the nests from poaching and help with research and tagging. Enclose $1 and a stamped, self-addressed business-size envelope with your request for information to help defray costs for this nonprofit organization. The CCC has an 18-minute video on the turtles of Tortuguero ($14.95).

The **Earth Island Institute**, 300 Broadway, San Francisco, CA 94133, tel. (415) 788-3666 or (800) 859-SAVE (800-859-7283), has a "Sea Turtle Restoration Project" in which paying guests count and tag turtles, take radio-transmitter readings, and perform other duties at Playa Nancite, Punta Banco, and Ostional. Trips usually last eight days.

Volunteers with the **Foundation for Field Research**, P.O. Box 2010, Alpine, CA 92001, tel. (619) 445-9264, help biologists in a leatherback turtle study program as well as patrol nesting beaches. Five- to 15-day programs are offered at selected times of the year.

Youth Challenge International, 11 Soho St., Toronto, Ont., Canada M5T 1Z6, tel. (416) 971-9846, accepts volunteers for its "Turtle Project" at Playa Ostional.

species increase in carapace length by less than three cm a year. In fact, little is known about the lives of adult marine turtles. In captivity, a turtle can grow to the size of the smallest fertile nester in about 10 years; in the wild, they grow much slower.

Turtles are great travelers capable of amazing feats of navigation. Greens, for example, navigate across up to 1,500 miles of open sea to return, like salmon, to the same nest site. Guided presumably by stars and currents, thousands of greens arrive at Tortuguero every year from their faraway feeding grounds. (Most Tortuguero greens apparently arrive from the Miskito Bank feeding area of Nicaragua.)

One of the few things known about the intervals between females' trips to the nesting beaches is that a lot of strenuous romance goes on out in the surf. There is no pair-bonding between individual turtles, and each female may be courted by as many as 10 males.

"Sea turtles in love are appallingly industrious," according to Archie Carr. "The male turtle holds himself in the mating position on top of the smooth, curved, wet shell of the wave-tossed female by employing a three-point grappling rig [consisting] of his long, thick, curved, horn-tipped tail and a heavy, hooked claw on each front flipper. . . . The female generally stays coy and resistant for what seems an unnecessarily long while. Other males gather, and all strive together over the female in a vast frothy melee." In the frenzy of mating, intelligence seems sadly lacking. Females have been mounted by a male who in turn is mounted by another male while several more jealous males jostle and bite one another to dislodge the successful Casanova.

Most females make their clumsy climb up the beach and lay their eggs under the cover and cool of darkness (loggerheads and ridleys often nest in the daytime, as they seem less timid). They normally time their arrival to coincide with high tide, when they can swim in over the coral reef and when they do not have to drag themselves puffing and panting across a wide expanse of beach. Their great weight, unsupported by water, makes breathing difficult. As a turtle drags her ponderous bulk up the beach, her progress is slow and punctuated by numerous halts to breathe. Some turtles even die of heart attacks brought on by the exertions of digging and laying.

Once she settles on a comfortable spot above the high tide mark, the female scoops out a large body pit with her front flippers. Then her amazingly dexterous hind flippers go to work hollowing out a small egg chamber below her tail and into which white, spongy, golf-ball-size spheres fall every few seconds. After shoveling the sand back into place and flinging sand wildly about to hide her precious treasure, she makes her way back to sea.

The eggs normally take 6-8 weeks to hatch, incubated by the warm sand. The sex of the hatchling is determined by the temperature of the sand: males are predominantly produced in cooler sand; a difference of 2-3 degrees Celsius will produce females. Thus, hatchlings from any one nest site are usually siblings of the same gender.

Note: When near nesting sites, respect the turtles' need for peace and quiet. Nesting turtles are very timid and extremely sensitive to flashlights, sudden movements, and noise, which will send a female turtle in hasty retreat to the sea without laying her eggs. Sometimes she will drop her eggs on the sand in desperation, without digging a proper nest.

Frogs and Toads

The amphibians are primarily represented by the dozens of species of frogs and toads, most of which you're probably more likely to hear than to see. That catlike meow? That's Boulenger's hyla, one of Costa Rica's more than 20 kinds of toxic frogs. That sharp tink, tink that is usually the most prominent sound on damp nights in Costa Rica's midelevation rainforests? That's the tiny tink frog, of course. That insectlike buzz is probably two bright-red poison-arrow frogs wrestling belly-to-belly for the sake of a few square meters of turf. And the deafening choruses of long loud whoops that resound through the night in Nicoya and the adjacent lowlands of Guanacaste? That's an orgiastic band of ugly, orange and purple-black Mexican burrowing toads doing their thing. Should you locate them—the sound carries for miles—don't be surprised to find the horny toads floating like balloons with legs outstretched, emitting their lusty whoops. Love's a strange thing!

Of all Central America's exotic species none are more colorful—literally and figuratively—than the **poison-arrow frogs,** of the type from which Indians extract deadly poisons with which to tip their arrows. Frogs are tasty little fellows to carnivorous amphibians, reptiles, and birds. Hence, in many species, the mucous glands common in all amphibians have evolved to produce a bitter-tasting poison.

In Central and South America at least 20 kinds of frogs have developed this defense still further: their alkaloid poisons are so toxic that they can paralyze a large bird or small monkey immediately. Several species—the dendrobatids, or poison-arrow frogs, which are confined to Costa Rica—produce among the most potent toxins known: atelopidtoxin, bufogenin, bufotenidine, and bufotoxin. Pity the poor snake that gobbles up *Dendrobatis granuliferus,* a tiny, bright green, red, and black frog that inhabits the lowland forests of the Golfo Dulce region (it is commonly seen on forest floors of Corcovado National Park). Another species, *Bufo marinus,* can even squirt its poison in a fine spray. And some species' eggs and tadpoles even produce toxins, making them unpalatable, like bad caviar!

Of course, it's no value to an individual frog if its attacker dies *after* devouring the victim. Hence, many have developed conspicuous, strik-

poison-arrow frog

JEAN MERCIER

ing colors—bright yellow, scarlet, purple, and blue, the colors of poison recognized throughout the animal world—and sometimes "flash colors" (concealed when at rest but flashed at appropriate times to startle predators) that announce, "Beware!" These confident critters don't act like other frogs either. They're active by day not night, moving boldly around the forest floor, "confident and secure," says one writer, "in their brilliant livery."

Perhaps the most famous poison frog species is the **golden toad**, found only in the Monteverde Cloud Forest Preserve. In fact, the montane rainforest reserve owes its existence in part to the discovery of *Bufo periglenes*. This brilliant, neon orange arboreal toad—discovered in 1964 and so stunning that one biologist harbored "a suspicion that someone had dipped the examples in enamel paint"—may now exist only on the cover of tourist brochures. The males are the orange ones; females are yellow and black with patches of scarlet.

April through May, toads go looking for love in the rainpools of scarlet bromeliads that festoon the high branches. Here, high in the trees, tadpoles of arboreal frogs wriggle about.

Adaptive Breeding: Few Costa Rican frog species breed in permanent bodies of water, where fish predation is intense. Above 1,500 meters, where there are no native fish species, stream breeding is more common, although the introduction in recent years of trout into upland streams already threatens whole frog populations.

The frogs instead have evolved away from dependence on bodies of permanent water. Many species, particularly the 39 species of hylids, spend their entire lives in the tree canopies where they breed in holes and bromeliads. The hylids have enlarged suction-cup pads on their toes. They often catch their prey in midair leaps: the suction discs guarantee surefooted landings. Others deposit their eggs on vegetation over streams; the tadpoles fall when hatched. Others construct frothy foam nests, which they float on pools, dutifully guarded by the watchful male.

Some rainforest species, such as the diminutive and warty eleutherodactylus—its name is longer than its body—live on the ground, where they lay their eggs in moist cups of leaves. The tadpole develops fully within the egg sac before emerging as a perfect, if tiny, replica of its parents:

it and 12 of its siblings could easily fit on a man's fingernail. Some tadpole species—the *Hyla zeteki*, for example—are cannibalistic: they eat other frogs' tadpoles. The carnivorous smoky frog *(Leptodactylus pentadactylus)*, an aggressive giant (adults can grow up to 20 cm long), can eat snakes up to 50 cm long. It, too, can emit a poisonous toxin, to which some snakes are immune. If the smoky frog's loud hissing, inflated body, and poisonous secretions don't manage to scare off its predator, it has another ingenious defense: when captured it emits a loud scream.

BIRDS

In William Henry Hudson's *Green Mansions,* his great romantic novel of the American tropics, the young hero Abel is lured into the jungle by the mysterious call of an unseen bird. So stirred is he by the siren song that he follows the haunting sound deeper and deeper into the forest until he eventually discovers the source: a lovely, half-wild girl called Rima, who has learned to mimic the sounds of the birds. The birdlife of Costa Rica is so rich and so varied—and often so elusive—that at times it seems as if Rima herself is calling.

With approximately 850 recorded bird species, the country boasts one-tenth of the world's total. More than 630 are resident species; the remainder are occasionals who fly in for the winter. Birds that have all but disappeared in other areas still find tenuous safety in protected lands in Costa Rica, though many species face extinction from deforestation. The nation offers hope for such rare jewels of the bird world as the quetzal and the scarlet macaw, both endangered species yet commonly seen in protected reserves.

It may surprise you to learn that in a land with so many exotic species the national bird is the relatively drab *yiguirro,* or clay-colored **robin,** a brown-and-buff bird with brick-red eyes. You may hear the male singing during the March-May breeding season when, according to *campesino* folklore, he is "calling the rains."

The four major "avifaunal zones" roughly correspond to the major geographic subdivisions of the country: the northern Pacific lowlands, the southern Pacific lowlands, the Caribbean lowlands, and the interior highlands. Guanacaste's dry habitats (northern Pacific lowlands) share relatively few species with other parts of the country. This is a superlative place, however, for waterfowl: the estuaries, swamps, and lagoons that make up the Tempisque Basin support the richest freshwater avifauna in all Central America, and Palo Verde National Park, at the mouth of the Tempisque, is a birdwatcher's mecca. The southern Pacific lowland region is home to many South American neotropical species, such as jacamars, antbirds, and, of course, parrots. Here, within the dense forests, the air is cool and dank and underwater green and alive with the sounds of birds.

Fortunately, Costa Rica's birds are not shy. Depending on season, location, and luck, you can expect to see many dozens of species on any one day. Many tour companies offer guided bird-study tours, and the country is well set up with mountain and jungle lodges that specialize in birdwatching programs. But the deep heart of the jungle is not the best place to look for birds: you cannot see well amid the complex, disorganized patterns cast by shadow and light. For best results, find a large clearing on the fringe of the forest, or a watercourse where birds are sure to be found in abundance.

The sheer size of Costa Rica's bird population has prompted some intriguing food-gathering methods. The **jacamar** snaps up insects on the wing with an audible click of its beak. One species of epicurean kite has a bill like an escargot fork, which it uses to pick snails from their shells. The **attila,** a ruthless killer like its namesake, devours its frog victims whole after bashing them against a tree.

Essential guides for serious birders are *A Guide to the Birds of Costa Rica,* by Gary Stiles and Alexander Skutch; *A Travel and Site Guide to Birds of Costa Rica,* by Aaron Sekerak; and *Birds of the Rainforest: Costa Rica,* by Carmen Hidalgo.

Anhingas and Cormorants

The **anhinga** (*pato aguja* to locals) and its close cousin, the **olivaceous cormorant** *(cormorán)* are sleek, long-necked, stump-tailed waterbirds with the pointy profile of a Concorde. Though they dive for fish in the lagoons and rivers of the lowlands, and are superb swimmers, their feathers lack the waterproof oils of other birds. You can thus often see them after a dousing, perched on a branch, sunning themselves in a vertical position with widespread wings, which are silvered against the bird's sleek black body and sinuous necks (tawny in the female) that have earned them the moniker, "snake-bird." These birds have kinked necks because they spear fish and use the kink as a trigger.

Aracaris and Toucans

The bright-billed **toucans**—"flying bananas"—are a particular delight to watch as they pick fruit off one at a time with their long beaks, throw them in the air and catch them at the back of their throats. Costa Rica's six toucan species (there

keel-billed toucans

JEAN MERCIER

are 42 neotropical toucan species) are among the most flamboyant of all Central American birds.

The gregarious **keel-billed toucan** *(tucan pico iris)* inhabits lowland and midelevation forests throughout the country except the Pacific southwest. This colorful stunner has a jet-black body, blue feet, a bright yellow chest and face, beady black eyes ringed by green feathers, and a rainbow-hued beak tipped by scarlet, as if it has been dipped in ink. Its similarly colored cousin, Swainson's or **chestnut-mandibled toucan.** (Ticos call is *dios tedé,* for the onomatopeic sound it makes), is the largest of the group—it grows to 60 cm long—with a two-tone yellow-and-brown beak. It is found in moist forests below 2,000 feet, notably along the coastal zones, including the Pacific southwest. Listen for a noisy jumble of cries and piercing creaks.

There are also two species of toucanets, smaller cousins of the toucan: the green **emerald toucanet,** a highland bird with a red tail; and the black **yellow-eared toucanet,** found in the Caribbean lowlands.

Aracaris *(tucancillos)* are smaller and sleeker relatives, with more slender beaks. Both the **collared aracari** (a Caribbean bird) and **fiery-billed aracari** (its southern Pacific cousin) boast olive-black bodies, faces, and chests, with a dark band across their rust-yellow underbellies. The former has a two-tone yellow-and-black beak; the latter's is also two tone—black and fiery orange.

Birds of Prey

Costa Rica has some 50 raptor species: birds that hunt down live prey seized with their talons. Though they rely on stealth and speed to capture their food, the birds are easily seen in the wild. The various species have evolved adaptations to specific habitats. For example, the large **common black hawk** *(gavilán cangrejero,* or "crab-hunting hawk" to Ticos) snacks on crabs and other marine morsels. And the **osprey** is known as *agula pescadora* ("fishing eagle") locally for the skill it applies to scooping fish from rivers or sea while on the wing. Hence, it has evolved especially long talons, barbed between the toes, all the better for snatching slippery fish. The bird is found throughout the world and, in Costa Rica, throughout the coastal and inland lowlands.

That lunatic laughter that goes on compulsively at dusk in lowland jungles is the **laughing falcon** (locally called the *guaco* for the repetitive "wah-co" sound it makes), which feeds on lizards and snakes. Its plumage is predominantly white, but with brown wings, a black-and-white banded tail, and black spectacles around its eyes.

Eagles: The endangered neotropical **harpy eagle** *(águila arpía)* at one-meter-long, the largest of all eagles, is renowned for twisting and diving through the treetops in pursuit of unsuspecting sloths and monkeys. Alas, sightings in Costa Rica—where in recent years it has been relegated to the Osa Peninsula and more remote ranges of the Talamancas—are extremely rare, and it may already be locally extinct.

Costa Rica's two species of caracaras are close cousins to the eagles, though like vultures they also eat carrion. Thus they are commonly seen; I have come across many of these large, fearsomely beaked, goose-stepping, long-legged birds picking at roadkill. The **crested caracara** is named for the black crown atop its bright red face. Its white neck fades into a black-and-white barred body and tail, though the wings and back are charcoal black. The name speaks for its buff-colored cousin, the **yellow-headed caracara.**

Hawks and Kites: Though in many regards virtually identical, hawks are physically robust, with broad wings and short, wide tails, compared to the sleeker kites, which have longer, slender tails and wings.

The most ubiquitous hawk is the small, gray-brown **roadside hawk** *(gavilán chapulinero),* commonly seen perched on telegraph poles and fence posts spying for mice and other potential tasty treats. Like many hawks, it has a yellow beak tipped by black, plus yellow feet and eyes, and is also distinguished by the thin rust-red bands down its chest. Its cousin, the larger, browner, migratory **broad-winged hawk** wings in for a visit Sept.-May and also favors a low perch from which to swoop in for a kill.

The white **black-shouldered kite,** as its name suggests, wears a black shawl across its back of white and light-gray feathers. It favors open habitat and is thus easily seen. You can't confuse it with the **black-chested hawk,** a predominantly black-plumed forest dweller with a white underbelly and telltale white tail band. Its polar opposite is the **white hawk** *(gavilán blanco),* sporting a *black* tail band.

You can't mistake the black **double-toothed hawk,** with its white-and-black banded belly and tail, bright-red chest, and white throat; nor the graceful, black-and-white **American swallow-tailed kite,** easily recognized by its long, deeply forked black tail. It takes insects in midair, as well as small lizards nabbed from branches.

Owls: Costa Rica's 17 species of owls are nocturnal hunters, more often heard than seen. An exception is the **spectacled owl** (Ticos call it *bujo de anteojos*), which also hunts by day. A large dark-brown owl, it is conspicuous for its yellow chest and white head with black eye patches and black crown.

Doves and Pigeons

Doves and pigeons—called *palomas* locally—are numerous (Costa Rica has at least 25 species, including endemic neotropical species and migratory visitors familiar to North Americans). The birds belong to the Columbiformes order characterized by the ability, unique in birds, to produce milk for the hatchlings. Remarkably, both genders do so. The secretions gradually diminish, replenished by regurgitated food.

Many neotropical species are far more colorful than their northern counterparts. The large **band-tailed pigeon,** for example, though predominantly gray, has a green nape with white band, blue wings tipped by brown, a yellow bill, and mauve chest and belly. The mauve-gray **red-billed pigeon** has a red nape, bright red feet and forewing, and pale-blue rear quarters fading to a black-and-gray tail. And the **ruddy pigeon** and its ground-dwelling cousin, the **ruddy ground-dove,** are flushed in various shades of rust and red.

Egrets, Herons, and Relatives

Some 25 or so stilt-legged, long-necked wading birds—members of the Ciconiiformes order—are found in Costa Rica. Most ubiquitous is the snowy white **cattle egret** whose numbers have exploded during the past four decades. Uniquely, its preferred turf is terrestial (it favors cattle pastures) and it can often be seen hitching a ride on the back of cattle, which are happy to have it picking off fleas and ticks. The males have head plumes which, along with the back and chest, turn tawny in breeding season. The species is easily mistaken for the **snowy egret,**

a larger though more slender bird wearing "golden slippers" (yellow feet) on its black legs. Largest of the white egrets is the **great egret,** which grows to one meter tall.

There are three species of brown herons—called "tiger herons" *(garza tigre)*—in Costa Rica, most notably the **bare-throated tiger heron.** The **little blue heron,** commonly seen foraging alongside lowland watercourses, is a handsome blue-gray with purplish head plumage (the female is white, with wings tipped in gray). The northern lowlands are also a good place to spot the relatively small **green-backed heron,** fronted by rusty plumage streaked with white. The dun-colored **yellow-crowned night heron** is diurnal, not nocturnal as its name suggests. It is unmistakable, with its black-and-white head crowned with a swept-back yellow plume. Another instantly identifiable bird is the stocky, gray **boat-billed heron,** named for the keel-shape of its abnormally wide, thick bill. It, too, wears a plumed crown (of black), and a rust underbelly.

Storks—notable for their fearsomely heavy, slightly upturned bills—also inhabit the lowland wetlands, notably in Caño Negro and Palo Verde National Parks, where the endangered **jabiru** can be seen. This massive bird (it grows to over one meter tall) wears snow-bright plumage, with a charcoal head, and a red scarf around its neck. Its relative, the **wood stork,** is also white, but with black flight feathers and featherless black head.

The **roseate spoonbill** *(Espátula rosada)*—also relegated to Caño Negro and Palo Verde National Parks—is the most dramatic of the waders, thanks to its shocking pink plumage and spatulate bill. Unlike its relatives, it feeds by sight, stirring up the bottom with its feet and disturbing tiny fish and other critters, then *snap!*

Costa Rica also has three species of ibis, recognizable by their long, slender, down-turned bills handy for probing muddy watercourses. Nicoya and Guanacaste are good places to spot the **white ibis,** with its startlingly red bill and legs; to see the green-black **green ibis,** head to the Caribbean.

Hummingbirds

Of all the exotically named bird species in Costa Rica, the hummingbirds beat all contenders. Their names are poetry: the **green-crowned brilliant, purple-throated mountaingem,** Buffon's plummeteer, and the bold and strikingly beautiful fiery-throated hummingbird. More than 300 species of New World hummingbirds constitute the family Trochilidae (Costa Rica has 51), and all are stunningly pretty. The **fiery-throated hummingbird**, for example, is a glossy green, shimmering iridescent at close range, with dark blue tail, violet-blue chest, glittering coppery orange throat, and a brilliant blue crown set off by velvety black on the sides and back of the head. Some males take their exotic plumage one step further and are bedecked with long streamer tails and iridescent mustaches, beards, and visors.

These tiny high-speed machines are named because of the hum made by the beat of their wings. At up to 100 beats per second, the hummingbirds' wings move so rapidly that the naked eye cannot detect them. They are often seen hovering at flowers, from which they extract nectar and often insects with their long, hollow, and extensile tongues forked at the tip. Alone among birds, they can generate power on both the forward and backward wing strokes, a distinction that allows them to even fly backward!

Understandably, the energy required to function at such an intense pitch is prodigious. The hummingbird has the highest metabolic rate per unit of body weight in the avian world (its pulse rate can exceed 1,200 beats a minute) and requires proportionately large amounts of food. One biologist discovered that the white-eared hummingbird consumes up to 850% of its own weight in food and water each day. At night, they go into "hibernation," lowering their body temperatures and metabolism to conserve energy.

Typically loners, hummingbirds bond with the opposite sex only for the few seconds it takes to mate. Many, such as the fiery-throated hummingbird, are fiercely territorial. With luck you might witness a spectacular aerial battle between males defending their territories. In breeding season, the males "possess" territories rich in flowers attractive to females: the latter gains an ample food source in exchange for offering the male sole paternity rights. Nests are often no larger than a thimble, loosely woven with cobwebs and flecks of bark and lined with silky plant down. Inside, the female will lay two eggs no larger than coffee beans.

Motmots

The motmot is a sickle-billed bird that makes its home in a hole in the ground. Of nine species of motmot in tropical America, six live in Costa Rica. You'll find them from humid coastal southwest plains to the cool highland zone and dry Guanacaste region and, yes, even San José. You can't mistake this gaily colored charmer: Motmots have a pendulous twin-feathered tail with the barbs missing three-quarters of the way down, leaving two bare feather shafts with disc-shaped tips resembling oval pendant earrings.

Two commonly seen species are the **blue-crowned motmot** and **turquoise-bowed motmot.** The former has a green-and-brown body with red belly, a scintillating turquoise head, and beady red eyes peeping out between a black Lone Ranger-style mask. The latter is similarly colored, but with a red back and a large black spot on its chest, plus longer bare "handles" on its racquet-like tail.

THE LEGEND OF THE BELEAGUERED MOTMOT

According to Bribrí legend, the god Sibo asked all the creatures to help him make the world. They all chipped in gladly except the motmot, who hid in a hole. Unfortunately, the bird left his tail hanging out. When the other birds saw this they picked the feathers from the motmot's tail but left the feathers at the tip.

When the world was complete, Sibo gave all the tired animals a rest. Soon the motmot appeared and began boasting about how hard he had labored. But the lazy bird's tail gave the game away, so Sibo, who guessed what had happened, admonished the motmot and banished him to living in a hole in the ground.

BOB RACE

Parrots

If ever there were an avian symbol of the neotropics, it must be the parrot. This family of birds is marked by savvy intelligence, an ability to mimic the human voice, and uniformly short, hooked bills hinged to provide the immense power required for cracking seeds and nuts. Costa Rica claims 16 of the world's 330 or so species, including six species of parakeets and two species of macaws, the giants of the parrot kingdom.

The parrots are predominantly green, with short, truncated tails (parakeets and macaws, however, have long tails), and varying degrees of colored markings. All are voluble, screeching raucously as they barrel overhead in fast-flight formation.

Macaws: Although macaw is the common name for any of 15 species of these large, long-tailed birds found throughout Central and South America, only two species inhabit Costa Rica: the scarlet macaw *(lapa roja)* and the great green or Buffon's macaw *(lapa verde)*. Both bird populations are losing their homes to deforestation and poaching. The macaw populations have declined so dramatically that they are now in danger of disappearing completely. (There are far more macaws in captivity than exist in the wild.)

What magnificent creatures these birds are! No protective coloration. No creeping about trying to blend in with the countryside. Instead, they posture like kings and queens. The largest of the neotropical parrots, macaws have harsh, raucous voices that are filled with authority. They fly overhead, calling loudly, their long, trailing tail feathers and short wings make it impossible to confuse them with other birds. They are gregarious and rarely seen alone. They are almost always paired male and female—they're monogamous for life—often sitting side by side, grooming and preening each other, and conversing in rasping loving tones, or flying two by two.

Macaws usually nest in softwood trees, where termites have hollowed out holes. April through July, you might see small groups of macaws clambering about the upper trunks of dead trees, squabbling over holes and crevices.

Many bird books mistakenly describe macaws as feeding on fruits—they get their names because they supposedly feed on the fruits of the macaw palms. In fact, they rarely eat fruit, but prefer seeds and nuts, which they extract with a hooked nutcracker of such strength that it can split that most intractable of nuts, the Brazil nut—or a human finger.

The **scarlet macaw** is a giant parrot—it can grow to 85 cm in length—that wears a dazzling rainbow-colored jackets of bright yellow and blue, green, or scarlet. Though the scarlet ranges from Mexico to central South America and was once abundant on both coasts of Costa Rica, today it is found only in a few parks on the Pacific shore, and rarely on the Caribbean side. Only three wild populations of scarlet macaws in Central America have a long-term chance of survival—at Carara Biological Reserve and Corcovado National Park in Costa Rica, and Coiba Island in Panamá—although the bird can also be seen with regularity at Palo Verde National Park, Manuel Antonio National Park, and Santa Rosa National Park. Even these are below the minimum critical size. An estimated 200 scarlets live at Carara and 1,600 at Corcovado.

It is impossible to tell male from female. The scarlet's bright red-orange plumage with touches of blue and yellow does not vary between the sexes or with aging.

The **Buffon's macaw** is slightly smaller than the scarlet. It has a pea-green body, with a white face spotted with red, blue wingtips, and red tail. Fewer than 50 breeding pairs of Buffon's macaw are thought to exist in the wild, exclusively in the Caribbean and northern lowlands. The bird relies on the almendro tree—a heavily logged species—for nest sites and calls have gone out for a ban on logging almendros. For more information on how you can help, contact George Powell, tel./fax 645-5024, e-mail: gpowell @sol.racsa.co.cr; or Vivienne Solis, World Conservation Union, Apdo. 1161-2150, Moravia, tel. 236-2733, fax 240-9934.

Macaw Protection: Several conservation groups are working to stabilize and reestablish the scarlet macaw population. Deep in the forest of the Carara Biological Reserve, Sergio Volio oversees a project to build artificial nests high up in jallinazo trees beyond the reach of poachers. Although macaws are the biggest attraction at Carara, they are threatened with extinction by poachers who take the chicks to sell on the black market. Most die, however, even before they are sold. Volio estimates up to 95% of natural nests at the reserve are poached. Volio's is the first project that will protect the birds' breeding grounds in their natural habitat. Your donations will help build the birdhouses, which cost about $100. Contact: **Geotur,** P.O. Box 469 Y Griega, San José 1011, tel. 534-1867, fax 253-6338.

Zoo Ave at La Garita, west of Alajuela, has the most extensive macaw breeding program in the nation.

Richard and Marge Frisius, two experienced aviculturists, have formed a nonprofit organization, **Amigos de las Aves,** Apdo. 2306-4050, Alajuela, tel./fax 441-2658, e-mail: richmar@ticonet .co.cr. The Frisius's have a macaw-breeding program on their three-hectare estate—Flor de Mayo—in Río Segundo de Alajuela. The Frisiuses have successfully raised scarlet baby macaws using special techniques and cages; in 1997 they also succeeded in a first-ever experiment to breed green macaws in captivity). The goal is to teach domestically raised macaws how to find native food and then release them into carefully selected wilds of Costa Rica with the intent of reestablishing flocks of these magnificent birds in parts of the nation where there is still appropriate habitat for viable populations to establish themselves. The Frisiuses had about 80 macaws at press time (including eight pairs of mature green macaws and 19 pairs of scarlets). The Frisiuses request donations.

Dr. Dagmar Werner—famous as the "Iguana Mama"—heads the **Macaw Program,** a captive breeding program run in collaboration with the World Wildife Fund and Costa Rica's National University's School of Medicine (see **Iguana Park** in the Central Pacific chapter).

Seabirds and Shorebirds

Costa Rica has almost 100 species of seabirds and shorebirds, including a wide variety of gulls, the most common being the **laughing gull** (gaviota reidora). Many are migratory visitors, more abundant in winter months, including the **sanderling,** a small light-gray shorebird that scurries along the surf line in a high-speed jittery gait, like a mechanical toy.

The large, pouch-billed **brown pelican** (pelicano) can be seen up and down the Pacific coast (and, in lesser numbers, on the Caribbean), where they can be admired gliding in superb formation over the water, diving like Stukas for fish, or lazing on fishing boats, waiting for the next catch to come in.

Boobies inhabit several islands off Nicoya, as do **storm petrels, jaegers,** the beautiful red-billed, fork-tailed **royal tern,** and a variety of other seabirds. **Oystercatchers, whimbrels, sandpipers** (often seen in vast flocks) and other shoreline waders frequent the coastal margins.

Frigate birds, with their long scimitar wings and forked tails, hang like sinister kites in the wind all along the Costa Rican coast. They hold a single position in the sky, as if suspended from invisible strings, and from this airborne perch harry gulls and terns until the latter release their catch (birders have a name for such thievery: kleptoparasitism).

Despite the sinister look imparted by its long hooked beak, the frigate bird is quite beautiful. The adult male is all black with a lustrous faint purplish-green sheen on its back (especially during the courtship season). The female, the much larger of the two, is easily distinguished by the white feathers that extend up her abdomen and the breast, and the ring of blue around her eyes.

Second only to a frigate bird's concern for food is its interest in the opposite sex. The females do the conspicuous searching out and selecting of mates. The hens take to the air above the rookery to look over the males, who cluster in groups atop the scrubby mangrove bushes. Whenever a female circles low over the bushes, the males react with a blatant display of wooing: they tilt their heads far back to show off their fully inflated scarlet gular pouches (appropriately shaped like hearts), vibrate their wings rapidly back and forth, and entice the females with loud clicking and drumming sounds.

Once the pair is established, a honeymoon of nest-building begins. In the structured world of the frigate birds it is the male's job to find twigs for the nest. The piratical frigates will not hesitate to steal twigs from their neighbors' nests, so the females stay home to guard them. The female lays a single egg, and each parent takes turns at one-week shifts during the eight-week incubation. They guard the chick closely, for predatory neighbors, hawks, and owls make quick feasts of the unwary young. For five months, the dejected-looking youngsters sit immobile beneath the hot sun; even when finally airborne, they remain dependent on their parents for more than a year while they learn the complex trade of air piracy.

Superb stunt flyers, frigate birds often bully other birds on the wing, pulling at the tails of their victims until the latter release or regurgitate a freshly caught meal. Frigate birds also catch much of their food themselves. You may see them skimming the water, snapping up squid, flying fish, and other morsels off the water's surface. (They must keep themselves dry, as they have only a small preen gland, insufficient to oil their feathers; if they get too wet they become waterlogged and drown.)

Tanagers and Other Passerines

Costa Rica boasts 50 species of tanagers—small, exorbitantly colored birds that favor dark tropical forests. Tanagers brighten the jungle, and you are likely to spot their bright plumage as you hike along trails. The tanagers' short stubby wings enable them to swerve and dodge at high speed through the undergrowth as they chase after insects.

Among the most astonishing is the **summer tanager,** flame-red from tip to tail. The black male **scarlet-rumped tanager** also has a startlingly flame-red rump (his mate—they travel together—is variegated orange and olive-gray). The exotically plumed **blue-gray tanager** is as variegated in turquoise and teal as a Bahamian sea, while the **silver-throated tanager** is lemon yellow.

Tanagers belong to the order Passerines— "perching birds"—that includes about half of *all* Costa Rica's bird species. It is a taxonomically challenging group, with members characterized by certain anatomical features: notably, three toes pointing forward and a longer toe pointing back. **Sparrows, robins,** and **finches** are Passerines, as are **antbirds** (30 species), **blackbirds** (20 species), **flycatchers** (78 species), **warblers** (52 species), and **wrens** (22 species).

Many tropical Passerines are more exuberantly liveried than their temperate counterparts. Look for the blue-black-and-red **blue-hooded euphonia,** the Day-glo green and yellow **golden-bowed chlorophonia,** and the black-and-flame orange **red-capped manakin.**

Trogons

Costa Rica has 10 of the 40 species of trogons: brightly colored, long-tailed, short-beaked, pigeon-sized, forest-dwelling tropical birds Most

QUETZAL CULTURE

Early Maya and Aztecs worshiped a god called Quetzalcoatl, the Plumed Serpent, and depicted him with a headdress of quetzal feathers. The bird's name is derived from *quetzalli,* an Aztec word meaning "precious" or "beautiful." The Maya considered the male's iridescent green tail feathers worth more than gold, and killing the sacred bird was a capital crime. Quetzal plumes and jade, which were traded throughout Mesoamerica, were the Maya's most precious objects. It was the color that was significant: "Green—the color of water, the lifegiving fluid. Green, the color of the maize crop, had special significance to the people of Mesoamerica," wrote Adrian Digby in his monograph *Mayan Jades,* "and both jade and the feathers of the quetzal were green."

During the colonial period, the indigenous people of Central America came to see the quetzal as a symbol of independence and freedom. Popular folklore relates how the quetzal got its dazzling blood-red breast: in 1524, when the Spanish conquistador Pedro de Alvarado defeated the Maya chieftain Tecun Uman, a gilt and green quetzal lit on the Indian's chest at the moment he fell mortally wounded; when the bird took off again, its breast was stained with the brilliant crimson blood of the Maya.

Archaeologists believe that the wearing of quetzal plumes was proscribed, under pain of death, except for Maya priests and nobility. It became a symbol of authority vested in a theocratic elite, much as only Roman nobility were allowed to wear purple silks.

trogons combine bodies of two primary colors— red and blue, blue and yellow, or green and some other color—with a black-and-white striped tail. The **orange-bellied trogon,** for example, is green, with a bright orange belly beneath a sash of white. The trogons are most dazzlingly represented by the quetzal.

Many birdwatchers travel to Costa Rica simply to catch sight of the **quetzal,** or resplendent trogon. What this bird lacks in physical stature it makes up for in audacious plumage: vivid, shimmering green that ignites in the sunshine, flashing emerald to golden and back to iridescent green. In common with other bird species, the male outshines the female. He sports a fuzzy punk hairdo, a scintillating crimson belly, and two brilliant green tail plumes up to 60 cm long, edged in snowy white and sinuous as feather boas.

Its beauty was so fabled and the bird so elusive and shy that early European naturalists believed the quetzal was a fabrication of Central American natives. In 1861, English naturalist Osbert Salvin, the first European to record observing a quetzal, pronounced it "unequaled for splendour among the birds of the New World," and promptly shot it. During the course of the next three decades, thousands of quetzal plumes crossed the Atlantic to fill the specimen cabinets of European collectors and adorn the fashionable milliners' shops of Paris, Amsterdam, and London. Salvin redeemed himself by writing the awesome 40-volume tome *Biología Centrali Americana,* which provided virtually a complete catalog of neotropical species.

The quetzal's territory spans a radius of approximately 300 meters, which the male proclaims each dawn through midmorning and again at dusk with a telltale melodious whistle—a hollow, high-pitched call of two notes, one ascending steeply, the other descending—repeated every 8-10 minutes.

Nest holes (often hollowed out by woodpeckers) are generally about 10 meters from the ground. Within, the female generally lays two light-blue eggs, which take about 18 days to hatch. Both sexes share parental duties. By day, the male incubates the eggs while his two-foot-long tail feathers hang out of the nest. At night, the female takes over.

Although the quetzal eats insects, small frogs, and lizards, it enjoys a penchant for the fruit of the broad-leafed *aguacatillo* (a kind of miniature avocado in the laurel family), which depends on the bird to distribute seeds. The movement of quetzals follows the seasonal fruiting of different laurel species. Time your birdwatching visit, if possible, to coincide with the quetzals' rather meticulous feeding hours, which you can almost set your watch by. It's fascinating to watch them feeding: an upward swoop for fruit is the bird's aerial signature.

Everywhere throughout its 1,000-mile range (from southern Mexico to western Panamá), the quetzal is endangered by loss of its cloud-forest habitat. This is particularly true of the lower

forests around 1,500 to 2,000 meters, to which families of quetzals descend to seek dead and decaying trees in which to hollow out their nests. This is the best time to see narcissistic males showing off their tail plumes in undulating flight, or launching spiraling skyward flights, which presage a plummeting dive with their tail feathers rippling behind, all part of the courtship ritual.

Despite its iridescence, the bird's plumage offers excellent camouflage under the rainy forest canopy. They also sit motionless for long periods, with their vibrant red chests turned away from any suspected danger. If a quetzal knows you're close by and feels threatened, you may hear a harsh "weec-weec" warning call and see the male's flicking tail feathers betray his presence. Quetzals are easily seen throughout highland Costa Rica at cloud forest elevations.

Waterfowl

Costa Rica lies directly beneath a migratory corridor between North and South America, and in the northern lowland wetlands, the air is always full of **blue-winged teals, shoveler ducks,** and other waterfowl settling and taking off amid the muddy, pool-studded grasslands. Most duck species are winter migrants from North America. Neotropical species include the **black-bellied whistling duck** and **Muscovy ducks.**

The wetlands are also inhabited by 18 species of the order Gruiformes: rails, bitterns, and their relatives, with their large, wide-splayed feet good for wading and running across lily- and grass-choked watercourses. Many are brightly colored, including **purple gallinule,** liveried in vivid violet and green, with a yellow-tipped red bill, bright yellow legs, and a blue dot on its forehead. The order includes many migrants, including the charcoal-gray, white-billed **American coot** and **sun-bittern,** a long-legged, multihued wader with bright orange legs and bill, and—when in flight—a dramatic sunburst pattern in white, black, and brown beneath the wings, like the markings of a military aircraft.

The widely dispersed *rascón* or **gray-necked wood rail** (common along lowland rivers and lagoons throughout the country) is easily spotted stalking the muddy watercourses in search of frogs and other tidbits. The dark olive-brown bird has a colorful bronze breast, gray neck, yellow legs, and red legs and eyes. The black-and-brown, yellow-beaked **northern jacana** is also easy to see, especially in the canals of Tortuguero, hopping about atop water lilies thanks to its long, slender toes—hence its nickname, the "lily-trotter." It has a strange yellow shield atop its bill, and yellow streaked wing feathers. The female jacana is promiscuous, mating with many males, who take on the task of nest-building and brooding eggs that may have been fertilized by a rival. Tortuguero is also a good place to spot the **sungrebe,** a furtive, brown waterbird with black-and-white striped neck and head and red beak; it has a habit—among the males—of carrying its young chicks in a fold of skin under its wing.

Vultures

You can't help but be unnerved at the first sight of scrawny black vultures picking at some roadside carcass, or swirling overhead on the thermals as if waiting for your car to break down. They look quite ominous in their undertaker's plumage, with bald heads and hunched shoulders. Costa Rica has four species of vultures (*zopilotes* to Ticos), easily identified by the color of the skin on their heads.

The grotesquely red-headed **turkey vulture** is common in all parts of Costa Rica below 2,000 meters, noticeably so in moister coastal areas where it hops about on the streets of forlorn towns such as Golfito and Puerto Viejo de Limón. The stockier **black vulture** has a black head (as do juvenile turkey vultures). Both are otherwise charcoal colored. The two adopt different flying patterns: the turkey vulture flies low, seeking out carrion with its well-developed sense of smell; the black vulture soars higher and uses its eyes to spot carrion and often drop in to chase off smaller vultures from carcasses they have claimed.

Count yourself lucky to spot the rarer **lesser yellow-headed vulture,** with its namesake yellow head; or the mighty **king vulture,** widely dispersed, but most frequent in Corcovado. The latter wears a handsome white coat with black wing feathers and tail, and a wattled head variegated in vermilion and yellow.

Other Notable Birds

The **three-wattled bellbird,** which inhabits the cloud forests, is rarely spotted in the mist-shrouded treetops, though the male's eerie call, described by one writer as a ventriloqual "bonk!" (it

is more like a hammer clanging on an anvil), haunts the forest as long as the sun is up. It is named for the strange pendulous wattles that dangle from its bill. The bellbird is one of the Cotinga family that includes many of Costa Rica's most exotically liveried species.

In the moist Caribbean lowlands (and occasionally elsewhere) you may spot the telltale, pendulous woven nests—often one meter long—of **Montezuma oropendolas,** a large bronze-colored bird with a black neck, head, and belly, a blue-and-orange bill, and bright yellow outer tail feathers. The birds nest in colonies. Their favored trees often look as if they have been hung with cheesesacks. The **chestnut-headed oropendola** is less commonly seen.

Nicoya and Guanacaste are good places to spot the **white-throated magpie jay,** a large and gregarious bird that often comes begging food from tourists. It is sky-blue above, with a snow-white throat and belly fringed by a dark blue necklace, and—unmistakably—has a tufted crest of black feathers curling forward.

The great **curassow,** growing as tall as one meter, is almost too big for flight and tends to run through the undergrowth if disturbed. You're most likely to see this endangered bird in Corcovado or Santa Rosa National Park.

All four New World species of kingfishers inhabit Costa Rica: the large red-breasted; the slate-blue **ringed kingfisher,** which can grow to 40 cm; its smaller cousin, the **belted kingfisher;** and the **Amazon kingfisher** and smaller **green kingfisher,** both being green with white and red underparts.

To my mind, the most dangerous creature in Costa Rica is the **common pauraque** (or *cuyeo*), a member of the Nightjar family—nocturnal birds that in flight are easily mistaken for bats. They like to sit on the roads at night, where they are well camouflaged (it is mottled gray, black, and brown), especially on bumpy, dusty roads. The first you know of it is when it suddenly decides to lift off as your car approaches, causing you at least a heck of a scare. Worse, if you hit it and drive on, there's the worry over the poor bird and about how much the car rental company will charge for the dent in the hood!

Another neotropical Nightjar is the odd-looking **great potoo** *(nictibio grande),* a superbly camouflaged bird that perches upright on tree stumps and holds its hawk-like head haughtily aloft. It's squat cousin, the **common potoo,** with its beady yellow-and-black eyes, resembles an owl.

Other birds you might expect to see include the 16 species of **woodpeckers, cuckoos,** any of 11 species of **swifts,** the **tinamou** (a large bird resembling a cross between a hen and a dove), and a host of birds you may not recognize but whose names you will never forget: scarlet-thighed dacnis, violaceous trogons, tody motmots, laneolated monlets, lineated foliage-gleaners, and black-capped pygmy tyrants.

The **Caribbean Conservation Corps,** CCC, P.O. Box 2866, Gainesville, FL 32602, tel. (352) 373-6441 or (800) 678-7853, fax (352) 375-2449, e-mail: ccc@cccturtle.org, needs volunteers for its year-round research into neotropical birds at Tortuguero. You might find yourself netting and tagging birds, or merely observing rare species.

INSECTS

The long history of the rainforest has enabled countless butterflies, moths, ants, termites, wasps, bees, and other tropical insects to evolve in astounding profusion. Ant species alone number in the many thousands. Corcovado National Park boasts at least 220 species of breeding butterflies, plus others that simply pass through. And there are so many species of beetles and grasshoppers that no one knows the true numbers. Many, many thousands of insect species still await identification.

The most brilliantly painted insects are the butterflies and moths, some quite tiny and obscure, others true giants of the insect kingdom, dazzlingly crowned in gold and jewel-like colors. In Guanacaste, hundreds of species of bees, moth larvae, and tiger beetles make an appearance in the early dry season. When the first rains come, lightbulbs are often deluged with adult moths, beetles, and other insects newly emerged from

leaf-cutting ant

their pupae. That's the time, too, that many species of butterfly migrate from the deciduous lowland forests to highland sites.

Many insect species are too small to see. The **hummingbird flower mite,** for example, barely half a millimeter long, is so small it can hitch rides from flower to flower inside the nostrils of hummingbirds. Other insects you may detect by their sound. Male **crickets,** for example, produce a very loud noise by rubbing together the overlapping edges of their wing cases.

Many exotic-looking species you can immediately recognize. The giant **Guanacaste stick insect** is easily spotted at night on low shrubs. The three-inch **rhinoceros beetle** has an unmistakable long, upward-curving horn on its head. And the number of spiders ornamented with showy colors is remarkable. Some even double themselves up at the base of leaf-stalks, so as to resemble flowerbuds, and thus deceive the insects on which they prey.

Of course, a host of unfriendly bugs also exist in great numbers: chiggers, wasps and bees (including aggressive African bees), ticks, mosquitoes, fire ants, and the famous "no-see-ums." All six insects can inflict irritating bites on humans.

Ants

There's something endearing about the **leaf-cutting ant** *(Atta cephalotes),* a mushroom-farming insect found in lowland forests throughout Costa Rica, carrying upright in its jaws a circular green shard scissored from the leaves of a plant. At some stage in your travels you're bound to come across an endless troop of "media" workers hauling their cargo along jungle pathways as immaculately cleaned of debris as any swept doorstep.

The nests are built below ground, sometimes extending over an area of 200 square meters, with galleries to a depth of six meters. Large nests provide a home for up to five million insects. All ant societies are composed entirely of females; males exist only to fertilize the queen and then die. And only the queen, who may boast a thousand times the body weight of a minor worker, is fertile. Hence, all other ants in the colony are her daughters. They set off from their nests, day and night, in long columns to demolish trees, removing every shoot, leaf, and stem section by tiny section and transporting them back to their underground chambers.

They don't eat this material. Instead, they chew it up to form a compost on which they cultivate a nutritional breadlike fungus whose tiny white fruiting bodies provide them with food. So evolved has this symbiosis become that the fungus has lost its reproductive ability (it no longer produces sexual spores) and relies exclusively on the ants for propagation.

The species has evolved different physical castes, each specializing in its own social tasks. Most of the workers are tiny minors ("minimas"), which tend the nest. The cutting and carrying are performed by intermediate-size workers ("medias"), guarded by ferocious-looking "majors" about two centimeters long.

The most terrifying ants of all are the **army ants,** which march through the forest with the sole intent of turning small creatures into skeletons in a few minutes. They produce a faint hissing sound and distinct ant-army odor. They're like a wolf pack, but with tens of thousands of miniature beasts of prey that merge and unite to form one great living creature.

Hollywood images of mammals and even humans fleeing madly before them are mostly imagination run wild. In truth, while the ants advance across the forest floor driving small creatures in front of them, humans and other large creatures can simply step aside and watch the column pass by—this can take several hours. Even when the ants raid human habitations, people can simply clear out with their foodstock while the ants clean out the cockroaches and other vermin as thoroughly as any exterminator might.

The army ants' jaws are so powerful that Indians once used them to suture wounds: the tenacious insect was held over a wound and its body squeezed so that its jaws clamped shut, closing the wound. The body was then pinched off.

Larvae carried by workers produce pheromones, which stimulate the army to keep on the move. When the larvae begin to pupate and no longer exude their chemical messages, the ants bivouac in a vast ball in a hollow. They actually cling to one another and make a nest of their bodies, complete with passageways and chambers where the eggs are deposited. Once the queen lays her eggs and these hatch as larvae, a new generation of workers and soldiers synchronistically emerges from the stored pupae. The larvae begin to secrete their characteristic pheromone, and the army is again stimulated to march off and terrorize the bush.

Butterflies
With nearly 1,000 identified species (approximately 10% of the world total), Costa Rica is a lepidopterist's paradise. You can barely stand still for one minute without checking off a dozen dazzling species: metallic gold riondinidae; delicate black-winged heliconius splashed with bright red and yellow; orange-striped paracaidas; and the deep neon-blue flash of morphos fluttering and diving in a ballet of subaqueous color. The marvelously intricate wing patterns are statements of identity, so that individuals may recognize those with whom mating may be fertile.

Not all this elaboration has a solely sexual connotation. Some butterflies are ornately colored to keep predators at bay. The bright white stripes against black on the **zebra butterfly** (like other members of the Heliconid family), for example, tell birds that the butterfly tastes acrid. There are even perfectly tasty butterfly species that mimic the Heliconid's colors, tricking predators to disdain them. Others use their colors as camouflage so that at rest they blend in with the green or brown leaves or look like the scaly bark of a tree. Among the most intriguing, however, are the **owl-eye butterflies,** with their 13-cm wingspans and startling eye spots. The bluegray *Caligo memnon,* the cream owl butterfly, is the most spectacular of the owl-eyes: the undersides of its wings mottled to look like feathers and boast two large yellow-and-black "eyes" on the hind wing, which it displays when disturbed.

The best time to see butterflies is in the morning, when most species are active. A few are active at dawn and dusk, and one species is even active by night. In general, butterfly populations are most dense in June and July, corresponding with the onset of the rainy season on the Pacific side. Butterfly migrations are also common. Like birds, higher-elevation species migrate up and down the mountains with changes in local weather. The most amazing

MORPHO BUTTERFLIES

Undoubtedly the Narcissus of the Costa Rican butterfly kingdom is the famous blue morpho, one of the most beautiful butterflies in the world. There are about 50 species of morphos, all in Central and South America, where they are called *celeste común*. The males of most species are bright neon blue, with iridescent wings that flash like mirrors in the sun. Sadly, this magnificent oversized butterfly—it grows to 13-20 cm—is not as common as it once was, thanks to habitat destruction.

"It used to be a backyard species; now it is found only in reserves," says Maria Sabido, cofounder of the Butterfly Farm, in La Guácima de Alajuela. Still, you can't miss them when they're around and active—particularly in November, when they are extremely common along riverbeds and other moist habitats.

The morpho is a modest, nondescript brown when sitting quietly with wings closed. But when a predator gets too close, it flies off, startling its foe with a flash of its beautiful electric blue wings. (Not that they are always successful. Biologist David Janzen reports that piles of morpho wings are often found under the perches of jacamars and large flycatchers, which are partial to the morpho.)

The subspecies differ in color: in the Atlantic lowlands, the morpho is almost completely iridescent blue; one population in the Meseta Central is almost completely brown, with only a faint hint of electric blue. One species, commonly seen gliding about in the forest canopy, is red on the underside and gray on top.

Showmen have always used mirrors to produce glitter and illusion. The morpho is no exception. Look through a morpho butterfly's wing toward a strong light and you will see only brown. This is because the scales *are* brown. The fiery blue is produced by structure, not by pigment (one consequence is that the color will never fade). Tiny scales on the upper side of the wing are laid in rows that overlap much like roof shingles. These scales are ridged with minute layers that, together with the air spaces between them, refract and reflect light beams, absorbing all the colors except blue. The Atlantic species have additional glassy scales on top of the others to reflect even more light and give the wings a paler, more opalescent quality.

migration—unsurpassed by any other insect in the neotropics—is that of the kitelike uranidae (this black and iridescent green species is actually a moth that mimics the swallowtail butterfly), in which millions of individuals pass through Costa Rica heading south from Honduras to Colombia.

The popularity and success of the **Butterfly Farm,** tel. 438-0115, at La Guácima, and **Spirogyra,** tel. 222-2937, a butterfly garden in San José, has spawned a dozen or more competitors in recent years; see regional chapters. Besides being able to walk inside netted butterfly gardens, you'll learn fascinating snippets of butterfly lore, such as that the butterfly's two antennae allow it to keep flying steady even when half its wings have been chomped by hungry predators, and that the male can detect a single molecule of female pheromone at two kilometers' distance.

Selva Verde Lodge, tel. 766-6800, fax 766-6011, e-mail: travel@holbrooktravel.com, offers butterfly-study workshops (1-9 days). The Butterfly Farm two- and five-day tours for butterfly lovers, with visits to local butterfly breeders plus other sites on a lepidoterous theme.

FISH

Costa Rica is as renowned for its marine life as for its terrestrial and avian fauna—most famously, perhaps, for the billfish (marlin and sailfish) that cruise the deep blue waters offshore, and for tarpon and snook, feisty estuarine and wetland game fish. The former swim seasonally as packed as sardines in the warm waters off the Golfo de Papagayo and Golfo Dolfo. The latter are particularly concentrated in the waters of the Río Colorado and Caúo Negro.

Costa Rica lacks substantial coral reefs, though reefs *can* be found offshore of Cahuita and Gandoca-Manzanillo, on the Caribbean, and Bahía Ballena, along the Central Pacific shore.

Sharks are forever present in Costa Rican waters. They seem particularly to favor waters in which marine turtles swim. Isla Cocos is renowned for its schools of hammerhead sharks as well as giant whale shark (the world's largest fish), which can also be found hanging out with giant grouper, jewfish, and manta rays in the waters around the Islas Murciélagos, off the Santa Elena peninsula of Guanacaste.

HISTORY

PRE-COLUMBIAN ERA

When Spanish explorers arrived in what is now Costa Rica at the dawn of the 16th century, they found the region populated by several poorly organized, autonomous tribes living relatively prosperously, if wanton at war, in a land of lush abundance. In all, there were probably no more than 200,000 indigenous people on 18 September 1502, when Columbus put ashore near current-day Puerto Limón. Although human habitation can be traced back at least 10,000 years, the region had remained a sparsely populated backwater separating the two areas of high civilization: Mesoamerica and the Andes. High mountains and swampy lowlands had impeded the migration of the advanced cultures. Though these cultures were advanced in ceramics, metalwork, and weaving, there are few signs of large complex communities, little monumental stone architecture lying half-buried in the luxurious undergrowth, no planned ceremonial centers of comparable significance to those elsewhere in the isthmus.

The region was a potpourri of distinct cultures divided into chiefdoms. In the east along the Caribbean seaboard and along the southern Pacific

JADE

Ancient Costa Ricans had a love affair with jade. The semiprecious stone first appeared in Costa Rica around 400 B.C., when the Olmecs of Mexico introduced it to the Nicoya Peninsula. It became more prized than gold.

Though early carvings were crude, quality pieces began to appear around A.D. 300, when the indigenous peoples developed the "string-saw" carving technique—involving drilling a hole in the jade, inserting a string, and sawing back and forth. Pendants, necklaces, and earrings appeared, exquisitely carved with reliefs of human faces and scenes of life. Painstakingly worked figurines of monkeys, crocodiles, anteaters, jaguars, reptiles, and owls (symbol of the underworld) appeared in jade. Most common of all was the eagle, worshipped by indigenous peoples throughout the isthmus.

Costa Rican jade comes in green, black, gray, and—the rarest—blue. Although the quarry for the famous blue jade has never been found, Fidel Tristan, curator of the Jade Museum, believes a local source exists. The nearest known source of green is at Manzanal, in Guatemala.

pre-Columbian jade figurines

shores, the peoples shared distinctly South American cultural traits. These groups—the Caribs on the Caribbean and the Borucas and Chibchas and Diquis in the southwest—were seminomadic hunters and fishermen who raised yucca, squash, *pejibaye* (bright orange palm fruits), and tubers supplemented by crustaceans, shrimp, lobster, and game; chewed coca; and lived in communal village huts surrounded by fortified palisades. The matriarchal Chibchas and Diquis had a highly developed slave system and were accomplished goldsmiths, for their habitat was abundant in gold ore. Amulets, awls, tweezers for plucking out facial hair, beads and baubles, pendants and religious icons decorated in fantastical animist imagery were among the many items of gold expertly worked through the "lost wax" technique. These people were famed for their simple clothwork, which was traded throughout the country. They were also responsible for the fascinating, perfectly spherical granite balls *(bolas)* of unknown purpose found in large numbers at burial sites in the Río Terraba valley, Caño Island, and the Golfito region. Tens of thousands have been unearthed. Some are the size of grapefruit. Others weigh 16 tons. One and all are as perfectly round as the moon. Like other indigenous groups, the people had no written language, and their names are of Spanish origin—bestowed by colonists, often reflecting the names of tribal chiefs.

The most interesting archaeological finds throughout the nation relate to pottery and metalworking. The art of gold working was practiced throughout Costa Rica for perhaps one thousand years before the Spanish conquest, and in the central highlands was in fact more advanced than in the rest of the isthmus. The tribes here were the Corobicís, who lived in small bands in the highland valleys, and the Nahuatl, who had recently arrived from Mexico at the time that Columbus stepped ashore. The largest and most significant of Costa Rica's archaeological sites found to date is here, at Guayabo, on the slopes of Turrialba, 56 km east of San José, where an ancient city is being excavated. Dating from perhaps as early as 1000 B.C. to A.D. 1400, Guayabo is thought to have housed as many as 10,000 inhabitants. Rudimentary though it is by the standards of ancient cities elsewhere in the isthmus, it is nonetheless impressive, with wide cobblestone walkways and stone-lined pools and water cisterns fed by aqueducts.

Perhaps more important (little architectural study has been completed) was the Nicoya Peninsula of what is today northwest Costa Rica. In late prehistoric times, trade in pottery from the Nicoya Peninsula brought this area into the Mesoamerican cultural sphere, and a culture developed among the Chorotegas—the most numerous of the region's indigenous groups—that in many ways resembled the more advanced cultures farther north. In fact, the Chorotegas had been heavily influenced by the Olmec culture, and may themselves have even originated in southern Mexico before settling in Nicoya early in the 14th century (their name means "Fleeing People"). The most advanced of the region's cultures, they developed towns with central plazas, brought with them an accomplished agricultural system based on beans, corns, squash, and gourds, had a calendar, wrote books on deerskin parchment, and produced highly developed ceramics and stylized jade figures (much of it now in the Jade Museum in San José) depicting animals, humanlike effigies, and men and women with oversized genitals, often making the most of their sexual apparati. Like the Olmecs, they filed their teeth; like the Mayans and Aztecs, too, the militaristic Chorotegas kept slaves and maintained a rigid class hierarchy dominated by high priests and nobles. Human sacrifice was part of the cultural mainstay. Surprisingly little, however, is known of their spiritual belief system, though the potency and ubiquity of phallic imagery hints at a fertility-rite religion.

Alas, the pre-Columbian cultures were quickly choked by the stern hand of gold-thirsty colonial rule—and condemned, too, that Jehovah might triumph over local idols.

Costa Rica is just beginning to open up its native culture to tourism. Plans are afoot to establish a "Petroglyph Trail," for example, plus a sound-and-light show at the Guayabo Monument with archaeo-astronomers to explain the pre-Columbians' sophisticated knowledge of the heavens, nighttime dramatizations of pre-Columbian mythologies atop Irazú Volcano, and explorations of the Pacific southwest to study the mysterious rock spheres found in the rainforests.

COLONIAL ERA

The First Arrivals

When Columbus, 51 years of age, anchored his storm-damaged vessels—*Captiana, Gallega, Viscaína,* and *Santiago de Palos*—in the Bay of Cariari, off the Caribbean coast on his fourth voyage to the New World in 1502, he was welcomed and treated with great hospitality by indigenous peoples who had never seen white men before. Columbus' son Ferdinand recorded that the coastal Indians sent out two girls, "the one about eight, the other about 14 years of age. The girls . . . always looked cheerful and modest. So the Admiral gave them good usage." In his *Lettera Rarissima* to the Spanish king, Columbus offered a different tale of events: "As soon as I got there they sent right out two girls, all dressed up; the elder was hardly eleven, the other seven, both behaving with such lack of modesty as to be no better than whores. As soon as they arrived, I gave orders that they be presented with some of our trading truck and sent them directly ashore."

The Indian dignitaries appeared wearing much gold, which they gave Columbus. "I saw more signs of gold in the first two days than I saw in Española during four years," his journal records. He called the region La Huerta ("The Garden"). Alas, the great navigator struggled home to Spain in worm-eaten ships (he was stranded for one whole year in Jamaica) and never returned. The prospect of vast loot, however, drew adventurers whose numbers were reinforced after Vasco Nuñez de Balboa's discovery of the Pacific in 1513. To these explorers the name Costa Rica would have seemed a cruel hoax. Floods, swamps, and tropical diseases stalked them in the sweltering lowlands. And fierce, elusive Indians harassed them maddeningly.

In 1506, Ferdinand of Spain sent a governor, Diego de Nicuesa, to colonize the Atlantic coast of the isthmus he called Veragua. He got off to a bad start by running aground off the coast of Panamá and was forced to march north, enduring a welcome that was less hospitable than the one afforded Columbus. Antagonized Indian bands used guerrilla tactics to slay the strangers and willingly burnt their own crops to deny them food. Nicuesa set the tone for future expeditions

by foreshortening his own cultural lessons with the musket ball. Things seemed more promising when an expedition under Gil González Davila set off from Panamá in 1522 to settle the region. It was Davila's expedition—which reaped quantities of gold—that won the land its nickname of Costa Rica, the "Rich Coast." Alas, the Indians never revealed the whereabouts of the fabled mines of "Veragua" (most likely it was placer gold found in the still-gold-rich rivers of the Osa Peninsula).

Davila's Catholic priests also supposedly managed to convert many Indians to Christianity with cross and cutlass. But once again, sickness and starvation were the price—the expedition reportedly lost more than 1,000 men. Later colonizing expeditions on the Caribbean similarly failed miserably; the coastal settlements dissolved amidst internal acrimony, the taunts of Indians, and the debilitating impact of pirate raids. When two years later Francisco Fernández de Córdova founded the first Spanish settlement on the Pacific at Bruselas, near present-day Puntarenas, its inhabitants had all died within less than three years.

For the next four decades Costa Rica was virtually left alone. The conquest of Peru by Pizarro in 1532 and the first of the great silver strikes in Mexico in the 1540s turned eyes away from southern Central America. Guatemala became the administrative center for the Spanish main in 1543, when the captaincy-general of Guatemala, answerable to the viceroy of New Spain (Mexico), was created with jurisdiction from the Isthmus of Tehuantepec to the empty lands of Costa Rica.

By the 1560s several Spanish cities had consolidated their position farther north and, prompted by an edict of 1559 issued by Philip II of Spain, the representatives in Guatemala thought it time to settle Costa Rica and Christianize the natives. By then it was too late for the latter. Barbaric treatment and European epidemics—opthalmia, smallpox, and tuberculosis—had already reaped the Indians like a scythe, and had so antagonized the survivors that they took to the forests and eventually found refuge amid the remote valleys of the Cordillera Talamanca. Only in the Nicoya Peninsula did there remain any significant Indian population, the Chorotegas, who soon found themselves chattel on Spanish land under the encomienda system whereby Spanish settlers were granted the right to forced Indian labor.

Settlement

In 1562, Juan Vásquez de Coronado—the true conquistador of Costa Rica—arrived as governor. He treated the surviving Indians more humanely and moved the few existing Spanish settlers into the Cartago Valley, where the temperate climate and rich volcanic soils offered the promise of crop cultivation. Cartago was established as the national capital in 1563. The economic and social development of the Spanish provinces was traditionally the work of the soldiers, who were granted encomiendas, landholdings that allowed for rights to the use of indigenous serfs. Coronado, however, to the regret of his subordinates, never made use of this system; in response, the Indians, led by chief Quitao, willingly subjugated themselves to Spanish rule. Coronado's successor allowed the Spanish to enslave the Indians. Soon, there were virtually no Indians left alive in the region.

After the initial impetus given by its discovery, Costa Rica lapsed into a lowly Cinderella of the Spanish empire. The gold was soon gone, shipped to Spain. Land was readily available, but there was no Indian labor to work it. Thus, the early economy lacked the conditions that favored development of the large colonial-style hacienda and feudal system of other Spanish enclaves. Without native slave labor or the resources to import slaves, the colonists were forced to work the land themselves (even the governor, it is commonly claimed, had to work his own plot of land to survive). Without gold or export crops, trade with other colonies was infrequent at best. The Spanish found themselves impoverished in a subsistence economy. Money became so scarce that the settlers eventually reverted to the Indian method of using cacao beans as currency.

A full century after its founding, Cartago could boast little more than a few score adobe houses and a single church, which all perished when Volcán Irazú erupted in 1723.

Gradually, however, prompted by an ecclesiastical edict that ordered the populace to resettle near churches, towns took shape around churches. Heredia (Cubujuquie) was founded in 1717, San José (Villaneuva de la Boca del Monte) in 1737, and Alajuela (Villa Hermosa) in 1782. Later, exports of wheat and tobacco placed the colonial economy on a sounder economic basis and encouraged the intensive settlement that characterizes the Meseta Central today.

Intermixing with the native population was not a common practice. In other colonies, Spaniard married native and a distinct class system arose, but mixed-bloods and ladinos (mestizos) represent a much smaller element in Costa Rica than they do elsewhere in the isthmus. All this had a leveling effect on colonial society. As the population grew, so did the number of poor families who had never benefited from the labor of encomienda Indians or suffered the despotic arrogance of criollo (Creole) landowners. Costa Rica, in the traditional view, became a "rural democracy," with no oppressed mestizo class resentful of the maltreatment and scorn of the Creoles. Removed from the mainstream of Spanish culture, the Costa Ricans became very individualistic and egalitarian.

Not all areas of the country, however, fit the model of rural democracy. Nicoya and Guanacaste on the Pacific side offered an easy overland route from Nicaragua to Panamá and were administered quite separately in colonial times from the rest of Costa Rica. They fell within the Nicaraguan sphere of influence, and large cattle ranches or haciendas arose. Revisions to the encomienda laws in 1542, however, limited the amount of time that Indians were obliged to provide their labor; Indians were also rounded up and forcibly concentrated into settlements distant from the haciendas. The large estate owners thus began to import African slaves, who became an important part of the labor force on the cattle ranches that were established in the Pacific northwest. The cattle-ranching economy and the more traditional class-based society that arose persist today.

Some three centuries of English associations and of neglect by the Spanish authorities have also created a very different cultural milieu all along the Caribbean coast of Central America. On the Caribbean of Costa Rica, cacao plantations—the most profitable of the colonial period—became well established. Eventually large-scale cacao production gave way to small-scale sharecropping, and then to tobacco as the cacao industry went into decline. Spain closed the Costa Rican ports in 1665 in response to English piracy, thereby cutting off seaborne sources of legal trade. Such artificial difficulties to economic development compounded those created by nature. Smuggling flourished, however, for the largely unincorporated Caribbean coast provided a safe haven to buccaneers and smugglers, whose strongholds became 18th-century shipping points for logwood and mahogany. The illicit trade helped weaken central authority. The illusion of Central American colonial unity was also weakened in the waning stages of the Spanish empire as interest in, and the ability to maintain, the rigid administrative structure declined.

THE EMERGENCE OF A NATION

Independence

Independence of Central America from Spain on 15 September 1821 came on the coattails of Mexico's declaration earlier in the same year. Independence had little immediate effect, however, for Costa Rica had required only minimal government during the colonial era and had long gone its own way. In fact, the country was so out of touch that the news that independence had been granted reached Costa Rica a full month after the event. A hastily convened provincial council voted for accession to Mexico; in 1823, the other Central American nations proclaimed the United Provinces of Central America, with their capital in Guatemala City.

After the declaration, effective power lay in the hands of the separate towns of the isthmus, and it took several years for a stable pattern of political alignment to emerge. The four leading cities of Costa Rica felt as independent as had the city-states of ancient Greece, and the conservative and aristocratic leaders of Cartago and Heredia soon found themselves at odds with the more progressive republican leaders of San José and Alajuela. The local quarrels quickly developed into civic unrest and, in 1823, to civil war. After a brief battle in the Ochomogo Hills, the republican forces of San José were victorious. They rejected Mexico, and Costa Rica joined the federation with full autonomy for its own affairs. Guanacaste voted to secede from Nicaragua and join Costa Rica the following year.

From this moment on, liberalism in Costa Rica had the upper hand. Elsewhere in Central America, conservative groups tied to the Church and the erstwhile colonial bureaucracy spent generations at war with anticlerical and laissez-faire liberals, and a cycle of civil wars came to dominate the region. By contrast, in Costa Rica colonial institutions had been relatively weak and early modernization of the economy propelled the nation out of poverty and laid the foundations of democracy far earlier than elsewhere in the isthmus. While other countries turned to repression to deal with social tensions, Costa Rica turned toward reform. Military plots and coups weren't unknown—they played a large part in determining who came to rule throughout the next century—but the generals usually were puppets used as tools to install favored individuals (usually surprisingly progressive civilian allies) representing the interests of particular cliques.

Early Liberalism

Juan Mora Fernández, elected the nation's first chief of state in 1824, set the tone by ushering in a nine-year period of progressive stability. He established a sound judicial system, founded the nation's first newspaper, and expanded public education. He also encouraged coffee cultivation and gave free land grants to would-be coffee growers. The nation, however, was still riven by rivalry, and in September 1835 the War of the League broke out when San José was attacked by the three other towns. They were unsuccessful and the national flag was planted firmly in San José.

Braulio Carrillo, who had taken power as a benevolent dictator, established an orderly public administration and new legal codes to replace colonial Spanish law. In 1838, he withdrew Costa Rica from the Central American federation and proclaimed complete independence. In a final show of federalist strength, the Honduran general Francisco Morazán toppled Carrillo in 1842. It was too late. The seeds of independence had taken firm root. Morazán's extranational ambitions and the military draft and direct taxes he imposed soon inspired his overthrow. He was executed within the year.

Coffee is King

By now, the reins of power had been taken up by a nouveau elite—the coffee barons, whose increasing prosperity led to rivalries between the wealthiest family factions, who vied with each other for political dominance. In 1849, the *cafetaleros* announced their ascendancy by conspiring to overthrow the nation's first president, José María Castro, an enlightened man who initiated his administration by founding a high school for girls and sponsoring freedom of the press. They chose as Castro's successor Juan Rafael Mora, one of the most powerful personalities among the new coffee aristocracy. Mora is remembered for the remarkable economic growth that marked his first term and for "saving" the nation from the imperial ambitions of the American adventurer William Walker during his second term. In a display of ingratitude, his countryfolk ousted him from power in 1859; the masses blamed him for the cholera epidemic that claimed the lives of one in every 10 Costa Ricans in the wake of the Walker saga, while the elites were horrified when Mora moved to establish a national bank, which would have undermined their control of credit to the coffee producers. After failing in his own coup against his successor, he was executed—a prelude to a second cycle of militarism, for the war of 1856 had introduced Costa Rica to the buying and selling of generals and the establishment of a corps of officers possessing an inflated aura of legitimacy.

The Guardia Legacy

The 1860s were marred by power struggles among the ever-powerful coffee elite, supported by their respective military cronies. General Tomás Guardia, however, was his own man. In April 1870, he overthrew the government, and he went on to rule for 12 years as an iron-willed military strongman backed by a powerful centralized government of his own making.

True to Costa Rican tradition, Guardia proved himself a progressive thinker and a benefactor of the people. His towering reign set in motion forces that shaped the modern liberal-democratic state. Hardly characteristic of 19th-century despots, he abolished capital punishment, managed to curb the power of the coffee barons, and tamed the use of the army for political means. He used coffee earnings and taxation to finance roads and public buildings. And in a landmark revision to the Constitution in 1869, he made "primary education for both sexes obligatory, free, and at the cost of the Nation."

Guardia had a dream: to make the transport of coffee more efficient and more profitable by forging a railroad linking the Central Valley with the At-

lantic coast, and thus with America and Europe. Fulfillment of Guardia's dream was the triumph of one man—Minor Keith of Brooklyn, New York—over a world of risks and logistical nightmares.

Guardia's enlightened administration was a watershed for the nation. The aristocrats gradually came to understand that liberal, orderly, and stable regimes profited their business interests while the instability inherent in reliance on militarism was damaging to it. And the extension of education to every citizen (and the arrival of thousands of European immigrants bringing notions of liberalism) raised the consciousness of the masses and made it increasingly difficult for the patrimonial elite to exclude the population from the political process.

Democracy

The shift to democracy was manifest in the election called by President Bernardo Soto in 1889—commonly referred to as the first "honest" election, with popular participation (women and blacks, however, were still excluded from voting). To Soto's surprise, his opponent José Joaquín Rodríguez won. The masses rose and marched in the streets to support their chosen leader after the Soto government decided not to recognize the new president. The Costa Ricans had spoken, and Soto stepped down.

During the course of the next two generations, militarism gave way to peaceful transitions to power. Presidents, however, attempted to amend the Constitution to continue their rule and even dismissed uncooperative legislatures. Both Rodríguez and his hand-picked successor, Rafael Iglesias, for example, turned dictatorial while sponsoring material progress. Iglesias's successor, Ascensión Esquivel, who took office in 1902, even exiled three contenders for the 1906 elections and imposed his own choice for president: González Víquez. And Congress declared the winner of the 1914 plebiscite ineligible and named its own choice, noncontender Alfredo González Flores, as president.

Throughout all this the country had been at peace, the army in its barracks. In 1917, democracy faced its first major challenge. At that time, the state collected the majority of its revenue from the less wealthy. Flores's bill to establish direct, progressive taxation based on income and his espousal of state involvement in the economy had earned the wrath of the elites. They de-

THE WILLIAM WALKER SAGA

William Walker was 1.65 meters (5 feet, 5 inches) and 55 kg (120 pounds) of cocky intellect and ego. Born in Nashville in 1824, he graduated from the University of Pennsylvania with an M.D. at the age of 19, then went on to study in Paris and Germany. Despite his illustrious start, Walker was destined for failure. He tried his hand unsuccessfully as a doctor, lawyer, and writer, and even joined the miners and panners in the California Gold Rush. Somewhere along the line, he became filled with grandiose schemes of adventure and an arrogant belief in America's "manifest destiny"—to control other nations. During the next decade the Tennessean freebooter went on to become the scourge of the Central American isthmus.

He dreamed of extending the glory of slavery and forming a confederacy of southern American states to include the Spanish-speaking nations. To wet his feet, he invaded Baja California in 1853 with a few hundred cronies bankrolled by a pro-slavery group called the Knights of the Golden Circle. Forced back north of the border by the Mexican army, Walker found himself behind bars for breaking the Neutrality Act. Acquitted and famous (or infamous, depending on point of view), he attracted a following of kindred spirits to his next wild cause.

During the feverish California Gold Rush, eager fortune hunters sailed down the East Coast to Nicaragua, traveled up the Río San Juan and across Lake Nicaragua aboard an exaggerated canoe called a bungo, and thence were carried by mule the last 12 miles to the Pacific, where with luck a San Francisco-bound ship would be waiting. In those days, before the Panamá Canal, wealthy North Americans were eyeing southern Nicaragua as the perfect spot to build a passage linking the Pacific and the Caribbean Oceans. The conservative government of Nicaragua decided that both the traffic and the proposed canal were worth a hefty fee.

Backed by North American capitalists and with the tacit sanction of President James Buchanan, Walker landed in Nicaragua in June 1855 with a group of mercenaries—the "fifty-six immortals"—and the ostensible goal of molding a new government that would be more accommodating to U.S. business ventures.

Perhaps some of Walker's men thought they were fighting simply to annex Nicaragua to the United States; others may have believed they were part of the great struggle to establish slavery in Central America. But Walker, it seems, had other ambitions—he dreamed of making the five Central American countries a federated state with himself as emperor. After subduing the Nicaraguans, he had himself "elected" president of Nicaragua, and promptly legalized slavery there.

Next, Walker looked south to Costa Rica. In March 1856, he invaded Guanacaste. President Mora, backed by the Legislative Assembly, called up an army of 9,000 to join "the loyal sons of Guatemala, El Salvador, and Honduras," who had combined their meager and bickering forces to expel the invaders. President Mora and his brother-in-law, José María Cañas, took personal charge of Costa Rica's band of campesinos and makeshift soldiers (Cornelius Vanderbilt, stung by Walker's seizure of his Trans-Isthmian Transit Company steamers, reportedly bankrolled the effort). Armed with machetes and rusty rifles, they marched for Guanacaste and routed Walker and his cronies, who retreated pell-mell the way they'd come. Costa Rica still celebrates its peasant army's victory. The site of the battle—La Casona, in Santa Rosa National Park—is now a museum.

Eventually, the Costa Rican army cornered Walker's forces in a wooden fort at Rivas, in Nicaragua. A drummer boy named Juan Santamaría bravely volunteered to torch the fort, successfully flushing Walker out into the open. His bravery cost Santamaría his life; he is now a national hero and a symbol of resistance to foreign interference.

With his forces defeated, Walker's ambitions were temporarily scuttled. He was eventually rescued by the U.S. Navy and taken to New York, only to return in 1857 with even more troops (filibusteros). The Nicaraguan army defeated him again, and Walker was imprisoned. Released three years later and unrepentant, he seized a Honduran customs house. In yet another bid to escape, he surrendered to an English frigate captain who turned him over to the Honduran army, which promptly shot him, thereby bringing to an end the pathetic saga.

creed his removal. Minister of War Federico Tinoco Granados seized power. Tinoco ruled as an iron-fisted dictator and soon squandered the support of U.S. business interests. More important, Costa Ricans had come to accept liberty as their due; they were no longer prepared to acquiesce in oligarchic restrictions. Women and high-school students led a demonstration which called for his ouster, and Tinoco fled to Europe.

There followed a series of unmemorable administrations culminating in the return of two previous leaders, Ricardo Jiménez and González Víquez, who alternated power for 12 years through the 1920s and '30s. The apparent tranquility was shattered by the Depression and the social unrest it engendered. Old-fashioned paternalistic liberalism had failed to resolve social ills such as malnutrition, unemployment, low pay, and poor working conditions. The Depression distilled all these issues, especially after a dramatic communist-led strike against the United Fruit Company, which had attained inordinate political influence, brought tangible gains. Calls grew shrill for reforms.

REFORMISM AND CIVIL WAR

Calderón
The decade of the 1940s and its climax, the civil war, marked a turning point in Costa Rican history: from paternalistic government by traditional rural elites to modernistic, urban-focused statecraft controlled by bureaucrats, professionals, and small entrepreneurs. The dawn of the new era was spawned by Rafael Angel Calderón Guardia, a profoundly religious physician and a president (1940-44) with a social conscience. In a period when neighboring Central American nations were under the yoke of tyrannical dictators, Calderón promulgated a series of farsighted reforms. His legacy included a stab at land "reform" (the landless could gain title to unused land by cultivating it), establishment of a guaranteed minimum wage, paid vacations, unemployment compensation, progressive taxation, plus a series of constitutional amendments codifying workers' rights. Calderón also founded the University of Costa Rica.

Calderón's social agenda was hailed by the urban poor and leftists and despised by the upper classes, his original base of support. His early declaration of war on Germany, seizure of German property, and imprisonment of Germans further upset his conservative patrons, many of whom were of German descent. World War II stalled economic growth at a time when Calderón's social programs called for vastly increased public spending. The result was rampant inflation, which eroded his support among the middle and working classes. Abandoned, Calderón crawled into bed with two unlikely partners: the Catholic Church and the communists (Popular Vanguard Party). Together they formed the United Social Christian Party.

The Prelude to Civil War
In 1944, Calderón was replaced by his puppet, Teodoro Picado Michalsky, in an election widely regarded as fraudulent. Picado's uninspired administration failed to address rising discontent throughout the nation. Intellectuals, distrustful of Calderón's "unholy" alliance, joined with businessmen, *campesinos,* and labor activists and formed the Social Democratic Party, dominated by the emergent professional middle classes eager for economic diversification and modernization. In its own strange amalgam, the SDP allied itself with the traditional oligarchic elite. The country was thus polarized. Tensions mounted.

Street violence finally erupted in the run-up to the 1948 election, with Calderón on the ballot for a second presidential term. When he lost to his opponent Otilio Ulate (the representative of *Acción Democrática,* a coalition of anti-calderonistas) by a small margin, the government claimed fraud. Next day, the building holding many of the ballot papers went up in flames, and the calderonista-dominated legislature annulled the election results. Ten days later, on 10 March 1948, the "War of National Liberation" plunged Costa Rica into civil war.

Don Pepe—Savior of the Nation
The popular myth suggests that José María ("Don Pepe") Figueres Ferrer—42-year-old coffee farmer, engineer, economist, and philosopher—raised a "ragtag army of university students and intellectuals" and stepped forward to topple the government that had refused to step aside for its democratically elected successor. In actuality, Don Pepe's "revolution" had been long in the planning; the 1948 election merely provided a good excuse.

COFFEE, BANANAS, AND MINOR KEITH

Costa Rica became the first Central American coutry to grow coffee when seeds were introduced from Jamaica in 1808. Coffee flourished and transformed the nation. It was eminently suited to the climate (the dry season made harvest and transportation easy) and volcanic soils of the central highlands. There were no rival products to compete for investments, land, or labor. And the coffee bean—*grano d'oro*—was exempt from taxes. Soon, peasant settlements spread up the slopes of the volcanoes and down the slopes toward the coast.

By 1829, coffee had become the nation's most important product. Foreign money was pouring in. The coffee elite owed its wealth to its control of processing and trade rather than to direct control of land. Small farmers dominated actual production. Thus, no sector of society failed to advance. The coffee bean pulled the country out of its miserable economic quagmire and placed it squarely on a pedestal as the most prosperous nation in Central America.

In 1871, when President Guardia decided to build his railroad to the Atlantic, coffee for export was still being sent via mule and oxcart 100 km from the Meseta Central to the Pacific port of Puntarenas, then shipped—via a circuitous, three-month voyage—around the southern tip of South America and up the Atlantic to Europe.

Enter Minor Keith, a former stockboy in a Broadway clothing store, lumber surveyor in the American West, and Texas pig farmer. In 1871, at the age of 23, Minor had come to Costa Rica at the behest of his brother Henry, who had been commissioned by his uncle, Henry Meiggs (the famous builder of railroads in the Andes), to oversee the construction of the Atlantic Railroad linking the coastal port of Limón with the coffee-producing Meseta Central. By 1873, when the railway should have been completed, only a third had been built and money for the project had run out. (The railroad was to have been financed by a loan of 3.4 million pounds issued by English banks; unscrupulous British bankers, however, took advantage of the Costa Ricans by retaining the majority of the money as commissions.) Henry Keith promptly packed his bags and went home.

The younger brother, who had been running the commissary for railroad workers in Puerto Limón, picked up the standard and for the next 15 years applied unflagging dedication to achieve the enterprise his brother had botched. In London, he renegotiated the loans and raised new money. He hired workers from Jamaica and China, and drove them—and himself—like beasts of burden. The Jamaicans, says one writer, were "a generation freed from slavery only in 1834 . . . proud new British subjects who profoundly identified with what seemed to them the imperial task at hand—so much so that they conferred honorary British citizenship on the white man Minor Keith."

A direct route to the Caribbean had never been surveyed, and as a result some stretches of railway had to be abandoned when progress turned out to be impossible. The workers had to bore tunnels through mountains, bridge numerous tributaries of the Reventazón River, hack through jungles, and drain the Caribbean marshlands. During the rainy season, mud slides would wash away bridges. And malaria, dysentery, and yellow fever plagued the workers (the project eventually claimed more than 4,000 lives). In December 1890, a bridge high over the turbulent waters of the Birris River finally brought the tracks from Alajuela and Puerto Limón together. It was a prodigious achievement.

For Keith, the endeavor paid off handsomely. He had wrangled from the Costa Rican government a concession of 800,000 acres of land (nearly seven percent of the national territory) along the railway track and coastal plain, plus a 90-year lease on the completed railroad. And the profits from his endeavors were to be tax-free for 20 years.

To help finance the railroad project, Keith planted his lands with bananas, a fruit of Asian origin called *Musa sapientum* (the "muse of wisdom"), which had been brought to the New World by the Spaniards. It was a popular novelty in North America, and Costa Rica became the first Central American country to grow them. Like coffee, the fruit flourished. Exports increased from 100,000 stems in 1883 to more than a million in 1890, when the railroad was completed. By 1899 Keith, who went on to marry the daughter of the Costa Rican president, had become the "Banana King" and Costa Rica the world's leading banana producer.

Along the way, the savvy entrepreneur had wisely entered into a partnership with the Boston Fruit Company, the leading importer of tropical fruits for the US market. Thus was born the United Fruit Company—La Yunai, as Central Americans called it—which during the first half of the 20th century was to become the driving force and overlord of the economies of countries the length and breadth of Latin America.

"Don Pepe" Figueres, leader of the 1948 revolution, at a victory parade

Don Pepe, an ambitious and outspoken firebrand, had been exiled to Mexico in 1942—the first political outcast since the Tinoco era. Figueres formed an alliance with other exiles, returned to Costa Rica in 1944, began calling for an armed uprising, and arranged for foreign arms to be airlifted in to groups being trained by Guatemalan military advisors. In 1946 he participated with a youthful Fidel Castro in an aborted attempt to depose General Trujillo of the Dominican Republic. (Figueres and Castro remained close friends. Years later, following the success of the leftist Sandinistas in Nicaragua, Castro initiated a Costa Rican guerrilla army to topple Costa Rican democracy and prepare for the "Vietnamization" of Central America. Surveying Costa Rica from across the Río San Juan, he is said to have scoffed, "A nurse's strike could bring that down.")

In 1948, back in Costa Rica, Figueres formed the National Liberation Armed Forces in the mountains of Santa María de Dota. Supported by the governments of Guatemala and Cuba, Don Pepe's insurrectionists captured the cities of Cartago and Puerto Limón from calderonistas (the government's army at the time numbered only about 500 men) and were poised to pounce on San José when Calderón, who had little heart for the conflict, capitulated. (The government's pathetically trained soldiers—aided and armed by the Somoza regime in Nicaragua—included communist banana workers from the lowlands; they wore blankets over their shoulders against the cold of the highlands, earning Calderón supporters the nickname mari-

achis.) The 40-day civil war claimed over 2,000 lives, most of them civilians.

THE MODERN ERA

Foundation of the Modern State

Don Pepe became head of the Founding Junta of the Second Republic of Costa Rica. As leader of the revolutionary junta, he consolidated Calderón's progressive social reform program and added his own landmark reforms: he banned the press and Communist Party, introduced suffrage for women and full citizenship for blacks, revised the Constitution to outlaw a standing army (including his own), established a presidential term limit, and created an independent Electoral Tribunal to oversee future elections. Figueres also shocked the elites by nationalizing the banks and insurance companies, a move that paved the way for state intervention in the economy.

On a darker note, Don Pepe reneged on the peace terms that guaranteed the safety of the calderonistas: Calderón and many of his followers were exiled to Mexico, special tribunals confiscated their property, and, in a sordid episode, many prominent left-wing officials and activists were abducted and murdered. (Supported by Nicaragua, Calderón twice attempted to invade Costa Rica and topple his nemesis, but was each time repelled. Eventually he was allowed to return, and even ran for president unsuccessfully in 1962.)

COSTA RICA
AND THE NICARAGUAN REVOLUTION

Costa Rica's relations with neighboring Nicaragua have always been testy. During the 1970s, the Nicaraguan revolution brought these simmering tensions to a boil, threatening to destabilize Costa Rica and plunge the whole of Central America into war. Costa Rica was led to the brink by a pathetically myopic U.S. foreign policy. That it was ultimately saved owes much to the integrity of Costa Rican president Oscar Arias Sánchez (1986-90), who earned the 1987 Nobel Peace Prize for bringing peace to the region.

Much of the post-1948 friction between the two nations stemmed from the personal rivalry between Costa Rica's "Don Pepe" Figueres and Nicaragua's strongman dictator, "Tacho" Somoza, who despised Figueres's espousal of social democracy and efforts to rid Central America of tyranny. In 1948, Figueres ousted the *calderonista* government and came to power with the backing of Nicaragua's anti-Somoza opposition. For the next two decades Figueres and the Somoza family conspired against each other.

During Figueres's second term as president (1970-74), relations with Nicaragua briefly improved—enough, in fact, for the Somoza family (now headed by Tacho's son, Anastasio or "Tachito") to acquire three vast properties on the Costa Rican side of the border. (The estates, equipped with airstrips suitable for large aircraft, became training grounds for Cuban exiles planning a military invasion of Cuba; in the 1980s, the lands became training grounds for the contras.)

The Carter administration brought new attitudes toward human rights. U.S. support for right-wing dictatorships temporarily waned, and countries with relatively democratic systems, such as Costa Rica, benefited from increased aid. Buoyed by the new moral stance, the Nicaraguan church and the Sandinista National Liberation Front (FSLN) stepped up their attacks on the tyrannical Somoza regime. Costa Rica was to play a pivotal role in the revolution and postrevolutionary war that followed.

Most Ticos were sympathetic to the Sandinista cause and supported their government's tacit backing of the anti-Somoza revolutionaries who established guerrilla camps in Costa Rica close to the Nicaraguan border. Many Costa Ricans even took up arms alongside the revolutionaries.

As relations worsened, Somoza launched retaliatory air strikes on Costa Rican border towns; Civil Guards came under attack, and the dictator threatened a full-scale invasion, prompting Costa Rica to break off diplomatic relations and seize the Somoza estates. As the Sandinistas became more radical, however, fears were raised that the revolution would have a destabilizing effect throughout the isthmus. President Rodrigo Carazo attempted to rid the northern border of guerrilla camps. Meanwhile, he allowed the FSLN to set up a government-in-exile in San José in the apparent hope that he could influence the Sandinistas into taking a more moderate stance.

The picture was reversed overnight. On 19 July 1979, the Sandinistas toppled the Somoza regime. Thousands of Nicaraguan National Guardsmen and right-wing sympathizers were forced to flee. Many settled in northern Costa Rica, where they were warmly welcomed by wealthy ranchers sympathetic to the right-wing cause. By the summer of 1981, the anti-Sandinistas had been cobbled into the Nicaraguan Democratic Front (FDN), headquartered in Costa Rica; contras roamed throughout the northern provinces, and the CIA was beginning to take charge of events. Costa Rica's foreign policy underwent a dramatic reversal as the former champion of the Sandinista cause found itself embroiled in the Reagan administration's vendetta to oust the Sandinista regime.

Costa Rica was in a bind. In February 1982, Luis Alberto Monge Alvarez was elected president. He originally tried to keep his country neutral. In the face of the Sandinistas' radical shift to the left, however, Monge found himself hostage to U.S. and domestic right-wing pressure to support the contras. As the economy slipped into crisis, he was forced to bow to U.S. demands in exchange for foreign aid. By 1984, when contra raids had begun to prompt Nicaraguan counterstrikes across the border, the CIA, Oliver North, and his cronies in the National Security Council were firmly in command; the Costa Rican Civil Guard was being trained in Honduras by U.S. military advisors; roads and airstrips were being built throughout the northern provinces; and the CIA was running drugs.

By the fall of 1984, Monge's administration, with right-wingers in ascendancy, was giving tacit support to newly formed paramilitary groups that began carrying out acts of domestic terrorism that were intended to implicate the Sandinistas and lead to a militarization of Costa Rica's security forces.

As the prospect of regional war increased, the Costa Rican people "stepped back from the brink" *(continues on next page)*

COSTA RICA
AND THE NICARAGUAN REVOLUTION
(continued)

and rallied behind peace advocate Oscar Arias Sánchez in the 1986 presidential elections. Arias had been outraged by U.S. attempts to undermine Costa Rica's neutrality and drag the tiny nation into the conflict. Once inaugurated, he immediately threw his energies into restoring peace to Central America.

In February 1987, Arias presented the leaders of the Central American nations a formal peace plan, which called for suspension of all military aid to insurrectionists, cease-fires to all conflicts, general amnesties for political prisoners and for guerrillas who laid down their arms, negotiations between governments and their opposition, and free and fair elections.

Ronald Reagan called the plan "fatally flawed," but, despite Washington's best efforts to sabotage it, all five Central American presidents—including Nicaragua's Daniel Ortega—signed it in August 1987, rejecting Reagan's inane military "solution" in favor of a solution in which all concerned committed themselves to fundamental reforms in their political systems. In a speech before the U.S. Congress the following month, Arias told Washington forthrightly that the Costa Rican people "are convinced that the risks we run in the struggle for peace will always be less than the irreparable cost of war."

"Although we are poor, we have so far been able to reach satisfactory goals," Arias told the U.S. Congress. "This is largely because we have no arms expenditures and because the imbedded practice of democracy drives us to meet the needs of the people. Almost 40 years ago we abolished our army. Today we threaten no one, neither our own people nor our neighbors. Such threats are absent not because we lack tanks, but because there are few of us who are hungry, illiterate, or unemployed."

Then, by a prior agreement that established the interim junta for 18 months, Figueres returned the reins of power to Otilio Ulate, the actual winner of the '48 election. Costa Ricans later rewarded Figueres with two terms as president, in 1953-57 and 1970-74. Figueres dominated politics for the next two decades. A socialist, he used his popularity to build his own electoral base and founded the Partido de Liberación Nacional (PLN), which became the principal advocate of state-sponsored development and reform. He died on 8 June 1990, a national hero.

The Contemporary Scene
Social and economic progress since 1948 has helped return the country to stability, and though post-civil war politics have reflected the play of old loyalties and antagonisms, elections have been free and fair. With only two exceptions, the country has ritualistically alternated its presidents between the PLN and the opposition Social Christians. Successive PLN governments have built on the reforms of the *calderonista* era, and the 1950s and '60s saw a substantial expansion of the welfare state and public school system, funded by economic growth. The intervening conservative governments have encouraged private enterprise and economic self-reliance through tax breaks, protectionism, subsidized credits, and other macroeconomic policies. The combined results were a generally vigorous economic growth and the creation of a welfare state which had grown by 1981 to serve 90% of the population, absorbing 40% of the national budget in the process and granting the government the dubious distinction of being the nation's biggest employer.

By 1980, the bubble had burst. Costa Rica was mired in an economic crisis: epidemic inflation, crippling currency devaluation, soaring oil bills and social welfare costs, plummeting coffee, banana, and sugar prices, and the disruptions to trade caused by the Nicaraguan war. When large international loans then came due, Costa Rica found itself burdened overnight with the world's greatest per-capita debt. In addition to tens of thousands killed, a decade of war in the region (and Monge's support for U.S. policy) had eroded international confidence in Costa Rica. Regional trade had declined 60%. There had been a capital flight from the country; by 1984, the national debt had almost quadrupled. And as many as 250,000 Nicaraguan exiles and refugees fled into Costa Rica, whose political stability had been seriously undermined.

In May 1984 events took a tragic turnn at a press conference on the banks of the Río San Juan held by Edén Pastora, the U.S.-backed leader of the Contras. A bomb exploded, killing foreign journalists (Pastora escaped). A general consensus is that the bomb was meant to blame the Sandinistas; the CIA has been implicated.

In February 1986, Costa Ricans elected as their president a relatively young sociologist and economist-lawyer called Oscar Arias Sánchez. Arias's electoral promise had been to work for peace. Immediately, he put his energies into resolving Central America's regional conflicts. Arias's tireless efforts were rewarded in 1987, when his Central American peace plan was signed by the five Central American presidents in Guatemala City—an achievement that earned the Costa Rican president the 1987 Nobel Peace Prize, and for which the whole nation is justly proud.

In February 1990, Rafael Angel Calderón Fournier, a conservative lawyer and candidate for the Social Christian Unity Party (PUSC), won a narrow victory with 51% of the vote. He was inaugurated 50 years to the day after his father, the great reformer, was named president. Restoring Costa Rica's economy to sound health in the face of a debilitating national debt was Calderón's paramount goal. Under the aegis of pressure from the World Bank and International Monetary Fund, Calderón initiated a series of austerity measures aimed at redressing the country's huge deficit and national debt. Indications were that the attempts were succeeding, although not without social cost.

In March 1994, in an intriguing historical quirk, Calderón, son of the president ousted by Don Pepe Figueres in 1948, was replaced by Don Pepe's youthful son, José María Figueres, a graduate of both West Point and Harvard. The Figueres period was bedeviled by problems, including the collapse of the Banco Anglo Costarricense in 1994, followed in 1995 by inflation, a massive teachers strike, and an antigovernment demonstration of 100,000 people. A slump in tourism (partly thanks to a massive price hike of $15 in national park entrance fees; since rescinded) and Hurricane César, which ripped the Pacific southwest in July 1996 causing $100 million in damage, worsened the country's plight. A month later the nation was rocked when a female German tourist and her tour guide were kidnapped, generating heaps of unwanted exposure in the European press. Tourism from Europe plummeted. The kidnappers were caught, but the affair took a strange twist when photographs appeared showing the woman French-kissing one of her captors. Ticos took solace in the gold medal—the first ever for the country—won at the 1996 Olympics by Costa Rican swimmer Claudia Poll. And President Clinton's visit to Costa Rica in May 1997—capped by a visit to Braulio Carillo National Park—during a summit of Central American leaders augered a new era of free trade and enhanced regional accord.

The Figueres administration was considered a bit of a flop by a majority of the electorate, who in February 1998, overwhelmingly voted for the Social Christian Unity Party. Figueres was replaced by Miguel Ángel Rogríguez, a wealthy businessman and economist whom Figueres had defeated in a run for president in 1994.

GOVERNMENT AND ECONOMY

Organization

Costa Rica is a democratic republic, as defined by the 1949 Constitution, which guarantees all citizens and foreigners equality before the law, the right to own property, the right of petition and assembly, freedom of speech, and the right to habeas corpus. As in the United States, the government is divided into independent executive, legislative, and judicial branches, with "separation of powers." In 1969 an amendment ruled that neither the incumbent president nor any subsequent president may be reelected (they must also be secular citizens; i.e. not a priest).

The **executive branch** comprises the president, two vice presidents, and a cabinet of 17 members called the Council of Government *(Consejo de Gobierno)*. Legislative power is vested in the **Legislative Assembly,** a unicameral body composed of 57 members elected by proportional representation. *Diputados* are elected for a four-year term and can be reelected only after four more. The Assembly holds the power to amend the president's budget and to appoint the comptroller general, who checks public expenditures and prevents the executive branch from overspending. Like its U.S. equivalent, the Assembly can override presidential decisions by two-thirds majority vote and reserves unto itself the sole right to declare war. The power of the legislature to go against the president's wishes is a cause of constant friction (Costa Rica is governed through compromise: a tempest may rage at the surface, but a compromise resolution is generally being worked out behind the scenes), and presidents have not been cowardly in using such tools as the executive decree to usurp power to themselves. The Oduber administration (1974-78), for example, issued 4,709 executive decrees; the legislature enacted just 721 laws in the same period.

The Legislative Assembly also appoints **Supreme Court** judges for minimum terms of eight years. They are automatically reappointed unless voted out by the Legislative Assembly. Twenty-four judges now serve on the Supreme Court. These judges, in turn, select judges for the civil and penal courts. Together, the courts have done much to enforce constitutional checks on presidential power. The courts also appoint the three "permanent" magistrates of the **Special Electoral Tribunal,** an independent body that oversees each election and is given far-reaching powers. The Tribunal appointees serve staggered six-year terms and are appointed one every two years to minimize partisanship (two additional temporary magistrates are appointed a year before each election). Control of the police force reverts to the Supreme Electoral Tribunal during election campaigns to help ensure the integrity of all constitutional guarantees.

The nation is divided into seven provinces—Alajuela, Cartago, Guanacaste, Heredia, Limón, Puntarenas, and San José—each ruled by a governor appointed by the president. The provinces are subdivided into 81 *cantones* (counties), which in turn are divided into a total of 421 *distritos* (districts) ruled by municipal councils. The provinces play only one important role: as electoral districts for the Legislative Assembly. The number of deputies for each province is determined by that province's population, with one member for each 30,000 people; seats are allotted according to the proportion of the vote for

each party. In the past three decades, the municipalities have steadily lost their prerogatives to central authority and now are relegated to fulfilling such functions as garbage collection, public lighting, and upkeep of streets—with a marked lack of success in some cases.

Political Parties

Costa Rica has no shortage of political parties. However, only two really count. The largest is the **National Liberation Party** (Partido de Liberación Nacional, or PLN), founded by the statesman and hero of the Civil War, "Don Pepe" Figueres. The PLN, which roughly equates with European social democracy and American-style welfare-state liberalism, has traditionally enjoyed a majority in the legislature, even when an opposition president has been in power. Its support is traditionally drawn from among the middle-class professionals and entrepreneurs and small farmers and rural *peones*.

PLN's archrival is the **Social Christian Unity Party** (Partido de Unidad Social Cristiana, or PUSC), which was formed in 1982, represents more conservative interests, and is a loose coalition of four different parties known as La Oposición.

Between them, the two parties have alternated power since 1949 (in every presidential election but two, the "ins" have been ousted). The margin is always narrow; in 1994, Figueres (PLN) defeated Miguel Ángel Rogriguez (PUSC) by only 20,000 votes, and in February 1998, a heavily disillusioned electorate replaced Figueres with Ángel by a one percent margin.

In addition, a number of less influential parties represent all facets of the political spectrum. Since Costa Ricans tend to vote for the man rather than the party, most minor parties form around a candidate and represent personal ambitions rather than strong political convictions. (Former president Figueres once accused Ticos of being as domesticated as sheep; they are not easily aroused to passionate defense of a position or cause.) However, in recent years, the marginal parties have attracted increasing attention as Ticos seem to be waking up to the fact that their nominally democratic system is debased by massive corruption and cronyism. The 1998 presidential elections fielded a large number of candidates from alternate parties.

Elections

Costa Rica's national elections, held every four years (on the first Sunday of February), reaffirm the pride Ticos feel for their democratic system. In the rest of Central America, says travel writer Paul Theroux, "an election can be a harrowing piece of criminality; in Costa Rica [it is] something of a fiesta. 'You should have been here for the election,' a woman told me in San José, as if I had missed a party." The streets are crisscrossed with flags, and everyone drives around honking their horns, throwing confetti, and holding up their purple-stained thumbs to show that they voted. (Cynics point out that most of the hoopla is because political favors are dispensed on a massive scale by the victorious party, and that it pays to demonstrate fealty.)

Costa Rican citizens enjoy universal suffrage—everyone over 18 has the vote—and citizens are automatically registered to vote on their 18th birthdays, when they are issued voter identity cards. Since 1959 voting has ostensibly been compulsory—it is a constitutional mandate—for all citizens under 70 years of age. After being ushered into voting booths by schoolchildren decked out in party colors, voters indicate their political preferences with a thumbprint beneath a photograph of the candidate of their choice. Splitting votes across party lines is common, as separate ballots are issued for the presidency, legislature, and municipal councils. If the president-elect fails to receive 40% of the vote, a special runoff election is held for the two top contenders.

The daily press is full of political messages for months preceding an election. Most papers take an overt partisan stance and journalists "print news stories that may be extremely biased, and allow supporters of opposing points of view to reply the next day," say the Biesanzes in their book, The Costa Ricans. As in the U.S., campaigns tend to stress personalities and the opponent's weaknesses rather than issues or suggested solutions. The Supreme Electoral Tribunal rules on campaign issues and can prohibit the use of political smears, such as branding an opponent as communist. Given the tone of the two most recent elections, when North American consultants introduced Machiavellianism into the arena, the Tribunal is in danger of losing hold of the reins.

All parties are granted equal air time on radio and television, and all campaign costs are largely drawn from the public purse: any party with five percent or more of the vote in the prior election can apply for a proportionate share of the official campaign fund, equal to 0.5% of the national budget. If a party fails to get five percent of the vote, it is legally required to refund the money, though this rarely happens.

Don't expect to buy a drink in the immediate run-up to an election: liquor and beer sales are banned for the preceding three days.

Bureaucracy

Little Costa Rica is big on government. Building on the reforms of the calderonista era, successive administrations have created an impressive array of health, education, and social-welfare programs plus steadily expanding state enterprises and regulatory bodies, all of which spell a massive expansion of the government bureaucracy. In 1949, the state employed only six percent of the working population; today the government pays the salaries of approximately 25%, or one in four employed people. For the nation, this represents a huge financial burden. Public employees are the best paid, most secure, and most highly unionized and vocal workers, and the supposedly neutral bureaucracy has become the largest and most insatiable pressure group in the country. Public employees' repetitive demands for higher pay, shorter hours, and greater fringe benefits (backed up by the constant threat of strikes) are so voracious that they eat up a vast proportion of the government benefits intended for the poor. "The state," says one Tican, "is a cow with a thousand teats and everyone wants a teat to suck."

Unfortunately, Costa Rica's government employees have nurtured bureaucratic formality to the level of art. Travelers may find a lot of their time being tied up in interminable lines. The problem has given rise to despachantes, people who make a living from their patience and knowledge of the bureaucratic ropes: for a small fee they will wait in line and gather the necessary documents on your behalf. Travel agencies can usually arrange a trustworthy despachante.

Armed Forces and Police

Simply put, Costa Rica has no army, navy, or air force. The nation disbanded its military forces in 1949, when it declared itself neutral. Nonetheless, Costa Rica's police force has various powerfully armed branches with a military capability. Throughout the country—especially near the Nicaraguan and Panamian borders—you'll see "soldiers" in army fatigues touting M-16 rifles. The "lower" branches are severly underfunded. Many community police stations lack a car! Costa Rica's police force has traditionally been underpaid and, as such, its ranks have suffered from being little-educated and prone to bribery and corruption. Many senior officers, too, have been political appointees rather than career men and women. The government recently tried to purge the force of its cancer (as a result, the traffic police are noticeably more professional than a few years ago).

Corruption and Cronyism

Despite the popular image as a beacon of democracy (*El Financiero* published a study in 1997 that found Costa Rica to be the least corrupt of all Latin American countries), nepotism and cronyism *is* entrenched in the Costa Rican political system, and corruption *is* part of the way things work. Political favoritism is endemic, as for example when the Figueres administration awarded a contract to build a geothermal plant to the *highest* bidder—a company represented by the president's father-in-law. The failure of the Banco Anglo Costarricense in 1994 is also attributed to massive fraud and corruption; the judge investigating the case narrowly escaped an assassination attempt in December 1997.

And if you've been wondering why the roads continue to deteriorate year-by-year, it's not simply because of the torrential rains or because there's no *plata* (money), though this is true. Often it is because money earmarked for municipalities for road repairs disappears into local pockets. The entrenched families who control local politics are powerful enough to prevent reform. The political system is too weak to resist the "bite," or bribery, locally called *chorrizo* (a poor grade of bacon).

Integridad Democrática, Apdo. 476-2100 San José, tel./fax 240-8292, is a non-governmental association of concerned citizens who banded together in 1997 to fight for a more democratic, open, and ethical government. **Centro de Amigos Para La Paz,** Apdo. 1507, San José 1000,

tel./fax 233-6168, at Calle 15, Ave. 6 bis., is a nonprofit Quaker-established association that promotes peace and social justice throughout Costa Rica and Central America. Its committees address issues such as adolescence, penal abolition, and community development.

ECONOMY

Costa Rica's economy this century has, in many ways, been a model for developing nations. Highly efficient coffee and banana industries aided by high and stable world prices have drawn in vast export earnings. Manufacturing has grown rapidly under the protection of external tariffs and the expanding purchasing power of the domestic market (per-capita income doubled between 1960 and 1979). And the nation long avoided amassing a crippling foreign debt.

Costa Rica's economy took a serious fall in 1978 when world coffee prices plummeted. The following year, oil prices rose sharply (Costa Rica spends the equivalent of its *total* coffee income for foreign oil every year) while foreign capital took to its heels with the outbreak of the Nicaraguan Revolution, which slowed commerce throughout the isthmus. Costa Rica is dependent on foreign investment. The welfare state established in the 1960s and 1970s was financed largely through foreign loans, and the industrialization policies of the 1970s based on import substitution were largely funded by foreign sources of investment capital. Locals taxes simply disappeared into private pockets (Ticos didn't seem to care because these were good times) while international funds paid the nation's way.

In 1980, a large part of the foreign loans came due. Starved for money, the government of President Rodrigo Carazo (1978-82) began to soak up domestic bank credit, devalued the *colón,* the nation's currency, and printed more money to meet its debts. Carazo's government was overwhelmed by the resulting crisis. Inflation soared to 100% by 1982. Industrial production went into decline. Official unemployment rose to 8.2%, with an additional 22.6% officially "underemployed" (unofficial figures were certainly higher). Real wages fell to pre-1970 levels, bringing impoverishment to much of the nation. By August 1981, when the nation's foreign debt reached US$4 billion, Costa Rica was forced to cease payment on its international loans.

The U.S. and International Monetary Fund (IMF) stepped in with a massive aid program that injected $3 billion into the economy between 1981 and 1984, equivalent to more than one-third of the Costa Rican government's budget and 10% of the nation's gross national product (GNP) for the period (Costa Rica was second only to Israel as the highest per-capita recipient of U.S. aid). Much of the U.S. government aid was tied to Costa Rica's support for the contra cause; IMF and World Bank assistance was tied to austerity measures designed to slash government spending, stimulate economic diversification, and sponsor competitive export industries. It was a boon to Costa Rica: many of the now dangerously deteriorated roads were laid during this period, although the surfeit of money fostered vast corruption (tax funds were craftily siphoned off into private pockets, while U.S. aid kept the country running).

Costa Rica *must* diversify to overcome reliance on a few agricultural products (earnings from coffee, for example, plummeted from $300 in 1990 to $180 in 1991) and a debilitating international debt which in 1998, at US$4.6 billion, is one of the world's highest per capita. And tourism, the lead industry, stalled in 1994-97. Although figures picked up in 1997 (both tourism and coffee have rebounded from recent slumps), Costa Rica faces increasing competition from its neighbors, all of whom are emerging tourism markets.

The Calderón administration (1990-94), under strong pressure from the IMF and World Bank, pledged to balance the budget and rectify Costa Rica's structural weaknesses. Albeit halfheartedly, state-owned enterprises were privatized, elements of the social welfare institutions were dismantled, some subsidies and tax exemptions—such as those for *pensionados* (foreign residents)—were rescinded, and new taxes were levied on income and savings. In the short run the social costs have been high. The Figueres administration (1994-98) continued the privatization mandate and warmly welcomed the arrival of Intel, the giant computer chip manufacturer, whose establishment in 1997 of a $500 million assembly plant in Costa Rica suggested that the country may blossom as a "Silicon Valley South."

The country's external debt peaked in 1989 at $4.7 billion and has since been reduced. Another bright note was the signing of a bilateral trade agreement with Mexico. Beginning 1 January 1995, 70% of customs duties between the two countries were eliminated (the remaining 30% will be phased out over 10 years). It's anticipated that this will vastly increase Mexican investment in Costa Rica's tourism industry. It also gives Costa Rica access to a Mexican market of 90 million people and represents a step toward Costa Rica's eventually joining the North American Free Trade Agreement (NAFTA), which has tempted many businesses to relocate to Mexico. That would be a culmination of the move, since the late 1970s, progressively away from a protectionist attitude and toward a more diversified trading economy (together, coffee, bananas, sugar, and beef represented almost 80% of exports in 1980, but less than 40% today).

But there is still trouble in paradise. Interest rates are in the 30% range. The Legislative Assembly failed to ratify constitutional reforms sought by the Figueres administration to privatize state behemoths such as the Banco de Costa Rica and Banco Internacional. The budget deficit grew to $3.6 billion in 1997. The economy has been moribund in the mid-1900s (the GNP, which averages about $2,700 per capita, actually fell 0.7% in 1996—Costa Rica placed last with Paraguay in Latin America for 1996 in economic growth indicators) but rebounded to 4.3% in 1997. The *colón* continues to decline in value. Consumption taxes add to the general inflation, while real wages remain basically stagnant (inflation was 12% in 1997, and unemployment 5.7%—a sure underestimate). And about 35% of the nation's families are officially below the poverty line, with 6.9% in "extreme poverty" in 1996 (up from 5.8% since 1994).

Manufacturing

Manufacturing still plays a relatively small part in the Costa Rican economy (in 1990 earnings from industrial manufacturing were US$398 million—21.6% of GNP), and there is little to suggest that industrialization is going to transform the essentially agricultural economy in the near future. Local industrial raw materials are restricted to agricultural products, wood, and a small output of mineral ores. Manufacturing is still largely concerned with food processing, although pharmaceutical and textile exports have risen dramatically in recent years. Major industrial projects also include aluminum processing, a petrochemical plant at Moín, a tuna-processing plant at Golfito, and an oil refinery at Puerto Limón. And Costa Rica is finding favor as a darling of high-tech industries: Intel and Motorola recently opened assembly plants, and other computer and telecommunications giants are slating investments.

Hydroelectricity, though well developed and concentrated in the Arenal area, is the only domestic power source of significance. Costa Rica's electricity needs are growing at six to seven percent annually. In 1997, the country has 1,300 megawatts capacity, but must grow 78 MW per year to meet demand. To meet it, a newly completed geothermal plant on Miravalles volcano, in Guanacaste, is anticipated to produce about 10% of the nation's electricity need, and massive HEP plants are being installed on rivers nationwide.

Agriculture

Noted Nicaraguan poet Rubén Darío once described Costa Rica as a nation of clerks, lawyers, and oxen. Indeed, while it might *appear* that bureaucrats and legal eagles have the upper hand, agriculture dominates the Costa Rican economy. The fact is obvious everywhere you go, particularly in the central highlands, where a remarkable feature of the land is the almost complete cultivation, no matter how steep the slope. Nationwide, some 12% of the land area is planted in crops, 45% is given to pasture, and only 27% is forested. Despite the ubiquitousness of small family farms, large-scale commercial agriculture is more important in terms of dollar value, even in coffee, where a relatively small number of large farms associated with the coffee *beneficios* (processing plants) have established their dominance.

Despite Costa Rica's reputation as a country of yeoman farmers, land ownership has always been highly concentrated, and there are parts, such as Guanacaste, where rural income distribution resembles the inimical patterns of Guatemala and El Salvador. In colonial days, agricultural land in the highlands, however, was relatively equally distributed among peasant smallholders. The situation began to change toward the end of the 19th century, when wealthy coffee

barons began to squeeze other farmers off their lands. Today, 71% of the economically active rural population is landless. The bottom 50% of all landholders own only three percent of all land. And the top one percent of farm owners own more than one-quarter of the agricultural land.

Coffee—the *grano d'oro,* or golden bean—is the most important crop in the highlands in terms of area. The mist-shrouded slopes of the Meseta Central and southern highlands are adorned with green undulating carpets of coffee. The large hacienda is foreign to the traditions of the Meseta Central, and the fabric of the rural landscape, with its thousands of small-size farmsteads, is reminiscent of certain parts of peasant Europe.

Houses, by their pattern and numbers, indicate that pressure on the land has mounted. Some relief has been found by intensifying cultivation of coffee and, west of Alajuela and at lower levels, sugarcane; elsewhere in the higher, more temperate areas, carnations, chrysanthemums, and other flowers grow under acres of plastic sheeting, and dairying is becoming more important in a mixed-farming economy that has been a feature of the Meseta since the end of the 19th century. The situation is a far cry from the very limited economy of the Altiplano at similar elevations in Guatemala.

The vast banana plantations that swathe the Caribbean plains produce some 50 million boxes of bananas per year, making Costa Rica the second-biggest exporter of bananas in the world, behind Ecuador. Sugarcane is grown by small farmers all over the country but becomes a major crop on plantations as you drop into the lowlands. Particularly rapid growth in sugar production occurred in the 1960s after the U.S. reassigned Cuba's sugar import quota; production has since gone into decline—in 1981 Costa Rica had to import sugar to meet domestic demand. And cacao, once vital to the 18th-century economy, is on the rise again as a major export crop; the trees, fruit hanging pendulously from their trunks, are everywhere, especially in large plantations around Limón and Upala and to a much lesser degree around Alajuela and increasingly around Golfito and the *llanuras.*

Recent attempts to stimulate nontraditional exports are paying dividends in agriculture. Cassava, papaya, the camote (sweet potato), melons, strawberries, chayote (vegetable pear), eggplant,

traditional Sarchí oxcart

curraré (plantain bananas), pimiento, macadamia nuts, ornamental plants, and cut flowers are all fast becoming important export items.

For tourists with an interest there are several farms where you can learn about agriculture firsthand. The Central American School of Animal Husbandry, for example, fosters agri-ecotourism on a working ranch near Atenas.

Bananas have been a part of the Caribbean landscape since 1870, when American entrepreneur Minor Keith shipped his first fruit stems—360 bunches—to New Orleans. In 1899, his Tropical Trading & Transport Co. merged with the Boston Fruit Co. to form the United Fruit Co., which soon became the overlord of the political economies of the "banana republics." By the 1920s, much of the chaotic jungle south of Puerto Limón had been transformed into a vast sea of bananas.

Although it was ousted in the mid-1990s by tourism as Costa Rica's number-one earner of foreign currency, the nation's banana industry continues to expand to meet the demand of a growing international market. By the time you read this, bananas will cover at least 45,000 hectares. Most growth is concentrated in the north Atlantic lowlands.

Then, as now in some areas, working conditions were appalling, and strikes were so frequent that when Panamá disease and then *sigatoka* (leaf-spot) disease swept the region in the 1930s and 1940s, United Fruit took the opportunity to abandon its Atlantic holdings and move to the Pacific coast, where it planted around Golfito, Coto Colorado, and Palmar (operated by United Fruit's subsidiary Compañía Bananera). Violent clashes with the banana workers' unions continued to be the company's nemesis. In 1985, after a 72-day strike, United Fruit closed its operations in southwestern Costa Rica. Many of the plantations have been replaced by stands of African palms (used in cooking oil, margarine, and soap); others are leased to independent growers and farmers' cooperatives who sell to United Fruit. Labor problems still flare: a telling tale of continued abuse by the banana companies (in 1994, riots ensued when the English company Geest hired illegal immigrants at below minimum wage levels. Geest is one of several companies that routinely flaut labor laws).

The Standard Fruit Co. began production in the Atlantic lowlands in 1956. Alongside ASBANA (Asociación de Bananeros), a government-sponsored private association, Standard Fruit helped revive the Atlantic coast banana industry. Much of the new acreage, however, has come at the expense of thousands of acres of virgin jungle. Banana export earnings—$482.9 million in 1992—surpassed tourism income for the country in 1996, when some 50,000 hectares planted in bananas and more than a billion kilos of the fruit exported.

By far the largest share of agricultural land (70%) is given over to **cattle** pasture. Despite its evolving complexion, Guanacaste remains essentially what it has been since midcolonial times—cattle country—and three-quarters of Costa Rica's 2.2 million head of cattle are found here. They are mostly humpbacked zebu, originally from India and now adapted over several generations; there are also herds of Charolais and Hereford. Low-interest loans in the 1960s and 1970s encouraged a rush into cattle farming for the export market, prompting rapid expansion into new areas such as the Valle de El General and more recently the Atlantic lowlands.

Although Costa Rica is today Latin America's leading beef exporter (it accounts for some five percent of U.S. meat imports), beef has never provided more than nine percent of Costa Rica's export earnings. Sadly, much of the land placed under cattle in recent decades has been on steep hill slopes that have been stripped bare of timber. The scoured slopes bear mute testimony to the greed and folly of man. Destructive floods now common in the *terra caliente* of the Pacific lowlands can be traced to "cattle mania." And the loss of the ready smile of the small farmers who have been driven from their land—cattle ranches need little labor—is a poignant reminder of a cancer that has slowly but inevitably eaten away at the land. All this so that North Americans can enjoy their hamburgers and TV dinners.

Costa Rica's Meseta Central possesses ideal conditions for **coffee production** (Costa Rica—which produces three percent of the world's coffee—has the greatest coffee productivity per acre in the world), and beans grown here are ranked among the best in the world. The coffee plant loves a seasonal, almost monsoonal climate with a distinct dry season; it grows best, too, in well-drained, fertile soils at elevations between 800 and 1,500 meters with a narrow annual temperature range—natural conditions provided by the Meseta Central. The best coffee—mild coffee commanding the highest prices—is grown near the plant's uppermost altitudinal limits, where the bean takes longer to mature. Coffee claims about 105,000 hectares of land. In 1997, some 80,000 small, medium, and large producers sold 2.5 million *fanegas* (46-kg bags) of green coffee to the country's 95 mills.

The first coffee beans were brought from Jamaica in 1779. Within 50 years coffee had become firmly established; by the 1830s it was the country's prime export earner, a position it occupied until 1991, when coffee plunged overnight to third place in the wake of a precipitous 50% fall

in world coffee prices after Brazil scuttled the International Coffee Agreement quota system in 1989. (Ticos can find satisfaction in the fact that their coffee has an unusually high—86%—content of "liqueur," or coffee essence; Brazilian coffee has a meager 29%.) The decline has caused widespread distress for small farmers and the 45,000 poorly paid laborers who rely on work in the harvest season. In 1994, however, international coffee prices skyrocketed after large crop losses in Brazil. The 1996-97 harvest increased nine percent and reaped $376 million.

Population pressure on the land has induced the adoption of the most modern and intensive methods of cultivation, including high-yielding plants. The plants are grown in nurseries for their first year before being planted in long rows that ramble invitingly down the steep hillsides, their paths coiling and uncoiling like garden snakes. After four years they fruit. In April, with the first rains, the small white blossoms burst forth and the air is laced with perfume not unlike jasmine. By November, the glossy green bushes are plump with shiny red berries—the coffee beans—and the seasonal labor is called into action.

The hand-picked berries are trucked to *beneficios* (processing plants), where they are machine-scrubbed and washed to remove the fruity outer layer and dissolve the gummy substance surrounding the bean (the pulp is returned to the slopes as fertilizer). The moist beans are then blow-dried or laid out to dry in the sun in the traditional manner. The leather skin of the bean is then removed by machine, and the beans are sorted according to size and shape before being vacuum-sealed to retain the fragrance and slight touch of acidity characteristic of the great vintages of Costa Rica.

A visit to a coffee *finca* (farm) is an interesting day-trip from San José. **Café Britt,** tel. 260-2748, in the U.S.A, tel. 800-GO-BRITT (800-462-7488), offers an hour-long "Coffeetour" of its *finca* and *beneficio* near Barva. At San Pedro de Barva, 10 km north of Heredia, is a coffee research station and the **Museo de Café,** tel. 237-1975. **Aventuras Turísticas de Orosí,** tel. 533-3030, fax 533-3212, offers an "Orosí Coffee Adventure" featuring a tour of a coffee farm and *beneficio*.

Tourism

Costa Rica is one of the world's fastest-growing destinations for adventure and nature travel, and

REDUCING YOUR PERSONAL ENVIRONMENTAL IMPACT

If you're camping, here are some ways to keep your impact on the environment to a minimum.

• Pick it up, pack it out. In addition, of course, to packing out any detritus you've packed in, try to leave a convenient pack pocket available for carrying out whatever litter you find along the trail.

• Give yourself enough time at the end of the day to find a camping site that will notice your presence the least.

• Bone up on the types of wildlife you're likely to meet. The more you know, the better you can observe without disrupting them.

• To lessen your visibility, use gear and wear clothing that blend in with the landscape.

• Read books on enjoying the outdoors in environmentally sensitive ways. *Soft Paths,* by Bruce Hampton and David Cole (Stackpole Books), and *Backwoods Ethics,* by Laura and Guy Waterman (Stone Wall Press), are two good choices.

travelers of every other persuasion are pouring in, too. The resort industry is blossoming as it realizes the seductive potentials. Even the cruise lines are taking notice. Above all the country has been adopted as the darling of the ecotourist: the just reward for two decades of foresight and diligence in preserving its natural heritage in national parks and wildlife reserves.

Costa Rica has had more and more fans every year through 1995, when 792,000 tourists arrived, spending about $661 million. Then tourism stalled (1996 actually posted a *drop* in arrivals, prompting a massive injection of promotion dollars by the ICT), before rebounding to 812,000 visitors in 1997, up four percent over 1996. About 850,000 tourist arrivals were predicted for 1998.

The nation's status as a "destination of the 1990s" is a boon. In fact, the government is relying on tourism dollars to help pull the country out of debt. In 1993, tourism overtook the banana industry to become the nation's prime income earner. About 14% of the labor force works in tourism-related activities. By 2000, the country hopes to receive 1 million visitors, when it is hoped revenues will surpass $1 billion. It's not simply a matter of tourist numbers: the average stay is up

from 6.9 days in 1988 to 11.2 days in 1995, while per diem expenditures per tourist are up, too.

Costa Rica is even looking to sponsor further growth in tandem with Cuba (with whom close ties have been developed; Havana is served by daily flights from San José) and its Central American neighbors, including easing immigration restrictions among the Central American nations, creating a Mayan Route for tourists, and even developing a regional tourism card. Five Central American airlines—Aviateca of Guatemala, COPA of Panamá, LASCA of Costa Rica, NICA of Nicaragua, and TACA of El Salvador—are being amalgamated and have a cooperative marketing effort that allows travelers to visit the entire region.

The Beach Resort Boom: In a recent study, more than 50% of visitors cited that they were visiting Costa Rica to pursue some interest in nature. Nonetheless, in its haste to boost the influx of tourist dollars, the government of Rafael Calderón began promoting large-scale resort development on the shores of the Pacific northwest. The government decided to position Costa Rica as a comprehensive destination for the whole family, and particularly as a beach resort contender to Mexico and the Caribbean.

Sprawling resort complexes began sprouting. Jacó Beach has been pinpointed for redevelopment, and Puerto Limón is expected to prosper as cruise tourism booms. Chief among the projects, however, is the Gulf of Papagayo project encompassing several beaches in Guanacaste. The megaresort, being constructed by a host of European and Mexican developers (initially led by the Spanish developers Sol Meliá), was initially conceived to be the largest "leisure city" in Central America with more than 20,000 rooms. The development covers 4,942 acres close to several national parks and wildlife reserves, and has stalled since coming under attack from conservation groups.

"We're really concerned about the direction tourism is taking in Costa Rica," says Kurt Kutay, a director of the Ecotourism Society and president of Seattle-based Wildland Adventures. "There's a place for Mexico-style developments, but it has to be done in a sensitive way, otherwise there's a threat Costa Rica could lose it all. Unfortunately, the [Calderón] government espoused ecotourism and then did the opposite."

The Down Side: There has been much debate about how to regulate the impact of tourism on Costa Rica. Concern about whether Costa Rica is growing too fast and shifting from its ecotourism focus toward mass-market tourism led, in 1993, to a threatened boycott of the country's annual travel trade show, Expotur, by environmentally responsible tour operators. Everyone agreed on one point: the nation was lacking any sort of coherent tourism development plan to control growth. Consequently, developers large and small were pushing up hotels along Costa Rica's 1,227 km (767 miles) of coastline in total disregard of environmental laws.

In 1977, the country adopted the Maritime Terrestrial Zone Law, which declares the country's entire coastline to be public property, prohibits construction within 50 meters of the point halfway between high and low tides, and restricts construction within 200 meters of the same spot. It was happening anyway, without punishment. The sheer volume of violations, said a report in the *Tico Times* (29 May 1992), "bespeaks a massive lack of political will. . . . Violations of the coastal law—most noticeably building within the 'inviolable' 50-meter tide line—are out of control."

Tax credits and other incentives for foreign investors were also pushing the price of land beyond reach of the local population. Up to 40% of Costa Rica's habitable coastline is now owned by North Americans and Europeans, according to Sergio Guillen, an information officer for the Ministry of Planning. "We are selling our land to the highest bidder," he says. "And the government doesn't seem to care."

How Bad is It?: Few people were shocked when, in March 1995, 12 ICT officials and even Manuel Chacó, the Minister of Tourism in the Calderón administration, were indicted on a variety of charges relating to violations at Papagayo (see below). Major corporations who look only at their balance sheets were paying off Costa Rican government officials to get permission to build. The Spanish developer Barceló was taken to court for flagrant breaches of environmental codes during construction of a 400-room resort at Playa Tambor, opened in 1992 (the Calderón administration sided with Barceló).

"The current atmosphere is to build first and deal with the legalities later," claims Michael Kaye, president of Costa Rica Expeditions. Ecoconscious tour operators express worry about the degree to which "big" money has begun to corrupt the democratic process in Costa Rica. "As long as nature unspoiled had the best bottom line, it had at least a fighting chance," noted an article on Costa Rica in *Condé Nast Traveler*, July 1993. "But in the end the big money would come, and what the big money wanted, the big money got, and what the big money wanted was *big*."

In October 1993 the Municipality of Liberia ordered Grupo Situr to stop construction of two resorts that were part of the government's Gulf of Papagayo Tourism Project. The Mexican developer lacked the necessary permits and was accused of violating environmental codes. Heeding the requests of local residents, the municipal government formed a special commission to assess complaints that Grupo Situr's subsidiary, Eco-Desarollo Papagayo, was causing environmental damage, including filling in a protected mangrove estuary.

"Plans in the works suddenly appear on the ground. The question is, have rigorous environmental reviews been done?" asks one ecotour operator. The government's independent ombudsman office thought not. In January 1994, it charged the Calderón administration of issuing a presidential executive decree granting permission for tourism infrastructure to be built inside areas previously defined as "inalienable" (protected); granting land concessions to foreign developers on preferential terms outside legal provisions; allowing resort development at Papagayo without permits; and ignoring destruction of natural resources at Papagayo.

In September 1994, tourism minister Carlos Roesch, together with developers and members of the local government, met with the ombudsman. They agreed that development should continue under a new master plan and guidelines that don't violate preservation laws. They also decided that local communities should participate in the monitoring process and should be guaranteed a large share of jobs and other benefits generated by the project. However, in March 1995, in the midst of an announcement that the government would move ahead with the project, 12 senior former ICT officials, including former tourism minister Luis Manuel Chacón, were indicted on charges of embezzlement, violating public trust, and dereliction of duty relating to Papagayo! Construction briefly stopped. At press time the indicators were that after going through the courts for two years, the project was set to move ahead.

Ecotour operators have warned that without a conscientious development plan, the government could kill the goose that lays the golden egg. Says Kaye: "The [Calderón administration's] policy [was] to use eco-development as a smoke screen to get as much foreign exchange as fast as possible without regard for the long-term consequences. . . . The [Calderón] policy [was] to talk appropriate-scale tourism and to foster mass tourism. People are *already* beginning to see too many other people," says Kaye, who points to the example of Manuel Antonio National Park, where the problem recently reached a crisis. The diminutive (682-hectare) park, midway down the Pacific coast, was averaging more than 1,000 visitors daily—three times more than it could withstand, according to park director José Antonio Salazar. The shallow lagoon that visitors wade to reach the park was polluted. Trails were showing wear and tear. And hotels had squeezed Manuel Antonio against the Pacific, cutting off migratory corridors for the park's 350 squirrel monkeys. "The day mass tourism gets the upper hand, we'll switch our groups to Panamá, Nicaragua, and Venezuela. They've got a tiger by the tail here. If they don't start dealing with it in an effective way, it's going to be a catastrophe," concludes Kaye.

The Up Side: Chacón claimed that opponents of large-scale resorts are afraid of losing their share of the market. The "greens" who denounce the government's policy, he said, are really leftists: "When you scratch them, the red begins to flow!" Chacón pointed out that surging tourism dollars could pull the country out of debt: "Larger projects represent significant investment that the country requires." Costa Rica stands to gain much more than cash from the current boom. Firstly, optimists suggest that the profit potential of tourism encourages private landowners to regard natural areas as long-term assets rather than a source of quick cash, and that resort developers realize that the added expense of building *around* rather than through a forest pays ample dividends in the end. And the employment opportunities are huge. Chacón claimed

the Gulf of Papagayo development alone could provide 30,000 jobs by the year 2000.

The government has also poured money into improving road access to along the Pacific coast. Unfortunately, where roads come so do the loggers. While many local residents welcome the potential development, others fear that if the roads that lead to more remote natural shrines are paved, more and more tourists will flock, thereby quickening the possible destruction of the very thing they come to worship; see, for example, Ostional National Wildlife Refuge.

Collaboration in monitoring tourism growth, as well as Costa Rica's environment in general, is growing. Before leaving office, tourism minister Chacón announced that the government was developing a blueprint for sustainable tourism, as well as a management plan and carrying capacity studies to determine the impact of visitors on protected areas. Carlos Roesch, tourism minister in the Figueres administration (1990-94) stated his commitment to launch an ambitious plan for "sustainable tourism development" that would include licensing of tourism companies and visitor quotas for national parks. Roesch unveiled a multifaceted plan to protect both the country's natural assets and the culture and character of the Ticos.

By 1997, it was clear that the country was steering away from the mass market it went after a few years ago and was reverting to a more educated traveler. A new emphasis was also being placed on the business and incentive travel market, supported by the arrival of large, world-class, chain hotels such as Marriott.

Ecotourism: Travel, like fashion, follows trends. In the 1990s the ecological movement has become something of a solar-powered steamroller, changing the way we travel. A 1986 study by the Costa Rican Tourism Institute found that 87% of tourists surveyed cited natural beauty as one of their main motivations for visiting Costa Rica, and 36% specifically cited ecotourism.

Ecotourism—defined as responsible travel that contributes to conservation of natural environments and sustains the well-being of local people by promoting rural economic development—has become to the 1990s what the European Grand Tour was to the 1930s and adventure travel was to the 1980s. Many adventure enthusiasts of the last decade have discarded their wetsuits, mountain boots, and whitewater rafts; they still want to explore exotic regions, to peer beneath the veneer of the normal mass tourist experience, but in a more relaxed and socially acceptable manner. Bringing only their curiosity, the new wave of ecotourists are leaving their footprints—and their cash.

Costa Rica practically invented the term. In October 1991 the country was chosen as one of three winners of the first environmental award presented by the American Society of Travel Agents (ASTA) and *Smithsonian* magazine. The award was designed to recognize a "company, individual or country for achievements in conservation and environmentalism."

Just because an excursion or expedition is labeled an "ecotour" doesn't mean that it is. The term has become catchy. The term has become prostituted and can have little meaning if a tour provider doesn't adhere to sound environmental principles. Fortunately, most tour operators are honorable role models. But what to make of such resorts as the ill-named Eco-Playa Resort, in Guanacaste, which planned on introducing jet skis (!) in an enclosed bay surrounding a protected bird sanctuary close to shore?

Filtering tourist dollars into the hands of locals is another problem. In January 1990, the World Wildlife Fund released a two-volume report that found that people interested in nature travel and in visiting fragile environments generally spend more money than other kinds of tourists. Yet Guillermo Canessa, a veteran conservationist and nature guide, found that less than three percent of the profits earned by the tour companies and hotels in Tortuguero actually benefited people of the local community. And conservationists claimed that neither the foreigners flocking to the nation's protected areas

nor the tour companies that bring them there had been contributing their share to maintaining the parks. The past few years, however, have seen solid efforts to place management of on-site tourism in the hands of local cooperatives whereby the local community gains the benefits (Playa Grande, in Nicoya, and Tortuguero, on the Caribbean, are good examples).

In support of regulated ecotourism and the Code of Environmental Ethics for Nature Travel, the Institute for Central American Studies has a Department of Responsible Tourism. The DRT monitors the compliance of tour operators according to the code of ethics, as well as the impact that tourism has on local communities and development in Costa Rica. Based on these investigations, the DRT can recommend "responsible" tour operators and can research complaints about those who are not complying. The DRT, in collaboration with the **Institute for Central American Studies,** Apdo. 1524, San Pedro 2050, tel. 223-7221 or 223-7112; in the U.S., c/o Mesoamerican Communications, P.O. Box 423808, San Francisco, CA 94142, has launched the "Partnership for Sustainable Tourism," which has resulted in a "Sustainable Tourism Ranking" for tour operators, hoteliers, etc.

In the U.S., contact **Ecotourism Society,** 801 Devon Place, Alexandria, VA 22314, tel. (703) 549-8979, fax 549-2920, a watchdog body comprising travel operators and conservationists. In Costa Rica, the **Eco-Institute of Costa Rica,** Apdo. 8080, San José 1000, tel. 233-2200, fax 221-2801, publishes the *Sustainable Tourism Newsletter.*

In 1997, the Figueres government initiated a "Certification for Sustainable Tourism" rating system to regulate the environmental impact of hotel development.

PEOPLE

POPULATION

The July 1989 census recorded a population of 2.92 million, more than half of whom live in the Meseta Central; the population in 1998 was thought to be about 3.4 million. Approximately 275,000 live in the capital city of San José (about three times that number live in the metropolitan region). Fifty-one percent of the nation's population is classed as urban. The country's annual population growth rate is 2.3% and gradually falling. As recently as the 1960s the rate was a staggering 3.8% per annum, a figure no other country in the world could then match. The impressive decline in recent decades has likewise been matched by few other countries.

All the municipalities of the Meseta Central have gained agricultural migrants for whom there is simply no more room. Hence, emigration from the Meseta Central in recent decades has taken people in all directions, assisted by government incentives. The most attractive areas of settlement in the past 35 years have been on the Nicoya lowlands on the drier part of the Pacific coast, on the northern lowlands, and on the alluvial soils of the Valle de El General in the south. The Pan-American Highway has attracted set-tlers, and the border between Panamá and Costa Rica is now quite densely settled, with colonists from Italy as well as the Meseta Central grafted onto the local population.

CLASS AND RACE

Most Costa Ricans—Las Costarricense—insist that their country is a "classless democracy." True, the social tensions of class versus class that characterize many neighboring nations are absent. Ticos lack the volatility, ultranationalism, and deep-seated political divisions of their Latin American brethren. There is considerable social mobility, and no race problem on the scale of the United States'. And virtually everyone shares a so-called middle-class mentality, a firm belief in the Costa Rican equivalent of "the American Dream"—a conviction that through individual effort and sacrifice and a faith in schooling every Costa Rican can climb the social ladder and better him- or herself.

Still, despite the high value Ticos place on equality and democracy, their society contains all kinds of inequities. Wealth, for example, is unevenly distributed (the richest one percent of families receive 10% of the national income; the poorest 50% receive only 20%; and at least one-fifth of the population remain *marginados* who are so poor they remain outside the mainstream of progress). And a small number of families—the descendants of the original *hidalgos* (nobles)—have monopolized power for almost four centuries (just three families have produced 36 of Costa Rica's 49 presidents, and fully three-quarters of congress-

JOHN ANDERSON

men 1821-1970 were the offspring of this "dynasty of conquistadors").

Urbanites, like city dwellers worldwide, condescendingly chuckle at rural "hicks." The skewed tenure of an albeit much-diluted feudalism persists in regions long dominated by plantations and haciendas. Tolerance of racial minorities is tenuous, with "whiteness" still considered the ideal (in more remote areas, blacks may experience the all-too-familiar cold shoulder). And the upwardly mobile "elite," who consider menial labor demeaning, prefer to indulge in conspicuous spending and, often, in snobbish behavior (several restaurateurs and hoteliers have told me that the Tico nouveau riche will, as a matter of course, complain about service, food, etc., and that they often treat waiters and service staff with such contempt that the latter may even refuse to serve them).

Though comparatively wealthy compared to most Latin American countries, by developed-world standards most Costa Ricans are poor (the average income is slightly less than US$3,000 per annum). Many rural families still live in simple huts of adobe or wood; the average income in the northern lowlands, for example, is barely one-seventh of that in San José. Although few and far between, shacks made from gasoline tins, old automobile tires, and corrugated tin give a miserable cover to poor urban laborers in small *tugurios*—illegally erected slums—on the outskirts and the riverbanks of San José. And a U.N. report on child labor issued in 1997 found that 120,000 Costa Rican minors aged 5-17 are exploited and are paid little or not at all.

However, that all paints far too gloomy a picture. In a region where thousands thrive and millions starve, the vast majority of Costa Ricans are comparatively well-to-do. The country has few desperately poor, and there are relatively few beggars existing on the bare charity of the world. The majority of Costa Ricans keep their proud little bungalows spick and span and bordered by flowers, and even the poorest Costa Ricans are generally well groomed and neatly dressed.

Overt class distinctions are kept within bounds by a delicate balance between "elitism" and egalitarianism unique in the isthmus: aristocratic airs are frowned on and blatant pride in blue blood is ridiculed; even the president is inclined to mingle in public in casual clothing and is commonly addressed in general conversation by his first name or nickname.

Costa Rican Ethnicity

Costa Rica is unquestionably the most homogeneous of Central American nations in race as well as social class. Travelers familiar with other Central American nations will immediately notice the contrast: the vast majority of Costa Ricans look predominantly European. The 1989 census classified 98% of the population as "white" or "mestizo" and less than two percent as "black" or "Indian." Native and European mixed blood far less than in other New World countries. There are mestizos—in fact, approximately 95% of Ticans inherit varying mixtures of the mestizo blend of European colonists with Indian and black women—but the lighter complexion of Old World immigrants is evident throughout the nation. Exceptions are Guanacaste, where almost half the population is visibly mestizo, a legacy of the more pervasive unions between Spanish colonists and Chorotega Indians through several generations. And the population of the Atlantic coast province of Puerto Limón is one-third black, with a distinct culture that reflects its West Indian origins.

Blacks

Costa Rica's approximately 40,000 black people are the nation's largest minority. For many years they were the target of racist immigration and residence laws that restricted them to the Caribbean coast (only as late as 1949, when the new Constitution abrogated apartheid on the Atlantic Railroad, were blacks allowed to travel beyond Siquirres and enter the highlands). Hence, they remained isolated from national culture. Although Afro-Caribbean turtle hunters settled on the Caribbean coast as early as 1825, most blacks today trace their ancestry back to the 10,000 or so Jamaicans hired by Minor Keith to build the Atlantic Railroad, and to later waves of immigrants who came to work the banana plantations in the late 19th century.

Costa Rica's early black population was "dramatically upwardly mobile" and by the 1920s a majority of the West Indian immigrants worked their own plots of land or had risen to higher-paying positions within the banana industry. Unfortunately, they possessed neither citizenship nor the legal right to own land. In the 1930s, when "white" highlanders began pouring into the lowlands, blacks were quickly dispossessed of land and the best-paying jobs. Late that decade, when the banana blight forced the banana companies to abandon their Caribbean plantations and move to the Pacific, "white" Ticos successfully lobbied for laws forbidding the employment of *gente de color* in other provinces, one of several circumstances that kept blacks dependent on the largesse of the United Fruit Company, whose labor policies were often abhorrent. Pauperized, many blacks migrated to Panamá and the U.S. seeking wartime employment. A good proportion of those who remained converted their subsistence plots into commercial cacao farms and reaped large profits during the 1950s and 1960s from the rise of world cacao prices.

West Indian immigrants played a substantial role in the early years of labor organization, and their early strikes were often violently suppressed (Tican folklore falsely believes in black passivity). Many black workers, too, joined hands with Figueres in the 1948 civil war. Their reward? Citizenship and full guarantees under the 1949 Constitution, which ended apartheid.

Costa Rica's black population has consistently attained higher educational standards than the national average and many blacks are now found in leading professions throughout the nation. They have also managed to retain much of their traditional culture, including religious practices rooted in African belief about transcendence through spiritual possession *(obeah),* their rich cuisine (codfish and akee, "rundown"), the rhythmic lilt of their slightly antiquated English, and the deeply syncopated funk of their music.

Indians

Costa Rica's indigenous peoples have suffered abysmally. Centuries ago the original Indian tribes were splintered by Spanish conquistadors and compelled to retreat into the vast tracts of the interior mountains (the Chorotegas of Guanacaste, however, were more gradually assimilated into the national culture). Today, approximately 9,000 Indian peoples of the Bribrí, Boruca, and Cabecar tribes manage to eke out a living from the jungles of remote valleys in the Cordillera Talamanca of southern Costa Rica, where their ancestors had sought refuge from Spanish muskets and dogs. Eight different Indian groups live on 22 Indian reserves.

Although various agencies continue to work to promote education, health, and community development, the Indians' standard of living is appallingly low, alcoholism is endemic, and they remain subject to constant exploitation. In 1939, the government granted every Indian family an allotment of 148 hectares for traditional farming, and in December 1977 a law was passed prohibiting non-Indians from buying, leasing, or renting land within the reserves.

Despite the legislation, a majority of Indians have gradually been tricked into selling their allotments or otherwise forced off their lands. Banana companies have gradually encroached into the Indians" remote kingdoms, buying up land and pushing *campesinos* onto Indian property. And mining companies are infiltrating the reserves along newly built roads, which become conduits for contamination, like dirty threads in a wound. In 1991, for example, an American mining company was accused of illegally exploring within the Talamanca Indian Reserve.

Indigenous peoples complain that the National Commission for Indigenous Affairs (CONAI) has proved ineffective in enforcing protections. "When the moment arrives for CONAI to stand up for the Indian people, they don't dare. They duck down behind their desks and wait for their paychecks to arrive," says Boruca Indian leader José Carlos Morales.

The various Indian clans cling tenuously to what remains of their cultures. The Borucas, who inhabit scattered villages in tight-knit patches of the Pacific southwest, have been most adept at conserving their own language and civilization, including matriarchy, communal land ownership, and traditional weaving. For most other groups, only a few elders still speak the languages, and interest in traditional crafts is fading. Virtually all groups have adopted elements of Catholicism along with their traditional animistic religions, Spanish is today the predominant tongue, and economically the Indians have for the most part come to resemble impoverished *campesinos.*

It is possible in towns such as San Vito and Ciudad Neily, in the Pacific southwest, to see Indian women and girls in traditional bright-colored garb—a beautiful sight!

Other Ethnic Groups

Immigrants from many nations have been made welcome over the years (between 1870 and 1920, almost 25% of Costa Rica's population growth was due to immigration). Jews are prominent in the liberal professions. A Quaker community of several hundred people centers on Monteverde, where they produce gouda, cheddar, and *monterico* cheeses. Germans have for many generations been particularly successful as coffee farmers. Italians have gathered, among other places, in the town of San Vito, on the central Pacific coast. Tens of thousands of Central American refugees from El Salvador, Guatemala, and Nicaragua still find safety in Costa Rica, where they provide cheap labor for the coffee fields. The Chinese man quoted in Paul Theroux's *Old Patagonian Express* is one of several thousand Chinese who call Costa Rica home. Many are descended from approximately 600 Asians who were imported as contract laborers to work on the Atlantic Railroad (an 1862 law prohibiting immigration by Asians had been lifted on the understanding that the Chinese would return home once the work was complete). The Chinese railroad workers were worked miserably and paid only one-fifth of the going wage. In recent years many *chinos* have immigrated freely and are now conspicuously successful in the hotel, restaurant, and bar trade (Theroux's Chinese man owned one of each), and in Limón as middlemen controlling the trade in bananas and cacao.

During the past decade, Costa Rica has become a favorite home away from home for an influx of North Americans and Europeans (predominantly Italian, German, and French, who concentrate in enclaves)—including a large percentage of misfits and malcreants evading the law! The largest body of recent immigrants, however, are *Nicas* (Nicaraguans); as many as 200,000 by one account. Although lauded by foreign hoteliers as conscientious, hard-working employees, Ticos have given the Nicas a somewhat cool reception. The Nicas often face overt discrimination and are held to blame for many of Costa Rica's current social ills. They are instantly recognizable, being shorter and darker, with more pronounced indigenous features than the average Tico.

THE TICAN IDENTITY

Every nationality has its own sense of identity. Costa Ricans' unique traits derive from a profoundly conscious self-image, which orients much of their behavior as both individuals and as a nation. The Ticos—the name is said to stem from the colonial saying "we are all *hermaniticos*" (little brothers)—feel distinct from their neighbors by their "whiteness" and relative lack of indigenous culture. Ticos identify themselves first and foremost as Costa Ricans and only Central Americans, or even Latin Americans, as an afterthought.

In general, Costa Ricans act with humility and judge as uncouth boasting of any kind. Above all, the behavior and comments of most Ticos are dictated by *quedar bien,* a desire to leave a good impression. Like the English, they're terribly frightened of embarrassing themselves, of appearing rude or vulgar (tactless and crude people are considered "badly educated") or unhelpful. As such, they can be exceedingly courteous, almost archaically so (they are prone, for example, to offer flowing compliments and formal greetings). It is a rare visitor to the country who returns home unimpressed by the Costa Ricans' cordial warmth and hospitality. However, this is not uniform and several readers have written expressing how much resentment from Ticos they felt in Costa Rica, especially in restaurants and other businesses that make a habit of ripping off tourists.

Some Tico characteristics can be tiresome. Ticos, for example, have a hard time speaking forthrightly. They can't say "no!" They're also "flakey." Thus, when a Tico makes a promise, don't expect him or her to come through. (A joke among foreign residents is: "How do you know when a Tico is lying? When they open their mouths.") What you see (or hear) is *not* what you get: Ticos have been called icebergs, for their tendency to conceal the real meaning of what they say or feel below the surface. How does this fit with *quedar bien?* Well, Ticos avoid the consequences of this glaring inconsistency by not even thinking about it. Raise the issue and all you get is a stony look and glazed eyes.

Nor can you count on a Tico's punctuality. Private companies, including most travel businesses, are efficient and to a greater or lesser degree operate *hora americana:* punctually. But don't expect it. Many Ticos, particularly in government institutions, still tick along on turtle-paced *hora tica*. *"¿Quien sabe?"* ("Who knows?") is an oft-repeated phrase. So too *"¡Tal vez!"* ("Perhaps!") and, of course, *"¡Mañana!"* ("Tomorrow!"). In fact, *mañana* is the busiest day of the week!

Ticos are also hard to excite. They are marshmallowy over issues. Violence is extremely rare and it is almost impossible to draw a Tico into a spirited debate or argument. They are loath to express or defend a position and simply walk away from arguments. (As such, resentments fester and sneaky retributions—such as arson—are common.) It has been said that the Ticos respect and have faith in their laws, their police force, and state institutions; but the frightening statistics on theft and fraud (and their in-your-face driving habits) suggest that this is baloney. Still, the *notion* of democracy and the ideals of personal liberty are strongly cherished. Costa Ricans are intensely proud of their accomplishments in this arena, and gloss over the glaring inadequacies such as endemic corruption, for example, or limited development of individualism and applied intelligence.

They are a progressive people in an isthmus of conservatism, and they revere education. "We have more teachers than soldiers" is a common boast, and framed school diplomas hang in even the most humble homes. Everyone, too, is eager for the benefits of social progress. However, Costa Ricans are also conservative, suspicious of experimentation that is not consistent with a loosely held sense of "*tico* tradition." Changes, too, supposedly should be made *poco a poco* (little by little). Ticos share the fatalistic streak common to Latin America, one that accepts things as they are and promotes resignation to the imagined will of God. Many North American and European hoteliers and residents have bemoaned the general passivity that often translates into a lack of initiative. At government levels, political contentious issues go unresolved for years.

The cornerstone of society is still the family and the village community. Social life still centers on the home and family bonds are so strong that foreigners often find making intimate friendships a challenge. Nepotism—using family ties and

connections for gain—is the way things get done in business and government. But traditional values are severely challenged. Drunkenness is common. Theft, fraud, and burglary are endemic. Drug abuse, previously unknown in Costa Rica, has intruded: Costa Rica has become a major trading zone for cocaine traffic and in 1997, the U.S. Drug Enforcement Agency identified Barra del Colorado, Cahuita, and Limón as "critical drug-trade areas." And though many Ticos display a genuine concern for conservation, the ethic is still tentative among the population as a whole, especially *campesinos*, who still regard wildlife and the wilderness as an economic resource to cull. There is no sentimentality towards pets, and one of the greatest dangers facing many endangered animals is the decimation caused by thoughtless Ticos seeking ocelots, scarlet macaws, etc. as showcase pets. Many people think nothing of cutting off a pet sloth's hands so that it won't claw the children, or of keeping a wild cat in a cage so small that it will never learn to walk.

SEX, MACHISMO, AND THE STATUS OF WOMEN

In October 1990 I had dinner in San José with a young North American friend who was studying for a year at the University of Costa Rica. She is tall and beautiful, with hair as blonde as flax and skin as white as fresh-fallen snow. She was tired, she told me. Tired of the attention-arresting "Ssssst!" of Tico men. Tired of the silent, insistent stares—of *dando cuerva,* "making eyes." Tired of leeringly being called *guapa, mi amor,* and *¡machita!* To her, Costa Rica was a land of unbridled and ugly machismo.

Everything in life of course is relative. Yes, Tico men make a national pastime of flirting. But by the standards of other Latin American countries— I am constantly assured—Costa Rican men are relatively restrained in their advances, and the nation is progressive and moderately successful in advancing the equal rights of women.

That said, legacies of the Spanish Catholic sense of "proper" gender roles are twined like tangled threads through the national fabric. Male and female roles are clearly defined. Machismo, sustained by a belief in the natural superiority of men, is integral to the Costa Rican male's way of life. It "justifies" why he expects to be given due deference by women, why he expects his wife or *novia* (girlfriend) to wait on him hand and foot, why he refrains from household chores, and why he is generally free to do as he pleases, particularly to sleep around. The sexual wanderings of married men are still tolerated by a remarkably high percentage of women, and the faithful husband and male celibate is suspect in the eyes of his friends. The Latin male expresses his masculinity in amorous conquests. In Costa Rica flirting has been taken to the level of art. "Making love is the number one pastime in Costa Rica, followed by drinking and eating," suggests writer Kent Britt. "*Fútbol* [soccer]—the so-called national sport—isn't even in the running."

But it always takes two to tango. San José's stylish young Ticas, with their unbelievably tight jeans and high heels, give as good as they get. Hip urban Ticas have forsaken old-fashioned romanticism for a latter-day liberalism that accepts short-term relationships and sexual pleasure. Even in the most isolated rural towns, dating in the Western fashion has displaced the *retreta*—the circling of the central plaza by men and women on weekend evenings—and chaperonage, once common, is now virtually unknown.

The rules of the mating game, however, are not the same as in Europe or North America. A gradual wooing is expected. Males are expected to adhere to traditional romantic roles; Sir Walter Raleigh would do well here with his cloak. And females can be both outrageously flirtatious and stand-offish as part of the ritual. Male suitors are expected to spend lavishly, often bearing gifts for women who will stand them up on dates as a matter of course; a woman's acceptance of a date does not mean that she will honor it (a result of *quedar bien*).

Costa Ricans are liberal in their sexual relations, even if some of the mental projections don't quite match up. Women are *supposed* to be loyal and chaste. Sexual freedom is the prerogative of males; sexually liberated women are still looked down on as "loose." You don't need to be Einstein to work out the mathematical inconsistencies and mental delusions this implies. In fact, almost 10% of all Costa Rican adults live to-

gether in "free unions," one-quarter of all children are *hijos naturales* (born out of wedlock; one in five of such births list the father as "unknown"), and one in five households is headed by a single mother. Many rural households are so-called Queen-bee (all-female) families headed by an elderly matriarch who looks after her grandchildren while the daughters work. Divorce, once a stigma, is now common and easily obtained under the Family Code of 1974, although desertion remains as it has for centuries "the poor man's divorce."

Compañeras, women in consensual relationships, enjoy the same legal rights as wives. In theory, the law, too, forbids sex discrimination in hiring and salaries, and women are entitled to maternity leave and related benefits. And urban women have attained considerable success in the political and professional arena: women outnumber men in many occupations and notably in university faculties, the nation's vice-president 1986-90 was a woman (Dr. Victoria Garron), and a recent president of the Legislative Assembly was Dr. Rosemary Karpinsky. The 1990 Law to Promote Women's Social Equality added one more steppingstone to real equality.

In reality, discrimination is ingrained. Low-level occupations especially reflect wide discrepancies in wage levels for men and women. The greater percentage of lower-class women remain chained to the kitchen sink and the rearing of children. And gender relationships, particularly in rural villages, remain dominated to a greater or lesser degree by machismo and *marianismo*, its female equivalent. Women are supposed to be bastions of moral and spiritual integrity (to call a wife and mother *abnegado*—'self-sacrificing"— is the ultimate compliment), to be accepting of men's infidelities, and to "accept bitter pride in their suffering."

RELIGION

Costa Ricans are said to be "lukewarm" when it comes to religion; the religious fervor common in Mexico and the Central American isthmus is unknown. Although more than 90% of the population is Roman Catholic, at least in name, almost no one gets riled up about his or her faith. Sure, Holy Week (the week before Easter) is a na-

Nuestra Señora de Los Angeles, Cartago

tional holiday, but it's simply an excuse for a secular binge. The passing of the parish priest inspires no reverential gestures. And most Costa Ricans respond to the bell only on special occasions, generally when the bell peals for birth, marriage, and maybe for Easter morning, when the mass of men mill by the door, unpiously half in and half out.

The country has always been remarkably secular, the link between Christianity and the state—between God and Caesar—always weak. The Costa Ricans' dislike for dictators has made them intolerant of priests. The feudal peasants of other Central American nations, miserably toiling on large estates *(latifundias)* or their own tiny plots, may have been poor and ignorant, but the Church offered them one great consolation. Theirs would be the kingdom of heaven. And in more recent times, when Catholic organizations attempted to address pressing social problems, they strengthened the Church's bond with the people. In Costa Rica, by contrast, the Church, from the earliest colonial times, had little success at controlling the morals and minds of the masses. While poor peasants can be convinced they'll become bourgeois in heaven, a rising class wants its comforts on earth. Costa Rica's modernity and "middle-class" achievements have made the Church superfluous.

Still, every village no matter how small has a church and its own saint's day, albeit celebrated with secular fervor. Every taxi, bus, government office, and home has its token religious icons. The Catholic marriage ceremony is the only church marriage granted state recognition. And Catholicism is the official state religion. The 1949 Constitution even provided for state contributions to the maintenance of the Church, and the salaries of bishops are paid by the state.

Catholicism, nonetheless, has only a tenuous hold; mass in some rural communities may be a once-a-year affair, and resignation to God's will is tinged with fatalism. In a crisis Ticos will turn to a favorite saint, one who they believe has special powers or "pull" with God, to demand a miracle. And folkloric belief in witchcraft is still common (Escazú is renowned as a center for *brujos*, witches who specialize in casting out spells and resolving love problems).

Protestantism has proved less spellbinding. The Catholic clergy has fiercely protected its turf against Protestant missionaries (even Billy Graham's tour in 1958 was blackballed by the local media), and the Protestant evangelism so prevalent in other parts of Central America has yet to make a dent in Costa Rica. A great many sects, however, have found San José the ideal base for proselytizing forays elsewhere in the isthmus. The nation's black population constitutes about half of Costa Rica's 40,000 or so Protestants, though the archbishop of Canterbury would be horrified at the extent to which "his" religion has been married with African-inspired, voodoo-like *obeah* and *pocomoia* worship.

EDUCATION

The briefest sojourn in San José makes clear that Costa Ricans are a highly literate people: the country boasts of 93% literacy in those 10 and over, the most literate populace in Central America. Many of the country's early father figures, including the first president, José María Castro, were former teachers and shared a great concern for education. In 1869, the country became one of the first in the world to make education both obligatory and free, funded by the state's share of the great coffee wealth (as early as 1828, an unenforced law had made school attendance mandatory). Then, only one in 10 Costa Ricans could read and write. By 1920, 50% of the population was literate. By 1973, when the Ministry of Education published a landmark study, the figure was 89%.

The study also revealed some worrying factors. More than half of all Costa Ricans aged 15 or over—600,000—had dropped out of school by the sixth grade, for example. Almost 1,000 schools had only one teacher, often a partially trained *aspirante* (candidate teacher) lacking certification. And the literacy figures included many "functional illiterates" counted by their simple ability to sign their own name. The boast of the highest literacy rate in Central America had blinded Costa Ricans to their system's many defects.

The last 20 years have seen a significant boost to educational standards. Since the 1970s the country has invested more than 28% of the national budget on primary and secondary education. President Figueres advocated a computer in each of the nation's 4,000 schools, plus mandatory English classes to coincide with the tremendous boom in tourism (the Program for Foreign Language Education for Development—involving the training of 500 teachers and 100,000 children—began three months later). A nuclearization program has worked to amalgamate one-teacher schools. And schooling through the ninth year (age 14) is now compulsory. Nonetheless, there remains a severe shortage of teachers with a sound knowledge of the full panoply of academic subjects, remote rural schools are often difficult to reach in the best of weather, and the Ministry of Education is riven with political appointees who change hats with each administration. As elsewhere in the world, well-to-do families usually send their children to private schools.

The country, with approximately 100 libraries, has a desperate need for books and for funds to support the hundreds of additional libraries that the country needs. Books (Spanish preferred) can be donated to the **National Library,** c/o Vera Violeta Salazar Mora, Director, Dirección Bibliotecas Públicas, Apdo. 10-008, San José, tel. 236-1828 or 221-2436.

The **Ministerio de Educación,** Departamento de Inglés, San José 1000, accepts volunteers to teach English. **World Teach,** Harvard Institute for International Development, 1 Eliot St., Cambridge, MA 02138, tel. (617) 495-5527, fax 495-1239, also places volunteers to teach English in schools that have requested assistance. The local school or community provides housing and a living allowance; you pay a participation fee that covers airfare, health insurance, training, and field support.

Universities

Although the country lacked a university until 1940, Costa Rica now boasts four state-funded schools of higher learning, and opportunities abound for adults to earn the primary or secondary diplomas they failed to gain as children.

The **University of Costa Rica** (UCR), the largest and oldest university, enrolls some 35,000 students, mostly on scholarships. The main campus is in the northeastern San José community of San Pedro (UCR also has regional centers in Alajuela, Turrialba, Puntarenas, and Cartago). The **National University** in Heredia (there are regional centers in Liberia and Perez Zeledon) offers a variety of liberal arts, sciences, and professional studies to 13,000 students. Cartago's **Technical Institute of Costa Rica** (ITCR) specializes in science and technology and seeks to train people for agriculture, industry, and mining. And the **State Correspondence University,** founded in 1978, is modeled after the United Kingdom's Open University and has 32 regional centers offering 15 degree courses in health, education, business administration, and the liberal arts.

In addition, there are also dozens of private "universities," though the term is applied to even the most marginal cubby-hole college.

HEALTH

Perhaps the most impressive impact of Costa Rica's modern welfare state has been the truly dramatic improvements in national health. Infant mortality has plummeted from 25.6% in 1920 to only 1.5% today. The annual death rate has dropped from 41 per thousand in 1894 to 3.9 per thousand. And the average Costa Rican today can expect to live to a ripe 73.2 years—longer than the average U.S.-born citizen. All this thanks to the Social Security system, which provides universal insurance benefits covering medical services, disability, maternity, old-age pensions, and death. These factors, together with considerations on levels of education and standard of living, have elevated Costa Rica to 28th on the United Nations" "Human Development Index." Despite this, nearly 121,000 Costa Rican families live in poverty, which creates its own health problems.

Costa Rica assigns about 10% of its GNP to health care. The result? A physician for every 700 people and a hospital bed for every 275. In fact, in some areas the health-care system isn't far behind that of the U.S. in terms of the latest medical technology, at least in San José, where transplant surgery is now performed. Many North Americans fly here for surgery, including dental work. And the Beverly Hills crowd helps keep Costa Rica's cosmetic surgeons busy.

One key to the nation's success was the creation of the Program for Rural Health in 1970 to ensure that basic health care would reach the furthest backwaters. The program, aimed at the 50% of the population living in small communities, established rural health posts attended by paramedics. The clinics are visited regularly by doctors and nurses, and strengthened by education programs stressing good nutrition, hygiene, and safe food preparation. Even a few years ago malnutrition reaped young Ticos like a scythe; in the last two decades infant mortality from malnutrition has fallen by more than 80%. In 1992, the Social Security service initiated a plan aimed at lowering infant mortality to one percent. It's a constant battle, however. Health standards slipped slightly in 1990-91 because of budget cutbacks: the tuberculosis rate doubled in 1991, for example, and that year the nation witnessed its first measles epidemic in many years (so did the United States). A major problem is the high incidence of smoking among Ticos—a cherished tradition in Costa Rica.

BOB RACE

ON THE ROAD
RECREATION

Costa Rica is a nirvana for active travelers with recreation or a specific adventure in mind. Virtually whatever your taste in recreation, Costa Rica has something for you. You can pursue your own thing, or book any of scores of organized excursions and tours on a particular theme.

BICYCLING

The occasional sweat and effort make Costa Rica's spectacular landscapes and abiding serenity all the more rewarding from a bicycle saddle. Sure, you'll work for your reward. But you'd never get so close to so much beauty in a car. Away from the main highways roads are little traveled. However, there are no bike lanes. Potholes are a persistent problem. And traffic can be hazardous on the steep and windy mountain roads. A helmet is a wise investment.

Costa Ricans are particularly fond of cycling, and bicycle racing is a major sport, culminating each December in the 12-day **Vuelta a Costa**

Rica, which crisscrosses the mountain chain from sea level to over 3,000 meters. Mountain-bike racing has become very popular, culminating in the **Trofeo Estrella,** the year's biggest race.

If you're planning your own trip, a good reference source is *Latin America on a Bicycle* by J.P. Panet (Champlain, NY: Passport Press, 1987), which has a chapter on Costa Rica. Airlines generally allow bicycles to be checked free (properly packaged) with one piece of luggage. Otherwise a small charge may apply. Leave your touring bike at home: bring a mountain bike or rent one once you arrive.

Many tour companies offer group tours. Most are suitable for all levels of competence, but check in advance about the kind of terrain and mileages involved. Don't be put off by the fact that the majority of tours involve cycling on the volcanoes: you usually ride down, not up! It helps to ride a bicycle regularly before such a tour. Even so, the pace is as leisurely or demanding as you wish to make it. You'll feel no pressure to conform to anyone else's pace. Armed with a route map and in-

SIGHTSEEING HIGHLIGHTS

SAN JOSÉ

National Theater: Historic landmark with magnificent murals and interior decoration. Classical music, opera, and other performances at night.

Fidel Tristan Jade Museum: Immense collection of jade utensils and jewelry and other artifacts recording Costa Rica's pre-Columbian history.

National Arts and Cultural Center: Housed in the former Liquor Factory, the Center embodies art, architectural and photo exhibitions, and performing arts theaters.

Pre-Columbian Gold Museum: Superb collection of pre-Columbian gold figurines, ornaments, etc.

Contemporary Art Museum: Proof that Costa Rica is *not* a cultural backwater; encompasses paintings, engravings, ceramics, and sculptures spanning the century.

Costa Rica Science and Cultural Center. This former prison houses the splendid National Gallery of Contemporary Art, plus a superb, interactive Children's Museum.

National Museum: Displays recording Costa Rica's history and cultures from pre-Columbian days to the contemporary setting. Housed in an old fort.

Pueblo Antigua: A marvelous re-creation of traditional Costa Rican settings; a living museum on a Williamsburg theme, also with fairground.

Spirogyra: Splendid collection of live butterflies flitting about inside a walk-through netted arena.

CENTRAL HIGHLANDS

Poás Volcano: Drive-up volcano with active fumaroles, viewing platforms, good geological displays, nature trails, and stunning views on clear days.

Butterfly Farm, La Guácima: Entertaining and enlightening breeding farm with walk-through display areas and guided tours.

Café Britt, Heredia: Working coffee *finca* with guided tours, folkloric show, and coffee tasting.

Guayabo National Monument: The nation's only pre-Columbian archaeological site of significance; an intriguing entrée into Costa Rica's Indian heritage. Good birding.

Irazú Volcano: The world's highest drive-up volcano. Stunning scenery en route.

Joyeros del Bosque Húmedos, Grécia: World's largest butterfly collection, magnificently displayed.

World of Snakes, Grécia: A large collection of endemic and exotic snakes, marvelously exhibited.

NORTHERN LOWLANDS

Caño Negro Wildlife Refuge: Remote lagoon surrounded by wetlands protecting vast quantities of birds and other wildlife. Fantastic fishing.

Arenal Volcano: An active volcano that throws out lava and breccia almost daily. Backed by beautiful Lake Arenal. Best enjoyed from Arenal Observatory Lodge or while soaking in thermal hot springs at Tabacón.

Tabacón Hot Springs, Fortuna: A kind of lush, open-air Roman baths, with waterfalls, chutes, and steaming pools fed by waters from Arenal volcano, which looms nearby.

CARIBBEAN COAST

Tortuguero National Park: Coastal jungle with vast numbers of birds and animals easily seen on guided boat trips. Turtles come ashore to lay eggs. Superb fishing.

Cahuita National Park: Pretty beaches, coral reefs (sadly depleted), and nature trails leading into coastal rainforest. Popular budget travelers' hangout.

Gandoca-Manzanillo National Park: Lonesome beaches plus a plethora of wildlife, including marine turtles and rarely seen manatees and freshwater dolphins.

Los Canales: A narrow canal linking Tortuguero National Park with Moín. Plentiful wildlife viewing en route.

Rainforest Aerial Tram: Dr. Donald Perry's innovative aerial tram provides a unique entrée to the wildlife-rich world of the canopy.

CENTRAL PACIFIC

Manuel Antonio National Park: Small rainforest preserve with diverse wildlife, good nature trails, and beautiful beaches. Popular and heavily visited.

Carara Biological Reserve: Easily reached reserve at the meeting point of moist and dry tropical ecosystems. Monkeys, crocodiles, and macaws virtually guaranteed.

Rainmaker Project: Boardwalks in the sky? Yes, elevated walkways lead you through the forest canopy.

Río Tácoles: The best site in the country for viewing crocodiles. *(continues on next page)*

SIGHTSEEING HIGHLIGHTS
(continued)

GUANACASTE

Monteverde Cloud Forest Biological Reserve: Plentiful wildlife and birds, including the quetzal. Lectures. Guided hikes. Superbly maintained reserve. Plus Butterfly Garden and other attractions nearby.

Sky Walk: Elevated walkways lead you through the cloud-forest canopy at Santa Elena Cloud Forest Reserve.

La Casona—Santa Rosa National Park: Costa Rica's most important historic site, this rustic farmstead, now a museum, has been the setting of three major battles. Nature trails and plentiful wildlife.

Lake Arenal: Scenery reminiscent of England, with quilted patchwork farmland and forest running down to the lake. A favored windsurfing spot, with smoldering Arenal volcano as a backdrop.

Rincón de la Vieja National Park: Remote, scenic volcano with fumaroles, boiling mud pots, and thermal springs reached by nature trails. Excellent hiking.

NICOYA PENINSULA

Playa Grande: Premier leatherback turtle nesting site. One of the prettiest beaches—great for surfing, too—in Costa Rica. Backed by a mangrove estuary replete with wildlife.

Cabo Blanco Absolute Nature Reserve: Remote rainforest preserve protecting rare flora and fauna.

Guaitil: Small village maintaining the Chorotega Indian pottery tradition. Beautiful earthenware for sale.

Ostional National Wildlife Refuge: One of two major nesting sites featuring *arribadas* (mass nestings) of the Pacific ridley turtle.

GOLFO DULCE AND PENINSULA DE OSA

Corcovado National Park: Remote pristine rainforest reserve harboring jaguars, macaws, and other rare species. Excellent hiking and camping for the hardy.

SOUTH CENTRAL

Wilson Botanical Gardens: Combines magnificent landscaped tropical gardens and protected rainforest with plentiful wildlife.

Chirripó National Park: Remote and rugged region surrounding Costa Rica's highest peak. Superb, yet strenuous hiking to the summit.

---

structions for safe riding, you can cycle alone if you wish. A support van ("sag wagon") follows in the group's wake to drop off and pick up those wishing to cycle only a part of each day's journey, or those short of breath or energy. And qualified bilingual guides cycle with you to cure any mechanical, physical, or psychological breakdowns. One-day bicycling tours generally cost $65-75, including lunch and bike rental.

Many hotels and local tour operators rent mountain bikes. See regional chapters. In San José try **Mountain Biking Costa Rica,** tel. 255-0914, or **Ríos Tropicales.**

Costa Rican Tour Companies
Aventuras Naturales, tel. 225-3939, fax 253-6934, offers one-day mountain biking tours of Irazú, Turrialba, and Guayabo, plus two- and three-day tours of both the Caribbean coast and Arenal Volcano. **Coast to Coast Adventures** has one- and three-day mountain biking trips ($85-350), plus longer trips combining biking with other activities.

Fiesta Tours International, tel. 233-8167, fax 222-2707, has a one-day "jungle mountain bike tour" from San José. **VRTour,** Apdo. 12850, 1000 San José, tel. 235-4982, fax 297-1993, also offers mountain bike tours.

Ríos Tropicales offers three- and four-day trips combining biking on Irazú and rafting on the Pacuare ($395 and $455). **Horizontes** has a one-day "Tapantí Cycling Adventure." **Tikal Tours** offers mountain biking trips.

North American Tour Companies
Backroads, 801 Cedar St., Berkeley, CA 94710-1800, tel. (510) 527-1555 or (800) 462-2848, fax (510) 527-1444, e-mail: goactive@backroads.com, runs a nine-day mountain-biking tour featuring La Fortuna, Monteverde, and the southern Nicoya Peninsula; plus a seven-day multisport trip featuring mountain biking, hiking, and rafting around

Turrialba and Osa Peninsula ($2,185, Jan.-March). **Mariah Wilderness Expeditions,** P.O. Box 248, Pt. Richmond, CA 94807, tel. (510) 233-2303, fax 233-0956, e-mail: rafting@mariahwe.com, features cycling on Orosí volcano as part of an eight-day "Tropical Adventure." **Lost World Adventures,** 220 Second Ave., Decatur, GA 30030, tel. (404) 373-5820, fax 377-1902, e-mail: lwa@lost-worldadventures.com, website www.lostworldadventures.com, offers a three-day mountain biking package, plus a five-day biking and rafting program.

Experience Plus!, 1925 Wallenberg Dr., Fort Collins, CO 80526, tel. (800) 685-4565, e-mail: tours@xplus.com, has nine-day guided tours of the highlands, Arenal, and Guanacaste ($1,595), plus an eight-day "self-guided solo tour" ($1,095).

Canadian BackRoutes, 597 Markham St., Toronto, Ont., Canada M6G 2L7, tel. (416) 588-6139, fax 588-9839, offers an eight-day tour taking in Lake Arenal, Poás Volcano, the Orosí Valley.

BIRDWATCHING

Costa Rica is to birders what Grand Central Station is to pickpockets. Few places in the world can boast so many different bird species in such a small area. Wherever you travel, you're sure to be surrounded by the calls and whistles of scores of exotic species.

Birding, like any outdoor activity, requires some knowledge of where you are going, what you're looking for, and the best season. No self-respecting ornithologist would be caught in the field without his copy of *A Guide to the Birds of Costa Rica* by F. Gary Stiles and Alexander Skutch (Ithaca, NY: Cornell University Press, 1989), or the *Birds of the Rainforest: Costa Rica* by Carmen Hidalgo (Trejos Hermanos, San José, 1997). Still, even with these in hand, your best bet for seeing and learning about different bird species is to hire a qualified guide or to join a birdwatching tour. A handy resource is the **Birding Club of Costa Rica,** tel. 267-7197.

Costa Rican Tour Companies
Costa Rica Temptations, Apdo. 1199-1200, San José, tel. 220-4437, fax 220-2792, e-mail: crtinfo@sol.racsa.co.cr, offers a birding tour aboard the M/V *Temptress.* **Horizontes,** Apdo. 1780-1002,

San José, tel. 222-2022, fax 255-4513, e-mail: horizont@sol.racsa.co.cr, offers one-day and multi-day guided birdwatching trips to selected national parks and reserves. It also offers a birdcount program in May—the breeding season for many species. Several companies, including **Geotur,** Apdo. 469 Y Griega, San José 1011, tel. 234-1867, fax 253-6338, offer one-day quetzal tours.

North American Tour Companies
Holbrook Travel, 3540 N.W. 13th St., Gainesville, FL 32609, tel. (352) 377-7111 or (800) 858-0999, fax (352) 371-3710, e-mail: travel@holbrooktravel.com, occasionally offers a midwinter "Costa Rica Birding Adventure" that includes Palo Verde, Monteverde, Arenal, and Selva Verde.

Preferred Adventures, One W. Water St., Suite 300, St. Paul, MN 55107, tel. (612) 222-8131 or (800) 840-8687, fax (612) 222-4221, e-mail: paltours@aol.com, has a 15-day birding trip in

---

GUIDES

To fully appreciate your time in the wilderness you need an outstanding guide—an experienced and well-read local who is part animal biologist, part ecologist, and part entertainer. (Hiring a guide is also one of the best ways to help benefit the people living near the parks and reserves.)

Costa Rica is home to scores of good guides. Standards are generally very high, and a handful have been truly outstanding. Bad guides tend to anthropomorphize; they're really chauffeurs who clutch a wildlife handbook and merely point at animals and identify them. A good guide provides a lucid, lively, and learned discussion that leaves you wide-eyed in wonder.

Ask for recommendations from local tour operators (ask for a "naturalist guide"—a more appropriate term for qualified, professional guides.)

Costa Rica Expeditions has some splendid guides and even publishes an extensive profile on each, including his or her specialty interest or unique approach to guiding. Recommended.

Also recommended is Federico Grant Esquivel, P.O. Box 1244-1000, San Jose, tel. 283-9152, pager 224- 2400, e-mail: advguide@sol.racsa.co.cr. Federico is a multilingual, go-getting, all-around natural history and adventure guide with an irrepressible character plus a 4WD and a minivan.

Jan.-Feb. taking in Carara, Tortuguero, La Selva, and Tiskita ($3,595). **Field Guides,** P.O. Box 160723, Austin, TX 78716-0723, tel. (512) 327-4953 or (800) 728-4953, e-mail: fgileader@aol.com, has a 16-day birding tour visiting five distinct areas (March only; $2,850). **Costa Rica Connection,** 975 Osos St., San Luis Obispo, CA 93401, tel. (805) 543-8823 or (800) 345-7422, fax 543-3626, e-mail: tours@crconnect.com, lists escorted birdwatching tours including a 12-day "Tropical Birding" tour. **Geostar Travel,** 4754 Old Redwood Hwy., Suite 650A, Santa Rosa, CA 95403, tel. (707) 579-2420 or (800) 624-6633, e-mail: mansellw@crl.com, has eight- and 10-day natural history tours. **Cheeseman's Ecology Safaris,** 20800 Kittredge Rd., Saratoga, CA 95070, tel. (408) 741-5330 or (800) 527-5330, fax (408) 741-0358, e-mail: cheesemans@aol.com, also features birding on its nature trips. Birdwatching tours are also a specialty of **Questers,** 257 Park Ave. S, New York, NY 10010, tel. (212) 673-3120.

Osprey Tours, P.O. Box 832, W. Tisbury, MA 02575-0823, tel./fax (508) 645-9049, e-mail: soosprey@aol.com, customizes birding tours for groups.

European Tour Operators
Journey Latin America 14-16 Devonshire Rd., Chiswick, London W4 2HD, tel. (0181) 747-3108, fax 742-1312, e-mail: tours@journeylatinamerica.com, offers a 16-day birdwatching tour.

CANOEING/KAYAKING

Anyone planning on kayaking rivers on his or her own (instead of joining an organized tour) should obtain a copy of *The Rivers of Costa Rica: A Canoeing, Kayaking, and Rafting Guide* by Michael W. Mayfield and Rafael E. Gallo, Menasha Ridge Press, 3169 Cahaba Heights Rd., Birmingham, AL 35243, which provides detailed maps plus a technical description of virtually the entire river system.

Costa Rican Tour Companies
Costa Sol Rafting, Apdo. 8-4390-1000 Cariari, San José, tel. 293-2151, fax 293-2155; in the U.S., tel. (800) 245-8420, fax (305) 858-7478, has a one-day kayaking school ($100).

Ríos Tropicales, Apdo. 472-1200, San José, tel. 233-6455, fax 255-4354, e-mail: info@riostro

THE FIGHT TO SAVE THE RÍOS PACUARE AND REVENTAZÓN

In 1985, the Costa Rican government recognized the Pacuare Gorge's scenic quality by making it a *zona protectora,* the first designated wild and scenic river in the country. But the national electricity agency, ICE, already had plans to dam the gorge—which is one of the country's best potential sites for hydroelectric power generation. As ICE has pursued feasibility studies on its dam site, the Pacuare has become the focus of a classic development-vs.-preservation face-off.

ICE has proposed three massive hydroelectricity dams on the Pacuare and Reventazón rivers. The Angostura Project is under construction on the latter and due for completion in 1999. The second project, known as the Guayabo-Siquirres Hydroelectric Project, will inundate a 14-km stretch of river and 1,250 hectares of surrounding wilderness. The project will cost an estimated $1 billion, presumably with a loan from the World Bank, and should be completed by 2008. The Pacuare Hydroelectric Project, sched-

uled for completion in 2015, will flood five square miles of class V rapids and primary rainforest.

The dams will devastate ecotourism and river-rafting activities on the rivers. The ICE dams have not yet been funded and approved. In the meantime, significant erosion and deforestation goes on as exploratory mining takes place.

If you're interested in helping save the Pacuare, contact the **Costa Rican Association for the Protection of the Rivers** (CRAPR), Apdo. 4600, San José 1000, tel. 223-1925, fax 222-9936, a non-profit group of concerned citizens trying to promote "positive, environmentally compatible and sustainable alternatives" to ICE's project; or the **Fundación Ríos Tropicales,** Apdo. 472-1200 Pavas, San José, tel. 233-6455, fax 255-4354, e-mail: frt@riostro.com, which welcomes donations payable in the USA to Friends of the River/Fundación Ríos Tropicales, 128 J St., Sacramento, CA 95814-2203.

.com, offers kayaking trips for experienced kayakers on the Sarapiquí, Sucio, Grande de Orosí, Peñas Blancas, Chirripó (all class IV), and the Pacuare (class V). **Aguas Bravas,** tel. 292-2072 or 479-9025, fax 229-4837, also offers kayaking. **Costa Rica Expeditions,** Apdo. 6941-1000, San José, tel. 257-0766, fax 257-1665, e-mail: crexped@sol.racsa.co.cr, rents kayaks and canoes, plus offers guided programs on the Chirripó, Reventazón, and Pacuare. And **Coast to Coast Adventures,** Apdo. 2135-1002, San José, tel./fax 225-6055, e-mail: ctocsjo@sol.racsa.co.cr, offers kayaking.

Kayak Jungle Tours, Rancho Leona, La Virgen de Sarapiquí, tel. 761-1019, offers five-day kayaking trips on the Sarapiquí River and through Caño Negro National Wildlife Refuge, in the northern lowlands.

North American Tour Companies
American Wilderness Experience, 2820-A Wilderness Place, Boulder, CO 80301-5454, tel. (303) 444-2622 or (800) 444-0099, fax (303) 444-3999, e-mail: awedave@aol.com, offers two 11-day canoeing trips—one in the Northern Lowlands, with stays at lodges; the other in the Talamancas, using lodges and a "safari-style" base camp ($1,750-1,850). **Battenkill Canoe,** P.O. Box 65, Historic Rt. 7A, Arlington, VT 05250, tel. (802) 362-2800 or (800) 421-5268, fax (802) 362-0159, e-mail: bcl@sover.net, has group trips throughout Costa Rica and arranges customized itineraries.

CANOPY TOURS

Hardly a month goes by without *another* "canopy tour" opening in Costa Rica. No experience is necessary for most such treetop explorations, which usually consist of a system of treetop platforms linked by horizontal transverse cables that permit you to "fly" through the treetops. The system uses techniques developed by cavers and canyon rappellers and allows you to ascend and explore life amid the canopy from a unique perspective.

It all began at Finca Valverdes in Monteverde, where Canadians Rick Graham and Darren Rennick founded a company called Canopy Tour (now The *Original* Canopy Tour) and created a transverse system through the treetops.

The **Original Canopy Tour,** Apdo. 751-2350, San Francisco de Dos Ríos, tel. 257-5149, fax 256-7626, e-mail: canopy@sol.racsa.co.cr, has facilities in Monteverde Cloud Forest Preserve, at Iguana Park, at Isla Tortuga, at Rainmaker, and at Thermales del Bosque near Ciudad Quesada (San Carlos). More facilities are under construction. The tour takes about three hours. It charges $45 walk-in ($55 Iguana Park), $35 students, $25 children. Package trips from San José are offered. No credit cards.

Warning: The success of The Original Canopy Tour company has spawned several copycat operations, not always with the same standards. Some are potentially unsafe. (In mid-1997 a U.S. woman died in a fall from a rope at La Fortuna by an outfit called Canopy Adventure Tours, which asks clients to *jumar*—an intermediate-level ascent by rope—to a tree platform. The woman had no rope-climbing experience. The Original Canopy Tour does not ask clients to do this.)

The **Rainforest Aerial Tram** provides a 90-minute, Disneyworld-like ride through the canopy aboard motorized trams in a private rainforest reserve on the fringe of Braulio Carrillo National Park. And the Santa Elena Cloud Forest Reserve's Skywalk and the Rainmaker Adventure Retreat offer the chance to walk through the canopy on elevated boardwalks.

CRUISES/YACHTING

Half- and full-day excursions and sunset cruises are offered from dozens of beaches along the Pacific coast.

Isla Tortuga
By far the most popular trip is that to Isla Tortuga. Several companies offer day-long excursions from Puntarenas (the cruises are also offered as excursions from San José) to Isla Tortuga in the Gulf of Nicoya. The cruise—1-2.5 hours each way, depending on the vessel—is superbly scenic, passing the isles of Negritos, San Lucas, Gitana, and Guayabo. En route you may spot manta rays or pilot whales in the warm waters. Even giant whale sharks have been seen basking off Isla Tortuga. You'll normally have about two hours on Isla Tortuga, with a buffet lunch served on the beach. Costs average $65 from

Puntarenas, $75 from San José. Check carefully to see what's included in the price.

Calypso Cruises, Apdo. 6941-1000, San José, tel. 256-2727, in the U.S. tel. (800) 948-3770, fax 233-0401, e-mail: calypso@centralamerica.com, initiated Tortuga Island cruises in 1975 aboard its 15-meter cruise yacht *Calypso.* In 1994, the venerable vessel was replaced by a huge catamaran, the *Manta Raya,* described as an "oceangoing spaceship" built of high-density, closed-cell waterproof PVC, with a bow of Kevlar (used in bulletproof vests), and fitted with $30,000 of NASA-type electronic equipment. It carries up to 100 passengers and features a fishing platform and underwater viewing platform, plus two jacuzzis, and the amazing ability to "drive" right up onto the beach. Daily departures are offered during dry season (15 Dec.-15 April), Wednesday, Friday, and Sunday in wet season ($94 from Puntarenas, $99 from San José). An "astronomy tour" is also offered (same price). These tours are great.

The *Calypso* now operates day-trips to the company's private island—Punta Coral—that likewise offers great hiking, sea kayaking, snorkeling, etc. (same price). Calypso Cruises also offers a three-day "Land-Sea Adventure" combining a cruise with two nights in Monteverde ($508 s, $710 d).

Bay Island Cruises, Apdo. 49, San José 1017, tel. 296-5544, fax 296-5095, offers cruises year-round aboard the *Bay Princess,* an ultramodern 16-meter cruise yacht with room for 70 passengers. The ship has a sundeck and music, and cocktails and snacks are served during the cruise.

Sea Ventures, tel. 257-3139, fax 239-4666, operates daily cruises to Tortuga Island aboard its sleek 29-meter namesake vessel. A three-day "Sailing/Nature Adventure" combines two days sailing in the Gulf of Nicoya and one day at Cabo Blanco National Reserve, with overnights on board (the trip departs and returns to Playa Herradura, north of Jacó; $445).

Other

The sleek *Star Chaser* catamaran operates day-trips from Punta Leona. **Pollux de Golfito,** Apdo. 7-1970, San José 1000, tel. 231-4055, fax 231-3030, has a range of day-long and multiday cruises aboard the sleek 16-meter-long S/Y *Pollux.*

Yacht Charters

Way To Go Costa Rica, P.O. Box 81288, Raleigh, NC 27622, tel. (800) 835-1223, fax (919) 787-1952, has four fully outfitted sailing vessels for rent for five or seven days. Calypso Cruises, Pollux de Golfito, and Sea Ventures (see above) also offer yacht charters. **Veleros del Sur,** Apdo. 13, Puntarenas 5400, tel. 661-1320, fax 661-1119, charters 14- to 19-meter yachts, with skippers and crew if needed.

DEEP-SEA FISHING

When your fishing-loving friend tells you all about the big one that got away in Costa Rica, don't believe it. Yes, the fish come big in Costa Rica. But *hooking* trophy contenders comes easy; the fish almost seem to line up to get a bite on the hook. The country is the undisputed sailfish capital of the world on the Pacific, the tarpon capital on the Caribbean. Fishing varies from season to season, but hardly a month goes by without some International Game Fish Association record being broken; the 1996 IGFA's World Record edition lists 18 all-tackle records for Costa Rica, 41 line test records, and 18 fly-fishing records. And 1997 went down as the best season on record.

Alas, the sportfishing industry is facing some sharp competition from illegal commercial harvesting. Fishing experts talk of a possible catastrophe, such as befell sportfishing in Puerto Rico and Baja California. Regulation is a problem for cash-strapped Costa Rica: it cannot police its 1,227 km (767 miles) of coastline. Fears escalated when a five-year slump set in following the 1991 success. But the game fish came back stronger than ever in 1996 and 1997, with giant marlin appearing in staggering numbers.

Boat charters run $250-400 a half day, and $350-650 for a full day for up to four people, with lunch and beverage included. Most fishing resorts are similar in their approach to servicing anglers, providing world-class boats and equipment; most operators now operate only catch-and-release.

Fishing expert Jerry Ruhlow has a column on fishing in the weekly *Tico Times* and *Costa Rica Today,* and also publishes *Costa Rica Outdoors,* a slick full-color bimonthly magazine dedicated to fishing and outdoor sports.

TYPES OF SPORTFISH

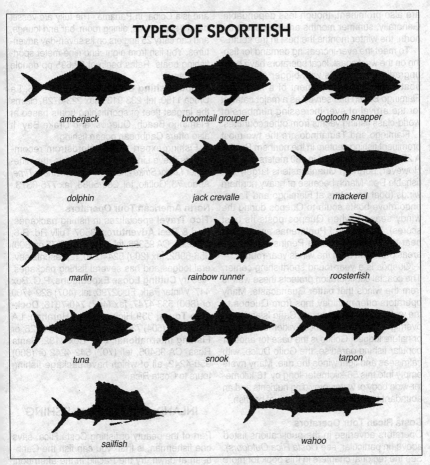

amberjack

broomtail grouper

dogtooth snapper

dolphin

jack crevalle

mackerel

marlin

rainbow runner

roosterfish

tuna

snook

tarpon

sailfish

wahoo

Carlos Barrantes, the "father of Costa Rican fishing" has a **tackle shop**, Gilca Casa de Pesca, in San José at Calle 1, Avenidas 16/19, tel. 222-1470, fax 223-8223.

The Pacific

No place in the world has posted more "super grand slams"—all three species of marlin and one or more sailfish on the same day—than the Pacific coastal waters of Costa Rica, where it's not unusual to raise 25 or more sailfish in a single day. In May 1991, fishermen posted the highest catch record in tournament history when 120

anglers caught and released 1,691 sailfish and marlin in the four days of the 13th Annual International Sailfish Tournament. And in early 1991, an angler out of Guanamar caught the first Pacific blue marlin taken on a fly (at 92 kg, it's also the largest fish ever caught on a fly).

The hard-fighting blue marlin swims in these waters year-round, although this "bull of the ocean" is most abundant in June and July, when large schools of tuna also come close to shore. June-October is best for dorado (another year-round fish). Then, too, yellowfin tuna weighing up to 90 kg offer a rod-bending challenge. Wahoo are also prominent, though less dependable. Generally, summer months are the best in the north; the winter months the best in the south.

To meet the ever-increasing demand for fishing on the west coast, local operators have been upgrading their fleets with bigger and better boats. And the development of a marina at Flamingo Beach has served as a major catalyst for the arrival of ever-increasing numbers of world-class fishing yachts from other countries.

Flamingo and Tamarindo are the two most prominent fishing centers in the northern Pacific. A 20-minute run puts you in 180 meters of water. However, northern Guanacaste is largely unfishable Dec.-March because of heavy northern winds (boat operators at Flamingo and Tamarindo move boats south to Quepos during the windy season, when Quepos posts its best scores). Boats out of Puntarenas and resorts near the tip of the Nicoya Peninsula can fish areas protected from the winds year-round.

Quepos is a year-round sportfishing center. The coastal configuration protects these waters from the winds that batter Guanacaste. Many operators offer multiday trips from Quepos to the waters off Drake Bay and Caño Island, with overnights at one of the local wilderness camps or nature lodges. Golfito is the base for another popular fishing paradise, the Golfo Dulce, with calm seas and light winds the rule. Many rivers empty into this 56-kilometer-long by 16-kilometer-wide body of water, providing nutrients and an abundant food source for a wealth of baitfish.

Costa Rican Tour Operators
Operators advertise in the publications listed above (in particular, see *Costa Rica Outdoors*). See the regional chapters in this book for more specific listings on operators and lodges.

Larger operators include **J.D.'s Watersports,** tel. 257-3857, fax 256-6391, e-mail: jdwater @sol.racsa.co.cr; in the U.S., tel. (970) 356-1028, fax 352-6324, e-mail: phoyman@aol.com; **Papagayo Excursions,** Apdo. 162, Santa Cruz, tel. 653-0227, fax 653-0254, e-mail: papagayo@sol .racsa.co.cr; **Costa Rican Dreams,** and **Costa Rican Sportfishing,** tel. 257-3553, fax 222-1760, in the U.S. tel. (800) 862-1003, which offers packages from Flamingo, Quepos, and Golfito. In 1994 it introduced the 35-meter *Coral Sea,* a "mother ship" for fishing packages to the Hannibal Bank

and Isla Coiba, in Panamá. The fully a/c vessel has 11 staterooms, dining room, bar and lounge, and can carry 25 anglers on its seven-day adventures. You fish from eight- and nine-meter sportfishing boats. Rates begin at $2,695 pp double occupancy.

Sportfishing Costa Rica, Apdo. 115, La Uruca 1150, tel. 233-9135, fax 223-6728, claims the largest fleet of sportfishing boats based at Flamingo Beach, Quepos, and Drake Bay. It also offers Caribbean ocean fishing.

Fishing expert Wayne Nordstrom recommends Steve Lino and his two boats, the nine-meter *Lucky Strike* and seven-meter *Show Time,* Apdo. 73, Golfito, tel. 288-5083, fax 775-0373.

North American Tour Operators
Tico Travel specializes in fishing packages. **Rod & Reel Adventures,** 3507 Tully Rd. B-6, Modesto, CA 95356, tel. (209) 524-7775 or (800) 356-6982, fax (209) 524-1220, represents several lodges and has several fishing packages. Also try **Cutting Loose Expeditions,** P.O. Box 447, Winter Park, FL 32790, tel. (407) 629-4700 or (800) 533-4747, fax (407) 740-7816; **Dockside Tours,** 339 Hickory Ave., Harahan, LA 70123, tel. (504) 734-5868 or (800) 235-3625; or **Fishing International,** P.O. Box 2132, Santa Rosa, CA 95405, tel. (707) 542-4242 or (800) 950-4242, all of which have package fishing tours to Costa Rica.

INLAND AND COASTAL FISHING

Part of the beauty of fishing Costa Rica, says one fisherman, is that "you can fish the Caribbean at dawn, try the Pacific in the afternoon, and still have time to watch a sunset from a mountain stream." Forget the sunset—there are fish in those mountains. A freshwater fishing license is mandatory; the limit is a maximum of five specimens (of any one species) per angler per day. The closed season runs September through December.

Lodges and outfitters provide the permit (license, not fish). Or, you can obtain one from the Department of Agriculture in San José, Ministerio de Agricultura, Calle 1 and Avenida 1, tel. 257-8066 or 223-0829. Reportedly, permits can also be obtained from the Banco Nacional de

Costa Rica, Avenida 1, Calles 2/4; weekdays 9 a.m.-3 p.m. Cost is approximately $12.

Lakes and Mountain Streams

More than a dozen inland rivers provide lots of action on rainbow trout, *machaca* (Central America's answer to American shad), drum, *guapote*, *mojarra* (Costa Rica's bluegill with teeth!), *bobo* (a moss-eating mullet that adapted to fresh water thousands of years ago), and other freshwater and tidal species in season. A good bet is the **Río Savegre** and other streams around San Gerardo de Dota, Copey and Cañon.

Caño Negro Lagoon and the waters of the Río San Juan are virtually untouched but represent fabulous horizons for snook and tarpon. Lake Arenal is famed for its feisty rainbow bass *(guapote)* running 3.5 kg or more. Lake Arenal boasts the world record for *guapote* (5.2 kg).

Caribbean

Costa Rica's northeastern shores, lowland lagoons, and rivers offer the world's hottest tarpon and snook action for the light-tackle enthusiast. At prime fishing spots, tarpon average 35 kg (sometimes reaching up to 70 kg). These silver rockets are caught in the jungle rivers and backwater lagoons, and ocean tarpon fishing just past the breakers is always dependable. Wherever you find them, you'll have your hands full; no other fish jumps, leaps, twists, and turns like the tarpon. Often, the fish will leap four meters and jump five or six times before you get it to the boat to be lipgaffed, hoisted for a photo, and released. When you tire of wrestling these snappy fighters, you can take on snook—another worthy opponent.

Fall, when the rain tapers down and winds swing onshore, flattening the rivermouths, is the best time to get a shot at the trophy snook that return to the beaches around the rivermouths to spawn. Anglers stand knee-deep in the surf and cast at five- to nine-kilogram snook. "Talk about excitement! There's nothing like it!" says Chet Young, owner of Angler's Connection. Snook will hit lures trolled or cast along the riverbanks, but the biggest fish are usually taken from the surf. The all-tackle IGFA record came from Costa Rica, which regularly delivers 14-kilogram fish.

Tarpon are caught year-round. Snook season runs from late August into January, with a peak Aug.-November. November through January the area enjoys a run of *calba*, the local name for small snook that average two kilograms and are exceptional sport on light tackle, with 20 or more *calba* per angler in a typical day's catch. Jacks are also common year-round in Caribbean waters. They are voracious predators, and because they are extremely strong and have great endurance, they can be a challenge for any fisher using light tackle.

The Río Colorado Lodge offers Caribbean offshore fishing, but most offshore fishing is relegated to the Pacific coast. In addition to the many fishing lodges, another option is the **Rain Goddess,** c/o Blue Wing International, Apdo. 850, Escazú 1250, tel. 231-4299, fax 231-3816; in the U.S., tel. (800) 308-3394, a luxurious 20-meter, a/c houseboat dedicated to fishing the San Juan and Colorado rivers on three- to seven-day excursions.

GOLFING

Costa Rica is putting itself on the golfing map. Before 1995, the country had just two courses, both associated with luxury resorts—the championship course at **Meliá Cariari and Country Club** outside San José, and the **Hotel Tango Mar,** overlooking the Gulf of Nicoya on the Pacific coast. The Tango Mar course is a nine-hole layout on 1,765 meters, but a good challenge for the average golfer.

The country is in the midst of a course-building binge in search of the birdie that lays the golden egg. By 1996 six courses had opened, nine more were set to open by 1999, and *two dozen* more on the books. (The new greens have environmentalist "greens" fuming. Most are located in Costa Rica's parched northwest and, in addition to contributing to the destruction of precious forests, tap the aquifers upon which surrounding regions rely—the courses consume millions of gallons of water.)

New 18-hole courses in Guanacaste include one at **Bahía Culebra,** a Robert Trent Jones, Jr., stunner at the Meliá Playa Conchal, and the **Rancho Las Colinas Golf and Country Club,** tel. 654-4089 or 293-4644, whose front nine feature gently rolling fairways surrounded by water hazards and whose back nine have steep fairways cut through rocky terrain demanding accuracy over length.

Another course was slated to open around press time as part of the Pueblo Real resort complex north of Quepos. The biggest development of all is a 27-hole resort—**La Roca Beach Resort and Country Club,** tel. 289-4313, fax 289-4247, e-mail: laroca@sol.racsa.co.cr—to be constructed two miles north of Puerto Caldera. At least three other courses—**Los Altos de Cacique, Resort Rancho Mary,** and **Monte del Barco**—are in construction in the Nicoya peninsula. And the Tamarindo Diría Hotel in Tamarindo had set aside land for an 18-hole course; Marriott was planning a course at Playa Herradura; and Vistas del Flamingo was planning a course at Potrero.

Elsewhere, Tulin Resort broke ground on a course near Jacó in 1997. And **Parque Valle del Sol,** tel. 282-9222, fax 282-9333, e-mail: habitasu@sol.racsa.co.cr, opened its front nine holes at Santa Ana, west of San José in late 1997.

Three other existing nine-hole courses are at the **Costa Rica Country Club** in Escazú; the **Los Reyes Country Club** in La Guácima, near Alajuela; and the **El Castillo Country Club** above Heredia.

Tour Companies
Costa Rican Golf Adventures, tel./fax 446-6489, e-mail: golf@centralamerica.com; in the U.S., Interlink 854, P.O. Box 02-5635, Miami, FL 33102; and **Morris Overseas Tours,** 418 4th Ave., Melbourne Beach, FL 32951, tel. (407) 725-4809 or (800) 777-6853, offer golfing adventures in Costa Rica.

HIKING

Surprisingly, organized hiking has only recently found its feet. Those that exist are mostly one-day hikes of the upland slopes of volcanoes. Half-day or full-day hiking tours with a professional guide can generally be arranged through nature lodges or local tour operators. Most major tour operators offer hiking trips. See the charts **North American Tour Companies** and **Costa Rican Tour Companies** in the appendix.

Be sure to prepare fully for your foray: a map, sunscreen, sun hat, insect repellent, and plenty of

water. Raingear and a warm sweater or jacket are essential for hiking at higher elevations. Most reserves and national parks maintain marked trails. However, hiking in the more remote high-elevation parks may require stamina, a high degree of self-sufficiency, knee-high rubber boots, and, says one writer, "a guide so comfortable with a machete he can pick your teeth with it." The hardy and adventurous might try a strenuous hike to the peak of Chirripó, Costa Rica's tallest mountain. If you plan on overnight hiking in the boondocks, the **Army & Navy Surplus Store** in Moravia, northeast of San José, can outfit you with lightweight thermal sleeping bags, hiking boots, water canteens, rain ponchos, and other hiking and camping equipment.

A word of warning for those setting out alone to hike through the mountain-forests of the Caribbean: the *duendes* dwell here—little men covered with long gray hair who will cut off your thumbs if they get a chance because they have none of their own. Many local *campesinos* firmly believe in their existence.

Costa Rican Companies
Coast to Coast Adventures, Apdo. 2135-1002, San José, tel./fax 225-6055, e-mail: ctocsjo@sol.racsa.co.cr, offers multiday adventure trips combining hiking in Valle Escondido with mountain biking, plus a one-day hiking and rock-climbing trip to Pico Blanco ($75). **Tourtech,** tel. 221-1895, fax 256-0120, offers a "Walk in the Clouds" in Bajo la Hondura Cloud Forest Reserve near Braullio Carrillo. **Jungle Trails,** Apdo. 2413, San José 1000, tel. 255-3486, fax 255-2782, specializes in hiking tours, including a "Walk in the Clouds" on Barva and Poás Volcanoes. **Camino Travel,** Apdo. 1049-2050, San Pedro, tel. 234-2530, fax 225-6143, e-mail: caminotr@sol.racsa.co.cr, also customizes hiking and trekking trips. **Para Las Orejas,** tel./fax 279-9752, offers treks using llamas as pack animals.

North American Companies
Wildland Adventures, 3516 N.E. 155th St., Seattle, WA 98155, tel. (206) 365-0686 or (800) 345-4453, fax (206) 363-6615, e-mail: wildadve@aol.com, offers a three-day Chirripó hike ($395), plus a one-day hike to La Paza waterfall ($155), and hiking is featured on several of its other natural history trips. **Above the Clouds**

Trekking, P.O. Box 398, Worcester, MA 01602, tel. (800) 233-4499, website www.gorp.com/ad-vclds.htm, features hiking on its Costa Rican programs, as does **Explore Earth,** P.O. Box 461562, Garland, TX 75046, tel. (972) 414-0627 or (800) 313-8264, fax (972) 530-9540, e-mail: exearth@airmail.net, which features a Chirripó climb.

Backroads, 801 Cedar St., Berkeley, CA 94710-1800, tel. (510) 527-1555 or (800) 462-2848, fax (510) 527-1444, e-mail: goactive@back-roads.com, offers a seven-day walking trip that includes Monteverde, the Arenal region, and Cabo Blanco Nature Reserve ($1,895, Dec.-April); plus hiking is featured on its seven-day multi-activity trip around Turrialba and the Osa Peninsula ($2,198, Jan.-March). It is also available through **American Wilderness Experience,** 2820-A Wilderness Place, Boulder, CO 80301-5454, tel. (303) 444-2622 or (800) 444-0099, fax (303) 444-3999, e-mail: awedave@aol.com.

Mountain Travel-Sobek, 6420 Fairmount Ave., El Cerrito, CA 94530, tel. (510) 527-8100 or (800) 227-2384, fax (510) 525-7710, e-mail: info@MTSobek.com, has a 10-day "Volcanoes and Rivers" adventure, with hiking around Monteverde and Arenal, plus rafting ($1,990).

For the truly hardy, **Outward Bound,** Route 9D, R2 Box 280, Garrison, NY 10524-9757, tel. (800) 243-8520, the organization that takes folks into the outdoors to toughen up and build self-confidence, offers courses—not "trips"—that include a hike up Chirripó and have been described by participants as having "fistfuls of experience mashed in your face." You get to teach in a rural orphanage prior to the outdoor adventure portion.

HORSEBACK RIDING

Horseback riding is very popular in Costa Rica, where the *campesino* culture depends on the horse for mobility. Wherever you are, horses are sure to be available for rent. Many tour operators in San José offer half- or full-day rides at ranches and mountain lodges throughout the country. Prices average $70 for a full-day tour, including lunch. (The native horse of Costa Rica is the *crillo,* a small, big-chested creature of good temperament.)

Hacienda Guachipelín offers horseback rides up Rincón de la Vieja.

In Santa Ana (about nine km west of San José), **Club Paso Fino,** tel. 249-1466, provides instruction in riding, and the **Club Hípico la Caraña,** tel. 228-6106, offers intensive riding clinics. The latter, known simply as La Caraña, boasts two covered exhibition and practice arenas, an open-air jumping ring, and more than 100 stables. The club also offers guided horseback tours into the Santa Ana mountains.

Scores of ranches offer trail rides, notably in Guanacaste; see regional chapters. At a few (such as La Enseñada Lodge), city slickers longing to be the Marlboro Man can pay perfectly good money to work hard and get coated with dust and manure alongside workaday cowboys. The chorus of mooing and slapping of Levis on leather saddles combines with a rest on the beach as you drive cattle to where the grass is greener, preparing them for American supermarkets.

Costa Rican Tour Operators
Horizontes, Apdo. 1780-1002, San José, tel. 222-2022, fax 255-4513, e-mail: horizont@sol.racsa

.co.cr, lists a one-day ride on Orotina Ranch, with lunch at a beach on the Pacific ocean. **Jungle Trails,** Apdo. 2413, San José 1000, tel. 255-3486, fax 255-2782, has a three-day program in Rincón de la Vieja National Park, and a one-day trip in the central Pacific. **Papagayo Excursions,** tel. 653-0227, fax 653-0254, e-mail: papagayo@sol .racsa.co.cr, and **Robles Tours,** tel. 237-2116, also offer riding adventures.

On the Atlantic coast, **Tropical Adventure Tours,** Apdo. 1362, San José 1000, tel. 222-8974, fax 255-0306, has a series of half-day guided horseback tours, including to the KekoLdi Indian Reserve and Gandoca-Manzanillo Wildlife Refuge.

North American Tour Operators
Rico Tours, 130809 Research Blvd., Suite 606, Austin, TX 78750, tel. (512) 331-0918, fax 331-8765, e-mail: lac@amtvl.com, offers a 10-day "Horse Trekking Adventure" and other horseback tours. **Wildlands Adventures,** 3516 N.E. 155th St., Seattle, WA 98155, tel. (206) 365-0686 or (800) 345-4453, fax (206) 363-6615, e-mail: wildadve@aol.com, offers horseback ride on Irazú ($75).

Mariah Wilderness Expeditions, P.O. Box 248, Pt. Richmond, CA 94807, tel. (510) 233-2303, fax 233-0956, e-mail: rafting@mariahwe.com, includes horseback riding on Barva Volcano as part of an eight-day adventure tour of Costa Rica, plus a full day on horseback at Gandoca-Manzanillo Wildlife Refuge during an eight-day "Jungles Off-the-Beaten-Track" tour of the Caribbean.

FITS Equestrian, 685 Lateen Rd., Solvang, CA 93463, tel. (805) 688-9494 or (800) 223-7728, has a 10-day horse-trekking adventure featuring rides at Quepos, Irazú, Monteverde, Arenal, and Braulio Carrillo. Trips are in February, March, July, August, November, and December; $1,995.

MOTORCYCLE TOURING

Motorbike enthusiasts haven't been left out of the two-wheel touring business. Two-wheel touring—which is growing in popularity—makes you sit up and take notice of the country far more than does touring by car. The potholes and dust can be a pain in the ass, but motocross machines take care of the former.

Costa Rican Companies
The highly respected **Costa Rican Trails,** Apdo. 2907-1000 San José, tel. 233-0557 or 221-5800, fax 257-4655, e-mail: crtrails@sol.racsa.co.cr, run by Wilhelm von Breymann, offers a 10-day "Trails' Fly-N-Ride" tour using BMW F650 Fonduros ($1,500). A 16-day tour of Costa Rica and Panamá is also offered, and a grand tour of Central America is planned.

In 1997, Californian Paul Bealey set up **Tour Harley of Costa Rica,** SJO 1235, P.O. Box 025216, Miami, FL 33102-5216, in Costa Rica tel. 253-3451 or 225-4938, in the U.S., tel. (800) 466-6069, e-mail: harleytr@sol.racsa.co.cr, website www.arweb.com/harleytours. Half-day ($90), full-day ($135), and four- to 10-day trips ($600-2,400) are offered using 1200cc Sportsters and 1340cc FXRs. All you need is a valid bike license and a credit card to cover the insurance. Beware, recently there's been rumors that the company may fold.

Motorcycles Costa Rica, Villas de la Colina, Atenas, tel./fax 446-5015; in the U.S., P.O. Box 56, Redwood, VA 24146, tel. (540) 489-9181, fax 228-6557, e-mail: fbrown@naxs.com, has six-night trips using dual-sport motorcycles, Jan.-May ($995). **Moto Aventura,** Apdo. 4188, San José 1000, tel. 255-4174, fax 221-9233, uses Husqvarna four-stroke 610s for enduro rides from one day ($50) to two weeks, all-inclusive. And **Eko-Alternativo Tours,** Apdo. 1287, San José 1002, tel. 221-6476, fax 223-7601, offers an eight-day motorcycle tour of the central highlands, Arenal, and Nicoya ($675).

North American Companies
Pancho Villa Moto-Tours, a highly respected operator, runs 10-day "Fly-n-Ride" motorcycle tours in Costa Rica using BMW F650 Funduros, with eight trips in 1997, Jan.-June ($2,295, $1,495 passenger). You can also choose the "El Vagabundo," a go-as-you-please program with four- to 11-night packages from $995 ($595 passenger) using the F650s. Highly recommended!

Lotus Tours, 1644 N. Sedgwick St., Chicago, IL 60614-5714, tel. (312) 951-0031, fax 951-7313, has an eight-day tour of Costa Rica each November ($2,700).

SCUBA DIVING

Less than a decade ago, Costa Rica was virtually unknown as a destination for diving. New facilities along the Pacific coast now offer first-class dive boats and fully stocked dive shops. And divers have the excitement of truly virgin diving in areas never before explored. Visibility, unfortunately, ranges only 6-24 meters, but water temperatures are a steady 24-29° C (75-85° F) or higher. If you're looking for coral, you'll be happier in Belize, the Bay Islands of Honduras, or in the Caribbean. Costa Rica's diving is for pelagics.

A wise investment is to join **Divers Alert Network,** P.O. Box 3823, Duke University Medical Center, Durham, NC 27710, tel. (919) 684-8111, which provides emergency medical evacuation, treatment, and referral services.

Pacific

Most dive-site development has been along the Pacific coast of Guanacaste Province. You'll see little live coral and few reefs. In their place divers find an astounding variety and number of fish, soft corals, and invertebrates—a result of the abundant plankton and other marine organisms that thrive in the warm tropical waters. Most diving is around rock formations: the typical site is alongside a rocky island or partially submerged rocky pinnacles a mile or more offshore. Visibility can often be obscured (particularly in rainy season, May-Nov., where rivers enter the ocean; where rivers are absent, visibility is *enhanced* during this period), but on calm days you may be rewarded with densities of marinelife that cannot be found anywhere in the Caribbean.

Favored dive destinations in the Pacific northwest include Islas Murcielagos and the Catalinas. Both locations teem with grouper, snapper, jacks, sharks, and giant mantas, as well as indigenous tropical species. Dozens of morays peer out from beneath rocky ledges. And schools of tang, Cortez angelfish, bright yellow butterflies, hogfish, parrot fish, giant jewfish, turtles, and an array of starfish, crustaceans, clown shrimp, and eagle rays are common. Great bull sharks congregate at a place called "Big Scare," at the farthest point of Murcielagos (the place is aptly named and is recommended only for advanced open-water divers). The two island chains are challenging because of their strong currents and surges.

At the Punta Gorda dive site, six km west of Playa Ocotal, thousands of eagle rays have been known to swim by in columns that take more than 10 minutes to pass from start to finish. And divers can drop into select spots where whale sharks bask on the bottom at a depth of 12 meters. Divers also report seeing black marlin cruising gracefully around pinnacle rocks; at Las Corridas, only one kilometer from El Ocotal, you're sure to come face to face with one of the 180-kilogram jewfish that dwell here.

Many hotels have dive shops. Larger, more respected Costa Rican companies include **Bill Beard's Diving Safaris,** Apdo. 121-5019, Playas del Coco, tel./fax 670-0012, e-mail: diving@sol .racsa.co.cr, website www.diving-safaris.com; in the U.S., tel. (800) 779-0055, fax (954) 351-9740, e-mail: billbeards@netrunner.net; **El Ocotal Diving Safaris,** Apdo. 1013-1002, San José, tel. 222-4259, fax 223-8483, e-mail: elocotal@sol.racsa .co.cr, website www.centralamerica.com/cr/hotel /ocodive.htm; and **Resort Divers de Costa Rica,** tel./fax 670-0421, e-mail: beckers@sol.racsa.co .cr, which maintains scuba centers in at least eight hotels in the Playas del Coco region and adjacent beaches.

Bahía Herradura has an area known as El Jardín, famed for its formations of soft coral and sea fans. Call **J.D.'s Watersports,** tel. 257-3857, fax 256-6391, e-mail: jdwater@sol.racsa.co.cr; in the U.S., tel. (970) 356-1028, fax 352-6324, e-mail: phoyman@aol.com. Charters operate from Puntarenas and Quepos.

Farther south, Caño Island, just off the Osa Peninsula, has a reef that hosts a large variety of tropical fish, as well as groupers, snappers, wahoo, roosterfish, jacks, and tuna. About two km out from Caño is a near-vertical wall and parades of pelagic fish, including manta rays. The island is serviced by dive boats out of Drake Bay and Golfito. Charters can also be arranged out of Quepos, and the *Temptress Explorer* offers scuba diving for certified divers at Caño during its one-week natural-history itineraries.

Cocos Island

This is the Mt. Everest of dive experiences in Costa Rica. Divers from around the world descend on Costa Rica to dive Cocos Island—the subject of a Jacques Cousteau special. Its reputation for big animal encounters—whale sharks, hammerheads (sometimes schooling 500 at a time), and mantas—have made it renowned. Cocos is 550 km southwest of Costa Rica, necessitating a long sea journey.

Live-Aboards: Four vessels are used for diving at Cocos Island, usually operating 10-day itineraries out of Puntarenas. The *Okeanos Aggressor* is a 34-meter, fully a/c, 10-stateroom ship with complete facilities for 21 divers, including an E-2 film processing lab and helicopter landing pad. It is operated by **Cruceros del Sur,** Apdo. 1198, San José 1200, tel. 220-1679, fax 220-2103; in the U.S., Aggressor Fleet Ltd., P.O. Drawer K, Morgan City, LA 70381, tel. (504) 385-2628 or (800) 348-2628, fax (504) 384-0817, website www.aggressor.com.

The *Undersea Hunter* is a 27-meter steel-hull ship with two compressors and 50 tanks, seven cabins, and a capacity for 14 divers. The *Sea Hunter* is a 38-meter steel vessel that accommodates 18 divers in eight cabins, all with private bath. There's a film processing lab and two eight-meter dive boats, plus a helicopter landing pad and movie theater.

The *Iznan Tiger* is a sleek 31-meter luxury motor yacht for six passengers in four staterooms, one with a king-size bed and jacuzzi. It can be used for custom itineraries up to 21 days.

All four vessels are utilized by **Tropical Adventures,** 111 Second N., Seattle, WA 98109, tel. (206) 441-3483 or (800) 247-3483, fax (206) 441-5431, e-mail: dive@divetropical.com, a leading North American dive specialist that offers 10-day packages ($2,495-3,595 depending on vessel).

The **Oceanic Society,** Fort Mason Center, Bldg. E, San Francisco, CA 94123, tel. (415) 441-1106 or (800) 326-7491, fax (415) 474-3395, offers a "Biodiversity Study" trip as part of its marine science research project. No research experience is necessary; basic scuba certification is required.

S/Y Pollux, Apdo. 7-1970, San José 1000, tel. 231-4055, fax 231-3030, offers eight- and 10-day Cocos Island diving adventures.

Caribbean

The Caribbean coast has yet to develop a serious infrastructure catering to sport divers, despite good coral reefs. At Isla Uvita, just offshore from

Limón, are tropical fish, sea fans, and a coral reef, plus the wreck of the *Fenix,* a cargo ship that sank about a mile off the island years ago. There is a compressor in Puerto Limón, and you can rent boats for the run out to the island.

Farther south, at Cahuita, is Costa Rica's most beautiful coral reef, extending 500 meters out from Cahuita Point. The fan-shaped reef covers 593 hectares and has 35 species of coral, including the giant elkhorn. Two old shipwrecks—replete with cannons—lie on the Cahuita reef, seven meters down, playgrounds for more than 500 species of fish. The reef has suffered significant damage in recent years from sedimentation running down from the banana plantations, and there is concern that rapidly expanding hotel development will do further damage.

If undersea caverns are your thing, check out Puerto Viejo, 20 km south of Cahuita. South of here, the Gandoca-Manzanillo Wildlife Refuge protects a southern extension of the Cahuita reef, and one in better condition! Best time for diving is during the dry season (Feb.-April), when visibility is at its best. Check with park rangers for conditions, as the area is known for dangerous tides. There's a full-service dive shop at Manzanillo.

Viajes Aventura Tropical (Tropical Adventure Tours), Apdo. 1362, San José 1000, tel. 222-8974, fax 255-0306, has full-day and half-day diving packages to Cahuita, Puerto Viejo, and Punta Uva. **Mutra Tours,** Sabana Sur, tel. 232-6324, fax 231-2145, also has diving trips to Punta Uva. See the Caribbean Coast chapter for local operators.

SEA KAYAKING

This sport is quickly catching on in Costa Rica, and no wonder. The sea kayak's ability to move silently means you can travel unobtrusively, sneaking close up to wildlife without freaking it out. Dolphins and even turtles have been known to surface alongside to check kayakers out. The long, slender one- and two-man craft provided are remarkably stable and ideally suited for investigating narrow coastal inlets and flat-water rivers larger vessels cannot reach. They allow you access to places you can't hope to reach by land.

The modern kayaks used for group-tour programs are seaworthy boats of fiberglass and plastic, with built-in watertight compartments to provide added buoyancy. And the basics of kayaking are easy to learn. Experienced guides give beginners introductory instruction on handling the craft, including a "dunk" test (deliberate rolling). The kayaks have rudders operated by foot pedals, which make steering in wind and waves remarkably easy. You'll paddle from one secluded beach to another or explore the shorelines of national parks. At night, you'll normally camp on an idyllic beach. An accompanying support boat generally carries the camping gear and personal belongings. The Gulf of Nicoya is particularly kind to sea kayakers, with sheltered waters and easily accessible parks to explore. Kayak trips are also particularly popular along the mangrove-lined tidal zone of the central Pacific.

Costa Rican Tour Operators

Ríos Tropicales, Apdo. 472-1200, San José, tel. 233-6455, fax 255-4354, e-mail: info@riostro.com, offers four-day kayaking trips at Curú ($600) and a nine-day trip in Golfo Duce ($1,370). **Costa Sol Rafting,** Apdo. 8-4390-1000 Cariari, San José, tel. 293-2151, fax 293-2155; in the U.S., tel. (800) 245-8420, fax (305) 858-7478, has an eight-day sea kayaking trip ($902).

North American Tour Operators

Wildlands Adventures, 3516 N.E. 155th St., Seattle, WA 98155, tel. (206) 365-0686 or (800) 345-4453, fax (206) 363-6615, e-mail: wildadve@aol.com, offers a four-day kayaking trip in the Gulf of Nicoya ($800) and a five-day trip to the Golfo Dulce featuring kayaking ($795). **Mariah Wilderness Expeditions,** P.O. Box 248, Pt. Richmond, CA 94807, tel. (510) 233-2303, fax 233-0956, e-mail: rafting@mariahwe.com, features sea kayaking as part of a multi-activity trip.

Baja Expeditions, 2625 Garnet Ave., San Diego, CA 92109, tel. (619) 581-3311 or (800) 843-6967, offers 10-day trips on the jungle-lined Río Cañas through Palo Verde National Forest and along the Pacific coast. Similar trips of Guanacaste and Nicoya are also available Oct.-May through **American Wilderness Experience,** 2820-A Wilderness Place, Boulder, CO 80301-5454, tel. (303) 444-2622 or (800) 444-0099, fax (303) 444-3999, e-mail: awedave@aol.com.

Gulf Island Kayaking, S-24, C-36, Galiano Island, BC, Canada V0N 1PO, tel. (604) 539-2442, has one-week guided kayaking trips out of Drake Bay Wilderness Camp.

SURFING

Dedicated surfers are constantly in search of the perfect wave. For many, the search has ended in Costa Rica (the "Hawaii of Latin American surf"), where uncrowded beaches and a tantalizing array of waves have convinced devotees that this is as close to nirvana as they'll ever get. Long stretches of beaches provide thousands of beach breaks. Numerous rivers offer quality sandbar rivermouth breaks, particularly on the Pacific coast. And coral reefs on the Caribbean coast, says Costa Rican surf expert Peter Brennan, "take the speed limit to the max." The reef breaks often hold more size and get more hollow (they're also shallower and more consistent) than the beach breaks.

If the surf blows out or goes flat before you are ready to pack it in for the day, you can simply jump over to the other coast, or—on the Pacific—head north or south. If one break isn't working, another is sure to be cooking. You rarely see monster-size Hawaiian waves—waves are generally smaller, although they occasionally grow to three-plus meters—but they're nicely shaped, long, and tubular, and in places never-ending—often nearly a kilometer! Many of the more popular surf spots are beginning to look crowded, but there is always another beach beyond the horizon.

Note: Beware riptides! Costa Rica's beaches are beautiful and the surf top-notch, but every year many tourists and surfers lose their lives to treacherous riptides. Lifeguards can be found at Jacó Beach and Manuel Antonio National Park. Elsewhere, you're on your own. A free 24-hour **Costa Rican Surf Report,** tel. 233-7386, provides information on the latest conditions. *Surf Guide* magazine provides information on virtually every beach in Costa Rica, and is published every six months by Consultoria Ecar Ltda., Apdo. 694, 1100 Tibas, San José, tel./fax 253-3966. Also see *Surfos: The Costa Rican Surfer's Guide,* a full-color magazine on sale nationwide; and *Costa Rica Outdoors,* Apdo. 199-6150, Santa Ana, tel./fax 282-6743; in the U.S., Dept. SJO 2316, P.O. Box 025216, Miami, FL 33102-5216, which has an update column on the surf scene. And look for the *Surfer's Guide to Costa Rica,* a detailed booklet by Mike Pariser (Surf Press Publishing, P.O. Box 492342, Los Angeles, CA 90049). Many hotels and car rental companies offer discounts to surfers.

The **Costa Rican Surf Association,** P.O. Box 393, Puntarenas 5400, tel. 661-0344, sponsors 4-6 competitions a year.

Generally, your double board bag flies free as a second piece of checked luggage on international airlines, but you are advised to gear your trip through Atlanta, Houston, Los Angeles, Miami, New York, Orlando, San Francisco or Washington, D.C. Domestically, SANSA airline's policy on carrying surfboards is subject to change. Airlines require that you pack your board in a board bag.

Where to Go

Caribbean: The Caribbean has fewer breaks than the Pacific, but still offers great surfing during winter and spring. Waves are short yet powerful rides with sometimes Hawaiian-style radical waves. Occasionally massive swells sweep over the coral reefs, creating demanding tubes. You'll also experience exciting offshore cloud breaks, reef breaks, point breaks, and more than 80 km of beach breaks.

Just north of Playa Bonita is Potrete, with a hollow right break at the south end of a small bay. It's very shallow. A 20-minute boat ride from Puerto Limón is Isla Uvita, with a strong and dangerous left. Farther south there are innumerable short breaks at Cahuita. Closing in on the Panamanian border, things really heat up! Puerto Viejo has the biggest rideable waves in Costa Rica (up to seven meters at times, mostly in December), although these have diminished in size because of coastal uplift caused by the April 1991 earthquake. The mecca for surfers is Salsa Brava (so named for the "juice" the huge, tubular waves contain). The waves are now said to be a lot "tubier" since the earthquake and offer a right slide that "pitches out in a nasty manner that surfers love." One expert recommends avoiding the Tortuguero region, where sharks are abundant.

The best time is late May through early September (hurricane season) and Dec.-March (when Atlantic storms push through the Caribbean, creating three-meter swells).

Guanacaste: You're spoilt for choice here. The Pacific northwest offers more than 50 prime surf spots. The best time is during the rainy season (May-Oct.), when the surf can build to three meters; there are large offshore winds thoughout the dry season (Nov.-April), but the waves are smaller. Tamarindo is the surfing capital, with lots of good surf spots within a short driving distance; it also offers good hotels and is an excellent jumping-off place for a surf safari south to more isolated beaches.

Hot spots such as Witch's Rock at Playa Naranjo (one of the best beach breaks in the country, with very strong offshore winds Dec.-March) require 4WD or boat for access. You can rent a boat from Playa del Coco and other beach resorts for visits to Naranjo and Potrero Grande (also in Santa Rosa National Park), which has a right break, very fast and hollow. Here you'll find Ollie's Point, named after Oliver North, who masterminded a secret airstrip nearby to ferry weapons to the Nicaraguan rebels in the 1980s. "What Ollie probably never knew," says Peter Brennan, "is that just off the coast there's a hot right point."

Just north of Tamarindo is Playa Grande, a five-km-long beach break acclaimed as Costa Rica's most accessible consistent break. Tamarindo itself has three main points, including Pico Pequeño, a rocky right point in front of the Hotel Tamarindo; El Estero, an excellent rivermouth; and Henry's Point.

There's fine surfing the whole way south from Tamarindo, including at Avellanas, with a "very hollow" beach break called "Guanacasteco," and breathtakingly beautiful Playa Negra, a narrow beach with very fast waves breaking over a coral- and urchin-encrusted shelf—definitely for experts only when the waves are big. Continuing south you'll find Nosara, Sámara, Camaronal, Coyote, Manzanillo, and Mal País, all with good surf and lively action and several surf camps.

Central Pacific: March through June are good. The best time, however, is during the heart of the rainy season (July-Dec.) when the Caribbean dies down and conditions along the central Pacific create a full spectrum of kilometer-long lefts, reef breaks, and powerful beach breaks.

The fun begins at Boca de Barranca, at the mouth of the Río Barranca, a few kilometers south of Puntarenas (it's the closest surfing spot to San José). Boca reportedly has one of the world's longest—albeit slowest—lefts, which can run Malibu-style for more than a kilometer! Unfortunately, it has lost some of its luster because of its polluted water, but a new sewage-treatment plant for Puntarenas should restore Boca's image. Two miles south is Caldera, with a very good left called "Jetty Break." Playa Tivives and Valor also offer good beach breaks.

Central Pacific surfing centers on Jacó, though the waves really appeal to beginners and intermediates. Farther south lie Playa Hermosa (known as Boom Boom Beach to the locals), which has miles of expert beach breaks and an international contest every August, plus Escondida, Esterillos Este and Oeste, and Boca Damas. The Esterillos playas are blossoming with surf camps. Manuel Antonio has beach breaks, lefts, and rights. What it lacks in consistency it more than makes up for in natural beauty. Farther south lies Playa Dominical, which has "militant" sandbars and long point waves in an equally beautiful and classically tropical setting.

Southern Pacific: The Osa Peninsula and Golfo Dulce have many virtually virgin surfing beaches. The cognoscenti head to Zancudo and Pavones, on the southern shore of the Golfo Dulce, to conquer, or at least encounter, what one writer calls the "temple of zoom." On a decent day, the very fast, nearly one-kilometer left break (one of the longest in the world) is "so long it will make your legs wobbly," according to Peter Brennan. Getting there in rainy season can be problematic. That doesn't stop the diehards, who pour in in droves. Then the waves are at their grandest, and the long left point can offer a three-minute ride.

Board Rentals

Surf shops are opening up throughout the country, and rentals are offered at all major surfing towns. Don't rely on being able to rent boards away from the most popular surf centers, however. If you have a board, bring it. Many surfers sell their boards in Costa Rica before returning home.

In San José, try **Mango Surf Shop,** tel. 225-1067, and **Keola Surf,** tel. 225-6041, both in San Pedro, and **EcoTreks,** tel. 228-4029, fax 289-8191, in Escazú. **Shaka-Bra Dake** is a surf information center, with offices in San Pedro, tel./fax

234-7508, and Escazú, tel. 289-8589, that rents and sells surf equipment and beachwear.

Costa Rican Tour Operators

Papagayo Escursiones, Apdo. 162, Santa Cruz, tel. 653-0227, fax 653-0254, e-mail: papagayo@sol.racsa.co.cr, offers surf tours, including to Witch's Rock and Playa Potrero.

Tricolor Rent-a-Car, tel. 222-3333 or (800) 949-0234, fax 221-4444, has a series of 11- and 16-day "4x4 Surfing Tours" promising "Good Waves, Good Climate, Virgins, and Wild Beaches."

North American Tour Operators

Tico Travel, 151 E. Commercial Blvd., Ft. Lauderdale, FL 33334, tel. (800) 246-2822, fax (305) 493-8466, e-mail: tico@gate.net, specializes in surfing packages and customized trips for surfers, as does **Worldwide Adventures** 599 Sherwood Ave., Suite 101, Satellite Beach, FL 32937, tel. (407) 773-4878, fax 773-4216, e-mail: surfer@surfingadventures.com, and **Surf Costa Rica,** P.O. Box 9009, Gainesville, FL 32607, tel. (904) 371-8124 or (800) 771-7873, which has "Surf Surfaris" packages (from about $450 for one week) that include roundtrip airfare, free board travel, the 24-hour Costa Rican Surf Report, hotel lodging at the surf break of your choice, and fully surf-rigged 4WD rental vehicle. Surf Costa Rica also offers a 14-day surf camp where you can learn to surf or learn to improve your technique.

Toucan Surf Tours, 2822 Newport Blvd., Suite 101, Newport Beach, CA 92663, tel. (714) 673-2785, fax 675-1331, also offers surf tours to Costa Rica.

WHITEWATER RAFTING

Whitewater rafting is the ultimate combination of beauty and thrill—an ideal way to savor Costa Rica's natural splendor, diverse ecosystems, and exotic wildlife, which have made river running here only slightly less popular than in the United States.

Tour operators offer a wide range of whitewater programs, with ground transportation from San José and professional, bilingual guides. Generally, no experience is necessary. Families are catered to. Guests' desire for comfort is

rafting on the Río Corobicí

met with quality meals, and roomy tents and thick pads for sleeping on overnight trips. And unlike most other places, Costa Rica regulates its tourist industry, so whitewater outfitters are held to strict standards.

Because the land is so steep, streams pass through hugely varied landscapes within relatively short distances. At high elevations, Costa Rican rivers closely resemble those of California. Farther downstream, the water is warmer and rainforest lines the riverbanks. You'll tumble through a tropical fantasia of feathery bamboos, ferns, and palms, a roller-coaster ride amid glistening jungle entwined with vines and perhaps a green python or two. The sense of isolation is complete. Everything is as silent as a graveyard, except for the chattering monkeys and birds. With luck, you may even see small caimans in pools and shallows at lower elevations.

Rafters are required to wear helmets and life jackets, which are provided by the tour operators. Generally, all you need bring is a swimsuit, a T-shirt, and tennis shoes or sneakers. Sunscreen is a good idea, as you are not only in the open all day but also exposed to reflections off the water. You'll also need an extra set of clothing, and

perhaps a sweater or jacket, as you can easily get chilled if a breeze kicks up when you're wet. And you *will* get wet. Most operators provide a special waterproof bag for cameras, though you may wish to buy a waterproof bag for your camera before leaving your home country. One-day trips start at about $70.

In San José, you can buy or rent rafting and kayaking equipment from **Centro de Aventuras Tropicales,** tel. 255-0618, fax 233-3031, at Paseo Colón and Calles 22/24.

When and Where
Generally, May-June and Sept.-Oct. are the best times for high water. Trips on the Reventazón, Pacuare, and Corobicí are offered year-round, although in dry season the latter can be barely runnable. Most other rivers are seasonal and become too low to paddle during dry season. Rivers are rated from class I to VI in degree of difficulty, with V considered for true experts only. The only class V river in the country is the Guayabo section of the Reventazón. Rafting experience is required for this trip; all other trips are generally offered to beginners and intermediates. New rivers are constantly being opened up and additional options may be available by the time you read this. The following are the most popular runs.

Río Chirripó: The majestic Chirripó (class III-IV) runs down the slopes of the southwest Pacific and is recommended for two- to four-day trips. The river, which tumbles from its source on Mt. Chirripó, has been compared to California's Tuolomne and Idaho's Middle Fork of the Salmon, with massive volumes of water and giant waves. It produces more than 100 class III and IV rapids in its first 65 kilometers. The river runs into the Río General. Trips are offered Aug.-December.

Río Corobicí: The Corobicí (class II) provides more of a float trip and makes an ideal half-day trip for families, with superb wildlife viewing and calms the whole way. The river is lined its whole length by a thin strip of tropical jungle, and howler monkeys, iguanas, coatis, boat-billed herons, egrets, and a host of other birds are common. The river flows westward through Guanacaste into the Gulf of Nicoya. It is runnable year-round.

Río General: This high-volume river is famous for its large, challenging rapids and big waves (including a six-meter wave at Chachala) ideal for surfing. Its "outlandish scenery" includes narrow, dramatic gorges and waterfalls, and giant iguanas by the score. Complex rapids follow in quick succession. Worth the trip in itself is The Whirlpool, which, say Mayfield and Gallo (authors of *The Rivers of Costa Rica: A Canoeing, Kayaking, and Rafting Guide*), "obligingly pulls entire boats underwater for several seconds before dissipating. Boats often spend two or three hours here spinning down the eddy line, giggling the afternoon away."

Río Naranjo: A recent addition to the rafting scene, this river in the mountains above Manuel Antonio, on the central Pacific coast, is a corker in high water. However, it's inconsistent, with dramatic changes in water level. During low water you'll need to look elsewhere for thrills. In high water, however, such rapids as Satan's Gut offer swirling class V action. The upper section runs through rainforest; lower down, it slows as it passes through ranchland before winding through Manuel Antonio National Park—what a bonus!—and exiting into the Pacific.

Río Pacuare: For an in-depth immersion in nature, the Pacuare (class III-IV) is the best choice, a stunner even among all the other beauties as it slices through virgin rainforest, plunging through mountain gorges to spill onto the Caribbean plains near Siquirres. Toucans, monkeys, and other animals galore make this journey unforgettable. Overhead loom cliffs from which waterfalls drop right into the river, drenching rafters as they pass. Black tongues of lava stick out into the river, creating large, technically demanding rapids such as Doble Piso, Pinball, and Huacas, and making great lunch beaches. And steep drops produce big waves. Best of all is the stunning Dos Montañas Gorge (the proposed site of a controversial dam project). Though run year-round, the best months are June and October.

Río Reventazón: Whitewater rafting enthusiasts will get more than their money's worth of excitement on the Reventazón (class II-V)—the name means "bursting" in Spanish. The river tumbles out of Lake Cachí and cascades to the Caribbean lowlands in an exciting series of rapids, plus stretches of tranquil waters that provide the perfect combination of soothing calm and adventure. Beginners can savor class II and III rapids on the "mid-section," the most popular run for one-day trips. The Guayabo section offers

extremely difficult class V runs. Constant rainfall allows operators to offer trips year-round; June and July are considered the best months.

Río Sarapiquí: The Sarapiquí (class III) runs along the eastern flank of the Cordillera Central and drops to the Caribbean lowlands. It is noted for its crystal-clear water, variable terrain, and exciting rapids. Trips are offered May-December.

Costa Rican Companies
Costa Rica Expeditions, Apdo. 6941-1000, San José, tel. 257-0766, fax 257-1665, e-mail: cr-exped@sol.racsa.co.cr, was the first whitewater company in Costa Rica, performing the exploratory expedition on most rivers. It remains the preeminent rafting operator and offers one-day and multiday trips on most major rivers, from class I (Corobicí) to class V (Reventazón-Guayabo section)

Ríos Tropicales, Apdo. 472-1200, San José, tel. 233-6455, fax 255-4354, e-mail: info@riostro.com, operates on the Corobicí, Sarapiquí, Reventazón, General, and Pacuare, including class V runs on the Peralta section of the Reventazón and the Upper Pacuare. Most trips are four-days ($380-440). It also has one-day tours on most rivers, and offers rafting in combination with mountain biking, as well as with kayaking.

Costa Sol Rafting, Apdo. 8-4390-1000 Cariari, San José, tel. 293-2151, fax 293-2155; in the U.S., tel. (800) 245-8420, fax (305) 858-7478, offers one day trips on seven rivers, plus multiday trips on the Pacuare and General. A large number of smaller companies offer whitewater trips regionally. **Dos Ríos Rafting,** tel. 556-1111 or 556-1575, website www.rockinr.com, has trips ($75-90) on the Sarapiquí, Reventazón, and Pacuare, as does **Aguas Bravas Rafting** tel. 292-2072 or 479-9025, fax 229-4837, website www.hway.com/arenas/abravas, and **Ticos River Adventures,** tel./fax 556-1231, which also offers trips on the Chirripó and Pejibaye.

North American Companies
Mariah Wilderness Expeditions, P.O. Box 248, Pt. Richmond, CA 94807, tel. (510) 233-2303, fax 233-0956, e-mail: rafting@mariahwe.com, offers a nine-day "Tropical Jungle Rafting" trip including trips on the Corobicí, Reventazón, and Pacuare year-round. Rafting is also included on an eight-day multi-activity program.

Pioneer Raft, P.O. Box 22063, Carmel, CA 93922, tel. (408) 648-8800 or (800) 288-2107, fax (408) 648-8300, e-mail: Lynn_D@ix.netcom.com, offers one-day tours on the Reventazón, Pacuare, Sarapiquí, and Corobici, and multiday tours on the Reventazón, Pacuare, and Chirripó.

Mountain Travel-Sobek, 6420 Fairmount Ave., El Cerrito, CA 94530, tel. (510) 527-8100 or (800) 227-2384, fax (510) 525-7710, e-mail: info@MT-Sobek.com, has a 10-day "Pacuare River Expedition" that also includes the Reventazón ($1,995).

WINDSURFING

Despite the strong winds that sweep along the coast of the Pacific northwest in summer, ocean windsurfing in Costa Rica has yet to take off. Bahía Salinas, in the extreme northwest, is recommended and has a windsurfing center. Inland, Lake Arenal is paradise, with 23-35 kph easterly winds funneling through a mountain corridor virtually year-round. Strong winds rarely cease during the dry season (Dec.-April). The lake has acquired an international reputation as one of the best all-year freshwater windsurfing spots in the world.

Windsurfing at nearby Coter Lake is also good. For taking off at high speed during the high-wind season (Nov.-April), experienced windsurfers can use four- to five-square-meter sails with short boards; even during the low-wind season, long boards with six- to 6.5-square-meter sails can give a good ride.

Rentals

See regional chapters. If you plan on testing ocean waters, equipment is in short supply. There are two dedicated windsurfing centers at Lake Arenal, where many of the hotels also rent equipment.

On the coast, **Aqua Sports** at Playa Hermosa rents windsurfers. If you rent at Arenal, try negotiating to use the same equipment at the coast.

Costa Rican Tour Companies
Destination Costa Rica, Apdo. 590, San José 1150, tel. 223-0676, fax 222-9747, offers three-day windsurfing packages from San José, with two nights at the Rock River Lodge. **Tikal Tour**

Operators, Apdo. 6398, San José 1000, tel. 223-2811, fax 223-1916, offers windsurfing at Lake Coter.

North American Tour Companies
Windsurf Costa Rica, P.O. Box 9009, Gainesville, FL 32607, tel. (904) 371-8124 or (800) 771-7873, offers windsurfing packages, including a budget "Paradise on a Shoestring" package. Also contact **Windsurfing Vacations,** tel. (800) 635-1155, fax (215) 348-2341, and **Windsurfing World Travel,** tel. (800) 936-3333.

MISCELLANEOUS

Ballooning
Serendipity Adventures, tel./fax 225-6055, offers seven- and 10-day adventures that combine ballooning with rafting and other active adventures. Customized balloon trips are also offered. Pilot **Roberto Kopper,** tel. 222-6722 or 450-0311, is said to offer balloon trips.

Bungee Jumping
Tropical Bungee, tel. 232-3956, offers bungee jumping year-round.

Parachuting
The **Asociación Costarricense de Paracaidismo,** tel. 257-5822 or 380-1217, offers courses in Spanish, English, and Italian. The first jump costs $200, then $30 for extra jumps.

Spelunking
Coast to Coast Adventures, Apdo. 2135-1002, San José, tel./fax 225-6055, e-mail: ctocsjo@sol.racsa.co.cr, offers caving in Barra Honda.

Horse Racing
The **Hipódromo del Sol,** tel. 441-4741, on the southern outskirts of San Rafael de Alajuela, 20 km west of San José, offers thoroughbred action every Saturday afternoon.

Motoring
Pro Motor, Apdo. 150, San José 1002, tel. 233-3166, fax 233-3341, offers tour packages to the **Costa Rica Grand Prix** (Formula 3), held at La Guácima Race Track.

Photography Tours
Close-Up Expeditions, 1031 Ardmore Ave., Oakland, CA 94610, tel. (510) 465-8955, fax 465-1237, offers tours for amateur photographers. **Photo Adventure,** P.O. Box 5095, Anaheim, CA 92814, tel. (714) 527-2918, fax 826-8752, offers eight-day photographers' workshops. **Rico Tours,** 130809 Research Blvd., Suite 606, Austin, TX 78750, tel. (512) 331-0918, fax 331-8765, e-mail: lac@amtvl.com, offers an eight-day Costa Rican "Photo Safari."

In Costa Rica, **Photo Safaris,** Apdo. 7812, San José 1000, tel. 267-7070, fax 267-7050, offers seven-day photo workshops.

Running
The Costa Rican International Marathon is held each December. Contact the **Costa Rican Marathon Reservation Center,** tel. 296-3896, fax 231-7089, e-mail: toptours@sol.racsa.co.cr.

ARTS AND CULTURE

Costa Rica has traditionally been relatively impoverished in the area of native arts and crafts. The country, with its relatively small and heterogeneous pre-Columbian population (devastated at an early stage), had no unique cultural legacy that could spark a creative synthesis where the modern and the traditional might merge. Postcolonial development, too, was benign, and the social tensions (often catalysts to artistic expression) felt elsewhere in the isthmus were lacking. And more recently, creativity has been stifled by the Ticos' desire to praise the conventional lavishly and criticize rarely.

In literature, Costa Rica has never fielded figures of the stature of Latin American writers such as Gabriel García Márquez, Octavio Paz, Jorge Amado, Pablo Neruda, Isabel Allende, or Jorge Luís Borges. Indeed, the Ticos are not at all well-read and lack a passionate interest in literature. And much of the modern art that exists has been coopted by the tourist dollar, so that art and craft shops now overflow with whimsical Woolworth's art: cheap canvas scenes of rural landscapes, rough-hewn macaws gaudily painted, and the inevitable cheap bracelets and earrings sold in market squares the world over.

In recent years, however, artists across the spectrum have found a new confidence and are shaking off rigid social norms to experiment with new paintings and sculptures and movements that metaphorically express the shape of their thoughts. It's exciting for a country long dismissed as a cultural backwater. The performing arts are flourishing. A young breed of woodcarvers and artists are tearing free from a straitjacket of conformity. And the National Symphony Orchestra sets a high standard for other musical troupes to follow. Ticos now speak proudly of their latter-day "cultural revolution."

The new sophistication in culture is amply demonstrated by the introduction of an **International Art Festival** in March 1992. Featuring dance troupes, theater, experimental music, puppets, jazz, folklore, classical music, etc., from around the world, the annual marathon event has already won a place among the arts festivals of the continent. When March comes around, you can almost feel the country's pulse begin to quicken. Then, theaters, parks, and plazas are flooded with color and motion. The festival has brought inspiration and new ideas while raising the quality of local groups by allowing them to measure themselves against international talent.

ART

Santa Ana and neighboring Escazú, immediately southwest of San José, have long been magnets for artists. Escazú in particular is home to many contemporary artists: Christina Fournier; the brothers Jorge, Manuel, Javier, and Carlos Mena; and Dinorah Bolandi, who was awarded the nation's top cultural prize. Here, in the late 1920s, Teodorico Quiros and a group of contemporaries provided the nation with its own identifiable art style—the Costa Rican "Landscape" movement—which expressed in stylized forms the flavor and personality of the drowsy little mountain towns with their cobblestone streets and adobe houses backdropped by volcanoes. The artists, who called themselves the Group of New Sensibility, began to portray Costa Rica in fresh, vibrant colors.

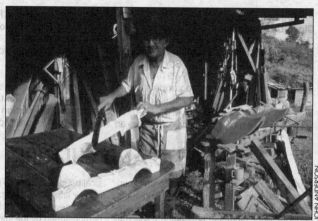

Craftsmen, such as this yoke-maker, still thrive in Sarchí.

JOHN ANDERSON

Quiros had been influenced by the French impressionists. His painting *El Portón Rojo* ("The Red Gate") hangs in the Costa Rican Art Museum. In 1994, aged 77, he was awarded the *Premio Magón* award for lifetime achievement in the "creation and promotion of Costa Rican artistic culture." The group also included Luisa Gonzales de Saenz, whose paintings evoke the style of Magritte; the expressionist Manuel de la Cruz, the "Costa Rican Picasso"; as well as Enrique Echandi, who expressed a Teutonic sensibility following studies in Germany.

One of the finest examples of sculpture from this period, the chiseled stone image of a child suckling his mother's breast, can be seen outside the Maternidad Carit maternity clinic in southern San José. Its creator, Francisco Zuñiga (Costa Rica's most acclaimed sculptor), upped and left for Mexico in a fit of artistic pique in 1936 when the sculpture, titled *Maternity,* was lampooned by local critics (one said it looked more like a cow than a woman).

By the late 1950s many local artists looked down on the work of the prior generation as the art of *casitas* (little houses) and were indulging in more abstract styles. The current batch of young artists have broadened their expressive visions and are now gaining increasing international recognition for their "eclectic speculations into modernist and contemporary art."

Many of Costa Rica's new breed of artists have won international acclaim. Isidro Con Wong, from Puntarenas but of Mongolian descent, is known for a style redolent of magic realism and has works in permanent collections in several U.S. and French museums. Once a poor farmer, he started painting with his fingers and *achiote,* a red paste made from a seed. "Children, drunk bohemians, or the mentally regressed—in other words the innocent chosen by God—are those who understand my works," he says. Imagine the Nicoya landscape seen on LSD! His paintings sell for about $35,000 each.

In Puerto Limón, Leonel González paints images of the Caribbean port with figures reduced to thick black silhouettes against backgrounds of splendid colors, "overtaken if not fully embraced by the design," says art critic Pau Llosa. The most irreverent of contemporary artists is perhaps Roberto Lizano, who collides Delacroix with Picasso and likes to train his eye on the pomposity of ecclesiastics.

Alajuelan artist Gwen Barry is acclaimed for her "Movable Murals"—painted screens populated by characters from Shakespeare and the Renaissance. Rafa Fernández is noted throughout the Americas; his work, heavily influenced by his many years in Spain, has been defined as "magic realism, where the beauty and grandness of women is explored with a sense of intimacy and suggestion." His ladies often appear in quasi-Victorian guise wearing floral hats. And Rolando Castellón, who won acclaim in the U.S. and was director of the Casa España de Bellas Artes and also a director of the New York Mu-

THE OXCARTS OF SARCHÍ

Sarchí is famous as the home of gaily decorated wooden *carretas* (oxcarts), the internationally recognized symbol of Costa Rica. The carts, which once dominated the rural landscape of the central highlands, date back only to the end of the 19th century. Sadly, they are rarely seen in use today, though they are a common decorative item.

At the height of the coffee boom and before the construction of the Atlantic Railroad, oxcarts were used to transport coffee beans to Puntarenas, on the Pacific coast—a journey requiring 10-15 days. In the rainy season, the oxcart trail became a quagmire. Costa Ricans thus forged their own spokeless wheel—a hybrid between the Aztec disc and the Spanish spoked wheel—to cut through the mud without becoming bogged down. In their heyday,

A Sarchí artisan paints an intricate design on a wooden oxcart.

some 10,000 cumbersome, squeaking *carretas* had a dynamic impact on the local economy, spawning highway guards, smithies, inns, teamsters, and crews to maintain the roads.

Today's pretty and superbly crafted *carretas* bear little resemblance to the original rough-hewn, rectangular, cane-framed vehicles covered by rawhide tarps. Even then, though, the compact wheels—about four or five feet in diameter—were natural canvases awaiting an artist. Enter the wife of Fructuoso Barrantes, a cart maker in San Ramón with a paint brush and a novel idea. She enlivened her husband's cart wheels with a geometric starburst design in bright colors set off by black and white. Soon every farmer in the district had given his aged *carreta* a lively new image.

Oxcart art evolved along established lines. By 1915, flowers had bloomed beside the pointed stars. Faces and even miniature landscapes soon appeared. And annual contests (still held today) were arranged to reward the most creative artists. The *carretas*, in fact, had ceased to be purely functional and had become every farmer's pride and joy. Each cart was also designed to make its own "song," a chime as unique as a fingerprint, produced by a metal ring striking the hubnut of the wheel as the cart bumped along. Supposedly, the intention was to allow the farm owner to hear his laborers. Once the oxcart had become a source of individual pride, greater care was taken in their construction, and the best-quality woods were selected to make the best sounds.

Today, the *carretas*, forced from the fields by the advent of tractors and trucks, are almost purely decorative, but the craft and the art form live on in Sarchí, where artisans still apply their masterly touch at *fábricas de carretas* (workshops), which are open to view. A finely made reproduction oxcart can cost up to $5,000.

The **Ox-cart Museum,** in Salitral de Desamparados, on the southern outskirts of San José, has displays of *campesino* life, including a collection of hand-painted oxcarts, in a typical old adobe house. Also, the Pueblo Antigua, outside San José, has a living museum featuring the carts.

seum of Modern Art before returning to Costa Rica in 1993, translates elements of indigenous life into 3-D art. His studio gallery in Zapote, Moyo Coyatzin, is named for the indigenous deity of creativity. Castellón was recently named curator of Costa Rica's Museum of Contemporary Art and Design. And you can't travel far in Costa Rica these days without seeing examples of the works of another Escazú artist, Katya de Luisa, whose stunning photo collages are complex allegories. Katya has recently initiated "Encounters With Art," a collaborative effort in which artists from different media contribute to a single work.

The government-subsidized House of Arts helps sponsor art by offering free lessons in painting and sculpture. The Ministry of Culture sponsors art lessons and exhibits on Sunday in city parks. University art galleries, the Museo de Arte Costarricense, and the many smaller galleries scattered throughout San José exhibit works of all kinds. The **Centro Creativo,** tel. 282-6556 or 282-8769, in Santa Ana, offers courses and studio space for local and visiting artists.

CRAFTS

Here's an example of what the tourism revolution can launch. As recently as 1993, I wrote that "Costa Rica doesn't overflow with native crafts. Apart from a few notable exceptions—the gaily colored wooden *carretas* (oxcarts) which have become Costa Rica's tourist symbol, for example—you must dig deep to uncover crafts of substance. And other than the *carretas,* there is little that is distinctly and recognizably *costarricense.*"

The tourist dollar, however, has spawned a renaissance in crafts, and many new forms (several of them experimental) have emerged in the past few years. The revival is most remarkable in the traditional realm. At Guaitil, in Nicoya, not only is the Chorotega Indian tradition of pottery retained, it is booming, so much so that neighboring villages are installing the potters' wheels, too. Santa Ana is also famous for its ceramics: large greenware bowls, urns, vases, coffee mugs, and small *típico* adobe houses fired in brick kilns and clay pits on the patios of some 30 independent family workshops, such as **Cerámica Santa Ana.** In Escazú, master craftsman

Barry Biesanz skillfully handles razor-sharp knives and chisels to craft subtle, delicate images, bowls as hemispherical as if turned with a lathe, and decorative boxes with tight dovetailed corners from carefully chosen blocks of tropical woods: lignum vitae (ironwood), *narareno* (purple heart), rosewood, satinwood, and tigerwood.

Many of the best crafts in Costa Rica come from Sarchí. Visitors are welcome to enter the *fábricas de carretas* and watch the families and master artists at work producing exquisitely contoured bowls, serving dishes, and—most notably—miniature versions of the *carretas* for which the village is now famous worldwide. Although an occasional full-size oxcart is still made, today most of the *carretas* made in Sarchí are folding miniature trolleys—like little hot-dog stands—that serve as liquor bars or indoor tables, and half-size carts used as garden ornaments or simply to accent a corner of a home. The carts are painted in dazzling white or burning orange and decorated with geometric mandala designs and floral patterns that have found their way, too, onto wall plaques, kitchen trays, and other craft items. Sarchí and the Moravia suburb of San José are also noted for their leather satchels and purses.

There's not much in the way of traditional clothing. However, the women of Drake Bay are famous for *molas,* colorful and decorative handsewn appliqué used for blouses, dresses, and wall hangings. Of indigenous art there is also little, though the Boruca Indians carve balsawood masks—light, living representations of supernatural beings—and decorated gourds, such as used as a resonator in the *quijongo,* a bowed-string instrument.

LITERATURE

Though the government, private donors, and the leading newspaper—*La Nación*—sponsor literature through annual prizes, only a handful of writers make a living from writing, and Costa Rican literature is often belittled as the most prosaic and anemic in Latin America. Lacking great goals and struggles, Costa Rica was never a breeding ground for the passions and dialectics that spawned the literary geniuses of Argentina, Brazil, Mexico, Cuba, and Chile, whose works, full of satire and bawdy humor, are clenched fists which cry out against social injustice.

Costa Rica's early literary figures were mostly essayists and poets: Roberto Brenes Mesen and Joaquín García Monge are the most noteworthy. Even the writing of the 1930s and 1940s, whose universal theme was a plea for social progress, lacked the pace and verisimilitude and rich literary delights of other Latin American authors. Carlos Luis Fallas's *Mamita Yunai*, which depicts the plight of banana workers, is the best and best-known example of this genre. Other examples include Fallas's *Gentes y Gentecillas*, Joaquín Gutierrez's *Puerto Limón* and *Federica*, and Carmen Lyra's *Bananos y Hombres*.

Much of modern literature still draws largely from the local setting, and though the theme of class struggle has given way to a lighter, more novelistic approach it still largely lacks the mystical, surrealistic, Rabelaisian excesses, the endless layers of experience and meaning, and the wisdom, subtlety, and palpitating romanticism of the best of Brazilian, Argentinean, and Colombian literature. An outstanding exception is Julieta Pinto's *El Eco de los Pasos*, a striking novel about the 1948 civil war.

A compendium of contemporary literature *on* Costa Rica is *Costa Rica: A Traveler's Literary Companion,* edited by Barbara Ras, which brings together 26 stories by Costa Rican writers spanning the 20th century. The essays have been selected to provide a sense for Costa Rica's national psyche and are arranged "according to the geographical allusions they contain." Says former President Oscar Arias, "This anthology offers an accurate synthesis of the literary perceptions that accompanied Costa Rica's transition from a rural, rather isolationist, society . . . to a highly urbanized society increasingly open to the cultural and commercial currents of the present decade of globalization." I found it to be dull reading!

MUSIC AND DANCE

Ticos love to dance. By night San José gets into the mood with discos hotter than the tropical night. On weekends rural folks flock to small-town dance halls, and the Ticos' celebrated reserve gives way to outrageously flirtatious dancing befitting a land of passionate men and women. Says *National Geographic:* "To watch the viselike clutching of Ticos and Ticas dancing, whether at a San José discotheque or a crossroads cantina, is to marvel that the birthrate in this predominantly Roman Catholic nation is among Central America's lowest." Outside the dance hall, the young prefer to listen to Anglo-American rock, like their counterparts the world over. When it comes to dancing, however, they prefer the hypnotic Latin and rhythmic Caribbean beat and bewildering cadences of *cumbia, lambada, marcado, merengue, salsa, soca,* and the Costa Rican swing, danced with sure-footed erotic grace.

Many dances and much of the music of Costa Rica reflect African, even pre-Columbian, as well as Spanish roots. The country is one of the southernmost of the "marimba culture" countries, although the African-derived marimba (xylophone) music of Costa Rica is more elusive and restrained than the vigorous native music of Panamá and Guatemala, its heartland. The guitar, too, is a popular instrument, especially as an accompaniment to folk dances such as the Punto Guanacaste, a heel-and-toe stomping dance for couples, officially decreed the national dance. (The dance actually only dates back to the turn of the century, when it was composed in jail by Leandro Cabalceta Brau.)

Costa Rica has a strong *peña* tradition, introduced by Chilean and Argentinian exiles. Literally "circle of friends," *peñas* are bohemian, international gatherings—usually in favored cafes—where moving songs are shared and wine and tears flow copiously.

On the Caribbean coast, music is profoundly Afro-Caribbean in spirit and rhythm, with plentiful drums and banjos, a local rhythm called *sinkit,* and the *cuadrille,* a maypole dance in which each dancer holds one of many ribbons tied to the top of a pole: as they dance they braid their brightly colored ribbons. The Caribbean, though, is really the domain of calypso and reggae, and Bob Marley is king.

Folkloric Dancing

Guanacaste is the heartland of Costa Rican folkloric music and dancing. Here, even such pre-Columbian instruments as the *chirimia* (oboe) and *quijongo* (a single-string bow with gourd resonator) popularized by the Chorotega Indians are still used as backing for traditional Chorotega dances such as the Danza del Sol and Danza de la Luna. The more familiar Cambute and Botijuela Tamborito—blurring flurries of kaleidoscopic, frilly satin skirts accompanied by tossing of scarves, a fanning of hats, and loud lusty yelps from the men—are usually performed on behalf of tourists rather than at native *turnos* (fiestas). The dances usually deal with the issues of enchanted lovers (usually legendary coffee pickers) and are mostly based on the Spanish *paseo,* with pretty maidens in white bodices and dazzlingly bright skirts being circled by men in white suits and cowboy hats.

A number of folkloric dance troupes tour the country, while others perform year-round at such venues as the Melico Sálazar Theater, the Aduana Theater, and the National Dance Workshop headquarters in San José. Of particular note is Fantasía Folklorica, a colorful highlight of the country's folklore and history from pre-Columbian to modern times.

Vestiges of the half-dead Indian folk dancing tradition linger (barely) elsewhere in the nation. The Borucas still perform their Danza de los Diablitos, and the Talamancas their Danza de los Huelos. But the drums and flutes, including the curious *dru mugata,* an ocarina (a small potato-shaped instrument with a mouthpiece and finger holes which yields soft, sonorous notes) made of beeswax, are being replaced by guitars and accordions. Even the solemn Indian music is basically Spanish in origin and hints at the typically slow and languid Spanish *canción* (song) which gives full rein to the romantic, sentimental aspect of the Latin character.

Classical Music

Costa Rica stepped onto the world stage in classical music with the formation, in 1970, of the **National Symphony Orchestra** under the baton of an American, Gerald Brown. The orchestra, which performs in the Teatro Nacional, often features world-renowned guest soloists and conductors. Its season is April through November, with concerts on Thursday and Friday evenings, plus Saturday matinees. Costa Rica also claims the only state-subsidized youth orchestra in the Western world. The **Sura Chamber Choir,**

founded in 1989 with musicians and vocalists from the country's two state universities, is the first professional choir in Central America, with a repertoire from sacred through Renaissance to contemporary styles. The **Goethe Institute, Alliance Française,** the **Museo de Arte Costarricense,** and the **Costa Rican-North American Cultural Center,** tel. 225-9433 for information on the Center's U.S. University Music Series, all offer occasional classical music evenings.

Costa Rica holds an **International Festival of Music** during the last two weeks of August. There's also an annual six-week-long **Monteverde Music Festival,** tel. 645-5125, each Jan.-Feb., combining classical with jazz and swing. It's held at the Hotel Fonda Vela, in Monteverde. Book early!

THEATER

A nation of avid theater lovers, Costa Rica supports a thriving acting community. In fact, Costa Rica supposedly has more theater companies per capita than any other country in the world. The country's early dramatic productions gained impetus and inspiration from Argentinian and Chilean playwrights and actors who settled here at the turn of the century, when drama was established as part of the standard school curriculum.

The streets of San José are festooned with tiny theaters—everything from comedy to drama, avant-garde, theater-in-the-round, mime, and even puppet theater. Crowds flock every night Tuesday through Sunday. Performances are predominantly in Spanish, although some perform in English. The English-speaking **Little Theater Group** is Costa Rica's oldest theatrical troupe; it performs principally in the Centro Cultural's Eugene O'Neill Theater. The prices are so cheap—you could go once a week for a year for the same cost as a single Broadway production—that you can enjoy yourself even if your Spanish is poor. Theaters rarely hold more than 100-200 people and often sell out early. Shows normally begin at 7:30 or 8 p.m. The *Tico Times* and *Costa Rica Today* offer complete listings of current productions and whether a play is in Spanish or English. Also see the "Viva" section in *La Nación.*

HOLIDAYS

Costa Rica is a Catholic country and its holidays *(feriados)* are mostly religious. Most businesses, including banks, close on official holidays. The country closes down entirely during the biggest holiday time, **Easter Holy Week** (Wednesday through Sunday). Buses don't run on Holy Thursday or Good Friday. Banks and offices are closed. And hotels and rental cars are booked solid months in advance as everyone seems to head for the beach. Avoid the popular beaches during Easter week. Most Ticos now take the whole **Christmas** holiday week through New Year as an unofficial holiday.

Easter is a tremendous opportunity to see colorful religious processions. Individual towns also celebrate their patron saint's day: highlights usually include a procession, plus bullfights (benign), rodeos, dancing, and secular parades. Fireworks and firecrackers *(bombetas)* are a popular part of local fiestas *(turnos)* and church celebrations. Often they'll start at dawn. Ticos can't resist sirens and horn-honking during celebrations. The *Tico Times* provides weekly listings of festivals and events nationwide.

ACCOMMODATIONS

Accommodations run the gamut from cheap *pensiones,* beachside *cabinas,* and self-catering *apartotels* to rustic jungle lodges, swank mountain lodges, homestays, and glitzy resort hotels with casinos. "Motels" are cheap hotels, usually on the outskirts of San José, used for sexual trysts. Cabinas range from truly horrendous, spartan, and ill-equipped hovels to upscale, fully equipped units that would do any hotelier proud. The moniker hides a lot; check around before making a reservation if at all possible. And don't be afraid of looking at several rooms in a hotel (particularly in budget hotels) before making your decision: this is quite normal and accepted in Costa Rica. Rooms in any one hotel can vary dramatically.

In 1997, Costa Rica had about 1,600 hotels and 25,000 hotel rooms. The ICT planned on introducing a star-rating system in 1998.

Reservations

Hardly a week goes by without two or three new hotels springing onto the scene; until recently it was hardly fast enough to keep pace with tourism growth. The sudden blossoming of inventory is beginning to ease booking headaches. Indeed, tourism officials are beginning to worry that the rapid growth of hotels will bring a new crisis—that of *too many* rooms!—as the tourism boom shows signs of slowing down (the unexpected drop in visitors in late 1994 left many hotels struggling to fill their rooms, and several hotels went out of business).

During dry season planning is recommended for popular destinations. Christmas, Easter week, and weekends in dry season (Dec.-April) are particularly busy. And nature lodges tend to be heavily booked May-Nov. too. Make your reservations well in advance for the busier months.

Virtually every hotel (except budget hotels) has a fax, so you can easily book directly from the United States. Take your fax copy with you and reconfirm reservations a few days before arrival.

Honor your reservations! Or at least call as far in advance as possible if you have to cancel. Someone else may have been turned away.

Rates and Facilities

Many hotels offer discounts of 20% or more off-season. Upscale properties also have shoulder-season rates. If no single rooms are available, you'll usually be charged the single rate for a double room. And couples requesting a *casa matrimonial* (i.e., wishing to sleep in one bed) will often receive a discount off the normal double rate. Rates are subject to fluctuation. A 15% tax and 3.4% ICT tax are added to your room bill.

The sudden downturn in tourism arrivals in late 1994 stalled increases in room rates. The law of supply and demand had come into effect: many hotels posted "specials." Others upgraded their properties and increased their rates. The situation is fluid. Every attempt has been made to ensure that prices given here are accurate at time of going to press.

ACCOMMODATIONS RATINGS CHART

Based on high-season, double occupancy rates:

Shoestring	under $15
Budget	$15-35
Inexpensive	$35-60
Moderate	$60-85
Expensive	$85-110
Premium	$110-150
Luxury	$150+

Rates are normally quoted for single or double. Rates for additional guests are shown in this book as "additional," e.g. "$10 s ($5 additional)."

In cheaper hotels, be prepared for cold-water showers (you'll soon get used to it and come to look forward to a refreshingly icy shower). In others, hot water, often little more than tepid, may be available only at certain times of the day. Shower units are often powered by electric heating elements, which you switch on for the duration of your shower (don't expect steaming-hot water, however). *Beware!* It's easy to give yourself a shock from any metal object nearby, including the water pipes. Upscale hotels usually have "U.S. standard" showers, plus flushing toilets capable of handling toilet paper. Cheaper hotels do not: trying to flush your waste paper down the toilet will cause a blockage. Waste receptacles are provided for paper. Unhygienic, yes, but use the basket unless you fancy a smelly back-up.

Though not as bad as in many countries, theft is a problem. Before accepting a room, ensure that the door is secure and that your room can't be entered by someone climbing through the window. Always lock your door. Never leave valuables in your room if you can avoid it and always lock your possessions in your baggage (many hotel workers are abysmally low-paid and the temptation to steal may be irresistible; I've had favorite shirts and other items "disappear" because I trustingly left them lying around). Take a padlock to use in cheaper hotels.

Those concerned to stay in "environmentally conscious" accommodations have been presented an easy means of identifying appropriate properties. In 1994, the government initiated an **Eco-Seal** program: a standardization system

for recognizing hotels that meet certain environmental standards.

HOTELS

Many of the bottom-end hotels (under $15), though often sparsely furnished with no more than a bed and a dresser, are usually clean and adequate. They can be great places to meet other budget travelers. The cheapest—often called *pensiones* or *hospedajes*—usually have communal bathrooms. There are some splendid bargains in the $20-35 range; generally, these will have private bathrooms, but don't bet on it. Standards vary markedly, with prices in direct relationship to a destination's popularity.

There's a wide and growing choice of upper-end hotels. Many properties can hold their own on the international hotel scene. Often what you're paying for, however, is the extra space and furniture. Shop around. Many expensive hotels can't justify their price: where this is the case, I've said so. Most of Costa Rica's luxury hotels ($150+) live up to expectations. They run the gamut from beach resorts, mountain lodges, and haciendas-turned-hotels to San José's plusher options.

About one dozen hotels proffer remarkable ambience; a fistful are truly superb. I've profiled these especially noteworthy cases in separate boxes, with the prefix, "Special Hotel."

APARTOTELS

The equivalent of drive-in motels in the U.S., apartotels offer rooms with kitchens or kitchenettes (pots and pans and cutlery are provided) and sometimes small suites furnished with sofas and tables and chairs. One- or two-bedroom units are available, and weekly and monthly rates are offered. Apartotels are particularly economical for families. In San José, they are concentrated in Los Yoses, 10 minutes' walk east of downtown. Most are characterless; it's all a matter of taste.

CAMPING

Costa Rica is not greatly endowed with established campsites. Still, that doesn't stop the locals, for whom camping on the beach during national holidays is a tradition. Several of the national parks have basic camping facilities. And there are a growing number of commercial camping areas at popular beach sites. At more remote beaches camping is the only option, even though there are often no facilities.

The nation's maritime zone law, which maintains 50 meters of beachfront in the public domain, means that you should be able to camp on any beach without permission. Ask locals if you're unsure; you may need to pass through private land to reach the beach. You may also need to pack everything in and out. *Leave only footprints.* Don't camp near riverbanks. And make sure you camp *above* the high-tide line.

Theft is a problem at many sites. If possible, camp with a group of people so one person can guard the gear. You'll need a warm sleeping bag and a waterproof tent for camping in the mountains, where you are more likely to need permission from local landowners or park rangers before pitching your tent. Generally, a Gore-Tex bivouac bag or even a tarp will suffice in the lowlands. You'll also need a mosquito net and plenty of bug repellent for many locations. If you really want the "local" flavor, buy a hammock (widely available) and sleep between two coconut trees. A hammock also suspends you safely beyond the reach of most creepy crawlies. Avoid grassy pastures: they harbor chiggers and ticks.

It is best to bring all your camping gear with you, as quality camping-supply stores are few and far between in Costa Rica.

Staying in National Parks

Most national parks and reserves permit camping ($1-3 pp). See **National Parks** in the Introduction. Others, such as Ballena Marine National Park, are now discouraging camping in the park in an attempt to have you support locals who offer cabins or camping.

NATURE LODGES

Costa Rica is richly endowed with mountain and jungle lodges, many in private reserves. Most have naturalist guides and arrange nature hikes, horseback riding, etc. Some offer basic facilities only. Others are relatively luxurious. Most

are moderately expensive—despite which they're heavily booked. Reservations are highly recommended in dry season (Dec.-April) well in advance.

HOMESTAYS AND BED AND BREAKFASTS

More and more bed and breakfasts are opening, with live-in hosts to cosset you. And more and more Costa Rican families are welcoming foreign travelers into their homes as paying guests. Staying with a local family provides a wonderful cross-cultural exchange and a great insight into the Tico way of life. It's also an opportunity to improve your Spanish. Many local hosts advertise in the *Tico Times* and *Costa Rica Today.* Also, contact the ICT office, tel. 222-1090. Judy Tattersall Ryan's book, *Simple Pleasures: A Guide to the Bed and Breakfasts and Special Hotels of Costa Rica,* has descriptions of select hostelries, Apdo. 2055, San José 1002, fax 222-4336.

Bell's Home Hospitality, Apdo. 185, San José 1000, tel. 225-4752, fax 224-5884, e-mail: homestay@sol.racsa.co.cr; in the U.S., P.O. Box 025216, Miami, FL 33102, run by Vernon and Marcela Bell, lists more than 70 host homes in the residential suburbs of San José, plus a few in outlying towns. Rates are $30 s, $45 d (dinners $5). The company arranges accommodations for singles, couples, and families of up to five people, and will match you with an English-speaking family if you wish. The Bells will also arrange airport transfers and offer a free information service. *Recommended* for a home-away-from-home!

Costa Rican Homestays Bed & Breakfast, Apdo. 8186, San José 1000, tel. 240-6829, also offers lodging in private homes. And **Costa Rica Home & Host,** 2445 Park Ave., Minneapolis, MN 55404, tel. (612) 871-0596, fax 871-8853, offers homestay packages with English-speaking families who also act as chauffeur-guides.

TurCasa, tel. 221-6161, represents hosts who take guests. They have uniform pricing and offer a variety of services, including airport transfers for stays of five nights or more. Soledad and Virginia Zamora, tel. 224-7937 or 225-7344, specialize in finding accommodations for **long-term renters** (expect to pay $250 monthly, including meals and laundry).

YOUTH HOSTELS

The following hotels and lodges are members of Hostelling International and offer discounts to members (few are true hostels). See regional chapters for details.

San José
Hostal Toruma
Hotel Don Paco Inn

Caribbean
Hotel Yaré, Playa Cocles
Samay Lagoon Lodge, Barra del Colorado

Northern Lowlands
Cabinas Rossi, Fortuna
Rara Avis, Las Horquetas

Guanacaste
Finca Valverde, Monteverde
Rincón de la Vieja Lodge, Rincón de la Vieja
San Isidro Hotel and Club, Puntarenas

Nicoya
Playa Hermosa Inn, Playa Hermosa

Central Pacific
Hotel Mar Paraíso, Jacó

Golfo Dulce and Peninsula de Osa
Estero Azul Lodge, Sierpe

The **Costa Rican Bed and Breakfast Group,** call Pat Bliss, tel. 228-9200, can provide information on where to stay, as can the **All Costa Rica Bed and Breakfast Reservation Service,** tel. 223-4168, fax 223-4157.

YOUTH HOSTELS

In Costa Rica, Hostelling International (the U.S. affiliate of the International Youth Hostel Federation, or IYHF) is represented by the Organized Touristi Network, or **RETO,** Apdo. 1355, San José 1002, tel. 224-4085, fax 234-8186, formerly the Costa Rican Youth Hostel Association, or RECAJ. Its headquarters and reservation center is the Hostel Toruma in San José, Avenida Central, Calles 29/31. It publishes a *Hostelling Centers Guide* with detail of the 14 properties that were participants at press time. Most of the hostels are actually standard hotels that honor hostel rates. Some offer horseback riding, windsurfing, hiking, and guided tours. A few also allow camping.

Reservations are recommended. RETO also has eight- to 22-day tour packages.

You can reserve youth hostel accommodations up to six months in advance through the **International Booking Network** ($2 booking fee), or any participating hostel or travel center worldwide. **Hostelling International,** 733 15th St., N.W. #840, Washington, DC 20005, tel. (202) 783-6161 or (800) 444-6111, fax (202) 783-6171, offers reservation services on the Internet at http://gnn.com/gnn/bus/ayh/.

HEALTH SPAS

Costa Rica offers several health spas. See regional chapters. The **Nosara Retreat** at Playa Nosara, in Nicoya, is an upscale holistic resort run by renowned yoga practitioners Amba and Don Stapleton, both teachers at the Kripalu Center for Yoga and Health in Massachusetts. Sunrise yoga on the beach, anyone? The most complete spa is **El Tucano** near Aguas Zarcas in the northern lowlands, and **Tara Resort Hotel & Spa** above Escazú in the central highlands.

Also in the central highlands are the **Healthy Day Inn** near Grecia, and **Hearty Hands Health Home,** Apdo. 185, Ipis, San José, tel. 253-1162, fax 234-9469, in San José's Barrio Escalante. The latter offers everything from mud baths and massages to herbal treatments to dietary programs, naturalist routines, and reflexology. Take your pick from residential courses from one week to one year, including programs for seniors and people with disabilities. Bedrooms with private baths are said to be "comfortable."

Centro Creativo, tel. 282-6556, fax 282-6959, near Santa Ana, offers residential holistic-living courses and treatments in massage, chiropractic, etc., as well as art, writing, and textiles.

Also to consider: **Costa Rica Rainbow Connection,** Apdo. 7323, San José 1000, tel./fax 240-7325, offers courses in Kripalu Yoga and the healing arts; **Centro de Balance Integral,** tel. 224-5806, and **Acu Yoga,** tel. 253-1614, offer short- and long-term yoga and massage courses; **Hare Krishna Farm,** tel. 551-6752 or 227-4505, holds meditation and yoga classes; and **Integree Clínica de Bienestar Corporal,** tel. 233-3839, and **Instituto Bienestar,** tel. 226-4975, have massage and spa facilities and beauty treatments.

FOOD AND DRINK

COSTA RICAN CUISINE

Generally speaking, Costa Rican food is frequently disappointing. The cuisine is simple, the chefs tend to shun spices, and Ticos are timid diners, generally loath to experiment. Says *Weissmann Travel Reports:* "It's almost easier to find an American fast food outlet than a restaurant serving good, native cuisine." *Comida típica,* or native dishes, rely heavily on rice and beans, the basis of many Costa Rican meals, and "home-style" cooking predominates. However, meals are generally wholesome and reasonably priced. *Gallo pinto,* the national dish of fried rice and black beans, is as ubiquitous, particularly as a breakfast staple, as is the hamburger in North America. I never tire of *gallo pinto* for breakfast *(desayuno).* Many meals are derivatives, including *arroz con pollo* (rice and chicken) or *arroz con tuna.* At lunch, *gallo pinto* becomes the *casado* (married): rice and beans supplemented with cabbage-and-tomato salad, fried plantains, and meat. Vegetables do not form a large part of the diet.

Food staples include *carne* (beef, sometimes called *bistek*), *pollo* (chicken), and *pescado* (fish). Beef and steaks are relatively inexpensive, but don't expect your tenderloin steak *(lomito)* to match its North American counterpart—in the worst case, you'll find yourself served a leathery slab cooked in grease. The beef is also quite lean—Costa Rican cattle is grass fed.

Although it possesses 1,227 km (767 miles) of coastline, Costa Rica exports most of its seafood. As a result, when you're actually in Costa Rica, seafood—especially shrimp *(camarones)* or lobster *(langosto)*—is expensive. Travelers on tight budgets should stick with the set meal—*casado*—on lunchtime menus ($2-3). **Sodas,** open-air lunch counters, also serve inexpensive snacks and meals ($1-3).

Eating in Costa Rica doesn't present the health problems that plague the unwary traveler elsewhere in Central America, but you need to be aware that pesticide use in Costa Rica is un-regulated. I've *never* become sick in Costa Rica. However, *always* wash vegetables in water known to be safe. And ensure that any fruits you eat are peeled yourself; you never know where someone else's hands have been. Otherwise, stick to staples such as bananas and oranges. If on a budget, eat where the locals eat. Usually, that means tasty, trustworthy food.

Dining in Costa Rica is a leisurely experience (so leisurely that you'll have to summon your waiter to bring the bill), befitting the relaxed pace of a genteel vacation. Restaurants normally stay open 11 a.m.-2 p.m. and 6 p.m.-11 p.m. or midnight. Some restaurants stay open 24 hours. If desperation sets in, you have plenty of fast-food options—McDonald's, Pizza Hut, KFC, and the like.

Now for the good news: In San José, many fine restaurants serve the gamut of international cuisines at reasonable prices. And though culinary excellence in general declines with distance from the capital city, a growing number of hoteliers and gourmet chefs are opening restaurants worthy of note in even the most secluded backwaters. Take the Caribbean coast, for example, where the local cuisine reflects its Jamaican heritage with mouth-watering specialties such as ackee and codfish (ackee is a small, pink-skinned fruit that tastes like scrambled eggs), johnnycakes, curried goat, curried shrimp, and pepperpot soup, with its subtle, lingering heat. Here, simple restaurants such as The Garden, in Puerto Viejo, are worthy of review in *Bon Appétit.* There are some other fabulous restaurants in Manuel Antonio and the Tamarindo area.

Many bars in Costa Rica have a delightful habit of serving *bocas*—savory tidbits ranging from ceviche to *tortillas con queso* (tortillas with cheese)—with each drink. Some bars provide them free, so long as you're drinking. Others apply a small charge. Turtle *(tortuga)* eggs are a popular dish in many bars.

If you wish to cook for yourself, the best places to buy fresh food are the Saturday-morning street markets *(ferias de agricultor).* Even the smallest hamlet has its *pulpería* or *abastacedor*—local grocery store.

FRUIT

Costa Rica grows many exotic fruits. The bunches of bright vermilion fruits on the stem found at roadside stalls nationwide are *pejibayes,* teeny relatives of the coconut. You scoop out the boiled avocadolike flesh; its taste is commonly described as falling between that of a chestnut and that of a pumpkin. The *pejibaye* palm (not to be confused with the *pejibaye*) produces the *palmito* (heart of palm), used in salads. *Guayabas* (guavas) come into season Sept.-Nov.; their pink fruit is used for jams and jellies. A smaller version—*cas*—finds its way into *refrescos* and ice cream. The *marañón,* the fruit of the cashew, is also commonly used in *refrescos. Mamones* are little green spheres containing grapelike

pulp. And those yellow-red, egg-size fruits are *granadillas* (passionfruit). One of my favorites— it comes both sweet and sour—is the "star fruit," or *carambeloa,* with the flesh of a grape and the taste of an orange.

Most of the tropical fruits you'll find in the stateside Safeway were grown in Costa Rica. The sweetest and most succulent *sandías* (watermelons) come from the hot coastal regions. Be careful not to confuse them with the lookalike *chiverre,* whose "fruit" resembles spaghetti! *Piña* (pineapple) is common. So too are *mélon* (cantaloupe) and mangos, whose larger versions are given the feminine gender, *mangas,* because of their size! Papayas come in two forms: the round, yellow-orange *amarilla* and the elongated, red-orange *cacho. Moras* (blackberries) are most commonly used for refrescos.

EATING COSTA RICAN: SOME SPECIALTIES

arreglados—sandwiches or tiny puff pastries stuffed with beef, cheese, or chicken. Greasy!

arroz con pollo—a basic dish of chicken and rice

casado—*arroz* (rice), *frijoles* (black beans), *carne* (beef), *repollo* (cabbage), and *plátano* (plantain). Avocado *(aguacates)* or egg may also be included.

ceviche—marinated seafood, often chilled, made of *corvina* (sea bass), *langostinos* (shrimps), or *conchas* (shellfish). Normally served with lemon, chopped onion, garlic, and sweet red peppers.

chorreados—corn pancakes, often served with sour cream *(natilla)*

elote—corn on the cob, either boiled *(elote cocinado)* or roasted *(elote asado)*

empañadas—turnovers stuffed with beans, cheese, meat, or potatoes

enchiladas—pastries stuffed with cheese and potatoes and occasionally meat

gallo—tortilla sandwiches stuffed with beans, cheese, or meat

gallo pinto—the national dish (literally "spotted rooster"), made of lightly spiced rice and black beans. Traditional breakfast *(desayuno)* or lunch dish. Sometimes includes *huevos fritos* (fried eggs).

olla de carne—soup made of squash, corn, *yuca* (a local tuber), *chayote* (a local pear-shaped vegetable), *ayote* (a pumpkinlike vegetable), and potatoes

palmitos—succulent hearts of palm, common in salads

patacones—thin slices of deep-fried plantain. A popular Caribbean dish. Served like French fries.

pescado ahumado—smoked marlin

picadillo—a side dish of fried vegetables and meat

sopa negra—a creamy soup, often with a hard-boiled egg and vegetables soaking in the bean broth

sopa de mondongo—soup made from tripe (the stomach of a cow)

tamales—boiled cornmeal pastries stuffed with corn, chicken, or pork, and wrapped in a banana or corn leaf. A popular Christmas dish.

tortillas—Mexican-style corn pancakes or omelettes

DESSERTS (POSTRES) AND SWEETS (DULCES)

cono capuchino—an ice-cream cone topped with chocolate

dulce de leche—a syrup of boiled milk and sugar. Also thicker, fudgelike *cajeta*—delicious!

flan—cold caramel custard

mazamorra—corn starch pudding

melcocha—candy made from raw sugar

milanes—chocolate candies

pan de maíz—corn sweet bread

queque seco—pound cake

torta chilena—multilayered cake filled with *dulce de leche*

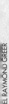

Heredia's Mercado Central rouses the senses.

DRINK

Costa Rica has no national drink, perhaps with the exception of **horchata**, a cinnamon-flavored cornmeal drink, and **guaro**, the *campesino*'s near-tasteless yet potent drink of choice. And **coffee**, of course, is Costa Rica's *grano d'oro* (grain of gold). Most of the best coffee is exported, so don't expect it consistently good everywhere you go. What you're served may have been made from preground coffee that has been in a percolator for an hour or two. Coffee is traditionally served very strong and mixed with hot milk (the ratio can sometimes be one to one). When you order coffee with milk *(café con leche)*, you'll generally get half coffee, half milk. If you want it black, you want *café sin leche* or *café negro*. Herb teas are widely available. **Milk** is pasteurized.

The more popular North American soda pops, such as Pepsi and Coca-Cola, as well as sparkling water (called *agua mineral* or *soda*) are popular and also widely available. Costa Rican refreshers are *refrescos*, energizing fruit drinks served with water *(con agua)* or milk *(con leche)* and usually heavily sugared. They're a great way to taste the local fruits, such as *tamarindo* (the slightly tart fruit of the tamarind tree), mango, and papaya. They come in cartons or made to order (in which case you may want to ask for your drink *sin azucar,* without sugar). Some are made from oddities such as *pinolillo* (roasted corn flour).

Sugar finds its way into all kinds of drinks, even water: *agua dulce,* another beverage popular with *campesinos* is boiled water with brown sugar—energy for field workers. Roadside stalls also sell *pipas*, green coconuts with the tops chopped off. You drink the refreshing cool milk from a straw.

Alcoholic Beverages

Imported alcohol is expensive in Costa Rica, so stick with the local drinks. Lovers of **beer** *(cerveza)* are served locally brewed pilsners and lagers that reflect an early German presence in Costa Rica. Imperial and Bavaria are the two most popular brews. If you're watching your diet, try Tropical, a low-calorie "lite" beer. Heineken is also brewed here under license. Bavaria is a flavorful dark beer. Cheaper bars charge about 60 cents for a local beer; fancy hotels charge about $2. Most bars charge $1. (Bars—other than in hotels and restaurants—close at midnight.)

Even the poorest *campesino* can afford the native red-eye, *guaro,* a harsh, clear spirit distilled from fermented sugarcane; a large shot costs about 40 cents. My favorite drink? Guaro mixed with Café Rica, a potent coffee liqueur akin to Mexican Kahlúa.

The national liquor monopoly also produces vodka and gin (both recommended), rum (so-so), and whiskey (not recommended). A favorite local cocktail is Cuba libre (rum and Coke). Imported whiskeys—Johnnie Walker is very popular—are less expensive than other imported liquors, which are very expensive (often $8 or more a shot).

Avoid the local wines. The most memorable thing about them is the hangover. Imported wines are expensive—except Chilean and Argentinian vintages, of which there are some superb options.

Costa Ricans deplore drunks; it goes against the grain of *quedar bien*. Still, drinking is not restricted to lunch and the evening hours. Don't be surprised to find the Tico at the table next to yours washing down breakfast with a little whiskey. On Friday, the streets are full of drunks and it is not uncommon in any town in the country to have to step over people sprawled across the sidewalks.

GETTING THERE

BY AIR

About 20 international airlines provide regular service to Costa Rica. Flights from the U.S. are either direct or have stopovers in Mexico, Nicaragua, Guatemala, Honduras, and/or El Salvador. Most flights land at San José's Juan Santamaría International Airport (19 km northwest of, and 20 minutes by taxi, from the city center). At press time, the airport was undergoing extensive expansion, including a new terminal to handle charter flights. The **Daniel Oduber International Airport,** six km west of Liberia in Guanacaste, accepts mostly charters (Costa Rica's national airline, LACSA, also stops here on route between North America and San José). The latter is perfect for anyone wishing to restrict their exploring to the northwest provinces. The **Tobías Bolaños Airport,** four miles southwest of San José, is for domestic flights only.

Fares

Airline fares are in constant flux in these days of deregulation. The cheapest scheduled fares are APEX (advance-purchase excursion) fares, which you must buy at least 21 days before departure and which limit your visit to 30 days (from U.S.). From Europe, you must stay a minimum of 14 days and return within 180 days. Penalties usually apply for any changes after you buy your ticket. Generally, the further in advance you buy your ticket, the cheaper it will be. Buy your return segment before arriving in Costa Rica, as tickets bought in the country are heavily taxed.

If you fly to a U.S. gateway on a carrier with no service to Costa Rica, try to have your ticket issued on the stock of the airline on which you'll fly to Costa Rica; the latter will have an office in San José, which makes having your ticket reissued much easier if needed.

Keep your eyes open for introductory fares. Central American carriers are also usually slightly cheaper than their American counterparts but stop over at more cities en route. The cheapest flights generally are via Miami. Midweek and low-season travel is often cheaper. And you may be able to obtain lower fares by changing planes and/or carriers in Mexico City. If you're flexible, consider traveling **standby,** where you do not make a reservation, but turn up at the airport and hope for an empty seat, preferably at a last-minute discount fare (if there's a seat). In the U.S., the **Last Minute Travel Club,** tel. (617) 267-9800, specializes in last-minute airfares.

A wise investment is *The Worldwide Guide to Cheap Airfares* by Michael McColl, $14.95 plus postage; Insider Publications, 2124 Kittredge St., San Francisco, CA 94704, tel. (510) 276-1532 or (800) 78-BOOKS (800-782-6657), fax (510) 276-1531, which gives a complete profile on how to travel the world without breaking the bank. **Consumer Reports,** 101 Truman Ave., Yonkers, NY 10703, publishes the *Travel Buying Guide* ($8.95, Ed Perkins, ed.), which provides information on "How to Get Big Discounts on Airfares, Hotels, Car Rentals, and More." Also of use is the monthly *Consumer Reports Travel Letter* ($37 annual subscription).

For Students, Teachers, and Budget Travelers
Council Travel, an affiliate of the Council on International Education Exchange (CIEE), 205 E. 42nd St., New York, NY 10017, tel. (212) 882-2600 or 888-COUNCIL (888-268-6245), fax (212) 822-2699, e-mail: info@ciee.org, website www. ciee. org, with a worldwide network of trav-

CIEE AND STA OFFICES IN THE U.S.

CIEE/COUNCIL TRAVEL SERVICES OFFICES

Arizona
Tempe . . . . tel. (602) 966-3544

California
Berkeley . . . . tel. (510) 848-8604
Davis . . . . tel. (530) 752-2285
Fresno . . . . tel. (209) 278-6626
Fullerton . . . . tel. (714) 278-2157
La Jolla . . . . tel. (619) 452-0630
Long Beach . . . . tel. (562) 598-3338
Los Angeles . . . . tel. (310) 208-3551
Northridge . . . . tel. (818) 882-4692
Palo Alto . . . . tel. (408) 325-3888
Pasadena . . . . tel. (626) 793-5595
San Diego . . . . tel. (619) 270-6401
San Francisco . . . . tel. (415) 421-3473
Santa Barbara . . . . tel. (805) 562-8080

Colorado
Boulder . . . . tel. (303) 447-8101
Denver . . . . tel. (303) 571-0630

Connecticut
New Haven . . . . tel. (203) 562-5335

District of Columbia
Washington . . . . tel. (202) 337-6464

Florida
Gainesville . . . . tel. (352) 371-4455
Miami . . . . tel. (305) 670-9261

Georgia
Atlanta . . . . tel. (404) 377-9997

Illinois
Chicago . . . . tel. (312) 951-0585
Evanston . . . . tel. (847) 475-5070

Indiana
Bloomington . . . . tel. (812) 330-1600

Iowa
Ames . . . . tel. (515) 296-2326

Kansas
Lawrence . . . . tel. (913) 749-3900

Louisiana
New Orleans . . . . tel. (504) 866-1767

Maryland
Baltimore . . . . tel. (410) 516-0560

Massachusetts
Amherst . . . . tel. (413) 256-1261
Boston . . . . tel. (617) 266-1926
Cambridge . . . . tel. (617) 497-1497

Michigan
Ann Arbor . . . . tel. (313) 998-0200

Minnesota
Minneapolis . . . . tel. (612) 379-2323

New Jersey
New Brunswick . . . . tel. (908) 249-6667

New York
Ithaca . . . . tel. (607) 277-0373
New York City . . . . tel. (212) 882-2700,
666-4177, or 254-2525

North Carolina
Chapel Hill . . . . tel. (919) 942-2334

Ohio
Columbus . . . . tel. (614) 294-8696

Oregon
Eugene . . . . tel. (541) 344-2263
or 346-5535
Portland . . . . tel. (503) 228-1900

Pennsylvania
Lancaster . . . . tel. (717) 392-8272
Philadelphia . . . . tel. (215) 382-0343
Pittsburgh . . . . tel. (412) 683-1881

Rhode Island
Providence . . . . tel. (401) 331-5810

Tennessee
Knoxville . . . . tel. (423) 974-9200

Texas
Austin . . . . tel. (512) 472-4931
Dallas . . . . tel. (214) 363-9941

Utah
Salt Lake City . . . . tel. (801) 582-5840

Washington
Seattle . . . . . . tel. (206) 632-2448 and 329-4567

STA OFFICES

Arizona
Scottsdale . . . . tel. (800) 777-0112

(continues on next page)

CIEE AND STA OFFICES IN THE U.S.

(continued)

STA OFFICES *(continued)*

California
Berkeley . . . . tel. (510) 642-3000
Los Angeles . . . . tel. (213) 934-8722
and (310) 824-1574
San Francisco . . . . tel. (415) 391-8407
Santa Monica . . . . tel. (310) 394-5126

District of Columbia
Washington . . . . tel. (202) 994-7800

Florida
Gainesville . . . . tel. (352) 338-0068
Miami . . . . tel. (305) 461-3444
Orlando . . . . tel. (407) 541-2000
Tampa . . . . tel. (813) 974-3380

Illinois
Chicago . . . . tel. (312) 786-9050

Massachusetts
Boston . . . . tel. (617) 373-7900
and 266-6014
Cambridge . . . . , ... tel. (617) 576-4623

Minnesota
Minneapolis . . . . tel. (612) 615-1800

New York
New York City . . . . tel. (212) 865-2700
or 627-3111

Washington
Seattle . . . . tel. (206) 633-5000

Wisconsin
Madison . . . . tel. (608) 263-881

el agencies, caters to students, teachers, and youths. Another CIEE affiliate, **Council Charter** sells discounted air tickets on scheduled flights. Council Travel issues the International Student Identification Card, good for special fares.

STA Travel, 5900 Wilshire Blvd., Los Angeles, CA 90036, tel. (213) 937-1150 or (800) 781-4040, fax (213) 937-2739, also caters to students. Its more than 120 offices worldwide offer low-price airfares, as well as the ISIC and a **STA Travel Card** good for travel discounts. Also try **International Student Exchange Flights,** 5010 E. Shee Blvd. A-104, Scottsdale, AZ 85254, tel. (602) 951-1177. I also recommend the *Alternative Travel Directory,* Transitions Abroad, P.O. Box 1300, Amherst, MA 01004, tel. (800) 293-9373, fax (413) 256-0373; $16.95, for practical information on travel, learning and working abroad.

Courier Flights
Here, you deliver or accompany a package on behalf of a company for a much-discounted ticket. Delivery of the package usually takes priority over your personal travel plans upon arrival. The *Air Courier Directory* lists courier companies; $5, Pacific Data Sales Publishing, 2554 Lincoln Blvd., Suite 275, Marina del Rey, CA 90291. Also look for *A Simple Guide to Courier Travel*

published by **Discount Travel,** P.O. Box 331, Sandy, UT 84091, and *Courier Air Travel Handbook,* by Mark Field.

The following companies offer courier flights: **Now Voyager,** 74 Varick St., Suite 307, New York, NY 10013, tel. (212) 431-1616; **Trans-Air System,** tel. (305) 592-1771, in Miami, and **Travel Unlimited,** P.O. Box 1058, Allston, MA 02134, which publishes a monthly schedule. Other courier companies advertise in the Sunday travel sections of major newspapers.

Special Considerations
Ensure that you make your reservation as early as possible (several months in advance would be ideal), especially for the dry season, as flights are often oversold. Always reconfirm your reservation within 72 hours of your departure (reservations are frequently canceled if not reconfirmed, especially during Dec.-Jan. holidays), and arrive at the airport with *at least* two hours to spare. Avoid reservations that leave little time for connections, as baggage transfers and customs and immigration procedures can be infuriatingly slow.

I recommend using a travel agent for reservations (most travel agents do *not* charge a fee, but derive their income from commissions already costed into the airlines' fares). The agent's computer will display all the options, including seat availability and current fares, and they have the responsibility to chase down refunds in the events of overbooking, cancellations, etc.

From the U.S.
Scheduled Carriers: American Airlines, tel. (800) 433-7300, has daily service to Costa Rica from both Miami and Dallas. Typical 30-day APEX fares—departing midweek—in high season 1998 began at $590 from Dallas, $490 from Miami, $670 from Los Angeles, and $640 from New York. **Continental,** tel. (800) 231-0856 or (800) 982-4600, flies daily from Houston to San José; sample high-season fares began at $407 from Houston, $535 from Los Angeles, and $514

from New York. **United Airlines,** tel. (800) 241-6522, serves Costa Rica daily from Los Angeles, with sample fares from $536, and Washington ($640). At press time, **Delta,** tel. (800) 221-1212, was planning on introducing daily service from Atlanta, Georgia.

Fares for weekend departures cost about $500-1,000 extra. Stays of more than 30 days cost about $100-200 more! The major American carriers prefer to fill their planes rather than fly with excess capacity. Seats are at a premium so book early! Schedules change frequently.

Costa Rica's national airline, **LACSA,** 1600 N.W. LeJuene Rd., Suite 200, Miami, FL 33126, tel. (800) 225-2272 or (305) 876-6583, offers daily

---

CIEE AND STA OFFICES WORLDWIDE

CIEE/COUNCIL TRAVEL SERVICES

France
16 rue de Vaugirard, 75006 Paris, tel. 1-44-41-89-89 or 0800-148-188

Germany
Graf Adolf Strasse 64, 40212 Dusseldorf, tel. (211) 36-3030

Adalbert Strasse 32, 80799 Munich, tel. (089) 39-5022

Japan
Cosmos Aoyama, 5-53-67 Jingumae, Shibuya-ku, Tokyo, tel. (3) 5467-5535

Singapore
110-D Killiney Rd., Tai Wah Bldg., Singapore 0923, tel. (65) 7387-066

Thailand
108, 12-13 Kaosan Rd., Banglampoo, tel. (66) 2-282-7705

United Kingdom
28A Poland St., London W1V 3DB tel. (0171) 287-3337 in Europe, tel. (0171) 437-7767 worldwide

STA

Australia
235 Rundle St., Adelaide, SA 5000, tel. (8) 223-2426

Brisbane Arcade, 111-117 Adelaide St., Brisbane, QLD 4000, tel. (7) 3229-2499

University of Canberra, P.O. Box 1, Belconnen, Canberra ACT 2166, tel. (6) 247-8633

Shop T17, Smith St. Mall, Darwin, NY 0800, tel. (9) 412-955

Box Hill Central, Melbourne, VIC 3218, tel. (3) 9349-2411

53 Market St., Fremantle, Perth, WA 6160, tel. (9) 227-7569

9 Oxford St., Paddington, Sydney NSW 2021, tel. (2) 93-68-1111

Germany
Berger Strasse 118, 60316 Frankfurt, tel. (69) 430-191

Marienstrasse 25, 10117 Berlin, tel. (30) 285-98264

Japan
Star Plaza Aoyama Bldg., 1-10-3 Shibuya-ku, Tokyo 102, tel. (3) 5391-2922

Honmacky Meidai Bldg., 2-5-5 Azuchi-machi, Chuo-ku, Osaka 541, tel. (6) 262-7066

New Zealand
Union Bldg., Auckland University, Princes St., Auckland, tel. (9) 309-0458

90 Cashel St., Christchurch, tel. (3) 379-9098

233 Cuba St., Wellington, tel. (4) 385-0561

Singapore
01-01 Science Hug, 87 Science Park Rd., Singapore 118256, tel. 737-7188

Thailand
Wall St. Tower Bldg., Room 1406, 33 Surawong Rd., Bangrak, Bangkok 10500, tel. (2) 236-0262

United Kingdom
Priory House, 6 Wrights Ln., London W8 6TA, tel. (0171) 361-6161 in Europe, tel. (0171) 361-6123 worldwide

flights from Los Angeles, Miami, New York, Orlando, and San Francisco; and five flights weekly from New Orleans. Some flights are nonstop; others make the "milk run" through Central America. Service is aboard Airbus Industries wide-body A310s (240 passengers) and narrow-body A320s (168 passengers). Service is excellent, with free beverages. Sample 30-day APEX fares, midweek, in high season were $525 from Los Angeles, and $397 from Miami. LACSA offers students a 40% discount with an International Student Identification Card, but you must buy your discounted ticket through a student travel agency. See **Notes for Students** later in this chapter.

In 1994, LACSA and four other Central American carriers—Aviateca, Guatemala, tel. (800) 327-9832; TACA, El Salvador, tel. (800) 535-8780; COPA, Panamá, tel. (800) 359-2672; and NICA, Nicaragua, tel. (800) 831-6422—formed a joint marketing company, America Central Corporation, which was superceded in 1997 by Grupo Taca, headquartered in El Salvador. LACSA's management has been taken over by Taca, and I anticipate that the LACSA logo will disappear entirely, to be replaced by the five golden macaws of Grupo Taca (a deterioration in service and management is already noticeable).

Grupo Taca, 5885 N.W. 18th St., Miami, FL 33159, tel. (305) 871-1587, fax 871-1359, offers a **Visit Central America Air Pass** valid with a roundtrip ticket from the United States. The fare allows purchase of 3-10 coupons (two to arrive and depart Central America) to cities throughout Central America over a 45-day period. Press-time prices started at $499 low season, $549 high season from Miami, Houston, Orlando, or New Orleans; and $699 low season, $759 high season from Los Angeles, with one stopover allowed. A fourth and fifth coupon cost $50 each (high season); a sixth and seventh cost $80 each. High season is 1 July-31 Aug. and 1 Nov.-31 December. A great bargain! You can combine services of participating carriers.

LACSA, TACA, and Aviateca have a similar deal called a **Mayan Airpass.** You must buy your ticket before arrival, buy a minimum of four coupons ($75 apiece), and arrive on any of the three airlines from any gateway city in the U.S. or Mexico. Call (800) 353-5430 for a brochure and details.

US Airways, tel. (800) 428-4322, and 12 Latin American carriers, including LACSA, have the **LatinPass** program, tel. (800) 44-LATIN (800-445-2846) or (305) 870-7500, fax 870-7676. This allows members of the individual carriers' frequent flyer programs to accrue miles on other LatinPass member airlines. (To enroll, mail your last statement from *any* US Airway's frequent flyer program and LatinPass will match the last three one-way flights between the U.S. and Latin America.)

SAHSA, tel. (800) 327-1225, the airline of Honduras, has a **Maya World Fare** from U.S. gateways that allows visits to five Central American destinations, including Costa Rica; it is valid for 21 days and you must make a minimum of three stopovers.

Aero Costa Rica, Costa Rica's other international carrier, discontinued service in October 1997. Keep your ears tuned for a potential resurrection.

Charters: Charter operators have only recently begun adding Costa Rica to their roster. In December 1997, **Apple Vacations,** tel. (800) 727-3550 east coast, (800) 363-2775 west coast, launched weekly charter service to Daniel Obuder Airport in Liberia from Philadelphia and Newark, high season only. In January 1998, **Funjet Vacations,** tel. (800) 558-3050, began offering charter packages using Continental Airlines' service via Houston.

Consolidators: You may save money by buying your ticket from a consolidator (similar to a "bucket shop" in England), which sells discounted tickets on scheduled carriers. Consolidators usually have access to a limited number of tickets, so book early. The Sunday travel sections of major city newspapers are the best source. The following offer cut-rate fares to Costa Rica: **Cut Rate Travel,** 1220 Montgomery Drive, Deerfield, IL 60015, tel. (800) 388-0575 or (847) 405-0575, fax 405-0587; **Buenaventura Travel,** 595 Market St., San Francisco, CA 94105, tel. (415) 777-9777 or (800) 286-8872, fax (415) 777-9871; **The Vacation Store,** tel. (800) 825-3633; and **UniTravel,** tel. (314) 569-2501 or (800) 325-2222. Many tour operators offer air and hotel packages that provide excellent bargains. Try **Costa Rica Connection,** 975 Osos St., San Luis Obispo, CA 93401, tel. (805) 54-8823 or (800) 345-7422, fax (805) 543-3626, e-mail: tours@crconnect.com, and **Costa Rica**

Experts, 3166 N. Lincoln Ave. #424, Chicago, IL 60657, tel. (312) 935-1009 or (800) 827-9046, fax (312) 935-9252, e-mail: crexpert@ris.net.

From Canada

LACSA, tel. (800) 225-2272, offers service between Toronto and Costa Rica three times weekly. Sample high-season fares are CAN$808 (US$558) midweek, CAN$838 (US$588) weekend. And **Air Canada,** tel. (800) 869-9000, flies three times weekly from Toronto via Havana, Cuba—a route I highly recommend as you can stop over and thrill to a country that is even more exhilarating than Costa Rica (see special topic, **Beyond Costa Rica? Try Cuba** and look for *Cuba Handbook,* one of Moon Travel Handbook's best-selling guides).

In winter, **Air Transat,** tel. (514) 987-1616, fax 987-9750, offers charter flights every Saturday from Montreal (from CAN$549 roundtrip). **Canada 3000** offers charters every Sunday from Toronto (from CAN$499). You'll need to book through a travel agent. **Conquest,** tel. (416) 665-9255, fax 665-6811, has charters to both San José and Liberia. **Tours Mont-Royal,** tel. (514) 342-6070, fax 342-3130, operates a charter Nov.-April. And the following companies also offer inexpensive charter packages: **Fiesta Wayfarer Holidays,** tel. (416) 498-556 in Toronto; **Fiesta West,** tel. (416) 967-1510, fax 967-5347, in Toronto, and **Go Travel,** tel. (514) 735-4526, in Montreal.

Canadian Universities Travel Service, Travel Cuts; 187 College St., Toronto, Ont., Canada M5T 1P7, tel. (416) 979-2406, which has 25 offices throughout Canada, sells discount airfares to students as well as the general public.

From the U.K.

There were no scheduled direct flights to Costa Rica at press time. However, **Voyages Jules Verne,** 21 Dorset Square, London NW1 6QG, tel. (0171) 723-5066, offers a weekly charter from Gatwick, Dec.-May. **Airtours Holidays,** Wavel House, Holcombe Rd., Helmshore, Rossendale, Lancaster BB4 4NB, tel. (0170) 623-2991, fax 623-2426, was slated to begin weekly charter flights to Liberia in May 1998.

American Airlines, British Airways, Continental, United Airlines, USAirways and Virgin Atlantic fly from London to Miami (or Washington), from where you can connect with an airline serving Costa Rica. You can also hop over to Europe, from where several airlines fly to Costa Rica, usually via circuitous routes.

Alternately, consider flying via Havana, Cuba, from where both LACSA, Cubana, and Air Canada offer three flights daily to Costa Rica (see special topic, **Beyond Costa Rica? Think Cuba**).

Typical APEX fares between London and Costa Rica begin at about £550 via the U.S.A. for stays of less than 30 days. However, you can buy reduced rate fares on scheduled carriers from "bucket shops," discount ticket agencies. "Bucket shops" advertise in London's *What's On* and *Time Out* plus leading Sunday newspapers. One of the most reputable budget agencies is **Trailfinders,** 42 Earl's Court Rd., London W8 6EJ, tel. (0171) 938-3366, which publishes *Trailfinder* magazine; it also lists fares. The company also has offices in Birmingham, Bristol, Glasgow, and Manchester. Another respected operator, is **Journey Latin America,** 16 Devonshire Rd., Chiswick, London W4 2HD, tel. (0181) 747-3108, fax 742-1312, e-mail: tours@journeylatinamerica.com, which specializes in cheap fares and tour packages.

Council Travel, 28A Poland St., London W1V 3DB, tel. (0171) 437-7767, specializes in student fares, as does **STA Travel,** Priory House, 6 Wrights Ln., London W8 6TA, tel. (0171) 361-6161 or 361-6262, website www.sta-travel.com, which has 25 offices throughout Britain.

From Continental Europe

Scheduled service between Europe and Costa Rica was in flux at press time, when **KLM** cancelled its service from Amsterdam and **LTU,** tel. 01-90-21-1767, fax 0211-9-27-0000, cancelled its charters from Dusseldorf. The only regular scheduled service in January 1998 was with **Iberia,** with a daily flight from Madrid via Puerto Rico or the Dominican Republic. **Condor,** tel. 061-07-755440, fax 061-07-7550, also flies charters direct from Dusseldorf and Munich. And **Viasa,** the Colombian airline, serves Costa Rica from Madrid via South America.

One of the best routes is **via Havana,** Cuba, where you can connect with daily flights to Costa Rica. Havana is served from Madrid daily by Iberia, and twice-weekly by Cubana, which also flies there twice-weekly from Frankfurt and Berlin, as well as from Lisbon, Moscow, Paris, and

Rome. LTU and Condor fly to Havana from Dusseldorf. KLM and Martinair both serve Havana from Amsterdam. Aeroflot flies to Havana three times weekly from Shannon, tel. 62-299; to Miami from Stockholm (Sveavagan 20, tel. 217-007), and Luxembourg (35 rue Glesener, L-1631, tel. 493-291); and to Nicaragua from Moscow.

Check with local travel agents for latest fares and schedules, which change frequently. The cheapest route may be to fly via London or Manchester using a "bucket shop" (usually you must pick up your ticket in person at the office, although you can book from abroad). Check to see if the fare includes a connecting flight via another UK city. Discount fares are available through **Council Travel** and **STA Travel,** both of which have offices throughout Europe.

In France, try **Uniclam,** 63 rue Monsieur Le Prince, Paris 75006, tel. 01-43-29-12-36, or **Voyages Découvertes,** 21 rue Cambon, Paris, tel. 01-42-61-00-01. In Germany, try **America Latina Reisen,** Conrad Strasse 16, Berlin D-140G1, tel. (308) 060-2460, fax 060-2461, e-mail: alr-travel@compuserve.com. In Italy, try Central America specialist **Marcelletti,** via Guiseppe Belluzzo 1, Rome 00149, tel. 6-559-9672, fax 6-558-1694. In Denmark, try **Euroamerica Travel,** Havnegade 28B, Frederikssund 3600, tel. 45-423-1779, fax 45-423-1779, e-mail: argeu-roamdk@dk-online-dk, specialists in Latin American travel. In Holland, call Latin America specialist **Thika Travel,** Kerkplein 6, Kochengen, utrecht 362ZN, tel./fax 34-62-4252, e-mail: thika@knoware.nt.ass.crent. In Switzerland, try **Globetrotter Travel,** Remweg 35, 8001 Zurich, tel. 01-211-7780, or **RDR Travel,** Hammer-strasse 11, Zurich 8034, tel. 1-389-9389, fax 1-383-9290, e-mail: rdrtravel@swissonline.ch, which specializes in travel to Costa Rica.

You can also purchase Grupo Taca's "Visit Central America Air Pass" in Europe: UK, tel. 01293-553-3330; France, tel. 01-4451-0165; Germany, tel. 49-6103-81061; Holland, tel. 23-291-723; Italy, tel. 6-559-4342.

From Latin America and the Caribbean

Costa Rica is served from all the Central American nations (see "From the U.S.," above). LACSA flies between Costa Rica and Brazil, Chile, Ecuador, Peru, and Venezuela. Aviateca flies from Colombia. And Ladeco links Costa Rica and

Chile. And American Airlines, Continental, and United Airlines' flights all connect Costa Rica with destinations throughout South America. There are few bargains, and if originating in the U.S.A., it pays to make reservations ahead (airline tickets are heavily taxed and subject to greater restrictions in South America; there are few APEX fares). **Aeroperlas,** tel. 440-0093, fax 442-9103, e-mail: aeroexp@sol.racsa.co.cr, flies direct between San José and Bocas del Toro in Panamá.

There are few flights between Costa Rica and its Caribbean neighbors, except for Cuba. Air Canada, Cubana, and LACSA all offer regular scheduled service between San José and Havana.

From Asia

The easiest and cheapest route from Asia is to fly to California, from where you can connect to flights to Costa Rica. From Hong Kong, an alternate route is with **Iberia** from Macau to Madrid and then to Costa Rica. A roundtrip ticket is about HK$17,000, but it pays to shop around. STA Travel and Council Travel offer the best fare; both have offices throughout Asia.

From Australia and New Zealand

The best route from Australia or New Zealand is via San Francisco or Los Angeles, from where you can connect to flights to Costa Rica (Qantas, United Airlines, Air New Zealand, and several other major airlines offer direct service to Los Angeles). A route via Santiago, Chile or Buenos Aires is also possible. Fares vary widely, beginning at about A$2,200 in low season (mid-October to mid-January, and February-April), rising to A$3,000 or so in high season (June-July and mid-December to mid-January).

Specialists in discount fares include **STA Travel,** with offices throughout Australia and New Zealand. To purchase the "Visit Central America Air Pass" from Grupo Taca (see "From the U.S.," above), call 03-654-3233.

BY LAND

By Bus

The overland route from North America is an attractive alternative for patient travelers who can take the rough with the smooth and for whom time is no object. Whether by bus or your own

*a macadamia farm in
the Central Highlands*

vehicle, allow at least three weeks (the journey is well over 3,500 km from the U.S. and the going is slow). Obtain all necessary visas and documentation in advance. Accommodations are plentiful all along the route.

Central America is well served with local bus systems. However, buses are often crowded to the hilt, and you may end up standing for parts of your journey. Rest stops are infrequent. You can travel from San Diego or Texas to Costa Rica by bus for as little as $100 (with hotels and food, however, the cost can add up to more than flying direct). Where possible, book as far ahead as you can—the buses often sell out well in advance.

Watch your baggage; consider keeping it with you on the bus. Passports are often collected by the driver to present en masse to immigration. You will need to provide passport and visas when buying your ticket.

Bus schedules are featured in *Mexico and Central American Handbook,* edited by Ben Box (Prentice Hall, New York). Vivien Lougheed's *Central America by Chickenbus,* (Repository Press, Quesnel, BC, Canada) may provide useful reading.

Buses serve Mexico City from the U.S. border points at Mexicali, Ciudad Juárez, and Laredo. **Cristóbal Colón** line serves Mexico City to Tapachula on the Guatemala border, where local buses connect to Guatemala City. **Tícabus,** also known as TICA, tel. 221-8954 in San José, provides direct service to San José from Guatemala City via Nicaragua (departs Managua on Tues-

day, Thursday, and Saturday; $25; 11 hours); **Sirca,** tel. 222-5541, offers service from Managua on Monday, Wednesday, and Friday ($5). TICA also offers service to San José from Tegucigalpa in Honduras daily. Most buses depart early morning. From Panamá, **Tracopa,** tel. 221-4214 in San José, buses depart David daily at 7:30 a.m. and noon; TICA operates buses from Panamá City daily at 11 a.m. Note that Panamá time is one hour ahead of Costa Rica!

Green Tortoise, 494 Broadway, San Francisco, CA 94133, tel. (415) 956-7500 or (800) 867-8647, fax (415) 956-4900, e-mail: info@greentortoise.com, website www.greentortoise.com, is an institution among hardy budget travelers seeking cheap passage down the Central American isthmus. Trips from San Francisco to Costa Rica take five weeks, with bunk beds on board and meals cooked roadside ($1,500).

See "Border Crossing," below, for details on buses between San José and the Nicaraguan and Panamian borders.

By Car
Many people drive to Costa Rica from the U.S.A. via Mexico, Guatemala, Honduras, and Nicaragua. It's a long haul, but you can follow the Pan-American Highway all the way from the U.S. to San José and into Panamá. Farther south, the road ends abruptly in southern Panamá; no road link exists into South America. It's 3,700 km minimum, depending on your starting point (the closest point to Costa Rica is Brownsville, Texas).

Experienced travelers recommend skirting El Salvador and the Guatemalan highlands in favor of the coast road. Allow three weeks at a leisurely pace. High ground clearance is useful. And be sure that your vehicle is in tip-top mechanical condition.

The roads are often full of hazards, such as potholes and livestock, so do *not* drive at night (Sanborn's insurance company reports that 80% of insurance claims are a result of nighttime accidents). You should plan your itinerary to be at each day's destination before nightfall. Be wary of theft. Always lock your car when parked. Do not leave *any* items in view in the car. U.S. license plates are a collector's item, and fancy mirrors and other shiny embellishments are likely to be ripped off (take off the plates and display them *inside* your car).

You can ship your vehicle as far as Honduras aboard the M/V *Regal Voyager,* a car ferry that makes a weekly journey between Puerto Isabel (near Brownsville, TX) and Puerto Cortés, Honduras. It has 112 comfy staterooms and a restaurant, bar, casino, and movie theater. It departs Texas early Sunday evening, arriving Honduras on Wednesday at noon. Contact **Isabel-Cortés Ferry Service,** 1200 W. Hwy. 100 #7-A, Box 7, Port Isabel, TX 78578, tel. (210) 943-2331, fax 943-2235.

Drive the Pan-American Highway is a guidebook that offers practical advice and tips; $17.95 plus $3 postage, Costa Rica Books, Suite 1, SJO 981, P.O. Box 025216, Miami, FL 33102-5216, tel. (800) 365-2342, fax (619) 421-6002.

Maps: The **American Automobile Association** (AAA) publishes a road map of Mexico and Central America (free to AAA members). Also consider the *Traveller's Reference Map of Central America* published by International Travel Map Productions, P.O. Box 2290, Vancouver, BC, Canada V6B 3W5.

Documentation: You'll need passport, visas, driver's license, and vehicle registration. It's also advisable to obtain tourist cards (good for 90 days) from the consulate of each country before departing. A U.S. driver's license is good throughout Central America, although an International Driving Permit—issued through the American Automobile Association—can be handy, too. You'll need to arrange a transit visa for Mexico in advance, plus car entry permits for each country (cars freely pass across international borders without paying customs duty; duty becomes payable, however, if your car is stolen). The AAA can provide advice on *carnets* (international travel permits), permits, etc., as well as a good area map. Also check with each country's consulate for latest information.

Insurance: A separate vehicle liability insurance policy is required for each country. Most U.S. firms will not underwrite insurance south of the border. **American International Underwriters,** 70 Pine St., New York, NY 10271, tel. (212) 770-7000, can arrange insurance; inquire several months in advance of your trip. **Sanborn's,** P.O. Box 310, McAllen, TX 78502, tel. (956) 686-0711, fax 686-0732, is a reputable company specializing in insurance coverage for travel in Mexico and Central America. They publish a very handy booklet, *Overland Travel,* which is full of practical information. The company has the Sanborn's Mexico Club. Reportedly you can buy insurance for Mexico at the border. Note, however, that insurance sold by AAA (American Automobile Association) covers Mexico only, not Central America.

Upon arrival in Costa Rica, foreign drivers *must* buy insurance stamps for a minimum of three months (approximately $15). There's also a $10 road tax payable upon arrival in Costa Rica. Vehicle permits are issued at the border for stays up to 30 days. You can extend this up to six months at the Instituto Costarricense de Turismo (travel agencies in San José can help with paperwork). Don't plan on selling your newer-model car in Costa Rica—you'll be hit with *huge* import duties.

Border Crossing

Visa requirements are always in flux, check in advance with the Nicaraguan or Panamanian embassies. Likewise, borders are open only at specific times and these, too, are subject to change.

Nicaragua: A **tourist visa** into Nicaragua costs $2 and is issued at the border. Everyone needs one. In addition, some nationalities ostensibly need **entry visas**, which cannot be obtained at the border (you have to get them in advance from a Nicaraguan embassy). Currently, British and U.S. citizens, plus some Western Europeans, are permitted to enter Nicaragua for stays up to 90 days without an entry visa.

However, entry visas are required of Canadians, Australians, New Zealanders, and citizens of other European nations (including France, Germany, and Italy), although there are reports that the Nicaraguan border officials often let these nationalities through with only a tourist visa. Entry visas cost $25 (good for 30 days; and take a minimum of 24 hours to obtain in San José. Contact the Nicaraguan Consulate, tel. 233-3479 or 233-8747, at Avenida Central, Calle 27, in the Barrio La California suburb, in San José, weekdays 8 a.m.-noon.

You can cross into Nicaragua for 72 hours and renew your 30- or 90-day Costa Rica visa if you want to return to Costa Rica and stay longer. A 72-hour transit visa for Nicaragua costs $15. If your visa has already expired, you will need to get an exit visa in San José, otherwise you may be turned back at the border. You can obtain the visa—$40 for exiting by land, plus $2.50 per month fine—from the immigration office at Calle 21, Avenidas 6/8 in San José, Mon.-Fri. 8:30 a.m.-3:30 p.m.

Virtually everyone arriving from Nicaragua does so at **Peñas Blancas,** in northwest Costa Rica. This is a border post, not a town. The Costa Rican and Nicaraguan posts are four km apart, with no-man's-land between. The border is open daily 8 a.m.-8 p.m.; southbound, it is open 7:30 a.m.-7 p.m. When you arrive at Peñas Blancas, you must get an exit form (at window #8), which you complete and return with your passport. It will be passed to window #6, where you pay about 35 cents. Then walk 600 meters to the Costa Rican border, where your passport will be validated (it must have at least six months remaining before expiry). After a short walk across no-man's-land to the Nicaraguan side, shuttle buses (50 cents) take you three km to the Nicaraguan immigration building. Here you'll pay about $7 for a 30-day tourist visa (officially it costs $2, so I guess the $5 is pocketed by corrupt immigration officials), plus $1 municipal stamp. Then complete a customs declaration sheet, present it with your passport, and proceed to the customs inspection (next building along). Then take your papers to the gate for final inspection. *Phew!* Welcome to Nicaragua.

Cross-border buses (70 cents) depart from here every hour for Rivas, a small town about 40 km north of the border. *Colectivo* (shared)

taxis also run regularly between the border and Rivas, the nearest Nicaraguan town with accommodations. Buses fill fast—get there early. There's a basic restaurant near the Nicaraguan immigration office.

Southbound you may be required to pay an **exit fee** ($1) leaving Nicaragua. (The Costa Rica tourist card is free.) If you're asked for proof of onward ticket when entering Costa Rica, you can buy a bus ticket—valid for 12 months—back to Nicaragua at the bus station at Peñas Blancas; the Costa Rican authorities will normally accept this, though they rarely ask for them.

TICA, tel. 221-8954, and **Sirca,** tel. 222-5541 or 223-1464, operate cross-border buses from San José. See chart, **Buses From San José,** in the San José chapter for schedules. Service on Sirca is reportedly unreliable, and tickets should be bought several days ahead. The TICA and Sirca buses between Managua and San José are often delayed for hours, as the bus usually waits for all passengers to be processed. Allow lots of time for border delays.

See **Peñas Blancas** in the Guanacaste chapter for details of services at Peñas Blancas, plus bus schedules and fares to/from Peñas Blancas.

There's also a border post at **Los Chiles,** in the northern lowlands. Until recently, foreigners were automatically turned away and had to enter Nicaragua via Peñas Blancas. When I visited in December 1997, foreigners were permitted to cross. The Costa Rican **Oficina de Migración,** tel. 471-1153, is open daily, 8 a.m.-4 p.m. There is no road crossing. You have to hire a boat or take a ferry across the Río San Juan, then take a bus 14 km to San Carlos, on the southeast shore of Lake Nicaragua; or hire a boat to take you downriver to San Carlos.

Panamá: Citizens of the UK and certain European nations do not require a visa but need a tourist card, issued at the border ($5, good for 30 days); however, don't count on tourist cards being available at Paso Canoas. Visas are required by citizens of Australia, Canada, New Zealand, some Western European nations, and the U.S., and must be obtained in advance of arrival (you cannot obtain a visa at the border). The cost varies according to citizenship. David and Panamá City each have a Costa Rican consulate. Both Costa Rican and Panamian officials often ask for proof of onward ticket before granting permission to enter (Costa Ricans also asked me to show that I had at least $200; Panamá requires that you show at least $300).

The main crossing point, **Paso Canoas,** is on the Pan-American Highway. The border posts have been open 24 hours, but are subject to change (at press time, they were open 6-11 a.m. and 1-6 p.m.). If you don't have a ticket out of the country, you can buy a Tracopa bus ticket in David to Paso Canoas and back (however, apparently you can't buy a ticket from Paso Canoas to David).

A bus terminal on the Panamanian side offers service to David, the nearest town (90 minutes), every hour or two until 7 p.m. Buses leave from David for Panamá City (last bus 5 p.m.; seven hours). **TICA,** tel. 221-8954, operates a/c buses from Panamá City direct to San José from the Hotel Ideal, Calle 17 Este, at 11 a.m. Panamá time ($25). **Transchiri,** Calle 17 Este and Balboa, has departures daily from Panamá City to David at noon and midnight ($11, or express $15; five hours); you can connect with **Tracopa,** tel. 221-4214 in San José, buses departing David at 7:30 a.m. and noon. Book at least two days ahead.

Panaline, tel. 255-1205, has express bus service to Panamá City from the Hotel Cocorí on Calle 16, Avenida 3, daily at 2 p.m. ($22), and via Sixaola to Changuinola on Panama's Caribbean coast, at 10 a.m. ($8, payable to the driver; 6-7 hours). Alfaro, TICA and Tracopa also have service from San José to Panamá: see chart, **Buses From San José,** in the San José chapter. Also see **Paso Canoas** in the Golfo Dulce and Peninsula de Osa chapter.

Sixaola, a rather squalid village on the Caribbean coast, sits on the north bank of the Río Sixaola. It's brighter, more lively counterpart is **Guabito,** a duty-free town on the Panamanian side of the river. The two are linked by a bridge. The Costa Rican Customs and Immigration offices—opposite each other—are ostensibly open daily 7 a.m.-5 p.m.; the Panamian office, tel. 759-7952, is open 8 a.m.-6 p.m. Reports are that officials occasionally take lengthy siestas (and may even not show up on certain days); they may also demand a malaria test or ask to see your malaria tablets. Minibuses operate a regular schedule from Guabito to Changuinola (16 km). A narrow-gauge cargo train also runs daily to Almirante (30 km), the end of both rail

and road; it leaves at 5 a.m. Taxis are available at all hours ($1 to Changuinola). For access to the rest of Panamá, you can either fly to David from Changuinola or take a boat from Almirante to Bocas del Toro ($2 by ferry; $10 by water taxi) and then Chiriquí Grande, where a road traverses the mountain to David.

There is another crossing between Costa Rica and Panamá at the remote mountain border post of **Río Sereno** east of San Vito, in the Pacific southwest, but it is not open to foreigners.

BY SEA

Costa Rica is appearing with increasing frequency on the itineraries of luxury cruise ships. However, stops are usually no more than one day, so don't expect more than a cursory glimpse of the country. Excursions are offered while ashore, typically to Carara Biological Reserve, Poás and Sarchí, and Palo Verde, or to Cahuita, Tortuguero, and the Rainforest Aerial Tram.

Cruises from Florida usually stop off at various Caribbean islands and/or Cozumel before calling in at Puerto Limón. Cruises from San Diego or Los Angeles normally stop off in Puerto Caldera. (A new port facility for international cruise lines at Puerto Caldera, near Puntarenas, has been touted for years, but remains a thing of the future. New—albeit meager—facilities for cruise ships have been added to Puerto Limón.) Many itineraries include the Panamá Canal and the San Blas Islands.

World Explorer Cruises, 555 Montgomery St., San Francisco, CA 94111, tel. (415) 393-1565 or (800) 854-3935, includes an overnight stop in Puerto Limón as part of a 14-day odyssey that is steeped in the allure of the old Spanish Main ($1,445-3,095). The cruise aboard the *Universe Explorer* begins and ends in Nassau, Bahamas, and includes Montego Bay, Cartagena, Puerto Cristóbal in Panamá, and other stops along Central America's Caribbean seaboard. An eight-day voyage is offered ($825-1,770). In 1998, **Dolphin Line,** tel. (888) 325-808, introduced a similar eight-day itinerary using its *Ocean Breeze,* beginning and ending in Montego Bay, Jamaica.

Tour options while in port (normally one or two days) usually include a San José tour, sight-

CRUISE LINES SERVING COSTA RICA

Crystal Cruise Line, 2121 Ave. of the Stars #200, Los Angeles, CA 90067, tel. (800) 446-6645

Cunard Lines, 6100 Blue Lagoon Dr. #400, Miami, FL 33126, tel. (305) 465-3000 or (800) 7-CUNARD (800-728-6273); in the U.K., tel. 1703-229933; in Germany, tel. 40-415-3330

Holland America, 300 Elliott Ave. W., Seattle, WA 98119, tel. (800) 426-0327

Norwegian Cruise Line, 95 Merrick Way, Coral Gables, FL 33134, tel. (800) 327-7030

Princess Cruises, 10100 Santa Monica Blvd., Los Angeles, CA 90067, tel. (800) 421-0522

Radisson Seven Seas Cruises, 600 Corporate Dr. #410, Ft. Lauderdale, FL 33334, tel. (800) 333-3333

Regal Cruise Lines, 4199 34th St., Suite B-103, St. Petersburg, FL 33711, tel. (800) 270-SAIL (800-279-7245)

Royal Caribbean Cruise Line, 1050 Caribbean Way, Miami, FL 33132, tel. (305) 539-6000

Silversea, 110 E. Broward Blvd., Ft. Lauderdale, FL 33301, tel. (800) 722-9955

seeing and shopping in Sarchí, a rafting expedition, a nature walk in Carara Biological Reserve, a banana plantation tour, maybe even golfing or horseback riding.

Freight Ships

Adventurous travelers might be able to book a passage on a "tramp" steamer plying ports up and down the Americas. Some have limited passenger accommodations. This can be tremendous fun, and passengers are normally fed and looked after very well. Itineraries, however, can change without notice, and your interests will always be secondary to commercial freight considerations.

Marcon Lines takes 10 passengers aboard the *Nedlloyd Hong Kong* on journeys from Lázaro Cárdenas (Mexico) and Puerto Caldera. The cruises, up to 150 days long, travel as far as Japan. Contact **Freighter World Cruises,** 180 South Lake Ave. #335, Pasadena, CA 91101, tel. (818) 449-3106, fax 449-9573, which

also books passage on the MV *Maya Tikal,* which has three-week roundtrip cruises between Long Beach and Central America, with room for five passengers in one double and three single cabins.

The semi-annual directory *Ford's Freighter Travel Guide,* 19448 Londelius St., Northridge, CA 91342, tel. (818) 701-7414, and *Ford's International Cruise Guide* (published quarterly) provide comprehensive listings on freighters that take passengers.

ORGANIZED TOURS

ICT surveys suggest that about 30% of North American tourists to Costa Rica arrived on package tours, and that a majority of the remaining 70% book some form of tour through a company in Costa Rica once they arrive.

A growing number of U.S. (and European) tour companies specialize in Costa Rica, and dozens of others offer group tours and/or prepackaged programs for independent travelers based on a wide range of special-interest themes. Joining a group tour offers many advantages over traveling independently, such as the camaraderie of a shared experience and the joys of discovery and learning passed along by a knowledgeable guide. Tours are also a good bet for those with limited time: you'll proceed to the most interesting places without the unforeseen delays and distractions that can be the bane of independent travel. Everything is taken care of from your arrival to your departure, including transportation and accommodations. And the petty bureaucratic hassles and language problems you may otherwise not wish to face are eliminated, too.

The majority of group tours to Costa Rica are operated by companies with a genuine concern for the quality of your experience and the impact on the local environment. That means relatively small groups of no more than 20 people, escorted by a trained guide, often a professional naturalist or other specialist who loves to share his or her knowledge.

Ask, too, about the "difficulty" level of particular tours. Many nature tours involve a certain amount of activity and even discomfort. Certain companies offer "soft adventure" tours that include a lesser degree of discomfort or difficulty than other tours that follow a similar itinerary. Don't be put off by a "hard" adventure unless you're an absolute couch potato or thoroughly detest the slightest physical discomfort, as the rewards of active adventures are truly immense: how otherwise might you see a quetzal in its natural environment, for example?

The overwhelming majority of tours focus on natural history. Nature tours are not for lounge lizards. They're often get-your-feet-wet tours. You may be expected to endure hard treks through rainforest. The line between athleticism and ecology in Costa Rica is tenuous at best. Just remember one caveat: you won't see much wildlife if you're moving quickly or noisily. Think slow, think small, think quiet.

North American Companies

Costa Rica Experts offers two- and three-day packages to various nature lodges, plus a 10-day "Costa Rica Explorer" (soft adventure) and 10-day "Odyssey" (hardy adventure) for nature lovers. Contact them at 3166 N. Lincoln Ave. #424, Chicago, IL 60657, tel. (312) 935-1009 or (800) 827-9046, fax (312) 935-9252, e-mail: cr-expert@ris.net. **Holbrook Travel** has a series of eight- to 16-day natural history trips, including a 12-day "Costa Rica's Ecozones" ($1,540), a 10-day "Viewing the Turtles of Costa Rica" tour ($1,335) and a nine-day "Turtle Tagging" tour (from $1,585). Contact 3540 N.W. 13th St., Gainesville, FL 32609, tel. (352) 377-7111 or (800) 858-0999, fax (352) 371-3710, e-mail: travel@holbrooktravel.com. **Earthwatch,** P.O. Box 9104, Watertown, MA 02272, tel. (800) 776-0188, fax (617) 926-8532, e-mail: info@earthwatch.org, also has 10-day turtle-tagging "tours" where participants assist research scientists.

Cheeseman's, 20800 Kittredge Rd., Saratoga, CA 95070, tel. (408) 741-5330 or (800) 527-5330, fax (408) 741-0358, e-mail: cheesemans@aol.com, has an annual 20-day natural history trip limited to 12 participants ($3,600), and the **Sierra Club,** Dept. 05618, 85 Second St., San Francisco, CA 94105, tel. (415) 977-5588, fax (415) 977-5795, has 10- and 14-day natural history trips. **Quest Nature Tours** has an annual 15-day nature trip, plus an eight-day trip to Tiskita Jungle Lodge. Contact them at 36 Finch Ave. W, Toronto, Ont., Canada M2N 2G9, tel. (416) 221-3000 or

(800) 387-1483, fax (416) 221-5730, e-mail: travel@worldwidequest.com. **Mountain Travel-Sobek,** 6420 Fairmount Ave., El Cerrito, CA 94530, tel. (510) 527-8100 or (800) 227-2384, fax (510) 525-7710, e-mail: info@MTSobek.com, has a 10-day "Natural History of Costa Rica" trip ($1,890). **Wilderness Travel,** 1102 Ninth St., Berkeley, CA 94710, tel. (510) 558-2488 or (800) 368-2794, fax (510) 558-2489, e-mail: info@wildernesstravel.com, has a 14-day "Costa Rica Wildlife" trip ($2,495). Also try **Eco-Travel Services,** 5699 Miles Ave., Oakland, CA 94618, tel. (510) 665-4054, fax 655-4566, e-mail: susanna.ecotravel@wonderlink.com.

For Orchid Lovers: Costa Rica Connection, has an annual Costa Rica National Orchid Show tour ($1,795 from Miami), including excursions to several national parks. Contact them at 975 Osos St., San Luis Obispo, CA 93401, tel. (805) 54-8823 or (800) 345-7422, fax (805) 543-3626, e-mail: tours@crconnect.com. **Geostar Travel** also offers both seven- and 10-day botanical trips to Costa Rica, with a special focus on orchids. Reach them at 4754 Old Redwood Hwy., Suite 650A, Santa Rosa, CA 95403, tel. (707) 579-2420 or (800) 624-6633, e-mail: mansellw@crl.com. The **Brooklyn Botanic Garden,** 1000 Washington Ave., Brooklyn, NY 11225, offers a 14-day Costa Rica trip for orchid lovers and botanists each January. Also see **Orchids** in the Introduction.

The Organization of Tropical Studies, Duke University, P.O. Box 90630, Durham, NC 27708-0630, tel. (919) 684-5774, fax 684-5661, offers annual nine-day **Rainforest Ecology Workshops** at La Selva and Tortuguero, and at Las Cruces and Corcovado ($1,840-1,999). You can book them through Preferred Adventures, One W. Water St., Suite 300, St. Paul, MN 55107, tel. (612) 222-8131 or (800) 840-8687, fax (612) 222-4221, e-mail: paltours@aol.com, and Wildlands Adventures, 3516 N.E. 155th St., Seattle, WA 98155, tel. (206) 365-0686 or (800) 345-4453, fax (206) 363-6615, e-mail: wildadve@aol.com.

British Tour Companies

The following companies offer group tours to Costa Rica from the U.K.: **Exodus Expeditions,** 9 Weir Rd., London SW12 0LT, tel. (0181) 675-5550, fax 673-0799, includes Costa Rica on its two-month overland itineraries through Central America by truck; **Explore Worldwide,** 1 Frederick St., Aldershot, Hants GU11 1LQ, tel. 01252-344161, fax 01252-343170, has budget 15-day tours taking in most of Costa Rica; **Journey Latin America,** 14-16 Devonshire Rd., Chiswick, London W4 2HD, tel. (0181) 747-3108, fax (0181) 742-1312, e-mail: tours@journeylatinamerica.com, has three-day packages, plus a 15-day birdwatcher's tour, but also specializes in airfares and trip planning; **Reef and Rainforest Tours,** 3 Moorashes, Totnes, Devon TQ9 5TH, tel. 01803-866965, fax 01803-865916; **South American Experience,** 47 Causton St., London SW1P 4AT, tel. (0171) 976-5511, fax 976-6908, offers customized itineraries plus its own tours; **Steamond Latin American Travel,** 278 Battersea Park Rd., London SW11 3BS, tel. (0171) 978-5500, fax 978-5603; **Trips,** 24 Clifton Wood Crescent, Bristol BS8 4TU, tel./fax 0272-292199, specializes in customized tours to Costa Rica, Belize, and Mexico; and **Voyages Jules Verne,** 21 Dorset Square, London NW1 6QG, tel. (0171) 723-5066, operates nine-day packages, with weekly direct flights from Gatwick airport to Costa Rica.

**Australian and
New Zealand Tour Companies**
In Australia, **Adventure Associates,** 197 Oxford St., Bondi Junction, Sydney NSW 2000, tel. 02-9389-7466, fax 02-9369-1853, e-mail: advassoc@ozemail.com.au, customizes trips to Costa Rica and offers guided trips; **Adventure Specialists,** 69 Liverpool St., Sydney, NSW 2000, tel. 02-9261-2927 or (800) 643-465, fax 02-9261-2907, offers one- to three-week adventure and nature tours; **Adventure World,** 73 Walker St., Sydney NSW 2000, tel. 02-9956-7766 or (800) 221-931, offers nature tours; **Contours,** 466 Victoria St., N. Melbourne, Victoria 3051, tel. 03-9329-5211, fax 03-9329-6314, also has adventure and nature tours; and **Surf Travel Company,** 25 Cronulla Beach, Suite 2, Sydney, tel. 02-9527-4722, offers surfing packages and customized itineraries.

In New Zealand, **Adventure World,** 101 Great South Rd., Remeura, Auckland, tel. 09-524-5118, fax 09-520-6629, and **Surf Travel Company,** 6 Danbury Dr., Torbay, Auckland, tel. 09-473-8388, have offices.

GETTING AROUND

BY AIR

Traveling by air in Costa Rica is easy and economical, a quick and comfortable alternative to often long and bumpy road travel—and a great way to nip back to San José between forays by road to other places. The government-subsidized domestic airline **SANSA,** tel. 221-9414, fax 255-2176, has inexpensive flights to points throughout Costa Rica. Flights are short—only 20-40 minutes. In 1996, SANSA replaced its aging fleet with sleek new Cessnas. However, planes are small (22-35 passengers) and sell out quickly. SANSA reservation staff reportedly often fill all the seats with people making over-the-counter bookings before honoring requests for reservations from travel agents. One-way tickets are $50 to all destinations except Barra Colorado and Tambor ($40). Book well in advance. Reservations have to be paid in full and are nonrefundable. Check in at the airport or SANSA's San José office on Paseo Colón (at Calle 24) at least an

hour before departure—it provides a free minibus transfer to Juan Santamaría Airport. SANSA baggage allowance is 11 kg (22 lbs). Delays and flight cancellations are common. And check the current schedules. *Schedules change frequently* as well as between seasons.

SANSA's rival, **Travelair,** tel. 220-3054, fax 220-0413, e-mail: airplane@sol.racsa.co.cr, flies from Tobías Bolaños Airport, near Pavas, three km west of San José. Its rates are higher than SANSA's, but unlike SANSA, you can confirm reservations without prepayment and the airline is somewhat more reliable. Baggage limit is 12 kg (25 lbs). A **Costa Rica Pass,** good for four one-way flights for $200, but two of the legs must be to Tortuguero or Quepos, is valid for 30 days from first flight.

Charters
You can charter small planes in San José from Tobías Bolaños Airport to fly you to airstrips throughout the country. Rates range from $150 per hour upward. The going rate is about $300

per hour per planeload (usually 4-6 people). Virtually everywhere is within a one-hour reach, but you'll have to pay for the return flight, too, if there are no passengers returning from your destination. Luggage space is limited.

Aero Costa Sol (c/o Costa Sol International, Apdo. 8-4390-1000 Cariari, San José, tel. 293-2151, fax 293-2155; in the U.S., tel. (800) 245-8420, fax (305) 858-7478) offers charter, ambulance, and executive flights to 23 destinations throughout Costa Rica using twin-engine five-passenger Aztecs, seven-passenger Navajos, and Lear Jets. **Aerolineas Turísticas de América,** tel. 232-1125, fax 232-5802, has charter service to almost 40 destinations throughout Costa Rica. Also try **Aeronaves de Costa Rica,** tel. 231-2541; **SAETA,** tel. 232-1474; **Aerobell Taxi,** tel. 290-000, fax 296-0460; **Taxi Aereo Centroamericano,** tel. 232-1317, fax 232-1469.

Aviones Taxi, tel. 441-1626, fax 441-2713, operates from Juan Santamaría International Airport. **Pitts Aviation,** Apdo. 1442-1250, Escazú, tel. 228-9912, fax 228-9912, e-mail: skytours@sol.racsa.co.cr, also offers charters as well as flightseeing excursions.

Flightseeing Excursions

Pitts Aviation, Apdo. 1442-1250, Escazú, tel. 228-9912, fax 228-9912, e-mail: skytours@sol.racsa.co.cr, offers a series of flightseeing excursions that include the "Dance of the Volcanoes" over the four central valley volcanoes (90 minutes; $99); "The Pirate Treasure," a 2.5-hour flight to Manuel Antonio and Corcovado ($165); "Pacific Islands" taking you across the Gulf of Nicoya (90 minutes; $99); and "Jungle Spirits," a half-day trip to Barra del Colorado and Tortuguero that includes a two-hour boat ride for wildlife viewing ($159). Passengers listen to the pilot's commentary and to New Age and classical music through stereo headphones. Binoculars are carried on board.

Helicopter: Yes, you can now get a bird's-eye view of Costa Rica by whirlybird, courtesy of **Helisa,** tel. 222-6867, fax 231-5885, based at Tobías Bolaños Airport. It offers air-taxi and charter service, as does **Servicio Nacional de Helicopteros,** tel. 232-1317, and **Helicopteros del Norte,** tel. 232-7534. **Helicopters of Costa Rica,** Apdo. 144, San José 2300, tel. 231-6564 or 232-1251 (24 hours), fax 232-5265, has flight-

seeing excursions (from $25 for a 10-minute tour of the Meseta Central to $300 for a two-hour tour of Nicoya). Air taxi and charter services are offered. **Helicopteros Turísticos,** tel. 220-3940, also offers helicopter sightseeing trips.

BY RAIL

Railway lines, originally built to serve the coffee and banana industry, run from San José to Puntarenas on the Pacific and Puerto Limón on the Caribbean. No scheduled passenger trains run along them. The train to Puntarenas stopped service in October 1991 after a locomotive was stolen and the hijacker ran it off the rails! Actually, that was just the final blow—the railroad had been running at a loss for years. And the infamous and highly popular Jungle Train to Puerto Limón—one of the world's wildest train rides—was discontinued in November 1990 after a massive landslide covered the track. Landslides during the April 1991 earthquake sealed its fate. There's been talk in recent years of an international consortium reopening the railway between Puntarenas and Puerto Limón.

Up until quite recently, you could still take part of the journey courtesy of **Swiss Travel Service,** Apdo. 7-1970-1000, San José, tel. 282-4898, fax 282-4890, which ran a day tour to Braulio Carrillo National Park, from where its private "Banana Train" ran to Siquirres. Lunch, a swimming stop, and a banana-plantation tour were included. In the same vein, **TAM Travel Co.** Apdo. 1864-1000, San José, e-mail: info@tamtravel.com, operated a "Green Train," featuring two fully restored 1930s-style carriages with air-conditioning. It followed the same route as the old Jungle Train, with a stop at Río Frío for a tour of the Dole banana plant. Neither is currently operating, but a resurrection of service is possible in the future.

Reportedly, local service on the Pacific Railroad is still offered between Salinas, Orotina, and Ciruelas, and on the Atlantic Railroad between Siquirres and Puerto Limón. A passenger train also still clunks between Limón and Estrella, a 55-km journey through banana country and a throwback to a more leisurely era. And the Pachuco Tico Tren Company may have reinstated service between Turrialba and Lake Bonilla by the time you

THE BANANA TRAIN

The defunct "Jungle Train" that ran between San José and Limón was closed in 1991 following the devastating earthquake of that year. **Swiss Travel Service** and **TAM Travel** revived a portion of the journey as the "Banana Train," taking passengers on a leisurely ride through the banana plantations near Guápiles with a visit to a banana packing plant included aboard air-conditioned vintage-1930s carriages. Then it, too, fizzled.

In 1998, plans were afoot to reintroduce the "Banana Train" once the expanded cruise terminal at Puerto Limón comes on line. Stay tuned.

read this. There's also local service from San José's Pacific Station to the western suburb of Pavas, Mon.-Fri. at 6 a.m., 12:15 p.m., and 5:15 p.m., Sunday 10 a.m. and 11:15 a.m.

The "Silver Train," a commuter train between Heredia, San José, and San Pedro had ceased operation at press time.

BY BUS

The Meseta Central is well provided with good roads and local transportation. Both diminish the farther you travel from San José, the hub for services to the rest of the nation. However, most Costa Ricans use the nation's comprehensive bus system as their daily transport, and buses generally serve even the most remote towns: generally, if there's a road there's a bus. They are almost always on time, they smooth out the potholed roads, and provide a close interaction with the Tico culture.

More popular destinations are served by both fast buses *(directo)* and slower buses *(normal* or *corriente),* which stop en route. You can travel to most parts of the country for less than $10. Some popular national parks are not included on bus schedules; take a bus as close as you can, then take a taxi.

Standards of service vary widely, from modern, ultracomfortable Volvos to smoking, run-down old-timers. Most buses serving major towns from San José are up to par with Greyhound. Farther afield, many local buses are old

U.S. high-school buses with arse-numbing seats.

Information about the bus system is fragmentary. Most bus stops are unmarked, and there are few published schedules (fewer still are reliable). The ICT information office in San José provides a relatively up-to-date (though not entirely trustworthy) fold-out bus schedule. Both *Costa Rica Today* and the *Tico Times* publish bus schedules.

Buses for Puerto Limón and the Caribbean region depart from a modern terminal—the **Gran Terminál Caribe**—on Calle Central, Avenidas 15/17. Otherwise, San José has no central terminal. Most buses leave from the Coca-Cola "terminal" (centered on Calle 16 and Avenida 1, but spread around many streets), named after the defunct Coca-Cola bottling factory. Beware pickpockets here, and avoid it at night if possible. Other buses leave from the bus company office or a streetside bus stop—*parada.* Many street departure points are unmarked: ask the locals. Buses from San José are particularly crowded on Friday and Saturday. So, too, are those returning *to* San José on Sunday and Monday.

Make reservations. Buy tickets in advance from larger bus companies (with smaller companies, you'll have to pay when getting aboard). Fare cards are posted near the driver's seat. Don't display wads of money. And *get there early* or your reservation may not be honored: at least an hour before departure for long-distance buses. Locals pack aboard until there isn't even standing room left and the rush for seats can be furious. Some buses have storage below; local buses do not. Luggage space inside is usually limited to overhead racks. Stops on normal buses are frequent—everyone seems to have a couple of boxes and perhaps a chicken or two to load aboard. Travel light. Consider leaving some luggage at your hotel in San José.

If possible, sit toward the front. Conditions on local buses can get very cramped and very hot; the back tends to be hottest. Aisle seats usually provide more leg room. Don't drink too much coffee or other liquids if you anticipate a long journey; toilet stops are few and far between. Often, the bus won't have a buzzer. To get off, whistle loudly or shout *"¡Parada!"* In the Meseta Central, bus stops are marked by yellow lines on the roadside, rectangular signs, or shelters. Elsewhere, you can usually flag down rural buses anywhere along their routes. Long-distance buses don't always stop when waved down. Locals will direct you to the correct bus stop if you ask.

Men and women relinquish their seats gladly to pregnant women, the handicapped, elderly people, and mothers with small children. Set a good example: do the same. (School children in uniform ride free, so buses are always stopping to pick up and drop off; saving the children awfully long walks between school and home.)

Tourist Buses

The tourist boom is spawning new bus shuttle services (most operated by specific tour companies) between points on the tourist circuit. **Interbus,** tel. 283-5573, fax 283-7655, e-mail: vsftrip@sol.racsa.co.cr, for example, operates daily shuttles with hotel pickups on four routes serving Manuel Antonio, Tamarindo, Fortuna, and Cahuita; see appendix.

BY CAR

Nearly half of all foreign tourists to Costa Rica rent a car. Exploring the country by car allows total freedom of movement. You can cover a lot of turf without the time delays of buses, and you can stop for sightseeing anywhere you want. The exception is San José, where a car can be a distinct liability in a setting where, says *National Geographic,* "Japanese compacts play daylong dodg'em with bullyboy buses."

Costa Rica has some 29,000 km (18,000 miles) of highway (14% paved). A two-lane "freeway" links many of the major towns in the Meseta Central (four-lane roads into San José are toll roads). Beyond San José, however, roads generally deteriorate with distance. Even much-traveled roads, such as those to Monteverde Reserve and Manuel Antonio National Park, are still not paved and can shake both a car and its occupants until their doors and teeth rattle. In the rainy season, many roads become totally flooded. Parts of the Nicoya Peninsula are often impenetrable by road during the rainy season, which does desperate damage to roads nationwide.

In 1994, the newly elected Figueres administration promised to invest one billion *colones* ($6.5 million) for road improvements nationwide,

with a large percentage dedicated to the Nicoya Peninsula. However, in 1997 construction was halted due to "irregularities" in the contractors' performance, and Figueres's promise has proved hollow. Allocated funds disappear into local pockets, and the MOPT (Ministry of Public Transport) planners—and road crews—are at times astonishingly inept—the result of their work is often as dangerous as the potholes, etc. they're supposed to be fixing! During my last research trip in late 1997 and early 1998, the roads were worse than ever (said the *Tico Times:* "The Figueres' administration's 'Zero Potholes' program could have been retitled 'Zero Potholes Filled'"). Do not underestimate the terrible condition of Costa Rica's roads.

Traffic Regulations

You must be at least 21 years old and hold a passport to drive in Costa Rica. Foreign driver's licenses are valid for three months upon arrival. For longer, you'll need a Costa Rican driver's license. Apply at Calle 5 and Avenida 18 in San José. The speed limit on highways is 80 kph (50 mph), and 60 kph on secondary roads. Speed limits are vigorously enforced on the Pan-Am Highway (Hwy. 1 between Nicaragua and San José; Hwy. 2 between San José and Panamá) and Guápiles Highway (Hwy. 32) which links San José with Puerto Limón, but rarely else-

---

TIPS FOR DRIVERS

- U.S. license plates are collectors' items—take them off and display them inside your vehicle.
- Good tires are a must, as is a sackful of spare parts.
- Make sure your car is in tip-top condition before leaving.
- Gas stations are few and far between—keep your tank topped up. Have a lock on your gas cap.
- Unleaded gas is hard to come by. Disconnect your catalytic converter.
- Be patient and obliging at customs/immigration posts.
- Never leave anything of value in your car.
- Always secure your parked vehicle with one or more anti-theft devices. Apply locking nuts to the wheels.

TRAFFIC SIGNS

NO VEHICULOS AUTOMOTORES

no motorized vehicles

18 m ANCHO MAXIMO

maximum width (number)

NO ESTACIONAR

no parking

60 KPH VELOCIDAD MAXIMA

maximum speed (number)

PARADA DE TAXIS

taxi stand

NO ADELANTAR

no passing

PEATONES POR LA IZQUIERDA

pedestrians to the left

SILENCIO

quiet

3 m ALTURA MAXIMA

maximum height (number)

NO VIRAR EN U

no U-turn

SE PERMITE VIRAR EN U

U-turn permitted

MANTENGA SU DERECHA

stay to right

CEDA EL PASO

yield

E ESTACIONAMIENTO UNA HORA 6 AM - 6 PM

parking permitted (hours)

ALTO

stop

COURTESY OF COSTA RICAN TOURIST BOARD

where. Seat belt use, alas, is no longer mandatory, but motorcyclists must wear helmets. Nonetheless, wear your seat belt! Insurance—a state monopoly—is also mandatory. Car rental companies sell insurance with rentals.

Note, too, that regulations make it illegal to 1) enter an intersection unless you can exit; 2) make a right turn on a red light unless indicated by a white arrow; and 3) overtake on the right—you may pass only on the left. Cars coming uphill have the right of way.

If you see a speed sign ahead, it's a good idea to slow down immediately. I once got a speeding ticket for exceeding 50 kph as I *approached* a 50 kph zone; the officer was standing by the sign, pointing his radar gun at traffic still in the 70 kph zone! He wanted me to pay a fine on the spot for his crafty subterfuge—an illegal act that you should *never* fall for.

Driving Safety

Costa Rica has one of the world's highest auto fatality rates—18 deaths per 100,000 km, compared to 2.7 per 100,000 km in the U.S. A sizeable share of Costa Ricans are appalling drivers capable of truly unbelievable recklessness. They drive at warp speed, flaunt traffic laws, hold traffic lights in total disdain, and love to crawl up your tailpipe at 100 kph. Worse, Ticos overtake at the slightest chance—Tico males live in a macho society and feel the need to assuage their feelings of inadequacy through displays of bravado. Too many Ticos can't stand the sight of a car in front of them. They will overtake on blind corners and narrow overhangs, so beep your horn before sharp bends. And keep your speed down, especially on rural roads, with their potholes from hell. Roads usually lack sidewalks, so pedestrians—and even livestock—walk the road. Be particularly wary at night. And treat mountain roads with extra caution: they're often blocked by thick fog, floods, and landslides. The two roads from San José to Puntarenas, the road linking San José to Guápiles, and the long and winding road between Cartago and San Isidro de El General are particularly bad: steep, fog-ridden, narrow, and as serpentine as coiled snakes. Still, that doesn't faze local drivers, who even in the worst conditions drive with an almost feline disdain for mortality.

Watch out for piles of leaves or boulders at the roadside—they indicate a stalled car ahead. Check old wooden bridges before crossing: you may need to go around if tire tracks lead into the watercourse. Narrow bridges *(puente angosto),* which usually accommodate only one vehicle at a time, are first-come, first-served. And slow down whenever you see the sign *topes* or *túmulos,* meaning "road bumps." The first time you barrel over them heedlessly will serve notice to respect the warning next time.

Potholes are a particular problem. "Hit a big one," says Bill Baker in *The Essential Road Guide for Costa Rica,* "and it's not unusual to damage a tire or even destroy a wheel. . . . Nor is it unusual to have a driver suddenly swerve to avoid one just as you're passing him." Beware buses, too. They'll often stop without warning. Drive slowly. And give everyone else on the road lots of room.

Another good tip is to drive with your lights on at *all times,* as they do by law in Scandinavia (where vehicular accidents have been significantly reduced as a consequence). Oncoming drivers will flash their lights at you in response, even in gloomy conditions, but so what: they've acknowledged your presence!

Accidents and Breakdowns

The law states that you must carry fluorescent triangles in case of breakdown. Locals, however, are more likely to make a pile of leaves, rocks, or small branches at the roadside to warn approaching drivers of a car in trouble. If your own car is involved, **Coopetaxi Garage,** tel. 235-9966, in San José, is recommended for towing and repair. If your car is rented, call the rental agency: it will arrange a tow.

After an accident, *never* move the vehicles until the police arrive. Get the names, license plate numbers, and *cedulas* (legal identification numbers) of any witnesses. Make a sketch of the accident. And call the **traffic police** *(tráfico),* tel. 222-9330 or 222-9245.

Do *not* offer statements to anyone other than the police. In case of injury, call the **Red Cross ambulance,** tel. 128 or 221-5818. Outside towns, call 911 for **emergency rescue.** Try not to leave the accident scene, or at least keep an eye on your car: the other party may tamper with the evidence. And don't let honking traffic—there'll be plenty!—pressure you into moving the cars.

Show the *tráfico* your license and vehicle registration. Make sure you get them back: he is not allowed to keep any documents unless you've been drinking (if you suspect the other driver has been drinking, ask the *tráfico* to administer a Breathalyzer test, or *alcolemia*). Nor can the *tráfico* assess a fine. The police will issue you a green ticket or "summons." You must present this to the nearest municipal office *(alcaldia)* or **traffic court** *(tribunal de tránsito)* within eight days to make your *declaración* about the accident. Wait a few days so that the police report is on record. Don't skip this! The driver who doesn't show is often found at blame by default. Then, take your driver's license, insurance policy, and a police report to the **INS,** the state insurance monopoly in San José, Avenida 7, Calles 9/11, tel. (800) 800-8000 or 223-5800, to process your claim. Car rental companies will take care of this if your car is rented.

Car Rentals

The leading U.S. car rental companies have offices in Costa Rica. You also have a wide choice of local rental companies (many reputable, many not), usually with slightly cheaper rates. I highly recommend **Prego Rent-a-Car,** tel. 221-8680, fax 221-8675, e-mail: pregomot@sol.racsa.co.cr, based on my own experiences and that of readers. Their staff have proved consistently professional, trustworthy, and gracious, and their vehicles have always been in good repair. I have yet to hear any complaints.

Most agencies are in San José, usually west of downtown. Some have offices at Juan Santamaría Airport and/or representatives at major hotels in more popular resort towns. Minimum age for drivers ranges 21-25. You'll need a valid driver's license plus a credit card. Without a credit card you'll have to pay a hefty deposit, normally around $700.

The government fixes a ceiling on rental rates. Most agencies charge the maximum during the high season (Nov.-April) and offer discounts during the low season (May-Oct.). You'll normally get better rates (up to 10% discount) by making your reservations in the U.S. at least one week before departure, though I've heard several reports of extra charges appearing and other

complications. Always leave one person with the car when you return it to the car rental office, especially if unforeseen billing problems arise (there are numerous examples of renters having their belongings stolen from the vehicle while their attention is distracted).

Reserve as far in advance as possible, especially in dry season and for Christmas and holidays. Make sure you clarify any one-way drop-off fees, late return penalties, etc. Take a copy of your reservation with you. And be prepared to defend against mysterious new charges that may be tagged on in Costa Rica (for example, I've heard reports of companies charging for a new tire after renters have had a flat tire fixed; you won't know about it until your credit card bill arrives). You must rent for a minimum of three days to qualify for unlimited mileage. Stick shift is the norm. Some agencies will rent camping and surfing equipment, too.

Rates: Small cars such as the Subaru Justy, Nissan 1300, or Toyota Starlet begin at about $30 daily/$200 weekly plus 21 cents per kilometer, or $38 daily/$228 weekly with unlimited mileage. **Economy** cars such as the Nissan Sentra and Toyota Tercel begin at around $35 daily/$225 weekly plus 29 cents per kilometer, or $42 daily/$252 weekly with unlimited mileage. **Mid-Size** cars such as the Toyota Corolla cost about $49 daily/$295 weekly with unlimited mileage. It behooves you to get unlimited mileage if you plan on driving more than 500 km per week.

Listen Up: Regardless of where you plan to go, forget about sedans and rent a 4WD! If you don't you'll regret it the first time you hit one of Costa Rica's gargantuan potholes or infuriating corrugations.

Four-Wheel Drive Vehicles: Most agencies offer a range of small-size to full-size 4WD vehicles. Four-wheel drives are essential for Nicoya and other off-the-beaten-path destinations. In fact, I recommend them, *period.* Some agencies will insist you rent a 4WD for specific regions, especially in rainy season. Fortunately, you may get an off-season discount then. The smaller models (Suzuki Sidekick, Samurai, etc.) begin at about $60 daily/$360 weekly with unlimited mileage and insurance. Rates rise to about $540 per week for larger models. The smaller 4WDs may be too lightweight for most rugged conditions, especially in wet season, although—believe me—I've put such little 'uns through hell without undue difficulty. If you intend exploring off the beaten track in wet season with complete assurance, a lightweight vehicle won't do. I strongly recommend a heavy-duty 4WD, such as a Toyota Land Cruiser, Nissan Pathfinder, or Isuzu Trooper—perfect for families. If you're alone or there are two of you, but with a minimum of luggage, consider the Suzuki X-90, a tiny but cozy 4WD with a pop-off roof, soft suspension, and a surprisingly sporty engine (it has far more "get up and go" than the Samurai or Sidekick, which also have detestable springing). The best medium-size 4WD is the Toyota Rav-4—a superb vehicle!

Most car rental companies offers a range of 4WD rentals, including family-size behemoths. Companies that specialize in these are **Jeeps R Us,** tel. 289-9920, and **Tricolor Rent-a-Car,** tel. 222-3333 or (800) 949-0234, fax 221-4444, which also offers a series of "4x4 Tours."

I've heard complaints regarding U-Haul Rent-a-Car (which is *not* affiliated with the U.S. company of that name) and numerous complaints about **Rent-a-Rover,** Apdo. 77, Paraíso de Cartago, tel./fax 533-3037, which rents 1970s-model Range Rovers for about $500 a week, including unlimited mileage. The vehicles are more than a decade old and although rebuilt and completely reupholstered, reliability is clearly an issue. The company provides a specialized technician on call 24 hours, as proved true in my case when my vehicle broke down.

Several companies offer 4WD tours. **Southern Horizons Travel,** 5315 Laurel Canyon Blvd. #210, Valley Village, CA 91607, tel. (818) 980-7011, fax 980-6987, e-mail: tripman@delphi.com, offers an eight-day 4WD package. **Costa Rica Experts,** 3166 N. Lincoln Ave. #424, Chicago, IL 60657, tel. (312) 935-1009 or (800) 827-9046, fax (312) 935-9252, e-mail: crexpert@ris.net, and **Costa Rica Temptations,** Apdo. 1199-1200, San José, tel. 220-4437, fax 220-2792, e-mail: crtinfo@sol.racsa.co.cr, have a 24-day 4WD tour following the "Route of Biodiversity" to remote national parks.

Fly-Drive Packages
Consider a pre-arranged package such as **Costa Rica Experts'** "Flexipak," which includes round-trip airfare from Miami, seven nights' accommodations, and choice of vehicle with unlimited mileage (from $715 double, pp). You can contact them at 3166 N. Lincoln Ave. #424, Chicago, IL 60657, tel. (312) 935-1009 or (800) 827-9046, fax (312) 935-9252, e-mail: crexpert@ris.net. **Adventure Vacations,** 10612 Beaver Dam Rd., Hunt Valley, MD 21030-2205, tel. (800) 638-9040, also offers a fly/drive program with two itineraries from $625 pp, double occupancy, including airport transfers, upscale accommodations, and car rental.

Escapes Ecológicos, Apdo. 531-2200 San José, tel. 257-7010, fax 257-7012, e-mail: escapes@ecologicos.lcr.co.cr, has an "open voucher" package that includes hotel, breakfast, and car rental (choice of Nissan Sentra or Suzuki Sidekick 4WD). Choose from six-, seven-, or 15-night packages. You must pre-book your first night's accommodations, after which you receive vouchers good for any of 22 hotels throughout Costa Rica. Just show up or reserve 24 hours ahead (rooms are subject to availability). Two children under 12 pay only for breakfast.

Camino Travel, Apdo. 1049-2050 San Pedro, tel. 234-2530, fax 225-6143, e-mail: caimotr@sol.racsa.co.cr, also has an "open voucher" using 40 hotels ($420 s/d per week low season, $504 high season plus $38-59 daily car rental depending on vehicle type).

The *Tico Times* and *Costa Rica Today* advertise private car rentals and guide services in the classified sections.

Recreational Vehicles
Siesta Campers, c/o Escazú Travel Service, tel. 228-4850, fax 228-4824, e-mail: siesta@sol.racsa.co.cr; in the U.S., 2271 W. 237 St., Torrance, CA 90501, tel. (310) 530-3737, offers fully equipped VW Westfalia campers with pop-top roofs ($450 weekly two-person camper; $500 four-person low season; $500 and $550 high season). **VW Campers,** tel. 232-7532 or 231-5905, has vehicles from $320 weekly.

ATA Motor Home Rentals, tel. 288-2011; in the U.S., c/o Dockside Tours, tel. (800) 235-3625, offers rentals with tax and insurance included. Prices based on two people begin at about $415 ($30 per day each additional person) for three days, and $895 seven days ($25 per day each additional person).

Motorcycles
Dirt Rider Rent-a-Moto, Apdo. 413-1007, San José, tel. 257-3831, fax 221-3509, rents Honda XL250s. **Motorcycles Costa Rica,** tel./fax 446-5015; in the U.S. tel. (540) 489-9181, fax 228-6557, rents Honda XR200s, 250s, 600s, and 650Ls and Suzuki 650s ($45-90 daily).

Fancy a Hog? **María Alexandra Tours,** Apdo. 3756-1000 San José, tel. 228-9072, fax 289-5192, e-mail: matour@sol.racsa.co.cr, rents Harley-Davidsons. A valid motorcycle license is required, and you must be 25 years old. The XL883 Sportster rents for $80 daily; $480 weekly; a XL1200 Sportster costs $100 daily, $600 weekly; a FXD Dyna SuperGlide costs $140 daily, $840 weekly. A $800-1,400 deposit is required.

Prego Rent-a-Motorcycle, tel. 265-1400, fax 257-1158, rents Honda XL125 trail bikes from $25 daily and Honda 200 Fourtrax from $35. **Moto Rental S.A.,** tel. 257-0193, has Honda XR200 motorcycles and Suzuki TS185s.

Insurance
Many rates quoted by rental agencies include insurance. However, if you make a reservation through a rental agency abroad and are told the rate includes insurance, or that one of your existing policies—such as American Express auto-rental insurance—will cover it, don't believe it! Once your arrive in Costa Rica, you may find that you have to pay the *mandatory* insurance fee. Check carefully. Because auto insurance is mandatory in Costa Rica, you will need to accept the obligatory C.D.W. (collision damage waiver) charged by car rental companies. It does not cover your car's contents or personal possessions, nor a deductible. Each company determines its own deductible—ranging $500-1,000—even though the INS sets this at 20% of damages. Rates are generally $12.50 per day.

Inspect your vehicle for damage and marks before departing, otherwise you may be charged for the slightest "damage" when you return. Note even the smallest nick and dent on the diagram you'll be presented to sign. And don't forget the inside, as well as the radio antenna. Heaters and defrosters often don't work (you'll need to bring a rag for your frequently steamed-up windows).

Note: *Don't* use your a/c to clear up condensation as it cools the windows and actually fosters condensation. Don't assume the rental

agency has taken care of oil, water, brakes, fluids, or tire pressures: check them yourself before setting off. Most agencies claim to provide a 24-hour road service.

Gasoline
Unleaded gasoline is called Super and is widely available (many rental cars take regular, although all cars imported to Costa Rica beginning 1 January 1995, had to use unleaded gas). Service stations *(bombas* or *gasolineras)* are far apart. Many are open 24 hours; in rural areas they're usually open dawn to dusk only. It's a wise idea to always fill up whenever you pass a service station. Gasoline cost 50 cents a liter ($1.90 a gallon). Expect to pay double at off-the-beaten-track spots where gasoline may be poured from a jerry-can. In the boondocks, there's sure to be someone nearby selling from their backyard stock.

Always stand next to the guy filling up your gas tank. There are several reports of attendants giving you cheap diesel or—*yikes!*—even water when you're not looking, then pocketing the profit.

Maps and Directions
The past few years have seen signposts erected in major cities and along major highways (I tip my hat to the Figueres administration), but don't count on a sign being there when you need it. Many signs are located where you'd never think of looking, or are otherwise obscured. Others lead you off on the longest route simply because they were placed by folks who want to direct tourists past their sundry business establishments. And many of the street signs point the wrong way (they were placed by crews who hadn't the foggiest idea which street was a Calle and which an Avenida; after all, they live in a society that uses landmarks, not street names).

Ask directions when in doubt. And check with locals about conditions down the road. Costa Ricans tend to be optimistic about whether roads are passable in excessive rain and fog, so double-check with foreigners if possible. Roadside ads for Delta cigarettes also include brief directions to major destinations.

You'll need the best map you can obtain. The **ICT** tourist information office has a basic road map, as do car rental agencies. They're accurate for San José and major cities, but are not much use for general touring. **World Wide Books And Maps,** 736A Granville St., Vancouver, B.C., Canada V6Z 1G3, tel. (604) 687-3320, fax 687-5925, sells the best map: the *International Travel Map of Costa Rica* (scale 1:500,000), showing minor roads and service stations. I recommend also buying a copy of the *Red Guide to Costa Rica* and/or the *Costa Rica Nature Atlas-Guidebook,* which have detailed 1:200,000 road maps; they're not always accurate, but they're the best around. (See the **San José** chapter for bookstores with map sections.)

Consider buying a copy of Bill Baker's *Essential Road Guide to Costa Rica.* An alternative is audiocassettes for the independent traveler produced by **Audio Turismo de Costa Rica,** Apdo. 1214, San José, tel. 233-8751; in the U.S., Interlink #217, P.O. Box 526770, Miami, FL 33152. It offers three tapes: one describes a self-drive tour from San José to Atenas, Orotina, Jacó, Parrita, Quepos, Manuel Antonio, and Dominical; another covers San José to Monteverde via Grecia and Sarchí; a third leads via Grecia and Sarchí to the beaches of Guanacaste. They give specific driving directions, plus driving tips, side trips, information on national parks, etc. en route. Each tape comes with a map of the route. Available in hotel gift stores ($15 each).

Traffic Police

Traffic police patrol the highways to control speeding drivers. They pull people over at random to check documentation. In the past they've been fond of rental cars (the TUR on rental car license plates gives the game away) in the hope of extorting bribes, but I've heard few reports in recent years of this occurring.

If you're stopped, the police will request to see your license, passport, and rental contract. *Tráficos* use radar guns and you will get no special treatment as a tourist if you're caught speeding. Speeding fines are paid at a bank; the ticket provides instructions. Don't think you can get away with not paying a fine. Delinquent fines are reported to the immigration authorities and people have been refused exit from the country (reportedly, police also have the right to take your license away until you pay the fine). Normally, the car rental agency will handle the tickets, although you remain responsible for pay-

ing the fine. The best way of avoiding this hassle, of course, is not to speed.

It's important to know your rights and respond accordingly. *Never* pay a fine to police on the road. The police cannot legally request payment on site. If he (I've never seen a female traffic cop) demands payment, note the policeman's name and number from his MOPT badge (he is legally required to show his *carnet* upon request). Report the incident to the Asesoría Legal de Tránsito of MOPT in San José, Calle 2, Avenida 20, tel. 227-2188 or 257-7798.

Traffic police cars and pickups are usually dark blue with white tops and doors (older), or light metallic blue (newer). Oncoming vehicles will often flash their lights at you to warn you of traffic police—or an accident or disabled vehicle—ahead.

HITCHHIKING

Hitchhiking is reasonably safe and straightforward, though it may be slow going; if buses don't go where you're going, cars aren't much more likely to. Ticos are used to picking up pedestrians in areas where bus service is infrequent, and locals often hitchhike in more remote regions. They'll also unabashedly ask you for a ride. However, simply sticking out your thumb won't do the trick; instead, try to wave down the car. Politely ask if there's room, as you've "been waiting for ages for a bus," etc. Politeness and gratitude, too, demand you offer to pay for your ride *("¿Cuanto le debo?")* after you're safely delivered.

Generally, Ticos are immensely civil and trustworthy and will go out of their way to help out of goodwill. Still, caution is always a watchword when hitchhiking, especially for women. I do not recommend that women hitchhike alone. Try to "get the measure" of the driver *before* getting in a car. If you feel uncomfortable, don't get in.

TAXIS

Costa Rica has an excellent nationwide taxi system. Taxis are inexpensive by U.S. standards, so much so that they are a viable means of touring for short trips, especially if you're traveling with two or three others. Generally, taxis will go wherever a road leads. Most taxis are radio dispatched. A white triangle on the front door contains the taxi's license plate number.

You can hire a taxi by the hour or half day; the cost normally compares favorably to hiring a car for the day. Many national parks are served infrequently by bus, or not at all; hence you may be inclined to take a taxi, for example, to Poás Volcano (110 km roundtrip), which should cost about $50 with perhaps two hours at the volcano. Jeep-taxis are common in more remote areas, particularly the Nicoya Peninsula.

Agree on the fare *before* setting off, as taxi drivers are notorious for overcharging. Don't be afraid to bargain. How you dress might make a difference: the more downbeat you dress the less likely it is that you'll receive an inflated price. Outside San José, few taxis are metered and taxi drivers are allowed to negotiate their fare for any journey over 15 kilometers.

Taxi drivers are required by law to use their meters *(marías)*. In San José, however, drivers rarely use them (many will do so in the morning; the later it gets, the less they like to do so). Insist on it being used. If there isn't one, agree on the rate before getting in the taxi. Check rates in advance with your hotel concierge. Official rates in 1997 were: 100 *colones* (60 cents) for the first kilometer, 45 *colones* (about 25 cents) each kilometer thereafter. Nighttime fares cost 20% more. Journeys longer than 12 km, or on unpaved roads outside San José, are charged at a previously agreed amount. Fares quoted by taxi drivers who don't use their meters tend to be inflated 20-30%. Consider getting out if after a few blocks the meter doesn't start advancing; taxi drivers are now being fined, so your ruse may work.

Outside San José, you'll usually find taxis around the main square of small towns. Here, you'll be dependent on taxis after, say, 10 p.m., about the time most rural buses stop running. Few taxis outside San José have *marías*. You'll get a better deal if you speak Spanish and know local customs. You do not tip taxi drivers.

FERRIES

On the Pacific, three ferries link the Nicoya Peninsula with mainland Guanacaste. Car/passenger ferres link Puntarenas to both Playa Naranjo and Paquera, on the southeastern corner of the Nicoya Peninsula. Farther north, the Tempisque Ferry crosses the Gulf of Nicoya from the mouth of the Tempisque River. Water-taxis also operate between key destinations on the Pacific coast.

ORGANIZED TOURS

The Costa Rican tour industry has grown rapidly in the past decade or so. In 1973 there were just 10 licensed tour and travel agencies in Costa Rica; in July 1997, there were almost 300! They're a close-knit, supportive, and thoroughly professional community. Many North American-based tour companies use the services of Costa Rican-based operators, or book their own clients into the latter's tour packages. The leading operators offer a complete range of tour options, including one-day and overnight excursions to all the major points of attraction. English-speaking guides, private transportation, meals, and accommodations are standard inclusions. This gives you the added flexibility of making your own tour arrangements once you've arrived in Costa Rica and have gained a better sense of your options and desires.

Many hotels in San José have tour information desks, where you can make inquiries and reservations. Most tours and excursions pick up group tour members at the major hotels, and drop them either at their hotels or outside the Gran Hotel in Plaza de la Cultura. On most day-trips, lunch is included; on longer trips, meals, accommodations, and any equipment are included as part of the package.

See the chart **Costa Rican Tour Companies** in the appendix for recommended Costa Rican tour operators. The **Asociación Costarricense de Operadores de Turismo** (Costa Rican Association of Tour Operators), Apdo. 1628, San Pedro de Montes de Oca 2050, tel./fax 250-5878, can provide a complete list and additional details.

Several private individuals offer tour services. One who is recommended by a reader is "Chepe" José Morales Corrales, tel./fax 442-1184, a Tico whose driving is "even-tempered." He offers excursions by bus to various spots. Most of his passengers are Tico families—a great opportunity to interact with locals. Chepe speaks only Spanish; his wife speaks English. They'll fax you a monthly schedule.

Natural History Trips

Costa Rica is replete with tour operators offering natural history programs to suit every interest, and the nation boasts scores of bilingual naturalist guides (Costa Rica has more American field biologists than anywhere else in the world). Professional guides generally know where the wildlife is at any given moment; they have an uncanny ability to identify the most well-camouflaged birds and beasts. Most nature tours are from one to four days; one-day tours typically cost $40-85, including lunch.

Costa Rica Expeditions (CRE), Apdo. 6941-1000, San José, tel. 257-0766, fax 257-1665, e-mail: crexped@sol.racsa.co.cr, has a complete range of natural history tour packages to destinations throughout Costa Rica. In addition to guided tours offered daily to eight prime forest habitats, the company offers specialist natural history and birding trips from its acclaimed Monteverde Lodge and Tortuga Lodge. CRE also offers "Women in Conservation," featuring field workshops to nature reserves such as Ostional, Monteverde, and Gandoca-Manzanillo Wildlife Refuge; trips are led by prominent female conservationists.

Horizontes, Apdo. 1780-1002, San José, tel. 222-2022, fax 255-4513, e-mail: horizont@sol.racsa.co.cr, has a wide range of tour options at nature lodges nationwide, including various cloud forest habitats, plus horseback riding and rafting; its brochure includes a handy "Key to Adventure" chart showing which programs highlight birdwatching, and other special activities.

Fantasía Ecológica, Apdo. 1500, San José 1002, tel. 220-2515, fax 222-3216, offers three- to 14-day ecological study tours in association with the International University of the Americas, with lectures provided by university faculty, who also act as guides.

The "Route of Biodiversity" is a 24-night comprehensive off-the-beaten-path tour to a variety of ecosystems, many quite remote, with travel by 4WD. It's the brainchild of **Costa Rica Temptations**, which divides the Route into regional sec-

tions; you can choose certain sections according to interest and schedule (in the U.S., contact **Costa Rica Experts**). The ratio of participants to guides is never more than six per guide. Lecturers accompany the tour. Cost is approximately $190 per day, all-inclusive.

Cultural Trips

Several local tour operators offer trips focusing on Costa Rican culture, particularly in Guanacaste. For example, **Papagayo Excursiones**, Apdo. 162, Santa Cruz, tel. 653-0227, fax 653-0254, e-mail: papagayo@sol.racsa.co.cr, has a "Typical Fiestas of Costa Rica" tour on weekends at 3 p.m. ($25). And **Caña Dulce**, tel. 258-3535, fax 222-0201, e-mail: canadulc@sol.racsa.co.cr, is a tour agency dedicated to cultural tourism, such as trips to local fiestas and immersion in the Caribbean culture.

Global Exchange, 2017 Mission St. #303, San Francisco, CA 94103, tel. (415) 255-7296, offers "Global Reality Tours" that provide an educational focus on local cultures, peering beneath the touristic veneer to appreciate often neglected aspects of real life for Costa Ricans.

VNA Humanitarian Tours, Gail Nystrom, Apdo. 458, Santa Ana Centro, tel. 282-7368, provides opportunities to explore the often troubling downside of Costa Rica, with day-trips to a women's prison, an orphanage, a girls' shelter, a boys' detention center, and a children's hospital. Longer, multiday trips include visits to indigenous people's reserves and even a street kids' project in Puerto Limón. Company owner Gail Nystrom also runs an annual Eco-Camp for children aimed at enriching the youngsters' perspectives and appreciation of Costa Rica's indigenous peoples.

Vantage Adventures, P.O. Box 5774, Greensboro, SC 29661, tel. (800) 826-8268, fax (803) 233-3864, offers an eight-day package with five days of "tropical gourmet" cooking classes hosted by Maria Batalla, a member of the prestigious Chaine des Rotisseurs (from $1,409).

Costa Rica Rainbow Connection, Apdo. 7323, San José 1000, tel./fax 240-7325, offers an "11-day journey through the wonders and wisdom of magical Costa Rica," focusing on healing arts, meditation, and more.

IMMIGRATION AND CUSTOMS

DOCUMENTS AND REQUIREMENTS

Tourist Cards, Passports, and Visas

Citizens of the following countries may enter Costa Rica for up to 90 days *without* a visa (a passport *is* required): Argentina, Austria, Canada, Colombia, Denmark, Finland, Germany, Israel, Italy, Japan, Luxembourg, Netherlands, Norway, Panamá, Romania, South Korea, Spain, United Kingdom, United States, and Yugoslavia. In addition, citizens of Canada, the U.S., and Panamá do not need a passport for stays of less than 30 days (you *do* need identification, however, such as driver's license or birth certificate); a passport is required for longer stays.

Citizens of the following countries may enter Costa Rica for up to **30 days** *without* a visa (a passport *is* required): Australia, Belgium, Brazil, Ecuador, Guatemala, Honduras, Iceland, Ireland (Eire), Liechtenstein, Mexico, Monaco, New Zealand, Sweden, Switzerland, Vatican, Venezuela.

Citizens of the following countries may enter Costa Rica for up to 30 days *with* a passport and a visa ($20), obtainable through any Costa Rican consulate: Andorra, Barbados, Belize, Bermuda, Bolivia, Chile, Cyprus, Dominican Republic, Grenada, Greece, Grenadines, Guadalupe, Guyana, Haiti, Jamaica, Malta, Martinique, Morocco, Paraguay, Peru, San Marino, St. Lucia, St. Vincent, Saudi Arabia, Surinam, Taiwan, Trinidad and Tobago, Uruguay.

Citizens of all other countries may be allowed entry into Costa Rica on a restricted visa subject to approval by a Costa Rican consulate (passports are required). This includes nationals of Cuba, former Soviet republics, and other countries with extremist governments.

Tourist cards (free) are issued during your flight or at the immigration desk upon arrival, or may be obtained in advance ($5) through any Costa Rican embassy or consulate. The card can be renewed monthly for up to three months from the immigration office in San José in the Irazemi Bldg. on Calle 21 and Avenidas 6/8 (open 8:30 a.m.-3:30 p.m. weekdays), but since this can be a time-consuming hassle, it's one more reason to take your passport. British citizens need a 10-year passport (a visitor's passport is insufficient); no visa is required.

The law requires that you carry your passport or tourist card with you at all times during your stay. It's a good idea in any case to make photocopies of all documentation and to keep them with you, separate from the originals.

Legal entry requirements often change, so contact your travel agent or the Costa Rican Tourism Institute or consulate before you leave home.

Visa Extensions

Extending your stay beyond the authorized time is like entering the Minotaur's maze. Anticipate bureaucratic headaches and a heavy toll on your time and patience. Permission to extend your 30- or 90-day stay *(prórroga de turismo)* must be requested from the immigration office (Migración) in the Irazemi Bldg. on Calle 21 and Avenidas 6/8, open 8:30 a.m.-3:30 p.m. weekdays, which may also require you to obtain an affidavit from the Justice Tribunal, Calle 17, Avenidas 6/8, stating that you have no dependents in Costa Rica. If they're busy, you could wait all day. Check first with a reputable local travel agent or tour operator: they can usually obtain what you need for a small fee. Be sure to begin the process *before* your 30 or 90 days are up. Since you'll need to allow three days minimum—plus an additional four days or more if you are asked to submit to a blood test for AIDS—it may be just as easy to travel to Nicaragua or Panamá for 72 hours and then reenter with a new visa or tourist card.

The following are required with your application for an extension via the immigration office: three passport-size photos, a ticket out of the country, and adequate funds in cash or traveler's checks. The processing fee is approximately $1.50 (revenue stamps to attach to your application are available outside the immigration office at a booth on Calle 21), plus $12 for the visa if you leave by air, $30 if you leave by land.

Note that the government began deporting foreigners who had been caught after staying

COSTA RICAN EMBASSIES AND CONSULATES ABROAD

UNITED STATES OF AMERICA

Embassy
2112 S Street NW, Washington, D.C. 20008, tel. (202) 234-2945, fax 234-2946

Consulates
Chicago, tel. (312) 263-2772

Denver, tel. (303) 377-0050, fax 777-5864

Houston, tel. (713) 266-0484, fax 974-6059

Los Angeles, tel. (213) 380-7915, fax 384-1245

Miami, tel.(305) 871-7485, fax 871-0860

Orlando, tel. (407) 422-4544, fax 422-5220

San Francisco, tel. (415) 392-8488, fax 647-4082

ELSEWHERE

Argentina: Ave. Callao 1103, CP 2023 Capital Federal, Buenos Aires, tel. (54) 1-814-1660, fax 1-815-8159

Austria: Scholeglasse 10/2, A-1120 Vienna, tel. (43) 1-804-0537, fax 1-804-9071

Belgium: 489 Ave. Louise, Boite 13, 1050 Brussels, tel. (32) 2-640-5541, fax 2-648-3192

Belize: 60 Ave. Orange St., Belmopan, Belize, tel. (501) 23801, fax 23805

Brazil: SHLS-QL10, Conjunto 4 casa 3, CEP 71-630-045, Lago Sur, Brasilia, tel. (55) 61-248-7656, fax 61-248-6234

Canada: 135 York St., Suite 208, Ottawa, Ont. K1N 5TA, tel. (613) 562-2855, fax 562-2582

Chile: Calle La Concepción #65, Oficinia 801, Providencia, Santiago, tel. (56) 2-235-1869, fax 2-236-1099

Colombia: Carrera 15 #102-25, Apdo. Aéreo 94795, Bogotá, tel. (57) 1-622-8830, fax 1-623-0205

Ecuador: Calle Rumipamba 692, Quito, tel. (59) 32-254-945, fax 32-254-087

El Salvador: Ave. Albert Einstein 11-A, Lomas de San Francisco, San Salvador, tel. (503) 273-3111, fax 273-1455

France: 79 Ave. Emile Zola, 75015 Paris, tel. (33) 1-45-78-96-96, fax 1-45-78-99-66

Germany: Langenbachstrasse 19, 53113 Bonn, tel. (49) 228-54-0040, fax 228-54-9053

Guatemala: Edif. Galerías Reforma 9 #902, La Reforma 8-60, Zona 9 Guatemala, tel. (502) 2-331-9604, fax 2-332-1522

Honduras: Colonia El Triángulo, Tegucigalpa, tel. (504) 321-768, fax 321-876

Israel: Rehov Deskin 13 #1, Jerusalem 91012, tel. (972) 2-566-6197, fax 2-563-2591

Italy: Via Bartolomeo Eustacho 22, Interno 6, Rome 00161, tel. (39) 6-4425-1046, fax 6-4425-1048

Japan: Kowa Bldg. #38, Nishi-Azuba 4, Chome Minato-ku, Tokyo, tel. (81) 3-3486-1812, fax 3-3486-1813

Mexico: Calle Río Poo #113, Colonia Cuactemoc, Mexico D.F., tel. (525) 525-7765, fax 511-9240

Netherlands: Statenlaan 28, 2582 GM DEW HAAG, The Hague, tel. (31) 70-354-0780, fax 70-358-4754

Nicaragua: Callejón Zelaya (two blocks north and one block east of the La Estatua de Montoya), Managua, tel. (505) 2-66-2404, fax 2-66-3955

Norway: Skippergaten 33, 0154 Oslo, tel. (47) 22-425823, fax 22-330408

Panamá: Edif. Miraflores, Calle Gilberto Ortega 51-B, Panamá, tel. (507) 264-2980, fax 2644057

Peru: Emilio Cavenecia, 175 Oficina 7-8-9, San Isidro, Lima, tel./fax (511) 4-409-982

Russia: Rublovshoe Shosse #26, Kv.23 Moscow, tel. (70) 95-415-4014, fax 95-415-4042

Spain: Paseo de la Castellana 164 #17-A, 28046 Madrid, tel. (34) 1-345-9622, fax 1-345-6807

Switzerland: Thunstrasse 150E, 3074 Muri, Bern, tel. (41) 31-952-6230, fax 31-952-6457

United Kingdom: Flat 1, 14 Lancaster Gate, London W2 3LH, tel. (44) 171-706-8844, fax 171-706-8655

Uruguay: Calle de Correos 12242, Montevideo, tel. (598) 2-783645, fax 2-718126

Venezuela: Edif. Davada Palace PH, Ave. San Juan Bosco, Transversal Altamira, Caracas, tel. (58) 2-267-1104, fax 2-265-4660

in the country indefinitely. Deportation means you're not allowed back in for 10 years!

You no longer need to show documentary proof that you owe no taxes, haven't sired or given birth to a child, and don't owe child support. Check to ensure these requirements have not been reintroduced. If the immigration authorities request that you submit to an AIDS test, the Ministerio de Salud, Ministry of Health, Calle 16

and Avenidas 6/8, can oblige. Exit visas take 48 hours or more to process.

Don't overstay your 30- or 90-day entry terms without obtaining an extension, as you will quite possibly end up at Migración anyway. Although the fine is small ($6 for each month or part of a month extra), you will not be allowed to leave without first obtaining an exit visa ($50), which means a trip back to the immigration office, plus

EMBASSIES AND CONSULATES IN COSTA RICA

The following nations have embassies/consulates in San José. Note, however, that phone numbers and addresses change frequently; check the phone book under "Embajadas" and "Consulados" to confirm addresses and numbers, and for additional embassies and consulates not listed below.

Argentina: Avenida 6, Calles 21/23, tel. 221-3438

Austria: Avenida 4, Calles 36/38, tel. 255-3007

Belgium: Calle 39, Avenidas Central/2, tel. 225-6255 or 225-0484

Belize: 400 meters east of Iglesia Santa Teresita, Barrio Escalante, tel. 234-9969, fax 222-6184

Bolivia: Avenida 2, Calles 2/4, tel. 255-1805

Brazil: Paseo Colón, Calles 20/22, tel. 257-5484 or 233-1544, fax 223-4325

Canada: Oficentro Ejecutivo La Sabana, Edificio 5, Sabana Sur (behind La Contraloria), tel. 296-4149, fax 296-4270

Chile: Barrio Dent, tel. 225-0413

China, Republic of (Taiwan): San Pedro, tel. 234-9959

Colombia: Calles Los Negritos, tel. 253-0819 or 221-0725

Denmark: Centro Colón, Paseo Colón, Calles 28/40, tel. 257-2695

Ecuador: Sabana Sur, tel. 232-1562

El Salvador: Calle 30, Avenida 1, tel. 224-9034

France: 200 meters south of Indoor Club, San Pedro, tel. 225-0733, fax 253-7027

Germany: 200 meters north, 75 meters west of ITAN, Rohrmoser, tel. 232-5533, fax 231-6403

Guatemala: Plaza del Sol, Curridabat, tel. 283-2290

Honduras: Los Yoses, tel. 234-9502, fax 257-0867

Israel: Calle 2, Avenidas 2/4, tel. 221-6011, fax 257-0867

Italy: Avenida 10, Calles 33/35, tel. 224-1082

Japan: 100 meters north, 400 meters west of La Nunciatura, Rohrmoser, tel. 232-1255, fax 231-3140

Mexico: Los Yoses, tel. 225-7284

Netherlands: Oficentro Ejecutivo La Sabana, Edificio 3, Sabana Sur (behind La Contraloria), tel. 296-1490, fax 296-2933

Nicaragua: Avenida Central, Calles 25/27, tel. 223-2373, fax 221-5481

Norway: Centro Colón, Paseo Colón, Calles 38/40, tel. 257-1414

Panamá: Centro Colón, Paseo Colón, Calles 38/40, tel. 257-3241, fax 257-4864

Peru: 200 meters south, 50 meters west of Auto Mercado, Los Yoses, tel. 225-9145, fax 253-0457

Poland: Calle 33, Avenida 9, tel. 225-1481

Romania: Rohrmoser, tel. 231-0742

Spain: Calle 32, Paseo Coló/Avenida 2, tel. 222-1933, fax 222-1480

Sweden: La Uruca, tel. 232-8549

Switzerland: Centro Colón, Paseo Colón, Calles 38/40, tel. 221-4829, fax 525-2831

United Kingdom: Centro Colón, Paseo Colón, Calles 38/40, tel. 221-5816, fax 233-9938

United States: in front of Centro Comercial, road to Pava, Rohrmoser, tel. 220-3939, fax 220-2305

Uruguay: Los Yoses, tel. 234-9909

Venezuela: Los Yoses, tel. 225-5813

Yugoslavia: Avenida 8, Calles 21/23, tel. 225-7362

a visit to the Tribunales de Justicia for a document stating you aren't abandoning any offspring or dependents in Costa Rica. The exit visa is valid for an additional 30 days' stay. Travel agencies in San José can arrange exit visas for a small fee.

Other Documentation

All tourists may be required to demonstrate adequate finances for their proposed stay upon arrival (at least $200). This is normally requested only of those travelers intent on staying 30 days or more. In addition, you may be asked to show a return or onward ticket. Technically, you must have an exit ticket out of the country, but immigration officials rarely request to see it. Airlines, however, frequently will not let you board without proof of a return or onward ticket.

If you're traveling overland you need an onward bus ticket (you can buy one at the border immigration office or even from the driver on TICA international buses), and you will need to show at least $200 in cash or traveler's checks. Check with other overland travelers you meet to see how they fared.

Note: Ease of entry may well depend on your looks. Costa Rican immigration officials—like Costa Ricans in general—are sensitive to appearance, so be aware that you can help your own cause by looking neat and tidy.

Immunizations

Costa Rican authorities do not require travelers to show proof of immunizations or an international vaccination card (see **Health and Safety,** below). However, if you plan on staying beyond 30 days, you may be required to show proof of being free from AIDS or its precursor, HIV positive status. Again, check with your travel agent or Costa Rican consulate for the latest updates. Travelers arriving from Nicaragua report being tested for malarial infection at the border.

To Nicaragua

Canadians and U.S. citizens, as well as citizens of Belgium, Denmark, Finland, the Netherlands, Norway, Spain, Sweden, Switzerland, and the United Kingdom, do not need visas; others—including French, Germans, Australians, and New Zealanders—do. This may have changed by the time you read this.

To Panamá

U.S. citizens, as well as citizens of the Dominican Republic, El Salvador, Germany, Honduras, Spain, Switzerland, and the United Kingdom, do not require visas; all others do. Do not rely on obtaining visas/entry permits at border crossings; obtain them in advance. Regulations for entry into Nicaragua and Panamá are subject to frequent change, so check in advance.

CUSTOMS

Travelers arriving in Costa Rica are allowed 500 cigarettes or 500 grams of tobacco, plus three liters of wine or spirits. You can also bring in two cameras, binoculars, electrical and video equipment, plus camping, scuba, and other sporting equipment duty-free. You may be asked to prove that your personal computer is for personal use. A nominal limit of six rolls of film per person is rarely enforced. If you wish to bring your dog, write the Jefe de Departamento de Zoonosis, Ministerio de Salud, San José 1000, for an importation form.

Exiting Costa Rica

Travelers exiting Costa Rica are currently charged $17 (or its equivalent in *colones*) departure tax on international flights out of San José. No departure tax applies for overland or sea. You may change no more than $50 worth of *colones* into U.S. currency at the airport. Costa Rica prohibits the export of pre-Columbian artifacts.

Returning to the U.S.

U.S. citizens can bring in $400 of purchases duty-free. You may also bring in one quart of spirits plus 200 cigarettes (one carton). Live animals, plants, and products made from endangered species will be confiscated by U.S. Customs (you'll also be fined for bringing in items made from endangered species). Tissue-cultured orchids and other plants in sealed vials are okay.

The Caribbean Basin Initiative scheme raised the customs exemption for member countries, including Costa Rica, to $600. Granting you the added allowance is at the discretion of the customs agent. Costa Rica is also listed under the U.S. Customs Service's Generalized System of Preferences (GSP) program, which provides for duty-free importation of arts, handicrafts, and other select items from Third World countries.

The U.S. Department of State, 2210 C St. NW, Washington, D.C. 20520, tel. (202) 647-4000, publishes *Your Trip Abroad;* and the U.S. Customs Service, Department of the Treasury, 1301 Constitution Ave. NW, Washington, D.C. 20229, tel. (202) 566-5286, publishes *GSP and the Traveler,* both of which outline what may and may not be brought into the United States.

Returning to Canada

Canadian citizens are allowed a $300 annual "exemption," or $100 per quarter for goods purchased abroad, plus 1.1 liters of spirits and 200 cigarettes.

Drugs

It goes without saying that trying to smuggle drugs through customs is not only illegal, it's stupid. Travelers returning from Central and South America are particularly suspect. Trained dogs are employed to sniff out contraband at U.S. airports as well as at Juan Santamaría Airport in San José. Be warned, too, that recent years have seen a concerted effort to stamp out drug trafficking and use within the country.

HEALTH AND SAFETY

Sanitary standards in Costa Rica are very high, and although occasional outbreaks of tropical diseases occur, the chances of succumbing to a serious disease are rare. As long as you take appropriate precautions and use common sense, you're not likely to incur serious illness. If you do, you have the benefit of knowing that the nation has a superb health-care system. There are English-speaking doctors in most cities, and you will rarely find yourself far from medical help. *Medical Systems of Costa Rica,* by Frank Chalfont, Dept. 257-SJO, P.O. Box 025216, Miami, FL 33102-5216, "gives English-speaking foreigners a feel" for Costa Rica's "interactive combination of socialist-private medical systems."

Dental and medical check-ups may be advisable before departing home, particularly if you intend to travel for a considerable time, partake in strenuous activities, or have an existing medical problem. Take along any medications, including prescriptions for eyewear; keep prescription drugs in their original bottles to avoid suspicion at customs. If you suffer from a debilitating health problem, wear a medical alert bracelet. Pharmacies can prescribe drugs (be wary of expiry dates, as shelf life of drugs may be shortened under tropical conditions).

A basic health kit is a good idea. Pack the following (as a minimum) in a small plastic container: alcohol swabs and medicinal alcohol, antiseptic cream, Band-Aids, aspirin or pain killers, diarrhea medication, sunburn remedy, antifungal foot powder, calamine and/or antihistamine, water-purification tablets, surgical tape, bandages and gauze, and scissors.

Information on health concerns can be answered by **Intermedic**, 777 3rd Ave., New York, NY 10017, tel. (212) 486-8974, and the **Department of State Citizens Emergency Center**, tel. (202) 647-5225. The **International Association for Medical Assistance to Travellers** (IAMAT), 417 Center St., Lewiston, NY 14092, tel. (716) 754-4883; in Canada, 40 Regal Rd., Guelph, Ont. N1K 1B5, tel. (519) 836-0102, publishes helpful information, including a list of approved physicians and clinics. An invaluable pocket-size book is *Staying Healthy in Asia, Africa, and Latin America,* Moon Publications, P.O. Box 3040, Chico, CA 95927, tel. (800) 345-5473, which is packed with first-aid and basic medical information.

Medical Insurance

Medical insurance is highly recommended. Check to see if your health insurance or other policies cover you for medical expenses and/or baggage loss while abroad. Your American Express credit card service may provide coverage too. Traveler's insurance isn't cheap, but it can be a sound investment. Travel agencies can sell you traveler's health and baggage insurance, as well as insurance against cancellation of a prepaid tour. The best coverage I've found is through **American Express**, tel. (800) 234-0375, and **Wallach and Company,** tel. (703) 687-3166 or (800) 237-6615. The following compa-

EMERGENCY TELEPHONE NUMBERS

NATIONAL

The national emergency numbers are slowly being expanded to cover the entire country.

All emergencies. 911
Air Ambulance 225-4502
(24-hour beeper, 225-2500)
Red Cross (Cruz Roja). 128
Police (Guardia rural). 127
Traffic police (Policía de tránsito) 117

Fire brigade (Bomberos) 118

Credit Cards
American Express 233-0044
MasterCard .253-2155
Visa International 223-2211

PROVINCE	RED CROSS	POLICE	TRAFFIC POLICE	OIJ (Crime Division)	FIRE
See regional chapters for local emergency numbers.					
San José	128	127	117	295-3339	118 or 223-8055
Alajuela	441-3939	441-6346	441-7411	442-2367	441-0789
Cartago	251-0421	551-1619	551-7575	551-6140	551-0513
Heredia	237-1115	237-0011	238-1966	260-7812	237-0561
Guanacaste	666-0994	666-9092	666-0649 (Caúas) 666-1116 (Liberia)	666-1143	666-0279
Puntarenas	661-0184	661-0640	663-1599 (Golfito 778-2078)	661-1539	661-0429
Limón	758-0125	758-0365	758-3943 (Guápiles 710-6994)	758-1865	758-0229

nies also offer travel insurance: **Travelers,** tel. (203) 277-0111 or (800) 243-3174; **Access America International,** P.O. Box 90315, Richmond, VA 23286, tel. (800) 284-8300; **International Underwriters,** 243 Church St. W, Vienna, VA 22180, tel. (703) 281-9500; **TravelGuard International,** 1145 Clark St., Stevens Point, WI 54481, tel. (715) 345-0505 or (800) 782-5151; and **Carefree Travel Insurance,** P.O. Box 310, 120 Meola Blvd., Mineola, NY 11501, tel. (516) 294-0220 or (800) 323-3149.

The **Association of British Insurers,** 51 Gresham St., London BC2V 7HQ, tel. (071) 600-3333, and **Europ Assistance,** 252 High St., Croyden, Surrey CR0 1NF, tel. (081) 680-1234, can provide advice for obtaining travel insurance in Britain.

Costa Rica's Social Security system (Instituto Nacional de Seguros) has a **Traveller's Insurance** program specifically for foreigners. As well as loss or theft of possessions, it covers emergency medical treatment (hospitalization and surgery, plus emergency dental treatment are covered; services for pre-existing conditions are not), plus repatriation of a body. You can choose coverage between 500,000-10 million colones for the number of weeks you desire (1-12 weeks). You can buy coverage at travel agencies or the Instituto Nacional de Seguros, tel. 223-5800.

MEDICAL EMERGENCIES

In emergencies, call 911. Alternately, call 128 for the Red Cross or Emergency Rescue Unit, or tel. 221-5818 in San José. For the police, outside San José call 127. No coin is required.

Many hospitals and private clinics offer 24-hour emergency care, X-rays, and more. Foreigners receive the same service as Costa Ricans in public hospitals. While the standard of service is generally good, lines are often very long. Private hospitals offer faster treatment. Use public hospitals for life-threatening emergencies only; private clinics and doctors are recommended for all other emergencies and health needs (a large deposit may be requested on admittance).

Private office visits are usually $20-30. Hospitals and clinics accept credit card payment. U.S. insurance is not normally accepted, but you can send your bill to your insurance company for reimbursement.

Doctors—many of them U.S.-trained—are listed by specialty in the Yellow Pages under "Médicos." *Living in Costa Rica,* a guidebook published by the United States Missions Association, provides a comprehensive listing of doctors by specialty.

See regional chapters for locations and telephone numbers of specific hospitals.

Air Ambulance, Apdo. 256, San José 1017, tel. 225-4502, fax 235-8264, 24-hour beeper 225-2500, offers 24-hour coronary and mobile critical care for surgical and medical emergencies, using either a twin Learjet or a helicopter. **Ambulancia Emerca,** tel. 256-6989, cellular tel. 383-0614, offers specialized ambulance service.

Medical Evacuation
Traveler's Emergency Network, P.O. Box 238, Hyattsville, MD 20797, tel. (800) 275-4836, provides worldwide ground and air evacuation and medical assistance, as does **International SOS Assistance,** P.O. Box 11568, Philadelphia, PA 19116, tel. (215) 244-1500 or (800) 523-8930, which for $55 offers a 14-day package including 24-hour medical assistance. Couples and families can buy the same package for $96 and $151. Longer packages are offered. The following companies also provide emergency evacuation and other services: Carefree Travel Insurance, Travel Guard, and Wallach and Company (see **Medical Insurance,** above).

VACCINATIONS

No vaccinations are required to enter Costa Rica. Epidemic diseases have mostly been eradicated throughout the country. However, a few isolated cases of cholera, measles, and tuberculosis are occasionally reported. Consult your physician for recommended vaccinations. Travelers planning to rough it should consider vac-

cinations against tetanus, polio, typhoid and infectious hepatitis. The Center for Disease Control and Prevention says that the risk of cholera to travelers is so low that it is questionable whether vaccination is of benefit.

Infectious hepatitis is endemic throughout Central America, although only infrequently reported in Costa Rica. Main symptoms are stomach pains, loss of appetite, yellowing skin and eyes, and extreme tiredness. Hepatitis A is contracted through unhygienic foods or contaminated water (salads and unpeeled fruits are major culprits). A gamma globulin vaccination is recommended. The much rarer hepatitis B is usually contracted through unclean needles, blood transfusions, or unsafe sex.

If you're traveling overland, it may be wise to carry an **International Certificate of Vaccinations,** available from the Superintendent of Documents, U.S. Government Printing Office, Washington, D.C. 20402, tel. (202) 783-3238, $2. The **Ministerio de Salud** (Ministry of Health), Calle 16 and Avenida 4, tel. 222-0333, can provide yellow fever vaccinations.

HEALTH PROBLEMS

Infection
Even the slightest scratch can fester quickly in the tropics. Treat promptly and regularly with antiseptic and keep the wound clean.

Intestinal Problems
Water is safe to drink virtually everywhere, although more remote rural areas, as well as Escazú, Santa Ana, Puntarenas, and Puerto Limón, are suspect. To play it safe, drink bottled mineral water *(agua mineral* or *soda).* Remember, ice cubes are water too. And don't brush your teeth using suspect water. Always wash your hands, too, before eating. A few areas, such as the waters around Puntarenas in particular, are too polluted for swimming.

Food hygiene standards in Costa Rica are generally very high. Milk is pasteurized, so you're not likely to encounter many problems normally associated with dairy products. However, the change in diet—which may alter the bacteria that are normal and necessary in the bowel—may cause **diarrhea** or **constipation.** (In case of the latter, eat lots of fruit.) Fortunately, the stomach usually builds up a resistance to unaccustomed foods. Most cases of diarrhea are caused by microbial bowel infections resulting from contaminated food. Common-sense precautions include not eating uncooked fish or shellfish (which collect cholera bugs), uncooked vegetables, unwashed salads, or unpeeled fruit (peel the fruit yourself). And be fastidious with personal hygiene.

Diarrhea is usually temporary and many doctors recommend letting it run its course. Personally, I like to plug myself up straightaway with Lomotil or a similar "solidifier." Treat diarrhea with rest and lots of liquid to replace the water and salts lost. Avoid alcohol and milk products while suffering from diarrhea. If conditions don't improve after three days, seek medical help. There are clinical laboratories *(laboratorios clínicas)* in most towns.

Diarrhea accompanied by severe abdominal pain, blood in your stool, and fever is a sign of **dysentery.** Seek immediate medical diagnosis. Tetracycline or ampicillin is normally used to cure bacillary dysentery. More complex professional treatment is required for amoebic dysentery. The symptoms of both are similar. **Giardiasis,** acquired from infected water, is another intestinal complaint. It causes diarrhea, bloating, persistent indigestion, and weight loss. Again, seek medical advice. **Intestinal worms** can be contracted by walking barefoot on infested beaches, grass, or earth.

Sunburn and Skin Problems

Don't underestimate the tropical sun! It's intense and can fry you in minutes, particularly at higher elevations. It can even burn you through light clothing or while you're lying in the shade. The midday sun is especially potent. Even if you consider yourself nicely tanned already, *use a suncream or sunblock*—at least SPF 15 or higher. Zinc oxide provides almost 100% protection. Bring sunscreen with you; it's expensive in Costa Rica. If you're intent on a tan, have patience. Build up gradually, and use an aloe gel after sunbathing; it helps repair any skin damage. The tops of feet and backs of knees are particularly susceptible to burning. Consider a wide-brimmed hat, too. Calamine lotion and aloe gel will soothe light burns; for more serious lobster-pink burns use steroid creams.

Sun glare—especially prevalent if you're on water—can cause **conjunctivitis** (eye infection). Sunglasses will protect against this. **Prickly heat** is an itchy rash, normally caused by clothing that is too tight and/or in need of washing. This, and **athlete's foot,** are best treated by airing out the body and washing your clothes. And the tropical humidity and heat can sap your body fluids like blotting paper. Drink regularly to avoid dehydration. Leg cramps, exhaustion, and headaches are possible signs of dehydration.

Snakebite

Snakes are common in Costa Rica. Fewer than 500 snakebites are reported each year, and less than three percent of these are fatal. The majority of bites occur from people stepping on snakes. Caution is always the watchword. Always watch where you're treading or putting your hands. Never reach into holes or under rocks, debris, or forest-floor leaf litter without first checking with a stick to see what might be quietly slumbering there. Be particularly wary in long grass. Avoid streams at night. And remember that many snakes are well-camouflaged arboreal creatures that snooze on branches, so never reach for a branch without looking. You should even be cautious when peering inside bromeliads: the dark-colored chunk-headed snake likes to doze inside the moisture-collecting plants during the dry season. If you spot a snake, keep a safe distance, and give the highly aggressive fer-de-lance a *very wide* berth.

Death from snakebite is extremely rare; fear of the consequences is one of your biggest enemies, so try to relax. Do not move unless absolutely necessary. Commercial snakebite kits are normally good only for the specific species for which they were designed, so it will help if you can definitively identify the critter. But don't endanger yourself further trying to catch it.

If the bite is to a limb, immobilize the limb and apply a tight bandage between the bite and body. Release it for 90 seconds every 15 minutes. Ensure you can slide a finger under the bandage; too tight and you risk further damage. Do *not* cut the bite area in an attempt to suck out the poison unless you are an expert. Many snake poisons are anticoagulants; cutting your blood vessels may cause you to bleed like a hemophiliac. Recommendations to use electric shock as snakebite treatment have gained popular favor recently in Costa Rica; do *not* follow this medically discredited advice.

Symptoms include swelling, bruising around the bite (which will show two puncture marks), soreness of the lymph glands, nausea, vomiting, and fever. Worst-case scenarios normally involve numbness and tingling of the face, muscular spasms, convulsions, and hemorrhaging. Seek medical attention without delay. Rural health posts and most national park rangers have antivenin kits on-site.

Insects and Arachnids

Sweet blood or sour blood, at some stage during your visit to Costa Rica, creepy crawlies may get you. Fortunately, only a few people will have fierce reactions. Check your bedding before crawling into bed. Always shake out your shoes and clothing before putting them on. Keep beds away from walls. And, for true paranoids, look underneath the toilet seat before sitting down.

Repellent sprays and lotions are a must. Apply regularly in jungle areas, marshy areas and coastal lowlands (particularly the Caribbean). Take lotion to apply to the body, and aerosol spray for clothing. Avon Skin-So-Soft oil is such an effective bug repellent that U.S. Marines use it by the truckload ("Gee, private, you sure smell nice, and your skin's so soft!").

Bites can easily become infected in the tropics, so avoid scratching! Treat with antiseptics or antibiotics. A baking-soda bath can help relieve itching if you're badly bitten, as can antihistamine tablets, hydrocortisone, and calamine lotion. Long-sleeved clothing and full-length pants will help keep the beasties at bay.

Chiggers *(coloradillas)* inhabit grasslands, particularly in Guanacaste. Their bites itch like hell. Mosquito repellent won't deter them. Dust your shoes, socks, and ankles with sulphur powder. Sucking sulphur tablets *(azufre sublimado)* apparently gives your sweat a smell that chiggers find obnoxious. Chigarid relieves chigger bites.

mosquito

Nail polish apparently works, too (on the bites, not the nails) by suffocating the beasts.

Ticks *(garrapatas)* hang out near livestock. They bury their heads in your skin. Remove ticks immediately with tweezers—grasp the head parts as close to your skin as possible and pull gently but steadily. Don't try to extract ticks by holding a lighted match near them or painting them with nail polish remover or petroleum jelly. If you get a tick out within 24 hours, you greatly reduce your risk of infection.

Tiny, irritating **no-see-ums** (truly evil bloodsucking sandflies about the size of a pinpoint, and known locally as *purrujas*) inhabit many beaches and marshy coastal areas: avoid infested beaches around dusk, when they appear out of nowhere. They're not fazed by bug repellent with DEET, but Avon's Skin-So-Soft works a treat. Sandflies on the Atlantic coast can pass on leishmaniasis, a debilitating disease: seek urgent treatment for non-healing sores.

Insect larvae, such as that of the botfly, can cause growing boils once laid beneath your skin (you'll see a clear hole in the middle of the boil or pimple). Completely cover with Vaseline and a secure Band-Aid or tape and let it dry overnight. All being well you should be able to squeeze the culprit out next day. If stung by a **scorpion**—not normally as bad as it sounds—take plenty of liquids and rest. If you're unfortunate enough to contract **scabies** (a microscopic mite) or **lice,** which is possible if you're staying in unhygienic conditions or sleeping with unhygienic bedfellows, use a body shampoo containing gamma benzene hexachloride. You should also wash all your clothing and bedding in very hot water, and toss out your underwear. The severe itching caused by scabies infestation appears after three or four weeks (it appears as little dots, often in lines, ending in blisters, especially around the genitals, elbows, wrists, lower abdomen, and nipples).

Avoid **bees'** nests. African bees have infiltrated Costa Rica in recent years. They're very aggressive and will attack with little provocation. Running in a zigzag is said to help in fleeing. If there's water about, take a dunk and stay submerged for a while.

Many bugs are local. The bite of a rare kind of insect found along the southern Caribbean coast and locally called *papalamoya* produces a deep and horrible infection that can even threaten a limb. It may be best to have such infections treated locally (and certainly promptly); doctors back home (or even in San José) might take forever to diagnose and treat the condition.

AIDS and Sexually Transmitted Diseases

AIDS is on the rise throughout Central America. The Costa Rican government conducted an exemplary anti-AIDS campaign (the Ministry of Health distributes 800,000 condoms a month in nationalized clinics) but, alas, Pope John Paul II's admonitions have led to removal of the billboards and TV ads that once promoted condom use.

Avoidance of casual sexual contact is the best prevention. If you succumb, use condoms. Though readily available, Costa Rican condoms tear easily; to be safe, bring your own. Prostitution is legal in Costa Rica, and though most licensed prostitutes have regular health checks, many prostitutes aren't registered and thereby constitute a particular risk. Blood transfusions and unclean needles, such as those shared in drug use, are other potential sources of HIV infection. Remember that gonorrhea, syphilis, and other sexually transmitted diseases are no less prevalent than elsewhere in the world. Practice safe sex!

Malaria

Malaria is not a serious problem. It is nonexistent in highland areas, and only a limited risk in the lowlands, although an increase in the incidence of malaria has been reported recently in the Caribbean lowlands, particularly the area south of Cahuita (the majority of cases were due to poor health practices on banana plantations). Consult your physician for the best type of anti-malarial medication. Begin taking your tablets a few days (or weeks, depending on the prescription) before arriving in an infected zone, and continue taking the tablets for several weeks after leaving the malarial zone. Malaria symptoms include high fever, shivering, headache, and sometimes diarrhea.

Chloroquine (called Alaren in Costa Rica) and Fansidar are both used for short-term protection. Chloroquine reportedly is still good for Costa Rica, although Panamanian mosquitoes have built up a resistance to the drug. Fansidar may be a safer bet for travel south of Puerto Limón. **Note:** Fansidar can cause severe skin reactions and

is dangerous for people with a history of sulfonamide intolerance. If you take Fansidar and suffer from such skin and mucuous-membrane ailments as itching, rash, mouth or genital sores, or a sore throat, seek medical help immediately.

The best mosquito repellents contain DEET (diethylmetatoluamide). Use rub-on repellent directly to the skin; use sprays for clothing. DEET is quite toxic; avoid using on small children. And avoid getting this on plastic—it melts it. Use mosquito netting at night in the lowlands; you can obtain good hammocks and "no-see-um" nets in the U.S. from **Campmor,** P.O. Box 700-H, Saddle River, NJ 07458, tel. (800) 526-4784. A fan over your bed and mosquito coils *(espirales)* also help keep mosquitoes at bay. Coils are available from *pulperías* and supermarkets (don't forget the metal stand—*soporte*—for them).

The Ministerio de Salud, Calle 16, Avenida 4, can supply free malaria tablets from the information desk to the left of the ministry. Long-sleeved shirts and long pants will help reduce the number of bites you collect.

Other Problems

Occasional and serious outbreaks of **dengue fever** have occurred in recent years, notably around Puntarenas and Caribbean coast (especially in areas hit by heavy rains). Transmitted by mosquitoes, the illness can be fatal (death usually results from internal hemorrhaging). Its symptoms are similar to malaria, with additional severe pain in the joints and bones (it is sometimes called "breaking bones disease"), but, unlike malaria, is not recurring. You can spray your clothing with the insecticide *permethrin.*

Rabies, though rare, can be contracted through the bite of an infected dog or other animal. It is always fatal unless treated. You're extremely unlikely to be the victim of a vampire bat, a common rabies vector that preys on cattle. If you're sleeping in the open (or with an unscreened window open) in areas with vampire bat populations, don't leave your flesh exposed! Their bite is said to be painless. They're particularly fond of toes.

You're not likely to suffer from **altitude-related problems** unless you intend climbing Chirripó (3,819 meters), in which case you should ascend slowly and take plenty of liquids. If you experience nausea, severe headaches, fatigue, a rapid pulse, and/or irregular breathing, you've probably got altitude sickness.

SAFETY

With common sense, you are no more likely to run into problems in Costa Rica than you are in your own back yard. The vast majority of Costa Ricans are honest and friendly. However, there is a growing problem of muggings and theft—especially along the Caribbean coast—and burglary is endemic. An average of five thieves are arrested daily in Parque Central in San José, where recent years has seen an increase in vi-olent youth gangs—*chapulines*—which operate like Fagin's urchins in Dickens' *Oliver Twist.* The name means "grasshoppers," because the gangs swarm their victims like locusts. Police crackdowns have arrested dozens of offenders, but their numbers are estimated at more than 400. Be cautious of overly friendly strangers. Remain alert!

Traffic is perhaps the greatest danger. Be especially wary when crossing the street in San José. Tico drivers do not like to give way to pedestrians and they give no mercy to those still in the road when the light turns to green. Stand well away from the curb, especially on corners, where buses often mount the curb. And sidewalks are full of gaping potholes and tilted curbstones. Watch your step!

Outside the city you need to be savvy to some basic precautions. Hikers straying off trails can easily lose their way amid the rainforests. And don't approach too close to an active volcano, such as Arenal, which may suddenly hiccup lava and breccia far and wide. Remember that atop the mountains, sunny weather can turn cold and rainy in seconds, so dress accordingly. And be extra cautious when crossing rivers; a rainstorm upstream can turn the river downstream into a raging torrent without any warning. Ideally, go with a guide.

If things go wrong, contact the U.S. embassy or consulate, Apdo. 10035, San José, tel. 220-3939, in front of the Centro Comercial, on the road to Pavas, in the western suburbs of San José. (Other nationalities should refer to the "Embassies and Consulates in Costa Rica" chart.) Consulate officials can't get you out of jail, but they can help you locate a lawyer, alleviate unhealthy conditions, or arrange for funds to be wired if you run short of money. They can even authorize a reimbursable loan—the Department of State hates to admit it—while you arrange for cash to be forwarded, or even lend you money to get home. Don't expect the U.S. embassy to bend over backward; it's notoriously unhelpful. The *Handbook of Consular Services,* Public Affairs Staff, Bureau of Consular Affairs, U.S. Department of State, Washington, D.C. 20520, provides details of such assistance. Friends and family can also call the Department of State's **Overseas Citizen Service,** tel. (202) 647-5225, to check on you if things go awry.

REPORTING CRIMES

Report theft and assault and similar crimes to the **Judicial Police,** Organismo de Investigación Judicial (OIJ), in the middle courthouse on Avenida 6/8, Calles 17, tel. 221-5337 or 222-1365. (If you're a U.S. citizen, call 220-3939 and ask a representative of the U.S. Embassy to accompany you.)

If you are sold counterfeit dollars or *colones,* contact the Crime Prevention Unit, UPD, tel. 233-5083.

Report complications with restaurants, tour companies, hotels, etc., to the main office of the **Costa Rican Tourism Institute (ICT)** at Avenida 4, Calles 5/7, tel. 223-1733.

Report theft or demands for money by traffic police to the **Ministry of Public Works and Transport** at Calle 9, Avenidas 20/22, tel. 227-2188. Report similar problems with Radio Patrulla police to the OIJ; then try to identify the policeman at the Radio Patrulla headquarters, tel. 226-2242, in front of Centro Comercial del Sur.

The U.S. State Department maintains a **Citizens' Emergency Center,** tel. (202) 647-5225, fax 647-3000, as well as a computer bulletin board, tel. (202) 647-9225.

If you need a lawyer *in* Costa Rica, Chris Howard's *Golden Door to Retirement and Living in Costa Rica* provides particularly valuable information on finding and dealing with lawyers, as does the *Legal Guide to Costa Rica,* by Roger Peterson.

THEFT AND DRUGS

Theft

A lot of tourists get ripped off in Costa Rica in all manner of crafty scams. Don't trust locals to handle your money. Be particularly wary of credit. And don't exchange money before receiving the services or goods you're paying for—I've heard more than once of locals saying they needed your money to pay someone in advance to arrange a boat ride or horse-back trip, then disappearing for a few days.

Watch, too, for petty theft and pickpocketing. Don't leave valuables in your room or on the beach. Armed holdups are rare but increasing in frequency. And there are reports of nighttime muggings in San José, Puerto Limón, and other select areas. Be cautious at night, particularly if you intend to walk on beaches or park trails. Stick to well-lit main streets if possible. Be aware that the cheaper the *cabinas,* the more susceptible you are to burglary. Make sure you have bars on the window (bringing your own lock for the door is a good idea) and that your room is otherwise secure.

A Sampler of Costa Rican Con Games

Here are a few special tricks of which to beware.

Guys, beware any amorous ladies who may approach you and start running their hands over your body. The bulge that has them most impressed is your wallet. They walk away giggling while you struggle to compose yourself. Only later do you realize that they walked off with your money. Also beware drinks offered by strangers; your beverage may be laced with a knock-out drug.

Be wary, too, of "plainclothes policemen." Ask to see identification, and never relinquish your documentation or give money. And be especially wary if he asks a third party to verify his own credentials; they could be in league.

Never allow yourself to be drawn into arguments (the Costa Ricans are so placid that anyone raising a temper is immediately to be suspected). And don't be distracted by people spilling things on you. These are ruses meant to distract you while an accomplice steals your valuables. An acquaintance of mine, a well-known travel writer to boot, fell for a beauty. She was hit on the head and shoulders by birdshit, and two young men, seeing her plight, came rushing to her aid with handkerchiefs, then lifted her wallet amid the pandemonium. The two

rogues had contrived the whole routine—including spattering her.

Remain alert to the dark side of self-proclaimed good samaritans. Another acquaintance of mine had her luggage neatly stolen by two men who offered to help as she struggled to cross a street in Puntarenas with two suitcases. Convinced of their samaritan nature, she went off to look for a taxi while they "looked after" her luggage. When she returned, they and her suitcases were gone.

By the same token, don't be too paranoid.

Drugs

Marijuana and cocaine are increasingly available in Costa Rica, which is a transshipment point between South America and the United States. Drug trafficking and laundering of drug money has increased markedly since the ouster of Manuel Noriega from Panamá. And traffickers have been able to entice impoverished farmers into growing marijuana and cocaine, notably in the Buenos Aires region of southern Puntarenas. The dramatic rise in car theft in Costa Rica is believed to be linked to drug trafficking, with stolen cars being used to ship goods.

The Costa Rican government and U.S. Drug Enforcement Agency (DEA) initiated an ongoing anti-narcotics campaign in 1986. Penalties for possession or dealing are stiff. If you're offered drugs on the street, be aware that you may be dealing with a plainclothes policeman. If caught, you will receive no special favors because you're foreign. A trial could take many months, in which case you'll be jailed on the premise that you're guilty until proven innocent. *Just say NO!*

Article 14 of the Drug Law stipulates: "A jail sentence of eight to 20 years shall be imposed upon anyone who participates in any way in international drug dealing." That includes anyone caught distributing, producing, supplying, transforming, refining, extracting, preparing, cultivating, transporting, or storing. The jail sentence also applies to anyone buying or otherwise involved in financial dealings involving drugs.

If you roll your own cigarettes, consider leaving your papers at home; they are considered highly suspect. Stick to commercial brands—or use it as an opportunity to give up smoking!

You need to be aware, too, that the State Department's **Travel Advisories,** which warn U.S. citizens about "danger" spots, are usually politically motivated (an advisory against travel in the Pavones region issued in 1997 devastated tourism to the region—there were almost no tourists when I visited in December 1997—but the place was totally safe; the advisory was issued as leverage to get the Costa Rican government to resolve a politically charged legal dispute; see **Pavones,** in the Pacific Southwest chapter).

Travelers venturing overland through Central America should contact the **Central American Resource Council,** 1407 Cleveland Ave. N, St. Paul, MN 55108. It publishes *Centroamérica: The Month in Review,* a digest of information not readily available or widely reported on current conditions in Central America. Suscriptions cost $25 a year.

Americans Traveling Abroad: What You Should Know Before You Go, by Gladson Nwanna, World Travel Institute Press, P.O. Box 32671-1A, Baltimore, MD 21208, is a good resource on safety, healthy, money tips, etc. It includes a chapter on Central America.

Theft

Costa Rica's many charms can lull visitors into a false sense of security. Like anywhere else, the country has its share of social ills, with rising street crime among them. An economic crisis and influx of impoverished refugees has spawned a growing band of petty thieves and purse slashers that blossomed into a sudden spree in winter 1994/5. And since the arrest of Noriega in 1990, Costa Rica has become a distribution point for cocaine, thereby fostering a concomitant increase in larger-scale crime. Still, most crime is opportunistic, and thieves seek easy targets. Don't become paranoid, but a few common-sense precautions are in order.

The Instituto Costarricense de Turismo publishes a leaflet—*Passport For Your Security*—listing precautions and a selection of emergency phone numbers. It's given out free at airport immigration counters. The ICT operates a 24-hour toll-free tourist information line—tel. (800) 012-3456—for **emergencies.**

Make photocopies of all important documents: your passport (showing photograph and visas, if applicable), airline ticket, credit cards, insurance policy, driver's license. Carry the photocopies with you, and leave the originals in the hotel safe where possible. If this isn't possible, carry the originals with you in a secure inside pocket. Don't put all your eggs in one basket! Prepare an "emergency kit," to include photocopies of your documents and an adequate sum of money to tide you over if your wallet gets stolen. If you're robbed, immediately file a police report. You'll need this to make an insurance claim.

For credit card security, insist that imprints are made in your presence. Make sure any imprints incorrectly completed are torn up. Don't take someone else's word that it will be done. Destroy the carbons yourself. And beware credit card "skimmers"—thieves who use a skimmer to make a copy of the magnetic code on the back of your card, then use it fraudulently; don't let store merchants or anyone else walk off with your card. Keep it in sight!

In San José, be especially wary in and around the Coca-Cola bus terminal and streets to the north (avoid the area altogether at night). Be wary, too, in the red light districts downtown. Don't use buses at night, and be alert if you use them by day. Crowded places are the happy hunting grounds of quick and expert crooks. If you sense yourself being squeezed or jostled, don't hold back—elbow your way out of there *immediately.* Better safe than sorry.

Be equally cautious of foreign residents. Costa Rica has attracted more than its fair share of misfits and miscreants, including many who are evading arrest warrants back home.

Large-scale scams are common. I know several foreigners who lost huge sums by investing in bogus macadamia farms and other schemes. I've heard cautionary reports that "Newcomers' Seminars" have shills in the audience to inspire attendees to part with their money.

If you pick up hitchhikers, *always* take the car keys with you if you get out of the vehicle. One of my friends had his rental car and possessions stolen by a local guide he had hired—after a full week together!

A few policemen are less than honest, and there have been reports of tourists being shaken down for money. Never pay a policeman money. If you are stopped by policemen wanting to see your passport or to search you, insist on its being done in front of a neutral witness—*"solamente con testigos."*

Don't expect the police to respond to a real emergency. I've heard countless stories of pleas for emergency help going unheeded—usually because the police are scared. One local expat suggests calling ICE (the state electricity company) and telling them your electricity has gone dead; they'll be around like a shot.

Precautions: Don't wear jewelry, chains, or expensive watches. They mark you as a wealthy tourist. Wear an inexpensive digital watch. Never carry more cash than you need for the day. The rest should be kept in the hotel safe. If you don't trust the hotel or if it doesn't have a safe, try as best you can to hide your valuables and secure your room. The majority of your money should be in the form of traveler's checks, which can be refunded if lost or stolen.

Never leave your purse, camera, or luggage unattended in public places. And always keep a wary eye on your luggage on public transportation, especially backpacks: sneak thieves love their zippered compartments.

Never carry your wallet in your back pocket. Instead, wear a secure moneybelt. Alternatively, you can carry your bills in your front pocket. Pack them beneath a handkerchief. Carry any other money in an inside pocket, a "secret" pocket sewn into your pants or jacket, or hidden in a body pouch or an elasticated wallet below the knee. Spread your money around your person.

Don't carry more luggage than you can adequately manage. Limit your baggage to one suitcase or duffel. And have a lock for each luggage item. Purses should have a short strap (ideally, one with metal woven in) that fits tightly against the body and snaps closed or has a zipper. Always keep purses fully zipped and luggage locked.

Don't leave anything of value within reach of an open window.

Don't leave anything of value in your car.

Don't leave tents or cars unguarded.

Be particularly wary after cashing money at a bank.

Riptides

On average, four people drown every week in Costa Rica. Rip currents are responsible for three-quarters of those ocean drownings. And most victims are caught in water barely deeper

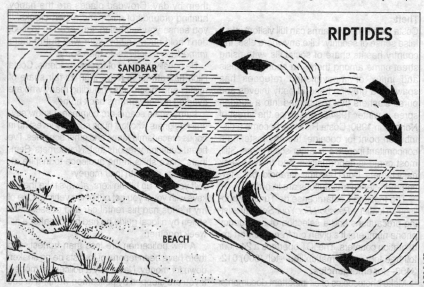

Never fight a riptide; it will always deliver you to calm water.

than waist-high. Most victims died because they *unnecessarily* panicked and struggled against the tide until they became exhausted. Yet surfers and strong swimmers rely on rip currents to carry them beyond the breakers. If you understand how rip currents function, you too can use their forces to get to safety.

Rip currents form where a large volume of wave-borne water attempting to return to sea is blocked by the mass of water coming ashore; the excess water rushes back to sea via a narrow fast-flowing "river" channel that relieves the build-up. Sometimes they run parallel to shore before turning out to sea. They can carry a swimmer out to sea for several hundred yards before they lose their strength. Remember: Rip currents will always deliver you to calm waters, the "head" (a mushroom-shaped plume of muddy water), a short distance from shore.

Call for help immediately if you sense something wrong. Don't try to swim against the current. It is far, far stronger than you, and you'll only exhaust yourself while being carried out. Float. Alternatively, gently swim or wade parallel to the shoreline (many victims are pulled out by rip currents while wading close to shore); with luck you may reach the edge of the rip current and break free. Conserve your energy. And above all, don't panic. Rip currents do *not* pull you under. Once the current subsides, you can

return to shore by swimming obliquely (at a 45-degree angle) to the beach.

Rip currents sometimes have a discolored brown surface; others may display a mirrorlike, deceptively smooth surface. An area of low incoming waves or a break in a surf line is another good indicator. Some rip currents migrate up and down a beach. They can also change location with the tides and weather. What seemed safe yesterday may not be today. Avoid wading or swimming on surf-swept beaches, where rip currents often occur during lulls in wave action. Also avoid rivermouths and jetties, which form their own rip currents.

The **Costa Rican Lifesaving Association,** tel. 777-0345, can provide more information. Remember: There are very few lifeguards on duty at Costa Rican beaches. Educate yourself, and always check the sea's behavior or ask about local conditions before venturing in.

Beaches to Beware: The following popular beaches are particularly renowned for their riptides:

• Cahuita National Park (beach near entrance)
• Espadilla (Manuel Antonio)
• Jacó Beach
• Playa Barranca (Puntarenas)
• Playa Bonita (Puerto Limón)
• Playa de Doña Ana (Puntarenas)
• Playa Savegre (Manuel Antonio)

MONEY

CURRENCY

Costa Rica's currency is the *colón* (plural *colones*), which is written ¢ and sometimes colloquially called a peso. Notes are issued in the following denominations: 20 (brown), 500 (purple), 1,000 (red), and 5,000 (blue) *colones;* coins come in one, five, 10, 25, 50, and 100 *colones.* Older 50 (light green) and 100 (gray) *colones* notes, and two-*colones* coins remain in circulation. The *colón* is divided into 100 *centimos,* though these coins are being taken out of circulation. You may hear money referred to colloquially as *pista* or *plata. Menudo* is loose change; *caña* is one *colón;* a 1,000-*colón* bill is called a *rojo.*

The five-*colones* bank note is considered obsolete as a form of currency and is popularly sold as a souvenir ($1). It's a beautiful note with a portrait of late-19th-century president Don Rafael Yglesia Castro on the face side and, on its reverse, a colorful reproduction of the pretty mural on the ceiling of the National Theater in San José.

Watch out: A large quantity of counterfeit 5,000-*colones* bills are in circulation. Look for the watermark above the 5,000 to the right of the official signature, absent on fakes. Be particularly wary if changing money on the street.

Most hotels will accept payment in U.S. dollars, as do car rental companies and taxis (for larger fares). For most other items, use *colones.* Other international currencies are generally not accepted as direct payment.

CHANGING MONEY

Dollars are widely accepted, and so there is no *urgent* need to convert. You can arrive in Costa Rica without local currency and function just fine. You can change money at Juan Santamaría Airport upon arrival; the bank is inside the departure terminal but service can be abominably slow and complicated; hours: Mon.-Fri. 8 a.m.-4 p.m., weekends and holidays 7 a.m.-1 p.m. Travelers arriving from countries other than the U.S. may find it easier to buy U.S. dollars before arriving in Costa Rica. Small towns may not have banks or moneychangers: change money beforehand. And travel with sufficient small bills.

Legally, money may be changed only at a bank or hotel cash desk. You are allowed to convert only $50 of *colones* to dollars when departing, so spend all your local currency before leaving.

Exchange Rates

The value of the *colón* has fallen steadily against the U.S. dollar over the past few years. At press time the official exchange rate was approximately 241 *colones* to the dollar. A yearly devaluation of 5-15% is expected (hence, a dollar will be worth about one *colón* more every week). All prices in this book are quoted in U.S. dollars unless otherwise indicated.

Banks

Banks are normally open 9 a.m.-4 p.m., but hours vary. Foreign-exchange departments are often open longer. There are many private banks with outlets throughout the country; many have 24-hour automated teller machines for cash advances using credit cards. Most towns have a branch of the state-run **Banco Nacional de Costa Rica,** the least efficient of the banks. Don't expect fast service. Costa Rican banks can be infernally slow. At many banks, you'll have to stand in two lines: one to process the transaction, the other to receive your cash. It can sometimes take more than an hour. Ask to make sure you're in the correct line. Banks close during Easter, Christmas, New Year's, and other holidays, so plan accordingly.

Banks are allowed to charge what they wish for foreign-exchange transactions. Shop around if changing a large amount.

Hotels

Most hotels will exchange dollars for *colones* for guests, although I've frequently changed money at hotels where I wasn't staying. Hotels offer similar exchange rates to banks. Understandably, hotels will only change small amounts, but at least you'll avoid the long lines that are the plague of banks.

Street Changers

Many hustlers offer money exchange on the street, although this is strictly illegal. At best, you'll get between perhaps five percent more than the official exchange rate (less for traveler's checks). It isn't worth it! Travelers caught illicitly changing money—as well as the vendors—can face heavy fines. (The moneychanger may even be an undercover policeman.)

The Judicial Police say they receive between 10 and 15 complaints every day from people who've been ripped off while changing money on the street. Not surprisingly, most victims are tourists. Some rip-off artists work in pairs. Tricks include going to a car to "change dollars"; instead of returning, they flee. Always count your money before handing over your U.S. dollars (street changers won't change other currencies).

Chris Howard, author of *The Golden Door to Retirement Living in Costa Rica*, recommends **Villalobos Brothers Money Traders,** tel. 233-0090, fax 223-8838, on the second floor of the Schyfter Bldg, 75 meters south of the post office, next to the Banco Lyon.

TRAVELER'S CHECKS

Traveler's checks can be readily cashed, though some banks may refuse or will change only a specific kind. You'll usually need your passport, and you may also need to show your proof-of-purchase slip. You'll receive one or two *colones* less per dollar than if changing cash. Take small-denomination checks, and stick to the well-known international brands, such as American Express, Citibank, Barclays, and Thomas Cook. Banks will deduct a small commission. **Thomas Cook Currency Services,** 630 5th Ave., New York, NY 10111, tel. (212) 757-6915, specializes in traveler's checks. The **American Express** office, located in the TAM Travel Agency, Calle Central, Avenida Central/1, tel. 256-0203, fax 222-8092, will also issue U.S.-dollar traveler's checks. Unlike the U.S., few stores will accept traveler's checks as currency.

CREDIT CARDS

Most larger hotels, car rental companies, and travel suppliers, as well as larger restaurants and stores, will accept credit card payment by Visa and MasterCard (American Express is not widely accepted). Conversion is normally at the official exchange rate, although a 6% service charge may be added. You can also use your credit cards to buy *colones* at banks (minimum $50); some banks will pay cash advances in dollars. Most banks accept Visa, but very few accept MasterCard. At least one bank in every major town now has a **Credomatic** (24-hour automatic credit) machine—but you'll need your PIN number. Credomatic, tel. 257-4744, has offices throughout San José; its main office is at Calle Central, Avenida 3/5.

The **American Express** Express Cash system, tel. (800) 227-4669 (for information), also links your AmEx card to your U.S. checking account. You can withdraw up to $1,000 in a 21-day period; a $2 fee is charged for each transaction and the money is usually issued in traveler's checks. The local American Express representative is **TAM Travel Agency,** Calle Central, Avenida Central/1, tel. 256-0203, fax 222-8092; open 8 a.m.-5:30 p.m. weekdays. Credomatic also has an American Express service, tel. 257-1646.

MONEY TRANSFERS

You can arrange immediate wire transfers through **Western Union,** tel. 283-6336 or (800) 777-7777, which has representatives throughout the country; its main office is at San Pedro in San José. Major banks in San José will also arrange cash transfers from the U.S. for a small commission fee. Ask your home bank for the name and details of a "correspondent" bank in San José. If you need money transferred while traveling, simply telex your home bank to arrange a wire transfer to the correspondent bank. You can also wire or receive up to $10,000 via **American Express MoneyGram** (to send, the full amount must be paid in advance; only $1,000 can be charged to a credit card). Call (800) 543-4080 for information.

In an emergency, you may be able to cull money on a Visa Gold or Business Card via the 24-hour **Visa Assistance Center,** call collect (919) 370-3203; in the U.S., tel. (800) 759-6262.

COSTS

Costa Rica may be more expensive than you thought, and certainly is more so than the rest of Central and much of South America. However, it should be possible to get by on $25 a day by being frugal. Budget hotels will cost $5-15 per night. A breakfast or lunch of *gallo pinto* will cost $1-4, and a dinner with beer at an inexpensive restaurant should cost no more than $5. I normally travel in a little more style and average $30-60 a day, depending on the standard of accommodations. Your mode of transportation will make a difference. Day tours featuring sightseeing and first-class hotels average $75-100, all-inclusive. Remember, too, you can fly anywhere in the country for $50, or travel by bus for less than $10. Renting a car will send your costs skyrocketing—a minimum of $40 a day, plus insurance and gas.

Bargaining
Haggling over prices is *not* a tradition in Costa Rica, except at streetside craft stalls.

Discounts
Many tour companies, hotels, car rental agencies, etc. offer discounts to members of **Hostelling International.**

Access Costa Rica Network, tel. 231-3637, fax 231-5221, produces a **Passport Discount Card** ($20) offering discounts of 10-30% on a wide range of tourist facilities.

The main ICT information office in San José distributes leaflets and coupons offering discounts at select hotels and other establishments. Also see ad coupons in the *Tico Times* and *Costa Rica Today.*

Tipping

Taxi drivers do not receive tips. Tipping in restau-

rants is *not* the norm—restaurants automatically add both a 15% sales tax and a 10% service charge to your bill. Don't add an additional tip except as a reward for exceptional service. Bellboys in classy hotels should receive 25 cents to 50 cents per bag. And don't forget your chambermaids—the often-forgotten workhorses who have worked hard on your behalf—when you leave. Tour guides normally are tipped $1-2 pp per day for large groups, and much more, at your discretion, for small, personalized tours. Again, don't tip if you had only so-so service, but be fair.

COMMUNICATIONS

BROADCASTING

Costa Rica has twelve TV broadcasting stations. Four TV channels provide 24-hour satellite coverage from the United States (many hotels that advertise "satellite TV" have access to only a few fuzzy stations). And cable TV is offered widely; thus many hotels provide North American programming from C-Span and CNN to ESPN and HBO.

There are about 120 radio stations. The vast majority play Costa Rican music, and finding Western music isn't easy. Classical music fans are served by **Radio Universidad**, 870 AM and 96.7 FM, and by **Radio FM 96**. For New Age and jazz, tune to **Radio Estereo Azul**, on 99 FM. BBC World Service and Voice of America provide English-language news, as does **Radio 2** on FM 99.5. The latter offers 24-hour, all-English-language programming, with trivia contests, weather, music, and a special Friday morning segment devoted to tourist information. There's an English-language station—**Radio Paladin**—at 107.5 FM with interesting and eclectic programing.

NEWSPAPERS AND MAGAZINES

Local Publications

Costa Rica has three major dailies. *La Nación* offers a distinctly right-wing bias. *La República* and *La Prensa Libre* offer slightly less biased news accounts. For a leftist perspective, read *Libertad.* I recommend the Spanish-language

weekly *Esta Semana* for its solid and clear-minded news coverage. The government has its own official organ: *La Gazette.*

No hablas español? The excellent, family-run, English-language *Tico Times* will edify you. It is consistently more analytical than its Costa Rican peers and diligently covers environmental issues. It's published each Friday and is a particularly good source of information on cultural events. It's sold at newsstands and in hotels nationwide (50 cents). A six-month subscription costs U.S. residents $26.50; one year costs $45. Contact *Tico Times,* Dept. 717, P.O. Box 025216, Miami, FL 33102, e-mail: ttimes@sol.racsa.co.cr.

In a similar, though lighter vein, look for *Costa Rica Today,* an English-language weekly newspaper geared specifically to foreign travelers and published in color. It's available free at hotels. U.S. subscriptions cost $32.95 for six months from Ediciones 2000, ACO-117, P.O. Box 0025216, Miami, FL 33102.

The German-language *Costa Rica aktuell,* Apdo. 3264, San José 1000, tel. 257-0232, fax 257-0237, is a superb monthly newspaper combining practical information for travelers with news and profiles on every aspect of the country. A subscription runs DM139 or US$79. The same company publishes a color magazine, *Focus Zentral-Amerika,* subscription DM139 or US$45, listing country profiles and essential telephone numbers for German travelers in Central America.

Costa Rica Outdoors, Dept. SJO 2316, P.O. Box 025216, Miami, FL 33102; in Costa Rica, Apdo. 199, Santa Ana 6150, tel. 282-6743, is a color magazine dedicated to fishing and outdoor sports, and published twice-monthly; annual subscription, $39.50.

The **Costa Rica Resident's Association,** Apdo. 232-1007 Centro Colón, San José, tel. 233-8068, fax 233-1152, e-mail: arcrsacc@sol.racsa.co.cr, publishes *La Voz,* a newsletter full of practical information.

Latin America Travel Tribune, Apdo. 661, Alajuela, costs $25 per year (in U.S.) and offers a strong focus on Costa Rica, with plenty of news features, tourism profiles, and tongue-in-cheek humor.

Green: For the New Age Traveler is a "Central American Environmental Travel Magazine," Apdo. 1290-1100 Tibas, tel. 236-1951, fax 235-8311, e-mail: greencorp@greenarrow.com, focusing on ecological issues. And *Welcome to Costa Rica,* tel. 221-3221, fax 258-1940, is a color travel magazine distributed free throughout the country.

Surfers are served by *Surfos: The Costa Rican Surfer's Guide,* Apdo. 1985-1100, San José, tel. 256-9455, fax 223-3336, e-mail: surfos@sol.racsa.co.cr, a slick full-color magazine published in Spanish and English; and by the newsletter style *Surf Guide Magazine,* Apdo. 694-1100, San José, tel./fax 289-6137.

International Publications

Adventures in Costa Rica, Starflame Productions, P.O. Box 508, Jackson, CA 95642, has lots of first-person reportage and a strong focus for would-be retirees to Costa Rica. Also new, *Costa Rica Adventure & Business,* 12416 Hymeadow Dr., Austin, TX 78750, tel. (512) 250-9023, is a quarterly full-color magazine ($19.95 a year), and includes features articles and news reports. The *Guide Magazine,* Guide Magazine, P.O. Box 025216-175, Miami, FL 33102-5216, is a slick English-language glossy magazine dedicated to tourism in Costa Rica. International subscriptions cost $35. **Costa Rica Advisor,** 8121 S. Yukon Way, Littleton, CO 80123, tel./fax (303) 973-2806, is a quarterly newsletter covering all aspects of Costa Rica. And in December 1997, *Premiere,* P.O. Box 69111, Orlando, FL 32869, tel. (407) 354-2694, fax 903-0531, e-mail: pandion@sol.racsa.co.cr, the "Premier Travel Magazine of Costa Rica," was initiated; the slick full-color quarterly is associated with the Grupo Barceló group of hotels.

International newspapers and magazines are available at a few newsstands, bookstores, and upscale hotels. The *Miami Herald* beams its Latin American edition to Costa Rica, where it is printed as a daily in English. However, Ticos are not passionate readers, and away from large towns you'll be hard-pressed to find *any* outlet selling magazines, Spanish-language or otherwise.

POSTAL SERVICES

The nation's mail service is inefficient and has faced some severe criticism for internal fraud in recent years. A recent investigation of CORTEL (the Costa Rica postal service) revealed a frightening degree of mail theft. Even when mailing out of Costa Rica, don't enclose anything of value. There is a post office in every town and most villages, and some larger hotels, plus the main post offices in San José, at Calle 2 and Avenida 1/3, have 24-hour postage machines. Many hotels can provide stamps and will often take care of mailing for you.

Airmail *(correo aereo)* to/from North America averages two weeks, though three or more weeks is not unknown. To/from Europe, anticipate a minimum of three weeks; sea mail *(marítimo)* takes anywhere from six weeks to three months. Postcards to North America cost 40 *colones* (approximately 15 cents); letters cost 50 *colones* (about 20 cents) for the first ounce. Add 10 *colones* to Europe. Registered mail costs 30 *colones* extra. Opening hours vary; most post offices are open Mon.-Fri. 7 a.m.-6 p.m. and Sat. 7 a.m.-noon.

Mailing packages overseas is expensive. *Don't* seal your package. You must first take it to the central post office for customs inspection. See the San José chapter for more information.

Receiving Mail

Street addresses are rarely used in Costa Rica. Most people rent a post office box (*apartado*—abbreviated Apdo.—but increasingly being written as "P.O. Box"). You may wish to do the same if you plan on staying a few months or more. Mailboxes are in short supply, so you may find an individual or company willing to share—it's common. Costa Rican postal codes sometimes appear before the name of the town, or even after the *apartado* number (e.g., Apdo. 890-1000, San José, instead of Apdo. 890, San José 1000). Embassies generally will not hold mail for you.

You can receive international mail c/o **Lista de Correos** at the central post office in San José (Lista de Correos, Correos Central, San José 1000), or any other large town. Each item costs 10 cents. You must pick up your mail in person at window 17 in the hall at the southern end of the building on Calle 2. Bring your passport; you won't get your mail without it.

Incoming letters are filed alphabetically. If the clerk can't find your name under the initial of your surname, try other initials—your first or middle name, for example. Tell anyone you expect to write to you to *print* your surname legibly and to include the words "Central America." Also tell them not to send money or anything else of monetary value.

Tell friends and family not to mail parcels larger than a magazine-size envelope. Receiving them is a hassle. You'll need to make two or more visits to the Aduana (Customs) in Zapote, on the outskirts of San José; one visit to declare the contents, the second to pay duty. The fee is hefty: at least equal to the value of the goods, however minor they may be.

Private Mail Services

The incidence of mail theft has spawned many private mail services. **DHL Worldwide Express** in San José, Calle 34, between Paseo Colón and Avenida 2, tel. 223-1423, offers express document and parcel service. It's open Mon.-Fri. 7:30 a.m.-7:30 p.m., and Saturday 8 a.m.-7 p.m. The main office, tel. 290-3020, is in the San José suburb of Pavas. Most major towns have a DHL office.

TELEX, FAX, AND TELEGRAMS

Most moderate and upscale hotels will send a fax or telex for you for a small fee. There's a public telex in San José at **Radiográfica Costarricense**, one block west of the National Theater, Calle 1, Avenida 5, tel. 287-0087 or 287-0462, fax 223-1609; it's open 7 a.m.-10 p.m. The telex number is Costa Rica 1050. It costs about 50 cents a word. You can also send and receive faxes via Radiográfica or **ICE** (Insituto Costarricense de Electricidad) offices nationwide. Most towns have one. The fax or telex must indicate your name and Costa Rica address or telephone number or you'll not be advised of its arrival; it's best to call anyway to check if you've received a fax or telex. Fax transmissions cost $7 per page to Europe, $5 to the United States. ICE also has a telegram service, which you can dictate by telephone, call 123.

Cheaper by far is CORTEL, the Costa Rican postal and telegraph system. Most post offices permit you to send telexes and faxes.

E-MAIL AND THE INTERNET

Sending and receiving e-mail via the World Wide Web is easy in Costa Rica. Many upscale hotels have telephone jacks for laptop plug-in (calls aren't cheap, however, as most hotels add a huge mark-up for calls). Well-known online companies such as America On-Line (AOL) have local access numbers that provide you instant access to the web; AOL's number is tel. 257-7898. Others do not. You can still access your e-mail account while in Costa Rica through one of the companies listed below.

Radiográfica Costarricense (RACSA), tel. 287-0087 or 287-0515, fax 223-1609, e-mail: mercadeo@sol.racsa.co.cr, is a branch of ICE and operates the major Web-site servers in Costa Rica. It has e-mail service: ptoventa@sol.racsa.co.cr. It offers Internet technical assistance, tel. 287-0300 or 287-0407, and via e-mail at asistenc@sol.racsa.co.cr, and can set you up with an e-mail address if you're in the country for a while.

It charges $30 monthly, including 30 hours online time ($1 extra per hour). It also charges $2 per hour for Internet access. It has a **telecommunications center** at Calle 1, Avenida 5 in San José.

Ticonet, tel. 280-0932, fax 280-0329, e-mail: mercadeo@tr.ticonet.co.cr or lance@mail.ticonet. co.cr, offers Internet services and e-mail rentals, plus access to your own e-mail account. Its office is in the ICE building (called the Equus Bldg.) in San Pedro.

Other such companies in San José include **Información Internacional,** tel. 256-3222, e-mail: iclayton@istar.com, and **KitCom,** Keep in Touch Communications, e-mail: kitcom@yelloweb. co.cr, which has e-mail, fax, and voice-mail services, as does **Inter@merica,** tel. 256-5811, fax 222-0331, e-mail: rarena@cool.co.cr. **ICE** also offers an Internet service.

TELEPHONES

Costa Rica has an efficient direct-dial telephone system under the control of ICE, which has offices in most towns. You can place calls from ICE offices, or (in San José) at **Radiográfica Costarricense,** one block west of the National Theater, Calle 1, Avenida 5, tel. 287-0087 or 287-0462, fax 223-1609. The country boasts more telephones per capita than any other Latin American nation. ICE offers the White Pages telephone directory on-line at www.ice.go.cr, or http://200.9.47.5/pgblancas.html. **Kitcom** (Keep in Touch Communications), e-mail: kitcom@yelloweb.co.cr, has a telephone message center.

Costa Rica converted from a six-digit to a seven-digit telephone system in 1994; some sources of information may still advertise the old numbers.

The Costa Rica **country code is 506.**

Public Phone Booths
Street signs with telephone symbols point the way to public phone booths, found throughout the nation in even the most extreme boondocks and implausible places. In more remote spots, the public phone is usually at the village *pulpería,* or store. Often the phone is the *only* phone in a village and there is often a lengthy line. If no one else is standing in line, the phone is probably *malo* (broken)!

IMPORTANT PHONE NUMBERS

Dictate telegrams and fax. 123
Directory Information 113
International information. 124
International operator. 116
Time 112

Direct dial to foreign operators:
Canada . . . . 161 or 0800-015-0161
France 0800-033-1033
Germany 0800-049-1049
Italy 0800-039-1039
Netherlands (Holland) 0800-031-1111
Spain 0800-034-1034
UK . . . . 167 or 0800-044-1044
U.S.
   AT&T 0800-011-4114
   MCI . . . . 162 or 0800-012-2222
   Sprint . . . . 163 or 0800-013-0123
   Worldcom 0800-014-4444

Public phones accept only the new five-, 10-, and 20-*colones* coins. You may need a stack of coins. Wait for the dial tone before inserting your coin. The dial tone is similar to that of U.S. phones. The coin will drop when your call is connected. Two *colones* gives you two minutes. Have your second and subsequent coins ready to insert immediately when the beep indicating "time up" sounds, or you'll be cut off. Some phones allow you to "stack" coins in an automatic feeder.

It's a good idea to give your phone booth telephone number to the person you're calling so he or she can call you back (it is usually indicated on a yellow sign above the phone). Phone booths do not have telephone books; your hotel front desk should have one.

Where public phones are absent, local hotels, corner stores, or *pulperías* will usually allow use of their phones for a charge. They'll dial for you and meter your call; you'll be charged by the minute.

Some phone booths accept only phone cards.

Local Calls
Local calls are very cheap. You can call anywhere in the nation for three minutes for 50 cents from public phone booths. Calls from your hotel room may be considerably more expensive than nor-

mal long-distance rates (the more expensive the hotel, the more they jack up the fee). There are no area or city codes; simply dial the seven-digit number. There is one telephone directory for the whole country, plus a separate directory for San José. In some villages you will reach the local operator, who will connect you with your party.

International Calls

When calling Costa Rica from North America, dial 011 (the international dial code), then 506 (the Costa Rican country code), followed by the seven-digit local number. AT&T has a "Language Line" that will connect you with an interpreter, (800) 843-8420 in North America, (408) 648-7174 in Costa Rica; interpreter time is billed at $3.50 per minute.

For outbound calls from Costa Rica, dial 00, then the country code and local number. You can dial direct to most countries from public phone booths, or via an English-speaking international operator (dial 116). You'll need to call 116 to make collect calls (reverse charges) or charge to a telephone credit card. The operator will call you back once he/she has connected you. Hotel operators can also connect you, although charges for calling from hotels are high. The easiest and least costly way, however, to make direct calls is to bill to your credit card or phone card by calling one of the operators listed in the accompanying chart, **Important Phone Numbers.**

USADirect phones automatically link you with an AT&T operator. You'll find them at Juan Santamaría Airport, in the lobbies of some top-class hotels, and at Radiográfica Costarricense in San José.

Direct-dial international calls to North America cost $2-3 per minute, depending on where you're calling. Calls to the UK cost $3-4 per minute; to Australia $5 per minute. The first minute costs extra. Cheaper rates apply between 8 p.m. and 7 a.m. and on weekends. Hotels add their own, often exorbitant, charges, plus government tax. From a coin box, calls to North America cost 65 cents-$1.60 per minute, depending on where you're calling. Calls to the U.K. cost $1.25-2 per minute, to Australia $1.75-2 per minute.

Phone Cards

You can buy a pre-paid telephone card for international direct-dial calls. The card is sold in denominations of $10, $20, and 3,000 colones at ICE telephone agencies, certain banks, calling card vending machines, and stores bearing the **Viajera Internacionál 199** symbol. You simply put the card in the telephone slot, dial 199, then 2 for instructions in English; then dial the card number, then 00, plus the country code, area code, and telephone number. The cost of your call is automatically deducted from the value of the card.

A similar card system—**Chip**—is available for both national and international calls. It is sold in units of 500, 1,000, and 2,000 colones. English-language instructions are provided.

Cellular Phones

The Costa Rican division of Millicom Corp., tel. 257-2527, offers cellular phone rentals for $7.50 per day. A fax attachment can also be rented (you provide the fax machine). Rentals can be charged to an American Express account.

OTHER PRACTICALITIES

INFORMATION

Tourist Information Offices

The **Costa Rican Tourism Institute (Instituto Costarricense de Turismo—ICT)** has a 24-hour toll-free tourist information line—tel. (800) 343-6332—in the United States. You can request brochures, but anticipate that it will take weeks or months before they arrive.

The ICT has a tourist office at 1101 Brickel Ave., Suite 801, Miami, FL 33131, tel. (305) 358-2150 or (800) 327-7033. There are no ICT offices in Canada or the United Kingdom. The Costa Rican embassies can provide limited tourist information (see the **Embassies and Consulates in Costa Rica** chart).

In Costa Rica, the ICT head office, Apdo. 777, San José 1000, tel. 223-1733, fax 223-5452, e-mail: promoict@tourism-costarica.com, is at Avenida 4, Calles 5/7, on the eleventh floor. The information office is open Mon.-Fri. 8 a.m.-4 p.m. (The office beneath the Plaza de la Cultura closed in 1996; word in early 1998 was that it may soon be reopened.) The ICT issues a road map (free) and a San José city map, plus other literature. It also has a Web page at www.tourism-costarica.com.

There's also an information booth and reservation center run by **INFOtur**, tel. 442-8632, fax 442-9417, outside Customs at Juan Santamaría Airport; open Mon.-Sat. 9 a.m.-10 p.m. (INFOtur is not appreciated by local tour operators, as it seems to operate as a travel agency with special concessions from the ICT that, it is claimed, were granted through nepotism.)

Futuropa (Fundación para la Promoción de Costa Rica en Europa) has a tourist informtion office in Cologne, Germany; more sites are to be added.

Telephone Information Services

A 24-hour, multilingual **Tourist Tele-Info Line**, tel. 257-4667, provides information on a wide range of tourist facilities that include restaurants, accommodations, adventures, etc. Only paying business subscribers are listed. The *Tico Times*

newspaper also operates a 24-hour bilingual **Tourist Information Line**, tel. 240-6373.

National Parks

You can receive toll-free information on national parks nationwide by calling 192 (a long-touted toll-free number had not been introduced at press time for worldwide calls). See **National Parks** in the "Conservation" section of the Introduction for information on the SPN's **public information office.**

Other Sources

Adams Enterprises, P.O. Box 18295, Irvine, CA 92713-8295, tel. (714) 857-8079, fax 786-8079, distributes a "Costa Rica Information Packet" containing dozens of brochures on hotels, tour packages, Spanish language schools, real estate, etc., as well as a video and a magazine on Costa Rican real estate ($9 postpaid, $10 California, US$11.50 Canada).

The **South American Explorer's Club,** 126 Indian Creek Rd., Ithaca, NY 14850, tel. (607) 277-0488, fax 277-6122, publishes the quarterly *South American Explorer* magazine, containing a list of guidebooks, maps, trip reports, and resources for sale, as well as feature articles and advice for travelers and explorers. Annual membership costs $40. The **South America Travel Association,** c/o Creative Resources, 12830 N.W. 9th St., Miami, FL 33182, is geared to travel industry personnel though it accepts memberships from anyone (rates vary); it publishes *The News of Latin America* ($20). Also try the **Asociación Costarricense de Agencias** (Costa Rica Travel Agents Association), Apdo. 8076, San José 1000, tel. 233-2921, for information on specific tour companies and tour options.

Lastly, of course, are a wide range of travel videos and guidebooks, including several of special-interest focus (see the **Booklist**). Make sure you obtain the latest edition. The *Pocket Traveler's Guide to Costa Rica,* American Research Service Corp., tel. 221-6408, fax 223-3811; in the U.S., P.O. Box 025216, Dept SJ-316, Miami, FL 33102-5216, is a 28-page pamphlet listing essential information and telephone numbers.

In Costa Rica, *Tico Times* reporter Peter Brennan, hosts "Costa Rica Update" at 7 p.m. every Thursday on Channel 19 (it's rebroadcast on Saturday at 1 p.m.). And **Radio 2** has a Friday-morning tourist information segment, broadcast in English on FM 99.5.

Online Information
Scores of Costa Rican hotels, tour operators, and other establishments have web-sites, in addition to the plethora of sites with generic information on Costa Rica. The ICT has a site at www.tourismcostarica.com. Other generic sites to try include: www.city.net/countries/costa_rica, www.cocori. com, www.crica.com, www.centralamerica. com, and www.tuanis.com/costarica.

Phil Greenspun's *Travels With Samantha* provides a fabulous information service on the **Internet's World Wide Web Travel Review,** http://www-swiss.ai.mit.edu/cr/, based largely on his own anecdotal travels. Much of the text from the *Costa Rica Handbook* is also on-line. Thanks, Phil!

For a range of travel information and further resources, remember Moon's own website: http://www.moon.com.

MAPS

The ICT issues a basic 1:1,000,000 ICT road map of the country (though this is not much use for driving beyond the Meseta Central) featuring more detailed inset maps of San José and major cities. One of the best road maps is a topographical 1:500,000 sheet published by **International Travel Map Publications,** P.O. Box 2290, Vancouver, B.C. V6B 2WF, Canada. The map features a 1:250,000 "Environs of San José" inset. It is available in the U.K. through **Bradt Publications,** 41 Nortoft Rd., Chalfont St. Peter, Bucks SL9 0LA, England, and at **Stanford's,** 12-14 Long Acre, London WC2E 9LP, tel. (0171) 836-1321, fax 836-0189. Most travel bookstores in the U.S. stock it or can order it.

Similar 1:500,00-scale maps of Costa Rica can be ordered from **South Trek,** 1301 Oxford Ave., Austin, TX 78704, tel./fax (512) 443-4533, e-mail: sotrek@onr.com; **Treaty Oak,** P.O. Box 50295, Austin, TX 78763-0295, tel. (512) 326-4141, fax 443-0973; or **Omni Resources,** P.O

Box 2096, Burlington, NC 27216, tel. (800) 742-2677, fax (910) 227-3748. The **Fundación Neotrópica** also publishes a superb topographical map with nature reserves and parks emphasized.

Jitan also publishes a reasonable quality 1:800,000 *General Map of Costa Rica* ($2) and a 1:670,000 road map ($4), available by mail order from Jiménez and Tanzi, Apdo. 2553, San José 1000, tel. 233-8033, fax 233-8294 (add $1 for postage and handling; do *not* send cash by mail).

The *Red Guide to Costa Rica: National Map Guide* (San José: Guías de Costa Rica), provides detailed regional maps, as does Wilberth S. Herrera's *Costa Rica Nature Atlas* (San José: Editorial Incafo), which has detailed 1:200,000 scale maps (it also has the advantage of providing detailed and lucid accounts of national parks and other sites. Also look for *Costa Rica Tourist Guide,* a compendium of hotels with 21 route maps showing locales of advertisers, Ruticas S.A., Apdo. 2063-2100 San José, tel. 283-1430, fax 283-5139, e-mail: ruticas@sol.racsa.co.cr.

Major bookstores in San José carry the above maps and books. **Chispas Books, Lehmann's,** and **Librería Trejos** (see **Publications** under "Shopping" in the San José chapter for addresses) have an excellent stock of maps; prices at Librería Trejos tend to be cheaper.

You can mail-order maps from **Jiménez & Tanzi, Ltda.,** Apdo. 2553, San José 1000, tel. 233-8033, fax 323-8294, with prepayment. Maps include: *General Map of Costa Rica* (1:800,000; $2), *Greater Metropolitan San José* (1:200,000; $1.50), a *Center of San José* map for walkers (1:10,000; $2), *Downtown San José,* more suited to drivers (1:12,500; $3), and a three-map *Road Map* ($4). Add $1 postage and handling for up to four maps. Postage is free for more than four maps.

A wide variety of accurate topographic maps and detailed city maps can be bought from the **Instituto Geográfica Nacional** in San José.

WHEN TO GO

Costa Rica has distinct wet and dry seasons. The best weather is during dry season (Dec.-April), with December, January, and February perhaps the ideal months. This is the busiest time, however, and many hotels and coastal resorts tend to be fully booked. Easter is the very busiest period, closely followed by Christmas and New Year's, when accommodations tend to be booked solid months in advance. Advance reservations—several months ahead—are strongly recommended for dry season.

Consider traveling off-season. The rainy season—now promoted as the "green season"—normally begins in late April or early May. While many dirt roads can be washed out, and many regions temporarily inaccessible by road, don't let this put you off. Advantages to green-season travel are many. Prices are often lower, and it is usually much easier to find vacant hotels rooms, especially in more popular destinations, which remain accessible by road at this time of year. The highlands can be especially delightful at this time of year (rain normally means short-lived afternoon and evening showers or rainstorms). The Golfito and Caribbean lowlands, both of which can be lashed by the whip of tropical storms in the wet season, don't have a distinct dry season anyway. Temperatures in any locale remain the same year-round; temperatures generally vary with elevation, not season.

WHAT TO BRING

Pack light! A good rule of thumb is to lay out everything you wish to take, then eliminate half. Remember, you'll also need some spare room for any souvenirs and books you plan on bringing home. *Leave your jewelry at home;* it invites theft. Most important, don't forget your passport, airline tickets, traveler's checks, and other documentation. You'd be amazed how many folks get to the airport before discovering this oversight.

One Traveler, One Bag
Space on buses and planes is severely limited. Limit yourself to one bag (preferably a sturdy duffel bag or internal-frame backpack with plenty of pockets), plus a small day pack or camera bag. Avoid backpacks with external appendages: they catch and easily bend or break. Believe me! One of the best investments you can make is a well-made duffel bag that can be carried by hand and on the back. A small day pack allows you to pack everything for a one- or two-day

journey. Then, you can leave the rest of your gear in the storage room of a San José hotel and return frequently as you travel around the country using the capital as a base.

Clothing Tips
Limit the number of changes of clothing. Pack items that work in various combinations—preferably darker items that don't show the inevitable dirt and stains you'll quickly collect on your travels. Note, though, that dark clothes tend to be hotter than khaki or light clothing. Bright clothing tends to scare off wildlife; pack khakis and subdued greens if you plan on serious nature viewing. Some people recommend packing just one set of clothes to wash, and one to wear. Two sets of clothing seems ascetic. Two T-shirts plus two dressier shirts, a sweatshirt and sweatpants, a polo shirt, a pair of Levi's, "safari" pants, two pairs of shorts, and a "safari" or photographer's jacket with heaps of pockets suffice me. Women may wish to substitute blouses and mid-length skirts. And don't forget your bathing suit.

Socks and Underwear
Pack plenty of socks and underpants. Socks get wet quickly and frequently in Costa Rica. You may need to change daily. Wash them frequently to help keep athlete's foot and other fungal growths at bay.

Packing for Temperature Variations
Remember, Costa Rica can be both hot and cold. If you plan on visiting a volcano or cloud forest, pack a warm sweater and/or a warm windproof jacket; you'll want one for San José and the highlands at night, anyway. In the mountains, cold winds are common, and it gets very chilly and wet when the clouds set in. The lowlands, of course, are humid and warm to hot. You'll want light, loose-fitting shirts and pants. And if you plan on hiking in the forests, loose-fitting cotton canvas shirt and pants will help protect against thorns and biting bugs.

Note: Here's a handy tip for handling changes in environment. Whenever you move from, say, the relatively cool central highlands to hot, dry Guanacaste, or from Guanacaste to the humid Pacific Southwest, *take a shower!* This leaves the human body at the local temperature.

local laundry, Cahuita

JOHN ANDERSON

Wet or Dry Season?

In the wet season, plan on rain—plenty of it! An inexpensive umbrella is best (you can buy one in San José). Raincoats are heavy and tend to make you sweat, although a hooded poncho can be an invaluable asset. Make sure it has slits down the side for your arms, and that it is large enough to carry your small day pack underneath. Breathable Gore-Tex rainproof jackets also work fine.

Denim jeans take forever to dry when wet, so also pack a pair of light cotton-polyester-blend safari-style pants, which are cooler, dry quickly, and have plenty of pockets. Ideally, everything should be drip-dry, wash-and-wear.

Jackets, Ties, and Cocktail Dresses

Most travelers will not need dressy clothes. However, many Costa Ricans love to dress up for dinner or the theater, as well as for business functions. You may wish to take a jacket and tie or cocktail dress for dinners in more expensive hotels and restaurants, and for the theater. Otherwise, Costa Ricans dress informally, but always very neatly. Knee-length shorts for men are becoming acceptable wear in San José. Save shorter style runner's shorts for the beach.

Footwear

A comfortable, well-fitting pair of sneakers will do double-duty for most occasions. In the wet season and any time in the rainforests, your shoes will get wet. Rubber boots (botas de hule)

are a godsend on tropical trails. They're standard wear for many rural dwellers. You can buy them in Costa Rica for about $10. (Ticos have small feet; if you take size 9 or above, plan on bringing your own.) If you go hiking, you'll also want a plastic water bottle and sturdy walking shoes. If hiking in the wet season or rainforest, protect your spare clothing in a plastic bag inside your backpack.

PHOTOGRAPHY

Equipment

You are allowed to bring two cameras and six rolls of film into Costa Rica (don't worry about the official film limit; I've never heard of it being enforced). Film is susceptible to damage by X-ray machines. You should always request that film (including your camera loaded with film) be hand-checked by airport security rather than having it go through the X-ray machine.

Try to figure out how much film you think you'll need to bring—then double it. I recommend one roll per day as a minimum, much more if you're even half serious about your photography. Film is expensive in Costa Rica. If you do need to buy in San José, check the expiry date; the film may be outdated. And the film may have been sitting in the sun for months on end—not good! Kodachrome 64 and Fujichrome 50 give the best color rendition in Costa Rica's bright, high-contrast conditions (Fuji is superior to Kodak), but you may need ASA 200 or 400 for the dark conditions typical within the gloomy rainforest sanctum.

Keep your film out of the sun. If possible, refrigerate it. Color emulsions are particularly sensitive to tropical heat and the colors will fade (Kodak film is far more likely to fade than Fuji's films). Film rolls can also soften with the humidity so that they easily stretch and refuse to wind in your camera. Pack both your virgin and exposed film in a Ziploc plastic bag with silica gel inside to protect against moisture. You can have Fuji processed in Costa Rica at one of its many outlets. For Kodak, wait until you get home (try to keep your film cool). Or buy film with prepaid processing. It comes with a self-mailer and you can simply pop it in a mailbox; the prints or slides will then be mailed to your home.

Bring extra batteries for light meters and flashes. Protect your lenses with a UV or skylight filter, and consider buying "warming," neutral-density, and/or polarizing filters, which can dramatically improve results. Your local camera shop can help you understand their applications. Keep your lenses clean and dry when not in use (believe it or not, there's even a tropical mildew that attacks coated lenses). Silica gel packs are essential to help protect your camera gear from moisture; use them if you carry your camera equipment inside a plastic bag. Never turn your back on your camera gear. Watch it at all times.

Fuji has air-conditioned outlets throughout Costa Rica, including most towns and resorts; call their central office for information, tel. 222-2222. They sell fresh film and instamatic cameras. In San José try **Equipos Fotográficos**, tel. 233-0176, on Avenida 3, Calles 3/5; or **Dima**, tel. 222-3969, on Avenida Central, Calles 3/5. If you need urgent repairs, **Taller de Equipos Fotográficos**, Avenida Central, Calles 3/5, tel. 223-1146, in San José is recommended. Kodak and Agfa have photographic labs in large cities throughout Costa Rica. And **Canon** has an authorized camera-repair shop on Avenida 3, Calles 3/5 in San José.

Shooting Tips

Don't underestimate the intensity of light. Midday is the worst time for photography. Early morning and late afternoon provide the best light; the wildlife is more active then, too. Use rubber hoods on all your lenses to screen out ambient light. And a good idea is to "stop down" one or two f-stops to underexpose slightly for better color rendition when photographing in bright sunlight. In the forest, you'll need as much light as possible. Remarkably little light seeps down to the forest floor; use a tripod, slow shutter speed, wide-open aperture, and higher-speed film. Use a flash in daytime to "fill in" shaded subjects or dark objects surrounded by bright sunlight.

Ticos enjoy being photographed and will generally cooperate willingly. Never assume an automatic right to take a personal photograph, however. Ask permission to take a photograph as appropriate. And respect an individual's right to refuse.

Two recommended books are *The Wildlife & Nature Photographer's Field Guide* by Michael Freeman (Cincinnati: Writer's Digest Books, 1984) and *The Traveler's Photography Handbook* by Julian Calder and John Garrett (New York: Fielding/Morrow, 1985). The *PhotoGuide: The Ticos,* Guide Magazine, P.O. Box 025216-175, Miami, FL 33102-5216, is a coffee-table book about the Costa Ricans. It may offer some ideas for improving your own photography.

Also see "photography tours" in this chapter.

WEIGHTS AND MEASURES

Costa Rica operates on the metric system. Liquids are sold in liters, fruits and vegetables by the kilo. Some of the old Spanish measurements still survive in vernacular usage. Street directions, for example, are often given as 100 *varas* (the Spanish "yard," equal to 33 inches) to indicate a city block. See the chart at the back of this book for metric conversions.

TIME

Costa Rica time is equivalent to U.S. central standard time (i.e., six hours behind Greenwich mean time, one hour behind New York, and two hours ahead of the U.S. west coast). Costa Rica has no daylight saving time, during which time it is *seven* hours behind Greenwich and *two* hours behind New York. There is little seasonal variation in dawn (approximately 6 a.m.) and dusk (6 p.m.).

BUSINESS HOURS

Businesses are usually open Mon.-Fri. 8 a.m.-5 p.m. A few also open Saturday morning. Lunch breaks are usually two hours; businesses and government offices may close 11:30 a.m.-1:30 p.m. Bank hours vary widely, but in general are open 9 a.m.-3 p.m. Most shops open Mon.-Sat. 8 a.m.-6 p.m., often with a lunch break. Some restaurants close Sunday and Monday. Most businesses also close on holidays.

ELECTRICITY

Costa Rica operates on 110-volts AC (60-cycle) nationwide. Some remote lodges are not connected to the national grid and generate their own power. Check in advance to see if they run on direct current (DC) or a nonstandard voltage. Two types of U.S. plugs are used: flat, parallel two-pins and three rectangular pins. A two-prong adapter is a good idea (most hardware stores in Costa Rica—ferreterías—can supply them). **Magellan's,** P.O. Box 5485, Santa Barbara, CA 93150, tel. (800) 962-4932, can supply appropriate plugs, as well as dozens of other handy travel items featured in a 36-page catalog.

Never allow your personal computer or disks to pass through an airport X-ray machine. The magnets can wipe out all your data and programs. Insist on having it hand-checked. You will need to turn your computer on to show that it's what you say it is and not a bomb.

SPECIAL NOTES

NOTES FOR MEN

The lure of women is the likeliest source of problems for men. Ticas are renowned for their beauty and a reputation for pampering their men; the classifieds in the Tico Times are full of advertisements from Europeans and North Americans seeking a pretty Tica (and vice versa) with whom to settle down in blissful union for a week or a lifetime. Many Ticas are simply seeking a foreign boyfriend (usually older and monied) for the duration of his visit, or in the hope that a longer relationship may develop. The scores of Ticas who hang out at tourist bars in San José are generally seeking invitations to be part of the high life (prostitution in Costa Rica is mostly an amateur affair). A recent study found that most women who form intimate relationships with tourists "have the benefit of extensive economic and educational opportunities. Most are not ashamed and [few] have low self-esteem. . . . What motivates these women . . . is the desire to go out, to enjoy themselves." A pretty Tica attached to a generous suitor can be wined and dined and get her entrance paid into the posher discos. Any financial transaction—assuredly more in one night than she might otherwise earn in a week—becomes a charitable afterthought to a romantic evening out. And who knows—he might even propose. Agencies that provide bilingual companions for dining and travel advertise in the Tico Times, Costa Rica Today, and other publications.

Forget everything you ever learned about romance, love, and lust in your homeland. The rules of the romance game are not the same in Costa Rica, and take some fathoming. You will be the moneybags in any relationship, and are expected to act as such. A book called Happy Aging With Costa Rican Women, by James I. Kennedy (Canoga Park, CA: Box Canyon Books), provides a feel for the trials and tribulations you, the amorous gringo, can expect if you lose your head and your heart to a Tica.

If a Tica isn't interested in you, she's not likely to tell you. Expect to be stood up on dates by Ticas who may express keen interest in you simply because they don't know how to say "no." Always it is because some family emergency—the mother usually had a headache!—arose.

Be careful of scams pulled by prostitutes, or other salacious Ticas, who may have a pecuniary gain in mind above any stated fees. And, by the way, that beauty giving you the wink near the Clínica Bíblica is probably a transvestite.

PROSTITUTION

Prostitution is legal in Costa Rica and looked upon with a general acceptance (many Latin American fathers still initiate sons into sex, for example, by introducing them to prostitutes), and many Costa Rican men use prostitutes as a matter of course. Almost every town and village has a brothel—and San José has dozens.

The government issues licenses for legal brothels and provides regular health checks for prostitutes, who are issued *carnets de salud* to attest to their cleanliness. Many prostitutes, however, are not registered. Be aware that AIDS cases are on the rise in Costa Rica, other venereal diseases are prevalent, and prostitutes pose a particular risk.

The women are independent (their legal status protects prostitutes from the development of pimping). As opposed to places in Asia, for example, where many prostitutes are underage or forced into prostitution, the women plying their bodies in Costa Rica are past the age of consent and do so of free will. However, sordid enterprises *do* exist—in 1997, four foreigners were arrested for operating brothels where minors under 16 were employed.

The **Instituto Eco de Costa Rica,** Apdo. 8080, San José 1000, tel. 221-2801, fax 222-3300, sponsors job training for youngsters and works to mitigate the negative impacts of tourism in promoting prostitution.

NOTES FOR WOMEN

Most women get great enjoyment from traveling in Costa Rica. The majority of Tico men treat foreign women with great respect. Still, Costa Rica is a *machismo* society and you may experience certain hassles. The art of gentle seduction is to Ticos a kind of national pastime: a sport and a trial of manhood. They will hiss in appreciation from a distance like serpents, and call out epithets such as *"guapa"* ("pretty one"), *"machita"* (for blondes), or *"mi amor."* Be aware that many Ticos think a gringa is an "easy" *conquista.* The wolf-whistles can grate but, fortunately, sexual assault of women is rare—though it *does* happen.

If you do welcome the amorous attentions of men, Costa Rica may be heaven. But take effusions of love with a grain of salt; while swearing eternal devotion, your Don Juan may conveniently forget to mention he's married. And when he suggests a nightcap at some romantic locale, he may mean one of San José's love motels. On the Caribbean coast are many "beach boys"—"Rent-a-Rastas"—who earn their living giving pleasure to women looking for love or lust beneath the palms.

If you're not interested in love in the tropics, unwanted attention can be a hassle. Pretend not to notice. Avoid eye contact. An insistent stare—*dando cuervo* (making eyes)—is part of their game. You can help prevent these overtures by dressing modestly. Shorts, halter tops, or strapless sundresses in San José invite attention (this despite the preference among young Ticas—who take great pleasure in knowing that they've been noticed—for skin-tight, shorter, and revealing clothing). And avoid deserted beaches, especially at night. Wearing a wedding band may help keep the wolves at bay. There have been reports of a few taxi drivers coming on to women passengers. Though this is the exception, where possible take a hotel taxi rather than a street cab. And beware unmarked "taxis" which may be cruising on the look-out for single women.

Women Travel: Adventures, Advice, and Experience, by Niktania Jansz and Miranda Davies (Real Guides), is full of practical advice for women travelers. So, too, *Gutsy Women,* by MaryBeth Bond (Travelers' Tales), a small-format guide with travel tips for women on the road. Likewise, the following magazines may be useful: the quarterly *Journeywoman,* 50 Prince Arthur Ave. #1703, Toronto, Canada M5R 1B5; the quarterly *Maiden Voyages,* 109 Minna St. #240, San Francisco, CA 94105, tel. (800) 528-8425, e-mail: info@maiden-voyages.com; and the monthly *Travelin' Woman,* 855 Moraga Dr. #14, Los Angeles, CA 90049, tel. (800) 871-6409, e-mail: traveliw@aol.com.

Resources in Costa Rica

A feminist center called **Casa Yemayá,** tel. 223-3652, fax 225-3636, in San José's Barrio Guadalupe, provides information for women. It also has accommodations from $15 with shared bath and kitchen privileges. Similarly, **Casa de la Nueva Mujer** (House of the New Woman), tel. 225-3784, provides a forum for women to meet and discuss issues ranging from arts and self-defense to women's issues. Accommodations are provided if needed ($9 per night). Located on Calle Sabanilla, about 250 meters north and 100 meters east of La Cosecha market. **CEFEMINA** (Centro Feminista de Información y Acción), Apdo. 5355, San José 1000, tel. 224-3986, and its offshoot, **Mujer No Estás Sola** (Woman, You're Not Alone), are feminist organizations that can provide assistance to women travelers. CEFEMINA publishes the quarterly *Mujer.* The **Women's Club of Costa Rica,** tel. 249-1069 or 239-3396, an English-speaking social forum, is a good resource.

NOTES FOR GAYS AND LESBIANS

San José has been described as a "very actively gay city." On the books, Costa Rica is tolerant of homosexuality and has laws to protect gays from discrimination. Although Costa Rica is nominally a Roman Catholic nation, you may be surprised to learn that homosexual intercourse is legal (the consensual age is 17—for heterosexuals it's 15). However, the Costa Rican government is zealous in protecting minors, and, since the age of majority is 18, gay travelers are advised against fraternizing with anyone under 18. And Costa Rica remains a *machismo* society. Despite legal protections, discrimination exists—for example, the police routinely raid and harass gay clubs, and employers routinely fire or refuse to hire gays—and for the most part, Costa Rican gays remain in the closet. There is even less tolerance of lesbians. Understandably, the climate of abuse and intolerance has resulted in a high level of alcoholism, drug abuse, and even suicide among Costa Rica's gays.

Only in 1986, when Costa Rican authorities attempted to tackle the AIDS problem by "harassing" gays, did the gay movement coalesce, resulting in the formation in 1992 of **Triángulo Rosa** (Pink Triangle), the most prominent gay organization in Central America and one dedicated to fighting human rights violations of gays.

Gay tourists should feel no discrimination "if you don't indulge in foolish [overt] behavior." These words of advice are from *Pura Vida!: A Travel Guide to Gay & Lesbian Costa Rica* by Joseph Itiel (Orchid House, 1993), a practical guidebook that also provides a no-holds-barred look at the author's experiences in Costa Rica.

To understand the sociology of Latino homosexuality, readers of Spanish may wish to browse *Hombres que aman hombres,* by Jacobo Schifter Sikora and Johnny Madrigal Pana (San José: Ediciones Illep-Sida, 1992).

Transvestis (transvestites) are part of the gay and prostitution scene, much more so in Latin American countries than, say, North America. Itiel describes a world of "brutal fights, drugs, unsafe sex, and robberies." A majority of *transvestis,* he says, are involved with drugs. Beware.

Gente 10 and *Confidencial* are gay magazines published in Costa Rica.

Organizations

The **International Gay Travel Association,** 4331 N. Federal Hwy., Suite 304, Ft. Lauderdale, FL 33308, tel. (800) 448-8550, fax (954) 776-3303, e-mail: glpa@aol.com, is one good resource and another is the **Lesbian & Gay Center,** 208 W. 13th St., New York, NY 10011, tel. (212) 620-7310, fax 924-2657, Internet: http://www.gaycenter.org; in Europe, 81 Rue Marche au Charbon, 1000 Brussels, Belgium, tel. 32-2-502-2471.

In Costa Rica: The most prominent organization is **Triángulo Rosa,** Apdo. 1619-4050, Alajuela, tel. 442-7375, Spanish, or tel./fax 234-2411 in English, which acts as an information center and provides a gamut of services: safe sex education, AIDS counseling, and fighting ongoing discrimination. It is staffed by volunteers, who can provide recommendations for gay-friendly bars, hotels, and more.

Other gay organizations include **Colectivo Gay Universitario,** tel. 222-3047, and **Las Entendidas,** tel./fax 233-9708, a local lesbian/feminist group that meets the last Wednesday of each month at La Avispa, Calle 1, Avenidas 8/10, tel. 223-5343. The **International Gay & Lesbian Association** has a local chapter, tel. 234-2411. There are several support groups for HIV-positive gays, including **Asociación de Lucha Contra el SIDA,** tel. 283-5305. Supposedly, there's even one for English-speaking foreign residents.

Meeting Places
Gay action is centered in San José. Wednesday is supposedly a "cruising day" at **Ojo de Agua,** a water park outside San José that is

also popular with families. **Troyanos** is a gym "with a gay reputation." Itiel recommends the following steam baths: **Leblon,** Calle 9, Avenidas 1/3; **Decameron,** Avenida 10, Calles 7/9; and **Jano,** Calle 1, Avenidas 4/6. **Soda La Perla,** Avenida Central, Calle 1, is supposedly a gay hangout after hours. Itiel strongly advises against "cruising" the parks where "you can get yourself into real trouble."

There are several gay bars and nightclubs. **Dejavú,** Calle 2, Avenidas 14/16, tel. 223-3758, is a disco—spacious, elegant, with two dance floors—for both men and women; don't go wandering alone around the run-down neighborhood. Better known to foreign gays is **La Torre,** also called "Tonite Disco," Calle 7, Avenidas Central/1. Open Wed.-Sun., it's popular with gays, lesbians, and straight couples. Its disco has flashing lights, smoke, and great music. **La Avispa,** Calle 1, Avenidas 8/10, tel. 223-5343, caters to both gays and lesbians with a popular disco playing mostly techno and Latin music, plus a pool room, a bar and a big-screen TV upstairs. Drag queens flock on show night. Two predominantly lesbian bars are **Unicornio,** Avenida 8, Calles 1/3, and, in Barrio San Pedro, **Bar De La Tertulia,** tel. 225-0250, a pleasant and sedate bar-cum-restaurant tucked away one block north of the San Pedro church. A mixed gay and straight crowd hangs out at **Risas,** Calle 1, Avenidas Central/1, and at **El Churro Español El Puchito,** Calle 11, Avenida 8. **Los Cucharones,** tel. 233-5797, at Avenida 6, Calle Central/1, is said to be a fast-paced disco for working-class gays.

Away from San José, Manuel Antonio is the gay meeting place of choice. Here, a tiny, nude beach north of Playa Espedilla, the main beach, is a gathering spot, especially during holidays.

Accommodations

San José: Triángulo Rosa recommends two gay-friendly guesthouses—**Casa Agua Buena** and **Casa Copa Buena**—both for long-term rentals. The city has at least two dedicated gay hotels. A U.S. travel agency, Colours Destinations, operates **Colours Costa Rica,** Apdo. 341, San José 1200, tel./fax 232-3504; in the U.S., 255 W. 24th St., #542, Miami Beach, FL 33140, tel. (800) 964-5622 or (305) 532-9341, fax 534-0362, e-mail: newcallers@aol.com, a small colonial-style property in the quiet residential Rohrmoser district. Most rooms have shared bath (more private baths are planned). The hotel hosts occasional social events. Women encouraged. Rates: $695-1,099 high season; $59-99 low season, including breakfast. **Casa Yemayá,** tel. 223-3652, fax 225-3636, in Barrio Guadalupe, though not overtly gay, is a hostel for women and a center for the feminist movement.

Apartamentos Escocia, in San José's Barrio La California ($495 per month), is owned by a trans-op, Gianna. Each apartment has a large living room with TV, and bedroom plus kitchenette. Itiel describes it as "rundown and dirty" but with a nice view. He lists the **Hotel L'Ambiance** and **Hotel Santo Tomás** as "gay-friendly." **Hotel Kekoldi** is also gay-friendly. The nicest gay-friendly place is **Hotel Grano de Oro.**

Elsewhere: In Manuel Antonio, Itiel lists the **Casa Blanca, Vela Bar Hotel,** and **Hotel Mariposa** (although the gay owners sold the property in 1995, many of the gay staff have been retained); and in Puntarenas, **Hotel Cayuga.**

Tours

Holbrook Travel, 3540 N.W. 13th St., Gainesville, FL 32609, tel. (352) 377-7111 or (800) 858-0999, fax (352) 371-3710, e-mail: travel@holbrooktravel.com, offers a one-week natural history trip six times annually, taking in the central highlands and Manuel Antonio ($869 land-only).

Way to Go Costa Rica, tel. (800) 835-1223, offers gay adventure tours and plans independent itineraries for gay travelers. **Colours Destinations,** 255 W. 24th St., #542, Miami Beach, FL 33140, tel. (800) 964-5622 or (305) 532-9341, fax 534-0362, e-mail: newcallers@aol.com, does the same. **Mariah Wilderness Expeditions,** P.O. Box 248, Pt. Richmond, CA 94807, tel. (510) 233-2303, fax 233-0956, e-mail: rafting@mariahwe.com, is a gay-friendly, women-owned company specializing in Costa Rica, with a roster of trip (for everyone) that includes whitewater rafting, sea kayaking, and nature cruises.

Odysseus: The International Gay Travel Planner, P.O. Box 1548, Port Washington, NY 11050, tel. (516) 944-5330 or (800) 257-5344, fax (516) 944-7540, e-mail: odymarket@aol.com, lists worldwide hotels, tours, etc. and publishes travel guides for gays and lesbians.

NOTES FOR TRAVELERS WITH DISABILITIES

You'll need to plan your vacation carefully, as few allowances have been made in infrastructure for travelers with disabilities. Fortunately, wheelchair ramps are now appearing on sidewalks, and an increasing number of hotels are provisioning rooms and facilities for the physically challenged.

In the U.S., the **Society for the Advancement of Travel for the Handicapped,** 347 5th Ave., #610, New York, NY 10016, tel. (212) 447-7284, fax 725-8253, publishes a quarterly newsletter, *Access to Travel.* Another handy newsletter is *The Wheelchair Traveler,* 23 Ball Hill Rd., Milford, NH 03055, tel. (603) 673-4539.

In Costa Rica, **Vaya con Silla de Ruedas** *(Go With Wheelchairs),* Apdo. 1146-2050 San Pedro, Montes de Oca, tel. 225-8561, fax 253-0931, e-mail: vayacon@sol.racsa.co.cr, is a specialized transport service for the ambulatory disabled. It operates a specially outfitted vehicle with three wheelchair stations, has 24-hour service, and offers overnight and multiday tours ($120 full day).

NOTES FOR STUDENTS AND YOUTHS

Student Cards

An **International Student Identity Card** could be the most valuable item in your wallet. The card entitles students 12 years and older to discounts on transportation, entrances to museums, etc. When purchased in the U.S. ($20), ISIC even includes $3,000 in emergency medical coverage, limited hospital coverage, and access to a 24-hour, toll-free emergency hotline. Students can obtain ISICs at any student union. Alternately, contact the **Council on International Educational Exchange** (CIEE), 205 E. 42nd St., New York, NY 10017, tel. (212) 822-2600 or 888-COUNCIL (888-268-6245), fax (212) 822-2699, e-mail: info@ciee.org, website www.ciee.org, which issues ISICs and also arranges study vacations in Costa Rica. (CIEE publishes a quarterly, *Student Travel,* and operates Council Travel, a travel agency for U.S. students, with offices at most major campus cities throughout the U.S.; see the chart **CIEE and STA Offices in the U.S.** in the "Getting There" section, this chapter.) In Canada, cards can be obtained from **Travel Cuts,** 187 College St., Toronto, Ont., tel. (416) 979-2406. In the United Kingdom, students can obtain an ISIC from any student union office.

In Costa Rica, **OTEC,** tel. 256-0633, fax 233-2321, e-mail: gotec@sol.racsa.co.cr, a student travel agency with agencies throughout Costa Rica, can arrange an ISIC for a small fee; you'll need two passport photos and proof of student status.

The **Youth International Educational Exchange Card** provides similar benefits for students and nonstudents under 26. In the U.S., contact CIEE; in Europe, contact **Federation of International Youth Travel,** 81 Islands Brugge, DK-2300, Copenhagen S, Denmark.

Travel and Work Study

Students wishing to study in Costa Rica have a wide choice of options. The **University of Costa Rica** offers special *cursos libres* (free courses) during winter break (Dec.-March). It also grants "special student" status to foreigners. Contact the Oficina de Asuntos Internacionales, tel. 207-4729. The **University for Peace** and **Organization for Tropical Studies** also sponsor study courses. Work abroad programs are also offered through **CIEE's Work Abroad Department,** which publishes a series of reference guides, including *Work, Study, Travel Abroad* and *The High School Student's Guide to Study, Travel, and Adventure Abroad.* Contact Council on International Educational Exchange, Publications Dept., 205 E. 42nd St., New York, NY 10017, e-mail: books@ciee.org, an invaluable resource for young travelers.

Holbrook Travel, 3540 N.W. 13th St., Gainesville, FL 32609, tel. (352) 377-7111 or (800) 858-0999, fax (352) 371-3710, e-mail: travel@holbrooktravel.com, offers an eight-day "Tropical Education Program" in Costa Rica for students and teachers ($825), providing an immersion in natural history. The **School for Field Studies,** 16 Broadway, Beverly, MA 01915-4499, tel. (508) 927-7777, fax 927-5127, e-mail: sfshome@igc.apc.org, has summer courses in sustainable development, with four academic courses, Spanish language lessons, and three case studies where students pursue direct research. **Costa Rica Study Tours,** 1182 Horn Beam Rd., Sabina, OH 45169, tel. (937) 584-2900, conducts tours and customizes travel for students of all ages.

Transitions Abroad, tel. (413) 256-0373, provides information for students wishing to study abroad, including advertisements from universities offering study programs in Costa Rica. The *Directory of Study Abroad Programs* (Renaissance Publications) lists university bodies that offer international study courses.

In Costa Rica, **Ecole Travel,** tel. 223-2240, fax 223-4128, e-mail: ecolecr@sol.racsa.co.cr, at Calle 7, Avenidas Central/1, specializes in student travel, including **international student exchange** programs that have a strong focus on ecology and include a visit to Panamá's San Blas islands. It also offers language study for students.

NOTES FOR SENIORS

The **American Association of Retired Persons** (AARP), 601 E St., Washington, D.C. 20049, tel. (202) 434-2277, has a "Purchase Privilege Program" offering discounts on airfares, hotels, car rentals, and more. Check also to see if any of the airlines serving Costa Rica are offering seniors discounts. The AARP also offers group tours for seniors. **Golden Circle,** 347 Congress St., Boston, MA 02210, tel. (617) 350-7500 or (800) 995-5689, fax (617) 423-0445, specializes in senior travel.

Elderhostel, 75 Federal St., Boston, MA 02116, tel. (617) 426-7788, also offers relatively inexpensive educational tours to Costa Rica for seniors, including ecological tours in which participants contribute to the welfare of Mother Nature. Toronto-based **ElderTreks,** 597 Markham St., Toronto, Ont., Canada M6G 2L7, tel. (416) 588-5000, fax 588-9839, e-mail: passages@inforamp.net, offers a 10-day "Nature & Adventure Tour" in Costa Rica for travelers 50 years of age and older, with six departures a year.

Useful information sources include *The Mature Traveler,* P.O. Box 50400, Reno, NV 89513, tel. (702) 786-7419 or (800) 460-6676, a handy monthly newsletter packed with tips for seniors; and *The International Health Guide for Senior Citizen Travelers,* by Robert Lange, M.D. (New York: Pilot Books).

Especially for Retirees

Thinking of retiring in Costa Rica? I recommend the "Live or Retire in Paradise Tour" offered by **Overseas Retirement Network,** 950 Surrey Dr., Edwardsville, IL 62025, tel. (888) 535-5289, fax (618) 659-0283, e-mail: orn@ilnet.com, led by Christopher Howard, author of the excellent book, *The Golden Door to Retirement and Living in Costa Rica,* Costa Rica Books, Suite I SJO 981, P.O. Box 025216, Miami, FL 33102-5216, tel. (800) 365-2342.You'll meet with retirees, get a thorough look at Costa Rica, and have a great time.

Another company specializing in tours especially for retirees considering living in Costa Rica is **Lifestyle Explorations,** World Trade Center, 101 Federal Ave., Suite 1900, Boston, MA 02210, tel. (617) 342-7359, fax (978) 369-9192.

TRAVELING WITH CHILDREN

Generally, travel with children poses no special problems, and virtually everything you'll ever need for younger children is readily available. Costa Ricans adore children and will dote on your youngsters. There are few sanitary or health problems to worry about. However, ensure that your child has vaccinations against measles and rubella (German measles), as well as any other inoculations your doctor advises. Bring cotton

---

SPECIAL NOTE FOR TRAVELERS WITH CHILDREN

Regardless of nationality, children under 18 who stay for more than 90 days in Costa Rica become subject to the nation's child-welfare laws and will not be allowed to leave unless both parents request permission to take the child out of the country. For this, contact the **National Child Protection Agency** (Patronato Nacional de Infancia), Calle 19 and Avenida 6, tel. 223-4219 or 221-3639.

If your child is traveling with only one parent or with someone other than his or her parent, then you must obtain notarized permission from the Costa Rican consulate in the child's country of residence. Two passport-size photos (Costa Rican size) plus the child's passport must accompany the application form.

swabs, Band-Aids, and a small first-aid kit with any necessary medicines for your child. The **Hospital de Niños** (Children's Hospital), tel. 222-0122, is at Paseo Colón and Calle 14 in San José. Proceeds from the **Pueblo Antigua and Parque Nacional de Diverciones,** tel. 231-2001—a children's amusement park in La Uruca, west of San José—go to the hospital.

Children under two travel free on airlines; children between two and 12 are offered special discounts (check with individual airlines). Children are also charged half the adult rate at many hotels, many of which feature children's facilities (amusements, babysitting, etc.). Cheaper hotels may charge an extra-bed rate. Baby foods and milk (radiated for longevity) are readily available. Disposable diapers, however, are expensive (consider bringing cloth diapers; they're ecologically more acceptable). Bring baby wipes. If you plan on driving around, bring your child's car seat—they're not offered for rental cars. Costa Rican TV features children's programs.

The **Children's Museum** has interactive exhibits, plus workshops on weekend mornings, call to register: 223-7003 or 233-2734—ask for the Education Department.

Great Vacations with Your Kids (New York: E.P. Dutton), by Dorothy Jordan and Marjorie Cohen, is a handy reference guide to planning a trip with children. *Let's Discover Costa Rica* is an educational "color and activity fun book" for children published by Bandanna Republica, P.O. Box 1-6100 Mora, Ciudad Colón, tel. 249-1179, fax 249-1107, e-mail: agingold@sol.racsa.co.cr; $5 plus $2.50 shipping.

Special Permits for Exit

If you plan on staying for more than 90 days, you will need special permits for your children to leave the country (see **Immigration and Customs,** above). This applies to all children under 18 years old.

Family-Friendly Tour Companies

Rascals in Paradise, 650 Fifth St., #505, San Francisco, CA 94107, tel. (415) 978-9800 or 800-U-RASCAL (800-872-7225), offers family trips to the tropics, including Costa Rica.

Temptress Adventure Cruises offers a "Family Adventure Program." Contact them at Apdo. 1198, San José 1200, tel. 220-1679, fax 220-2103; in the U.S., 351 N.W. LeJeune Rd., Suite 6, Miami, FL 33126, tel. (305) 643-4040 or (800) 336-8424, fax (305) 643-6438, e-mail: temptress@worldnet.att.net. **Wildland Adventures,** 3516 N.E. 155th St., Seattle, WA 98155, tel. (206) 365-0686 or (800) 345-4453, fax (206) 363-6615, e-mail: wildadve@aol.com, offers a 10-day "Family Adventure," as does **Preferred Adventures,** One W. Water St., Suite 300, St. Paul, MN 55107, tel.

ETHICAL TOURISM

The **North American Center for Responsible Tourism,** P.O. Box 827, San Anselmo, CA 94979, suggests travelers abide by the following Code of Ethics for Tourists:

- Travel with a spirit of humility and a genuine desire to meet and talk with local people.
- Be aware of the feelings of others. Act respectfully and avoid offensive behavior, particularly when taking photographs.
- Cultivate the habit of actively listening and observing rather than merely hearing and seeing. Avoid the temptation to "know all the answers."
- Realize that others may have concepts of time and attitudes which are different—not inferior—to those you inherited from your own culture.
- Instead of looking only for the exotic, discover the richness of another culture and way of life.
- Learn local customs and respect them.

- Remember that you are only one of many visitors. Do not expect special privileges.
- When bargaining with merchants, remember that the poorest one may give up a profit rather than his or her personal dignity. Don't take advantage of the desperately poor. Pay a fair price.
- Keep your promises to people you meet. If you cannot, do not make the promise.
- Spend time each day reflecting on your experiences in order to deepen your understanding. Is your enrichment beneficial for all involved?
- Be aware of why you are traveling in the first place. If you truly want a "home away from home," why travel?

Costa Rica has developed its own set of guidelines for tourists. Contact the **Department of Responsible Tourism,** Apdo. 1524, San Pedro 2050, tel./fax 224-8910, for its leaflet *Code of Ethics for Sustainable Tourism.*

(612) 222-8131 or (800) 840-8687, fax (612) 222-4221, e-mail: paltours@aol.com. **LAPA Vacations,** 13260 S.W. 131st St., #123, Miami, FL 33186, tel. (305) 255-8140, fax 255-8143, offers family ranch vacations at various haciendas; children under 12 are free.

PERSONAL CONDUCT

Generally, Costa Ricans are respectful and courteous, with a deep sense of integrity. Politeness is greatly appreciated, and you can ease your way considerably by being both courteous and patient. Always greet your host with *"Buenas días"* or *"Buenas tardes"* (or the colloquial *"Adios"*). And never neglect to say *"gracias"* ("thank you"). Honor local dress codes as appropriate. Don't flaunt flesh off the beach! Nude bathing is neither allowed nor accepted. Short shorts should generally be relegated to beaches.

Costa Ricans have an understandable natural prejudice against anyone who ignores personal hygiene.

spider monkey

DIANA LASICH HARPER

CATHY CARLSON

SAN JOSÉ

San José, the nation's capital, squats on the floor of the Meseta Central, a fertile upland basin 1,150 meters (3,773 feet) above sea level in the heart of Costa Rica. The basin is a tectonic depression some 20 km wide and 70 km long, with volcanoes forming a meniscus on three sides, their slopes quilted with dark green coffee and pastures as bright as fresh limes. It's a magnificent setting, and nature is never far away (this isn't always a good thing: earthquakes regularly give San José a shaking; the last major temblor, in April 1991, did significant damage to the Teatro Nacional).

San José—or "Chepe," as Ticos call it (using the diminutive for the name José)—dominates national life. Two-thirds of the nation's urban population lives in greater or metropolitan San José, whose population of 1.3 million represents 30% of the nation's total (central San José had an official population of 278,373 in the last census, in 1991). The city's pull continues to attract those from outlying regions in search of a better life. Nearby towns such as Heredia have become virtual dormitory towns from which many people commute daily into San José.

San José's central position makes it an ideal base for forays into the countryside—virtually every part of the country is within a four-hour drive—applying the "hub and spoke" system of travel. Just as well, for there is little to hold your attention in San José.

THE FEEL OF THE CITY

San José is compact, congested, bustling, and noisy, yet still manageably "small town" in scale and feel. One of the first things you note is the relative lack of a colonial or even a pre-20th-century legacy. Sure, its chaos of architectural styles is part Spanish, part Moorish, and many streets in the older neighborhoods are still lined with one- or two-story houses made of wood or even adobe, with ornamental grillwork abutting the sidewalk and opening onto inner patios in the colonial style. But what few older structures remain are of modest interest. If it's colonial quaintness that you're seeking, skip San José.

Also absent is any vestige of an Indian heritage, such as gives Guatemala its characteristic feel. Almost every street, though, has its lottery vendors, hawkers, and carts bursting with mangos, bananas, coconuts, pineapples, and papayas. And the neighborhood corner store *(pulpería)* remains the locus of social life.

Far more, however, San José mirrors North America: its commercial center dominated by hotels, offices, and countless shops stocked with the latest fashions; its narrow streets clogged with cars, trucks, and buses kicking out palls of oily smoke; its ugly modern high-rise architecture; and its neon signs advertising Kentucky Fried Chicken, McDonald's, and Pizza Hut contending with billboards touting condoms, Mercedes-Benzes, and the Moulin Rouge-style lures of "gentlemen's nightclubs."

The Josefinos (as San José residents like to be called) have a passion for motor vehicles—which has exacerbated the effects. Despite staggering import duties that can boost the cost of a Japanese compact to $30,000, the cramped city streets grow more choked every year with honking cars, buzzing mopeds, and trucks and gaily painted buses spewing diesel. In 1997 the situation was improved markedly when traffic was rerouted along several major roads downtown, including rerouting buses and the elimination of traffic lights at certain junctions to keep the traffic flowing.

Despite its working-class tenor, the city has a relatively progressive and cosmopolitan middleclass. "Shopping," says one commentator, "is a social pastime," and on weekends suburbanites flock into San José to stroll Avenida Central. Businessmen sport expensive suits that rival those you might see in San Francisco. Women make a contemporary statement with tight miniskirts and high heels. And the city is large enough, and its middle-class cosmopolitan enough in outlook, to support a vital cultural milieu and vivacious nightlife.

Fortunately, though the city is not without its share of homeless and beggars, there are very few of the ghoulish *tugurios* (slums) that scar the hillsides of so many other Latin American cities. The modest working-class *barrios* (neighborhoods), such as the newer regions of Hatillo, San Sebastian, and Zapote to the southwest, are almost everywhere clean and well ordered. And the tranquil residential districts such as Sa-

bana Sur, San Pedro, and Rohrmoser, and more so the burgeoning middle-class suburbs of La Granja and Peralta with their gracious houses, green lawns, and high metal fences, have come to resemble those of Miami or outer Los Angeles.

San José has undergone a facelift in recent years under a Ministry of Culture concerned to improve the city's image. The first tuck-and-lift was to Parque Morazán which, like a butterfly, metamorphosed from blight to beauty. Next came Parque La Merced (also known as Parque Braulio Carrillo), then Parque Central, an erstwhile eyesore that has emerged as a point of pride. At press time, the Catedral Metropolitan was receiving cosmetic surgery. And 1998 was scheduled to see the removal of many power poles downtown as telephone wires are replaced by underground optic fibers; and the down-at-the-heels and dangerous red-light district known as Coca-Cola, centered on Mercado Borbón, is to be transformed.

CLIMATE

For first-time visitors the mild climate is surprising in a place so tropical. The weather is refreshingly clear and invigorating. Affectionately referred to by locals as "perpetual tropical spring," San José's climate earned the approval of *National Geographic,* which decleared it one of the best three in the world.

There's never a need for air-conditioning. San José's daily temperatures are in the 70s virtually year-round, with very little monthly variation; the average annual temperature is 20° C (68° F). A heat wave is when the mercury reaches the 80s; if it falls below 65° F, it's considered cold. The record high for San José is only 92° F; record low is 49° F. It has never snowed in San José. Nights are usually in the 60s year-round, so bring a sweater. But rest assured, there's never a frost.

However, there *is* a distinct wet season—May to October—when rain can be expected at some time almost every day. Bring your umbrella during these months. Rain generally falls in midafternoon and evening, and long rainy days are a rarity. November through April are dry months when rain virtually never falls.

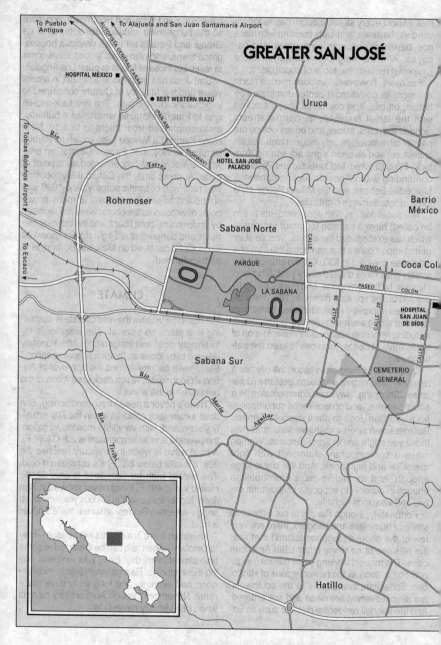

GREATER SAN JOSÉ

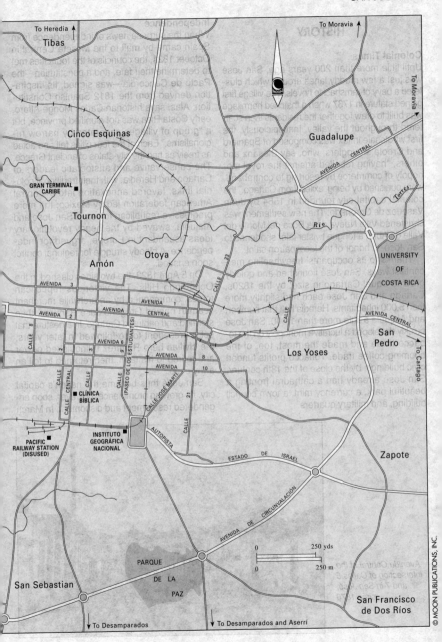

To Heredia
Tibas
To Moravia

To Moravia

Cinco Esquinas

Guadalupe

GRAN TERMINAL
CARIBE

AVENIDA CENTRAL

Tournon

Río

Amón

Otoya

Calle 23

Calle 37

UNIVERSITY
OF
COSTA RICA

AVENIDA 3

AVENIDA 2

AVENIDA
CENTRAL

AVENIDA 1

AVENIDA CENTRAL

San
Pedro

CALLE 8

CALLE 2

AVENIDA 6

AVENIDA
CENTRAL

Los Yoses

To Cartago

CALLE 2

CALLE 3

CALLE 9

CALLE (PASEO DE LOS ESTUDIANTES)

AVENIDA 8

AVENIDA 10

CALLE CENTRAL

CALLE

CLÍNICA
BÍBLICA

CALLE 21

CALLE JOSÉ MARTÍ

Zapote

PACIFIC
RAILWAY STATION
(DISUSED)

INSTITUTO
GEOGRÁFICA
NACIONAL

AUTOPISTA

ESTADO DE ISRAEL

AVENIDA DE CIRCUNVALACIÓN

San Sebastian

PARQUE
DE LA
PAZ

250 yds

250 m

San Francisco
de Dos Ríos

To Desamparados

To Desamparados and Aserrí

© MOON PUBLICATIONS, INC.

HISTORY

Colonial Times

Until little more than 200 years ago, San José was just a few muddy lanes around which clustered a bevy of ramshackle hovels. The village first gained stature in 1737 when a thatched hermitage was built to draw together the residents then scattered throughout the valley. Inauspiciously, the first wholesale influx was composed of Spaniard and Creole smugglers, who, say Biesanz and others, "having rebelled against the royal monopoly of commerce by resorting to contraband, were punished by being 'exiled' from Cartago," the colonial capital city founded in 1564 by Juan Vásquez de Coronado. The new settlement was christened Villa Nueva de la Boca del Monte del Valle de Abra, a tongue twister later shortened to San José, in honor of the local patron saint.

Thanks to its occupants' freewheeling mercantilist ways, San José flourished and quickly grew to equal Cartago in size: by the 1820s, Cartago and San José each had slightly more than 5,000 inhabitants, Heredia half that number, and Alajuela a little more than 1,800. San José quickly developed a lucrative monopoly on the tobacco trade and made the most, too, of the booming coffee trade. Tobacco profits funded civic buildings; by the close of the 18th century, San José already had a cathedral fronting a beautiful park, a currency mint, a town council building, and military quarters.

Independence

When the surprise news of independence from Spain came by mail to the Meseta Central in October 1821, the councils of the four cities met to determine their fate, and a constitution—the Pacto de Concordia—was signed, its inspiration derived from the 1812 Spanish Constitution. Alas, says historian Carlos Monge Alfaro, early Costa Rica was not a unified province, but a "group of villages separated by narrow regionalisms." Each of the four cities felt and acted as freely as had the city-states of ancient Greece. The conservative and aristocratic leaders of Cartago and Heredia, with their traditional colonial links, favored annexation into a Central American federation led by Mexico; the more progressive republican forces of San José and Alajuela, swayed by the heady revolutionary ideas ascendant in Europe, argued for independence. A bloody struggle for regional control soon ensued.

On 5 April 1823, the two sides clashed in the Ochomogo Hills. The victorious republican forces, commanded by an erstwhile merchant seaman named Gregorio José Ramírez, then stormed and captured Cartago. In a gesture that set a precedent to be followed in later years, the civilian hero Ramírez relinquished power and retired to his farm, then returned to foil an army coup.

San José thus became the nation's capital city. Its growing prominence, however, soon engendered resentment and discontent. In March

Avenida Central at the intersection of Calles 5 and 7 in San José, circa 1870

DISTRICTS (BARRIOS) OF SAN JOSÉ

The names of San José's most important neighborhoods—or barrios—will come in handy if you plan on extensive sightseeing. Here are the most important:

Barrio Amón

Between Avenidas 3-11 and Calles Central and 17, northeast of downtown, this historic neighborhood is replete with San José's most venerable buildings. It is in the midst of revival after going to seed. It makes for an interesting walking tour—as does the contiguous Barrio Otoya.

Barrio México

To the north of Avenida 7, west of Calle 16, this working-class area provides a slice of local color. Few tourist facilities, but an important church. Be cautious at night.

Desamparados

A working-class suburb on the south side of San José, with one of the most impressive churches in the city, plus a museum honoring traditional life in Costa Rica.

Los Yoses

East of downtown, Avenida Central leads to this bustling residential and commercial center that is off the tourist path, yet contains some fine historic bed-and-breakfast hotels, restaurants, and upscale shopping malls.

Moravia

Strictly a separate entity from San José, this quiet residential suburb (officially known as San Vicente de Moravia), six km northeast of downtown, is the undisputed center for art and handicrafts.

Pavas and Rohrmoser

These contiguous upscale neighborhoods, due west of Sabana Park, are the setting for fine mansions, a growing number of quality restaurants, and several embassies.

San Bosco

Although rarely referred to as San Bosco, its main thoroughfare—Paseo Colón—is the vitally important western extension of Avenida Central. A large number of car rental and airline companies have headquarters here. The area contains several select restaurants and hotels.

San Pedro

Beyond Los Yoses, about three km east of downtown, this residential enclave replete with bohemian nightclubs and restaurants owes its vitality to the presence of the University of Costa Rica. It offers some fine bed-and-breakfast hotels.

Tibas

About three km north of downtown, this important residential suburb—officially called San Juan de Tibas—is replete with restaurants and nightclubs. It is off the tourist track.

1835, in a conciliatory gesture, San José's city fathers offered to rotate the national capital among the four cities every four years. Unfortunately, the other cities—Alajuela included—had a bee in their collective bonnet. In September 1837 they formed a league, chose a president, and on 26 September attacked San José in an effort to topple the Braulio Carrillo government. The Josefinos won what came to be known as La Guerra de la Liga ("The War of the League"), and the city has remained the nation's capital ever since.

By the mid-1800s the coffee boom was bringing prosperity, culture, and refinement to the once-humble backwater. San José developed a substantial middle class eager to spend its new-found wealth for the social good. The mud roads were bricked over and the streets illuminated by kerosene lamps. Tramways began to appear. The city was the third in the world to install public electric lighting. Public telephones appeared well ahead of most cities in Europe and North America. By the turn of the century, tree-lined parks and plazas and sumptuous buildings catering to a burgeoning bourgeoisie—libraries, museums, the Teatro Nacional, and grand neoclassical mansions and middle-class homes—graced the city. Architects, influenced by the Paris and Crystal Palace Expositions and aided by coffee income, were erecting great monuments and schools built of imported prefab metals. Homes and public buildings, too, adopted the in-vogue, French-inspired look of New Orleans and Martinique. The city became respectable!

Of course, the city had its slumlike suburbs of *puertas ventanas,* tiny workers' houses in which several families often lived side by side. Industrial zones rose on the periphery of the urban center. And isolated sections were populated by blacks who had defied segregationist laws and settled in the Meseta Central.

Modern Times

Still, as recently as the 1940s San José had only 70,000 residents—a mere tenth of the country's population. After WW II ended, however, the capital city began to mushroom, growing haphazardly, encroaching on neighboring villages such as Guadalupe and Tibas. Sadly, many of the city's finest buildings felt the blow of the demolition crane in postwar years. In their stead have monstrous examples of modern architecture. Uncontrolled rapid growth in recent years has spread the city's tentacles farther afield

until the suburban districts have begun to blur into the larger complex, and neighboring towns such as Heredia and Alajuela are threatened with being engulfed. At night the surrounding hills twinkle with the lights of suburban villages that are slowly being drawn into the city's fold.

FESTIVALS

The **Festival de las Carretas,** begun in 1996, celebrates traditional rural life with a parade of dozens of oxcarts *(carretas)* from throughout the country. It's held in November in downtown San José, passing along Paseo Colón and Parque Central.

The **Festival de la Luz** was also initiated in 1996 as a Christmas parade highlighted by the "Parade of Lights" from Parque Sabana along Calle 42, Paseo Coló, and Avenida 2 to Calle 11, with floats trimmed with colorful Christmas lights (6-10 p.m.). In 1997, RECOPE, the state petroleum company, had a "locomotive" with 38,000 lights!

SIGHTSEEING

As a drawing card in its own right, the capital has been subject to regular disparagement. Even Anthony Trollope, passing through in 1858, observed that "there is little more interest to be found in entering San José than in driving through . . . a sleepy little borough town in Wiltshire." Things have improved since then (and continue to do so).

While San José has nothing to compare with the Smithsonian or the Louvre, it does have a number of excellent museums that provide a good perspective on the history and culture of Costa Rica. Baroque or Renaissance-style buildings are few. And excepting the Teatro Nacional, San José's late-19th-century belle-epoque theater, the city is wholly lacking the grand colonial structures of, say, Mexico City or Havana, Cuba. Thus, I've often heard tourists say that San José can be "done" in two days. That is true—bona fide tourist attractions can be counted on two hands—although you can cer-

tainly occupy a third day. After two or three days you'll know it is time to move on.

Although San José lacks a predominant central square such as Mexico City's *Zócalo,* several

SIGHTSEEING HIGHLIGHTS OF SAN JOSÉ

The following are the main attractions not to be missed.

Teatro Nacional
Pre-Columbian Gold Museum
National Museum
Fidel Tristan Jade Museum
Mercado Central
Serpentario
Spirogyra
Costa Rican Art Museum

small parks and plazas lie at the city's heart, oases of calm amid the incessant hubbub of traffic. The once-nondescript parks have been given spic-and-span liveries in recent years. (Some of the parks had developed a reputation for muggings at night; leave your jewelry in the hotel safe, and carry your wallet and money in a money belt.) The capital city also has a block-square Mercado Central (Central Market), a dark, century-old maze of stalls where vendors hawk everything from T-shirts and chickens to medicinal herbs and Christ figurines. At sunset on a Sunday evening, San José's small parks fill with strolling families and youths.

A handy pocket-size guide is *Vern Bell's Walking Tour of Downtown San José, With Some Glimpses of History, Anecdotes, and a Chuckle or Two,* available at hotel gift stores in San José, or directly from Mr. Bell, tel. 225-4752, fax 224-5884, who leads you by the hand, providing erudition and tongue-in-cheek humor along the way.

Sightseeing Buses

A free sightseeing tour of San José is offered by the Hotel Del Rey, tel. 221-7272, ext. 444. The one-hour tour includes most major places of historic interest downtown, and departs Hotel Del Rey at 9:20 and 11:20 a.m., and on Avenida 2 in front of the Teatro Nacional at 9:30 and 11:30 a.m. And the **Discover San José Pass,** tel. (800) 565-6565, is a tour bus that operates a circuit eight times daily, passing by most museums and sites of interest in downtown, with calls at all major hotels as far afield as Sabana and San Pedro ($10); you can alight and get on as you wish.

ORIENTATION

Theoretically, San José's grid system should make finding your way around easy. In actuality, it can be immensely frustrating.

Streets and Avenues

Streets *(calles)* run north to south. Avenues *(avenidas)* run east to west. Downtown San José is centered on **Calle Central** and **Avenida Central.** To the north of Avenida Central, *avenidas* ascend in odd numbers: Avenida 1, Avenida 3,

etc.; to the south they ascend in even numbers: Avenida 2, Avenida 4, etc. West of Calle Central, *calles* ascend in even numbers: Calle 2, Calle 4, etc.; to the east they ascend in odd numbers: Calle 1, Calle 3, etc. The main thoroughfare is **Paseo Colón,** running east from Parque Sabana 2.5 kilometers to the **central business district** downtown, where the main thoroughfare is Avenida 2. Avenida Central (the easterly extension of Paseo Colón) is closed to traffic between Calles Central and 11.

Almost all streets are one-way. Often, no sign indicates which direction the traffic is flowing. If you're walking, be particularly wary before stepping off the sidewalk.

Street names usually hang on buildings at street corners, about five meters off the ground. Many streets have no signs. And although buildings have official numbers, they're rarely posted and almost never used, so it's difficult to tell which side of the street the building you're seeking is on.

Addresses are written by the nearest street junction. Thus, the Bar Esmeralda, on Avenida 2 midway between Calles 5 and 7, gives its address as "Avenida 2, Calles 5/7." In telephone directories and advertisements, *calle* may be abbreviated as "c," and *avenida* as "a."

Landmarks

That said, Josefinos rarely refer to street addresses by *avenida* and *calle*. Instead, they usually give a distance in meters *(metros)* from a particular landmark—"100 meters north and 300 meters west of Auto Mercado," for example. If you state a specific street address, you may receive a confused look (an amazing number of Josefinos have no idea what street they live on). To make matters worse, many reference landmarks still in common use disappeared years ago. Most are not marked on maps. The edifice may have disappeared, but the "landmark" remains. For example, the Coca-Cola factory near Avenida Central and Calle 14 was long ago replaced by a "bus terminal," but the area is still called "Coca-Cola."

Distances are sometimes expressed in *varas,* an antediluvian Spanish measurement roughly akin to 100 meters *(cien metros).* Fortunately, *"cien metros"* usually refers to one block. *"Cinquenta metros"* (fifty meters) is sometimes used to mean half a block.

(continues on page 206)

SAN JOSÉ

Rohrmoser

JAPANESE EMBASSY

INTERNET DE CENTROMEDIA

BUSES TO DOWNTOW

ANTOJITOS

CANAL 7 TV

MARISQUERIA LA PRINCESA MARINA

LA GAUCHO

MUSEO LA SALLE DE CIENCIAS NATURALES

GIARDINA

HOTEL RINCON DEL VALLE

Río María

Río

Río Tiribí

Aguilar

To Juan Bolaños Airport

To Escazú

To Escazú

AVENIDA DE

CIRCUNVALACION

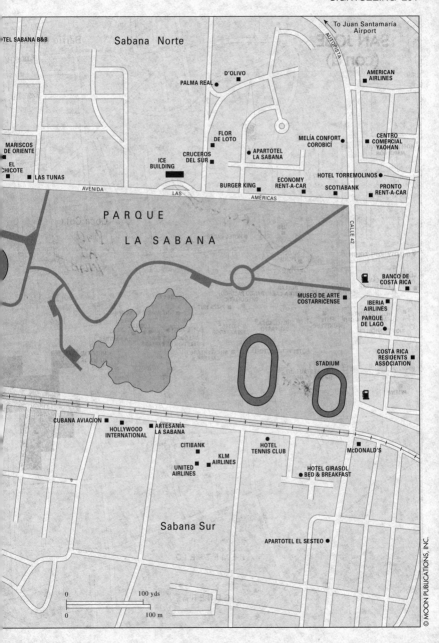

To Juan Santamaría Airport

Sabana Norte

TEL SABANA B&B

D'OLIVO

PALMA REAL

AMERICAN AIRLINES

FLOR DE LOTO

CRUCEROS DEL SUR

MELÍA CONFORT COROBICÍ

CENTRO COMERCIAL YAOHAN

MARISCOS DE ORIENTE

ICE BUILDING

APARTOTEL LA SABANA

EL CHICOTE

LAS TUNAS

BURGER KING

ECONOMY RENT-A-CAR

HOTEL TORREMOLINOS

SCOTIABANK

PRONTO RENT-A-CAR

AVENIDA

LAS

AMÉRICAS

PARQUE

LA SABANA

CALLE 42

BANCO DE COSTA RICA

MUSEO DE ARTE COSTARRICENSE

IBERIA AIRLINES

PARQUE DE LAGO

COSTA RICA RESIDENTS ASSOCIATION

STADIUM

CUBANA AVIACIÓN

HOLLYWOOD INTERNATIONAL

ARTESANÍA LA SABANA

CITIBANK

HOTEL TENNIS CLUB

McDONALD'S

KLM AIRLINES

UNITED AIRLINES

HOTEL GIRASOL BED & BREAKFAST

Sabana Sur

APARTOTEL EL SESTEO

0   100 yds

0   100 m

© MOON PUBLICATIONS, INC.

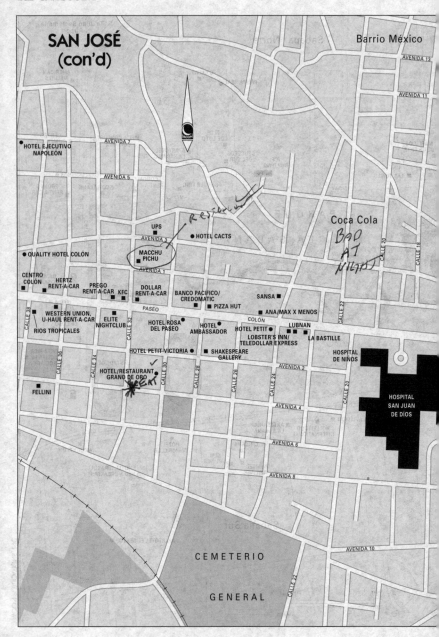

SAN JOSÉ (con'd)

Barrio México

AVENIDA 13

AVENIDA 11

AVENIDA 7

Moon

HOTEL EJECUTIVO NAPOLEÓN

AVENIDA 5

UPS

Restaurant

AVENIDA 3

HOTEL CACTS

Coca Cola

BAD AT NIGHT

QUALITY HOTEL COLÓN

MACCHU PICHU

AVENIDA 1

CALLE 20

CALLE 18

CENTRO COLÓN

HERTZ RENT-A-CAR

PREGO RENT-A-CAR

KFC

DOLLAR RENT-A-CAR

BANCO PACIFICO/ CREDOMATIC

SANSA

PIZZA HUT

PASEO

ANA/MAX X MENOS

CALLE 22

CALLE 38

WESTERN UNION, U-HAUL RENT-A-CAR

RIOS TROPICALES

ELITE NIGHTCLUB

CALLE 32

HOTEL ROSA DEL PASEO

HOTEL AMBASSADOR

COLÓN

HOTEL PETIT

LUBNAN

LOBSTER'S INN/ TELEDOLLAR EXPRESS

LA BASTILLE

HOTEL PETIT VICTORIA

SHAKESPEARE GALLERY

HOSPITAL DE NIÑOS

CALLE 36

CALLE 34

HOTEL/RESTAURANT GRANO DE ORO

CALLE 30

CALLE 28

CALLE 24

AVENIDA 2

FELLINI

EAT

AVENIDA 4

CALLE 20

HOSPITAL SAN JUAN DE DÍOS

AVENIDA 6

AVENIDA 8

AVENIDA 10

CEMETERIO

GENERAL

CALLE 22

GRAN TERMINAL
CARIBE ■

Tournon

R MÉXICO

CENTRO COSTARRICENSE
DE CIENCIAS Y CULTURA/
MUSEO DE LOS NIÑOS ■

Río

CENTRAL

Torres

JOSEPHINE'S ■

Amón

■ CAFÉ GOURMET

AVENIDA 7

NIGHT CLUB OLYMPUS ■

■ RESTAURANTE TASKA

AVENIDA 5

■ BENNY'S

RAINFOREST AERIAL ■
TRAM OFFICE

RADIOGRÁFICA ■

AVENIDA 3

McDONALD'S CREDOMATIC

PARQUE
MORAZAN

■ BANCO DE SAN JOSE

■ COSTA RICA EXPEDITIONS

AVENIDA 1

BANCO NACIONAL ■

MUSEO POSTAL,
TELEGRÁFICO, Y
FILATÉLICO/
POST OFFICE

NASHVILLE SOUTH ■

KEY
LARGO

AVENIDA
CENTRAL

MERCADO
CENTRAL

McDONALD'S ■

RESTAURANTE
EL ESCORIAL ■

HAPPY DAYS ■

COMPANIA
FINANCIERA
DE LONDRES ■

BANCO DE
COSTA RICA ■

LIBRERÍA ■
UNIVERSAL

■ VISHNU
■ TAM TRAVEL

BANCO NACIONAL ■

MONPIK ICE CREAM ■

■ LEHMANN'S

CHIAPAS BOOKS ■

LUCKY'S PIANO BIANCO BAR, ■
EL TUNEL DE TIEMPO

PARQUE
BRAULIO CARILLO
(LA MERCED PARK)

TEATRO
MELICO SALAZAR ■

SODA PALACE ■

SODA
LA PERLA

BANCO
METROPOLITAN

PLAZA DE LA
CULTURA

CHELLE'S BAR ■

♦ IGLESIA LA MERCED

BURGER
KING ■

EDIFICIO LAS ARCADAS ■

TEATRO
NACIONAL

LA HACIENDA, ■
L'ÎLE DE FRANCE

PARQUE
CENTRAL

BANCO
POPULAR ■

LA ■
ESMERALDA

ARCHBISHOP'S
PALACE

TIKAL TOURS ■

METROPOLITAN
CATHEDRAL

ICT HEADQUARTERS OFFICE/
TOURIST INFORMATION

WESTERN UNION ■

IGLESIA SOLEDAD ♦

FOR ACCOMMODATIONS FROM CALLES 10-19, SEE "DOWNTOWN SAN JOSÉ ACCOMMODATIONS" MAP

CALLE 12

CALLE 10

CALLE 8

CALLE 6

CALLE 4

CALLE 2

CALLE CENTRAL

CALLE 1

CALLE 3

CALLE 5

CALLE 7

PASEO DE LAS ESTUDIANTES

CALLE 9

MANSION DE BRAULIO ●

LA GEMA ●

0   100 yds

0   100 m

To Clínica Bíblica ▼

© MOON PUBLICATIONS, INC.

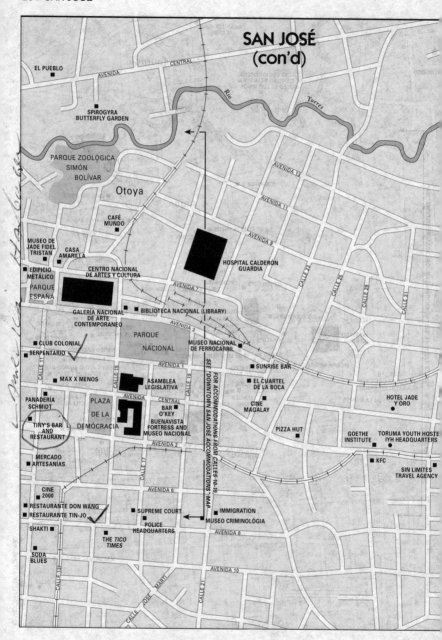

SAN JOSÉ
(con'd)

EL PUEBLO

AVENIDA   CENTRAL

SPIROGYRA
BUTTERFLY GARDEN

Río   Torres

PARQUE ZOOLÓGICA
SIMÓN BOLÍVAR

Otoya

AVENIDA 13

AVENIDA 11

CAFÉ
MUNDO

AVENIDA 9

MUSEO DE
JADE FIDEL
TRISTAN

CASA
AMARILLA

CENTRO NACIONAL
DE ARTES Y CULTURA

HOSPITAL CALDERÓN
GUARDIA

CALLE 23

CALLE 25

CALLE 29

CALLE 31

EDIFICIO
METÁLICO

PARQUE
ESPAÑA

AVENIDA 7

GALERÍA NACIONAL
DE ARTE
CONTEMPORANEO

BIBLIOTECA NACIONAL (LIBRARY)

AVENIDA 3

CLUB COLONIAL

PARQUE
NACIONAL

MUSEO NACIONAL
DE FERROCARRIL

SERPENTARIO

CALLE 1

AVENIDA 1

CALLE 15

CALLE 19

SUNRISE BAR

MAX X MENOS

ASAMBLEA
LEGISLATIVA

EL CUARTEL
DE LA BOCA

PANADERÍA
SCHMIDT

PLAZA
DE LA
DEMÓCRACIA

AVENIDA

CENTRAL

BAR
O'KEY

CINE
MAGALAY

HOTEL JADE
Y ORO

TINY'S BAR
AND
RESTAURANT

BUENAVISTA
FORTRESS AND
MUSEO NACIONAL

PIZZA HUT

GOETHE
INSTITUTE

TORUMA YOUTH HOSTEL
IYH HEADQUARTERS

MERCADO
ARTESANÍAS

AVENIDA 2

CALLE 17

KFC

SIN LIMITES
TRAVEL AGENCY

CINE
2000

AVENIDA 6

RESTAURANTE DON WANG

SUPREME COURT

IMMIGRATION

RESTAURANTE TIN-JO

POLICE
HEADQUARTERS

MUSEO CRIMINOLÓGIA

SHAKTI

AVENIDA 8

THE TICO
TIMES

SODA
BLUES

CALLE 13

CALLE JOSÉ MARTÍ

CALLE 21

AVENIDA 10

SEE DOWNTOWN SAN JOSE ACCOMMODATIONS MAP
FOR ACCOMMODATIONS FROM CALLES 10-19

PLAZA DE LA CULTURA
AND VICINITY

San José's unofficial focal point is the Plaza de la Cultura, bordered by Calles 3/5 and Avenidas Central/2. It's a popular hangout for tourists and young Josefinos alike. Musicians, jugglers, and marimba bands also entertain the crowds, especially on Sunday. Tourists gather to absorb the vibrant and colorful atmosphere while enjoying a beer and food on the open-air terrace of the venerable Gran Hotel, fronted by a little plaza named **Parque Mora Fernandez.**

Museo del Oro Pre-Columbiano

Given the paucity of pre-Columbian sites in Costa Rica, the Pre-Columbian Gold Museum run by the state-owned Banco Nacional comes as a pleasant surprise. The more than 2,000 glittering pre-Columbian gold artifacts (frogs, people, etc.) weigh in at over 22,000 troy ounces. If anything will inspire lustful greed, this is it. A collection of old coins is also displayed in an adjoining room in the **Museo Numismática** and **Museo de Arquitectura,** while a small exhibit hall features works from the bank's art collection.

The museum is in the basement beneath the plaza; the entrance is the east, on Calle 5. An audio-taped self-guided tour costs $2. Free guided tours presented by bilingual guides are offered Tuesday and Thursday at 2 p.m., and on weekends at 11 a.m. and 2 p.m. Bring your passport or other identification for the security check upon entry. Hours: Tues.-Sun. and holidays 10 a.m.-4:30 p.m.; admission $4 tourists, $2 residents, $1.50 students, 75 cents children; tel. 223-0528, fax 257-0651, e-mail: museooro@sol.racsa.co.cr.

Teatro Nacional

Truly a national treasure and unquestionably the nation's most impressive architectural showpiece, the National Theater, on the south side of Plaza de la Cultura, on Avenida 2 between Calles 3 and 5, is a study in harmony and regal splendor, and justifiably a source of national pride.

The theater was conceived in 1890 when a European opera company featuring the prima donna Adelina Patti toured Central America but

DOWNTOWN SAN JOSÉ ACCOMMODATIONS

PLaza LA ESQUINA del cafe

Galeria

Bishop Castle

RADISSON EUROPA

Tournon

HOTEL VILLA TOURNON

Rio

Torres

PARQUE ZOOLÓGICO SIMÓN BOLÍVAR

HOTEL LA AMISTAD INN

To D'Raya Vida Villa

HOTEL VESUVIO

Otoya

TAYLOR'S INN

HOTEL HILDA

HOTEL VENEZIA

Amón

BEST WESTERN SAN JOSÉ DOWNTOWN

AVENIDA 9

BRITANNIA HOTEL

HOTEL MARLYN

HOTEL GALAAD MOUNT INN

60 places

AVENIDA 7

HOTEL AMÓN PARK PLAZA

DUNN INN

JOLUVA GUESTHOUSE

LA CASA VERDE AMÓN

HEMINGWAY INN

HOTEL L'AMBIANCE

CINCO HORMEGAS ROJAS

HOTEL AMÉRICA

HOTEL KEKOLDI

LA CASA MORAZAN

HOTEL DON CARLOS

HOTEL EDELWEISS

PENSIÓN OTOYA

HOTEL SANTO TOMÁS

HOTEL ASTORIA

HOTEL REY AMÓN

HOTEL COMPOSTELA

AVENIDA 5

HOTEL EUROPA

HOTEL AUROLA HOLIDAY INN

PARQUE ESPAÑA

Congo Gulca

HOTEL CENTRAL

HOTEL CAPITAL

AVENIDA 3

PENSIÓN OTOYA

PARQUE MORAZÁN

DIANA'S INN

COSTA RICA INN

HOTEL MORAZÁN

PARQUE NACIONAL

AVENIDA 1

HOTEL AMSTEL MORAZÁN

HOTEL DEL REY

57

HOTEL LA GRAN VÍA

HOTEL DIPLOMAT

HOTEL PLAZA

HOTEL ROYAL GARDEN

HOTEL BALMORAL

PENSIÓN DE LA CUESTA

GRAN HOTEL ROAMERICANO

HOTEL ROYAL DUTCH

GRAN HOTEL

PENSIÓN AMERICANA

PLAZA COLONIAL

HOTEL PRESIDENTE

AVENIDA

HOTEL GALILEA

PLAZA DE LA DEMÓCRACIA

NUEVO HOTEL TALAMANCA

HOTEL PARK

PARQUE CENTRAL

PENSIÓN ARAICA

HOTEL DORAL

HOTEL TICA LINDA

AVENIDA 2

HOTEL AVENIDA SEGUNDA

PENSIÓN SUPER FAMILIAR

HOTEL NICARAGUA

HOTEL FLEUR DE LYS

APARTOTEL SAN JOSÉ

CASA 429

CASA LEO

HOTEL DOÑA INES

HOTEL FORTUNA

HOTEL PRINCIPE

HOTEL BOSTON

HOTEL BERLIN

AVENIDA 8

RITZ/PENSIÓN CENTRO CONTINENTAL

CASA RIDGEWAY

AVENIDA 10

AVENIDA 12

national—see Trecter

1. 24 Hours

Latres

AVENIDA 14

Cappuccino

2. Also Blue Marlin Bar

AVENIDA 16

24 Hr. Hot Spot/Tica

AVENIDA 18

3. Plaza de la Cultura

Sunday entertainment

© MOON PUBLICATIONS, INC.

El Teatro Nacional

was unable to perform in Costa Rica because there was no suitable theater. Jilted, the ruling *cafelateros* (coffee barons) voted a tax on coffee exports to fund construction of a theater, and craftsmen from all over Europe were imported. It was inaugurated on 19 October 1897 to a performance of *Faust* by the Paris Opera and its great Ballet Corps.

Outside, the classical Renaissance facade is topped by statues symbolizing Dance, Music, and Fame. Inside, the foyer, done in pink marble, rivals the best of ancient Rome, with allegorical figures of Comedy and Tragedy, stunning murals depicting themes in Costa Rican life and commerce (if the giant mural showing coffee harvesting looks familiar, it's probably because you've seen it on the old five-*colón* note), and triptych ceiling supported by six-meter-tall marble columns topped with bronze capitals.

Art and good taste are lavishly displayed on the marble staircase, with its gold-laminated ornaments sparkling beneath bronze chandeliers. A grandiose rotunda painted in Milan in 1897 by Arturo Fontana highlights the three-story auditorium, designed in a perfect horseshoe and seating 1,040 in divine splendor. The ceiling fresco depicts naked celestial deities surrounding a giant crystal chandelier.

Magnificent frescoes abound. Much of the mahogany furniture is gold-leafed, and the floor is fashioned in local hardwoods. Uniquely, the auditorium floor was designed to be raised to stage level by a manual winch so that the theater could be used as a ballroom. Downstairs, to the left of the entrance foyer, is a coffee shop no less resplendently gilded than the theater itself.

The theater was fully reopened in early 1995 after a four-year restoration to repair damage sustained in the April 1991 earthquake. You can buy tickets for performances at a ticket booth next to the entrance (expect to pay $3-15). Be sure to dress for the part: Josefinos treat a night at the National Theater as a distinguished social occasion.

Hours: Mon.-Sat. 9 a.m.-5 p.m., Sunday 10 a.m.-noon and 1-5 p.m.; entrance: $2.50; tel. 223-1690 or 223-1086. Guided tours are offered. *A must see!*

PARQUE CENTRAL AND VICINITY

In colonial days this small park, between Calles Central/2 and Avenidas 2/4, was San José's main plaza and market square. Today it is popular with Josefinos who congregate beneath the looming palms. The noisy park is replete with a fountain, a bronze statue, hardwood sculptures, and venerable guachipelín, *guanacaste,* and higueron trees. At its center is a raised platform with a large domed structure supported by arches where the municipal band plays concerts on Sunday. The **bandstand**—a bit of an ugly duckling—stands proudly in the center of this urban jewel. Hunkered beneath the bandstand is the **Carmen Lyra Children's Library** (named after a Costa Rican writer famous for her children's stories).

Across Avenida 2 is the popular **Soda Palace,** which is open 24 hours a day; and the **Teatro Melico Salazar,** dating to the 1920s, with its fluted Corinthian columns, high balconies, and gilding providing a study in understated period detail.

The area immediately south and west is rough: beware pickpockets, and be especially wary at night.

Catedral Metropólitan

Dominating the east side of Parque Central is the city's modest, Corinthian-columned cathedral: whitewashed, with a blue domed roof more reminiscent of a Greek Orthodox church than a Catholic edifice. The original cathedral was toppled by an earthquake in 1821; the current structure dates from 1871. The interior is unremarkable, bar its lofty barrel-arched ceiling, and there is little of the ostentatious baroque influence found in cathedrals elsewhere on the continent. Tucked neatly in its shadow to the south is the marvelously mellowed **Archbishop's Palace,** dating from the 18th century and one of the few colonial structures of note in San José.

PARQUES ESPAÑA AND MORAZÁN AND VICINITY

Pretty **Parque Morazán** is overshadowed by the looming Aurola Holiday Inn, between Calles 5/9 and Avenida 3/5. The park's four quadrants surround the domed **Temple of Music,** which was supposedly inspired by Le Trianon in Paris. A small Japanese garden lies in the northeast quadrant, which also contains a children's playground. The infamous Key Largo night spot sits on the southeastern corner.

Parque Morazán merges east into diminutive **Parque España,** a secluded place to rest your feet. Its tall and densely packed trees have been adopted by birds, and their chorus is particularly pleasing just before sunrise and sunset. Note the quaint, colonial-style tiled "pavilion" on the northeast corner. A colorful outdoor art market is held here on Sunday. On the north side of the park you will see an old, ornately stuccoed, ocher-colored colonial building, **Casa Amarilla,** which once housed the Court of Justice and today is the Chancellery, or State Department (no entry).

Centro Nacional de Artes y Cultura (CENAC)

On the east side of Parque España is the erstwhile Liquor Factory (Fábrica Nacional de Licores), now housing a permanent collection of national art, ceramics, and architecture in the Museum of Contemporary Art and Design. The name is a little misleading as exhibits extend all the way back to pre-Columbian days. Note the old sun clock and exemplary decorative stonework on the west side. The building dates to 1887 and though drained of alcohol, relics of the distilling days linger. The museum spans art from throughout Latin America, much of it very forceful. The National Dance Company, National Theater Company, Cultura Hispánica, Casa de la Cultura Iberoamericana, and the Colegio de Costa Rica are all housed here, too, in a complex comprising two theaters, three art galleries, a library, and live cultural activities. Hours: Tues.-Sun. 10 a.m.-5 p.m.; tel. 255-2468. The library is open Mon.-Fri. 8 a.m.-4:30 p.m. Entrance is free.

Edificio Metálico

One of San José's more intriguing edifices, this ocher-colored prefabricated building is made entirely of metal. Designed by the French architect Victor Baltard (some attribute it to Charles Thirio), who also designed Les Halles in Paris, the structure was shipped piece by piece from Belgium in 1892 and welded together in situ. The facade is dressed with a bust of Minerva, the "goddess of wisdom." The building, on the northwest corner of Parque España, is now a school.

Museo de Jade Fidel Tristan

San José's world-famous Jade Museum houses the largest collection of jade in the Americas. The museum, on the 11th floor of the INS (Instituto Nacional de Seguro) Building at Calle 9 and Avenida 7, displays a panoply of pre-Columbian artifacts (mostly carved adzes and pendants) and reconstructions. They're well-organized, with some mounted pieces backlit to show off the beautiful translucent colors of the jade to best effect. The museum also displays a comprehensive collection of pre-Columbian ceramics and gold miniatures organized by culture and region, as well as special exhibits of jewelry by important national and foreign artists.

Humankind's eternal preoccupation with sex is evidenced by the many enormous clay phalluses and figurines of men and women masturbating and copulating. The museum's 11th-floor vantage point offers splendid panoramic views over the city through the large windows: bring your camera. Hours: Mon.-Fri. 8 a.m.-4:30 p.m.; entrance $2, tel. 223-5800, ext. 2581.

Serpentario

This is a good place to get a close-up look at some of Costa Rica's most colorful reptiles. The small but interesting collection is quite impressive, despite its peculiar location on the second floor of the Radamida building, opposite the Hotel Del Dey on Avenida 1, Calles 9/11. The displays include poison-arrow frogs, iguanas, and many of Costa Rica's poisonous species—including the much-feared fer-de-lance—safely on view behind glass cages. Signs are offered in English for some exhibits, others only in Spanish. Hours: Mon.-Fri. 9 a.m.-6 p.m., weekends 10 a.m.-5 p.m.; admission $4; tel. 255-4210, fax 233-5520.

PLAZA DE LA DEMOCRACIA AND VICINITY

This uninspired square, between Avenidas Central/2 and Calles 13/15 was built in 1989, reportedly to receive visiting presidents attending the Hemispheric Summit. Dominating the dreary plaza, which rises to the east, is the crenel-

lated historic **Bellavista Fortress,** which today houses the Museo Nacional. On the west from the plaza is a bronze statue of **Don "Pepe" Figueres,** completed in 1994. Note the etchings of some of the former president's favorite sayings. To the south are the buildings of the "Judicial Circuit," including the Supreme Court and Immigration buildings.

Asamblea Legislativa

The pretty white Moorish structure on the north side of the plaza, on Calle 15, was originally the Presidential Palace, built in 1912 by presidential candidate Máximo Fernández in anticipation of victory in the 1914 elections. He lost. Nonetheless, he lent his home—known as the Blue Castle (Castillo Azul)—to President-elect Alfredo González Flores as his official residence. The Tinoco brothers (Federico and Joaquín) ousted Flores in a coup in 1917 and took possession of the home. Eventually it was returned to Fernández, who sold it to the U.S. State Department as the site of the U.S. Diplomatic Mission. It was a private residence between 1954-89, when the Costa Rican government bought it. Today it houses the Legislative Assembly (or Congress) and features a tiny library and history exhibit open to the public via a side door.

Museo Nacional

A large collection of pre-Columbian art (pottery, stone, and gold) and an eclectic mix of colonial-era art, furniture, costumes, and documents

Museo Nacional, San Jose

highlight the National Museum, in the old Bellavista Fortress on the east side of Plaza de la Democracia at Calle 17 and Avenida Central/2. Separate exhibition halls deal with history, archaeology, geology, religion, and colonial life. Only a few exhibits offer translations in English. The National Institute of Biodiversity also has a small but interesting display of insects downstairs. The towers and walls of the fortress, an old army barracks, are pitted with bullet holes from the 1948 civil war. The museum surrounds a beautiful landscaped courtyard featuring colonial-era cannons. There's a small gift shop. The main entrance is on the east side of the fortress. However, you may also enter by ascending the steps on the west side. Hours: Tues.-Sat. 8 a.m.-4 p.m., Sunday 9 a.m.-4:30 p.m.; entrance $1, students free; tel. 257-1433.

PARQUE NACIONAL AND VICINITY

The largest and most peaceful of the city's central parks graces a gentle hill that rises eastward between Calles 15/19 and Avenidas 1/3. At the park's center, under towering, shady trees, is the massive **Monumento Nacional,** one of several statues commemorating the War of 1856. The statue depicts the spirits of the Central American nations defeating the American adventurer William Walker. Like several other San José edifices, the monument originated in France: it was made in the Rodin studios. On Parque Nacional's southwestern corner is a statue of **Juan Santamaría,** the national hero. Avoid this area at night.

Galería Nacional de Arte Contemporaneo
Costa Rica has a thriving community of artists, producing some stunning work. The National Gallery of Contemporary Art shows revolving displays by leading Costa Rican artists. It's in the basement on the west side of the National Library, on the north side of the park, at Avenida 3, Calle 15. Hours: Mon.-Sat. 10 a.m.-1 p.m. and 1:45-4 p.m.; admission is free; tel. 233-4919.

Museo Nacional de Ferrocarril
The ornate, pagodalike Atlantic Railway Station on Avenida 3 and Calle 21, was built in 1907 and now houses the National Railroad Museum tracing the history of railroads in Costa Rica.

It displays a small collection of memorabilia plus old photographs and even vintage rolling stock and an old steam locomotive, Locomotora 59 (or Locomotora Negra), imported from Philadelphia in 1939 for the Northern Railway Company. One room traces the history of railway development. Note the beautiful if aged tile floor and ornately carved ceiling. The museum seems to keep irregular hours (perhaps because it is severely underfunded) and was closed for "restoration" in early 1998, as it had been for over a year. Hours: Mon.-Fri. 9 a.m.-4 p.m.; entrance costs 60 cents; tel. 221-0077.

BARRIO AMÓN AND VICINITY

Barrio Amón and **Barrio Otoya,** north of Parques Morazán and España, with the Río Torres as its northern border, form an aristocratic residential neighborhood founded at the end of the last century by a French immigrant, Amón Fasileau Duplantier, who arrived in 1884 to work for a coffee enterprise owned by the Tournón family, which lent its name to an adjacent region. Until recently, it had suffered decline and stood on the verge of becoming a slum. The restoration of Parque Morazán prompted investors to refurbish the neighborhood's grand historic homes, helped along by the Barrio Amón Conservation and Development Association. A burst of newfound civic pride is leading to a renaissance of the area as the region of choice for intellectuals and nouveau riche. Of particular note are the **Bishop's Castle,** Avenida 11, Calle 3, an ornate Moorish, turreted former home of Archbishop Don Carlos Humberto Rodriguez Quirós, and Avenida 9 between Calle 7 and 3, which is now lined with beautiful ceramic wall murals depicting traditional Costa Rican scenes.

Centro Costarricense de Ciencias y Cultura
The prominent building atop the slope on the west side of Barrio Amón, at the north end of Calle 4 (reached via Avenida 9), looks like an old penitentiary, and indeed that's what it was from 1910-79. Today the former prison houses the Costa Rican Science and Cultural Center, comprising a library and auditorium, plus the following two gems.

Galería Nacional: The superb National Gallery (not to be confused with the National Gallery of Contemporary Art) is dedicated to contemporary art displayed in splendidly lit and airy exhibition halls conjured from former jail cells and watchtowers. Some of the work is stupendous, representing Costa Rica's new breed of forceful artists, such as Francisco Zúñiga. Hours: Wed.-Fri. 8 a.m.-4 p.m., weekends 10 a.m.-5 p.m.; tel. 223-7003.

Museo de Niños: The Children's Museum lets children touch science and technology, with exhibits that include a planetarium and rooms dedicated to astronomy, planet earth, Costa Rica, ecology, science, human beings, and communications. A guided tour is given weekdays at 9 a.m.-noon and 1:30-5 p.m., and weekends at 10 a.m.-1 p.m. and 2-5 p.m. You have to buy tickets for the Children's Museum the day before

El Pueblo

Centro Comercial El Pueblo, tel. 257-0277, in Barrio Tournón on the north side of the Río Torres, is an entertainment and shopping complex designed to resemble a Spanish colonial village. El Pueblo's warren of alleys harbors art galleries, quality craft stores, and restaurants specializing in typically Costa Rican country meals.

You can walk from downtown in 15 minutes. The Calle Blancos bus departs from Calles 1/3 and Avenida 5. Get off a half a kilometer after crossing the river. Use a taxi by night. Taxis to and from El Pueblo often overcharge: settle on a fee before getting into your cab ($1 to downtown hotels, $2 to Sabana would be appropriate at night; slightly more after midnight). There's free parking and 24-hour security.

Parque Zoológico Simón Bolívar

This 14-acre zoo proves the adage that there's no joy in seeing animals caged. Until recently, the zoo was truly appalling, reflecting a severe shortage of funds that has resulted in understaffing and an inability to provide the animals with adequate facilities, nutrition, or veterinary care. A Friends of the Zoo and Adopt an Animal program, **FUNDAZOO,** Apdo. 11594, San José 1000, tel. 223-1790, fax 223-1817, were initiated in 1993 with the aim of collecting money to improve conditions in a five-stage project. A Nature Center, for example, opened in 1994, containing

a video room, library, and work area for schoolchildren. The amphibians and reptiles recently received a new home—the Joyeros del Bosque Húmedos—designed by the Baltimore Aquarium. And the alligators and tapirs are slated to receive a new lagoon, and other beasts will get their own new enclosures. But when I visited, the zoo retained many dismal elements.

The native species on display includes spider and capuchin monkeys, most of the indigenous cats, plus a small variety of birds, including toucans and tame macaws. The zoo's finest exhibits, surprisingly, are a male lion and a handsome Bengal tiger. Sadly, they and the other cats are housed in tiny, depressingly austere metal cages fouled with urine (the zoo was founded in 1916 and retains too many of its original, despairingly small cages; even the new cages for the native animals are small and dour). The lion had to be rehoused after he had learned to piss on people passing his cage. Who can blame him! Maybe they'll have more pleasing new homes by the time you visit.

Facilities include a **McDonald's,** a small *soda,* and a souvenir store. The zoo's entrance is hidden away at Calle 7 and Avenida 11, turn right at Avenida 11 and follow the curving road for 100 meters. Avoid the zoo on weekends if possible, when the locals flock in droves. Hours: Tues.-Fri. 8 a.m.-4 p.m., weekends and holidays 9 a.m.-5 p.m.; entrance is $1.50.

Spirogyra Butterfly Garden

Butterfly lovers no longer have to venture beyond San José to see butterflies in their natural setting. This small butterfly garden and farm is 100 meters east and 150 meters south of El Pueblo. Bilingual tours are offered every half-hour, or you can opt for a 30-minute self-guided tour; an educational video is shown prior to the tour. More than 30 species flutter about in the 350-square-meter garden, which is sheltered by a net. In the center is a small waterfall surrounded by orchids, heliconias, and trees. A separate section houses cages where eggs and caterpillars develop, protected from nature's predators. The small natural forest is being protected as a private botanical garden. Hummingbirds abound! A restaurant is planned. Hours: Mon.-Sat. 8 a.m.-4 p.m.; $6 admission, $5 students, $3 children; tel./fax 222-2937, e-mail: parcar@sol.racsa.co.cr.

MERCADO CENTRAL AND VICINITY

Mercado Central

San José's most colorful and authentically Central American market, between Avenidas Central/1 and Calles 6/8, is heady on atmosphere nonetheless. Everything but the kitchen sink seems on offer within its dark warren of alleyways: baskets, flowers, hammocks, spices, meats, vegetables, souvenirs. There are fish booths selling octopus, dorado, and shrimp; butchers' booths with oxtails and pigs' heads on display; flower stalls, saddle shops, and booths selling medicinal herbs guaranteed to cure everything from sterility to common colds. Outside, street hawkers call out their wares sold from brightly colored barrows. The market is a good place to order *olla de carne,* a steaming beef-and-vegetable stew, at a bustling *soda.* Pickpockets thrive in crowded places—watch your valuables. Closed Sunday. *A must see!*

Museo Postal, Telegráfico y Filatélico

On the second floor of the main post office at Calle 2, Avenidas 1/3, the Postal, Telegraphic, and Philatelic Museum features old telephones, philatelic history displays, and postage stamps including Penny Blacks. Costa Rica's oldest stamp—dating from 1863—is also represented. Hours: Mon.-Fri. 8 a.m.-4:30 p.m.; entrance free; tel. 223-9766, ext. 269.

Parque Braulio Carrillo

This tiny park (not to be confused with Braulio Carrillo National Park), between Avenidas 2/4 and Calles 12/14, is also known to Josefinos as La Merced Park, because it faces La Merced church. Highlights include a gothic arch-shaped fountain to match the arched windows of La Merced church and a monument honoring the astronomer Copernicus.

WEST OF DOWNTOWN

Cemeterio General

When you've seen everything else, and before heading out of town, check out the final resting place of Josefinos, with its many fanciful marble mausoleums of neo-classical design. The cemetery, on the south side of Avenida 10 between Calles 20/36, is particularly worth seeing 1 and 2 November, when vast numbers of people go to leave flowers at the tombs of their relatives.

Museo de Arte Costarricense

Founded in 1977, the museum, facing Paseo Colón, on the east side of Sabana Park, houses a permanent collection of some of the most important works in the history of the fine arts in Costa Rica. Besides a diverse, robust, and outstanding permanent collection of woodcuts, wooden sculptures, and 19th- and 20th-century paintings, revolving exhibitions of contemporary native artists are also shown. The Golden Hall (Salón Dorado) on the second floor depicts the nation's history from pre-Columbian times through the 1940s. Done in stucco and bronze patina, the resplendent mural was constructed during Costa Rica's "muralist" period by French sculptor Louis Feron. Lovers of chamber music will also appreciate free concerts occasionally given in the Salón Dorado. Hours: Tues.-Sun. 10 a.m.-4 p.m.; entrance $1.50, free on Sunday; tel. 222-7155.

Museo de la Empresa Nacional

A motley yet interesting collection of printing presses, typesetting machines, typefaces, and other print-related objects represent the history of printing in Costa Rica during the last 150 years. Founded in 1985, the National Printing Office Museum is in the La Uruca district, just behind the Capris S.A. Corporation Complex. Tours are guided. Hours: Tues.-Fri. 8 a.m.-3 p.m.; admission is free.

Museo La Salle de Ciencias Naturales

The La Salle Museum of Natural Sciences proffers the bounty of the Central American tropics. Reputed to have among the most comprehensive collections in the world, the museum houses more than 22,500 exhibits (mostly stuffed animals and mounted insects) covering zoology, paleontology, archaeology, and entomology. Some of the stuffed beasts have been ravaged by time and are a bit moth-eaten; other displays simulating natural environments are so comical one wonders whether the taxidermist was drunk. A coterie of caimans and crocodiles that live on a small island in the *museo* patio are the only live animals.

The museum is administered by the Ministry of Agriculture and is in the old Colegio La Salle on the southwest corner of Sabana Park. Hours: Mon.-Fri. 7 a.m.-3 p.m., Saturday 7.30 a.m.-noon; admission $1; tel. 232-1306. If it looks closed, simply ring the buzzer and hope that the curator appears to open the door and switch on the lights. The Sabana-Estadio bus, which departs from the Catedral Metropolitana on Avenida 2, passes Colegio La Salle.

Parque la Sabana

The only park of any real scale in San José, this favorite weekend getaway for Josefinos used to be the national airport (the old terminal now houses the Costa Rican Art Museum). It's one mile west of the city center, at the west end of Paseo Colón. Today, it's a focus for sports and recreation and one of the few places within San José where you may jog without being hassled by traffic. Sabana Park contains both the Estadio Nacional (on the northwest corner) and the National Gymnasium (southeast corner), which features an Olympic-size swimming pool. There are also basketball, tennis, and volleyball courts, a baseball diamond and a soccer field, and tree-lined paths for jogging and walking. A small lake on the south side is stocked with fish, and fishing is permitted. And a small hill has been piled up from Sabana ("Flatlands") for kite flyers. The Sabana-Cemeterio bus, which leaves from Calle 7 and Avenida Central, will take you there. Otherwise, it's a pleasing, brisk, 30-minute walk.

Pueblo Antiguo and Parque Diversiones

This splendid 12-acre Disney-style attraction, three km west of downtown in La Uruca, is the Williamsburg of Costa Rica. The theme park recreates the locales and dramatizes the events of Costa Rican history. Buildings in traditional architectural style include a replica of the National Liquor Factory, Congressional Building, church, market, fire station, and the Costa Rican Bank. The place comes alive with oxcarts, horse-drawn carriages, live music, folkloric dances, and actors dramatizing the past. The park has three sections: the capital city, coast (including a replica of the Tortuguero Canals), country (with original adobe structures moved to the site, including a sugar mill, coffee mill, and milking barn). The venture is operated by the Association

for the National Children's Hospital and profits fund improvements to the hospital. There are craft shops and a restaurant serves typical Costa Rican cuisine. A four-hour "Costa Rica Experience" tour is offered Saturday and Sunday at 10 a.m. ($28). It hosts "Costa Rican Nights" with traditional entertainment Fri.-Sun. 6-9 p.m. ($28 including dinner). Hours: Mon.-Fri. 9 a.m.-5 p.m., weekends 9 a.m.-9 p.m. Entrance: $6, or $20 including historic show; Apdo. 730, San José 1150, tel. 231-2001, fax 296-2212. There are no signs; it's about 200 meters east of Hospital México on the road that runs along the west side of the Autopista.

SOUTH OF DOWNTOWN

There's an **artisans' market** on the east side of **Iglesia Soledad,** a pretty, ocher-colored church fronting a tiny plaza at Avenida 4 and Calle 9, Paseo de los Estudiantes. Paseo runs south to **Desamparados,** a working class suburb on the southern outskirts of San José. Its superb church is one of the most impressive in the country, and the **Museo de Joaquín García Monge** is dedicated to the Costa Rican author and intellectual. Hours: Mon.-Fri. 1-4 p.m.; tel. 259-5072.

Museo Criminología

Reflecting a national concern with public awareness and responsibility, the ostensible purpose of the Criminology Museum, in the Judicial Police headquarters in the Supreme Court Building at Calle 17/19 and Avenida 6, is to prevent crime through education. The museum attempts to achieve this by featuring pictures and displays of Costa Rica's more famous crimes, along with weapons involved in the diabolical deeds, a jar containing an embalmed severed hand, and an illegally aborted fetus. The stuff that good nightmares are made of, in other words. Hours: Monday, Wednesday, and Thursday 1-4 p.m.; tel. 223-0666, ext. 2378.

Museo de las Carrateras y Vida Rural

The Oxcart and Rural Life Museum, in a venerable home in Desamparado, displays artifacts profiling the traditional peasant lifestyle. The most impressive exhibits are the rustic oxcarts span-

ning the decades. Hours: Tues.-Sun. 8 a.m.-
noon and 2-6 p.m.; entrance $1; tel. 259-7042.

Parque de la Paz

This huge park, two km due south of the city
center, is the most peaceful retreat within the
city bounds. Like Sabana, the Peace Park is a favorite of Josefinos on weekends. It has an artificial lake with boats, plus horseback rides, kite-fly-
ing, sports fields, and even horse-drawn car-
riage rides. You can walk there by following Calle
9 (Paseo de los Estudiantes) to **Parque Gonzalez Viquez,** then follow Calle 11 south to the
Peace Park, which is also bisected by the *autopista* (the freeway, or "ring-road," that skirts
the city).

EAST OF DOWNTOWN

Moravia

Moravia—properly San Vicente de Moravia (it
appears as San Vicente on maps)—lies five km
northeast of San José and is renowned as the
center of handicrafts; the main street is known as
"Calle de los Artesanías." The village moves at a
slower pace than the capital city and is an alternative to touristy Sarchí for craft bargains,
especially leather and wicker furniture. The
town's pretty plaza is sleepily suburban. Note
that its street signs are all messed up!

Museo de Arte Indígena

The Indigenous Art Museum, 100 meters west of
Spoon, in Los Yoses, about one km east of
downtown, boasts a fine collection of pre-
Columbian jewelry, art, ceramics, and artifacts.
It's forte seems to be a sales pitch—gold, emeralds, and semi-precious stones sold on site.
Hours: Mon.-Sat. 8 a.m.-6 p.m., and Sunday 8
a.m.-3 p.m.; tel. 234-1858, fax 253-4764. Free
transportation.

Museo de Entomología

There's no explaining why this museum—one
of the largest collections of insects in the world—
is housed in the basement of the School of Music

(Facultad de Artes Musicales) of the University of
Costa Rica. The Entomology Museum features
an immense variety of Costa Rican and Central
American insects, including a spectacular display of butterflies. Knowledgeable guides are
available, but call ahead to check availability
and opening times, which reputedly vary. Don't
be discouraged if the door is locked. Ring the
bell for admission. You can take a bus from the
National Theater on Avenida 2 and Calle 5 to
the church in San Pedro, from where the faculty
and museum are signposted; a taxi from downtown San José will cost approximately $1.50.
Hours: Mon.-Fri. 1-5 p.m.; admission is free; tel.
207-5318.

Parque del Este

On the outskirts of the city, in the hills three km
east of San Pedro, this rural retreat provides a
close-at-hand escape from the city. Trails lead
through landscaped grounds to a panoply of facilities: children's playhouses, basketball courts,
volleyball nets, two pools, and clearings with
barbecue pits and benches. Trails lead uphill
into wild woodlands, where you may settle beneath tall pines and listen to the needles and
branches sighing in the wind. Josefinos flock at
weekends. You reach it via the suburb of Sabanilla, turn north—left—at the large roundabout
in San Pedro, then right at the road immediately
before Friday's restaurant. Beyond Sabanilla
the road ends; turn left and head uphill to the
park. Open daily except Monday 8 a.m.-4 p.m.
Entrance: 60 cents.

University of Costa Rica

The university campus, in the suburb of San
Pedro, about two km east of downtown, is a fine
place to take in Costa Rica's youthful bohemi-
anism. UC Berkeley it's not, but the plentiful
sodas and bars and bookstores nearby hint at
Berkeley's famed Telegraph Avenue. Concerts,
exhibitions, and more are given at the gallery of
the Facultad de Bellas Artes (College of Fine
Arts). The last week of March, during **Semana
Universitaria,** students shirk studies for a ram-
bunctious fiesta.

ACCOMMODATIONS

Travelers to Costa Rica have long bemoaned the lack of charming boutique hotels in the nation's capital city. Of late, however, a new breed of intimate and gracious hotel has emerged to blow the dust off San José's dowdy hotel scene. And the recent arrival of Intel and other multinational companies has helped foster the arrival of large name-brand hotels. Budget hotels, however, are for the most part still uninspired, though a few gems shine.

San José is a noisy city; it is always wise to ask for a room away from the street. Also, consider staying outside San José, where you'll find dozens of superb options close enough for forays into the capital and farther afield.

Christmas and Easter are particularly busy periods. If you'll be in San José during these times, plan on making reservations several months in advance. Reservations are also strongly advised for dry-season months (Dec.-April). Don't rely on mail to make reservations; it could take several months to confirm. Instead, call direct, send a fax, e-mail, or have your travel agent make reservations for you. It may be necessary to send a deposit, without which your space may be released to someone else. Check on this when you make your reservation. The ICT office, tel. 222-1090, provides a list of recommended hotels. The information booth at the airport can help with reservations. For private houses and rooms, check the classified ads in the back of the *Tico Times* or *Costa Rica Today*.

Most hotels supply towels and soap, but unless you're staying in the upscale hotels, you may need to bring your own shampoos and conditioners. Bringing a sink plug is also a good idea if you plan on using budget accommodations. If you anticipate carousing until midnight or later, make sure in advance that the hotel provides late access. Many of the better hotels discourage unregistered guests.

Hotels are arranged below by area, then by price category, and then by type (e.g., hotel, hostel, bed and breakfast, etc.). Prices were as accurate as possible at press time. Please bear in mind that prices may have increased by the time you read this book. A 15% sales tax and 3% ICT tax are added to all hotel bills. Some hotels charge extra (as much as six percent) for paying by credit card.

San José has lots of budget hotels. Most are dirty and bug-ridden, or just plain dark and dingy, and usually noisy. It's difficult to find a really good one at a fair price. A number of super-cheap hotels (below $10) can be found in the unsavory area near the Coca-Cola bus station, Calle 16, Avenidas 1/3. Caution is needed here at night, as with the cheap hotels between Calles 6/10 and Avenidas 3/5. Both areas boast plenty of drunks and cheap hookers, and many of the hotels themselves are little more than brothels. Since walls in budget hotels are often merely wooden partitions, noise can be a major problem. Don't take cleanliness and comfort for granted. Compare. Hot (more likely, heated) water is never guaranteed.

Apartotels: A hybrid of hotels and apartment buildings, apartotels resemble motels on the European and Australian model. These self-catering units come fully furnished, with kitchenette and TV. Most offer daily maid service and are available for rent by the day, week, or month. Weekly and monthly rentals get substantial discounts. They are particularly popular with Ticos. Decor ranges from upscale to dingy and austere. Most are on the fringe of the city, with many concentrated in Los Yoses.

Guesthouses: "Guesthouse" refers to a bed-and-breakfast hotel in a family-run home where you are made to feel like part of the family, as opposed to hotels that include breakfasts in their room rates (such hotels are not what people traditionally mean when they speak of a "bed and breakfast"—i.e., a small, atmospheric hotel with a homey ambience and congenial, often live-in, hosts). The **Bed and Breakfast Association** can provide recommendations, tel. 223-4168 or 228-9200. Michael Long of the Raya Vida operates the **All Costa Rica Bed & Breakfast Reservation Service,** tel. 223-4168, fax 223-4157.

Homestays: Another option is to stay with a Costa Rican family—an ideal way to experience the legendary Tico hospitality and warmth, and a pleasing opportunity to bone up on your Spanish.

You may choose English-speaking hosts if you wish. Dinners ($5) are not included. Two companies that specialize in this are **Bell's Home Hospitality,** run by Vernon and Marcela Bell, Apdo. 185, San José 1000, tel. 225-4752, fax 224-5884, e-mail: homestay@sol.racsa.co.cr, and Steve Beaudreau's **Costa Rican Homestays,** tel. 240-6829. The Bells offer a selection from 70 homes in the San José area, most in the suburbs ($30 s, $45 d or twin share, with breakfast; $5 extra for private bath; monthly rates are available). Beaudreau offers two classes of accommodations in and around San José: "A" class in upper-middle-class homes, with private baths ($28 d per day up to 15 days, less after that); and "B" class in more humble homes, with shared baths. Families also advertise rooms for rent in the classifieds of the *Tico Times* and *Costa Rica Today.*

Private Apartments: The *Tico Times, Costa Rica Today,* and *Adventures in Costa Rica* all publish ads listing private apartments for rent. Usually these are on the outskirts of town and in adjacent towns.

Motels: In Costa Rica, as throughout Latin America, "motels" are explicitly for lovers. Rooms—complete with adult movies and, sometimes, jacuzzis and ceiling mirrors—are rented out by the hour (about $20). Originally aimed at providing privacy for young couples, today's motels more commonly serve as meeting places for adult trysts. Hence, they're usually hidden behind high walls with private garages for each room to protect guests from inquisitive eyes and chance encounters with the neighbor or spouse. Many of the patrons are married . . . sometimes to each other. Motels concentrate in the southeast suburb of San Francisco de Dos Ríos.

SHOESTRING

Downtown

Hotels: There are several super-cheap hotels along Avenida 2. **Hotel Tica Linda,** Calles 5/7, tel. 233-0528, fax 255-0444, is one of the cheapest places in San José. This basic hostel next to La Esmeralda has bare-bones private rooms plus shared bedrooms—alas tiny, noisy, and dingy—a small garden and, amazingly, a jacuzzi.

It's popular with backpackers. Rates: $3.50 dorm; $5 d private. **Hotel Avenida Segunda,** Calles 7/9, tel. 222-0260, fax 223-9732, is also popular, despite reportedly doing double-duty as a "love shack." It's almost always full. The 10 rooms are well-lit, with shared baths with warm water. Those facing the road are noisy. Rates: $8 s, $12 d. Next door is the equally popular **Pensión Super Familiar,** tel. 223-1102 or 257-0486, a favorite of penny-pinchers and Central Americans. The 14 rooms are clean but spartan. Shared bath. Rates: about $5. On the same block are the **Hotel Lilimani,** tel. 222-0607, and **Pensión Salamanca,** next door to Tiny's Bar and Restaurant, with tiny rooms with cold showers for $4. One block east is **Pensión Araica,** Calles 11/13, tel. 222-5233. Rate: $2.50. Between Calles 13 and 15 is the family-operated **Hotel Nicaragua,** tel. 223-0292, with clean and quiet, though somewhat dingy, rooms popular with Central American travelers. Cold-water showers. Rate: $7. The **Hotel Generaleño,** Avenida 2, Calles 8/10, tel. 233-7877, has 45 large but dingy, basic rooms with cold showers. Rates: $5 s, $8 d with communal shower, from $14 d with private shower.

North of Avenida 2, **Pensión Otoya,** Calle Central, Avenidas 5/7, tel. 221-3925, comes recommended as "good value for money." The 14 rooms are clean but dark. There's a TV in the lobby. The owner says it's a "family hotel"—no unregistered guests. Rates: $7 s, $12 d shared bath; $10 s, $14 d private bath. **Pensión Villa Blanca,** Avenida 7 and Calles 2/4, tel. 223-9088, has 12 spotless rooms, some with private bath with cold water for $6. Reportedly, owner Don Sergio turns away "undesirables" but gets rave reviews for being friendly and helpful.

Hotel Galaad Mount Inn, Avenida 9, Calles Central/1, tel. 222-6395, is recommended by a reader as "very clean and comfortable." It has sparsely furnished but clean rooms, most with shared baths. A jacuzzi spa hints—along with the girls hanging out in the lobby—that the place may double as a brothel. Rooms cost $7 s, $15 d, $19 t. Across the way, the **Hotel Venezia,** 25 meters east of Josephine's nightclub, is the **Hotel Venezia,** with 25 simple, clean rooms for $10 pp, with free parking. There's a laundry. Some rooms have a double bed, others have three singles. There are no fans or a/c.

The **Hotel América,** Avenida 7, Calles 2/4, tel. 221-4116, has 11 clean rooms. Reportedly it accepts hourly guests. Rates: $6 s, $8 d. The **Hotel Asia,** Calle 11, Avenida Central/1, tel. 223-3893, is clean and well-lit. Rooms have communal showers and thin particle-board walls; downstairs is a haven for prostitutes and their johns. One room has private bath. Rates: $6 s, $8 d. The **Hotel Astoria,** Avenida 7, Calles 7/9, tel. 221-2174, fax 221-8497, is popular for its airy, albeit spartan rooms with private bathrooms and hot showers. Some rooms have communal baths. Rates: $8 s shared bath, $10 d; $12 d private bath. The **Hotel Compostela,** Calle 6, Avenidas 3/5, tel. 257-1514, is family run and quiet. Rates: $6 pp in dorms with dingy shared bath; $15 s/d rooms with private bath. The **Hotel Marlyn,** Calle 4, Avenidas 7/9, tel. 233-3212, has small, dark, but clean rooms with hot water. Rates: $6 s communal bath, $10 private bath. The **Hotel Morazán,** Avenida 3, Calles 11/13, tel. 221-9083, has clean and large but spartan rooms from $5 s in low season, $8/15 s/d in high season. The **Hotel Rialto,** Calle 2, Avenida 5, has clean bare-bones room with occasional hot water for $5 pp shared bath, $7 private bath. **Pensión Americana,** Calle 2, Avenidas Central/2, tel. 221-9799, has large albeit dingy rooms with cold showers. Rates: $7.

South of Avenida 2, the **Hotel Aurora,** Avenida 4, Calle 8, has clean rooms with hot showers from $10 s/d. The **Pensión Centro Continental,** above the Hotel Ritz, has basic rooms with communal showers for $8 pp.

In the Coca-Cola district, **Gran Hotel Imperial,** Calle 8, Avenidas Central/1, tel. 222-7899, is a favorite of the backpacking crowd. Step down the stairwell and you'll find basic yet clean rooms for $5 a night. Communal showers have tepid water. The restaurant offers filling meals for a pittance. No room in the inn? Step north a few meters to **Hotel Moderno,** tel. 221-2572, where basic rooms with cold water cost $4 pp.The **Hotel Boruca,** Calle 14, Avenidas 1/3, tel. 223-0016, fax 232-0107, has clean rooms with shared bath, plus a restaurant, and is popular with Peace Corps volunteers. Rates: $7 s, $12 d. The **Hotel Roma,** Calle 14, Avenidas Central/1, tel. 223-2179, has clean but bare-bones rooms with cold water for $4.

BUDGET

Downtown

Hostels: The **Casa Ridgeway,** tel./fax 233-6168, hostel is attached to the Friends Peace Center (Centro de los Amigos Para La Paz) in a cul-de-sac (Calle 15 bis) between Avenidas 6/8. Four small, well-lit dorms and private rooms provide clean accommodations in a relaxed and friendly environment. It has a laundry, basic kitchen facilities, and shared showers. No alcohol or smoking. Rates: dorm $8 pp; $10 s, $20 d/t private room.

A friendly German named Andrea runs **Casa Leo,** tel. 222-9725, tucked away on Avenida 6 bis, Calles 13/15, and a favorite of the backpacking crowd and conservationist volunteers, including the overflow from Casa Ridgeway. It's a great meeting place. It has two clean, simple, well-lit dorm rooms which share showers with hot water, plus three private rooms (one with private bathroom). Guests have kitchen and laundry privileges. Andrea makes "kick-ass coffee" (her words). Rates (pp): $8 dorm; $12 s, $22 d private room.

Hotels: North of Avenida 2, the **Pensión de la Cuesta,** Avenida 1, Calles 11/13, tel. 256-7946, fax 255-2896, e-mail: ggmnber@sol.racsa.co.cr, is clean, cozy, charmingly eccentric, and ideal for those who like offbeat hotels. Nicola Bertoldi, the Italian manager, presides over this 1930s house full of antiques and potted plants. It's owned by local artists Dierdre Hyde and Otto Apuy, whose original artworks adorn the walls. There are nine rooms plus a furnished apartment for up to six people. The shared baths are clean. There's a TV room and self-service laundry. Guests get free use of the kitchen. Coupons good for a 20% discount are available at the ICT. Rates: $19 s, $27 d low season; $23 s, $31 d high season, including breakfast; $10 extra person.

A reasonable option is the **Hotel Capital,** Apdo. 6091, San José 1000, Calle 4, Avenidas 3/5, tel. 221-8583, fax 221-8497, offering 15 completely remodeled rooms with tiled bathrooms. Eight rooms have king-size beds; some have no windows. No TVs or phones. Antique photographs adorn the walls. Rates: from $20. A nearby alternative is the **Hotel Central,** Avenida 3, Calle 6, tel. 222-3509, with 45 spacious rooms from $8 s with shared bath; $17 d with private bath.

The **Hotel Johnson,** Apdo. 6638, San José 1000, Calle 8, Avenidas Central/2, tel. 223-7633, fax 222-3683, has long been a favorite of budget travelers, Peace Corps volunteers, and Central American businessmen. Rooms—57 in all—are moderately clean, but timeworn and spartan. There's a restaurant/bar. Rates: $16 s, $20 d. Larger rooms cost $30 for up to six people.

The **Costa Rica Inn,** Apdo. 10282, San José 1000, Calle 9, Avenidas 1/3, tel. 222-5203, fax 223-8385; in the U.S., tel. (800) 637-0899, erstwhile home of former president Tinoco, has decor that has been described as resembling "a '50s horror movie—not gothic, just cheesy." The 35 rooms are small and dingy yet clean, comfortable, and quiet. Each has private bath, hot water, and telephone. Rates: from $25 s, $30 d. The **Hotel Galilea,** Avenida Central, Calle 13, tel. 233-6925, fax 223-1689, has 23 basic rooms with private bath with hot water. Discounts are offered for students and week-long stays. The Dutch owner speaks English, German, French, Dutch, and Malay! Rates: $26 s, $30 d. The **Hotel El Crucero** , Calle 4, Avenidas 7/9, tel. 233-3124, has 12 simple rooms with private bath and hot water for $15 s, $23 d.

The pleasing **Hotel Plaza,** Apdo. 2019, San José 1000, Avenida Central, Calles 2/4, tel. 222-5533, fax 222-2641, has 40 rooms from $20 s, $28 d. The '70s-era **Hotel Diplomat,** Apdo. 6606, San José 1000, Calle 6, Avenida Central/2, tel. 221-8133, fax 233-7474, has 29 rooms with TVs and private baths with hot water from $21 s, $30 d. There's a restaurant.

South of Avenida 2, the **Hotel Principe,** Avenida 6, Calle Central/2, tel. 222-7983, fax 223-1589, has 34 spacious rooms with private bath with hot water for $12 s, $16 d. Popular **Hotel Gran Hotel Centroamericano,** Avenida 2, Calles 6/8, tel. 221-3362, fax 221-3714, which has 45 small, cell-like rooms with telephone, and private bath with hot water. There's a laundry, a TV in the lobby, and a self-service restaurant. It's noisy and musty. Rates: $15 s, $24 d, $29 t, $35 quad. The recently renovated **Hotel Fortuna,** Apdo. 116, San José, Avenida 6, Calles 2/4, tel. 223-5344, fax 221-2466, e-mail: fortuna@habitat.co.cr, is a good bargain, clean and quiet, with 32 large rooms plus a restaurant and bar. It was being remodeled at press time. Rates: $22 s; $28 d.

The **Ritz,** Apdo. 6783, San José 1000, Calle Central, Avenidas 8/10, tel. 222-4103, fax 222-8849, has 25 modest rooms with private baths with hot water. It looked relatively clean and well-run, albeit simply furnished, but a reader says it's "musty and dark." A second-floor lounge has TV, and breakfasts are served in a well-lit restaurant. Rates: $18 s, $24 d shared bath; $21 s, $29 d private bath. The **Hotel Berlin,** tel. 255-0388, cater-corner to the Ritz, has 19 basic, clean rooms with fans, firm mattresses, and private bath with hot water for $13 s/d. The **Hotel Boston,** next door on Avenida 8, tel. 257-4499, fax 221-0563, is less appealing (one reader calls it a "flophouse"), but the staff are lauded for helpfulness. Rooms with private baths have hot water and black and white TVs. Rates: $10 s, $16 d. The **Hotel Park,** Avenida 4, Calles 2/4, tel. 221-6944, fax 233-7602, is a clean hotel with 16 rooms with hot water, and a bar. It does a brisk business off the red-light district. Rates: $24 s, $30 d.

In the Coca-Cola district, try the **Hotel Bienvenido,** Calle 10, Avenida 1/3, tel. 233-2161, fax 221-1872, has 44 clean rooms with private bath and hot water. There's a small restaurant. Rates: $18 s, $22 d (don't believe the advertisements for cheaper rates). Hookers and crack addicts hang out on the streets outside. The **Hotel Cocorí,** Avenida 3, Calle 16, tel. 233-0081, with 26 rooms with private baths and hot water, and the recently renovated **Hotel Musoc,** Calle 16, Avenidas 1/3, tel. 222-9437, fax 255-0031, with 45 rooms, both charge about $10 s, $16 d with communal bath; $14 s, $18 d private bath.

West of Downtown

Hotels: The **Hotel Petit,** Apdo. 357, San José 1007, Paseo Colón and Calle 24, tel. 233-0766, fax 233-1938, has 15 basic rooms, all with hot showers and electric stoves. Kitchen facilities and laundry service are available. It's a very popular hotel which I find musty and overpriced. There's laundry, secure parking, and a cable TV in the lounge. Rooms vary markedly. Rates: $17 s, $27 d, $38 t, including breakfast.

The **Kalexma Inn,** Apdo. 6833-1000 San José, tel./fax 232-0115, e-mail: kalexma@n.s.goldnet. co.cr, website www.goldnet.co.cr/kalexma, in La Uruca, opposite the Irazú Hotel, has 12 simply furnished rooms with hot water, plus a lounge featuring cable TV, laundry service, and kitchen facilities. It operates a Spanish language school. Rates: $15-20 s, $20-30 d including breakfast.

Guesthouses: La Aurora de Heredia, tel. 293-1655, is a private home with a bed-and-breakfast service, about two km east of Ciudad Cariari and seven km west of San José. It offers kitchen privileges and cable TV. Rates: $25 d, $250 a month. **Mondorama Guesthouse,** tel./fax 232-0304, is a neoclassical home in Rohrmoser.

East of Downtown

Hostels: Headquarters of the Costa Rican Youth Hostel Association is the **Toruma** hostel, RECAJ, Apdo. 1355, San José 1002, tel./fax 224-4085, a beautiful old colonial-style structure sitting above Avenida Central, Calles 29/31, about a half-kilometer east of the National Museum. No age restrictions. Segregated dormitories accommodate 95 beds in 12 well-kept rooms. Family rooms are available. Advance booking required, weeks ahead in peak season. Laundry and restaurant. It's popular with the backpacking crowd and a great place to meet other travelers. Hours: 7 a.m.-10 p.m. You can stay out later with a pass. Rates: from $10 pp IYH cardholders; $13 nonmembers; breakfast included. Private rooms cost $26 s/d. Guests are permitted 24 hours.

Hotels: The popular **Bella Vista,** Avenida Central, Calles 19/21, tel. 223-0095, in the U.S. tel. (800) 637-0899, is described as being as close as you get to a "surfers' hangout" in San José. The 30 carpeted rooms with private bathrooms are spic-and-span, albeit small and stuffy. There's a *soda* attached, plus a laundry. Rates: $20 s, $26 d.

The intimate **Hotel Aranjuez,** Apdo. 457, San José 2070, in Los Yoses at Calle 19, Avenidas 11/13, tel. 223-3559, fax 223-3528, e-mail: aranjuez@sol.racsa.co.cr, has been recommended as a good place to meet local expats and for families with kids. It has 23 admirably and eclectically decorated rooms with cable TV, phones, and hair dryers. Some rooms have shared bath; all baths have hot water. It's formed of four contiguous houses, each with its own personality; the original home is Caribbean in style. Relax on wicker and rattan furniture in the inner courtyards or shady patios, enjoying the limes and heliconias adorning the grounds. Guests have kitchen privileges. Rates: $16 s, $20 d shared

bath; $25 d, $30 d private bath, including buffet breakfast. Nearby on Avenida 2 and Calles 19/21, is the English-owned **Hotel Troy,** tel. 222-6756. You can't miss its blue-and-ocher exterior. Inside, there's lots of bamboo and tropical colors. Rates: $15 s/d.

INEXPENSIVE

Downtown

Hotels: North of Avenida 2 in Barrio Amón, at Avenida 7, Calles 7/9, is the **Hotel Rey Amón,** Apdo. 7145-1000 San José, tel. 233-3819, fax 233-1769, a refurbished centenarian mansion with original tile floors and high ceilings. The 12 rooms all have cable TV and private bath with hot water. None have fans, a/c, or telephone. They're small, but well-lit, clean, and pleasant. There's secure parking, plus a TV lounge and a tiny breakfast area. Rates: $25 s, $35 d low season; $35 s, $50 d high season, with breakfast and airport pick-up.

For atmosphere, try the **Hotel Don Carlos,** Apdo. 1593, San José 1000, tel. 221-6707, fax 255-0828, e-mail: hotel@doncarlos.co.cr, website www.cool.co.cr.usr.don-carlos/doncarlos.htm; in the U.S., SJO 1686, P.O. Box 025216, Miami, FL 33102-5216. Founded by pre-Columbian art expert Don Carlos Balser in an aged colonial-style mansion, the homey, well-run hotel, at Calle 9 and Avenidas 7/9, is replete with Sarchí oxcarts and archaeological treasures. Magnificent wrought-iron work, stained-glass windows, stunning artwork, and bronze sculptures abound—one wall is covered with 272 hand-painted tiles showing San José at the turn of the century. Some of the 15 rooms and suites are long in the tooth, with drab decor and furniture, though the noise of passing vehicles—once a problem—has abated since traffic was rerouted. Newer rooms at the back, reached by a rambling courtyard, are more pleasing. Rooms have cable TV. The Boutique Annemarie has a splendid collection of artwork and souvenirs, and there's a full tour service. The hotel has live marimba music, plus a small gym, and a restaurant lit by an atrium skylight. It offers free e-mail service on a computer in the lobby. Rates: from $40 s, $50 d, including continental breakfast, English-language newspaper, and welcome cocktail.

Splendidly situated on a corner of Parque Morazán, Calle 5, Avenida 3, is the no-frills **Diana's Inn,** tel. 223-6542, fax 233-0495, with a/c rooms with private bath, phone, and color TV. They're basic, as are the public arenas, but clean and well-lit. The three-story pink building was once home to an ex-president of Costa Rica, but has lost its lustre. Rates: from $25 s, $35 d, including tax and breakfast.

The **Hotel La Amistad Inn,** Apdo. 1864, San José 1002, tel. 221-1597, fax 221-1409, e-mail: wolfgang@sol.racsa.co.cr, website www.central america.com/cr/hotel/amistad.htm, at Avenida 11, Calle 15—a quiet location, just east of the zoo on the edge of the historic Barrio Otoya district—is a restored old mansion with 22 rooms, each featuring two queen-size beds with orthopedic mattress, a ceiling fan, a telephone, a cable TV, a security box, and a black marble bathroom. The hotel has a small garden. It's under multilingual German ownership (the influence is evident in the breakfasts). Take a room in the old wing upstairs; readers report newer rooms downstairs are noisy. Rates: from $25 s, $35 d, $50 suites.

Hotel Vesuvio, Apdo. 477, San José 1000, Avenida 11, Calles 13/15, tel. 221-7586, fax 221-8325, is a modern structure that hints at Spanish colonial. The 20 rooms have spic-and-span, if soulless, all-pink decor, with remote control TV, safety deposit box, telephone, and private bath. It has an intimate restaurant and a pleasing tiled patio out front for literally watching the world go by. There's private parking. Rates: $40 s, $50 d, $60 t, $75 deluxe, including breakfast. It offers a 15% discount with this guide.

Nearby is **Hotel Kekoldi,** Apdo. 12150, San José, tel. 223-3244, fax 257-5476, e-mail: kekoldi@sol.racsa.co.cr, on Avenida 9 and Calle 3 bis, in Barrio Amón. The jade-green wooden house was built in 1914 and today, after restoration, offers 14 large though spartan rooms with king-size beds, polished hardwood floors, and private baths; the rooms are all fantastically decorated from head to toe in a rainbow of tropical Caribbean hues. The place reminds me of something you might see in a painting by David Hockney. It offers free breakfast after three days stay, free laundry after two days, and a 15% discount with the *Costa Rica Handbook*. Rates: $29 s, $39 d, $49 t low season; $30 s, $42 d, $55 t high season.

The **Hotel Amstel Morazán,** Apdo. 4192, San José 1000, Calle 7, Avenida 1, tel. 222-4622, fax 233-3329, website www.centralamerica.com/cr/hotel/amamon.htm, is a popular albeit modest downtown option, with 52 a/c rooms with TV. Its bar/restaurant is a popular lunch spot for the city business crowd. One plus: Breakfasts and lunches are among the best bargains in San José. Rates: from $23 s, $25 d.

The **Hotel Europa,** Apdo. 72, San José 1000, Calle Central and Avenidas 3/5, tel. 222-1222, fax 221-3976, e-mail: europa@sol.racsa.co.cr; in North America, tel. (800) 222-7692, has 72 spacious a/c rooms and two suites with cable TV, private bath, direct dial telephones, and safety deposit box. Avoid lower-floor rooms facing onto the noisy street (quieter, inner-facing rooms are more expensive). The tiny pool is for dipping only. The hotel restaurant and efficient service make amends. Rates from $50 s/d, $10 extra person.

Another pleasing alternative is the **Best Western San José Downtown,** Apdo. 1849, San José 1000, tel. 255-4766, fax 255-4613, e-mail: garden@sol.racsa.co.cr; in the U.S. tel. (800) 272-6654; in Canada, tel. (800) 463-6654, formerly the Garden Court Hotel, at Avenida 7, Calles 6/8. It has 70 clean and comfortable, recently remodeled a/c rooms with cable TV and phones. It has a swimming pool and a self-service restaurant. One major drawback: Immediately to the west is a terrible (albeit steadily improving) area full of cheap bars-cum-brothels. At least you receive 100% satisfaction guarantee! Rates: $37 s, $45 d, $55 t, including full breakfast and airport transfers.

Alternatively, try the soulless **Hotel Royal Garden,** Apdo. 3493, San José 1000, Calle Central, Avenidas Central/2, tel. 257-0022, fax 257-1517, with dowdy utility furniture. The 54 recently decorated rooms come with a/c and TV. The hotel's saving graces are its convenient location one block from Parque Central, and a Chinese restaurant serving dim sum breakfasts. Gamblers may appreciate the 24-hour casino. Rates: $35 s, $40 d.

Also in the center, the **Hotel La Gran Vía,** Apdo. 1433, San José 1000, Avenida Central, Calles 1/3, tel. 222-7737, fax 222-7205, has 32 rooms with twin double beds, TV, and safety box. Some have a/c. Those with balconies overlooking the street can be noisy; inside rooms are quieter. There is a restaurant and coffee shop. Rates: $35 s, $45 d low season; $45 s, $55 d high season. The **Hotel Royal Dutch**, on the corner of Avenida 2 and Calle 4, tel. 222-1414, fax 233-3927, has 26 modestly furnished, spacious, well-lit a/c rooms with fan, cable TV, telephone, security box, and private bath with hot water. There's a small streetfront restaurant and a casino. Rates: $35 s, $45 d, $55 t.

The **Hemingway Inn**, Apdo. 1711, San José 1002, tel. 257-8630, fax 221-1804; in the U.S., Interlink 670, P.O. Box 025635, Miami, FL 33102, in a twin-story colonial-era building at Calle 9, Avenida 9, in Barrio Amón, has nine small and sparely furnished rooms, albeit with bright floral decor, ceiling fans, and security box. Some have hardwood walls. The Hemingway Suite has a canopied bed and pleasing maroon decor plus a spacious bathroom. Full breakfast is served on a small patio that has a jacuzzi. Rates: $30 s, $40 d, $50 t.

Nearby, on Avenida 9, Calles 13/15, is the **Hotel Edelweiss**, tel. 221-9702, fax 222-1241, with floors of hardwood and tile, and 16 clean, comfortable rooms with telephones and private bath with hot water (three rooms have a TV). Rates: $45 s, $55 d, including breakfast.

The popular **Dunn Inn**, tel. 222-3232, fax 221-4596, in a restored 19th-century home on Calle 5, Avenida 11, is operated by Patrick Dunn, a Texan who used to run the old Nashville South bar. Rooms—13 in the original Spanish-colonial home, 17 in a newer addition—are simple and small but clean, and have cable TV and telephone. Some have a refrigerator. Older brick-lined rooms downstairs have atmosphere, albeit little light. The hotel features a jacuzzi and a sky-lit patio restaurant lush with greenery, including a philodendron that climbs to the second floor. There's a barber's shop on site. Rates: from $47 one double bed, $59 two doubles, $94 suite with jacuzzi bathtub.

The **Hotel Hilda**, Apdo. 8079, San José 1000, Avenida 11, Calles 3/3 bis, tel. 221-0037, fax 255-4028, is a refurbished home with clean, airy rooms featuring private bath and hot water. Massage is offered. Rates: $25 s, $30 d.

South of Avenida 2, the **Mansion de Braulio,** Apdo. 276-1002, San José 1000, tel. 222-0423, fax 222-7947, e-mail: mansion@sol.racsa.co.cr, formerly Hotel Mansion Blanco, at Calle 9 and Avenida 10, is handily located on a busy street corner five blocks from the National Theater. A beautiful hardwood staircase leads to a reception lounge festooned in plants and cascades of curtains. There's a TV and phone in the lounge, Delightful touches include walls decorated with oil paintings of Costa Rican scenes. The 11 adequately sized bedrooms are pleasingly decorated in muted pastels, with comfy beds, but tiny sinks, minimal shelf space, and teeny mirrors in the bathrooms. Room 9 is much larger, with two double beds and TV, but the bathroom has the same deficiencies. Secure parking, and the Restaurante Sant Jordi is attached. Rates: $28 s, $40 d.

Casa 429, Calle 5, Avenidas 4/6 (direct postal address), tel. 222-1708, fax 233-5785, is just two blocks from Plaza de la Cultura. Czech-born George Aron offers six rooms with rattan furniture and maroon-and-sea-green curtains, lampshades, and cushions on the sofas and chairs. Throw rugs adorn the colonial-tiled and lacquered hardwood floors. Ceiling fans keep things cool. Original paintings adorn the walls. Some rooms have shared baths, albeit spacious and beautifully tiled. The single suite opens onto its own patio—an excellent spot for sunbathing. Another has French doors onto a narrow veranda. Avoid the two dank downstairs rooms with no outside windows (one reader says they're "damp and smell sour"). The dining area features a jacuzzi with a waterfall-fountain. Rooms have VCRs. Drawbacks? Noise from the traffic outside, and George tends to hang out wearing only a towel and his pet snake, which can appear intimidating. Rates: from $50 s/d, $75 suite.

The **Hotel Doral,** Apdo. 55-30, San José 1000, Avenida 4, Calle 8, tel. 233-0665, fax 233-4827, offers 42 clean, bright rooms with TV, telephone, and private bath with hot water. Rates: $30 s, $40 d.

Also worth considering is the small and homey **Hotel Doña Inés,** tel. 222-7443 or 222-7553, fax 223-5426, behind the Iglesia la Soledad, on Calle 11, Avenidas 2/6. It's a good bet—luxury bathrooms with full-size tubs, TVs, phones, and reproduction antique furnishings in the 19 carpeted bedrooms. Rates: from $40 s, $50 d, $60 t, including breakfast and tax.

La Gema, Apdo. 1127-1000 San José, Avenida 12, Calles 9/11, tel. 257-2524, fax 222-1074, is a two-story colonial home on a quiet downtown street, with 28 rooms surrounding a sky-lit atrium courtyard which has a colonial tile floor. They're dark and basically furnished but have private bath with hot water, plus telephone and color TV. There's a bar and small restaurant with pool table and large-screen TV. Rates: $25 s, $35 d, $45 t, including continental breakfast.

Guesthouses: In Barrio Amón is the gay-friendly **Joluva Guesthouse,** tel./fax 223-7961; in the U.S., tel. (800) 296-2418 or (619) 294-2418, on Calle 3 bis, Avenidas 9/11. The eight rooms have private baths and cable TV. Rates: $35 s, $45 d, including continental breakfast.

Madeleine's Bed & Breakfast, Apdo. 1478-2050 San Pedro, tel. 283-0158, fax 285-3520, cater-corner to Super Málaga, in Residencial Málaga, in San Pedro, is a small family-run guesthouse. Rooms have hot water. There's a TV room, secure parking, and guests can use the kitchen. Directions are complicated: from Sabanilla church, it's 400 meters (four blocks) west, one block north, and one block west. Rates: $25 s, $30 d low season; $25 s, $35 d high season.

The strangely named **Cinco Hormigas Rojas** (Five Red Ants), on Calle 15 and Avenidas 9/11, tel. 257-8581, is a small, six-room bed and breakfast run by local artist Mayra Guell. The place vibrates with Mayra's paintings and drawings. Not content to simply display her works, she applied her talent to even the enamel toilet seat and other mundane objects, turning them into riots of color. It looks like a transplanted Haight-Ashbury commune. The simply furnished yet pleasing rooms have their own color schemes, and shared baths with hot water. Hardwood floors gleam. There are thick patterned curtains and rattan furnishings. A Costa Rican breakfast is served in a dining area described as "a jungle in miniature." Rates: $25 s, $30 d low season, $27 s, $37 d high season. Also to consider is **Doña Merced Bed and Breakfast,** Apdo. 3660, San José 1000, tel. 223-1582, fax 233-1909, on Avenida 14, Calles 13/15.

West of Downtown
Hotels: The popular **Hotel Cacts,** Apdo. 379, San José 1005, Avenida 3 bis, Calles 28/30, tel. 221-2928, fax 221-8616, e-mail: hcacts@sol.racsa.co.cr, website www.tourism.co.cr/hotels/cacts.htm, has 25 spacious, nonsmoking rooms, including 12 modest "deluxe" rooms with telephone and satellite TV, and private bath with hot water. Standard rooms have no telephone or TV (four have shared bath). It offers a swimming pool, gift store, and tour agency, provides airport pick-up, and has secure parking. Rates: $31 s, $40 d, standard; $50 s, $60 d deluxe, including breakfast.

The **Belmundo Hotel,** tel. 222-9624, is a restored mansion at Calle 20 and Avenida 9. There's a dorm, plus private rooms with cable TV and private baths. Dinners are served. Rates: $18 pp dorm; $30 s, $40 d private rooms, including breakfast.

The pretty daffodil-yellow exterior of the **Hotel Petit Victoria,** Calle 28, Avenida 2, tel. 233-1813, fax 233-1812, resembles a New England home. The intriguing entrance hall—approached through a Chinese-style circular doorway with intricate woodwork—has fancy colonial tiles and a venerable chandelier. Despite the hotel's popularity, the 13 basically appointed bedrooms are disappointing—made more so by the melancholy blue color scheme, although each has TV, fan, and small refrigerator. Bathrooms are spacious and airy. There's a kitchen, plus a skylit cafe and TV lounge. It's overpriced at $45 s, $50 d, including breakfast and tax.

The **Hotel Ritmo del Caribe,** tel./fax 256-1636, opened in mid-1997 in a 1950s art deco home on Paseo Coló at Calles 32/34. The German-Tico owners bill it as an "upscale backpackers'" place for Europeans. It has 11 rooms (2-6 beds) with orthopedic mattresses, soundproof double-pane windows, wooden floors, and modern art. Some have a TV (by request) and balcony. It rents Suzuki 350 motorcycles and offers motorcycle tours to Irazú. Rates: $35-45 d, including buffet breakfast in the garden courtyard.

You don't have to be a member or even a tennis fan to check into the **Hotel Tennis Club,** Apdo. 4964, San José 1000, tel. 232-1266, fax 232-3867, on the south side of Sabana Park. The 27 spacious rooms, each with king-size beds, cable TVs, and pleasing bathrooms, are complemented by 11 tennis courts, a gym, a pool, a spa, and a sauna. Hotel guests get free use of sports facilities. Some rooms have kitchenettes. Secure parking; childcare includes a children's playground. A bargain! Rates: $40 s, $50 d, $55 suite.

The Italian-owned and operated **Hotel Siena,** tel./fax 231-1791, in La Uruca, needless to say, has a strong Italian following.

Guesthouses: The small, family run **Hotel Sabana B&B,** Apdo. 91-1200 Pavas, San José, tel. 296-3751, fax 232-2876, e-mail: sabanabb@sol.racsa.co.cr, website www.online.co.cr/sabana, offers four simple yet cozy rooms with parquet wooden floors, fans, 52-channel cable TVs, and private baths with hot water. Internet and e-mail service is offered, and there's a tour desk. Breakfast is served in a tiny upstairs restaurant. It's one block north, 25 meters west, and two blocks north of Restaurant El Chicote, on the north side of Sabana. Rates: $45 s, $55 d, $75 t, $85 quad, including airport pickup and breakfast ($10 less in low season).

In residential Rohrmoser, west of Sabana Park, try the Canadian run **La Casita Inn #2,** tel./fax 231-6304, recommended by a reader. There are four rooms with private baths and two with shared bath. It has wood floors and walls and "lovely bedding and decor." There's a lounge and dining room and courtyard garden, plus laundry. Rates: from $25 s, $45 d low season; $30 s, $50 d high season, including full breakfast and airport pickup. Nearby, in the same price range is the **Majestic Inn,** tel. 232-9028, fax 296-3967, with seven spacious, nicely decorated rooms. It has a bar and restaurant, plus library and TV room. Nearby, and not reviewed, on Sabana Sur, is **Hotel Girasol Bed & Breakfast,** Apdo. 97-1225, San José, tel. 290-7982, fax 290-5587, pmgras@sol.racsa.co.cr.

In Barrio México, at Avenida 7 and Calles 18/20, is **Hotel Surú,** tel. 222-4151, fax 221-7917, featuring seven rooms with private bath. There's a TV room, plus a bar and a terrace with cafe. Rates: $30 s, $40 d, $50 t.

Apartotels: The **Apartotel Castilla,** Apdo. 944, San José 1007, Calle 24, Avenidas 2/4, tel. 222-2113, fax 221-2080, offers 15 spacious one- and two-bedroom units with pleasingly simple decor and color TVs. Free parking. Rates: $40 s, $50 d. Farther west, the **Apartotel Ramgo,** Apdo. 1441, San José 1000, tel. 232-3823, fax 232-3111, two blocks west and one block south of Hotel Tennis Club on Sabana Sur, has 16 rooms, each with two double beds and cable TV. Rates from $55 d.

On the north side of Sabana Park, the clean and modern **Apartotel Cristina,** Apdo. 1094, San Pedro 2050, tel. 220-0453 or 231-1618, fax 220-2096, 300 meters north of ICE, Sabana Norte, has 25 furnished apartments, each with cable TV. Swimming pool, garage parking, laundry, and free continental breakfast. Also in Sabana Norte is **Apartotel La Sabana,** Apdo. 11400, San José 1000, tel. 220-2422, fax 231-7386. It has a/c rooms and apartments with cable TV and telephone, plus a pool and sauna. Rooms vary in size, from doubles to large units for six people. Rates: $40-100, including breakfast. Nearby, too, is the **Apartotel El Sesteo,** Apdo. 1246-1007 San José, tel. 296-1805, fax 296-1865, e-mail: sesteo@sol.racsa.co.cr, 200 meters south of McDonald's and centered on a beautiful garden with pool. It has 36 simple yet clean, well-maintained one- and two-bedroom units. Twenty feature a kitchen, and dining and living areas; the other 16 are hotel-style rooms. All have cable TV and direct-dial telephone. It offers a jacuzzi, laundry, and secure parking. Room rates: $45 low season, $50 high season for rooms; $55/75 low season, $60/75 high season for one- and two-bedroom apartments. Rates include continental breakfast. Weekly and monthly rates.

Apartments Intertex, tel. 232-9620, in La Uruca near the Hotel Irazú, has small furnished apartments, plus a TV room and small pool. Monthly rates: $250 s, $300 d.

About three km north of Sabana is **La Perla,** east of Hospital México on Autopista General Cañas, Apdo. 2148, San José 1000, tel. 232-6153, fax 220-0103. The 14 one- and two-bedroom apartments come with living and dining rooms, kitchen, cable TV, phone, and fax. Rates: from $40.

East of Downtown

Hotels: Casa Las Orquideas, P.O. Box 1101-2050 San José, tel. 283-0095, fax 234-8203, in Los Yoses, is an attractive option done up in pea-green and walls festooned with murals of tropical scenes. The 16 rooms have tile floors and New Mexico-style bedspreads. Upstairs rooms have more light plus king-size beds. There's a small yet elegant restaurant, plus secure parking. Rates: $35 s, $45 d, $55 t low season; $45 s, $55, d, $66 t high season.

Guesthouses: Being Home Bed & Breakfast, tel. 283-0101, fax 225-3516, in the former Dutch embassy one block south and one block west of the Automercado Los Yoses, has a/c rooms with private bathroom, and cable TV and telephone from $22, including full breakfast. The interior is adorned with local artwork. Secure parking. Not inspected.

Nearby is **Tres Arcos,** Apdo. 161, San José 1000, tel./fax 225-0271, a pleasing B&B run by longtime residents Eric and Lee Warrington in an area of old houses on Avenida 10, 200 meters south and 50 meters west of the Auto Mercado. Individually styled rooms all have large windows overlooking the southern mountains beyond a large walled garden with trees festooned with orchids, bromeliads, and fruits. The living room has a stone fireplace plus cable TV. Breakfast is served on the outside "birdwatching terrace." Rates: $45 d with shared bath, $55 with private bath; minisuites for four cost $90.

Bamboo and rattan abounds in the **Ara Macao Inn,** Apdo. 839, San José 2050, tel. 233-2742, fax 257-6228, a recently restored early-century house 50 meters south of Pizza Hut, at Calle 27 and Avenidas Central/2 in Barrio La California. The eight sunny rooms have ceiling fans, cable TV, and radios. A singular attraction: poison-arrow frogs in specimen tanks! Rates: $38 s, $48 d, $58 t, including breakfast.

Also to consider are the **Hotel Amaranto Inn,** Apdo. 230, San Pedro 2010, tel. 225-0542, fax 224-5747, in Zapote, 12 rooms, some with shared bathroom; and nearby, in Barrio La Granja, near the university, **Maripaz Bed & Breakfast,** tel./fax 253-8456; in Canada, tel. (613) 747-7174, with either private or shared bath (from $20 pp).

In Moravia, the **Victoria Inn,** Apdo. 6280, San José 1000, tel. 240-2320, fax 323-7932, three blocks east of the town hall, is a bed and breakfast in a large home with an atrium lounge and wicker furniture and potted plants in profusion. Of the five rooms, two have private bath and kitchen and private garden in their own apartment. Romantic touches include lace bedspreads. Rates: $25 s, $30 d shared bath; $30 s, $40 d private bath, including breakfast. **El Verolis,** Apdo. 597, Moravia 2150, San José, tel. 236-0662, is a bed and breakfast with seven comfortable rooms featuring cable TV. Rates: $40 d shared bath; $60 private bath. Also recommended is **Casa Rosa Inn,** Apdo. 155, Moravia 2100, tel./fax 236-6105, e-mail: crosa@vanweb.com; in the U.S., SJO 667, P.O. Box 025240, Miami, FL

33102, a charming bed and breakfast run by live-in owners, Arturo and Vanessa. It's in a quiet residential neighborhood one block south of La Guaria Club, to which guests have privileges. The seven rooms include a large unit for up to five people (three have private bath). There's cable TV in the lounge. Two rooms are small singles. Several rooms have private balconies. Strictly nonsmoking! No children under 14. Secure parking. Rain Forest Tours is based here. Rates: $36-65 s, $55-75 d.

Apartotels: The **Apartotel Los Yoses,** Apdo. 1597, San José 1000, tel. 225-0033, fax 225-5595, 25 meters east of the Pollos Kentucky, has 23 rooms, swimming pool, free parking, and daily housekeeping. Rates: from $50 s/d. Adjoining it is **Apartotel Don Carlos,** Apdo. 1593, San José 1000, Calle 29, Avenidas 6/8, tel. 221-6707, fax 255-0828, e-mail: hotel@doncarlos.co.cr; in the U.S., Dept. 1686, P.O. Box 025216, Miami, FL 33102, offering rooms with satellite TV for $350 weekly, $900 monthly. **Apartotel Llama del Bosque,** tel. 283-0709, 100 meters south and 50 meters west of Plaza del Sol shopping center, in the southern suburb of Curridabat, is one of the better options. A reader liked it. Rooms surround a lush patio and pool and have cable TV. Rates: from $45.

In San Pedro, **D'Galah,** Apdo. 208, San José 2350, tel. 234-1743, faces the gardens of the University of Costa Rica and absorbs noise from the street. Some rooms are suites with fully equipped kitchenette and loft. Sauna bath, swimming pool, and coffee shop. Rates: from $40. Alternately, try **Apartotel The Palm Trees,** 200 meters west, 100 meters north, then 100 meters east of San Pedro church, tel. 253-0182. Units have color TV and phone; there's a jacuzzi and pool on site. Rates: from $50 daily, $1,000 monthly.

The Suburbs

Hotels: The **Hotel Dulce Hogar,** Apdo. 343-1150 San José, tel. 239-2633, fax 293-2778, e-mail: dulceh@sol.racsa.co.cr, is a modern, modest-size hotel outside Residencial Los Arcos at Ciudad Cariari. The 31 a/c rooms and three junior suites all have cable TVs, telephones, and safety boxes. The airy bathrooms have small showers; the suites have jacuzzi bathtubs. Rates: $40 s, $50 d, $10 extra person, including breakfast served in a Tico-style bar/restaurant. Dis-

SPECIAL HOTEL: THE GRANO DE ORO

This gracious turn-of-the-century mansion turned thoroughly modern hotel has acquired a staunch clientele. The guestbook is a compendium of compliments. "What charm! What comfort!" "The best hotel we've stayed in—ever!" "We would love to keep it a secret, but we promise we won't." And no wonder—the Grano de Oro, a member of the organization Small Distinctive Hotels of Costa Rica, exudes charm and superlative service. Unquestionably my hotel of preference whenever I stay in San José.

The hotel, in a quiet, tree-lined residential neighborhood, Calle 30 and Avenida 2, off Paseo Colón and a pleasing 20-minute walk from the bustling city center, offers the best of both worlds—the tranquility of a residential setting and the uproar of San José close at hand, proving that a fine house, like a jewel, is made complete by its setting. It is operated by Canadians Eldon and Lori Cooke, who are congenial hosts. Together, they have overseen the creation of a real home away from home.

Comfort is the keynote. In the 36 faultlessly decorated guest rooms, orthopedic mattresses and plump down pillows guarantee contented slumber beneath sturdy beamed ceilings. Each is done up in flattering combinations of soft gray, peach, and coral, with Latin American watercolors and tapestries adorning the walls. Locally handcrafted furniture and gleaming hardwood floors add to the sense of elegant refinement. And bedside lamps you can actually read by, satellite TV (four channels only, including CNN), and direct-dial telephones reflect North American savoir-faire. A downstairs suite features mahogany wall panels, jacuzzi bathtub, and French doors that open onto a private garden.

Extravagant bathrooms are adorned with hand-painted colonial tiles, brass fittings, fluffy towels, torrents of piping-hot water, and cavernous showers and deep bathtubs where one can relax with bubbles up to the nose.

Consider the mammoth, rooftop Vista de Oro suite for its plate-glass window running the full width of one wall, providing views of three volcanoes; its jacuzzi, elevated, nose-up to the window with one of two TVs at hand; king-size bed; and sofas lushly decorated in Turkish fabrics. All rooms—which were to be enhanced with a more elegant motif in 1998 (including drape curtains, and rooms with king-size canopied beds)—are non-smoking. And no request is too much for the mustard-keen, English-speaking, ever-smiling staff. The impeccable service is friendly but stops short of familiarity, relaxed but always professional. Soothing classical, South American, and Peruvian flute music, the sound of trickling water from a patio fountain, and soft choral chants from the chapel next door waft through the hallways, lounge, and courtyard restaurant lush with palms, orchids, ephiphytes, and yucca—a perfect place to eat. In fact, the restaurant could well be San José's finest, too. Meals—stylish and light on the palate—are inventive, assured, and presented with flair. If you're not staying here, you owe it to yourself at least to eat here.

Hotel Grano de Oro, Apdo. 1157, San José 1007, Costa Rica, tel. 255-3322, fax 221-2782, e-mail: granoro@sol.racsa.co.cr, website www.centralamerica.com/cr/hotel/granodeoro.htm; in the U.S., SJO 36, P.O. Box 02516, Miami, FL 33102-5216. Rates (double): $72 standard, $88 superior, $98 deluxe, $125 suite, $155 Vista de Oro suite; singles $5 less, triples/quads $5 more. A bargain.

counts for longer stays and larger groups. Airport transfers are offered.

Guesthouses: The **Versalles Inn,** tel./fax 235-3735, is in Tibas, about five km north of downtown, with rooms from $25 s, $40 d.

MODERATE

Downtown

Hotels: The **Nuevo Hotel Talamanca,** Apdo. 11661, San José 1000, Avenida 2, Calles 8/10, tel. 233-5033, fax 233-5420, e-mail: talamanc@ sol.racsa.co.cr, is an elegant option on the city's main drag. The 46 a/c rooms and four junior suites (with jacuzzis and minibars) are tastefully appointed and have TVs and telephones. The four junior suites have been described as "a vision in chrome and black, emphasizing sharp lines and minimalist furnishings." Other rooms are done in cool slate greens. It has already established itself as a popular business hotel. Rates: $50 s, $60 d, $70 t, $90 suite, including tax and breakfast. It offers a five-day package combining a night at the Nuevo Talamanca and three nights at a sister resort property on the Caribbean coast ($249 pp, double occupancy, including meals).

The **Gran Hotel,** Apdo. 527, San José 1000, Avenidas 2 and Calle 3, tel. 221-4000, fax 221-3501, website www.centralamerica.com/cr/hotel/gran.htm; in the U.S., tel. (800) 949-0592, dates from 1930. Its 105 a/c rooms were recently renovated and vary from spacious to small. All have telephones and cable TVs. Rooms facing the plaza can be noisy. Junior suites are very elegant. It has a small but lively casino on the ground floor, plus the basement Bufo Dorado Restaurant. The Gran enjoys a superb position in front of the Teatro Nacional, where the hotel's Café Parisienne is a favorite hangout for tourists. Rates: $54 s, $71 d, $78 t; $69-189 for suites.

Another steps-to-everything option downtown is the **Hotel Balmoral** Apdo. 3344, San José 1000, one block east of Plaza de la Cultura, on Avenida Central, Calles 7/9, tel. 222-5022, fax 221-7826; in the U.S., tel. (800) 327-7737. The Balmoral offers 116 a/c rooms and four suites with appealing modern decor, and cable TVs and safety deposit boxes. However, rooms are small, bathrooms are very small, and walls are so

thin you can hear your next-door neighbor brushing his/her teeth. A sauna and mini-gym, plus a restaurant and casino, are on the ground floor. You'll find a tour desk and car rental agencies in the lobby. Rates: $65 s/d, $10 extra person.

Opposite the Balmoral on Avenida Central is the **Hotel Presidente,** Apdo. 2922, San José 1000, tel. 222-3022, fax 221-1205, e-mail: hot-pres@sol.racsa.co.cr; in the U.S. (800) 972-0515, with 110 a/c rooms, each with a direct-dial telephone, safety box, and cable TV. The older rooms are spacious but dowdy. Otherwise pleasant. The hotel has a jacuzzi and sauna, a discotheque, a casino, and a bar, plus a restaurant serving Italian cuisine. Free airport pickup. Rates: $50 s, $55 d, $60 standard; $65 s, $75 d, $85 junior suite; $70 s, $80 d, $90 t suite.

Nearby on Avenida 1, Calle 9, is the **Hotel Del Rey,** Apdo. 6241, San José 1000, tel. 221-7272, fax 221-0096, e-mail: delrey@ticonet.co.cr, a renovated neoclassical building long on history (many of the bullet holes on the face of the Bellavista Fortress were fired from this building in the 1948 revolution). The five-story, 104-room structure is a National Heritage Treasure. Seventeen rooms are deluxe (five with balconies); all rooms are large, newly carpeted, and come with a king-size beds and cable TV. Rooms range from singles to suites for six people. Those facing the street can be noisy. Note the superb handcrafted wooden doors, to which electronic locks are slated to be added. The Del Rey boasts a lively 24-hour casino, 24-hour cafe/restaurant, full-menu room service, well-stocked gift shop, and a full-service sportsfishing desk and travel agency. It's superbly run by an English diamond in the rough, Timothy Johnson, and has become a favorite of gringos, especially fishermen and single males keen to be chatted up by local beauties in the Blue Marlin Bar who, ahem, may invite you to your room. An added bonus is the unique free guided city tour aboard the hotel's own modern tour bus. There's secure parking. Rates: $55-75 s, $68-75 d, $125 suites with living rooms and balconies.

There are many smaller, more intimate offerings in centenary homes. Try the **Hotel Santo Tomás,** Avenida 7, Calles 3/5, tel. 255-0448, fax 222-3950, e-mail: hotelst@sol.racsa.co.cr, a fine, albeit aloof, bed and breakfast with 20 nonsmoking rooms in an elegant turn-of-the-century plantation home built, Carolina-born owner Thomas Douglas stresses, from a termite-proof mahogany. The high vaulted ceiling and original hardwood and colonial tile floors are impressive. Rooms vary (some are huge), but all have cable TV and direct-dial phones, queen-size beds and orthopedic mattresses, antique reproduction furniture, throw rugs, watercolors by a local artist, and a large-scale touring map on the wall. Room 7 has its own patio. There are three separate TV lounges and a full-service tour planning service. Thomas was planning to add car rental on site. The place is a lot quieter than it used to be now that the traffic along Avenida 7 flows more smoothly, and since Thomas bought the raucous bar-cum-disco next door and closed it down. Laundry service. The all-male staff are bilingual. No guests at night. Rates from $50-80 d, including breakfast served in an airy patio conducive to mingling.

One of the best options is the Swiss-owned and -operated **Hotel Fleur de Lys,** Apdo. 10736, San José 1000, Calle 13, Avenidas 2/4, tel. 223-1206, fax 257-3637, e-mail: florlys@sol.racsa.co.cr. This marvelously restored mansion offers guests a choice from the 19 individually styled rooms, each named for a species of flower. All have private baths with hot water, plus phones and cable TVs, sponge-washed pastel walls, patinated wrought-iron or wicker beds with crisp linens. A restaurant serves Italian cuisine. Its enviable location, one block from the National Museum, is a plus. Rates: $50/60 s, $60/70 d low/high season; suites from $70 low season, $80 high season, including breakfast.

La Casa Verde de Amón, Calle 7, Avenida 9, tel./fax 223-0969, e-mail: casaverde@sol.racsa.co.cr; in the U.S., P.O. Box 025216, Dept. 1701, Miami, FL 33102-5216, is another elegant Victorian mansion, once the home of Don Carlos Saborio, an influential figure in turn-of-the-century Costa Rica. The building, constructed in red pine, was traded for coffee and imported from New Orleans! It was restored by American Carl Stanley, who runs it as an inn. The Victorian lounge is lit by a soaring *tragaluz* (skylight) and features Chinese rugs, silk wallpaper, and a resplendent centenary grand piano. Lots of antique detailing. Breakfast is served on a small garden patio, and there's a glassed-in veranda. There are three suites and five deluxe rooms, all huge and handsomely appointed with furnishings from grandma's parlor. Hangar-size suites are replete with living rooms and king-size canopy beds, and bathrooms feature Victorian claw-foot tubs. Rates: $55-65 s/d deluxe rooms, $65-72 junior suites, $72-96 suites, $72-116 family rooms, low season; $72-86, $86-96, $106-126, and $86-126, respectively, high season. It offers special weekly and monthly rates in low season.

A stone's throw away is **La Casa Morazán,** tel. 257-4187, fax 257-4175, another colonial mansion at Calle 7 and Avenidas 7/9. It boasts antique furnishings and modern art, plus original (rather stained) tile floors. The 11 a/c rooms all have cable TV, old-style telephones, large bathrooms, and 1950s-style furniture. Dowdy, yet possessing its own charm. Breakfast is served on a small patio. The cook will prepare lunch and dinner upon request. Rates: $35 s, $45 d, low season; $55 s, $65 d, high season, including breakfast.

Taylor's Inn, Avenida 13 and Calles 13/15, tel. 257-4333, fax 221-1475, has 12 nonsmoking rooms with cable TV and private bath with hot water. Note the pretty ceramic tiles on the exterior of this 1908 property, and the modern art within. Rates: $45 s, $60 d low season; $55 s, $60 d high season, including "tropical" breakfast served in a breezy, skylit courtyard.

The very *moderne* **Hotel Villa Tournon,** Apdo. 6606, San José 1000, tel. 233-6622, fax 222-5211, e-mail: hvillas@sol.racsa.co.cr, is brimful with artwork and sculpture and is a favorite of North American tourists. It's situated opposite the copper-windowed COFISA Building, in Barrio Tournón, 200 meters from El Pueblo. The 84 mammoth rooms are graciously appointed. The restaurant offers fireside dining but the food is said to be ho-hum. A jacuzzi and swimming pool in a splendidly decorated garden round out the offerings. It's noisy. Ask for rooms off the street. Rates: $64 s, $69 d standard; $74 s, $79 d, $89 t superior.

Also try the **Hotel Boulevard Ejecutivo,** Apdo. 3258, San José 1000, tel./fax 232-9839, in Rohrmoser. Not inspected. The hotel's brochure suggests exquisite decor. Rates: $55 s, $68 d, from $85 suites.

Guesthouses: The homey **D'Raya Vida Villa,** Apdo. 2209-2100 San José, tel. 223-4168, fax 223-4157; in the U.S., P.O. Box 025216-

1638, Miami, FL 33102-5216, is a lovely restored two-story mansion—described as "antebellum"—tucked in a cul-de-sac in Barrio Otoya, behind the tall black gate at the end of Avenida 11 and Calle 17. The live-in owner, Michael Long, rents four rooms, each delightfully done up in individual decor; the Pineapple Room upstairs has a four-poster bed (the two upstairs rooms share a large bath) There's a small patio with fountain, and an exquisite TV lounge and reading room with fireplace and chandeliers. The place is secluded and peaceful. Dogs and other pets swarm. Rates: $50 s, $65 d low season; $65 s, $85 d high season, with full breakfast and airport pick-up; $20 extra person. Every seventh night is free. Michael will prepare lunch ($7.50) and dinner ($15) on request.

Apartotels: The modern **Apartotel San José,** Apdo. 688-1250 Escazú, tel. 256-2191, fax 221-6684; in the U.S., tel. (800) 575-1253, across from the National Museum at Avenida 2, Calles 17/19, offers 12 small one- and two-bedroom suites with living rooms and fully equipped kitchenettes, cable TVs, phones, and parking. Rates: from $60 s, $70 d, one bedroom; $70 s, $80 d, two bedroom

West of Downtown

Hotels: I like the **Hotel Rosa del Paseo,** Apdo. 287, San José 1007, tel. 257-3213, fax 223-2776; in the U.S., 2011 N.W. 79th Ave., SJO 1162, Miami, FL 33122, which has 18 nicely decorated rooms plus one suite in a completely remodeled century-old residence on Paseo Colón at Calles 28/30. Architectural details combine parquet and tile floors, original artwork, and art-nouveau flourishes with "Victorian Caribbean." All rooms have handsome modern decor, plus beautiful white-tiled private bathrooms with hot water, cable TV, safety deposit boxes, and ceiling fans. A master-suite has a large jacuzzi tub. Secure parking. Rates: $65 s/d, $95 suite, including breakfast, served in the garden courtyard on tables made of old sewing treadles.

The **Hotel Ambassador,** Apdo. 10186, San José 1000, tel. 221-8155, fax 255-3396; in North America, tel. (800) 709-2806, on Paseo Colón offers a good location within a 20-minute walk of both the city center and Sabana Park. The 74 a/c rooms are clean and spacious, if uninspired, with minibar, security box, and cable TV. Amenities include a restaurant, a coffee shop, and a bar with dance floor. Rates: from $60 s/d for standard rooms with a choice of king-size bed or twins, including continental breakfast.

The **Quality Hotel Colón,** 10750 Columbia Pike, Silver Spring, MD 20901, tel. (301) 236-5032 or (800) 228-5151; in Costa Rica, Apdo. 433, San José 1007, tel. 257-2580, fax 257-2582, on Avenida 3 and Calle 38, is in one of the two towers of the Centro Colón complex on Paseo Colón, near La Sabana. It's operated by Choice Hotels. The 124 a/c rooms (including 42 suites) are "extra-large" and come with cable TVs, safety boxes, hair dryers, and telephones. There's also a restaurant, a casino, and a nightclub/bar done up in dazzling eye-popping pink and neon! All very contemporary. Rates: $69 s/d standard; $82 junior suite; $90 suite.

The **Hotel Ejecutivo Napoleón,** Apdo. 8-6240, San José 1000, tel. 258-0772, fax 222-9487, e-mail: napoleon@sol.racsa.co.cr, website www.octarica.tourism.co.cr, on the corner of Avenida 5 and Calle 40 near Sabana Park, is a splendid modern hotel popular with businessfolk. The lobby sets the tone with its rich mahogany and deep-green color scheme, as well as the fake stream and bridge leading to a well-stocked dining area. The 26 spacious rooms—each with two double beds, cable TV, and direct-dial phone (downstairs rooms have fans; upstairs rooms have a/c)—boast attractive modern decor and are arrayed around an outdoor swimming pool with open-air bar. Beware the phone charges ($2 just to connect you to ATT). Rates: $53 s, $60 d; $62 s, $70 d with a/c, including continental breakfast.

One block away at Avenida 5, Calle 40 is the **Hotel Torremolinos,** Apdo. 114-1107, San José 2000, tel. 222-5266, fax 255-3167, e-mail: torremolinos@centralamerica.com, website www.centralamerica.com/cr/hotel/torrem.htm, now owned by Sol Melié. Its 70 rooms in contemporary style are modest in size but handsomely furnished, with lots of hardwoods and an Egyptian motif. All have cable TVs, carpeting, alarm clock radios, direct-dial telephones, and hair dryers. Suites have glassed-in balconies. It offers a pool and a jacuzzi, plus a courtesy bus to downtown and car rental service. The beautiful restaurant has hints of Italian and Japanese decor. Rates: $45 s, $55 d, $75 t, $75-85 suites low season; $50 s, $60 d, $70 t, $80-90 suites high season.

In a similar vein is the stylish **Palma Real,** Apdo. 694-1005, San José, tel. 290-5060, fax 290-4160, e-mail: fiesta@sol.racsa.co.cr, an upscale, contemporary boutique hotel with sharp angles and rounded columns, a surfeit of marble and autumnal colors, in a quiet residential area 200 meters north of the ICE in Sabana Norte. Its focus is on business travelers. It features 67 carpeted, tastefully decorated a/c rooms, with mini-bars, bathtubs, cable TVs, telephones, huge windows, orthopedic mattresses, and hair-dryers in the well-lit marble-lined bathrooms. Suites have king-size beds and jacuzzi bath-tubs. There's a state-of-the-art gym and a large open-air jacuzzi, plus a business center, a bar, and an elegant restaurant serving *típico* and continental cuisine for $6-15 (good restaurants are a stone's throw away). Rates: $69 s, $79 d, $115 suite.

The **Hotel Rincón del Valle,** Apdo. 422-1007, San José, tel. 231-4927, fax 231-5924, e-mail: susana@sol.racsa.co.cr, next to the Colegio de Médicos on the south side of Sabana Park, is a contempo stunner, uniformly done up in rich pol-ished hardwoods, maroons, black, and deep sea-greens. The decor is lively, blending modern with traditional styles. It has 20 carpeted rooms with cable TVs, hair-dryers, telephones, and safety deposit boxes. Some rooms are a bit dingy. There's a 24-hour cafe, plus restaurant and laundry, and guests have use of nearby ten-nis courts and swimming pool. Rates: $55 s, $70 d standard; $71 s, $82 d superior; $82 s, $93 d junior suite, including breakfast.

East of Downtown

Hotels: The **Hotel Don Fadrique,** Apdo. 1754-2050, San José, at Calle 37 and Avenida 8, tel. 225-8186, fax 224-9746, e-mail: fadrique@ centralamerica.com, website www.centralamerica. com/cr/hotel/fadrique.htm, claims 20 "luxuriously furnished rooms" and "lush tropical gardens." The rooms are decorated in tropical pastels (some have Guatemalan bedspreads), with origi-nal modern art on the walls. Each has parquet wood or tile floor, telephone, cable TV, safety deposit box, and fan. Take an upstairs room, with heaps of light. There's a charming patio where you can enjoy breakfast beneath the shade of a mango tree. Rates: $45 s, $55 d, $65 t low season; $55 s, $65 d, $75 t high season, in-cluding full breakfast.

Hotel Americano del Este, tel. 224-2455 or 225-3022, fax 224-2166, 200 meters north of Agencia Subaru in Los Yoses, is a lovely prop-erty with 29 large and comfortable bedrooms with cable TVs and direct-dial phones. There is also a swimming pool, a bar, and a cafe. Rates: $65 s, $75 d, including buffet breakfast.

Hôtel Le Bergerac, Apdo. 1107, San José 1002, tel. 234-7850, fax 225-9103, is a pretty colonial home in Los Yoses, on Calle 35, 50 meters south of Avenida Central, with views south toward the Cordillera Talamanca. Le Berg-erac is a full-service hotel that serves breakfast, *not,* the owners hasten to add, a bed-and-break-fast hotel. To prove the point, it features a se-questered conference room complete with video, bar, telephone and fax service, computer hookups, and rooms with private gardens for solace and quiet contemplation. Business trav-elers and guests of the diplomatic missions here-abouts gravitate to this piece of the Parisian Left Bank. The French influence originates in Québec with its two French Canadian owners, James Elhaleh and Diane-Alexis Fournier. Service is discreet, the atmosphere a curious blend of aloofness and warmth enhanced by the deep maroon/rust and gray color scheme. The hotel has 18 rooms in three buildings (five in the origi-nal home, reached via a sweeping spiral stair-case), all with cable TVs, direct-dial telephones, and safety boxes, plus hardwood floors and clas-sical furniture. Rooms vary in size. **Aux Fines Herbes,** the airy dining terrace, serves gourmet French cuisine, along with *bocas* and drinks in the evening. Rates: $58 s, $68 d, $78 t stan-dard room; $68 s, $78 d, $88 t deluxe.

Guesthouses: Hotel Milvia, Apdo. 1660, San Pedro 2050, tel. 225-4543, fax 225-7801, e-mail: hmilvia@novanet.co.cr, website www.novanet. co.cr/milvia/index.html; in the U.S., Costa Rica Connection, 975 Osos St., San Luis Obispo, CA 93401, tel. (805) 543-8823 or (800) 345-7422, fax (805) 543-3626, e-mail: john@crconnect.com, in San Pedro, offers a discreet yet sophisticated European charm. The Caribbean-style wooden home has been restored to its original turn-of-the-century splendor by offspring of the original family. Relaxed intimacy is the watchword, aided by soothing classical music. Oriental throw rugs abound. Walls are festooned with family portraits and original paintings. There are four rooms upstairs in the original home, five more downstairs in a contemporary add-on built around a tiny garden courtyard. Hardwood floors glisten downstairs (rooms upstairs are carpeted). The spacious, individually styled rooms are furnished with tasteful fabrics. You'll find a fresh rose in your bathroom, along with cookies on your table, and a chocolate on your pillow with nightly turndown service. Bathrooms gleam (the decoratives tiles were hand-painted by Milvia). There are fluffy towels, and baskets replete with toiletries. Fans and phones are standard. There's a dining room, lounge with TV and VCR, and boutique. Upstairs, a terrace perfect for alfresco breakfasts provides views over the garden full of bright yellow lirios. And no words can praise highly enough the caring concern of live-in owners, Milvia and Mauricio. Milvia, a former tour guide, is Italian, and the hotel is popular with Italians. Follow Avenida 2 east from San José, turn left 100 meters beyond Centro Comercial M&N in San Pedro (you'll see the hotel signed here), then the first right. The hotel closed in 1996, but was reopened in early 1998. Rates: $65 s, $70 d, $75 t, including continental breakfast.

Another intriguing and tasteful conversion is the **Don Paco Inn,** Apdo. 29-2970, Sabanilla, San José, tel. 234-9088, fax 234-9588; in the U.S., tel. (800) 288-2107, a cozy bed and breakfast blending *moderne* decor into the setting of a colonial-style mansion. The hotel—in a quiet residential area at Calle 33 and Avenidas 9/11—has 10 comfortable bedrooms decorated in light and cheery colors, with plump comforters, fluffy pillows, and cable TVs. The hotel has a small souvenir shop. Full breakfast included. Rates: from $50 s, $60 d.

Health Homes, tel. 253-1162, fax 234-9469, on Avenida 1, Calles 33/35, has rooms with private bath with hot water, laundry service, and professional massage on site. Rates: $100 three nights, including breakfast.

The **Hotel Jade y Oro,** Apdo. 4988-1000 San José, tel. 225-3752, fax 233-6397, e-mail: jade@cool.co.cr, at Avenida 1 and Calles 31/33 in the quiet residential neighborhood of Barrio Escalante, is a beautiful little colonial-style residence boasting 10 simply yet handsomely appointed rooms (three are junior suites). Each room has hardwood floors, private bath, hot water, ceiling fan, telephone, and cable TV. Exquisite *rejas* (turned wooden grills) and tilework abound, including in the bathrooms. Most rooms have windows that open to small gardens, and there's a patio garden done up in Tico fashion and where a happy hour of wine and cheese is hosted nightly. The handsome lounge has a soaring ceiling and fireplace, the original tile floor, and ceramic mosaics in the walls. Rates: $55 s, $65 d, $75 d junior suite; $10 extra person, including *tico* breakfast. It offers a weeklong package with sightseeing excursions for $470 pp, double occupancy.

The **Casa de Finca,** Apdo. 1071, San Pedro 2050, tel./fax 225-6169, is farther out, surrounded by coffee plantations and tropical gardens on the outskirts of San Pedro. This beautifully restored and elegant 1926 mansion features splendid tile floors, hardwoods, and king-size beds in bright pastel-colored bedrooms. Rates: $63 s, $73 d, $83 t.

The Suburbs

Hotels: The **Vista de Golf,** Apdo. 379, San Antonio de Belén 4005, tel. 293-4330, fax 293-4371, 200 meters southeast of the Meliá Cariari, is a quiet, modern hotel offering a jacuzzi, heated swimming pool, and access to the Cariari Hotel and Country Club, with golf course and tennis courts. Most of the 35 rooms have king-size beds; some have singles. It also has self-catering "studios" with fully equipped kitchens. Rates: $70/75 standard/large double, breakfast included; $80 junior suite; $100 master studio. Low-season discounts.

Hotel Residencias de Golf, Apdo. 5548, San José 1000, tel. 239-2272, fax 239-2001, residgo@sol.racsa.co.cr, immediately southeast of the Meliá Cariari, is a reclusive complex offering a jacuzzi, a heated swimming pool, and access to the adjacent Cariari Country Club. It has standards, doubles, and suites, all with fans, a/c, safety boxes, cable TVs, and radios. Most rooms have king-size beds and resemble apartments; some have singles. Suites have kitchenettes. There's a restaurant and bar. Rates: $73 s, $78 d; $110 suite.

EXPENSIVE

Downtown

Hotels: The 24-room **Britannia Hotel,** Apdo. 3742, San José 1000, tel. 223-6667, fax 223-6411, e-mail: britania@sol.racsa.co.cr, website www.centralamerica.com/cr/hotel/britania.htm; in the U.S., tel. (800) 263-2618, is a neoclassical Victorian-style mansion built in 1910 in Barrio Amón, at Calle 3 and Avenida 11. A new block has 14 standard rooms, all with cable TVs, telephones, safety deposit boxes, a king-size or two twin beds, plus a private bathroom with tub. The five deluxe rooms and five junior suites in the old house boast high ceilings, stained glass, arches, ceiling fans, mosaic tile floors, and English-style furniture. The boutique hotel features "tropical courtyards," a restaurant converted from the old cellar, a coffee shop, and room service. Rates: $77 s, $89 d standard; $93 s, $105 d deluxe; $106 s, $117 d junior suite.

Hotel L'Ambiance, Apdo. 1040, San José 2050, tel. 222-6702, fax 223-0481; in the U.S., Interlink 179, P.O. Box 526770, Miami, FL 33152, at Calle 13 and Avenida 9 in the historic Barrio Otoya district, offers a tranquil setting a stone's throw from downtown. Alas, though American owner William Parker restored the former colonial mansion with the same attention for period detail that he lavished on his previous success, Shiretown Inn in Martha's Vineyard, he has since let L'Ambiance decay. Six individually styled bedrooms and one suite—with names such as Esperanza and Amor—come with cable TVs, ceiling fans, and colonial furnishings: massive antique wardrobes and gilt-framed mirrors. Genuine Currier and Ives prints decorate the dirty bathrooms. The hub is the open-air Spanish-style colonial courtyard, also in need of a spruce-up. The restaurant—once acclaimed—is now closed. And supercilious service is a concern. No children under 15. No credit cards. Room rates: $70 s, $90 d; $140 s/d presidential suite. The hotel is gay-friendly.

West of Downtown

Hotels: Parque de Lago, Apdo. 624, San José 1007, Avenida 2, Calles 40/42, tel. 257-8787, fax 223-1617, e-mail: parklago@sol.racsa.co.cr; in the U.S., Dept. 1634, P.O. Box 025216-1034, Miami, FL 33102, has 39 exquisitely decorated, a/c rooms, plus suites with kitchenettes, all with a maroon-and-green color scheme. Woods, ceramics, plants, and Costa Rican artworks combine to create a nostalgic ambience. Sound-insulated windows, cable TVs, direct-dial phones with fax, and coffeemakers are standard. There's a restaurant and bar. The public areas have original colonial tile. Rates: $85 s, $95 d; suites from $120 s, $130 d. Children under two stay free.

Looking a little like a set from *Star Trek* is the **Meliá Confort Corobicí,** Apdo. 2443-1000 San José, tel. 232-8122, fax 231-5834, e-mail: corobici@sol.racsa.co.cr; in the U.S., tel. (800) 336-3542, fax (305) 530-1626, on the northeastern corner of Sabana Park. Its angled exterior is ungainly, but its soaring atrium design, with tier upon tier of balconies festooned with ferns, is impressive. The 200 spacious rooms and eight suites boast handsome furnishings. All have a/c, safety deposit boxes, mini bars, and cable TVs. There's a 24-hour cafeteria, plus Italian and Japanese restaurants. The Confort's spa is one of the best in the country. It's within walking distance of downtown (30 minutes), and there's a courtesy shuttle. It offers a nightclub and casino for those who don't want to wander far at night. Rates: from $100 s/d; suites from $120.

The **Best Western Irazú,** tel. 232-4811, fax 231-6485, e-mail: htlirazu@sol.racsa.co.cr, website www.centralamerica.com/cr/hotel/irazu.htm; in the U.S., tel. (800) 272-6654; in Canada, tel. (800) 463-6654, has 350 rooms, including a nonsmoking floor. Most rooms have a balcony overlooking the pool or gardens, plus direct-dial telephone, cable TV, and a/c. The hotel features all the amenities of a deluxe property: tennis courts, sauna, swimming pool, restaurant, Costa Rica's largest casino, plus a small shopping mall. It is popular for tour groups. Its out-of-the-way location has little to recommend it, although there's an hourly shuttle bus to downtown. Rates: $65-80 s, $75-90 d, $85-110 t.

PREMIUM

Downtown

Hotels: Dominating the downtown skyline is the sophisticated **Hotel Aurola Holiday Inn,** Apdo. 7802, San José 1000, tel. 233-7233, fax 255-

1036, e-mail: aurola@ticonet.co.cr, website www.ticonet.co.cr/hotel/aurola/aurola.html; in the U.S., tel. (800) 465-4329, with its bronze-tinted windows. The modern high-rise overlooking Parque Morazán, at Avenida 5 and Calle 5, offers sumptuous accommodations, with 201 a/c rooms featuring cable TVs and all modern conviences. Topping off the hotel's attractions is the *mirador* restaurant on the 17th floor, adjacent to the casino. The hotel contains a gym, a sauna, and an indoor pool. However, Gregg Calkin describes it as "a giant hermetically sealed container with windows that don't open." Rates: from $128 s, $140 d.

A handsome recent addition is the **Hotel Amón Park Plaza**, Apdo. 4192, San José 1000, tel. 257-0191, fax 257-0284, e-mail: amonpark@ sol.racsa.co.cr; in North America, tel. (800) 575-1253, on Avenida 11, Calle 3 Bis, in the historic Barrio Amón area downtown. The modern four-story, "neo-Victorian" hotel has 90 rooms, including 24 junior and six deluxe suites. Rooms have a/c, telephones, cable TVs, coffee-makers, safety deposit boxes, and hair dryers. An unusually elegant marble lobby decorated with artwork hints at the upscale decor throughout. It features an office center with computers, plus conference center, spa, casino, and underground parking. The Danubio Restaurante is *muy elegante*. Overpriced? Rates: from $110 d for a standard to $205 for a luxury suite with living room and jacuzzi.

The **Radisson Europa Hotel & Conference Center**, Apdo. 538-2120 San José, tel. 257-3257 or (800) 333-3333, fax 257-8221, e-mail: eurohot@sol.racsa.co.cr, near El Pueblo at Calle 3 and Avenida 15, is a thoroughly modern five-star hotel with 107 "superior" rooms, six executive suites, and one presidential suite, all with a/c, 24-hour room service, direct-dial telephones, cable TVs, mini-bars, and safes. It has a restaurant, cafe, and bar, plus a full-serve business center (hence, it's popular with businessfolk). It also offers a pool and spa with jacuzzi, plus a small gym, an art gallery and shops, and the inevitable casino. The decor is beautiful. Rates: $130 s, $140 d; $10 extra person.

West of Downtown
Hotels: The **Hotel San José Palacio**, Apdo. 458, San José 1150, tel. 220-2034, fax 231-1990, has 254 rooms flush with hardwoods and

pleasing decor. It offers a large swimming pool, tennis and racquetball courts, health spa and gym, sauna and jacuzzi, plus a casino popular with the San José elite. A lively casino and elegant and reasonably priced restaurant are countered by a drab bar. The hotel is out on a limb, one mile north of Sabana Park on the Autopista General Cañas—an awkward location that necessitates a taxi, despite its proximity to Sabana. Rates: from $115 s, $135 d.

Between San José and the Airport
For those who want the convenience of both the city and the airport close by, consider the hotels at Ciudad Cariari, eight km west of San José and a similar distance from the airport, which is immediately south of Alajuela.

Hotels: Two deluxe properties stand adjacent to each other at Ciudad Cariari, on the General Cañas Highway about 10 km northwest of San José, a 20-minute taxi journey to downtown and about five minutes from Juan Santamaría Airport. The first is the **Meliá Cariari Hotel and Golf Club**, Apdo. 737-1007 San José, tel. 239-0022, fax 239-2803, e-mail: cariari@sol.racsa.co.cr website www.centralamerica.com/cr/hotel/cariari.htm; in the U.S., tel. (800) 336-3542, fax (305) 530-1626, offering deluxe resort facilities, including access to the Cariari Country Club (next door) featuring a championship golf course, 10 tennis courts, and an Olympic pool. The 196 spacious, handsomely appointed rooms and 24 suites are arrayed around an outdoor swimming pool with swim-up bar. There's a casino and small disco. Rates: from $115 s/d low season, $130 s/d high season; suites from $200 low season, $220 high season.

The **Hotel Herradura**, Apdo. 7-1880, San José 1000, tel. 239-0033, fax 239-2292, e-mail: hherradu@sol.racsa.co.cr, website www.west-net.com/costarica.herra.html; in the U.S., tel. (800) 245-8420, fax (305) 539-1123, offers impressive entertainment facilities, including the Krystal Casino and a 51,000-square-foot conference center. There is a jacuzzi and a spa, plus an outdoor swimming pool. Magnificent hardwoods abound. The 234 elegantly furnished, a/c rooms (including 28 suites) have cable TVs, direct-dial telephones, and 24-hour room service. Some have a patio or a balcony. The Herradura is replete with restaurant options: Sakura for Japanese, Bon Vivant for international cuisine, Tiffany's 24-hour coffee shop, the Sancho Panza serving Spanish dishes, and the Tropicana health food restaurant. A "San José by Night" *folklórico* show is presented on weekends in the Bon Vivant. A shuttle runs to downtown. Rates: from $120 s, $130 d standard; $150 s, $160 d deluxe; from $210 for suites. Children under 17 stay free with parents.

One km west, near San Antonio de Belén, is the colonial-style **Costa Rica Marriott Hotel and Resort**, tel. 298-0000, fax 298-0011; in the U.S., tel. (800) 831-1000, fax (800) 325-9714, which opened in 1996 on a 30-acre site commanding panoramic views over the valley. This showy jewel sits amid a coffee plantation at Ribera de Belén and boasts sweeping views down through lush landscaped grounds to distant mountains. All 252 rooms and seven suites are exquisitely decorated, with French doors opening to a patio or balcony. The decor fits the bill: in public areas, evocative antiques and stressed timbers and stone floors, while the humongous bedrooms boast regal furnishings and fabrics and a full complement of modern amenities. It features a ballroom for 1,000 people, a golf practice range, a horizon swimming pool, three restaurants, three tennis courts, and a gym, plus 200 square meters of retail space and a business center. The buffet meals are superb, though otherwise the cuisine is a letdown.

FOOD

A cosmopolitan range of cuisines awaits in San José. Recommended restaurants are listed below according to ethnicity and proximity. Don't neglect the many fine hotel restaurants, such as the Hotel y Restaurante Grano de Oro—for my mind, the *best restaurant in San José*. Eat here once and you may decide to stay.

Breakfast: San José is sadly lacking in good breakfast haunts. The Hotel Grano de Oro is justifiably popular with Tico businessfolk for intimate breakfasting on the outdoor patio. Try the superb gringo or *tico* breakfasts (the "Gringo"— a large bowl of granola with bananas, and thick slices of freshly baked whole-wheat toast— should see you through the day).

Hearty Lunches Under $2: Many eateries serve a hearty, all-inclusive *almuerzo ejecutivo*, or businessman's lunch special, on which you can fill your stomach for 250-500 *colones* ($1-2). Look for a hand-lettered sign in the window announcing an *almuerzo, plato del día,* or *casado*. Lunch specials normally contain vegetables, plus a meat, fish, or chicken dish, and most often a natural fruit drink. You have dozens of inexpensive restaurants and *sodas* to choose from. Most big corporations and government buildings also have cafeterias for their staffs. Many are open to the public and offer a *plato del día* for as little as $1.

Smoking is treated as a national right in Costa Rica. Few restaurants boast a nonsmoking section, and few Costa Ricans would give a second thought to lighting up while you're still eating, even if you're at the same table. You might politely ask smokers around you to refrain. Failing that, you could grab your throat and fall to the floor in a histrionic choking fit.

Service, Service Charges, and Tipping: Upscale restaurants automatically add a 10% service charge (plus tax) to your bill. Refreshingly, tipping is not expected. A small tip is generally appreciated as a reward for good service and is sure to be remembered if you return. However, service is usually slow and uncaring. As one reader wrote: "If you're in a hurry, you're screwed." Gouging of tourists is common, especially in cheaper *sodas*. And far too many proprietors and their staff don't seem to care for your business. In these circumstances, no tip is deserved.

RESTAURANTS

Many fine restaurants can be found in Escazú, within a 15-minute drive of San José. Hours are typically generally 11 a.m.-3 p.m. and 6-10:30 p.m. *Sodas* generally stay open throughout the day.

Costa Rican Nouvelle
West of Downtown: You can't go wrong at the **Restaurante Grano de Oro,** tel. 255-3322, in the splendid hotel of the same name on Calle 30, Avenidas 2/4. Chef Francis Canal (formerly of

Chalet Tirol and Fleur de Lys) has successfully merged Costa Rican into nouvelle, conjuring the tropical into a European context. Creative interpretations include spicy enchilada pie ($5), poached mahi mahi ($8), tenderloin in green peppercorn sauce ($11), and sweet curry chicken sprinkled with coconut ($8). The menu is vast; the prices exceedingly fair. So, too, the specialty cocktails and an array of desserts (you *must* try the sublime Pie Grano de Oro). You can dine within, or alfresco on an intimate patio festooned with epiphytes. The Junta Asesora Gourmet Centroamericana recently chose it as one of the top 25 restaurants in the region. Open 6 a.m.-10 p.m.

East of Downtown: A recent addition is **Bijahua,** tel. 225-0613, 300 meters south of Mas x Menos in San Pedro, also serving "nueva cocina Costarricense" and claiming to have rescued grandma's recipes and lent them an international flair, using exquisite local ingredients and a creative aesthetic. Open Mon.-Fri. noon-2:30 p.m. and 7-10:30 p.m., Saturday 7-11 p.m., and Sunday noon-5 p.m.

Costa Rican Traditional

Downtown: The **Centro Comercial El Pueblo,** in Barrio Tournón, has several restaurants renowned for traditional Costa Rican fare. **La Cocina de Leña,** tel. 255-1360, is one of the best. Here, you'll dine by candlelight, surrounded by the warm ambience of a cozy rural farmhouse. Dishes include Creole chicken, *olla de carne* soup, and square *tamales* made with white corn meal, mashed potatoes, and beef, pork, or chicken, wrapped tightly in a plantain leaf. Entrées average $10. Its sister restaurant next door, **El Fogón de Leña,** tel. 233-9964, offers slightly more exotic Costa Rican fare in a setting that resembles a farmhouse ($5-20). The open-air **Restaurant Lukas,** tel. 233-8145, serves familiar local cuisine with a dashing touch and stays open until dawn to capture the danced-out patrons of the discos. Light jazz and a guitarist strumming Latin melodies accompanies such dishes as mixed tacos and *picadillos* (small chopped-vegetable platter), fried pork, mixed meats, and grilled corvina in garlic butter. Most dishes are prepared al dente over a large grill. Lukas offers a **Pasaporte** ($33) good for a complete dinner (including wine, dessert, and cof-

fee), plus free admission with drinks and snacks to both Chavetas nightclub and Cocoloco discotheque, next door.

Roasted chicken is the name of the game at **Restaurante Campesino,** Calle 7, Avenidas 2/4, tel. 222-1170, where you can watch your bird being cooked Tico-style over wood coals, then served with mashed potatoes (optional). Down-home ambience and good food for less than $4. Chinese dishes are also served.

If you're pinching pennies, try **La Vasconia,** Avenida 1, Calle 5, good for an extensive menu of local fare for $2 or less; or **El Cuartel de la Boca del Monte,** Avenida 1, Calles 21/23, tel. 221-0327, popular as a lively bar by night but an excellent source of good food, reasonably priced. A *corvina al ajillo* (garlic sea bass) or *lomito* (tenderloin) costs $5. I've also heard good things of **Restaurante Bratsi,** in the Nuevo Talamanca Hotel, Avenida 2, Calles 8/10, tel. 233-5033.

Restaurante El Escorial, Calle 3, Avenida 5, tel. 221-3756, is a pleasant albeit earthy place with booths with curtains. It serves *bocas* (from $1.50) and international Latin dishes, including churrasco ($7). A "plate of the day" costs $5.

The **Poás Taberna y Restaurant,** Avenida 7, Calles 3/5, tel. 221-7802, specializes in the "native platter" ($5), including excellent soups and regional dishes from Central America. Exotic tropical foliage and live birds surround diners. The setting truly is a piece of the urban jungle. A waterfall is even planned inside! Amid the palms is a wooden dance floor, and a romantic ill-lit bar upstairs is a great place for sneaking kisses.

The **Café Parisienne,** the terrace cafe fronting the Gran Hotel, besides snacks and coffee, serves simple Costa Rican fare—*arroz con pollo* (rice with chicken; $4) and more—at a reasonable price. The hustle and bustle of the Plaza de la Cultura, my favorite daytime hangout, provides good theater, as do the aging North American expats of modest means accompanied by or trolling for *chicas* one-third their age. And though the food is bland, the newly remodeled **La Esmeralda,** Avenida 2, Calles 5/7, tel. 221-0530, is still a great place to dine at night, if only to hear the mariachis.

West of Downtown: Restaurante Regio, on the west side of the Estadio Nacional in Sabana Park, tel. 232-2887, serves rack-roasted meats, chicken, and fish. There's also a *chorizo* (carvery). Nearby is **Bembec,** tel. 221-8631, in a columned colonial house at Calle 40 between Paseo Colón and Avenida 4. Popular as both cafe and bar, Bembec serves excellent sea bass in garlic ($5), Mexican dishes ($2 and up), and such simple fare as *montaditos,* a filling tortilla sandwich of miscellaneous fillings, including beans and cheese, and meats and salad.

Costa Rican *Sodas*—Inexpensive Dining
Sodas—cheap snack bars serving typical Costa Rican fare—are a dime a dozen. They serve "working class" fare, such as tripe soup and rice-and-beans dishes. You can usually fill up for $2-4. They're good for mixing with the "working classes."

Downtown: My favorite *soda* is the 24-hour **Soda La Perla,** tel. 222-7492, on an always-lively junction facing Parque Central, Avenida Central, Calle 1. It's popular with the after-theater crowd. Basic but good-value fare, from a refreshing *refresco* to *gallo pinto, arroz con pollo,* and *torta española,* an inch-thick omelette with everything but the kitchen sink. Soups are outstanding. Free *bocas* are served with drinks. One block west on Avenida 2 is the **Soda Palace,** highly popular with both locals and budget travelers. The garish lighting is enough to scare me off. Often noisy. Mariachis sometimes appear impromptu. It's open 24 hours.

Also nearby, at Avenida Central and Calles Central/2, is **Manolo's.** Try the *churros,* greasy Mexican donuts, at the streetside stall. Upstairs you can fill up on sandwiches and other fare; the third story is more elegant and double the price.

For atmosphere, check out the Mercado Central, Avenidas Central/1 and Calles 6/8, which has dozens of inexpensive *sodas,* which get packed at lunchtime. Late afternoon is a good time to sit down. Beware pickpockets! Closed Sunday.

Spanish
Downtown: Old wooden wine casks and Moorish screens are part of the appealing decor at **Casino Español,** Calle 9, Avenidas Central/1, tel. 222-9440. The menu contains more than 150 options: everything from octopus in ink sauce ($5) and tongue in prune sauce ($5.50) to more traditional classics such as chateaubriand flambé ($12 for two), lobster thermidor ($21),

and Spanish dishes such as *zarzuela de mariscos* and paella a la Valenciana.

One of my down-to-earth favorites is **Restaurante Taska,** Calle 3 and Avenidas 7/9, tel. 257-6556, with suitably Manchegan (from La Mancha) decor—oak barrels and the like—and a menu featuring such items as paella ($20), rice and rabbit ($15), and flambé steak ($11). The atmospheric **Goya,** Avenida 1, Calles 5/7, tel. 221-3887, provides generous *bocas* as well as excellent Spanish cuisine, including a splendid paella plus rabbit in wine ($9), at moderate prices (entrées begin at $5).

West of Downtown: Restaurant Reggio, tel. 232-2887, opposite the Estadio Nacional in Sabana West, is an elegant place with large horseshoe booths. It's run by Spaniard José Luis Garcia, who boasts among his 70 dishes a famous paella. The special lunch will cost you $4. **La Masia de Triquell,** Avenida 2, Calle 40, tel. 296-3528, is recommended for its Catalonian-inspired paella and steak-in-garlic ($10 average); closed Sunday. It also has a restaurant in Rohrmoser, tel. 232-3584.

East of Downtown: Chef Emilio Machado works wonders at the small but beautifully appointed **Marbella Restaurant,** tel. 228-0180, in the Centro Comercial de la Calle Real in San Pedro. The large selection of seafood dishes includes paella Marbella (shellfish and sea bass) and paella Valenciana (chicken and seafood). The paella Madrilena (rabbit, chicken, and pork) is particularly good.

Mexican
There's no shortage of choice. One of the best is **Antojitos,** inexpensive yet classy, and justifiably popular with Ticos. Meals cost from $4; a grilled tenderloin costs $10. It has four outlets in San José: west of Sabana Park, in Rohrmoser, tel. 231-5564; east of downtown in Los Yoses, tel. 225-9525, in Centro Comerciál del Sur, in San Pedro, tel. 227-4160; and north of town on the road to Tibas, tel. 235-3961. It sometimes has mariachi.

Downtown: Huaraches, south of downtown at Avenida 22, Calles 5/7, tel. 222-7714, serves fast-food *comida auténtica.*

West of Downtown: Restaurante El Tapatio, in the San José 2000 Shopping Center, 100 meters north of Hotel Irazú, offers a $14.50 special: margarita, beer or wine, plus house filet or Mexican entrée, coffee, and dessert.

Bar México, Calle 16 and Avenida 13, tel. 221-8461, is a modestly upscale favorite. Live mariachi music forms a backdrop for excellent Mexican cuisine. Generous *bocas* are offered with drinks at the bar.

Las Tunas, tel. 231-1802, in a large log cabin overlooking Sabana Park, 500 meters west of the ICE Building, in Sabana Norte, is Costa Rica's answer to Tex-Mex for those seeking Tico-Mex fare (tacos, for example, offer shredded beef rolled in a tortilla and deep fried). Las Tunas has drive-in service. A bar-disco next door stays open until 4 a.m. on weekends. Also to consider is **Sus Antonos,** tel. 222-9086, on Paseo Colón and Calles 24/26.

East of Downtown: The spot to try is **La Hacienda de Panchos,** tel. 224-8261, 200 meters east of the La Rotunda de Zapote (roundabout) in San Pedro. It's open 11 a.m.-11 p.m.

French

Downtown: El Jardín de Paris, Avenida 10, Calle 21, tel. 222-6806, is located in the Casa Matute Gómez, a venerable downtown mansion turned into a complex of bars and eateries. Chef Vincente Fromont whips up classic French dishes that will set you back more than $20 per head for dinner. Casa Matute was closed at press time (ostensibly for restoration), with plans to reopen.

Other highly recommended options for those feeling flush are the cozy **L'Ile de France,** Calle 7, Avenidas Central/2, tel. 222-4241, run by Chef Jean Claude Fromont (vichyssoise, tournedos, and regional dishes are typical); the **Restaurant El Mirador,** on the top floor of the Hotel Aurola Holiday Inn, tel. 233-7233; and **Bromelias,** Calle 23, Avenida 3, tel. 221-3848, with a wide menu, elegant decor, and live music in the executive bar of an old customs building. A jacket is in order. Main entrées start at around $10 at all three.

West of Downtown: La Bastille, Paseo Colón, Calle 22, tel. 255-4994, is the oldest French restaurant in San José. Chef Hans Pulfer produces superb French cuisine. It's elegant and expensive. Closed Sunday.

East of Downtown: Cognoscenti craving classical French head to **Le Chandelier,** tel. 225-3980, in a restored Mediterranean-style

mansion complete with beamed ceiling and fireplace, just behind the high-rise ICE Building in San Pedro. It has 10 separate dining areas, including a sculpture garden. Chef Claude Dubuis conjures up imaginative cuisine, stunning sauces, and even Dubuis's own version of typical Costa Rican fare: roasted heart of palm, cream of *pejivalle* soup, *gratin* of corvina with avocado. The restaurant is adorned with murals and the chef/owner's own works of art. Appetizers average $4; entrées range $8-15. Closed Sunday.

In San Pedro, the tiny and moderately priced **Le Bistro,** tel. 253-8062, 200 meters north and 100 meters east of San Pedro church, serves French cuisine Dijon style. Closed Monday.

Italian

Downtown: The **Balcón de Europa,** Calle 9, Avenidas Central/1, tel. 221-4841, is a revered culinary shrine where Chef Franco Piatti presents moderately priced cuisine from central Italy in an appropriately warm, welcoming setting with wood-paneled walls festooned with historic photos and framed proverbs. Try *pasta a la boscaiola* with tuna, tomatoes, and mushrooms. Even a steak costs less than $10. Closed Saturday.

West of Downtown: The popular **La Piazzetta,** Paseo Colón, Calle 40, tel. 222-7896, is acclaimed for such decadent dishes as risotto with salmon and caviar, and filet mignon in white truffle sauce, served in atmospheric surroundings illustrated by authentic Italian paintings. Closed Sunday. **Emilia Romagna,** tel. 233-2843, 25 meters west of Pollo Kentucky on Paseo Colón, is a romantic restaurant that doubles as San José's hippest jazz club. The elegant **D'Olivo,** tel. 220-0453, next to Hotel Palma Real on Sabana Norte, serves pastas and seafoods ($4-10).

Three inexpensive options on Paseo Colón are **Ana,** Calles 24/26, tel. 222-6153, with pleasing ambience and the usual Italian fare of lasagne, spaghetti, and veal; **Piccolo Roma,** Calle 24, with home-style cooking; and **Giardina,** on the south side of Sabana Park. Nearby, too, is **Il Bel Paese,** tel. 232-5119, 400 meters east of Pops, on Sabana Sur.

One of my more moderately priced favorites is **Peperoni,** tel. 232-5119, in Rohrmoser/Sabana East, on the road to Pavas, serving superb pastas, pizzas, and roasted meats. Hidden away in the freezer and known only to the cognoscenti is the house liqueur, *eneldo verde,* a tasty, bright-green knock-you-down concoction distilled from sweet green peppers! Try it. It's better than it sounds. **Fellini,** Avenida 4 and Calle 36, tel. 222-3520, has also been recommended.

East of Downtown: Il Ponte Vecchio, tel. 283-1810, 200 meters west and 25 meters north of San Pedro church, serves moderately priced, tasty cuisine cooked with imported Italian ingredients: sun-dried tomatoes, porcini mushrooms, and basil. Pastas are homemade by chef Antonio D'Alaimo. A Roman arch doorway and a mural of Venice's famous Ponte Vecchio add to the ambience. Open 11:30 a.m.-2:30 p.m. and 5:30-10:30 p.m.; closed Sunday. In the same area is **Ristorante Caruso,** Centro Comercial de la Calle Real in San Pedro, tel. 224-4801, with gnocchi, homemade pastas, and vegetarian dishes.

Il Pomodoro, tel. 224-0966, 100 meters north of San Pedro church, is a popular hangout for university types who favor the pizzas ($4-8). And **Miro's Bistro** is also recommended for its mix of Italian and Hungarian dishes. This cozy and inexpensive restaurant is next to the railroad tracks, 300 meters west of Pulpería La Luz in Barrio Escalante.

The Suburbs: Out of town, at Ciudad Cariari, is **Antonio's,** tel. 293-1613, 100 yards east of the Hotel Herradura, and serving exquisite cuisine. Try the melazane—baked eggplant topped with mariana sauce, parmigiano, and mozarella cheese ($7). There's an "executive lunch" special ($4).

Others to consider include the elegant **Via Veneto,** tel. 234-2898, which one reader thought "overpriced," and **Restaurante Italiano Il Bagatto,** tel. 224-5297, both in Curridabat.

German, Russian, and Swiss

Downtown: The "Switzerland of the Americas" lost its finest Swiss restaurant in 1997, when Chalet Suizo closed, but **Zermatt,** Calle 23 and Avenida 11, tel. 222-0604, still offers its famous *fondue bourguignonne* and Chicken Supreme Zermatt. Closed Saturday. Expensive.

East of Downtown: La Galería, tel. 234-0850, 125 meters west of the ICE Building in San Pedro, is famed for its sauces complementing continental cuisine with a heavy Teu-

tonic slant ($6-15). There's soothing classical music. Reservations are essential. It's closed Sunday. **Rossia,** tel. 225-2690, 500 meters north of the Costa Rican-North American Cultural Center, whisks you to the Ukraine. Run by three Russians and a Tico, the restaurant offers a suitably *dacha* ambience and tasty Russian fare, such as *borscht, buzhenina* (thinly sliced oven-cooked pork), and spongy chocolate cake; $4-8.

The Suburbs: The **Hotel Marriott,** outside town, tel. 298-0000, offers an Oktoberfest special during October, with German specialties such as *Rippli mit sauerkraut* (smoked pork chop with sauerkraut).

Chinese

There's no shortage of Chinese restaurants. Most serve a bland cross between Chinese and Tico fare. If you want chopsticks, ask for *palillos.*

Downtown: My favorite Chinese restaurant is the popular **Tin Jo,** Calle 11, Avenidas 6/8, tel. 221-7605. The decor is quaintly colonial Costa Rican, but the food is distinctly Asian: exquisitely tasty Mandarin and Sichuan specialties at moderate prices. The booths have waiters' bells. It also serves Thai food! Next door is the more homey **Don Wang,** tel. 223-6484, serving generous, reasonably priced portions, although the quality isn't up to par with Tin Jo. It offers Taiwanese dishes and small *bocas.* Seafoods are a particular bargain ($4-6). Pleasing classical music and attentive Chinese owner.

Penny pinchers might try the **Restaurant Kian Kok,** Calle 1, Avenida Central/2, on the same block as Soda La Perla. The decor and cuisine are uninspired, but the portions are hefty—ask for it spicy if that's how you like it. The **Lai Yuin** restaurant in the Hotel Royal Garden, Calle Central, Avenida Central, tel. 257-0023, serves dim sum on weekends.

West of Downtown: Flor del Loto, tel. 232-4652, opposite the ICE Building in Sabana Norte, is the place if you like your Chinese food hot and spicy. Mouth-searing Hunan and Sichuan specialties include *mo-shu-yock* (Shi Chuen-style pork) and *ma po tofu* (vegetables, bamboo shoots, and tofu stir-fried in a sizzling hot-pepper oil). Dishes average $7.

Another acclaimed option is **King's Garden,** tel. 255-3838, on the second floor of the Centro Comercial Yaohan, opposite the Hotel Corobicí.

The head chef is from Hong Kong; the menu features many favorites from the city, as well as Cantonese and Sichuan dishes. A set dinner for two costs about $14.

Mariscos de Oriente, tel. 232-2973, on Sabana Norte, specializes in seafoods.

East of Downtown: Ave Félix, tel. 225-3362, 200 meters west of the San Pedro church, is a very popular Chinese restaurant acclaimed for its original sauces: soy sauce spiced with crushed garlic, minced onion, and sesame oil; and sweet-and-sour sauce with lemon juice and the juice of maraschino cherries. The Taiwanese chef conjures more than 100 entrées that include some exotic offerings as well as staples ($4-8) such as bird's nest sliced beef ($6). Portions are huge. Open 11 a.m.-3 p.m. and 6-11:30 p.m., Sunday 11 a.m.-9:30 p.m. In the same area is **Nueva China,** Avenida Central, tel. 224-4478, an elegant favorite of aficionados of Chinese cuisine. Among its specialties is dim sum (served on weekends) and garlic-honeyed chicken. Quintessential Asian decor. It was closed for remodeling at press time.

The Suburbs: Another good option is **Restaurante Palacio Real,** tel. 235-4487, in Tibas.

Other Asian Cuisines

Downtown: Tin Jo Calle 11, Avenidas 6/8, tel. 221-7605, serves Thai food. I tried the *pad thai,* which proved different from Thai food I'd experienced previously, but was, after I got used to it, quite excellent.

West of Downtown: Fuji, tel. 232-8122, in the Hotel Corobicí, has tatami-covered private dining rooms for six. My favorite spot—thanks to Michael Kaye, who turned me on to it—is the cozy **Arirang,** in Centro Colón on Paseo Colón, Calles 38/40, tel. 223-2838. It caters to those who love grilled eel, *kimch'i, chu'sok,* and other Korean specialties cooked on a hibachi at your table. It also has sushi specials. Most dishes cost less than $10. Open Mon.-Fri. 11:30 a.m.-3 p.m. and 5:30-9:30 p.m., Saturday and holidays 11:30 a.m.-9:30 p.m.

For Thai and Indonesian food, try **El Exótico Oriente** in Sabana West, serving all the classics: *rystaffel, pad thai,* and more. Li-ket, the chef, is Thai, and his dishes have all the sweet zing you expect of Thai cuisine. Top it off with delicious homemade coffee ice cream.

The Suburbs: The **Sakura,** tel. 239-0033, ext. 33, a sushi bar and restaurant in the Japanese-owned Hotel Herradura, is expensive, but offers superb Teppani-style Japanese cooking.

Steaks

Most seafood restaurants also serve steaks and other dishes.

Downtown: Recommended for charbroiled surf-and-turf for less than $10 is **La Hacienda,** Calle 7, Avenidas Central/2, tel. 223-5493, a renovated barn with rough-hewn beams, walls decorated with sombreros, horseshoes, and paintings, and a fountain fashioned from an antique *paila* (sugar cauldron).

"TR's," or **Tony's Ribs,** Avenida 6, Calles 11/13, tel. 223-2957, offers Texas barbecue, marinated beef and pork ribs, and finger-food appetizers. Also downtown is **Kamakiri Steak House,** Calle Central and Avenidas 9/11, tel. 257-8133. **Lancer's Steak House,** tel. 222-5938, in the El Pueblo shopping center, Barrio Tournón, has Texas-style cuts from $6, plus seafoods.

West of Downtown: El Chicote, tel. 232-0936, 400 meters west of ICE in Sabana Norte, is noted for its chateaubriand, shrimp-stuffed tenderloin, and filet mignon basted with honey and served with breaded bananas and mashed potatoes. Steaks are cooked over a large open fire. Palms and ferns abound. It has a drive-in next door. Open daily 11 a.m.-midnight. Nearby is **Los Ranchos,** tel. 232-7757, serving prime ribs, meats, and seafood dishes, beginning at around $6. Meats are served Argentinian-style—*chimichurri.* **La Gaucho,** on Sabana Oeste, is also known for its Argentinian *empeuadas.*

East of Downtown: Friday's Restaurant, tel. 224-5934, in the suburb of La Paulina, east of San Pedro, bills itself as the "Great American Bistro." Tex-Mex and steaks here, folks, plus seafood, salads, chicken, burgers, and your favorite cocktails. It's very popular with the younger crowd. Open daily noon-11:30 p.m. The **Cocina de Borodlino,** Calle 21, Avenidas 6/8, serves excellent, cheap Argentinian empanadas to the local crowd.

Seafood

Downtown: A favorite, **Restaurante Bratsi,** in the Nuevo Hotel Talamanca, Avenida 2, Calles 8/10, tel. 233-5033, offers up lobster and shrimp for $12. **Rias Bajas,** tel. 233-3214, in El Pueblo, serves a splendid seafood paella and fish casserole. **Richard's Seafood House** in the Hotel Morazán has been recommended. Like most seafood restaurants, it also serves prime ribs.

West of Downtown: One of my favorite restaurants is **Macchu Pichu,** Calle 32, Avenidas 1/3, tel. 222-7384, with delicious authentic Peruvian seafoods and *spicy* sauces! Try the superb ceviches ($2.50-5) or the *picante de mariscos* (a seafood casserole with onions, garlic, olives, and cheese), enjoyed in a suitably nautical ambience. Moderately priced (some potato entrées are less than $4; garlic octopus is $5). The "pisco sours" are powerful. The place is always full with Ticos. Across the way is **Tierras Peruanos,** also serving Peruvian food.

For a cheap meal, check out **Marisqueria La Princesa Marina** (The Mermaid), tel. 232-0481, fax 296-3739, 150 meters south of Canal 7 on Sabana Oeste. This canteen-like seafood spot is a favorite of Ticos at lunchtime. It serves from a wide menu and wins no gourmet prizes, but at least you fill up. Most dishes cost $1-5.

A celebrated seafood restaurant is the posh **Lobster's Inn,** Paseo Colón and Calle 24, tel. 223-8594, with fresh fish dishes from $8, namesake lobsters more than twice that. Chicken and beef dishes, too.

Another recommended spot is **La Fuente de Los Mariscos,** tel. 231-0631, in Centro Comercial San José adjacent to the Hotel Irazú in La Uruca, with seafood at moderate prices. It's open daily 11:15 a.m.-10:30 p.m.

The Suburbs: Consider **Las Malvinas,** tel. 224-3131, in Curridabat. It features live music and free hotel transfers.

Vegetarian

Downtown: San José is well blessed with monuments to healthy, meat-free dining. Most cater to the budget crowd. The best known is **Restaurante Vishnu,** Avenida 1, Calles 1/3, tel. 222-2549, serving superb health-food breakfasts, lunches, and dinner. Meals are generous in size and low in price (a *casado* costs $2.50). Get there early for a seat. Vishnu has smaller outlets at Calle 14, Avenida Central/2, and at Calle 1, Avenida 4.

Barbara and Helga whip up creative vegetarian dishes at the **Café Amón,** Avenida 11, Calles

3/5; and **Gavinda's Vegetarian Restaurant,** Avenida 2 and Calles 8/11, tel. 256-7392, has macrobiotic lunch specials for $2.

Don Sol, Avenida 7, Calle 15, is an inexpensive macrobiotic *soda* with a pleasing ambience and a filling *plato fuerte* (lunch of the day). The delicious fruit salad is particularly recommended.

Also try **La Macrobótica,** Avenida 1, Calles 11/15; **Soda Yure,** Avenida 2, Calle 3; **La Nutrisoda,** Calle 3, Avenida 2, tel. 255-3959; and **Shakti,** Calle 13, Avenida 8.

East of Downtown: La Mazorca, tel. 224-8069, 100 meters north and 200 meters east of San Pedro Church, San Pedro, is a bohemian macrobiotic restaurant and a favorite of the university crowd. You can feast on superb health food and fresh-baked breads and desserts for $5. Try the Friday fish special ($4). Closed Sunday. Nearby is **San Pedro Vegetarian,** tel. 224-1163, which has a *casado* with juice for $2. At cozy **Ambrosia,** tel. 253-8012, 75 meters east of Banco Popular in San Pedro, chef Janie Murray conjures up soufflés, quiches, and other moderately priced vegetarian and nonvegetarian dishes.

Pizza

Ticos are fond of pizza, and there are dozens of pizzerias. **Pizza Hut** alone has more than 30 outlets in San José! And **Domino's** is making inroads. Your hotel concierge is sure to be able to recommend his or her favorite.

West of Downtown: Pizza Pizza, tel. 258-2828, is housed in a beautiful, ocher-colored Georgian-style building at the end of Paseo Colón, opposite the Hotel Corobicí. **Pizzería da Pino,** Avenida 2, Calle 24, tel. 223-4985, also serves a range of tasty Italian dishes in a downhome Italian setting.

East of Downtown: Pizzeria Il Pomodoro, tel. 224-0966, in San Pedro, is recommended.

Other

Lubnan, tel. 257-6071, a Lebanese restaurant on Paseo Colón and Calles 22/24, brings a taste of the Levant to San José with noteworthy Middle Eastern specialties such as shish kebob, falafel, *michi malfuf* (stuffed cabbage) and *kafta naie* (marinated ground beef). On a similar theme are **Las Pirámides,** on Paseo Colón, tel. 257-8818, serving Lebanese and Middle Eastern dishes; and **Beirut,** Avenida 1, Calle 32, tel.

257-1808, open Tues.-Sat.; there's a belly-dancing show nightly at 8 p.m.

Craving a good burger? Then head to **Tiny's Bar & Restaurant,** Avenida 2, Calles 9/11, where a *real* American burger is served by real American hands. Another good bet is the **Lone Star Grill,** tel. 229-7597, in Coronado, run by Texan Judy Heidt.

Bromelias Cafe and Grill, cater-corner to the old Atlantic Railway Station, Calle 23, Avenida 3, tel. 221-3848, is also much more than a cafe. Creative dishes—corvina with avocado and beurre blanc, and steak Diane with a green pepper sauce light on the palate—rival those of the better restaurants.

CAFES AND PASTRY SHOPS

The coffee renaissance is catching up with Costa Rica. My favorite spot is the **Café Havana** a refined and cozy cafe in Escazú.

San José has dozens of pastry shops (*pastelerías*). **Spoon** has burgeoned over the past decade from a small take-out bakery one block off Avenida Central in Los Yoses, tel. 224-0328, into a chain with outlets on Avenida Central near the Plaza de la Cultura, tel. 221-6702, and throughout the city. In addition to desserts, Spoon serves sandwiches, salads, lasagnes, soups, empanadas (pastries stuffed with chicken and other meats), and *lapices*, a Costa Rican equivalent of submarines. **Musmanni,** tel. 296-5750, is a national *pastelería* chain selling pastries and fresh breads. It has about one dozen outlets in San José.

Downtown: One of the best coffee shops in town is the **Café Ruiseñor** inside the foyer of the National Theater. Marble-topped tables, magnificent tilework, a gilded and mirrored serving counter, classical music, and artwork adorning the walls are topped by tempting desserts.

For a good cappuccino ($1) or espresso ($1.58), head to **La Esquina del Café,** Avenida 9, Calle 3 bis., tel. 257-9868, serving gourmet coffees sold by region of the country. It also serves pastries, sandwiches, soups, salads, and killer desserts. It has free tastings and an excellent selection of pastries. The 24-hour cafe in the **Hotel Del Rey** serves a wide range of lattes, cappuccinos, etc.

Another of my favorites is **Café Mundo,** at Avenida 9 and Calle 15, tel. 222-6190. This handsome remake of a colonial mansion has open patios and several indoor rooms. Persian rugs and contemporary art on the walls add to the warm mood. A capuccino costs $1.75. It sells pastries, pizzas, salads, and desserts. It's a popular gay hangout.

If you've a sweet tooth, check out **La Miel,** Avenida 6, Calles 13/15, tel. 223-3193, a delightful pastry shop offering cheap yet delicious desserts and pastries. Likewise, try **Panadería Schmidt,** Avenida 2, Calle 4 and Avenida Central, Calle 11, while **Churrería Manolo's,** Avenida Central, Calles Central/2, tel. 221-2041, is known for its *churros,* greasy, cream-filled doughnuts.

East of Downtown: La Maga de los Artes, tel. 280-9361, one block east of the church on the main road in San Pedro, is a trendy cafe that serves coffee to an art-thirsty crowd. Magazines from around the world keep the literary crowd happy. The cafe shows films and rents videos and CDs, and even has an experimental theater and art workshop. And the cafe offers computer buffs access to the Internet over a cup of fine blend. The members-only ($25) cafe is so popular that lines form to get in. Yes, sandwiches and desserts are served. Also in San Pedro, try **Kira,** tel. 253-9417, a sublime little two-story bakery, pastry shop, and cafe with a tasteful ambience. It's 50 meters west and 20 south of Mas x Menos.

Also in Los Yoses is **Café Ruiseñor,** tel. 256-6094, a trendy spot serving all range of coffee drinks including lattes ($1.25), but also serving sandwiches ($3) and entrées such as curried chicken ($6). If you're staying at the Toruma youth hostel, there's tiny **Café Giratablas** next door. It serves a *casado* lunch special with juice for $2.

FAST FOOD

There's no shortage of Yankee (and U.S.-style) fast-food joints for those who hanker for a taste of back home. Inevitably, they have become icons for Tico teenagers, who pay homage here. McDonald's and KFC have become San José landmarks known by everyone in town.

Hamburgers: McDonald's, tel. 257-1112, has more than a dozen outlets in San José, including on the north side of the Plaza de la Cultura. After touring Costa Rica for a few weeks, you may be ready for a good ol' Big Mac. Its Costa Rican clones are **Archi's** (serving fried chicken as well as burgers), also with an outlet on the north side of the plaza; **A/S,** open 24 hours on Calle 1 and Avenida 2; **Woopy's,** on Avenida 2 and Calle 2; and **Hardee's** at Calle 1 and Avenidas Central/1. **Burger King** has an outlet on the east side of Plaza de la Cultura, opposite the entrance to the Gold Museum, and another next to Soda Palace, on Avenida 2 and Calle Central.

Chicken: Fried chicken is a Costa Rican staple, and most restaurants sell it. **KFC,** Pollo Kentucky, tel. 224-1796, had 10 outlets at press time, as did both the Nicaraguan equivalent, **Rosti Pollo,** tel. 290-1595, and the homegrown **Restaurantes Delipollo,** tel. 256-7732.

Mexican: Every city should have a **Taco Bell** and San José is no exception, with outlets at Calle 5 and Avenidas Central/2, tel. 233-2607, and in San Pedro and Curridabat. The local equivalent is **Don Taco,** at Avenida 1, Calle 2.

ENTERTAINMENT, SHOPPING, AND RECREATION

Whatever your nocturnal craving, San José has something to please, if you don't seek sophistication. Look for a copy of *Info-Spectacles,* tel. 223-3520, which lists forthcoming music and entertainment events; it's published each Tuesday and can be obtained at bars, nightclubs, and from the ICT office. The *Tico Times, Costa Rica Today,* and the "Viva" section of *La Nación* have comprehensive listings of what's on in San José, from classical symphony and theater to cinema showings, concerts, and disco.

With the exception of one or two areas (particularly around the Coca-Cola bus station and any of the city parks), walking at night is generally safe. Be aware, however, that muggings are on the increase and you should always use common-sense caution. If you have any qualms, consider using the **Night Life Tour Service,** tel. 256-3807, which has guided excursions.

BARS AND NIGHTCLUBS

There's a bar on every block, or at least it seems that way. The local *pulpería* often doubles as a combination of bar, family room, and front porch. The tourist bars are found in "Gringo Gulch," Calles 5/9, Avenidas Central/3. Bars in San Pedro are the most bohemian, catering to the university crowd and upscale Ticos. Many of the class acts are in Escazú, about four miles west of town. It's generally quite acceptable for women to drink at bars and nightclubs—at least until midnight, when many local women slip home for an un-

written curfew. Many bars stay open until the last bleary-eyed patrons go home—which could be about the time the sun comes up. Unless you want local color, avoid the spit-and-sawdust working men's bars where women are few and drunks are many. However, prostitution is a staple of San José life, and dozens of bars double as cheap strip clubs and brothels. Women entering may be mistaken for "working girls."

All but the fancier bars offer locally brewed beers for about $1 (prices are generally higher in Gringo Gulch), and Heineken and other imported beers are usually available for $1.50-2. *Bocas* (bar snacks) are often served free; sometimes a small charge applies. Don't be afraid to ask. Penny-pinchers should stay away from hard liquors and foreign wines, which carry a hefty price tag, and stick with *guaro,* the local sugarcane firewater that has been likened to everything from a cross between tequila and vodka to a mix of nail-polish remover and turpentine. I like it, particularly chilled or with Café Rica (coffee liqueur) on the rocks. Funnily, I don't recall having had a hangover from it, but the lack of recollection may be one of its side effects.

Downtown
La Esmeralda, Avenida 2, Calles 5/7, tel. 221-0503, is an institution, and a *must visit!* This lively 109-year-old restaurant and bar—with a brand new livery in 1997—is headquarters of the mariachis' union. On any night, you may count 50 flamboyantly dressed mariachis hanging out in the high-ceilinged room open to the street. They

warm up to applause from the diners while await-ing calls to action to serenade on some lover's behalf or to enliven a birthday party or other event: the telephone rings, a mariachi band is requested, and off the band goes. The bands expect tips or will charge a set fee per song. It is perfectly accept-able to decline a song if a band ap-proaches your table. A house specialty is the mixed *boca* plate. La Esmeralda doesn't get in the groove until after 9 p.m., and stays open past 4 a.m.

The **Casa Matute Gómez,** tel. 222-6806, fax 257-9752, a com-plex of bars—including a wine bar and a whiskey bar—and restaurants in a beautiful building on the corner of Aveni-da 10 and Calle 21, was closed at press time following a mur-der. Maybe it will reopen.

Gringo Gulch: Many bars in the touristy area downtown known as Gringo Gulch are run by North Americans. Virtually every bar that attracts gringos also attracts its share of prostitutes and Ticas trolling for sugar dad-dies. The liveliest spot—and the only 24-hour bar in town—is the **Blue Marlin Bar** in the Hotel Del Rey, Calle 9, Avenida 1. It's packed day and night. Fishermen particularly gather here to tell each other big lies, but the biggest lure seems to be as a pickup spot for the flirtatious local lasses and out-of-town girls making good. Who's picking up whom? ESPN and MTV are shown on the TV, and the adjacent casino is just as lively. **Tiny's Bar & Restaurant,** Avenida 2, Calles 7/9, also shows ESPN and CNN on three large TV screens and is understandably popular with North American tourists and expat residents. It gets packed during major sporting events. It has darts, and the St. Patrick's Day party is legendary.

Key Largo, Calle 7, Avenidas 1/3, tel. 221-0277, lost its lustre a few years ago but seems to have regained a second wind. A cross between an elegant Victorian bordello and a raffish Western saloon, this lively bar, housed in a handsome colo-nial mansion, is a favorite of voyeuristic tourists and anyone with prurient interests (most of the female patrons are part-time prostitutes). Each of three

large rooms has a dark-wood oval bar. There's live music, dancing, and cable TVs above the bars. Many of the characters propping up the bar could have stepped straight out of a Hemingway novel. Old ladies move among the crowd selling roses. Rife with at-mosphere. Open through 5 a.m. Cover charge $2.50 (Sunday free). Beers cost around $2.

The equally salacious **Happy Days** is a narrow unattractive bar on two levels, next door to Key Largo. The bar gets lively enough on weekends, but Key Largo has more atmosphere. A reader warns that the girls who hang out here are "fast and smooth" pickpockets. The gar-ishly lit **Chelle's Bar,** Calle 9 and Avenida Central, tel. 221-1369, is open 24 hours. **Chelle's Taber-na,** around the corner on Avenida Cen-tral, is marginally more appealing. One block away is **Lucky's Piano Blanco Bar,** Aveni-da Central, Calle 7, tel. 222-8385, with ESPN on TV and live piano music. **Nashville South,** Calle 5, Avenidas 1/3, tel. 233-1988, caters to country-and-western fans. Around the corner on Avenida 1, Calles 5/7, is **Pat Dunn's Bar,** for-merly "The New Nashville South," whose claim to fame is that it possesses the longest bar in Costa Rica. Saloon-style swinging doors and Jimmy Buffett tunes give it its down-home feel. Two blocks east and south is **Charleston,** Calle 9, Avenidas 2/4, offering pleasant 1920s quasi-Deep South decor replete with a stereo pumping out jazz classics and live jazz on weekends ($2). One block south of Key Largo is the **Bikini Club.** A narrow bar at the front shows risqué movies on TV screens above the bar. The bar-maids, appropriately, wear bikinis. Upstairs has striptease. No cover charge; beers $2.

If this is all too much, check out the **Amstel Hotel Bar,** Calle 7, Avenidas 1/3, tel. 222-4622, a comfortable place for a quiet drink; or **Roger's Bar,** an intimate and popular drinking joint op-posite the Hotel Del Rey. One block west, be-tween Calles 5/7, is **Yesterday's,** tel. 233-1988, where you can play darts or backgammon, watch a weekly comedy and magic act, or listen to the '60s and '70s oldies over a drink or two.

Where the Locals Go: Soda Palace, on Avenida 2 opposite Parque Central, is popular with locals and budget travelers as well as the odd bohemian intellectual. I find its garish fluorescent lighting and cold ambience unappealing. It's noisy with debate, arguments, and mariachi music. Supposedly, the 1948 Revolution was planned here over beers and *bocas*.

The best place for miles is the hip **El Cuartel de la Boca del Monte,** Avenida 1, Calles 21/23, tel. 221-0327, a popular hangout for young Josefinos and the late-night, post-theater set who crowd elbow to elbow. The brick-walled bar is famous for its 152 inventive cocktails, often served to wild ceremony and applause. It's also a restaurant. It has live music on Monday and Wednesday. A great place for singles who wish to meet Ms. or Mr. Right. Don't bother before 9 p.m., when folks begin to gravitate from **Sunrise,** another lively bar across the road. Close by is **Akelarre,** Calle 21, Avenidas 4/6, tel. 223-0345, a sprawling old house with several rooms and a backyard garden, and a venue for live bands on weekends.

Farther Afield
West of Downtown: Cocktail's, run by Soley and Mayra Starson, from Sweden, is cater-corner to Super Triangulo, in Pavas, and attracts an intellectual crowd. It's open Tues.-Sunday.

Bar México, tel. 221-8461, cater-corner to the Barrio México church, on Calle 16 and Avenida 13, serves excellent *bocas* and margaritas, and has mariachi music. The surrounding area is rundown, but the bar and restaurant is full of life. Thursday is Singles' Night. Music videos light up a giant screen. Nearby is **Disco Castro's,** tel. 256-8789, with karaoke and *bocas*. Playing '50s and '60s oldies and closer to town is **Rock Cafe** on Paseo Colón.

East of Downtown: Intellectuals also gather at **La Villa,** tel. 225-9612, in San Pedro. The atmospheric bar drips with political posters and understandably draws leftists who will massage your brain with a healthy discourse on the contemporary political scene. Also in San Pedro, there's **El Cocodrilo,** tel. 225-3277, a popular hangout for university students. A stuffed crocodile presides menacingly over the bar. If you tire of the video screen, don't be too shy to step onto the dance floor. **Río** is also popular, with hip music and a chic crowd, but otherwise devoid of character. **Los Andes,** opposite the entrance to the University of Costa Rica, in San Pedro, offers South American folk music.

Nearby in Los Yoses is **Benigan's,** one of San José's trendiest spots for the younger crowd. It's noisy and *very* lively. Also in Los Yoses is **Río,** tel. 225-8371, a lively place with TVs showing music videos. No dancing, but a hip young crowd gathers, especially for occasional all-day musical events when the street outside is closed and the party spills out onto the road. Often open until the last guest goes home.

Heavy-metal fans should head to **Bar Rock,** in San Pedro.

The **Habanos Smoking Club,** in the Calle Reál Shopping Center in San Pedro, tel. 224-5227, fax 283-4593, offers climatized smoking rooms, and an elegant bar serving Cuban cocktails. It's open Mon.-Sat. 10 a.m.-2 a.m.

"Gentlemen's Nightclubs"
San José has acquired a no-holds-barred nightlife in recent years, notably in a burgeoning number of strip and sex clubs. The clubs are popular with foreign businessmen, monied Ticos, and even Tico couples (proving that Ticos—male and female alike—enjoy celebrating the body as much as the mind). The places are as discreetly respectable and as hassle-free as these places can be. Stick to beers ($3-4), as hard liquor is inordinately expensive. Lap dances cost about $8. Scrutinize your bill thoroughly, and avoid paying with credit cards (the clubs tend to inflate the prices vastly). Take a calculator to check conversions to dollars. Most clubs have "VIP" rooms for "private entertainment" (i.e., intercourse).

Josephine's, Avenida 9, Calles 2/4, tel. 256-4486 or 256-4396, Costa Rica's original answer to the Moulin Rouge, promises the "splendor of Paris with a Latin flavor." It's the classiest act with the most beautiful women (who charge accordingly) and most colorful floor shows, which have grown more risque of late. Hours: 9 p.m.-2 a.m. nightly except Sunday. Don't be fooled by the "free admission" coupon in the English-language newspapers; admission costs $16. An open-bar costs $20. There's valet parking.

The same company recently opened **Elite,** on Paseo Colón and Calle 32, tel. 256-4486 or 256-4396. It has a "champagne saloon" for executives. Entrance costs $16 with two drinks, or $25 for all-you-can-drink.

Night Club Olympus, Calle Central, Avenida 5, tel. 223-4058, is perhaps the most risqué (and popular) of the bunch. The $16 admission includes two drinks. Not to be outdone, **Hollywood International,** tel. 232-8932, fax 296-1483, 400 meters west of McDonald's La Sabana, boasts the "best show in Latin America"—a parade of strippers, one on stage and another in a glass shower booth. Entrance: $2, plus two drink minimum. Open Mon.-Sat. 9 p.m. to 4 a.m.

Three less swanky exotic-dance clubs in the genre are **Casa de Muñecas** ("Doll's House"), at Avenida 15 and Calle 3; **Benny's,** opposite Olympus at Calle Central, Avenida 7; and **Nightclub Key West,** tel. 293-5009, with "grand shows," near Mall Cariari. The U.S.-owned **Arte Sauna,** tel. 222-2881, 50 meters west of Benny's, is favored for therapeutic massage for men and women and is considered an institution by local gringos.

The so-called red-light districts south of Parque Central, between Calles Central/8 and Avenidas 6/10, and east of Coca-Cola, are the preserve of working-class Ticos. The former is modestly rundown; the latter is *very* rundown and to be avoided. Flashing neon signs advertise strip shows at **Tabernas Juniors,** Calle 2, Avenida 8/10, the most substantial of the strip joints. Half a block south is the **Night Club Molino Rouge.** You'll find several more, including **Femme Internacional,** with a naked lady on the sign in case you miss the idea, Avenida 8, Calles 2/4, and **Arcadas,** Calle 2, Avenidas 8/10, which on Wednesday nights is women-only.

Strictly for Women: Male strip shows, called *maripepinos* (a play on words combining the Spanish word for "cucumber" with the name of the cabaret dancer Maripepa), are offered on Saturday at **Kilates Discoteque,** in Tibas. Male strippers are not for hire at the end of the show, nor do they remove their G-strings. However, for a bill slipped into a bikini, eager women may hop on stage to dance with the macho men of their choice.

DISCOS

Josefinos love to dance. Their first love is *salsa,* but you'll find a gamut of discos playing hip-hop, rap, new wave, reggae, and almost any other

DANCE LESSONS

Ticos can sometimes seem to have been born on the dance floor. But their mellifluous moves come through practice and tuition. Several dance academies welcome foreigners and can teach you the basics of dancing *a la Costarricense,* the better to prepare you for the nightlife. Expect to pay about $25 per month for weekly two-hour sessions, or $5-15 per hour for private lessons.

Danza Viva, tel. 253-3110, in San Pedro, offers courses in salsa and merengue, the two dances most popular at discos, as well as the *lambada,* the more formal *bolero* and *marcado,* the Caribbean mambo, and ballet, jazz, and modern dance. An offshoot of Danza Viva is **Merecumbé,** tel. 224-3531, fax 225-7687, in San Pedro, which specializes in popular dancing. It also has an outlet next to the U.S. Embassy in Rohrmoser, tel. 231-7496.

Academia de Bailes Latinos, tel. 233-8938 or 221-1624, fax 233-8670, in the Costa Rican Institute of Language and Latin Dance, Avenida Central, Calles 25/27, also conducts intensive courses in ballroom and formal dancing, as well as teaching you the latest disco moves. **Kinesis,** tel./fax 440-0852, in Alajuela, and the La Maga Bar in San José both teach tango.

dance music that gets you on your feet. Discos often stay open until dawn. Most apply some sort of dress code. Shorts are never allowed. Call ahead to check. Most discos charge a cover, generally about $2-5. Many bars—notably El Cuartel de la Boca—also have music and dancing.

Club Panda, on Paseo Colón, is popular with the surfing set because of the screen showing surfing videos; no cover charge except when live bands play. Also on Paseo Colón is **Members,** tel. 223-4911, in Centro Colón, which plays everything from rock to salsa, plus live music by the band Los Bandoleros. The dark and moody **Bar O'Key,** Calle 4, Avenidas 6/8, is also new. **New Leonardo's,** tel. 223-7310, is in the same building.

A favorite of the younger crowd is **Disco Salsa 54,** Calle 3, Avenidas 1/3, tel. 233-3814, with two discos in one. One favors romantic Latin sounds; the other is World Beat and techno. Live bands on Monday. The same owners operate **Zadidas,** tel. 221-4454, 200 meters north of the National Theater, playing techno and reggae. If Caribbean riffs are your thing, check out the **Showbar,** Calle 7 and Avenidas 1/2, which has reggae on Wednesday. **Dynasty,** Centro Comercial del Sur, near the Pacific Railway Station, tel. 226-5000, also plays reggae. This is the place to get down to James Brown, Hammer, and funk. **Parthenon** is another disco in Centro Comercial del Sur. Also downtown is **El Tunel de Tiempo,** Avenida Central, Calles 11/13, with a light show as loud as the music.

La Torre, Calle 7, Avenidas Central/1, also known as Tonite, is for the gay crowd, although everyone else is welcome. It's a popular dance spot, too, for women who don't want to be hassled by men trying to pick them up. Musical taste is heavy on funk and rap. High energy and fun!

The Centro Comercial El Pueblo, in Barrio Tournón, boasts several bars and discos. **Bar Tango Che Molinari,** tel. 226-6904, is a tiny, smoke-filled hole-in-the-wall that features hot-blooded Argentinian tangos. Opens at 8:30 p.m.; closed Sunday. **El Escondite de Morgan,** otherwise known as Jerry Morgan's Piano Bar, has—you guessed it—live piano music. **Los Balcones,** tel. 223-3704, is a barbecue restaurant that features live music. The Bolivian folk group Khrisol, the Peruvian group Musica Andea, and the Cuban group Nueva Trova often play in the small bar. No cover.

Cocoloco, tel. 222-8782, is one of the hottest spots in town, with two dance floors and live bands on weekdays. A two-hour comedy show is offered nightly at 6 p.m. Closed Monday and Sunday. **Visa a Cocoloco,** tel. 233-8145, 233-2309 or 222-8782, fax 233-6410, is a "passport" ($33) good for free admission to Chavetas (including beverages and snacks), Lukas (including dinner with wine), and Cocoloco (including beverages). Virtually next door is **Infinito,** tel. 223-2195, with a choice of three dance floors playing salsa, rock, and Latin sounds. **La Plaza Disco Club,** tel. 233-5516, in front of El Pueblo, has live music every Thursday, where you can practice merengue and salsa on its massive dance floor.

CINEMAS

More than a dozen movie houses show American and other foreign movies—often in English with Spanish subtitles, although many are dubbed into Spanish. (Movies with Spanish soundtracks are advertised as *hablado en Español*.) *La Nación* and the *Tico Times* list current movies. Most movie houses charge $1.50-4. They generally have large screens and—good news for nonsmokers—are just about the only places in San José where smoking is not permitted.

The cinema in Multi-Plaza near Escazú has alternate hours, such as mornings and midnight. **Sala Garbo,** Calle 28 and Avenida 2, shows avant-garde international movies. **Metro Metropolitan,** Calle Central, Avenidas 6/8, and **Cine 2000,** Calle 9, Avenidas 8/10, screen adult movies ($2.50).

THEATER

Theatergoing is still light years from the status-mongering of Broadway, but San José is a theatrical cornucopia, with a score of professional theaters putting on original plays as well as classics and traditional Spanish productions. Josefinos' support a viable fringe—often called "theater-in-the-round"—serving more controversial fare.

By Broadway standards, prices are ludicrously low—rarely much more than $2. Theaters are tiny and often sell out early. Book early. Performances normally run Thurs.-Sun. and begin at 7:30 or 8 p.m. Most performances are in Spanish. The **Little Theater Group,** tel. 234-3643, supposedly the oldest English-language theatrical group in Latin America, presents English-language musicals and comedies throughout the year in the Centro Cultural's Eugene O'Neill Theater and occasionally at the Teatro Laurence Olivier.

The *Tico Times* offers a complete listing of current productions, including whether they're in Spanish or English; also see the "Viva" section in *La Nación*.

MUSIC, DANCING, AND *FOLKLÓRICA*

Folklórica

One of the most colorful "cabaret" shows in town is the **Fantasía Folklórica,** which depicts the traditions, legends, and history of Costa Rica's seven provinces. The spectacular dance program blends traditional Costa Rican dances with avant-garde choreography and stunning stage backdrops. Every Tuesday, 8 p.m., at the Melico Salazar Theater, Avenida 2, Calle Central, tel. 222-2653. Tickets at the door: $3-9.

A similar show—**Folklórico**—is put on by the Compañía de Danza Folklórica Zurquí every Thursday at 9 p.m. at the Bon Vivant Restaurant in the Hotel Herradura, tel. 239-0033.

Pueblo Antigua, tel. 231-2001, fax 296-2212, hosts a "traditional Costa Rica evening" every Fri.-Sun. at 6:30 p.m., with marimba music and folkloric dancing ($28, or $35 with hotel transfers).

Classical
April through December is the season for the **National Symphony Orchestra,** which performs at the Teatro Nacional on Thursday and Friday (8 p.m.) and Sunday mornings (10:30 a.m.). You can hobnob with cafe society at the symphony or opera for as little as $2, or as much as $20 for the best seats.

The Centro Cultural Costarricense Norteamericano, tel. 225-9433, presents the **U.S. University Musicians Series,** with concerts each month. The **National Lyric Opera Company** (Compañía de Lírica Nacional), presents operas, June through mid-August, in the Teatro Melico Salazar.

Live Music
Popular local bands to watch out for include Cantoamerica, a fusion band blending salsa, calypso, and reggae. Jaque Mate, La Mafia, Los Bandoleros, La Pandilla, and Marfil are also popular salsa bands. For jazz lovers, there's Oveja Negra, which blends jazz with a Latin beat. The most well-known and well-loved rock band is Liverpool.

Jazz: The nascent jazz scene is now fairly robust. In addition to places mentioned above, check out the **Shakespeare Gallery,** next door to Sala Garbo on Calle 28 and Avenida 2. The cognoscenti head to **Emilia Romagna,** tel. 233-2843, an elegant restaurant-cum-jazz club 25 meters west of Pollos Kentucky on Paseo Colón; open Mon.-Sat. from 8 p.m.; no cover, two-drink minimum). **Charleston,** Calle 9, Avenidas 2/4, features live jazz on weekends. Bambu Jazz plays at **El Tablado,** opposite Pollos Kentucky on Avenida Central) on Monday; weekends feature live Latin jazz (Nueva Canción). And

Bromelia's Cafe and Grill, Calle 23 and Avenida Central, tel. 221-3848, offers live jazz nightly 8-11 p.m.; no cover. **La Habanera,** tel. 233-8383, features live jazz and classical music in a suitably jazzed-up classical colonial structure on Avenida 9 and Calles 11/13, behind Casa Amarilla; 8:30 p.m. until the last guest leaves. And **El Caracol,** on Calle 16 between Avenidas 1/3, tel. 253-4407, offers occasional jazz in a laid-back and often crowded atmosphere.

Soda Blues, Calle 11, Avenidas 10/12, tel. 221-8368, features blues, jazz, and R&B sponsored by a zany Brit-Yank duo, Jimmy Forstner and David Scott, horn-tooting owners. Dave and Jim have been in the music business for more than 30 years (Scott opened London's infamous Pink Panther Club at the tender age of 16!). The club is already one of the most happenin' scenes in town.

Other Music: Boleros de Rafa, Centro Cocorí, Los Yoses, tel. 225-6259, has *bolero* singers and dancing, Wed.-Saturday. For rock, head to **Classic Rock and Roll,** 50 meters north of Antojitos restaurant in Tibas, which bills itself as the only rock and roll bar in Costa Rica. **Aida's Sala Musical,** opposite the Barrio California's Pizza Hut, has traditional Costa Rican serenades.

You can sing your own song at **King's Garden Restaurant,** tel. 255-3838, where *karaoke* is going down big with the local yuppie crowd.

Something Different
Candil Cultural Center, Calle 13, Avenida 7 bis, offers a medley of entertainment: everything from poetry readings, art classes, and New Age workshops to live music and screenings of hit movies (7 p.m.), preceded by coffee hour; it's open Mon.-Fri. 2-9 p.m., Saturday 9 a.m.-9 p.m.

Boliche, tel. 234-2777, one block south of the Centro Cultural Norteamericano in San Pedro, has 10-pin bowling for $7 per hour. And the **Centro Cultural Norteamericano** hosts conferences, English-language films, and miscellaneous entertainment.

And **Formula 1,** tel. 285-2371, fax 285-2413, is an indoor adults-only go-kart track (with cafe and video game room) in Alto de Guadelupe, northeast of San José, on the road to Coronado. The go-carts have four-speed 160-cc engines and reach 60 kph. Open weekdays 4-11 p.m.

and weekends noon-11 p.m. ($2 entrance, $6 per 10 minutes race).

CASINOS

If two fiery-throated hummingbirds move roughly in the same line, Costa Rica punters are likely to place a bet on which one will reach a certain point first. Gambling is second nature in Costa Rica. Every street corner has two or three touts selling tickets for the national lottery. And virtually every major hotel is home to a small casino. They're not the sophisticated palaces of Monte Carlo or the massive establishments of Las Vegas, but the familiar sounds of roulette, craps, and blackjack continue well into the night.

Rummy, canasta (a form of roulette, but with a basket containing balls replacing the roulette wheel), craps, and *tute* (a local variant of poker) are the casino games of choice. Slot machines, once prohibited by law, have grown popular, too. Bingo is a favorite pecuniary pursuit in less cos-

JOHN ANDERSON

flirting with Lady Luck at the Club Cariari

CASINOS

Casino Amstel, Hotel Amstel, Calle 7, Avenidas 1/3, tel. 222-4622, ext. 32

Casino Aurola, Hotel Aurola, Calle 5, Avenida 5, tel. 233-9490

Casino Aurora, Avenida 5, Calles 5/7l, tel. 257-6344

Casino Club Colonial, Avenida 1, Calles 9/11, tel. 258-2807

Casino Concorde, Best Western Irazú, La Uruca, tel. 232-7910

Casino Gran Hotel, Gran Hotel, Avenida Central, Calles 1/3, tel. 223-2573

Casino Real, Camino Real Inter-Continental, Escazú, tel. 289-7000

Club Domino, Hotel Balmoral, Avenida Central, Calles 7/9, tel. 222-1103

Hotel Del Rey, Avenida 1, Calle 9, tel. 221-7272

Hotel Herradura, Ciudad Cariari, tel. 239-3022

Hotel Royal Garden, Avenida 2, Calle Central, tel. 257-0022

Meliá Cariari, Ciudad Cariari, tel. 233-0022

Meliá Confort Corobicí, Sabana Norte, tel. 232-8122

Quality Hotel Centro Colón, Avenida 1, Calles 38/40, tel. 257-2580

San José Palacio, Hotel San José Palacio, La Uruca, tel. 220-2034

mopolitan terrain. Government oversight supposedly remains relatively weak, and house rules and payoffs are stacked far more heavily in the house's favor than they are in the United States.

The atmospheric casinos of **Club Colonial** and **Royal Garden** will evoke images of a Humphrey Bogart movie. Some, such as **Club Domino,** serve free drinks and *bocas.* That of the **Hotel Del Rey** is the liveliest (open 24 hours). Plusher casinos in the expensive hotels have dress codes.

SHOPPING

With the exception of arts and crafts, shopping in San José lacks scope. If you want to live like a local, head for the Mercado Central, San José's answer to London's Petticoat Lane. Shop hours are usually Mon.-Sat. 8 a.m.-6 p.m. Many places close at noon for a siesta; a few stay open until late evening. Most shops close on Sunday, and many on Saturday, too.

Photography and Film

A **Kodak** office is next to U-Haul Rent-a-Car, on Paseo Colón.

For specific locations of air-conditioned **Fuji** outlets, which sell fresh film and instamatic cameras, call the central office at 222-2222. Or try **Equipos Fotográficos**, tel. 233-0176, on Avenida 3, Calles 3/5; or **Dima**, tel. 222-3969, on Avenida Central, Calles 3/5.

If you need urgent repairs, **Taller de Equipos Fotográficos**, Avenida Central, Calles 3/5, tel. 223-1146, is recommended. And **Canon** has an authorized camera-repair shop on Avenida 3, Calles 3/5. Kodak and Agfa have photographic labs in large cities throughout Costa Rica.

If you need to buy film in San José, check the expiry date; it may be outdated or may have been sitting in the sun for months on end.

See the On the Road chapter for general advice on photography and film in tropical Costa Rica.

Books

Chispas Books, Calle 7 and Avenida Central/1, tel. 223-2240, fax 224-9278, has the widest variety of books in English, emphasizing travel, nature, and science books—including Moon Travel Handbooks—but also with novels and nonfiction. Also check the **Travelers Stores,** Calle Central, Avenida 3, tel. 257-0766; **Librería Trejos,** Avenida Central, Calle 13/13 bis, tel. 256-2942, which stocks many travel guidebooks at prices generally 25% below those elsewhere in town; and **Mora Books,** in the Omni Building on Avenida , Calles 3/5, tel. 383-8385, which also sells magazines and maps.

Also check out **Librería Internacional** with locations in San Pedro, tel. 253-9553, and at Multi-Plaza near Escazú; it has a good range of nature books and guidebooks plus general reading in several languages.

The largest book selection in Spanish is at **Librería Lehmann,** Avenida Central and Calles 1/3, tel. 223-2122. Also try **Librería Universal,** Avenida Central and Calles Central/1, tel. 222-

2222. **Staufer Books** has two stores, one in La Uruca, tel. 232-0810, the other on Calle 37 in Los Yoses, tel. 224-5170.

There are plenty of bookstores (most dealing in academic texts written in Spanish) on Calle José Maró Muúoz leading to the university in San Pedro. **Gambit Books,** tel. 283-0603, nearby at Calle 37, has books in English. The Multi-Plaza Mall in Escazú has two good bookstores upstairs.

The Bookshop closed its doors in 1997, as did Book Traders.

Newspapers and Magazines

Most major hotel gift stores sell international favorites. Adolescents hawk the day's *Miami Herald, New York Times,* and *USA Today* at the Café Parisienne, in front of the Gran Hotel. Once you've finished reading, they'll buy the paper back from you for half price. The **Candy Shop,** around the corner on the north side of the Plaza de la Cultura, sells a range of English-language newspapers and magazines, as does **Librería Lehmann** on the second floor (see above). **La Casa de las Revistas** has outlets at Calle Central, Avenidas 4/6, and Calle 7, Avenidas 1/3, selling a wide range of Spanish and English-language magazines. **Chispas Books** and **Mora Books** also sell English-language magazines (see above).

Maps

Check the bookstores listed above for a variety of tourist maps, notably Chispas, Lehmann's, Librería Universal, and Librería Trejos. You can also obtain detailed topographical and city maps from the **Instituto Geográfica Nacional** (National Geographic Institute), Avenida 20, Calles 9/11, tel. 257-7798, ext. 26-30. The Institute is to the left inside the gates of the Ministerio de Obras Públicas, with a sign reading Mapas. Hours: Mon.-Fri. 8:30-11:30 a.m. A bus marked "Barrio La Cruz" departs from Avenida 2 at Parque Central.

Food

Within the warren of the **Mercado Central,** Calles 6/8, Avenidas Central/1, are stands selling poultry, flowers, meat, fish, medicinal herbs, fresh produce, coffee, etc. (closed Sunday). An equally colorful alternative across the way is **Mercado Borbón,** Calle 8, Avenidas 3/5. A farmers' market

SHOPPING WITH A CONSCIENCE

Think twice before buying something exotic: the item may be banned by U.S. Customs and, if so, you could be fined. Even if legal to import, consider whether your purchase is an ecological sin. In short, shop with a conscience! Don't buy:

- Combs, jewelry, or other items made from tortoise shells.
- Coral, coral items, or shells. Costa Rica's coral reefs are being gradually destroyed. And every shell taken from a beach is one less for the next person to enjoy.
- Jewelry, artwork, or decorated clothes made of feathers. The bird may well have been shot simply for its plumage—and it may well be endangered.
- Furs from jaguars, ocelots, etc. Such furs are illegal. Your vanity isn't worth the life of such magnificent and endangered creatures.
- Think twice, too, about buying tropical hardwood products. Help protect Costa Rica's forests.

For more information, contact the **U.S. Fish and Wildlife Service,** Dept. of the Interior, Washington, D.C. 20240, which puts out a booklet, *Buyer Beware;* or the **U.S. Customs Service,** 1301 Constitution Ave., Washington, D.C. 20229.

(feria del agricultor) is held every Saturday morning on the west side of Plaza Víquez, Calles 7/9, Avenidas 16-20. Try to get there before 7 a.m. for the best buys.

Bakeries

San José is replete with good bakeries. **Pastelería Francesca,** Calle 30 and Paseo Colón; **Giacomin,** Calle 2 and Avenidas 3/5; and **Pastelería Don Simon,** Calle 28 and Paseo Colón, are among the best. Also see **Cafes and Pastry Shops** under "Food," above.

Coffee

You're gonna want to take coffee home. Every souvenir stores sells premium packaged coffee. When buying these, make sure the package is marked *puro.* Otherwise the coffee will already be laced with enough sugar to make even the most ardent sugar-lover turn green. **La Esquina del Café,** Avenida 9, Calle 3 bis, tel. 233-4560, fax 221-1048, sells a wide variety of gourmet coffees as well as roasters, *chorreadors,* traditional cotton strainers on a wooden frame), and other paraphernalia. Free tastings to go with pastries! You can also buy whole beans—albeit not the finest export quality—roasted before your eyes at the Mercado Central and at **El Trebol,** Calle 8, Avenidas Central/1. Ask for whole beans, otherwise you'll end up with superfine grounds. One pound of beans costs about $1. **Café Gourmet,** Avenida 9, Calle 3, also specializes in all things coffee-related.

Liquor

I always save space in my rucksack for a bottle of Café Rica, the local equivalent of Kahlúa, and *guaro,* the local sugarcane drink that makes another great souvenir. Prices at *pulperías* per bottle are four or five times more than you'll pay at a supermarket such as Mas x Menos.

Handicrafts

San José is replete with arts and crafts, such as reproduction pre-Columbian gold jewelry, hammocks, woodcarvings, and the famous brightly painted miniature oxcarts. Most hotels of substance have gift stores. One of the best is the **Boutique Annmarie** in the Hotel Don Carlos, tel. 221-6063, an Aladdin's Cave of quality arts and crafts, including Panamanian *molas* and silk-screen scarves by Bandanna Republic.

The Plaza de la Cultura no longer has a crafts market. Instead, the "unlicensed" vendors have been moved to **Mercado de Artesanías Nacionales** behind the Iglesia Soledad on Calle 11, Avenidas 4/6, which teems with colorful stalls selling T-shirts, paintings, trinket jewelry, and superb-quality hammocks (excellent bargains at $20-30). Sundays are best. Another craft market is supposedly held daily at **Parque de las Garantías Sociales** on Calle 5. Many of the items—from jewelry and miniature oxcarts to chairs and carved gourds—are sold by the artists themselves. And the **Mercado Central** has a panoply of leatherwork and other artisans' stalls.

Specialty handicraft stores include **Atmósfera,** Calle 5, Avenidas 1/3, tel. 222-4322, where a gallery on the second floor displays fantastic Indian masks, carved fantasy beasts, and paintings. Among my favorite items are the brightly painted ceramic buses laden with people (about $7). Next door, **Suríksa Gallery,** Calle 5, Avenida 3, tel. 222-0129, sells top-quality woodcarvings and furniture, including the works of renowned North American artists/carpenters Barry Biesanz and Jay Morrison. The upscale **La Galería,** Calle 1, Avenidas Central/1, tel. 223-2110, has a fine selection of quality handicrafts and also features Barry Biesanz woodworks along with reproduction pre-Columbian 14-karat gold jewelry. Also good is the artisan's guild, **Artesanía CANAPI,** Avenida 2, Calle 11, tel. 221-3342.

A handful of handicrafts stores cluster together on two levels at **La Casona,** a complex at Calle Central and Avenidas Central/1. The cross-section of crafts include Guatemalan textiles, woodcrafts from Honduras, and the popular Costa Rican nativity figures and Christmas crèches in ceramics and wood. **ANDA,** Avenida Central, Calles 5/7, tel. 233-3340, also has a fine collection of Indian artifacts—gourds, pottery, maracas, and fantastic balsa-wood masks—as well as native Costa Rican weavings and ceramic tea sets. **Sol Maya,** Avenida Central, Calles 18/20, tel. 221-0864, specializes in Guatemalan textiles and other Mayan crafts.

Centro Comercial El Pueblo has many high-quality art galleries and crafts stores. **Alba Art Gallery,** tel. 239-4324, sells fabulous pieces by Central America's leading painters (works run up to $10,000). The **Galería Valanti,** tel. 253-1659, specializes in Latin American art.

Farther out, in the Los Yoses district, is **Galerías Casa Alameda,** a touch of Beverly Hills come to the tropics. Fine art mingles with fashion in this upscale commercial center that includes **Galería Real** art gallery and **Villa del Este,** tel. 224-1261, selling Peruvian and Mexican silver work, pewter, Turkish rugs, and more.

There are many other places to consider, including the **Tienda de la Naturaleza,** Calle 20, Avenidas 3/5, operated by the Fundación Neotrópica; and **Costa Rica Expeditions Travelers Store,** Avenida 3 and Calle Central.

The suburb of Moravia, five km northeast of downtown, is a major center for arts and crafts, with a wide array of shops. **Las Garzas Handicraft Market,** tel. 236-0037, 100 meters south of the Red Cross Station, contains 28 indoor craft

stores. The **Caballo Blanco,** tel. 235-6797, on the plaza, is also recommended. Also try **La Rueda** and **La Tinaja,** tel. 325-7787, as well as the **Palette Souvenirs** arts-and-crafts gallery, tel. 235-3464. Most stores close on Sunday. If you need cash, you can get an advance against your Visa or MasterCard at **Credomatic,** half-a-block south of St. Francis College, tel. 235-3184. A bus departs San José from Avenida 3, Calles 3/5; a microbus reportedly departs from Avenida 7, Calle 6.

To watch a jigsaw puzzle of stained glass being magically turned into art, head to **Gunter Noah Poppe's workshop,** tel./fax 253-8574, 200 meters north of La Luz restaurant in the Barrio Escalante suburb; or **Talleres de Participación Creativos,** tel. 244-0451, in Santo Domingo de Heredia, 75 meters east of Rayo Azul supermarket. Poppe's work, which graces the windows of many churches, sells for about $1,000 per square meter.

And *do* buy a pair of comfy rope sandals made by Sandalias de Costa Rica, tel./fax 433-9317, e-mail: poppyg@sol.racsa.co.cr, and sold at outlets nationwide.

Clothing

If you admire the homely Tico look, check out the **Mercado Central** on Calle 6 and Avenida 1, where you'll find embroidered *guayabero* shirts and blouses and cotton *campesino* hats. **La Choza Folklórica** at Avenida 3, Calle 1, specializes in replicas of national costumes. You can also buy Costa Rican dresses (bright red, blue, and green designs on white cotton) at **Bazaar Central Souvenir,** Calle Central, Avenida 3. A good place to find the handmade appliquéd blouses and fabrics—*molas*—from the Drake's Bay region and the San Blas Islands of Panamá is **Antic,** Edificio las Arcadas, Avenida 2 and Calle 1, next door to the Gran Hotel, tel. 233-4630.

Leather: Costa Rica produces high-quality leatherwork, including purses, attaché cases, and cowboy boots. The suburb of Moravia is well-known for producing leather goods. If you're shopping in town, try **Galería del Cuero,** Avenida 1, Calle 5, tel. 223-2034; **Marroquinería Del Río,** Calle 9, Avenidas Central/2, tel. 238-2883; and **Artesanías Malety,** Avenida 1, Calles 1/3, tel. 221-1670.

You may well be tempted, too, to buy a snazzy pair of handmade leather boots. Shoemakers abound in San José, and almost everywhere downtown you can come upon rows of boots made from 50 or so different leathers, including dandy two-tones. Stay clear of snakeskin and crocodile skins. A bevy of high-quality shoemakers can be found on Paseo Colón and Avenida 3 between Calles 24 and 26.

The best places for upscale clothing are **Mall San Pedro** in San Pedro, and the **Multi-Plaza** in Escazú. Both are replete with upscale, brand-name boutiques.

Jewelry

Here are trustworthy places selling Colombian emeralds and semiprecious stones, 14-carat gold earrings, brooches, and more, along with fabulous pre-Columbian re-creations: **Esmeraldas y Diseños,** in Sabana Norte; **La Casa del Indio,** Avenida 2, Calles 5/7, tel. 223-0306; and **Esmeraldas y Creaciones,** tel. 280-0808, near Spoon's restaurant in Los Yoses.

Artisan's markets sell attractive ethnic-style earrings and bracelets. Here, much of what you'll see on the street is actually gold-washed, not solid gold. For semiprecious stones check out **Blue Diamond,** on the south side of Parque Morazán.

Cigars

Costa Rica is a prime spot to buy Cuban cigars. (The best option, of course, is just to fly to Havana and buy your cigars at the source.) Otherwise, head to **Café Havana,** tel. 228-6735, in the Centro Montealegre in Escazú. It has a wide selection of choice Cuban cigars, a cozy lounge where you can enjoy your smoke over a compatible drink, and educational cigar nights on Tuesday. **Havanas de Costa Rica,** tel. 383-6835, fax 221-8690, one block north of Parque Morazán, is a modestly well-stocked store run by Cuba's own Habanos S.A. corporation. It also has an outlet, tel. 224-1769, 50 meters east of Centro Comercial. They sell individual Cohibas for $15 (Siglo Uno's) or $26 (Lancero); a box of Montecristo Uno's costs $300. However, I've heard reports that some of the brands sold may not be the real McCoy.

The **Cigar Shoppe,** tel. 257-5021, fax 256-4306, in the foyer of Diana's Inn at Calle 5 and

Avenida 3, has premium Cuban cigars, but at slightly higher prices. Here you'll pay $122 for a box of 25 Romeo y Julieta Flores and $595 for Romeo y Julieta Churchill's—about the cost of airfare to Havana *and* the same cigars purchased there!

The **Habanos Smoking Club** in the Calle Reál Shopping Center in San Pedro, tel. 224-5227, fax 283-4593, also sells premium Cuban cigars. It has a walk-in humidor and a cocktail bar, and offers seminars. It's open Mon.-Sat. 10 a.m.-2 a.m.

Never buy cigars on the streets. They're almost assuredly fakes, however impressive the sealed box.

Miscellaneous

Rugs: Cecilia Tristán Telles and her sister Ana Gabriela Tristán custom-make rugs at their **C-Tris Alfombras factory,** tel. 273-3554 or 273-3594, fax 273-3624, 100 meters east of Plaza del Sol, in the hills of San Ramón Tres Ríos, in Curridabat. The two can make superb, heavy-duty rugs to match any design you give them, with a 3-D effect to boot, for less than $200 per square meter.

Guitars and Violins: Guzman Mora conjures classical compositions from wood. His Spanish-style guitars sell for about $80. You can try them out in his showroom—**Aristides Guzman Mora, Ltd.,** tel. 223-0682—in Tibas. Alternately, **Martin Prada,** tel. 221-8870, continues a family heritage of handcrafting world-class violins in his San José studio (many members of Costa Rica's acclaimed National Symphony play Prada instruments).

SPORTS AND RECREATION

Sabana Park has baseball diamonds, basketball courts, jogging and walking trails, soccer fields, tennis and volleyball courts, plus an Olympic-size swimming pool (open noon-2 p.m.; $3) and showers.

Bowling

El Boliche, tel. 234-2777, is the local bowling alley in Los Yoses. It's 100 meters south of the Centro Cultural Norteamericano. It costs $8 per hour.

Gyms and Health Clubs

Most upscale hotels have Nautilus and spa facilities: Hotel Confort Corobicí and Hotel Palma Reál are noteworthy. Most gyms are for private membership only. See "Gimnasios" in the telephone directory.

Racquetball/Squash

Club Squash Monterreal, tel. 232-6777, in Sabana Norte; **Club Olímpico,** tel. 228-7017, in Escazú; **Top Squash,** tel. 220-1108, in Sabana Sur; and **San José Indoor Club,** tel. 225-9344, in San Pedro all have racquetball courts. You'll need to become a member.

Bicycling

Contact the Federación Costarricense de Ciclismo, tel. 222-1568, which organizes group cycling. You rarely see bicycles in use on San José's streets, with good reason. It's plain suicide! **Mountain Biking Costa Rica,** tel. 255-0914, rents mountain bikes for those heading out of town. There are numerous bicycle shops concentrated in San Pedro and on the road to Pavas, in Rohrmoser.

Golf

The **Meliá Cariari Hotel & Country Club,** tel. 239-0022, fax 239-2803, has a championship 18-hole golf course hewn from a former coffee plantation about 10 miles west of town. Nearby, the **Marriott** has a driving range and putting green. A new course was slated to open at Santa Ana, west of San José in 1998-99.

Running

Sabana Park's trails provide a peaceful, traffic- and pollution-free environment for running. It has showers. Avoid the streets. San José has a chapter of the internationally famous Hashhouse Harriers, tel. 228-0769, which organizes cross-country runs.

Tennis

You'll find public courts in Sabana Park. You must be a guest to play on hotel courts, or a member to play at private clubs. Private clubs include the Costa Rica Country Club, tel. 228-9333; Costa Rica Tennis Club, tel. 232-1266; and San José Indoor Club, tel. 225-9344.

Spectator Sports

Soccer: Watching a soccer game in Costa Rica is quite an experience. Ticos are passionate and fanatically partisan about soccer. On the day of a major game, Josefinos throw their usual decorum out the window. The San José team plays at the Estadio Nacional, in Sabana Park; call 221-7677 for a schedule of games. Its archrival, Saprissa, plays in Tibas; call 235-3591.

You can ask to join in a soccer game in Sabana Park, but be aware that Ticos—who are skilled players almost to a man (women's soccer is unheard of in Costa Rica)—take no prisoners. The aim is to win.

Softball: *Bolo lento* or *sofbol* games are played each weekend in Sabana Park; see the "Síntesis Deportiva" section of *La Nación* for schedules. You're free to join in.

SERVICES AND INFORMATION

MONEY

San José has no shortage of **banks,** but they're hardly worth the hassle for small sums (for speed and ease, I recommend using your hotel cashier, which gives about the same exchange rates). Hours vary. Most banks have a separate foreign exchange counter, usually guaranteeing speedier service. The **Banco de San José,** Calle Central, Avenidas 3/5, tel. 256-9911, is the swiftest and most efficient place to change money or cash traveler's checks. The notori-

ously slow state-run **Banco Nacional de Costa Rica,** tel. 287-9000, with branch banks scattered throughout the city, will change German deutsche marks. **Banco Metropolitan,** Avenida 2, Calle Central, also specializes in foreign currency transactions, as does the **Compañía Financiera de Londres,** Calle Central and Avenida Central, tel. 222-8155. You'll need your passport and a good deal of patience for all bank transactions, especially at the Banco Nacional de Costa Rica. **Citibank,** tel. 296-1494, has an office in Sabana, as does **Scotiabank,** tel. 257-6868.

Credit Card Cash Advances: Most banks will give cash advances against your Visa card, and many banks now have **ATM machines** that issue cash advances against Visa. **BanCrecen,** tel. 296-5301 or (800) 882-2626, has ATMs throughout the city. However, very few will grant a cash advance for MasterCard. An exception is the **Banco de San José. Credomatic,** tel. 257-4744, with outlets citywide, and **TAM Travel Agency,** Calle 1 and Avenidas Central/1, also pay against MasterCard and American Express. **American Express,** tel. 257-1646, 257-0155 or 800-TAR-JETA (800-827-5382), has an office at Calle Central, Avenidas 3/5; open Mon.-Fri. 8 a.m.-7 p.m., Saturday 9 a.m.-1 p.m.

The Credomatic office, Calle Central, Avenidas 3/5, tel. 257-0155, is the only branch that will assist you with card replacement for Visa/MasterCard. It's open Mon.-Fri. 8 a.m.-7 p.m., Saturday 9 a.m.-1 p.m. It's a time-consuming process. **Diner's Club International** is represented by Scotiabank, tel. 257-2351 or 24 hours at 257-7878, at the corner of Avenida 1, Calle 2; open Mon.-Fri. 8 a.m.-5 p.m.

Exchange houses *(casas de cambio)* were closed down several years ago. **Moneychangers,** though illegal, congregate around Calle Central and Avenida Central. They'll call out "dólares" or "cambio" (change) in hushed tones as you pass: moneychanging is strictly illegal, and there are regular police sweeps. Beware of fake notes, and always count your money when it's given to you. It's not worth the hassle!

You can send and receive money by wire transfer via **Western Union,** tel. 283-6336, which has offices throughout the city, including Calle 9, Avenidas 2/4, and Paseo Colón, Calles 36/38. Alternately, you can send and receive international money orders via **GIRO** at the main post office at Calle 2, Avenidas 1/3.

LAUNDRIES

Self-service laundromats *(lavanderías)* are still few and far between. Most laundries offer a wash and dry service (about $4 per load). Downtown, try **Sixaola,** Avenida 2, Calles 7/9, tel. 221-2111, or **Lavamex,** Calle 8, Avenidas Central/1, tel. 258-2303. Sixaola, central office tel.

225-5333, has outlets elsewhere in the city. Also try **Sol y Fiesta Lavaropa,** Calle 9, Avenidas 8/10, tel. 257-7151; open Mon.-Sat. 8 a.m.-7 p.m. American-owned **Lavanderías de Costa Rica,** tel. 237-6273, will pick up and deliver ($4.50); cold wash costs $1.75, hot wash $2.25, dry $1.75.

East of downtown, **Betamatic,** Calle 47, Avenida 2, near Burger King in Los Yoses, offers both self-service or drop-off and pickup service ($1.50 per kg). It closes at 4:30 p.m. for self-service, though you can drop off laundry until 6 p.m. (closed Sunday). **Lavandería Lava-Mas,** in San Pedro, tel. 225-1645, is on the same street, between Calles 43 and 45, next to Spoon's. Nearby, too, is **Burbujas,** tel. 224-9822, with coin-operated machines.

West of downtown, on Paseo Colón, is **La Margarita,** tel. 222-5094, at Calle 36. To the north, in Tibas, is **Lavandería Americana,** tel. 236-8724.

Dry cleaning is a more risky business: you drop off your clothes and keep your fingers crossed. Most *lavanderías* offer dry cleaning.

Most hotels can arrange to do your laundry with 24 hours notice—usually as much for two or three items as a whole load will cost elsewhere! Many budget hotels have a laundry sink and drying area (don't wash your clothes in the large water tank; instead draw water from the tank and wash your clothes in the sink).

LIBRARIES

The National Library or **Biblioteca Nacional,** at Avenida 3, Calles 15/17, tel. 221-2436, has more than 100,000 volumes. It is open to foreigners. The main index and information desk is upstairs on the second floor. The national newspaper collection is here. Another useful source is the **Biblioteca Universidad de Costa Rica,** tel. 225-7372, at the university in San Pedro. The **Mark Twain Library** part of the Centro Cultural Norteamericano, tel. 225-9433, on Calle Negritos in Los Yoses has English-language books and reference materials. You must be a member to check books out, but it's open to the public for reference; Mon.-Fri. 9 a.m.-7 p.m., Saturday 9 a.m.-noon.

MAIL AND TELECOMMUNICATIONS

The main post office, tel. 223-9766, or **Correo Central,** is on Calle 2 between Avenidas 1 and 3. Take the middle entrance to buy stamps; the postal slots are on the left. It's open Mon.-Fri. 8 a.m.-5 p.m. It has a 24-hour stamp machine. You can also buy stamps and post your mail at front desks at upscale hotels. There are no other mail boxes in San José to my knowledge.

Getting incoming mail is very time consuming. To collect incoming mail, go to window 17 through the entrance nearest Avenida 1. You'll need to bring identification. Mail should be addressed to you using your name as it appears on your passport or other I.D., c/o Lista Correos, Correos Central, San José. There's a small charge (about 25 cents) per letter.

You can send faxes and telegrams at the main post office, at the booth marked CORTEL Fax. After filling out a fax form, take it to the main lobby and follow the arrow marked Servicio de Fax upstairs to the telex office. The fax office is in an anteroom. A clerk will send your fax. **KitCom** (Keep In Touch Communications), kitcom@sol.racsa.co.cr, on the second floor of the OTEC Building, on Calle 3, 175 meters north of the Plaza de la Cultura, has a message board. You can send or receive by e-mail, fax, or telephone. Alternately, to send and/or receive a telegram or fax, go to the ICE's **Radiográfica** office, one block west of the National Theater, at Calle 1 and Avenida 1; or RACSA's **Telecommunications Center,** tel. 287-0515, fax 223-1609, at Calle 1 and Avenida 5. You can also send faxes from most hotels.

American Express cardholders can have mail sent to them c/o the **American Express** office, tel. 257-1646 or 800-TARJETA (800-827-5382) at Calle Central, Avenidas 3/5. In the U.S., call (800) 528-2121. **Trans-Air Express Interlink,** tel. 232-2544, lets you mail or receive up to four

pounds of mail a month for $15; the **Costa Rica Residents Association,** tel. 233-8068, offers a courier service to Miami; and **Aerocasillas,** Apdo. 4567, San José 1000, tel. 255-4567, fax 257-1187, also offers courier service ($25 per month for accounts).

Business Centers

The **Executive Center,** tel. 290-5501, fax 290-5502, e-mail: solution@sol.racsa.co.cr, at La Sabana Bldg. 7, offers full business services, including office and meeting room rental, computer rental, photocopying, and secretarial services. You can also make discounted telephone calls, and receive and send faxes and e-mail messages. There are showers. Open Mon.-Fri. 8:30 a.m.-5:30 p.m.; other times by appointment.

The **Business Center,** tel. 257-1138, fax 257-1345, has a message service; you can send or receive mail, faxes, or phone messages. It offers complete business services, including secretaries.

MEDICAL SERVICES

There are plenty of hospitals and clinics to choose from. The privately run **Clínica Bíblica** is the best hospital in town, and is recommended. The public **Hospital San Juan de Dios,** Paseo Colón and Calle 16, is the most centrally located medical facility. The **Children's Hospital** (Hospital Nacional de Niños) is adjacent, to the west. Many private clinics are concentrated around the hospitals.

Emergencies

The following **private hospitals** have emergency medical facilities available for foreigners at reasonable rates: Clínica Bíblica, Clínica Católica, Clínica Americana, and Clínica Santa Rita. Clínica Bíblica reportedly accepts U.S. Medicare.

The following **public hospitals** can provide free emergency health care on the Social Security system: Calderón Guardia, Children's Hospital, Hospital Mexico, and San Juan de Dios.

TOURIST INFORMATION

ICT operates tourist information offices both in San José and the at airport. The ICT head office,

Apdo. 777, San José 1000, tel. 223-1733, fax 223-5452, e-mail: promoict@tourism-costarica. com, is at Avenida 4, Calles 5/7, on the eleventh floor. The information office is open Mon.-Fri. 8 a.m.-4 p.m. (The office beneath the Plaza de la Cultura closed in 1996; word in early 1998 was that it may soon be reopened.) In addition, dozens of hotels and travel and tour agencies throughout the city provide free tour information services.

TRAVEL AGENCIES

You'll find dozens of English-speaking travel agencies in central San José and in the lobbies of moderate and upscale hotels. They can arrange city tours, one- and multiday excursions, beach resort vacations, air transportation, etc. Most tours and excursions are operated by local tour companies, in which case you may wish to make your reservations direct. I've found **Costa Rica Expeditions,** tel. 257-0766, fax 257-1665, e-mail: crexped@sol.racsa.co.cr, at Avenida 3, Calle Central, to be very knowledgeable, helpful, and efficient.

Two recommended travel agencies of note are **Swiss Travel,** tel. 282-4896, and **TAM Travel,** tel. 256-0203, fax 221-8092. **Sin Limites,** tel. 280-5182, fax 225-9325, 200 meters east of Pollos Kentucky in Los Yoses, specializes in cheap airfares; it advertises the following sample one-way fares: Chicago ($250), Frankfurt ($382), Guatemala City ($170), London ($382), Los Angeles ($252), Mexico City ($170), and New York ($230).

TRANSPORTATION

GETTING THERE AND AWAY

By Air
See the accompanying chart **Juan Santamaría International Airport** for information on arriving at and departing from the San José's International Airport, 19 km west of town.

Pavas Airport (Tobías Bolaños), about four km southwest of town, is used for most domestic flights. Bus 14B runs from Avenida 1, Calles 16/18, and stops in Pavas, a short walk from the airport. A taxi will cost about $8 between the airport and downtown.

By Bus
Most provincial cities and towns are linked to San José by bus. Most buses to the outlying regions leave from the area referred to as Coca-Cola, centered on Calle 16 and Avenidas 1 and 3 (this is a rough area; be cautious). Buses for the Caribbean lowlands depart from the Gran Terminal Caribe, a splendid new bus station on Calle Central, between Avenidas 15/17.

By Car
Westbound from downtown San José, Paseo Colón feeds right onto the Pan-American Highway (Hwy. 1), which leads to Alajuela, Puntare-nas, and the Pacific coast. A tollbooth just east of the airport charges 60 *colones* (25 cents) per vehicle for westbound traffic only.

Eastbound from downtown, Calle 3 leads directly from the Guápiles Highway (Hwy. 32) for Puerto Limón and the Caribbean. Avenida 2 leads east via San Pedro to Cartago and the southern section of the Pan-Am Highway (Hwy. 2). There's a toll-booth (60 *colones*) about three km east of the suburb of San Pedro.

GETTING AROUND

Taxis
You can travel virtually anywhere within the city for less than $4. Fares are fixed by the government at 150 *colones* (60 cents) for the first km, and 65 *colones* for each additional kilometer. Rates are periodically adjusted. There's a 20% surcharge after 10 p.m.

By law taxi drivers must use their meters—*marias*—for journeys of less than 12 kilometers. Hardly anyone does, although most taxi drivers are fair. To be sure, establish the fare before getting in the cab or setting off. You're well within your rights to demand that the taxi driver use his meter. You do not tip taxi drivers in Costa Rica.

BEYOND COSTA RICA? THINK CUBA

So you want to explore farther afield? Guatemala? Panamá? Forget them. Try Cuba, a country as different from Costa Rica as chalk from cheese, and exhilarating to a degree that Costa Rica is not. Cuba is remarkably easy to get to from Costa Rica, with whom it has amicable ties.

Five hundred years after Christopher Columbus appeared on the horizon—and four decades after Cuba closed its doors to foreign tourists—tourism in the island nation is booming again. In 1997, about 1.3 million foreigners flocked to this Caribbean island of socialism and sensuality (far more visitors, in fact, than Costa Rica). Of those, at least 50,000 were U.S. citizens.

Cuba is made for tropical tourism: the diamond-dust beaches and bathtub-warm seas the colors of peacock feathers; the bottle-green mountains and jade valleys full of dramatic formations; the ancient cities (especially Havana—indisputably the most fascinating city between Miami and Maracaibo—and Trinidad) with their flower-bedecked balconies, rococo cathedrals, and elegant plazas; its cigar factories permeated with intoxicating aromas; and, above all, the sultriness and spontaneity of a country called "the most emotionally involving in the Western hemisphere."

Walking Havana's streets you sense you are living inside a romantic thriller. You don't want to sleep for fear of missing a vital experience. Before the Revolution, Havana had a reputation as a place of intrigue and tawdry romance. The whiff of conspiracy, the intimation of liaison, is still in the air.

Your first sense is of being caught in an eerie colonial-cum-1950s time warp. Fading signs evoke the decadent period when Cuba was a virtual colony of the United States. Finned gas guzzlers dating back to Detroit's heyday are everywhere, conjuring images of dark-eyed temptresses and men in Panama hats and white linen suits. Havana, now communist but still carnal, is peopled in fact by characters from the novels of Ernest Hemingway and Graham Greene. All the glamour of an abandoned stage set is there, patinated by age. For foreign visitors, it is heady stuff.

All this and more sends visitors into flights of ecstasy. Cuba is still intoxicating, still laced with the sharp edges and sinister shadows that made Federico García Lorca, the Spanish poet, write to his parents, "If I get lost look for me in Cuba," and that made Ernest Hemingway want "to stay here for ever."

What Uncle Sam Says

Most *yanquis* harbor the misimpression that it's illegal for U.S. citizens to visit Cuba. It's not. It's merely illegal to spend dollars there. In any event, no U.S. tourist has ever been prosecuted merely for visiting Cuba. Cubans have an open-door policy and play their part by abstaining from stamping passports, so Uncle Sam need never know. (The Cuban people welcome U.S. visitors with a warmth that transcends differences in ideology. For all the fist-shaking against Uncle Sam, there's no personal animosity.) In any event, taking a prepaid tour excursion to Cuba is entirely *legal!*

You won't be long in Costa Rica before noticing posters advertising excursions to Cuba. For example, **Tikal Tours** offers a three-night Havana package from $592 s, $517 d, with city tour and a visit to Varadero, Cuba's main beach resort. A week-long Havana package costs as little as $582 s, $505 d, depending on hotel. At press time, Tikal charged $399 roundtrip, San José-Havana, airfare only. Tikal has an office in the Hotel Habana Libre, tel. 537-33-3114, fax 537-33-3728. **Costa Rica Trails** plans to introduce motorcycling tours in Cuba.

LACSA flies to Havana on Monday, Wednesday and Friday. **Cubana** has flights on Wednesday and Sunday. And **Air Canada** flies to Havana from San José three times weekly.

All you need to enter Cuba is a passport and a tourist visa (issued on the spot by any of the airlines or tourist companies that offer excursions). You can travel freely throughout Cuba without restriction using rental cars or other means.

Complete information is provided in Christopher P. Baker's *Cuba Handbook*.

In mid-1995 the government set strict regulations. Taxi drivers must now have a business card with name, license plate, and other details.

Finding a taxi is usually no problem (there are more than 3,000), except during rush hour and when it's raining. One of the best places to find a taxi is Parque Central, where they line up on Avenida 2, and in front of the Gran Hotel and National Theater two blocks east (from where taxi drivers not using their meters may charge

JUAN SANTAMARÍA INTERNATIONAL AIRPORT

San José's Juan Santamaría International Airport, tel. 442-0241 or 441-0744, isn't in San José at all! It's on the ouskirts of Alajuela, 17 km west of San José. (Small charter planes and air-taxis use **Tobías Bolaños Airport**—tel. 232-2820—in Pavas, about four km west of San José).

At press time, a four-year airport expansion program was underway, to include the relocation of the airline check-in counters (renowned for their notoriously cramped quarters), a new terminal, new boarding arms, and a reorganization of passenger arrival and departure routes. A new terminal for charter flights was slated.

Arrival
Immigration proceedings take no more than 10-15 minutes, though the wait for baggage can be considerably longer.

Downstairs, immediately beyond Customs, is a **tourist information booth** run by CANATUR. The Instituto Costarricense de Turismo (ICT) has a more substantial **tourist information,** tel. 442-8632, fax 442-9417; Mon.-Sat. 9 a.m.-10 p.m.) to the left at the top of the stairs beyond Customs. Both booths provide maps and other literature. The staff can also recommend hotels and make reservations.

There's a **Banco Nacional,** hours: Mon.-Fri. 5:30 a.m.-8 p.m., weekends and holidays 7 a.m.-1 p.m.) in the departure terminal. Ticos use the bank (which has a single teller) for their own purposes, too, and the wait can be a grim experience. Taxis happily accept dollars, so save changing money until you arrive at your hotel. You'll need local currency if you plan on taking the public transport into San José.

Getting into Town
Some upscale hotels and most language schools will pick you up free at the airport; you'll need to prearrange before arriving.

Taxis: Taxi drivers will hustle you for your patronage as you exit Customs. Taxis that operate between the airport and downtown are orange (local San José taxis are red). The legally sanctioned daytime fare into downtown San José is $13 (slightly more late at night). It normally takes 20-30 minutes to reach downtown, depending on traffic.

Buses: A Tuasa, tel. 222-5325, bus from Alajuela runs about every 15 minutes via the airport into downtown San José (via the Herradur and Meliá Cariari hotels) until 11:30 p.m. The bus stop is opposite the departure terminal (to the left when you exit Customs) between the two entrance points to the parking lots, and is clearly marked: turn. The fare is 65 *colones* (30 cents). The driver will make change, but you'll need small bills or change. The journey takes about 30 minutes, and ends downtown at Avenida 2, between Calles 10 and 12. Luggage space is limited.

Car Rental: Several car-rental companies have offices at the airport. Some are in mobile units on the far side of the taxi car park at the top of the stairs after you exit customs; additional ones face the departure terminal. If you plan on spending a few days in San José before heading off to explore the country, you'll be better off using taxis and local buses in San José. Rental cars are in very short supply. Make your reservations as soon as you arrive, or much better yet, make reservations *before* departing home. (See the "Car-Rental Agencies in San José" chart). Economy, Pilot, Poás, Tropical, Thrifty, and U-Haul operate a free minibus shuttle from the airport to theire offices about 800 meters away. They'll also return you to the airport at the end of your trip. Tricolor and Dollar also have offices nearby. See chart: "Car Rental Companies."

Departure
Getting to the Airport: The San José-Alajuela **bus** stops at Juan Santamaría Airport. It departs from Avenida 2 and Calles 10/12 every 15 minutes or so. Any **taxi** will take you to the airport. To order an airport taxi in advance, call Taxis Unidos, tel. 221-6865.

Departure Tax: At press time, the departure tax cost $16.50 (or $2 for 48-hour transit) or 3,550 *colones,* payable in either currency. It changes frequently . . . upwards!

Facilities: There's a **post office** and a bank (see "Arrival") in the departure lounge. The bank will give no more than $50 in dollars for *colones.* Change the rest before you arrive at the airport. There are several gift shops, snack bar, plus a full-service restaurant and bar on the second floor. You can spend your last *colones* here. The **duty-free stores** beyond the immigration post prefer payment in dollars.

slightly higher rates). Penny-pinchers should consider walking one or two blocks before hailing a taxi. Likewise, when traveling *to* a deluxe hotel, name a location one or two blocks away.

Taxis are painted bright red (airport taxis are orange). If it is any other color, it is a "pirate" taxi operating illegally. There are reports of taxi drivers making sexual advances toward single women; this is more likely to happen with pirate taxis, which you should avoid.

Buses

San José has an excellent network of local bus services, though there is no central bus station (instead, buses leave from widely dispersed sites). Buses are ridiculously cheap: fares are about 40 *colones* (15 cents) downtown and under 60 *colones* elsewhere within the metropolitan area. The standards, however, may not be quite what you're used to back home. While some routes are served by slick new Mercedes, other buses are decrepit old things belching fumes, with wooden, uncushioned seats. But most are clean and comfortable enough for short journeys. And since almost all Josefinos use them, they play every note on the social scale: a bus journey in San José is a kaleidoscopic vignette of social life. I've found it virtually as quick as the bus and far more pleasant to walk downtown if a journey is less than three kilometers.

Most buses begin operating at about 5 a.m. and run until at least 10 p.m. The frequency of bus service is determined by demand. Downtown and suburban San José buses leave their principal *paradas* (bus stops) every few minutes. The wait is rarely very long, except during rush hours (7-9 a.m. and 5-7 p.m.), when there are often long passenger lines and buses can get woefully crowded. Also, buses to outer suburbs often fill up straightaway: I recommend boarding at their principal downtown *parada,* designated by a sign, Parada de Autobuses, showing the route name and number. General *paradas*—where all buses may stop—do not usually display any signs (you may need to ask locals): once they leave the downtown area buses will usually stop at any *parada,* assuming they have space.

The ICT publishes a listing of current bus schedules, including the bus company and telephone numbers. It also provides a listing of out-of-town services. Another information source for both San José and provincial bus routes is *The Essential Road Guide* by Bill Baker, which provides detailed route maps plus a complete listing of metropolitan bus stops and services.

A sign in the windshield tells the route number and destination. Fares are marked by the doors and are collected when you board. Drivers provide change and tend to be scrupulously honest. Buses—most of them garishly painted, with improbable names such as *Guerrero del Camino* ("Road Warrior"), *Desert Storm, Tico Tex,* and *Titanic*—are equipped with turnstiles.

Private or cooperative bus services operate across the city from east to west, linking the center with Sabana Park and San Pedro, and north and south, from Guadalupe, Moravia, San Juan, and other nearby towns. Many take a circular routing that can provide a good introductory sightseeing experience. From the west, the most convenient bus into town is the Sabana-Cementerio service (route 2), which runs counterclockwise between Sabana Sur and downtown along Avenida 10, then back along Avenida 3 (past the Coca-Cola bus station) and Paseo Colón. The Cementerio-Sabana service (route 7) runs in the opposite direction along Paseo Colón and Avenida 2 and back along Avenida 12. Both take about 40 minutes to complete the circle.

Note: Be wary of pickpockets on buses, especially in crowded situations. Be especially suspect of anyone pushing you or pushing against you.

Driving

There are about 50 car rental agencies in San José. Many are along Paseo Colón and parallel streets west of downtown. However, don't even think about it for travel *within* San José. Traffic jams are frequent. The traffic lights will give you a neckache. The one-way system can run you ragged (note that Paseo Coló is one-way only—eastbound—weekdays 6:30-8:30 a.m.). The competitive, free-for-all mentality of Josefino drivers can fray your nerves. And, anyway, most places are quickly and easily reached by taxi, bus, or on foot.

A peripheral highway *(circunvalación)* passes around the south and east sides of San José. The northern and western extensions completing the circle are light years away. Bill Baker's book

BUSES FROM SAN JOSÉ

TO; DAYS; TIMES; DURATION; COMPANY; DEPARTURE POINT
IN COSTA RICA

Alajuela (and airport); Daily; every 10 min. 4:50 a.m.-11 p.m.; 25 mins; Tuasa; Ave. 2, Calles 10/12

Arenal Volcano NP (see Fortuna)

Braulio Carrillo NP (see Guápiles)

Cahuita; Daily; 6 a.m., 1:30 and 3:30 p.m.; 4 hrs; Autotransportes Mepes; Calle Central, Ave. 13/15

Cañas; Daily; 8:30 and 10:30 a.m. and 1:30, 2:15, and 4:30 p.m.; 3 hrs; Transportes la Cañera; Calle 16, Ave. 3/5

Caño Negro NP (see Los Chiles)

Carara Biological Reserve (see Jacó)

Cartago; Daily; every 10 min. 5 a.m.-7 p.m.; 45 min.; SACSA; Calle 5, Ave. 18

Chirripó NP (see San Isidro)

Ciudad Quesada (San Carlos); Daily; hourly 5 am.-7:30 p.m.; 3 hrs; Autotransportes Ciudad Quesada; Calle 16, Ave. 1/3

Corcovado NP (see Puerto Jiménez)

Dominical; Daily; 1:30 and 3 p.m.; 8 hrs; Transportes Muse; Calle 14, Ave. 5

Fortuna; Daily; 6:15, 8:40 a.m. and 11:30 a.m.; 4.5 hrs; Barquero; Calle 16, Ave. 1/3

Golfito; Daily; 7 a.m. and 3 p.m.; 8 hrs; Tracopa; Calle 14, Ave. 5

Guápiles; Daily; every 30 min. 5:30 a.m.-7 p.m.; 60 min.; Coopetragua; Calle 12, Ave. 7/9

Guayabo National Monument (see Turrialba)

Heredia; Daily; every 15 min. 5:25 a.m.-midnight; 25 min.; Microbuses Rápidos; Calle 1, Ave. 7/9

Irazú Volcano NP; Saturday and Sunday; 8 a.m.; 90 min.; Buses Metropoli; Ave. 6, Calle 1/3

Jacó; Daily; 7:30 and 10:30 a.m. and 3:30 p.m.; 2.5 hrs; Transportes Morales; Calle 16, Ave. 1/3

Liberia; Daily; 6 a.m., 7 a.m., 8 a.m., 9 a.m., 10 a.m., and 11:30 a.m. and 1 p.m., 2 p.m., 3 p.m., 4 p.m., 5 p.m., 6 p.m., and 8 p.m.; 4 hrs; Pulmitán; Calle 14, Ave. 1/3

Los Chiles; Daily; 5:30 a.m. and 3:30 p.m.; 5 hrs; Autotransportes Ciudad Quesada; Calle 16, Ave. 1/3

Manuel Antonio (see Quepos)

Monteverde; Daily; 6:30 a.m. and 2:30 p.m.; 3.3 hrs; Autotransportes Tilarán; Calle 14, Ave. 9/11

Nicoya; Daily; 6 a.m., 8 a.m. and 10 a.m., and noon, 1 p.m., 2:30 p.m., 3 p.m. and 5 p.m.; 6 hrs; Empresa Alfaro; Calle 14, Ave. 3/5

Nosara; Daily; 6:15 a.m.; 6 hrs; Empresa Alfaro, Calle 14, Ave. 3/5

Palmar; Daily; 5 a.m., 6:30 a.m., 8:30 a.m. and 10 a.m. and 2:30 p.m. and 6 p.m.; 5 hrs; Tracopa; Ave. 18, Calles 2/4

Playa Brasilito; Daily; 8 a.m. and 11 a.m.; 6 hrs; Tralapa; Calle 20, Ave. 3

Playa del Coco; Daily; 10 a.m.; 5 hrs; Pulmitán; Calle 14, Ave. 1/3

Playa Flamingo; Daily; 8 and 11 a.m.; 6 hrs; Tralapa; Calle 20, Ave. 3

Playa Hermosa; Daily; 3:20 p.m.; 5 hrs; Empresa Esquivel; Calle 12, Ave. 5/7

Playa Junquillal; Daily; 2 p.m.; 5 hrs; Tralapa; Calle 20, Ave. 3

Playa Panamá (see Playa Hermosa)

Playa Potrero; TBA

Poás Volcano NP; Daily; 8:30 a.m.; 1.5 hrs; Tuasa; Calle 12, Ave. 2/4

Puerto Jiménez; Daily; 6 a.m. and noon; 8 hrs; Transportes Blanco; Calle 14, Ave. 5

Puerto Limón; Daily; every 30 min. 5 a.m.-7 p.m.; 2.5 hrs; Coopelimón and Coopecaribeúos; Calle Central, Ave. 13/15

Puerto Viejo de Limón (see Cahuita)

Puerto Viejo de Sarapiquí; Daily; 8 a.m., 10 a.m. and 11 a.m. and 3 p.m. and 4 p.m.; 4 hrs; Calle 12, Ave. 7/9

Puntarenas; Daily; hourly 6 a.m.-7 p.m.; 2 hrs; Empresarios Unidas; Calle 16, Ave. 10/12

Quepos/Manuel Antonio; Daily; 6 a.m., noon, and 6 p.m.; 3.5 hrs; Transportes Morales; Calle 16, Ave. 1/3

Sámara; Daily; 8 a.m. and 3 p.m. and 4 p.m.; 6 hrs; Empresa Alfaro; Calle 14, Ave. 3/5

San Isidro; Daily; 6:30 a.m. and 9:30 a.m. and 12:30 p.m. and 3:30 p.m.; 3 hrs; Transportes Musoc; Calle 16, Ave. 1/3

Santa Cruz; Daily; 7:30 a.m. and 10:30 a.m. and 2 p.m., 4 p.m. and 6 p.m.; 5 hrs; Tralapa; Calle 20, Ave. 1/3

Sarchí; Daily; every 30 min. 5 a.m.-10 p.m.; 1.5 hrs; Tuan; Calle 8, Ave. Central/1

Tamarindo; Daily; 3:30 p.m.; 5.5 hrs; Alfaro; Calle 14, Ave. 5

Turrialba; Daily; hourly 5 a.m.-10 p.m.; 1.5 hrs; Transtusa; Calle 13, Ave. 6/8

Zarcero; Daily; hourly 5 a.m.-7:30 p.m.; 1.5 hrs; Autotransportes Ciudad Quesada; Calle 16, Ave. 1/3

INTERNATIONAL BUSES

Guatemala City and Tegucigalpa; Daily; 6 a.m. and 7:30 a.m.; 60 hrs; Tica; Ave. 4, Calles 9/11

Managua, Nicaragua; Mon., Wed., Fri. and Sun.; 5:45 a.m.; 11 hrs; SIRCA; Calle 7, Ave. 6/8

Managua, Nicaragua; Daily; 6 a.m. and 7:30 a.m.; 60 hrs; Tica; Ave. 4, Calles 9/11

Managua, Nicaragua; Daily; 5:30 a.m.; 10 hrs; Transnica; Calle 14, Avenida 3

Changuinola, Panamá; Daily; 10 a.m.; 8 hrs; Alfaro; Calle 14, Ave. 3/5

David, Panamá; Daily; 7:30 a.m. and noon; 9 hrs; Alfaro; Calle 14, Ave. 3/5

David, Panamá; Daily; 7:30 a.m. and noon; 9 hrs; TRACOPA; Avenida 18, Calle 4

Panamá City, Panamá (via David); Daily; 6 a.m. and 10 p.m.; 20 hrs; Tica; Ave. 4, Calles 9/11

Panamáa City, Panamá; Daily; 2 p.m.; 15 hrs; Panaline; Calle 16, Ave. 3

The Essential Road Guide provides detailed directions for navigating by car around San José.

Parking spaces are at a premium and you may end up having to park so far away you may as well have walked in the first place. Parking meters take five-*colón* coins (30 minutes) as well as tokens *(ficas)*. Forget the tokens! If you really love waiting in line, however, you can obtain these at the Departamento de Parquémetros, in the administrative offices of the Mercado Central, Calle 6, Avenidas Central/1, second floor; or at the Banco de Costa Rica, at the window where municipal taxes are paid. Never park in a no-parking zone, marked Control por Grúa ("Controlled by tow truck"). Regulations are efficiently enforced.

Break-ins and theft are common (rental cars are especially vulnerable; make sure your in-surance covers loss). Never leave anything of value in your car, even in the trunk. Many **public parking lots** offer secure 24-hour parking. You must leave your ignition key with the attendant (it's not necessary to tip except in special circumstances). Elsewhere, young men and boys may offer to watch your car for 40 or 50 *colones.* Usually, it's a worthwhile investment.

Motorcycle Rental: As a motorcyclist, I can assure you that motorcycling in San José is suicidally foolish.

Walking

San José is ideal for walking. The city is compact, with virtually everything of interest within a few blocks of the center. However, sidewalks are in horrendous repair. Use the same philosophy as in the rainforests: when walking, look

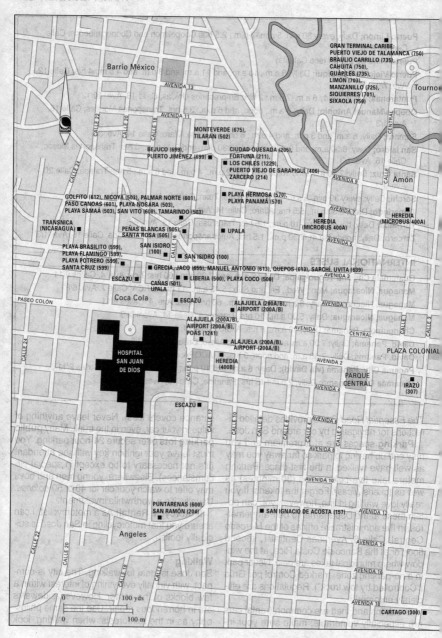

Barrio México

AVENIDA 13

AVENIDA 11

MONTEVERDE (675),
TILARÁN (502)

BEJUCO (699),
PUERTO JIMÉNEZ (699)

CIUDAD QUESADA (205),
FORTUNA (211),
LOS CHILES (1229),
PUERTO VIEJO DE SARAPIQUÍ (406)
ZARCERO (214)

AVENIDA 9

PLAYA HERMOSA (570),
PLAYA PANAMÁ (570)

GOLFITO (612), NICOYA (503), PALMAR NORTE (601),
PASO CANOAS (601), PLAYA NOSARA (503),
PLAYA SAMAÁ (503), SAN VITO (608), TAMARINDO (503)

TRANSNICA
(NICARAGUA)

PEÑAS BLANCAS (505),
SANTA ROSA (505)

UPALA

PLAYA BRASILITO (599),
PLAYA FLAMINGO (599),
PLAYA POTRERO (599),
SANTA CRUZ (599)

SAN ISIDRO
(100)

SAN ISIDRO (100)

ESCAZÚ

GRECIA, JACÓ (655), MANUEL ANTONIO (613), QUEPOS (613), SARCHÍ, UVITA (639)

CAÑAS (501),
UPALA

LIBERIA (500), PLAYA COCO (500)

ESCAZÚ

ALAJUELA (200A/B),
AIRPORT (200A/B)

PASEO COLÓN

Coca Cola

ALAJUELA (200A/B),
AIRPORT (200A/B),
POÁS (1241)

ALAJUELA (200A/B),
AIRPORT (200A/B)

HOSPITAL
SAN JUAN
DE DÍOS

HEREDIA
(400B)

ESCAZÚ

PUNTARENAS (600)
SAN RAMÓN (204)

Angeles

SAN IGNACIO DE ACOSTA (157)

GRAN TERMINAL CARIBE:
PUERTO VIEJO DE TALAMANCA (750),
BRAULIO CARRILLO (735),
CAHUITA (750),
GUÁPILES (735),
LIMÓN (703),
MANZANILLO (725),
SIQUIERRES (701),
SIXAOLA (750)

Tournon

Amón

HEREDIA
(MICROBUS 400A)

HEREDIA
(MICROBUS 400A)

AVENIDA 7

AVENIDA 8

AVENIDA 5

PLAZA COLONIAL

PARQUE
CENTRAL

IRAZÚ
(307)

AVENIDA 1

AVENIDA 2

AVENIDA 3

AVENIDA 4

AVENIDA 6

AVENIDA 10

AVENIDA 12

AVENIDA 14

AVENIDA 16

AVENIDA 18

CARTAGO (300)

0   100 yds

0   100 m

SAN JOSÉ BUS TERMINALS

Río Torres

PARQUE ZOOLÓGICA SIMÓN BOLÍVAR

Otoya

PARQUE MORAZÁN

PARQUE ESPAÑA

PARQUE NACIONAL

CALLE 5
CALLE 9
CALLE 11
CALLE 15
CALLE 17

PLAZA DE LA DEMÓCRACIA

TICA (GUATEMALA, HONDURAS, NICARAGUA, PANAMÁ)

TURRIALBA (302)

SIRCA (NICARAGUA)

CALLE 13

© MOON PUBLICATIONS, INC.

down; look up when standing still. You'll need to keep an eternal vigil for great potholes, tilted flagstones, and gaping sewer holes.

And pedestrians and automobiles mix about as well as oil and water. Says *National Geographic:* "Rush hour is a bullfight on the streets, with every car a blaring beast and every pedestrian a torero." Josefinos treat both pedestrians and traffic lights with total disdain. They love to jump the gun on green lights and sail through heedlessly on red. Don't expect traffic to stop for you if you get caught in the middle of the road when the light changes; drivers will expect you to act like a local—run! To make matters worse, a single stoplight usually hangs above the center of the narrow junctions, where it is far too high for pedestrians to see. Watch the cars, not the lights. Don't take your eyes off the traffic for a moment.

Other than traffic hazards, walking is generally safe everywhere, although pickpockets and muggings are on the increase. Avoid the parks at night, and use particular caution if exploring the district bordered by Calles Central and 8, and Avenidas 6 and 10, or the streets around—particularly north and east of—the Coca-Cola bus terminal.

TAM Tours, Apdo. 1864-1000, San José, email: info@tamtravel.com, offers a three-hour guided walking tour daily at 9 a.m., taking in sites as diverse as the Mercado Central and Teatro Nacional. Vernon Bell publishes the *Walking Tour of Downtown San José,* Dept. 1432, P.O. Box 025216, Miami, FL 33102, tel. 225-4752, fax 224-5884. It's a whimsical guide to exploring the city, with all the main sites included.

CATHY CARLSON

CENTRAL HIGHLANDS

The Central Highlands region is stunningly beautiful and replete with sights to see. The large, fertile central valley—sometimes called the Meseta Central ("Central Plateau")—is held in the cusp of verdant mountains that rise on all sides. Almost 70% of the nation's populace lives here, concentrated in the four colonial cities of San José, Alajuela, Cartago, and Heredia, though settlements are found far up the mountain slopes. Though variations of climate exist—the valley floor has been called a place of "perpetual summer" and the upper slopes a place of "perpetual spring"—an invigorating, salubrious climate is universal.

The marvelous beauty owes much to the juxtaposition of valley and mountain. The ethereal landscapes—the soaring volcanoes and impossibly green coffee terraces—lift the spirits. The serenity beguiles. You can reach virtually any point within a two-hour drive of San José; roads are narrow, unlit, and poorly marked, though almost all are paved and in reasonably good condition. Many fine hotels, lodges, and bed and breakfasts are scattered throughout the highlands, so that you can spend a week or more touring the region without having to retire to San José to rest your head.

The Meseta Central is really two valleys in one, divided by a low mountain ridge—the **Fila de Bustamente** (or Cerro de la Carpintera)—which rises immediately southwest of San José. West of the ridge is the larger valley of the Poás and Virilla rivers, with flanks gradually rising from a level floor. East of the ridge the smaller Valle de Guarco (containing Cartago) is more tightly hemmed in, and falls away to the east, drained by the Río Reventazón.

Volcanoes of the Cordillera Central frame the valley to the north, forming a smooth-sloped meniscus. To the south lies the massive, blunt-nosed bulk of the Cordillera Talamanca. The high peaks are generally obscured by clouds for much of the "winter" months (May through November). When clear, both mountain zones offer spectacularly scenic drives, including the chance to drive to the very crest of two active volcanoes: Poás and Irazú.

When the Spaniards arrived, broad-leafed evergreen forest covered the valley floor. Pine forests blanketed the slopes. Not so today. Sugarcane, tobacco, and corn smother the valley floor, according to elevation and microclimate. Dairy farms rise up the slopes to over 2,500 meters. Small coffee *fincas,* too, are everywhere on vale and slope, the dark green, shiny-leafed bushes often shaded by *erythrina* trees, which can be planted simply by breaking off a branch and sticking it in the ground; every manicured row flows into the next like folds of green silk, with blazing orange flame-of-the-forest and bright red African tulip adorning the hedgerows. Pockets of natural vegetation remain, however, farther up the slopes and in protected areas such as Braulio Carrillo National Park and the Tapantí National Park, lush nurseries where quetzals, tapirs, pumas, ocelots, monkeys, toucans, and other treasured species can be seen in the wild.

Refreshingly clear and invigorating, the weather of the Central Highlands has been termed idyllic. As a rule of thumb, mornings are clear and the *meseta* and adjacent valleys bask under brilliant sunshine. In the dry season, things stay this way all day. In the wet ("green") season, clouds form over the mountains in the early af-ternoon, announcing the possible arrival of rain. Temperatures average in the mid-20s C (mid-70s F) year-round in the valley and cool steadily as one moves into the mountains, where coniferous trees lend a distinctly alpine feel. The valley—with an average high of 25° C (77° F) and average low of 16° C (61° F)—has a pronounced dry season Dec.-April, with monthly rainfall averaging less than one inch. Monthly rainfall May-Oct. averages 25-30 cm, when moist westerlies begin bearing in from the Pacific. Long rainy days are a rarity.

Things are different on the mountain slopes. Western-facing slopes have a distinct dry season that roughly corresponds to North America's winter months; temperatures increase, however, peaking in February, March, and April, when temperatures are generally 3-5 degrees C (5-10 degrees F) warmer than in cooler months. The eastern-facing—windward—slopes receive considerably more rainfall any time of year thanks to convective cooling of moist air moving in from the Caribbean. Braulio Carrillo and Tapantí National Parks, for example, are generally always wet.

ESCAZÚ AND VICINITY

The old road to the Pacific coast once led through this area, full of small farming communities, charming old villages, and wilderness reserves.

It's remarkable that a place such as Escazú can be found so close to the capital city. The town, only four km west of San José's Parque Sabana and a virtual suburb of San José, is one of the oldest settlements in the country, with a host of superb bed and breakfast inns adding to its many charms. "Maybe," says author and local resident Harvey Haber, "it is just what you were hoping to discover in a small Latin country, but really did not dare hope that it would exist."

Escazú's tempting climate, its views, and sleepy *campesino*-town ambience go hand-in-hand with fancy homes and condos, chic restaurants and nightclubs, and ultrachic shopping plazas that have drawn scores of English-speaking expatriates (there's good reason that the U.S. embassy and ambassador's home are here). The town's oh-so-chic side is exemplified by **Multi-Plaza,** Costa Rica's largest shopping mall, two km northwest of town alongside the **Carratera Prospero Fernández** (Hwy 27), an expressway that runs from Sabana, passes north

ESCAZÚ—WITCH CAPITAL OF COSTA RICA

Escazú is famous as the *bruja* (witch) capital of the country. The Río Tiribi, which flows east of Escazú, is said to be haunted, and old men still refuse to cross the Los Anonos Bridge at night for fear of La Zegua and Mico Malo (the magic monkey). Some 60 or so witches are said to still live in Escazú, including Doña Estrella, who says that "any woman who lives in Escazú long enough eventually becomes a *bruja*." Amorous tourists should beware La Zegua—an incredibly beautiful enchantress. When the (un)lucky suitor gets her to bed, she turns into a horse.

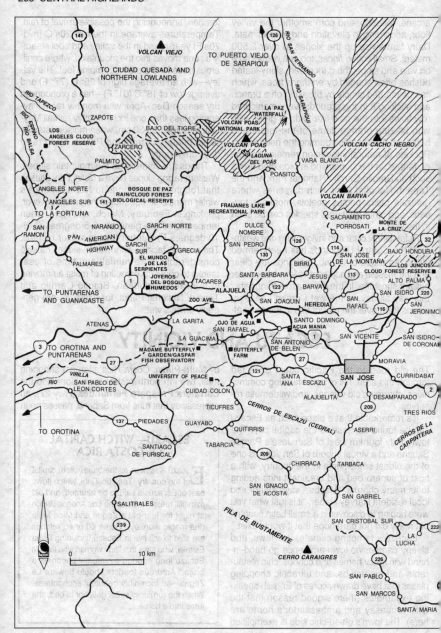

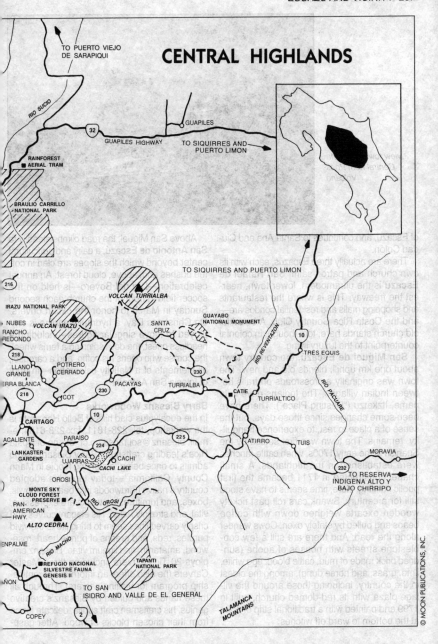

CENTRAL HIGHLANDS

TO PUERTO VIEJO
DE SARAPIQUI

RIO SUCIO

GUAPILES

32

GUAPILES HIGHWAY

TO SIQUIRRES AND
PUERTO LIMON

RAINFOREST
AERIAL TRAM

BRAULIO CARRILLO
NATIONAL PARK

TO SIQUIRRES AND PUERTO LIMON

216

VOLCAN TURRIALBA

IRAZU NATIONAL PARK

SANTA
CRUZ

GUAYABO
NATIONAL MONUMENT

NUBES
RANCHO
REDONDO

VOLCAN IRAZÚ

218

POTRERO
CERRADO

RIO REVENTAZON

10

TRES EQUIS

LLANO
GRANDE

ERRA BLANCA

218

PACAYAS

230

TURRIALBA

RIO PACUARE

COT

230

CATIE

TURRIALTICO

RIO REVENTAZON

CARTAGO

10

PARAISO

224

225

ATIRRO

TUIS

MORAVIA

ACALIENTE

LANKASTER
GARDENS

UJARRAS

CACHI

CACHI LAKE

232

TO RESERVA
INDIGENA ALTO Y
BAJO CHIRRIPO

OROSI

MONTE SKY
CLOUD FOREST
PRESERVE

RIO OROSI

PAN-
AMERICAN
HWY.

ALTO CEDRAL

ENPALME

RIO MACHO

REFUGIO NACIONAL
SILVESTRE FAUNA
GENESIS II

TAPANTI
NATIONAL PARK

TALAMANCA
MOUNTAINS

ÑÓN

COPEY

2

TO SAN
ISIDRO AND VALLE DEL GENERAL

© MOON PUBLICATIONS, INC.

view toward Meseta
Central from Poás
Volcano

of Escazú, and continues to Santa Ana and Ciudad Colón.

There are actually three Escazús, each with its own church and patron saint. **San Rafael de Escazú** is the ultramodern, lower town, nearest the freeway. This is where the restaurants and shopping malls and residential condos are—and the Costa Rica Country Club. A beautiful old church stands here, too, though, in colonial counterpoint to the luxury living.

San Miguel de Escazú, the country town about one km uphill, blends old and new. The town was originally a crossroads on trails between Indian villages. The Indians gave it its name, Itzkatzu ("Resting Place"). There have been some changes since those days, but the sense of a place to rest, to experience tranquility, remains. The town was first settled by the Spanish in the early 1700s, when cattle ranches were established in the highlands. A small chapel constructed in 1711 became the first public building. Here, time seems to have stood still for a century. Swank cars roll past rickety wooden oxcarts weighed down with coffee beans and pulled by stately oxen. Cows wander along the road. And there are still a few cobblestone streets with houses of adobe (sundried brick made of mud, cattle blood, egg white, lime, grass, and horse dung), among the oldest in the country, including those around the village plaza with its red-domed church, built in 1799 and painted with a traditional strip of color at the bottom to ward off witches.

Above San Miguel, the road climbs steadily to **San Antonio de Escazú,** a dairy and agricultural center beyond which the slopes are clad in coffee bushes and, above, cloud forest. An annual celebration—Día del Boyero—is held on the soccer field in front of the church each second Sunday in March to honor the oxcart drivers. On Christmas Day, a hydraulic engine is employed to move singular figures—including a headless priest, the devil spinning a ferris wheel, the corpse who opens his coffin, and a carousel, all elements of a Nativity celebration—in front of Iglesia San Antonio.

Barry Biesanz Woodworks

In the eucalyptus-clad hills of Bello Horizonte is the workshop, tel. 228-1811, fax 228-6184, e-mail: biesanz@sol.racsa.co.cr, of one of Costa Rica's leading craftsmen. Barry Biesanz—who admits to once being "a starving hippie in Marin County, California"—today turns his adopted country's native hardwoods into beautiful bowls, boxes, and furniture. His works are expressive, vital, and strongly Asian. His elegant curves and crisply carved lines seem to bring life to the vivid purples, reds, and greens of purple heart, rosewood, amaranth, and lignum vitae. Biesanz employs 20 Tico carvers, including three Master Carvers (he also offers an informal apprenticeship program for visiting carvers). Through all these hands and guided by Biesanz's creative genius, his craftsmen craft subtle, delicate forms from their chosen blocks of wood. After gasping in disbelief, you'll immediately appreciate why his boxes and bowls grace the collections of three U.S. presidents and assorted European royalty. Don't fuss over the demise of the rainforest. Biesanz's source is gnarly, dead trees from local farmland. Visitors are welcome by appointment, Mon.-Fri. 8 a.m.-5 p.m.

Reaching Biesanz's shop is a little tricky. Biesanz recommends showing the taxi driver these instructions: *Tome la primera entrada a Bello Horizonte y siga los rótulos de nuestra empresa por 3.5 kms. Son seis rótulos con la leyenda Biesanz Woodworks y flechas. Estamos 400 mts sur del antiguo Hotel Los Portales, casa residencial mano izquierda con muro de piedra.*

Mountain Hikes

The clear mountain air and sense of tranquility owe much to Escazú's lofty position. The town climbs up the lower slopes of soaring mountains, including La Cruz (topped by an imposing 15-meter-tall iron cross), Piedra Blanca, Cerro Rabo de Mico (the tallest at 2,455 meters), and Cerro de Escazú, fluted with waterfalls. You can hike to the La Cruz cross from the small pueblo of Poás

wooden bowls by Barry Biesanz

de Aserrí (one km west of Aserrí, four km south of San José), ending in Alajuelita or Escazú. A bus to Poás leaves from Avenida 6, Calles 10/12 in San José; from Poás you walk across a river to the trailhead, about one km beyond the footbridge and marked by a large iron gate. The hike, popular on weekends, is steep in parts but offers staggering views of the valley and mountains. Locals sell food and drinks along the trail.

Escazú Hills Sanctuary

This private reserve south of San Antonio de Escazú ascends to 2,400 meters and includes more than 1,900 hectares of primary cloud forest on a large dairy farm in the El Cedral area of the Escazú Hills. The property is co-owned by Don Alvaro Riba and his Canadian partner John Boden, who have formed the nonprofit Riba Foundation to manage and direct the Escazú Hills Sanctuary. Much of the cut land has been reforested with trees native to the hills. Another 400 hectares will gradually become part of the reserve.

Cedars, oaks, and laurels—all dominant giants of the mountaintops—tower in splendor, waving beards of Spanish moss. There are stands of jaul, the tall slender coffin tree, and a dense understory of bamboo. For the last few years there have been a breeding pair of pumas. No monkeys have returned yet. However, a pair of young white-faced monkeys have been introduced with the hope that they'll spawn offspring. Two-toed sloths are common. Poaching is a recurring problem.

Don Alvaro and Boden also operate the five-room **Hacienda Cerro Pando,** Apdo. 586, San José 1000, tel./fax 253-8726 or 224-9405, in Cedral de Acosta. Horseback rides are available over mountain trails into cloud forest, and you can also explore on little all-terrain four-wheelers.

National Boyero's Day

Held every second Sunday of March since 1983, this festival pays homage to the *boyeros,* the men who guide the traditional oxcarts to market. More than 100 *boyeros* from around the country trim their colorful carts and gather for this celebration, which includes an oxcart parade helped along by a supporting cast of women and children in traditional garb, plus a musical accompaniment of *cimarronas,* the traditional instrument mandatory for popular feasts. Lencho Salazar, a local folklorist, regales crowds with tales of *brujas.*

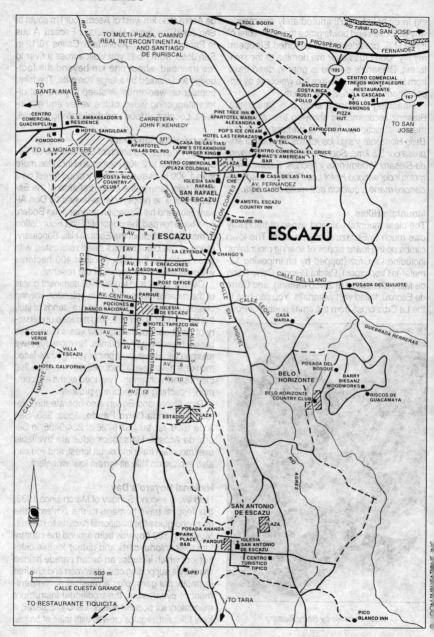

TO MULTI-PLAZA, CAMINO REAL INTERCONTINENTAL AND SANTIAGO DE PURISCAL

TOLL BOOTH
AUTOPISTA
RIO TIRIBI TO SAN JOSE
PROSPERO FERNANDEZ

TO SANTA ANA

CENTRO COMERCIAL GUACHIPELIN
U.S. AMBASSADOR'S RESIDENCE
IL POMODORO
HOTEL SANGILDAR

CARRETERA JOHN F. KENNEDY

TO LA MONASTERE

COSTA RICA COUNTRY CLUB

APARTOTEL VILLAS DEL RIO

CASA DE LAS TIAS/ LAMM'S STEAKHOUSE BURGER KING

CENTRO COMERCIAL PLAZA COLONIAL

IGLESIA SAN RAFAEL

SAN RAFAEL DE ESCAZU

CENTRO COMERCIAL TREJOS MONTEALEGRE
RESTAURANTE LA CASCADA
BBQ LOS ANONOS
PIZZA HUT
CAPRICCIO ITALIANO

BANCO DE COSTA RICA ROSTI POLLO

PINE TREE INN
APARTOTEL MARIA ALEXANDRA
POP'S ICE CREAM
HOTEL LAS TERRAZAS
McDONALD'S
Q'TAL
CENTRO COMERCIAL EL CRUCE
MAC'S AMERICAN BAR
CASA DE LAS TIAS
AV. FERNANDEZ DELGADO

EL CHE

PLAZA

TO SAN JOSE

AMSTEL ESCAZU COUNTRY INN
BONAIRE INN

ESCAZÚ

ESCAZU

AV. 9
AV. 7
AV. 5
AV. LA CASONA
LA LEYENDA
CREACIONES SANTOS
CHANGO'S

CALLE DEL LLANO

POSADA DEL QUIJOTE

POST OFFICE

AV. CENTRAL
POCIONES
BANCO NACIONAL
PARQUE
IGLESIA DE ESCAZU
HOTEL TAPEZCO INN

CALLE LEON CORTES
CALLE CHUGUERO
CALLE LEON
CALLE SAN MIGUEL
CASA MARIA

QUEBRADA HERRERAS

COSTA VERDE INN
VILLA ESCAZU
HOTEL CALIFORNIA

AV. 2
AV. 4
AV. 6
AV. 8
AV. 10
AV. 12

CALLE 8
CALLE MONTE
CALLE 4
CALLE 2
CALLE CENTRAL
CALLE 3
CALLE 5

POSADA DEL BOSQUE
BARRY BIESANZ WOODWORKS
RISCOS DE GUACAMAYA

BELO HORIZONTE
BELO HORIZONTE COUNTRY CLUB

ESTADIO
PLAZA

RIO AGRES

SAN ANTONIO DE ESCAZU

POSADA ANANDA
PARK PLACE B&B
PARQUE
IGLESIA SAN ANTONIO DE ESCAZU
CENTRO TURISTICO TIPICO
UPE!

0   500 m
CALLE CUESTA GRANDE
TO RESTAURANTE TIQUICITA

TO TARA

PICO BLANCO INN

Grupo Auténtico Tradicional Tiquicia treats on-lookers to much-loved local melodies. And young girls perform ancestral dances.

ACCOMMODATIONS

You're spoiled for choice. Many of Escazú's bed and breakfasts are exemplary of the hotel genre. Most are gringo-owned and gringo-run. Competition has winnowed the chaff in recent years. And the highly rated Puesta del Sol closed its doors in late 1997.

Lower Down (San Rafael and San Miguel)
Budget: Hotel La Terraza, Apdo. 1574, Escazú 1250, tel. 228-6937, fax 289-9867, opposite the Shell gas station in San Rafael, is run by a Taiwanese family who operate the Chinese restaurant adjacent. The eight rooms are clean. Some have shared bathrooms. There's a cable TV in the lobby. Rates: $15 s, $20 d, including breakfast.

Inexpensive: The **Pine Tree Inn,** Apdo. 1516-1250 Escazú, tel. 289-7405, fax 228-2180, e-mail: pinetree@sol.racsa.co.cr; in the U.S., P.O. Box 40-2151 Miami Beach, FL 33140, in the heart of San Rafael, has 15 rooms, some with king-size beds and spacious bathrooms; all have parquet floors, cable TVs, telephones, and safety boxes. The inn has a pool and solarium and parking, plus a large lounge with fireplace. Rates: $45 s, $50 d, including breakfast.

The **Hotel Tapezco Inn,** tel. 228-1084, fax 289-7026, one block south of the main square in San Miguel de Escazú, is a contemporary colonial-style property with 15 charmless, simply furnished rooms, each with hot water, telephone, TV, and fan. It offers a jacuzzi and sauna, plus a small restaurant. Rates: $35 s, $45 d, $68 t, including breakfast and tax.

Bonaire Inn, tel. 228-0866 or 228-0764, fax 289-8107, is dour and disappointing and in need of a good scrubbing and makeover. It has seven basically furnished rooms, some with a/c. Four rooms share a bathroom. A lounge has cable TV. It is 350 meters south of El Cruce shopping center. Rates:$25 s/d with shared bath, $35 s/d with private bath. The owner prefers longer rentals: $200 per week, $450 monthly.

Posada del Bosque, Apdo. 669, Escazú 1250, tel. 228-1164, fax 228-2006, is another

excellent bed and breakfast. The irrepressibly animated Gilbert Aubert and his charming wife Elza run this intimate home away from home—once the residence of the U.S. commercial attaché. The beautiful lounge has a large open fireplace, a bamboo-lined roof, a terra-cotta tiled floor, and a wide veranda overlooking the expansive garden, which has a barbecue pit. Since I last visited, the couple have taken over most of the spacious bedrooms in the house for themselves (only one is now rented), and added four less appealing yet still handsome rooms in a new building centered on a small patio and that features a common kitchen and lounge. The rooms are well lit and ventilated, with plenty of closet space and large tiled showers. A full breakfast is served in a quaint gazebo decorated Tico-style. Guests have free access to the nearby Bello Horizonte Country Club. Fruit trees in the garden attract lots of birds, including motmots. Lunch and dinner cost $6. No smoking, but children are welcome. Rates: $45 d low season; $55 d high season; $10 extra person.

Nearby, **Riscos de Guacamaya Country Inn,** Apdo. 351, Escazú 1250, tel. 228-9074, fax 289-5776, is a homey option with one suite, two double rooms (two with shared bath), and three single rooms, most of which have beautiful parquet floors, and all of which have cable TV and private bath with hot water. The huge suite has a double and two single beds and a massive bathroom. There's a restaurant (plus 24-hour room service), and a brick sundeck around a pool with fine views. Rates: $45 s/d; $60 suite, including breakfast.

My favorite hotel is the **Casa de Las Tías,** Apdo. 295-1200 San José, tel. 289-5517, fax 289-7353, e-mail: casitas@yellowweb.co.cr; in the U.S., SJO-478, P.O. Box 025216, Miami, FL 33102, one block east of El Ché; it bills itself as a "country bed and breakfast in town." This exquisite yellow-and-turquoise, southern plantation-style wooden home has five airy, wood-panelled rooms, all with polished hardwood floors, wooden ceilings, wicker and antique furniture, ceiling fans, and Latin American art and other tasteful decor. One room has a balcony with chaise longue and rocker. The suite is beautiful, and boasts a king-size bed and heaps of light pouring in from wide windows facing the back garden. All have private bath and ceiling fan. Breakfast is served on the garden patio. Your delightful hosts, Xavier and Pilar Vela, are planning to convert two garden cottages for rental. Rates: $49 s; $59 d; $70 suite; $10 extra person, including full breakfast. Airport pickups with advance notice.

Villa Escazú, Apdo. 1401, Escazú 1250, tel./fax 228-9566, boasts stunning hardwood interiors mixed with rusticity and tasteful modern decor in a pretty Swiss-style chalet. A "minstrel's gallery" balcony overhangs the lounge, with its fireplace and wide chimney of natural stone. Five rooms include a deluxe room with private bath, and two bedrooms with shared bath on both the main and third floors. The solid and superbly crafted house is enhanced by an all-around outside veranda with chunky wicker chairs for enjoying the view. Landscaped lawns cascade downhill to a fruit orchard. There's an open barbecue at the back, and a stone patio with outdoor seating out front. Villa Escazú is run by friendly Floridians Mary-Anne and Inez, who prepare full American breakfasts in the large kitchen. Rates: $40 s, $57 d, $74 t; $68 d, $80 t, deluxe, including breakfast.

Moderate: The **Amstel Country Inn Escazú,** Apdo. 668-1250, San José, tel. 228-1764, fax 228-0620, e-mail:escazu@sol.racsa.co.cr; in the U.S., tel. (800) 575-1253, 200 meters south of the El Cruce shopping mall, has 14 well-lit albeit characterless, carpeted rooms and two deluxe suites, all with telephones and cable TVs; some have a/c and king-size beds. The large bathroom in the suite has a sunken jacuzzi bathtub and mirrored walls on all sides. There's a swimming pool with its own fountain in nicely landscaped grounds. Rates: $45 s/d standard, $65 suite low season; $55 s/d, $75 suite high season. Breakfast included.

The **Costa Verde Inn,** SJO 1313, P.O. Box 025216, Miami, FL 33102-5216; in Costa Rica, tel. 228-4080, fax 289-8591, is a very beautiful, atmospheric, and peaceful bed and breakfast long on creature comforts. The lofty-ceilinged house is creatively conceived. Hardwoods abound, including a stunning hardwood floor. Walls are adorned with hand-colored historic photos. Decor is simple, romantic, and bright, the furnishings tasteful. The lounge has a plump leather sofa, an open fireplace, and a large-screen TV. Twelve individually styled bedrooms

come with king-size beds, built-in hardwood furniture, and huge, beautifully tiled bathrooms. Room 6 has a bathroom in natural stone with an open pit shower at its center. There's not a room I wouldn't want to sleep in. Economy rooms have small singles and shared bath. Outside are a tennis court and a shaded terrace with rough-hewn supports and open fireplace. Added in 1994 were a swimming pool, sundeck, and outdoor gym. A solid bargain. Rates: from $45 (single with shared bath) to $70 (suite), including breakfast and tax. *Recommended!*

Also recommended is the American-run **Posada El Quijote,** Apdo. 1127, Escazú 1250, tel. 289-8401, fax 289-8729, e-mail: quijote@sol.racsa.co.cr; in the U.S., Dept. 239-SJO, P.O. Box 025216, Miami, FL 33102, tel. (800) 570-6750, ext. 8401, in the Bello Horizonte hills. This beautiful Spanish colonial home has been totally renovated, exquisitely decorated, and stocked with modern art. The eight tastefully appointed rooms look out over beautiful gardens, and have queen- or king-size beds, telephones, cable TVs, and private baths with lots of high-pressure hot water. Two "superior" rooms have a patio. Breakfast is served under an arbor on the intimate patio, and you can order light lunches and dinners, and take a nip at the bar. Room 25 has a bathroom that you won't be able to tear yourself away from. Rates: $50 s, $60 d standard, low season; $60 s, $70 d high season ($5 extra for superior; $10 extra for deluxe), including full breakfast. Add seven percent for credit card transactions. No children under 12.

Apartotel María Alexandra, Apdo. 3756, San José 1000, tel. 228-1507, fax 228-5192, e-mail: matour@sol.racsa.co.cr, a quiet and comfy retreat away from the main road, offers 14 fully furnished, elegant, luxury a/c one- and two-bedroom apartments, each with king-size bed, telephone, cable TV, private parking, and full kitchen. There are also twin-level townhouses that sleep up to five people. I consider them the finest apartments in the region. Facilities include a lounge and restaurant, a pool, a sauna, and mini-golf. A reader praised the attentive and superlative service. There's a tour and travel operation on site. Rates: $63-70 one-bedroom; $76-85 two-bedroom; $90-100 townhouse.

Apartotel Villas del Río, Apdo. 2027, San José 1000, tel. 289-8833, fax 289-8627, was near completion at press time on the south side of the Costa Rica Country Club, with one-, two-, and three-bedroom a/c apartments, plus suites and penthouses, each with cable TV and VCR, a fully equipped kitchen, and a computer message center. Other features include a children's playground, plus a pool with swim-up bar, a gym and sauna, and a rental car and tour agency.

Expensive: Hotel Sangildar, Apdo. 1511, Escazú 1250, tel. 289-8843, fax 228-6454, e-mail: pentacor@sol.racsa.co.cr; in the U.S., tel. (800) 758-7234, set in lush grounds adjoining the Costa Rica Country Club on the western outskirts of Escazú, is a very handsome contemporary Spanish-style building named for San Gildar, the Father of Triumph, whose effigy was placed in a private chapel in Escazú in 1834 (today it can be seen in the parish church). A plaque in the lobby tells his tale. Hardwoods and stonework abound, and the 30 luxurious rooms (each with cable TV, plus a telephone in both the bedroom and bathroom, and hair dryer) reflect tasteful decor. Amenities include a swimming pool, a small shop, a bar, and the elegant Terraza del Sol restaurant, which is earning its own acclaim. Airport transfers are provided. You can rent the hotel minivan. Rates: $98 s/d; $125 suite; $15 extra person, including continental breakfast.

Luxury: The **Camino Real,** Apdo. 11856, San José 1000, tel. (800) 521-5753 or 289-7000, fax 289-8998; in North America, tel. (800) 722-6466, opposite the Multi-Plaza two km west of Escazú, is a classy option for those who prefer large-scale hotels with contemporary opulence. The hotel is set in landscaped grounds including a clover-shaped pool with swim-up bar. Each of the 261 a/c rooms is luxuriously carpeted, with a 25-inch TV, electronic key lock, direct-dial telephone with voice mail, safety box, hair dryer, and other niceties that include a king-size bed with orthopedic mattress, plus a lounge chair and writing desk with classical hints. Bathrooms are magnificent—magnesium-bright lighting and marble. Go on, indulge—wallow in the deep, deep bathtub. The top floor—the Camino Real Club—has 54 rooms, all with bathrobes, daily newspaper, concierge and valet services, and a daily cocktail party. Here, too, are five junior suites and the posh presidential suite. The hotel—centered on a five-story atrium lobby—has a fully equipped business center and a con-

ference center. The Azulejo Café serves reasonably priced meals. Contemporary fades to classical in the Restaurant Mirage, with a splendidly Baroque feel and a pianist to add mood; French-inspired gourmet cuisine costs $5-20. A health and fitness center, massage parlor, beauty center, stores, car rental agency, and travel agency complete the picture. A shuttle runs between the hotel and downtown San José. And a public bus runs nearby. If driving from Escazú, take the Santa Ana road to Centro Comercial Guachipelín, turn right, and right again after 800 meters. Rates: $150 standard; $180 Club; $325-540 suites.

The aptly named **Alta,** tel. 282-4160 or 888-388-ALTA (888-888-2582), fax 282-4162, e-mail: hotlalta@sol.racsa.co.cr; in the U.S., Interlink 964, P.O. Box 025635, Miami, FL 33102, tel. (888) 388-2582, on a hillside three km west of Escazú on the "old road" to Santa Ana, offers the best of both worlds: the tranquility of an out-of-town setting as well as the uproar of San José close at hand. The thoroughly contemporary hotel, which opened in late 1997, is lent a medieval monastical feel by its gently curved arches, hand-forged ironwork, whitewashed narrow corridors, cathedral ceiling, and a stairway cascading down between lofty columns and palms. New York designer Keller Henderson has lent her aesthetic sensibility to the five-story hotel's 23 deluxe rooms (including four suites and a staggering Penthouse suite with three guest rooms), with real ocher walls, terracotta tile floors, hardwoods stained with sienna, and subdued autumn colors. The splendid bathrooms have bathtubs inset in Romanesque alcoves and kimono-style robes. The result is understated elegance. Some rooms proffer modest views from private balconies; others hug the oval, glass-tiled swimming pool in the shade of a spreading guanacaste tree. The top-floor suite is sublime and even has its own library and *mirador* courtyard with fountain. The La Luz restaurant serves some of the best cuisine in the central valley. It has a full-service spa with sauna and massage, plus executive services for businessfolk. Rates: $130 s ($150 deluxe); $190 s, $220 d (suite) low season; $180 s, $210 d (deluxe), $240 s, $270 d (suite) high season. The Penthouse Suite costs $1,450 nightly year-round. Recommended.

In The Hills

Budget: The rustic **Linda Vista Lodge**, Apdo. 785, Escazú 1250, tel. 228-5854, fax 228-8010; in the U.S., SJO 998, P.O. Box 025216, Miami, FL 33106, is okay for those who don't mind things rough around the edges. It has nine all-hardwood rooms, some with a stone fireplace and all with tin roofs. Some share baths. There are also more charming and cozy stone cabins with kitchenettes and simple stone walls. There's a huge lounge with a stone fireplace. It offers a wonderful view. Rates: $25 s, $30 d, or $60 d for a three-day special, including breakfast.

Inexpensive: The **Pico Blanco Inn**, Apdo. 900, Escazú 1250, tel. 228-1908 or 289-6197, fax 289-5189, is a bed and breakfast at the end of a cobbled drive in San Antonio de Escazú. The English owner has stamped a very British imprint: lots of wicker furniture and a cozy Georgian-style bar-cum-restaurant. The 20 comfortable rooms all feature private balconies with fantastic views, plus terra-cotta tile floors, Peruvian wall-hangings, carved hardwood headboards, and small bathrooms with hot water. There's a swimming pool, and a disco was to be added in 1998. There are also two two-bedroom cottages. Rates: $35 s, $45 d, $55 t, $65 quad. Reduced rates for longer stays.

Park Place, Apdo. 1012, Escazú, tel./fax 228-9200, is a modern, 370-square-meter bed and breakfast with four rooms and two shared bathrooms. A huge lofty-ceilinged lounge with tall windows lets in a lot of light. You can warm yourself on cool evenings beside the small open-hearth fireplace, prepare a do-it-yourself breakfast in the full kitchen, and admire the view out over the valley from the interior veranda upstairs. Bedrooms are very homey, with hardwood floors and ceilings and mammoth walk-in showers. Bus service to San José is right outside the door. Rates: $45 s/d, $176 weekly. At press time, a new owner was unsure if he would continue to operate as a hotel.

Las Golondrinas, Apdo. 672-1250 Escazú, tel. 228-6448, fax 228-6381, is a secluded "B&B cabaña" amid a half-hectare orchard with panoramic view in the hills above San Antonio. The rustic cabin has a kitchenette and bathroom. Rates: $50 d ($210 weekly, $600 monthly).

The **Parvati Mountain Inn**, Apdo. 20, Escazú 1250, tel. 228-4011, has four rooms with shared bath. Yoga and meditation classes are given.

Expensive: Rhett and Scarlett would be aghast to find **Tara**, 1459, Escazú 1250, tel. 228-6992, fax 228-9651, e-mail: tarasp@sol.racsa.co.cr, website www.magi.com/crica/hotels/tara.html; in the U.S., Interlink 345, P.O. Box 025635, Miami, FL 33152. a bed and breakfast. But there it is, foursquare on the hill above Escazú. Who said the South's plantation lifestyle has gone with the wind? The Greek-revival plantation mansion—complete with Corinthian columns, period-piece furnishings, dark hardwoods, and 15 resplendent bedrooms with antique rosewood tester beds and private verandas—makes it easy to sense the whole opulent antebellum mystique. There are also 26 two-bedroom villas in classical style, all with fax, printer, and computer systems with Internet access. Tara offers a completely equipped workout room, pool and gazebo with jacuzzi and recently added barbecue terrace, and black-and-white-tiled pavilion patio and croquet lawn with staggering views over the central valley, with the meniscuses of Poás and Barva Volcanoes in full view. You'll like Tara's orderliness and its lush gardens with tropical plants perfuming the air. Guests eat in a formal dining room, set with silver, crystal, candles, and fresh flowers. And health nuts will love **Scarlett's Fountain of Youth Spa**, with gym, aerobics rooms, saunas, steam rooms, massage, and a wide range of inclusive programs from the "Jetlag Special" to "Bonnie's Beauty Bounty." The basic "Novia" program includes aerobics class, sauna, body polish, body cocoon, and manicure ($59). Professional staff offer a range of fitness programs. Also available are reflexology, lymphatic drainage, eye-lifting, acupuncture, aromatherapy, mud treatments, and therapies for cellulite and stress. A conference center was recently added, too. Alas, the place is aloof and lacks welcoming warmth. Room rates: $72-90 single room; $100-125 standard suite; $124-155 junior suite; $152-190 superior suite; $190 poolside bungalow; $250 villa, including continental breakfast. Special spa packages are offered. Apdo.

FOOD

Costa Rican

Chango, tel. 228-1173, in San Rafael, serves Tico and Cuban fare with a Yankee twist, mainly steaks, seafoods, and grilled pork dishes (entrées from $7-12). For a totally rustic adobe eatery in the hills, head to Cuesta Grande de San Antonio de Escazú and the **Restaurante y Mirador Tíquicia,** tel. 289-5839, where the views are mesmerizing. The hacienda has a glassed-in terrace and an open patio. Your meal is prepared over charcoal. It mostly caters to groups and hosts folkloric dancing on Wednesday evenings ($28 including dinner and transfers from San José). A minimum $4 is charged.

Costa Rican Nouvelle

At **La Luz** in the Hotel Alta, on the old road to Santa Ana, American-born chef Sherman Johnson conjures up dishes reaching toward sublime heights: Johnson fuses Costa Rican ingredients with "Pacific rim, California, Southwest, and Caribbean with a touch of the Mediterranean thrown in for balance." The setting—a contemporary remake on a Tudor theme, including fleur-de-lys fabrics—is classy, the views splendid, and the service exemplary. Prices are very fair. Try the macadamia nut-crusted chicken in *guaro*-chipotle cream, or fiery garlic prawns in tequila lime-butter sauce ($12), followed by killer desserts such as chocolate macadamia tart. Breakfast—accompanied by New Age or jazz music—options include pulled pork, potato hash, and poached egg and *salsa cruda* ($7).

Continental

The **Restaurante María Alexandra,** tel. 228-4876, offers reasonably priced European cuisine in a warm, friendly ambience enhanced by a lush courtyard and floodlit pool. The **Terraza del Sol** restaurant, tel. 289-8843, in the Hotel Sangildar serves international cuisine with a strong French and Italian flair. Choose to dine in or out to a backdrop of classical music. Great desserts. A good place for Sunday champagne buffet brunch. Also try **Café el Sol Restaurant,** tel. 228-1645, two blocks east of the church in central Escazú. It serves a wide range of salads, seafoods, sandwiches, pastas, and fish and meat dishes.

The Tara hotel's **Atlanta Restaurant,** tel. 228-6992, offers grand elegance, spectacular views, and such dishes as grilled beef with shrimp and bernaise sauce ($11), and lobster bisque ($5). It has an all-you-can-eat Pasta Night each Sunday, and a Family Fun Sunday brunch (11 a.m.-2 p.m.) with free balloons and a magician.

Le Monastère, tel. 289-4404, fax 228-6370, has been called a "religious dining experience," not for the cuisine but for the venue—a restored chapel amid gardens in the hills east of town. You can't miss it. It has a tall cross in electricneon green. The waiters are dressed like monks, and you'll dine to gregorian chants as background music. The menu includes grilled lamb chops, and *vol au vent* of asparagus. Expect to pay $30 pp. Dinner only. Closed Sunday; reservations recommended. Turn south at Paco Factory on the Santa Ana road from Escazú and follow the green crosses.

Other top-notch choices are the **Restaurant Pociones,** next to the plaza in San Miguel; **Lukas** and **El Capriccio** in San Rafael; and the exclusive and expensive **Arlene Restaurant,** tel. 228-0370, opposite the Costa Rica Country Club.

Italian

The fashionable place for Italian is the handsome, atmospheric **Hostaria Cerutti,** tel. 228-4511, 200 meters south of El Cruce, offering elegance and such specialties as squid in red wine ($7) and taglioni lobster ($14). You'll find a **Pizza Hut** in the Los Anonos Shopping Center.

Mexican

The upscale **La Leyenda,** tel. 228-6846, on the hill half-a-mile south of El Cruce, serves "high Mexican" nouvelle cuisine indoors and on an outdoor patio overlooking a small pool. Fashionable decor appeals to the in crowd. The menu includes molé ($7) and sweet peppers stuffed with sirloin, almonds, and raisins ($8). The **Restaurante Tapatio,** a Mexican steak house in Plaza Colonial Escazú, is also recommended.

Asian

The highly acclaimed **Restaurant Beijing City,** tel. 228-6939, is on the road to Santa Ana; closed Monday.

Seafood and Steaks

Órale, tel. 228-6438, in Centro Comercial Trejos Montealegre, specializes in seafoods. It's a nocturnal hot spot, with lively music and an outdoor bar that claims the "best margaritas south of Mexico." At **El Ché Restaurant,** tel. 228-1598, you can watch traditional Argentinian delicacies being prepared in front of your eyes on an open barbecue rotisserie. A churassco costs $8. It also serves a charcoal-grilled corvina al ajillo (sea bass with garlic; $10). El Ché has rustic yet endearing ambience—a piece of the pampas transplanted. Alternately, for steak and seafood, try **La Cascada,** tel. 228-0906, or **Barbecue Los Anonos,** tel. 228-0180, in San Rafael de Escazú. The latter is *the* place for barbecued meats ($6-12). Closed on Monday. **Lamm's** is a venerable steak house in San Rafael.

Cafes

Don't leave Escazú without checking out **Rincón de la Calle Real,** a bookshop-cum-cafe run by American artist Meredith Paul. The place looks as if it just fell from a painting of a *campesino* home, and is replete with fine works of art. You can sip coffee and read your favorite newspaper or a good book (Meredith stocks leading U.S. journals and best-sellers) at wrought iron tables, and even enjoy live jazz and classical music on full moon nights. The turnoff is on the road to Santa Ana, next to Pizzeria Il Pomodoro.

You can buy gourmet foods at **Ritmo Culinarios,** tel. 228-7978, 300 meters south of El Cruce (closed Sunday).

ENTERTAINMENT

Escazú is a happenin' spot for chic Ticos, who warm-up with drinks at **Fandango,** then head next door to **Babu,** a fun, hip-hoppin' place in the Centro Comercial Trejos Montealegro. **Q'tal,** tel. 228-4091, opposite El Cruce shopping plaza, has a piano bar. Every Wednesday is rock 'n' roll night, and there's a talent spotting show every Wednesday, Thursday, and Friday 6-8 p.m.

Café Havana Coffee & Cigar Bar, tel. 228-6735, in Centro Comercial Trejos Montealegro, is *the* spot to plop into a soft sofa and enjoy the aromas of a damn good Cuban stogie upstairs in the smoker's lounge, accompanied by Cuban music. It offers educational evenings on Tuesday, and serves espresso (75 cents) and lattes ($1.20). Hours: Mon.-Wed. 7 a.m.-7 p.m.; Thurs.-Sat. 7 a.m. until closing.

Escazú took a cue from the pool-hall craze that swept the United States a few years ago. **Bola Ocho** ("Eight Ball") is an upscale hall in the Plaza Colonial Escazú. No floor-spitting, cigar-sucking pool sharks here, thank goodness. The place gets crowded weekdays and weekends with upscale young Ticos; even women are trading discos for pool on Saturday night (I like the sensual way they purse their lips when they chalk up and blow the powder off the tips of the cues—suddenly, pool seems so sexy). Another option is **Mac's American Bar,** tel. 228-2237, a sports bar—popular with expat gringos—opposite the El Cruce Shopping Center. The place is run—surprise—by two Brits. It has four pool tables upstairs; they rent for $2 for 30 minutes, or $3 an hour. Burgers, hot dogs, and fries are served. A great place for a break.

Russel's, tel. 228-6740, in the Centro Comercial Trejos, has musicians to entertain while you eat. **Vivaldi,** tel. 228-9332, features an Argentinian guitarist, plus karaoke (and the antipasto bar is recommended). Or hop down the road to Santa Ana on Wednesday to hear an irreverent expat blues band, Blind Pig, at the **Cebolla Verde,** tel. 282-8905. How irreverent? Well, lead guitarist Fat Boy Fowler, "though a thin man," reportedly "takes his name from the way his guitar emulates the moans and groans of large-bodied women, for whom he has a fondness."

There's a two-screen cinema in Plaza Colonial Escazú.

THINGS TO BUY

Check out the superb stained-glass windows and wares at **Creaciones Santos,** tel. 289-6555, at the entrance to San Miguel de Escazú off Calle L Cortes. **El Sabor Tico,** tel. 228-7221, souvenir and gift store has a large collection of fine crafts from Costa Rica, Guatemala, and El Salvador.

For Barry Beisanz's exquisite handcrafted hardwood items, go right to the source (see above).

INFORMATION, SERVICES, TRANSPORTATION

You can rent or buy surf and mountain bike equipment at **EcoTreks Adventure,** tel. 228-4029, tel./fax 289-8191, website www.ecotreks.com, in

Centro Comercial El Cruce. It also sells beachwear but, more important, offers a wide range of biking, scuba, and adventure packages.

María Alexandra Tours, tel. 228-9072, fax 289-5192, e-mail: matour@sol.racsa.co.cr, in Centro Comercial Trejos Montealegro, offers a tour of Escazú visiting churches, sugarcane mills, coffee plantations, etc. with lunch at a *típico* restaurant. Horseback tours and a nocturnal "Typical Nights" tour are also offered.

Getting There and Away
Buses depart San José from Avenida 6, Calle 14, every 15 minutes. Minibuses leave from Avenida 6 near the San Juan de Dios Hospital. The "Bebedero" bus departs San José from Calle 14 and Avenida 6 for San Antonio de Escazú.

SANTA ANA

Santa Ana is a sleepy town set in a sunny mountain valley about five km west of Escazú and one km south of the Carretera Prospero Fernandez. It was named after the daughter of an early landowner and was previously known as the "Valley of Gold," apparently because local Indians mined gold here. The church dates from 1870, and there are still many old adobe homes and old wooden houses clad in bougainvillea. Many of the patrician houses hark to a time when Santa Ana was *the* place to live and vacation. Back then it was known as "sin city," since many of the secluded country villas were used for illicit trysting. Today it is more famous for ceramics and its onions and garlic and locally made honey. Look for braided onions hanging from restaurant lintels and roadside stands.

Tierra Rica is a large *cerámica artística* workshop midway between Escazú and Santa Ana. In town, the artisans of **Cerámica Santa Ana** still use an old-fashioned kick-wheel to fashion the pots. You'll find some 30 independent potteries in the area.

The **Cerro Pacacua** is an 8,000-hectare forest preserve and bird sanctuary that sits above the town. Mineral springs bubble up from the ground at **El Centro Turístico El Salitral** in the mountains three km south of Santa Ana. It's popular with Ticos on weekends. There's a children's playground, exotic birds in cages, and mediocre

fare is served at a rustic *bohio*. The **Centro Ecuestre Valle de Yos-Oy,** tel. 282-6934, is a riding school near Salitral.

Accommodations
Llama de Bosque, tel. 282-6342, one block north of Santa Ana church, is a venerable house of traditional Costa Rican design run by brother and sister Miguel and Katia Obregon, who were raised here and have turned their childhood home into a rustic bed and breakfast. The 10 sparsely furnished rooms have wood-lined walls, tile floors, and small tiled bathrooms, and are surrounded by a wraparound veranda. The place is popular with backpackers. A souvenir shop specializes in locally made crafts. Out back, amid a riot of bougainvillea and heliconias, is the offbeat Bosque Café, with hammocks and chairs for relaxing; it's known for its *refrescos,* pizzas, and *típico* cuisine. One of Costa Rica's most notable jazz musicians, Manuel Obregon, plays nightly. Rates: $27 s, $32 d, including breakfast.

Apartotel Paradiso Canadiense, Apdo. 68-6151, Santa Ana 2000, tel./fax 282-5870, is a Canadian-run unit with one two-bedroom and four one-bedroom apartments. Each is fully furnished and has a TV lounge. Daily rates are $50-60; weekly rates are $225-250.

For those seeking a healing retreat there's the **Centro Creativo,** tel. 282-8769, fax 282-6959, which offers yoga, meditation, and art classes, along with basic accommodations. Four basic rooms share baths. Predictably, it serves health food. Rates: $18 s, $28 d, including breakfast.

Food
Tony's Ribs, tel. 282-5650, at the west end of the Santa Ana shopping center, fires up its grill nightly. Ribs, chicken, seafood, and steaks—and *bocas* with drinks (including exotic cocktails)—are accompanied by music and views of the valley from the open-air terrace. If you're passing through on Sunday, call in for the grand buffet lunch at **Casa Quitirrisi,** tel. 282-5441, a venerable adobe house with outside dining patio. I hear rave reviews about the food. Open for dinner only, Tues.-Sat., with live music on Friday and Saturday.

Rancho Macho, tel. 228-7588, in the hills above town serves Tico fare such as sweet fried onion, barbecued chicken *(la plancha de gallo)* and the like, cooked over a coffee-wood fire. Typical meals cost about $6. There's often live music, and always great views from the terrace. It's very popular with locals.

A good place to try roasted onions is the down-to-earth, open-air **El Estribo,** an Argentinian restaurant on the west side of the ridge dividing Escazú from Santa Ana, on the old Santa Ana road on the east edge of town. You can watch your fare being prepared over a blazing open grill behind a sturdy wall of logs. The restaurant serves *típico* dishes, including *punta de lomito El Estribo,* steak permeated with a coffee-smoked flavor. The locals wash their meals down with rum; the wine is considered cheap plonk. Roberto entertains with guitar and song.

Getting There
Buses depart San José from Calle 16, Avenida 1, every 15 minutes. Driving, take the Santa Ana exit off the Carretera Prospero Fernandez freeway; or, from Escazú, take the road west from El Cruce in San Rafael (this road has some steep hills and windy bends).

PIEDADES

Piedades is a peaceful agricultural village—coffee is important hereabouts—with a beautiful church boasting impressive stained-glass windows and a jade-green exterior.

The town is famous as the home of American craftsman Jay Morrison, who turns out fine furniture—chests, desks, mirrors, tables, and chairs—rendered with forceful majesty from cristóbal, cenizaro, cocobolo, and lace wood from hardwoods. Morrison owns two large plots of land at Tárcoles and Turrúcares that he is reforesting in native timber. His showroom, **Tierra Extraña,** tel. 282-6697, is three km west of Santa Ana; turn left at Bar la Enramada as you enter Piedades. From here, signs direct you to the showroom.

Horseback Riding
Club Hípico La Caraña, tel. 282-6106 or 282-6754, a highly regarded equestrian club, offers classes in dressage and jumping, as well as horseback tours in the mountains south of Santa Ana. You can also rent horses ($2) at **Rancho

Macho,** tel. 228-7588, in the hills southeast of town (the turnoff is just east of the Red Cross).

Accommodations
A few kilometers west of Piedades, in the hillside hamlet of La Trinidad, is **Albuergue El Marañon,** Apdo. 1880, San José 1000, tel. 249-1271, fax 249-1761, surrounded by an orchard and with views toward Poás. This simple yet tasteful and utterly reclusive place has eight rooms (two triples)—four in the garden with private patios and bathrooms with solar-heated water. Hammocks are slung beneath ranchitas in the garden. There's also a three-room apartment with kitchen. The place is popular with Germans. Children welcome. Rates: $22 s, $30 d with shared bath, including breakfast; $28 s, $40 d with private bath. Your German and Costa Rican hosts, Frank Doyé and Anabelle Contreras Castro, run Cultourica, a tour company offering three- to 20-day excursions throughout the country. They also host two-week Spanish language courses.

Splendid is the word for **Hotel Posada Canal Grande,** Apdo. 84, Santa Ana, tel. 282-4089, fax 282-5733, website www.novanet.co.cr/canal, in the heart of an old coffee *finca,* 800 meters north of the church in Piedades. The two-story villa-hotel is operated by a Florentine art collector and is popular with Italians. The lodge boasts an old terra-cotta tile floor, rustic antique furnishings, plump leather chairs, and a fireplace. The 12 bedrooms have parquet wood floors, exquisite rattan-framed queen-size beds with Guatemalan bedspreads, cable TV, and wide windows offering views toward the Gulf of Nicoya. Italian taste is everywhere, from the ultra-chic furniture and halogen lamps to the classical vases overflowing with flower bouquets, the ceramic bowls full of fruit, and the antique Italian prints gracing the walls. The hotel embraces a large pool. The grounds are mantled in groves of grapefruit, bananas, mango, and coffee trees in rows that undulate like a long, swelling sea. It has a restaurant, sauna, and tour agency, and massage and horseback rides are offered. Airport transfers provided. Rates: $55 s, $65 d, $85 t low season; $60 s, $70 d, $90 t high season, including breakfast.

Food
The elegant **Restaurante Canal Grande** at the Hotel Posada Canal Grande attempts ambitious

Italian fare, such as scallops al vino ($6) and pastas from $5.

CIUDAD COLÓN

Ciudad Colón, about eight km west of Santa Ana, is a pretty and neat little town spoilt by an ugly modern church—a true carbuncle. Coffee is an important crop here. Retired Chicagoan, Jim Moberg, lovingly maintains a menagerie of more than 140 **tropical birds,** including toucans and macaws. The "Birdman of Colón" welcomes visitors by advance arrangement, tel. 249-1402.

Reserva Forestal el Rodeo

Supposedly, this reserve—in the hills three km west of town and part of a cattle estate called Hacienda el Rodeo—protects the largest remaining tract of virgin forest in the Meseta Central. In the late 1970s, Emilio Ramírez Rojas and his uncle Cruz Rojas Bennett, two conservationists, philosophers, and idealists, donated 350 hectares of primary forest on an untouched part of their estate to the nation. You can rent horses for $3 per hour at **Hacienda el Rodeo,** tel. 249-1013, which is popular with Ticos on weekends. There's a rustic restaurant here, where a simple meal costs $2.

The family also donated an adjoining 100 hectares to the United Nations. From that well-spring came the **University for Peace,** where students from many lands come to pursue disciplines designed to make the world a better place. Visitors are welcome.

Getting There

A bus marked "Ciudad Colón" runs from the Coca-Cola bus terminal in San José.

QUITIRISSI TO SAN IGNACIO DE ACOSTA

South of Cuidad Colón the road climbs past the hamlet of Ticufres to **Quitirissi,** where you crest the ridge of **Cerro de Cedral Escazú.** Suddenly the Talamancas spring into view, wildly scenic, forested and unfarmed, sculpted and scalloped in rugged relief.

If you turn south two km beyond Quitirrisi, you can enjoy one of the most splendid drives in

toucan

the country, perfect for an afternoon journey from San José. Follow the road south to **Tabarcia,** and turn left for **Chirraca** and the **Balneario Valle Cantado,** with swimming pools fed by hot springs (open Fri.-Sun.). East of the *balneario,* the road is unpaved all the way to San Ignacio de Acosta, from where you can return to San José via Aserrí or turn south and follow the "Route of the Saints" (see below).

The rough roads are little traveled. And the landscapes are truly spectacular. Despite some steep, enduring grades, the circuit grants a joyous communion with one of Costa Rica's most splendid regions.

SANTIAGO DE PURISCAL AND VICINITY

Santiago de Puriscal (called Puriscal by locals), 20 km west of Ciudad Colón, is a quiet yet important agricultural town noted for its intense seismic activity and as a center for a major reforestation project—**Arbofilia,** tel. 235-5470—which involves local *campesinos* and which you can visit for educational tours (contact Jungle Trails, tel. 255-3486). Santiago is centered on a large square with lots of "monkey puzzle" trees (araucaria pine) and overlooked by a large and pretty if threadbare church surrounded by bougainvillea. Jeep-taxis line the south side of the square. An orchid hobbyist, Eugenio Esquivel, tends a nursery (300 meters north of the post office) with more than 350 orchid species. Visitors are welcome. There's a **Banco Nacional** one block east of the plaza.

Midway between Ciudad Colón and Santiago, at Km 30, is the entrance for the **Guayabo Indian Reserve,** protecting the land of the Quitirrisi Indians on the slopes of Cerro Turrubares. This remnant indigenous community lives relatively marginalized (reportedly, many of its members can barely speak Spanish), though several members eke out livings as weavers; you may see some of their fine baskets on sale at roadside stalls.

From Santiago you can turn north and follow a dirt road to Turrúcares and La Garita or follow a paved road southwest to Salitral and thence follow a little used but scenic route to the Quepos and the Central Pacific coast.

Getting There
Buses depart San José for Santiago de Puriscal from Calle 16, Avenidas 1/3 hourly. Bus no. 613 leaves for Quepos from the east side of the church in Santiago.

SALITRALES AND VICINITY

Salitrales, 18 km west of Santiago, nestles atop the southwesternmost flank of the highlands. From here the road descends steeply to the Pacific coast, crossing the Fila Coyolar and Fila Cangreja mountains and meeting the coast road just north of Parrita. Beyond Salitrales the paved road ends, but the dirt road is in reasonably good condition, with little traffic. It's 99 km from Santiago to Quepos. A long-touted paved highway linking the central valley with Orotina, the gateway to the central Pacific, remains far from complete.

La Cangreja Reserve
This reserve is part of Finca Mastatal, a farm where guests can stay in a century-old farm-

house (c/o Puesta del Sol Country Inn, Dept. 305, P.O. Box 025216, Miami, FL 33102, e-mail: puestasol@aol.com; in Costa Rica, tel. 289-6581, fax 289-8766). It lies in the midst of a peaceful pastoral area, with quiet lanes leading through rural hamlets, and wilderness trails leading through pristine forest to waterfalls. Horses can be rented ($9 with guide), with miles of trails leading through forest and along riverbanks with tumbling cascades. The jungle is home to monkeys, parrots, toucans, and countless butterflies. The reserve is about 15 km beyond Salitrales; the turnoff is about 11 km south of Salitrales and leads east to the village of **Mastatal.** The La Cangreja farmhouse is here, with an iron gate. Rates for the farmhouse: $60 d, including refreshments and guide; $90 d, including transportation, day-trip with driver/guide, and lunch or breakfast

SAN ANTONIO DE BELÉN AND VICINITY

This small town, five km north of Santa Ana and two km south of the Juan Santamaría International Airport (and two km west of Ciudad Cariari), lies in the midst of coffee fields but has taken on new importance since the recent opening nearby of the Marriott Hotel and Intel's microprocessor assembly plant. The town has a sleepy provincial feel. Several attractions popular with Ticos lie close at hand. The road system hereabouts is convoluted, however, and finding them isn't easy.

Acua Mania
This 12-hectare aquatic amusement complex, tel. 293-2033, is 500 meters west of the exit for San Antonio de Belén on Autopista General Cañas at Ciudad Cariari, and made a big splash when it opened in January 1995. The open-air water park is centered on a massive 1,300-square-meter pool with volleyball, water slide, and rope swing, plus underwater cave. You'll find at least one dozen water slides, an artificial river, a wave pool, and other attractions to keep kids and kids-at-heart amused. Watch out for the water guns. The grounds have been landscaped with tropical foliage and include picnic areas, miniature golf, go-kart track, plus play

areas for children. Acua Mania also has a video arcade and, appropriately, a swimwear shop plus restaurant. Additional theme settings are in the works. Hours: Tues.-Thurs. and Sunday 10 a.m.-5:30 p.m., Fri.-Sat. 10 a.m.-10 p.m. Admission: $9 adults, $6 children.

Ojo de Agua

Ojo de Agua ("Eye of Water") is a swimming resort, tel. 441-2808, or *balneario*, three km west of San Antonio at San Rafael de Alajuela. The popular resort features a series of swimming pools, a smaller children's pool, and a natural lake fed by a subterranean river. There's also a waterfall surrounded by forest, plus picnic areas, sauna, bar and restaurant, and volleyball, tennis, and soccer facilities. You can hire boats on the lake. Ticos flock on weekends. Entrance: $1 (plus 60 cents for parking).

Accommodations

Villa Belén, tel./fax 239-0740; in the U.S., Villa Belén, Interlink 899, P.O. Box 02-5635, Miami, FL 33102, is an exquisite, American-owned and -run historic hacienda-style villa about three km south of San Antonio de Belén, midway to Santa Ana. This charmer is centered on a courtyard with a swimming pool, and it's surrounded by acres of tropical gardens. Each of the nine rooms is distinct, with dainty furnishings, terra-cotta tile floors, regal drapes, plus cable TVs. A separate two-bedroom apartment is very homey. Facilities include a sauna and colonial-tiled jacuzzi (defunct at last visit), an outdoor barbecue pit, and a large, cozy lounge. Breakfast is served on the patio. The owner, Ginger, is a gung ho gringa who tends her nursery with loving care. Rates: $50 s/d, including continental breakfast and airport pickup. There's also a two-bedroom apartment with kitchen for $70. No children. *Recommended!*

The gringo-owned **Belén Trailer Park,** tel. 239-0421, fax 239-2578, on the north side of San Antonio de Belén on the road to/from Ciudad Cariari, is Costa Rica's only fully equipped RV and camper site. It has hookups with electricity and water for 30 vehicles, plus a dump station, shady lawns for camping, a washing machine, and hot showers (mornings only). The owner was considering converting an old house on the premises into a bed and breakfast with communal kitchen. They permit camping: $5-7 daily,

depending on tent size. Rates: $10 RV per night; $60 weekly; $200 monthly.

Food

Restaurant Rancho Guaitíl, tel. 239-1106, west of San Antonio, is a popular restaurant under a large *palenque* roof. It serves a good choice of salads, seafood dishes, and meats at reasonable prices. In town, try the colonial-style **Restaurant Las Tajiles** and the **Marlin Marisquería,** which has very good Italian seafoods.

Getting There

Buses for Ojo de Agua depart San José from Avenida 1, Calles 20/22, hourly on the half hour, every quarter hour on weekends. Buses also depart Alajuela from Calle 10, Avenida Central.

LA GUÁCIMA

The road west from San Antonio de Belén continues to La Guácima, known on the tourist circuit for the Butterfly Farm, an essential visit on a day-trip from San José and among socialites at the **Los Reyes Country Club,** tel. 438-0004, where on weekends (and occasionally midweek) you may settle with champagne and cucumber sandwiches to watch a chucker or two of polo, a game introduced to Costa Rica in 1898 by the British who came to build the Atlantic Railroad. November through August is polo season, when six national teams compete; the club also hosts international competitions. The social scene here is quite the thing. Pip-Pip! Los Reyes and the Butterly Farm are opposite each other two km south of La Guácima, and are clearly signed from San Antonio de Belén (look for the flying morpho logo, as competing butterfly farms try to divert you by posting their own signs).

La Guácima Race Track has motor races on weekends and hosts the Grand Finale of the International F3 Championship; a Costa Rica Grand Prix (Formula 3) is held in December. **Pro Motor Costa Rica,** Apdo. 150, San José 1002, tel. 233-3166, fax 233-3341, offers tourist packages.

The Butterfly Farm

The Butterfly Farm, Apdo. 2132, Alajuela 4050, tel./fax 438-0115, established in 1983 by Joris

Brinkerhoff and his wife María Sabido as the first commercial butterfly farm in Latin America, has grown to be the second-largest exporter of living pupae in the world. An educational two-hour tour begins with a video documentary introducing the world of butterflies, followed by a guided tour through the gardens and laboratory, where you witness and learn all about each stage of the butterfly life cycle. Hundreds of butterflies representing 60 native species flit about in an endless ballet. Educational signs are posted throughout the garden. Serpentine paths lead to a miniature waterfall where many of the butterflies mate. Photographers should bring a macro lens.

In the wild, the survival rate to adult phase is estimated to be only two percent. Raised under controlled conditions within the netted garden, the survival rate on the farm is 90%, ensuring an ongoing supply for the 30,000 pupae exported annually. Eggs are harvested daily by farm employees. The guides will show you the tiny eggs and larvae which, you're informed, are coded to "eat and grow, eat and grow." The guide will thrust out a fat, four-inch caterpillar to show the point. If a newborn human baby ate at the same rate it would grow to the size of a double-decker bus in two months. You'll also see the pupae hanging in stasis and, with luck, witness a butterfly emerging to begin life anew. Occasionally, butterflies are released into the wild. Because of their relatively short lifespan—an average of 2-3 weeks after becoming butterflies—there's an ongoing demand for replenishment among zoos and butterfly gardens worldwide. Although butterfly activity is greatly reduced in late afternoon, that's the time to enjoy the spectacular show of the *Caligo memnon* (giant owl butterfly), which fly only at dawn and dusk.

Alas, a real honey of an attraction—a bee farm that allowed you to discover what's buzzing in the bee world—closed in 1997 with no plans to reopen. A souvenir store sells items on a lepidopterian theme. A restaurant serves snacks and lunch.

Hours: daily 9 a.m.-5 p.m. Guided tours last two hours; the last tour starts at 3 p.m. Entrance: $14 adult, $7 residents and children (children under four free), and $20 and $14 respectively with transfers. Monday (and Thursday, March-Aug.) is export day, when visitors can watch pupae being packed.

Madame Butterfly Garden and Gaspar Fish Observatory

Copying the Butterfly Farm, this garden, Apdo. 91-1150 San José, tel. 255-2031, fax 255-1946, e-mail: mitour@sol.racsa.co.cr, about five km northwest of the Butterfly Farm, also has trails through netted enclosures where butterflies flit and fleet. You can also see the gaspar fish, a living fossil with an unaltered heritage dating back 180 million years. Hours: daily 8 a.m.-4 p.m. Guided tours are offered.

Accommodations

Hotel Costa Rica Country Inn, Apdo. 807, Alajuela 4050, tel. 438-0179, fax 221-8245, at La Guácima, is a small bed and breakfast with two rooms with private bath for $60 d. It has a pool and jacuzzi.

Getting There

The Butterfly Farm offers direct bus service from major San José hotels daily (by reservation, tel. 438-0400) at 7:30 a.m., 10 a.m., and 2 p.m. and twice daily May-November. Alternately, public buses marked "La Guácima" depart at 11 a.m. and 2 p.m. (except Sunday) from the stop marked "San Antonio/Ojo de Agua" on Avenida 1, Calles 20/22. Take the bus until the last stop (about 60 minutes), from where you walk—follow the signs—about 400 meters. The bus to San José departs at 3:15 p.m.

From Alajuela, buses marked "La Guácima Abajo" depart from Calle 10 and Avenida 2 at 6:20, 9, and 11 a.m., and 1 p.m.; and return at 9:45 and 11:45 a.m., and 1:45, 3:45, and 5:45 p.m. Ask the driver to stop at La Finca de Mariposas.

ALAJUELA AND VICINITY

A mini version of San José with a warmer climate, Alajuela (pop. 35,000) rises gently up the lower slopes of Volcán Poás. The town is 20 km northwest of San José and two km north of Juan Santamaría Airport and the Pan-American Highway. First named La Lajuela in 1657, the town's name was changed several times and finally to Alajuela in 1825, though it's also known locally as "La Ciudad de los Mangos" for the mango trees around the main square. Today, Costa Rica's "second city" is a modestly cosmopolitan town with strong links to the coffee industry. On weekends Alajuela is congested. Saturday is market day, and hundreds of people gather to buy and sell produce fresh from the farm. Soccer is played in the city stadium (home of La Liga soccer team) most Sunday.

SIGHTS

Memories of Juan Santamaría—or "Erizo" (meaning "hedgehog," referring to Santamaría's bristly hair)—the homegrown hero of the Battle of 1856, figure prominently in Alajuela, notably in the **Museo Cultural y Histórico Juan Santamaría,** tel. 441-4775, housed in the former colonial city jail on the northwest corner of the Parque Central, on Avenida 3, Calles Central/2. This small but interesting museum tells the story of the War of 1856 against the no-good American adventurer William Walker (see special topic, "The William Walker Saga" in the Introduction). The two rooms of permanent exhibits are full of maps, paintings, cannons, and other war-era mementoes relating to Alajuela's drummer-boy hero. There's also an exhibit room for local handicrafts. The museum has a good library, plus an auditorium where historical films and cultural programs are offered. Call ahead to arrange a screening of an English-language film. Guided tours are given Tues.-Fri. 9 a.m.-4:30 p.m. Hours: Tues.-Sun. 10 a.m.-6 p.m. Entrance free.

At the heart of town is **Parque Central,** officially called Plaza del General Tomás Guardia. This hub of social activity is a popular hangout for retired men of a certain age—many of them grin-

gos. They sit under the mango trees (favored by blue-gray tanagers), watching the pretty girls and giving nicknames to the passersby (the old men's presence has inspired local wags to dub the park, with pointed metaphor, El Parque de las Palomas Muertas—Park of the Dead Doves). Some of the park benches have chess sets built into them. Twice weekly, classical—and sometimes pop—music is played in the domed bandstand. Any day, look for the resident sloths. Notice, too, the pretty 19th-century structures with fancy iron grilles surrounding the park.

The square is backed by a red-domed colonial-era **cathedral,** simple within, where the bodies of ex-presidents Tomás Guardia and León Cortés Castro are buried. The cathedral was badly damaged by an earthquake in December 1990 and reopened after repairs in 1993. It has

JOHN ANDERSON

monument to the hero Juan Santamaría in Alajuela, inaugurated September 1891

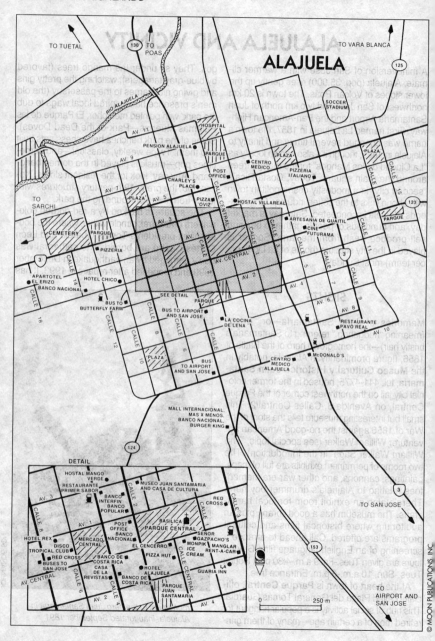

ALAJUELA

TO TUETAL

130 TO POAS

TO VARA BLANCA

125

SOCCER STADIUM

RIO ALAJUELA

AV. 11

HOSPITAL

PENSION ALAJUELA

AV. 9

PARQUE

PLAZA

PLAZA

CENTRO MEDICO

POST OFFICE

PIZZERIA ITALIANO

AV. 7

CHARLEY'S PLACE

PLAZA

AV. 5

CALLE CENTRAL

PIZZA OVIZ

HOSTAL VILLAREAL

TO SARCHI

CALLE 13

CALLE 15

123

PARQUE

3

AV. 3

ARTESANIA DE GUAITIL

CINE FUTURAMA

CEMETERY

PARQUE

AV. CENTRAL

PIZZERIA

AV. 2

CALLE 5

CALLE 7

3

APARTOTEL EL ERIZO

HOTEL CHICO

BANCO NACIONAL

CALLE 14

BUS TO BUTTERFLY FARM

SEE DETAIL

PARQUE

AV. 4

AV. 6

AV. 8

RESTAURANTE PAVO REAL

BUS TO AIRPORT AND SAN JOSE

LA COCINA DE LENA

AV. 10

CALLE 8

CALLE 6

CALLE 18

CALLE 12

PLAZA

CALLE 10

BUS TO AIRPORT AND SAN JOSE

CENTRO MEDICO ALAJUELA

McDONALD'S

MALL INTERNACIONAL, MAS X MENOS, BANCO NACIONAL, BURGER KING

124

3

TO SAN JOSE

153

DETAIL

HOSTAL MANGO VERDE

RESTAURANTE PRIMER SABOR

AV. 3

MUSEO JUAN SANTAMARIA AND CASA DE CULTURA

CALLE 2

RED CROSS

CALLE 3

BANCO INTERFIN BANCO POPULAR

AV. 1

HOTEL REX

CALLE 8

POST OFFICE BANCO NACIONAL

MERCADO CENTRAL

BASILICA

PARQUE CENTRAL

SENOR GAZPACHO'S MONPIK ICE CREAM

MANGLAR RENT-A-CAR

DISCO TROPICAL CLUB

RED CROSS

BUSES TO SAN JOSE

EL CENCERRO

BANCO DE COSTA RICA

PIZZA HUT

CALLE CENTRAL

CALLE 1

CASA DE LA REVISTAS

HOTEL ALAJUELA

GUARIA INN

BANCO DE COSTA RICA

AV. CENTRAL

CALLE 6

AV. 2

PARQUE JUAN SANTAMARIA

AV. 4

CALLE 4

0   250 m

MOON

TO AIRPORT AND SAN JOSE

© MOON PUBLICATIONS, INC.

some impressive religious statuary, including a glass cabinet brimful of eclectic and macabre offerings to La Negria.

Two blocks south of Parque Central is **Parque Juan Santamaría,** a tiny concrete plaza with a dynamic statue of the national hero rushing forward with flaming torch and rifle to defend the country against the American invader William Walker. A rumor suggests that the statue is actually that of a French soldier and looks nothing like Santamaría. The French manufacturer, it is said, sent the wrong statue, but the city fathers put it up anyway.

Alajuela has several other appealing churches, including a simple baroque structure five blocks east of the main plaza.

At Río Segundo de Alajuela, three km southeast of Alajuela, Richard and Margot Frisius breed scarlet macaws for eventual release into the wild. Their home and breeding center—**Flor de May,** Apdo. 2306-4050 Alajuela, tel./fax 441-2658, e-mail: richmar@ticonet.co.cr—features two 33-meter-long aviaries where pairs of breeding macaws are housed plus a flyway where they can fly and learn to flock. Dozens of other birds have been welcomed into the Frisius' beautiful home, surrounding a lush botanical garden: the estate was owned and landscaped by the famous botanist and orchid lover, Sir Charles Lankaster. A clinic, laboratory, nursery, and educational visitor's center is planned. The Frisiuses have formed a nonprofit organization—**Amigos de las Aves**—and welcome donations.

FESTIVALS

Every year, **Juan Santamaría Day** (11 April) is cause for serious celebration, with parades, bands, dancing, and arts-and-crafts fairs lasting a full week. The town also hosts the annual nine-day **Mango Festival** in July.

ACCOMMODATIONS

In Town
Shoestring: Hotel Rex, tel. 441-6778, Avenida 1, Calles 6/8, is a bottom-tier place to rest your head. Communal bathrooms—none too clean—have cold showers. Rates: $4 d. In a similar vein,

Hotel Chico, tel. 441-0572, at Calle 10 and Avenidas 1/Central, has 11 clean but basic rooms (some are dingy) with minimal furniture and shared baths ($12 s, $15 d). **Hostal Villa Real,** tel. 441-4022, in an old wooden home at Avenida 3, Calle 1, has five simple rooms (two have shared bathroom) for $10 pp. All are close to the bus terminal. The **Hotel Moderno,** nearby, has also been recommended for budget travelers.

Budget: A good bet, the **Mango Verde Hostel,** tel. 441-6330, fax 442-6527, 50 meters west of the Museo Juan Santamaría, has six rooms with private baths, hot water, fans, plus a shared kitchen and TV lounge. The old house has terracotta tile and wood floors. Rates: $14 s, $26 d, $33 t, including tax.

Pensión Alajuela, tel. 441-6251, Calle Central, Avenida 9, is simple yet appealing, with 10 clean rooms with small, tiled private bathrooms with hot water. There's a snack bar, book exchange, and laundry service. Rates: $10 s, $17 d, shared bath; $15 s, $20 d, private bath. **Hospedaje La Posada,** at Avenida 3, Calle 5, is a bed and breakfast, recommended but not reviewed. Also not reviewed is **Los Andes,** another bed and breakfast that was slated to open as I prepared this book; it's associated with the Peruvian restaurant at Avenida 1 and Calle 4.

The **Colón Mini Hotel** reportedly has spacious rooms with a/c, two double beds, and private baths with hot water. It's run by the same folks who operate Colón Rent-a-Car, tel. 441-1661. Rates: $15 s, $20 d.

I also recommend **La Rana Dorada,** tel. 442-5360, a bed and breakfast with private baths, cable TV, and laundry service; rates: $25. And the spic-and-span **La Guajira Inn** at Avenida 2, Calles 3/5, has five simple rooms with hardwood floors and colorful bedspreads, fans, and private bathrooms with hot water. There's a TV lounge. Rates: $25 s, $30 d, including breakfast.

Inexpensive: Hotel Alajuela, Apdo. 110, Alajuela 4050, tel. 441-1241, fax 441-7912, on the southwest corner of Parque Central, has 50 clean and nicely furnished rooms, with private baths with hot water. Apartment rooms with kitchens in the old section are dark. Laundry service. No restaurant. Rates: $35 s, $40 d, $43 t.

Another good bet, popular with backpackers, is **Charly's Place,** Avenida 5, Calles Central/2, tel./fax 441-0115, with 11 simply yet romantically appointed rooms—hardwood floors and private baths with hot water. The upstairs rooms are well-lit; some rooms downstairs are dingy. Guests can use the kitchen. There's an attractive patio dining area, plus laundry and secure parking. Rates: $18 s low season, $25 high season (shared bath); $25 s, $30 d low season, $30 s, $40 d high season (private bath).

Moderate: The **Hotel Airport Guest House,** Avenida 3 and Calle 4, tel. 442-0354, a colonial-style hostelry, has 24 a/c, carpeted rooms with cable TV and real bathtubs. The hotel is set in beautiful grounds with a pool and a restaurant. Rates: $55-75 d.

The **Apartotel El Erizo,** tel./fax 441-2840, has eight fully furnished apartments with full kitchens and cable TVs, laundry service included. It also has four rooms ($54, up to three people). No restaurant. It's on the western outskirts of town, off the road for Grecia. Rates: $84 for 2-4 people (seventh night free).

Outside Town

Shoestring: The very popular Canadian-run **El Tuetal Lodge,** Apdo. 1346, Alajuela, tel./fax 442-1804, e-mail: tuetal@sol.racsa.co.cr, website www.IslandNet.com/~tuetal, at Tuetal about three km north of Alajuela, has 30 **campsites**—$7 each, plus $3 for a second person and additional people. Campers have access to toilets, showers, and laundry. You can even curl up in your sleeping back in a basic open-sided bamboo-framed "tree house" ($9 s, $12 d). Bunk beds were to be added to form an upscale hostel ($10 pp). The eight-acre grounds include an orchard and a large swimming pool plus a handsome **rancho cafe** where vegetarian and North American meals are served. Horseback rides ($10), ping-pong, and darts are offered.

Inexpensive: El Tuetal Lodge also offers six spacious albeit simple cabins, including three with kitchenettes, private baths, and solar-heated water. Rates: $30 s, $35 d; $10 more with kitchenette.

Another recommended hostelry at Tuetal is **Pura Vida Bed and Breakfast,** Apdo. 1112, Alajuela, tel./fax (800) 585-8943, set amid 24 acres, including beautiful gardens. The handsome old home has five well-lit, well-ventilated rooms with hardwood floors and simple furnishings. Three modest bungalows are below in the garden; all have bathrooms, hot water, kitchenettes, and

two beds. Rates: $45 d, including breakfast for rooms; $65-75 for bungalows. Each has a patio, fireplace, kitchen, and maid service. There's a pool and jacuzzi. New owners had just taken over when I called in November 1997.

Paradise Tropical Inn, tel. 441-4882, 400 meters north of town on Calle 2, has six rooms facing spacious gardens. They're furnished simply, apartment-style, with plump sofas, wood ceilings, and clean bathrooms with hot water. Some smell of cigarette smoke. It has secure parking. Rates: $40 s, $45 d, $50 t, including tax and airport transfers. Low rates are offered for monthlong stays.

El Avión Hotel, Apdo. 43-4003, Alajuela, tel. 441-2079, fax 443-3447; in the U.S., P.O. Box 50612, Lighthouse Point, FL 33074, between Alajuela and the airport, has 10 clean rooms for $30 d with shared bath, $35 d with private bath, including airport transfers. The soulless **Hotel Aeropuerto,** Apdo. 20-4050 Alajuela, tel. 442-0354, fax 441-5922, e-mail: hotelaer@sol.racsa.co.cr, on the Autopista four km west of the airport, has 24 a/c but musty rooms with carpets, fans, telephones, and TVs, plus large, attractive bathrooms with hot water. Airport transfers are offered. It is set back from the freeway and does not get the noise. There's a large-screen TV in the lounge. Rates: $53 s, $65 d, including tax and breakfast. *Overpriced!* A more intimate option is the **Posada Aeropuerto,** tel./ fax 441-7569; in the U.S., tel. 800-330-HOME (800-330-4663), about two km south of the airport. Not inspected. Rates: $38 d, including breakfast. And **Hotel La Cabaña 1863,** tel. 442-9936, fax 441-7242, 200 meters north of the Hampton Inn, 500 meters east of the airport, is a private home with a TV lounge, and rooms with private bath and hot water.

Moderate: The **Hampton Inn,** Apdo. 962, San José 1000, tel. 442-0043, fax 442-9532, e-mail: hampton@sol.racsa.co.cr, website www.centralamerica.com/cr/hotel/hampton.htm, or Resertel, tel. (800) 272-6654, fax 232-3159, is a "two-minute" drive east of the airport terminal. It's perfect if you have tight flight transfers and don't mind charmless motel-style Americana. The 100 a/c rooms (75% nonsmoking) are soundproofed and feature king or two double beds, cable TV with in-room movies, telephones, and lighting you can actually read by. It offers a fully accessible room, airport transfers, and runs to nearby

restaurants. The hotel guarantees "100% satisfaction" or your money back. Rates: $61 s, $67 d
green season; $65 s, $69 d high season; $7
extra person, including continental breakfast
(children under 18 free).

FOOD

Señor Gazpacho, tel. 441-9681, is the happenin' spot. This lively Mexican *tapas* bar on
Avenida Central, Calles Central/1, is popular
with aging gringos (possibly because the wait-
resses are in mini-skirts) and good for nachos, frijoles, burritos, spaghetti dishes (from $3), and
Mexican breakfasts (from $3). Alajuela's small
but lively colony of Peruvians add a touch of au-
thenticity to the **Rincón Peruano Restaurant,**
tel. 442-3977, a favorite hangout of locals at
Avenida 1 and Calle 4. For less than $5 you can
feast on Peruvian dishes, including the restaurant's famous *papa relleno.* Dancing on Tuesday.
The chef, intriguingly, is Russian; she'll make
Russian dishes upon request.

Try **El Cencerro** ("The Cowbell"), facing the
plaza on Avenida Central, for inexpensive charbroiled steaks ($6), special burgers ($4), and
even shish kebab; or **Don Hernán,** tel. 441-
4680, next to the Hotel Alajuela, for hamburgers
and hot dogs. Vegetarians should head to **Soda
Alberto** on Calle 4, Avenidas 1/3.

Las Cocinas de Leña, Calle 2, Avenida 6,
tel. 442-1010, prepares *típico* dishes over coffee-
wood fires and has an extensive beef and
seafood menu. An abundance of potted plants,
but basic decor. **La Esquina de los Mariscos,**
tel. 433-8077, on the south side of the main
square, has seafood at budget prices. For
seafood, also try **Restaurante Turístico Ceviche del Rey,** on Calle 2, one km north of town.
Soda El Parque, on the same block, is recommended for inexpensive, filling breakfasts.

Recommended for Asian fare is **Restaurant
El Primer Sabor,** Avenida Central, Calles Cen-
tral/2, tel. 441-7082, a classy restaurant which
also serves meat dishes such as *lengua en
salsa* (tongue in sauce, $4). For pizzas try **Pizza
Oviz,** Calle Central, Avenida 3, tel. 441-4328;
Pizzeria Italiano, Calle 9, Avenida 3, tel. 442-
0973; or **Pizza Hut,** Avenida 2, Calle Central, tel.
441-2222.

Almibar coffee and pastry shop, Calles 1/3,
Avenida Central, has a fine selection of desserts,
gourmet cakes, and breads and rolls, as does
Trigo Miel. The ice-cream addict should head to
Mönpik, located on the southeast corner of the
main square.

For fast food, try **McDonald's** on Avenida 2,
one block east of the plaza.

ENTERTAINMENT AND SHOPPING

Señor Gazpacho is lively at night; it receives
ESPN on the TV. **Bar Evelyn,** Calle Central,
Avenida 1/3, tel. 441-2867, has live guitar music
daily except Friday. **Disco Tropical Club** is at
Calle 6, Avenidas Central/1. More down-to-earth
local color is provided at **Indianapolis Taberna,**
Calle 8, Avenidas 1/3, where the scene report-
edly can get fairly rowdy. Movies are shown at
Cine Milan on the south side of Parque Central
($1.50), and **Cine Futurama,** Avenida Central,
Calles 7/5.

Artesanías Guaitíl, at Avenida 1, Calle 5, tel.
441-0640, sells pottery, carvings, earthenware,
and other artwork. **Fujifilm,** tel. 441-5251, has an
outlet at Calle Central, Avenidas Central/2.

INFORMATION AND SERVICES

There's a **tourist information booth,** tel. 442-
8632, fax 442-9417, in the airport. The **Alajuela
Welcome Center,** on Avenida 2, Calles 2/4,
tel./fax 441-1141, supposedly provides travelers' information and acts as a full-service travel
agency, but I couldn't find it.

Banks: The Banco Nacional has two branches along Avenida Central at Calle 12 and Calle 2.
There are several other banks downtown. You
can get a cash advance against Visa or MasterCard at Credomatic, Avenida 3, Calles Cen-
tral/2, tel. 441-2080.

Medical: Medical clinics downtown include the
Clínica Medical Juan Santamaría, tel. 441-6284;
Laboratorio Biopsias, tel. 221-4545, opposite the
statue of the national hero; and the Centro Medical, tel. 441-1971, at Calle 3, Avenidas 5/7. Hospital San Rafael, tel. 441-5011, is at Avenida 9,
Calles Central/1. There are plenty of pharmacies
in town.

Police: The Guardia Rural, tel. 441-5277, is at Calle 2, Avenida 1. For the local traffic police—"highway patrol"—call 441-7411.

Getting There and Around
By Bus: TUASA, tel. 222-4650, buses depart San José from Avenida 2, Calle 10/12, every 10 minutes, 5 a.m.-midnight; and every 40 minutes from Calle 2, Avenida 2, midnight-4:20 a.m. Return buses depart from Calle 8, Avenidas Central/1. The buses run past the airport.

By Car: Manglar Rent-a-Car, tel. 442-1534, fax 442-6789, has an office at Calle 3 and Avenida 2.

ALAJUELA TO VARA BLANCA

Above Alajuela, coffee plantations give way to dairy farms and fields of ornamental plants, ferns, and strawberries separated by forests of cedar that form important watersheds and edge up the slopes of Volcán Poás (to the west) and Barva (to the east). From Alajuela, Avenida 7 exits town and turns uphill via Carrizal and Cinco Esquinas to **Vara Blanca,** a village nestled just beyond the saddle between the volcanoes on the edge of the Continental Divide about 25 km north of Alajuela. The drive is marvelously scenic. At Vara Blanca, you can turn west for Poás Volcano National Park, or turn south and descend via the **La Paz Waterfall** to the northern lowlands. La Catarata la Paz—the "Peace Waterfall"—is a pencil-thin fall that attracts Ticos en masse on weekends. A trail leads you behind the cascade.

Accommodations
La Rana Holandesa, tel. 483-0816, one km above Carrizal, about 15 km northeast of Alajuela, is the home of Dutch-Tica owners—John and Vicky Dekker—who offer three simple rooms (two share a large bathroom) with hot water. The larger room with small private bath has two bunks and a single bed. There's laundry service. The Dekkers provide free airport pickup plus guided tour for $70. Rates: $17 s, $25 d including full breakfast served on the backyard patio; dinners are $3 extra. A seven-night all-inclusive package costs $650 d, $900 t, $1,200 quad, including dinners and four sightseeing trips.

The hillside **Strawberry Farm Bed & Breakfast,** tel. 483-1012, three km above Carrival, is surrounded by pastures with spectacular views down over the valley enjoyed through picture windows. The place is simply furnished in Midwest-style Americana and is run by a charming and lively hostess, Claudia Grimm, from Pennsylvania. She bakes dessert cakes and makes homemade strawberry jams and has a pack of German shepherds (which she breeds) that swarm at your heels. The three rooms have tile floors, throw rugs, large windows, and wheelchair-accessible private bathrooms. There's a lounge with library, plus a stable for guided horseback rides ($50). Children are welcome. Rates: $35 s/d including breakfast; a weekend package costs $120, including dinner on Friday, breakfast Saturday, and a horseback ride.

At Vara Blanca, **La Suiza,** tel. 225-3243, has *cabinas* and offers horseback rides and birding; it's 500 meters east of the gas station. A new restaurant and more *cabinas* are under construction nearby.

Food
Bar/Restaurante Rancho Axelu, tel. 483-0841, one km above Cinco Esquinas, is a popular upscale restaurant view marvelous views and rustic decor. It serves *comida típica* and has live music Friday and Saturday nights. Trails lead through landscaped grounds and woodland.

The **Restaurant Vara Blanca,** tel. 482-2193, behind the gas station at Vara Blanca, is an atmospheric eatery of volcanic stone and timbers serving *comida típica*.

ALAJUELA TO POÁS

The scenic drive up Poás Volcano takes you through quintessential coffee country, with rows of shiny dark-green bushes creating artistic patterns on the sensuous slopes. Farther up, coffee gives way to fern gardens and fields of strawberries grown under black shade netting, then dairy pastures on steeper slopes. En route, you'll pass several stalls selling fresh strawberries *(fresas)* and freshly baked cookies.

There are two routes from Alajuela. The first leads directly from downtown Alajuela via Calle 2. The second leads north from San José de

Alajuela (see "Western Outskirts of Alajuela," below) via San Pedro and Sabana Redondo. The two roads merge at the hamlet of **Fraijanes**, about 20 km north of Alajuela.

Alvaro Alfaro, a primitivist peasant painter, has an **art studio** on the grounds of Xandari plantation, above Tacacori, about five km north of Alajuela. **La Casa del Café**, tel. 449-5014, fax 449-5142, three km north of San Isidro de Alajuela and three km east of Fraijanes, is a cafe and coffee shop perched above the coffee fields, with a wooden balcony from which to admire the views or watch the pickers at work. **Parque Laguna Fraijanes**, tel. 448-5322, one km east of Fraijanes, is an 18-hectare recreation area of forested parkland round a 1.5-hectare lagoon popular with Ticos on weekends for fishing and swimming. You'll find basketball courts,

a volleyball court, a soccer field, a children's playground, picnic tables and grills, plus horses for rent ($3 per hour). Alcohol is not allowed. The park is run by the Ministry of Culture, Youth, and Sport. Hours: Tues.-Sun. 9 a.m.-3:30 p.m. Entrance: $1, kids 50 cents.

Poasito, two km above Fraijanes, is the uppermost village on the mountain and a popular way station for hungry sightseers. The road to the right leads east four km to Vara Blanca.

Accommodations

You really shouldn't miss Xandari, if you have—and are willing to spend—the money.

Lower Down: The modern and elegant albeit soulless **Hotel Buena Vista,** six km north of Alajuela at Las Pilas de San Isidro, tel. 442-8585, fax 442-8701, e-mail: bvista@sol.racsa.co.cr; in

---

SPECIAL HOTEL: XANDARI

This strangely named hotel, Apdo. 1485, Alajuela 4050, tel. 443-2020, fax 442-4847, e-mail: paradise@xandari.com; in the U.S., Box 1449, Summerland, CA 93067, tel. (805) 684-7879 or (800) 686-7879, fax (805) 684-4295, is a supremely conceived contempo stunner that looks like it fell from its own picture postcard. Or perhaps a David Hockney painting. Actually, it's the masterful product of owner/architect Sherrill Brody's harmonious aesthetic vision.

Xandari is loftily perched amid folds of coffee fields in the hills above Tacacori, five km north of Alajuela. The views are ripe indeed through the vast picture windows and from the graciously curved terraces overhanging the *finca*. Rippling ceilings of polished hardwoods and voluptuously curving walls merge mellifluously with the soft-contoured hills. Ecclesiastical whites are balanced by warm tropical pastels and brilliantly colored stained-glass windows in dramatic counterpoint. The furniture is space-age stylish. When I visited, chorale music was playing softly.

The 16 private villas (16 more are to be added) are set atop a ridge, with miraculous views toward San José. Decor defines understated elegance—dark hardwood furniture with colorful fabrics, modern works of art and gallery pieces, soft-cushioned rattan chairs, sponge-washed walls, Guatemalan bedspreads and plump down pillows, and wave-form hardwood ceilings and tall stained-glass windows

echo the theme in the public lounge. Each has a kitchenette, its own expansive stone terrace with shady *ranchita,* and a voluminous bathroom with heaps of fluffy towels, bathrobes, theater-dressing-room lighting, and a cavernous walk-in shower backed by a floor-to-ceiling window facing onto a private courtyard garden with lounge chairs. Take your pick of king-size or two full-size beds.

The restaurant serves macrobiotic meals and creative Tico specialties (three entrées nightly): my tomato soup and penne pasta *a la arriabiata* ("angry"—spicy—vegetarian pasta) were exquisite. And the healthy breakfasts are filling to say the least.

There are two lap pools with jacuzzis, plus—*get this!*—a soundproofed TV lounge with VCR, well-stocked video library, and plump leather sofas. A crafts store and full-service spa and gym were planned. The staff are all locals. There are no pretensions. Service comes from the heart. And Sherrill and his artist wife Jacquelyn—the theme decor is hers—are gracious in the extreme.

Xandari is a working coffee plantation (once owned by, uh, Robert Vesco). Scenic trails lead through the coffee fields and bamboo groves to hidden waterfalls in the valley bottom.

Rates: $105 prima villa, $165-185 ultra villa, low season; $135 and $195-225 respectively, high season, including breakfast delivered to your room (single costs $20 less; extra people cost $20 more).

the U.S., tel. (800) 506-2304, ext. 1234, has 25 carpeted rooms, each with abundant tilework and hardwoods, two queen-size beds, color TV, and telephone. There's a pool, a bar, and Quetzal restaurant. Rates: $55 s, $65 d low season; $60 s, $70 d high season; $10 extra person. Larger rooms with views cost $85 d. It offers a full-day excursion for $99.

Higher Up: Cabinas Doña Miriam, on a coffee *finca* at Sabana Redonda, has four rooms in a two-story house, with shared bathrooms and hot water. Rates: $8 pp. **Bar/Restaurant Las Fresas,** tel. 661-2397, between Sabana Redonda and Fraijanes, has six octagonal *cabinas* made of red volcanic stone, with hardwood interiors. They're nicely but simply furnished and have clean tiled bathrooms with hot water ($30 s/d). Nearby, **Jaulares Restaurant,** tel./fax 482-2174, e-mail: jaulares@usa.net, has five basic and rustic wooden *cabinas* overlooking a river accessible by trails; each features a fireplace. Rates: $20 s, $25 d. A larger cabin costs $40 for six people.

At Poasito, the well-run and clean **El Churasco,** tel. 482-2135, has four rooms in a house next to the restaurant; all have private baths with hot water ($25 s/d). Two km east of Poasito are two handsome alpine-style *cabinas* for rent in the midst of a pasture, tel. 239-0234. Lauren Fonseca, who owns the Restaurant Vara Blanca, also has two *cabinas* for rent: one for six people, the other for two, and each with fireplace, kitchen, and hot water. Rates: $30 d; $35 cabin for six.

Above Poasito, **Lo Que Tu Quieros,** tel. 482-2092, has four *cabinas* with private baths and hot water. Rates: $12.50. Camping is also allowed, with hot water showers; $5. A short distance beyond is **Lagunillas Lodge,** tel. 448-5506, two km below the park entrance, with eight simple cabins that proffer splendid views down the mountainside. Rates: $16 d with shared bathroom. There are trails for horseback rides, plus a homey Hansel-and-Gretel-type restaurant. Access is by 4WD only.

Poás Volcano Lodge, Apdo. 5723, San José 1000, tel./fax 441-2194, four km east of Poasito, near Vara Blanca, gets two thumbs up. The magnificent rough stone mountain lodge, stunningly situated amid emerald-green pastures at 1,900 meters, the midpoint between Poás and Barva Volcanoes, might have been conceived by Frank Lloyd Wright. Actually, it was built as a farmhouse by an English family that still owns the dairy farm, El Cortijo. The unusual design lends immense atmosphere to the lodge. Centerpiece is a timber-beamed lounge with walls hung with Indian weavings and sunken chairs in front of a massive open fireplace. French doors open onto a patio with fabulous views over the Caribbean lowlands. The nine bedrooms are rustic yet comfortable, with thick down comforters. The large suite has a stunning bathroom with a fathoms-deep stone bathtub shaped like a pool; the bedroom has its own fireplace, plus two bunks and a double bed of rough timbers. Smaller rooms in the house have shared but voluminous baths. Rooms in an adjacent block have the advantage of reliable piping-hot water. Trails lead into the forest, which is a good spot for birding. Guests commonly see quetzals. The lodge serves filling breakfasts, and dinners by request. Horseback rides cost $15, three hours. Rates: $35-45 s, $55-65 d; $80 suite, including breakfast.

Above Poasito, **Albergue Ecológico La Providencia,** tel. 232-2498, fax 231-2204, immediately below the park entrance, is a rustic jewel with six lonesome cabañas spread out among 50 hectares of forested hillside pasture on the upper flanks of Poás at 2,500 meters. You can hike or take a horse or a traditional cart to the huts. Views are fantastic. Each cabin has a small kitchenette with plus hot water from a hydroelectric power generating plant. There's no heating, and it gets cold up here, so come prepared. Meals are cooked on a traditional stove in a rustic little restaurant. Horseback rides ($25) lead to sulfur springs and waterfalls. The property even has a small dairy for those who want to pull their own pints of warm milk. The staff do not speak English. It is accessed via a rugged dirt road (4WD recommended). Rates: $40 d, $53 quad, $100 up to 10 people. Breakfasts cost $6; lunches and dinners cost $10.

Food

Bar/Restaurant Las Fresas is justifiably renowned for its Italian specialties. You can't go wrong with the calzones, hamburgers, or pizzas (anticipate up to a 30-minute wait for pizza; call ahead to order). It's very popular with Ticos and can get full. A short distance down the hill is **L'Aldea,** a family-run restaurant serving quality

Costa Rican dishes for less than $3. Trails lead through a patch of primary forest.

The atmospheric **Jaulares Restaurant** serves meals cooked on an open wood-burning stove. It's a popular spot at night, when it has live music. One km east of Fraijanes is another popular *típico* restaurant—**Chubascos, alias Restaurant Poás,** tel. 441-1813, fax 253-4320)—whose menu includes *gallitos* (tortillas with various toppings), *refrescos* made from strawberries, and even homemade cheesecake. Closed Monday. Also at Fraijanes is **Restaurant El Recreo,** tel. 482-2063, a down-to-earth place serving superb *típico* cuisine cooked in an open kitchen ($1-3), plus *batidos* and homemade drinks such as barley with milk (75 cents).

At Poasito, the **Steak House El Churrasco** is a popular spot for tenderloins, *lengua en salsa,* and other meat dishes ($4 and up). Try the bean dip with tortillas and jalapeños, followed by tiramisu. The tiny **Soda Familiar Poasito** next door is more rustic but less expensive.

Above Poasito, **Rancho Fiesta del Maíz** specializes in maize (corn) dishes. Farther up, **Lo Que Tu Quieras** has *típico* dishes ($3 for *casados*) served at rough-hewn benches and tables overlooking the whole valley.

Getting There

Buses for Poasito depart Alajuela from Avenida Central, Calle 10 (three blocks west of the Mercado Central) Tues.-Fri. at 9 a.m., 1 p.m., 4:15

p.m., and 6:15 p.m. Return buses depart at 6 a.m., 10 a.m., 2 p.m., and 5 p.m. Call 449-5141 for more information. Buses operate hourly, 9 a.m.-5 p.m. weekends.

PARQUE NACIONAL VOLCÁN POÁS

Few volcanoes allow you to drive all the way to the rim. Poás does—well, at least to within 300 meters, from where a short stroll puts you at the very edge of one of the world's largest active craters (1.5 km wide). The viewing terrace gives a bird's-eye view not only 320 meters down into the hellish bowels of the volcano, with its greenish sulfuric pool, but also magnificently down over the northern lowlands.

Poás (2,708 meters) is a restless giant with a 40-year active cycle. It erupted moderately in the early 1950s and was briefly active in 1989, when the access road was closed, and again in May 1994, when the park was temporarily closed. In July and August 1994 it rumbled dramatically. The park is frequently closed to visitors because of pungent and irritating sulfur gas emissions—many plants bear the scars of acid attacks.

Over the millennia it has vented its anger through three craters. Two now slumber under a blanket of vegetation; one even cradles a lake. But the main crater bubbles persistently with active fumaroles and a simmering lake. The sulfuric pool frequently changes hues and emits a

the Poás Volcano,
as seen from
lookout point

geyser up to 200 meters into the steam-laden air. The water level of the lake has gone down about 15 meters during the past decade, one of several indications of a possible impending eruption. In the 1950s a small eruption pushed up a new cone on the crater floor; the cone is now 200 feet high and still puffing.

Oft as not it is foggy up here and mist floats like an apparition through the dwarf cloud forest draped with bromeliads and mosses. Clouds usually form midmorning. Plan an early-morning arrival to enhance your chances of a cloud-free visit. Temperatures vary widely. On a sunny day it can be 21° C (70° F). On a cloudy day, it is normally bitterly cold and windy at the crater rim. Dress accordingly.

Poás is popular at weekends with local Ticos who arrive by the busload with their blaring radios. Visit midweek if possible. Hours: daily 8 a.m.-3:30 p.m. The gates close promptly at 3:30 p.m.

Trails
The **Botos Trail** just before the viewing platform leads to an extinct crater filled with a cold-water lake—Botos. This and the **Escalonia Trail**, which begins at the picnic area, provide for pleasant hikes. The park protects the headwaters of several important rivers, and the dense forests are home to emerald toucanets, coyotes, resplendent quetzals, sooty robins, hummingbirds, frogs, and the Poás squirrel, which is endemic to the volcano.

Information and Services
Poás National Park is the most developed within the Costa Rican park system. It offers ample parking, toilets, and an exhibit hall and auditorium, where audiovisual presentations are given on Sunday. Upstairs is the **Heliconia Nature Store** run by the Fundación Neotrópica. There's wheelchair access to the exhibits and trails. The **Soda El Volcán**, to the left beyond the car park, serves snacks. The park has no accommodations, and camping is not permitted (check with the National Park headquarters—tel. 233-5284—as camping has reportedly been allowed in prior years). Hours: 8 a.m.-3:30 p.m. Entrance: $6.

Tours
Most tour operators in San José offer day-trips to Poás (average $30 half day, $50 full day). Many arrive fairly late in the morning, which reduces the chances of seeing anything before the clouds set in. Try to get a tour that arrives no later than 10 a.m.

Getting There
A TUASA, tel. 233-7477, bus departs San José daily at 8:30 a.m. from Avenida 2, Calles 12/14 ($2). Buses also leave from the plaza in Alajuela at 9 a.m, tel. 441-0631. Buses fill quickly; get there early. The bus makes a short rest stop at Poasito. You arrive at the volcano about 11 a.m. and depart at 3 p.m.

If driving, there's a gas station at Poasito.

WESTERN OUTSKIRTS OF ALAJUELA

From Alajuela, Avenida 3 leads west six km to the Pan-American Highway (Autopista General Cañas) at **Coyol**. Here, on the south side of the highway, is **Rodeo Jaiza**, Apdo. 469, San José 1007, tel. 232-8480, fax 231-4723, a "Typical Rodeo and Costa Rican Fiesta" where *sabaneros* (cowboys) demonstrate deep-rooted traditions of Costa Rican culture: bullriding, bronco riding, Tico bullfighting, fancy rope tricks, and demonstrations of the Costa Rican saddle horse. It's great fun to watch the cowboys ride bareback and hang on to angry, jumping, twisting, 700-kg bulls with only one hand or none at all (freestyle). Quieter interludes include the music of a "Cimarrona" band and a folkloric show by dancers in traditional costume. There's a swimming pool and restaurant. Alas, it accepts groups only.

Two km east of Coyol, the Alajuela-Coyol road divides. The turn to the west leads one km to **San José de Alajuela**, a small town with a historic church, where the main road (Hwy. 3) divides again for La Garita (see below) to the west and, to the northwest Grecia, Sarchí, and San Ramón. At Cruce de Grecia y Poas, one km along the road to Grecia, a sideroad leads uphill via Tambor to Poás Volcano via the pretty little village of **San Pedro**, highlighted by its blue church. One km south of San Pedro the Costa Rica Tourism Institute (ICT) has a lookout point situated where the Ríos Carracha and Poás join; you'll have reasonable views of two waterfalls. A trail—**Sendero Carracha**—follows the river to picnic tables in the forest.

Accommodations

Bar/Cabinas La Sirena, tel. 433-2222, on the west side of San José de Alajuela, has simple roadside cabins for $15 s/d.

Villa Dolce Hotel and Villas, tel./fax 433-8932, at Coyol, offers six spacious rooms, each with telephone, TV, fan, and tiled bathroom. There's a pool, and a restaurant serves predominantly home-cooked Italian meals. Rates: $32 s, $46 d.

Hotel el Colibri, Apdo. 64, Alajuela 4030, tel./fax 441-4228, is a pretty family-operated bed and breakfast in San José de Alajuela. Its 11 rooms in four bungalows are set in tropical gardens and modestly yet elegantly furnished. Each has TV, fan, private bath, and terrace. Breakfast is served in a garden pavilion. Rates include use of a pool and tennis court and free airport transfer.

The German-run **Michele's Hotel,** tel./fax 433-9864; in the U.S., SB-106, P.O. Box 025292, Miami, FL 33102-5292, at Cruce de Grecia y Poas, has 14 large a/c rooms with two double beds (one room has a king-size bed; all have orthopedic mattresses), tile floors, patios, screened windows granting cross ventilation, and private bathrooms. Upstairs rooms offer views from the balcony. A garden falls to a river. The owner was adding 18 more rooms, plus a restaurant, pool, and gym. Rates: $40 s, $50 d, including breakfast.

The **Orquídeas Inn,** Apdo. 394, Alajuela, tel. 433-9346, fax 433-9740, e-mail: orchid@sol.racsa. co.cr, below Michele's, is a gringo-owned gem run by charming hosts and, understandably, has become a kind of home away from home for local expat gringos who pop in and out (famous figures such as Charlie Sheen and Jimmy Buffet are also regulars). The home—vaguely hacienda in style—is set amid five acres of landscaped grounds and fruit orchard. There's a swimming pool in an enclosed courtyard. The 12 tile-floored rooms have arched windows, arched doors hand-carved with orchid motifs, and matching arched bed heads. A sky-lit geodesic dome in the garden offers luxury perfect for lovers: a sunken tub and a spiral staircase to the king-size bed. Vases full of orchids and stunning Guatemalan bedspreads and paintings add a note of bright color. Breakfast is truly superb: toast and jam to die for, and spicy *gallo pinto* with *huevos rancheros* and marinated red pep-pers. A late afternoon coffee tasting energizes tourists en route to Poás. Guests are given kitchen access and encouraged to conjure their favorite recipes for other guests. The hotel's famous Marilyn Monroe Bar, open to the breezes on three sides, is festooned with posters, T-shirts, and photos immortalizing the pinup queen. Buffalo wings and popcorn are on the house. A souvenir store stocks fine national artisan work. The inn offers limousine service to/from the airport. The place is a menagerie. Friendly toucans, parrots, and a scarlet macaw fly free and play tricks on the guests. And there's a butterfly garden and very popular thatch-roofed **Restaurant Típico las Tinajitas,** tel./fax 433-8668. Rates: $55 s, $65 d, $120 mini-suite, $130 geodesic dome. The road to the left leads to La Garita.

The somewhat decayed **Hotel Monte del Mago,** no telephone, one km west of Cruce de Grecia y Poas, has five large but gloomy, simply furnished rooms with fans, TV, refrigerator, patio, and clean bathrooms with hot water. Rates: $31 d. The atmospheric but run-down restaurant—replete with horsedrawn carraige—was being restored at press time.

Food

Orquídeas Inn is a great place to stop for lunch or dinner. Alternately, stop off for refreshments at the **Russian Tea Terrace,** tel. 433-9257, in Tambor, seven km beyond Orquídeas Inn on the road to San Pedro. Here, Johanna Sosenskay serves a healthy dose of Russian culture along with borscht, strudel, and Russian tea served from a genuine *samovar*. Turn right at Bar Veranera to reach the place. Dinners are offered at 5 p.m.

LA GARITA

La Garita, spanning the Pan-Am Highway (at its junction with Hwy. 3 from Alajuela) about 12 km west of Alajuela, is important for its central location at the road junction for Atenas, Orotina, and Puntarenas. The area has a distinct climate; *National Geographic* claims that it's the third best in the world. Hence the area is popular among the well-to-do. Roads and gardens are fringed with bougainvilleas of carnal plum purples and reds, and La Garita is famed for ornamental-plant farms known as *viveros*. Group tours can be arranged to the nursery of **Orchid Alley,** tel. 487-7086, which grows more than 100,000 orchids on site. It sells blooms packaged in plastic boxes, plus live *guaria morada* orchids (the national flower) in sealed vials suitable for import into the United States.

Zoo Ave

This splendid zoo, tel. 433-8989, fax 433-9140, e-mail: ZooAve@sol.racsa.co.cr; in the U.S., Dept. 280, P.O. Box 025216, Miami, FL 33102, at Dulce Nombre, 3.5 km east of the Pan-Am Highway, is a *must see!* It covers 59 hectares of landscaped grounds and is a wildlife rescue center for injured and confiscated wildlife. The fantastic bird collection (the largest in Central America) includes dozens of toucans, cranes, curassows, and parrots, and a veritable Pantone chart of more than 100 other Costa Rican bird species. Zoo Ave is one of only two zoos in the world to display aptly named resplendent quetzals. Lots of macaws fly free. And peacocks strut their stuff on the lawns. You'll also see crocodile, deer, turtles, and all four species of indigenous monkeys in large enclosures. Noah would be proud: most creatures are in pairs or groups. The scrawny birds you see near the entrance were confiscated from owners who had taken them illegally from the wild; the birds developed behavioral problems, such as plucking their feathers until they look like they've been in a tumbler.

The goal is to breed national species for reintroduction into the wild. The zoo has successfully bred the scarlet macaw (200 are scheduled for release into the wild over a 15-year period), curassow, green macaw, the guan, and about 50 other native bird species with the help of a human-infant incubator. The breeding center is off-limits.

Zoo Ave has a small *soda* and bathrooms, and a visitor's center with video presentations and educational events twice monthly. Hours: daily 9 a.m.-5 p.m. Entrance: $3.50.

Getting There: Take either the Atenas or the La Garita bus from Alajuela. Both pass by the zoo.

Accommodations

Club Martino Hotel and Spa is an upscale bed and breakfast hotel that was due to open in late 1998 opposite Zoo Ave, with tennis and squash courts, a solarium, pool, gym, and gourmet restaurant.

Villa Raquel, tel. 433-8926, is a bed and breakfast country inn with a tennis court and large swimming pool, with lots of fresh-cut flowers, wicker and antique furniture, spacious living areas, and 12 bedrooms tastefully decorated in lively pastels. A large, modern kitchen is open to guests, and the pleasing grounds are good for relaxing. Rates: $65 d. There are no signs; both La Piña Dorado and Villa Raquel are hard to find. Call ahead.

Chatelle Country Resort, Apdo. 755, San José 1007, tel. 487-7781, fax 487-7095, at Turrúcares, one km south of Fiesta del Maíz, though pleasant, is not quite the exclusive country club that the brochure proclaims. First the good points. The hexagonal rooms—spaced amid landscaped grounds—are very cozy, atmospheric, and large, with TVs, lofty, radial-beamed ceilings, and two supremely comfortable queen-size beds. The complex is quiet and relaxing. Owner Arturo Otero is from Bolivia, has lived in Argentina, Canada, Mexico, and the U.S., and has tried to combine hints of each. The amalgam is an eclectic jumble. Newer rooms around a swimming pool and sundeck are in more traditional style. Most rooms have views over the mountains. There's a conference center and tennis court. A reader reports "poor service." On my last visit I concurred; it seems badly managed. Rates: $60 d small, $75 d large, including continental breakfast and airport transfers.

Food

Some acclaimed eateries serving traditional Costa Rican fare are located here. **Centro Turístico Mi Quinta,** tel. 487-7065, on Hwy. 3 one km west of the Pan-Am Hwy, has a *mirador* lookout and serves wood-roasted *pollo mi quinta.* Nearby, and equal to it, is the **Fiesta del Maíz,** tel. 487-7057, a large, cafeteria-style restaurant famous for its very tasty corn meals: *chorreadas* (corn fritters), tamales (corn pudding), corn on the grill, very tasty rice with corn and chicken, and other tempting morsels. Free tastings are offered. No plate costs more than $2.75. It's open daily. The marvelously atmospheric **Delicias del Maíz,** half a km east of Zoo Ave, is another rustic corn restaurant serving full meals for $3.

The road south from Fiesta del Maíz leads to Turrúcares, where the **Restaurant Las Campañas,** tel. 487-7021, fax 487-7020, serves seafood and international dishes to the accompaniment of live music.

Farther west along Hwy. 3 are **La Casita de Campo Steak House,** tel. 487-7408, and the **Green Parrot,** La Lora Verde, tel. 487-7846, a more elegant eatery specializing in barbecued meats: Caribbean chicken, T-bone, filet mignon, grilled chicken, and Southwest dishes and burgers. There's an open-air dining terrace, plus a dance floor with live music on Friday and Saturday.

For gourmet Italian fare, check out **Restaurant la Lucia,** an upscale Italian-run eatery one km east of Zoo Ave. You'll dine on outside terraces in lush orchid gardens, or inside in an elegant lounge. The inexpensive, wide-ranging menu includes fettuccine, gnocchi, smoked fish, and roast porcetta ($5-10).

Getting There

Buses for La Garita and Atenas depart San José from the Coca-Cola bus terminal, and from Alajuela from Avenida Central, Calle 10.

ATENAS

Balmy Atenas, five km west of La Garita, is an agricultural town renowned for its quality fruits and perpetually springlike climate (in 1994, *National Geographic* declared it the best climate in the world). It's popular with Josefinos on weekends but thus far has been bypassed by tourists. Watch for the statue of the Virgin Mary on a hill one km east of town, which has a beautiful church (unusual for its north-facing orientation) surrounded by palms in the plaza, two blocks south of Hwy 3, which dips and rises dramatically through steep river valleys. Drive carefully.

The **Central American School of Animal Husbandry,** tel. 446-5050 or 446-5250, one km east of Atenas, is pioneering agri-ecotourism and welcomes visitors, who get a firsthand look at dairy operations, reforestry programs, iguana farming, and more, on the 530-hectare property. Besides its own research, the center teaches courses in environmental studies, reforestry, natural history, and more, to farmers interested in hosting tourists. You can saddle up for full-

Richard Frisius and macaws

day guided rides into the mountain forests. Fee: $60, including lunch at an old hacienda; reservations must be made a week in advance.

Accommodations

Ana's Place, Apdo. 66, Atenas, tel. 446-5019, is a cozy and quiet home away from home on the east side of town. Italianate steps lead up to the house, with its spacious lounge and beautiful hardwood parquet floors. The 11 modestly furnished rooms vary markedly; some have shared baths. There are also two apartments with kitchenettes. Macaws, parrots, and a toucan fly free in the back lawn, which has an outside restaurant and a small swimming pool. Turn left opposite the gas station as you enter Atenas from the east; follow the signs from here. Rates: $25 s, $35 d, including breakfast (lunch and dinner are served by request). Weekly and monthly discounts.

Villa Tranquilidad, Apdo. 28, Alajuela 4013, tel. 446-5460, lives up to its name. This Canadian-run ranch-style bed and breakfast, surrounded by coffee bushes on a private *finca,* has four pleasant rooms with private baths and soft couches, plus a swimming pool set in grounds full of bougainvilleas and orchids. Local monkeys and other wildlife think the inn is a cool place to visit. Rates: $50 d, including breakfast.

The German-run **Aparamentos Atenas,** Apdo. 88-4013 Atenas, tel./fax 446-5792, e-mail: apatenas@sol.racsa.co.cr, on the western outskirts of Atenas, has two- and four-person bungalows with kitchen and hot water set amid lush gardens. The modestly furnished bungalows have hardwood ceilings and mosquito nets over the beds. There's a pool, plux fax and e-mail service, car rental, horseback and mountain bike tours, and airport transfers are all offered. Rates: $30 s, $35 d, $55 t, $60 quad, daily; $175 s, $210 d, $315 t, $350 quad, weekly.

Hotel Colinas del Sol, Apdo. 164, Atenas, tel./fax 446-6847, is a handsome upscale complex with eight red-tile-roofed bungalows and three smaller cabañas amid lush, beautifully landscaped grounds on a breezy hillside in the midst of the *campo* two km southeast of town. The spacious units are well-lit and nicely appointed, with kitchenettes, attractive tiled bathrooms, and French doors opening to wide patios facing a large pool and sundeck. All have fans and hot water. An open-sided restaurant higher up has views towards Volcán Poás. Hiking trails, tennis, and horse rentals were to be added. The place is German-run, but has no hints of anything Teutonic; the feel is contemporary Spanish. Rates: $35 s/d daily, $240 weekly low season; $45 s/d daily, $300 weekly high season. *A bargain!*

El Cafetal Inn, Apdo. 105, Atenas, tel. 446-5785, fax 446-7028, e-mail: cafetal@yellowweb.co.cr, website www.yellowweb.co.cr/cafetal.html, is an elegant bed and breakfast on a small coffee and fruit *finca* cascading down the side of a valley in Santa Eulalia, about five km north of Atenas. The erudite, warm-hearted, and super-friendly owners Lee and Romy Rodríquez (he's Salvadoran, she's Colombian) run their 10-bedroom hostelry like a true home away from home. The open-plan lounge has marble floors and cascading fountains and thick white pillars; light

streams in through glass doors and huge bay windows that proffer marvelous valley and mountain vistas. The upstairs rooms (some quite small) are modestly appointed, with wafer-thin particleboard walls. Outside, a patio and steps lead down to a large, tiled swimming pool (shaped like a four-leaf clover) and a thatched coffee bar where hearty meals are served. Or you may dine on the patio, but be prepared for a brisk, warm wind predicatably after dawn and at dusk. Howler monkeys hang out in the trees nearby. Two pet toucans are kept in a walk-in cage. Tyson, the collie, loves to play with his best pal, the free-roaming parrot, Lolita. There's even a cow, called Panchita. Fancy a tour? Romy and Lee offer 15 options ($25-45 depending on number of people). Airport tranfers cost $25 d ($2.50 additional). Rates: $50 or $65 d (with luxury bathroom), including breakfast. *Recommended!*

American Kevin Hill, tel./fax 446-5055; in the U.S., SJO 1858, P.O. Box 025216, Miami, FL 33102-5216, offers two one-bedroom ($675 per month on a six-month basis) houses and one two-bedroom ($775) house built "Spanish colonial/Costa Rican rustic" style with antique colonial furniture, plus a swimming pool on his 10-acre farm property. Rates are higher on a month-by-month basis.

Food
The rustic **Don Tadeo Restaurant Parrilla,** on the west side of the park, has lots of ambience. Also recommended is **Ekalís Pizzeria,** on the park's east side, serving whopping pizzas and milkshakes. There's another pizzaeria on the west side.

Services
There are two **banks** in town. A **post office** stands one block west of the church. There's a local **Red Cross,** tel. 446-5161.

Getting There and Away
See **La Garita,** above, for bus schedules. The **taxi** stand is one block south and one block west of the plaza.

SARCHÍ AND THE NORTHWEST

The Pan-American Highway slices west through wide-open coffee country and begins a gradual rise up the western rim of the highlands before dropping sharply to Puntarenas and the Pacific lowlands. Important agricultural market towns—Palmares, Naranjo, and San Ramón—line the route. A scenic secondary road leads west from San José de Alajuela to Naranjo, paralleling the Pan-Am to the north via Grecia and Sarchí, center of crafts in Costa Rica.

ROSARIO

This small mountain hamlet is hidden away just west of the Pan-Am Highway, about five miles northwest of La Garita and eight km southeast of Palmares. It's the gateway to Grecia (eight km northeast) and to the **Río Grande Canyon Nature Reserve,** a 3,700-acre nature reserve flanking a dramatic gorge west of the highway. Access is via the Vista del Valle hotel, whose owners created the reserve; the exit is two km west of the Grecia turnoff from the Pan-American Highway. The valley is thickly forested with bamboo and has a series of waterfalls, one of which tumbles 100 meters.

Thrill seekers can leap off the 83-meter Puente Negro bridge over the Río Colorado, one km east of Rosario. **Tropical Bungee,** tel. 232-3956, offers bungee jumps under the guidance of "jump masters" using an 11-meter bungee. The company charges $45 for the first jump ($25 subsequent jumps), $55 for two jumps and students. Anyone with back, neck, or heart problems is advised not to jump. Hours: Sat.-Sun. 9 a.m.-3 p.m., weekdays by reservation (low season); daily 9 a.m.-3 p.m. (high season). There's a *soda.*

The San José-Puntarenas bus from Calle 12 and Avenida 7 or San José-Naranjo bus from Calle 16 and Avenida 1 will drop you off at Salon Los Alfaro, from where it is a short walk north to the bridge.

Accommodations
Definitely check out the Vista del Valle.

GRECIA AND VICINITY

Grecia is an important market town. Its claim to fame is its unique, rust-red, twin-spired **metal church** made of steel plates imported from Belgium in 1897. The church is an intriguing amalgam, with steps of pumice, a wooden interior, and a white, arched wooden ceiling with glass chandeliers, a beautiful tiled floor, stained-glass windows, and an all-marble altar that rises fancifully like one of Emperor Ludwig's fairy-tale castles. Birds fly in and out through open doors. The church is fronted by a pretty park with tall palms, an obelisk erected to commemorate the foundation of Grecia in July 1864, fountains, and a domed music temple.

The **Museo de Cultural,** tel. 444-6767, on the park's northwest corner, houses a regional museum tracing the development of the area during the last 200 years.

Joyeros del Bosque Húmedos
The Museo de Cultural also houses this collection of more than 50,000 butterflies—truly "Jewels of the Rainforest"—from around the world; this is the accumulation of Richard Whitten's more than 50 years of collecting. It claims to be the largest collection of butterflies in the world. It surely is the most colorful—a veritable calliope of shimmering greens, neon blues, startling reds, silvers, and golds. The collection has been split between the Museo de Cultura and the Posada Mimosa, tel. 494-5868, six km south of Grecia in the hamlet of Ricon de Salas, where Richard and his wife Margaret now live. The Posada Mimosa exhibit is open only to hotel guests and special groups (4-6 p.m.).

The truly stunning displays make the Smithsonian's collection look moth-ridden by comparison. The creativity is sheer choreography. At Posada Mimosa, exhibits glitter against a background of opera and classical music, the climactic highs of the arias and ponderous lows of the cellos seemingly rising and falling to the drama of the displays. Part of the exhibit is dedicated to a collection of every species in the country. Other exhibits include shimmering beetles displayed against black velvet, like opal jewelry, and boxes of bugs majestically turned into caskets of gems. Some beetles are bigger than your fist; some moths outsize a salad plate. An unexpected treat may be an impromptu performance by Whitten (a former professional concert performer) displaying his talents on the glockenspiel, accordina, piano, or organ.

Los Chorros

Los Chorros ("The Spouts") is a 38-hectare recreational park with trails leading into a forest preserve where the lucky hiker might spot porcupines, opossums, armadillos, and even margays and jaguarundis. The entrance is in the Quebrada del León Quarry, three km north of the Corazón de Jesús Church in Tacares, about five km southeast of Grecia. You'll pass **Bar Los Chorros** on the right. The road turns into a rocky path and ends at a fence. A path leads from here down to the quarry where the park is signed. Trails lead to two waterfalls and a *mirador* (lookout point) but are slippery and not well maintained. A rickety rope bridge leads to one of the waterfalls. The place is popular on weekends. Hours: 7 a.m.-5 p.m. Entrance: 60 cents.

Nearby are **Balneario Victoria**, a popular swimming spot at Santa Gertrudis, eight km northeast of Grecia; and **Complejo Turístico Los Trapiches**, tel. 444-6656, another tourist haunt popular with Ticos. A restaurant, lawns, a children's pool, picnic sites, and playing fields surround a duck pond and *trapiche* (traditional sugarcane press) powered by an equally venerable waterwheel.

El Mundo de las Serpientes

The World of Snakes, tel./fax 494-3700, run by Austrians Nikolaus Schwabe and Robert Meindinger, displays a collection of more than 300 live snakes from around the world, including many of Costa Rica's most beautiful critters. Schwabe and Meindinger breed 40 different species for sale and for reintroduction to the wild. They hope, too, to educate visitors and dispel the negative image with a clear message—don't harm snakes! For example, you'll learn how snakes are vital to helping keep rodent populations in check, thus preventing plagues. The critters live behind glass windows in re-creations

of their natural habitats. You can touch harmless snakes. A snack bar and cafe are to be added. Open daily 8 a.m.-4 p.m. Entrance costs $11 ($6 children). It's just east of Grecia, opposite the sawmill on the old Alajuela road that leads to Poro. *A must see!*

Accommodations

A cheap option in town is **Pensión Familiar**, tel. 444-5097. Not inspected. I've also heard reports of two inexpensive options nearby: Cabañas Los Cipreses and the basic Pensión Quirís.

Healthy Day Inn, tel./fax 444-5903, on the western edge of town, is described as a "naturistic health home." Tastefully decorated rooms have parquet floors with throw rugs (carpets in upstairs rooms), hardwood ceilings, cable TVs, telephones, and private baths with hot water. The hotel offers therapeutic massage, reflexology, facials, sauna, hydrotherapy, and supervised macrobiotic diets. Amenities include a jacuzzi, a swimming pool, and a lighted tennis court. The inn offers car rental ($20 daily) and tour guides. Rates: $40 s, $45 d, $60 suite, including breakfast and airport transfers.

Posada Mimosa, Apdo. 135-4100 Grecia, tel./fax 494-5868, e-mail: mimosa@sol.racsa.co.cr, in the hamlet of Ricon de Salas, is an exquisite bed and breakfast run by Germans Tessa and Martin Bürner. Set amid seven hectares of landscaped gardens and privately owned forest—sugarcane and coffee—the modern hillside home has five modestly furnished yet appealing rooms, all with private baths, a guesthouse with two fully equipped suites, and a four-bedroom casa with kitchenette and two bathrooms for longer stays. There's a swimming pool. Part of the Whitten Collection is here; Richard Whitten leads butterfly walks on the property. Rates: $40 s, $55 d, $70 suite, $140 guesthouse low season; $45 s, $59 d, $80 suite, $160 guesthouse high season.

Food

The south side of the park in Grecia has several pleasant-looking restaurants. **Pollos a la Lena** serves chicken roasted over coffee-wood ($2-4). It also has ceviche, tortillas, and papas. The **Oásis** serves *típico* dishes and burgers and is popular with locals.

Services

There's a **Banco Nacional** on the northwest corner of the square, and a **Banco de Costa Rica** facing the church, on the south side. You can make international calls from the **ICE** office on the north side of the square; Mon.-Fri. 8 a.m.-3:30 p.m. There's also a **hospital,** San Francisco de Asis, tel. 444-5045, and **Red Cross,** tel. 444-5292.

Getting There

Buses depart San José hourly from the Coca-Cola bus terminal. The bus station in Grecia is at Avenida 2, Calles 4/6.

SARCHÍ

Sarchí, 29 km northwest of Alajuela, is Costa Rica's crossroads of crafts and famous for the intricately detailed, hand-painted oxcarts that originated here in the middle of the 19th century. Handcrafted souvenirs—from chess sets and salad bowls, leather sandals and rockers, to miniature oxcarts decorated in traditional geometric designs—are sold at shops all along the road of Sarchí Sur, which sits atop a steep hill about one km east of the much larger Sarchí Norte. Many of the town's whitewashed buildings are painted with the town's own floral motif trim.

The setting is fabulous. The town is surrounded by steep-sided valleys reminiscent of Bali, with row upon row of coffee bushes cascading downhill like folds of green silk. Sarchí Norte's **church,** done up in bright pink with turquoise trim and stuccoed motifs, is one of the most beautiful in the nation and has a vaulted hardwood ceiling and carvings—a gift of devotion from local artisans.

Another sight of interest is **Butterfly Valley,** tel. 454-4050, fax 454-4300, where you can learn about the life cycles of the more than 40 species that flutter by. The 1.6-hectare butterfly garden is on the main road in Sarchí Norte, next to the Coopearsa artisan's cooperative. It has a *trapiche* (traditional sugar mill). Entrance: $6; children $3, including tour, which runs continuously; open daily 8:30 a.m.-4:30 p.m.

The name Sarchí, according to writer Carlos Gagini, comes from the Aztec name Xalachi, which means "Under the Volcano." Sarchí is on virtually every package-tour itinerary. Avoid at weekends. At **Fábrica de Carretas Joaquín Chaverrí,** tel. 454-4412, fax 454-4421, in Sarchí Sur, you can see souvenirs and oxcarts being painted in workshops at the rear. Joaquín's grandfather "invented" the 16-pie-wedge-piece wheel bound with a metal belt that has become the traditional oxcart wheel. The factory was founded in 1903 and now has 15 owner-partners, most of them Chaverrí family members. The family still makes working oxcarts of sturdy wood, with mahogany wheels, a body of cedar, coachpole of ironwood, and braces of lagarto.

oxcart

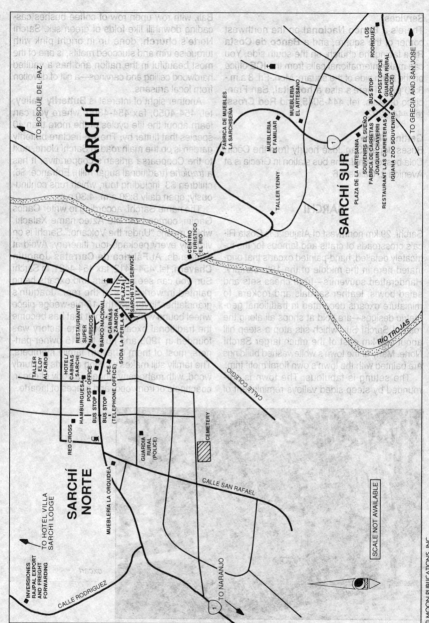

© MOON PUBLICATIONS, INC.

Commercialized Sarchí Sur may strike you as kitschy, despite the quality of the crafts. For the real McCoy, check out **Taller Eloy Alfaro,** a traditional workshop in Sarchí Norte where Señor Alfaro can be seen making yolks and oxcarts in age-old manner.

The town celebrates its colorful fiesta each first week of February, featuring bull-riding, amusement rides, and, of course, a parade of oxcarts.

Spanish Language Programs

Villa Sarchí Lodge (see below) has a language course.

Accommodations and Food

The only budget hotel is the **Cabinas Sarchí,** tel. 454-4425, which has four simple but clean rooms, each with a double bed and bunk, plus private bath and hot water. Rates: $12.50 s/d. It's one block west of the square. Around the corner is the slightly more appealing **Cabinas Zamora** with three simple, clean rooms with small TVs and private baths with hot water. Rates: $17 d.

Villa Sarchí Lodge, Apdo. 34, Sarchí Norte, tel./fax 454-4006, one km northwest of Sarchí Norte, has 11 simple, well-lit cabins with tile floors, clean private baths and hot water, and hammocks and rockers on the porch. Some rooms have cable TV and views toward Volcán Poás. There's a small swimming pool, plus restaurant and bar. Airport transfers are provided, and car rental and local tours are offered. Rates: $30 s, $40 d, $60 t, including breakfast.

For eats in Sarchí Norte try **Restaurante Super Mariscos,** tel. 454-4330, behind the Banco Nacional, for seafood. In Sarchí Sur there are several eateries in the Plaza de la Artesanía, including **La Troja del Abuelo,** tel. 454-4973, with a large menu of *típico* dishes and Mexican fare ($3-5). The **Restaurant Helechos** has a *plata del día* for $4.50. There's also an ice cream store.

Next door to Fábrica de Carretas Joaquín Chaverrí is the **Restaurant Las Carrateras,** with a shaded patio out back; its serves *típico* dishes plus chicken parmegiana ($5), pastas ($4), salads, and burgers.

Souvenirs

There are dozens of places to choose from. The largest is Fábrica de Carretas Joaquín Chaver-

rí. Next door, **Iguana Zoo Souvenirs** has iguanas in a pit at the front. One hundred meters west of Fábrica de Carretas Joaquín Chaverrí is the **Plaza de la Artesanía,** a modern complex with 34 showrooms, souvenir stores, and restaurants. You'll find mostly upscale, quality goods, including one shop selling expensive leather goods by Del Rio, another dedicated to Guatemalan clothing and textiles, and the **Galeria de los Habanos** selling Cuban cigars.

You can order custom-made furniture from any of dozens of *tallers,* including **Cooperativa de Artesanos Coopearsa,** tel. 454-4050. **Inversiones Rajpal S.A.,** tel. 454-3250, west of town on Calle Rodriguez, can arrange freight forwarding. It will also recommend where to have furniture made and will inspect for high quality before shipping.

Services

There are **Banco Nacional** outlets in the Plaza Artesanía and one block west of the square in Sarchí Norte; both are open 8:30 a.m.-3 p.m., weekdays. The **post office,** 50 meters west of the square, is open weekdays 7 a.m.-5 p.m. The **police** (Guardia Rural) station is on the southwest corner of the soccer field in Sarchí Norte, as well as across from Fábrica de Carreta Joaquín Chaverrí.

Getting There and Around

By Bus: Buses depart Alajuela every 30 minutes, 5 a.m.-10 p.m., from Calle 8, Avenidas Central/1 (Tuan, tel. 441-3781). An express Tuan bus departs San José from Calle 16, Avenidas 1/3, at 12:15 and 5:30 p.m.; returning 5:30 a.m., 6:15 a.m., and 1:45 p.m. You can also take a San José bus to Naranjo and change there.

By Taxi: Taxis wait on the west side of the square in Sarchí Norte, or call Sarchí Taxi Service, tel. 454-4028.

PARQUE NACIONAL JUAN CASTRO BLANCO AND BOSQUE DE PAZ RAIN/CLOUD FOREST BIOLOGICAL RESERVE

North from Sarchí a road climbs up the mountain slopes via Luisa and Angeles to the saddle between Poás and Platanar volcanoes—you are now high amid the cloud forest—before dropping sharply to **Bajos del Toro,** a tranquil Shangri-la hidden at the head of the valley of the Río Toro. The route is incredibly scenic, and at times daunting as you weave along a road that clings precariously to the face of the cloud-shrouded mountains. You can also reach Bajos del Toro via a rough dirt road from Zarcero.

Parque Nacional Juan Castro Blanco, one of Costa Rica's youngest national parks, was created in 1995 to protect the vital watershed on the slopes of Volcán Platanar (2,183 meters), about five km northeast of Zarcero. Several endangered species, including the quetzal, curassow, red brocket deer, and black guan exist in the 14,258-hectare park, which is covered in mixed primary forest and clearings in the process of regeneration. Most notable species are lancewoods, oaks and *yayo.* At higher elevations the vegetation is stunted and, given the moister climate, epiphytes abound.

Bosque de Paz Rain/Cloud Forest Biological Reserve is a 400-hectare reserve nestled in a reclusive valley west of Bajos del Toro at the foot of Parque Nacional Juan Castro Blanco. It is a favorite of birders. The reserve boasts several hiking trails (2-6 km) leading to waterfalls, a botanical garden, hummingbird gardens, and lookout points. The forests are replete with exotic wildlife, including howler, capuchin, and spider monkeys, cats, and—according to the owner—more bird species than anywhere else in the nation, not least quetzals, which hover near the lodge. Two streams tumble through the beautiful gardens.

Accommodations and Food
Bosque de Paz, Apdo. 130-1000 San José, tel. 234-6676, fax 225-0203, e-mail: bosque@sol. racsa.co.cr, has a rustic stone and log lodge with a handsome restaurant serving *típico* food, plus two rooms with private baths and hot water, and each for four people ($10 pp; groups only, no individuals). A one-day excursion from San José includes lunch. However, call-in visitors are not accepted; you *must* make reservations. **Café Britt** offers a one-day tour combining a visit to their coffee *finca* and processing plant with a visit to Bosque de Paz. **Viajes Sin Frontera,** fax (800) 585-8943, offers an excursion ($65).

Bosque de la Paz is not signed from Bajos de Toro. The dirt road leads west from opposite

Valle de Truchas, a trout farm at Bajos del Toro that offers fishing on weekends.

NARANJO TO ZARCERO

Naranjo, five km west of Sarchí and three km north of the Pan-American Highway, is an important agricultural center with a pretty, twin-towered, cream-colored, red-roofed baroque church worth a stop. Within, thick limestone Corinthian columns support a fine ceiling. Notice the splendid religious paintings to the sides. Otherwise the city is one to pass through en route to Zarcero and the northern lowlands.

North of Naranjo, a road leads to the northern lowlands. It is one of the most scenic drives in the country. Midway between Naranjo and Zarcero you'll pass through **San Juanillo.** Beyond, the scenery becomes distinctly alpine, with black-and-white dairy cattle munching contentedly on the emerald mountain slopes. Higher up, beyond the hamlet of Llano Bonito, there are many tight hairpin bends. Drive carefully.

Zarcero is a pleasant mountain town with an impressive setting beneath green mountains. Dominating the town, though, is the whitewashed church fronted by a **topiary park.** The mark of the scissors is on every plant and bush. The work is that of Evangelisto Blanco, who has unleashed his wildest ideas in leafy splendor: a cat riding a motorcycle along the top of a hedge; an elephant with lightbulbs for eyes; corkscrews whose spiral foliage coils up and around the trunks like serpents around Eden's tree; even a bullring complete with matador, charging bull, and spectators. On virtually any day you can see Blanco snapping his pruning shears, evenly rounding off the rabbits and clipping straight the great cascading archway arbor that leads to the steps of the church. Zarcero is also famous for its fresh cheese—called *palmito*—and peach preserves.

North of Zarcero you reach the Continental Divide, with sweeping vistas of the northern lowlands far below.

A road to the left just beyond the hamlet of **Palmita,** about three km south of Zarcero, leads west to San Ramón. The drive is as lovely as a fairy tale. Topiary hedges begin to appear. And the brooding scenery reminds me of the Eng-

Zarcero church and
topiary garden

lish Lake District—without the lakes. A dirt road just beyond Alto Villegas leads northwest to Villablanca and the Los Angeles Cloud Forest Reserve (4WD only).

Accommodations and Food
Hotel Don Bosco, tel. 463-3137, facing the church on the north side, has eight clean, modestly furnished rooms with hot water for $20 d (shared bath) and $35 (private).

There are several *típico* restaurants around the plaza in Zarcero, including **Pizzeria/Restaurant Casa el Campo,** opposite the Banco Nacional. Next door is a *panadería* selling wonderful breads, scones, and sticky buns.

At San Juanilla the rustic **Soda el Mirador** proffers views over the valley and good *típico* food that'll fill you up on a dime and that should be washed down with a refreshing fresh-fruit *refresco.*

Services
Zarcero has two **banks:** Banco Nacional, one block north of the church, next to the Red Cross; and Banco de Costa Rica, two blocks north of the church. You'll find **public telephones** on the west side.

Getting There and Away
Buses for Zarcero depart San José hourly 5 a.m.-7:30 p.m. from Calle 16, Avenidas 1/3, tel. 255-4318; and from San Ramón at 5:45 a.m., 8:30 a.m., noon, 2:30 p.m., and 5 p.m. Buses for

San Ramón depart from the southwest corner of the park at 7 a.m., 9:40 a.m., 1 p.m., 3:40 p.m., and 6:45 p.m. The bus stop for San José faces the church. Buses depart Zarcero for Ciudad Quesada.

PALMARES

Palmares, 10 km west of Naranjo and 1.5 km south from the Pan-Am Highway, is renowned for its lively weeklong agricultural and civic **fiesta** held each mid-January, with bullfights, carnival rides, and general merriment. The stone village church, built in 1894, is attractive in its ornamental setting. Venture within to inspect the impressive mosaic floor and stained-glass windows.

At Cocaleca, one km south of Palmares, is **Jardín de Las Guarias,** tel. 452-0091, a private orchid collection and the largest such in the country. Owner Javier Solórzano Murillo has more than 180 orchid species on display, but it is Costa Rica's national flower, the violet *guaria morada* orchid, that blossoms most profusely—more than 40,000 of them. Javier planted his first orchid here in 1941. At least a dozen species are always in bloom. Best time, however, is January to April. A small restaurant (closed Monday) serves Costa Rican dishes, which you can enjoy beneath a shady *amate* tree. A butterfly garden may be completed by the time you read this. Open: 8 a.m.-5 p.m. Entrance: $2.

Accommodations and Food

Hotel Rancho Mirador, tel. 451-1301, fax 451-1302, on a coffee *finca* beside Hwy. 1, three km east of Palmares and four km west of Naranjo, is a soaring restaurant boasting stupendous views east along the valley with the four volcanoes—Poás, Barva, Irazú, and Turrialba—magnificently aligned. It serves *comida típica* and is open 3 p.m.-midnight. It also has six rooms arrayed down the hillside perpendicular to the valley. They are clean, carpeted, and pleasingly furnished, with TV, fan, and mini-refrigerator. Incredibly, the architect put the windows facing *west*—into the driveway. At least each room has a tiny balcony facing east. There's a small swimming pool. Rates: $50 s/d, including tax and breakfast.

SAN RAMÓN

San Ramón, about 12 km due west of Naranjo, and one km north of Hwy. 1, is an agricultural town known for its Saturday *feria del agricultor* (farmer's market). The impressive church on the main square is built of steel manufactured by the Krups armament factory in Germany and has a beautiful colonial tile floor and stained-glass windows. The **San Ramón Museum,** on the north side of the plaza, focuses on local history; it features a re-created turn-of-the-century *campesino* home. It was closed for restoration in December 1997. Hours: Mon.-Fri. 1-5 p.m.; Wednesday and Saturday 8:30-11:30 a.m. The **Mercado Central,** one block north of the plaza, is also worth a visit.

Balneario Las Musas, about three km north of town, on the road to Piedades Sur, is a swimming complex with a water slide and a waterfall reached by a trail that continues into primary forest. It has a restaurant and dance hall, which are open on weekends. The last two kilometers are rough dirt road. Entrance: $1.75.

San Ramón is a center for cigar production. There are at least three **cigar factories:** Tabalera de Occidente, Fábrica Don Pedro, and Fábrica San Lazaro.

Accommodations and Food

La Posada Bed and Breakfast, tel./fax 445-7359, 50 meters east of the hospital, is a beautiful home furnished with antique reproductions;

it has a soft green decor and polished hardwood ceiling. The six rooms surround a tiny courtyard and are modestly yet pleasingly furnished and let in tons of light. Three have private bathrooms and some have magnificent Louis XIV-style beds. Room #1 also has a huge walk-in shower; a large room upstairs has French doors opening to the veranda. It has a small gift store and laundry. *Recommended!* Rates: $25 s, $40 d, including tax and breakfast.

Hotel Gran, tel. 445-6363, is a modern building with a strange, ill-conceived design around an atrium. The 22 rooms differ markedly, but most are dingy. Some have shared baths. There's a TV lounge. Rates: $8 s, $12.50 d, shared bath; $16 s/d, private bath. Also consider the budget **Hotel El Viajero,** tel. 445-5580.

Restaurant Han Bin serves Chinese; it's a block southwest of the plaza. **Greco's,** four blocks south of the plaza, is a class-act with contempo decor and a cafe below and restaurant upstairs. And **Il Giardino** steakhouse and pizzeria is recommended (a huge chateaubriand with black pepper sauce for two costs about $14), with salad and garlic bread.

Services

There are several banks, including **Banco del Comercio,** on the west side of the plaza, and **BanCrecen,** three blocks north on Calle 3 Norte.

Getting There and Around

Buses depart San José hourly from Calle 16, Avenidas 3/5, 6 a.m.-10 p.m. (one hour). **Taxis** operate from the main plaza, or call Taxis San Ramón, tel. 445-5966, or Taxis Unidos San Ramón, tel. 445-5110.

SAN RAMÓN TO LA TIGRA

San Ramón is a gateway to the northern lowlands via a lonesome mountain road that crests the cordillera, then begins a long sinuous descent to La Tigra and the northern lowlands. Just north of the ridge crest, tucked dramatically into the head of the a valley about 20 km north of San Ramón, is the **Valle Escondido Lodge,** Apdo. 452, La Uruca 1150, tel. 231-0906, fax 232-9591, reached via a steep and rugged dirt road that winds dramatically downhill through a working *finca.* I highly recommended a stop for a drink, meal, and/or overnight. All around are mountain cleaves clad in dark forest primeval, often shrouded in wispy clouds. Guided horseback riding and hiking are offered on the 60-hectare plantation and 400 hectares of ranchland and primary forest. There's an artificial lake for trout fishing. Mountain bikes can be rented. Trails lead down to the Río La Balsa, a good spot for swimming. Note the tiny butterfly and insect collection, and it is tantalizing to join the workers moving among the rows of citrus and ornamental plants.

At **Angeles Norte,** about four km north of San Ramón, a road leads east nine km to the Los Angeles Cloud Forest Reserve.

Los Angeles Cloud Forest Reserve

This relatively unknown 800-hectare reserve provides the same experience as Monteverde Cloud Forest Preserve without the crowds or the quetzals. The reserve is part of the Villablanca *finca,* a cattle ranch owned by former president Rodrigo Carazón, who often gives lectures to guests at the Hotel Villablanca. It begins at 700 meters' elevation and tops out at 1,800 meters (when the clouds clear—not often—you can see Volcán Arenal). The hills are covered with thick cloud forest, with the calls of howler monkeys emanating from its shrouded interior. Some 210 bird species were identified in the first 12 months, including bellbirds, trogons, and aricaris. Laureles trees have been planted to lure quetzals. Monkeys—howlers, capuchins, and spiders—abound, and other mammals such as ocelots, jaguars, and jaguarundis, are there in abundance for the lucky hiker.

Two short though fairly demanding trails (1.5 and two km) have wooden walkways with nonslip surfaces. A third, hard-hiking trail (6-9 hours) descends past waterfalls and natural swimming pools to the junction of the Ríos Balsa and Espino. A **canopy tour** is offered using a 300-meter-long cable slung between seven treetop platforms.

No bags are allowed on the trail, as fanatical horticulturalists have been stealing orchids. Forest entrance is $14 pp, a guided walk $7 more. Horseback rides cost $9 per hour.

Accommodations

Hotel Villablanca, tel. 228-4603, fax 233-6896, a reclusive hacienda, sits atop a hill—the very rim of the Continental Divide—on the edge of the reserve. Features include a restaurant, a lounge with TV, a lecture room, antique furnishings, and a mammoth open kitchen that could feed all the guests at the Ritz. The main lodge resembles a colonial farmhouse and has five guest rooms upstairs. A separate lodge has bunk beds for 30 people, plus its own kitchen and ping-pong table. The 49 cozy chalets (sleeping 2-6 people) surround the hacienda and feature rocking chairs and other dainty decor befitting Hansel and Gretel. A small fireplace decorates one corner and swinging saloon-style doors open onto a colonial tiled bathroom. Rain ponchos, flashlights, and umbrellas are provided. The buffet-style meals are tasty and filling. *Bocas* are served at the bar in the evening, and informal barbecues are hosted outside. There's a tiny chapel open for view by request. Volleyball and basketball courts are to be added. Rates: $77 s, $101 d *casitas;* $59 s, $83 d hotel rooms; $17 each additional person, including full breakfast.

Valle Escondido Lodge has 25 elegant, spacious *cabinas* with handsome, handcrafted hardwood furniture, plus a terrace for enjoying the magnificent setting and tallying the many bird species. The restaurant serves *típico* cuisine with a European flair (my sea bass with garlic was splendid; $7). Cool off in the swimming pool, warm up in the jacuzzi, or linger at the cocktail bar, which features live musicians and draws a local crowd on weekends. Roundtrip transfers from San José are offered ($25). Rates: $55 s, $66 d, $77 t.

Getting There

Interbus stops at Los Angeles on its daily shuttle between San José and La Fortuna.

HEREDIA AND VICINITY

Heredia (pop. 32,000) is 11 km northwest of San José, surrounded by coffee fields on the lower slopes of Volcán Barva. A pleasant, slow-paced, nostalgic atmosphere pervades the neat and orderly grid-patterned town with its old adobe houses with tile roofs and corridors. It has undergone several name changes from its inception in 1706 as Barrio Lagunilla. It is colloquially known as La Ciudad de las Flores ("City of the Flowers"). The **National University**—famed particularly for its veterinary courses—is here, on the east side of town. It enrolls many foreign students, giving the city a cosmopolitan feel.

Downtown streets are narrow and jam-packed with jostling traffic.

Sights

Heredia is centered around a weathered colonial cathedral—the **Basílica de la Inmaculada Concepción**—containing beautiful stained-glass windows as well as bells delivered from Cuzco, Peru. The church was built in 1797. It is squat and thick-walled and has withstood many earthquakes. The church faces west onto lively **Parque Central,** shaded by large mango trees and more Latin in feel than anything San José has to offer. Concerts are held on Thursday evenings in the peculiarly shaped music temple.

The streets have other fine examples of colonial architecture, notably **El Fortín,** a circular fortress tower bordering the north side of the central plaza. A curious piece of military-textbook heresy are the gun slits that widen to the outside. In a classic piece of military ineptitude, eccentric president Alfredo González Flores (1914-17) got the gun-ports so wrong that they allow bullets in easily but made it difficult for defenders to shoot out.

The **Casa de la Cultura,** next to El Fortín, contains a small art gallery and historic exhibits. It was once the residence of González Flores, who was exiled in 1917 after a coup d'etat. He was later welcomed back and ran much of his presidency from his home, where he lived until his death in 1962. Flores is the father of social reform in Costa Rica, and the founder of its income tax and the state-run insurance system. The house was declared a National Historic Monument in 1981, when it was refurbished. Hours: daily 8 a.m.-9 p.m.; free.

The **Mercado Central** (Central Market) is a must-visit, brimming with locally grown produce. The School of Marine Biology at the National University houses the **Marine Zoological Museum,** tel. 277-3240, with 1,900 specimens of native marine flora and fauna. Hours: Tues.-Fri. 8 a.m.-4 p.m.; free.

Heredia's stout Basílica de la Inmaculada Concepción, built in 1797, has survived several earthquakes.

MICHAEL RAYMOND GREER

HEREDIA

CALLE 11

TO SAN RAFAEL

■ HOTEL VALLADOLID
■ LA RAMBLA
■ RESTAURANTE EL
   GRAN PAPA

TO APARTOTEL ROMA

■ BAR/RESTAURANTE
   COWBOY

Verano Calle

AV. 9

TO SAN JOSE

CALLE 9

■ FRESAS
■ RESTAURANTE
   VEGETARIANO
   VISHNU
■ LA CHOZA

NATIONAL
UNIVERSITY

112

■ McDONALD'S
   ■ POP'S
      ICE CREAM

3

TO SAN JOSE

CALLE 7

■ LIBRARY

■ RESTAURANTE
   EL PRINCIPE

■ PIZZERIA LA
   TARTARUGA

■ WESTERN UNION

CALLE 5

■ AGENCIAS
   VIAJES
   COLON

■ LE PETIT
   PARIS

3

CALLE 3

□ PARQUE

150 m
0

126

TO BARVA

AV. 9
AV. 7
AV. 5
AV. 3

CALLE CENTRAL

□ PARQUE

■ BANCO
   POPULAR

■ CASA DE LA
   CULTURA

† BASILICA DE
   LA CONCEPCION

■ TAXIS
■ HOTEL
   AMERICA

PLAZA

■ PIZZA HUT

■ BANCO DE
   COSTA RICA

■ BUS TO
   SAN JOSE

AV. 1

CALLE 1

AV. 3

CALLE 3

■ RED
   CROSS

■ BUS TO
   BARVA

■ EL
   FORTIN

■ BANCO INTERFIN

■ FUJIFILM
■ CASA
   DE LAS
   REVISTAS

■ MONPIK
   ICE CREAM

■ MERCADO
   CENTRAL

■ BUS TO SAN JOSE

CALLE CENTRAL (RAFAEL MOYA)

■ TOWN HALL AND
   POST OFFICE

■ POLLO
   FRITO RAIMY

■ AZZURRA

PARQUE
CENTRAL

■ HOTEL VERANO

CALLE 2

CALLE 4

■ T.J.
   STEAK HOUSE

■ HOTEL
   COLONIAL

■ HOTEL OJO
   DE AGUA
■ HOTEL EL
   PARQUE

AV. CENTRAL (RAFAEL MOYA)

■ HOTEL
   HEREDIA

■ INSTITUTO
   DE LENGUAJE
   PURA VIDA

CALLE 6

AV. 2

■ BANCO
   NACIONAL

TO SAN JOSE

AV. 4

CALLE 8

AV. 6

■ PARQUE

AV. 8

CALLE 10

AV. 10

■ CASA DE
   HUESPEDES
   RAMBLE

AV. 12

CALLE 12

■ GYM STEVEN'S
   (CAMPING/FISHING GEAR)

■ BANCO
   NACIONAL

CALLE 14

HOSPITAL
SAN
VICENTE

CALLE 16

3

TO ALAJUELA

■ HOTEL LAS FLORES

© MOON PUBLICATIONS, INC.

INSET

TO SAN
RAFAEL

113

112

TO SAN JOSE

3

TO BARVA

126

AV. 13
AV. 11
AV. 1
AV. 15

AREA OF MAP COVERAGE

CALLE

CENTRAL

TO ALAJUELA

3

AV. 14

SOCCER
STADIUM

Accommodations

Don't neglect the several superb hotels that lie in the hills outside Heredia.

Budget: The **Hotel Verano,** Calle 4, Avenida 6, tel. 237-1616, upstairs on the west side of the market, has clean rooms with shared baths and cold water. Disturbed by the noise of love-making? Don't worry; most likely your neighbors took a room for only an hour. Rates: $15 s, $20 d. Some rooms have private baths for $18. The **Hotel Colonial,** Avenida 4, Calles 4/6, tel. 237-5258, is of a similar standard. It has hot water and charges $7-10. A less attractive, but not unappealing, alternative is the **Hotel Heredia,** tel. 237-1324, on the north side of town at Calle 6, Avenida 3/5. It has 10 rooms with private baths and hot water. Rates: $12 s, $20 d.

Casa de Huéspedes Ramble, Avenida 8, tel. 238-3829, also has 15 small but clean wood-paneled rooms with private baths (some have shared bath) for $15 s, $25 d. The best bargain is **Hotel Las Flores,** Avenida 12, Calles 12/14, tel. 382-3418. It's run by the folks who have Casa Ramble. The 20 rooms are modern, tiled, spacious, and well-lit, and private bathrooms have hot water. Rates: $11 s, $17 d. It has secure parking.

A more basic option is **Hotel Parque,** on Calle 4, tel. 238-2882, on the west side of the Mercado Central. Its dingy rooms cost $5 pp, shared bath; $10 s, $17 d, private bath.

Inexpensive: The modern **Hotel América,** Apdo. 1740, Heredia 3000, tel. 260-9292, fax 260-9293, 50 meters south of Parque Central, is a good bargain. It features 36 a/c rooms and four suites, all with cable TVs, telephones, and private baths with hot water, plus laundry service and a souvenir shop. Decor (mauves, blues, and creams) is pleasing. It has a steak house restaurant, and offers 24-hour room service. The glassed-in rooftop provides city and mountain vistas. Tours of Heredia are offered by the owner, in his Mercedes. Rates: $25 s, $35 d, $45 t.

The **Apartotel Vargas,** Apdo. 87, Heredia 1300, tel. 237-8526, fax 223-9878, has eight fully equipped apartments with private baths in a residential setting opposite coffee fields. It's 800 meters north of Colegio Santa Cecilia near Sacramento, north of Heredia (take Calle 12). Rates: $45 s, $55 d. **Apartotel Roma,** tel. 260-0127, fax 260-6339, has small but nicely decorated one- and two-bedroom suites with kitchenettes, TVs, and hot water. Rates: $35 s, $40 d.

Moderate: The class act in town is the remodeled **Hotel Valladolid,** Apdo. 1973-3000, Heredia, tel. 260-2905, fax 260-2912, at Avenida 7, Calle 7, with 11 a/c rooms featuring cable TVs, phones, and kitchenettes. The hotel has a sauna, a jacuzzi, a rooftop solarium with great views, plus a bar and a restaurant, as well as its own travel agency. Rates: $58 s, $62 d, $72 t, $71 suite.

Food

First and last, head to **Le Petit Paris,** tel./fax 238-1721, on Calle 5, Avenidas Central/2, an exquisite French restaurant with a patio. The menu features salads, sandwiches, soups, omelettes, pastas, and two dozen kinds of crepes ($2-5), plus special entreés such as chicken Normande and steak in pepper sauce ($4-5), and fondue bourguignonne ($11). A barbecue is offered on Sunday. The mood is enhanced by world music. Each month features a rotating art exhibition, plus slide shows.

El Gran Chaparral in the Casa de la Cultura serves traditional Costa Rican fare. **Restaurante El Gran Papá,** tel. 237-4432, on Calle 9, Avenidas 5/7, and **Restaurante El Príncipe,** tel. 238-1894, at Calle 5, Avenida Central/2, have also been recommended for *típico* food. **Fresas,** tel. 238-4074, Calle 7, Avenida 1, serves all things strawberry as well as meals for less than $5.

For surf and turf check out **T.J. Steak House,** tel. 237-9115, at Avenida 3, Calle 4/6. **La Rambla,** tel. 238-3912, opposite the Hotel Valladolid, serves spaghettis, steaks ($5), and shrimp dishes ($15), plus *típico* fare.

Azzurra, an Italian restaurant on the west side of the plaza, is also known for its ice creams. **Pizzería La Tartaruga,** Calle 7 and Avenida Central, has a *plata del día* for $2.50. One block north is the clean **Restaurante Vegetariano Vishnu,** tel. 237-2527, serving sandwiches (from $1.50), veggie burgers ($1.50), *batidos* (75 cents), and the like. There are several Chinese restaurants on the south side of the plaza.

Pizza Hut, Calle 3, Avenida 6, and **McDonald's,** Calle 9, Avenida 6, offer you know what. For fried chicken, try **Pollo Frito Raymi,** tel. 328-3828, on Calle 2, Avenidas Central/2.

Entertainment

Several bars are popular with students. Try **Bar/Restaurant Cowboy,** at Calle 9, Avenida 5; and **La Choza,** at Calle 7, Avenida Central. The **Oceanos Bar,** on Calle 4, Avenidas Central/2, is also a favorite of students, who warm up here before heating up the dance floor (sometimes until dawn) at **Miraflores Disco.**

Information and Services

The *biblioteca* (library) is on Avenida 7, Calle 7. **La Casa de las Revistas,** Calle Central, Avenidas 4/6, sells English-language magazines. **Fujifilm,** tel. 237-8188, has an outlet at Avenida 4, Calles Central/2. You can buy basic **fishing and camping gear** at Gym Steven's on Calle 10, Avenidas 8/10.

There are branches of **Banco Nacional** at Calle 2, Avenidas 2/4, and Calle 12, Avenida 6; a Banco de Costa Rica at Calle 1, Avenida 6; and a Banco Popular at Avenida Central, Calle 3. You can get a cash advance against Visa or MasterCard at Credomatic, tel. 260-2000, on Calle 9 at Avenida 6. **Western Union** has an office at Calle 7 and Avenida 2.

Hospital San Vicente, tel. 237-1091, is situated at Calle 14 and Avenida 8. There are plenty of **pharmacies** in the downtown area. Lavandería La Margarita, tel. 237-0529, Avenida 6, Calles Central/2, offers **laundry** and dry-cleaning service. Need a travel agent? Try **Agencías Viajes Colón,** tel. 260-8989, at Avenida Central, Calle 3.

Getting There and Away

By Bus: Microbuses Rápido, tel. 238-8392 or 238-0506, offers bus service from San José every 10 minutes 5 a.m.-10 p.m., from Calle 1, Avenidas 7/9. Other microbuses depart San José from Avenida 2, Calles 10/12 every 15 minutes, and hourly midnight-6 a.m. from Avenida 2, Calles 4/6. Heredia has no central terminal: buses depart for San José from both Calle Central and Avenida 4.

Buses to Barva depart Heredia every 30 minutes from Calle Central, Avenidas 1/3; to Ojo de Agua from Avenida 6, Calle 6; to Puerto Viejo de Sarapiquí at 6:30 a.m., noon, and 3 p.m. from the west side of Parque Central; to Sacramento (and Braulio Carrillo National Park) at 6:30 a.m.,11 a.m., and 4 p.m. from Avenida 8, Calles

2/4; and hourly to San José de la Montaña from Avenida 8, Calles 2/4.

By Taxi: Taxis wait on the south side of Parque Central, or call Taxis Coopemargarita, tel. 238-3377, or Taxis Coopetico, tel. 237-6163.

SAN JOAQUÍN

San Joaquín de las Flores, four km west of Heredia, has a pretty colonial-era church still in use. It is famous for its colorful **Easter-week procession.** The village is a popular upscale residential area replete with villas hidden behind bougainvillea hedges.

Butterfly Paradise, tel. 224-1095 or tel./fax 221-2015, is a live butterfly "museum" and farm—pupae are exported to zoos in Europe— one km to the north of San Joaquín, on the road to Santa Bárbara. Here, you can observe the life cycle of the butterfly in the breeding laboratory. Your visit begins with an educational video and an exhibit of live butterflies emerging from their cocoons like folded hankerchiefs. Guided tours are offered in six languages. Morning is best, when butterflies are emerging from cocoons. Hours: daily 9 a.m.-4 p.m.

Accommodations and Food

A reader recommends a "comfortable *pensión*" in San Lorenzo de Flores, one km north of San Joaquín, run by Jorge Meza, tel. 265-6253, e-mail: fmulate@sol.racsa.co.cr. It has eight rooms, some bunk-style. Students pay $10 including breakfast.

Galería Vivero is an elegant restaurant with alfresco dining.

BARVA

Barva, about two km north of Heredia amid superb coffee country, is as quaint as any town in Costa Rica. A major restoration has spruced up one of the oldest settlements in the country, with Barva and Poás Volcanoes behind creating a sublime setting. The **Basílica de Barva,** which dates back to 1767, sits atop an ancient Indian burial ground and faces onto a square surrounded by red-tiled colonial-era adobe houses built of cane, wood, brick, animal dung, and mud using a pre-Columbian method called *bahareque.* On one side of the church is a grotto dedicated to the Virgin of Lourdes. Many of the buildings open onto pretty inner courtyards with fountains and fruit trees hidden behind thick walls. One of these—the former home of Cleto Gonzalez Víquez, twice president of Costa Rica—was declared a national landmark in 1985. The place is best experienced at sunset, when slanting rays gild the square like burnished copper.

The **Museum of Popular Culture,** tel. 260-1619, fax 261-3462, 1.5 km southeast of Barva at Santa Lucía de Barva, presents a picture of rural life at the turn of the century. It is housed in a renovated, red-tile-roofed, mustard-colored home dating from 1885 and once owned by former president Alfredo González Flores; the house has been kept as it was when he died. The landscaped gardens include a fruit orchard. Guided tours are offered for groups only, but individuals can explore at will. The museum is signed on the road. Open Mon.-Fri. 8 a.m.-4 p.m., Saturday 10 a.m.-5 p.m., and Sunday 9 a.m.-6 p.m. Entrance: $1.50. An adjacent wattle-and-daub farmstead was being restored to house a **Museo del Peón,** dedicated to the farm worker.

Café Britt

Midway between Heredia and Barva is the *finca* and *beneficio* of Café Britt, Apdo. 528, Heredia 3000, tel. 260-2748, fax 238-1848, e-mail: info@cafebritt.com; in the U.S., tel. 800-GO-BRITT (800-462-7488), where you can learn the story of Costa Rican coffee. The company, which roasts, packs, and exports to specialty stores around the world, has opened its factory and farm to visitors. The two-hour "Coffeetour" ($15, or $20 with transfers) includes an educational tour of the *finca* and roasting plant, complete with live-theater skit (very commercial, but amusing) telling the history of coffee. You conclude in the tasting room, where you are shown how experts taste coffee. The factory store, where coffee goes for a song, can arrange mail-order delivery to the United States. Tours are daily at 9 a.m. You can combine the Coffeetour with a visit to the Museum of Popular Culture, Nov.-March ($20, or $25 with transfers). A full-day "Organic Coffee Farming Tour" is also offered, Nov.-March ($75). Other combined tours are offered. Café Britt picks up

tour guests in San José with the Britt Bus, colorfully decorated with coffee themes. Call for locations and times.

Watch for El Castillo, a castlelike house on the left, about two km north of Heredia; Café Britt is immediately beyond, on the left.

Accommodations and Food

On the outskirts of Barva, in Santa Lucía, is **Los Jardines,** Apdo. 64, Barva de Heredia 3011, tel. 260-1904, a Canadian-run bed and breakfast in a contemporary home with four rooms and two baths. Not reviewed. Rates: $20 s, $32 d. Long-term discounts.

There are several restaurants around the plaza. Try **Pollo de Pastor Barva** on the north side for fried chicken; or **Pollo Pepe** on the south.

Information

There's a **Centro de Información Turística** on the west side of the plaza.

Getting There

By Bus: Buses depart Heredia for Barva from Calle Central, Avenidas 1/3. Buses drop off and depart from the south side of the plaza.

By Car: If driving from Heredia, Calles Central and 2 lead north to Barva.

NORTH OF BARVA

Half a kilometer north of Barva, the road forks. The road to the right leads uphill to **San José de la Montaña** (1,550 meters), known for its pretty church and mountain resorts in the midst of pine forests. It's popular with Ticos. Beyond San José de la Montaña, the air becomes decidedly chilly and the road decidedly steeper. Five km above San José de la Montaña, is the hamlet of **Porrosatí** (also known as Paso Llano), where a turnoff to the left from the Guardia Rural post leads to **Sacramento,** but a 4WD vehicle will get you all the way to the **Parque Nacional Braulio Carrillo** ranger station (three km) along a very steep (first gear), deeply rutted rock road. The entrance gate is open Tues.-Sun. 8 a.m.-4 p.m.; entrance $6.

The left fork at the Y-junction 600 meters north of Barva leads to the village of **Birrí** and con-

SPECIAL HOTEL: FINCA ROSA BLANCA

Imagine if Gaudi and Frank Lloyd Wright had combined their talents and visions. The result might be an architectural stunner as eclectic and electrifying as Finca Rosa Blanca, Apdo. 41, Santa Barbara de Heredia 3009, tel. 269-9392, fax 269-9555; in the U.S., SJO 1201, PO Box 025216, Miami, FL 33102-5216, tel. (800) 327-9854, e-mail: rblanca@sol.racsa.co.cr, website www.finca-rblanca.co.cr. This is one of Costa Rica's preeminent boutique hotels. Inspired by Gaudi's architectonics and the Santa Fe style, the family-run hotel is conceived as if from a fairy tale. *Que linda!*

Its hillside position one km northeast of Santa Barbara de Heredia offers vistas as romantic and visionary as the house itself, with row upon row of coffee plants cascading down the slopes, and mountains almost mauve in the distance. Tall 200-year-old higuerones trees and effusive tropical plants—bougainvilleas and fuchsia—provide a magnificent frame for the snow-white house with its bridge-of-the-Starship-*Enterprise* turret (actually, the honeymoon suite).

Upon entering via the hand-carved wooden front door, it feels like walking into the pages of *Architectural Digest*. Focal-point is an open-plan, circular atrium lounge with wraparound deep-cushioned sofas and a huge open-hearth fireplace that—imagine!—resembles a mushroom. Light pours in through countless windows to feed the profusion of tropical plants. Flowers and creeping vines are everywhere, as is the dramatic artwork of Glenn Jampol, live-in owner, who has his art studio and wood workshop in the grounds (all hardwood furnishings are crafted on-site).

The whole is contrived by the genius of architect Francisco Rojas in a surfeit of voluptuous curves and finely crafted hardwoods, not least the magnificent dining table and uniquely curled diners and leather casual chairs. The place is like a museum, with imaginative and tasteful statuettes, prints, and New Mexican artifacts in every delightful nook and cranny.

There are six suites and a master suite, plus a three-bedroom "colonial cottage"and two villas on the resplendent grounds. Each room is as distinct as a thumbprint. Genuine hardwood antiques stand on rough stone floors. Walls are painted with trompe l'oeil landscapes; mine was of an idyllic coffee *finca*. The stylish "Blanco y Negro" Room has a black-and-white checkerboard floor and a black bed made of coffeewood. The honeymoon suite—a fantasy come true—has a bathroom with walls painted to resemble a tropical rainforest, with water that tumbles down a rocky cascade into the fathoms-deep tub shaped liked a natural pool. A hardwood spiral staircase—each step shaped like a petal—twists up to the coup de grâce: a rotunda bedroom that caps the building's turret, with a canopied bed and wraparound windows. All rooms have a patio or voluptuous deck. And bathrooms are like miniature free-form pools.

Exceptional cuisine (using organic, estate-grown produce) comes with service to match. Four-course dinners ($25) are served with candlelight and soothing classical music, with free-flowing wines poured in generous portions.

There's an exquisite horizon swimming pool fed by a cascade, gardens (including an organic vegetable garden), and a calming library, plus a stable for guided rides as far as Volcán Barva ($15 per hour). A minibus provides transfers to the airport and throughout the Meseta Central.

It's impossible not to fall head-over-heels in love with this fantasy in stone conjured from the remains of an abandoned farm.

Rates: from $104 s, $122 d; $190 two-bedroom villa; $183 s, $204 d for the Rosa Blanca Suite. Includes full American breakfast.

tinues to Vara Blanca on the ridge of the Continental Divide. In Birrí, a road to the right at Restaurante Las Delicias leads uphill via the hamlets of Guacalillo to Porrosatí. The Hotel Chalet Tirol offers a three-hour guided excursion to a local farm noted for its forest of giant Spanish cedar and ficus cathedral trees; it costs $50 including transport from San José plus gourmet lunch at the hotel.

A separate road leads northwest from Barva two km to **San Pedro de Barva** and, three km beyond to **Santa Barbara de Heredia,** a lively and compact town with colonial-era adobe houses set amid colorful gardens in the heart of coffee country. San Pedro is home to the Instituto de Café research laboratory and **Coffee Museum,** tel. 237-1975, 400 meters north of the San Pedro church. The museum building is an adobe house dating from 1834. Inside are displays of antique coffee-making paraphernalia: pulp extractors, toasters, grinders, etc. Hours: Mon.-Fri. 7 a.m.-4 p.m. Café Britt has stolen the museum's thunder and the latter may be closed by the time you read this.

Accommodations

San José de la Montaña: You'll find *cabinas* for rent about 400 meters below Hotel Cypresal (take the right fork at the sign for Urbanización El Cypresal), and others, tel. 238-4242, opposite El Portico. **Mountain Cabins La Catalina,** Apdo. 12742, San José 1000, tel. 233-6108, fax 233-6293, has 13 modern cottages, each with a small living room and two bedrooms, plus volleyball, swimming pool, and gardens. Rates: $42 s, $45 d, $55 t.

Porrosatí: Cabañas Laudriana, tel. 219-4175 or 219-4050, amid the pines, has rustic A-frame wooden cabins with fireplaces, kitchens, and private bathrooms with hot water. There are beds downstairs and in a mezzanine. Two rustic restaurants are at hand. Rates: $37 d, $58 quad, $67 six people. North of Porrosatí, **Restaurante La Campesina** (three km) and **Restaurante Sacramento** (four km) have basic *cabinas.* **Sacramento Lodge,** tel. 237-2116, fax 237-1976, six km north of Porrosatí, has comfortable and rustic rooms on the family farm run by gracious hosts. It has fabulous views down through the pine forest, plus *típico* cuisine, and hiking and horseback rides. Rates: $40 pp.

Birrí to Porrosatí: Cabañas Don Gollo, five km north of Birrí, is a simple homey place with three rustic Swiss-style cabins, each with fireplace and kitchenette. Rates: $29 s/d.

Just up the road, the **Hotel Cypresal,** Apdo. 7891, San José 1000, tel. 223-1717 or 237-4466, fax 221-6244, has 24 rooms, 13 with fireplaces (which you'll be glad for). The log cabins are very pleasant; other brick structures have ugly terraces and are more basic. Rooms have tiled floors, small TVs, and telephones. There is a volleyball court, a small and grungy swimming pool, and a modestly elegant restaurant and bar at which I enjoyed a curry chicken ($5). Rates: $35 s, $43 d, $50 t.

A better bet is **Hotel El Portico,** Apdo. 289, Heredia 3000, tel. 260-6000 or 237-6022, fax 260-6002, 200 meters above Cypresal and set in a six-hectare farm with forest trails. The atmospheric lodge has 18 rooms with rough-stone tiled floors and private bathroom. There's a beautiful and spacious lounge with leather sofas and a large stone fireplace and vast windows proffering views down the mountainside. There's also a separate TV lounge, a sauna and jacuzzi, plus an atmospheric Swiss-style restaurant with bar. Beautiful artwork abounds. Landscaped grounds contain a small swimming pool and lake. Rates: $50 s, $60 d, $70 t, including tax.

Las Ardillas Resort Health Spa, tel./fax 260-2172, e-mail: verasol@sol.racsa.co.cr, opposite the Cypresal, has 15 rustic log-and-brick cabins, each with fireplace, kitchenette, and private bathroom. There's a game room, a bar and restaurant, a children's play area, and a simple spa with a large Italian-tiled jacuzzi and pinewood sauna. A professional masseuse and holistic health practitioner offer massage ($25 per hour), plus mud wraps, herbal wraps, hydrotherapy, and aromatherapy. Horseback riding and hiking are offered. High fiber/low fat meals are prepared on a wood-burning stove using organic, homegrown produce. A musician plays marimba at meal times. Rates: $35 d. Special packages are offered.

Associated with Las Ardillas is **Cabañas La Milenas,** Apdo. 44, Heredia 3009, tel./fax 260-2172, with romantic, rustic log cabins 500 meters above Cypresal. It, too, offers "stress management," massage, hydrotherapy, mud baths, tai chi, and horseback riding. It's reminiscent of a log cabin in the California Sierras.

Santa Barbara de Heredia: La Casa Que Canta, tel. 238-2536, is an American-run hostelry on five acres of lawns and orchards in Barrio Jesús, on the road from Santa Barbara to Barva. Loftily perched at 4,250 feet, it offers views over San José and the valley. Brian Mathews rents rooms (two fully equipped), roomy two-bedroom cottages with kitchens, plus his own fully equipped two-bedroom home. Rates: from $40.

Finca Rosa Blanca, one km east of Santa Barbara, is one of the most spectacular boutique hotels in the country.

Food

Most of the hotels listed above have restaurants. The road from Porrosatí to Sacramento is lined with rustic *sodas* and restaurants: Chago's Bar, Restaurant El Ranchito (with an open fireplace), Bar y Restaurant La Campesina (with outdoor tables), Bar y Restaurant Sacramento, and Soda El Bosque.

El Banoco de Mariscos, in Santa Barbara, is a popular seafood restaurant; the owners catch their own fish and ship it fresh daily under ice.

Getting There

Buses marked "Paso Llano" depart Heredia at 6:30 a.m., noon, and 3 p.m. for San José de la Montaña, Porrosatí, and Sacramento from Avenida 8, Calles 2/4. Hourly buses also go to San José de la Montaña (on Sunday you may need to alight here and take a 7 a.m. bus to Porrosatí). The last bus from Porrosatí departs for Heredia weekdays at 5 p.m. and Sunday at 4 p.m.

A bus for Santa Barbara de Heredia departs Heredia from Avenida 1, Calles 1/3 every 15 minutes Mon.-Friday.

VOLCÁN BARVA

Barva Volcano (2,906 meters), on the western extreme of Braulio Carrillo National Park, sleeps placidly in majestic surroundings. The mountain's botanical treasures range from mosses to giant oaks, cypress, and cedar. A loop trail leads to the summit from Porrosatí (the trail is marked as BCNP Sector Barva) and circles back to the ranger station three km northeast of Sacramento (four or five hours hiking, roundtrip). The summit is three km from the ranger station. The trail

leads up through cloud forest—good for spotting resplendent quetzals and black-faced solitaires—to the crater and a lookout point from which, on a clear day, you can see forever. Fog, however, is usually the order of the day.

You can also follow marked trails on a four-day hike from the summit all the way to Puerto Viejo de Sarapiquí, in the northern lowlands. Apparently there are huts en route. Check with the National Parks headquarters, tel. 257-0922. Take an Instituto Geográfica map and a compass, plus high-quality waterproof gear and warm clothing, and—of course—sufficient food and water. Several people have been lost for days in the park. You can camp beside the crater lake, behind the ranger station, or at two picnic areas with barbecue grills on the trail (no facilities).

Tours

Jungle Trails, Apdo. 2413, San José, tel. 255-3486, fax 525-2782, offers a "Walk in the Cloud Forest" hiking tour on Barva Volcano, including tours of Heredia, Barva, and a coffee plantation. It's four hours of hiking, with picnic lunch served in a spot favored by quetzals.

EAST OF HEREDIA

Santa Domingo de Heredia, three km southeast of Heredia and three km north of San José, has two handsome historic churches plus many colonial houses restored to creamy grandeur, as does **San Isidro,** eight km due east of Heredia. San Isidro (not to be confused with San Isidro de Coronado) is known for its landmark white church, very Gothic, with lots of pointed spires (English in inspiration). The town is known for its **Easter procession.**

In San Isidro, check out **Cerámica Chavarris,** tel. 268-8455, where Doña Frances makes "California-style" ovenproof pottery. Cross the narrow iron bridge on the northeast corner of the plaza and head uphill to the left (look for the little white sign on the right); the road eventually loops back to Heredia via San Rafael.

Accommodations

Budget: Rancho de Wicho, tel. 268-8279, beside the river one km north of San Isidro, is a popular fiesta spot on weekends. It has cages full of song birds (80 species), and there's an A-frame hut with kitchen and bathroom with hot water. Rates: $21 daily; $300 monthly. (A *wicho* is a friendly person.)

Hotel y Restaurante Penguin's, on Avenida 7 in Santo Domingo, has simple rooms.

Inexpensive: La Posada de la Montaña, Apdo. 1-3017, San Isidro de Heredia, tel./fax 268-8096, e-mail: cwatz@sol.racsa.co.cr, website www.bhw.com/costarica; in Germany, tel. 49-2154-87699, 400 meters north of Cerámica Chavarris, is a relaxing, 16-bedroom bed and breakfast set amid five acres of landscaped gardens and orchards at 1,500 meters elevation. The place, which is German-run, is spacious and spic-and-span, with lots of light and closet space. Hardwoods abound. Guests have full access to the large living-dining area with TV. Thin partition walls in small economy rooms with shared bath may create a noise problem. All rooms have double beds. Three twin-bedroom suites at the bottom of the garden have large kitchens and dining rooms with fireplaces. Guests can use the barbecue pit in the garden, which also has a small swimming pool and *rancho*. Guided two-hour horseback rides cost $25. The owners will meet you at the airport or arrange a taxi. *Good bargain!* Rates: $20 s, $40 d standard; $35 s, $50 d, $60 t deluxe; $70-135 suites. Rates, which include family-style breakfasts, are about 25% less in low season.

Debbie King's B&B, Apdo. 465, Heredia 3000, tel. 268-8284, is a small bed and breakfast on a coffee *finca* with great views over San José. Two large wood-paneled bedrooms have private baths. Upper rooms have wraparound balconies. Two cottages have kitchens and private baths and sleep four. Dinners on request. The hotel's greatest asset is Debbie, an erstwhile Beverly Hills restaurateur, and her equally affable husband. Rates: $20 s, $35 d, $49 *cabinas*.

Moderate: The delightful, superbly run, Dutch-owned **Hotel Bougainvillea,** Apdo. 69, San José 2120, tel. 244-1414, fax 244-1313, e-mail: bougainvillea@centralamerica.com, website www.centralamerica.com/cr/hotel/bougain.htm, about 800 meters east of Santo Domingo, is a splendid option. This contemporary three-story hotel is set in vast landscaped grounds surrounded by a sea of coffee plants, with a beautiful view of the mountain ranges and San José.

The 82 spacious rooms each have a/c, two double beds, TV, and balcony, plus luxurious bathrooms in the newer rooms. Sarchí oxcarts, local handicrafts, and abundant modern artwork decorate the public areas. There is a gift shop, swimming pool, tennis court, and an elegant restaurant. A shuttle service runs into San José. Rates: $55 s, $65 d, $75 t, $95 quad. *Recommended!*

Food

The **Hotel Bougainvillea** is known for its excellent cuisine, including *corvina* and *lomito*. It offers a *plato fuerte* (entrée, dessert, and coffee) for $10—good value. **Al Piel del Monte** is a short walk from Debbie King's B&B—you can enjoy a delicious *casado* here for $3.

Getting There

Buses depart San José from Calle 4, Avenidas 7/9 every half hour.

SAN RAFAEL TO MONTE DE LA CRUZ

Two km northeast of Heredia lies **San Rafael.** A medieval stonemason would be proud of the town's stunning, recently restored, cream-colored Gothic church, with its buttresses and magnificent stained-glass windows. The church, completed in 1962, is visible from throughout the Meseta Central and bears strong hints of Notre Dame.

North of San Rafael, the land begins to rise up the slopes of Volcán Barva, the temperatures begin to drop, and the first hints of the Swiss Tyrol begin to appear, with pine and cedar forests and emerald-green pastures grazed by dairy cattle. Many expensive mansions line the road or lie hidden deep in the forest. Remnants of ancient oaks and other primary forests remain on the higher reaches: a San Rafael community group had campaigned for more than a decade in an effort to save the forests that protect the water supply for Heredia. In 1995 their efforts were rewarded with creation of the 100-hectare **Chompipe Biological Reserve** and construction of a environmental education center—**The Center for Earth Concerns,** Apdo 2042, San Rafael de Heredia 3000, tel./fax 267-7215—aimed primarily at school age children. Tapirs, deer, coyotes, sloths, and kinkajous are among the wildlife species that inhabit the mountainside forests.

Hotel Chalet Tirol

The area is popular with Ticos, who flock on weekends and holidays to a series of recreation areas. **Complejo Turístico Aúoranzas,** tel./fax 267-7406, three km above San Rafael, offers a kids' playground, trails, and a bar and restaurant (*típico* dishes, $3-6) with views over the valley. About 100 meters uphill is **Ponte Vedra,** a rustic restaurant with live bands midweek. One km uphill, a turn off to the left leads to **Centro Turístico las Chorreras,** which has hiking trails through the forests.

The largest and most popular recreation spot is the upscale **Club Campestre El Castillo,** or El Castillo Country Club, tel. 267-7111, with stunning views over the central valley. Recreational possibilities include basketball, soccer, sauna, swimming pool, go-carts, and the country's only ice rink. A restaurant serving *típico* cuisine is warmed by logs flaming in a large hearth. The club has camping and picnic tables. It hosts ice-skating *espectáculos* (shows) and a regular program of activities for adults and kids. It's a members-only club, but guests can be invited. Entrance: $3.50 pp weekends, $2.50 weekdays.

The right-hand fork two km north of El Castillo leads to **Monte de la Cruz Reserve,** popular with weekend hikers from San José. This 15-hectare private forest reserve eight km north of San Rafael is superb for nature hikes along trails choked with ferns and wild orchids through pine forest and cloud forest great for birding, including a chance to spot quetzals. One trail along the Río Segundo leads to Braulio Carrillo National Park, another leads to a complex of waterfalls. It is often cloudy and usually exhilaratingly crisp, if not cold and wet; bring warm waterproof clothing (also bring binoculars—the birding is superb). Hours: Mon.-Fri. 8 a.m.-4 p.m., weekends 8 a.m.-5 p.m. Entrance: 75 cents. The road—climbing steeply and deteriorating the while—continues two km to **Refugio de Vida Silvestre Cerro Dantas,** part of Braulio Carrillo National Park.

The fork to the left north of El Castillo leads to the **Parque Residencial del Monte,** an exclusive residential area amid the pines with the **Hotel Chalet Tirol** at its heart. The hotel—which resembles a Swiss village—offers a full-day guided cloud-forest birding trip in search of quetzals, trogons, toucanets, and more; it's $75, including pick up in San José and lunch at the hotel. The trip penetrates the **Tirol Cloud Forest** on the upper reaches of Volcán Barva.

Festival
The **International Music Festival** is hosted at Hotel Chalet Tirol each July and August in the Salzburg Café Concert Dinner Theater, looking like a set for *The Sound of Music*. The classical concerts cost $14 each.

Accommodations
Hotel Chalet Tirol, Apdo. 7812, San José 1000, tel. 267-7371, fax 267-7050, e-mail: tirolcr@sol. racsa.co.cr, website www.arweb.com/tirol, is a delightful Tyrolean-style place with a superb French restaurant. The hotel is at 1,800 meters

(5,900 feet), within a 15-hectare private cloud forest reserve. Ten rustic yet charming twin-level alpine cabins—handpainted in Tyrolean fashion—surround a small lawn. There are also 20 modern hotel rooms, each with a TV, fireplace, spacious bathroom, and furnishings from a Hansel-and-Gretel story. One suite has a spiral staircase to a mezzanine bedroom. There's a pool, sauna and massage/fitness room, plus two tennis courts. The lodge was owned by a former Costa Rican president, Alfredo González Flores (1914-17) and is worth a visit just to eat in the rough-hewn timbered dining room, with its pretty curtains, window boxes, blazing log fire in an old-world fireplace, brass chandeliers, and romantic candlelight. The hotel offers a wide selection of tours, including horseback riding ($65 with gourmet lunch). Concerts are given in the Salzburg Café Concert Dinner Theater. Rates: Chalets $53 s/d cabins midweek; $66 cabins Fri.-Sun.; $10 each additional person; $70 suites midweek; $85 suites weekends. An International Music Festival special costs $62, including breakfast, dinner, room, and performance.

The Spanish-run **Hotel Occidental La Condesa**, tel. 267-6000 or 261-2000, fax 261-3000, e-mail: condesam@sol.racsa.co.cr, immediately above El Castillo Country Club, opened in early 1998 at San Rafael de Heredia. It is a total remake of a failed project—Hotel Monte Alpino—that had been closed for 24 years. A soaring sky-lit atrium lobby with dramatic cascade, plus classical stonework and terra-cotta tiles, hints at the overall splendor. It has 60 spacious, beautifully furnished double rooms and 37 suites, the latter with king-size beds. The mammoth executive and presidential suites (with their own hearths) are truly deluxe. All rooms have minibars, direct-dial telephones, cable TVs, and security boxes, plus hair-dryers in the stylish marble bathrooms. One of the two restaurants specializes in Italian cuisine. Facilities include a heated indoor pool, children's pool, sauna, jacuzzi, jogging track, squash court, gym, and free shuttles to San José. Rates: $105 s/d standard, $165 junior suite, $190 executive suite, $525 presidential suite in low season; $120 s/d standard, $180 junior suite, $210 executive suite, $585 presidential suite in high season.

Food

About two km north of San Rafael are **Pollos del Monte**, an open-air roadside *soda* with grilled and roasted chicken, and **Complejo Turístico Bar y Restaurant Añoranzas**, tel. 267-7406, in a wooded park setting with views down the mountain. Two km farther, a road to the left leads uphill to **El Expresso del Bosque**, a rustic restaurant with children's playground and a small, narrow-gauge steam engine, and, beyond, to **Los Peroles**, a tiny restaurant in a meadow, with rustic log tables and seats. The main road from San Rafael continues past **Stein Biergarten**, tel. 267-7021, which specializes in German cuisine. The **Bugatti** pizza parlor serves pizza prepared on a wood-fired oven. The **Bar/Restaurant Taberna Chalet**, on the road to Monte de la Cruz, is a dark, moody, rustic Swiss chalet stuffed with fantastical eclectic decor (tree-stumps, anvils, farm implements). It serves *bocas*.

The best meals for miles, however, are at the **Hotel Chalet Tirol**, serving superbly executed French nouvelle cuisine, such as rabbit marinated in prune sauce, sea bass with melted avocado, and shrimps in fennel Pernod sauce (from $8). The hotel also has a **Biergarten**. The road to Monte de la Cruz leads past the equally impressive **Restaurant Le Barbizón**, tel. 267-7449, fax 267-7451, in a marvelous Spanish colonial-style lodge with views toward cloud-shrouded Barva. Rough-hewn timbers re-create the feel of an English country inn. Tasteful art decorations, expensive furnishings, and stained glass abound. The elegant dining room is centered on a mammoth open-hearth fireplace. The menu includes fondues, *corvina* in curry ($12), oysters ($20), and tenderloins ($12).

Hotel Occidental La Condesa also offers upscale dining in **La Florencia**, its signature Italian restaurant.

Getting There

Buses for San Rafael depart Heredia from the Mercado Central hourly 8 a.m.-8 p.m. Buses to El Castillo and Bosque de la Hoja depart Heredia from the Mercado Central hourly 8 a.m.-8 p.m. For Monte de la Cruz, take a bus departing 9 a.m., noon, or 4 p.m.

NORTHEAST FROM SAN JOSÉ

A fistful of charming little towns and villages nestle on the lower slopes of Volcán Barva and Volcá Irazú to the northeast of San José. The roads are a maze, however, and finding your way isn't easy.

SAN JOSÉ TO BRAULIO CARRILLO

The Guápiles Highway (Hwy. 32) climbs up the saddle between the volcanoes, cuts through the Zurquí tunnel and enters Parque Nacional Braulio Carrillo before descending to the Caribbean lowlands. Climbing uphill, you'll enjoy views of the volcanoes and valley.

At **San Jerónimo,** about 15 km northeast of San José and four km east of Hwy. 32, there begins a cobblestone road: the remains of the old **Carretera Carrillo** that still runs, in much-dilapidated condition, via Alto Palma to Bajo Hondura and Braulio Carrillo National Park and was once used by oxcarts carrying coffee to the railway line that ran to Puerto Limón. (Turn left by the church on the small village green in San Jerónimo: the paved road eventually becomes the *carretera*.)

The Alto Palma entrance to Braulio Carrillo is 10 km northeast of San Jerónimo along the tormenting cobbled paving.

Accommodations and Food

Hotel Villa Zurquí, Apdo. 11534, San José, tel. 268-5084, fax 268-8856, alongside Hwy. 32 two km below the Zurquí tunnel is a rustic A-frame alpine lodge with 20 rooms in eight spacious, modern chalet-style cabins spread throughout the gardens. Each has a stove, refrigerator, and hot water. It's popular with Tico families on weekends. It's cool up here, and the air is laced with piney scents. Horseback riding takes you into the surrounding forest, or along trails through the orchard. Rates: $50 s, $65 d standard; $65 s, $80 d, superior, including breakfast.

San Jerónimo Lodge, Apdo 88, 2200 Coronado, tel. 292-3613, fax 292-3243, e-mail: jeronimo@sol.racsa.co.cr, one km northeast of the San Jerónimo church, is a "tropical forest mountain retreat" run by a Liverpudlian and her husband. This stunning Colorado-style lodge hewn of timber and natural stone boasts a warm, cozy ambience aided by a log-burning hearth. Picture windows proffer dramatic views. Nine spacious, tastefully decorated rooms have beamed ceilings, stone or hardwood walls, tiled bathrooms, telephones, and satellite TVs. One hangar-sized suite has its own fireplace, and a magnificent bathroom big enough for a Roman orgy. Trails lead into 50 acres of farmland and private forest featuring waterfalls and pools. There's even a stable. Rates: $40 s/d standard, $80 deluxe, $96 suite in low season; $64, $100, and $120 respectively in high season, including full breakfast.

Complejo Turístico El Valle de las Tejas, at Trinidad, between Moravia and San Jerónimo, is a rustic country-style restaurant popular with Ticos on weekends.

A gamut of restaurants along Hwy. 32 let you soak in the views over a soda or beer. **Las Orquídeas Restaurante,** tel. 268-8686, fax 268-8989, at San Luis on the Guápiles Highway, is a rustic yet elegant and charming eatery with a large international menu.

Getting There

Buses depart San José for San Jerónimo from Avenida 3, Calles 3/5. You can walk or take a taxi to Alto Palma from here. Inquire about local buses. If driving, take the Guápiles Highway or, via Moravia, follow the signs for Trinidad from Mall Don Pancho.

PARQUE NACIONAL BRAULIO CARRILLO

Rugged mountains, dormant volcanoes, deep canyons, swollen rivers, and seemingly interminable clouds, torrential rains, and persistent drizzle characterize Braulio Carrillo National Park, 20 km northeast of San José. The park was established in 1978 as a compromise with environmentalists concerned that the construction of the Guápiles Highway to the Caribbean

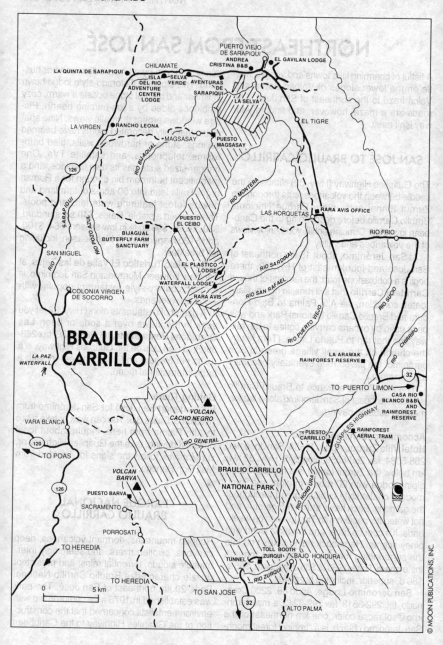

THE RAINFOREST AERIAL TRAM

The Rainforest Aerial Tram, on a 354-hectare private nature reserve on the northeastern boundary of Braulio Carrillo National Park, is a must-experience! Constructed at a cost of more than $2 million by Dr. Donald Perry, author of the fascinating book *Life Above the Jungle Floor,* the tram takes visitors on a guided 90-minute excursion through the rainforest canopy, home to two-thirds of all rainforest species. The mysteries of the lush canopy unfold with each passing tree.

Your ride is preceded by an instructional video. Then it's a 1.3 km ride on any of 20 cable cars that travel 150 meters apart (each holds six people, including a guide armed with a walkie-talkie to communicate with other cars) in the manner of a ski-lift, giving you a truly unique vantage of the "spectacular hanging gardens of the rainforest roof." The 30-meter F-shaped towers were lifted into place by helicopters of the Nicaraguan Air Force, which removed their machine guns and pitched in.

The tram, the first of its kind in the world, serves Perry in his continued scientific investigations, but, most important, it is an educational vehicle, so to speak. Perry hopes that by showing people the wonders of the rainforest, the tram will inspire people to help save the forests (he originated the concept after building the Automated Web near Rara Avis to support his research). "We liked the idea of putting people in cages, rather than animals," he says. There are short loop trails for hikes. Bird excursions are also offered (bring a flashlight for nocturnal outings).

Tram hours: Monday 9 a.m.-3:30 p.m.; Tues.-Sun. 6 a.m.-3:30 p.m. Entrance: $50, children half price (no children under five). The fee includes as many tram rides as you wish. Expect a wait of up to one hour, as the lines are long (coffee, fruit drinks, and cookies are served). A restaurant serves breakfast, lunch, and dinner (about $7).

The office in San José, Apdo. 1959-1002 San José, tel. 257-5961, fax 257-6053, e-mail: doselsa @sol.racsa.co.cr, website www.rainforest.co.cr, is on the corner of Avenida 7 and Calle 7.

Getting There: The tram is on Hwy. 32. The parking lot is on a dangerously fast bend, eight km east of the Río Sucio (four km past the ranger station, 15 km west of Guápiles). Keep your speed down or you could leave tire marks as you brake hard into the parking lot! The Guápiles bus will drop you off at Chichorronera la Reserva or "El Teleférico" ($1.50). You're driven from the parking lot 1.5 km along a gravel road to the visitor center (you must walk a brief trail and rope bridge over a river).

would lead to deforestation of the important watershed region. It was named in honor of the president who promoted the cultivation of coffee.

The 44,099-hectare park (84% of which is primary forest) extends from 2,906 meters above sea level atop Volcán Barva down to 36 meters at La Selva, in Sarapiquí in the Caribbean lowlands. This represents the greatest altitudinal range of any Costa Rican park.

Temperature and rainfall vary greatly and are extremely unpredictable. At higher elevations, temperatures range from 15° to 22° C. At the Carrillo, Magsasay, and El Ceibo biological stations, in the Atlantic lowlands, the average temperature is much warmer, ranging from 22° to 30° C. Annual rainfall is between 400 and 800 centimeters. Rains tend to diminish in March and April. With luck, you might even see the sun.

Encompassing five life zones ranging from tropical wet to cloud forest, Braulio Carrillo provides a home for 600 identified species of trees, more than 500 species of birds, and 135 species of mammals, including howler and capuchin monkeys, tapirs, jaguars, pumas, ocelots, deer, pacas, raccoons, and peccaries. Highlights include hundreds of butterfly species and excellent birding. Quetzals are common at higher elevations. The rare solitary eagle and umbrella bird live here. And toucans, parrots, and hummingbirds are ubiquitous.

The park protects several tree species fast disappearing elsewhere from overharvesting: among them, the palmito, valued for its "heart," and the *tepezcuintle,* which has been chosen as the park's official mascot. Those elephant-ear-size leaves common in Braulio Carrillo are *sombrilla del pobre* (poor man's umbrella).

Entrances
The main entrance is approximately 19 km northeast of San José, where there is a tollbooth (200 *colones*—$1.20) on the Guápiles Highway.

Zurquí, the main ranger station, is described in most literature as being 500 meters south of the Zurquí tunnel. If so, it eluded me. Instead, I found it on the right two km north of the tunnel. Drive slowly; you come upon it suddenly on a bend. The station has maps (not much good) for sale, and a basic information center. The **Puesto Carrillo** ranger station is 22.5 km farther down the road. It has a tollbooth in the center of the road for those entering the park from Limón; it's several kilometers inside the park boundary.

Two other stations—**Puesto El Ceibo** and **Puesto Magsasay**—lie on the remote western fringes of the park, reached by rough trails from just south of La Virgen, on the main road to Puerto Viejo de Sarapiquí. You can also enter the Volcán Barva sector of the park via the **Puesto Barva** ranger station three km northeast of Sacramento, and via Alto Palma and Bajo Hondura, accessible from San José via San Vicente de Moravia or from the Guápiles Highway at a turnoff about three km south of the main park entrance. Entrance costs $6.

Trails and Facilities

Two short trails lead from Puesto Carrillo: **Los Botarramas** is approximately 1.6 km; **La Botella,** with waterfalls and views down the Patria Canyon, is 2.8 kilometers. Says the national park trail map: For additional exercise as you head down La Botella, turn left at a sign labeled Sendero. This path takes you 30 minutes deeper into the forest to the Río Sanguijuela. South of Puesto Carrillo is a parking area on the left (when heading north) with a lookout point and a trail to the Río Patria, where you can camp (no facilities). Another parking area beside the bridge over the Río Sucio ("Dirty River") has picnic tables and a short loop trail.

A one-km trail leads from south of the Zurquí Tunnel to a vista point. The entrance is steep, the rest easy. Another trail—the **Sendero Histórico**—is shown on the national park map as following the Río Hondura all the way from Bajo Hondura to the Guápiles Highway at a point near the Río Sucio. Check with a ranger.

A trail from Puesto Barva leads to the summit of Volcán Barva and loops around to Porrosatí (no ranger station). From the summit, you can continue all the way downhill to La Selva in the northern lowlands. It's a lengthy and arduous hike that may take several days. Recommended only for experienced hikers with suitable equipment. There are no facilities. You can join this trail from Puesto El Ceibo and Puesto Magsasay; you can also drive in a short distance along a 4WD trail from Puesto Magsasay.

Bring sturdy raingear, and preferably hiking boots. The trails will most likely be muddy. Several hikers have been lost for days in the fog and torrential rains. Remember: It can freeze at night. If you intend to do serious hiking, let rangers know in advance, and check in with them when you return.

Note: There have been armed robberies in the park. Hike with a park ranger if possible. Thefts from cars parked near trailheads have also been a problem. Watch for snakes!

Tours

Most tour operators in San José can arrange half-day or full-day tours. **Jungle Trails,** Apdo. 2413, San José 1002, tel. 255-3486, fax 255-2782, has a full-day guided birdwatching tour departing at 5:30 a.m.

Getting There

Buses for Guápiles and Puerto Limón drop off and pick up at the Zurquí and Puesto Carrillo ranger stations. Buses depart several times per hour from the Gran Terminal Caribe, Calle Central, Avenidas 15/17. For Alto Palma, take a bus from San José for San Jerónimo from Avenida 3, Calles 3/5. You can walk or take a taxi to Alto Palma from here (there also may be local bus service).

SAN ISIDRO DE CORONADO AND VICINITY

San Isidro de Coronado is a somnolent country town six km northeast of Moravia. It's popular as a summer escape with Josefinos. The Gothic church is impressive. A **fiesta** is held here each 15 February.

Coronado is most famous as the site of the **Instituto Clodomiro Picado**—the "snake farm"—of the University of Costa Rica, which is dedicated to snake research. You'll see snakes of every kind, including the fearsome and infamous fer-de-lance, or *terciopelo.* The institute was founded by Clodomiro Picado Twight, a Costa Rican genius born in 1887 and educated in Paris, where he later worked at the Pasteur Institute before returning home to work on immunizations, vaccinations, and serums. Evidence suggests he may have discovered penicillin before Alexander Fleming, the British scientist to whom its discovery is credited. Visitors are welcome (hours: 8 a.m.-noon and 1-4 p.m.). Particularly interesting is to watch snakes being milked for venom (Friday afternoons only). Snake-feeding time is not for mice-lovers. The institute is about one km southwest of Coronado.

From the church in San Isidro de Coronado, Calle Central leads uphill past cloud-shrouded pasture and strawberry fields to **Los Nubes,** where you can sample strawberry desserts as well as pizzas and *típico* dishes at **Cronopios,** tel. 229-0517, a cozy restaurant warmed by an open fire, with splendid views over the valley. The last few miles, the road is rock and dirt.

Los Juncos Cloud Forest Reserve

Los Juncos, 14 km beyond Los Nubes, is a 200-hectare reserve area of virgin cloud forest straddling the Continental Divide on the Caribbean slopes of Irazú Volcano, in the mist-shrouded mountains above San Isidro. Its node is a metal-walled farmhouse once the home of Presidents Federico Tinoco and Mario Echandi. Trails through Los Juncos forest connect with the adjacent Braulio Carrillo National Park. Guides lead hikes, followed by a home-cooked lunch served family style at the farmhouse (where overnight stays can be arranged). Rubber boots and raingear are provided for hikes. The trails have been left in a semi-natural state. It's very misty up here, with everything covered in spongy moss and epiphytes. Quetzals are among the many bird species you may see if the magical mists aren't too dense.

Guided hikes are offered by **Green Tropical Tours,** tel./fax 292-5003, which owns the reserve and manages a biological station with rustic accommodations for up to 20 in a combination of single and bunk beds.

Accommodations and Food

Lone Star Grill, tel. 292-1207, offers "A Taste of Texas"—including "the best fajitas south of the Río Grande"—with Texan-size margaritas and other drinks to match. Choose from charbroiled meats, salads, burgers, soups, and "delectable desserts." Alternately, try the **Club Mediterráneo,** tel. 229-0661.

Getting There

Buses marked "Dulce Nombre de Coronado" depart San José from Calle 3, Avenidas 5/7.

Gothic church in San Isidro

BOB RACE

SOUTH OF SAN JOSÉ~
THE "ROUTE OF THE SAINTS"

South of San José lies a Shangri-la region perfect for a full-day drive along the fabulously scenic "Route of the Saints." The roads rise and fall, sometimes gently, sometimes steeply. The tiny villages cling precariously to the steep mountainsides; others nestle in the valley bottoms. The route is virtually unsullied by tourist footprints.

An alternate and popular approach to exploring these saintly villages is to drive south from Cartago along the Pan-Am Highway—Hwy. 2—and to turn east at Enpalme or Cannon.

SAN JOSÉ TO SAN IGNACIO DE ACOSTA AND SAN GABRIEL

From San José's southern suburb of Desamparado, Hwy. 209 begins to climb into the Fila de Bustamante mountains via **Aserrí,** a very pretty hillside town famed for its equally pretty church, for its simplistic handcrafted dolls, and for La Piedra de Aserrí—a massive boulder with, at its base, a cave once inhabited by a witch. The gradient increases markedly to the crest of the mountains just north of **Tarbaca.** En route you gain a breathtaking view of Volcán Irazú. Three km south of Tarbaca is a Y-junction. The road to the right (Hwy. 209) drops westward to **San Ignacio de Acosta,** a charming little town nestled on a hillside. You can see its whitewashed houses for miles around. The sun sets dramatically on its steep west-facing slopes, and if approaching from Ciudad Colón you should time your drive for sundown.

The road to the left at the Y-junction (Hwy. 222) leads to **San Gabriel,** gateway to the "Route of the Saints."

Accommodations
An unnamed, fully furnished **mountain chalet,** tel. 259-0840, is available for rent ($1,000 per month) above Desamparados; it includes a pool, phone, and panoramic view.

Food
Mirador Ram Luna is in a similar vein: fireplace, hanging plants, fantastic views, and heaps of warm rusticity to go with the *típico* fare (heavy on Mexican-style steaks). Farther south, **Restaurant Chicharronera La Tranca,** high on the mountain road above Aserrí, has a breezy outdoor patio with stunning views down over San José and the far-off volcanoes. The rustic restaurant serves food prepared on an open hearth grill. **Las Doñitas Restaurant,** tel. 230-2398, in Tarbaca, also serves traditional Costa Rican cuisine cooked on a woodstove. **Praga,** in Tarbaca, is a popular steak house.

Entertainment
In Aserrí **Chicharroenera Cacique Aserrí,** tel. 230-3088, has an "Aserriceñas" night featuring marimba music and traditional dancing every Friday and Saturday.

Getting There
Buses from San José depart, for Aserrí from Calle 2, Avenidas 6/8; and for San Ignacio from Calle 8, Avenida 12 hourly 5:30 a.m.-10:30 p.m. There's bus service for San Ignacio from Aserrí.

SAN GABRIEL TO
SANTA MARÍA DE DOTA

Route 222 leads east from San Gabriel, dropping and rising through river valleys, via Frailes to **San Cristóbal Sur,** another important market town better known to Ticos for **La Lucha Sin Fin** ("The Endless Struggle"), the *finca* (two km east of San Cristóbal) of former president and national hero Don "Pepe" Figueres, who led the 1948 revolution from here. There's a **museum** in the high-school; open weekends only. Entrance is free. The only monument—the rusting remains of an engine, with a plaque bearing the words Remember the fallen of both sides, 1948—is hardly worth seeking out; if you insist, it's halfway downhill to the Colegio Técnico Profesional Industrial José Figueres Ferrer, one km west of La Lucha. East of La Lucha, the road clambers precipitously through pine forests three km to the Pan-Am Highway.

You can turn south from San Cristóbal and follow a scenic route via San Pablo de León Cortes to **San Marcos de Tarrazú,** dramatically situated over coffee fields and dominated by a handsome white church with a domed roof. **Balnearios Los Sances,** two km east of San Marcos, has swimming pools fed by stream water, plus a small zoo.

From San Marcos, the main road climbs east to **Santa María de Dota,** a tranquil village with (in the main plaza) a small but dramatic granite monument honoring those who died in the 1948 revolution. There's a lake nearby full of waterbirds. From Santa María, the roads east snake steeply to Enpalme and Copey, on the Pan-Am Highway, with dramatic views en route.

Accommodations and Food
In San Marcos, the **Hotel Zacatecas,** tel. 546-6073, on the south side of the church, looks well-kept. It has a lively bar and restaurant downstairs. **Hotel Tarrazu,** tel. 546-6161, fax 546-7711, is two blocks north; it, too, looks okay and

has a *soda* attached. **Hotel Marylú,** tel. 546-6110, between the two, is a budget option.

In Santa María, the inexpensive **Hotel Santa María,** tel. 541-1193, has rooms with private bath; the **Hotel Marieuse,** tel. 541-1176, has rooms with shared bath; the dour **Hotel Dota,** tel. 541-1193, adjacent to the plaza, has nine rooms and a restaurant-cum-bar ($10 pp). For other eats, try **Restaurante As del Sabor** cater-corner to the church. **El Arbolito,** tel. 541-1111, on the southwest corner of the plaza, or **Las Tejas,** 200 meters east of the church.

Services
In San Marcos, the Red Cross and the ICE telephone office are both one block north of the church. There's a Banco Nacional at Avenida 2, Calle 0, cater-corner to the church; and a gas station two blocks north. In Santa María, for the local Red Cross, call 541-1037; for the local police, call 541-1135.

Getting There
Autotransportes Los Santos, tel. 227-3597, buses to San Marcos and Santa María depart San José from Avenida 16, Calles 19/21, at 6 a.m., 9 a.m., 12:30 p.m., 3 p.m., and 5 p.m. Return buses San José depart Santa María at 5 a.m., 6 a.m., 9 a.m., 1 p.m., and 4 p.m.

EAST OF SAN JOSÉ

East of San José, the Autopista Florencio del Castillo freeway passes through the suburb of Curridabat, climbs over the ridge known as Cerros de la Carpintera, then drops steeply to the colonial capital, Cartago. Just west of the ridge, at **Tres Ríos,** eastbound traffic must pay a 60-*colones* toll.

From Tres Ríos, you can follow a road uphill to **Rancho Redondo,** on the lower western flanks of Volcán Irazú. You can also take a scenic drive due east from San José via Guadelupe. A bus departs San José from Avenida 5, Calle Central.

Accommodations
If Costa Rican hospitality, Texas-style, is your thing, then check into the **Ponderosa Lodge,** tel./fax 273-3818, a magnificent bed and breakfast across from La Campina Country Club, in San

Ramón de Tres Ríos, a village in the hills north of Tres Ríos. The wood-and-stone lodge sits on 12 acres and abounds with hardwoods and Southwestern furnishings. Six individually decorated rooms provide American-standard amenities, including orthopedic mattresses, oodles of closet space, plus color TVs and VCRs (with 200 movies to choose from). There's a honeymoon suite. The lounge, which offers marvelous views over the central valley, has a TV, soaring stone fireplace, deep leather sofas, and beautiful artwork. Gourmet meals are served on a massive eight-foot-long solid hardwood dining table. The peaceful gardens have quiet "privacy parks" where you can relax and meditate. The lodge sits at 1,300 meters: perfect for wandering the paths through the adjacent forest. The hotel offers limousine service from the airport. Rates: $70 s, $80 d, including tax and full breakfast.

Bello Monte, Apdo. 8-5630, San José 1000, tel./fax 273-3879, also in San Ramón de Tres Ríos, has rooms for $40 and up.

Hacienda San Miguel, tel. 229-5058, fax 229-1094, is a rustic yet modern and atmospheric lodge at Rancho Redondo. The lounge boasts a fireplace, plump sofas, and a TV/VCR. There's also a jacuzzi, and a game room with pool table. Rooms of stone-and-timber have stone-walled bathrooms, plus electric blankets for chilly nights. The hacienda is a working dairy farm on 480 hectares. Horseback rides and guided hikes lead through the pastures to forests and waterfalls. Rates: $60 pp, including breakfast.

Mountain Garden Hostel, tel. 229-3541, has pleasant rooms for $5. Free pickup in San José.

CARTAGO

Cartago (pop. 120,000), about 21 km southeast of San José, is a chaotic parochial town founded in 1563 by Juan Vásquez de Coronado, the Spanish governor, as the nation's first city. Cartago—a

Spanish word for Carthage, the ancient North African trading center—reigned as the colonial capital until losing its status to San José in the violent internecine squabbles of 1823. In 1841 and again in 1910 earthquakes toppled much of the city. Virtually no old buildings are extant: the remains of the ruined cathedral testify to Mother Nature's destructive powers. Volcán Irazú looms over Cartago and occasionally rubs salt in the wounds by showering ash on the city.

Despite its woes, Cartago has kept its status as the nation's religious center and home of

Costa Rica's patron saint: La Negrita, or Virgen de los Angeles. Fittingly, she "lives" in the most impressive church in the nation—one of only a fistful of sights in Costa Rica's second-largest city. Excepting the cathedral, the city is a place to pass through and at press time had the worst roads of any city in the nation.

Las Ruinas

Cartago's central landmark is the ruins of the **Iglesia de la Parroquia,** Avenida 2, Calle 2, fronted by lawns and trees shading a statue of

© MOON PUBLICATIONS, INC.

Las Ruinas, Cartago

Manuel Salazar Zunca, the "immortal tenor." Completed in 1575 to honor Saint James the Apostle, the church was destroyed by earthquakes and rebuilt a number of times before its final destruction in the earthquake of 1910. Today, only the walls remain. The interior is now a garden (closed to the public).

Basílica de Nuestra Señora de los Angeles
The gleaming blue-and-white Byzantine, cupola-topped Cathedral of Our Lady of the Angels, 10 blocks east of the main plaza, at Avenidas 2/4 and Calles 14/16, is one of Costa Rica's most imposing structures. There's a unique beauty to the soaring, all-wooden interior, with its marvelous stained-glass windows, its columns and walls painted in floral motifs, and its miasma of smoke rising from votive candles and curling about the columns like an ethereal veil.

The basilica houses an eight-inch-high black statue of La Negrita, embedded in a gold- and jewel-encrusted shrine above the main altar. According to superstition, in 1635 a mulatto peasant girl named Juana Pereira found a small stone statue of the Virgin holding the Christ child. Twice Juana took the statue home and placed it in a box, and twice it mysteriously reappeared at the original spot where it was discovered. The cathedral marks the spot (the original cathedral was toppled by an earthquake in 1926). Beneath the basilica is the rock where the statue was supposedly found, plus a small room full of ex-votos or *promesas:* gold and silver charms, sports tro-

phies, and other offerings for prayers answered, games won, amorous conquests, etc. Many are in the shape of various human parts, left by devotees seeking a cure for afflictions or in thanks for a miraculous healing. Outside, a spring that flows beneath the basilica is thought to have curative powers. You can buy a receptacle at a shop across the street and take home a vial of holy water if so inclined; you can also buy ex-votos and other religious trinkets here.

Museo de Etnografía
This Elias Leiva Museum of Ethnography, tel. 551-1110, at Calle 3, Avenida 3/5, displays pre-Columbian and colonial artifacts.

San Rafael de Oreamuno
This village on the northeastern outskirts of Cartago is the site of Costa Rica's venerable if diminutive cigar-making industry. Chircagres cigars have been made hereabouts since the 17th century from locally grown tobacco. The indigenous population had been growing it since pre-Columbian days, of course. Columbus himself recorded how in September 1502, an Indian maiden had blown smoke in his face when he anchored at Cariay—now Puerto Limón—on his fourth voyage to the New World. You can watch cigars being hand-produced in the time-honored fashion. It is a treat to watch the workers and to marvel at their manual artistry and dexterity as their highly skilled fingers conjure yet one more perfect cigar with their *chavetas,* rounded, all-pur-

pose knives for smoothing and cutting leaves, tamping loose tobacco, and snipping the tips. You will forever remember the pungent aroma.

Aguacaliente

Aguacaliente, about three km south of Cartago, beyond Tejar, is named for the *balneario* (swimming pool) fed by hot springs and surrounded by an exotic plant collection. Local tours operate from San José and include Cartago, Lankester Gardens, the Orosí valley, a coffee plantation, and Aguacaliente hot springs, tel. 221-3778, fax 257-2367.

Accommodations

The best spot is **Los Angeles Lodge,** tel. 551-0957, on Avenida 4, facing the Plaza de la Basílica. Simple rooms with private bath with hot water cost $20 s, $34 d. Also try the **Hotel Dinastica,** tel. 551-7057, on Calle 3, 50 meters north of the market. It has rooms with shared bath ($18 s, $30 d) and private bath ($28 s, $40 d).

A palmful of cheap and grungy hotels—the **Hotel Venecia, Pensión El Brumoso,** and **Familiar Las Arcadas**—straggle Avenida 6 near the market. Rooms are often rented by the hour; the particle-board walls guarantee you'll hear every moan. Definitely a refuge of last resort for those stranded.

Food

There are several Chinese restaurants on Avenida 2. Best bet is the **Restaurante City Garden,** Avenida 4, Calle 2/4. **Puerta del Sol,** Avenida 4, Calle 16, is the best of several eateries near the

basilica. There's a **Pizza Hut** at Calle 2, Avenidas 2/4. East of town, on the road to Paraíso, is a reasonable *soda* called **Casa Vieja.**

Services

There's no longer a tourist information office. The **post office** is at Calle 1, Avenida 2/4. There are several **banks** in the town center, and Credomatic, tel. 552-3155, has a cash-advance booth one block west of El Carmen Church.

Hospital Dr. Max Peralta, tel. 551-0611, is at Avenida 5, Calle 3/5. Many **medical clinics** and doctors' offices are nearby. There are several **pharmacies** and more **dentists** than you would care to count.

Getting There

By Bus: SACSA's, San José tel. 233-5350, Cartago tel. 551-0232, express buses depart San José from Calle 5, Avenida 18 several times per hour 5 a.m.-midnight, and hourly midnight-5 a.m. (50 cents). Buses will drop you along Avenida 2, ending at the Basílica. Return buses to San José depart Cartago from Avenida 4, Calles 2/4 on a similar schedule.

Buses to several destinations around Cartago depart from Avenida 3. TRANSTUSA, tel. 591-4145, buses for Turrialba depart Avenida 3, Calles 8/10 every 30 minutes 6-10:30 a.m. and hourly thereafter until 10:30 p.m. Hourly buses also serve the following destinations, with departure points in parentheses: Aguacaliente (Calle 1, Avenida 3); Cachí (Calle 6, Avenidas 3); Lankester Gardens and Paraíso, (Avenida 1, Calles 2/4); Orosí (Calle 4, Avenida 1); and Tierra Blanca (Calle 4, Avenida 6/8), on Volcán Irazú, at 7 a.m. and 9 a.m.

By Taxi: Taxis hang out on the north side of Las Ruinas. Otherwise, call Taxis El Carmen, tel. 551-0247, or Taxis San Bosco, tel. 551-5151. A *colectivo* taxi from San José costs about $2 from Avenida Central, Calles 11/13.

THE LA NEGRITA PILGRIMAGE

Every 2 August, hundreds of Costa Ricans walk from towns far and wide to pay homage to the country's patron saint, La Negrita, at Cartago's Basílica de Nuestra Señora de la Concepción. The event attracts pilgrims from throughout Central America. Many *crawl* all the way from San José on their knees, starting at dawn! Others carry large wooden crosses. On any day, you can see the devout crawling down the aisle, muttering their invocations, repeating the sacred names, oblivious to the pain.

PARQUE NACIONAL VOLCÁN IRAZÚ

The slopes north of Cartago rise gradually up the flanks of Volcán Irazú. The views from on high are stupendous. Every corner reveals another picture-perfect landscape. You'll swear they were painted for a Hollywood set. The

main crater,
Volcán Irazú

slopes are festooned with tidy little farming villages with brightly painted houses of orange, yellow, green, and light blue. Dairying is an important industry, and you'll pass by several communities known for their cheese. Many of the vegetables that end up on your plate originate here. The fertile fields around Cot look like great salad bowls—carrots, onions, potatoes, and greens are grown intensively.

Volcán Irazú, about 21 km northeast of Cartago, tops out at 3,432 meters. Its name comes from two Indian words: *ara* (point) and *tzu* (thunder). The volcano has been ephemerally active, most famously on 13 March 1963, the day that U.S. President John F. Kennedy landed in Costa Rica on an official visit, when Irazú broke a 20-year silence and began disgorging great columns of smoke and ash. The eruption lasted two years. At one point, ash-filled vapor blasted up into overhanging clouds and triggered a storm that rained mud up to five inches thick over a widespread area. No further activity was recorded until December 1994, when Irazú unexpectedly hiccuped gas, ash, and breccia. It is still rumbling occasionally.

The windswept 100-meter-deep Diego de la Haya crater contains a sometimes-pea-green, sometimes-rust-red, mineral-tinted lake. Fumaroles are occasionally active. A larger crater is 300 meters deep. Two separate trails lead from the parking lot to the craters. Follow those signed with blue-and-white symbols (*don't* follow other trails made by irresponsible folks whose feet destroy the fragile ecosystems). The crater rims are dangerously unstable. Keep your distance.

A sense of bleak desolation pervades the summit, like the surface of the moon. It is often foggy. Even on a sunny day expect a cold, dry, biting wind. Dress warmly. The average temperature is a chilly 7.3° C (45° F). Little vegetation lives at the summit, though stunted dwarf oaks, ferns, lichens, and other species are making a comeback. Best time to visit is March or April, the two driest months.

Don't be put off if the volcano is shrouded in fog. Often the clouds lie below the summit of the mountain—there's no way of telling until you drive up there—and you emerge into brilliant sunshine. On a clear day you can see both the Pacific and Atlantic oceans. The earlier in the morning you arrive the better your chances of getting clear weather.

The ranger booth (two km below the summit) is open 8 a.m.-3:30 p.m., but you can visit at any time. A mobile *soda* serves food and drinks on weekends, and the site has toilets and picnic benches beside the crater, but no camping or other facilities. Entrance: $6.

The **Reserva Forestal Prusia** (Prusian Forestry Reserve), on the southwest flank of Irazú, five km north of Potrero Cerrado, is a reforestation project with a recreation area—Ricardo Jiménez Oreamuno—which features hiking trails and camping and picnic sites set amid pines. There's a "mushroom forest" here, too.

Tours

Most tour operators in San José offer half-day or full-day tours to Irazú (about $30 half day; $50 full day, including Orosí and/or Lankester Gardens). **Universal Tropical Nature Tours,** Apdo. 4276, San José 1000, tel. 257-0181, fax 255-4274, offers tours of Irazú and the Prusia Forestry Reserve.

Accommodations and Food

Restaurant/Hotel Gestoria Irazú, tel. 253-0827, in the former home of ex-president Ricardo Jiménez at San José de Chicua, has 20 very basic wood-paneled rooms that may appeal to the most hardy budget traveler. Overpriced at $2 s/d. The pleasant restaurant, replete with fireplace, offers sandwiches and *platos especiales* ($3).

About one km uphill is **Bar/Restaurante Linda Vista,** tel. 225-5808, which, as its name suggests, offers magnificent views. It claims to be the highest restaurant in Central America (2,693 meters). Take your business card to add to 30,000 others pinned on the walls. It serves *típico* dishes (average $6) and sandwiches. There's also a simple A-frame cabin that sleeps five people, with hot water and fabulous views. Rates: $17 s, $25 d, $40 five people.

Hacienda Retes, a centennial oak-log farmhouse bordering the Prusia Reserve, has accommodations for special-interest groups as well as horseback and hiking tours.

Getting There

By Bus: Buses Metrópoli, tel. 272-0651, operates a special bus to the park from San José from opposite the Gran Hotel on Avenida 2, Calles 1/3, at 8 a.m. on weekends and holidays (and Wednesday Nov.-April), returning at 12:15 p.m. ($5). You can also hop aboard this bus in Cartago on Avenida 2, by Las Ruinas. There's no public bus service, but you can take a bus to Tierra Blanca or Linda Vista, and from there walk (18 km) or take a taxi. Buses to Linda Vista depart Cartago at 5:45 a.m. Buses to Tierra Blanca depart Cartago from one block north of the ruins Mon.-Thurs. at 7 a.m., 9 a.m. and 1 p.m., Sunday at 7 a.m.

By Taxi: A taxi from Cartago will cost upward of $20.

By Car: If you drive, the most scenic route east from San José is via the suburb of Guadalupe, then Vista de Mar, and Rancho Redondo, flanking the mountain. Splendid! If you drive via Cartago, the road leading northeast from the Basílica continues to Irazú. At a Y-junction just below Cot, seven km northeast of Cartago, is a **statue of Jesus,** his arms outstretched as if to embrace the whole valley. The road to the right leads to Pacayas, Santa Cruz, and Guayabo National Monument. That to the left leads to Volcán Irazú National Park (turn right before Tierra Blanca; Irazú is signed). The paved road leads all the way to the mountaintop via Potrero Cerrado.

PARAÍSO AND VICINITY

Paraíso, a small town eight km east of Cartago, is the gateway to the Orosí valley (turn right at the town square) and Ujarrás (keep straight ahead). Just east of Paraíso is the **Auto Vivero del Río,** featuring a private zoo. It charges no fee to see the coatimundis, agoutis, pizotes, and bird collection—but donations are gratefully accepted. Closed Monday.

Two km south of Paraíso on the road to Orosí, is the **Mirador Orosí,** an ICT park with lawns and picnic tables overlooking the valley. Steps lead up to a riot of shrubbery that, with the views, lures Ticos on weekends. Entrance is free.

Lankester Gardens

Covering 10.7 hectares of exuberant forest and gardens, Lankester Gardens, Apdo. 1031-7050 Cartago, tel. 551-9877, seven km east of Cartago, just before Paraíso, is one of the most valuable botanical centers in the Americas, with about 700 native and exotic orchid species, plus bromeliads, a tropical forest, and palms. Species flower throughout the year, with peak blooming in February, March, and April.

The garden attracts a huge number of butterflies and birds and has been declared a refuge for migratory birds. The gardens were conceived by an Englishman, Charles Lankester Wells, who arrived in Costa Rica in 1898 to work in coffee production. Wells also dedicated himself to the conservation of the local flora and the preservation of a representative collection of Central American species. He established the garden in 1917 at a site called Las Cóncavas. After his death, the garden was acquired by the

North American Orchid Society and the English Stanley Smith Foundation. It was donated to the University of Costa Rica in 1973. Hours: every hour on the half-hour, 8:30 a.m.-3:30 p.m. After an orientation, you're allowed to roam freely. Entrance: $4.

Buses, tel. 574-6127, depart Cartago for Paraíso from the south side of Las Ruinas on Avenida 1 every 30 minutes 4:30 a.m.-10:30 p.m. Get off at the Camp Ayala electricity installation and walk approximately 600 meters to the south.

Accommodations

The **Sanchiri,** tel./fax 533-3210, has six basic yet delightful hillside *cabinas* of various sizes made of rough-hewn logs and bamboo, with telephones and views over the valley. Bathrooms of natural stone have hot water. Rates: $40 d, $60 t, including tax and breakfast. A larger cabin costs $70 for 2-6 people, or $90 for six. **Motocross bikes** can be hired ($40 per day), and a "Safari Tour" of the valley is offered. There's a playground for kids.

Hacienda del Río, tel./fax 533-3308, sits beside the Orosí River and is reached via a steep dirt road that begins about 400 meters beyond Mirador Orosí. This Spanish colonial-style stone lodge—once a den of iniquity for a drug baron—is the home of professional hoteliers, Sonya Hayward and her son Mark. Ponds and pools, including a fish-filled moat, abound. Its surrounded by palm trees. Each of seven rooms is unique in shape, size, and character. Upstairs, you may laze in soft-cushioned sofas in the vast lounge, boasting a huge stone fireplace in the center. Downstairs are a restaurant and bar. There's a stable on-site. Don't mind the pheasants, geese, chickens, and dogs—they're part of the family.

Rosie the puma, you'll be glad to know, is caged. But the horses run free and may carry you on rides farther afield along trails that lead through the 36-hectare property and into surrounding fruit orchards and forest. Rates: $60 s, $70 d, including breakfast.

Also nearby, but up high, is **Orosí Valley Inn,** tel./fax 574-7893, a bed and breakfast operated by a hospitable gringa, Julia Green, atop a perch overlooking her 12-hectare farm-cum-private reserve (with nature trail), which slopes down toward the valley and Bridal Veil waterfall. The five rooms with shared bath have picture windows and private patios with great vistas (the corner room proffers a magnificent view down over the waterfall). Rates: $30-50 d, including breakfast.

Food

In Paraíso, the **Restaurante Continental** dishes up reasonable seafood and homemade strawberry mousse. One km south of Paraíso are the open-air **Restaurant Las Encinas,** surrounded by pines, and **Parque Doña Anacleto** (closed Monday), with magnificent views over the Orosí Valley. One hundred meters beyond, a dirt road on the right leads to the **Bar/Restaurant Mirador Sanchiri,** serving *comidas típica* ($6-10) and featuring stunning vistas through plate-glass windows. The **Lost in Paradise Cafe,** tel. 574-6047, run by Americans-in-exile Karen and Jim Read at the Mirador Orosí, is the place to stock up on homemade chocolate chip cookies and cakes before exploring farther.

Complejo Turístico Picacho, tel./fax 574-6322, offers Costa Rican cuisine, and has jazz and blues on Wednesday, Friday and Saturday nights.

OROSÍ-CACHÍ VALLEY

South of Paraíso, you drop steeply into the gorge-like Orosí valley, with several sites of interest: coffee *fincas,* hot springs, a large lake for fishing, two stunning colonial churches (Ujarrás and Orosí), trout ponds, a private nature reserve, and an important national park (Tapantí). The valley (pop. 14,000) is a self-contained world dedicated to raising coffee and centered on a huge man-made lake drained by the Río Reventazón.

Two roads drop into the valley from Paraíso and loop around Lake Cachí: one drops to Orosí, the other to Ujarrás. Thus the valley makes a fine full-day circular tour. About three km south of Orosí village, at **Río Macho,** the road divides: the main road crosses the river and turns north then east around the lake's southern shore via the village of Cachí. The road via Ujarrás runs along the lake's northern shore. South of Río Macho, a side road leads nine km to Tapantí past undulating rows of coffee plants.

OROSÍ AND VICINITY

The village of Orosí is the center of the coffee growing region, which was originally settled by Indians forced from the central valley by the Spaniards. Its main claim to fame is its charming **Church of San José de Orosí,** built by the Franciscans in 1735 of solid adobe with lime-covered walls, rustic timbered roof, and terra-cotta tiled floor. The church is adorned with gilt icons. The altar moved even this atheist to reverence. The recently restored church has withstood earth tremors with barely a mark for nigh three centuries. Note the old bell in the cracked church tower. The church adjoins a small **religious art museum,** tel. 533-3051, located in what were once living quarters for the friars. The museum houses furniture, paintings, icons, and even a monk's cell. Photography is not allowed without prior permission. Hours: 9 a.m.-5 p.m. Closed Monday. Entrance: 50 cents.

About one km south of Orosí is **Los Patios Balnearios,** with simple thermal mineral pools (50° C), changing rooms and showers, and a bar and restaurant. Hours: 8 a.m.-4 p.m. En-

trance: $1.50. Another hot springs, **Balnearios Termales,** is two blocks from the plaza in town. Hours: Wed.-Mon. 7:30 am.-4 p.m. Entrance: $1.25.

Literally a stone's throw south of Los Patios is a **coffee mill** *(beneficio),* where a three-hour "Orosí Coffee Adventure" is offered through Aventuras Turísticas de Orosí, Apdo. 45, Paraíso 7100, tel. 533-3030, fax 533-3212, and **Orosí National Tours,** tel. 265-5484, fax 265-4385, e-mail: orosina@sol.racsa.co.cr, website www.arweb.com/orosi. The basic plantation and *beneficio* tour costs $15 ($20 with lunch at the Balneario/Motel Río Palomo); a full-day option combines the coffee tour with a horseback tour of Tapantí National Park ($45). Other tour options are offered.

At **Purisil,** four km south of Orosí, a dirt road leads west two km to **Truchas de Purisil,** tel. 533-3333, which offers trout fishing, trails, and barbecue pits. You pay ($5 per kg) for what you catch, which the owners will prepare on-site.

Monte Sky Cloud Forest Preserve

This 500-hectare private reserve, tel. 533-3333, is on the flanks of the Talamancas, near the village of Purisil. Its main focus has been environmental education and tree-planting. Trails lead through the cloud forest, good for birding. Guided hikes cost $8. **Ríos Tropicales,** Apdo. 472-1200, San José, tel. 233-6455, fax 255-4354, e-mail: info@riostro.com, offers tours from San José.

Accommodations

Albergue Montaña Orosí, tel. 533-3028, fax 228-1256, has basic rooms with shared bath and hot water in an old house. Rates: $15. You can also rent two cabins with cold water for $15 (for four people) at **Hotel Orosí,** attached to Supermercado Orosí, tel. 533-3032. **Montaña Linda,** Apdo. 1180, Cartago, tel. 533-3640, fax 533-3132, next to Balnearios Termales, is a rustic yet homey and welcoming place run by a Dutch and Canadian couple. There are seven double rooms with hot water, and two dorms that looked like the aftermath of a student's frat party when I was there ($5 pp), plus a bamboo rancho with hammocks ($2). It accepts campers

($3) and features a shared kitchen plus jacuzzi. It has massage ($3.50 one hour), and horseback rides ($12 half-day), and can arrange whitewater rafting. Mountain bike rentals cost $5 daily. Meals are provided, but guests get kitchen privleges ($2).

The **Hotel Río Palomo,** Apdo. 220, Cartago 7050, tel. 533-3128, fax 533-3173, or tel./fax 533-3057, has 16 modest *cabinas* with private baths and hot water, some with kitchenettes ($10 pp). It's immediately east of a suspension bridge over the Río Orosí—a small toll is collected on Sunday—two km south of Orosí. The

two cold water swimming pools are open to nonguests. **Sabadito Alerre,** tel. 533-3254, 400 meters north, has basic *cabinas* beside the river.

Monte Sky Albergue Ecológico, tel. 533-3333, in the Monte Sky Cloud Forest Preserve, has a double room and an eight-bed dorm with cold water in a rustic pink house. Rates: $30 pp including all meals. You can camp here.

Alburgue Turístico Kiri Tapantí, tel. 284-2024, eight km east of Orosí and 800 meters west of the national park, sits beside a river at the base of the forested mountain. Trails lead into the forest reserve. It has six basic cabins

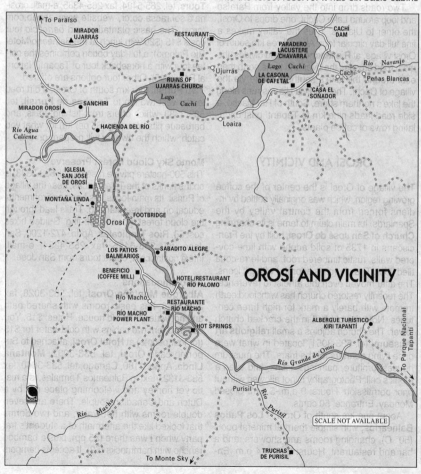

OROSÍ AND VICINITY

SCALE NOT AVAILABLE

with handsome stone-walled showers. Rates: $30 d, including tax and breakfast. Some rooms have bunk beds. It offers fishing ($4), and a restaurant specializing in trout culled from its own trout ponds. It's open 7 a.m.-9 p.m.; dishes run $3-4.

Food
Take your pick from several *sodas,* including **Soda El Gallo Pinto** and **Centro Social Reventazón,** one block east of the soccer field. The hot spot in town is the **Balneario Termal Orosí,** a large restaurant and bar with small pools filled with thermal water—a good spot for kids. A better bet is the **Balneario/Motel Río Palamo,** with an elegant and popular riverside bamboo restaurant. The restaurant hosts free coffee tastings.

Entertainment
You can sup with locals at several *pulperías* in Orosí, where the **Safari Disco,** tel. 533-3422, gets in the groove.

Tourist Information
Orosí Turismo, tel. 533-3456, fax 533-3333, has a tourism office opposite Los Patio, in Orosí. It offers guided mountain hikes ($10) and tours to Irazú.

Spanish Language Classes
Montaña Linda offers Spanish language classes. Courses cost $97 for five days, $120 for a week, $190 for 14 days, and $200 for two weeks.

Organized Tours
Most tour operators in San José offer day tours. **Tours Colón,** tel. 221-3778 or 233-1090, offers a tour that includes visits to Cartago, Lankester Gardens, Mirador de Orosí, Orosí church, a tour of Las Chucaras coffee *finca,* and lunch at Las Chucaras restaurant, with time to bathe in the hot springs. Rate: $60. **Rainforest 4x4 Adventures,** tel. 574-6171, cellular 383-7127, fax 574-6010, offers a five-hour tour by jeep departing Cartago at 8:30 a.m. Rate: $55.

Montaña Linda offers a wide range of tours locally, as does **Orosí National Tours** and **Orosí Turismo,** with everything from a coffee tour ($10) and petroglyph tour ($10), to a horse-and-buggy ride ($3) and cloud-forest hikes ($8).

Getting There and Around
By Bus: Buses, tel. 551-6810, depart Cartago for Orosí from Calle 4, Avenida 1/3, every hour on the hour 8 a.m.-10 p.m. (25 cents). A microbus operates at 1 p.m. and 3:30 p.m. (40 cents). Buses stop at Mirador Orosí. Return buses depart Orosí 4:30 a.m.-10:30 p.m. The bus stop in Orosí is by the soccer field.

By Taxi: Servicios de Jeep Trans Orosí, tel. 533-3451 or 284-2483, has jeep-taxi service to/from Orosí. It charges $5 for pickup in Cartago.

PARQUE NACIONAL TAPANTÍ

Tapantí National Park, 27 km southeast of Cartago, sits astride the northern slopes of the Cordillera Talamanca, which boasts more rain and cloud cover than any other region in the country. Average rainfall for the Orosí region is 324 cm (128 inches); Tapantí gets much more—almost 800 cm (330 inches) of rain at the intermediate peaks. February through April are the driest months. Not surprisingly, there are many fast-flowing rivers and streams excellent for fishing, permitted in designated areas April through October.

The 6,080-hectare park (formerly Tapantí Wildlife Refuge), on the headwaters of the Río Reventazón, climbs from 1,200 to 2,540 meters above sea level and forms a habitat for resplendent quetzals (often seen on the western slopes near the ranger station), toucans, parrots, great tinamous, squirrel cuckoos, and more than 260 other bird species, plus mammals such as Neotropic river otters, tapirs, jaguars, ocelots, jaguarundis, howler monkeys, silky anteaters, and multitudinous snakes, frogs, and toads. Birdwatching is tops, particularly at dawn.

The park possesses two life zones: lower montane rainforest and premontane rainforest. Terrain is steep and rugged and prone to landslides. Well-marked trails begin near the park entrance ranger station, which has a small nature display. The Oropendola Trail, which begins about 800 meters from the ranger station, leads to picnic shelters and a deep pool by the Río Macho where the hardy can swim in ice-cold waters. There's a vista point—a short trail leads from here to a waterfall viewpoint—about four km along. A trailhead opposite the beginning of the Oropendola

Trail leads for miles into the mountains. Hours: daily 6 a.m.-4 p.m. Check to see if the park is open on Thursday and Friday. Entrance: $6.

Tours
Aventuras Turísticas de Orosí, Apdo. 45-7100, Paraíso, tel. 533-3030, fax 533-3212, offers a three-hour horseback tour to Tapantí ($25). **GeoVenturas,** tel. 221-2053, fax 282-3333, has a mountain-biking tour of Tapantí and the Orosí valley. Most other tour operators in San José can arrange guided tours.

Accommodations
The ranger station has a *hospedaje* with a kitchen and bunk beds ($7.50 per day, students $2). You'll need your own sheets and blankets or sleeping bag.

Getting There
Buses depart Cartago at 6 a.m. and go via Orosí as far as Purisil, five km from the park entrance. You can hike or take a jeep-taxi from here with Co-Opetaca, tel. 533-3087; $5 each way. Later buses go only as far as Río Macho, nine km from Tapantí. If you befriend the park ranger before setting off to explore, he or she may call for a taxi to pick you up at a prearranged time.

LAGO CACHÍ

Lake Cachí was created by a dam across the Río Reventazón at its eastern end. About 13,000 years ago a lava flow blocked the Ríos Reventazón and Orosí to form a natural lake. Over the years, the rivers found a way through the natural dam. Thousands of years later, the Instituto Costarricense de Electricidad built the Cachí Dam in the same place to supply San José with hydroelectric power.

On the southern shore, just east of Cachí village, is **La Casona del Cafetal,** tel. 533-3280, a coffee *finca* with bar and restaurant. It has horseback riding ($10), mountain biking, and boating on the lake ($3.50), plus buggy rides ($2.50). Open 11 a.m.-6 p.m. low season, until 9 p.m. on weekends and during high season.

A short distance east, is **Casa El Soñador** ("Dreamer's House"), the unusual home of woodcarver Hermes Quesada, who carries on his father Macedonio's tradition of carving crude figurines from coffee plant roots. The house—with carved figures leaning over the windows (these, apparently, represent the town gossips)—is made entirely of rough-cut wood, with carvings adorning the outside walls. Upstairs is decorated with historical relics. Check out the *Last Supper* on one of the walls. Macedonio, who died in 1996, once taught at the University of Costa Rica though he had not even had an elementary education. His work adorns galleries throughout San José. Take time to read the newspaper clippings on the walls that tell about his life.

Paradero Lacustere Chavarra is an ICT recreational complex on the north shore of the lake, one km east of Ujarrás. A basketball court, soccer field, and swimming pools are set amid

*Macedonio Quesada's
Last Supper, Cachí*

*colonial church
at Ujarrás*

landscaped grounds. It has camping areas (50 cents pp) plus picnic tables ($1), bathrooms, and a restaurant and bar. Hours: Tues.-Sun. 8 a.m.-5 p.m. Entrance: 80 cents ($1.50 extra for autos).

Accommodations and Food

Peñas Blancas Bed & Brunch, tel. 551-9701, has two cabins near the hamlet of Peñas Blancas, about five km east of Cachí. It offers tours and horseback riding. Rates: $60 d. **La Casona del Cafetal** serves *típico* and international dishes ($5-12) in pleasing surroundings on the shores of the lake, Mon.-Sat. 11 a.m.-10 p.m. and Sunday 11 a.m.-8 p.m.

UJARRÁS

Ujarrás, on the north shore of the lake, seven km east of Paraíso, is famous as the site of the ruins of the **Church of Nuestra Señora de la Limpia Concepción,** built out of limestone between 1681 and 1693 to honor the Virgen del Rescate de Ujarrás. The church sits on the same site as a shrine built after an Indian fisherman saw an apparition of the Virgin in a tree trunk. When he attempted to carry the trunk to Ujarrás, it became so heavy that a team of men couldn't move it, a sign that the local priests interpreted as an indication from God to build a shrine where the trunk lay.

The church, however, reportedly owes its existence to another "miracle." In 1666, the pirates Mansfield and Morgan led a raiding party into the Turrialba valley to sack the highland cities. They were routed after the defenders prayed at Ujarrás (there was more bluff than blunderbuss on the part of the defending forces). The victory was thought to be a miracle worked by the Virgin. The church was abandoned in 1833 after the region was flooded. A pilgrimage is held mid-March from Paraíso to commemorate how the Virgin saved Ujarrás from the pirate invasion. The ruins—set in a beautiful walled garden and surrounded by coffee and banana plants—are open daily. There's a bathroom. Entrance is free.

Opposite the entrance to the church is Balnearios de Ujarrás, with a small swimming pool. For eats, try the **Restaurante Típico la Pipiola** at the entrance to the ruins.

Stop at the Ujarrás Lookout Point southeast of Paraíso for a stunning view of the valley and the hamlet of Ujarrás, one of the earliest Spanish settlements in the country.

Getting There

Buses do not complete a circuit of Lake Cachí; you'll have to backtrack to Paraíso to visit Ujarrás and the Cachí dam by public bus. Buses depart Cartago for Cachí via Ujarrás from one block east and one block south of Las Ruinas.

TURRIALBA AND VICINITY

East from Cartago, vast carpets of sugarcane swathe the rolling landscape. The main road via **Pacayas** falls gradually eastward before a final steep descent into Turrialba. Another, lower, route leads from Paraíso via **Cervantes,** where you might eat at **La Posada de la Luna.** The restaurant is chock-a-block with intriguing bric-a-brac from around the world. Homemade specialties include *tortilla de queso* (cheese tortilla) and *cajeta* (fudge) washed down by hot *agua dulce con leche* (a sugarcane drink with hot milk).

You can also reach Turriabla via Lake Cachí from the north side of the dam, where a badly pot-holed road winds east through the mountains.

TURRIALBA

Turrialba, a small town 65 km east of San José, was until recently an important stop on the old highway between San José and the Caribbean. The road still snakes down through the valley of the Río Reventazón but is little used since the Guápiles Highway via Braulio Carrillo National Park was opened two decades ago. Turrialba—once an important railroad stop—was further insulated when train service to the Caribbean was ended in 1991. (The **Pachuco Tico Tren Company** has touted plans to operate a small locomotive from Turrialba to Lake Bonilla, but nothing had evolved at press time.) The now-rusted tracks still dominate the town, which squats in a valley bottom—thought to have been a lake bed millennia ago—on the banks of the Río Turrialba at 650 meters above sea level.

There's nothing to see in town, which is centered on the **Parque la Dominica. Balneario Las Américas,** just east of town, has two large swimming pools ($1). Turrialba is popular among kayakers and rafters as a base for whitewater adventures on the Ríos Reventazón and Pacuare.

La Casa de la Sukia, tel. 556-1231, one km east of town, sells pre-Columbian stone figurines.

Accommodations

Shoestring: Two run-down and dingy hotels lie on the south side of the railway tracks: **Hotel Clen** ($3 shared bath, $3.75 private bath with cold water) and the **Hotel Chamanga,** tel. 556-0623 ($2 with shared bath with cold water). Much better is the **Hotel Interamericano,** tel. 556-0142, next door, with clean rooms and a large restaurant and bar. Rates: $10 s/d, shared bath; $10 s, $12 d, private bath with cold water. Kayakers and rafters congregate here. Three other low-cost options are the **Hospedaje Primavera**—very basic, but a friendly hostess—with shared bath with hot water ($3 pp); the **Hotel La Roche,** tel. 556-1624, with shared bath with cold water, and a tidy restaurant with TV downstairs ($8 s/d); and—opposite La Roche—the **Wittingham Hotel,** tel. 556-6013, which has seven clean rooms with TVs, fans, and hot water ($8 s, $10 d, shared bath).

The newly built **Hotel La Roche Anexo,** tel. 556-7915, at the north end of Calle 3 is much better, with simple yet clean and spacious, albeit meagerly furnished, rooms with private bath (no hot water). Rates: $10 s/d.

Hotel Turrialba, tel. 556-6396, on Avenida 2 at Calle 4, has 11 simple but clean wood-paneled rooms with fans, TVs, and private baths with hot water for $13 s, $19 d.

Inexpensive: The pleasant **Hotel Wagelia,** Apdo. 99-1750 Turrialba, tel. 556-1566, fax 556-1596, is the only class act in town. It has 18 rooms with a/c, private baths, TVs, and telephones. The well-lit rooms surround a lush courtyard and are modestly decorated with pleasant fabrics. The hotel offers tours locally. The restaurant is one of Turrialba's best. Rates: $30 s, $40 d, $50 t.

Food

Kingston's, tel. 556-1613, on the right as you exit town heading east, is a large, renowned restaurant with a breezy outdoor dining terrace. A reader has recommended **El Caribeño,** one block south of the railway tracks on the road to CATIE. Lacking in ambience, but great food. Owner Lazel Loyt Lanis—"El Rey del Buen Sabor"—cooks up spicy Caribbean dishes. **Bar/ Restaurante La Garza**—good for seafood— and the **Hotel Wagelia** are also good. There

are several Chinese options. Try **Restaurante Hong Kong,** tel. 556-0286, and **Nuevo Hong Kong,** tel. 556-0593. The **Panadería Merayo** sells fresh-baked breads and cookies. Fancy pizza? Try **Pizzería Julian,** tel. 556-1155.

Waira Macrobiótica, tel. 556-7463, sells health foods. **Café Gourmet,** opposite the Hotel Wagelia, looks interesting but was closed when I passed by; open 2-7 p.m.

Entertainment
The town boasts three cinemas, one showing adult movies. If you have to dance, try **Taberna Faro.**

Services
Banks include Banco de Costa Rica, Avenida Central, Calle 3, and Banco Nacional, Avenida Central, Calle 1.

For **medical** help, you'll find a Centro Médico, tel. 556-0923, and clinical laboratory, tel. 556-1516, (open 7 a.m.-noon and 2-6 p.m.) on Calle 3, and another around the corner on Avenida Central (open 3-7 p.m., Saturday 11 a.m.-1 p.m.).

Tico River Adventures, tel. 556-1231, rents kayaks and horses and offers guided hikes and rafting; it's run by Robert ("Tico"), a guide beloved on the river. The **Hotel Wagelia** runs tours. **COSASA Travel Agency,** tel. 556-1513, acts as a tourist information office and offers birdwatching and nature tours for five people minimum.

Getting There and Around

By Bus: Buses, tel. 556-0073, depart San José from Calle 13, Avenidas 6/8 hourly, 5 a.m.-midnight via Cartago. Buses depart Cartago for Turrialba from Avenida 3, Calle 4. In Turrialba, buses for San José depart hourly from Avenida 4, Calle 2. Buses for nearby towns and villages, including to Guayabo, Santa Cruz, Santa Teresita, and Tuís, leave from Avenidas 2/4, Calle 2.

By Taxi: For a taxi, contact Taxis Don Carlos, tel. 556-1593.

MONUMENTO NACIONAL GUAYABO

Guayabo, on the southern flank of Volcán Turrialba, 19 km north of Turrialba, is the nation's only archaeological site of any significance. Don't expect anything of the scale or scope of the Maya and Aztec ruins of Guatemala, Honduras, Mexico, or Belize. The society that lived here between 1000 B.C. and A.D. 1400, when the town was mysteriously abandoned, was far less culturally advanced than its northern neighbors. No record exists of the Spanish having known of Guayabo. In fact, the site lay uncharted until rediscovered in the late 19th century. Systematic excavations—still under way—were begun in 1968. The excavations are partly funded by a tax of one *colón* on each box of bananas exported. The site received national monument status in 1973.

The 218-hectare monument encompasses a significant area of tropical wet forest on valley slopes surrounding the archaeological site. Well-maintained trails lead to a hilly lookout point from where you can surmise the layout of the pre-Columbian village, built between two rivers. To the south, a wide and impressive cobbled pavement resembling a Roman road and estimated to be at least eight km long—most of it still hidden in the jungle—leads past ancient stone entrance gates and up a slight gradient to the village center, which at its peak housed an estimated 10,000 people. The total area of the city was perhaps 20 hectares.

Conical bamboo living structures were built on large circular stone mounds *(montúculos),* with paved pathways between them leading down to aqueducts—still working after 2,000 years—and a large water tank with an overflow so that the water was constantly replenished. About four hectares have been excavated and are open to the public via the Mound Viewing Trail. Note the square tombs, plundered years ago, now covered with mosses and encroached by slithering tree roots. The cobbled pavement *(calzada),* which is lined with impatiens, is in perfect alignment with the cone of Volcán Turrialba. It is being relaid in its original form. Maps are sometimes available from the ranger booth. A large map shows the layout. Nearby is a monolithic rock carved with petroglyphs of an alligator and a jaguar. You can buy a pamphlet at the ticket booth describing sites along the self-guided walk.

Birding is superb, but it helps to have a guide versed in birdlife. Oropendolas and aricaris are everywhere, as are hummingbirds.

Opposite the ranger booth are a picnic and camping area with shelters, an exhibition and projection hall, a miniature model of the site, plus a hut stuffed to the rafters with pre-Columbian finds. Many of the artifacts unearthed here are on display at the National Museum in San José.

Accommodations and Food

Albergue Montaña La Calzada, Apdo. 260, Turrialba 7150, tel. 556-0465, about 500 meters below the park entrance, has four rooms, each with a table and twin beds. The lodge hints of the Alps and is surrounded by trickling water. A rustic restaurant serves *típico* meals, including organic, homegrown produce. The lodge's friendly owner, José Miguel, offers tours to a local *trapiche* (oxen-powered sugar mill), a coffee *finca,* and a cheese factory. There's a children's playground. Expect a wake-up call from the resident roosters, and beware the vicious goose. Rates: $20 s/d (less with International Youth Hostel card). Reservations are required. José will meet the bus if you call ahead.

The monument's eight campsites (see above; $3 pp) feature access to flush toilets, cold-water showers, and barbecue pits.

Soda La Orquídea, Salon Cacique Acoyte, and **Bar Calipso** are simple restaurants in the hamlet of Guayabo, two km downhill from the monument. Salon Cacique is also a dance hall.

Getting There

Buses depart Turrialba for Guayabo village from Avenida 4, Calle 2 (from 100 meters south of the main bus terminal), Mon.-Fri. at 11 a.m. and Mon.-Sat. at 5 p.m. Return buses depart 6 a.m. and 1 p.m. You can also take a "Santa Teresita" bus from Turrialba—it departs daily at 10:30 a.m., 1:30 p.m. and, possibly, 6:30 p.m.—from where it's a three-mile uphill walk to the monument. You'll need to overnight if you take the 5 p.m. bus from Turrialba. Otherwise, **Taxis Don Carlos,** tel. 556-1593, will take you from Turrialba for about $30 roundtrip.

The steep road from Turrialba deteriorates to a rough dirt and rock about four km below Guayabo. Be prepared for a rough ride.

VOLCÁN TURRIALBA

Volcán Turrialba (3,329 meters), the country's most easterly volcano, is part of the Irazú massif. It was very active during the 19th century but today slumbers peacefully. Exploring Turrialba is as rewarding as any hike or drive in the country for the beauty and serenity. It can be very cold and rainy up here—bring sweaters and raingear.

A rough road for 4WD vehicles only—first gear in places—winds north from **Santa Cruz,** about 12 km north of the town of Turrialba, to Bar Canada (three km), where a sign next to the bar marks the beginning of the trail. It's a beautiful, hour-long ascent that deteriorates all the way. Just when you see a *finca* beneath a forested volcanic cone and you think you've arrived at the summit, your gratitude is shattered by a sign reading Volcán Turrialba Lodge 3 km. Here the track *really* begins to deteriorate.You can also hike from the hamlet of Santa Teresa, reached by direct bus or car from Cartago via Pacayas, on the southwestern slope (this route is far easier than that from Santa Cruz).

The hiking trail climbs through cloud forest to the summit, which features three craters, a *mirador* (lookout point), and guard house topped by an antenna. You'll find a campsite and additional trails at the summit, including one that leads to the crater floor. You can follow a path all around the summit (there are active sulfur emissions on the western side).

Queseria El Cypresal, a cheese factory 800 meters east of Santa Cruz, welcomes visitors. The road continues to Guayabo National Monument. It's easy to get lost trying to find Guayabo via this route. An easier option for reaching Guayabo is via the recently paved road that snakes northeast from Turrialba (signs mark the way).

Accommodations

Camping: Several local farmers, including La Central dairy farm, will let you camp on their property. Ask. You can also buy fresh homemade tortillas and cheese but are best advised to bring provisions.

Lodges: Volcán Turrialba Lodge, Apdo. 1632, San José 2050, tel./fax 273-4335, e-mail: volturri@sol, is set magnificently in the saddle between Irazú and Turrialba Volcanoes at 2,800 meters elevation, about three km north of Esperanza and eight km northwest of Santa Cruz. The setting is enhanced by the two sensual volcanic cones rising to each side. The remote, rustic lodge—built from an old milking shed on a working farm—nestles deep in the middle. The twelve rooms each have private baths. Costa Rican meals are cooked over a wood fire and served in a cozy lounge heated by a woodstove. Guided hikes and horseback rides are offered (Turrialba's crater is about one hour away, and thermal pools are nearby, too), or you can choose a mountain bike or ox-drawn cart for exploration. Guides at the lodge speak only Spanish but are super friendly (you are welcomed with a cup of warm *aguadulce*). Rates: $40 pp, including taxes and all meals. Transfers by 4WD from San José are $25.

Guayabo Lodge, tel. 556-0133 or 234-2878, fax 234-2878, 400 meters west of Santa Cruz on the grounds of Finca Blanco y Negro, is basic but a pleasant and homey atmosphere pervades. It has four double rooms of earthtone cinder block and hardwood construction, with airy and light bathrooms, plus laundry and kitchen. When not exploring the 80-hectare *finca,* settle yourself in a hammock on the patio and enjoy the superb views down across to the Cordillera Talamanca. The *finca* has its own dairy and cheese factory. Rates: $30 s, $40 d.

Food

Casa Bene, 100 meters west of Guayabo Lodge, is a rustic yet appealing wayside stop with valley views. It serves *típico* dishes and has kids' swings. **La Cocina de Lena,** nearby, serves breakfasts.

Getting There
Buses depart Cartago for Pacayas and Santa Cruz from south of Las Ruinas, and from the bus center at Calle 2, Avenidas 2/4, in Turrialba. You can take a jeep-taxi from Santa Cruz or Pacayas.

Rainforest 4x4 Adventures, tel. 574-6171, cellular 383-7127, fax 474-6010, offers a full-day tour of the volcano by 4WD, departing Mon.-Sat. at 8 a.m. ($100).

CATIE

The Centro Agronómico Tropical de Investigación y Enseñanza, four km east of Turrialba, is one of the world's leading tropical agricultural research stations. It was established in the 1930s and today covers 880 hectares of magnificent landscaped grounds surrounding a lake full of waterbirds. CATIE is devoted to experimentation and research on some 335 species of tropical plants and crops, including more than 2,500 coffee varieties. Besides conducting experiments into breeding tropical plants, animals, and crops, CATIE contains the largest library on tropical agriculture in the world.

Several trails provide superb birding, and the laboratories, orchards, herbarium, and husbandry facilities are fascinating. Individual visitors are allowed on a limited basis. Sign up for a group tour with any travel agent or tour operator in San José. Alternatively, call the chief of administration, tel. 556-6431, ext. 206, fax 556-8470, to arrange a personal visit. Guided five-hour tours (for groups only) cost $5, but individual visitors can explore alone.

Accommodations and Food
There's a modest 50-room hotel used by researchers but open to the public. Rates: $30 s, $38 d, $45 t. You can also rent apartments—**Casa del Café**—with kitchens and beds for two people. A cafeteria serves lunch (from buffet to a la carte service) for $5-15.

Getting There
Buses depart for CATIE from the railroad tracks near Taberna Faro in Turrialba. You can also catch the bus to Siquirres from Avenida 4, Calle 2, and ask to be dropped off at CATIE.

RÍO REVENTAZÓN

About five km southeast of Turrialba and one km east of CATIE, you cross the Río Reventazón ("Exploding River"). Here, from the bridge, you can watch kayakers running the rock-strewn slalom course. This is the traditional put-in point for rafting trips on the Río Reventazón, a spectacular river that begins its life at the Lake Cachí

whitewater rafting on the Reventazón

COCO VO/RÍOS TROPICALES

dam and cascades down the eastern slopes of the Cordillera Central to the Caribbean plains, a drop of more than 1,000 meters. On a good day it serves up class III-IV rapids, with the rainy season understandably providing the most exciting run (June-Oct. are considered the best months). Highlights include waterfalls and wildlife galore.

Many companies offer one- to three-day trips on the Reventazón. Typical prices are $65-95 for one-day, $200-250 two-day, depending on which section you choose to run. Several companies have facilities on the eastern bank, but they are *not* sales offices. You'll need to arrange your trip in advance.

ICE, the state-owned electricity company, sees another kind of gold in these waters: electricity! ICE is moving ahead with the **Proyecto Hidroelectrico Angostura**, which will create the largest hydroelectricity generating plant in the country, producing a whopping 177 megawatts of electricity. The ambitious plan, which is well-advanced, calls for damming the river about two km upstream of the bridge to create a 256-hectare (450,000-cubic-meter) lake. Canals are also being cut to feed water from the Turrialba and Tuís rivers. The lake will mostly inundate farmland presently belonging to Hacienda Atirro, but the plan calls for the planting of natural forest and regeneration of wetland habitats on its borders.

TURRIALTICO TO SIQUIRRES

The road east of the Río Reventazón continues one km to a Y-junction and veers left for Siquirres and the Caribbean (the road straight ahead leads to Tuís). The road switchbacks steeply uphill to tiny **Turrialtico**, eight km east of Turrialba. There's nothing of note here, but the views over Turrialba toward Volcán Turrialba and the Talamancas are superb.

Parque Vibarona, tel. 381-4781, is a serpentarium near Chitaria, beyond Turrialtico. It's run by herpatologist Minor Camacho Loaisa, his wife Fanny Fuentes, and their daughter, Noelia. About 100 snakes are displayed in cages (the labels are in Spanish). You can even enter the large boa pit. It's quite safe (boas are non-venomous), but be warned: the females won't take kindly to it, and their kettle-like hiss can be very

frightening. Your visit begins in the open-air lecture room. This place is not for the squeamish—cute little chickens and rabbits are dropped into the cages as snake snacks. Trails laced with plastic snakes lead into the forest. Hours: daily 8 a.m.-5 p.m. Entrance: $3.

There's also a private institution at **Chitaria** that breeds toucans and other endangered birds. It's not open to the public, but you can arrange visits through Bongo Benny's.

East of the hamlet of Tres Equis, the road begins its fall to Siquirres and the Caribbean lowlands. It's not a particularly scenic drive, but is a far less trafficked and challenging to the Caribbean than the road from San José via Braulio Carrillo for those with time to spare.

Accommodations and Food
Albergue Montaña Turrialtico, Apdo. 121-7150, Turrialba, tel. 556-1111, at Turrialtico, is a pleasant restaurant-cum-lodge amid landscaped grounds with views over the Reventazón Valley, and tables made from Sarchí oxcart wheels. They are beautiful. The 12 rustic and basically furnished rooms are atmospheric (but have "yucky" beds, according to one reader) and have private baths with hot water. Rates: $29 s, $34 d, $40 t; or $40 s, $60, d, $80 t including breakfast, dinner, and taxes. Another kilometer brings you to the **Pochotel Hotel/Restaurant,** Apdo. 333, Turrialba 7150, tel. 556-0111, fax 556-6222, on the right. A dirt road climbs steeply to a basic but pleasant restaurant (popular with whitewater rafters) with wide-open vistas and a tall *mirador* from which to admire the volcanoes and Talamanca mountains, with drinks served on a pulley-system. The *casados* are only $4. The eight cabins, each of a different size, have private baths with hot water. A reader describes them as "freezing" and "very drafty." Two newer cabins—#5 and #6—have splendid views through picture windows. Rates: $30-35 d, $10 extra person.

The oddly named **Bongo Benny's,** Apdo. 343, Turrialba, tel. 383-4965, fax 556-0427, just west of Chitaria, between Turrialtico and Tres Equis, is a small bed and breakfast whose owners James (an erstwhile California hippie and an accomplished carpenter) and Vikki (an erudite Mexican) Woods provide an effusive, unpretentious welcome. The five-bedroom home sits amid a 10-acre coffee and fruit plantation surrounded by

cloud forest on the edge of the Parque Internacional de la Amistad. Rooms are spacious and
nicely, albeit sparsely, furnished (two share a
bathroom). There's also a bunk room. There's a
separate dining room and a lounge with fireplace,
plus laundry and gardens. Views across the valley towards Irazú and Turrialba Volcanoes are
splendid. Varied organic fare—oriental, Mexican,
Italian—is whisked up in the kitchen, which guests
can use on the honor system. Hiking, birding,
fishing, and kayaking trips are offered. Reservations only. Rates: $30 pp, including breakfast;
$800 per week for the whole house.

Getting There

Buses for Siquirres depart Turrialba from Avenida 4, Calle 2; ask to be let off at Turrialtico.

TUÍS TO RESERVA
INDÍGENA CHIRRIPÓ

A branch road two km east of CATIE leads to
Hacienda Atirro, Tuís, Bajo Pacuare, and the
off-the-beaten-track hamlet of Moravia before
petering out in the foothills of the Cordillera Talamanca.

Hacienda Atirro is a huge *finca* planted in
sugarcane, macadamia nuts, and coffee (the
famed Café Britt coffee uses Atirro beans), and
dominating the flatlands of the Reventazón and
Atirro rivers south of Turrialba. Much of the land
is to be flooded as part of the Proyecto Hidroelectrico Angostura. The Rojas family, owners of
Atirro, plan to develop watersports and are active
supporters of the reforestation project—as stip-
ulated under the terms of international funding—
that will create ecological corridors linking the
lakeside forests with the forests of the Talamanca massif. A fascinating **plantation tour**
($18) includes a visit to the coffee mill, sugar
mill (in season), and macadamia processing
plant; choose either car or horseback.

Moravia del Chirripó is the gateway to the
Reserva Indígena Chirripó, a remote Indian
reserve that receives few visitors. Few of the
residents speak Spanish. They live a very reclusive life and I was told by a local evangelist that
they are not particularly welcoming. "It's an im-
position to visit unless you're bringing medicines
and medicinal aid," she explained. (She, of

course, had been bringing "enlightenment.") The
locals may also appreciate blankets and warm
clothes. If she is to be believed, they don't like
having their photos taken and are "fearsome of
foreigners." Moravia has no tourist facilities. You
may be able to hire guides in Moravia for excursions into the Talamancas and **La Amistad
International Peace Park.** Jay or Lisa at Rancho
Naturalist will guide you by prior arrangement. So
will James at Bongo Benny's, whose hiking trips
include nights at a rustic camp with hammocks.

Bajo Pacuare is a traditional starting point for
whitewater rafting trips on the **Río Pacuare,** a
thrilling river that plunges through remote
canyons and rates as a classic whitewater run.
The river is protected as a wild and scenic river,
but nonetheless faces the threat of being
dammed for its hydrolectric potential.

Accommodations

Rancho del Sol at La Suiza, two km west of
Tuís, has simple but clean, pleasing rooms for
about $4. There's a bathing pool and a restaurant.

Albergue de Montaña, Apdo. 364, San José
1002, tel. 267-7138; in the U.S., Dept. 1425,
P.O. Box 025216, Miami, FL 33102, one km beyond Tuís, is a surprisingly elegant if rustic hilltop
hacienda-lodge (owned by American evangelists, Kathleen and John Erb) on a 50-hectare
ranch—**Rancho Naturalista**—surrounded by
premontane rainforest at 900 meters' elevation at
the end of a steep dirt-and-rock road that is "not
user-friendly." The mountain retreat is popular
with nature and birding groups (more than 410
bird species have been recorded by guests).
Five spacious rooms have heaps of light (three
have private baths). Upstairs rooms open
through French doors onto a veranda—tele-
scopes and Sarchí leather rockers provided—
with sweeping views down over the Reventazón
Valley to Irazú. One room has a canopy bed
and a bathroom large enough to wash a Boeing
747. The upstairs also has a lounge with library.
Outside are four newer cabins with hammocks
on the verandas. Decor is of hardwoods, with
beamed ceilings. Horseback riding is included.
The ranch has an extensive trail system. You
can also see a small *trapiche* (ox-powered sugar
mill) on a neighboring *finca*. You can stay one
night, but there's a four-night minimum with transport. Rates: $125 pp, including three meals,

SPECIAL HOTEL: CASA TURIRE

Stay once at Casa Turire and you may decide next time that if you can't get a room here, you just won't bother visiting the region. Quiet, relaxing, romantic, and upscale without being pretentious, Casa Turire, Apdo. 303, Turrialba 7150, tel. 731-1111, fax 731-1075, e-mail: turire@ticonet.co.cr, a member of the Small Distinctive Hotels of Costa Rica, is my number-one choice for miles around. *Hideaways Reports* agreed: it named Casa Turire Country House Hotel of the Year.

The hotel—marvelously presided over by Michele de Rojas, a witty and erudite Cuban woman—is built on the right bank of the Río Reventazón on the grounds of Hacienda Atirro, about 15 miles southeast of Turrialba, at the foot of the Talamancas. Follow the road for La Garita and Tuís; turn right at the sign for Hacienda and continue past fields of lime-green sugarcane until you reach the driveway lined with palms and bougainvillea.

The classical-styled Casa Turire is the jewel in the crown of a working coffee, sugarcane, and macadamia plantation that commands magnificent views of the mist-haunted Talamanca massif. A trail through primary forest leads down to the river; horseback rides and bike rental are also offered ($15 half day).

You sense the sublime moment you enter the breathtaking atrium lobby of the modern Spanish-cum-California plantation home, with its colonial-tiled floors, Roman pillars, and sumptuous contemporary leather sofas and chairs. Upstairs, 12 spacious, lofty-ceilinged, deluxe rooms with TVs

and direct-dial telephones, each bespeak romantic indulgence, with divinely comfortable mattresses, sleek tiled bathrooms with thick towels, toiletries, and hair dryers, and decor that reflects exceptional taste. Three regal suites have wide French doors opening onto spacious private verandas.

The dining room proffers artistic food. Culinary treats include fresh homemade bread, spicy *gallo pinto,* and sublime coffee from the estate. An intimate bar has Edwardian hints. Further pluses? Soothing music echoes softly. And a gift store sells gold jewelry of stunning quality.

Outside, a wide, colonial-tiled, wraparound veranda supported by eucalyptus columns opens onto manicured lawns and a small lake out front, a small figure-eight pool and sunning deck surrounded by palms and an arbor of hibiscus, and—out back—a putting green and driving range. Mountain bikes are available; tours of the hacienda are offered, including the macadamia nut processing plant; and river-rafting trips are offered on the Río Reventazón, which at press time was due to be dammed, creating a lake that the hotel owners hope will provide an opportunity for a prime watersports center.

One guest from California wrapped herself around a lamppost in the atrium lounge and refused to leave. Could that be you?

Rates: $95 s, $110 d; $125 junior superior suite; $150 junior suite; $200 master suite. Breakfast $6, lunch $13, dinner $15.

guided hikes, and horseback riding. One-week packages are offered.

Reserva Esperanza, tel. 223-7074, fax 233-5390, squats on the flanks of the Río Atirro, with spring waters diverted into the pools of the *cabinas.* The renovated farmhouse also has rooms with private baths and hot water. Hiking and horseback riding are offered. Rates: $100, including meals.

Ríos Tropicales, Apdo. 472-1200, San José, tel. 233-6455, fax 255-4354, e-mail: info@ riostro.com, has a lodge and "Cabecar Indian-style" bungalows with electricity from its own self-sufficient hydro plant on the Pacuare. Likewise,

Costa Rica Expeditions, Apdo. 6941-1000, San José, tel. 257-0766, fax 257-1665, e-mail: crexped@sol.racsa.co.cr, maintains a rustic and isolated lodge at the head of the Pacuare Canyon, with rooms in Indian-style ranchos and flush toilets. Those who've stayed here on rafting trips report "superb meals." You have to be a participant in one of the companies' river trips to stay here.

The most outstanding hotel for miles is Casa Turire, in the midst of Hacienda Atirro.

Getting There

Buses for Tuís depart from the bus center at Calle 2 and Avenida 2/4 in Turrialba.

CARTAGO TO CERRO DE LA MUERTE

South of Cartago, the Pan-Am Highway (Hwy. 2) begins a steep and enduring ascent over the Talamanca mountains, cresting the range at Cerro de la Muerte ("Death Mountain") at 3,491 meters before dropping down into the Valle de El General and the Pacific southwest. The route is fantastically scenic. The vistas are staggering and opportunities for hiking, horseback riding, trout fishing, and birding are many. The region is clad in native oak and cloud forest, and you may leave your vehicle by the roadside and hike in search of resplendent quetzals, which are common hereabouts. Toucanets, hummingbirds, orioles, and collared trogons are all commonly seen. Few tourists seem to venture to this easily accessible yet remarkable region, which only now is being "discovered." Kilometer distance markers line the route.

Drive carefully! The road takes you up through the cloud forests and is always fog-bound (early to mid-morning are best, before the clouds roll in). It also zigzags, sometimes greatly turning, at other times continuing in a predictable line for a distance only to trap the unwary driver with a sudden, vicious turn. Plus, the route is badly potholed and washed out in places. And buses and big trucks use the road. The climate is brisk, so take a warm jacket if you want to go hiking or in the event of a breakdown.

CARTAGO TO CAÑON

The only gas station between Cartago and San Isidro de El General is at Enpalme, 30 km south of Cartago, where a road descends sharply in a series of spectacular switchbacks to **Santa María de Dota**. At **Vara de Roble** (two km north of the Enpalme gas station), a road leads west to San Cristóbal via La Lucha Sin Fin.

You can also reach Santa María de Dota from **Cañon,** five km south of Enpalme at Km 58 (where a yellow church perches over the roadside) via a dirt road that descends steeply to **Copey.** Copey is a small agricultural village at about 2,121 meters, eight km southwest of Cañon and five km east of Santa María de Dota.

The area is famous as a center for trout fishing. **La Cima de Dota el Remanso,** 1.5 km downhill from the Pan-Am Highway on the road to Copey, has trout fishing, horseback rides, plus camping and a bar and restaurant. In Copey, there's a trout farm run by Don Fernando Elizondo. Most accommodations listed below also offer trout fishing.

Refugio Nacional de
Vida Silvestre Fauna Genesis II

Genesis II Cloud Forest Reserve and National Wildlife Refuge, Apdo. 655, Cartago 7050, tel. 381-0739, fax 551-0070, e-mail: genesis@yellowweb.co.cr, website www.yellowweb.co.cr/genesis, the creation of Englishman Steve Friedman, and his Dutch-born wife Paula, protects 38 hectares of primary forest on the slopes of the Talamancas. The forest, which includes rare tropical white oaks, borders the Tapantí National Forest near the village of La Damita, at an elevation of about 2,360 meters. One-third lies within the Río Macho Forest Reserve. It's a great spot for sighting resplendent quetzals, trogons, toucanets, hummingbirds, and other birds (more than 200 species have been recorded). You can even see quetzals from the porch March-June. The superb trail system covers 20 km and is well-maintained by volunteers from all over the world.

The Friedmans run a **volunteer program** for people willing to assist in trail building, reforestation, general maintenance, and research into flora and fauna. Month-long programs cost $600 including accommodations and meals. If requesting details by mail, enclose three international reply coupons, which you can obtain at any post office.

Several people have gotten lost trying to hike to Tapantí National Park: if you go, take a guide. And bring a warm jacket and raingear—even in the so-called dry season (Nov.-May).

The reserve is three km east of Cañon. If driving southbound, turn left at the yellow Cañon church and then right at the Y-fork by La Damita School. The trail is steep and very rough—you'll need a 4WD vehicle. Day visits cost $8 (students $4).

Accommodations and Food

Hotel Cerro Alto, tel. 710-6852 or 382-2771, four km north of Enpalme, is a rustic log-and-bamboo lodge with panoramic views towards Irazú. It has eight serviceable A-frame chalets for four persons each, with heaters, kitchenettes, fireplaces, and private baths with hot water. There's a bar and restaurant, plus a tiny "swimming" pool and trails. Rates: $36 1-4 people. **Cabinas La Montaña** has cheap *cabinas,* 0.5 km north of Enpalme.

Genesis II, Apdo. 655, Cartago 7050, tel. 381-0739, fax 551-0070, e-mail: genesis@yellowweb.co.cr, 3.5 km east of Cañon, offers five small, clean, carpeted bedrooms (one with double bed, the rest single) with quilted comforters, electric heaters and hot water bottles (by request), and shared bathrooms with hot showers. Two rustic cabins in the lush gardens each sleep up to four people and share the bathrooms and toilets in the house. The cozy rough-hewn lodge has a cast-iron, wood-fired stove, a library, and a welcoming homey feel. The views through the forest are fabulous. Reader Yvonne Hodges reports the food (organic) is "excellent." Rates: $75; $35 students with ID, including all meals and guides (10% discount for weeklong stays). The owners recommend a three-night minimum stay.

At Copey, Don Elizondo's neighbor, Chema, has a single room with stained-glass window and shared bath. Rates: $7, with breakfast. He also rents horses and may guide you on horseback or foot to the Río Macho Reserve. The **Cabinas Copey,** tel. 541-1177, has three spartan and drafty concrete *cabinas* with kitchenette and private bath. Two North Americans, Dennis and Ana Wirth, have a one-bedroom cottage—**Cloud Forest Hideaway,** tel. 541-1485, fax 541-1437, e-mail: fintluni@sol.racsa.co.cr—with queen-size bed, kitchen, and hot water on a 275-acre fruit farm, 2.5 km from Copey; the property has 190 acres of cloud forest with hiking trails. Rates: $45/55 daily low/high season; $295/365 weekly low/high season. Horseback rides cost $20-40. **El Toucanet Lodge** is also nearby.

For eats in Copey, try **Pulpería y Cantina El Jilcuer** or **Restaurant Los Lagos,** a handsome restaurant that offers trout fishing ("you catch it, we'll cook it").

CAÑON TO CERRO DE LA MUERTE

At Trinidad, five km south of Cañon, you pass through the **Río Macho Forest Reserve,** comprising more than 80,000 hectares of critical forest. Seven of the 12 life zones classified by biologist L.H. Holdridge have been documented here. Together they provide a vital habitat for the quetzal, the Holy Grail for birders in the tropical cloud forest, and such endemic species as the copper-headed emerald hummingbird, silky flycatcher, cerise-throated hummingbird, red-billed finch, the *cipresillo* oak, the mountain-needle, and the blueberry.

Farther south, at Tres de Junio at Km 71, is **Iyöla Amí Cloudforest Reserve** adjacent to the Río Macho Forest Reserve and boasting equally good birding and splendid 500-year-old trees such as oaks, *cipresillos,* and aguacatillos.

At Km 76 you'll pass a refuge hut—**Casa Refugio de Ojo de Agua**—built for early pioneers who had to cross the mountains before a road existed to bring their produce to market in San José. The adobe hut is now the home of a small museum displaying maps and historical information.

At the Km 80 marker, 30 km south of Enpalme, a turnoff—easy to miss—leads downhill (west) to the hamlet of San Gerardo de Dota.

Cerro de la Muerte

The summit is at Km 85, where you may rest at **Las Torres,** a truck stop and restaurant. From here, a path leads uphill to communications towers from where you may enjoy commanding views through the stunted trees on a clear day. It gets its name not from the dozens who have lost their lives through auto accidents, but from the many poor *campesinos* who, often shoeless and in nothing more than shirt and pants, froze to death in days of yore while carrying sacks of wild blackberries, dried corn, and rice to trade in San José.

The actual summit is marked by a forest of radio antennae at Km 89, where you'll find the suitably named restaurant Las Torres ("The Towers"). A dirt road leads up to the antenna, from where you'll have miraculous views, weather permitting, and a strong feel for the damp forest conditions and stunted flora. At 3,000 meters the vegetation is Andean *páramo,* complete with wind-sculpted shrubs, peat bogs, and marshy grasses. Be prepared for high winds. The vegetation changes as you descend from the heights past great stands of bamboo and oak forest, good for spotting quetzals and other birding, and past plantations of agaves *(cabuya),* from which sisal fibers are extracted for twine.

Trout Fishing

Salmon-trout can be caught in the Ríos Pedregoso, Savegre, and other rivers, as well as at about a dozen trout farms with lakes. **Finca Los Prados,** 2.5 km west of the turnoff at Trinidad, has trout fishing ($3.50 per kg) plus a cafe. **Madre Selva Finca los Lagos** is two km east of the highway at Km 64. It has seven lakes, plus barbecue pits, and trails into the forest. The owners will prepare your fish ($5.50 per kg). Entrance costs $1.

Accommodations

Six km south of Cañon, at Km 62 at Macho Gaff, one km north of Trinidad, is **Tapantí Lodge,** Albergue de Montaña Tapantí, Apdo. 1818, San José 1002, tel. 231-3332, fax 232-0436, a small chalet-style hotel with 10 *cabinas* on a grassy ridge merging into cloud forest and Tapantí National Park. The rustic but cozy cabins sleep two, three, or five people, with private bathroom with hot water, plus electric heater, living room, and balcony. A lounge has a TV, fireplace, bar, and rather worn deep-cushioned chairs. The hotel offers a small conference room with a library, and a bar-cum-restaurant serving Costa Rican meals and the lodge's specialty, "Tapantí Trout." There are trails for hiking and horseback riding. Also available are a trout-fishing special, quetzal hikes, and tours to Tapantí, several hours' hike away. Rates: $45 s, $55 d, $75 t, $80 quad, including breakfast.

Nearby, at Km 70 on the Pan-Am Highway, is **Albergue Mirador de Quetzales,** tel. 381-8456, 771-6096, or 454-4746, fax 771-2003, also called "Finca Eddie Serano." This rustic yet cozy lodge is set amid cloud forest at 2,600 meters where quetzals congregate to nest. Eddie Serrano and his wife and three children were pioneers, settling in this area more than 45 years ago. He and his family continue to work their 100-hectare dairy farm, cut decades ago from virgin forest, while collecting wild blackberries for sale in San José and raising trout for local hotels. There are seven rooms, plus four A-frame log cabins boasting marvelous views; all have one double and one single bed (some also have a bunk bed plus), and a private bath with hot water. Up to 20 pairs of quetzals have been seen feeding in treetops near the *finca.* "We can almost guarantee that visitors will see quetzals," says Serrano. You can even see them while dining—you, not the birds—on the veranda of the homey rough-hewn lodge. Rates: $27, including breakfast, dinner, and quetzal tour. Recommended.

Iyöla Amí Cloudforest Reserve, Apdo. 335-2100 San José, has a lodge with views towards Turrialba and Irazú Volcanoes. Rates: $15 including breakfast. Volunteers pay $500 monthly to help maintain trails and teach English in local schools.

El Quetzal, tel. 771-2376, is another option. The remote and spartan concrete cabin sleeps up to eight and has a veranda with hammocks, plus bath. Meals included.

Tours

Costa Rica Expeditions, Apdo. 6941-1000, San José, tel. 257-0766, fax 257-1665, e-mail: crexped@sol.racsa.co.cr, offers a "Cerro de la Muerte Tropical Forest Adventure" ($65). **Horizontes,** Apdo. 1780-1002, San José, tel. 222-2022, fax 255-4513, e-mail: horizont@sol.racsa.co.cr, also has one-day and overnight trips to Cerro de la Muerte. **San José Travel,** Apdo. 1237, San José 1002, tel. 231-4808, fax 232-7284, offers a "Quetzal Tour," including lunch ($65). **Geostar,** 4754 Old Redwood Hwy., Suite 650A, Santa Rosa, CA 95403, tel. (707) 579-2420 or (800) 624-6633, e-mail: mansellw@crl.com, features two nights at Cabinas Chacón (aka Albergue de Montaña Savegre) during a 10-day "Birdwatcher's Paradise" tour (from $1,460). **Bio Tours,** tel. 272-4211 or 541-1034, offers "Dota Green Valley" packages.

Getting There

The San Isidro bus from San José, Calle 16, Avenidas 1/3, will drop you or pick you up anywhere along the Pan-Am Highway. Most hotel owners will pick you up with advance notice.

SAN GERARDO DE DOTA

San Gerardo de Dota, nine km west from the Pan-Am Highway at Km 80, is an exquisitely neat village tucked at the base of a narrow wooded valley at 1,900 meters—a true Shangri-la. It's a magnificent setting. The valley is a center for apples and peaches fed by the waters of the Río Savegre. It is also high enough to attract a healthy population of resplendent quetzals, especially during the April and May nesting season. Albergue de Montaña Savegre hosts the **Quetzal Education Research Complex** operated in association with the Southern Nazarene University of Oklahoma. The road (well-paved, but with a few tricky, washed-out sections) is snaking, steep, and breathtakingly beautiful (4WD vehicle recommended). **Paradero Lacustre Los Ranchos,** 400 meters downstream, has trout in a lake with rowboats, plus barbecue pits and trails leading to waterfalls. **Quetzales Home Trailriders,** tel. 771-1732, offers horseback rides from Albergue de Montaña Savegre.

You can also hike or ride by horse to **Olla Quemada Caverns.**

Accommodations

Trogon Lodge, Grupo Mawamba, Apdo 10980-1000 San José, tel. 223-7490, fax 222-5463, mawamba@sol.racsa.co.cr, website www.crica.co/mawamba, enjoys a beautiful and reclusive setting at the head of the San Gerardo valley, beside the burbling river tumbling through exquisitely landscaped grounds. There are 10 attractive, simply appointed, two-bedroom hardwood cabins with green tin roofs, each with tasteful fabrics, heater, bedside lamps, and private bathroom with hot water, plus veranda. Meals (the quality is said to be good) are served in a rustic lodge overlooking a trout pond. Trout fishing is available. Trails lead to waterfalls. Guided horseback tours ($10 per hour) and quetzal tours ($15) are offered. Rates: $71 pp.

Albergue de Montaña Savegre, Apdo. 482, Cartago, tel./fax 771-1732, e-mail: ciprotur@sol.racsa.co.cr, alias Cabinas Chacón, has 20 rustic *cabinas* on a family farm owned by Don Efraín Chacón. The handsome, all-wood cabins are basic but clean, with blankets, heaters, and private baths with hot water. There are trails (4-8 km), plus the *finca.* Offered are birding trips ($50 half-day), cloud-forest hiking ($70, six hours), horseback riding ($10 per hour), plus trout fishing ($50 half-day) in the Río Savegre (bring your own tackle), but don't expect prize-size fish. Rates: $65 pp, including three meals. Special packages are available.

Another Chacón family member, Rodolfo, and his wife Maribel, have three cabinas—**Cabinas El Quetzal,** tel. 771-2376—nearby on the banks of the river. One has four bedrooms. All have hot water. There's a children's playground. "We slept so well there with the wood stove going," reports one reader. Rates: $25 pp, including three meals.

The more rustic **Albergue Naturista de Montaña el Manantial,** tel. 771-0255, has 10 small, clean, but bare-bones rooms with private bath, plus a dormitory with eight double bunks. Plentiful blankets are provided. There's a small solar-heated pool and a sauna, plus a no-frills lounge with fireplace. A basic restaurant serves vegetarian meals. Rates: $31 pp, including three meals.

Food

Restaurant El Valle del Quetzal is seven km north of the summit, 0.5 km south of the turnoff for Albergue Mirador del Quetzales, which also has a marvelous rustic restaurant with fantastic views.

Sarchí oxcart wheel

BOB RACE

CATHY CARLSON

THE CARIBBEAN COAST

Part of the Mosquito Coast, Costa Rica's Caribbean coast extends some 200 km south—from Nicaragua to Panamá. The zone—wholly within Limón Province—is divided into two distinct regions. North of Puerto Limón is a long, straight coastal strip of broad alluvial plain separated from the sea by a series of freshwater lagoons and extending to Tortuguero ("Land of the Turtles") and the Río Colorado. South of Puerto Limón is the Talamanca coast, a narrow coastal plain broken by occasional headlands and coral reefs and backed by the looming Cordillera Talamanca, whose mountains encroach progressively southward. *Talamanka* is a Miskito Indian word meaning "place of blood," referring to the seasonal slaughter of turtles.

Life along the Caribbean coast of Costa Rica is fundamentally—almost comically—different than in the rest of the country. What few villages and towns lie along the coast are ramshackle, browbeaten by tropical storms and the curse of an ailing economy recently assuaged by a tourism boom. Here, among the swamps and jungles, life itself has been perceived as altogether too melancholy to take seriously. It has

been said that the people are more sullen, less friendly than elsewhere in Costa Rica. Whatever, much is a cameo of West Indian life for Afro-Caribbean influences are strong—notably in regional cuisine, and the local dialect is richly spiced with a parochial patois English.

Limón Province boasts a higher percentage of its area preserved in national parks and reserves than any other region of Costa Rica; almost half its coast is protected. The coastal city of Puerto Limón is the gateway to **Tortuguero National Park** and **Barra del Colorado National Wildlife Refuge** via the Tortuguero Canals, an inland waterway that parallels the coast all the way to the Nicaraguan border. Crocodiles, caimans, monkeys, sloths, and exotic birds can be seen from the tour boats that carry passengers through the jungle-lined canals and lagoons. Tortuguero is famed as the most important nesting site in the western Caribbean for the Pacific green turtle (leatherback and hawksbill turtles also nest here); Barra del Colorado, farther north, is acknowledged for the best tarpon and snook fishing in the world, with many lodges catering to anglers.

South of Puerto Limón are **Cahuita National Park,** protecting Costa Rica's only true coral reefs (backed by rainforests full of howler monkeys), and **Gandoca-Manzanillo Wildlife Refuge** and **Hitoy-Cerere Biological Reserve,** on the slopes of the Talamanca mountains; the refuge and reserve preserve some of the nation's finest rainforest and swamplands. Further delights include miles of black- and white-sand beaches and the funky, laid-back hamlets of **Cahuita** and **Puerto Viejo,** popular with surfers and others seeking an immersion in Creole culture.

Warning: The Caribbean region has a higher incidence of crime against tourists than any other region. Theft, muggings, even rape occur here with a frequency that calls for vigilance—especially south of Limón. Hoteliers in the region keep claiming that the bad reputation is all a sad misrepresentation, but I keep getting letters from readers who've been victims. Don't let this put you off visiting, however—the negativity is more than counterbalanced by the scores of wonderful, welcoming souls.

CLIMATE

The Caribbean coast is generally hot and exceedingly wet (averaging 300-500 cm annually); in the swamps the still air clings like a damp shawl. Fortunately, light breezes blow consistently year-round on the coast, rustling the mangroves and helping keep things relatively cool along the shores. It can be surprisingly cool when cloudy, and you may even find a sweater necessary.

Practically speaking, the region has no real dry season and endures a "wet season" during which the rainfall can exceed 100 cm per month. Rains peak May-Aug. and again Dec.-Jan., when polar winds—*nortes*—bear down on the Caribbean seaboard and sudden storms blow in, bowing down the coconut palms. (The Pacific coast receives almost no rain during these months and is blessed with fine, clear weather.) The heaviest rain falls inland on the eastern slopes of the Talamancas.

Regional microclimates exist even within the lowlands. Puerto Limón's two distinct dry periods (Feb.-March and Sept.-Oct.) are shorter than those farther north, where the dry seasons can

> ## NO-SEE-UMS
>
> I have been lucky on my visits to the Caribbean and suffered few mosquito attacks. However, the insect population is formidable. Chiggers and mosquitoes flourish here, and their hordes have been reinforced by truly evil little sandflies—no-see-ums—that you don't even know are on you until you rub an idle hand across your thigh and swatches of blood appear (later come the red lumps that can drive you crazy with itching). No-see-ums have shaped the architecture of the coast: since they fly only a few feet above the ground, houses (generally rickety, jerry-built shacks) are built on stilts—which happens to be a good precaution against snakes, too.

last into May and November. Whereas Tortuguero has shorter rainy seasons, it suffers through considerably more rain during the rainiest months: an average of 61 cm in January and 97 cm in July (by contrast, Puerto Limón's peak month is December, which averages 46 cm).

Although hurricanes may form in the Caribbean during late summer and fall, they're definitely not something to worry about: only one hurricane—Martha, which rushed ashore on 21 November 1969—has hit this coast during the last 100 years.

HISTORY

This was part of the Spanish Main of the conquistadors. It was also the haunt of rumrunners, gunrunners, mahogany cutters, and pirates, mostly British, attracted by the vast riches flowing through colonial Central America. Between raids, buccaneers found safe harbor along the wild shorelines, where they allied themselves with local Indians. Because of them, the Caribbean coast was never effectively settled or developed by the Spanish.

In 1502, Columbus became the first European to set foot on this coast when he anchored at Isla Uvita on his fourth and last voyage to the New World. Navigating off these shores, hopelessly lost, half a millennium ago, Columbus had assumed that the region was really Siam. Columbus's son Ferdinand, 14 at the time, described the area as "lofty, full of rivers, and abounding in very tall trees, as also is the islet [Uva Island] where they grew thick as basil. . . . For this reason the Admiral [Columbus] called it La Huerta [The Garden]."

Twenty-two years later, Hernán Cortés mapped the coast. The records the early Spaniards left tell of contact with indigenous tribes: subsistence hunters and farmers, and skilled seamen who plied the coastal waters and interior rivers in carved longboats in excess of 12 meters (Cortés even mentioned Aztec traders from Mexico visiting northern Costa Rica in search of gold). Recent evidence suggests that settlement along the coast dates back almost 10,000 years. The indigenous culture was condemned, however, that Jehovah might triumph over local idols; Spanish priests rabidly destroyed much of the documentation and tangible evidence of the indigenous realms of gods and deities. One group, the Votos, apparently had female chiefs. Shamans, too, were an important part of each tribal political system. Their influence is seen today in the National Museum in San José, where pottery from the region bears unusual symbols believed to have been painted by shamans under the influence of hallucinogens.

Cacao was grown here in the late 17th century and was Costa Rica's first export, an activity financed by well-to-do citizens of Cartago. This made now-derelict Matina such an important town that Fort San Fernando was built here in 1742. Despite this, the region remained virtually uninhabited by Europeans until the Atlantic Railroad was built in the 1880s and a port at Limón was opened for coffee export. Jamaican laborers were brought in in significant numbers.

In 1882, the government began to offer land grants to encourage migration. The cultivation of bananas was also encouraged, and the plantations prospered until the 1930s, when they were hit by disease: Panamá blight, mold, and sigatoka.

By the end of the 19th century development began to take hold. Bananas and cacao for export brought a relative prosperity. With the demise of the banana industry beginning in the 1930s, the region went into decline. During the 1960s, plantations were revived using more advanced technologies, and the industry now dominates the region's economy. The government has assisted these efforts with new infrastructure and services, resulting in a rapid population increase during 1960-90.

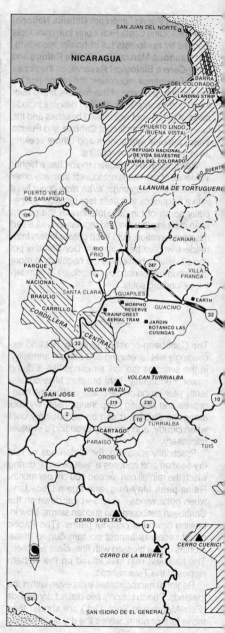

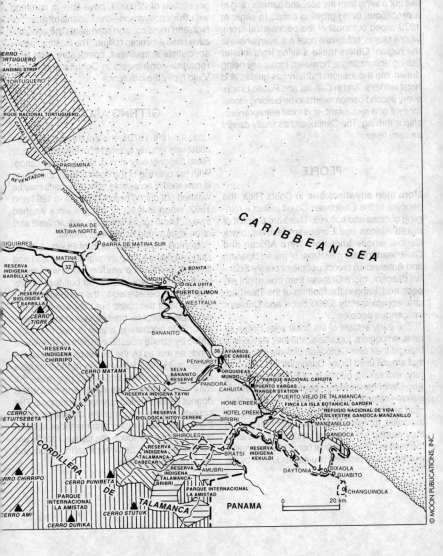

The port in Puerto Limón, along with its sister port of Moín, is the chief driving force of the urban economy. Beyond the city's hinterland, most people make their livings from farming or as plantation laborers, and there are few and only small industries: sawmills, ceramics, cabinet-making, bakeries. A few small-scale fishermen eke out a living from the sea, and farmers cling to a precarious living growing cacao (a blight in 1979 wiped out most of the commercial crop), whose plump, bobbinlike pods are everywhere in the region. Others make a living from lobster fishing. Increasingly, however, locals are being drawn into the tourism industry, as guides and hotel workers. And in Cahuita and Puerto Limón, every second person seems to be building rooms for rent or a restaurant, and local entrepreneurship is thriving. The Caribbean has finally caught tourism fever.

PEOPLE

More than anywhere else in Costa Rica, the peoples of the Caribbean Coast reflect a mingling of races and cultures. There are Creoles of mixed African and European descent; black Caribs, whose ancestors were African and Caribbean Indian; mestizos, of mixed Spanish and Amerindian blood; people of purely Spanish descent; more Chinese than one might expect; and, living in the foothills of the Talamancas, approximately 5,000 Bribrí and Cabecar indigenous peoples.

The early settlers of the coast were British pirates, smugglers, logcutters, and their slaves who brought their own Caribbean dialects with words that are still used today. During the late 19th century, increasing numbers of English-speaking Afro-Caribbean families—predominantly from Jamaica—came to build and work the Atlantic Railroad and banana plantations. They settled along the coast, grouping themselves into regions that they named after natural landmarks and after themselves. They built their homes by the creeks, which became property boundaries known by the family name (Ben Humphries, Kelly, Duncan, Louis Hudson, and so on). Their dialect is replete with lilting phrases familiar to travelers in the West Indies. "Whoppen" is a common greeting, "all right" or "okay" are farewells.

The black costeños (coast dwellers), who form approximately one-third of Limón Province's population of 220,000, have little in common with the sponyamon—the "Spaniard man," or highland mestizo, who represents the conservative Latin American culture. The Rastafarians—specialists in coolness, composure, and witty repartee—one meets in Cahuita and Puerto Viejo typify the difference.

GETTING AROUND

Until the late 1970s, the southern Caribbean coast was virtually isolated from the rest of Costa Rica; the only way in was slow train or canoe. With the opening of the coastal road, the region is now readily accessible, although roads may be washed out during heavy rains (as in 1991 and 1992, when at least 17 bridges were washed away). Local roads are quite deteriorated and often impassable because of flooding.

Behind the shores north of Puerto Limón, sluggish rivers snake through swampland and flooded forests. The winding inland waterways have stymied would-be road builders (a few roads have penetrated to the northern frontier far inland of the coast but they are often impassable except for brief periods in the dry season). Safe anchorage is also denied to marine traffic by strong coastal currents and onshore winds as well as by the lack of protective banks or reefs. Hence, travel is via outpost traders resembling the *African Queen* (they make the mail and *pulpería* runs daily) and motorized dugout canoes called *cayucos* or *canoas.* The canoes are the main means of getting about the swampy waterways that meander from lagoon to lagoon through the dense, mostly uninhabited jungles between Puerto Limón and the Nicaraguan border.

HIGHWAY 32 TO PUERTO LIMÓN

Highway 32 (the Guápiles Highway) runs east-west 104 km from the foot of the Cordillera Central at Santa Clara, 50 km east of San José, to Puerto Limón on the coast. The road runs along the base of the Cordillera Central and Talamanca mountains, passing sugarcane fields and cattle ranches and, increasingly eastward, banana plantations and, occasionally, farms cultivating macadamia nuts. Here and there, nestled in the bush, are zinc-roofed houses built on stilts with wide verandas and shuttered windows, and adjacent shacks where cacao beans are spread out to dry. In quiet little villages—Las Lomas, La Junta, Cimarrones (the Spanish word for intransigent runaway slaves)—black people begin to appear with greater frequency, letting you know you are now in the Caribbean proper. Once you reach the flatlands, watch your speed. It's easy to go zooming along above the speed limit. Speed cops laze beneath shade trees in wait of heedless tourists.

There are plenty of gas stations.

GUÁPILES AND VICINITY

Guápiles, 14 km east of Santa Clara, is a large town and a center for the Río Frío banana region to the north. There is no reason to visit, although the **Pococí Regional Tourist Association**, tel. 710-2323, has an information office here.

There are several local attractions, however, not least the **studio and gallery** of acclaimed artist Patricia Erickson, in a storybook pink house on the banks of the Río Blanco, six km west of town. Her vibrant paintings dance with brilliant Caribbean colors, many of them portraying her trademark faceless Limonense women of color with long floating limbs expressing the langor of the Atlantic coast and vividly capturing woman's connectedness to land and life. Her husband, Brian, designs and creates bamboo furniture.

Morpho Reserve

One km east of Santa Clara you cross the Río Corinto, where a turnoff leads south 800 meters (4WD only) to the Morpho Reserve, a private rainforest reserve with a butterfly garden where

you can watch *mariposas* of a thousand hues flitting about the heliconias and other luxuriant plants. Swimming and fishing are other options.

The reserve doubles as a science center, where courses in medicinal plant science and guide-training are among the dozens of courses offered. Rattan and other products "harvested" on the reserve are sold to locals to foster crafts and conservation. It's popular with schoolchildren and students, some of whom are researching an inventory of species. A "frog garden" and organic farm were planned. A Frog Trail is one of many that lace the reserve.

A one-day all-inclusive tour from San José costs $60. Entrance: $10; guided tours, $10 extra. Morpho Reserve, Apdo. 3153, San José 1000, tel. 221-9132, fax 257-2273, has an office in San José on the third floor of Edificio Murray, at Calle 7, Avenidas 1/3. There's a lodge and camping.

JOHN ANDERSON

Bosque Lluvioso

About six km west of Guápiles at Km 56, and 400 meters east of the bridge over the Río Costa Rica, a road to the right leads three km via Rancho Redondo to Bosque Lluvioso, Apdo. 10159, San José 1000, tel. 224-0819, fax 225-1297, a private 170-hectare rainforest reserve, reached via a rope bridge, with well-manicured trails that provide a chance to see poison-arrow frogs, sloths, oropendola birds and other arboreal critters without any of the discomforts associated with more rugged locales. Guided walks are offered, but you can walk yourself (none of the trails are strenuous): the trails are fitted with self-guided information posts that correspond to information in a guide booklet ($2). One trail leads past herbs: lemongrass, rosemary, etc. Another—the Hidden Pond Trail—leads to a pool. The ranch also has a fruit plantation and orchid garden, plus a visitor's center and a restaurant where you may regain your strength (lunch, $8). Admission: $12; children $6. Closed Wednesday in low season.

Jardín Botánico Las Cusingas

The Las Cusingas Botanical Garden, tel. 710-0114, two km east of Guápiles and four km south, preserves a region of tropical wet forest, undertakes medicinal plant and other botanical research, and raises ornamentals. You can hike the trails and bathe in the waters of the Río Santa Clara. Horseback rides are available to the village of Buenos Aires. The birding is excellent. Accommodations are provided (see below). Turn south at Soda Buenos Aires, from where it's four km by dirt road (4WD recommended). Entrance: $5.

Accommodations

West of Guápiles: The very rustic 10-room **Morpho Lodge** is on the rocky banks of the Río Corinto, a sometimes turbulent river that forms a natural swimming pool in front of the lodge. Rates: $20 pp. Meals cost $7. Two-day/one-night packages cost $99, including transportation and meals. Also, a **tent-camp** offers top-quality tents (lamp-lit at night) on wooden platforms and shaded from rain. No sleeping bags here; instead, beds with fresh cotton sheets and night tables. A "backpackers' special" ($15) includes lodging, guided tour, and use of a kitchen.

David and Dalia Vaughan, tel./fax 750-0012, offer lodging at **La Dante Salvaje,** their 410-hectare private reserve bordering Braulio Carrillo; it's a tough slog by 4WD, then a stiff hike to the mountainside property. The couple lives in Puerto Viejo de Limón and offers four-day, three-night trips ($190) from Puerto Viejo to La Dante.

Bosque Lluvioso has been planning to build *cabinas.* And **Hotel Huetar,** two km down a dirt road that leads north from Hwy. 32 at Flores, has five simple rooms and a little bar on a working cattle *finca* run by a charming old *campesino* called Teoro Reyes. Trails leads into nearby forests. Rates: $12.50.

One of my favorite places in Costa Rica is **Casa Río Blanco B&B and Rainforest Reserve,** Apdo. 241-7210, Guápiles, tel./fax 382-0957, or c/o the local Post Office, tel./fax 710-6161, on the banks of the turbulent Río Blanco about two km east of the Río Costa Rica (turn right and follow the dirt road 1.5 km) and only 12 km from the Rainforest Aerial Tram. It has six pleasant rooms—two in the main lodge, plus four "Cabañas-in-the Clouds"—with private baths with hot water. The rooms perch atop the river canyon so that you can look directly out into the rainforest canopy and the river, bubbling away below. The new owner, Donna "Miss D" Bocock, will make you feel right at home. She'll also happily lead you by the hand on birding and nature hikes (including a nocturnal frog walk) to hidden waterfalls and a cave full of bats. It's popular with birders and has nesting hummingbirds on the grounds, and motmots, aracaria, and kingfishers are common. Sloths hang about on the property. The only noise you'll hear is the rush of the river—and birds, of course. The simple and charming all-hardwood cabins have screened windows to all sides and a small raised porch. Each is a different size, with beds to match (one has a metal, king-size four-poster). All are decorated with twee Guatemalan bedspreads and handicrafts, and speakers—which you can turn off—pipe in New Age music. Bathrooms have plenty of light pouring in from above and *real* hot water systems using natural spring water. Solar lamps mark pathways at night. A marvelous curiosity is the collection of pickled insects, snakes, and creepy miscellany—part of what Donna calls her "Rain Forest Education Center." From the patio bar, you can watch the fireflies flit by and bats in pursuit. There's a souvenir store stocked with Guatemalan items. Marco, the in-house guide, offers tree-climbing lessons and a 45-

minute climb so you can peek into the forest canopy ($45), and you can take a waterfall hike ($25), or horseback rides and whitewater trips. Guests receive discounts up to 20% off the Rainforest Aerial Tram and other local attractions. Rates: $42 s, $58 d, $73 t, including American breakfast (lunches and dinners—$5—by advance notice) and rainforest tour. Guests get kitchen privileges. A jacuzzi is planned. Donna (who, in contrast to the prior owners, appears to be adored by her neighbors) takes in volunteers willing to work in the reserve or teach in local schools.

Happy Rana Lodge, Apdo. 348-7210 Guápiles, tel. 385-1167, fax 710-6794; in the U.S., tel. (520) 743-8254, is one km farther up the dirt road (4WD recommended), above the riverbank deep in the forest; there's a diving platform for plunging into a deep river pool. The place is dark and damp and a perfect retreat for anyone wishing a back-to-basics escape in the heart of nature (it's in the midst of a 15-hectare privately owned patch of forest). The four rustic wooden cabins—spaced well apart—are on stilts and meagerly furnished, with a double and two single beds, screened windows all around, huge walk-in showers with hot water, and electricity provided by a generator. It offers hikes, including a tough all-day hike to a 100-meter waterfall ($10), and arranges whitewater rafting and boat trips on the Río Sarapiquí. Rates: $40 s, $50 d, $60 t, $70 quad, including breakfast served on a veranda in the main lodge. Monkeys, sloths, and other critters abound. Transfers ($75 roundtrip) are provided for stays of three nights or longer.

The **Restaurante Río Blanco,** tel. 710-7857, 200 meters east of the river, also has *cabinas,* as does **Centro Turístico Río Blanco** one km to the east.

In Guápiles: The pickings are slim. **Hotel Keng Wa,** tel. 710-6235, is described by one reader as a "disgusting hovel! Filthy, dead cockroaches on the floor, dirty dishes left in the rooms. I won't mention the bathroom . . ." You may have better luck at **Hotel As de Oro** or **Hotel Hugo Sanchez,** tel. 710-6197, each charging about $5 pp. The **Hospedaje Guápiles,** tel. 710-6179, offers clean rooms. There are other cheap hotels.

The **Hotel Suerre,** Apdo. 25, Guápiles 7210, tel. 710-7551, fax 710-6376; in the U.S., tel. (800) 758-7234, at the east end of town, is an elegant,

modern hacienda-style property with 36 spacious, a/c rooms, beautifully appointed with hardwoods. Each has satellite TV. The hotel features a swimming pool with a water slide, tennis, basketball, and volleyball courts, a restaurant, two bars, a jacuzzi and sauna, and a poolside cafe. Hence it is popular with Tico families, and always lively. *Overpriced!* Rates: $72 s, $90 d, $120 suite. Dayguests can use the facilities for $4.

East of Guápiles: Jardín Botánico Las Cusingas (see above) has a rustic two-bedroom cabin complete with a kitchen, bathroom with hot water, woodstove, and "the best cotton sheets we saw the whole trip," reports one reader (who was also "fed very inexpensively and deliciously"). Rates: $30 up to four people.

Food
Restaurante Ponderosa, tel. 710-7144, one km west of the Río Blanco, specializes in smoked meats. **Centro Turístico Río Blanco** serves *típico* dishes.

The handsome **Restaurante Río Danta,** tel. 223-7490 or 223-2421, fax 222-5463, e-mail: mawamba@sol.racsa.co.cr, 0.5 km farther east—five km west of Guápiles—serves *típico* meals and has short trails leading into the adjacent forest (good for spotting poison-arrow frogs). The property is actually within the boundaries of Braulio Carrillo National Park.

The **Los Lagos,** on the main road as you enter Guápiles, is recommended by a reader.

Getting There
Buses from San José depart the Gran Terminal del Caribe, tel. 257-1961, fax 256-4246, on Calle Central, Avenidas 15/17 every 45 minutes between 5:30 a.m. and 7 p.m. ($1.50). Buses from Puerto Limón depart hourly from Calle 2 and Avenidas 1/2 ($1.20). Buses for Río Frío and Puerto Viejo de Sarapiquí depart Guápiles daily at 4:30 a.m., 7:30 a.m., and 2 p.m. A daily train service also reportedly operates to Siquirres and Puerto Limón.

GUÁCIMO AND VICINITY

Guácimo is a small town and important truck stop about 12 km east of Guápiles. Signs point the way north to **Costa Flores,** Apdo. 4769, San

José 1000, tel. 716-5047 or 220-1311, fax 220-1316, a tropical flower farm said to be the largest in the world, with more than 600 varieties of plants blossoming gloriously across 120 blazingly colorful hectares. Day visitors are welcome. A restaurant sits amid beautifully laid-out pathways. **Siempre Verde** is another horticultural farm nearby (ask for details at Las Palmas).

EARTH (Escuela de Agricultura de la Región Tropical Húmeda), tel. 255-2000, fax 255-2726, one km east of town, is a university that teaches agricultural techniques to students from Latin America. It specializes in researching ecologically sound, or sustainable, agriculture. EARTH has its own banana plantation and 400-hectare forest reserve with nature trails. Visitors are welcome. **Costa Rica Expeditions,** Apdo. 6941-1000, San José, tel. 257-0766, fax 257-1665, e-mail: crexped@sol.racsa.co.cr, offers a full-day guided tour ($69 including lunch).

About four km east of Guácimo a roadside hut sells wicker swing chairs, seats, and more.

Accommodations

Cabinas la Higuito, tel. 716-5025, 500 meters before the turnoff for Guácimo, has simple rooms. Alternately, you can stay overnight at **EARTH,** tel. 255-2000 (ask for *relaciones externas*), in any of 32 double rooms with private baths and hot water. Rates: $30 s, $40 d. Meals are in the campus refectory.

The nicest place along Hwy. 32 is **Hotel and Restaurant Las Palmas,** P.O. Box 6944-1000 San José, tel. 760-0330 or 760-0305, fax 760-0296, 400 meters east of EARTH. It sits amid lush gardens shaded by tall trees on the banks of the Río Dos Novillos, a pool of which has been stocked with tasty tilapias (African bass). Catch your own and the chef will happily prepare it to order. The American-run hotel has 32 rustic yet cozy rooms with private baths and hot water. There's a laundry, plus a figure-eight swimming pool. Trails lead into the nearby 200-hectare reserve, a good place to spot poison-arrow frogs (a stiff 1.5-hour hike leads to waterfalls). Kayak trips are offered. Rates: $32 s, $37 d standard; $39 s, $44 d superior.

Food

The **Restaurant Las Palmas** is open 6 a.m.-10:30 p.m.

Getting There and Away

Buses for Guácimo leave San José from Gran Terminal del Caribe on Calle Central, Avenida 15/17 ($1.75) at 5:30 a.m., 7 a.m., 8:30 a.m., 10 a.m., 10:30 a.m., 11:30 a.m., 1:30 p.m., 3 p.m., and 6 p.m.

SIQUIRRES AND VICINITY

Siquirres, 25 km east of Guácimo and 49 km west of Limón, is also a major railroad junction, echoing to the clanging of bells on locomotives pulling freight cars leased by the banana companies. The tumbledown town has a **monument** to Mártires del Codo del Diablo in honor of those who lost their lives in the revolution of 1948. There's a lively **Mercado Central** facing the railway station. Otherwise, as one reader states, "Yuck! Don't bother" (with Siquirres).

The town is two km east of the Río Reventazón and one km west of the Río Pacuare, one km east of which a road leads south to **Reserva Biológica Barbilla.** Whitewater rafters traditionally take out at Siquirres.

You can drive to the southern edge of Tortuguero (45 km) from Siquirres; the roads are signed from town. East of Siquirres, other dirt roads lead south to the **Parque Nacional Barbilla,** a 12,000-hectare national park formed in 1997 on the northeast flank of the Talamanca mountains to the north of Reserva Indígena Chirripó. Its creation in the face of heavy logging is a testament to the efforts of the **Fundación Nairi,** which has built a small field station and hopes to add tourist facilities.

Accommodations and Food

The **Hotel Alcenar,** tel. 768-8157, has 23 small, clean rooms with fans and shared bath with cold water. There's a TV lounge and a small restaurant. Rates: $3 s, $5.50 d. The **Hotel Río,** tel. 768-8178, opposite, is of a similar standard. Across from the railway station is the **Hotel Garza,** above the **Restaurant Vidal** with rooms for $10 d. On the other side of the market is the **Hotel Las Brisas,** with rooms in need of a good scrubbing. Rates: $5 s, $10 d. A bit nicer in the same price range, is the **Hotel Central,** tel. 768-8113. The **Hotel Mireya,** tel. 768-8178, is on the same block; **Henry's Bar** is adjacent. Both offer basic rooms for \$4-6. Also to consider are **Cabinas Las Palmas,** two km east of the turnoff for Siquirres.

Siquirres has plenty of basic restaurants and *sodas,* including in the colorful Mercado Central. It's a case of potluck. The **Los Castellanos Restaurant** facing the soccer field offers good-quality Tico food at reasonable prices.

The **Caribbean Dish Restaurant,** immediately west of Siquirres, is popular with rafters on the Reventazón. I also recommend the seafood at the **Brisas del Pacuare** east of town on the banks of the Río Pacuare, and **Café Ellis,** on Hwy. 32, 0.5 km east of town and serving an excellent hot buffet (\$4 full plate, \$ 2.50 *casado*).

Christopher Columbus

Services
The tiny **police** (Guardia Rural) post is a adjacent to the railway tracks facing the *mercado*. There's a **Banco de Costa Rica.**

Getting There and Away
Buses for Siquirres leave San José hourly from Gran Terminal del Caribe on Calle Central, Avenida 15/17 (\$1.50). Buses from Siquirres depart hourly for Guápiles, Puerto Limón, and San José from two blocks south of the railway station. Trains to Guápiles reportedly depart daily at 3:20 p.m. (\$1).

MATINA

Matina, about 28 km east of Siquirres, is a banana town on the banks of the Río Matina four km north of Hwy. 32 (the turnoff is at Bristol). It's the traditional beginning and end point for boat trips to Tortuguero; the wharf is in the heart of a banana processing plant near **Barra de Matina Norte,** about eight km northeast of Matina. A *lancha* (boat) to Tortuguero costs locals \$2.

Sea turtles come ashore to nest at Playa Barra de Matina, where an English scientist, John Denham, has **Mondongillo Endangered Wildlife Trust,** tel. 233-0451, fax 221-2820; in the U.K., 16 Brook Green, London W6 7BL, tel. (0171) 602-8002, fax 603-2853, along seven km of privately owned shoreline. John needs student volunteers to assist with turtle research and to help protect the hatcheries.

Las Ruedos del Mariscos on Hwy. 32 east of town is a rustic log structure with funky decor but good seafood. Try the caramel flan.

Reportedly a bus from Matina journeys as far as San Rafael (also called Freeman) and Parismina, on the Caribbean coast.

PUERTO LIMÓN

Puerto Limón, (pop. 65,000), is an important maritime port, the only large town on the Caribbean, and gateway to all other points. Except for Carnival, when it gets in the groove, Puerto Limón is merely a jumping-off point for most travelers; tourist facilities are limited and there is little of interest to see, although the colorful street life may pique your interest.

Puerto Limón has been described as a town of "sleazy charms." Until a few years ago it had more sleaze than charm. The earthquake of 22 April 1991 dealt Puerto Limón a serious blow—buckling pavements, toppling houses, and generally adding to the city's gone-to-seed appearance.

But since I first visited, in 1992, the city has come a long way, reflected in the razing of decrepit buildings and a sense of newfound prosperity. True, many of its decayed buildings with ironwork balconies are still badly in need of a paint job and vultures still pick on the streetside garbage, but the sewers have been relaid, and the roads and even the sidewalks have been properly paved and are now the best in the nation. And a three-block-long landscaped boulevard is planned. Despite this, many Limonenses (predominantly black) still claim that they are neglected by federal officials and continue to display a lingering resentment at having been treated as second-class citizens.

The name Puerto Limón goes back to when a big lemon tree grew where the town hall is today. The town, which is usually referred to simply as "Limón," was originally built in a swampy area (yellow fever was once rampant) near the site of an ancient Indian village, Cariari; it was later moved to rocky terrain in front of La Uvita islet, the only island on Costa Rica's Caribbean side and a pleasant place for a hiking excursion while killing time in Puerto Limón. The town is centered on a lively market, Avenida 2, Calles 3/4, focus of Puerto Limón's social action. There are many Limonenses of mixed Chinese-black blood, and many black and white couples can be seen walking hand in hand.

The harbor (there are four docks) handles most of the sea trade for Costa Rica and, with Moín, its sister port to the west, is the only seaport offering direct docking and ferrying. The city has never fully recovered from the slump in the banana industry in the 1950s and still moves with the lassitude of a tropical port. Many bars—some stay open 24 hours—are colorful hangouts for sailors and prostitutes. A new cruise port funded with Taiwanese money is in the works in the hope of attracting 100 cruise ships a year.

Warning: Because of the rising influence of drug traffic flowing from Panamá, the city has a bad reputation among Ticos and is often referred to as Piedropolis ("Crack City"). It's true that you should beware of pickpockets by day and muggings at night. But reports of Limón's evils have been greatly inflated.

Sights

There's not much to hold you in town, although the **Mercado Central** is worth a browse, and the **Catholic church** (three blocks west of the *mercado*) is worth seeing for its beautiful stained glass.

The most commonly touted attraction is **Parque Vargas** at Calle 1, Avenida 2, literally an urban jungle, with palm promenades, looming hardwoods, and a tangle of vines and bromeliads centered on a crumbling bandstand from which paths radiate like the spokes of a wheel. Three-toed sloths move languidly among the high branches. There's a beautiful mural showing life in Limón since pre-Columbian days on the north side. A bronze bust of Christopher Columbus and his son Fernando, erected in 1990 for the 500th anniversary of their landing, faces the sea.

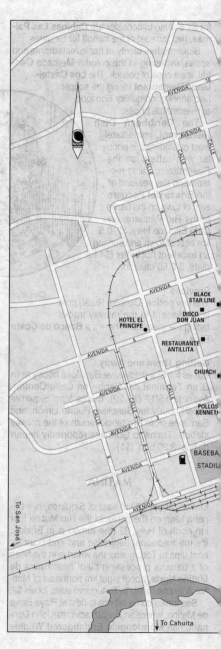

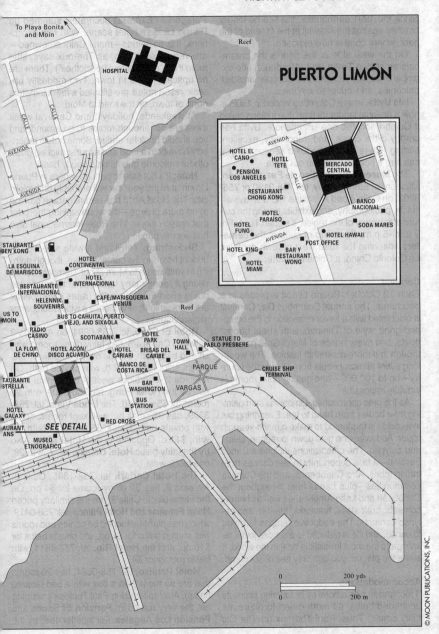

To Playa Bonita
and Moín

Reef

HOSPITAL

PUERTO LIMÓN

CALLE

AVENIDA
8

CALLE

AVENIDA

HOTEL EL
CANO

HOTEL
TETÉ

AVENIDA
3

CALLE
3

PENSIÓN
LOS ANGELES

RESTAURANT
CHONG KONG

MERCADO
CENTRAL

CALLE
2

BANCO
NACIONAL

RESTAURANTE
BEN KONG

LA ESQUINA
DE MARISCOS

HOTEL
CONTINENTAL

HOTEL
PARAISO

HOTEL
FUNG

AVENIDA
2

SODA MARES

HOTEL HAWAII

POST OFFICE

RESTAURANTE
INTERNACIONAL

HOTEL
INTERNACIONAL

HOTEL KING

BAR Y
RESTAURANT
WONG

HELENNIK
SOUVENIRS

CAFÉ/MARISQUERIA
VENUS

HOTEL
MIAMI

Reef

US TO
MOÍN

RADIO
CASINO

BUS TO CAHUITA, PUERTO
VIEJO, AND SIXAOLA

HOTEL
PARK

TOWN
HALL

STATUE TO
PABLO PRESBERE

SCOTIABANK

LA FLOR
DE CHINO

HOTEL ACÓN/
DISCO ACUARIO

HOTEL
CARIARI

BRISAS
DEL
CARIBE

PARQUÉ

BANCO DE
COSTA RICA

VARGAS

CRUISE SHIP
TERMINAL

TAURANTE
STRELLA

BAR
WASHINGTON

HOTEL
GALAXY

BUS
STATION

AURANT
ANS

SEE DETAIL

RED CROSS

MUSEO
ETNOGRÁFICO

0   200 yds

0   200 m

© MOON PUBLICATIONS, INC.

Since the 1991 earthquake, the sea no longer crashes against the seawall at the far end of the park, where coral is now exposed.

On the west side of the park is the cream-colored stucco **Town Hall** (Alcadía), a fine example of tropical architecture, with open arcades, balconies, and louvered windows.

Isla Uvita, where Columbus landed in 1502, is now a national landmark park (the Indians called it Quiribrí) located one km offshore. Uvita has craggy cliffs, caves, and, reportedly, excellent surfing. There is no scheduled service but you can hire a boat to take you out there.

The **Museo Ethnográfico de Puerto Limón,** Museum of Ethnography, tel. 758-2130 or 758-3903, on Calle 4 and Avenidas 1/2, displays artifacts, photography, and exhibits tracing the culture and history of the region; it's open Tues.-Fri. 9 a.m.-5 p.m. Speaking of culture, the **cemetery** spanning the road west of town contains La Colonia China, a Chinese quarter.

Carnival

Each 12 October, Puerto Limón explodes in a bacchanal. The annual Columbus Day Carnival is celebrated with a fervor more akin to the bump-and-grind style of Trinidad, with street bands, floats, and every ounce of Mardi Gras passion, though in a more makeshift fashion. The week-long event attracts people from all over the country—up to 100,000—and getting hotel rooms is virtually impossible.

As the date approaches, Limonians start painting their bodies from head to toe. Everything but insecticide is fermented to make napalm-strength liquor. And everyone gets down to reggae, salsa, and calypso. The celebrations include a Dance Festival—a rare opportunity to see dances from Indian tribes, Afro-Caribbeans, and the Chinese communities—plus bands from throughout the Caribbean and Latin America, as well as beauty contests, craft stalls, fireworks, theater, and calypso contests. The seductive tempos lure you to dance, and life is reduced to a simple, joyful response to the most irresistible beat in the world. It is like the plague: you can only flee or succumb.

Accommodations

"I recognized it as a hotel by its tottering stairs, its unshaded bulbs, its moth-eaten furniture, its fusty smell." Thus, Paul Theroux (in *The Old Patagonian Express*) accurately summed up Puerto Limón's hotel scene. With few exceptions, the hostelries—many Chinese-owned—are very basic (often, as Theroux says, little more than "nests of foul bedclothes"). There are no upscale hotels in town. Two modestly upscale resort hotels are situated a few kilometers north of town, on the road to Moín.

At weekends, holidays, and Carnival week there are not enough rooms to go around, and you should book far ahead. Some hotels reportedly have both a local and a tourist (higher) price; others welcome guests on an hourly basis.

Note: It's not safe to park anywhere in Puerto Limón at night; your car will probably be broken into. The Hotel Acón has secure garage parking at no extra charge—it's worth staying there for that reason alone. The Hotel International also has secure parking.

Shoestring: You'll find a wide selection of budget hotels in the center of town, though nothing to write home to Mum about. Compare before taking a room; many hotels cater to prostitutes doing short-time business (rates given below are for overnight), and there's a wide discrepancy in cleanliness.

Hotel El Caño, tel. 758-0894, on Avenida 3 between Calles 4/5, has fairly dingy rooms with shared bathroom, but the owner otherwise runs a tight ship. Rates: $9 d, with private bath. On Avenida 2, one block west of the central market, try the **Hotel Fung,** tel. 758-3309, with 22 rooms for $5 s, $10 d. The **Linda Vista,** tel. 758-3359, has 35 small but well-kept rooms, some with private bath. Rates: $5 s without bath, $8 with; $11 d. Opposite is the **Hotel King.** Also try the fairly basic **Hotel Galaxy,** tel. 758-2828, one block west.

The **Hotel Cariari,** tel. 758-1395, Calle 2, Avenida 3, has 30 dingy rooms for $4 pp. On the same block, Calle 2, are the similarly priced **Hotel Familiar** and **Hotel Palace,** tel. 758-0419, which has plant-festooned balconies and rooms with shared baths for $5 pp, and private baths for $10 pp; and the **Hotel Río,** tel. 758-4511, with basic rooms for $4.

Hotel Paraíso, tel. 758-0684, has 26 rooms that are no more than a box with a bed (shared baths). Also epitomizing Paul Theroux's warning are the very run-down **Pensión El Sauce** and **Pensión Los Angeles.** For a better deal, try the

Hotel El Principe, a little out of the way on Calle 7, but with nine small but clean rooms with overhead fans and communal bath. Rates: $5 pp.

Up the price scale, **Hotel Continental,** tel. 798-0532, Avenida 5, Calles 2/3, has 20 rooms with private baths and hot water. It's Chinese-run and spotlessly clean. Rooms are simple but spacious. Rates: $8 s, $11 d, $16 t. The spotless **Hotel Internacional,** tel. 758-0434, across the road, has 24 newly tiled rooms of similar standard and is recommended for its price range. Rates: $6 s, $9 d with fans; $8 s, $11 d with a/c.

the **Hotel Miami,** Apdo. 266, Puerto Limón, tel./fax 758-0490, between Calles 4/5 on Avenida 2, offers well-kept if sparsely furnished rooms with overhead fans and private baths. Rates: $12 s, $18 d; $15 s, $20 d with a/c. The restaurant serves Chinese food.

Budget: The best bet in town is the four-story **Hotel Acón,** Avenida 3, Calle 2/3, Apdo. 528, Puerto Limón, tel. 758-1010, fax 758-2924, popular with businessmen from San José. Rooms have a/c and are clean and spacious, though dowdy. The hotel has a reasonable restaurant. Take a fourth-floor room: Thursday through the weekend there's a disco on the second floor. Reservations are advised. Rates: $18 s, $23 d.

Another popular hotel is the **Hotel Park,** Apdo. 35, Puerto Limón, tel. 758-3476, fax 758-4364, with 30 rooms featuring private baths and overlooking the ocean at the corner of Calle 1 and the frontage road. Prices vary according to room standard and view. More expensive ocean-view rooms catch the breeze and, hence, are cooler. Rates: $13-17 s, $20-25 d.

Also consider **Hotel Tete,** Apdo. 401, Puerto Limón, tel. 758-1122, with 14 nice rooms featuring modern, private bathrooms with hot water, and balconies with chairs. Rates: $11 s, $18 d.

Food
One of the pleasures of the Caribbean coast is the unique local cuisine: *pan bon* (good bread) laced with caramelized sugar and a very sharp yellow cheese, banana brownies, fresh ginger cookies, fresh ice cream flavored with fresh fruits, and ceviche made with green bananas. You can sample many of these at the open-air *sodas* in and around the Mercado Central and offering filling meals for $2.

Soda Mares on the market's south side is popular. *Gallo pinto* here costs about $1.50, and you can have a shrimp dish and beer for $5. Also recommended is the **Restaurant Doña Toda,** around the corner on the east-facing side of the market; and the modestly upscale **Restaurante Brisas del Pacifico,** tel. 758-0138, on the west side of the park, serving *típico* and Chinese dishes ($1-5).

The ground-floor restaurant in the **Hotel Acón** offers reasonably priced meals (average $5), including basic American breakfasts. The restaurant in the **Hotel Park** is also recommended. For seafood, try the modestly elegant **La Esquina de Mariscos** at Calle 3 and Avenida 5. Cater-corner to it is the **International Restaurant,** which has appealing decor and hearty meals from $3. And the **Café/Marisqueria Venus** at Calle 2, Avenida 4, is a pleasant seafood restaurant serving staples such as octopus and shrimp cocktails, and *corvina al ajillo* (average $4). The cafe is in an adjoining courtyard.

One of the best places for Caribbean dishes is the popular **Black Star Line** in an old wooden structure at Calle 5 and Avenida 5. It has a limited menu, with *casados* for $2.50.

There's no shortage of clean, inexpensive Chinese restaurants. The **Restaurant Chong Kong,** facing the market on the west side, is one of the best. Around the corner on Avenida 2 is **Restaurant Wong** and, on the next block, **Soda Happy Landing, Palacio Encantador,** and the popular **Soda Restaurante Yans,** all offering meals for $2 and up. Two other reasonably priced restaurants to consider are **Restaurante Chong,** Avenida 3, Calles 6/7, and **Restaurante La Flor de China,** Avenida 4, Calles 4/5. More expensive is elegant **Restaurant Sien Kong,** Calle 3 and Avenida 6, with meals from $5.

Restaurante Estrella, a tiny and pleasing open-air restaurant behind wrought-iron grilles on the corner of Calle 5 and Avenida 3, offers inexpensive burgers and *típico* dishes (average $2), plus tasty *batidos* (75 cents). **Pollos Kenneth,** Calle 6, Avenida 3, is the local counterpart of Colonel Sanders. Hankering for pizza? Try **Pizza Mia** on Calle 5 and Avenida 3. Lastly, **Café Verde,** Avenida 3, Calles 19/21, serves from a truly international menu that features Italian, German, and Tican cuisines.

There's a lively **fruit market,** on Avenida 4 between Calles 4/7, on weekends. **Baloons,** on the north side of the *mercado,* and **Mönpik,** opposite the Hotel Acón, can satisfy your ice cream craving, as can **Pops,** on the corner of Calle 2 and Avenida 4.

Restaurant Springfield, tel. 758-1203, one km north on the road to Moín, is a favorite of locals. It has zesty Caribbean dishes from $4, including garlic shrimp and fish in curry sauce (*please* refrain from ordering turtle meat). The **Restaurante Arrecife,** 100 meters farther north, is also good for seafood.

Entertainment

Most bars—of which there's no shortage—have a decidedly raffish quality, and an aura of impending violence pervades many by night. The colorful but basic **Bar Washington** at Calle 1 and Avenida 2, is awash with prostitutes and tropical vagabonds. **Bar Mamajora** on Avenida 2 between Calles 1/2, is popular with locals, as is the lively **Bar Mamón.** Both look safe.

The weekend disco in the **Hotel Acón** is jam-packed, fun, safe, and sweaty, with a pulsing Latin beat (admission $1, free to hotel guests). For calypso and reggae check out **Discoteque Roxelle** above Soda Mares, or **Springfield,** on the road to Moín (the disco is unseen, at the back of the restaurant). A bit farther out, **Disco Tico Loco** features live bands. Just up the road, at Potrete, the seafront, open-air **Johny Dixon Bar** can get equally lively. In town, the **Mark 15 Disco** is also recommended.

The **Cine Ancón** at the south end of town offers American movies for $1. For theater, try the **Teatro Hong Kong** on Calle 9 and Avenida 1, tel. 758-0034.

Tourist Information

There's no tourist office. **Helennik Souvenirs,** tel. 758-2086, on Calle 3 and Avenidas 4/5, acts as an informal information office.

Services

There's a **Banco de Costa Rica,** tel. 758-3166, on Calle 1 and Avenida 2; a **Banco Nacional de Costa Rica,** tel. 758-0094, next to the Puerto Limón-San José bus terminal, Calle 2, Avenida 1; a **Banco de San José,** Calle 2, Avenida 4; and a **Scotiabank** at Calle 2 and Avenida 3.

There's only one bank south of Puerto Limón (at Bribrí), and none to the north; if you're spending more than a few days on the coast, change as much as you'll need here, as the bank in Bribrí is a long drive and can take hours to change money.

The **Hospital Dr. Tony Facio,** tel. 758-2222, for **emergencies,** tel. 758-0580, is at the north end of the seafront *malecón.* There's also a small clinic—**Clínica Santa Lucía,** tel. 758-1286—in the town center on Calle 2 and Avenidas 4/5. Dr. Eric Castro Vega has a **clinical laboratory,** tel. 758-3106, on Calle 4 and Avenidas 3/4. There are several **dental clinics** and no shortage of **pharmacies.**

The **post office** is cater-corner to the plaza, on the corner of Calle 4 and Avenida 2. The **Surf Shop** on Calle 6, Avenida 3, sells boogie boards.

Getting There and Away

By Air: **Travelair** and **SANSA** offer scheduled service to the recently built airport two km south of Limón.

By Bus: Direct buses depart the Gran Terminal Caribe, tel. 257-1961, fax 256-4248, in San José at Calle Central, Avenidas 15/17 at 5:30 a.m., 6:45 a.m., 7:30 a.m., 10:30 a.m., 11:30 a.m., 12:30 p.m., 2:30 p.m., 3:30 p.m., 4:30 p.m., 5:30 p.m., and 6:30 p.m. ($3; 2.5 hours). Buses to San José depart Puerto Limón on a similar schedule from Calle 2 and Avenida 2, one block east and half a block south of the municipal market ($2). Buses also serve Cahuita, Manzanillo, and Sixaola from San José stopping at Puerto Limón en route.

Buses depart Limón for Cahuita (85 cents), Puerto Viejo ($1.25), and Sixaola ($2) from opposite Radio Casino on Avenida 4 daily at 5 a.m., 10 a.m., 1 p.m., and 4 p.m. Buy tickets in advance at the *soda* beside the bus stop, as buses get crowded (advance tickets are reportedly only offered for the 10 a.m. and 4 p.m. departures). Buses also serve Penshurst and the Valle de Estrella regularly throughout the day from Calle 2. Around the corner on Calle 4 to the north is the bus stop for Playa Bonita and Moín.

Interbus stops at Limón on its daily shuttle between San José and Puerto Viejo (see **appendix**).

By Train: Train service to San José was suspended after the April 1991 earthquake. However, you can savor a down-to-earth journey by "rustic rail" to Estrella.

Getting Around

From San José you enter town along Avenida 1, paralleling the railway track that runs to the cruise port. The *avenidas* (east-west) are aligned north of Avenida 1 in sequential order. The *calles* (north-south) are numbered sequentially and run westward from the waterfront. Few locals know the streets by numbers; instead they refer to "landmarks" and call the streets by colloquial names such as "Market Street" (Avenida 2). Most addresses and directions are given in direction and distance from the market or Parque Vargas. Most streets are one-way.

You can walk anywhere in town (be cautious at night). You'll find plenty of **taxis** on the south side of the market. Expect to pay $20-25 for a taxi to Cahuita.

To reach Moín, take Calle 2 or Avenida 6, which merge into the coast road heading north. For Cahuita, turn south from Avenida 1 at the junction with Calle 9.

The town has three **gas stations:** on the corner of Calle 3 and Avenida 6, at Calle 7 and Avenida 2, and one km west of town on the

Guápiles Highway. Fill up here as there are only two gas stations south of Puerto Limón (one at Estrella, and the other near the Panamanian border, halfway between Bribrí and Sixaola).

PORTRETE AND PLAYA BONITA

Playa Bonita, four km north of Puerto Limón, boasts an attractive golden sand beach encusped by palms and popular with Limonenses. Reportedly, swimming is safe only at the northern end. The surf is good, but unreliable; it can be excellent on a good swell, or flat calm for weeks. The headland to the north features **Parque Recreativo Cariari,** an overgrown and untended public park with little to recommend it; trails reportedly offer sightings of sloths, toucans, iguanas, and parrots and the place was supposedly being spruced up in late 1997, but has a long way to go.

Adjoining Playa Bonita to the north is **Portrete,** an unsightly bay interesting only for the flocks of vultures that gather to feed on lobster scraps left by the local fishermen. The cove supposedly has good right points for surfers at its southern end.

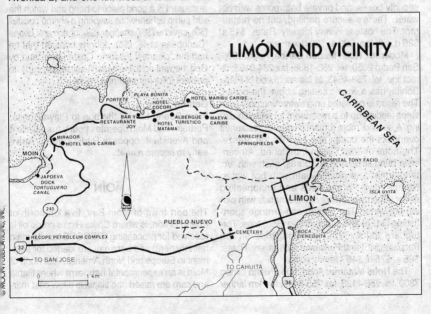

LIMÓN AND VICINITY

Accommodations

Shoestring: Apartotel La Cueva, tel. 798-0579, three km north of Limón, has modern self-catering units on the coral shore. The tiny, bare-bones **Cabinas Mar Bella,** just south of Playa Bonita, has basic rooms for $10. Also try **Cabinas Getsemani,** tel. 758-1123, which reportedly has cabins with a/c and bath. The dour **Nuevo Motel** is surely a brothel or love shack.

Budget: Cabinas Maeva Caribe, tel. 758-2024, is a bit run-down. It has 56 sparsely furnished rooms in 17 bamboo-lined octagonal cabins set in a lush hillside garden full of palms. The swimming pool was empty at press time. There's a basic open-sided restaurant. Rates: $27 d. Two km farther north, overlooking Playa Bonita, is **Hotel Cocori,** tel. 758-2930 or 257-4674, a modern clifftop complex with a pleasing ocean-view terrace restaurant—**Bar/Restaurante Tía María**—open to the breezes. It fills with Ticos on weekends, when the disco pumps out tunes loud enough to wake the dead. It has 25 simple but pleasing rooms with a/c. Rates: $14 s, $17 d; $45 apartments for six.

The **Albergue Turístico,** tel./fax 798-3090, is an attractive modern place with seven spotless albeit simply furnished and dark rooms with TVs, security boxes, and private bathrooms with hot water. There's secure parking, but no restaurant. The hostess is very friendly. Rates: $15 s, $25 d with fan; $20 s, $30 d with a/c.

Moderate: Hotel Maribu Caribe, Apdo. 1306, San Pedro 2050, tel. 253-1838, fax 234-0193; direct line, tel. 758-4543, at the south end of Playa Bonita, has a scenic setting above the ocean. The resort is centered on a swimming pool, with steps leading up to a restaurant for alfresco dining. A second, more romantic open-air restaurant overlooks the ocean and catches the breeze. The hotel offers 17 round, thatched, African-style bungalows and 56 rooms, each with a/c, telephone, and private bath with hot water. Rooms have narrow beds and unappealing decor. Roomy showers make amends with piping hot water. The Maribu can arrange sportfishing ($125) and scuba diving ($50) trips, Tortuguero tours ($70), and boat trips on the Pacuare ($45) and Parismina ($60) rivers. Rates: $65 s, $75 d, $107 family suite.

The **Hotel Matama,** Apdo. 606, Puerto Limón 7300, tel. 758-1123, fax 758-4499, two km farther

north, has rooms and four-person and six-person villas with loft bedrooms, set in 22 hectares of landscaped gardens and forest with trails on a rise set back from the shore. Rooms are spacious with wicker furniture, a/c, and large showers along with their own solarium gardens. Some have lofts. Mine was long past its prime and desperately in need of renovation in December 1997. The wide open-air restaurant overlooks the gardens and handsome swimming pool (with swim-up bar) and specializes in seafood. Live music is hosted on weekends. It has a lagoon with some caimans, plus caged animals, but the jaguar is gone (eaten by the boa constrictor, I was told). Overpriced? Rates: $50 s, $55 d low season; $55 s, $65 d high season.

Villas Cacao, Apdo. 3565, San José 1000, tel. 223-1126, fax 222-0930, is a resort development of villas and condominiums.

Food

Hotel Maribu Caribe and Hotel Matama both have reasonably good restaurants. **Restaurant Joy,** on the beachfront at Playa Bonita, is run by an outspoken character, Johnny Dixon, a former musician who says he's "as well known throughout Costa Rica as *gallo pinto.*" His breezy bar and restaurant is a good place to hang and watch the surf pump ashore while savoring a shrimp cocktail ($9), ceviche ($6), snapper ($9), or rice and beans "Caribbean style" ($6). Johnny boasted that he had the "cleanest toilets in Costa Rica," and by God, he was right. He doesn't sell plastic cups, to prevent folks from littering the beach.

Getting There

From Puerto Limón, the bus to Playa Bonita, Portrete, and Moín operates hourly from Calle 4 and Avenida 4, opposite Radio Casino. Arrive early to secure a seat.

MOÍN

The port town of Moín Bay, five km north of Puerto Limón, is where Costa Rica's crude oil is received for processing (RECOPE has its main refinery here) and bananas are loaded for shipment to Europe and North America. Just north of Moín is an experimental **fish farm** where tilapia and carp are raised (the tilapia is a low-cost market fish; the carp, it is hoped, will help control the growth of water hyacinth that clogs Los Canales).

The only reason to visit Moín is to catch a boat to Tortuguero. The dock (unsigned) is north of the railway tracks at the base of the hill below Hotel Moín (after crossing the track, follow the sinuous dirt road to the left). You pass through a security checkpoint. Inside the compound, touts will descend on you to offer rides on canopied boats.

Accommodations
Hotel Moín Caribe, Apdo. 483, Moín, tel. 758-2436, fax 758-1112, atop the hill above the dock to Tortuguero, is the only place around. It has 15 modestly furnished rooms (some are quite dark despite being large, so check several rooms before choosing; room 204 is well-lit). A veranda has sofas. There's a steak house restaurant

downstairs, plus private parking and laundry service. The **Banana Power** disco downstairs opens on weekends. The hotel seems to have reverted to its former status as a spawning ground for sailors and prostitutes. Rates: $18 s, $22 d.

Getting There and Away
The turnoff from Hwy. 32 is three km west of Puerto Limón, just past the RECOPE storage tanks on your left.

Boats to Tortuguero: Boats leave from the JAPDEVA dock (see above) and vary in size from eight- to 20-passenger vessels. Most are canopied. Some (but not all) provide rain ponchos. Come prepared for rain. If you're on a smaller boat (without a window), it will be a *very* cold ride zipping along in the rain. Expect to pay $50 pp for four people roundtrip for transport and tour ($100 if you're alone; $150 for two people), returning the same day or any other day.

THE NORTHERN CARIBBEAN

Lagoons and swamps dominate the coastal plains north of Limón. Many rivers meander through this region, carrying silt that the coastal tides conjure into long, straight, brown-sand beaches. These shores, which are pounded by wild surf, are the ideal places for sea turtles to lay their eggs. The 35-km beach of Tortuguero is favored by hawksbill, Pacific green, and leatherback turtles; the leatherback is the world's largest sea turtle. Tortuguero National Park and Barra del Colorado Wildlife Refuge protect these turtles, as well endangered manatees and a vast diversity of other critters in the rainforests and swamps backing the shore. Barra is a center for sportfishing.

PARISMINA

This small, haphazard village on a small strip of land at the mouth of the Río Parismina, 45 km north of Moín, is popular year-round with North American anglers. Parismina suffered severely in the April 1991 earthquake, however, and has had a hard time recovering. The spring tarpon season runs mid-January through May, with giant schools of tarpon, good offshore reef fishing, and some snook. The summer season runs June

through mid-August. Mid-August through November is the peak time for giant snook. Tuna, wahoo, King mackerel, snapper, and other gamefish await offshore. Wildlife viewing is good in the rainforests and wetlands around Parismina.

Accommodations
Serving the budget-conscious is the **Parismina Lodge,** tel. 768-8636, which offers basic accommodations in a twin-story waterfront structure; six of the nine rooms share bathrooms.

Caribbean Expedition Lodge, tel./fax 232-8118; in the U.S., tel. (512) 884-4277, fax 884-6740, opened in 1997 with modern bungalows with ceiling fans and private bathrooms and hot water, and center console boats with T-tops, radio, and fish-finder. There's a "free open rum bar." A one-day "Jungle Safari" to Tortuguero is offered ($79 from San José; $169 including lodging and meals).

The newly built **Río Parismina Lodge,** c/o Fishing Tours International, P.O. Box 460009, San Antonio, TX 78280, tel. (210) 824-4442 or (800) 338-5688, fax (210) 824-0151; in Costa Rica, tel. 222-6633, fax 221-9127, is a sportfishing lodge with an inventory of ten 21-foot V-hulls for handling choppy offshore waters. It has 12 attractive

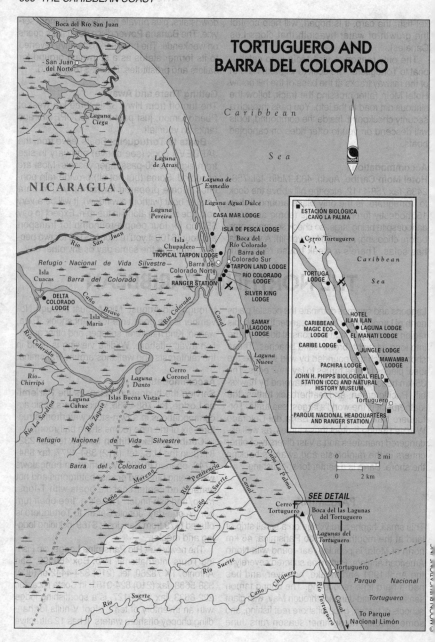

TORTUGUERO AND
BARRA DEL COLORADO

Boca del Río San Juan

San Juan
del Norte

Laguna
Ciega

Caribbean

Sea

NICARAGUA

Laguna
de Atrás

Laguna de
Enmedio

Laguna
Pereira

Laguna Agua Dulce

CASA MAR LODGE

ISLA DE PESCA LODGE

Isla
Chupadero

Boca del
Río Colorado

TROPICAL TARPON LODGE

Barra del
Colorado Sur

Refugio Nacional de Vida Silvestre

Barra del
Colorado Norte

TARPON LAND LODGE

Isla
Cuacas

Barra del Colorado

RÍO COLORADO
LODGE

RANGER STATION

SILVER KING
LODGE

DELTA
COLORADO
LODGE

Caño Bravo

Isla
María

SAMAY LAGOON
LODGE

Laguna
Nueve

Cerro
Coronel

Río
Chirripó

Laguna
Danto

Islas Buena Vistas

Laguna
Cahue

Refugio   Nacional   de   Vida   Silvestre

Barra   del   Colorado

Caño Penitencia

Caño Moreno

Caño La Palma

Caño Suerte

SEE DETAIL

Cerro
Tortuguero

Boca del las Lagunas
del Tortuguero

Lagunas del
Tortuguero

Río Suerte

Río   Suerte

Caño Chiquero

Río Tortuguero

Parque   Nacional

Tortuguero

To Parque
Nacional Limón

Detail map:

ESTACIÓN BIOLÓGICA
CAÑO LA PALMA

Cerro Tortuguero

TORTUGA
LODGE

Caribbean

Sea

HOTEL
ILAN ILAN

CARIBBEAN
MAGIC ECO-
LODGE

LAGUNA LODGE

EL MANATI LODGE

CARIBE LODGE

JUNGLE LODGE

PACHIRA LODGE

MAWAMBA
LODGE

JOHN H. PHIPPS BIOLOGICAL FIELD
STATION (CCC) AND NATURAL
HISTORY MUSEUM

Tortuguero

PARQUE NACIONAL HEADQUARTERS
AND RANGER STATION

0   2 mi

0   2 km

© MOON.COM/AVALON TRAVEL

rooms in modern bungalows, plus a swimming pool, jacuzzi, and airy, screened dining room and bar. The lodge is closed in July. Rates: from $60 pp including meals. Most people arrive on fishing packages; sample rates are $1,850 s, $3,300 d for the three-night "Long Weekend" with three full days fishing. Extra fishing days cost $400 pp.

The **Parismino Tarpon Rancho** was flattened by the earthquake and reopened in 1994. It closed again several years later but may reopen. Stay tuned.

Food

For those journeying to Tortuguero on the canals, a relaxing midway port-of-call—**Rancho Turístico el Tres,** also known as Armando's Bar—features tree trunks as tables to complement the rustic bamboo restaurant. Local dishes (about $3) include shrimp and rice, breaded fried fish, chicken, and *gallo pinto.*

For hungry and thirsty boaters traveling the canals on a dime is **Bar y Cabinas Madre de Dios,** a popular open-air eatery a few kilometers south of Parismina.

PARQUE NACIONAL TORTUGUERO

Tortuguero National Park extends north along the coast for 22 km from Jaloba, six km north of Parismina, to Tortuguero village. The 19,000-hectare park is basically a mosaic of deltas on an alluvial plain nestled between the Caribbean coast on the east and the low-lying volcanic hills of Coronel, Caño Moreno, and 300-meter-high Las Lomas de Sierpe—the Sierpe Peaks—on the west. The park protects the nesting beach of the green turtle, the offshore waters to a distance of 30 km, and the wetland forests extending inland for about 15 kilometers.

The park—one of the most varied within the park system—has 11 ecological habitats, from high rainforest to herbaceous marsh communities. Fronting the sea is the seemingly endless expanse of beach. Behind that is a narrow lagoon, connected to the sea at one end and fed by a river at the other, which parallels the beach for its full 35-km length. Back of the lagoon is a coastal rainforest threaded by an infinite maze of serpentine channels and streams fed by rivers flowing from the central mountain ranges and

by the torrential rains that fall in the area (the rains can last for days at a time, usually subsiding briefly in March). On the periphery of the forest lies a complex of swamps.

Drenched by 500 cm of rain a year, Tortuguero shelters a fabulous array of wildlife, including more than 300 bird species, among them the great green macaw; 57 species of amphibians and 111 of reptiles, including three species of marine turtles; 60 mammal species, including 13 of Costa Rica's 16 endangered species, not least jaguars, tapirs, ocelots, cougars, river otters, and manatees. Commonly seen birds include toucans, aricaris, oropendolas, swallow-tailed hawks, several species of herons, kingfishers, anhingas, parrots, and jacanas. The wide-open canals with their great forested walls make viewing easier than at many other parks—superb for spotting crocodiles, giant iguanas and basilisk lizards basking atop the branches, swallow-tailed hawks and vultures swooping over the treetops, and caimans luxuriating on the fallen raffia palm branches at the side of the river. At night you can shine halogen searchlights on the riverbanks seeking the reflections of crocodilian eyes in the inky-black night. One of my favorite pastimes is to watch bulldog bats skimming through the mist that rises from the water and scooping up a fish right on cue. Amazing! That hair-raising roar? A male howler monkey that has misjudged a leap and hit a tree with legs spread apart (this, at any rate, was the explanation given by one irrepressible guide).

The western half of the park is under great stress from logging and hunting, which have increased in recent years as roads are cut into the core of the rainforest from the west, north, and south. The local community and hotel and tour operators are battling a proposed highway sponsored by banana and logging interests into the region between Tortuguero and Barra del Colorado. The **Tortuguero Conservation Area Project,** Area de Conservación y Desarrollo Sostenible de las Llanuras del Tortuguero, Apdo. 338, Guápiles, tel. 710-2929, fax 710-7673, works to protect the region and publishes literature on local ecology. Particularly threatened is the large mammal population.

Every hotel and tour company in San José pushes Tortuguero, with good reason. About 50,000 tourists a year come here to explore the forests and swamps of Tortuguero National Park and to see any of four species of turtles that nest on the beach. The recent boom had spawned fears that the park was becoming overloaded with tourists (there were only 240 visitors in 1980). Help out by carrying out anything you bring in. Rubbish disposal is a serious problem at Tortuguero: leave no trash.

Entrance is $6, payable at the **Cuatro Esquinas** ranger station (park headquarters) at the southern end of Tortuguero village, or at **Estación Jalova**, at the park's southern end (45 minutes by boat from Tortuguero village). There's no fee to travel along the canals via the park en route to/from Tortuguero village.

Manatees

Tortuguero's fragile manatee population is endangered and was thought to be extinct until a population was located in remote lagoons within Tortuguero. Traditionally they have been hunted for their flesh, reputedly tender and delicious, and for their very tough hides, but the greatest threat of late has been chemicals and sediments washing into the waterways from banana plantations. Ironically, ecotourism is taking a toll, with increasing boat traffic. Manatees have moved west toward more remote lagoons seeking quiet places to mate and are rarely seen. Dr. Bernie Nietschmann of the University of California, Berkeley, runs a research program to count and study the manatees, and to provide environmental education to the local community.

Turtles

The park protects a vital nesting ground for green sea turtles, which find their way onto the brown-sand beaches every year June-Oct. (the greatest numbers arrive in September). Mid-February through July, giant leatherback turtles also arrive to lay their eggs (with greatest frequency April-May), followed, in July, by female hawksbill turtles. Tortuguero is the most important green-turtle hatchery in the western Caribbean. An estimated 30,000 turtles came ashore in 1997. Each female arrives two to six times, at 10- to 14-day intervals, and waits two or three years before nesting again.

During the 1950s, the Tortuguero nesting colony came to the attention of biologist-writer Archie Carr, a lifelong student of sea turtles.

Carr enlisted sympathy through his eloquent writing, particularly *The Windward Road* (Gainesville: University of Florida Press, 1955). His lobby—originally called the Brotherhood of the Green Turtle—worked with the Costa Rican government to establish Tortuguero as a sanctuary where the endangered turtles could nest unmolested. The sanctuary was established in 1963 and the area was named a national park in 1970. The Brotherhood, now the **Caribbean Conservation Corps,** CCC, Apdo. 246-2050 San Pedro, tel. 224-9215 or 238-8069, fax 225-7516, e-mail: baulas@sol.racsa.co.cr; in the U.S., P.O. Box 2866, Gainesville, FL 32602, tel. (800) 678-7853 or (904) 373-6441, e-mail: ccc@cccturtle.org, maintains the John H. Phipps Biological Station and a Natural History Visitor's Center (locals still call it by its old name—Casa Verde), five minutes' walk north of the village. The CCC also publishes *Velador,* a quarterly update on turtle projects in the region. You can also **adopt a turtle** for $35 by calling the CCC.

Turtle Walks: *No one is allowed on the 22-mile nesting sector without a guide after 6 p.m.* Limits were established in 1994 to control visitor impact. Only 350 people are allowed on the beach per night, apportioned by sector. Local guides—trained by the National Parks Service and organized into a local cooperative—escort walks at 8-10 p.m. and 10 p.m.-midnight each evening in turtle-nesting season ($5; you can buy tickets in advance at the information kiosk in the village center, on the north side of the soccer field). Strict rules and guidelines are enforced for turtle watching: no cameras or flashlights are permitted (they'll be confiscated); keep quiet, as the slightest noise can send the turtle hurrying back to sea; and keep a discreet distance. A conservationist ethic is still tenuous among the local population (including, alas, guides), and you still find turtle meat and eggs for sale, while school books continue to teach that turtles are an economic resource to harvest. Many environmentalists are in despair; it is impossible to turn around ingrained attitudes within one generation. You are asked to report any guide who digs up turtle hatchlings to show you—this is absolutely prohibited. Turtles are endangered; respect them.

Volunteers: The CCC needs volunteers to assist in research, including during its twice-yearly turtle tagging and monitoring programs.

See the chart **Volunteer Programs to Save the Turtles** in the Introduction. You should be willing to patrol up to five miles of beach nightly for 8-15 nights. Programs start at $1,495, including airfare, meals, and lodging at the John H. Phipps Biological Field Station.

When to Go
Rain falls year-round. The three wettest months are January, June, and July. The three driest are February, April, and November. Monsoon-type storms can lash the region at any time; rain invariably falls more heavily in the late afternoon and at night. August through November are best for turtlewatching. The interior of the park is hot, humid (*very* humid on sunny days), and windless. Bring good raingear; a heavy-duty poncho is ideal. **Note:** It can be cool enough for a windbreaker or sweater while speeding upriver under cloudy weather. Take insect repellent—the mosquitoes and no-see-ums (you'll need Avon's Skin-so-Soft for these) can be fierce.

COSTA RICA'S AQUATIC COASTAL "HIGHWAY"

During the Trejos administration (1966-70), four canals were dug from solid ground to link the natural channels and lagoons of the coastal swamplands stretching north of Moín to Tortuguero and the Río Colorado. Today, these canals form a connected "highway"—virtually the only means of getting around along the coast—and one can now travel from Siquirres eastward along the Río Pacuare to Moín, then northward to Tortuguero, and from there to the Río Colorado, which in turn connects with the Río San Juan, which will take you westward to Pavas and Puerto Viejo de Sarapiquí.

The three-hour journey from Moín (or Parismina) to Tortuguero provides a superb experience. All along the riverbanks are the ramshackle shacks of settlers who come and go with the river level, subsisting on corn and the canal's swarming fish, such as tarpon and gar. Mingling with the tour boats and puttering tug-like launches are slender nine-meter-long canoes—each carved from a single log—powered by outboard motors and sometimes piled high with bananas.

The easygoing waterway is lined with rainforest vegetation in a thousand shades of green. The deep verdure of the foliage, the many brilliant flowers, the graceful festoons of the vines and mosses intertwining themselves make for an endlessly fascinating journey. Noisy flocks of parrots speed by doing barrel rolls in tight formation. Several species of kingfishers patrol the banks; the largest, the Amazon kingfisher, is almost 30 cm long. In places the canopy arches over the canal and howler monkeys sounding like rowdy teenagers may protest your passing. Keep a sharp eye out, too, for mud turtles and caimans absorbing the sun's rays on logs.

JEAN MERCIER

*Los Canales,
Tortuguero
National Park*

Exploring Tortuguero

Hiking: You can walk the entire length of the beach. Trails into the forests—frequently waterlogged—also begin at the park stations at both ends of the park. The 2-km-long El Gavilán Trail leads south from the Cuatro Esquinas ranger station south of Tortuguero village and takes in both beach and rainforest. A trail that begins north of Tortuga Lodge leads to Cerro Tortuguero (119 meters), two km north of Tortuga Lodge; from here—the highest point for miles around—you have a superb perspective over the swamps and coastline from the rusting WWII-era lookout tower at the top. Short hikes from Estación Jalova provide a satisfying adventure for those with only limited time.

Canoes And Boats: You can hire dugout canoes (*cayucas* or *botes)* in Tortuguero village ($6 pp the first hour, $3 each additional hour, without a guide). Give the canoe a good inspection before shaking hands on the deal: paddle around until you feel comfortable and have ascertained that there are no leaks and that the canoe is stable. Alternately, consider a *panga,* a flat-bottomed boat with outboard motor, or a *lancha* (with inboard motor), which will cost more. It's also a good idea to check on local currents and directions, as the former can be quite strong and it's easy to lose your bearings amid the maze of waterways. And don't forget to pay your park entrance fee before entering Tortuguero National Park.

Guided Tours

If you want to see wildlife you *absolutely* need a guide, as otherwise you'll not see 10% of the wildlife you'll see in their company. Guides have binocular eyes: in even the darkest shadows, they can spot caimans, birds, crocodiles, and other animals you will most likely miss. Many local villagers also hire out as guides. You can hire guides in the village for about $5 pp, per hour (tours usually last two or three hours); try Ernesto at Cabinas Sabina (he charges $10 for 3-4 hours). The best guides are employed by the local lodges and are more versed in wildlife lore. You can book guided trips at any of the lodges or through tour companies in San José.

The guides will lead you deep into the narrow *caños* and chug up the side streams where the vegetation narrows down to a murky closeness

and he is forced to cut the motor and pole to make headway. On a guided three-hour tour from Tortuga Lodge, I saw crocodiles, caimans, howler monkeys, sloths, green macaws, turtles, toucans, herons, a diminutive pygmy kingfisher, river otters playing tag alongside the boat, and dozens of other species. The succession of creatures—some virtually at arm's reach—seemed almost to have been installed for my benefit. I felt as if we were in a museum instead of a wilderness. Exploring at night is no longer permitted.

The following companies offer guided tours. **Costa Rica Expeditions,** Apdo. 6941-1000, San José, tel. 257-0766, fax 257-1665, e-mail: crexped@sol.racsa.co.cr, operates a variety of quality tours with overnights at its Tortuga Lodge. It provides rain ponchos, plus lunches for daytrips to Barra del Colorado. Three-day/two-night packages with private flight from San José to Tortuguero cost $299 pp (based on a four-person minimum); boat tours into the park are extra. It has the best guides in the area. *Recommended!*

Cotur, Apdo. 26-1017, San José 2000, tel. 233-6579, has a three-day/two-night package from San José, including a bus ride to Moín, then a journey to Tortuguero aboard either the *Miss Caribe* or the *Miss América.* A half-day tour of the park is included. Accommodations are at the Jungle Lodge. Departure on Friday, return Sunday. **Agencia Mitur,** Apdo. 91, San José 1150, tel. 255-2031, fax 255-1946, e-mail: mitour@sol.racsa.co.cr, operates a daily "Tortuguero Jungle Adventures" aboard the *Colorado Princess,* with accommodations at the Hotel Ilan Ilan ($160 two days/one night; $215 three days/two nights). The **Mawamba Lodge,** in San José, tel. 233-9964, or in Puerto Limón, tel. 758-1564, operates a launch—the *Mawamba*—twice weekly from Puerto Limón to Tortuguero. **Tico Tours** has a one-day "Tortuguero Monkey Jungle Tour" from San José.

Laura's Tropical Tours, tel. 758-2410, and **Caribbean Magic,** tel./fax 758-1210, offer Tortuguero tours from Puerto Limón. Willie Rankin of **All Rankin' Tours,** tel. 798-1556, has trips from Moín for $50, as does **Caribbean Comfort,** tel. 758-1210. Most other hotels in Puerto Limón can arrange tours.

Ecole Travel, tel. 223-2240, has special trips during turtle-nesting season ($85, including one night lodging and the canal trip).

green macaw
at Tortuguero

TORTUGUERO

Somnolent, funky Tortuguero (pop. 550) is an 80-km, three-hour journey upriver from Moín; by small plane from San José, it's a 30-minute flight that sets you down on a thin strip of land between canal and ocean. The higgledy-piggledy village, a budget traveler's paradise, is a warren of rickety wooden houses linked by narrow sandy trails (there are no roads) and sprawling over a spit of sand that extends north six km to the mouth of **Laguna del Tortuguero,** with the ocean crashing on one side and the lagoon and the jungle on the other. Tortuguero sits at the southern end of Laguna del Tortuguero at its junction with **Laguna Penitencia,** another pencil thin waterway west of and parallel to Laguna del Tortuguero. Laguna Penitencia leads to Barra del Colorado and is the favored waterway for nature tours.

The waters here are not safe for swimming because of rip currents and the large number of sharks (mostly nurse sharks) in the two-meter range. Barracudas—silvery assassins, terrifyingly dentured—also abound in the warm, shallow waters. That rusting hulk of saw blades and metal framework was once a lumber mill that between the 1940s and 1972 provided steady work to the villagers, who supplemented their meager income selling turtle meat and shells, as had their forebears (many of whom came from San Andreas, Colombia). When the mill closed the population began drifting away. Now

tourism is booming and so is the local population (evidenced by the modern cement houses that locals are building), which, despite its ostensible stake in protecting turtles, still takes them illegally for meat. (Also, though the local lodges have placed trash cans around town, the locals don't use them—they still think the ground is the best receptacle.) Old habits die hard.

The village center is the **community center** and **Super Morpho,** the "supermarket" with the public telephone, tel. 710-6716. There's a **John B. Powers Information Kiosk** *(kiosko de información)* on the north side of the soccer field: it provides an excellent educational take on local ecology and the history of Tortuguero.

Telephone lines arrived in 1997. A few places had numbers at press time, with most of the community members scheduled to receive their own lines in 1998.

Natural History Visitor's Center

The CCC operates this splendid museum at the **John H. Phipps Biological Field Station.** It features turtle exhibits and educational presentations, including a video about turtle ecology and a fantastic life-size 3-D model of turtles hatching, and another of a turtle laying her eggs. The superb displays include aspects of rainforest ecology. It has a gift store well stocked with natural history books. Open daily 10 a.m.-noon and 2-5:30 p.m., Sunday 2-5:30 p.m. Entrance: $1.

The CCC also invites volunteers to join its fall and spring bird-research projects at Tortuguero.

It involves mist-netting, identifying, banding, and studying resident and migrant birds during their ancient treks north and south (Tortuguero is along a prime migration flyway). No experience is needed. The fieldwork is complemented by guided hikes, boat tours, etc.

Accommodations in the Village

Camping: You can camp at the **John H. Phipps Biological Field Station,** and at the **park headquarters** at the southern end of the village. Remember, it rains torrentially at Tortuguero, the ground is often waterlogged, and fer-de-lance snakes are abundant at night—hardly ideal conditions for camping.

Tortuguero sometimes fills up. You can reserve in advance by calling Olger Rivera at the community phone at Super Morpho, tel. 710-6716; you'll need to provide a return telephone number so that hotel owners can confirm your reservation. If you arrive without reservations, make it a priority to secure accommodations immediately. The **John H. Phipps Biological Field Station** has dormitory accommodations for up to 24 people, with communal kitchen and bathroom. Priority goes to researchers, students, and volunteers.

Shoestring: The **Cabinas Tortuguero,** adjacent to the beach, has simple but clean hostel-style rooms with communal outdoor bathroom. Rates: $5 pp. Another option is **Cabinas Meryscar,** tel. 290-2804, where 23 clean yet tiny bare-bones rooms with fans and shared bathrooms cost $5 pp. Cabins with hot water are slightly better—$19 d.

Tropical Lodge, tel. 710-2323 or 710-2608, 100 meters south of Super Morpho, has five very basic cabins with two single beds for sole furnishings, plus shared bath. Rates: $5 pp. It has a small restaurant over the water ($3 breakfast, $5 lunch or dinner). Patricio, the owner, was planning improvements. He also operates Arenas Tours.

Cabinas Aracari Lodge, tel. 798-3059, beside the soccer field 100 meters east of Super Morpho, has six nice little cabins with private bath with cold water. Rates: $7.50 pp. Nearby is **Cabinas Pancana** with seven bare-bones rooms in a two-story house. Rooms with private bath are gloomy and hot, despite having fans, and greatly overpriced at $12.50 s, $19 d. Rooms with shared bath cost $5 pp.

As a last resort, try **Cabinas Sabina,** with 35 basic rooms, plus a bar and rudimentary restaurant, and three newer rooms with private baths and fans facing the beach. Sabina, says another guidebook author, is not "the friendliest of souls." I found her surly. Rates: $4 pp; $7 with bath.

Budget: Miss Junie's, tel. 710-0523, at the north end of the village, has 24 clean and simply, albeit nicely, furnished rooms in a two-story unit, each with tiled floor, ceiling fan, screened windows, and large private bathroom with hot water. Rates: $17 pp. **Brisas del Mar** has a five-person room and offers live music in the bar on Wednesday and Saturday nights. Rates: $15.

The **Cabinas Tortuguero,** beeper tel. 223-3030, across the way, is run by friendly Italians Pepe and Morena. It has five simple rooms each with three single beds, ceiling fan, and private bath and hot water. Rates: $15 s, $20 d, $30 t. A small restaurant was to be added.

To the south is **Cabinas Riversal,** with four cabins with bathroom for $20 (available through the grocery next to Soda Caribbean).

Accommodations outside the Village

Most visitors arrive on tour packages and stay at one of several lodges along the lagoons beyond the village. Since several lodges are owned by tour companies, priority goes to people on the companies' own package tours You may be able to secure last minute reservations if room is available.

The **Canadian Organization for Tropical Education and Rainforest Conservation** (COTERC), P.O. Box 335, Pickering, Ont. L1V 2R6, tel. (416) 683-2116; or, in Costa Rica, beeper tel. 296-2626, has a research field station at Caño la Palma, about eight km north of Tortuguero. A dorm has bunk beds. You may also camp or sleep in hammocks. Rates: $40 including all meals and a guided walk on trails into the rainforest and swamps.

There are two lodges on the spit north of the village. About 800 meters north of Tortuguero is the **Mawamba Lodge,** tel. 223-7490, fax 222-5463, e-mail: mawamba@sol.racsa.co.cr, with 36 attractive rooms with private baths, fans, and rocking chairs reached by canopied walkways. The family-style restaurant and bar is airy and spacious. There's a swimming pool and sundeck with lounge chairs, plus a jacuzzi and a nature trail; natural history presentations are given each evening. A two-day/one-night package costs $243 s, $201 pp for two or more, high season; $201 and $159 respectively, low season. Other packages are offered.

Almost identical to Mawamba, the **Laguna Lodge,** tel./fax 225-3740, lies between the village and airstrip amid spacious landscaped grounds. The 26 modestly elegant, simply furnished rooms—in eight hardwood bungalows—have heaps of light, ceiling fans, and spacious private baths plus verandas. If you wish to relax in the grounds, simply hop into a hammock beneath thatched shade umbrellas. The lodge serves basic *típico* cuisine family style in a handsome *ranchito* restaurant. A swimming pool was to be added. It has 10 boats for nature trips, including one for 42 passengers. The owner lives on-site. Rates: $30 s, $45 d year-round; $219 for three days/two nights.

The **Pachira Lodge,** Apdo. 1818-1002 San José, tel. 256-7080, fax 223-1119, facing Mawamba two km north of Tortuguero on the west side of Laguna del Tortuguero, has thatched cabins of rough-hewn logs with polished hardwood floors. The cabins are connected by thatched walkways leading through lush grounds with trails that go into a 15-hectare patch of forest. All rooms have two double beds (made of bamboo), fans, attractive private tiled bathrooms, and verandas. There's a very attractive dining room serving buffet meals, plus a gift store, and a small bar with a TV/VCR. Guests get free use of canoes, and a pool was to be added. A slide show is given nightly at 6:30 p.m. Rates: $60 s/d room only; $176 for two days/one night; $239 for three days/two nights, including all meals.

The **Jungle Lodge,** about 400 meters north, is owned and operated by Cotur, Apdo. 26-1017, San José, tel. 233-0133, fax 233-0778, which promotes its three-day/two-night package featuring guided tours aboard the *Miss Caribe* and *Miss América* tour boats. Accommodations are in 50 rustic yet handsome, cross-ventilated *cabinas,* all with a double and a single bed, fans, large private bathrooms; they're linked by covered walkways. Oropendolas nest on the grounds. There's a small gift store, a game room, and a nice little bar and restaurant serving buffet meals. You can hire canoes *(cayucas)* for $5. Trails lead

into the forest. Hiking tours cost $15; fishing tours cost $40. Rates: $99, including meals. Packages are offered, and reservations are required.

The more basic and dull **El Manatí Lodge,** tel. 221-6148 (or through Ecole Travel, tel. 223-2240), three km north of the village, has six simply furnished rooms with floor fans and small private bathrooms with hot water, including two-room suites with bunks. There's a charmless bar with ping-pong. You can rent canoes and kayaks ($5). Rates: $17 s; $35 d including breakfast; $53 including breakfast and dinner; $200 for two-night stay, including transfers. **Viajes Río Tortuguero,** Apdo. 264-2050 San Pedro, tel./fax 225-1905, has a three-day, two-night package at Manatí Lodge for $200 pp.

The **Hotel Ilan Ilan,** 400 meters north of Manatí, has 28 large and comfortable but relatively spartan rooms, which feature private baths, fans, and ice coolers. The small but pleasant dining room serves *típico* meals. The lodge is owned and operated by Agencia Mitur, Apdo. 91, San José 1150, tel. 255-2031, fax 255-1946, e-mail: mitour@sol.racsa.co.cr, which offers two- and three-day packages ($160/215 including transfers, meals, and guided tours aboard the *Colorado Prince* or *Tortuguero Prince*.) Rates: $30 pp.

The basic **Caribe Lodge,** Apdo. 7433, San José 1000, beeper tel. 223-3333, formerly the Tatane Lodge, is one km from the village on the west bank of Laguna Penitencia. It has five small, A-frame, sparsely furnished bamboo huts with three beds and mosquito nets. The shared showers and toilets are in a separate hut. Plans were afoot to give two cabins their own private bathrooms. There's an atmospheric rustic restaurant and bar with hammocks. Rates: $85 pp, including transport to/from Moín, lodging (one night), and jungle excursions.

Half a kilometer along Laguna Penitencia is **Caribbean Magic Lodge,** tel. 235-0701. It features 12 spacious, thatch-roofed, modestly furnished cabins (painted jade-green), spaced a good distance apart amid gardens with trails lined by bougainvillea. Each has three beds, ceiling fan, veranda, and a clean tiled bathroom with hot water. A rustic lounge with lofty bamboo ceiling has a TV/VCR. There's a pool and wooden sundeck, plus fishing boats and tour boats (one for 14 passengers). You can visit on a one-day tour from San José, with lunch at the lodge. Rates:

$45 d, including breakfast. A three-day/two-night package costs $224 including transport.

The most appealing place is **Tortuga Lodge,** owned and operated by Costa Rica Expeditions, Apdo. 6941, San José 1000, tel. 257-0766, fax 257-1665. The lodge, which sits directly opposite the airstrip four km north of town, includes park visits in its room rates. It has 24 spacious and comfortable riverfront rooms surrounded by 20 hectares of landscaped grounds and forest. The wharf is a preferred spot for watching fishing bats that swoop and scoop in the wharf lights, and a short (albeit muddy) circular nature trail that leads from the gardens offers good sightings of poison-arrow frogs and other wildlife. You almost expect Tarzan and Jane to swing down from the trees and greet you as you dock. Standard and "deluxe" rooms (each with ceiling fans plus fully equipped bathrooms) are in handsome lodges made of hardwoods and fronted by wide verandas with leather rocking chairs. Each has comfy beds, huge screened windows, and splendid bathrooms with modern facilities and plenty of hot water. A recent upgrade has added an upscale restaurant serving excellent meals family style (outside on the veranda when its not raining), and a swimming pool and water-garden are planned. English-speaking staff and superb guides are under assured management. Rain ponchos are provided for boat tours (available 6:30 a.m.-5:30 p.m.; boats cost $40 per hour up to four people). Tortuga is also the only fishing lodge in Tortuguero. The lodge also offers hikes up Cerro Tortuguero ($11), turtle walks ($20), and boat transfers to Tortuguero village ($8-12 per boat), Barra del Colorado ($30 pp), and Matina or Moín. Both world-record snook and tarpon have been taken a short distance from Tortuga Lodge, and a former lodge manager, Eduardo Silva, holds the world's cubera snapper record. Rates: $97 s, $117 d, $135 t. Meals cost $13-21. Highly recommended!

Food

Not to be missed is dinner at **Miss Junie's,** whose mother, Sibella, used to feed the famed turtle-conservationist Archie Carr (in a grim irony, his favorite dish was green turtle soup). Today, $5 will buy you a platter of fish, chicken, or steak, with rice and beans simmered in coconut milk, plus fruit juice and dessert. **Soda Lilliana,** adja-

cent, offers *típico* Costa Rican meals for $1-3. You can buy breads, cakes, cinnamon rolls, omelettes, and lasagne at **Pancaca Restaurant.** And Evelyn, in the **Restaurant Caribeña,** 20 meters east of Super Morpho, proffers *típico* dishes including *casados* for $3, plus *batidos* and juices (50 cents-$1).

Entertainment

For night owls tired of turtlewatching and stargazing, there's **Bar La Culebra,** a really funky rough-hewn bar hanging over the water, where the local menfolk hang out supping one too many beers while the womenfolk are tending home. Decor is limited to girlie pictures. It's a colorful spot—when the *guaro* takes effect, your neighbor may decide to dive into the lagoon for the hell of it. There's dancing at **Disco El Bochinche** in the Salon Brisas del Mar, 100 meters north of Cabinas Sabina. Fancy a game of eight ball? Try the funky **pool hall** 150 meters south of Paraíso Tropical.

Shopping

For T-shirts and souvenirs, check out the **Jungle Shop** in the village center, or—better still—**Paraíso Tropical,** tel. 710-0323, 50 meters farther north by the main dock. The latter has a surprisingly large selection of shirts, swimwear, posters, jewelry, hammocks, etc. Owner Antoinette Gutierrez donates 10% of her profits to the local school. She may be able to cash traveler's checks.

Services

The **park headquarters office**—Cuatro Esquinas—is 200 meters south of the village. Super Morpho has the community **telephone,** tel. 710-6716. The **post office** and **police station** are in the village center.

Getting There and Away

By Air: **Travelair** and **SANSA** both operate scheduled daily flights between San José's Pavas Airport and the landing strip four km north of Tortuguero village (see the charts, "Travelair Schedule" and "SANSA Schedule"). **Costa Rica Expeditions,** Apdo. 6941, San José 1000, tel. 257-0766, fax 257-1665, operates a private plane. Tour members get priority, but you might get a spare seat ($60 one-way). Other tour operates arrange charter flights for about $280 per plane, one-way. There are no facilities at the airstrip.

By Boat: A colorful variety of private boats run from the JAPDEVA dock, tel. 758-1106, 758-3286, or 758-3417, in Moín to the rickety JAPDE-VA dock in Tortuguero. The *Riverboat Francesca*, piloted by Modesto Watson, Apdo. 218, San Francisco de Dos Ríos, San José, tel. 226-0986, is recommended; for $70 he'll take you to Tortuguero and back, with lunch and snacks and a guided cruise of the park. Carlos Bruno, Apdo. 2482, San José 1000, tel. 758-1210, offers a similar service from Limón. No reservations are needed. Cargo-cum-passenger boats also run irregularly via Parismina—3-10 hours, depending on vessel—but are not legally permitted to take passengers.

By Organized Tour: Most tour companies in San José and jungle lodges in Tortuguero offer tour packages featuring air charter or boat transfers via Moín.

REFUGIO NACIONAL DE VIDA SILVESTRE BARRA DEL COLORADO

One of the biggest of Costa Rica's wildlife preserves, Barra del Colorado National Wildlife Refuge (91,200 hectares) protects the vast rainforests and wetlands extending north from the estuary of Lagunas del Tortuguero to the Río San Juan, the international border with Nicaragua. About 30 km from the sea, the Río San Juan divides, with the San Juan flowing northeast and the main branch—the Río Colorado—flowing southeast to the sea through the center of the reserve. Dozens of tributaries form a labyrinth of permanent sloughs and ephemeral waterways that have made the region inaccessible to all but boat traffic. A series of finger-like lagoons span north from the lower reaches of the Río Colorado.

In many ways it is a replica of Tortuguero National Park—to which it is linked by the **Canal de Tortuguero**—on a larger scale and protects a similar panoply of wildlife. Great green macaws wing screeching over the canopy, mixed flocks of antbirds follow advancing columns of army ants, and jabiru storks with two-meter wingspans circle above, flying so high that they are no more than white motes in the sun. Cruising the small sloughs you might see caimans, manatees, peccaries, sloths, three species of monkeys, pacas, and, deep in the shadows, perhaps a jaguar or

tapir. Large crocodiles inhabit the rivers and can be seen basking on mudbanks.

The park is one of Costa Rica's wettest: the interior receives upward of 600 cm of rain a year. The Río Colorado branches from the Río San Juan some 30 km before its mouth and crosses a wide marshy region. The waterways are lined with ancient raffia palms. Riverside vines, too, grow more densely than the shaded vines deep in the forest, their host trees so thickly festooned with cascades of greenery that they resemble great walls of clipped and sculpted topiary. In the early winter, the tree-lined lagoons north of Barra are ablaze with the blossoms of bright yellow allamandas. No turtles nest here.

Barra del Colorado is a model for other parks because of the many small communities with roots in the region: although it is virtually without roads, a maze of navigable waterways has spawned tiny farmsteads and communities along the rivers. Conservationists are struggling to protect the wildlife refuge from illegal logging. Though plans exist to link Barra del Colorado and Tortuguero to form a continuous, protected corridor, the Rafael Calderón administration gave Geest, the British banana company, permission to log the interceding forest.

There's a ranger station west of Silver King Lodge. Entrance costs 75 cents (200 *colones*) payable at the ranger station, or at the Cuatro Esquinas ranger station in Tortuguero village.

Sportfishing "Paradise"

The rivers hereabouts are famous for their game fishing. There are several sportfishing lodges within the refuge, concentrated in the village of Barra del Colorado. They are perfect oases after a day in the sun fighting tarpon and snook. Tarpon are so abundant and feisty hereabouts that a two-meter whopper might well jump into your boat. Gar—one of the oldest fish on earth, with an ancestry dating back 90 million years—is also common; growing up to two meters long, these bony-scaled fish have long, narrow, crocodile-like snouts full of vicious teeth. A recently discovered blue-water fishery is "offering some big surprises."

In 1994 Nicaraguan authorities began charging for use of the Río San Juan at $5 pp, plus $7 per boat *(you must now carry your passport on the river)*.

In addition to the sportfishing lodges, a 20-meter a/c houseboat—the *Rain Goddess,* Blue Wing International, Apdo. 850, Escazú, tel. 231-4299, fax 231-3816, e-mail: bluewing@ticonet.cr; in the U.S., tel. (800) 308-3394—offers fishing on the San Juan, Colorado, and adjacent Nicaraguan rivers. Six cabins each have a queen-size and single bed, sink, and vanity. Three shared bathrooms have hot water and showers. It has an observation deck and dining room, plus TV and VCR. Two outboards are towed for fishing otherwise inaccessible areas. Rates: $1,350 pp, five-day package including all meals plus air transportation from San José. Guided nature trips are also offered.

Barra del Colorado Village
Unexciting and ramshackle Barra sits astride the mouth of the 600-meter-wide Río Colorado. **Barra del Norte,** on the north side of the river, has no roads (just dirt paths—littered with trash—and a broken concrete walkway down its center between cabins made of corrugated tin and wooden crates). The all-important soccer field is here, however. The slightly more salubrious **Barra del Sur** has the airstrip and most of the hamlet's few services. The locals are aloof and wary of strangers. (Many of them have rheumy eyes—too much ganja?)

The village once prospered as a lumber center but went into decline during two decades of Nicaraguan conflict, when the village became a haven for Nicaraguan refugees. Barra's fortunes are slowly returning as cargo traffic with Nicaragua increases. Locals predominantly rely on lobster fishing or serving as guides for the half-dozen sportfishing lodges. Beside being a sportfishing center, it is also a splendid base for nature trips upriver, and for spotting crocodiles, which lounge on the sandbars of the wide and murky Río Colorado.

Despite the end to the conflicts, tensions with Nicaragua run high, not least because Nicaraguan disputes Costa Rica's territorial rights to land north of the Río Colorado and because the Río San Juan is entirely Nicaraguan territory (when you are on the water you are inside Nicaragua). Ostensibly Costa Ricans have right of use. Nonetheless, in May 1994 a Nicaraguan navy gunboat arrested five U.S. sportfishermen and three Costa Rican guides at the mouth of the river for "violating Nicaraguan territorial waters." Those arrested claim they were inside Costa Rican waters. An agreement signed in 1994 between Presidents Figueres and Chamorro was aimed at more convivial relations.

Accommodations
Most lodges hereabouts rely on group business. When there are no groups in, they can be lonely places.

Budget: Supposedly, **Cabinas Leo** offers cheap and very basic accommodations in Barra del Norte. Also for hardy budget travelers is **Tarponland Lodge,** tel. 710-6917, in Barra del Sur. It offers 12 bare-bones, dingy *cabinas* with fans but no hot water. Some have shared bathrooms. There's a basic restaurant. The swimming pool was empty when I visited. In 1996, the place was bought by Eduardo Silva, former manager of Tortuga Logde in Tortuguero, but at press time no improvements had been made. Eduardo arranges fishing trips and nature tours. Rates: $25 d; $45 with three meals. *Overpriced!*

At the east end of Barra del Norte is the spartan **Tropical Tarpon,** tel. 225-2336; in Canada tel. (514) 469-4861, with five basic cabins on swampy land crossed by narrow raised walkways. There's a basic restaurant and bar, and a decrepit dock. The manager is surly.

Moderate: The German-run **Samay Lagoon Lodge,** Samay Tours, tel. 284-7047, fax 383-6370 or tel./fax 236-7154, e-mail: samaycr@sol. racsa.co.cr, website www.cool.co.cr/samay, on the south shore of Laguna Samay, six km south of Barra del Colorado, claims to be the "only lodge in the area located right at the Caribbean waterfront." It's 100 meters from the ocean. It has 22 rooms, modestly furnished, with ceiling fans, mosquito nets, and tiled bathrooms with hot water. There's a handsome restaurant. It offers canoe tours, and you can rent fiberglass canoes. It's not a fishing lodge, but fishing can be arranged. Rates: $75 pp including all meals and canoe use. It has a three-day "Samay Lagoon Safari" from San José with roundtrip boat trip via Puerto Viejo de Sarapiquí and canoeing in the lagoons, plus accommodations and all meals ($278 pp). There's also a "Deluxe Safari" package with air instead of boat transport ($375).

The attractive **Isla de Pesca,** Apdo. 8-4390, San José 1000, tel. 223-4560, fax 221-5148; in the

U.S., Costa Sol International, 1717 N. Bayshore Dr., Suite 3333, Miami, FL 33132, tel. (800) 245-8420 or (305) 539-1632, fax (305) 539-1123, on the east shore of Laguna Agua Dulce, 1.5 km north of Barra del Norte, has a South Seas feel. The 20 thatched A-frame cabins—a bit mildewed and in need of a face-lift—are raised on stilts amid clipped lawns. They're painted an appealing yellow with blue trim. Each has two double beds, a porch, ceiling fan, and hot water. It's open year-round and offers three-, five-, and seven-day packages for $999-1,375.

About 600 meters farther north is the **Casa Mar Fishing Lodge,** Apdo. 825, San José, tel. 441-2820, fax 433-9287; or, in the U.S., Bob Marriott's Travel Center, 2634 W. Orangethorpe #6, Fullerton, CA 92833, tel. (714) 578-1881 or (800) 543-0282, fax (800) 367-2299, which offers 12 comfortable, spacious, thatched and rustic duplex cabins set in attractive landscaped grounds. Each has screened windows, fans, and clean bathrooms. There's a handsome restaurant with wraparound windows, and a bar with leather Sarchí rockers, a dartboard, and large-screen TV/VCR. It's open only during fishing season, Sept.-Oct. and Jan.-May. Rates: $320-395 per fishing day, including lodging, all meals, and open bar. Packages begin at $960-1,185 for three nights including fishing.

The venerable **Río Colorado Lodge,** Apdo. 5094, San José 1000, tel. 232-8610 or 232-4063, fax 321-5987; in the U.S., 12301 N. Oregon Ave., Tampa, FL 33612, tel. (813) 931-4849 or (800) 243-9777, fax (813) 933-3280, at Barra del Sur, is unmistakable with its blue-and-white striped paintjob and a bright yellow roof. Its 18 comfortable rooms are open to the breeze and have private baths, hot showers, electric fans; daily laundry service provided. The rooms, plus dining and recreation areas, are connected by covered walkways perched on stilts (when the river rises the lodge extends only a few inches above the level of the water). The lodge contains a small zoo featuring an aviary with toucans and macaws, plus deer, spider and capuchin monkeys, and "Baby," a tapir that is let out to wander the bar and beg for scratches and bananas. The lodge features a main thatch-roofed bar and restaurant, plus an open-air restaurant-cum-bar on the riverfront, complete with hammocks. The lodge is equipped with a complete tackle shop, plus a large fleet of 5.5-meter boats with two fighting chairs. The lodge offers five-, six-, and seven-night packages, including air transfers from San José ($1,275-1,945). Extra fishing days are $375. Rates: $390 pp daily including fishing and all meals; $75 for nonfishing guests.

The German-run **Delta Colorado Lodge,** c/o José Rosello, tel. 257-8866, is about 20 km upriver, on the north shore of Isla Brava (a huge island bounded by the Ríos Caño Bravo and Colorado). This venerable lodge has 12 simple cabins with mosquito nets and private bath with cold water. Trails lead into the forest, and guided hikes and boat rides are offered (but not sportfishing).

Expensive: Upriver 300 meters is the **Silver King Lodge,** tel. 281-1403, fax 381-0849, slvrkng@sol.racsa.co.cr; in the U.S., Dept. 1597, P.O. Box 025216, Miami, FL 33102, tel. (813) 942-7959 or (800) 847-3474, fax (813) 943-8783, with 10 spacious duplexes, widely spaced and linked by covered catwalks. All cabins are modestly furnished, with queen-size beds with orthopedic mattresses, plus private baths with their own water heaters and large showers. Other features include a small swimming pool and sundeck with hammocks, a huge colonial-tiled indoor jacuzzi, well-equipped tackle shop, plus a spacious bar and restaurant (with "gourmet chef," they say) done in hardwoods with a wide-screen TV and VCR. Free beer, rum, and soft drinks are included. Fishing is from 10 six-meter Carolina skiffs and offshore boats (and five-meter aluminum canoes for rainforest fishing). Rates: $107 pp including meals. Package prices—from $1,815 s, $1,495 pp d for three days fishing, to $2,615 s, $2,080 pp d for five days—include roundtrip airfare from San José, alcoholic drinks, meals, transfers, and laundry service. Extra fishing days cost $401 s, $375 pp d. Ray Barry is the friendly manager. *Outside* magazine ranks it one of the top 50 lodges in the world.

Food

You're restricted to the lodges above—or, in Barra del Sur, to the quaint **Soda Fiesta** in the pink two-story building on the east side of the airstrip; it serves burgers ($1.50), hot dogs ($1), and chicken and fries ($2). Another restaurant is under construction 50 meters away.

Services

In Barra del Sur, the **Salon Los Almendros** is a small grocery and bar 100 meters east of and behind the Río Colorado Lodge. The heart and soul of things is **C y D Souvenirs,** tel. 710-6592, run by a Canadian, Diana Graves, who offers fax and photocopying services and acts as the post office, public telephone, tourist information service, and Travelair ticket rep. There's another public telephone in the bar of the Tarponland Lodge. The tiny **police station** is wharfside at the end of the airstrip.

Barra del Norte has two *pulperías* and not much else.

Getting There and Away

By Air: SANSA flies daily from San José. You can also charter a light plane from San José.

By Boat: Transportes Cocodrilo, based at the Hotel Bambú in Puerto Viejo de Sarapiquí, operates scheduled boat service to Barra del Colorado from Puerto Viejo on Tuesday and Friday at 9 a.m. ($35), continuing to Tortuguero at 12: 30 p.m. ($20). The boat departs Tortuguero on Thurs-

day and Sunday at 9 a.m. for Barra del Colorado, continuing to Puerto Viejo at 10:30 a.m.

You can also hire private boats from Tortuguero, Moín, Los Chiles, and Puerto Viejo de Sarapiquí. A rough road leads from Puerto Viejo de Sarapiquí to Pavas (at the juncture of the Ríos Toro and Sarapiquí rivers), where you can also charter a boat.

Do not attempt to reach Barra by boat without a guide, as there are several braided channels to negotiate and it is easy to get lost. A local guide and canoe cost $3 pp per hour.

By Road: Some of the plantation villages southwest of Barra del Colorado have bus service. Reportedly, buses depart Guápiles to Cariari (21 km north), from where in dry season another bus journeys to a place called Puerto Lindo, on the Río Colorado. According to some sources a boat leaves Puerto Lindo for Barra at 4:50 a.m.

Tours: The **Río Colorado Lodge** (see above) offers a two-day, one-night package from San José, including bus to Moín, canal cruise to Barra del Colorado, and return flight to San José.

jade amulet

BOB RACE

THE SOUTHERN CARIBBEAN

South from Puerto Limón, a succession of sandy shores leads the eye along the Talamanca coast toward Panamá. The beaches are popular with surfers and offbeat adventurers, but have now been discovered by mainstream tourists. Eight of Costa Rica's 34 "protected zones" lie in Talamanca, including the nation's only true coral reef. The coast is sparsely settled, with tiny villages spaced far apart.

The region, a mellow melting pot, has long been a cultural bastion for Bribrí and Cabecar Indians, who lived in the mountains, and English-speaking black immigrants from the Caribbean islands who settled along the coast and centered on a village originally called The Bluff. In 1915, a presidential decree changed the name to Cahuita, a combination of the Miskito Indian words *cawi*—a small tree with red wood that flourishes in coastal lowlands and is used to make dugouts—and *ta,* which means point of land. Hence, "mahogany point." A decade ago, the *Monilia* fungus destroyed the cacao plantations which had sustained the region for generations.

It has traditionally been hard to get to Talamanca, which remained isolated from national commerce before the opening of the coast road in the late 1970s. Life along the southern Caribbean is still lived at an easy pace. Making a public telephone call can take all afternoon. Services are minimal. And locals complain of being neglected by government. Paula Palmer's book *What Happen* depicts the traditional lifestyle of the Talamanca coast.

The paved—but badly potholed—road hugs the shore as far south as Puerto Viejo before continuing inland to Bribrí, from where another dirt road extends south from to Gandoca-Manzanillo National Park and to Sixaola, on the Panamanian border while others reach into the Talamancas. From Puerto Viejo, a dirt road runs to Manzanillo.

The weather is almost always humid. Though the region is slightly drier than the northern Caribbean, heavy rains can fall virtually any time of year. Then, the sea and sky are whipped into blending shades of gray, horses and cows stand about aimlessly, and water lies everywhere. The April 1991 earthquake and a series of devastating floods that same year struck the region a severe blow, wiping out half a dozen bridges on the road south from Limón. February to March and Sept.-Oct. are the driest months.

Talamanca Voice, Apdo. 7043-1000 San José, tel. 233-6613, fax 223-7479, e-mail: wolf-biss@sol.racsa.co.cr, is a quarterly regional newspaper published by Wanda Bissinger.

Remember that the Caribbean region has more crime against tourists than any other region. Especially south of Limón, be careful and avoid situations that might leave you vulnerable to theft, muggings, even rape.

PUERTO LIMÓN TO ESTRELLA

South of Puerto Limón, the shore is lined by brown-sand beach fringed by palms. The road makes brief forays inland to cross the Río Banano and, about 30 km south of Limón, the Río Estrella a few km north of the village of **Penshurst,** from where a branch road leads into the Valle del Río Estrella. Near the coast, the Río Estrella gives rise to a dense network of channels and lagoons that provide shelter for 180 species of birds, including great flocks of snow-white cattle egrets, which roost at dusk on the riverbanks. **Rancho del Sol,** immediately north of Aviarios del Caribe, offers birdwatching and fishing and has boats for rent.

Orchid-lovers may thrill to **Orquídeas Mundo,** Apdo. 575, Puerto Limón 7300, fax 758-2818, a botanical nursery where French-Canadian botanist Pierre Dubois hybridizes rare orchid species. Pierre will happily give you a tour, or guide you on a nature hike into nearby forests ($5). Turn west at the sign for Penshurst after crossing the Río Estrella. The nursery, based around an old school bus-turned-home, is on the right after 500 meters.

Aviarios del Caribe

This privately owned 75-hectare wildlife sanctuary and sloth refuge, also known as the **Caribbean Biological Bird Station,** Apdo. 569-7300 Puerto

Limón, tel./fax 382-1335, one km north of the Río Estrella, protects a marshland ecosystem of freshwater lagoons threatened by the effects of fertilizers washing down from nearby banana planta- tions (the fertilizers have caused the marsh grass- es to bloom prodigiously). The lagoons are a haven for caimans, river otters, and river turtles, as well as more than 300 bird species, plus mon-

YES, WE HAVE PROBLEMS WITH BANANAS

In 1967, banana plantations covered some 10,000 hectares of Costa Rica, and about nine million bunches a year were being exported. By 1995, more than 40,000 hectares were given to bananas and Costa Rica was well on its way to overtaking Ecuador as the world's largest banana exporter. So what's wrong with that?

Let's start with soil productivity. Banana production is a monoculture that causes ecological damage. Banana plants deplete ground nutrients quickly, re- quiring heavy doses of fertilizer to maintain produc- tivity. Eventually, the land is rendered useless for other agricultural activities. Fertilizers washed down by streams have been blamed for the profuse growth of water hyacinths and reed grasses that now clog the canals and wildfowl habitats, such as the estuary of the Río Estrella. And silt washing down from the plantations is acknowledged as the principal cause of the death of the coral reef within Cahuita Nation- al Park and, more recently, of Gandoca-Manzanillo.

Bananas are also prone to disease and insect assault. Pesticides such as the nematocide DBCP (banned in the U.S. but widely used in Costa Rica) are blamed for poisoning and sterilizing plantation workers, and for major fish kills in the Tortuguero canals. Even marine turtles are threatened. Plastic bags are wrapped around the fruit stems and filled with insecticides and fungicides, which kill the fungus responsible for the black marks on skins. Once the stems are cut, the banana companies have tradi- tionally dumped the plastic bags in streams—you can see them washed up at flood levels on tree branches throughout the lowlands—to be washed out to sea, where turtles mistake them for jellyfish, eat them, and suffocate.

Campaigns by local pressure groups and the threat of international boycotts are beginning to spark a new awareness among the banana com- panies. The plastic bags are now supposedly being saved for recycling (for every ton of bananas, 2.14 tons of waste is produced). A project called "Ba- nana Amigo" recommends management guidelines. Companies that follow the guidelines are awarded an Eco-OK seal of approval to help them export bananas; companies continuing to clear forests are

not. The Eco-OK program is a joint project of the Costa Rican environmental group Fundación Ambio and the international Rainforest Alliance. (The stick- er shows a yellow sun rising behind a map of the world.) The government-backed National Banana Corporation (CORBANA) has mounted a campaign to prove that it is cleaning up its act. The banana in- dustry, it claims, is turning green.

In 1994, the Río Sixaola plantation in Bribrí be- came the first Costa Rican producer to receive an Eco-OK label. Owner Volker Ribniger uses a mini- mum of pesticides and herbicides; contaminated water is run through a special filtering system; or- ganic wastes are recycled; and plastic bags are collected for recycling.

Green or not, massive tracts of virgin forest contin- ue to be put to the blade to meet the expansion of banana plantations. In mid-1992, for example, Chiquita Brands International announced a massive banana expansion of 6,000 hectares in the economically de- pressed areas of Limón, Sarapiquí, and Sixaola. Ba- nana producers assert that the industry provides badly needed jobs. Environmentalists claim that devastating environmental effects are not worth the trade-off for a product for which demand is so fickle. The multina- tional corporations, too, are hardly known for philan- thropy. Workers' unions, for example, have histori- cally been pushed out of the banana fields, and some banana companies—most recently the British com- pany Geest, in 1996—have been accused of operat- ing plantations under virtual slave-labor conditions.

The Calderón administration sided with the ba- naneros and supported expansion by improving the infrastructure in areas desirable for banana planta- tions. This, despite pleas from the local government of Limón—which derives its greatest source of in- come from bananas—to stop banana companies from clearcutting the forests of the Caribbean zone. The pleas have fallen on deaf ears. The Limón gov- ernment and environmentalists, for example, recently denounced Geest's clearcutting of forests separating Barra del Colorado and Tortuguero National Parks. The fragile region was supposedly protected by a management plan. But the Ministry of Natural Re- sources issued permits to Geest anyway.

keys and sloths; jungle trails lead to a lookout blind. You don't even need to head off into the sloughs, however, to spot wildlife—the owners have a veritable menagerie on-site, including Buttercup, an orphaned sloth, Pink Cheeks the boa constrictor, Coco the crocodile, a couple of tame toucans, and dozens of poison-arrow frogs spawned in the hatchery. Guided canoe trips cost $30 pp. Trips up the Río Estrella are also offered.

Accommodations and Food

Cabinas Westfalia, four km south of Limón, is basic. There's a modest house on stilts—**Beachhouse Bed & Breakfast**—400 meters farther south, but I haven't tried it.

Rancho Típico Viscaya (no telephone), one km south of the Río Viscaya, has three modest beachfront *cabinas* with private bathroom and cold water for $6 s, $11 d, $21 t/quad.

Selvamar Hotel & Club Campestre Cahuita, tel. 758-2861 or 233-1911, 22 km south of Puerto Limón, is a modestly attractive albeit slightly run-down resort 200 meters from a lonesome beach that seems to stretch to eternity. The lobby provides a touch of Tahiti with its attractive bamboo furnishings in bright floral prints and soaring *palenque* roof. The restaurant is similar. There's a large swimming pool. Choose from a/c *cabinas* or more basic rooms (52 in all) set amid shade trees and boasting color TVs. Some have kitchenettes. Rates: $15 s, $30 d, $35 t, $40 quad.

Cabinas Lemari, tel. 758-2859, five km farther south, has six very basic *cabinas* with cold water, plus a bar, a roadside *soda,* and a public telephone; fishing trips can be arranged. Rates: $8.

Aviarios del Caribe, Apdo. 569-7300 Puerto Limón, tel./fax 382-1335, one km north of the Río Estrella, offers one of the best bargains on the Caribbean coast. The beautiful modern lodge has five spacious, superbly furnished rooms featuring tiled floors, king-size beds, and ultramodern bathrooms. There's also a small gym, laundry service, a TV and video room with library, and a screened upstairs restaurant with beautiful hardwood floors. The friendly and erudite owners, Luis and Judy Arroyo, can arrange tours into the Talamanca mountains. *Highly recommended!* Rates: $50 s, $55 d low season; $60 s, $65 d high season, including breakfast. First-come, first-served.

Getting There and Away

The direct San José-Sixaola bus (Autotransportes MEPE) leaves from Gran Terminal del Caribe, tel. 257-1961, fax 256-4248, on Calle Central, Avenidas 15/17 daily at 6 a.m. and 3:30 p.m., passing Penshurst, Cahuita, and beyond (you may hop off the bus at any point that takes your fancy). A regular bus departs the same terminal on weekends at 8 a.m. Local buses depart Puerto Limón, Calles 3 and 4 and Avenida 4, for the Valle de Estrella and Pandora every two hours 5 a.m.-6 p.m.

VALLE DEL RÍO ESTRELLA

The Valle del Río Estrella is a wide basin blanketed by banana plantations of the Dole Standard Fruit Company—you'll gain no idea of the vastness of these plantations driving along Hwy. 36. The Río Estrella is spawned in the foothills of the Matama mountains (part of the Talamanca massif), where it collects the runoff of some 700 cm of rainfall and irrigates the banana plantations as it crosses the broad plains in search of the Caribbean. The banana plantations are an interesting study.

To the west rise the steep-sided, heavily forested Talamancas protected within the Parque Internacional La Amistad, but severely threatened by illicit logging.

Selva Bananito Reserve

This 950-hectare privately owned reserve, run by Conselvatur, Apdo. 801, San José 1007, tel./fax 253-8118, e-mail: costari@netins.net, website www.netins.net/showcase/costarica; in the U.S., 850 Juniper Ave., Kellogg, IA 50135-8677, tel./fax (515) 236-3894, on the edge of the Parque Internacional La Amistad, protects primary rainforest on the slopes of the Talamancas. Two-thirds is rainforest. The rest is devoted to low-impact agriculture and cattle management. A wide range of hiking (from $10) and horseback riding (from $20) options are offered, as are tree-climbing using rope-and-saddle ($20-50), mountain biking (from $20), overnight camping ($60), birding ($30), and other excursions. You can rent also bikes ($3 per hour; $12 per day). A trip to a Dole banana packing plant is offered.

The reserve, 15 km inland from Bananito (five km inland from the coast road), is a harpy to get to—but great fun in a high-clearance 4WD (absolutely essential) along a muddy track churned into a Somme-like assault course by logging trucks. There are no signs. Ask in the village of Bananito, where you cross the railway lines and keep going straight; take the right fork at a Y-junction. Eventually you'll get to a metal gate with a sign reading "No entrance. Private Property." You've arrived. There are two more barbed wire gates to pass through, then you have to drive along a riverbed to cross to the lodge (or you can park at the farm facing the lodge).

Accommodations

Selva Bananito Lodge, (see above), cellular tel. 284-4278, has seven simple yet elegant cabins on stilts on a ridge with views down the valley and towards the surrounding mountains. Each has a queen- and full-size bed, large, reading lamps, tiled bathroom and solar-heated water (there's no electricity), and deck with hammocks for enjoying the splendid view. The lodge is eco-sensitive in every way (the cabins are even made of salvaged wood). Dining is family style. Per person rates: $85 s, $65 d, $55 t, $50 q; $15 children under 12. A guided tour is included for stays of two nights or more. Ten percent of all revenues are donated to the Fundación Cuencas de Limón, a nonprofit organization dedicated to the protection of watersheds in Limón province.

Getting There

Local "Banana Train:" A fascinating way to get close to the locals is to ride on the local passenger service—not to be confused with the famous but defunct "Banana Train" that once operated from San José to Limón—that operates daily at 4 a.m. and 2:30 p.m. from Puerto Limón ($1.20 each way; tel. 758-3314). The roundtrip journey takes about five hours. Don't expect comfort. Seats are of the old-school-bus variety, bolted to the floors. Your companions will be local plantation workers and perhaps the odd backpacker. The weary iron horse groans along past ramshackle villages and lonesome corrugated-tin shacks interspersed between row upon row of banana plants and orderly plantation villages with names such as Finca 6 and Finca 8, where it lurches to a stop before jerking along

past Penshurst, winding west down the valley of the Río Estrella. The train returns for Limón at 6 a.m. and 4:30 p.m. If you want to take it one way only and continue to Cahuita or Puerto Viejo, get off at Bonifacio, 38 km south of Limón; from here, it's a 10-minute walk to the coastal highway, where you can hail any passing buses.

RESERVA BIOLÓGICA HITOY-CERERE

Virtually undeveloped and distinctly off the beaten track, the 9,050-hectare Hitoy-Cerere Biological Reserve is the nation's least visited park. It is surrounded by three indigenous reservations—Talamanca, Telire, and Estrella—and backed by the steep and rugged Talamanca mountains, which make the reserve seem all but inaccessible. Dense evergreen forests are watered by innumerable rivers, including the Hitoy, an Indian name for a moss-bedded stream, and the Cerere, meaning "River of Clear Waters."

Take your pick of arduous trails or moderately easy walks from the ranger station along the deep valley of the Río Hitoy-Cirere to waterfalls with natural swimming holes. Large sections of the park's western and southern flanks have not been explored, and trails into the interior are overgrown, unmarked, and challenging (Indian guides are available for local hikes). The park is a starting point for trans-Talamanca journeys to the Pacific via a trail that leads south to the Indian village of San José Cabecar and up the valley of the Río Coén and across the saddle between Cerro Betsú (2,500 meters) and Cerro Arbolado (2,626 meters) to Ujarrás, in the Valle de El General.

Rainfall is prodigious: seven meters a year is not unknown. When the sun shines, the park is spectacular. However, there is no defined dry season (March, September, and October are usually the driest months; July-Aug. and Nov.-Dec. are marked by torrential rains and storms). The result: one of the best specimens of wet tropical forest in the country. Large cats are also found throughout the reserve, as well as healthy populations of margays, tapirs, peccaries, agoutis, pacas, otters, and monkeys. The park is one of the last remaining strongholds of the harpy eagle. And Montezuma oropendolas, rare blue-headed parrots, toucans, and squirrel cuckoos are common.

margay

BOB RACE

Entrance: $6. Contact the Servicio de Parques Nacionales, tel. 259-2239 or call toll-free 192, for information.

Accommodations
You can reserve basic lodging at the ranger station, tel. 233-5473; researchers get priority. Most likely, you'll not be able to get through to the ranger station microwave telephone, so check with the National Parks Service headquarters in San José, tel. 233-4160. Camping is permitted, but there are no facilities.

Organized Tours
Javier Martín, tel. 758-1123, fax 758-4409, a naturalist guide, offers packages that include a night at the Hotel Matama in Puerto Limón, plus three meals, transport to Hitoy-Cerere, and guided hikes.

Getting There
By Car: From Puerto Limón, turn right at Penshurst and follow the unpaved road via Pandora. The road is reportedly passable even in rainy season, though a 4WD is needed even in dry season. Still, you may not be able to make it all the way. It's a 90-minute drive from both Puerto Limón and Cahuita. Jeep taxis from Cahuita cost about $30 each way (you will need to arrange your return pickup in advance if you stay overnight in the park). Reportedly, the local banana company, tel. 587-0753, may be able to provide transport.

By Bus: A local bus departs every two hours 5 a.m.-6 p.m. from Puerto Limón (Calles 3/4, Avenida 4) to the Estrella Valley Standard Fruit Co. banana plantation, 10 km from the park en-

trance. Taxis from Finca 6 in the Estrella Valley cost about $5.

CAHUITA

This offbeat village (pop. 3,000), 45 km south of Puerto Limón and one km east of Hwy. 36, is an in-vogue destination for the young backpacking crowd and others for whom an escapist vacation means back to basics. It gets very crowded on holidays but for much of the rest of the year is free from the hordes that descend on, say, Manuel Antonio National Park (typically, no more than 50 people a day enter Cahuita National Park, which abuts the village). Cahuita is totally laid-back and definitely not for those seeking luxuries. The village is no more than two parallel dirt streets crossed by four rutted streets overgrown with grass, with ramshackle houses spread apart throughout.

What you get is golden and "black" sand beaches backed by coconut palms, an offshore coral reef (now severely depleted, thanks to effluents washing out from the banana plantations), and an immersion in Creole culture. One of the most endearing aspects of life on the southern Caribbean coast is the large number of Rastafarians, with their broad smiles, dreadlocks, and a lifestyle that revolves around reggae, rasta, and—discreetly—ganja. Bob Marley is God in Cahuita. Even the postmaster has dreads.

The April 1991 earthquake raised the coast hereabouts, exposed most of the coral reef and dealt a devastating blow to the local economy. Though visitors are returning to Puerto Viejo (eight km south), once-popular Cahuita has not yet recovered—a fact not helped by a lingering negative perception fed by a brief series of robberies and a murder in 1994 at Estrella (the gang was caught). Cahuita also received the short end of the stick from the government following the Park Service uproar over increased park visitation fees to $15 in 1994. Since Cahuita relies on budget travelers, local hotels and businesses challenged the fee increase in the Supreme Court and soon found themselves in a surreal battle with the Minister of Natural Resources (MINEREM), who urged a boycott of Cahuita. The ministry even refused to sell tickets for Cahuita National Park at its San José headquarters, and stopped staffing the park entrance booths (proof that bureaucrats are experts at cutting off their own noses to spite their faces). Worse, MINEREM officials began playing up the robberies and murder at Estrella while insultingly implying that Cahuita's low-budget visitors are drug-crazed dropouts. True, drugs here are an easy purchase, but the statement was an affront to the majority of tourists. Fortunately,

the town and the ministry resolved their differences, resulting in a joint administrative committee to administer the park.

The locals have formed a committee to police the community, keep the beaches clean, and generally foster improvements. And in 1998 plans were also afoot for a community center, while the main road into Cahuita will be turned into a palm-lined boulevard, with interlocking-

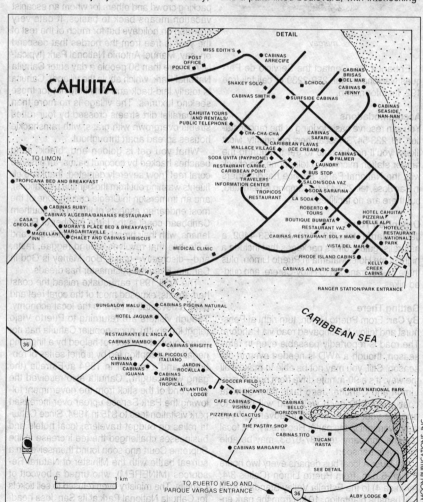

CAHUITA

TO LIMON

DETAIL

MISS EDITH'S
POST OFFICE
POLICE
CABINAS ARRECIFE
CABINAS BRISAS DEL MAR
SNAKEY SOLO
SCHOOL
CABINAS JENNY
CABINAS SMITH
SURFSIDE CABINAS
CABINAS SEASIDE/NAN-NAN
CAHUITA TOURS AND RENTALS/PUBLIC TELEPHONE
CHA-CHA-CHA
CABINAS SAFARI
CARIBBEAN FLAVAS (ICE CREAM)
WALLACE VILLAGE
CABINAS PALMER
SODA UVITA (PAYPHONE)
RESTAURANT CARIBE, CARIBBEAN POINT
LAUNDRY
TRAVELERS INFORMATION CENTER
BUS STOP
SALON/SODA VAZ
SODA SARAFINA
TROPICOS RESTAURANT
LA SODA
ROBERTO TOURS
HOTEL CAHUITA/PIZZERIA DELLE ALPI
BOUTIQUE BUMBATA
RESTAURANT VAZ
HOTEL/RESTAURANT NATIONAL PARK
CABINAS /RESTAURANT SOL Y MAR
VISTA DEL MAR
MEDICAL CLINIC
RHODE ISLAND CABINS
CABINAS ATLANTIC SURF
KELLY CREEK CABINS
RANGER STATION/PARK ENTRANCE

TROPICANA BED AND BREAKFAST
CABINAS RUBY
CABINAS ALGEBRA/BANANAS RESTAURANT
CASA CREOLE
MAGELLAN INN
MORAY'S PLACE BED & BREAKFAST/MARGARITAVILLE
CHALET AND CABINAS HIBISCUS

PLAYA NEGRA

CARIBBEAN SEA

BUNGALOW MALU
CABINAS PISCINA NATURAL
HOTEL JAGUAR
RESTAURANTE EL ANCLA
CABINAS MAMBO
CABINAS BRIGITTE
IL PICCOLO ITALIANO
CABINAS NIRVANA
CABINAS IGUANA
JARDIN ROCALLA
CABINAS JARDIN TROPICAL
ATLANTIDA LODGE
SOCCER FIELD
EL ENCANTO
CAHUITA NATIONAL PARK
CAFE CABINAS VISHNU
CABINAS BELLO HORIZONTE
PIZZERIA EL CACTUS
THE PASTRY SHOP
CABINAS TITO
TUCAN RASTA
CABINAS MARGARITA
SEE DETAIL

36

TO PUERTO VIEJO AND PARQUE VARGAS ENTRANCE

36

ALBY LODGE

MOON

0   1 km

© MOON PUBLICATIONS, INC.

brick paving for the other roads (the first hint that the government may be beginning to invest in Cahuita's fortunes and future).

Beaches

Three slender beaches lie within a short walking distance of Cahuita village. North of Cahuita is a black-sand beach (Playa Negra) that runs for miles. Cahuita's more famous beach is a two-km-long scimitar of golden sand that stretches south from the village along the shore of the national park; in 1997 the beach won two of 10 Bandera Azul awards for environmental quality. Beware riptides at the northern end of this beach. A second pale-sand beach lies farther along, beyond the rocky headland of Punta Cahuita. The latter is protected by an offshore coral reef and provides safer swimming in calmer waters.

Do not leave possessions unattended while swimming; they may not be there when you return. Also, nude bathing is not allowed.

Carnavalitos Cahuita

Cahuita hosts a five-day mini-Carnival in early December, when theater comes to town, the calypso and reggae is cranked up, and locals and tourists let their hair down.

Samasati Retreat Center

This holistic retreat, Apdo. 203-2070, San José, tel. 224-1870, e-mail: samasati@samasati.com; in the U.S., 721 Mountain View Ave., Petaluma, CA 94952, tel. (888) 867-4397, is hidden amid 100 hectares of private rainforest nudging up to the BriBrí and Cabecar indigenous reserves on the slopes behind Cahuita. It specializes in classes in yoga, shiatsu, reflexology, astrology, and other meditative practices, and offers a wide range of daily, weekly, and monthly workshops and sessions, plus hikes, horseback rides, and other excursions. It also hosts a music workshop. Accommodations are in 10 handsome Japanese-style log cabins with ocean and jungle vistas, all with verandas and loft bedrooms. There is also a five-room guest house with shared bathroom, and three two-bedroom *casas* with living rooms and kitchens. Vegetarian meals are served buffet-style, with seafood on request. Rates: $50 s, $84 d guest house; $90 s, $120 d cabin; $90 s, $134 d *casa,* including all meals and taxes.

Accommodations

Cahuita offers lots of options, mostly in the budget category. Choose carefully as there is great variety in standards. Although at press time, tourist numbers in Cahuita were low, hotel rooms may be in short supply on weekends and holidays; call ahead if possible (or visit midweek). Check that windows are secure. And bring your own soap and toiletries (many properties don't provide them). Prices are in flux; many hotels have lowered their rates since the last edition of this book, when there was only one telephone number for the whole village (the operator would then connect you to a particular extension). Telephone lines have since arrived, and most hotels have their own direct line.

Playa Negra: The following accommodations are arranged in order, north to south.

On the shorefront road about three km north of the village is **Cabinas Algebra,** leave messages c/o tel. 587-2861, run by a grumpy German named Alfred, who offers three double cabins and a four-person unit with kitchen. I liked the offbeat restaurant with its veranda festooned with epiphytes; Alfred cooks tasty, wholesome dishes. Rates: $15 cabins; $26 four-person unit.

Opposite Algebra is a pretty green cottage housing the very basic **Cabinas Ruby,** with three basic rooms with shared bath for $10. Ruby is a charming old dear. Next door is **Cocal Cabinas** (closed out of season). A short distance south is **Moray's Place Bed & Breakfast,** a romantic stone-and-hardwood two-story house. One bedroom has a king-size bed and private bathroom and wide windows. Four rooms are below, each with beautiful stone walls, fan, and private bath (except one room) with hot water. Rates: $25 s/d including breakfast. Moray's allows camping. The second-floor Margaritaville restaurant posts a meal of the day.

A stone's throw south is **Chalet & Cabinas Hibiscus,** Apdo. 943, Puerto Limón, tel. 755-0021, fax 755-0015, one of the best places in Cahuita, with four pleasing *cabinas* and three chalets for up to six people. There's no restaurant, but the chalets and one *cabina* each have a kitchen and refrigerator. All have ceiling fans and hot water. The chalets have a spiral staircase up to the second floor, where rockers and hammocks allow a balcony siesta. There's a swimming pool, volleyball court, and game room. The manager, Pius Graf, is a Ringo Starr look-alike. Rates: $30-40 s low season, $40-50 d high season, cabins; $40-75 s low season, $50-100 d high season, chalets.

Next is **Cabinas Piscina Natural,** run by a friendly chap called Walter and named for the natural seawater coral cove with sandy bottom (good for swimming). It's a modest place with five small cabins (each has a double bed and bunk) with private baths and hot water, plus patios. There's a shady veranda over the pool. Rates: $15 s/d.

Farther along is **Bungalow Malu,** a pretty thatched *cabina* enclosed in landscaped grounds. It's closed out of season. Farther south, a dirt road leads to **Cabinas Brigitte,** run by Swiss-born Brigitte. Two run-down rooms are somewhat dingy and have shared bath. She cooks, offers horseback tours ($19, half day), and supposedly has a large collection of poison-arrow frogs. Rates: $11 d. Opposite Brigitte's is **Cabinas Mambo,** a handsome two-story hardwood structure with four large rooms, each with mosquito nets, fan, and hot water, and spacious veranda. Fishing, horseback rides, etc. are offered. For information, see Cabinas Jardín Tropical. Rates: $20 s/d.

Fifty meters brings you to **Cabinas Iguana,** Apdo. 1049, Cahuita, tel. 755-0005, fax 755-0054, run by a Swiss-Tico couple. Three all-hardwood budget rooms share toilets and shower outside but are handsome; at $15 d, a bargain. Larger cabins are very attractive and have mosquito nets and kitchenettes (the owner provides fruits free) for $30-40, up to four people. Houses cost $40-50. All have verandas with hammocks. It offers a laundry service, plus large book exchange, and you can rent horses. There's a small pool with cascade. Nearby is **Cabinas Jardín Tropical,** offering two simple but charming and homey albeit simple and rustic *cabinas* plus a two-bedroom house with a big kitchen. The cabins each have a kitchenette, hot water, and hammocks. Guests get free use of bicycles. (Recommended for an offbeat escape.) Rates: $20 per cabin; $10 pp for the house.

Also here is **Cabinas Nirvana,** tel. 755-0110, a handsome two-story hardwood structure with five *cabinas* (two with private bath) with hot water. Breakfast is served on a terra-cotta patio.

Fifty meters south is **Jardín Rocalla,** which has an open-air restaurant serving Italian dishes,

and attractive stone-and-hardwood, two-story, Swiss-style cabins ($12 pp). Upstairs rooms have balconies.

South of the soccer field, a dirt road leads to **Cabinas Margarita,** tel. 755-0205, with 10 double cabins, each with fans, hot water, and tiled floors ($8 pp). Owner John Henry Lewis is a friendly soul. Continuing south is **El Encanto,** Apdo. 1234, Limón, tel./fax 755-0113, a bed and breakfast run by live-in owners Michael and Karen Russell, who offer three *cabinas* in a pretty garden. It's modern and pleasing, with lots of hardwoods, queen-size orthopedic mattresses, ceiling fans, private baths, and hot water. It also has a small patio restaurant and secure parking. Rates: $30 s, $35 d, including breakfast and taxes. **Café Vishnu** also has cabins for $18 d. Next, you'll come to **Cabinas Bello Horizonte,** tel. 755-0206, 200 meters north of the village. It has five simple *cabinas* with private bathrooms on the beach, plus four rooms with communal baths. Rates: $15 d shared bath; $20 d private bath. The very basic-looking **Cabinas Tito** is opposite.

The prettiest place in Cahuita is the romantic **Magellan Inn,** Apdo. 1132, Puerto Limón, tel./fax 755-0035, website www.web-span.com/tropinet/magellan1.htm, as intimate and warm as a grandfatherly hug. Six spacious, carpeted rooms are done up in mauves, with plentiful hardwoods in counterpoint. The bathrooms provide piping hot water. French doors open onto private patios with cozy bamboo and soft-cushioned seats overlooking magnificently lush landscaped grounds. A sunken swimming pool is cut into an uplifted (and therefore deceased) coral reef. Live-in owner Elizabeth Newton is a friendly soul. A restaurant offers candlelit elegance and there's a small bar (try the killer cocktails, such as Rasta's Revenge) for guests only. The lounge, with its Oriental rugs and sofas, is an admirable atmospheric place to relax with jazz and classical music adding just the right notes. Rates: $55 s/d ($10 extra person: third and fourth people can be accommodated on a foldaway bed), including continental breakfast.

Tropicana Bed and Breakfast, tel./fax 755-0059, e-mail: borgato@sol.racsa.co.cr, is an Italian-run hardwood two-story structure with four large, clinically clean rooms with king-size beds, private baths with large showers and hot water. They're set amid lawns and landscaped grounds. Two more buildings are being considered. Breakfast is served on an upstairs veranda. Guests have e-mail access. You have to love dogs, which swarm at your heels. Rates: $30 s, $35 d, $45 t.

The **Hotel Jaguar,** Apdo. 7046, San José 1000, tel. 755-0238 or 226-3775, fax 226-4693, website www.centralamerica.com/cr/hotels/jaguar.htm, is set in seven hectares of modestly landscaped grounds, and has 45 beachfront rooms: spacious and light, with screens and "thermo-cycling ceiling vents" to aid cooling, firm queen-size beds, fans, and private bathrooms with hot water. The breezy atrium bar and restaurant is renowned for its breakfasts.

Self-guided trails (there's a guidebook for $9) behind the hotel lead through the fruit farm into the nearby rainforest. You can rent boogie boards and snorkeling equipment in the souvenir shop, run as a separate business. There's a large swimming pool and tennis court. Rates: from $30 s, $55 d standard; $40 s, $70 d superior, including full breakfast and tax.

The German-run **Atlántida Lodge,** tel. 755-0115, fax 755-0213, e-mail: atlantic@sol.racsa. co.cr, has 15 pleasing bamboo-roofed duplex cabins amid lush landscaped grounds with a little arched bridge spanning a pool filled with carp. Each has tile floors, a private terrace, fan, and private bathroom with hot water. There's a restaurant under thatch with hammocks, a simple bar, plus a "boutique" and book exchange, a small exercise room, e-mail service, secure parking, and above all, a friendly, "home-with-the-family" ambience. *Highly recommended!* Tours are offered. Rates: $40 s, $50 d, $60 t low season; $55 s, $65 d, $75 t high season.

Cahuita Village: A good option is the **Hotel Cahuita,** tel. 755-0233, one block north of the park entrance. The place is well managed by Ingo and Cora Kolonko, and offers 12 spacious motel-style *cabinas* with fans but no hot water, plus two "houses," one for four people and one for six. The hotel has a small swimming pool, a bar (live music Friday and Saturday) and restaurant, plus hammocks. Rooms above the restaurant have balconies and communal bath. Rates: $10 s *cabinas;* $15 s house.

A tad more sophisticated is the **Hotel National Park,** tel. 755-0245, directly in front of the park entrance. The 15 rooms are pleasant: clean and bright, with private baths and hot water. Rates: $15 s, $20 d.

Cabinas Vaz, tel. 755-0218, has a clean restaurant popular with locals. The accommodations could use a damn good clean out. It's closed off-season. Rates: $12 s, $15 d. Next door, and of similar quality and price, is **Cabinas Sol y Mar,** tel. 755-0237, with eight basic rooms for 4-6 people, with pleasing private bathrooms but no hot water. Rooms upstairs catch the breeze. Rates: from $13 d.

Past Cabinas Sol y Mar, the side road leads to the **Rhode Island Cabins,** tel. 755-0866, with eight small rooms ($10-15), and **Cabinas Atlantic Surf,** tel. 755-0086, with six rooms in a two-story building (reception is in a cottage on the right, 20 meters beyond Sol y Mar).

On the east side of the village are several reasonable options beginning with **Cabinas Arrecife,** tel./fax 755-0081, whose 10 rooms have breezy verandas and are clean and roomy if gloomy. Bathrooms have hot water. Rates: $15 s, $20 d low season; $20 s, $35 d high season. Fifty meters west is **Cabinas Smith,** tel. 755-0068, with six pretty little rooms with fan and hot water and patios with seats. Miss Smith will sometimes cook for guests, and entertains with lively conversation while she rocks on the porch. Rates: $10 s/d, including taxes.

Cabinas Jenny, tel. 755-0256, has 15 basic rooms on two levels, all with comfy mattresses, mosquito nets, and fans plus private bathrooms with cold water. Seven rooms face the beach. Upstairs rooms have balconies. Rates: $16-26. Nearby, **Cabinas Seaside Nan-Nan,** tel. 755-0210, alias "Spencer Seaside Lodging," has a superb location only 20 meters from the waves with marvelous views along the shoreline. Hammocks are strung between the palms. It has 15 rooms, some in small *cabinas,* others in a two-story building. They're handsome, if simple, with hardwoods and a bright New Age motif, plus verandas or balconies with hammocks. Rates: $14-20 s, $16-25 d, $5 extra person. *A bargain!* You can rent a small two-story house with kitchen.

Also on the shore is **Cabinas Brisas del Mar,** tel. 755-0011, with clean and modest *cabinas* with private baths. Rates: $15 d, cold water; $20 d, hot water.

Surfside Cabinas, tel. 755-0246, has 12 modern and clean yet basic rooms, each with refrigerator, louvered windows, fan, and private bath. You can choose between doubles, bunks, and twin beds. Rates: $12 d. The restaurant offers meals from $2.50 and up and is popular with the locals.

One block toward the beach from the bus stop is **Cabinas Palmer,** Apdo. 123, Puerto Limón, tel./fax 755-0243, which has 20 rooms (13 with hot water) that include small but clean rooms with fans, plus three larger four-person rooms with refrigerator and kitchenette. The friendly owner Rene accepts credit cards. There's parking, and a sunny garden out back. Rates: $15 s, $20 d. Opposite is **Cabinas Safari,** tel. 755-0078, with seven clean and pleasant rooms, each with a tiny garden. Rates: $8 s, $12 d, $15 t.

The most charming option is **Kelly Creek Cabins,** tel. 755-0007, behind a white picket fence immediately overlooking the park entrance. Four very large rooms are in a single, handsome, all-hardwood Thai-style structure with heaps of light pouring in through tall jalousied (louvered) windows. Elegant bed linens add a bright note. A second, similar, structure houses the restaurant (serving Spanish cuisine). Tables on the lawn overlook the beach. Rates: $35 s/d low season; $40 s/d high season, $10 extra persons.

Another romantic gem is the private and peaceful German-run **Alby Lodge,** tel. 755-0031, with four beautiful, thatched, Thai-style cabins sitting on stilts and widely spread apart amid lawns and bougainvillea. All have tons of character, with high-pitched roofs, screened and louvered windows, hardwood floors, mosquito-net pendants on the ceiling, nice bathrooms, and private patios with hammocks and marvelous tables hewn from logs. Rates: $36 s/d, $41 t, $46 quad, including tax.

Near Parque Vargas: About 1.5 km south of Cahuita, on the road to Puerto Viejo, is **Hotel Playa Blanca,** with six clean cabins in a field backing onto Cahuita National Park. **Albergue Gandoka** is about 200 meters west of the Parque Vargas entrance gate. It has a rustic restaurant and a pool table. **Cabinas Amapola** ($10 pp) is also here. There's a bungalow called **Quetzal Jardín** ($25, four people) 400 meters north on Hwy. 36.

Camping

Cabinas Seaside allows camping on the shore beneath palms for $2.50 pp, including use of showers and toilets. **Vishnu's Camping Inn** ($1.50 to camp) is one-half km north of Cahuita. You can also reportedly camp at **Cabinas Brigitte.**

Don't pitch your tent too close to the beach; the no-see-ums there are vicious.

Food

There's excellent eating in Cahuita, but the scene is ever-changing and many places are open only in season (Dec.-May). Some relocate each new season.

For delicious and healthy breakfasts head to **Cafetería Vishnu,** tel. 755-0263, where a Vishnu Breakfast of Indian bread, juice, granola, herb tea, and fruit costs $2.50. Omelettes, pancakes, and American breakfasts are served, as are burgers, sandwiches, and fruit salads with yogurt for lunch and dinner. **The Pastry Shop,** nearby, sells homemade pastries, banana pancakes, cheesecake, lemon meringue pie, and the like. On the Playa Negra road, the **Hotel Jaguar** also serves filling breakfasts and "gourmet French Caribbean meals" such as sea bass steamed in banana leaf with hot spicy guanábana sauce, and tenderloin with spicy cashew fruit sauce ($6-10). **Bananas Restaurant** at Cabinas Algebra on Playa Negra is also recommended. Also check out **Restaurante El Ancla,** a colorful hangout for local Rastas with a good selection of basic Italian and local dishes, enjoyed to the accompaniment of reggae music.

The most creative cuisine is at the **Casa Creole** at the Magellan Inn, with such zesty fare as a garlic papaya appetizer, spiced shrimp martinique in creole spice ($10), sautéed steak marinated in ginger ($10), and punch coco casa creole. Be sure to start out with the paté maison ($4) and, to end, profiteroles to fatten a pig. It serves breakfast 8-10 a.m. and dinner 6-9 p.m.

Also don't leave Cahuita without having dinner at **Margaritaville,** also on Playa Negra, where Sandra Johnson offers a set dinner special ($5 for salad, main course, bread, dessert, and coffee) each evening—no breakfasts or lunches—washed down with piña coladas and killer margaritas. Jimmy Buffett riffs mingle with the rush of the waves. Sandra offers taxi service from Cahuita.

On a par is **Miss Edith,** who with her two daughters creates inexpensive, spicy, aromatic Caribbean specialties such as "Rundown" (a

Salon Vaz, Cahuita

spiced stew of fish, meat, and vegetables simmered in coconut milk) at lunchtime and dinner. She also serves breakfast 7-10 a.m. Meals are complemented by Miss Edith's own herbal teas. She offers a vegetarian menu. And weekend meals are highlighted by homemade ice cream. Her home-cum-restaurant is a charming little place. Expect to pay $5-10.

The **Il Piccolo Italiano** along Playa Negra is a rustic eatery serving Italian fare. The **Pizzeria Delle Alpi,** at Hotel Cahuita, serves pizzas and spaghettis for $4-6—as does **Pizzeria Cactus,** opposite Café Vishnu on Playa Negra.

By the beach, **Restaurant Sol y Mar,** and **Vista del Mar** (with Chinese dishes) are popular, as is the **Restaurant National Park.** All serve sandwiches, seafood, and *típico* dishes. Another favorite with locals is the restaurant at **Cabinas Surfside** (meals from $2.50), where games of dominoes stir quite a noise. **Cha Cha Cha** is a rustic, gaily painted spot serving international dishes, with specials of the day such as orange chicken breast, and corvina with shrimp and basil sauce ($5-12). Opposite, **Wallace Village** sells 35 types of fruit juices, 16 of salads, 20 of ice cream, 15 of sandwiches, and 10 spaghetti dishes. The rustic **Restaurant Caribe,** next door, and **Caribbean Point,** its nieghbor, serve seafood and steaks ($5-15).

Snakey Solo, opposite Cabinas Smith, also dishes up delightful fare from pastas and spiced-up fish to lobster ($10). Also with plenty of am-

bience is the tiny, rustic **Restaurante Trópicos** (opposite Soda Vaz), which also doubles as a bakery and serves delicious *refrescos* and crab dishes from $8, but you can dine on a filling *casado* special for $3. The **Kelly Creek** restaurant is a winner with its salad, garlic shrimp, beer and refesco special for $8. It also has paella and *sangria.*

The rustic **La Soda** in town serves a vegetarian plate, plus ceviche and other seafoods. Sometimes a fruit-and-vegetable stand sets up in front of the National Park Restaurant. There's a small bakery next to the small "park" opposite Salon Vaz on the main road where you can stock up on delicious pies, breads, and corn pudding, all for less than $1. You can also buy inexpensive foodstuffs and meals at **Soda Jardín Cervecero,** at the junction of the dirt road to the Puerto Vargas entrance.

Entertainment

There's not much night action in Cahuita. **Salon Vaz,** a laid-back bar with a plank-floored disco complete with flashing lights at the back, was closed for remodeling. It's a popular hangout for dreadlocked Rastas, who also favor **Soda Sarafina** across the street. Many people hop down to Puerto Viejo, where the discos pack them in more tightly.

Jardín Tropical has a small bar with a pool table (50 colones a game). **Cafetería Vishnu** also has a pool table, darts, and sports TV.

Tours and Activities

The **Cahuita Tourist Information Center,** tel. 755-0071, offers a panoply of tours and activities, including fishing ($35), birding, and even whitewater trips on the Pacuare ($85) and trips to Boca del Toro, in Panamá. **Cahuita Tours,** tel. 758-1515, ext. 232, fax 758-0652, has similarly varied offerings, including tours by jeep to Indian villages, and glass-bottomed boat tours to the reef ($10 for four hours, drinks included). You can also arrange boat trips up the Río Estrella, guided hikes, and trips to Tortuguero. **Tortuguero Green Tours,** tel. 758-1310, fax 758-0824, offers trips to Tortuguero ($50 transport only, $65 full-day tour, $80 overnight, $130 "deluxe").

José McCloud, a local guide trained by the Talamanca Association for Ecotourism and Conservation (ATEC), can also take you snorkeling on the reef; and Walt Cunningham, also trained by ATEC, offers guided hikes in the park and local cacao plantations (his house is the blue one next to the soccer field on Playa Negra).

Bike Rental: The **Cahuita Tourist Information Center** rents bikes for $35 per day. Cahuita Tours has bicycles for $1.25 per hour or $6 a day.

Horseback Riding: You can rent **horses** from Cabinas Brigitte for $6 a day, or take a half-day guided ride into the mountains ($35) or along the beach ($25). **Cahuita Tours** has three-hour horseback rides ($25 beginners, $35 experienced riders).

Scuba Diving and Snorkeling: Cahuita Tours charges $75 for six hours' guided scuba diving, with tanks included. It also rents scuba gear, plus snorkeling masks and fins (approximately $5 a day), as do many hotels. **Cahuita Tourist Information Center** offers guided snorkeling trips ($15). Roberto Smikle Smikle of **Roberto Tours,** tel./fax 755-0117, also offers boat trips and diving.

Shopping

Tucan Rasta, 400 meters north of the village, sells hip clothing—Guatemalan vests, Ecuadorian shirts ($18), and more—plus hammocks, jewelry, and Bob Marley paintings. Cahuita Tours sells T-shirts, postcards, postage stamps, etc. A store next door is fully stocked with clothing, hammocks, embroidered vests, sandals, carvings, and model ships made of wicker, and features a Guatemalan room and a Costa Rican room.

Boutique Bumbata is a good spot to select a sensual batik wrap and resort wear. It also has jewelry and souvenirs.

Letty Grant of Cabinas Bello Horizonte runs the **Tienda de Artesanía,** a women's cooperative crafts shop selling T-shirts and other souvenirs. Other little stalls are by the Kelly Creek park entrance.

Services

The tiny **police station** (Guardia Rural) at the north end of the village speaks of the difficulties the police face in fighting the rising drug trade. It doesn't even have a car. The **post office,** tel. 755-0096, is next door; it's open Mon.-Fri. 8 a.m.-noon and 1:30-5 p.m. There's a new **medical center** at the entrance to town, on the main road from Hwy. 36.

There are no **banks;** the nearest one is in Bribrí, about 20 km farther south. Cahuita Tours, however, offers dollar exchange, as will most hotels. You can pay almost everywhere with dollars. There's a **public phone** at Soda Uvita, opposite the bus stop, and at Cahuita Tours, tel. 755-0340 and 755-0355.

Many women wash clothes; look for **Laundry** (Lavandería) signs. There's a laundry 100 meters south of Cabinas Piscina and one next to Hotel Cahuita.

Getting There and Away

By Bus: Autotransportes MEPE, tel. 221-0524, operates direct buses to Cahuita ($4.50; four hours) and Puerto Viejo from San José, departing the Gran Terminal del Caribe, tel. 257-1961, fax 256-4248, on Calle Central, Avenida 15/17. Buses leave daily at 6 a.m. (continuing to Sixaola), 10 a.m. (continuing to Manzanillo), 1:30 p.m. (to Manzanillo), and 3:30 p.m. (to Sixaola). A regular bus also departs on weekends at 8 a.m. The buses will drop you off in Cahuita village center or at the road leading to the Parque Vargas park entrance.

Buses depart Puerto Limón from Radio Casino, one block north of the municipal market, Avenida 4, Calles 3/4, at 5 a.m., 10 a.m., 1 p.m., and 4 p.m. daily (one hour). Buses are usually crowded; get to the station early.

Buses depart Cahuita for San José at 7:30 a.m., 9:30 a.m., 11:30 a.m., and 4:30 p.m. from opposite Soda Vaz; and for Limón at 6:30 a.m.,

10 a.m., 1:30 p.m., 3 p.m., 4:30 p.m., 5:30 p.m., and 7 p.m. Buses for Puerto Viejo, Bribrí, and Sixaola depart at 6 a.m., 9 a.m., 11 a.m., 2 p.m., 5 p.m., and 7 p.m.

Interbus stops at Cahuita on its daily shuttle between San José and Puerto Viejo.

By Car: There's no gas station (the nearest one is at Bribrí), but several locals sell gas (petrol) from jerry cans. Ask around.

Getting Around

You can walk everywhere in town, although in the withering heat it can be a tiring walk along the Playa Negra road. Three local concerns—Enrique, Cabinas Palmas, and Cahuita Tours—operate impromptu taxis that should be booked in advance.

There are no car rental agencies, but Cahuita Tours rents **dune buggies.**

CAHUITA NATIONAL PARK

Cahuita's 14 km of beaches are shaded by palm trees, lush forests, marshlands, and mangroves. Together they make up Cahuita National Park (1,067 hectares), created in 1970 to protect the 240 hectares of offshore coral reef that distinguish this park from its siblings. Animal life abounds in the diverse habitats behind the beach—an ideal place to catch a glimpse of tamanduas, pacas, coatis, raccoons, tree-dwelling sloths, agoutis, armadillos, iguanas, and, of course, troops of howler and capuchin monkeys that come down to the shore.

The park is a good place, too, to focus your binoculars on a green ibis, rufous kingfisher, or low swooping Swainson and keel-billed toucans. Other birds include the Central American

---

THE DESTRUCTION OF COSTA RICA'S CORAL REEFS

The most complex and variable community of organisms in the marine world is the coral reef.

Corals are animals that secrete calcium carbonate (better known as limestone). Each individual soft-bodied coral polyp resembles a small sea anemone and is surrounded by an intricately structured calyx of calcium carbonate, an external skeleton that is built upon and multiplied over thousands of generations to form fabulous and massive reef structures.

The secret to coral growth is the symbiotic relationship with single-celled algae—zooxanthellae—that grow inside the cells of coral polyps and photosynthetically produce oxygen and nutrients, which are released as a kind of rent directly into the coral tissues. Zooxanthellae must have sustained exposure to sunlight to photosynthesize. Hence, coral flourishes close to the surface in clear, well-circulated tropical sea water warmed to a temperature that varies between 21° and 27° C (70° and 80° F).

The reef is a result of the balance between the production of calcium carbonate and a host of destructive forces. Though stinging cells protect it against some predators, coral is perennially gnawed away by certain snails and fish, surviving by its ability to repair itself and at the same time providing both habitat and food for other fauna.

Twenty years ago, Cahuita had a superb fringing reef—an aquatic version of the Hanging Gardens of Babylon. Today, much of it is dead—smothered by silt from mainland rivers. Coral growth is hampered by freshwater runoff and by turbidity from land-generated sediments, which clog their pores so that zooxanthellae can no longer breathe. Along almost the entire Talamanca coast and the interior, trees are being logged, exposing the topsoil to the gnawing effects of tropical rains. The rivers bring agricultural runoff, too: poisonous pesticides used in the banana plantations and fertilizers that are ideal for the proliferation of seabed grasses and algae that starve coral of vital oxygen. It is only a matter of time before the reef is completely gone.

Prospects for the reef at Gandoca-Manzanillo are equally grim. The region's isolation is already a thing of the past, and hotel developers are moving in fast. Ronal Umana, a marine biologist with the conservation group ANAI, fears that sedimentation and pollution could devastate the reef and tarpon and lobster nurseries.

Coral is a very resilient creature: a coral reef will grow back again if left alone. Alas, the Costa Rican government must move more quickly and conscientiously than it has to date if it is to save what little coral remains.

curassow and large groups of nesting parrots (and even, Dec.-Feb., macaws). Cahuita's freshwater rivers and estuaries are also good places to spot caimans and herons. Snakes—watch your step!—are commonly seen along the trail. And red land crabs and bright blue fiddler crabs—the latter with oversized claws—inhabit the shores.

The reef off Punta Cahuita protects the northern stretch of the beautiful scimitar beach to the south. Smooth water here provides good swimming; it's possible to wade out at knee level. At the southern end of the park, beyond the reef, huge waves lunge onto the beach—a nesting site for three species of turtles—where tide pools form at low tide. Check with rangers about currents and where you can walk or snorkel safely.

The coral reef lies offshore north off Puerto Vargas. Snorkelers can try their luck near Cahuita Point or Punta Vargas (you must enter the water from the beach on the Punta Vargas side and swim out to the reef); you can also hire a local resident to take you out farther by boat. On the sea floor are the massive brain corals and the delicate, branching sea fans and feathers; nearer the surface are elkhorn corals, frond-like gorgonians spreading their fingers upward toward the light, lacy outcrops of tubipora—like delicately woven Spanish mantillas—and soft flowering corals swaying to the rhythms of the ocean currents. Up to 500 species of fish gambol among the exquisite reefs. Here, amid sprawling thickets of bright blue staghorn, great rosettes of pale mauve brain coral, and dazzling yellow tubastras almost luminescent in the bright sunlight, a multicolored extravaganza of polka-dotted, piebald-dappled, zebra-striped fish protect their diminutive plots of liquid real estate among the reef's crowded underwater condominiums.

Besides what remains of the beautiful coral, there are two old shipwrecks about seven meters below the surface, both with visible ballast and cannons; one wreck has two cannons, and the second, a more exposed site, has 13. The average depth is six meters. The best time for diving and snorkeling is during the dry season, Feb.-April; water clarity during the rest of year is not very good beacause of silt brought by rivers emptying from the Talamanca mountains.

Trails

A footbridge leads into the park from the **Kelly Creek Ranger Station** (run by a local committee) at the southern end of Cahuita village. Kelly Creek is shallow and easily waded. A shady seven-km nature trail leads from the Kelly Creek Ranger Station to the **Puerto Vargas Ranger Station** (run by MINAE, the latest successor to MINEREM), three km beyond Cahuita Point at the southern end of the park. The nature trail walk takes about two hours including time to stop for a refreshing swim. You must wade the Perozoso ("Sloth") River—its waters stained dark brown by tannins—just west of Punta Cahuita. You can either walk along the beach to Puerto Vargas, or walk or drive to Puerto Vargas half a kilometer east from the entrance gate off Hwy. 36, about three km south of Cahuita (the Sixaola-bound bus will drop you off near the entrance). The Puerto Vargas entrance gate is locked after hours.

Both entrance stations are open 8 a.m.-4 p.m. Entrance costs $6 at Parque Vargas, and by donation at Kelly Creek. Don't forget your insect repellent and sunscreen.

Facilities

You can stay at a camping area with picnic tables, water, toilets, and showers at the **administrative center** beside the beach, one km north of the Puerto Vargas Ranger Station ($1 pp per day). A **museum** was planned here.

PUERTO VIEJO AND VICINITY

About 13 km south of Cahuita the road forks just after Home Creek (also spelled Hone Creek). The paved road turns east toward Bribrí; the bumpy unpaved road leads three km to Playa Negra, a stunning black-sand beach that curls east to Puerto Viejo, enclosing a small bay with a capsized barge (now sprouting a tree) in its center. The tiny headland of Punta Pirikiki at its eastern end separates Puerto Viejo from the sweep of beaches—Playa Pirikiki, Playa Chiquita, etc.—that run all the way to Manzanillo and Panamá. You can walk along the beach from Cahuita at low tide.

Lately, Puerto Viejo is the most happenin' spot in Costa Rica. The discos were hopping, and,

Puerto Viejo

while hoteliers in Cahuita were virtually begging visitors to stay, you couldn't find a room here to save your soul.

The population is mostly black, intermingled exotically with Bribrí Indian. Until very recently, most of the people lived a subsistence life of farming and fishing as generations had done before them. Before the growth of tourism, 95% of the area's income was derived from lobster fishing, which is highly seasonal. A few farmers still grow cacao; the coconut palm, too, is the "tree of life." Sweet and juicy citrus fruits fill the gardens, lobsters are plentiful, and large, tasty shrimp live in the rivers that rush down from the mountains. Few children stay in school beyond 13 years of age.

The laid-back way of life is still almost innocent, though changing fast as the surfer, backpacker, and counter-culture crowds (mostly Europeans and young North Americans) have firmly rooted here. Indeed, they dominate the scene, having settled and established bistros and restaurants alongside the locals. Telegraph poles and high wires today import the power of the 20th century (the supply is still not reliable; bring a flashlight), telephones arrived in 1997, and the sudden influx of tourists threatens to sweep away the last of the old ways.

Puerto Viejo is very low-key, very funky (vultures hop around lethargically on the streets, taking reluctant flight only when you approach within a meter or two). Everyone walks around barefoot, and clothing (at least for visitors) is

very casual—tie-dyed batik, cut-off Levi jeans, even (in one case to which I was personal witness) Day-Glo hot-pants and low-cut push-up bra beneath see-through chiffon. Many European and North American women descend on Puerto Viejo, and the "rent-a-Rasta" syndrome engendered by these foreign women with local gigolos in tow (along with Puerto Viejo's laissez-faire attitude) has inspired a reputation for "free love" that other women travelers must contend with. Be prepared for persistent overtures, from subtle entreaties to almost pornographic invitations. Drugs—cocaine and marijuana—are discreetly abundant.

Paula Palmer's *What Happen: A Folk History of Costa Rica's Talamanca Coast* (Ecodesarrollos, 1977) and *Wa'apin Man* (Editorial Costa Rica, 1986) provide insight into the traditional Creole culture of the area. Another useful reference is *Welcome to Coastal Talamanca,* published by Talamanca Association of Ecotourism and Conservation (ATEC).

It should take you at least three or four days to get in the groove. Don't expect things to happen at the snap of your fingers.

Finca la Isla Botanical Garden

This five-hectare botanical garden and farm, tel. 750-0046, one km west of town, is a treat for anyone interested in nature. Here, Lindy and Peter Kring grow spices, exotic fruits, and ornamental plants for sale. The couple have acres of native and introduced fruit trees. You can sample the fruits and even learn about chocolate production. There's also a rainforest loop trail with self-guided booklets. Toucans, sloths, and other animals are commonly seen—I saw a vine snake at arm's length—and there are scores of poison-arrow and "harlequin" frogs that make their homes in the row upon row of bromeliads grown for sale. The *finca* is 400 meters from the road (200 meters west of El Pizote Lodge) and is signed. Entrance: $3, or $8 with guided tour. Hours: Fri.-Mon. 10 a.m.-4 p.m. Lunches are offered by arrangement.

Surfing

Puerto Viejo is legendary among surfers. December through April the village is crowded with surfers, who come for a killer six-meter storm-generated wave called La Salsa Brava that washes ashore in front of Stanford's Restaurant. November and December are supposedly the best months, though I've seen it cookin in March. Beach Break is good for novices and intermediates.

Surfboards and surfing equipment can be rented, and you can buy boards from surfers

PUERTO VIEJO DE TALAMANCA

DETAIL

- JOHNNY'S PLACE
- POLICE
- PULPERÍA MANUEL LEÓN
- TORTUGUERO TOURS
- CABINAS TAMARA/ATLANTICO TOURS
- PIZZERIA CARAMBA
- ATEC (TOURIST INFORMATION, TELEPHONE)
- SODA TAMARA
- HOTEL MARITZA
- MADAME OUI OUI
- BUS STOP
- RESTAURANTE Y PIZZERIA MARCOS
- HOTEL PUERTO VIEJO/RESTAURANTE MEXI-TICO
- CABINAS DITI/TABU GIFT SHOP
- PIZZERIA CORAL
- SUNSET REGGAE BAR
- COLOR CARIBE
- MISS PATTY'S (BAKERY)
- SODA RITZ
- CABINAS GRANT
- CABINAS RITZ
- CABINAS JACARANDA/GARDEN CAFÉ
- SUPERMARKET
- CASA MAXIMO
- ANIMODO RISTORANTE
- HOTEL PURA VIDA
- RESTAURANTE TUNO CANARIO

Playa Negra

- LA PERLA NEGRA
- CABINAS BLACK SANDS
- MAURICIO'S CABINAS
- CABINAS ZULLY
- BAR RANCHO TÍPICO

Playa Negra

- CABINAS AZULILA
- CABINAS MARIBE PAN DULCE
- EL PIZOTE LODGE
- CABINAS PLAYA NEGRA
- CABINAS CHIMURI
- FINCA LA ISLA BOTANICAL GARDEN

To Home Creek

© MOON PUBLICATIONS, INC.

closing out their vacations (many surfers find it easier to sell their boards rather than carry them back home). Kirk, a Yank who owns the Hotel Puerto Viejo, is a surfing aficionado and can repair broken boards.

Accommodations

There are plenty of cabins to choose from. A few have hot water. You'll want a room with a ceiling fan (otherwise, make sure that the hotel provides mosquito nets). Ownership is fluid; the names and ownership may have changed by the time

you arrive. Demand is high. Secure your room in advance or as soon as you arrive. If the hotel you wish to stay at does not have a telephone, you can call ATEC, tel./fax 750-0188, e-mail: atec-mail@sol.racsa.co.cr, and leave a message for the owner of the hotel of your choice to call you back. There are several dozen *cabinas* and hotels south of town, many within walking distance.

Camping: You can pitch your tent at a funky campground next to Cabinas Soda Brava, southeast of town. It has basic shared toilets and is popular with surfers. Rates: $2 nightly. Hotel Puerto Viejo allows tents in its backyard.

Budget: In **Playa Negra**, nature lovers will enjoy the Indian-style **Cabinas Chimurí**, tel./fax 750-0119, e-mail: atecmail@sol.racsa.co.cr, on a 20-hectare farm and private rainforest reserve—Chimurí Nature Reserve—on a hill 400 meters from Playa Negra on the road from Hone Creek. A trail leads uphill to four small, charming A-framed thatched cabins with private balconies. Each has two single beds with mosquito nets. There's also an eight-bed dorm with bunks. Bring mosquito repellent. A small kitchen and airy, attractive open-air communal area provide for dining alfresco on organic food grown on-site. The place is managed by Anne Lewis and Bruce Peterson from Minnesota. Owners Mauricio and Colocha Salazar offer guided day-trips into the KekoLdi Indigenous Reserve (seven hours, $25 pp, including box lunch and a contribution to the Indian Association). Day and night walks at Chimurí—a Bribrí word for "ripe bananas"—are also offered ($12.50, three hours). Nearby are a waterfall and a pool, good for a refreshing dip. The birding is fabulous, and when I last visited, poison-arrow frogs were hopping about. Rates: $15 s, $20 d, $30 t/quad for cabins; $8 pp dorm.

Cabinas El Monte is also near Playa Negra on the road from Hone Creek; it advertises trips to Talamanca. Nearby, too, 200 meters before Playa Negra, is **Cabinas Azulil**, tel. 228-6748; in San José, tel. 255-4077, with self-catering accommodations and a good deal for a family or group. Two two-story family-size "cabins" have lots of light, beamed ceilings, and attractive hardwoods, with two bedrooms and two bathrooms upstairs, and two bedrooms and a shower downstairs. Rates: $10 s; $50 for up to eight people.

Cabinas Zully, on the beachfront, has basic rooms in a two-story house. Farther west along

Playa Negra is **Mauricio's,** with two very nice log-and-thatch cabins set in pleasant grounds. Pity about the caretaker, a feisty gringo who needs to chill out. Rates: $20 low season; $25 high season.

You'll receive a warmer reception next door at **Cabinas Black Sands,** tel. 750-0124, with four simple rooms, each with twin beds, in a two-story bamboo-and-thatch hut with communal bathroom. One room has a double bed, another has two singles, and two rooms each have a single bed. Owner Alexis Coto Molina is very friendly. The dirt road is often very muddy. The turnoff is opposite Pulpería Violeta, which also advertises rooms for rent. Rates: $10 pp; $50 for the entire hut.

Closer to town, 200 meters inland of the beach, **Cabinas Maribe Pan Dulce,** tel. 750-0182, has seven spacious, simply furnished rooms (each for four people) with fans and private bath with cold water. Rates: $6 s, $12.50 d low season; $8 s, $15 d, $17 t, $21 quad high season. Nearby, **Cabinas Playa Negra,** tel. 750-0063, has four small, well-maintained villa-style units, plus fully equipped apartments for up to six people. The latter have downstairs lounges, kitchens with refrigerators, and bathrooms and, upstairs, two bedrooms and a screened veranda. Rates: $12.50 d villa unit; $29 apartment.

In town, among the cheapest options is the all-hardwood **Hotel Puerto Viejo,** above the Restaurant Mexi-Tico. It has 40 small and spartan rooms with fans (upstairs rooms are preferable) and shared newly remodeled tiled bathrooms. There are also newer, pleasant cabins sleeping up to five at the rear. It is run by two friendly Americans, Jim and Kirk, and is popular with surfers, but I've received reports of theft and "unresponsive management." Jim and Kirk have seemed very conscientious when I've visited. Rates: $5 pp d; $20 for a large room with private bath.

A five-minute walk uphill from the soccer field (follow the sign) leads to **Kiskadee's,** a fairly basic but popular dormitory-style hotel run by an American, Alice Noel. One room has double beds. Bird lovers can admire the brightly colored tanagers and kiskadees that throng hereabouts. Don't forget your flashlight, and be prepared to get muddy hiking to and fro. Rates: $4, or $5 with use of the kitchen. Nearby, down the hill near the soccer field, is **Cashew Jungle Lodge,**

with *cabinas* plus a dorm room in the family home of two friendly Americans, Amy and Mike.

Cabinas Ritz has seven basic rooms with fans and hot water. Rates: $8 s, $15 t/quad; $20 for a large room for six. **Cabinas Diti** has three *cabinas* opposite the bus stop (contact Taverna Popo for information). Rates: $10 s/d, $12 t. **Cabinas Tamara** also has four basic *cabinas* with private bath with cold water, plus porches. Rates: $6 s, $12 d. Some have stoves. Basic, too, at a lonesome location on the south edge of town, is **Cabinas y Restaurante Rico Rico.**

Just east of Restaurante Bambú is **Salsa Brava Café y Cabinas,** right on the beachfront and a favorite of surfers. Simple, dark, dingy rooms have private bath and fans and veranda. Rates: $15 s/d. The very Caribbean-style restaurant is a cool place to hang.

The **Hotel Maritza,** tel. 750-0003, on the beachfront has 10 rooms with private bath with hot water; some have a/c, others fans. All have private bathrooms with hot water. On weekends, the bar and disco downstairs make the walls throb. It also has 14 simple but comfortable *cabinas* with fans and private baths with hot water. There's parking. Rates: $10 s/d rooms; $25 d, $30 t *cabinas.*

Up the price ladder, the clinically clean, Swiss-run **Cabinas Casa Verde,** Apdo. 1115, Puerto Limón, tel. 750-0015, fax 750-0047, sets a standard. It has 12 large rooms in three units, each with fans, mosquito nets, and lots of light, plus hot water. Four rooms share two spotlessly clean showers and bathrooms. Wide balconies have hammocks. Owner Renée, who mixes his time between lazing in a hammock and fussing over running his place, has maps and an info service. Features include a laundry, secure parking, and a book exchange, plus a tiny poison-frog garden and a tour booth (you can arrange horseback rides); a cafe was planned. There's also a small bungalow, romantic as all get-out, for a family or small group. Rates: $14 s, $26 d with shared bath; $30 s/d, $35 t with private bath; $25 pp for the bungalow.

Cabinas Jacaranda has four cabins set in a pretty landscaped garden; three with shared bathroom. Japanese paper lanterns, mats, and mosquito nets are nice touches. The fourth cabin is for four people. Best yet, it's a 10-second walk to the Garden Restaurant. *Highly recommended!* Rates:

$9 s, $17 d, or $20 d with fully equipped kitchen. The **Hotel Pura Vida,** around the corner from the Garden Restaurant, is nice: well-kept, with large, pleasing rooms for $13 s, $18 d. An airy outside lounge has hammocks and easy chairs.

The friendly, German-run **Cabinas Tropical,** c/o tel. 750-0012 (leave a message), has five pleasing rooms: clean and airy, with ceiling fans, huge showers, and wide French doors onto little verandas. Smaller single rooms are dingier. It's quiet and secure. There's also a restaurant. Rates: $15 s, $20 d, low season; $20 s, $25 d high season.

Cabinas Grant, tel. 758-2845, has also been recommended. It has 11 *cabinas* with private bath and cold water, plus hammocks on patios under eaves. Rates: $10 s, $15 d, $19 t, $20 quad.

Casa Máximo Bed and Breakfast, is a clean little house owned by Max, a Southern California surfer who rents four rooms (three with shared bath with hot water). There's a laundry and a small lounge plus a backyard with ping-pong. Rates: $10 pp shared bath; $15 private bath.

Unequivocally my favorite place to rest my head is **Coco Loco,** with just three handsome Polynesian-style *cabinas* raised on stilts and reclusively nestled amid lawns on the edge of town south of the soccer field. The log-and-thatched huts are simply furnished but crafted with exquisite care. They have mosquito nets over the beds, and hammocks on the porches. A fourth *ranchito* was planned for breakfasts. The charming owners are Austrian and live on-site. Rates: $20 s, $25 d, $30 t. A bargain.

East of town, several choices are within one km of Puerto Viejo along the dirt road that leads to Punta Cocles. About 100 meters along the road is **Cabinas Yucca,** with four cabins with private bath and a veranda facing the beach. A plus is the king-size beds, though the rooms are rather dark. Rates: $20 s/d, $30 t. **Cabinas David,** across the road, has six cabins in the same price range. Next door, **Coconut Grove,** tel. 750-0093; in the U.S., tel. (408) 423-9907, has rooms in a two-story house shaded by trees. Rates: $25 d. There's hot water, and guests get use of the kitchen. The rustic but attractive **Cabinas Billares Talamanca,** a stone's throw south, has six cabins with tiled private bathrooms for $6 pp. It gets its name from the four pool tables that are there to keep guests amused.

Calalú Cabinas, tel. 750-0042, off the road behind Billares Talamanca, has handsome little A-frame thatch huts in a compact garden, each with a hammock on the porch. Its neighbor, **Monte Sol,** has six rooms with heaps of light and a tasteful offbeat motif (colored ceramic tiles and sponge-washed walls like swirled ice cream). Screened windows, mosquito nets, and fans are standard. The German owners were planning to add a bar, a fountain and pool-garden with poison-arrow frogs, and a six-person house. Rates: $15-25 d. *A bargain!*

Hotel Casablanca, tel. 750-0001, 800 meters east of town, is a ho-hum place with four small rooms with tin roofs and private bathrooms with hot water. Each has a rustic four-poster bed with mosquito net, and hammock on the porch. Rates: $21 s, $28 d, $34 t low season; $25 s, $33 d, $40 t high season. It offers scuba diving.

Nearby is **Cabinas Casas Risas,** a quartet of small, hardwood cabins on stilts with floor-to-ceiling glass windows to three sides (three more were being added). Each comes with ceiling fan, little refrigerator, and heated water. They're clean, attractive, and peaceful, and have verandas with hammocks and tables. Rates: $30 s/d/t, $40 quad.

Inexpensive: El Pizote Lodge, Apdo. 1371-1000 San José, tel./fax 750-0088, about 400 meters before Playa Negra, is set in nicely landscaped grounds complete with giant hardwoods and sweeping lawns—a fine setting for eight small but clean and atmospheric rooms with shared bathrooms with huge screen windows. There are also six bungalows and a two-bedroom bungalow. Units have overhead fans and bedside lamps you can actually read by. The lodge even has a volleyball court. The restaurant gets good reviews. Six luxury bungalows, a swimming pool, and hot water were to be added. Rates: $50 d shared-bath rooms; $66 bungalows; $70-110 two-bedroom bungalow. Lower rates apply for walk-ins.

La Perla Negra, tel. 750-0111, fax 750-0114, e-mail: perlaneg@sol.racsa.co.cr, on Playa Negra, has 24 spacious rooms in a two-story all-hardwood structure cross-ventilated with glassless screened windows, charming albeit minimally appointed bathrooms with large walk-in showers, and bare-bones furnishings. Some rooms have a separate mezzanine bedroom.

Alas, the sponge mattresses won't do your bad back any favors. The grounds have a beautiful lap pool and sundeck and bar. The place is owned and run by a friendly Polish couple, Marlena and Julian Grae, who run their place like a home. Horseback rides and jungle tours are offered, as are banana-boat rides. Rates: $30 s, $40 d low season; $40 s, $65 d high season; $15 extra person, including hearty breakfasts.

About 400 meters east of town is the Italian-run **El Escape Caribeño,** tel./fax 750-0103, featuring 11 attractive hardwood cabins with double beds and bunks with mosquito nets, plus clean bathrooms with hot water, mini-bars, fans, and hammocks on the porch. They're widely spaced amid landscaped gardens and reached by raised wooden walkways. The brick-and-stucco bungalows across the road are also attractive, with raised ceilings, tile floors, and kitchenettes—each a true home-away-from-home. There's also a wood-paneled house at the end of the garden for four people ($55 per day, one-week minimum). Gloria and Mauro are delightful hosts. There's a large library. Rates: $35 d lowseason; $45 high season, cabins; $85 for up to six people low season, $95 high season, bungalows.

Food

Puerto Viejo is blessed with a surprisingly cosmopolitan range of eateries and even gourmet cuisine. At the **Garden Restaurant** at Cabinas Jacaranda, Vera Khan—a charming and vivacious Trinidadian—makes superb curries, vegetarian, Thai, and Caribbean dishes ($3-8) to true international standard, with flower petals and sauces artistically flourished for flair. Try the vindaloo curry chicken ($7) or Thai yellow curry kingfish ($8). Wolfgang Puck would be proud. And the candlelit setting is romantic and tranquil. Expect to wait at peak hours. The large cocktails—$2—could fuel a Mars mission. To finish, there's self-service coffee. Open 5-9:30 p.m. *Great value!*

The **Café Pizzeria Coral,** on the same block, serves good Italian fare ($6 and up for dinners), as does **Pizzeria y Restaurante Marcos,** cellular tel. 284-5130, with pizzas (from $3), pastas ($5), gnocchi ($6), calzone ($5), and other fare, including a large dessert menu. I also recommend the colorful **Restaurante Tuno Canario,** run by a Spaniard from the Canary Islands. It has great music to accompany such dishes as *pulpo* (octopus) *a la vinagreta* ($2) and *croquettes de pollo* ($1.50).

Soda Tamara, tel. 750-0148, is another popular place: clean, pleasant, and with a shaded patio. The menu runs from full breakfasts (including granola with yogurt) to burgers and *típico* dishes such as fried fish with *patacones* (plantain). Most meals cost $4 or less. It gets busy. Hours: 7 a.m.-9 p.m.; closed on Tuesday. **Soda Irma,** at the east end of town, is one of the cheapest options, with fried yucca ($1), *casados* for $3, and spaghetti with garlic bread for $4.

There are several tiny *sodas* on the waterfront, including **Soda Rita** with the best burgers in town ($1.50), plus sandwiches and pizzas. Next door, the German-run **Old Harbor's Fresco Shop** has health foods such as granola with fruit and yogurt ($2), plus daily specials such as pargo with salsa caribeña ($6) and chicken stroganoff ($5).

Good bets for seafood are **Cabinas Grant,** tel. 758-2845, and **Stanford's Restaurant Caribe,** on the beachfront. The latter has a highly regarded upstairs restaurant with ocean views. A vegetarian meal here will cost $2. Also on the beach nearby are the ramshackle **Restaurante Bambú** and **Salsa Brava Café,** both serving budget fare to the surf crowd; and the **Parquecito,** popular with local Rastas.

For Asian food, check out **Johnny's Place,** serving voluminous meals at a fair price. The **Restaurant Mexi-Tico** offers genuine Mexican food and food off the grill, steak burritos ($3), a veggie burrito supreme ($3.50), and healthy breakfasts. Around the corner, one block east, is **El Café Rico,** (the Dutch owner was still putting on the finishing touches when I popped by) promising gourmet European fare on the palm-fringed veranda surrounded by lush bougainvillea.

If you want to try local Caribbean fare, have one of the resident women cook for you (you'll need to give at least a day's notice). Miss Biggy makes steak and chips (French fries) in true English fashion (she has a kitchen at the back of the Taverna Popo); Miss Dolly makes delicious ginger biscuits and bread, plus Caribbean dishes such as "rundown" stew; Miss Sam bakes tarts and bread; while Miss Daisy is renowned for her *pan bon,* ginger cakes, and meat-filled patties. Ask around.

If you're cooking for yourself, a vegetable truck reportedly parks opposite the Soda Tamara every Wednesday afternoon. Watch for Yvette ("Boy Boy") wandering around town selling veggie and meat patties (75 cents) from a basket. There are several well-stocked groceries, including **Abastacedor Manuel León** (aka "Chino's") and **Super El Buen Precio,** at the entrance to town.

Entertainment

What Cahuita lacks in raging nightlife Puerto Viejo more than makes up for. It's well known for its hopping discos nightly (the bars and discos rotate duty), and folks travel from as far afield as Limón to bop. The prize contenders are **Stanford's**—reggae! reggae! reggae!—and **Johnny's Place,** which plays reggae and rock hits and has the craziest bar staff in the world. Wear your tank top, because you're gonna sweat. Another favorite is the **Sunset Reggae Bar,** which has live bands, plus darts, backgammon, and a large-screen TV. Stanford's also has live music on Wednesday (Caribbean Night). **Bambú** is the "in" spot on Monday. **Lapa Lapa,** at Playa Cocles south of town, also has a lively disco plus music videos.

To get your steps down, you can sign up for a dance class with **Escuela de Baila,** c/o tel. 750-0188.

By day, you can challenge someone to a game of backgammon or draughts on the shorefront outside Sunset Reggae Bar.

Spanish Language Courses

The **Center for Learning,** Centro de Aprendizaje, tel. 750-0004, e-mail: atecmail@sol.racsa.co.cr, offers Spanish language courses and individual tuition, with ongoing three- and four-week courses for children and adults (18 hours; tuition, $75). Weekend intensives are offered by request.

ATEC

The grassroots Asociación Talamanca de Ecoturismo y Conservación (Talamanca Association of Ecotourism and Conservation), or ATEC, tel. 750-0191 or tel./fax 750-0188, e-mail: atecmail@sol.racsa.co.cr, the region's environmental "chamber of commerce," was formed to promote cultural activities and sponsor ecological tourism and environmental education for the local community as well as visitors. Its office in the center of Puerto Viejo is the informal node of local activity. Visitors are welcome to attend the association's weekly meetings in the Hotel Maritza (Monday 6 p.m.), when development and conservation issues are discussed. The destruction of forests is a particuar concern. Another is that the bulk of tourist dollars are flowing into the more upscale resorts south of town, bypassing the local community. To help counter this, they train locals as approved guides to lead trips into the jungle. One of the best guides is "Juppy" (Roberto Hansel), a dreadlocked local who speaks English, German, and Spanish and grew up learning animal and plant lore.

Tours and Activities

Hiking and Nature Excursions: ATEC sponsors environmental and cultural tours of the Talamanca coast using local guides ($12.50 half-day, $25 full-day) in an effort to promote "ecologically sound tourism and small-scale, locally owned businesses." Options include "African-Caribbean Culture and Nature Walks," trips to the KekoLdi Indigenous Reserve that include the Iguana Farm, rainforest hikes, snorkeling and fishing, bird and night walks, and overnight "Adventure Treks" into the Gandoca-Manzanillo reserve. Trips to the remote Talamanca indigenous reserves require one week's notice (groups only). Trips are limited to six people. Be prepared for rain.

Mauricio Salazar at Cabinas Chimurí also offers hikes into the KekoLdi Indigenous Reserve (seven hours; $25 pp, including box lunch and a contribution to the Indian Association). Physically grueling three-day trips can be arranged (with several days' notice). He also offers night walks (three hours; $10). A percentage of his fee is given to the Indians. Mauricio also organizes education programs for students.

Other locals will take you hiking in Gandoca-Manzanillo Wildlife Refuge or into one of the nearby Indian reserves. Ask around. Also, check the notice boards in the Hotel Maritza and Pulpería Manuel León.

Atlantico Tours offers trips to as far afield as Tortuguero, Barra del Colorado, and Braulio Carrillo. Also try **Tortuguero Tours** next to Abastacedor Manuel León, which charges $55 for a two-day Tortuguero trip, plus $35 for trips to Gandoca-Manzanillo.

Deep-sea fishing can be arranged with advance notice through Earl Brown, Daniel Brown at Soda Acuario, or "Papi" Hudson. The El Pizote Lodge also offers boat trips and snorkeling. Rumor has it that a powerful fishing boat is available for charter trips to offshore reefs and to Bocas del Toro, in Panamá.

Bicycle Rental: You can rent mountain bikes at **Madame Oui Oui Boutique** and from Cabinas Diti's **Tabu Gift Shop.** Both charge $5 per day.

Horseback Riding: Don Antonio's stables, 600 meters south of town, rents horses for $5 per hour. He has trips to Punta Uva, and a special trip to the mountains ($20). You'll see lots of other signs advertising horse rentals.

Scuba Diving, Snorkeling, and Watersports: Buceo Aquatour, five km south of town at Punta Uva (no telephone), offers scuba diving, including four-day PADI certification courses ($350); also, kayaking to Gandoca, snorkeling, and river excursions. Two-tank morning dives cost $60; one-tank afternoon dives cost $40. Night dives are $60. "Virgin" dives ($35) are also offered for the novice diver. **Wet Nature Tours,** tel. 750-0001, at Hotel Casablanca, offers scuba dives ($35 per dive, or $225 for PADI certification) and snorkeling ($5), plus kayaking ($25). **Madame Oui Oui Boutique** rents snorkel gear.

Tourist Information
ATEC runs an excellent tourist information bureau, plus a gift store selling maps and stationery. It has a fax service and public telephone, and acts as the local **post office.** You can send and receive e-mail: atecmail@sol.racsa.co.cr ($1 each send; 75 cents first receive, plus 20 cents each additional). On-line use costs $6 per hour, or $1 for 10 minutes. Open Mon.-Fri. 7 a.m.-9 p.m., except Wednesday (7 a.m.-noon and 2-9 p.m.), Saturday 8 a.m.-noon and 1-9 p.m., and Sunday 8 a.m.-noon and 4-8 p.m.

Soda Tamara, opposite, has a bulletin board with tourist information, including private house rentals.

Shopping
Color Caribe, tel. 750-0075, stocks a great selection of clothing, jewelry, and souvenirs, including their trademark hand-painted and silk-screened clothing. You'll also find hand-painted T-shirts and jewelry on sale at stalls along

the beachfront. **Madame Oui Oui Boutique,** opposite ATEC, has similar offerings. Look, too, for custom crafted backgammon sets made by a Swiss chap named Urs.

Services
Puerto Viejo has no banks—the nearest is in Bribrí—but you can cash traveler's checks and change dollars for *colones* at Pulpería Manuel León, Johnny's Place, and Stanford's.

The **police station** is next to Johnny's Place. There are only three public **telephones** in town: at the Hotel Maritza, tel. 750-3844; Pulpería Manuel León, tel. 750-0854; and outside the ATEC office, tel. 750-0188, opposite Soda Tamara. You have to ask the operator to connect you. You can have incoming messages left here. Direct-dial coin-operated call-boxes and phonecard telephones were to be introduced.

There's a **doctor**—Dr. Rosa León—and health clinic in Hone Creek, tel. 750-0136; it's open Mon.-Fri. 7 a.m.-4 p.m. For serious problems you should visit the Red Cross evacuation center in Bribrí.

Getting There and Away
By Bus: The bus fare from San José to Puerto Viejo is $5.25. Return buses depart Puerto Viejo for San José at 7 a.m. and 4 p.m.; and for Limón at 6 a.m., 1 p.m., 4 p.m., and 5 p.m. The Puerto Limón-Puerto Viejo buses are usually crowded; get to the station early. **Interbus** has a daily shuttle between San José and Puerto Viejo.

By Taxi: Juan Lopez Andrea, tel. 750-0141, operates a taxi service, as do "Bull," tel. 750-0112; Spence, tel. 750-0008; and Pancho, tel. 750-0067.

PLAYA COCLES, PLAYA CHIQUITA, AND PUNTA UVA

"Where the road ends and the jungle begins," says a sign for Hotel Playa Chiquita on the potholed dirt road that leads east from Puerto Viejo via Punta Cocles and Punta Uva to Manzanillo, a fishing village at the end of the road, 13 km southeast of Puerto Viejo. The sign's *almost* right. While the potholed road is still an ordeal in places (most locals use horses), buses ply the route daily, and hotels are sprouting all the time. No wonder—the beaches are marvelous. Long, lonesome, and breathtakingly beautiful in a South Pacific kind of way. The road runs inland of the coast for most of the way, with very few views of the ocean.

The very beautiful coral-colored **Playa Cocles** runs southeast for four km from Puerto Viejo to the rocky point of Punta Cocles. Another stunning beach—**Playa Chiquita**—runs south four km to Punta Uva. From here, a five-km-long gray-sand beach curls gently southeast to Manzanillo, with dramatic ridgeback mountains in the distance. At Punta Cocles you enter **Gandoca-Manzanillo National Park,** and *cabinas* and hotels thin out. Coral reefs lie offshore, offering good snorkeling and diving. And you can explore the swampy estuary of the Río Uva, where caimans can be seen in channels resembling Tortuguero.

There are no settlements (except the teeny hamlet of Punta Uva), just a string of *cabinas* along the dirt road. The majority are run by Europeans (Italians predominate) drawn to a life of idyll as laid-back hoteliers.

howler monkey

KekoLdi Indigenous Reserve

The 3,547-hectare KekoLdi reserve, in the hills immediately south of Puerto Viejo, extends to the borders of the Gandoca-Manzanillo refuge. It is home to some 200 Bribrís and Cabecar people. Apparently, aerial surveys used to demarcate the reserve failed to take into account pre-existing cacao plantations on land later sold to private developers, to whom titles have reverted. Less than half of the reserve land is in Indian hands today. To protect their land, they formed ATEC and are preparing their reserves as tourist destinations. Reforestation and other conservation projects are ongoing. Gloria Mayorga, coauthor of *Taking Care of Sibo's Gift,* educates tourists on indigenous history and ways. Gloria and Juana Sanchez run the **Iguana Farm,** an experimental project to raise green iguanas and other endangered species (entrance: $1 pp).

ATEC arranges visits ($13 half-day; $19 full-day) to KekoLdi, with Gloria and her brother Lucas as guides (Spanish only). Hiking and horseback trips into KekoLdi are offered by Mauricio Salazar, who leads trips from Cabinas Chimurí in Puerto Viejo; his *cabinas* feature a trail directly into the reserve. The demanding trips (one-day trips cost $22; three-day trips cost $140, including overnight stays with the Indians) require notice.

Accommodations

You can rent private houses (advertised on noticeboards in Puerto Viejo), such as a rustic hilltop cottage with ocean views near Punta Uva (in the U.S., tel. 408-625-0424), or a fully equipped luxury home for $500 monthly, tel. 750-0012. The ultra-budget lineup has changed dramatically since I did the research for the previous edition of this book and now stands as follows from Punta Cocles eastward, arranged separately by category.

Camping: You can camp at **Tuanis** (one km south of Punta Cocles) for $5 pp. **Irie,** at Playa Chiquita, also offers camping.

Budget: Cabinas El Tesoro, about one km from Puerto Viejo, looks basic. I didn't stop by. About 600 meters south is the modest **Cabinas Surf Point,** with hot water and laundry; and, 200 meters beyond, a funky house called **Cabinas Garibaldi.**

It's another two km to the next budget property—**La Manda Cabinas.**—and a further 1.5 km to **Villas Paraíso,** tel. 798-4244, a rather grandly named budget establishment with 12 *cabinas,* eight with private baths and hot showers, and small decks facing tropical gardens. There's laundry, boogie board and bike rentals, a book exchange, and a hammock movie lounge. The Paloma Café is here. It caters to surfers. Rates: $10 s/d shared bath; $25 s/d private bath.

Other options include **Cabinas Selwyn** (with four cabins and a small open-air restaurant), **Casa del Sol,** and **Walaba Lodge,** tel. 234-2467 or 225-8023, all at the south end of Playa Chiquita. Walaba Lodge is a delightful three-story lodge with large carved sea-horse motifs on the facade. It sits in pleasing landscaped grounds. Owner Alejandro Rodriguez rents four airy rooms ($15 pp) with fans, plus beds in a dorm ($10).

You could also try **Cabinas Punta Uva** (not inspected).

Inexpensive: La Isla Inn, tel./fax 750-0109, 600 meters south of town, is a two-story all-hardwood structure with five rooms (three up, one down) just 50 meters from Playa Cocles. The wide, upper-story veranda replete with hammocks grants views over the ocean. Rooms are large, with lots of light pouring in through screened windows, plus fans and nets to keep mosquitoes at bay, orthopedic mattresses, and private bathrooms with hot water. Rates: $20 s, $30 d low season; $25 s, $40 d high season; $10 extra person; $50 for a big room sleeping four.

Two km south of Puerto Viejo is **Cariblue Bungalows,** tel./fax 750-0057, with six handsome hardwoodbungalows of different sizes (from 2-6 people) amid lawns with shade trees. Some have king-size beds. All have fans, private bathrooms with mosaic tiles and hot water, plus a porch with hammock. Simple meals are served under thatch. Rates: $40-50 d, including tax.

La Costa de Papito, c/o ATEC, tel. 750-0191 or tel./fax 750-0188, e-mail: atecmail@sol.racsa.co.cr, website www.greenarrow.com/x/papito.htm, 200 meters south, is run by Eddie Ryan, a New York hotelier, who has conjured six rustic, handsome, and simply yet tastefully decorated bungalows at the jungle edge in a lush five-acre garden. Each has ceiling fan, exquisite tiled bathrooms, and shady porches with hammocks under thatch. There's a laundry, and massage, bike rentals, and free transfers are offered. Rates: $35 d low season; $50 d high season, including taxes; $5 extra person.

Hotel y Restaurante Yaré, tel./fax 750-0106, at Punta Cocles, is a very atmospheric place with beautiful all-hardwood two-story houses set magnificently amid towering trees with flowering vines. Canopied, raised wooden walkways with

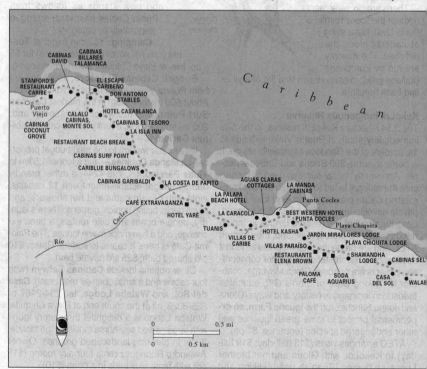

ship's hawsers as rails lead to tall cabins painted in terrific tropical pastels with V-shaped verandas. Each unit is a different combination of colors, spacious within, with bright floral curtains and covers (I find the festive Caribbean colors inside rather insipid), two double beds, and private bath with hot water. The smaller rooms are dark. Four *cabinas* are equipped with kitchenettes. A forest looms behind, and birdcall is everywhere. The restaurant is a popular dining spot. The hotel offers a wide range of tours. Rates: from $23 s, $32 d standard; $46 s, $65 d superior; $28 s, $55 d, $74 t family size ($10 extra for kitchenette).

La Palapa Beach Hotel, Apdo. 459, San José 1000, tel. 221-9592, fax 255-3941, a short distance east, is set in lush grounds. It has very attractive rooms 100 meters from the beach, with private bath and hot water. There's a popular bar and disco. Rates: $20 pp including continental breakfast and drinks.

La Caracola, between Punta Cocles and Punta Uva, has 10 colorfully painted cabins with screened windows and private bath with hot water. They're raised on stilts with parking beneath. It has a simple beachside cafe. Rates: $30 d with two single beds ($10 extra person); $40 d with double bed; $50 with kitchen (for four people). There are pretty cottages for rent next door at **Aguas Claras.**

At Playa Chiquita, on Punta Uva, is **Hotel Kasha,** tel. 284-6908, a comfortably attractive establishment with six bungalows set back from the road amid the forest. The handsome hardwood units are spacious, with plenty of light, screened windows, ceiling fans, two double beds, and pleasant bathrooms with heated water and beautiful Italian ceramics. The hotel boasts a small *ranchito* restaurant and a basic gym and jacuzzi. Rates: $42 d, including tax and breakfast.

PUERTO VIEJO TO MANZANILLO

Sea

Punta Uva

PALM BEACH
BEACH & TENNIS RESORT

RESTAURANTE
ARECIFE

HOTEL TALAMANCA
CARIBE

EL DUENDE FELIZ

ALMONDS & CORALS
LODGE TENT CAMP

CABINAS MAXI/
BAR MAXI

AQUAMORE

ALBERGUE
MANZANILLO

Manzanillo

To Sixaola

© MOON PUBLICATIONS, INC.

Next door is **Jardín Miraflores Lodge,** SJO 2385, P.O. Box 025216, Miami, FL 33102-5216; or Apdo 6499, San José 1000, tel./fax 233-2822 or direct tel. 750-0038, a true nature lover's paradise. It has a basic six-bed dormitory with outside bathrooms, double rooms with shared bathroom or private bathroom and balcony with hammock, and suites with king-size beds, private bathrooms and living areas. Downstairs rooms are dingy. Mosquito nets hang above the beds. The charming hotel—a combination of indigenous Bribrí and Caribbean architecture of wood and bamboo—is adorned with Latin American fabrics, masks and art, and bamboo vases full of fresh tropical blooms. Upstairs, cool breezes bearing hummingbirds flow through the rooms. Throw open your window shutters and sleep the full sleep of childhood to the calliope of insects and birds. Health-conscious breakfasts and Caribbean dinners are served in a tiny, rustic, charming Indian-style rancho. The place is surrounded by exotic plants, as Miraflores raises ornamentals for export. Heliconias abound. Pamela Carpenter, the erudite owner, is on the board of ATEC, tel. 750-0191 or tel./fax 750-0188, e-mail: atecmail@sol.racsa.co.cr, and arranges visits to the KekoLdi Indigenous Reserve, Manzanillo, and Panamá. You can also arrange boating, and rent bikes. Pamela will meet you with advance notice if you arrive by bus (the Limón-Manzanillo bus will also drop you at the gate). Rates include a hearty breakfast. Seventh day free. Rates: $15 s dorm rooms; $40 s, $50 d double rooms; $45-60 d suites.

Playa Chiquita Lodge, tel. 750-0062 or 233-6616, fax 223-7479, e-mail: wolfbiss@sol.racsa.co.cr, three km south of Punta Cocles, is appealing for its jungly ambience although one reader—a travel agent to boot—reports that cleanliness is an issue. Eleven spacious "bungalows" offer sunken bathrooms (no hot water), fans, and Sarchí's famous leather rocking chairs on a wide veranda. Three houses have been added across the road (one has two bedrooms and a kitchen). And a bathhouse-sauna was planned, offering massage and herbal therapy. You can dine alfresco under thatch in the restaurant. Narrow walkways lead through landscaped gardens to the golden sand beach. Bright blue sand crabs the size of dessert plates defend the terrain with fearsome claws. The lodge

arranges diving and snorkeling trips, boat trips to Punta Mona, plus bike and horse rentals. Rates: $22 s, $32 d low season, $29 s, $39 d high season bungalows; $50 d low season, $60 high season villas.

Somewhere on Playa Cocles, but not reviewed, is **Casa Camarona,** Apdo. 2070-1002, San José, tel. 224-3050, fax 222-6184, e-mail: camarona@ticonet.co.cr, with 18 rooms, a restaurant, bar, beach bar, laundry, safe parking, bicycles, kayaks, and tours. The facilities are wheelchair-accessible. The brochure hints at rustic elegance.

Moderate: About two km east of Punta Cocles is the relatively upscale **Villas del Caribe,** Apdo. 8080, San José 1000, tel. 381-3358 or 233-2200, fax 221-2801, with a superb location in the cusp of the bay. It has eight attractive rooms in a two-story complex in landscaped gardens 50 meters from the beach. Fully equipped kitchen, hot water, and fans are standard. The hotel is eco-conscious—even the soaps and toiletries are biodegradable. There's an ox-driven sugarcane mill and an oxcart for rides on-site. Rates: $50 d low season; $70 d high season, including tax. Possibly overpriced.

The most upscale place around is **Best Western Hotel Punta Cocles,** Apdo. 11020, San José 1000, tel. 234-8055, fax 234-8033; in the U.S., tel. (800) 325-6927, an oasis of tranquility five km south of Puerto Viejo. Set 500 meters back from the beach, it sprawls over gently rising gardens covering 10 hectares, all but 2.4 of them still forested. The only sounds are the buzz of insects, the call of birds, and the hushed sound of distant waves. Access to Punta Uva beach is via a path that leads past towering tropical trees. Nature trails lead into the private reserve. The hotel's 60 modern a/c cabins (some with kitchenettes) are spaced wide apart. They're spacious, with hot water, ceiling fans, large closets, and comfortable—but noisy—beds. Wide porches are good for armchair birdwatching. Facilities include an open-air restaurant overlooking a swimming pool and sundeck for alfresco dining, a jacuzzi, plus TV lounge. Guided tour programs include the "Cocles Indian Reserve Jungle Tour" ($45), "Hitoy-Cerere Reserve Jungle Hike" ($60), "Cahuita National Park" ($60), "Punta Mona Walking Tour" ($45), plus snorkeling ($45). Room rates: $60 s/d low season, $70 high season, standard (up to four people); $80 low season, $90 high season with kitchenette (up to six people).

I love the French-owned **Shawandha Lodge,** tel. 750-0018, fax 750-0037, farther south at Playa Chiquita. It has 12 spacious, thatched, hardwood cabins hidden amid tall ceibas and merging seamlessly into the jungle. Each is marvelously furnished, with lofty wood-and-thatch ceilings and simple yet beautiful modern decor, including four-poster beds, screened windows, and large verandas with hammocks. The bathrooms are splendid, boasting large walk-in showers with exquisite tilework from the hand of French ceramist, Filou Pascal. A restaurant serves breakfast and dinner, and there's a splendid open-air lounge with contempo decor and plump bamboo-framed sofas. Rates: $52 s, $62 d low season; $70 s, $80 d high season, including American breakfast. *Recommended!*

About two km farther, east of Punta Uva (take the side road to Punta Uva and continue along a rough track), is **Palm Beach Beach and Tennis Resort,** Apdo. 6942, San José 1000, tel. 750-0049 or 255-3939, fax 750-0079 or 255-3737, an expansive resort—originally called Las Palmas—claimed with undue bravado to be the "only full-service beach and jungle resort on the Caribbean." It nestles up to a stunning white-sand beach with hammocks in the palms. A reef lies just offshore. The resort has a small discotheque and shopping center. The rooms are modestly, though nicely appointed. An open-air restaurant overlooks the grounds and a large octagonal swimming pool with swim-up bar. The hotel rents snorkeling and diving equipment, and has horses on site. Rates: $60 s, $70 d, $85 t. Two-night packages with roundtrip transportation cost $150 pp; three nights $185. The Palm Beach offers full-day excursions from San José ($60). Las Palmas was built within Gandoca-Manzanillo without permits and the place has had an ongoing battle with conservationists (the government even ordered buildings to be razed and damaged ecosystems to be restored, although the Supreme Court later ruled for the hotelier). And the owner, a Czech, was ordered deported.

In 1997, a portion of the troubled Las Palmas property was sold and became the **Hotel Talamanca Caribe,** P.O. Box 11661-1000 San José, tel. 750-0181, fax 750-0196, e-mail: talamanc@sol.racsa.co.cr, which has 40 a/c rooms in Western-style bungalows, each with mini-bar, TV, hot water, and a terrace facing the sea. There's a pool and a children's pool and a kids' playground, plus a restaurant and bar, and a sports court; raised walkways lead through landscaped grounds to the beach. I found the property soulless, partly because the bungalows—though well-appointed—are entirely devoid of local character. Rates: about $70 pp. The company offers a five-day package with one night at the Hotel Nuevo Talamanca in San José for $249 pp double occupancy, including most meals. Transfers to/from San José cost $35.

The **Almonds & Corals Lodge Tent Camp,** c/o Geo Expediciones, Apdo. 681, San José 2300, tel. 272-2024, fax 272-2220, e-mail: almonds@sol.racsa.co.cr, is three km north of Manzanillo, with a lonesome setting a few leisurely steps from the beach. Each of 24 tent-huts is raised on a stilt platform, is protected by a roof, and features two singles or one double bed, a locker closet, night lamps, table and chairs (with reading light), plus mosquito nets and deck with hammock—a touch of Kenya come to the Caribbean. Very atmospheric. Each cabin has its own shower and toilet in separate washhouses (an environmentally friendly "bio-digester" gobbles up your waste, which reappears as light from methane lamps lining the walkways). Trees tower over the tent-huts. Raised walkways lead between the huts and also to the beach, pool, snack bar, and restaurant serving Costa Rican food. You can rent kayaks ($5 s, $8 d), bicycles ($10), and snorkeling ($5) gear, and take guided trips into Hitoy-Cerere Biological Reserve and the Indian village of Volio. Rates: $35 s, $40 d low season; $45 s, $60 d high season.

Food
The following spots are listed from Puerto Viejo eastward.

Restaurant Beach Break, two km east of Puerto Viejo, serves American breakfasts ($3), sandwiches ($2), and *batidos* (milk shakes). **Café Extravaganza** is a simple spot at Punta Cocles. It serves pizzas. **Hotel y Restaurante Yaré** is a good option; so, too, **Restaurante La Palapa,** a stone's throw away, strongly recommended for its corvina and *típico* dishes with a nouvelle twist and doubling as a disco after 10 p.m. Nearby, **Restaurante Elena Brown,** I'm informed, offers Caribbean dishes that border on gourmet. There are several basic *sodas* nearby south of Punta Cocles.

French-run **Paloma Café** at Playa Chiquita merges European into Caribbean, with such specialties as vegetarian lasagne, curried rice pilafs, pineapple chicken, and fresh fruit muffins served in an open-air dining room with chairs in bright tropical colors. It serves American breakfasts and features a chess night, video night, and backgammon night. Next door, try **Soda Aquarius** a tiny place where a German host serves omelettes, waffles, crepes, and fruit plates for breakfast, plus sandwiches, pasta, and seafood dishes for lunch.

One km farther, at Punta Uva, is **El Duende Felíz,** a cool and shady Italian restaurant serving salads and pastas (from $3), and a house specialty of lomito mediteraneo ($6). There's a seafood restaurant—**Restaurante Arecife**—400 meters south, along a side road that leads to the shore at Punta Uva.

MANZANILLO

This lonesome hamlet sits at the end of the road, 13 km south of Puerto Viejo. Manzanillo hardly deserves the moniker of "village," being just a few wooden shacks and houses. The primarily black and Indian population has lived for generations in what is now the wildlife refuge, living off the sea and using the land to farm cacao until 1979, when the *Monilia* fungus wiped out the crop. Electricity was a major change, arriving in Manzanillo for Christmas 1989. An even greater change is now underway: tourism. The hamlet has suddenly become a darling of the offbeat, alternate travel set. Expect things to happen around here in coming years.

From Manzanillo, a five-km coastal trail leads to the fishing hamlet of **Punta Mona** ("Monkey Point") and the heart of Gandoca-Manzanillo National Park. According to local legend, Christopher Columbus himself named Monkey Point—for the population of howler monkeys that still inhabits the swampy area—and Manzanillo, for a great old manzanillo tree that once towered over the coast. The tree died in the 1940s and finally toppled into the sea in 1957.

Accommodations and Food

Albergue Manzanillo has three large, a/c, carpeted, albeit soulless rooms with private bath. One has a king-size bed; another has two singles; the third has three singles. There's a shared veranda with hammock and sofa, plus a popular restaurant. Rates: $20 d. **Cabinas Maxi**—next to Bar Maxi—has five basic rooms facing the beach. Rates: $8.

Restaurant/Bar Maxi serves *típico* dishes and seafood, such as *pargo rojo* (red snapper) and lobster ($4-9). Several local ladies will cook meals with advance notice. Ask for Miss Alfonsina, Miss Edith, Doña Cipriana, and Miss Marva.

Entertainment

Bar Maxi is the only place in Manzanillo that remotely resembles action. The gloomy bar downstairs is enlivened by the slap of dominoes and the blast of Jimmy Cliff and Bob Marley, and the dancing spills out onto the sandy road. The upstairs bar (decorated with carved wooden motifs and wind chimes) has a breezy terrace. The place was jammin'—in the middle of the day—when I called by.

Tours and Activities

Aquamore, e-mail: aquavent@sol.racsa.co.cr, is a full-service dive shop offering dives ($30-40), PADI certification course ($200), and snorkeling ($5-35). It rents scuba and snorkel equipment, plus kayaks ($5 per hour). It also offers **kayak** trips up the Río Uva, into Gandoca lagoon, has open-kayak surf instruction, and features a "Dolphin Observation and Aquatic Photo Safari" ($25) into Gandoca-Manzanillo. Hours: daily 6:30 a.m.-8 p.m.

You can rent **horses** from Jácamo. Willie Burton arranges boat rides and snorkeling; Miss Alfonsina offers guided botany tours; and local guides for hikes into Gandoca-Manzanillo can be arranged through Florentino Renald, who acts as park administrator. He'll also help arrange a boat ride to the beaches at the southern end of the park.

Getting There and Away

By Bus: The bus fare from San José to Manzanillo is $6.25. Buses depart Puerto Limón for Manzanillo (two hours) via Puerto Viejo at 6 a.m. and 2:30 p.m., and from Puerto Viejo (45 min-

THE SOUTHERN CARIBBEAN 407

utes) for Manzanillo at 7:15 a.m. and 4 p.m. Return buses depart Manzanillo at 8:30 a.m. and 5 p.m. Check for current schedules.

By Car and Bike: Hitchhiking from Puerto Viejo is relatively easy; an informal pickup and delivery service operates among drivers. Just wave and they'll stop. Locals would appreciate a ride if you're driving. Alternatively, rent a bicycle, but be prepared for a hot, bumpy ride.

REFUGIO NACIONAL DE VIDA SILVESTRE GANDOCA-MANZANILLO

One of Costa Rica's best-kept secrets, 9,446-hectare Gandoca-Manzanillo National Wildlife Refuge protects a spectacularly beautiful, palm-fringed, nine-km-long, crescent-shaped beach where four species of turtles—most abundantly, leatherback turtles—come ashore to lay their eggs (Jan.-April is best). Some 4,436 hectares of the park extends out to sea, protecting the shore breeding grounds for turtles. Playa Gandoca is brown sand and littered with logs washed ashore, but I've nonetheless seen it referred to as Costa Rica's most beautiful beach, perhaps because of its lonesome setting. The ocean has rip tides and is not safe for swimming.

The reserve—which is 65% tropical rainforest—also protects rare swamp habitats, including the only mangrove forest on Costa Rica's Caribbean shores, two holillo palm swamps (important habitats for tapirs), a 300-hectare cativo forest, and a live coral reef 200 meters offshore. The reef system covers five square kilometers and is rarely dived by outsiders because of the difficulty of reaching the refuge. The hill forests, with their thick understories, harbor many tall mahoganies.

The large freshwater **Gandoca Lagoon**, one km south of Gandoca village, runs up to 50 meters deep and has two openings into the sea. The estuary comprises red mangrove trees: a complex world braided by small brackish streams and snakelike creeks, which sometimes interconnect, sometimes peter out in narrow cul-de-sacs, and sometimes open suddenly into broad lagoons that all look alike. The mangroves shelter both a giant oysterbed and a nursery for lobster and the swift and powerful tarpon. Manatees also swim and breed here. With luck, too,

you'll be able to spot crocodiles and caimans. The park is also a seasonal or permanent home to at least 358 species of birds (including toucans, red-lored Amazon parakeets, and hawk-eagles) as well as margays, ocelots, pacas, and sloths. And a rare estuarine dolpin—the *tucuxí*—was recently discovered in the lagoons. It is not a true riverine dolphin (such as the Amazonian and Ganges dolphins), although the *tucuxí* also swims in the mouth of the Río Sixaola. It is most commonly seen offshore and has been found as far north as Laguna Leimus, in Nicaragua.

The hamlets of Punta Uva, Manzanillo, Punta Mona, and Gandoca form part of the refuge. Because local communities live within the park, it is a mixed-management reserve; the locals' needs are being integrated into park-management policies. The tiny coastal hamlet of **Gandoca** is about five km south of Manzanillo.

In 1991, the cacophony of chainsaws began in earnest on the western side of Gandoca-Manzanillo, followed by the roar of flatbed trucks loaded with cativo and cedar logs. Independent loggers are reportedly buying trees from local farmers, then cutting them down and carrying them off to sell to lumber companies. Many trees—particularly the fine mahoganies—are being cut illegally on the borders of, and even within, the refuge itself. And banana plantations are pushing up against the refuge from the west (two banana companies, País and Chiriqui, have bought land rights on the park border).

ASACODE (Asociación Sanmigueleña de Conservación y Desarrollo), Apdo. 170-2070 San José, tel. 745-2165, c/o Teodoro, who speaks only Spanish; or Apdo. 170-2070 Sabanilla, tel. 224-6090, fax 253-7524, is a *campesino* organization that operates a private reserve within the reserve at the hamlet of **San Miguel**, deep in the forest on the western edge of Gandoca-Manzanillo. ASACODE fights to save the forest and other natural resources threatened by logging, and to evolve a sustainable livelihood through reforestation, and other earth-friendly methods. It welcomes visitors. Another association, **ADE-COMAGA** (Asociación de Desarrollo Ecológico de Cocles, Manzanillo y Gandoca), has similar objectives, including the implementation of a management plan for the region; the plan will involve expansion of telephone lines, drainage systems, storm-proof bridges, etc.

green turtle

WILDLAND ADVENTURES, INC.

Turtle Patrol

Volunteers are needed for the **Marine Turtle Conservation Project,** which conducts research and protects the turtles from predators and poachers. The tour of duty is one week. You patrol the beach at night, measuring and tagging turtles, camouflaging their nests, and discouraging egg-bandits. Conditions are harsh: lots of rain and insects, and long hours walking the beach. Lodging is either in your own tent or in closely packed bunk beds in a small earthen-floored rancho that acts as refuge headquarters. It has no electricity or running water. Mosquitoes will eye you greedily, awaiting a signal to pounce (bring a mosquito net). Local families prepare meals. Contact either **ATEC,** tel. 750-0191 or tel./fax 750-0188, e-mail: atecmail@sol.racsa.co.cr; or Jesús Valenciano, tel. 224-3570, fax 253-7524. Non-volunteers: $15 for accommodation.

Exploring the Park

The park is easily explored simply by walking the kilometers of white-sand beaches; trails also wind through the flat, lowland rainforest fringing the coast. A coastal track that skirts the swamps leads south from the west side of Manzanillo village to Gandoca village (two hours), from where you can walk the beach one km south to Gandoca Lagoon, virtually within a stone's throw of the Panamanian border. Beyond the lagoon, a trail winds through the jungle—thick, hot, and teeming with monkeys, parrots, sloths, and snakes—ending at the Río Sixaola and the

Panamá border. Trails are often obscure and slippery with mud. A guide is recommended.

You can hire a guide and boat in Sixaola to take you downriver to the mangrove swamps at the rivermouth (dangerous currents and reefs prevent access from the ocean). If you pilot yourself, stay away from the Panamanian side of the river, as the Panamanian border police are said to be very touchy.

The ranger station is ostensibly in Manzanillo, where refuge manager Florentino Renald can describe in glowing detail the reserve's treasures. Entrance: $1. Call the park service at 192 or (800) 012-3456 for information.

Accommodations and Food

Evaristo and Corea María have three basic rooms at **Cabinas Corea** in Gandoca for $15 with breakfast and lunch (volunteers who protect the turtles get first pick). The showers and toilet are in the backyard, which you share with pigs and fowl. The couple also have a tiny *abastacedor,* or village store.

ASACODE Lodge is a rustic *albergue* at San Miguel run by the local farmers' association. The simple lodge accommodates groups ($7 pp; $5 per meal).

Camping is permitted in the park, but there are no facilities.

Getting There

If you don't want to hike, you can easily drive to Gandoca village via a 15-km pebble-and-dirt road (in reasonable condition) that leads east from the Bribrí-Sixaola road; the turnoff is about three km south of Sixaola. Keep left at the crossroads 1.5 km down the road. Conditions may vary, but an ordinary car could have made it easily when I tried. Still, I recommend a 4WD.

BRIBRÍ AND VICINITY

From Hone Creek, Hwy. 36 (badly potholed during my last visit) winds uphill through the foothills of the Talamancas and descends to Bribrí, a small town 60 km south of Puerto Limón, and the administrative center for the local banana industry and nearby Indian reserves. It is surrounded by bright green banana plantations spread out in a flat valley backed by tiers of far-off mountains with veils of courtesan clouds drifting among the valleys and shrouding the peaks. The Indian influence is noticeable. Look for the studio of **primitivist painter** Fran Vasquez east of town.

The paved road ends in Bribrí, but dirt roads lead south to Sixaola, and west through the gorge of the Río Sixaola and the village of **Bratsi,** where the vistas open up across the wide, wide **Valle de Talamanca** surrounded by soaring mountains—a region known as **Alta Talamanca.** The United Fruit Company once reigned supreme in the valley and the history of the region is a sad tale of false promises (many of the Indians who opposed destruction of their forests at the turn of the century were hunted and jailed). The fight continues today against mining companies.

Dirt roads wind into the mountains and the Talamanca Indigenous Reserves.

Talamanca Indigenous Reserves
The **Reserva Indígena Talamanca-Bribrí** and **Reserva Indígena Talamanca-Cabecar** are incorporated into La Amistad International Peace Park, on the slopes of the Talamanca mountains. The parks were established to protect the traditional lifestyle of the indigenous people, though the communities and their land remain under constant threat from loggers and squatters (the tragically farcical story of the creation of the reserves is told in Anachristina Rossi's novel, *La Loca de Gandoca*).

The Indians have no villages of any substance as they prefer to live apart. Though the Indians speak Spanish and wear Western clothing, what the reserves offer is a rewarding insight into a lifestyle in harmony with nature, including customs and beliefs passed down through millennia. Their philosophy that all living things are the work of Sibô, their god of creation, and therefore sacred has traditionally pitted the Indians against pioneers, for the Indians see themselves as custodians of the land.

Government proposals to build a trans-Talamanca Highway and a hydroelectricity dam are being fought by the Indians, who are well aware that their fate hangs in the balance. The communities supplement their income by selling baskets and other crafts, and organically grown cacao is an increasingly important source of revenue.

"Capital" of the Talamanca-Bribrí reserve is **Shiroles,** public tel. 754-2064, little more than a Guardia Rural station, a couple of *sodas,* a U.S. missionary station and a few tumbledown houses, with banana plantations that provide employment down by the Río Sixaola. You can walk 15 minutes uphill to **La Finca Educativa Indígena,** an administrative center for the Bribrí people, who hash out their differences and plan their futures here. It has a 44-bed dorm and cafeteria.

In contrast, the Cabecar Indians remain cautious of any tourist influx. Any visit to Calveri or other remote Cabecar villages must be by invitation or prior permission. **Amubri,** eight km west of Bratsi, is the "capital" and gateway to the reserve. If you go, enter with a sense of humility and respect. Do not attempt to treat the community members as a tourist oddity. Remember: You have as much to learn from the indigenous communities as to share. Gifts for the locals would be appreciated—blankets and medicines are preferred.

Permits are necessary to enter the parks, although things are easing and this may have changed; contact ATEC, tel. 750-0191 or tel./fax 750-0188, e-mail: atecmail@sol.racsa.co.cr, which arranges visits to the reserves with one-week's notice, including possible overnights with a Bribrí family. Mauricio Salazar, a Bribrí Indian who owns the Cabinas Chimurí in Puerto Viejo, can arrange permits. The journey can be arduous, and the accommodations are very, very basic. Buses depart Bribrí for Shiroles at 8 a.m., noon, and 5:30 p.m. It's a bumpy ride along an unpaved road. Get off at Abastacedor El Cruce;

turn left at the *soda* and walk 200 meters to a path that leads uphill to the Iguana Farm.

American Wilderness Experience, 2820-A Wilderness Place, Boulder, CO 80301-5454, tel. (303) 444-2622 or (800) 444-0099, fax (303) 444-3999, e-mail: awedave@aol.com, offers a 10-day journey through the Talamancas using canoes (hiking and horseback riding are also featured) and native guides ($1,676 land only). You can also arrange canoe trips through ATEC.

Aerovías Talamanqueñas Indígenas reportedly flies to Amubri, where local nuns run the Casa de Huéspedes.

Accommodations and Food

Cabinas El Mango, tel. 754-2253, on the right as you enter town, has 12 pleasant albeit basic modern units with private bathrooms and cold water. Rates: $4 pp. Its **Bar/Restaurant Mango** has a pool table and serves *típico* fare. **Cabinas Picuno,** tel. 258-2981, has basic rooms with private bathrooms. Rates: $7.

Just east of Bribrí is the **Restaurant El Socia** and **Restaurant Mango,** tel. 258-3353; the latter has dancing. In town are the **Restaurante King-Giang** and **Restaurante Bribrí.** The **Bar Tiliri Bribrí** looks like the most "happening" place.

Services

The town has a **Banco Nacional** (open 10 a.m.-noon and 1-3:45 p.m.) and **post office.** The bank offers a discounted exchange rate (eight percent less than in San José) but has a $100 limit. It gets crowded and can take half a day to get money changed. There's also a **medical clinic** opposite the bank, and a **Red Cross** evacuation center, tel. 758-0125, for emergencies, plus a **police station,** tel. 758-1865.

Getting There

By Bus: The San José-Sixaola bus passes through Bribrí. Buses depart Puerto Viejo for Bribrí (30 minutes) and Sixaola at 6:30 a.m., 9:30 a.m., 11:30 a.m., 5:30 p.m., and 7:30 p.m. Buses depart Bribrí for Limón at 6:30 a.m., 9 a.m., 11:30 a.m., 12:30 p.m., and 4 p.m.; for San José at 6 a.m., 9 a.m., 11 a.m., and 4 p.m.; and for Sixaola at 7:30 a.m., noon, 3 p.m. and 5:30 p.m.

Buses drop off and depart from the Restaurant Bribrí. Buses run from there to the Indian villages of Amubri and Shiroles.

SIXAOLA AND VICINITY

Sixaola, 34 km southeast of Bribrí, is on the north bank of the 200-meter-wide, fast-flowing Río Sixaola, forming the border with Panamá. The town is divided into Sixaola Oeste and Sixaola Este by a raised railway embankment. There is no central plaza, although the soccer field in Sixaola Este is a focal point. You reach the dour, gutsy border town along a deeply rutted dirt road with banana plantations to the left and right. Like Sixaola, the graceless hamlets along the way exist only to serve the banana industry.

The turnoff for the hamlet of Gandoca and the Gandoca-Manzanillo Reserve is at **Noventa y Seis,** three km west of Sixaola. You can hire a boat in Sixaola to take you on a river trip with notice.

Crossing into Panamá

Unless you want to visit Boca del Toro, there's little reason to cross into Panamá here, as links with the rest of the country are tenuous. Most international travelers cross into Panamá at Paso Canoas, on the Pacific coast. You can walk or drive across the border at the bridge in Sixaola.

The Costa Rican Immigration and Customs posts face each other atop the railway embankment on the west side of the metal bridge. Both are open daily 7 a.m.-5 p.m. Remember to advance your watches by one hour.

If you want to go to Guabito (or Changuinola, farther down the line) to shop, you can do so without getting exit stamps from Costa Rica (the bus from the Panamanian side of the border to Changuinola costs $1). You will have to leave your bags at Panamanian customs after walking across the bridge. There are no hotels in Guabito.

Accommodations and Food

The **Hotel el Imperio,** tel. 754-2289, is on the left as you come into Sixaola. Its sole room costs $5. **Hotel Doris** is a ramshackle two-story house one block east of the soccer field. **Cabinas Sánchez** has basic *cabinas* on the southwest side of the railway. **Cabinas La Union** has six pleasant little *cabinas* with private bathrooms and cold water opposite the Texaco station at La Union, 10 km east of Bribrí (ask at Finca La Union, 100 meters farther east). Rates: $8 s/d.

THE SOUTHERN CARIBBEAN 411

The Chinese-run **Restaurant Central,** just before the ramp up to the border post, has a large menu and reportedly offers very basic accommodations. On the same block are the **Restaurant China, Restaurant Yeleski** (with discotheque), and **Restaurant Hang Wung.** Also in town is the **El Siquerreno.**

Getting There and Away
By Bus: The bus fare from San José to Puerto Viejo is $7. Return buses depart Sixaola for Puerto Limón at 5 a.m., 8 a.m., 10 a.m., and 3 p.m.; for San José at 6 a.m. and 2:30 p.m.

By Car: There's a Texaco **gas station** about 10 km east of Bribrí. Lots of people walk the road, including children who have to walk kilometers to school; help them out with a ride if you have room. You'll be stopped at the *comando* (military checkpoint) as you enter and depart Sixoala.

BOB RACE

CATHY CARLSON

NORTHERN LOWLANDS

With all the hyperbole about Costa Rica's magnificent beaches and mountains, the northern lowlands have until recently gotten short shrift from tourists. During the colonial period the region was a no-man's land marked only by murky rivers cutting through the vast forested plains that sweep across most of northern Costa Rica, forming a huge triangle-shaped plain as green and as flat as a billiard table.

Any ho-hum first impression is not a fair one. Skirting the foothills of the cordillera, the vistas southward are as grandiose as any in the country. From below, Costa Rica's ethereal volcanic landscapes remind me of Bali. Pastures tumble down the mountainsides like folds of green silk. The plains are thick with chartreuse wands of rice. And the colors are like a painting by Matisse: emerald greens flowing into burning golds, soft pastels, and warm ochers relieved periodically by brilliant tropical colors, houses as blue as the morning sky and flower petals and rich soils as red as ripe, luscious tomatoes.

For the naturalist there are some splendid sites: crocodile farms, remote national parks, and plenty of private reserves superb for birding.

For the explorer with time to spare, there are trails to off-the-beaten-track treasures: caves, waterfalls, and rivers for rafting and kayaking. Arenal Volcano looms magnificently and well within reach. And the past few years have seen a blossoming of marvelous hostelries. With good reason, the northern lowlands are finally on the tourist map—and the ritzy new look of Fortuna, the region's most important town, further reflects the newfound popularity.

Most places of greatest tourist interest can be reached along well-paved roads. More remote spots are approached along appallingly potholed roads, but the routes are comparatively straightforward. Most places of interest are within a short drive of one another, and all are readily accessible on a day's journey from San José.

Many roads slice through the cordillera and drop sharply down the steep north-facing slopes onto to the plains. The one you choose may depend on your destination in the lowlands.

CATUZON, the Northern Zone Tourism Board, Apdo. 258-4400 Ciudad Quesada, tel. 460-1672, fax 460-0391, provides an information and hotel reservation service.

THE LAND

The lowlands constitute a 40,000-square-kilometer watershed drained by the Ríos Frío, San Carlos, and Sarapiquí and their tributaries, many of which are navigable by shallow-water craft. They extend north to the Río San Juan and beyond into southern Nicaragua, where much of the fighting took place during the 1980s. This border zone is now an agrarian front in the battle to establish the Si-a-Paz transnational park.

The region is made up of two separate plains (llanuras): the **Llanura de los Guatusos** (formed by sediments washed down from the Cordillera de Guanacaste and Cordillera de Tilarán and deposited as part of the Lake Nicaragua basin millions of years ago) in the west, and the **Llanura de San Carlos** (formed of fluvial sediments from the basins between the San Carlos and Chirripó rivers) farther east.

These rivers meander like restless snakes and commonly flood in the wet season, when much of the landscape is transformed into swampy marshlands epitomized by Caño Negro National Wildlife Refuge, southwest of Los Chiles, near the Nicaraguan border. Such terrain provides perfect conditions for rice cultivation, and much of the rice that is the staple of the Costa Rican diet is grown here.

These plains were once rampant with tropical forest. During recent decades the western lowlands have been transformed into a geometrical patchwork of scraggly cattle pastures, fruit fincas, and rice paddies. Farther east, much of the land was cleared early in this century to make way for bananas, a crop especially suited to the region. Deforestation continues apace, and sawmills and huge piles of logs stacked ready for transportation line the routes every few kilometers. Yet, there is still plenty of rainforest—much of it protected as private reserves—extending for miles across the plains and clambering up the north-facing slopes of the cordillera whose scarp face encusps the lowlands. Allen M. Young's *Sarapiquí Chronicle: A Naturalist Guide in Costa Rica* (Washington, D.C.: Smithsonian Institution Press, 1991), is a splendid book telling of 20 years of natural history study in the region.

There are few towns, with many miles between lodgings. Buses serve most destinations.

Climate

The climate bears much in common with the Caribbean coast: warm, very humid, and consistently wet. Temperatures hover at 25-27° C year-round. The climatic periods are not as well defined as those of other parts of the nation, and rarely does a week pass without a prolonged and heavy rain shower (it rains a little less from February to the beginning of May). Annual rainfall can exceed 450 cm in some parts. Precipitation tends to diminish and the dry season grows more pronounced northward and westward.

HISTORY

Corobicí Indians settled the western lowland region several thousand years ago and were divided into at least 12 distinct tribes. This indigenous population was decimated by internecine warfare with Nicaraguan tribes in the early Spanish colonial period.

As early as the 16th century, Spanish vessels were navigating the Río San Juan all the way from the Caribbean to Lake Nicaragua, a journey of 195 kilometers. Pirates also periodically sailed up the river to loot and burn the lakeside settlements. One of the very few colonial remains in the region is El Castillo de la Concepción, a fort erected by the Spanish in 1675 to keep English pirates from progressing upstream (the ruins are in Nicaragua, three km west of where the Costa Rican border moves south of the river).

This early exploration was limited to the broad river channels, and colonization of most of the region has only occurred within this century. Only between 1815 and 1820 was the first access link with the Río Sarapiquí made, via a mud-and-dirt trail that went from Heredia via Vara Blanca. The river, which descends from Barva Volcano, became in the early heyday of coffee the most traveled route for getting to the Caribbean Sea from the central highlands.

The Spanish first descended from the central highlands on a foray into the lowland foothills in 1640. They called the region San Jerónimo de los Votos. But almost 200 years were to pass before the foothills were settled. The first pioneers—the Quesada family from San Ramón—formed a village, then known as La Uniá and today called Ciudad Quesada (colloquially called San Carlos). The Quesadas contributed greatly to the rapid development.

The area remained isolated for years. About 40 years ago the first organized farming reached below Ciudad Quesada onto the edge of the flatlands. Beginning in the 1950s the government, as part of its policy to promote new set-

tlements outside the Meseta Central, helped finance small cattle farmers, and settlement began to edge slowly north. Meanwhile, construction by banana companies of new feeder railways in the eastern lowlands opened up unexplored, virgin land for production. Much of the magnificent forests has since given way to great cattle *fincas* and sweeping banana plantations.

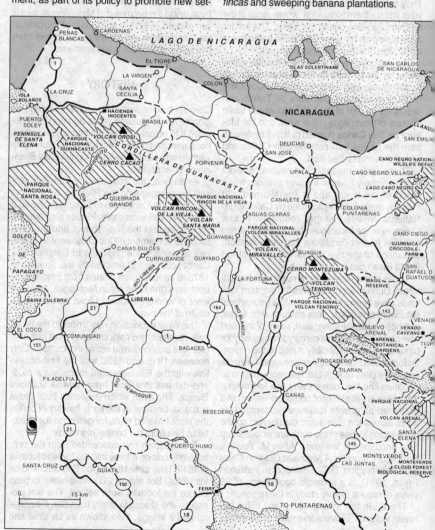

Only in 1948 was a highway built that reached the Río Cuarto (a little over 48 km due north of San José). The road didn't reach Puerto Viejo de Sarapiquí until 1957. And places such as Upala and Los Chiles continued to use rivers for transportation to Limón until the late 1970s, when the construction of paved highways and bridges granted access to the rest of the country.

ECONOMY

The northern lowlands have been called the breadbasket of the nation, and most of the working population is employed in agriculture.

Along the cordillera foothills, the lands are dedicated to cattle farming. The plain of San

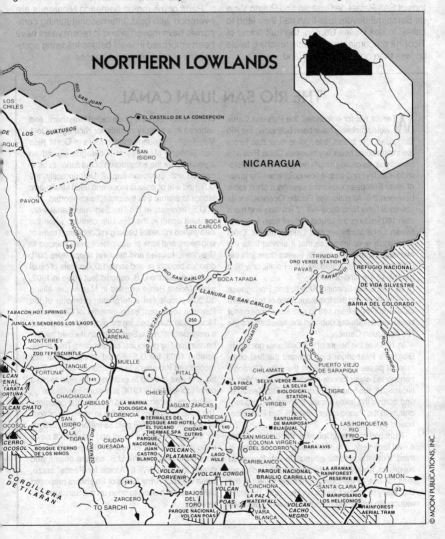

Carlos, centered on Ciudad Quesada, devotes almost 70% of its territory to cattle and produces the best-quality milk in the nation. In the lowlands proper, dairy cattle give way to beef cattle, and other agricultural products predominate the farther one travels from the foothills: plantations of *pejibaye* palm and pineapples, bananas in the east, and citrus fruits farther north. The cantons of San Rafael de Guatuso and Puerto Viejo de Sarapiquí devote less than half their land to cattle. In Los Chiles Canton, the fruit *fincas* of TicoFrut predominate and cattle ranching takes up less than one-third of farmland.

Many farmers in Guatuso, Upala, and Los Chiles cantons are little more than subsistence farmers who make their livings raising corn, beans, tubers, cacao, rice, and a few head of livestock. Nicaraguans have traditionally moved freely across the border by plying their watercraft upriver; today, they help sustain agriculture by working as cheap farm labor.

Parts of the region bordering Nicaragua are even rich with gold. International mining companies have moved in and in recent years have been embroiled in legal battles following accusations of environmental abuses.

THE RÍO SAN JUAN CANAL

Were it not for volcanoes, the Panamá Canal would probably have been built along the Río San Juan, the broad, easygoing river that forms the international boundary between Costa Rica and Nicaragua. Its gaping mouth (where Barra del Colorado is today) and ample flow quickened the pulse of early European explorers seeking a short route between the Atlantic and Pacific Oceans, for its source is Lake Nicaragua—at 72 km wide and more than 160 km long, the largest body of fresh water between Lake Michigan and Lake Titicaca. Lake Nicaragua is so immense that it almost links the two oceans, and although its waters drain into the Caribbean, it is separated from the Pacific only by a narrow 17-km strip of land.

By 1551, the Spanish, Dutch, and Portuguese were all surveying this fortuitous piece of real estate for a direct route from sea to sea. For the next four centuries, engineers debated the feasibility of the Río San Juan Canal.

In 1850, at the height of the California gold rush, Gordon's Passenger Line opened the first commercial passenger service on the river. Gordon's transported eager fortune-seekers from New York to Nicaragua, then ferried them up the Río San Juan and across the lake. A mule then carried the argonauts to the Pacific coast, where a San Francisco-bound ship waited.

Transport magnate Cornelius Vanderbilt opened a rival ferry service in 1851 with a grander vision in mind: a canal across the isthmus. Events forestalled his dream, however. The Nicaraguans levied transit fees for use of the river. Vanderbilt called in the U.S. Navy to "protect American interests." The Navy reduced to rubble the unfortunate rivermouth town of San Juan del Norte (then called Greytown), and ushered in a century of strife for Nicaragua. On 1 May 1858, President Juanito Mora of Costa Rica and General Martínes of Nicaragua signed an agreement for the construction of the canal, to be financed with European capital. Unfortunately, the U.S. had a fit of jealous pique and used strong-arm tactics to ensure that the project was aborted.

U.S. interests in the Río San Juan canal were aroused again in the late 19th century, when the idea gained influential backing in Congress. Teams of engineers and tons of equipment were shipped to Greytown, railroad and machine shops were built, dredges brought in, and some 1,000 meters of canal were dug. But the U.S. got cold feet again in 1902, when Mount Pelée erupted in Martinique, killing 30,000 people (an enterprising promoter of the Panamá route sent each member of Congress a Nicaraguan stamp bearing the picture of a volcano as a reminder that a Río San Juan canal would forever be menaced by geological catastrophe). Thus in November 1903, the U.S. signed an agreement that recognized Panamá's independence from Colombia and was granted in exchange the right to dig a canal (completed in 1914) at a much inferior site.

Even this fait accompli did not deter the dreamers. The fickle Americans tried twice to revive the project: in 1916, when the U.S. paid $3 million to Nicaragua for the right to build a canal and establish a naval base in the Gulf of Fonseca (Nicaragua's neighbors protested and the U.S. backed down); and during the post-WW II "Atoms for Peace" craze, when the U.S. Army Corps of Engineers proposed using nuclear bombs to open up the San Juan waterway!

COSTA RICA AND CATTLE RANCHING

"There was so much jungle 20 years ago; individual farmers had no concept of the cumulative damage," Jim Hamilton told me over a beer at the Tilajari Resort Hotel, which he owns. Though an American, Jim was once typical of the small-scale farmers who have turned the lowlands from jungle into Costa Rica's breadbasket in all of 20 years. Contrary to a popular perception, the story is not one of cattle barons and rapacious greed.

Jim was an atypical American, a poor gringo who started with nothing. He came to Costa Rica with the Peace Corps in 1969 and carried out the first census in Upala Province. After his work was finished he decided to clear a few acres and farm, "for the unique experience." He cleared his own land, milked his own cows, cooked his eggs on hot rocks, and learned his cattle skills from the locals.

Back then, the region was served only by horse trails and an airstrip often inoperable for days on end because of weather. It used to take Jim three days by river and horseback to travel between his two plots of land; in 1992, I made the same journey by road in two hours. "Cattle was the only type of product that could be got to market. Cattle can walk," Jim explained. "There was no other way of making money." Hence, the land was cleared by hundreds of impoverished squatters and homesteaders like Jim who each raised a few head and grew corn to feed pigs, which could also be walked to market.

Cattle brought in cash but condemned the rainforests. "Poor farmers can't make a living by holding their land in jungle," Jim said ruefully. The initial ranchers were forced to sell their lumber to pay for the cost of their land and loans. (Interest rates for cattle farmers 20 years ago were subsidized by the World Bank, as agricultural economists saw the most hopeful future for Central American economies in beef.)

Once the area was developed, the government eventually brought in roads and electricity. Suddenly, other alternatives were possible. Since beef farming is the least remunerative agribusiness (the return per hectare from cattle farms is only about one-quarter that from growing produce), very little land has been cleared for cattle within the last decade. Tropical fruits began to oust the hooved locusts. Alas, citrus fruits and bananas, which take up the best agricultural land in the lowlands, have pushed up land values enormously, and land is increasingly passing out of the hands of small-scale farmers and into those of the large fruit companies.

brown Swiss cow

BOB RACE

CIUDAD QUESADA AND VICINITY

Ciudad Quesada (pop. 30,000), known locally as San Carlos and denoted on bus routes as such, hovers above the plains at 650 meters elevation on the north-facing slope of the Cordillera de Tilarán, with the northern lowlands spread out at its feet. Despite its mountain-town airs, the bustling market town and transportation node is the hierarchial center of the entire northern region, and the main gateway to Fortuna, Volcán Arenal, and Parque Nacional Caño Negro. It is surrounded by lush pasture—some of the richest and most developed in the country—grazed by prize-specimen dairy cattle. The town slopes downhill northward.

The tree-shaded **main plaza** is a good place to sit on a bench and watch the bustling activity. You may find the **main church** of interest; so, too, the lively **mercado central** on the northwest corner featuring colorful fruit and vegetable stalls and an *artesanía* cooperative selling local arts and crafts. There are *talabarterías* (saddle shops), too, redolent of hides and tannins, where you can

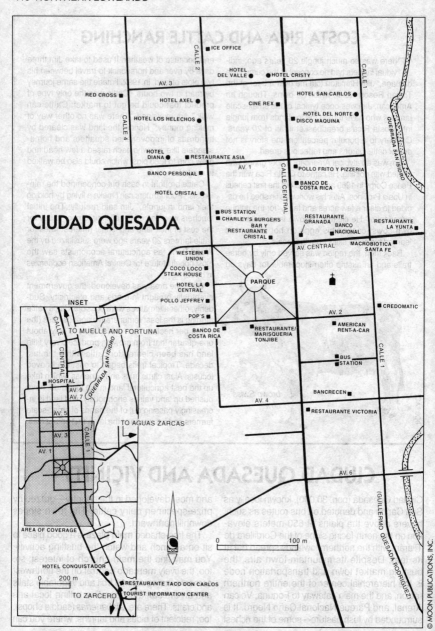

CIUDAD QUESADA

ICE OFFICE

HOTEL DEL VALLE • • HOTEL CRISTY

AV. 3

RED CROSS ■ HOTEL SAN CARLOS
HOTEL AXEL • CINE REX ■ HOTEL DEL NORTE •
HOTEL LOS HELECHOS • DISCO MAQUINA •

HOTEL DIANA • ■ RESTAURANTE ASIA

AV. 1

BANCO PERSONAL ■ POLLO FRITO Y PIZZERIA ■
BANCO DE COSTA RICA ■
HOTEL CRISTAL •

■ BUS STATION
■ CHARLEY'S BURGERS RESTAURANTE
BAR Y GRANADA ■
RESTAURANTE RESTAURANTE
CRISTAL ■ BANCO LA YUNTA ■
NACIONAL ■

AV. CENTRAL
MACROBIOTICA
WESTERN SANTA FE ■
UNION ■
COCO LOCO
STEAK HOUSE ■
HOTEL LA PARQUE
CENTRAL ■
POLLO JEFFREY ■
CREDOMATIC ■
POP'S ■ AV. 2
BANCO DE RESTAURANTE/ AMERICAN
COSTA RICA ■ MARISQUERIA RENT-A-CAR ■
TONJIBE ■
■ BUS
STATION
AV. 4 BANCRECEN ■
■ RESTAURANTE VICTORIA

AV. 6

CALLE 2 CALLE 1 CALLE CENTRAL CALLE 1

(GUILLERMO QUESADA RODRIGUEZ)

INSET

TO MUELLE AND FORTUNA

■ HOSPITAL
AV. 9
AV. 7
AV. 5
AV. 3
AV. 1

TO AGUAS ZARCAS

AREA OF COVERAGE

HOTEL CONQUISTADOR ■

0   200 m

■ RESTAURANTE TACO DON CARLOS
■ TOURIST INFORMATION CENTER

TO ZARCERO

0   100 m

© MOON PUBLICATIONS, INC.

watch elaborately decorated saddles being crafted. The annual **Cattle Fair** (Feria del Ganado) in April is one of the largest in the country, with a horse parade *(tope)* and general merriment. Otherwise there's nothing here of tourist concern.

Accommodations
Shoestring: Several hotels in the below-$10 category are found north of the plaza. The best is probably **Hotel San Carlos** with six spic-and-span rooms for $4 pp shared bath, $10 s/d private bath with hot water. There's a laundry. The **Hotel Cristal,** tel. 460-0541, has very basic rooms. Rates: $3.50 s, $5 d shared bath; $5 s, $8 d private bath. Across the road is **Hotel Ugalde,** tel. 460-0260, with rooms with private baths for $3 s, $5 d. In a similar price bracket and one block north is the **Hotel Axel Alberto,** tel. 460-1423, with private bathrooms and fans. Rates: $10 s/d. Between the blocks is the **Hotel Diana,** tel. 460-3319, which charges $3 s, $6 d. **Hotel Cristy,** tel. 460-4533, three blocks north of the plaza on Avenida 3, Calles 0/1, has basic rooms with shared bath for $3 pp. **Hotel del Valle,** tel. 460-0718, two blocks northwest of the square, is of a similar standard and price. Other budget hotels include **Los Fernandos; Lily,** tel. 460-0616; the very basic **Hotel Los Helechos;** and **Hotel Terminal,** tel. 460-2158, the latter conveniently located in the bus terminal, southwest of the plaza, and thereby noisy.

I recommend the **Hotel Del Valle,** tel. 460-0718, with 10 clean, carpeted rooms with wood ceilings, fans, and private bathrooms with hot water. There's a TV lounge. Rates: $7 s, $13 d, $16 t. Likewise, **Hotel del Norte,** tel. 460-1959, is a good bet, with 18 well-kept albeit simple rooms with cable TVs (some rooms), fans, and hot water in the clean tiled bathrooms. Rates: $4 pp shared bath; $8 s, $13 d private bath. It has a laundry and weight machine.

Budget: Climbing the scale, the **El Retiro,** tel. 460-0463, has clean and comfortable rooms with baths overlooking the main plaza. Rates: $10 s, $18 d. The **Hotel La Central,** Apdo. 345-4400 Ciudad Quesada, tel. 460-0301, fax 460-0391, is on the west side of the plaza. It has 48 clean, meagerly furnished rooms (some with balconies), with fans, TVs, and hot-water showers. There's a casino and restaurant. Rates: $15 s, $28 d. Nearby is the **Hotel Don Goyo,** tel.

460-1780, fax 460-6383, offering clean rooms in bright pastels, each with private bath, hot water, and heaps of light. Rates: $15 s, $19 d. Another acceptable bet is the **Hotel Conquistador,** tel. 469-0546, fax 460-6311, behind the tourist information center half a kilometer south of the plaza, with a restaurant, secure parking, and 45 sparely furnished rooms with clean private baths and hot water. Rates: $10 s, $16 d, $21 t. TVs were to be added. **Balneario San Carlos,** tel. 460-0747, on the northern outskirts, has a restaurant, weekend entertainment, and basic cabins with baths but no fans, and a swimming pool that doubles as a skating rink. Rates: $20 d.

The best bargain lies four km north of Quesada, where the **Hotel La Mirada,** tel. 460-2222, sits atop the scarp face overlooking the plains. The sweeping vistas from the open-air restaurant are truly stupendous; travelers familiar with Tanzania's Ngorongoro Crater will feel a touch of déjà vu as they look along the forested flanks of the escarpment. Each of the 13 rooms has a carport, a telephone, hot water, and a private bath. Rates: $15 s/d.

Food
The clean and modern **Coca Coca Steak House,** tel. 460-3208, on the west side of the plaza specializes in *lomitos* (from $5). **La Jarra Restaurant,** on the southeast corner, is a good alternative for meat dishes. So is **Restaurante Marisquería Tonjibe,** on the south side of the plaza, which also specializes in seafood. Owner Victor Murillo hosts music nightly and talent contests on weekends. Also try **Coca Loca** for steaks; it's inside the Centro Comercial on the town square.

Next door to the Hotel La Central is **Pop's,** for ice creams, and **Pollo Jeffrey,** for fried chicken. **Charlie's Burger Restaurant,** one block north, offers reasonable American fare. **Restaurante Asia,** next to Hotel Cristal, serves basic Chinese fare, as does **Restaurante Victoria.**

Restaurante Los Parados, 50 meters on the right on the road to Aguas Zarcas, specializes in chicken dishes cooked in front of you. For Mexican, try **Antojitos,** 400 meters east of the plaza, or **Restaurante Taco Don Carlos** near the the tourist information center. **Restaurant Aramacao** is a fancy *típico* restaurant on the mountainside one km south of town.

Tourist Information

CATUZON, the Cámara de Turismo de la Zona Norte (Northern Zone Chamber of Tourism), Apdo. 256, Ciudad Quesada 4400, tel. 460-1672, has a tourist bureau at the Y-junction two blocks south of the main square, where the road from Zarcero enters town. It sells a map of the region. Hours: Mon.-Sat. 8:30-11:30 a.m. and 1:30-5 p.m.

Services

There are four **banks** in the center of town. **Credomatic,** on Avenida 2 two blocks east of the square, has automatic credit machines (one for Visa, one for MasterCard). **BanCrecen,** Avenida 4 and Calle 1, also has a credit machine for Visa . **Western Union** has an office on the west side of the plaza; open Mon.-Fri. 8 a.m.-5 p.m. **Budget Rent-a-Car** has an office here, tel. 460-0650.

Getting There and Away

By Bus: Express buses depart San José every hour 5 a.m.-7:30 p.m. from the Coca-Cola bus station at Calle 16, Avenidas 1/3 (three hours via Zarcero; Autotransportes, tel. 255-4318). Slower buses for Ciudad Quesada and Fortuna also depart Coca-Cola at 6:15 a.m., 8:40 a.m., and 11:30 a.m. ($1.50; Garaje Barquero, tel. 232-5660). Buses to San José depart Ciudad Quesada hourly 5 a.m.-7 p.m.

In Ciudad Quesada, the two bus terminals are on the blocks immediately northwest and southeast of the plaza. Buses serve Arenal and Tilarán (via Fortuna) at 6 a.m. and 3 p.m.; to Fortuna at 5 a.m., 9:30 a.m., 1 p.m., 3 p.m., and 10 p.m.; to Los Chiles every two hours, 5 a.m.-5 p.m.; and to Puerto Viejo, tel. 460-0630, daily at 6 a.m., 10 a.m., and 3 p.m. **Interbus** stops at San Carlos on its daily shuttle between La Fortuna and San José.

By Car: American Rent-a-Car, tel. 460-0650, has an office on Avenida 2, 50 meters east of the plaza.

AGUAS ZARCAS AND VICINITY

Aguas Zarcas ("Blue Waters"), an important agricultural town at the foot of the cordillera, 15 km east of Ciudad Quesada, gets its name for the mineral hot springs that erupt from the base of the mountain. **Parque Nacional Juan Castro Blanco** flanks the slopes. Several spas—notably **El Túcano**—and *balnearios* take advantage of the thermal waters. **Termales del Bosque,** tel./fax 460-1356, about five km east of Ciudad Quesada, is billed as an "ecological park" with hiking trails through botanical gardens, plus horseback rides ($15-30) and bathing in thermal mineral springs. It offers aromatic and mud applications. Entrance costs $8 adults, $5 children. There's a coffee shop and lockers, a riverside restaurant, and the "Canopy Challenge Tour"—a treetop expedition that whisks you through the forest canopy using suspension bridges, nets, and gliding cables ($48). It's run by The Original Canopy Tour, Apdo. 751-2350, San Francisco de Dos Ríos, tel. 257-5149, fax 257-7626, e-mail: canopy@sol.racsa.co.cr.

Parque de Recreación Agua Caliente, tel. 460-0891, about 400 meters east, also has hot springs, swimming pools, forest trails, and tours.

At the community of **La Gloria de Aguas Zarcas,** a local cooperative—Coopesanjuan—of 12 families offers guided hikes, fishing, river rafting, and farm tours in an attempt to turn its 416-hectare property into a sustainable rural community. For information, contact Cooprena, Apdo. 6939-1000 San José, tel. 259-3401, fax 259-9430, cooprena@sol.racsa.co.cr.

From town, a paved road runs northwest to Muelle (22 km). The road from Ciudad Quesada continues east via **Venecia** and the hamlet of **Río Cuarto** to a T-junction at **San Miguel,** 24 km east of Aguas Zarcas. The road to the right leads south to San José via Vara Blanca, nestled in the saddle of Poás and Barva Volcanoes; the road to the left leads to Puerto Viejo de Sarapiquí. Two km east of Venecia, a dirt road (accessible by hiking or 4WD) leads to **Ciudad Cutris,** an archaeological site with pre-Columbian tumuli and hints that this was once a settlement with wide, well-ordered streets. The site has yet to be excavated and restored. From Río Cuarto, a rugged dirt road leads south uphill to an impressive waterfall.

La Marina Zoológica

This private zoo, tel. 460-0946, opposite the gas station three km west of Aguas Zarcas, houses jaguars, tapirs, agoutis, peccaries, badgers, monkeys, and other mammal species, as well as birds from around the world. The owner, Alba María Alfaro, has been taking in orphaned animals for three decades, and she now has more than 450 species of animals and birds, many confiscated by the government from owners who lacked permits to keep them. Señora Alfaro even has a Bengal tiger. The zoo, on a working cattle *finca* spread throughout five hectares, is nonprofit; donations are appreciated. A cafe is open on weekends. Hours: daily 8 a.m.-4 p.m. Entrance: $2.

Accommodations

Shoestring: Budget travelers might try **Cabinas Adriana,** tel. 474-4312, up the hill on the right immediately east of the church in the center of town. Basic rooms with shared bath cost $4 pp. **Hospedaje Hidalgo,** tel. 474-4154, is 20 meters up the hill and has similarly priced basic rooms. The **Hotel La Violeta,** tel. 474-4015, is similarly priced for rooms with shared bath, but has private baths, too, for $8

In Venecia, seven km east of Aguas Zarcas, **Hospedaje Torre Fuerte,** tel. 472-2424, has five clean, modern cabins with private bath and hot water on the main road. Rates: $6.50 pp.

Inexpensive: Coopesanjuan has a rustic **Ecolodge** at La Gloria de Aguas Zarcas, with three two-bedroom units—each room sleeps up to four people—with private bath and hot water. More rooms were to be added. Rates: $40 s, $60 d/t; $10 extra person, including breakfast.

Hotel y Restaurante Río Mary, tel. 474-4080, 200 meters east of the Río Aguas Zarcas, has 10 modestly furnished rooms with fans, a double and a single bed, and private baths with hot water showers.

Termales del Bosque, tel. 460-1356, fax 460-0311, has 10 appealing modern cabins with hot water. Rates: $30 d shared bath; $28 s, $35 d private bath; $32 s, $40 with terrace, including breakfast.

Villas Cristina, tel. 460-0767, fax 460-5689, has pleasing *cabinas* plus a swimming pool and jacuzzi in a lush garden at Vuelta de Kopper, eight km north of Aguas Zarcas. It permits **camping.**

Moderate: The beautiful **Hotel El Tucano Thermae Spa,** tel. 460-6000, fax 460-1692; in San José, tel. 221-9095, fax 221-9095, e-mail: tucano@centralamerica.com, website www.centralamerica.com/cr/hotel/tucano.htm, eight km east of Ciudad Quesada, promises healing for those dipping their toes into the thermo-mineral waters (hot springs) that hiccup out of clefts in the rocks on which the hotel is built. The riverside hotel—built around a courtyard patio and large open-air swimming pool—is styled loosely as a Swiss chalet complex, with wrought-iron lanterns and window boxes full of flame-red flowers. Peaceful and elegant, the hotel has gained popularity as a gathering place for San José's elite. The 59 guest rooms reflect European savoir faire in exquisite contempory decor, including beautiful hardwoods and soothing pink pastels, king-size beds, and Egyptian motifs on the walls. Luxury suites accommodate up to five. A four-story addition includes nine suites, a casino, plus 20 additional rooms. The hotel has built its reputation on health tourism. El Tucano boasts the **Thermae Spa,** Costa Rica's only full-service spa, replete with hot-spring jacuzzi, therapeutic mineral pool, four massage treatments, state-of-the-art physiotherapy, aromatherapy and other treatments, forest trails, and a gym. "Mark Twain and Freud," G.Y. Dryansky once wrote, "and Gogol and Nietzsche lost their skepticism in the steam room"—and so may you. Other facilities include tennis, miniature golf, horseback riding ($5 per hour), and a restaurant known for its Italian cuisine. A variety of tours are available. Rates: $55 s, $66 d, $77 t, $88-175 suites low season; $65 s, $75 d, 85 t, $105-185 suites high season.

Services

There's a gas station, plus a Banco Nacional at the east end of town.

Getting There

Buses between Ciudad Quesada and San Miguel and Puerto Viejo stop along the route; or take the 3.5-hour bus ride from San José ($2.50).

LAGUNA DEL LAGARTO

This private reserve is about 45 km northeast of Aguas Zarcas (turn right just north of Chiles, three km north of Aguas Zarcas; the gravel road leads via the hamlet of Boca Topada, seven km southwest of Laguna del Lagarto). You can reach Lagarto by ordinary car, but 4WD is recommended. The reserve protects 500 hectares of virgin rainforest and bayou swamps harboring crocodiles, caimans, turtles, thousands of red-and-green poison-arrow frogs, as well as ocelots, sloths, and all kinds of colorful bird species, including the rare green macaw. The University of Science and Technology of Latin America helps maintain the ecology of the area and uses the reserve for research.

Accommodations

The **Laguna del Lagarto Lodge,** Apdo. 995, San José 1007, tel. 289-8163, fax 289-5295, offers 20 rustic yet comfortable rooms in two separate buildings (18 with private baths, two with shared bath; hot water was being installed) on a hillock overlooking the lagoon, which resembles the bayous of Louisiana. Each has a large terrace with a view overlooking the San Carlos River and forest. A natural lake surrounds the lodge, which has two large decks where you can relax and sip cocktails (canoes are available, as are boat trips on the Río San Juan). There are miles of forest trails for hiking and horseback rides, plus a restaurant serving hearty Costa Rican meals. Crocodiles can be seen at night in the lagoon, waiting for something tasty to pass by. Rates: $53 pp, including three generous buffet-style meals. Transfers are offered. (The lodge gained unwelcome fame in 1996 when a German tourist and her Swiss guide were kidnapped from there and held for ransom.)

Getting There

A **bus** for Pital departs the Coca Cola terminal in San José at 12:30 p.m. Several buses depart Ciudad Quesada for Pital, from where buses run twice daily to Boca Tapada. A taxi from Pital costs about $25 one-way.

MUELLE AND VICINITY

This important crossroads is 21 km north of Ciudad Quesada, at the junction of Hwy. 4 (running east-west between Upala and Puerto Viejo de Sarapiquí) and Hwy. 35 (north-south between Ciudad Quesada and Los Chiles). There's a Texaco gas station and a store. The hamlet of Muelle is one km to the north.

Dropping down from Ciudad Quesada, the switchback road deposits you on the flat (the road is prone to landslides during rains) at the small town of **Florencia.** Here, turn right (north) at the stop sign for Muelle; the road to Fortuna and Arenal veers left.

The landscape, you'll note, has dramatically changed. Mountain cedars and oaks have given way to palms and wispy bamboos, which reflect the warmer, humid, "more tropical" climate. And holstein and Brown Swiss dairy cattle have been replaced by Brahmas and zebus attended by snow-white cattle egrets.

River trips down the Ríos San Rafael and San Carlos are popular. I took a half-day kayaking trip on the San Carlos courtesy of Tilajari Resort and had the good fortune to see howler monkeys and crocodiles almost in reaching distance. Tilajari also has a **butterfly garden** where guests may walk inside the netted garden to learn about lepidopterous lore.

Accommodations

Shoestring: The basic **Cabinas La Violeta** is two km north of the Muelle intersection (100 meters beyond the Bar Los Tres Gatos, immediately before the bridge over the Río San Rafael). Rates: $4.50. I've heard an unconfirmed report that it rents rooms by the hour. **Cabinas Las Iguanas** and **Cabinas Kambara,** tel. 469-1000, are nearby. **Cabinas Beitzy,** tel. 469-9153, 200 meters north of the Muelle gas station, has *cabinas* in gardens on a *finca* with trails and horseback riding.

Budget: The **Complejo Hotel y Piscinas Huetar,** tel. 474-4497, at Vacablanca, five km east of Muelle, has five attractively appointed cabins, with two double beds, wooden ceilings, and large private baths and hot water. The rooms surround a large swimming pool—popular with day visitors on weekends—and *ranchito* restaurant. Rates: $12 s, $21 d.

Inexpensive: La Quinta Inn, Apdo. 11021-1000 San José, tel./fax 761-1052 or 475-5260, at Platanar, four km south of the Muelle crossroads, is a very pleasant if modestly furnished hotel run by Ticos Jeanette and Bill Ugalde. Accommodations include two *cabinas,* each with hostel-style bunks for 10 people, with shared baths/showers;

a spacious triple room with attractive wood paneling and a roomy shower; and, upstairs, two triples with private baths and lounges. The Ugaldes also rent a two-room apartment with a double bed and four bunks in the house. Meals are cooked and served in an open-air restaurant overlooking a swimming pool. Outdoors you'll find a sauna and basketball and volleyball courts, and plenty of birds and iguanas. Fishing trips are arranged. Rates: $12 pp *cabinas;* $35 s/d/t triple rooms; $60 apartment (up to six people).

Moderate: Hotel La Garza, Apdo. 100-2250 Tres Ríos, tel. 475-5222 or 222-7355, fax 475-5015 or 222-0869, also at Platanar, has 12 beautifully kept cabins with polished wood floors, ceiling fans, Guatemalan fabrics and bamboo furnishings, heaps of potted plants, and verandas with tables and chairs overlooking the Río Platanar. Additional cabins were being added, along with a pool, restaurant, and a three-km hiking/jogging trail. The hotel is part of a 600-hectare working cattle and horse farm where you can hop in the saddle to explore the private lands, or opt for trips to Caño Negro National Wildlife Refuge, and more. Meals (pastas, sandwiches, and *típico* dishes) are served in a charming old farmhouse restaurant reached by a suspension bridge over the river. Delightful. Rates: $55 s, $64 d. Day visitors are welcome to use the pool and facilities.

At Boca Arenal, six km north of Muelle, is the **Río San Carlos Lodge,** Apdo. 345, Ciudad Quesada 4400, tel. 469-9179 or 460-0766, fax 460-0391, hidden on the left, 100 meters after the blue hotel sign, on the banks of the Río San Carlos. The old *quinta,* or country home, is built of dark hardwoods. Five handsome, individually decorated rooms (some with a/c) overlooking the river have private baths, hot water, fans, and hammocks that beg to be used. One room has a sunken tub. The lodge has a restaurant and a swimming pool plus children's pool. Rates: $60 d, including breakfast.

Tilajari Resort Hotel and Country Club, Apdo. 81, Ciudad Quesada, San Carlos, tel. 469-9091, fax 469-9095, one km west from the Muelle crossroads, is ideally situated for exploring throughout the lowlands. You don't have to travel far, however, to get your wildlife thrills. Crocodiles sun themselves on the banks of the Río San Carlos in plain view of guests, waiting (no doubt) for a tidbit thrown from the dining room terrace or a careless guest to lean a little too far over the rail. Iguanas roost in the treetops. Hummingbirds feed at the trumpet vines and hibiscus that emblazon the 16 hectares of groomed gardens replete with tropical fruit trees. Tilajari has 56 a/c, double rooms and four family suites, with beautiful hardwoods and private terraces overlooking the river. It offers three tennis courts, a swimming pool, children's pool, two racquetball courts, a sauna, a hot tub, and a jacuzzi. There's an open-air bar and lounge with satellite TV, an open-sided riverside restaurant, plus the Jacaré Discotheque. The hotel offers tour packages throughout the lowlands, including horseback riding through Jim Hamilton's 240-hectare cattle ranch, tours to Volcán Arenal and the Fortuna waterfall, as well as river trips to Caño Negro and a kayaking trip down the Río San Carlos to visit Don Pedro Carrillo Cruz, a wiry old *campesino,* and his family on their remote farm. The latter is marvelous, providing a rare opportunity to appreciate a tough homesteading subsistence lifestyle far from the trappings of the modern world. Ticos flock to Tilajari on weekends (Sunday is "tennis day"), when the place draws lots of kids—a good day for touring. Rates: $63 s/d, $70 t, $80 suite low season; $72 s, $82 d, $93 t, $110 suite high season.

Food
The Tilajari serves *típico* and international fare. There are several good eateries in Muelle. My favorite is **Bar y Restaurante Juana La Cubana,** serving Tico dishes with a zesty Cuban flare. **Soda Isla Canarias,** beside the bridge over the river in Muelle, is a good place to watch iguanas basking in the trees.

Getting There
Buses to/from Los Chiles and San Rafael can drop you in Muelle. **Interbus** stops at Muelle on its daily shuttle between La Fortuna and San José (see **Appendix**).

LOS CHILES

Los Chiles is literally a small frontier town on the Río Frío, about 100 km north of Ciudad Quesada and four km south of the Nicaraguan border. This was a sensitive region during the Nicaraguan conflicts of the 1980s—the Río Frío was a contra supply line, and for a while Los Chiles was a boomtown flush with CIA dollars and littered with MRE wrappers. Many local residents fled the fighting and only in the past few years have begun to drift back. Water-taxis ply to and from Los Chiles loaded with trade goods and families traveling downriver to the Nicaraguan town of San Carlos, which sits at the point where the Río Frío empties into Lake Nicaragua and the Río San Juan flows out.

Since 1996, foreigners have been permitted to cross into Nicaragua here. Otherwise, there's only one reason to travel the road to Los Chiles: to visit Caño Negro National Wildlife Refuge, about 25 km southwest of town. The town developed as a minor river port for traffic on the Ríos San Juan and Frío, but today derives much of its income from tourism.

The ruler-straight drive north from Muelle is modestly scenic, with the land rolling endlessly in a sea of lime-green pastures and waves of citrus—those of the TicoFrut company, whose *fincas* stretch all the way to the Nicaraguan border—with tidy little hamlets in between. The colors are marvelous, the intense greens made more so by soils as red as bright lipstick. The road fizzles out a few hundred meters beyond Los Chiles, about one km south of the Nicaraguan border. The road had a "military" barrier and civil guard checkpoint at the entrance to town, and you are likely to see U.S. Special Forces troops driving around in Humvees. Don't be fazed by the camouflage jackets and M-16s. Stop and show your papers, and all will be fine.

The wetlands east of Los Chiles, in an area surrounding the Río Medio Queso, are also superb for wildlife viewing.

Crossing into Nicaragua

In June 1994, Costa Rican President José María Figueres and his Nicaraguan counterpart Violeta de Chamorro signed an agreement to establish a new border crossing at Los Chiles (and 14 km inside Nicaragua, at San Pancho). These are now operating. Note, though, that this is a sensitive area and the situation fickle. There's a *migración* office, tel. 471-1153, by the riverside wharf; open daily 8 a.m.-4 p.m.

U.S. and U.K. citizens can cross into Nicaragua without a visa. Citizens of Canada, France,

and Germany *do* need a visa, as do Costa Ricans. Everyone is charged 100 *colones* for an exit visa from Costa Rica, and $5 for a tourist permit to enter Nicaragua. There's no cost to enter Costa Rica from Nicaragua.

A return boat excursion from Los Chiles to San Carlos de Nicaragua costs $100 (for up to 10 passengers). A one-way journey costs $75.

Accommodations and Food

The dour **Hotel Río Frío,** tel. 471-1127, between the park and river, has 10 rudimentary rooms with cold-water showers. Rates: $2.25. Just around the corner is the equally dismal **Apartamientos Onasis,** on the west side of the soccer field in the village center. **Las Carolinas Hotel,** tel. 471-1151, one block west of the police station near the entrance to town, is an improvement but, says local fishing authority Jerry Ruhlow, "It's not the Sheraton." Basic rooms are clean and have fans plus private bathrooms. Rates: $6 pp. You might also try the **Los Chiles Hotel** (not inspected).

In town, the nicest place is **Cabinas Jabirú,** tel. 471-1055, 50 meters north of Servitur, with simply furnished but clean rooms. Rates: $11 s, $15 d.

There are two lodges beside the road about one km south of town. **Cuajipal Lodge** has 12 spacious, clean, but meagerly appointed rooms with private baths and hot water, plus a bar and restaurant. Rates: $15 pp. Next door, the **Complejo Turístico El Gaspar,** tel./fax 471-1173, is *the* place to be if your budget permits. This handsome property has a *ranchito* restaurant and lively bar and three small swimming pools in its landscaped grounds. The 12 cabins are nicely appointed, with cool tile floors, fans, and lofty ceilings to combat the heat. It offers tours. Rates: $25 s, $40 d, $55 t.

At Pavón, 22 km south of Los Chiles, **Cabinas Manitas** has eight simple cabins with private bathrooms and four without. Rates: $6 s, $8 d.

The **Restaurant El Parque,** opposite the soccer field, serves basic Costa Rican fare and open 6 a.m.-9 p.m. Better yet is **Los Petates.**

Tourist Information and Tours

Servitur, tel. 471-1211, fax 471-1055, two blocks east of the soccer field, is a full-service touring information and tour agency that also acts as a post office. Nelson Leitón is super-friendly and offers a wide range of tours locally, including to Caño Negro and into Nicaragua, to the wetlands of the Río Medio Queso (southeast of Los Chiles), plus the "Green Heart Expedition" to the Eco Directa Reforestation project, a Dutch-owned teak project. A Nicaraguan tour operator, **Careli Tours,** has an office down by the wharf.

Services
The **police station,** tel. 471-1103, is on the main road from Muelle as you enter town. There's a **Banco Nacional** in the village center. There's a **gas station** one km south of town, and another 22 km south of Los Chiles at Pavón.

Getting There
By Air: The small airstrip has no scheduled air service and is used mostly by military aircraft. You can charter flights from San José or elsewhere.

By Buses: Buses run between Ciudad Quesada and Los Chiles frequently throughout the day. Express buses depart San José from Calle 16 and Avenidas 1/3 at 5:30 a.m. and 3:30 p.m. (return buses same time).

REFUGIO NACIONAL DE VIDA SILVESTRE FAUNA CAÑO NEGRO

Caño Negro National Wildlife Refuge is a remote tropical everglade teeming with wildlife.

The 9,969-hectare reserve protects a lush low-land basin of soft, knee-deep watery sloughs and marshes, *holillo* groves, and tan carpets of sturdy sedge. Life here revolves around **Lago Caño Negro,** a seasonal lake fed by the fresh waters of the Río Frío, which snake down from the flanks of Volcán Tenorio and collect in this basin, where they slow almost to a standstill.

In the wet season, when the region is flooded and great pools and lagoons form, vast numbers of migratory waterfowl flock in, turtles, crocodiles, and caimans in abundance bask on the banks, and as you look down into waters as black as Costa Rican coffee you may see the dim forms of big snook, silver-gold tarpon, and garish garfish lurking in the shadows. In February, the dry season sets in (it generally lasts through April), Caño Negro dries out, and the area is reduced to shrunken lagoons. Caiman gnash and slosh out pools in the muck, and wildlife congregate in abundance along the watercourses.

Caño Negro is a birdwatcher's paradise. The reserve protects the largest colony of neotropic cormorants in Costa Rica and the only permanent colony of Nicaraguan grackle. Cattle egrets, wood storks, anhingas, roseate spoonbills, and other waterfowl gather in their thousands. The bright pink roseate spoonbill is one of Caño Negro's most spectacular wading birds. It is named for its spatulate bill, some 15-19 cm long, which it swings from side to side as it munches insects or small shellfish. Another of my favorites is the anhinga, a bird as adept underwater as in the air

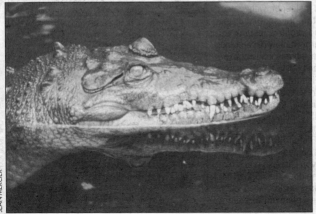

crocodile, Caño Negro

JEAN MERCIER

(it goes by three aliases: snakebird, for its serpentine neck; American darter, for its jerky movements; and water turkey, for the way its tail spreads in flight). You can see it solo or by the dozen, preening way up in the cypress trees.

The reserve is remarkable, too, for its healthy population of endangered mammal species, including jaguars, cougars, tapirs, ocelots, and tayras. There are always sure to be plenty of monkeys playacting. And the crocodile colony of Caño Negro is perhaps the best-protected in Costa Rica, though caimans are far more numerous and easily seen.

The mosquitoes—though tiny—eye your arrival greedily, awaiting the right moment for attack. Bring plenty of repellent.

The Río Frío, which cuts through the refuge, makes an ideal waterway for guided boat tours into Caño Negro.

Caño Negro Village

The hamlet of Caño Negro, 23 km southwest of Los Chiles, nestles on the northwest shore of Lago Caño Negro, at the edge of the refuge. Locals make their living from fishing and guiding. The **park ranger station**—Sitio Ramsar—is here, 400 meters inland from the dock.

Fishing

The Río Colorado may steal the show when it comes to hooking that feisty freshwater gargantuan "silver rocket," the tarpon, but the secret is finally leaking out: Caño Negro and the Río Frío are just as good. A handful of anglers have long known that the region is a sleeper, with waters that almost boil with tarpon, snook, drum, *guapote, machaca,* and *mojarra* jostling for space. Fishing expert Jerry Ruhlow says, "Most tarpon will jump three to five times, often coming 12 feet out of the water and doing a 360-degree twist in the process." Fishing season is July-March and licenses are required.

Organized Tours: Fishing trips on the Río Frío are offered by most hotels and tour companies in Fortuna, Los Chiles, and throughout the lowlands. In San José, Richard Krug, tel. 228-4812 or 289-8139, offers guided "No-Frills" fishing trips from San José; you can also reach him c/o Dunn Inn Hotel in San José, tel. 222-8134, fax 221-4596 ($300, including tackle, lunch, etc.). Krug has reportedly been planning to build a

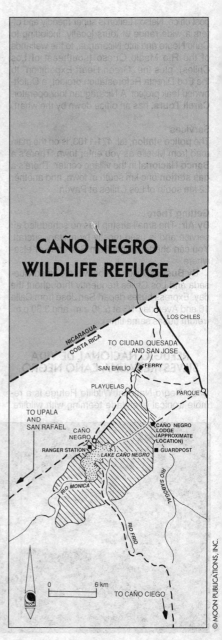

CAÑO NEGRO
WILDLIFE REFUGE

NICARAGUA
COSTA RICA

LOS CHILES

TO CIUDAD QUESADA
AND SAN JOSE

SAN EMILIO — FERRY

PLAYUELAS

PARQUE

TO UPALA
AND
SAN RAFAEL

CAÑO
NEGRO

CAÑO NEGRO
LODGE
(APPROXIMATE
LOCATION)

RANGER STATION — LAKE CAÑO NEGRO — GUARDPOST

RÍO SABOGAL

RÍO MONICA

RÍO FRÍO

0   6 km

TO CAÑO CIEGO

© MOON PUBLICATIONS, INC.

fishing lodge with a/c *cabinas* and a swimming pool in Los Chiles; stay tuned. **Americana Fishing Charters,** tel. 222-8134, fax 221-4596, run by Americans Martin Bernard and John Mills, also offers a "No-Frills" fishing package with transfers from San José, boat, guide, tackle, and accommodations ($400 for two days); a "Full Frills" package with nights at Tilajari Resort Hotel costs $550.

Alvaro Arguillas of Caño Negro Ecological Garden & Touristic Resort offers fishing trips, as does Colibri Tours.

Accommodations and Food

Camping is allowed, but there are no facilities inside the refuge. The grandly named **Caño Negro Ecological Garden & Touristic Resort** in the hamlet of Caño Negro permits camping on lawns beneath fruit trees. There are camping tables and barbecue pits. Owner Alvaro Arguillas also offers two rustic, bare-bones, two-story cabins on stilts, with screened windows, electricity, porches, and shared toilets and bathrooms beneath. Each unit has two-bedrooms with a double and two single beds. Rates: $2 pp campsite; $8 pp cabin.

Cabinas Machón, also in Caño Negro, has two simple cabins, each sleeping three people.

You can also stay overnight in the Caño Negro ranger station if space is available. You'll need a sleeping bag and, ideally, a mosquito net. Spanish speakers may be able to get through to the refuge by calling the public telephone in Caño Negro, tel. 460-1301, or via channel 38 on the National Parks Service radio-telephone, tel. 233-4160. Rates: about $7 (meals $5).

On the east shore, the **Albergue Caño Negro Lagoon,** tel. 460-0124 or 240-5460, fax 234-1676, 15 km south of Los Chiles, is reached by boat or via a very rough six-km-long dirt road from the El Parque on the Muelle-Los Chiles highway. The thatched lodge and 10 simple yet spacious and comfortable rooms (with private bath) sit on an artificial island on the banks of the Río Frío, and are built entirely of bamboo and rich red hardwoods with blue bedspreads and curtains in counterpoint. The restaurant, open to all sides, has a rustic elegance. Rates: $42 d.

Soda La Palmera is a quaint little restaurant by the boat dock in Caño Negro. **Restaurante Machón** is 50 meters away.

Tours

Most tour operators in San José and throughout the lowlands offer guided day-trips to Caño Negro (prices depend on number of people; average price is $45, including lunch). In Caño Negro village, Alvaro Arguillas of Caño Negro Ecological Garden &Touristic Resort offers three- to four-hour tours by canopied boat ($10-15 pp depending on group size). Trips are led by trained guides. **Colibri Tours,** beeper tel. 225-2500, facing the grassy plaza down by the river, also offers boat and fishing tours.

Getting There

By Road: Some maps show a road leading west from Los Chiles into the park. However, you cannot drive from Los Chiles, as there's no bridge across the Río Frío. A water-taxi will ferry you across—1,500 colones for a car, 200 for a passenger—to the other side, where you can catch a bus (infrequent) or hitch a ride to the village of Caño Negro. However, a new road (prone to flooding in the west season) from El Parque, 10 km south of Los Chiles, runs 10 km west to a bridge at San Emilio, from where you can reach Caño Negro village via a dirt road that continues to Colonia Puntarenas, on the main Fortuna-Upala road (Hwy. 4).

The road from Colonia Puntarenas (10 km southeast of Upala) is bone-jarring and, in the wet season, slipperier than a greased pig; it runs northeast 26 km to Caño Negro (the turnoff is signed). It's usually passable by car in the dry season but a sturdy 4WD is recommended; and in the wet season even this may prove inadequate. A bus runs daily from Upala to Caño Negro village via Colonia Puntarenas when conditions allow.

By Boat: A *colectivo* (water-taxi) reportedly departs Los Chiles each Monday afternoon for the hamlet of Caño Negro ($3). Alternately, you can rent a boat at the dock in Los Chiles for $40-90, depending on the size and type of boat. Canopied boats that provide shade are usually the most expensive. Typically, a four-hour boat tour to Caño Negro costs $50 for up to 10 passengers.

CIUDAD QUESADA TO FORTUNA

West from Ciudad Quesada the road zigzags past lime-green pastures, with the great bulk of

Volcán Arenal always looming magnificently to your left. At **Jabillos,** nine km west of Florencia, the road swings north to **Tanque,** 37 km from Ciudad Quesada, where a road to the right leads northwest to Upala. Continue straight for Fortuna (five km) and Volcán Arenal. Alternately, at Jabillos you can continue west to San Isidro and follow the road to Fortuna via Chachagua.

Interbus stops at Florencia on its daily shuttle between La Fortuna and San José.

Accommodations and Food

The **Hotel Rancho Corcovado,** tel. 479-9300, fax 474-4090, is a *cabina*-style property with pool and souvenir store about 200 meters west of Tanque. The 30 rooms and five suites are clean and cheery, and an open-air restaurant overlooks two swimming pools and a small lake. There's a small animal refuge. Rates: $37 s, $50 d, $62 t, $72 quad. A private airstrip was planned.

El Catalán, northeast of Tanque on the Muelle road looks down-at-heels but serves excellent Spanish cuisine. Owner Alex Castellón boasts that his paella is the "number one in Costa Rica," and well it may be. He even serves real *sangría.*

LA TIGRA AND VICINITY

You can reach Fortuna directly from the central Highlands via a road that transcends the mountains north from San Ramón and drops through the Valle Escondido to the hamlet of **Bajo Rodríguez,** at the foot of the mountains, and **La Tigra,** seven km west. The Eco-Tourist Project Valle Azul, on the banks of the Río Azul, between Bajo Rodríguez and La Tigra, has *cabinas,* camping, a restaurant, and swimming, but was put up for sale in late 1997.

La Tigra is a gateway to the **Bosque Eterno de los Niños** (Children's Eternal Forest) and **Monteverde Cloud Forest Biological Reserve;** you'll see a sign about 800 meters south of La Tigra and an **information office** one km north of town.

You'll cross a high suspension bridge before arriving, about three km north of La Tigra, in **San Isidro,** where you can turn right (east) at the T-junction in town for Jabillos (four km) and Ciudad Quesada. The paved road northwest from San Isidro leads to Fortuna via **Chachagua,**

where there's a gas station. About one km east of Chachagua, a dirt road leads west and dead-ends at the **Chachagua Rainforest Lodge,** a 50-hectare private forest reserve abutting the Children's Eternal Rainforest.

Bungee Jumping

Several companies in Fortuna offer bungee-jumping from the bridge over the Río Peñas Blancas at San Isidro.

Accommodations and Food

Cabañas Los Ríos (not reviewed) offers basic rooms in La Tigra, as does **Hotel Chachagua,** with simple, clean rooms in the $10 range.

Chachagua Rainforest Lodge, Apdo. 476-4005 San José, tel. 239-1164, fax 239-1311, is a tranquil getaway on a 80-hectare cattle ranch nestled at the foot of the Tilarán mountain range, with a gurgling brook cascading down through the property. The 23 spacious, simply appointed wooden cabins each have two double beds and a deck with a picnic table and benches for enjoying the lush greenery and forest close at hand. You'll shower under a skylight in front of one-way mirrored windows with bromeliads and potted plants sharing the waters. The atmospheric natural-log restaurant looks out upon a corral where, occasionally, *sabaneros* are testing their skills in the saddle or even riding bulls bareback. Alas, I thought the food to be mediocre. There's a swimming pool designed to resemble a natural pool, plus horseback riding, and nature and birding hikes led by an on-site naturalist guide. White-faced monkeys, toucans, poison-arrow frogs, peccaries, and ocelots all inhabit the surrounding terrain. Ducks and geese waddle freely through the grounds, and macaws swing on perches in the restaurant. The country hacienda also produces yucca, banana, papaya and pineapple, and has an experimental fish farm (the fish—tilapia, an East African species much favored for its delicate flavor—find their way onto your dinner plate). Rates: $76 s/d, $86 t.

Getting There

A bus runs between Chachagua and Fortuna. **Interbus** stops at San Lorenzo (Valle Escondido) on its daily shuttle between San José and La Fortuna.

FORTUNA TO UPALA

Fortuna is a pleasant and picturesque little town dominated by perfectly conical Volcán Arenal, which looms six km to the southwest. From Fortuna you can follow the road as it ascends gradually around the north side of the volcano to Tabacón Hot Springs and Lake Arenal. Fortuna is thriving on the tourist traffic, and the growing choice of decent hotels includes budget options and some great bargains. It gets crowded on weekends, so it's wise to book ahead.

In town there's nothing whatsoever to see except, perhaps, the village church on the west side of the soccer field. The Albergue Ecoturística La Catarata, run by the local farmers' cooperative, Asociación Proambiente y Desarrollo de Zefa Trece (ASPROADES), has a **butterfly garden** and **Zoo Tepescuintle,** where agoutis—charming dog-sized rodents—are raised for release into the wild; entrance $1.

About five km east of town is the **Catarata Fortuna,** a pretty waterfall in the care of a local community development group—the Asociación de Desarollo de Fortuna. The turnoff for the falls—popular with locals on weekends—is two km southeast of town, from where a rocky road (slippery as ice when wet; 4WD recommended) leads uphill 2.5 km to the entrance, where there's an information bureau. From here you have to negotiate a slippery and precipitous trail (20 minutes' walk) that leads down a steep ravine to the base of the cascade. Entrance: $1.50. There's a roadside cafe serving breads, muffins, and wholesome veggie burgers, on the road to the falls; **Gabino Tours** is here. Several guides and tour operators in Fortuna offer horseback trips (typically $15 for four hours). I recommend Alberto Serrano, tel. 479-9043. You can also reach La Catarata from the Fortuna-Arenal road but you must ford a river—a high 4WD is essential.

Jungla y Senderos Los Lagos, tel. 479-9126, three km west of town on the Arenal road, is a small private nature reserve and quasi-theme park: a large *finca* that includes 400 hectares of primary forest through which five km of trails wind intestinally, providing views of Arenal, Tenorio, and Miravalles Volcanoes. A massive water slide whorls down to a large cold-water swimming pool (be careful not to overshoot, as there are crocodiles and caimans in nearby ponds). Guided horseback rides ($12.50, five hours) are offered, and paddle boats or water bicycles ($1.50 per hour) can be rented. A *soda* serves food on weekends. Entrance: $1.

Accommodations

More hotels come on line every year, and older properties continue to upgrade.

Camping: In town, you can camp at **Fiesta del Mar** restaurant, opposite the cemetery. West of town, **Arenal Outdoor Center** permits camping. **Jungla y Senderos** charges $6 pp for camping ($2 each additional night), with use of showers and toilets. You can also camp at **Ojo de Agua** and also at **Finca de Cito,** one km west of Fortuna. About five km west is **Casa de Campo** ("Camping House") tel. 479-9006, surrounded by cattle pasture. You can rent horses here. A little farther uphill, on the right, is the **Centro Campero las Palmas,** tel. 479-9106, with camping and rooms for five people.

In Town: The **Burio Inn,** tel./fax 479-9076, on the main street, one block east of the soccer field, has eight rooms with private bathrooms and hot water; some have bunk beds. Rates: $8.50 pp (children under nine get a 50% discount). Fishing trips, horseback rides, birding trips, and tours of Arenal are offered. The Burio Inn has laundry service.

Hotel La Fortuna, tel. 479-9197, is very popular with Europeans, although the 10 rooms (each with a double and two single beds) are basic and small, with fans and private bathrooms with hot water. Larger rooms are better. There's a pleasant open-air restaurant. The old place burned down in 1997 and has been replaced. There's a popular and inexpensive restaurant, and horseback tours are offered. Rates: $8 pp.

Cabinas Sissy, tel. 479-9256 or 479-9356, has eight rooms with private bath and hot water for, plus a house for 11 people. It has secure parking and offers tours. Rates: $10 pp rooms; $4 pp house. **Cabinas Montreal,** tel./fax 479-9243, has three clean, modestly furnished *cabinas* (one with a/c) with refrigerators, verandas, and pri-

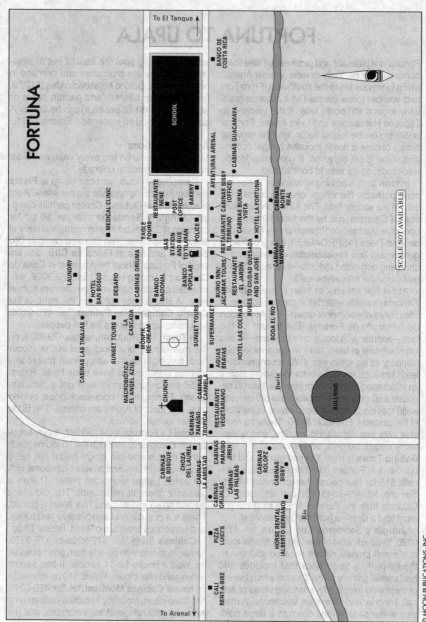

FORTUNA

To El Tanque ↑

SCHOOL

SCALE NOT AVAILABLE

Banco de Costa Rica

Cabinas Guacamaya

Aventuras Arenal

Restaurante Cabinas Sissy (office)
Cabinas Buena Vista
Cabinas Monte Real

Hotel La Fortuna

Restaurante Nene
Post Office
Bakery

Medical Clinic

Eagle Tours
Gas Station and Bus to Tilarán
Police

Restaurante El Terruño

Cabinas Mayor

Hotel San Bosco
Cabinas Oruma
Desafio

Banco Nacional
Banco Popular

Burio Inn / Jacamar Tours
Restaurante El Jardín
Buses to Ciudad Quesada and San José

Soda El Río

Laundry

Cabinas Las Tinajas

La Cascada
Sunset Tours
Monpik Ice Cream

Macrobiotica El Angel Azul
Sunset Tours

Supermarket

Aguas Bravas

Hotel Las Colinas

Burio

CHURCH

Cabinas Paraiso Tropical
Restaurante Vegetariano
Cabinas Carmela

BULLRING

Cabinas El Bosque
Choza del Laurel
Cabinas La Amistad
Cabinas Grijalba
Cabinas Las Palmas

Cabinas Paraiso Jireh

Cabinas Rolopz

Cabinas Sissy

Pizza Luici's

Horse Rental (Alberto Serrano)

Rio

Cali Rent-A-Bike

To Arenal ↓

© MOON PUBLICATIONS, INC.

vate bathrooms and hot water. There's secure parking and a garden. Rates: $25 d. **Cabinas Mayol,** tel. 479-9110, has eight small rooms with a bed as the only furniture, but hardwood walls and ceilings, pretty bedspreads, fans, and small private baths and hot water. Rates: $8 pp. A swimming pool and restaurant were to be added.

Cabinas Carmela, tel. 479-9010, has 10 clean rooms with hardwood walls, orthopedic mattresses, patios with hammocks and Sarchí rockers, plus private sky-lit bathrooms with hot water. There's secure parking. A small swimming pool was planned. Rates: $15 s, $20 d, including taxes. **Cabinas La Ribera,** tel. 479-9048, east of town, is recommended. There are six cabins, each with three rooms with hot-water shower, and 2-4 beds. Rates: $10 pp. The pleasant and roomy **Cabinas Oriuma,** tel./fax 479-9111, has seven large rooms for four people, plus two doubles with private baths, hot water, fans, and a common balcony with views of the volcano. Rates: $10 pp.

Others to consider are the **Hotel El Bosque,** tel. 479-9365, with six rooms for $6.50 pp shared bath, $8.50 private bath. Nearby, **Cabinas Grijalba,** tel. 479-9129, has basic but comfortable rooms, private baths and hot water. Rates: $6.50 pp in older cabins; $20 s/d; $25 t/quad are in newer, more appealing cabins. Next door, **Cabinas La Amistad,** tel. 479-9364, has 13 well-lit rooms with large windows and private bath with hot water. There's private parking and a laundry, plus rental bikes ($1 per hour). Rates: $25 d ($35 larger rooms).

In the higher price bracket, try the **Hotel Las Colinas,** tel./fax 479-9107, which has 17 clean rooms (mine was tiny, however, with a bed and sheets more fitting for a doll's house) with basic furniture, and private baths with hot water. Visa/MasterCard are accepted. Rates: $10 s low season; $12 s, $25 d, $40 t high season. **Cabinas Rolopz,** tel. 479-9058, has seven basic but clean rooms with private bath and showers. The Nicaraguan owners are friendly. There's a *soda* attached. Rates: $10 s, $15 d.

Cabinas Las Tinajas, tel. 479-9145 (leave a message), has four very handsome rooms with attractive tiled floors. Modern and clean, with lots of light and private baths with hot water. Beds boast beautiful hardwood frames and headboards. Rates: $25 s, $30 d, including tax.

Cabinas Las Palmas, tel. 479-9379, has horseback tours.

Cabinas Guacamaya, tel./fax 479-9087, is a modern house with 11 very clean, roomy a/c *cabinas* with refrigerators, private baths with hot water, and patios with rockers. (Watch your step upon entering; I almost broke my neck.) Parking is secure. Rooms sleep three people. Rates: $25 s, $40 d, $10 extra person.

Cabinas Paraíso Tropical, tel. 479-9222, has six new, spacious, modestly elegant cabins with private bath and hot water. There's secure parking. Refrigerators and TVs were to be added, plus a swimming pool and restaurant. Rates: $35 d low season; $40 s, $48 d high season, including tax and breakfast.

Hotel San Bosco, tel. 479-9050, fax 479-9109, e-mail: sanbosco@ns.goldnet.co.cr, 200 meters north of the soccer field, has 27 a/c rooms (11 are cabins) with private baths and hot water, plus two fully equipped homes for eight ($68) and 14 people ($104). A two-story annex offers verandas, plus a *mirador* above for viewing the volcano. It has a swimming pool and a jacuzzi. Some of the rooms are *very* small and overpriced. Rates: $25 s, $30 d, $35 t, $40 quad with fan low season ($5-20 more for a/c); $30 s, $35 d, $45 t, $60 quad high season ($10-35 more with a/c), including tax and breakfast.

About 400 meters east of town is **Villa Fortuna,** tel./fax 479-9139, has clean, modern rooms with refrigerators and private baths with hot water. The landscaped grounds include caged toucans. Rates: $30 s/d, $40 with a/c.

Las Cabañitas Resort, Apdo. 5, San Carlos 4417, tel. 479-9400, fax 479-9408, e-mail: gasguis@sol.racsa.co.cr, is an elegant, modern-style hotel with 30 cozy and comfortable wooden *cabinas* surrounded by lawns with trim borders, about one km east of Fortuna. Each bungalow has two double beds or one queen-size bed, private bathroom with hot water, and private porch with volcano vista. There's a swimming pool, tennis court, laundry service, and bar and *ranchito* restaurant. Rates: $75 d. Attractive, but overpriced?

West of Town: The following are in order, on the road to Tabacón and Arenal. **Arenal Outdoor Center,** tel. 479-9508, has three *cabinas* with queen-size beds, fans, and private baths and hot water. Rates: $25 s/d, $30 with breakfast.

The secluded **Albergue Ecoturística La Catarata,** tel. 479-9522, e-mail: wwfcii@sol.racsa. co.cr, one km west of town, has eight attractive hardwood cabins with dainty pink decor, fans, verandas, and private baths and hot water. There's a restaurant, butterfly garden, an orchid garden, and small zoo. It's run by a local cooperative of farmers. Rates: $15 pp, including breakfast. There's a canopied restaurant. Nearby, the modern **Cerro Chato Lodge Bed & Breakfast,** cellular tel. 284-9280, has two rooms in a bungalow

The well-run **Cabinas Rossi,** tel. 479-9023, fax 479-9414, e-mail: cabrossi@sol.racsa.co.cr, website www.cmnet.co.cr/rtossi/, about two km west, offers 20 simple but pretty white-and-blue *cabinas* with refrigerators and private baths with hot water. One has a full kitchen and sky-lit bathroom. Three have a/c. Rooms vary in size. "Immaculate and comfortable," reports a reader, but walls are thin. There's a tiny restaurant plus kids' pool and swings, and a souvenir store. Tours are offered. Rates: $20 s, $30 d, $40 t, including tax and breakfast.

The modern **Hotel La Flores,** tel. 479-9307, next door, has eight clean rooms with private baths and hot water. Rates: $12 s, $20 d low season; $15 s, $22 d high season. A stone's throw west, **Hotel Rancho La Pradera,** tel. 479-9167, is an attractive place with a good restaurant and 10 modern rooms with private baths and hot water. **Cabinas Los Guayabos,** tel. 479-9453, almost at Tabacón, has modest cabins.

Jungla y Senderos Los Lagos has 19 cabins with private baths and hot water. Rates: $35 d standard, $45 superior low season; $45 standard, $55 superior high season; $10 more for a/c. It also has a simple four-bed cabin, but you need to provide your own bedding—$20 d low season, $25 high season. **Miradores Arenal** is in construction nearby, with what looked like attractive wooden cabins.

Cabinas Arenal Paraíso, tel./fax 479-9006, cellular tel. 385-5058, about five km west of town, has 20 very pretty all-hardwood *cabinas* with porches offering volcano vistas. There's a small restaurant. Rates: $46 s/d, $55 t, $68 quad, standard; $52 s/d, $64 t, $76 quad "luxe." Half a kilometer farther is **Montaña de Fuego,** tel. 382-0759, fax 479-9579, e-mail: monfeugo@asstcard.co.cr, website www.asstcard. co.cr/guia/homp/monfuego.htm, where 20 handsome hardwood *cabinas* sit on a hillock with splendid views of the volcano from a veranda enclosed in glass. All have fans, private bathrooms with hot water, and terraces. A restaurant was to be added. Horseback trips and other tours are offered. Rates: $50 d; $81 quad.

Food

I like the quaint **Choza de Laurel,** tel. 479-9077, fax 479-9178, a rustic Tican country inn with cloves of garlic hanging from the roof and an excellent *plato especial*—mixed plate of Costa Rican dishes ($4). Grilled chicken ($2-6) and *casados* ($3) are other good bets.

At the popular **Restaurant El Jardín,** you'll find *casados* for $2.50. The thatch-roofed **Rancho La Casada Restaurant** on the town square serves *típico* dishes, plus pastas ($3) and burgers ($2), and filling breakfasts. For pizza, try **Pizzeria Luigis** two blocks west of the plaza. **Soda El Río** is popular with locals.

West of town are **Restaurante Vaca Mundo** serving good *típico* dishes (average $5); **Pizzeria Vagabondo;** the **Hotel Rancho La Pradera** restaurant, with a soaring *ranchito* and a wide-ranging menu with sandwiches, *típico* dishes, and pastas ($3-8); and the **Restaurante Marisquería Los Lagos,** with dining alfresco under a canopy.

Macrobiótica El Angel Azul is a health-food store. **Mönpik** sells ice-cream; it's on the north side of the park.

Entertainment

The ritzy **Volcán Look Disco,** tel. 479-9690, two km south of town is a contempo spot with flashing lights and a/c. There's a restaurant. It teaches Latin dance classes every Tuesday evening; month-long courses cost $17.

Tours and Activities

Many places in town have signs reading Tourist Information; most offer hiking, horseback riding, fishing and other guided trips. An increasingly popular trip is a horseback ride to Monteverde. **ASPROADES** offers horseback rides and tours.

Sunset Tours, tel./fax 479-9099, has full-day trips to Caño Negro ($40), evening trips to Tabacón ($25), sportfishing at Lake Arenal ($135-250), plus hiking and horseback trips, and trips to Monteverde ($45) and Venado Caves ($30).

Arenal Outdoor Center, tel. 479-9508, one km west of town, has bungee-jumping at Peñas Blancas ($25), kayaking on class I-III rivers ($50 all-day including lunch), rafting on the Ríos Sarapiquí or Peñas Blancas, and float trips. It's run by savvy U.S. college kids. U.S.-owned **Desafío Ríos y Montañas,** tel. 479-9464, fax 479-9178, e-mail: desafio@sol.racsa.co.cr, on the northeast side of the plaza, offers whitewater trips on the Sarapiquí and Peñas Blancas ($37-80) and horseback trips as far afield as Monteverde ($65 one-way, $110 return).

Aventuras Arenal, Apdo. 13-4417 Fortuna, tel./fax 479-9133, two blocks east of the plaza, specializes in trips to Caño Negro ($40) and fishing in Lake Arenal ($60), but also has tours to Venado Caves ($30) and La Catarata ($15), plus mountain biking ($45) and horseback riding trips ($25) as well as to the volcano.

Aguas Bravas, tel. 479-9025, fax 229-4837, specializes in whitewater rafting. Half-day trips on the Peñas Blancas typically cost $35/50 (class III/IV); full-day trips on the Sarapiquí cost $60/80 (class III/V). It, too, offers mountain biking, horseback rides, and bungee trips. **Arenal Bungee** also offers bungee jumps at Peñas Blancas.

Jacamar Tours, tel./fax 479-9458, in front of the Hotel Burio claims to have the only ICT-licensed guides. It replicates the tours above, but also has a "Safari Float" on the Peñas Blancas ($35), an early morning birding walk ($30), a "Canopy Adventure" where you ascend to treetop platforms at Finca de Orquideas ($45), and mountain biking to La Catarata ($35).

Jessica at **La Fortuna Horseback Riding Center,** tel./fax 479-9197, offers horseback tours, including farm rides ($20) and a one-way trip to Monteverde ($70, including a boat trip across Lake Arenal and a visit to the Skywalk at Santa Elena). Another local company is **Eagle Tours,** tel. 479-9091, fax 479-9073.

AveRica, tel. 479-9076 or 479-9447, offers birding trips (from $15 including use of binoculars) led by Aaron Sekerak, author of *A Travel and Site Guide to Birds of Costa Rica.*

You may be approached on the street by so-called guides. The local chamber of commerce warns tourists "not to take tours or information off the street." Instead, it urges you to use tourist offices, hotel services, etc. If you need recommendations, contact **AMITUFOR,** tel. 479-9077,

fax 479-9091, the Association of Small Tourist Businesses of Fortuna.

Services

There's a **Banco Nacional** on the northeast side of the soccer field, a **Banco Popular** one block southeast, and a **Banco de Costa Rica** as you enter town from Tanque. **Souvenirs La Cascada,** tel. 479-9351, changes dollars. The **police station** is one block east of the soccer field. **Massages Genesis,** next door, offers professional massage and body treatments. The **Clínica Fortuna** is two blocks northeast of the gas station. A laundry service operates opposite Hotel San Bosco. Restaurant El Jardín has a **public phone** with international access. **Desafío** has a book exchange and e-mail service.

Getting There

Garaje Barquer, tel. 232-5660, buses depart San José via Ciudad Quesada daily at 6:30 a.m., 8:40 a.m., and 11:30 a.m. from the Coca-Cola bus station (Calle 16, Avenida 1/3). Buses from Ciudad Quesada depart from the Parada Municipal, tel. 460-0326, at 6:30 a.m., 9:30 a.m., 11:40 a.m., 1 p.m., 3 p.m., 3:30 p.m., 4:45 p.m., and 6 p.m.

Buses depart the gas station in front of Restaurant El Jardín in Fortuna for San José at 12:45 p.m. and 2:35 p.m.; for Ciudad Quesada at 5:15 a.m., 6 a.m., 9:30 a.m., 10 a.m., and 3:30 p.m.; for San Ramón at 5 a.m.; and for Tialarán at 8 a.m. and 5 p.m.

Interbus has a daily shuttle between San José and La Fortuna. Sunset Tours offers transfers to Monteverde ($45 pp, one-way).

TABACÓN HOT SPRINGS

At the base of Arenal Volcano, 13 km west of Fortuna and six km east of Lake Arenal, is Tabacón Hot Springs, where the steaming waters of the Río Tabacón tumble from the lava fields and cascade alongside the road. A dip here is supposedly good for treating skin problems, arthritis, and muscular pains. You can either experience this in style at the Tabacón Resort, or try the more simple pools 100 meters downhill from the resort, where entrance costs $5, granting access to a 100-meter section of the river where shallow bathing pools are backed

TABACÓN HOT SPRINGS;

Tabacón Hot Springs and Arenal Volcano

by rainforest. There are toilets, changing rooms, and towels.

Balneario Tabacón

This delightful Spanish colonial-style *balneario* (bathing resort) features five natural mineral pools with temperatures of 27-39° C (80-102° F) and natural hot springs set in exotic gardens. The main stream (hot) and a side stream (cool) have been diverted through the grounds in a series of descending pools of varying temperatures. Steam rises moodily amid lush, beautifully landscaped vegetation. Even adults laugh as they whiz down the water slide. You can sit beneath a 20-meter-wide waterfall—like taking a hot shower—and lean back inside, where it feels like a sauna (however, warns Gregg Calkin, "Ladies often misjudge the force of the falls and if they are wearing suits without straps they can find their tops joining their bottoms very quickly, making a clean breast of things, so to speak"). The complex also has an indoor hot tub, plus a restaurant (meals $5-12) and three bars, including a swim-

up bar in the main pool. Towels, lockers, and showers are available for a small deposit. Massages ($26 for 45 minutes) and mud pack treatments ($9) complete the picture. You'll fall in love with Tabacón by night, too, when a dip becomes a romantic indulgence (and a jaw-dropping experience if the volcano is erupting). It's a staple with tour groups. *A must visit, but overpriced.* Entrance: $14 ($13 after 6 p.m.), children $7. Hours: 10 a.m.-10 p.m.

Warning: I've received two reports from readers of theft from both the parking lot and lockers. The management doesn't seem to care. Don't trust to the fact that there's supposedly a security guard on duty.

Accommodations and Food

Tabacón Lodge, tel. 233-0780 or 222-1072, fax 221-3075, e-mail: tabacon@sol.racsa.co.cr, part of Tabacón Resort, was almost complete in late 1997, half a kilometer north of the *balneario*. The long-awaited property has 42 a/c rooms, each with two double beds, TV, patio affording a volcano view, large bathrooms, and upscale decor— exquisite hardwood furnishings, silent a/c, and intriguing artwork. Some are in bungalows, others are in a three-story property. Rates: $75 s, $88 d, $100 t, $105 suite low season; $85 s, $100 d, $115 t, $120 suite high season, including buffet breakfast and unlimited access to the *balneario*.

There's no entrance fee to eat at the **Balneario Tabacón** restaurant, which serves good Tico and creative continental fare (French onion soup, $3; salads $3; pastas $5); open noon-9:30 p.m.

EL VENADO CAVERNS

At **Jicarito,** about 25 km northwest of Tanque and 15 km southeast of San Rafael, a paved road leads south, dipping and looping seven km to the mountain hamlet of **Venado,** nestled in a valley bottom and famous for the **Venado Caverns,** two km farther west. The limestone chambers, which extend 2,700 meters and are replete with stalactites, stalagmites, and underground streams, weren't discovered until 1945, when the owner of the farm fell into the hole. The main mouth is on the farm of Julio Solis, reached via a mud-and-gravel road that leads south from Venado uphill to Lake Arenal You'll park at the farm, where a guide will lead you on a two-hour exploration of the caverns. Entrance: $1.50. You'll need sturdy footwear, a flashlight, and a safety helmet (obligatory), which you can rent for $3.50, plus 75 cents for rubber boot rental. Bats and tiny, colorless frogs and fish inhabit the caves, which also contain seashell fossils, and a "shrine" that glows luminously. Expect to get soaked and covered with ooze. The farm has a rustic *soda*, a swimming pool, and changing rooms. You need to call ahead for food, beeper tel. 296-2626, then enter code 900-556.

You can reach Venado via a rough dirt road from the north shore of Lake Arenal.

Accommodations and Food
Hospedaje Las Brisas, tel. 460-1954, in the hamlet of Venado, has six very basic albeit clean and appealing rooms, with pastel wooden walls and shared bathrooms with cold water. It is run by a delightful old lady, María Nuñoz, who you may join on rockers on the patio. Rates: $3.50 s, $6 d.

Across the road is **Salon Odanev.**

Getting There
A **bus** departs Ciudad Quesada for Venado daily at 2 p.m.

SAN RAFAEL DE GUATUSO

San Rafael de Guatuso is a mundane agricultural town on the Río Frío, 40 km northwest of Tanque. There is little of interest in San Rafael (often called Guatuso), the center of the local canton, which subsists largely on cattle ranching and rice farming. Still, you can rent boats and guides here for trips down the Río Frío to the Ujuminica Crocodile Farm, Caño Negro National Wildlife Refuge, and other points of interest nearby, not least local Indian villages. You'll note

THE GUATUSO INDIAN CULTURE

"We were of 12 communities until the Nicaraguans searching for rubber came to our land and fought with us," Eliécer Velas Alvarez, a member of the El Sol tribe of the Guatuso clans of Corobicí Indians, told reporter Wendy Schmidt.

Only three of the tribal communities—El Sol, La Margarita, and Tongibe—survived the withering encroachments of the last few centuries. Today, about 400 of the natives survive on the Tongibe reservation *(palenque)* on the plains at the foot of Volcán Tenorio, near San Rafael de Guatuso, on land ceded to them by the government in the 1960s. Today, they are mostly farmers who grow corn and a type of root called *tiquisqui*.

Only one generation ago, Guatuso Indians strolled through San Rafael wearing only loincloths made of cured tree bark, called *tana*. These lowlands once rang with the sound of women pounding away at soggy *tana* bark, like metal-beaters hammering gold.

"When I was a little girl, we used *tana* cloth and nothing else," recalls Rebecca Lizondo Lizondo, a full Tongibe, who learned the art from her mother (who, in turn, had learned from *her* mother). "This is how my grandmother would have made *tana*," Rebecca explains, as she reaches for a slender strip of moist bark, lays it across a small wooden block, and raises a heavy mallet to beat the bark into thin tissue. Stripped of its outer casing, the bark is first soaked in a stream to render it soft and malleable. "The strips are then hammered to any degree of thinness desired," says Rebecca, striking quickly with a resounding rat-a-tat-tat. When the bark felt like soft corduroy, it was ready to be spread out to bleach and dry in the strong sun, then stitched together like leather.

Of course, no one wears *tana* these days. But the Guatuso Indians take great pride in their heritage. Most continue to speak their native dialect, Maleku. Radio Sistema Cultural Maleku airs programs and announcements in Maleku, and Eliécer Velas Alvarez instructs the youngsters in Maleku at the elementary school in Tongibe. Alvarez, reports Wendy Schmidt, "has to buy chalk and books and erasers from his own pocket," and when it rains the schoolroom floods.

The Guatusos developed jade ornaments and carvings, bowls of terra-cotta, and bows and arrows of *pejibaye*, a tree of the palm family. The San Rafael area has many ancient tombs, and jade arrowheads and other age-old artifacts are constantly being dug up.

distinctive features among the cowboys roaming this snoozy town—a mix of Maleku and Guatuso Indian, Nicaraguan, and Spanish. The locals have formed the Asociación de Microempresarios Turísticos to put Guatuso on the map.

La Paz Waterfall and El Arbol de la Paz

This narrow waterfall plunges 50 meters into the jade-colored Río Celeste, whose waters are "dyed" a jewel-like turquoise by volcanic minerals. Be prepared for an exhilarating though daunting hike. Guides in San Rafael will take you on horseback through primary forests until you reach the towering El Arbol de la Paz ("Peace Tree"), one of the oldest and largest trees in the nation, dedicated by former President Oscar Arias Sánchez in 1989 as a symbol of peace. Two hours into your journey you reach a tiny hamlet where Doña Marielos Villalobos will refuel you with steaming coffee, tortillas, and fruit under a *ranchito* for the uphill hike through dripping forest to the waterfall.

Accommodations and Food

Albergue Tío Henry, tel. 464-0211, is a 10-room hotel two blocks southwest of the soccer field in the center of town; each room has a double bed or two single beds and a balcony. Rates: $4 pp with shared bath; $10 s, $12.50 d with a/c and private bath.

There are at least three other basic places to stay: **Hotel Las Brisas,** tel. 464-2087, **Cabinas El Gordo,** tel. 464-0009, and **Cabinas Shirley,** tel. 464-0045.

The **Bar/Restaurante Turístico** is in the center of town and has been recommended for its *casado* set lunch for $2. **Restaurante Río Celeste,** 50 meters north of Albergue Tío Henry, looks okay.

Tours and Activities

Uncle Henry is a friendly fellow who offers full-day tours to Caño Negro ($75, including two nights at Albergue Tío Henry, plus breakfasts and a lunch), the Río Celeste, Venado, and Ujuminica.

Services

There's a **gas station** plus a **Banco de Costa Rica** and **Banco Nacional,** four blocks southwest of the soccer field and church. The **medical** clinic is one block east of the heavily guarded Banco Nacional; there's a well-stocked **pharmacy** next to Albergue Tío Henry.

Getting There and Away

Buses depart Tilarán and Ciudad Quesada every two hours for San Rafael de Guatuso.

UJUMINICA CROCODILE FARM

This crocodile farm recently moved to Los Lagos, near Fortuna, from its former home on the banks of the Río Frío, north of San Rafael. You can see young caimans and crocodiles swimming around in pens. They're not raised for commercial reasons but will instead be released into the wild as adults. *Ujuminica* is a Maleku Indian word meaning "crocodile fell in the trap." Until a few years ago, the area was favored as a place to shoot crocodiles; only a few of the antediluvian beasts survived the slaughter. The farm attains a hatch and brood survival rate of 95%.

Two garfish, examples of another antediluvian species, swim in an upturned boat that serves as a tank. Tours can be arranged at hotels in Fortuna or in advance by calling La Central Hotel, tel. 460-0766, or ARA Agencia de Viajes, Apdo. 799, San José 1007, tel. 222-2900, fax 222-5173, which offers a choice of two three-day/two-night tours from San José, including visits to Ujuminica and Caño Negro. You can rent boats at Ujuminica for the journey downriver to Caño Negro.

MAGIL RESERVE

Magil is a 414-hectare reserve protecting more than 280 hectares of virgin cloud forest on the flanks of Volcán Tenorio near Río Celeste de Guatuso. The property, 19 km southwest of San Rafael, was recently incorporated into Tenorio National Park. The forests provide a precious habitat for poison-arrow frogs, monkeys, oropendolas, toucans, and at least 250 other bird species, including the very rare white eagle, which has found a safe refuge in the Magil forest. The especially lucky guest may spot a black leopard, a jaguar, or even a tapir.

Only 50 meters downhill from the lodge is an interesting stone formation believed to be a collection of ancient tombs of Indian chiefs. The giant rocks have been cut into surreal shapes and slotted together like pieces of some great three-dimensional jigsaw puzzle. The stonemasons' precision was such that it is virtually impossible to slide a knife blade between the stones. A small museum was being created to house the finds. Archaeology students from the National Youth Movement and the Canadian-based Youth Challenge International have begun excavations. The **Magil Archaeological Excavation Project** welcomes donations.

Magil Forest Lodge, Apdo. 3404, San José 1000, tel. 221-2825, fax 233-5991, still in construction at press time, offers five rooms. It has electricity. Horseback rides and hikes are offered. The owner, Dr. Manuel Emilio Montero, former president of the Costa Rican Tourism Institute (ICT), had difficulties and forfeited the old eco-lodge to the national park service. A reader advises against sending deposits.

Getting There
You reach Magil by a rough road that begins 20 meters west of the steel bridge over the Río Frío on the road to Upala in San Rafael. It's 19 km from here to the reserve, with the road deteriorating all the while. The last kilometer is through pasture along a thin muddy trail that had me convinced I had lost my way (don't attempt this drive without a 4WD with high ground clearance). Keep going; you'll crest a hill with what looks like a simple farmstead to your right halfway up a slope. That's the old lodge; the new lodge is beside the river, closer to San Rafael. There is no bus service.

UPALA AND VICINITY

Upala, 40 km northwest of San Rafael de Guatuso, is an agricultural town sitting at the center of the local rice and dairy industries. Upala is only 10 km south of the Nicaraguan border. Dirt roads lead north to Lake Nicaragua, but for-eigners are not allowed to enter Nicaragua at this point. If you wish to enter Nicaragua, you'll have to continue west via Brasilia—where there's an armed police checkpoint—and Santa Cecilia to La Cruz (81 km), in Guanacaste. A dirt road leads north from Santa Cecilia (51 km west of

Upala) seven km to the hamlet of **La Virgen,** where you have stupendous vistas down over Lake Nicaragua, with classically conical volcanoes in the distance.

At **Colonia Puntarenas,** 10 km southeast of Upala on the San Rafael road, a dirt road leads north to Caño Negro.

Accommodations and Food
The **Cabinas y Restaurant Buena Vista,** tel. 470-0186 or 470-0063, immediately north and west of the bridge as you enter town from the south, has 15 basic rooms with private bath and hot water, plus a large open-air restaurant overlooking the river. The cabins are two blocks west of the bridge, on the left as you enter town from La Cruz and Bijagua. Rates: $7 pp. Across the road from the restaurant is the **Hotel Rosita,** tel. 470-0198, which also has basic rooms for the same price. The **Hotel Restaurante Upala,** tel. 470-0169, also has basic rooms with private baths but cold water only. Rates: $5 s, $7 d. It's near the bus station, as is **Cabinas del Norte,** tel. 470-0061. Another budget option includes the very basic **Hospedaje Rodriguez.**

The only place to stay in Santa Cecilia is the **Hotel/Bar/Restaurante Chuli,** with five clean, simple, and breezy rooms (no fans) with large beds and shared bath. Rates: $5 pp. The **Centro Social La Favorita** is a lively nocturnal spot on the north side of the plaza and the **Restaurant Las Brisas** and **Rancho Mary** are both attractive *ranchito* eateries on the outskirts of Santa Cecilia; the latter even has cable TV at the bar.

Services
There's a **Banco Nacional** five blocks north of the bridge in Upala. The **police station** (Guardia Rural), tel. 470-0134, is 100 meters north and west of the bridge. There's a **gas station** in town, and another just west of Santa Cecilia.

Getting There and Away
By Bus: Upala is served daily by express bus (5-6 hours) from San José via Cañas and the Pan-American Highway; it departs Calle 16 and Avenida 3/5 at 6:30 a.m. and 3 p.m. (call CNT, tel. 255-1932). Return buses depart Upala at 5 a.m., 9 a.m., 2 p.m. and 3:30 p.m. Local buses also link Upala with San José via San Rafael and Ciudad Quesada (departs Ciudad Quesada

at 3:30 p.m.; returns from Upala at 9 a.m.); and from Cañas at 5:45 a.m., 9 a.m., 11 a.m., 2 p.m., and 5 p.m. (returning from Upala at 6 a.m., 9 a.m., 11 a.m., 1 p.m., and 4:30 p.m.). Buses also run daily to Caño Negro Wildlife Refuge when conditions permit.

The bus station in Upala is one block north and one west of the bridge.

A bus departs La Cruz for Santa Cecilia daily at 5 a.m., 10:30 a.m., 1:30 p.m., 7 p.m., and 7:30 p.m.

By Air: Although there's no scheduled air service, there's an **airstrip** east of town just before the bridge over the Río Zapote; you can charter an air taxi from San José.

By Car: The paved road between Upala and San Rafael is in relatively good condition. It continues west in good condition as far as Brasilia (42 km), where the paving ends. Upala is also linked to the Pan-American Hwy. from north of Cañas by a little-trafficked and well-paved road (via Bijagua) that slices between Miravalles and Tenorio Volcanoes; and by the dirt road west of Brasilia via Santa Cecilia and, from there, by paved road linking La Cruz, in the extreme northwest.

Taxis wait by the bus station.

PUERTO VIEJO DE SARAPIQUÍ AND VICINITY

The Llanura de San Carlos comprises the easternmost part of the northern lowlands. The Ríos San Carlos, Sarapiquí and others crawl sinuously across the landscape, vast sections are waterlogged for much of the year, and the waterways to this day remain a vital means of communication. Much of the community today is dependent on the banana industry that extends eastward almost the whole way to the Caribbean. The railways of the big banana companies opened up this region decades ago. The map tells the story. From Puerto Viejo east to Tortuguero National Park is a gridwork maze of dirt roads and rail tracks linking towns named Finca UCR, Finca Paulina, Finca Agua, Finca Zona Siete, and Fincas 1, 2, 3, etc.

Much of the area is still covered with tropical rainforest that stretches north to the Río San Juan, linking the northern arm of Braulio Carillo National Park with the rainforests of the Nicaraguan lowlands. That are several private reserves offering nature lovers as rewarding experiences as any in the nation. Fishing is good, and there are plenty of crocodiles and river turtles, plus sloths, monkeys, and superb birdlife to see.

The area is one of the last refuges for the endangered green macaw, which is threatened by loss of habitat. The **Sarapiquí Conservation Association** is working to purchase lots along the rivers to secure nesting areas and, specifically, to protect individual trees upon which the bird depends for food and nests.

The town of Puerto Viejo de Sarapiquí is the major town, and the only one of consequence.

Routes from San José
There are two routes to Puerto Viejo from San José. Both are splendidly scenic. The routes meet up in Puerto Viejo, forming a perfect loop.

The **western route** is via Vara Blanca, between the saddle of Poás and Barva Volcanoes, then dropping down to San Miguel and La Virgen.

The **easterly route** traverses the saddle between Barva and Irazú Volcanoes, dropping down through Braulio Carrillo National Park then via Las Horquetas.

Buses from San José to Puerto Viejo will stop at any of the lodges in the circle along the way.

VARA BLANCA TO LA VIRGEN

The route via Vara Blanca is marvelous on a clear day as you descend the switchbacks via the **La Paz Waterfall.** Watch for pedestrians on the road as you approach the bridge on the hairpin bend. From here the road drops through the valley of the Río Sarapiquí. There's a toll booth (50 cents, voluntary) at **Cinchona.**

About six km south of San Miguel is **Laguna Hule,** just before the hamlet of Cariblanco, which has a gas station. The lake, set in a dormant volcanic crater and reached via a rough dirt road, is surrounded by lush forest. Fisherfolk should bring their tackle. Four-wheel drive is recommended. Of interest to birders is the dirt road—some seven km north of La Paz—that leads east to **Colonia Virgen del Socorro** (Costa Rica Expeditions offers one-day guided birding trips: $65 pp; see Appendix for contact information).

North of San Miguel, the road drops onto the plains at **La Virgen,** where the land flattens out and tropical fruit farms and banana plantations appear. Be sure to call in at **Rancho Leona** for a meal, or to request permission to visit the

---

SHARKS IN THE RÍO SAN JUAN

If you see a shark fin slicing the surface of the Río San Juan, you will be forgiven for thinking you've come down with heat stroke. In fact, there *are* sharks in the freshwater river! The creatures, along with other species normally associated with salt water—tarpon and sawfish, for example—migrate between the Atlantic Ocean and the crystal-clear waters of Lake Nicaragua, navigating 169 km of river and rapids en route. All three fish are classified as euryhaline species—they can cross from salt water to fresh and back again with no ill effects.

For centuries, scientists were confounded by the sharks' presence in Lake Nicaragua. The lake is separated from the Pacific by a 19-km chunk of land, and, since rapids on the Río San Juan seemingly prevent large fish from passing easily from the Caribbean, surely, the thinking went, the lake must have once been connected to one or the other ocean. Uplift of the Central American isthmus must have trapped the sharks in the lake.

Studies in the early 1960s, however, showed that there were no marine sediments on the lake bottom. Thus, the lake was never part of the Atlantic or the Pacific. (It was actually formed by a huge block of land falling between two fault lines; the depression then filled with water.)

Then, ichthyologists decided to tag sharks with electronic tracking devices. It wasn't long before sharks tagged in the Caribbean turned up in Lake Nicaragua, and vice versa. Incredibly, the sharks—and presumably the tarpon and sawfish—are indeed able to negotiate the rapids and move back and forth between lake and sea.

---

stained-glass studio where fabulous windows and other master-quality glasswork is conjured. (You can place orders; $80-125 per square foot. A lamp typically costs $300-1,000).

Just south of La Virgen, a side road leads east via a suspension bridge over the Río Sarapiquí and climbs eight km to **San Ramón** and (four km farther along a muddy dirt road that requires 4WD) **Santuario de Mariposa Bijagual** (Bijagual Butterfly Sanctuary). This small netted butterfly garden is on a small, simple farm run by Elgar Corrales and Virginia Cascante Ramón. Trails lead into the nearby forest, and family members lead horseback rides. It's a hard uphill journey but, heck, the views are worth it. Entrance: $5.

La Finca Lodge, tel./fax 284-5904, four km west of La Virgen at Los Angeles de Río Cuarto, is a wildlife shelter where tapirs, peccaries, white-tailed deer, monkeys, macaws, and other animal and bird species are bred and raised for introduction to the wild. The Río Sardinal flows through the property, which has a traditional sugar press *(trapiche)* and a dairy farm where you can help milk the cows. Horseback riding is offered. You can even ride a tame buffalo.

Spanish Language Course
Leona Wellington, at Rancho Leona, tel./fax 761-1019, or—if the line is down—c/o tel. 269-9410, offers a two-week Spanish course that includes hiking and practical settings, such as in the kitchen with local women, for language classes. She takes groups of five minimum ($1,900 pp including airfare, classes, accommodations, and meals; less for more people). As with their stained-glass work, Ken and Leona apply the profits to the purchase of forest lands for preservation.

Accommodations
Hotel Claribel Cabinas, tel. 761-1190, in the center of La Virgen has six basically furnished cabins with fans, private bath and cold water. Rates: $10 d. Nearby is **Cabinas del Río. Green Tortoise Bed and Breakfast,** tel./fax 761-1035, at La Virgen is a funky house where the famous Green Tortoise bus *(la Tortuga Verde)* is based. There was no one there when I called. It offers rafting, kayaking, and mountain biking. You can camp here.

Rancho Leona, tel./fax 761-1019, or—if the line is down—c/o tel. 269-9410, is recommended for its family coziness and delightfully funky ambience. The rooms, in a wooden lodge, are very rustic but appealing, with fans and stained-glass skylights. Leona Wellingon and Ken Upcraft are the charming hosts. Both are artists, as the stained-glass work attests. Ken is also a kayaker and offers full-day kayaking trips. When you return, hop into the stone and timber riverside sweat lodge ("big enough for 16 people") or the cooling tub. There's a splendid restaurant. Rates: $9 pp.

Leona and Ken also have a rustic **geodesic dome** surrounded by forest beside the Río Peje on the edge of Braulio Carrillo National Park, 14 km east of La Virgen. The place sleeps 11 people and has cooking facilities, candles, safety radio, water and a self-composting toilet, but no electricity. There are two concrete slabs for tents. A swimming hole is nearby. Rates: $80 pp, two nights including roundtrip transportation from Rancho Leona (additional nights are free until other folks want to use it). You have to hike in (one hour minimum) from Comunidad de San Ramón.

La Finca Lodge, tel./fax 284-5904, four km west of La Virgen at Los Angeles de Río Cuarto, has two old country houses featuring nine rooms with shared baths, hot water, and wrap-around verandas. Meals are served buffet-style in a rustic dining room.

Food
The **Rancho Leona** has a surprisingly cosmopolitan menu, and eclectic decor that includes stained-glass windows, homemade Tiffany lamps, oropendola nests hanging from the roof, and cushioned tree stumps for stools. Rancho Leona serves wholesome health food, including, brown rice, eggplant parmesan, French onion soup, vegetarian dishes, and home-baked whole wheat bread.

La Virgen has a couple of other good restaurants, including **Restaurant Tía Rosarita** and the **Centro Turisto Los Venados**—about one km north of La Virgen—which has a popular restaurant specializing in *chicharrones,* plus music nightly (it also has a small swimming pool and nature trails leading into a nature reserve).

Getting There
The Río Frío bus departs San José from Avenida 11, Calles Central/1, at 6:30 a.m., noon, 1 p.m., 3 p.m., 3:30 p.m., and 4 p.m.

LA VIRGEN TO PUERTO VIEJO

From La Virgen, the road slopes north seven km to **Chilamate** then swings east to Puerto Viejo (13 km farther). The road parallels the Río Sarapiquí, which here offers kayaking and whitewater rafting. There's a **butterfly garden** at La Quinta de Sarapiquí and another at Selva Verde.

Selva Verde
Selva Verde, Chilamate de Sarapiquí, tel. 766-6800, fax 766-6011, e-mail: travel@holbrooktravel.com, website www.holbrooktravel.com; in the U.S., contact Costa Rican Lodges, 3540 N.W. 13th St., Gainesville, FL 32609, tel. (904) 373-7118 or (800) 451-7111, fax (904) 371-3710, on the banks of the Río Sarapiquí at Chilamate, is a private reserve protecting some 192 hectares of primary rainforest adjacent to Braulio Carrillo National Park. The reserve is renowned for its birdlife, including oropendolas, motmots, parrots, jacamars, and other exotic lowland tropical birds. Poison-arrow frogs are common and easily spotted amid the leaf litter. Walking trails lead through the forests: trail maps are provided, and the lodge has a fine staff of naturalist guides. Guided hiking cost $15 three hours, $25 six hours.

Selva Verde also offers trips up the river by canopied boat ($25), guided canoe trips ($45 half-day), horseback trips ($20 pp, three hours), and a banana plantation visit ($25 pp). Mountain bikes are also available. Access to the butterfly garden costs $5.

Selva Verde—not to be confused with La Selva, farther east—is owned by U.S.-based Holbrook Travel, which operates a nature lodge on the property. Also here is the **Sarapiquí Conservation Learning Center** (Centro de Enseñanza) with a lecture room, library, and accommodations on stilts. Selva Verde is popular with academic and tour groups, so book well in advance.

Whitewater Trips on the Río Sarapiquí
Aventuras de Sarapiquí, at Chilamate, offers class III/V trips for $35 pp, half-day, plus flatwater trips farther downriver for birders. It also runs the Ríos Toro and Peñas Blancas. **Rancho Leona** in La Virgen, offers kayak trips for beginners and advanced kayakers ($75 including two nights' accommodations).

Costa Rica Expeditions, Apdo. 6941-1000, San José, tel. 257-0766, fax 257-1665, e-mail: crexped@sol.racsa.co.cr, has a one-day whitewater trip (class III), May through mid-December, on the upper Sarapiquí; $65 pp. **Ríos Tropicales,** Apdo. 472-1200, San José, tel. 233-6455, fax 255-4354, e-mail: info@riostro.com, also offers whitewater trips (classes I-II and class III).

Accommodations and Food
La Quinta de Sarapiquí Lodge, Apdo. 11021, San José 1000, tel./fax 761-1052, is a family-run venture on the banks of the Río Sardinal. This handsome hacienda-style property is surrounded by lush landscaped gardens full of *baston de emperador* and ginger. Hummingbirds abound. It has 15 widely spaced, clinically clean, well-lit cabins with contemporary furnishings, ceiling fans, and private baths with hot water. A swimming pool and deck are suspended over the river. An open dining room and bar, a well-stocked gift store, plus a riverside trail for hikes and mountain bikes or horseback rides complete the picture. Birding is particularly good (there are even endangered green macaws locally), and past guests speak well of the food and "congenial atmosphere." Rates: $35 s, $45 d, $60 t.

One km east, **Islas del Río Adventure Center Lodge,** tel./fax 766-6574, at Bajos de Chilamate, sits on seven hectares of forested property divided into tiny islets along the banks of the Río Sarapiquí. Owners Dr. Sonia Ocamp and Dr. Arturo Salazar offer 15 simple hardwood rooms in a lodge, each with fans and private bath with hot water. There are also cement *cabinas* plus an open-air restaurant with a riverside patio. Rates: $20 s/d low season; $40 s/d including breakfast. Guided hikes and horseback trips are offered. IYH members receive discounts.

Selva Verde, Chilamate de Sarapiquí, tel. 766-6800, fax 766-6011, e-mail: travel@holbrooktravel.com; in the U.S., contact Costa Rican Lodges, 3540 N.W. 13th St., Gainesville, FL 32609, tel. (904) 373-7118 or (800) 451-7111, fax (904) 371-3710, has a 45-room lodge—divided into the River Lodge and the Creek Lodge—set in 20 acres of landscaped grounds on the banks of the Río Sarapiquí. It has a very comfortable, manicured feel. Thatched walkways lead between the luxury cabins, which are raised on stilts and constructed of beautiful hardwoods. All rooms are large, airy, and screened, with verandas for wildlife viewing. You have a choice between cabins with private baths at the River Lodge and no less appealing rooms with shared baths at the Creek Lodge. Each room has two large single beds. Highlights include a large library and game room, a conference room with scheduled lectures, and a large dining room. Meals are served buffet-style at set times. The lodge offers laundry service and provides rubber boots and oversized umbrellas. Rates: $59 s, $86 d, $120 t, $132 quad low season; $75 s, $120 d, $150 t, $172 quad high season, including all meals and tax. Deduct $24 pp for a room only. There are also five four-person bungalows across the street ($74).

tamandua anteater

ERIN DWYER

PUERTO VIEJO

Unbelievably, this small landlocked town—at the confluence of the Ríos Puerto Viejo and Sarapiquí—was, in colonial times, Costa Rica's main shipping port. It still derives much of its income from river traffic (most of it touristic), but today the economy is dominated by a sea of banana plantations. There's nothing in town of interest, but a waterborne nature-viewing or fishing trip is a must, and several nature lodges lie close at hand.

El Gavilán, Apdo. 445-2010, San José 2010, tel. 234-9507, beeper tel. 223-3030, fax 253-6556, e-mail: gavilan@sol.racsa.co.cr, website costarica.tourism.co/hotels/gavilan/lodgegav.htm, is a 180-hectare private forest reserve on the east bank of the Río Sarapiquí. The lodge has horses for rent ($15 pp) and guided hikes along the forest trails. Boat rides cost $20; or $50 down the Río San Juan to Barra del Colorado. Fishing trips and a panoply of excursions are available, including boat trips to Tortuguero.

Five km south of Puerto Viejo, at **El Tigre** on the well-paved road to/from Horquetas, is **MUSA** (Mujeres Unida de Sarapiquí), Apdo. 91-3069, Puerto Viejo de Sarapiquí, a women's cooperative that sells native medicinal herbs, *afrodisiacas,* teas claiming remedies for everything from arthritis and anemia to PMS, and herb products such as chamomile and rosemary shampoos, soaps, and skin creams. You can tour their farm.

La Selva Biological Station

La Selva, tel. 710-1515, fax 710-1414, or OTS, Apdo. 676, San Pedro 2050, tel. 240-6696, fax 240-6783, e-mail: reservas@ns.ofs.ac.cr; in the U.S., tel. (919) 684-5774, fax 684-5661, four km south of Puerto Viejo, is a biological research station run by the Organization of Tropical Studies (OTS). The station, which includes laboratories, teaching facilities, and experimental plots, is centered on a 1,500-hectare biological reserve—mostly premontane rainforest but wtih varied habitats—linked to the northern extension of Braulio Carrillo National Park and extending from 35-150 meters above sea level. La Selva ("The Jungle") is the most important of OTS's stations worldwide, and leading scientists and graduate students work here year-round.

Birds are particularly profuse: more than 420 species have been identified here. Several birders have seen more than 100 species in a single day—an astonishing number considering the difficulty of spotting birds in the dank forest. An annual Audubon Society "Birdathon" is held, with money for each species seen in the one-day event pledged to a fund aimed at protecting Braulio Carrillo. More than 500 species of butterflies have been spotted, as have 120 species of mammals, and 55 species of snakes. The arboretum displays more than 1,000 tree species.

Almost 60 km of trails snake through the reserve. Many are no more than dirt trails, which deteriorate to muddy quagmires after heavy rain. Annual precipitation is over 400 cm; even the driest months (February and March) each receive almost 20 cm of rain. Rubber boots or waterproof hiking boots are essential. So, too, is adequate raingear (an umbrella is extremely useful for photographers wishing to protect their cameras). Some trails have boardwalks, and most are marked with distance markers at regular intervals. The gift shop sells maps, as well as *Walking La Selva* (R. Whittall and B. Farnsworth), a handy guide to the trails. Keep a wary eye out for snakes. Half-day guided nature walks are offered daily at 8 a.m. and 1:30 p.m. ($20 adults; $10 children 5-12). You are not allowed to explore alone.

Both day and overnight visitors are welcome with notice: impromptu appearances are not welcome. Only 65 people at a time are allowed in the reserve, including scientists. It is often booked solid months in advance. Hence, reservations are essential, even for day visits.

The OTS operates a shuttle van from San José on Monday, Wednesday, and Friday ($10), space permitting (researchers and students have priority). A van shuttle also operates between La Selva and Puerto Viejo Monday through Saturday. Taxis from Puerto Viejo cost about $4. Buses from San José will drop you off at the entrance to La Selva. You'll need to walk from the road to La Selva (two km). There are no bellhops: pack light.

Accommodations

Budget: Cabinas and Restaurant Monteverde, tel. 766-6236, opposite the soccer field, has six very simple rooms with fans and hot water. Rates: $6 s, $7.50 d. **Cabinas Laura,** 50 meters east of the Banco Nacional, has simple, clean rooms with fans but grungy private bathrooms. Rates: $8 d. **Hotel Gonar,** tel. 766-6196, above Ferretería Gonar, has basic rooms. Rates: $6 d without bath; $9 d with bath. **Restaurant/Cabinas La Paz,** tel. 766-6257, offers a choice of funky older rooms and nicer, newer rooms, both with private bath. Rates: $6 s, $10 d older rooms; $8 s, $12 d newer rooms. **Hotel Santa María** is a basic *pensión.* Rates: $4 pp.

Immediately west of the soccer field is the modern **Mi Lindo Sarapiquí,** tel. 766-6074, with 14 clean rooms with private baths and hot water plus a pleasing open-air restaurant. Rates: $8.50 s, $15 d, $19 t. Also consider **Cabinas Restaurant Jacaré,** three km west of town at Guaria.

Inexpensive: The best place in town is **Hotel Bambú,** Apdo. 1518, Guadalupe 2100, tel. 766-6005, fax 766-6132, facing the soccer field, with nine clean, modern rooms with ceiling fans, TVs, and private baths with hot water. Rates: $45 d, including breakfast. It also has two self-sufficient apartments, plus a restaurant. Transfers ($20 pp) from San José can be arranged.

Andrea Cristina Bed & Breakfast, tel./fax 766-6265, half a kilometer west of town on the road to La Virgen, is a pleasing place with four rooms with various combinations of beds, lofty wooden ceilings, tile floors, and private baths with hot water. Two simple yet appealing A-frame bungalows at the bottom of the garden share a bathroom. There's a restaurant with patio in the garden, which attracts sloths and kinkajous. It's run by friendly owners, Alexander and Floribell Martinez, who arrange nature and birding tours, plus tours to Nicaragua. A reader raves about the breakfast and coffee. Rates: $25 s, $40 d, including breakfast.

About four km east of Puerto Viejo is the peaceful **El Gavilán Lodge,** Apdo. 445-2010, San José 2010, tel. 234-9507, beeper tel. 223-3030, fax 253-6556, e-mail: gavilan@sol.racsa.co.cr, owned by Mariamalia Bissinger. The lodge is set in five hectares of lush landscaped grounds beside the river at the edge of the private forest reserve. It's splendid for birding: wild birds flock in and out. There are four rooms in the main two-story structure, with hardwood verandas and rockers, plus bungalows with 13 simply appointed rooms with private bathrooms and hot water. Simple meals are served in an open-air restaurant beneath a bamboo roof (no alcohol; bring your own). It has a playground for the kids. There is no telephone on the property. A variety of boating, hiking, and tour excursions are offered. Rates: $35 s, $40 d/t low season; $40 s, $50 d/t high season, including breakfast. Lunches cost $9; dinners cost $12. Meal plans are offered. You can take a boat to El Gavilán from the wharf in Puerto Viejo. If driving, the access road is three km *south* of Puerto Viejo, off the road to/from Las Horquetas. Transfers from San José cost $30 each way.

Moderate: La Selva has comfortable dormitory-style accommodations with communal bathrooms, some fitted to accommodate visitors with wheelchairs. It has a few singles and doubles, but researchers and students get priority. Tourists are allowed to stay here only on a space-available basis. Reservations are essential. Rates: $88 pp, including three meals served family style in the dining room (researchers half-price, students less). Word is that meals are served bang on time and latecomers get the crumbs. Laundry service is offered. Contact La Selva Biological Station, tel. 710-1515, fax 710-1414, or OTS, Apdo. 676, San Pedro 2050, tel. 240-6696, fax 240-6783, e-mail: reservas@ns.ofs.ac.cr, website www.ots.ac.cr; in the U.S., tel. (919) 684-5774, fax 684-5661.

The Murrillo family offers very rustic lodging in male and female dorm beds at **Sarapiquí Ecolodge,** tel. 766-6122, fax 766-6247, a ranch house on an 80-hectare farm across the river from La Selva. A female reader reports a problem with a Peeping Tom peering into the woman's dorm through wall slats. Rates: $15 pp, including three meals. Hiking, horseback riding ($5 per hour), and boating ($20 per hour) are available. Shared bathrooms.

Food

The restaurant at **Mi Lindo Sarapiquí** has an extensive menu. **Pip's Restaurant** is also reportedly good. And the **Hong Kong Restaurant** in Cabinas Monteverde, and that of the **Hotel Bambú** have been recommended.

There's a dockside *soda*—Servicentro el Río Sarapiquí—open 5:30 a.m.-6 p.m.

Services

Everything is on the main street. There's a **Banco Nacional** opposite the soccer field. The **post office** is 100 farther east, with the **police** (Guardia Rural) opposite. **MINAE** (the ministry in charge of national parks) has an office next to the police station, but it is *not* a tourist information office. The **Red Cross,** tel. 710-6901, ext. 212, is at the west end of town.

Getting There

By Bus: Buses (four hours) from San José depart from Avenida 11, Calles Central/1 daily at 7 a.m., 9 a.m., 10 a.m., 1 p.m., 3 p.m., and 4 p.m., via the Guápiles Highway and Horquetas. You can also take a slower bus through Heredia from the same bus stop at 6:30 a.m. and noon (this bus returns to San José via La Selva and continues to Rara Avis). Buses also reportedly leave from Calle 12, Avenidas 7/9 at 6:30 a.m. and 2 p.m., returning at 7:30 a.m. and 12:30 p.m.

By Taxi: Taxis line the main street.

ALONG THE RÍO SARAPIQUÍ

Before the advent of the Atlantic Railroad linking the central valley with Puerto Limón on the Caribbean, cargo boats ferried bananas and other goods down the Río Sarapiquí to Barra del Colorado and Puerto Limón. Now that the contras' and Sandinistas' guns lie silent, you can follow the same route as colonial traders (the Río Sarapiquí was once considered the contras' Ho Chi Minh Trail) aboard long narrow boats that ply the river and that will take you all the way to Barra del Colorado and Tortuguero. The nature viewing is fantastic, with birds galore, monkeys and sloths in the trees along the riverbank, and crocodiles and caimans poking their nostrils and eyes above the muddy waters.

The hamlet of **La Trinidad** lies at junction of the Río Sarapiquí and Río San Juan. Rough dirt roads push north from Puerto Viejo to **Pavas,** 10 km south of Trinidad and—perhaps—as far as Trinidad itself.

Accommodations

Oro Verde Station, tel. 233-6613, fax 223-7479, beside the Río Sarapiquí 3.5 km south of its confluence with the Río San Juan, is a rustic lodge surrounded by a 2,500-hectare reserve. Indian-style thatched huts offer simple accommodations for up to 40 people. One unit has four small dorm-style rooms with shared bathroom but no electricity: candles and kerosene lamps add to the reclusive and rustic atmosphere. Four two-room family-size cabins with private baths have kitchens, including propane stoves. Simple but tasty meals are served on an open-air dining terrace. Guides lead fishing trips, trail walks, and explorations by dugout canoes through the rainforests, lagoons, and on the Ríos Sarapiquí and San Juan. Rates: $195 pp, three-day package including meals, transportation, and lodging. It's a two-hour journey from Puerto Viejo to Transportes ($40).

The **Trinity Lodge,** tel. 259-1679, website www.online.co.cr/sarap.html, at La Trinidad, has clean albeit spartan *cabinas* with private baths on a working *finca* with a "deliberate pace." Electricity is supplied by generator until 9 p.m. Meals are served in a large *ranchito* restaurant. Forest walks are offered. Rates: $20 pp, including meals.

Las Oropendolas is a simple place with cabins somewhere upriver. It has a bar and restaurant, plus a pool. Rates: $25.

Tours on the Río Sarapiquí

A regular water-taxi departs the dock (at the far east end of Puerto Viejo) at 11 a.m. for Oro Verde and the Río San Juan ($2). Several dozen water-taxis are also for hire, from slender motorized canoes to canopied tour boats for 8-20 passengers. William Rojas, tel. 766-6260, has been recommended, and has a boat for up to 10 passengers. Trips cost $20 per hour for up to five people. A full-day trip to the Río San Juan and back costs $125 per boat. Expect to pay $200-300 for a journey all the way down the Río San Juan to Barra del Colorado and Tortuguero National Parks. However, **Transportes Cocodrilo** (based at the Hotel Bambú) operates a scheduled water-taxi to Barra del Colorado from Puerto Viejo on Tuesday and Friday at 9 a.m. ($35), continuing to Tortuguero at 12:30 p.m. ($20). The boat departs Tortuguero on Thursday and Sunday at 9 a.m. for Barra del Colorado, continuing to Puerto Viejo at 10:30 a.m.

Transportes Acuático Oasis, tel. 766-6108 or 766-6260, offers boat transfers and tours. And all the lodges locally offer trips. For example, El Gavilán has boat trips on the Ríos Sarapiquí ($20 pp) and San Juan ($60), plus a one-day boat trip to Tortuguero via the San Juan ($85, minimum four people). **Peace Rainbow Travel,** tel. 234-9507, fax 253-6556, associated with El Gavilán, offers boat trips on the Ríos Sarapiquí and San Juan, plus packages combining a night or more at El Gavilán with a boat trip and visit to Poás Volcano. **Tropical Canoeing,** tel./fax 285-1007, e-mail: gemtour@nexos.co.cr, has three-hour canoe trips from El Tigre.

Arenas Tours, tel. 221-6839, fax 257-7735, e-mail: larenas@sol.racsa.co.cr, offers trips from San José ($74).

American Wilderness Experience, tel. (303) 444-2622 or (800) 444-0099, fax (303) 444-3999 in the U.S., e-mail: awedave@aol.com, offers a 10-day paddling trip through the northern lowlands. **Swiss Travel Service,** tel. 231-4055, in San José offers a two-hour boat trip on the Río Sarapiquí, ending with lunch and a nature hike at Selva Verde Lodge. **Turavia,** Apdo. 458, San José 1150, tel. 296-1223, fax 220-2197, offers a similar boat tour ending at El Gavilán Lodge. **Blue Wing Tours,** tel. 231-4299, fax 231-3816, offers a three-day rainforest cruise aboard the *Rain Goddess,* a 65-foot cruise vessel with two double and four triple cabins. The cruise follows the Colorado and San Juan Rivers to Tortuguero.

Other tour operators in San José also offer river trips.

BRAULIO CARRILLO TO PUERTO VIEJO

The most dramatic route to Puerto Viejo from San José is through Braulio Carrillo National Park on the Guápiles Highway (Hwy. 32), built in 1987. Drive carefully! The road coils steeply 28 km downhill and is usually fog-bound for much of the way; landslides are frequent; and even in the worst conditions, Costa Rican drivers display insane recklessness. With luck, there'll be no clouds; if that's the case, you'll be blessed with one of the most scenic drives in the country. The road spills onto the northern lowlands at **Santa Clara,** where there's a gas station and handsome restaurant—**Rancho Robertos**— serving *típico* dishes.

Highway 4 leads north from Santa Clara to Puerto Viejo (34 km). The main highway continues east for Puerto Limón.

About four km west of Santa Clara, immediately east of Braulio Carrillo's Quebrada González ranger station, is **Mariposario Los Heliconios,** tel. 226-2570, beeper tel. 224-2400, cellular tel. 382-3953, a butterfly farm and nature reserve where you can walk inside the netted butterfly garden. It also has a poison-arrow frog garden, and trails lead to a river (30 minutes away) good for spotting frogs, monkeys, and birds. Hours: daily 8 a.m.-4 p.m. Entrance: $5.

You can experience much the same environment as you'll find in Braulio Carrillo, but this one for "wimps," at **La Arawak Rainforest Reserve,** tel. 289-7364, a lowland private reserve at the base of Braulio Carrillo, 2.5 km north of Hwy. 32. It has five km of easily negotiated self-guided trails good for birding and spotting monkeys, sloths, and other fauna. There is a swimming pool and a river pool for dips, plus showers and toilets, and a restaurant (it caters mostly to groups, but individuals are welcome to bring

their own food). There's secure parking. *Cabinas* were to be added. Entrance: $6.

Somewhere nearby is a tall circular column of rock called **Piedra Alegre** that local *campesinos* claim has never been climbed because it is protected by magic.

Accommodations and Food
Mariposario Los Heliconios has modern *cabinas* with private baths and hot water for $5 ($10 with tour). There's also a restaurant.

LAS HORQUETAS AND VICINITY

Las Horquetas, 17 km north of the Guápiles Highway and 17 km south of Puerto Viejo, is a sleepy little one-street hamlet about 500 meters west of the road. The forested slopes of Braulio Carrillo rise to the west. The flatlands to the east are carpeted with banana plantations. Rutted dirt roads and rail-tracks criss-cross the land, connecting plantation settlements and processing plants with names such as Finca UCR, Finca 1, Finca 3, etc., including **Río Frío,** two km south and four km east of Horquetas.

Las Horquetas is also the gateway to one of Costa Rica's most famous private reserves.

Rara Avis
This unique 1,280-hectare rainforest reserve abutting Braulio Carrillo National Park, 15 km west of Las Horquetas, contains two lodges, a biological research station, and a host of novel projects designed to show that a rainforest can be *economically* viable if left intact, not cut down. Projects include producing exportable orchids and ornamental air plants, seedlings of popular timber trees for reforestation projects, macadamias, the rare *Geonoma epetiolata* palm, philodendrons for wicker, *pacas* for meat, and ecotourism. And there's a **butterfly farm** and **orchid garden.**

"The objective," says founder Amos Bien, "was to demonstrate that we could take a piece of rainforest and make it economically productive and safe from the chainsaw for the indefinite future. We hope to be a model for many other similar projects, but more importantly to change the way people think about endangered resources." Bien hopes to show the surrounding communities that a cottage industry can be borne by the forest, so

three-toed sloth

GERRY ELLIS/SOCIETY EXPEDITIONS

that they see the forest not "as something they must cut down in order to earn a living, but rather as the source of that living." You, too, can support the project by buying shares in Rara Avis SA Corporation ($1,800 for three shares; it hopes eventually to pay dividends).

The area has remained pristine because of its inaccessibility, and the rewards are tremendous. More than 360 bird species—including snowcap hummingbirds, great green macaws, toucans, blue-and-gold tanagers, and umbrella birds—inhabit the reserve. There are jaguars, tapirs, monkeys, anteaters, coatimundis, butterflies galore, and a zillion other wildlife species. Rara Avis gets up to a phenomenal 5.5 meters of rain a year; it has no dry months.

There's an **office,** tel. 764-3131, fax 764-4187, in Las Horquetas; open daily 6 a.m.-6 p.m. Rara Avis is not a place for a day visit. Plan on at least one overnight.

Activities: Until recently you could thrill to the experience of dangling six stories high in the air, marveling at the superabundance of species in the forest canopy from Dr. Donald Perry's "Automated Web for Canopy Exploration," a radio-controlled aerial tramway designed for treetop exploration. (See Perry's book, *Life Above the Jungle Floor;* Simon & Schuster, 1986.) Alas, the tram no longer operates but you *can* view the canopy from two platforms ($35, including two-hour guided hike), including one at the foot of a spectacular double waterfall. A trained instructor will teach you how to use rappelling gear.

The miles of **hiking** trails range from easy to difficult. Rubber boots are highly recommended: hiking the muddy trails is akin to wading through soup (the lodge has boots to lend for those with U.S. shoe sizes of 12 or smaller). Recently, many of the trails have been improved so as to prevent the erosion and root damage prevalent in earlier years. You can explore alone or on guided hikes.

Note: You can swim at the waterfalls, but be aware that flash floods can pour over the break unannounced. When this happened in the spring of 1992, three Canadians were swept to their deaths.

Getting There: Driving there used to be a harpy. (Even 4WDs couldn't make it uphill when the road was halfway bad. Then, guests were transported either on a cart pulled by a tractor, or on horseback. Sometimes even the tractor got bogged down or was unable to cross the two rivers that were often so high you had to cross on a swinging rope bridge. Then, sometimes, even the horses couldn't make it, and guests had to hike.) The journey still isn't comfortable. Some people I've spoken to consider the experience of getting there part of the fun, others have stated that no reward is worth hours of bumping about on the back of an open flatbed followed by an hour tramping knee-deep in mud in the pouring rain. The good news is that the road to El Plástico lodge was upgraded in 1997 and a smooth dirt road should have been completed by the time you read this.

Buses from San José depart Calle 12 and Avenida 9 daily at 7 a.m. via the Guápiles Highway (do *not* take the bus via Heredia). Buses also run later, but you'll need the 7 a.m. bus to meet the transfer to Rara Avis from Las Horquetas. Get off at **El Cruce para Horquetas,** where a taxi—arranged through Rara Avis's San José office—will take you to Las Horquetas. If driving, you can leave your car in a parking lot at the Rara Avis "office" in Las Horquetas.

The transfer to Rara Avis leaves Las Horquetas daily at 9 a.m. You should be in Las Horquetas by 8:30 a.m. It's a three-hour journey (less once the new road is complete). You can rent horses ($10) for later arrivals, but not after noon; you must walk the last three kilometers. The vehicle leaves Rara Avis for Las Horquetas at 2 p.m., arriving in time for the 6 p.m. bus to San José. Buses for San José also leave Las Horquetas throughout the day.

Accommodations

The **Hotel Buenos Aires** in Las Horquetas is very basic (about $5). There are simple *cabinas* at the gas station seven km north of Horquetas. In Río Frío, there's the basic **Pensión Ana.** Not reviewed.

Rara Avis, Apdo. 8105, San José 1000, tel. 253-0844, fax 257-4876, e-mail: raraavis@sol.racsa.co.cr, website www.cool.co.cr/raravis/rar-avis.html, has two lodges at about 600 meters elevation, plus you can stay in **Dr. Perry's Tree-Top Cabin** 30 meters up in the crown of a tree; or in the two-room **River Edge Cabin,** ideal for birders and honeymooners, and replete with hammocks on a balcony, solar lighting, and private bath with hot water. **El Plástico,** the more rustic of two lodges (ideal for budget travelers and backpackers), is named for an abandoned jungle prison colony where the prisoners slept under plastic tarps. The lodge was formerly the penal-colony headquarters. Restored and upgraded, it now features kerosene lamp lighting, flush toilets and showers, plus accommodations for 30 people in bunk beds in seven rooms. Rates (two nights): $90 pp; $30 a night students; $36 extra nights. Costa Rican citizens and International Youth Hostel members receive a 30% discount. A little more comfortable is the **Waterfall Lodge,** three km farther into the forest at the end of the dirt road. It features eight corner rooms, each with a private bathtub and hot water, and a wraparound balcony overlooking the rainforest and lowlands. Only 200 meters away is a spectacular 55-meter double waterfall—the site of the canopy tramway. Rates: $85 pp d, $75 t, $65 quad. Room rates include lodging, meals, naturalist guide, and transport from Las Horquetas. A two-night minimum stay is required. You can rent horses ($20). Reservations are essential.

CATHY CARLSON

GUANACASTE AND THE NORTHWEST

Travelers who emerge from the verdant central highlands or southern Pacific and enter the arid northwest might think they're in a new country. For the most part the region is a vast alluvial plain of rolling hills—the southern extent of the Mesoamerican plain—broadening to the north and dominated by giant cattle ranches interspersed with smaller pockets of cultivation. To the east rises a backbone of mountains—the Cordillera de Guanacaste and Cordillera de Tilarán, separated by Lake Arenal—and, farther north, symmetrical volcanic cones spiced with bubbling mud pits and steaming vents. Rivers cascade down the flanks and slow to a meandering pace, halted—it seems—by the ravaging heat.

The name Guanacaste derives from *quahnacaztlan*, an Indian word meaning "place near the ear trees," for the tall and broad *guanacaste* (free ear or ear pod) tree—the national tree—whose seedpods spiral gracefully to the earth.

The tree spreads its gnarled branches long and low to the ground, and all that walks, crawls, or flies gathers in its cool shade in the heat of midday. Then, too, people take shady siestas or sit around drinking beer; local activity revolves around the cooler hours of early morning and late afternoon.

Recent years have seen a great emphasis on promoting tourism to the region in support of the opening of the new international airport at Liberia.

The **Pan-American Highway** (Hwy. 1) cuts northwest through the heart of Guanacaste, following the foothill contours of the cordilleras, ruler-straight almost all the way to the Nicaraguan border. North of Liberia the route becomes superbly scenic. Almost every site of importance lies within a short reach of the highway. If traveling by bus, sit on the right northbound for the views of the volcanoes.

A PALETTE IN BLOOM

In the midst of dry-season drought, Guanacaste explodes in Monet colors. Not wildflowers, but a Technicolor blossoming of trees as fervent flowers burst open on bare branches. In November, the saffron-bright flowering of the *guachipelín* sets in motion a chain reaction that lasts for six months. Individual trees of a particular genus are somehow keyed to explode in unison, often in a climax lasting as little as a day. Two or three bouquets of a single species may occur in a season. The colors are never static. In January, it's the turn of pink *poui* (savannah oak) and yellow *poui* (black bark tree). By February, canary-bright *Corteza amarillo* and the trumpet-shaped yellow blossoms of *Tabebuia chrysanta* dot the landscape. In March, it's the turn of delicate pink *curao*. As *curao* wanes, *Tabebuia rosea* bursts forth in subtle pinks, whites, and lilacs. The *malinche*—royal poinciana or flame tree—closes out the six-month parade of blossoming trees with a dramatic display as red as bright lipstick.

CLIMATE

It's no coincidence that the majority of Costa Rica's resort hotels are nestled along the shores of the Pacific northwest, where sun is the name of the game. Guanacaste's climate is in total contrast to the rest of the country. For half the year (Nov.-April) the plains and rolling hills receive no rain, it's hotter than Hades, and the sun beats down as hard and sharp as a driven nail. Fortunately, cool winds bearing down from northern latitudes can lower temperatures pleasantly along the coast Dec.-February. The dry season usually lingers slightly longer than elsewhere in Costa Rica. The province averages less than 162 cm (65 inches) of rain a year. Certain rain shadows receive much less: the Tempisque Basin is the country's driest region and receives less than 45 cm (18 inches) of rain in years of drought, mostly in a few torrential downpours during the six-month rainy season. In the wet season, everything turns green and the air is freshly scented.

HISTORY

The Guanacaste-Nicoya region was the center of a vibrant pre-Columbian culture—the Chorotegas. Descended from the Olmecs of Mexico, they arrived in Costa Rica around the 8th century and soon established themselves as the most advanced group in what would be Costa Rica. They alone, for example, developed art and writing schools. Their culture was centered on *milpas,* or cornfields. Many of the stone metates (small stool-like tables for grinding corn) on display in the National Museum in San José are from the region; elaborately carved with turtles, crocodiles, monkeys, and jaguars, they speak of the culture's strength. Some of the most beautiful pieces were delicately shaped into anthropomorphic axe-gods and two-headed crocodiles—totems derived from the Olmec culture.

The Chorotegas were particularly skilled at carving jade, and traded with the Mayan and Olmec empires to the north. They achieved their zenith in working jade between the last century B.C. and the 5th century A.D. Blue jade was considered the most precious of objects. Archaeologists, however, aren't sure where blue jade came from. Interestingly, there are no known jade deposits in Costa Rica, and the nearest known source of green jade, supposedly, was more than 800 km north, at Guatemasal, in Guatemala.

Archaeologists continue to unearth ancient gravesites. Although the culture went into rapid decline with the arrival of the Spanish, the Chorotega weren't entirely decimated as were indigenous cultures elsewhere in the region and today one can still see deeply bronzed wide-set faces and pockets of Chorotega life.

Between 1570 and 1821 Costa Rica was part of the Captaincy General of Guatemala, a federation of Spanish provinces in Central America. In 1787, Guanacaste—then an independent province—was annexed to Nicaragua; in 1812 Spain awarded the region to Costa Rica. In 1821, when the Captaincy General was dissolved and autonomy granted to the Central American nations, Guanacaste had to choose between Nicaragua and Costa Rica. Rancor between Liberians—cattle ranchers with strong Nicaraguan ties—and

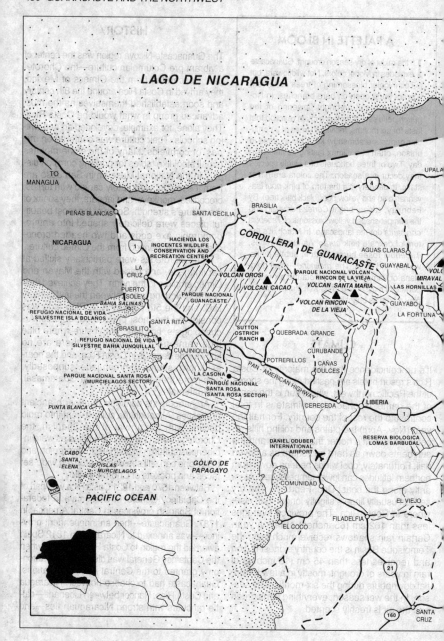

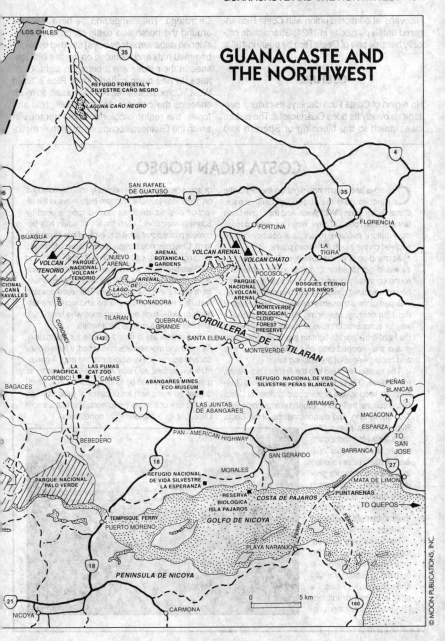

GUANACASTE AND THE NORTHWEST

LOS CHILES

35

4

REFUGIO FORESTAL Y
SILVESTRE CAÑO NEGRO

LAGUNA CAÑO NEGRO

SAN RAFAEL
DE GUATUSO

4

35

FLORENCIA

BIJAGUA

FORTUNA

LA
TIGRA

NUEVO
ARENAL

ARENAL
BOTANICAL
GARDENS

VOLCAN ARENAL

VOLCAN
TENORIO

PARQUE
NACIONAL
VOLCAN
TENORIO

VOLCAN CHATO
Y
POCOSOL

BOSQUES ETERNO
DE LOS NIÑOS

ARQUE
CIONAL
CAN
AVALLES

RIO COROBICI

LAGO
DE
ARENAL

TRONADORA

PARQUE
NACIONAL
VOLCAN ARENAL

MONTEVERDE
BIOLOGICAL
CLOUD
FOREST
PRESERVE

TILARAN

QUEBRADA
GRANDE

142

SANTA ELENA

CORDILLERA DE TILARAN

MONTEVERDE

BAGACES

LA
PACIFICA
COROBICI

LAS PUMAS
CAT ZOO

CAÑAS

ABANGARES MINES
ECO-MUSEUM

REFUGIO NACIONAL DE VIDA
SILVESTRE PEÑAS BLANCAS

MIRAMAR

PEÑAS
BLANCAS

1

MACACONA

ESPARZA

TO
SAN
JOSE

LAS JUNTAS
DE ABANGARES

1

PAN - AMERICAN HIGHWAY

BEBEDERO

18

SAN GERARDO

BARRANCA

27

PARQUE NACIONAL
PALO VERDE

REFUGIO NACIONAL
DE VIDA SILVESTRE
LA ESPERANZA

MORALES

RESERVA
BIOLOGICA
ISLA PAJAROS

COSTA DE PAJAROS

MATA DE LIMON

PUNTARENAS

TO QUEPOS

TEMPISQUE FERRY
PUERTO MORENO

GOLFO DE NICOYA

FERRY

FERRY

18

PENINSULA DE NICOYA

PLAYA NARANJO

21

NICOYA

CARMONA

0   5 km

160

© MOON PUBLICATIONS, INC.

Nicoyans who favored union with Costa Rica lingered until a plebiscite in 1824. Guanacaste officially became part of Costa Rica by treaty in 1858.

CULTURE

No region of Costa Rica displays its cultural heritage as overtly as does Guanacaste. The culture owes much to the blending of Spanish and Chorotega. The *campesino* life here revolves around the horse and cattle ranch, and dark-skinned *sabaneros* (cowboys) shaded by wide-brimmed hats and mounted on horses with lassoes at their sides are a common sight. Guanacaste has been called Costa Rica's "Wild West." Come fiesta time, nothing rouses so much cheer as the *corridas de toros* (bullfights) and *topes,* the region's colorful horse parades in which the Guanacastecans show off their metic-

COSTA RICAN RODEO

Cowboys are a common sight on the big cattle ranches (and the streets) of Guanacaste, Costa Rica's grassy Wild West. And they have been since Spanish colonial days, when a *sabanero* (cowboy) culture evolved, much as a cowboy culture evolved on the North American plains.

At round-up time, the cowboys of various ranches would get together to gather in the cattle. The round-up usually closed with a wild party and cowboy competitions. Breaking wild broncos, of course, was part of the *sabanero*'s daily work. By the turn of the 19th century, bull-riding had developed as a way for *sabaneros* to prove who was the toughest of the hard-drinking, fist-fighting breed. Fortified with *guaro,* they hopped onto wild bulls to pit their wits and courage against the bucking fury.

The tradition evolved into the *festejos populares,* folk festivals. These festivals, held throughout Guanacaste, keep alive a deep-rooted tradition of Costa Rican culture: bull-riding, bronco riding, homestyle Tico bullfighting, and demonstrations of the Costa Rican saddle horse. Today's festivals—more commonly called *fiestas cívicas*—usually raise revenue to finance community projects. People travel from miles around to attend the *recorridos de toros* (bull rodeos) that are the staples of *fiestas cívicas*.

The bulls are enraged before being released into the ring, where *vaqueteros* are on hand to distract the wild and dangerous animals if a rider is thrown or injured. (Their title comes from *va-* *queta,* a piece of leather originally used by cowboys on haciendas to make stubborn bulls move in the direction desired, much as the red cape is used by Spanish matadors.) Over time, bull-riding has become a professional sport and evolved into its modern form. Cowboys ride bareback and hang onto angry, jumping, twisting, 680-kg bulls with only one hand (or "freestyle"—i.e., with *no* hands), while the *vaqueta* has given way to red cloth (called a *capote* or *muleta*) or even the occasional clown. The *recorridos* also feature "best bull" competitions and incredible displays of skill—such as *sabanareos* who lasso bulls with their backs turned to the animals.

The events are a grand excuse for inebriation. As more and more beer is consumed, it fuels bravado, and scores of Ticos pour into the ring. A general melée ensues as Ticos with insecure egos try to prove their manhood by running past the bull, which is kept enraged with an occasional prod from an electric fork or a sharp instrument. The bull is never killed, but it's a pathetic sight nonetheless.

JOHN ANDERSON

ulously groomed horses and the horses' fancy footwork. Guanacastecans love a fiesta: the biggest occurs each 25 July, when Guanacaste celebrates its independence from Nicaragua.

Costa Rica's national costume, music, and even the national tree—the *guanacaste*—all emanate from this region, as does the *punto guanacasteco,* the country's official dance. Even the regional foods of Guanacaste have made their way into the national fare. Local specialties include *frito guanacasteco* (a local version of *gallo pinto*), *sopa de albondigas* (spicy meatball soup, with chopped eggs), and *pedre* (carob beans, pork, chicken, onions, sweet peppers, salt, and mint), plus foods based on corn, such as tortillas, *rosquillas,* corn rice, and the famous *yoltmatal.* And the regional heritage can still be traced in the creation of clay pottery and figurines.

SIGHTS

The country's first national park, Santa Rosa, was established here, the first of more than a dozen national parks, wildlife refuges, and biological reserves in the region. Santa Rosa National Park and Monteverde Biological Cloud Forest Preserve—one a parched dry forest environment on a coastal plateau, the other a cool misty cloud forest that straddles the Continental Divide—are the most visited, although other protected areas are coming on strong. The array of ecosystems and wildlife in the region is quite astounding and ranges from volcanic heights to pristine shores, encompassing just about every imaginable ecosystem within Costa Rica. The newly created Arenal National Park is one of several recent additions.

The coast is indented with bays, peninsulas, and warm sandy beaches that are some of the least visited, least accessible, and yet most beautiful in the country. No surprise, then, that sea turtles use many as their nurseries. The resort beaches lie south of Santa Rosa and, being more accurately considered part of the Nicoya Peninsula, are described in that chapter.

Most tour operators in San José operate tours to Guanacaste, but several companies specialize in tours of the region: **CATA Tours,** tel./fax 669-1203; **Frontera Tours,** Apdo. 1177, Tibas 1100, tel. 670-0472, fax 670-0403; **Guanacaste Eco Adventure Travel,** Apdo. 238-5000 Liberia, tel. 380-4036, fax 670-0012, e-mail: billbeard's@ netrunner.net; and **TAM,** Apdo. 1864, San José 1000, tel. 256-0203, fax 221-6465, in Guanacaste, tel. 667-0098, fax 667-0133.

THE SOUTHERN PLAINS

ESPARZA

The Pan-Am Highway (Hwy. 1) descends from the central highlands to the Pacific plains via Esparza, at the foot of the mountains about 15 km east of Puntarenas. The town has an impressive **colonial church** (on the plaza) of weathered pink stone, and is a good place to stop for a soda, fruits, and/or *gallo pinto.* Buses operate hourly between Esparza and Puntarenas.

Accommodations and Food
The **Motel Calypso** and **Cabinas El Mirador Alisa,** both on the mountainside near Angostura, about five km east of Esparza, are the only accommodations between the central highlands and Esparza. In Esparza, try the motel-style **Las Castañuelas,** tel. 635-5105, on the left at the turnoff into town: it has basic a/c rooms for about $10 s, $12 d. Other budget options include the **Hotel Cordoba,** tel. 635-5014, and **Pensión Fanny,** tel. 635-5158.

Services
There's a **Red Cross** post, tel. 635-5172, a **Banco Nacional,** plus a **taxi** service, Taxis de Esparza, tel. 635-5810.

PUNTARENAS

What to make of this sultry, slightly sleazy port town, 120 km west of San José? Five km long but only five blocks wide at its widest, the town is built on a long narrow spit—Puntarenas means "Sandy Point"—running west from the suburb of

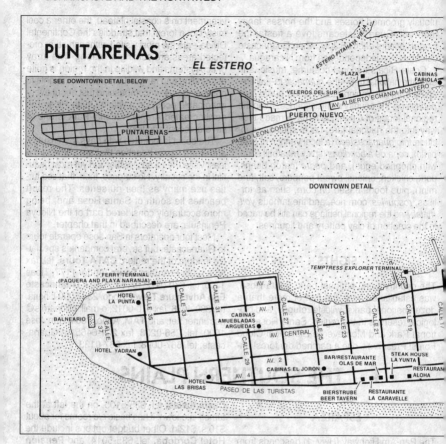

PUNTARENAS

EL ESTERO

SEE DOWNTOWN DETAIL BELOW

PLAZA
CABINAS FABIOLA
VELEROS DEL SUR
AV. ALBERTO ECHANDI MONTERO
PUERTO NUEVO
PASEO LEON CORTES
PUNTARENAS
ESTERO PITAHAYA VIEJA

DOWNTOWN DETAIL

FERRY TERMINAL
(PAQUERA AND PLAYA NARANJA)

TEMPTRESS EXPLORER TERMINAL

HOTEL LA PUNTA

BALNEARIO

HOTEL YADRAN

HOTEL LAS BRISAS

CALLE 37
CALLE 35
CALLE 33
CALLE 31
CALLE 29
CALLE 27
CALLE 25
CALLE 23
CALLE 21
CALLE 19
CALLE 17

AV. 3
AV. 1
AV. CENTRAL
AV. 2
AV. 4

CABINAS AMUEBLADAS ARGUEDAS

BAR/RESTAURANTE OLAS DE MAR
CABINAS EL JORON

STEAK HOUSE LA YUNTA
RESTAURAN ALOHA

PASEO DE LAS TURISTAS
BIERSTRUBE BEER TAVERN
RESTAURANTE LA CARAVELLE

Cocal and backed to the north by a mangrove estuary; to the south are the Gulf of Nicoya and a beach cluttered with driftwood. In past years there were health warnings against bathing in the estuary; the gulf waters were once considered unsafe. Fortunately, both have been cleaned up.

Puntarenas, the preeminent town on the Pacific coast, and the closest one to San José, has long been favored by Josefinos seeking R and R. Why is a mystery. The town is hot, modestly decayed, and boasts more than its fair share of bar-girls, drunks, and petty crime. The old wharves on the estuary side feature decrepit fishing boats leaning against ramshackle piers popular with pelicans. Ernest Hemingway, you

sense, would have loved the local color—the old women rocking under shade eaves, the men lolling about in shorts and flip-flops, the prostitutes beckoning from balconies at the occasional drunk staggering home.

You'd never guess from all this at the town's prior glory. The peninsula was colonized by the Spaniards as early as 1522. The early port grew to prominence and was declared a free port in 1847, a year after completion of an oxcart road from the Meseta Central. Oxcarts laden with coffee made the lumbering descent to Puntarenas in convoys; the beans were shipped from here via Cape Horn to Europe, launching Puntarenas to relative prosperity. At its height Puntarenas had

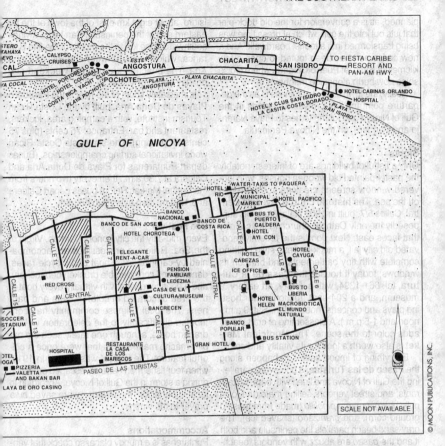

GULF OF NICOYA

SCALE NOT AVAILABLE

© MOON PUBLICATIONS, INC.

streetcars like those of San Francisco. It remained the country's main port until the Atlantic Railroad to Limón, on the Caribbean coast, was completed in 1890; the railroad between San José and Puntarenas would not be completed for another 20 years. Earlier this century, Puntarenas also developed a large conch-pearl fleet. Pearlers would spend months at sea earning money to spend on women and booze. Some 80% of Porteños, as the inhabitants of Puntarenas are called, still make their livings from the sea, often going out for days at a time to haul in corvina, wahoo, dorado, shrimp, lobster, and tuna.

Secure as the country's principal port, Puntarenas even enjoyed favor as a *balneario*—a place

for Josefinos to sun and bathe on weekends. It was "New Jersey to San José's New York or Brighton to its London," says writer Michael Tunison. Alas, when international tourists began to arrive in numbers in the 1970s, and resorts sprang up elsewhere to lure them, Puntarenas was left behind in the tourism sweepstakes.

In 1993 the city fathers initiated efforts to boost Puntarenas' fortunes by giving it a facelift. The kilometers-long beach has been transformed from a dump to a pleasant stretch of sand with the aid of a mechanized cleaner that makes regular forays. The Rotary Club has planted trees and installed a fountain near the newly opened Casa de Cultura. An aquarium and artisans' market are planned, as is a conversion for the old dock-pier that juts out into the gulf, which at press time was being transformed into a tourist boardwalk. And a new cruise port has been touted to open a few kilometers south, at **Puerto Caldera,** where cruise ships now berth alongside freighters.

Really, the town's only usefulness is as the departure point for day cruises to islands in the Gulf of Nicoya and for the ferries to Playa Naranjo and Paquera, on the Nicoya Peninsula.

Sights
Only a fistful of buildings are of interest, notably the pastel-painted old wooden houses, with louvered window screens creaking in the breeze off the sea. The **historic church,** Avenida Central, Calles 5/7, built in 1902 of flagstones is supposedly the only Catholic church in the country that faces east. Next door is the recently renovated old city jail, a mock-fortress-style building complete with tiny battlements and bars on its windows; today it houses the **Casa de la Cultura,** tel. 661-1394, with a library, art gallery, a museum, and a 204-seat auditorium for hosting plays and concerts (hours: Mon.-Sat. 9 a.m.-noon and 1-5 p.m.). A blossoming of craft stores adds color to the scene. The **Municipal Market** is also worth a look for its vitality and color.

Everything of import seems to happen along the **Paseo de las Turistas,** a boulevard paralleling the Gulf of Nicoya and lined with bars, restaurants, and street vendors selling *mató* (the local milkshake), creamy *pinolillo* (made from toasted ground corn), and *granizado* (shaved ice). The gray-sand beach parallels the peninsula and both it and the *paseo* are abuzz with vendors, beachcombers, and Costa Rican vacationers flirting and trying to keep cool in the waters. On the north side of the peninsula, the sheltered gulf shore—the "estuary"—is lined with fishing vessels in various states of decrepitude. Roseate spoonbills, storks, and other birds pick among the shallows. You can watch the locals, too, knee-deep in mud, hunting for *chuchecas*—clams—amid the mangroves. And the estuary is busy with boats zipping up and down, including the sleek motor yachts toing and froing on day-trips for Tortuga Island.

Playa San Isidro and Playa Doña Ana
The gulf-side beach of Puntarenas widens and improves to the east, notably so at Playa San Isidro, about eight km east of the town at the far eastern end of the peninsula. San Isidro swings southward three km to the mouth of the Río Barranca, which slices between the Playas Doña Ana. The beaches are popular weekend and holiday spots for Ticos.

Immediately south of the river is the **Paradero Playas de Doña Ana,** built by the Costa Rican Tourism Institute, with a camping area, lockers, restaurant and bar. Entrance: 75 cents (plus 75 cents for parking). The site hosts Costa Rican world invitational surfing championships. (Buses depart Puntarenas for Playa de Doña Ana and Caldera at 7:30 a.m., then every two hours from the Central Market. Return buses depart Caldera at 8:15 a.m. then every two hours.)

Sea Festival
Every mid-July the city honors Carmen, Virgin of the Sea. Religious processions are accompanied by carnival rides, boat and bicycle races, dancing and considerable drunken debauchery, and a boating regatta with virtually every boat in the area decorated in colorful flags and banners. The local Chinese community has contributed significantly to the celebration with its dragon boats, although one rarely sees the papier-mâché marine birds that were once a colorful feature. The festival was started in 1913, when four fishermen narrowly escaped drowning during a storm in the Gulf of Nicoya. According to local superstition, the seamen were saved by a prayer to the virgin.

Accommodations
Puntarenas is a muggy place, so check that ventilation is efficient (this is one place in Costa Rica where you'll be glad for a/c). If possible, take a hotel on the gulf side to catch the breezes. Hotels have lower rates off-season (May-November). Many of the low-end hotels downtown double as love motels. The worst are volatile refuges of drunks and cheap hookers. Caveat emptor. Things improve west of downtown.

Puntarenas: Casa Yemaya, Apdo. 258-5400 Puntarenas, tel./fax 661-0856, offers clean, safe lodging for women. Rates: $11-35. It's open Dec.-June only.

Hotel Ayi Con, Apdo. 358, Puntarenas, tel. 661-0164, has 44 clean though basic and dingy rooms. Twenty have private baths with cold water, well-situated for the market and docks. It's one of the better budget bargains in town. Rates: $6 s, $10 d shared bath; $9 s, $14 d with private bath. **Hotel El Prado** has 42 very shabby rooms with fans, and shared bath with cold water; last time I passed by, prostitutes beckoned from the upstairs windows. Rates: $5.

Hotel Helen, tel. 661-2159, has 16 basic but clean rooms with fans and private baths with cold water. Rates: $4.50. **Hotel Río,** tel. 661-0331, on the waterfront, has 91 rooms with fans and cold water. Rates: $4 small, $6 large with shared bath; $7 small, $11 large with private bath.

Other low-end budget hotels include **Hotel Zagala, Hotel Cabezas,** tel. 661-1045, recommended by another author as "one of the best choices in this price range," and **Pensión Montemar,** tel. 661-2771. **Hotel de Verano,** tel. 616-0159, is very basic and unclean; rooms can be rented by the hour. Rates: $12 d. The **Ledezma,** tel. 661-1468, next door, is a better bet in the same price range.

Very basic options include **Hotel Condor** with shared bath; **Hospedaje Castillo,** tel. 661-0771; **Pensión Juanita,** tel. 661-0096, on Avenida Central and Calles Central/1; and **Pensión Gutierrez,** on Calle 4. **Hotel Imperial,** Apdo. 65, Puntarenas, tel. 661-0579, is grim. The funky Caribbean architecture with high ceilings and wide halls belies its seedier side: sailors and hookers rent rooms by the hour. Likewise, the **Hotel Pacific Palms** is to be avoided.

Moving up the ladder, **Cabinas Fabiola,** tel. 661-0046, facing the sea in Cocal, has four two-bedroom units with kitchen, TV, and refrigerator. Rates: $25 low season; $29 high season. A small patio opens to the beach.

In town, **Hotel y Restaurant Cayuga,** Apdo. 306, Puntarenas, tel. 661-0344, fax 661-1280, is pleasant, clean, and well kept; a bargain popular with gringos. The 31 rooms have a/c and private baths with cold water. There's a restaurant and secure parking. Rates: $14 s, $20 d, $25 t; $35 d, $43 t with TV and telephone.

The rambling, ramshackle **Gran Hotel,** tel. 661-0998, next to the bus terminal on Paseo de las Turistas and Calle Central, has 36 basic rooms (13 with private bath) with hot water. Take an upstairs room with balcony and light (downstairs rooms are dingy). Rates: $8 pp, shared

bath; $11 s, 24 d, $27 t, private bath. Nearby, in the same price range and standard, is **Cabinas Central,** tel. 661-1484, at Calle 7 and Paseo de las Turistas.

Cabinas Amuebladas Arguedas, tel. 661-2146 or 661-3508, at Avenida Central, Calles 27/29, has secure parking, plus 12 clean, simple rooms with two fans, and private baths with cold water. Rates: $20-25. **Cabinas El Jorón,** tel. 661-0467, on Calle 25 and Avenidas 2/4, has rather gloomy rooms with a/c, hot water, and kitchenettes. It has a restaurant. Rate: $20 d. **Hotel Chorotega,** tel. 661-0998, on Calle 1 and Avenida 3, once popular with the backpacking crowd, has rooms with shared or private bath. Rates: $16 d shared bath; $25 d private bath.

The American-run **Hotel La Punta,** Apdo. 228, Puntarenas, tel. 661-0696, at Avenida 1, Calles 35/37, is a good place to rest your head if you want to catch the early-morning ferry to Nicoya. The 10 pleasant if spartan rooms have fans and spacious private baths with hot water. The hotel has a small pool and a breezy restaurant, plus indoor parking. Upper rooms have balconies. Rates: $21 s, $29 d, including tax; $7 each additional person.

The venerable **Hotel Tioga,** Apdo. 96, Puntarenas 5400, tel. 661-0271, fax 661-0127, has 46 rooms surrounding a pleasing but very compact courtyard with tiny swimming pool graced by its own tiny palm-shaded island. Rooms vary in size and quality; some have hot water. There's a small casino. Rates include breakfast in the fourth-floor restaurant, with views over the gulf. Rates: $35 s, $43 d with cold water; $43 s, $57 d with a/c and hot water; $57 s, $67 d with balcony.

Hotel Las Brisas, Apdo. 83, Puntarenas 5400, tel. 661-4040, is a modern hotel near the end of Paseo de las Turistas. The 19 spacious, a/c rooms are clean but spartan and soulless. Some face the Gulf of Nicoya. Cold water bath only. The hotel has an open-air bar and restaurant, plus a small pool. Rates: $42 s, $50 d low season; $50 s, $60 d high season. Also on Paseo de las Turistas, at Calles 3/5, is **Hotel Oasis del Pacífico,** tel. 661-0209, fax 661-0745, a Tico favorite with 18 funky-looking cabins and an open-air restaurant and disco under thatch, plus a pool. Rates: $25 s, $35 d.

The **Yacht Club,** tel. 661-0784, fax 661-2518, at Cocal, offers accommodations for yachters and others in 27 rooms with a/c, private baths, and hot water. There's an open-air restaurant-cum-bar, plus a pool spanned by a bridge. Often full. You may find a vacancy on a space-available basis, especially on weekdays. Rates: $23 s, $31 d standard; $29 s, $41 d economy; $41 s, $59 d superior (with a/c, TV, and mini-fridge); $31 s, $39 d villas.

Hotel Portobello, Apdo. 108, Puntarenas, tel. 661-1322, fax 661-0036, a stone's throw west, has 35 nicely decorated high-ceilinged rooms with a/c and private baths with hot water. Private patios and balconies open onto lush grounds with a nice pool beneath shade trees. A pleasing restaurant serves grilled meats and seafoods. The Italian owners hauled in tons of sand to create an artificial beach. Rates: $40 s, $50 d, $60 t.

The jaded **Hotel Colonial,** Apdo. 368, Puntarenas, tel. 661-1833, fax 661-2969, next to the Yacht Club at Cocal, has 56 modestly decorated rooms with a/c, balconies, and hot water. There's live mariachi music on weekends in El Bambú restaurant, plus a delapidated tennis court, a pleasing pool, mini-golf, and a dock for yachts. Lots of shade trees. It hints at Spanish colonial. Rate: $58 s, $72 d, including breakfast and tax. *Overpriced!*

Hotel Yadran, Apdo. 14, Puntarenas 5400, tel. 661-2662, fax 661-1944, at the breezy tip of the peninsula, provides views across the bay to Nicoya. The 42 rooms have private baths, hot water, a/c, cable TVs, and balconies or verandas. The hotel has two small pools, a discotheque, and an upstairs restaurant with bay vistas. One reader thought it "seedy," but I disagree. Nonetheless, it *is* overpriced. Rates: $60 s, $67 d estuary view; $73 s, $90 d sea view.

Playas San Isidro and Doña Ana: At Playa San Isidro, **Hotel Cabinas Orlando,** tel. 663-0064, has roomy but rather run-down cabins under shade trees. **La Casita Costa Dorado** is another option.

At Doña Ana, **Cabinas Oasis** and **Hotel Río Mar,** tel. 663-0158, are uninspired budget hosteleries.

Hotel y Club San Isidro, Apdo. 4674, San José 1000, tel. 663-0031 or 233-2244, has 50 two-bedroom *cabinas* (for eight people each) with rather grubby kitchens and small bathrooms.

They're laid out barracks-style in shady land-scaped grounds. Take a newer unit. Scattered around the complex are five pools, a children's playground, a volleyball court, and soccer and basketball courts. The place is part of the International Youth Hostel Association. Rates: $41 s, $54 quad, $75 six, $95 up to nine people. The **Villas del Mar/Las Chalets,** Apdo. 1287, San José 1000, tel. 663-0150, across the street, is virtually identical.

Casa Canadiense, Apdo. 125, Puntarenas, tel./fax 663-0287, 400 meters west of Fiesta, offers self-contained "deluxe" units, plus a pool. Nearby are the **Oceano Bed and Breakfast** and **Villa del Roble.**

Fiesta Caribbean Village, Apdo. 171, Puntarenas 5400, tel. 663-0808 or 239-4266, fax 663-1516 or 239-0217; in the U.S., tel. (800) 662-2990; in Canada, tel. (800) 264-1952, was recently taken over by Allegro Resorts. This attractive all-inclusive resort has 174 spacious and modestly furnished a/c rooms with TVs, plus five master suites, 120 junior suites, and the opulent presidential suite. Facilities include two restaurants, a seafood bar—the El Mastil (shaped like an old square-rigged schooner)—an a/c gym, an immense and beautiful free-form swimming pool with island bar, plus two other sizeable pools (one with jacuzzi jets). The expansive grounds contain volleyball and tennis courts. Lady Luck beckons in the casino (gamblers get free drinks), after which you can hit the disco; and nightly skits are offered in the theater. Sea kayaking, windsurfing, scuba diving, and jet-skiing are offered, as are tours. The resort is popular with unsophisticated, mass-market package-tour groups, Tico families (there are children's activities throughout the day), and young Ticos who know a good thing when they see it. It's a good choice for the gregarious who like things organized. Rates (s/d): $99 standard, $109 deluxe, $109-119 suites, $155 junior suite (six people), $350 presidential suite (six people). A "Green Season Deluxe Special" (from $369 pp) includes three nights' accommodation at Cariari or Corobicí hotels in San José, three nights at the Fiesta, plus transfers, breakfasts, and taxes.

Food

The best options are along Paseo de las Turistas, including the best restaurant in town: **La**

Caravelle, Calles 19/21, a very pleasant wood-paneled restaurant with outside terrace, serving French cuisine. Closed Monday and Tuesday. Next door is the **Bierstrube Beer Tavern,** tel. 661-0330, where a huge beam-ceilinged room tries to replicate the beer halls of Munich.

Also nearby on Paseo are the open-air **Restaurant Aloha,** tel. 661-0773; the charming **La Casa de los Mariscos,** serving good seafood; the lively, atmospheric **Bar/Restaurante Olas de Mar;** the rustically elegant **Steak House La Yunta** in a historic two-story seafront house; and **Pizzeria Valetta** at Calle 15. The **Restaurant Cayuga** is also a pizzeria.

There's no shortage of Chinese restaurants, concentrated at the junction of Calle Central and Avenida Central, with one on each corner. Cheap *sodas* abound near the Central Market and along the Paseo de las Turistas, between Calles Central and 3. **Bar Mar-Marina Restaurant,** tel. 661-3064, on the second floor, 50 meters east of the ferry terminal and handy for a meal if you're catching the ferry, serves Spanish paella and Costa Rican seafood specialties; it's open 6 a.m.-8 p.m. **Restaurante Italiano La Terraza,** in a pretty wooden building painted yellow, has been recommended.

You can buy health foods at **Macrobiótica El Mundo Natural** at Avenida Central, Calles 2/4.

Entertainment

In summer, concerts and plays are put on at the Casa de la Cultura. There are **discos** at Hotel Yadran and at the Oasis del Pacífico on Paseo de las Turistas. There's also a Saturday night disco party at Hotel Colonia. The small, unsophisticated **Playa de Oro Casino,** on Paseo at Calle 15, is hardly likely to deliver gold. Next door, the **Bakan Bar,** above Pizzeria Valetta, is a modestly elegant option for cocktails. Otherwise, the local bars provide plenty of color (guard against pickpockets).

The **Cine Central** reportedly shows movies in English; and **Cinema del Pacífico,** at Avenida 1, Calles 4/6, shows movies in Spanish.

By day you can swim at **Balneario Municipal,** the public swimming pool set amid lawns on Paseo de las Turistas at the end of the peninsula. Hours: Tues.-Sun. 9 a.m.-4:30 p.m. ($1 adults, 50 cents children).

Tours and Activities

Several cruise companies offer popular day-trips across the Gulf of Nicoya to Isla Tortuga and other, lesser-visited islands. Leading the cruising pack is **Calypso Cruises,** tel. 661-0585, at Calle 66 in Cocal. They originated day cruises aboard their motor yacht *Calypso.* Today the company operates Tortuga Island trips aboard the 21-meter *Manta Ray,* a space-age catamaran that goes like the wind ($84 day-tour). The venerable *Calypso* now operates cruises farther afield.

Veleros del Sur, tel. 661-1320, fax 661-1119, between Cocal and downtown, offers sailboat charters, sportfishing, and birdwatching trips.

Pacific Ocean Winds, c/o Fiesta Caribbean Village, tel. 663-0808, ext. 472, operates a high-tech catamaran, the *Lohe Lahi,* from the pier of the Hotel Fiesta. The 18-meter cat zips through two-hour cruises Wed.-Sat. at 11 a.m., 1:30 p.m., and 4 p.m.

Fred's Folly, tel. 288-2014, offers sportfishing trips; $275 per day for two people. **Sportfishing Costa Rica,** tel. 255-0791 or 661-0697, also offers fishing tours.

Information

La Cámara Puntarenense de Turismo, tel. 661-1985, which offers local tourist information, is in the Casa de la Cultura on Avenida Central and Calle 3. You can call AT&T USADirect here.

Services

Banco Nacional, tel. 661-0233, Avenida Central, Calle Central; **Banco de Costa Rica,** tel. 661-0444, Calle Central, Avenida 3; and **BanCrecen,** Avenida 2, Calles 3/5, all have branches. BanCrecen has a 24-hour auto-credit machine (Visa), as does Banco de San Jose (Visa and MasterCard) at Avenida 3, Calle 3.

The **Monseñor Sanabria Hospital,** tel. 663-0033, is eight km east of town, at the west end of San Isidro. There's a branch hospital at Paseo de las Turistas and Calle 9. You'll find plenty of pharmacies in town.

The **post office** is 50 meters south and 50 meters west of the Casa de la Cultura.

Getting There and Away

By Bus: Bus schedules change frequently; the following applied at press time. Empresarios

Unidos (in San José tel. 222-0064, in Puntarenas tel. 661-2158), buses depart San José from Calle 16, Avenidas 10/12 daily every hour 6 a.m.-7 p.m. ($3). Direct buses depart Puntarenas from Calle 2 and Paseo de las Turistas for San José at 5:30 a.m. and 7 p.m.; indirect buses depart at 4:15 a.m., 6:15 a.m., 8:10 a.m., 10:45 a.m., 1 p.m., 2:50 p.m., 5 p.m., and 8 p.m. Buses depart for Cañas and Tilarán at 11:30 a.m. and 4:15 p.m.; Monteverde at 2 p.m.; Jacó and Quepos at 5 a.m., 11 a.m., and 2:30 p.m.; and Liberia at 5 a.m., 7 a.m., 9:30 a.m., 11 a.m., 12:30 p.m., and 3 p.m.

By Air: You can charter an air-taxi to Chacarita Airport, east of town. There are no scheduled services.

By Ferry: The ferry to/from Playa Naranjo, tel. 661-1069, on the east coast of the Nicoya Peninsula, holds 50 vehicles and 500 passengers. It departs Puntarenas from Avenida 3, Calles 33/35, daily at 3:15 a.m., 7 a.m., 10:50 a.m., 2:50 p.m., and 7 p.m. (90 minutes). Fares: $1.50 passengers; $3 motorbikes; $10 car and driver. Get there early—two hours ahead is not unwise on weekends and holidays. Ferry times change, so check schedules in advance. Buses marked "Ferry" operate along Avenida Central to the Playa Naranjo ferry terminal ($2).

The **La Paquereña ferry,** tel. 661-3034 or 661-2830, to Paquera, at the southeastern tip of the Nicoya Peninsula, departs Puntarenas from Avenida 3, Calles 33/35, daily at 4:15 a.m., 8:45 a.m., 12:30 p.m., 4 p.m., and 7 p.m. ($1.50

pedestrians; $9 car and passengers). A **lancha** (water-taxi) operates to Paquera from the Muelle Banana dock, Avenida 3 and Calle 9, at 6:15 a.m., 11 a.m., and 3:15 p.m.

The **Costa Rica Yacht Club and Marina,** Apdo. 151-5400 Puntarenas, tel. 661-0784, fax 661-2518, offers a safe anchorage ($6 per foot, including use of swimming pool, bathrooms, and showers) and has a lift and dry dock, electricity, compressor, gas and diesel, fax and telephone, and rooms.

Getting Around
Buses ply up and down Avenidas Central and 2. Coopepuntarenas, tel. 663-0053 or 663-1635, offers **taxi** service. **Discovery Rent-a-Car,** tel. 661-0328, and **Elegante Rent-a-Car,** tel. 661-1958, opposite Banco Nacional, have offices.

MATA DE LIMÓN

Mata, facing onto the Bahía de Caldera, about 15 km southeast of Puntarenas, was one of the country's original beach resorts despite being built on the east side of an estuary—the **Boca del Caldera**—surrounded by mangroves. It is still favored by budget-minded Ticos, who flock on weekends. The beach is a reasonable surf spot, with good tubular waves at the jetty. Not my first choice for a beach vacation, but the mangrove swamps harbor scarlet macaws, caimans, and crocodiles. You can charter a boat in the

traditional carreta (oxcart), Guanacaste

WILDLAND ADVENTURES, INC.

village to go birding and looking for crocs. A wooden bridge leads across the estuary to another part of the village.

Accommodations and Food

The oceanside **Bar y Restaurante Caldera,** sitting over the mouth of Boca del Caldera, is a modern eatery with *cabinas,* plus live music and dancing. Rates: $10. In Mata, **Cabinas Puerto Nuevo,** tel. 634-4083, has four pleasing modern *cabinas* with a/c and TVs (one has hot water). Rates: $26 s/d/t. **Cabinas y Restaurante Leda,** tel. 634-4087, also overlooks the estuary. There are several other budget options.

The nicest place is the well-run **Marina Resort,** tel. 634-4194, with 10 a/c rooms with cable TVs, private baths with hot water, and verandas facing a small swimming pool in a courtyard with secure parking. Each room has a double, single, and bunk bed. The English-speaking owner rents jet skis, and there's a popular bar and restaurant. Rates: $42 s/d, $50 up to five people.

For atmosphere, check out the **Restaurante Tabaris Caldera,** with a breezy outside patio over the mouth of the river.

Getting There

Buses pass Mata regularly en route to and from Puerto Caldera.

REFUGIO SILVESTRE DE PEÑAS BLANCAS AND VICINITY

Eleven km north of Esparza on Hwy. 1, a side road winds east to the village of **Miramar,** on the western slopes of the Cordillera Tilarán. En route, one km uphill, is **Secado Ecológico del Café,** a coffee-processing facility that you can tour. Gold has been mined hereabouts since 1815; you can still visit **Las Minas de Montes Oro** (ask in the village). Eighteen km northeast of Miramar, in an area known as Tajo Alto, is **Zapotal,** gateway to the **La Mancuerna Private Ecological Reserve,** tel. 661-0976, at 1,500 meters elevation and offering horseback riding and hiking in cloud forests good for spotting quetzals, toucans, and a panoply of other wildlife.

Zapotal is also gateway to Refugio Silvestre de Peñas Blancas.

Refugio Silvestre de Peñas Blancas

This 2,400-hectare wildlife refuge, 33 km northeast of Puntarenas, protects the watersheds of the Ríos Barranca and Ciruelas, on the forested southern slopes of the Cordillera de Tilarán. The mountain slopes rise steeply from rolling plains carved with deep canyons to 1,400 meters atop Zapotal peak. Vegetation ranges from tropical dry forest in the southerly lower elevation to moist deciduous and premontane moist forest higher up. The region has been extensively deforested, however, but there remains plenty of wildlife. I saw a coatimundi, which bounded across the road like a cat. You may be lucky enough to see howler or white-faced monkeys, red brocket deer, kinkajous, and any of 70-plus species of birds, including toucans and quetzals at the highest elevations.

Peñas Blancas refers to the "white cliffs" of diatomaceous rocks that lend the park its name. The sedimentary rocks were laid down before the Central American isthmus rose from the sea and, like limestone, originated from the "skeletal" remains of subaqueous creatures—in this case microscopic algae.

Steep trails follow the Río Jabonal. Camping is permitted. There are no visitor facilities—and, perhaps consequently, very few visitors.

Accommodations and Food

Hotel Miramar is a small, basic option in the center of Miramar, where you can also try **Cabinas Katya Carolina,** tel. 639-9055.

Vista Golfo de Nicoya Lodge, tel. 382-3312, fax 639-9312 or tel./fax 639-8303, is an atmospheric modern hotel on a 27-hectare ranch and fruit farm—Finca Daniel—in the hills four km north of Miramar at Tajo Alto, boasting great views over the Gulf of Nicoya. It has rooms and apartments for 2-8 people (one has a kitchenette) with modest but pleasant decor and balconies. There's a swimming pool fed by spring water and a hot tub in a small garden. There are trails, and horseback rides ($10 one hour, $7 each additional hour) lead to the nearby gold mines ($20 two hours) and cloud forest ($29). It features the **Bar y Restaurant El Túcano,** where you can dine beneath the shade of a huge spreading tree. Day visitors are welcome ($5 to use the swimming pool, including towels). Rates: $29 s, $34 d bunk with shared bath; $40 s, $44 d shared bath; $51 s, $55 d, private bath; $15 extra person.

At Zapotal, Omar León has basic huts called **Cabinas las Orquídeas,** tel. 661-0976, with shared bath and hot water. Rates: $6 d, $8 quad. Nearby, **Albergue La Mancuena** offers three chalets (including one for six and another for eight people), including breakfast. It has laundry and horseback rides. Rates: $6 pp.

You can also dine beneath shady trees at **Restaurant 4 Cruces,** on the Pan-Am Highway on the corner of the turnoff for Miramar.

Services
There's a **Banco Nacional,** tel. 639-9090, on the plaza in Miramar. If you need medical assistance, call the **Red Cross,** tel. 639-9060. For the **police** (Guardia Rural), call 639-9132 or 117 (emergencies).

Getting There
Buses depart San José for Miramar at 5:30 a.m., 7:30 a.m., and 12:30 p.m., returning at 7 a.m., 12:30 p.m., and 4:45 p.m. Buses depart Puntarenas for Miramar throughout the day; direct buses leave at 7:15 a.m., 10 a.m., 2 p.m., and 4:30 p.m., returning at 6:30 a.m., 9 a.m., noon, and 3 p.m.

COSTA DE PÁJAROS

At San Gerardo, on the Pan-Am Highway, 40 km north of Puntarenas, a paved road leads west to Punta Morales and the Golfo de Nicoya. There's fabulous birding among the mangroves that line the shore—known as the Costa de Pájaros—stretching north to **Manzanillo,** the estuary of the Río Abangaritos, and, beyond, to the estuary of the Río Tempisque. The mangroves are home to ibis, herons, pelicans, parrots, egrets, and also harbor crocodilian caimans. You can follow this coast through cattle country via a road north from four km east of Punta Morales (a dead-end) to Hwy. 18, five km east of the Tempisque ferry.

Refugio Nacional de Vida Silvestre La Enseñada is near Abangaritos, two km north of Manzanillo, 17 km from the Pan-Am Highway. The 380-hectare wildlife refuge is part of a family-run cattle *finca* and salt farm (papayas and watermelons are also grown), with nature trails and a lake—Laguna Agua Dulce—replete with waterfowl and crocodiles.

The **Reserva Biológica Isla Pájaros** is about 600 meters offshore from Punta Morales. The 3.8-hectare reserve protects a colony of brown pelicans and other seabirds that live on this scrub-covered rocky islet rising 45 meters above the Gulf of Nicoya. Supposedly, it can be reached at low tide via a rocky platform, but access is restricted to biological researchers. You can hire a local fishing boat and guide in Morales to take you there, but you are not allowed to step ashore.

Accommodations
La Enseñada Lodge, Apdo. 318-1250 Escazú, tel. 289-6655, fax 289-5281, enjoys a breezy location at the heart of La Enseñada Wildlife Refuge, with tremendous views down the bougainvillea splashed lawns to the mangrove-lined gulf. It has 20 rustic yet spacious, comfortable wooden *cabinas* with two double beds, private baths with cold water, cross-ventilated by screened windows, and verandas with hammocks. Meals are served in a thatched restaurant played upon by the breezes. The Italian-owned property is fronted by mangroves and *salinas* (salt pans) and has a tennis court and a swimming pool. The lodge offers boat trips to Palo Verde, a tractor tour of the *finca,* plus horseback tours, including to Monteverde and Arenal. Rates: $30 pp, including breakfast, $38 with lunch, $47 with dinner.

Los Vaqueros, Apdo. 627, San José 2100, tel. 221-8051, fax 221-5884, a former cattle ranch five km west of San Gerardo is the planned site of a "Wild West" village, with a saloon and 20 colonial-era bungalows, plus a water slide and other attractions.

Universal Tropical Nature Tours, Apdo. 4276, San José 1000, tel. 257-0181, fax 255-4274, offers a three-day "Cowboy Country and Chira Island Adventure," which includes a boat trip to **Isla Chira** and two nights' accommodations at La Enseñada Lodge ($295, including roundtrip transfers from San José).

LAS JUNTAS DE ABANGARES

Las Juntas is one of Costa Rica's prettiest villages, splashed with colorful flowers and trim pastel-painted houses, at the base of the

Cordillera Tilarán about 50 km north of Esparza and six km east of Hwy 1 (the turnoff is at Km 164, about 12 km north of the Río Lagarto and the turnoff for Monteverde). A tree-lined main boulevard and streets paved with interlocking stones add to the orderliness.

Small it may be but Las Juntas once figured big in the region's history. When gold was discovered in the nearby mountains in 1884 it sparked a gold rush. Hungry prospectors came from all over the world to sift the earth for nuggets. Las Juntas was a Wild West town. The locals' facial features play every note on the racial calliope—a reflection of the disparate peoples who have flocked, rooted, and produced offspring in this remote quarter. Inflated gold prices have lured many *oreros* (miners) back to the old mines and streams, but today the pickings are thin.

That pint-size locomotive—the *María Cristina*—that sits in the town plaza once hauled ore for the Abangares Gold Fields Company. Minor Keith was the major shareholder and the train is named for his wife. The *oreros* are honored with a fine bronze statue in a triangular plaza on the other side of an arched bridge at the northeast corner of town (turn left about 100 meters beyond the park).

The road east from the triangular plaza leads into the Cordillera Tilarán via **Candelaria** and (to the right) Monteverde or (to the left) Tilarán; it is rough and relatively untraveled; 4WD is recommended. In places the views are fantastic. Three km east of Las Juntas, a side road leads to the hamlet of **La Sierra,** then drops sharply, in appalling condition, into the valley of the Río Aguas Claras and the tiny open-air **Abangares Mines Eco-Museum,** tel. 662-0129, displaying mining equipment and the ruins of a turn-of-the-century mining center. Trails run through tropical dry forest. Hours: 6 a.m.-5 p.m. Entrance: $1.25.

Nearby, at **Boston,** a cooperative of *oreros* may be happy to lead you down the dank candlelit tunnels to show you their operation. You can also take **The Gold Tour** from a rustic bar and restaurant opposite the eco-museum; the two-day horseback tour includes an overnight camping in Boston before continuing to Monteverde ($40). **Mina Tours,** tel. 662-0753, in Las Juntas also offers tours.

Accommodations and Food

Cabinas Cayuco, tel. 662-0868, 100 meters west of the *orero* statue, has eight cabins on the tree-shaded hillside, with fans and private baths with cold water. Rates: $6. There's a small pool, children's swings, and a rustic bar popular with locals. **Hospedaje El Elcanto,** tel. 662-0677, next to the lively **Bar Las Vegas,** 100 meters northeast of the triangular plaza, has nine clean, simple, modern rooms with private baths and cold water. Rates: $6. A stone's throw northeast is the older, less appealing **Hotel Abangares,** tel. 662-0257.

Near the main plaza, **Cabinas Las Juntas,** tel. 662-0069 or 662-0153, has basic rooms with cold water. Rates: $8. In Sierra, **The Gold Tour** has four modern, simple concrete riverside *cabinas* with hot water; there's a volleyball court. Rates: $20 s/d.

The best eatery in town seems to be **Pizzería La Cascada** by the bridge. **Restaurante Ji Lam Mun,** tel. 662-0005, has reasonable Chinese food.

Be sure to check out the **Cantina Caballo Blanco** facing the triangular plaza: it's as colorful a bar as can be found in Costa Rica, with pool tables painted in lively motifs, and walls festooned with paraphernalia of the *oreros'* life.

Services

There's a branch of **Banco Nacional,** tel. 662-0172, in the center of town. You can hire **horses** and 4WD **taxis** in Las Juntas.

Getting There

Buses depart San José for Las Juntas from Calle 12, Avenida 9, tel. 222-1867, daily at 11 a.m. and 5 p.m.; and from Cañas at 9:30 a.m. and 2:50 p.m. Return buses to San José depart Las Juntas at 6:30 a.m. and 12:30 p.m.

TEMPISQUE FERRY

The turnoff for the Tempisque ferry, tel. 685-5295, leads west from Km 168 on Hwy. 1, four km north of the turnoff for Las Juntas and 20 km south of Cañas. The road is brutally deteriorated. The ferry crosses to Puerto Moreno on the Nicoya Peninsula. It takes vehicles and passengers and runs back and forth across the wide

Tempisque ferry

Río Tempisque (400 *colones*—$2.50—per car; 200 *colones*—$1.25—passengers). It sails daily westbound every 30 minutes past the hour (6 a.m.-7 p.m.), and eastbound on the hour. Weekends and holidays are busy and delays can be two hours or more. Get there early. There's a small **tourist information office,** plus a shady *soda* and a *mirador* restaurant on a high bluff overlooking the river, 500 meters before the ferry wharf. If you're traveling by bus, you'll still need to buy a ferry ticket before boarding. (*Ganado sin guia no pasa,* reads one sign: No cattle allowed without guide.)

CAÑAS AND VICINITY

Cañas is a modest-sized town and a pivotal point for exploring Palo Verde National Park (west) or Lake Arenal (east), and for rafting trips on the Río Coribicí. The city is known as Ciudad de la Amistad ("City of Friendship") for the white-flowered wild cane that still grows in patches hereabouts. It is indisputably a cowboy town, as the many tanned *sabaneros* shaded by wide-brimmed hats attest.

A paved road runs west from Cañas 14 km to the depauperate village of **Bebedero,** a gateway to Palo Verde and a stone's throw away on the west bank of the Río Tenorio. Bebedero is dependent on sugarcane and was for many years a river port; reportedly, there's been talk for years of turning it into a tourist center, though

nothing to date has been done. There's no road access to the park from here, as the land all around is private haciendas. However, boats will take you across the wide Río Tenorio. **Bebedero and Tempisque Wildlife Adventures** has an office in Bebedero; it offers birding and wildlife trips by canopied boat.

Accommodations

Hotel Corral, tel. 669-0622, has 27 clean and spacious rooms with a/c and private baths with cold water; three rooms have TVs. It's on a noisy junction. Rates: $12 pp. **Cabinas Corobicí,** tel. 669-0241, has 12 small and basic but very well-kept *cabinas* with fans and private baths with cold water. Take the two *cabinas* on the left: they're larger. Rates: $6 pp. Cheaper yet are the **Hotel Parque** and **Hotel Guillén,** tel. 669-0070, on the southeast of the park. Both are basic. Rates: $4 pp. Budget hounds might also try the **Gran Hotel,** on Avenida 2 and Calle 5, but the surly owner refused me information about her run-down property.

The **Nuevo Hotel Cañas,** tel./fax 669-0039, on Calle 2 and Avenida 3, is popular with Tico families, who flock to the swimming pool. It has 48 clean, simple *cabinas,* some with a/c, all with private baths with hot water. An atmospheric restaurant features cowboy paraphernalia on the walls. Rates: $22 s, $40 d, including tax.

Food

There's half a dozen or so Chinese restaurants to choose from in Cañas. Take your pick.

Restaurante Panchito and **Bar y Restaurante Central** both have reasonable local fare. And there are several undistinguished places serving burgers and fried chicken.

Services

There are two **banks** in town: Banco de Costa Rica, tel. 669-0066, is on the southeast corner of the plaza; Banco Nacional, tel. 669-0128, has a branch on the northeast corner. There's a pharmacy—**Farmacia Cañas,** tel. 669-0748)—on Avenida 1, two blocks east of the plaza. **Dr. Juan Acon,** tel. 669-0139, has an office in the center of town. **Taxis Unidos de Cañas,** tel. 669-0898, has taxis on call.

Getting There

Buses depart San José for Cañas from Calle 16, Avenidas 3/5 (Transportes La Cañera, tel. 222-3006 or 669-0145), daily at 8:30 a.m., 10:30 a.m., 1:30 p.m., 2:15 p.m., and 4:30 p.m. Trala-

pa, in San José, also operates buses from Calle 20, Avenida 3 (three hours; $3). An express bus departs Puntarenas for Liberia via Cañas at 5:30 p.m. (Empresa Arata, tel. 666-0138). **Interbus'** daily shuttle bus stops in Cañas en route between San José and Tamarindo and back (see the Appendix).

Buses for San José depart from the new terminal in Cañas at Calle 1, Avenidas 9/11 at 4:30 a.m., 5:25 a.m., 9:15 a.m., 12:30 p.m., and 2 p.m. (5:30 p.m. on Sunday). Buses depart Cañas for destinations throughout Guanacaste from the new terminal, including to Arenal and Tilarán (6 a.m., 9 a.m., 10:30 a.m., 1:45 p.m., 3:30 p.m., and 5:30 p.m.); Bebedero (5 a.m., 9 a.m., 11 a.m., 1 p.m., 3 p.m., and 5 p.m.); Las Juntas (9:30 a.m. and 2:50 p.m.); Puntarenas (6 a.m., 6:40 a.m., 9:30 a.m., 11 a.m., 12:30 p.m., 1:30 p.m., and 4:15 p.m.); and Upala (5:45 a.m., 9 a.m., 11 a.m., 2 p.m., and 5 p.m.). Check against current schedules.

CORDILLERA DE TILARÁN

MONTEVERDE AND SANTA ELENA

About seven km north of San Gerardo on the Pan-American Highway (100 meters before the bridge over the Río Lagarto), 37 km north of Esparza, a road to the right leads 35 km uphill to a secluded 1,400-meter-high plateau in the Cordillera de Tilarán. The gut-jolting, vertiginous dirt road is almost as famous as the place it leads to: **Monteverde.** Take it slowly and enjoy the spectacular mountain scenery. En route, about four km east of Lagarto, you'll pass **Bosque Caliente,** a lowland forest reserve with soda springs, trails, and camping.

Monteverde means "Green Mountain," an appropriate name for one of the most idyllic pastoral settings in Costa Rica. Cows munch contentedly, and horse-drawn wagons loaded with milk cans still make the rounds. Monteverde is actually a sprawling agricultural community; the **Monteverde Cloud Forest Biological Reserve,** which is what visitors come to see, is a few kilometers southeast and higher up.

Monteverde is populated by North American Quakers and their Tico-born offspring. Mon-

teverde has no village to speak of; most of the homes are hidden from view in the forest, accessible by foot trail. It is scattered along the dirt road that leads to Monteverde Biological Cloud Forest Preserve from the village of **Santa Elena,** a community of Tico families that is the center of things hereabouts: the bank, stores, bars (these being absent, of course, in a Quaker community) and other services are here. Santa Elena is about six km from Monteverde Biological Cloud Forest Preserve.

The fame of the preserve has spawned an ever-increasing influx of birders and nature-loving tourists. There are now more than 30 lodges catering to visitors; most line the route to the reserve, but a growing number are found north of Santa Elena, which has its own cloud forest reserve and attractions. Community members are divided about the issue of tourism growth, and there is vociferous opposition to plans to pave the road from the Pan-Am Highway. Nonetheless, when I last visited, Santa Elena's dirt roads were being paved with interlocking blocks—a major enhancement.

Although the Monteverde Cloud Forest Biological Reserve steals the limelight, it isn't the

MONTEVERDE—COSTA RICA'S QUAKER VILLAGE

Monteverde was founded in 1951 by a group of 44 North American Quakers—most from Fairhope, Alabama—who as a matter of conscience had refused to register for the draft. Led by John Campbell and Wilford "Wolf" Guindon, they chose Costa Rica for a new home because it had done away with its army. With the help of their Costa Rican neighbors, the Quakers began developing the community that exists today. They built roads and cleared much of the virgin forest for dairy farming. They decided to make cheese because it was the only product that could be stored and moved to market (without spoiling) along a muddy oxcart trail. Cheese is still a mainstay of the local economy, and the Quaker organization is still active in Monteverde (it meets every Wednesday morning at the Friends' Meeting House; visitors are welcome).

The area had been heavily deforested when Guindon and company arrived. Monteverde's founders, however, were environmentally conscious and set aside a heavily timbered region near the headwaters of the Río Guacimal to be held undisturbed and in common to safeguard the water source for their small hydroelectric plant. The area attracted scientists, especially after a small brilliantly colored frog—the golden toad—was discovered in 1964. In 1972, under threat of homesteading in the surrounding cloud forest, visiting scientists George and Harriet Powell joined forces with longtime resident Wilford Guindon and, overcoming local resistance, established a 328-hectare wildlife sanctuary. In 1975, the 554-hectare community watershed reserve was annexed with the aid of a $40,000 grant from the World Wildlife Fund. Together they formed the initial core of the Monteverde Biological Cloud Forest Preserve.

Don't expect to find the Quakers walking down the road dressed like the chap off the oatmeal box. *Cuaqerismo* (Quakerism) in Monteverde is a low-key affair.

only site of interest hereabouts. Consider the other options, listed below.

Art Galleries
A path just west of La Lechería (the cheese factory) leads 400 meters uphill to **Sarah Dowell Watercolor Gallery,** where the local artist displays her distinctive artwork. Her watercolors decorate the walls of many local hotels. Admission is free.

The **Hummingbird Gallery** (Galería Colibrí), tel. 645-1259, is 100 meters below the entrance to the Monteverde Biological Cloud Forest Preserve. It features the photography of Monteverde residents Michael and Patricia Fogden. Prints, slides, T-shirts, and handicrafts from throughout Central America are for sale. Feeders outside the gallery attract a wide variety of hummingbirds.

Bajo del Tigre (Jaguar Canyon)
This private 30-hectare preserve, contiguous with the Monteverde Reserve and administered by the Monteverde Conservation League, is at a lower elevation than the Cloud Forest Preserve and thus offers a different variety of plant and animal life. Quetzals are more easily seen here, for example, than higher up in the wetter, mistier cloud forest. The same is true for the three-wattled bellbird and long-tailed manikin.

The preserve is crisscrossed by a network of easy trails and has strategically located picnic spots. Access is off the main road, near the Pensión Quetzal. Facilities include a Children's Nature Center designed to help kids discover and appreciate the wonders of the tropical rainforest; a self-guided interpretative trail; an arboretum; and a visitor's center and library. Guided tours are offered Mon.-Wed. at 7 a.m. and 1 p.m., plus guided night tours Thurs.-Sun. at 7 p.m. Hours: daily 8 a.m.-4 p.m. Entrance: $5, including map. For more information call 645-5003 orf fax 645-5104.

Bird Sanctuary: Paradise for Bellbirds
This private reserve, tel. 284-8590, fax 645-507, e-mail: heliconi@sol.racsa.co.cr, has seven km of trails. Bellbirds are common, staying in the sanctuary for eight months of the year. Guided birding tours are offered, including one beginning at 5 a.m. (you are picked up at your hotel) and including breakfast and slide show. Natural history walks are also offered, and a three-hour night hike begins at 7 p.m. There's a visitor's center and gift shop.

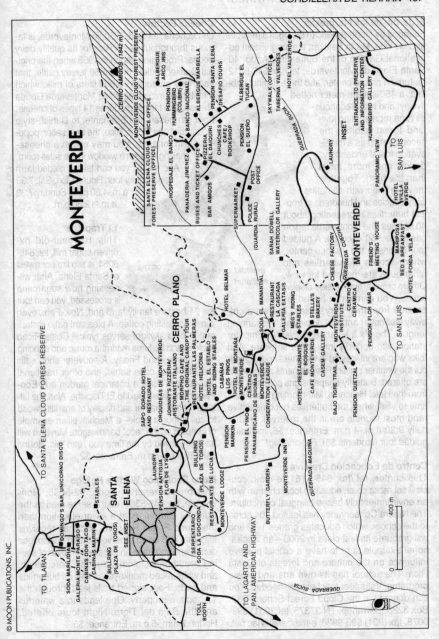

© MOON PUBLICATIONS, INC.

TO SANTA ELENA CLOUD FOREST RESERVE

TO TILARAN

SODA MARILIDIA
GALERIA MONTE PARAISO
CABINAS DON TACO
CABINAS MARÍN

DOMINGO'S BAR, UNICORNO DISCO
STABLES

LAUNDRY
PENSION ANTIGUA
FLOR DE LYS
SANTA ELENA
SEE INSET
BULLRING
(PLAZA DE TOROS)
SERPENTARIO
SODA LA GIOCONDA
RESTAURANTE DE LUCIA
MONTEVERDE LODGE
BULLRING
(PLAZA DE TOROS)

TOLL
BOOTH

TO LAGARTO AND
PAN - AMERICAN HIGHWAY

QUEBRADA SUCIA

400 m

CERRO PLANO

SAPO DORADO HOTEL
AND RESTAURANT
ORQUIDEAS DE MONTEVERDE
JOHNNY'S PIZZERIA
RISTORANTE ITALIANO
MORPHO CAFE AND
THE ORIGINAL CANOPY TOUR
RESTAURANTE LAS PALMERAS
HOTEL HELICONIA
HOTEL EL ESTABLO
AND RIDING STABLES
CABAÑAS
LOS PINOS
HOTEL DE MONTAÑA
MONTEVERDE
CENTRO
MONTEVERDE
PANAMERICANO DE IDIOMAS
CONSERVATION LEAGUE
PENSION EL PINO
PENSION MANIKIN

MONTEVERDE INN

QUEBRADA MAQUINA

HOTEL BELMAR

SODA EL MANANTIAL
RESTAURANT
LA CASCADA
GALERIA EXTASIS
MEG'S RIDING
STABLES
STELLA'S
BAKERY
HOTEL/RESTAURANTE
EL BOSQUE
CAFE MONTEVERDE
CASEM GALLERY
BAJO TIGRE TRAIL
PENSION QUETZAL

MONTEVERDE
INSTITUTE
CENTRO
CERAMICA
PENSION FLOR MAR

TO SAN LUIS

SARAH DOWELL
WATERCOLOR GALLERY

POLICE
(GUARDIA RURAL)

CHEESE FACTORY

QUEBRADA CUECHA

FRIEND'S
MEETING HOUSE

MONTEVERDE

MARIPOSA
BED & BREAKFAST
HOTEL FONDA VELA

QUEBRADA SUCIA

SANTA ELENA CLOUD
FOREST PRESERVE (OFFICE)

ICE OFFICE
HOSPEDAJE EL BANCO
PANADERIA JIMENEZ
BUSES AND TICKET OFFICE
BAR AMIGOS

ALBERGUE
ARCO IRIS
PENSION HUMMINGBIRD
(COLIBRI)
BANCO NACIONAL
ALBERGUE MARBELLA
PENSION SANTA ELENA
DESAFIO TOURS
PIZZERIA
EL DAIQUIRI
CHUNCHES
CAFE/
BOOKSHOP
PENSION
EL SUEÑO
ALBERGUE EL
TUCAN

SUPERMARKET
POST
OFFICE

CERRO AMIGOS (1842 m)
MONTEVERDE CLOUD FOREST PRESERVE

MONTEVERDE

SANTA ELENA

QUEBRADA SUCIA

INSET

SKYWALK (OFFICE)
TABERNA VALVERDES
HOTEL VALVERDE

ENTRANCE TO PRESERVE
AND INFORMATION CENTER
HUMMINGBIRD GALLERY

LAUNDRY

PANORAMIC VIEW

HOTEL
VILLA
VERDE

TO
SAN LUIS

El Jardín de las Mariposas

Founded by North American biologist Jim Wolfe and his wife, Marta Salazar, the magnificent educational Garden of the Butterflies, Apdo. 40, Sante Elena de Monteverde, tel./fax 645-5512, features a nature center, and three distinct habitats: a 450-square-meter netted flyway, and two greenhouses (one representing lowland forest habitat, the second set up as a midelevation forest understory, darker and more moist than the first). Together, they are filled with all-native plant species and hundreds of tropical butterflies representing about 40 species (the Monteverde region has some 550 species). A guided tour begins in the visitor's center, where scores of butterflies and other bugs are mounted for view. *emerald toucanet* Others crawl around inside display cases. You can watch butterflies emerge from their chrysalises. There's a cut-away leaf-cutter ant nest displaying ants farming fungus. There's a library and even a computer station with butterfly interactive software. And folks who are interested in weather should check out the weather station. Refreshments and snacks are offered. Butterfly-shaped signs point the way from the Hotel Heliconia. Mid-morning is the best time to visit, when the butterflies become active (and most tourists are in the reserve). Hours: daily 9:30 a.m.-4 p.m. Entrance: $6, including guided tour (students $5). *Fascinating!*

Centro de Educación Creativa

This center, tel./fax 645-5161, e-mail: ccc-clc@sol.racsa.co.cr, educates local children with an environmentally based bilingual curriculum. The Nature Conservancy has leased 104 acres to the school, which educates grades 1-12 and will graduate its first class in 2003—an inspirational example sure to have a crucial positive influence on the culture and forests of Costa Rica. The school has its own arts and music programs. Volunteer teachers are needed. You can donate via the Cloud Forest School, P.O. Box 3223, Sewanee, TN 37375, tel. (931) 598-0078, fax (931) 598-9936, e-mail: shill@iac.net.

Cheese Factory

La Lechería, tel. 645-2850, in Monteverde, is famous throughout Costa Rica for its quality dairy goods. Production began in 1953 when the original Quaker settlers bought 50 jersey cattle; that year they produced 76,000 liters of milk, which they turned into pasteurized Monteverde Gouda cheese. The factory produces 14 types of cheese, from parmesan and Emmantel to Danish-style "dambo" and Monte Rico, the best seller, popular in fondues. You may observe cheese-making through a window in the sales room. Alternately, you can take a guided farm and factory tour. Hours: Mon.-Sat. 7:30 a.m.-4:30 p.m., Sunday 7:30 a.m.-12:30 p.m.

BOB RACE

El Trapiche

This 100-year-old ox-driven sugar mill, tel. 645-6054, is two km northwest of Santa Elena. After witnessing how sugarcane is processed, you can tour the 24-hectare family farm and, Nov.-Feb., even join in harvesting coffee. A pleasant patio restaurant lit by a skylight serves typical Costa Rican cooking and features marimba music and dancing on Thursday and Friday. A souvenir shop sells T-shirts, fresh cane sugar, and other traditional dishes. You'll see a botanical garden and **Eco-Park** immediately next to El Trapiche. Alas, the latter is merely a rather sad display of animals caged to cull a tourist buck—a Machiavellian example of jumping on the "eco" bandwagon. Maybe it will have improved by the time you read this. Hours: daily 10 a.m.-7 p.m. Entrance: $2.

Finca Ecológico Wildlife Refuge

This private reserve, Apdo. 92-5655, Monteverde, tel. 645-5363, on the same road as the Butterfly Garden, is at a lower elevation than the Cloud Forest Reserve, and thus receives less rain and cloud. The vegetation is also less dense and you have an excellent chance of seeing coatimundis, sloths, agoutis, porcupines, and white-faced monkeys, as well as butterflies and birds. Four signed trails lead through the 17-hectare property. One leads to a waterfall and the Bajo del Tigre. Night tours offered. Hours: 7 a.m.-5 p.m. Entrance: $5.

Heliconia Cloud Forest Reserve

This private 284-hectare reserve, owned by the Hotel Heliconia, was still being prepared for the public at press time. It is near the Santa Elena Cloud Forest Reserve and has trails and two-hour guided horse rides ($24). I was quoted an $8 entrance fee.

Orquídeas de Monteverde

It took five years of arduous work to collate this collection, but now you can admire the results of the Monteverde Orchid Investigation Project, an ongoing effort to document and research local orchids. Short paths wind through the compact Monteverde Orchid Garden, tel. 645-5510, displaying almost 500 species native to the region and arranged in 22 groups ("sub-tribes"), each marked with an educational placard. Miniatures are preponderant, including the world's smallest flower, *Platystele jungermanniodes,* about the size of a pinhead (fortunately, you are handed a magnifying glass upon arrival). Hours: daily 8 a.m.-5 p.m. Entrance: $5.

Reserva Sendero Tranquilo

This 200-hectare reserve is operated by the Lowthers, one of the original Quaker families, whose home is beside the Quebrada Cuecha stream behind the cheese factory. Only 12 people at any time are allowed on the trail, led by guides who give detailed explanations of the habitats and wildlife ($15). Make reservations through the Hotel Sapo Dorado, tel. 645-5010.

Serpentario Monteverde

This den of snakes, tel. 645-5772, fax 645-5236, in Santa Elena village, lets you get up close and personal with a repertoire of coiled constrictors and venomous vipers and kin, as well as their prey: frogs, chameleons, and the like. The dreaded fer-de-lance is here, along with 20 or so other species separated from you, fortunately, by thick panes of glass. Guided tours cost $3. Hours: daily 9 a.m.-5 p.m.

Accommodations

Monteverde is a *very* popular destination. Accommodations may be difficult to obtain in dry season, when tour companies block space. Book well ahead if possible, especially for Christmas and Easter. A deposit may be required. Unless otherwise noted, mail all correspondence to the generic Monteverde postal box number: Apdo. 10165, San José 1000.

Camping: You can camp at **Albergue Arco Iris** ($3 pp) in Santa Elena. The campers' bathroom is magnificent, stone inlaid with blue mosaic tile. **Hotel Fonda Vela** has a shady camping area. Also try Hotel Villa Verde, Cabinas El Bosque, and Pensión Flor Mar.

Budget—Santa Elena and North: The **Pensión Santa Elena,** tel. 645-5298, fax 645-5148, has 10 clean though small and basic rooms of varying sizes (some dark). Some have private baths, others share, with separate baths for men and women. Very colorful decor and super-friendly hosts. There's a TV in the small reception lounge. The hotel provides free use of kitchen services, plus laundry service and a slide and video show. It also offers horseback riding. Rates: $10 pp; $15 with breakfast. **El Tucán,** tel. 645-5017, fax 645-5462, has 11 rooms—seven with shared bath, four with private baths. There's a large but dingy restaurant. Rates: $7 shared bath; $10 private bath. **Pensión Colibrí,** tel. 645-5067, has very basic rooms with shared bath. Rates: $5. Horse rentals are offered. Also consider the basic **El Tauro,** opposite Pensión Santa Elena, with rooms with shared bath. Rates: $4. **Pensión Hummingbird,** tel. 645-5682, has four small but pleasing rooms (two doubles, two triples) with hot-water shared bath. A budget bargain. Rates: $4 pp.

Hospedaje Esperanza, tel. 645-5068, above the *pulpería* opposite the police station, has 10 clean rooms with shared bath with hot water. Rates: $5 pp. **Hospedaje El Banco,** tel. 645-3204, behind Banco Nacional, has seven small, simple rooms with communal bath and hot water. Home-cooked meals are served in a tiny restaurant. The small lounge has a TV. Rates: $6 pp. **Pensión El Sueño,** tel. 645-5021, has nine double rooms with private but basic baths with hot water. There's a TV in the lounge, plus a small restaurant. Rates: $10 pp. **Soda La Gioconda** has small rooms, plus a *soda* selling *casados* for $3. Rates: $4 pp. **Cabinas Marin,** tel. 645-5279, on the hill north of the village center, has six clean but dingy rooms with shared (three with private) baths and hot water. Rates: $9 shared bath; $14 private bath. Next door, **Cabins Don Taco,** tel. 645-6023, has six spacious, well-lit, all-wood rooms with private, hot water baths including breakfast in a *mirado* restaurant with views over the Gulf of Nicoya. More cabins were planned. Rates: $10 pp.

Cabinas Las Cañitas, tel. 458-4133, two km northwest of Santa Elena, is another option. A dirt road about two km west of Santa Elena leads uphill to **San Gerardo Abajo** (three hours by horse from Santa Elena), where you can reportedly stay in basic *cabinas* (I didn't inspect them) offered by the Quesada family, tel. 645-2757. Four-wheel drive required. Also at San Gerardo Abajo, and accessible only in rainy season only by horseback, is **El Mirador,** tel. 645-5087, a rustic lodge with a large dormitory with shared baths, plus private rooms with baths. Home-cooked meals are provided, as are horseback rides. The lodge offers views towards Arenal Volcano.

Budget—On the Monteverde Road: Pensión Antigua Flor de Lys has seven small, simple rooms with large baths and hot water. Rates: $7 shared bath; $10 private bath. There's a small restaurant and tour information kiosk. The uninspired **Monteverde Inn,** tel. 645-5156, tucked at the bottom of the road past the Butterfly Garden, has 10 basic *cabinas* (four doubles, six singles), all except two with private baths with hot water, plus hardwood floors and sponge mattresses. A redeeming factor is the view out across the Gulf of Nicoya. Rates: $10 s, $18 d. Meals are available. **Pensión Manikin,** tel. 645-5080, is a basic bed and breakfast with nine rooms with bunk beds and hot water. Rates: $6 shared bath; $10 private bath. It also has two cabins for six people ($25 d). Breakfast is served in the stone-and-timber lounge. Land Rover tours are offered for groups. Next door is **Pensión El Pino,** tel. 645-5130, not to be mistaken for Cabañas los Pinos, with five simple wood-lined rooms with bunk beds and shared, skylit bath. Rates: $5 pp ($7 with private bath). It has a laundry, plus horses, a jeep, and a restaurant. *A bargain!*

There's a small single *cabina* 50 meters south of El Bosque restaurant, owned by Enrique Hurtado, which rents for $15 a day. It has a small kitchenette, plus a laundry sink outside. Call the restaurant for reservations. **Pensión Quetzal,** tel. 645-0955, is a popular though rustic lodge with 10 rooms (seven with private bath) featuring wood-paneled walls. It offers a small library and family-style dining. Hummingbirds gather in the flower-filled gardens. Rates: $25 pp; $35 private bath and hot water. **Pensión Flor Mar,** tel. 645-5009, fax 645-5580, has three rustic but clean rooms with private baths (one with double bed, one with two bunks, a third with double and bunk), plus nine rooms with shared bath. Some rooms are dark. It's popular with scientists and student groups. There's a laundry and a small restaurant. It's owned by Marvin Rockwell—one of the original Quaker settlers—and his wife Flory (hence the hotel's name). Rates: $10 pp shared bath ($26 with tax and meals); $13 private bath ($30 with tax and meals). **Bed and Breakfast Mariposa,** tel. 645-5013, has three very simple cabins, each with a double and a single bed and a private bath with hot water. Rates: $20 s, $25 d, including breakfast.

Inexpensive—Santa Elena and North: The splendid, German-owned **Albergue Arco Iris,** Apdo. 003-5655, Santa Elena de Monteverde, tel. 645-5067, fax 645-5022, is run with Teutonic efficiency. It has seven roomy rooms in a two-story unit amid a spacious garden with deck chairs on a hillside. The rooms differ in size; one has four bunk beds. Six handsome stone-and-hardwood *cabinas* have been added, featuring terra-cotta tile floors and Guatemalan prints on the sofas. All have clean, private baths and hot water. The airy restaurant is open Nov.-Easter and July-August, and offers a large menu of organic *típico* dishes at low cost. Horses can be rented, and there's a library, laundry, and safety deposit box. Rates: $30-50 d for rooms and cabins according to room size.

Hotel Finca Valverde, Apdo. 2-5655, Monteverde, tel. 645-5157, fax 645-5216, amid a setting of forest and pasture on the east side of Santa Elena, has 18 cozy if spartan double-unit wooden cabins with single beds in lofts and spacious bathrooms with bathtubs marvelous for soaking after a crisp hike. Rates: $35 s, $50 d. Its atmospheric Restaurant Don Miguel has plate-glass windows, and you can rent horses ($7 per hour). The attractive **Hotel Miramontes** is two km northwest of Santa Elena, on the road to Las Juntas. Cabinas surround an attractive wooden lodge on a hillside. It has mountain bike rental ($5 per day).

The German-run **Sunset Hotel,** tel. 645-5048, fax 645-5344, one km northeast of Santa Elena, has seven attractive, brightly lit, wood-trimmed rooms with private baths with hot water. It was adding more when I visited. You have panoramic views from your veranda and the restaurant. Rates: $18 s, $28 d, $36 t low season; $24 s, $36 d, $46 t high season, including tax and breakfast. Three km farther along the steep and eroded dirt road, beyond the Santa Elena Cloud Forest Reserve, is **Vista Verde Lodge** and **Mirador Lodge San Gerardo,** tel. 645-5087.

Inexpensive—On the Monteverde Road: Hotel El Establo, Apdo. 549, San Pedro 2050, tel. 645-5033 or 645-5110, fax 645-5041, offers traditional Quaker hospitality, dude-ranch style. The modestly attractive two-story wood-and-stone structure is set on a private 48-hectare farm. The 20 carpeted rooms have cinderblock walls. Rooms on the ground floor open onto a wood-floored gallery lounge with deep-cushioned sofas and an open fireplace. Each room has a double and a single bed, plus a pleasing bathroom with hot water. Heaps of light from the wraparound windows. There's a TV lounge, and El Establo has its own horse stable (see "Activities," below). Rates: $48 s, $58 d, $65 t, $70 quad; breakfasts $5, lunch and dinner $8. **Cabañas Los Pinos,** Apdo. 70, San José, tel. 645-5005 or 645-5252, has five *cabinas* in an alpine setting with lots of cedars. Each unit has a kitchenette and a private bath with hot water. Varying sizes sleep up to six people. Rates: $34 d, $42 t, $60 quad, $85 for a three-bedroom unit, including tax.

Hotel El Bosque, tel. 645-5158, fax 645-5221, has 21 fairly simple and soulless cabins surrounded by open lawns, each with private bath and hot water. The modest restaurant appeals. Rates: $25 s, $35 d, $45 t. Camping is allowed. **Hotel Villa Verde,** Apdo. 16 C.P., Monteverde 5655, tel. 645-5025, fax 645-5115, has compact, rustic *cabinas,* plus new apartment rooms with hardwood floors, roomy kitchenettes, a small lounge with fireplace, and large bedrooms, each with four beds (one double, three singles). Suites have fireplaces and tubs. Voluminous tiled bathrooms have hot water. The stone-and-timber lodge and restaurant offer a homey atmosphere. Two new blocks feature 18 rooms, plus an atrium restaurant and bar. Rates: $38 s, $49 d, $61 t, including American breakfast.

Moderate—On the Monteverde Road: Sapo Dorado, Apdo. 9, Monteverde 5655, tel. 645-

5010, fax 645-5180, e-mail: elsapo@sol.racsa. co.cr, website www.cool.co.cr/usr/sapodorado, run by descendants of the original Quakers, has 20 large rooms in 10 handsome stone-and-timber duplex cabins spread apart on the hillside, with great views. There are two types—"classic suite" (older, with fireplaces) and "sunset suite"—each with private bath, two queen beds, orthopedic mattresses, fireplace, and private balcony. Small bathrooms. Gregg Calkins reports that the older units are "simply built and very noisy when the neighbors so much as coughed." The hotel rules do prohibit "moving of furniture or gymnastics after 9 p.m." Chalets are spread through landscaped, hilly grounds. The acclaimed restaurant with open-air terrace and views out across the gulf is famous for its vegetarian and natural-food meals. Classical music accompanies dinner. Five km of self-guided trails lead through pastures and forest. There's professional massage, too, and transfers to places throughout the northwest. Rates: $45 s, $55 d "classic," $55 s, $65 d "sunset" green season; $70 s/d "classic," $80 s/d "sunset" high season.

Hotel Heliconia, Apdo. 10921-1000 San José, tel. 645-5109, fax 645-5007, is an appealing Swiss-style chalet built almost entirely of lacquered cedar. Rooms, too, have abundant hardwoods and lots of light. Home-style comforts include deep-cushioned sofas in the lobby, hand-painted curtains, and double and single beds with orthopedic mattresses in the 22 bedrooms, which have rocking chairs on the veranda. Otherwise basically furnished. Private bathrooms have hot water. There's a spacious and elegant restaurant, a jacuzzi, and potted plants abound. It is set in pretty landscaped grounds at the foot of the sloping 10-hectare Finca Heliconia, which boasts virgin forest at its upper elevations. Rates (pp): $65 s, $66 d, $73 t.

Hotel de Montaña Monteverde, Apdo. 2070-1002 San José, tel. 645-5046 or 224-3050, fax 645-5320 or 222-6148, is set in expansive grounds, which include a lake and 15-hectare private reserve. Spacious rooms—30 doubles and suites, each with private bath with hot water—have hardwood floors and verandas with rockers. Otherwise sparsely furnished. Rooms in the newer block are slightly more elegant. Suites get higher marks for their fireplaces and king-size beds. The hotel has a jacuzzi and a sauna, plus a large restaurant, a bar, and a lounge with TV and veranda offering views over the gulf. Rates: $45 s, $65 d, $76 t, $120 honeymoon suite, with its own jacuzzi.

Hotel Belmar, Apdo. 17-5655, Monteverde, tel. 645-5201, fax 645-5135, e-mail: belmar@sol.racsa.co.cr, website www.centralamerica.com/cr/hotel/belmar.htm, is a beautiful, ivy-clad, Swiss-style hotel with 34 clean, comfortable, atmospheric rooms, each with private bath and hot water. There are also four family rooms. French doors in most rooms and lounges open onto balconies with grand views over the valley. A west-facing glass wall catches the sunset. Spacious, modestly elegant, wood-paneled rooms in a new addition offer splendid views, plus large bathrooms. The large and breezy restaurant serves good hearty meals and also has a veranda with a lookout over the gulf. The hotel offers tours, and will prepare box lunches for hikers. The road up to the hotel is very steep. Rates: $40 s, $50 d low season; $50 s, $60 d high season, including tax.

Hotel Fonda Vela, tel. 257-1413 or 645-5125, fax 257-1416 or 645-5119, website www.centralamerica.com/cr/hotel/fondavel.htm, has 23 rooms, including five master suites. Hardwoods abound. Some rooms have hardwood floors; others have flagstone floors. Most have views over the Gulf of Nicoya. All are wheelchair accessible. A highly recommended restaurant with an open-air balcony overlooks forested grounds, through which a narrow trail leads to a Swiss-style chalet. Rates: $59 s, 68 d, standard; $66 s, $75 d junior suites; $74 s, $82 d master suite.

Expensive—Santa Elena and North: The **Cloud Forest Lodge,** tel. 645-5058, fax 645-5168, 1.5 km northeast of Santa Elena, earns raves from readers. It is set on a 25-hectare private forest reserve. The 18 wood-and-stone *cabinas* are clean and spacious, with large clerestory windows, peaked ceilings, and large bathrooms. There's a large-screen TV and VCR. It has lawns, a duck pond, and five km of trails into the nearby forests. There are views of Nicoya from the deck. No smoking. You can climb the huge strangler figs out back. Rates: $45 s, $55 d low season; $70 s, $88 d high season. Breakfast $7, dinner $11. The Canopy Tour is here.

Expensive—On the Monteverde Road: The moderne **Monteverde Lodge,** Costa Rica Expeditions, Apdo. 6941, San José 1000, tel. 257-0766, fax 257-1665; direct line, tel. 645-5057, fax 645-5126, is the most outstanding hotel and also a good bargain. A cavernous entrance foyer leads up to a spacious and elegant open-plan dining room with a soaring beamed ceiling, and a cozy bar with leather chairs from Sarchí around an open hearth, which has a log fire blazing at night. Chessboards and backgammon are at hand. The bar looks down on a large jacuzzi (open 24 hours) enclosed by a glass atrium that complements the red-brick and timber lodge. Wraparound windows offer wonderful views over the landscaped grounds and forested valley. Rooms are spacious and elegant, with large windows, two double beds, and well-lit bathrooms stocked with fluffy towels. Snacks are served in the bar at 5 p.m. Smoking is allowed in the bar and a designated smoking wing only. The lodge, which is set amid beautifully lanscaped gardens, is operated by Costa Rica Expeditions and is very popular with birding and nature groups. Transportation to the Cloud Forest Preserve is offered with notice ($4 one-way). Cuisine is superb. Rates: $89 d, including all meals. A three-day package with personal guide and transfers from San José costs $499 pp double, $349 quad. Recommended.

Food

Monteverde Lodge offers excellent, inexpensive cuisine (breakfast $6.50, lunch and dinner $11). The **Sapo Dorado** is recommended for vegetarian dishes, including whole-grain pizza, banana bread, and tofu with vegetarian primavera ($7); plus baked orange chicken with peppercorn ($7). Classical music is played at sunset, followed by live music and dancing.

A reader reports that the **Pizzeria El Daiquiri** "has the *best vegetarian pizza* in all Costa Rica." The pizzas cost $5-9. There's a nonsmoking cafe adjacent. **Johnny's Pizzeria and Café Neotrópica,** tel. 645-5066, is simple yet classy. The menu ranges from pizza ($3.50-10, small-large) and burritos to daily specials such as *pollo al dijon* ($7); open 7 a.m.-3 p.m. and noon-9:30 p.m. It also has a cafe menu, as does **Morpho Café,** tel. 645-5607, serving coffees and *batidos*. **Restaurant Las Palmas,** tel. 645-5450, also has pizzas plus steaks and chicken dishes; its neighbor, the **Restaurant de Lucía,** tel. 645-5337, is genuinely Italian, with cappuccinos, lasagnas, and vegetarian dishes.

Restaurant El Bosque, tel. 645-1258, is good for basic *típico* fare (average $5), as is **Restaurant La Cascada,** a pleasant little restaurant in landscaped grounds with a small waterfall and balcony for dining alfresco (most dishes below $10). Music and dancing follow. **Bar y Restaurante Miramonte,** 400 meters north of the turnoff for the Santa Elena reserve, has views over the gulf.

The **cheese factory,** of course, sells cheeses; Mon.-Sat. 7:30 a.m.-4:30 p.m. You can also buy homemade cookies and bread, and gouda and jack cheese at a dairy store next to the police station in Santa Elena. **Stella's Bakery,** tel. 645-5052 (open 6 a.m.-6 p.m.), next to the CASEM gallery, sells homemade bread, cookies, granola, sticky buns, doughnuts, sandwiches, and killer milk shakes ($3). The breakfast menu includes pancakes and omelettes, and granola with homemade yogurt ($2).

There are two well-stocked supermarkets in Santa Elena.

Entertainment

A **slide show**—*Natural History of Cloud Forest Animals*—is offered daily at 11 a.m. at the Hummingbird Gallery ($3; reservations required: tel. 645-5122, fax 645-5034); groups of four people or more can arrange an afternoon viewing. A **multimedia show**—*Sounds and Scenes of the Cloud Forest*—is also offered nightly at 6:15 p.m. at the Monteverde Lodge. And the Hotel Belmar has a slide show nightly (except Friday) at 8 p.m. ($5).

The **Monteverde Music Festival,** each January and February, features live music to accompany the sunset offered by members of the National Symphony Orchestra and other leading artists at a villa above the Hotel Belmar (5 p.m. daily except Sunday and Wednesday; $7). A festival shuttle bus departs Santa Elena at 4:20 p.m. and runs between the hotels. Call or fax 645-5125 or 645-5114 for reservations. You can buy tickets in advance at the Monteverde Lodge. Dress warmly and bring a flashlight.

Monteverde is a Quaker community: hence, there are no bars. Most hotels, however, have bars. For a taste of local color, wet your whistle at the **Taberna Valverdes,** tel. 661-2557, or **Bar Amigos** in Santa Elena, and **Domingo's Bar and Unicorno Disco** facing the soccer field north of the village. Bar Amigos and Domingo's

have pool tables. The **Sapo Dorado** also has dancing and live music at night.

Need to boogie? **La Cascada Disco** offers mostly salsa and reggae; doors open at 7 p.m. (closed Monday).

Activities

An intriguing way to explore the Santa Elena Cloud Forest Reserve is by ascending into the forest canopy on a **Canopy Tour,** tel. 645-5243, e-mail: canopy@sol.racsa.co.cr. You'll ascend to the treetops, then traverse from platform to platform using pulleys on horizontal cables before finally rappeling back to earth, all in the company of an experienced guide. The two-hour tours are offered daily at 7 a.m., 10 a.m., and 2 p.m. ($45 adults, $30 students, $25 children).

An alternate and more accessible option is the **Sky Walk,** Apdo. 57-5655, Monteverde, tel./fax 645-5238, which offers a monkey's eye view of things on a "sky walk" through the canopy of Santa Elena Cloud Forest Reserve. You walk along five suspension bridges and platforms and 1,000 meters of pathways permitting viewing from ground level to the treetops, where you are right in there with the epiphytes. No more than 50 people at a time. Contact the Sky Walk office in Santa Elena. Open daily 7 a.m.-4 p.m. The two-hour walk costs $8, students $6, including boots and poncho; it's $12 with a guide.

Meg's Stables, tel. 645-5052, has guided horseback tours ($23 for two hours); it also rents horses ($7 per hour). Notice is usually required. **Hotel El Establo** rents horses for $7 per hour with guide. **La Estrella,** tel. 645-2751, has 30 horses, with guided tours from one hour to a full day ($7 per hour). Also try **Rancho Verde,** tel. 645-1003, and **Establo Pepe Ginna,** tel. 645-5087, with trips as far afield as Arenal.

Educational Courses

The **Centro Panamericano de Idiomas,** tel./fax 645-5441, fax 645-5441, e-mail: info@cpi-edu.com, offers Spanish language courses. Rates—$370-720 (two weeks), $555-1,050 (three weeks), $660-1,300 (month)—depend on hours of tuition and whether you opt for homestay or not.

The **Monteverde Studios of the Arts,** Apdo. 6-5655 Monteverde, e-mail: mstudios@sol.racsa.co.cr; in the U.S., P.O. Box 766, Narberth, PA

19072, tel. (800) 370-3331, hosts one-week workshops June-August. Classes include ceramics, leatherwork, collage, wood-turning, painting, weaving, basketry, photography, stained glass, cooking, and a dozen other themes ($235 per week).

The **Monteverde Institute,** Apdo. 69-5655, Monteverde, tel. 645-5053, fax 645-5219, e-mail: mviimv@sol.racsa.co.cr, offers short and long-term courses for international students in fields such as biology, ecology, agriculture, and natural history. It also has programs catering to local needs, such as sustainable development, conservation, and courses on domestic violence and sexual abuse. It works with the Council for International Educational Exchange.

Shopping

The **Artisans' Cooperative of Santa Elena and Monteverde** (CASEM), tel. 645-5190, fax 645-5006, features the handmade wares of 140 local artisans whose work focuses on the natural beauty of the area. Sales directly benefit the artists (closed Sunday May-Nov.). Next door is the coffee roaster of **Café Monteverde,** where you can taste locally produced coffee and watch beans being roasted and packaged ($2 per half-pound). Roaster Victorina Molina will be happy to tell you all about the local coffee cooperative.

The **Extasis Gallery,** tel./fax 645-5548, sells exquisite paintings, hardwood sculptures, jewelry, bowls, and other creative art by gifted artist Marco Tulio Brenes. The **Hummingbird Gallery** is well-stocked with souvenirs—locally made hand-carved wooden pieces, embroidered placemats, wall hangings, and blouses—plus posters, postcards, and color transparencies. The **visitor center** at the Monteverde Biological Cloud Forest Preserve also sells posters, books, and T-shirts. The **Monteverde Conservation League** also sells videos, booklets, T-shirts, and posters.

And check out the **Monteverde Studios of the Arts** and the **Centro Cerámica,** both selling works by local artists. In Santa Elena, head to **Selva Paraíso** for Guaitil pottery and Guatemalan clothing.

Information

The Monteverde Tourist Board, Apdo. 10165, San José 1000, tel. 645-1001, has an information center opposite the bus stop in Santa Elena. It's closed half the time. In any event, you'll find the two Oregonians who run the sandwich shop next door to be far more informative. **Chunches** is a cafe and bookstore in Santa Elena; it sells U.S. and English magazines and newspapers, and has a vast selection of books on natural history.

Services

The **post office** is next door to the **police** (Guardia Rural) in the center of Santa Elena. Lavandería Patricia, tel. 645-2653, offers **laundry** service, as does a *lavandería,* tel. 645-5468 (open 8 a.m.-9 p.m.), opposite Pensión Antigua Flor de Lys. There's a small **health clinic,** tel. 645-1156, in Santa Elena.

Getting There and Away

By Car: The drive from Lagarto takes 1.5-2 hours. You'll stop at a tollbooth operated by the Monteverde Road Commission just before Santa Elena (the 50-*colones* fee goes to help maintain the road). Another road to Monteverde (35 km) leads via Sardinal; the turnoff from the Pan-Am Highway is about 10 km south of San Gerardo. Drive slowly through Santa Elena and Monteverde. There are a lot of pedestrians, horses, and children playing along the road, which has many blind bends. Speed limit in the area is 20 kph.

By Bus: Autotransportes Tilarán, tel. 222-3854 in San José, tel. 645-1152 in Santa Elena, operates an express bus from San José, Calle 14, Avenidas 9/11, daily at 6:30 a.m. and 2:30 p.m. (four hours; $4.50). Buses for Monteverde depart Puntarenas from the beachfront stop between Calles 2 and 4 at 2 p.m. (you can pick it up at the Río Lagarto turnoff for Monteverde); from Tilarán at 11:30 a.m. and 2 p.m.; and from Las Juntas at 1 p.m. and 2 p.m. A bus to Tilarán departs San José from Calle 12, Avenidas 9/11, tel. 222-3854, at 12:45 p.m. and usually arrives at Río Lagarto around 3:15 p.m., in time to connect with the bus from Puntarenas.

The cheese factory (about 2.5 km before the reserve) is the end of the route and beginning point for buses. Buses originating here pick up in Santa Elena at the Banco Nacional. Return buses depart for San José at 6:30 a.m. and 2:30 p.m.; for Puntarenas at 6 a.m.; for Tilarán at 7 a.m. and 2 p.m.; and for Las Juntas at 5 a.m. and 6 a.m. Buses will pick up passengers along the road.

Watch your luggage. Buses will drop you by your hotel. Buy your return bus ticket from the Transmonteverde ticket office (open daily 5:45-11 a.m. and 1-4 p.m.) as soon as you arrive in Santa Elena, otherwise you might be out of luck.

Evelio Fonseca Mata, tel. 645-0958, runs a private **minibus** service to and from San José for four people for around $200 roundtrip. Several folks offer rides to Fortuna. Try Leonel Quesada at Bar y Restaurante Don Taco, tel. 645-5087, who charges $75 s/d, $114 t/quad.

Getting Around
You can walk around Santa Elena and, if hale and hearty, to the Monteverde Cloud Forest Biological Reserve (although you should note that it's uphill all the way).

MONTEVERDE CLOUD FOREST BIOLOGICAL RESERVE

The 10,500-hectare Reserva Biológica Bosque Nuboso Monteverde, Apdo. 55-5655, Monteverde, Puntarenas, tel. 645-5122, fax 645-5034, e-mail: montever@sol.racsa.co.cr, is acclaimed as one of the most outstanding wildlife sanctuaries in the New World tropics. It extends down both the Caribbean and Pacific slopes and encompasses eight distinct ecological zones. Temperature and humidity change dramatically over relatively short distances, producing a great diversity of forest types with little change in elevation. Wind-battered elfin woods on exposed ridges are spectacularly dwarfed, whereas more protected areas have majestically tall trees festooned with orchids, bromeliads, ferns, and vines. Poorly drained areas support swamp forests, huge philodrendrons, tall bamboos, and giant tree ferns from the age of the dinosaurs. Humid trade winds blowing in off the sea shroud the forest in a veil of mist. Clouds sift through the forest primeval.

The preserve, which is owned and administered by the Tropical Science Center of Costa Rica, protects more than 100 species of mammals, more than 400 species of birds, and more than 1,200 species of amphibians and reptiles. It is one of the few remaining habitats of all five species of the cat family: jaguar, ocelot, puma, margay, and jaguarundi. Insects include over 5,000 species of moths. Bird species embrace black guan, emerald toucanet, the three-wattled bellbird (an endangered species whose metallic "BONK!" call carries for almost two miles), and 30 local hummingbird species. Feeders hang at the trailhead near the visitor center, where you will be sure to see violet saber-wing, as well as fiery-throated, rufous-tailed, and purple-throated hummingbirds; the latter are the most common at this elevation. Hundreds of visitors come to Costa Rica to visit Monteverde in hopes of seeing a resplendent quetzal (approximately 100 pairs nest in Monteverde). The quetzal is far from safe, however, for its habitat extends past the boundaries of the reserve, into forests threatened with deforestation.

Trails
The preserve has kilometers of trails, sections of which are not for the weak-hearted. Parts ooze with mud; other sections have been magnificently covered with raised wooden walkways. Knowledgeable locals wear rubber boots. Because of the fragile environment, the preserve allows a maximum of 120 people on the trails at any one time. The paths are strewn with exotic blossoms, such as "hot lips." Shorter nature trails are concentrated in an area called "The Triangle."

The **Sendero Chomogo** trail leads steeply uphill to a wide clearing ringed with thousands of pink and white impatiens, where a *mirador* (lookout) straddles the Continental Divide. Rivers to the north flow to the Caribbean, those to the south flow to the Pacific. On a clear day—a rarity in the cloud forest—you can see both bodies of water. The Sendero Chomogo then drops a short distance down the Pacific slope before looping back via the **Sendero Río** (3.2 km), where a platform hangs over the waterfall, or the **Sendero Pantanoso** and **Sendero Bosque Nuboso** ("Cloud Forest Trail"), which has educational stops corresponding to a self-guide booklet.

Longer trails lead down the Pacific slopes. **Sendero Valle** leads to **La Cascada**, a triple waterfall, and continues via the valley of the Río Peñas Blancas to **Pocosol**, about 20 km south of Fortuna. It's a full-day hike (20 km). Alternately, you can follow a three-km-long trail that begins behind Hotel Belmar and hike to the top of **Cerro Amigos** (1,842 meters).

Bring warm clothing and raingear. You may rent boots in many hotels and at the visitor cen-

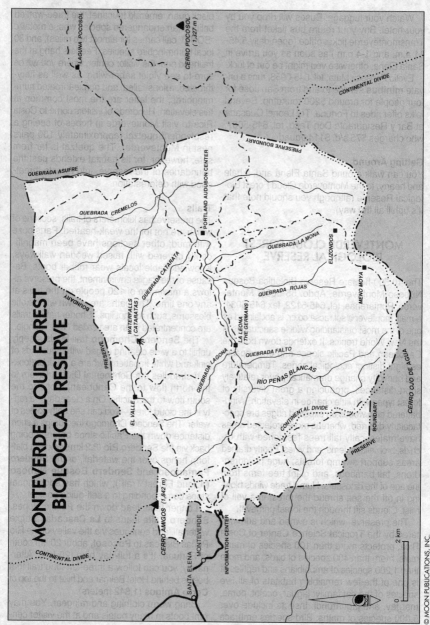

MONTEVERDE CLOUD FOREST
BIOLOGICAL RESERVE

© MOON PUBLICATIONS, INC.

0   2 km

THE DISAPPEARANCE OF THE GOLDEN TOAD

One of Monteverde's several claims to fame is the inch-long golden toad, an endemic species that is supposedly both deaf and dumb. Monteverde is the only known home of this brilliant neon-orange toad—supposedly the brightest toad in the world. But don't expect to see one. It may already be extinct. Although in 1986 it could be seen in large quantities, by 1988 very few remained. To my knowledge, no confirmed sightings have been made since. No one is sure whether or not the demise of *sapo dorado (Bufo periglenes)* is related to the global diminution of frog populations during the last decade.

BOB RACE

ter ($1), or you may buy a pair in Santa Elena for about $10. You can rent binoculars at the visitor center for $10 per day (plus deposit).

When to Visit

Temperatures range 13-24° C (55-75° F). Average annual rainfall is 242 cm (97 inches), falling mostly between June and November. A drier climate prevails Dec.-April, though windswept mists remain common and driving rain a possibility. However, strong winds push in, especially Dec.-February. February-May, quetzals are in the cloud forest. Later, they migrate downhill, where they can be seen around the hotels of Monteverde. The wet season is one of best times to visit: there are fewer people—a vital consideration, for the reserve limits entry to only 100 people every three hours.

Early morning and late afternoon are the best times to see birds, including hummingbirds, which can be seen feeding outside the information hut. Just after dawn is a good time to spot quetzals, which are particularly active in the early morning,

especially in the mating season (April and May). Midmorning peak hours are to be avoided.

Guides and Guided Tours

Hike with a guide. Although you can hike through the preserve on your own, you increase your chances of seeing quetzals and other wildlife if you hike with a guide. Guided tours *(caminatas)* are offered daily at 7:30 a.m., 8 a.m., 8:30 a.m., and 1 p.m. (minimum three people, maximum nine people; $15 pp plus entrance, including 40-minute slide show). A half-day birding tour leaves from the cheese factory at 6 a.m. ($25, including entrance). You can make reservations a day in advance—tel. 645-5112. Tours at other times may be arranged through your hotel or directly with guides (upward of $12 pp, half-day). A night hike is offered at 7:30 p.m. ($13); call 645-5118 or 645-5311 for reservations.

You can arrange a guide at the information center or through your hotel. Most are fluent in English. Recommended guides include: Samuel Arguedas, tel. 645-5112; Erick Bollo, tel. 645-5291; Pedro Bosque, tel. 645-5268; Gary Diller, tel. 645-5045; Debra Dorusior, tel. 645-5220; Marc Egar, tel. 645-5187; Ricky Guindon, tel. 645-5280; Tomas Guindon, tel. 645-5118; Koki Quesada, tel. 645-5220; Alex Villegas, tel. 645-5343.

Information

The park is open daily 7 a.m.-4 p.m. Entrance costs $8 adults, $4 students (with student card only), $2 residents, $1 national students, free for children under 12. A store at the entrance offers a self-guide pamphlet and trail map; you can also buy more detailed maps plus wildlife guides. If you want to hike alone, buy your ticket the day before and set out before the crowds. You can rent rubber boots at the store. There's a restaurant and hostel here, too.

Accommodations

The visitor's center and field station includes simple laboratory facilities and dormitory-style lodging and kitchens for up to 30 people (call 645-5276 for reservations). Of course, scientists and students get priority. Rates: $21, including all meals. Three basic backpacking shelters are located throughout the preserve. They have showers and hydro-electricity, plus propane stoves, pots, pans, and bunks, but you'll need to bring food and sleep-

MONTEVERDE CONSERVATION LEAGUE

Monteverde provides an excellent example for the Costa Rican government to learn how to make money from tourists while protecting an area from the adverse impacts of tourism. Despite its success, however, the preserve needs a bigger area to protect many animal species. The fact that the majority of sites used by local quetzals are outside the reserve shows the importance of protecting adjacent lands threatened by loggers and farmers. Recent efforts have gone into expanding the protected area. The Monteverde Conservation League—a nonprofit community conservation organization founded in 1986—is gradually buying back deforested land and virgin rainforest on the slopes of Monteverde. Since 1988, the reforestation program has helped almost 200 farmers plant more than 300,000 trees as windbreaks for pasture and crops, as well as supplying firewood, fence posts, and lumber.

Land purchase is only the first step toward long-term forest preservation. The next is to provide an al-

ternative means for local communities to earn money. The league—which has 40 employees, 90% of them Costa Rican—is developing programs to train local residents to become naturalist guides so that the surrounding community can profit from tourism. It is also using tourism as a focus for educating local children, including taking youngsters into the reserve for natural-history education. The environmental-education staff works in 10 primary schools in Monteverde and La Tigra to implement ecological programs. Training for teachers as well as community leaders and organized women's groups is also under way. The league is seeking an easy and effective method of teaching English and needs better materials than government schooling provides. Suggestions and assistance are welcomed.

The League's office, Apdo. 10165, San José 1000, tel. 645-2953, fax 645-1104, is opposite the gas station in Monteverde; here you can pick up the League's bimonthly newsletter *Tapir Tracks* (free with donations of $25 or more).

ing bag. Trail crews and researchers get priority. Rates: $3 nightly. Reservations are advised, especially for weekends; contact the Monteverde Biological Cloud Forest Preserve, Apdo. 10165, San José 1000, tel. 645-5212. A deposit is required, 45 days in advance. A wide range of accommodations are available in Santa Elena and along the road to the reserve. The closest hotel is about 1.2 km below the reserve.

Getting There
A bus departs the Banco Nacional in Santa Elena for the reserve at 6:20 a.m. and 1 p.m., returning at noon and 4 p.m. (80 cents each way). A bus for local workers departs from the Hotel Imán at 6:15 a.m. and goes all the way to the reserve, stopping en route for anyone flagging it down (tourists pay about $1). The return bus departs the reserve at 1 p.m. and 4 p.m.

There's parking near the entrance. Most hotels can also arrange transportation. Otherwise you can walk up the hill: muddy when wet, dusty when dry. A taxi from Santa Elena will cost about $5 one-way, but there are reports of gouging in recent years (one reader says he was charged $15 roundtrip).

Donations
The reserve relies on private funding. Donations should be sent to the Tropical Science Center, P.O. Box 8-3870, San José 1000; in the U.S., to Friends of the Monteverde Cloud Forest, P.O. Box 6255, Zephyrhills, FL 33540, tel./fax (813) 780-1946. You may also make contributions c/o the Tropical Science Center, Apdo. 8-3870, San José 1000. United States citizens wishing to make tax-deductible donations should make checks payable to the National Audubon Society, earmarked for the Monteverde Biological Cloud Forest Preserve, National Audubon Society, 950 Third Ave., New York, NY 10022.

For more donation information, call the Monteverde Cloud Forest Ecological Center, tel. 645-3550.

SANTA ELENA CLOUD FOREST RESERVE

This 600-hectare cloud forest reserve is five km northeast of Santa Elena, at a slightly higher elevation than the Monteverde Biological Cloud Forest Preserve (4WD required). The reserve is owned by the Santa Elena community. It boasts virtually all the species claimed by its eastern neighbor—quetzals, deer, sloths, ocelots, and howler and capuchin monkeys—plus spider monkeys, which are absent from the Monteverde reserve. It receives far fewer visitors: it may thus be easier to see a greater diversity of birds. It has four one-way trails (from 1.4 to 4.8 km) and a lookout point with views toward Volcán Arenal. At a higher elevation than Monteverde, it tends to be cloudier and wetter.

The reserve is the site of the **Monteverde Cloud Forest Ecological Center,** tel. 645-3550, a forest farm started in March 1992 to educate youngsters and local farmers on forest ecology and conservation. There's also a visitor/information center. Guides are available. Dormitory accommodations for students are under construction. Organizers hope to expand this to include a laboratory, library, and kitchen. The accommodations will eventually be available to tourists. The Santa Elena community continues to raise money to buy land adjacent to the reserve and to reforest this area to create a buffer zone, prevent hotel development, and protect the vital nesting areas for endangered species. Donations are welcome (call the center for details) The foundation is appealing to high schools to "adopt" the project.

Information

The foundation offers three-hour guided tours, including night tours ($13 pp). For information, visit the Santa Elena Reserve office in Santa Elena, or contact Monteverde Cloud Forest Ecological Center Foundation,, Apdo. 75, Santa Elena 5655, Monteverde, tel. 645-5390, fax 645-5014. Hours: daily 7 a.m.-4 p.m. Entrance: $7, $3.50 students. You can buy trail maps, a self-guided trail booklet, and rent rubber boots at the information center.

There's a cafe. A *hospedaje* is soon to be added; it will feature bunk beds and provide meals.

BOSQUE ETERNO DE LOS NIÑOS

A Monteverde Conservation League project that has caught the imagination of children and adults around the world is the Children's Eternal Forest, the first international children's rainforest in the world and the largest private reserve in Central America. It abuts Monteverde Biological Cloud Forest Preserve to the north and east. The dream of a rainforest saved by children began in 1987 at a small primary school in rural Sweden. A study of tropical forests prompted nine-year-old Roland Teinsuu to ask what he could do to keep the rainforest and the animals who live in it safe from destruction. Young Roland's question launched a group campaign to raise money to help the Monteverde Conservation League buy and save threatened rainforest in Costa Rica. With the guiding hand of teacher Eha Kern and her husband Bernd, and the assistance of tropical biologist Sharon Kinsman, who introduced the Monteverde project to the school, Roland and his classmates raised enough money to buy six hectares of rainforest at a cost of $250 per hectare, including surveying, title search, and legal fees connected with purchase.

Out of this initial success a group of children dedicated to saving the tropical rainforest formed Barnens Regnskog ("Children's Rain Forest"). The vision took hold. As the spirit sweeps across other lands, groups are forming to send contributions from the far corners of the globe. Fundraising projects have been as varied as a child's imagination. Children have collected aluminum cans and glass, baked cookies for sale with rainforest ingredients (ginger, chocolate, vanilla), or asked for a parcel of rainforest as a Christmas or birthday gift (land-purchase cost is $100 per 0.4 hectare). One-fifth of every donation goes into an endowment fund for protection and maintenance of the forest.

The original six-hectare preserve, established near Monteverde in 1988, has grown to more than 18,652 hectares and counting, bordering three sides of the Monteverde Biological Cloud Forest Preserve. More land awaits purchase. Donations should be sent to the following addresses:

In Costa Rica: Bosque Eterno de los Niños, c/o Monteverde Conservation League, Apdo. 10165, San José 1000; **in the U.S.:** The Children's Rainforest, P.O. Box 936, Lewiston, ME 04240; **in Canada:** World Wildlife Fund, 60 St. Clair Ave. E., Suite 201, Toronto, Ont. M4T 1N5; **in the U.K.:** Children's Tropical Forests U.K., The Old Rectory, Church St., Market Deeping, Peterborough PE6 8DA; **in Sweden:** Barnens

Regnskog, Pl 4471, Hagadal, 137 94 Väster-haninge; **in Japan:** Nippon Kodomo no Jungle, 386-22 Minenohara-Kogen, Suzaka, Nagano.

Information and Facilities

There are rustic cabins with fully equipped kitchens and showers, and three meals are served daily. Guides are available by request. There are two field stations: at **Poco Sol**, on the lower eastern slopes, with accommodations for 20 people and 10 km of hiking trails; and **San Gerardo**, at 1,220 meters elevation, a 3.5-km walk from the Santa Elena Cloud Forest Reserve, with accommodations for 26 people and six km of trails.

For information contact the Monteverde Conservation League, Apdo. 10165, San José 1000, tel. 645-2953, fax 645-1104.

ECOLODGE SAN LUÍS AND BIOLOGICAL STATION

This ecolodge, Apdo. 36, Santa Elena de Monteverde, tel./fax 645-5277, cellular tel. 380-3255, e-mail: smithdp@ctrvax.vanderbilt.edu, website www.greenarrow.com/nature/san_luis.htm; in the U.S., tel./fax (615) 297-2155 or tel. (800) 699-9685, doubles as an integrated tourism, research, and education project on a 70-hectare working farm at San Luís. Resident biologists work with members of the San Luís community to develop a model for sustainable development. There are fruit trees, vegetable gardens, coffee fields, and large stands of wildlife-rich primary and secondary forest, including cloud forest.

The station—the brainchild of Drs. Diana and Milton Lieberman—offers a wide range of activities: from horseback rides, birdwatching, cloud-forest hiking, and night walks to hands-on laboratory study (there's even a computer lab). All the while you get to intermingle with scientists, students, and community members. Guided hikes lead to Monteverde and to swimming holes in the Río San Luís. Open-air classes are given, with slide presentations and seminars, including an intensive seven-day tropical biology course ($130). And you can even help farm or participate in scientific research. It's one of the best models I know for getting to experience and appreciate Costa Rica's *campesino* culture.

Accommodations

Accommodations are in a cozy wood-paneled 30-bed bunkhouse—a former milking shed—with shared baths, and four rooms with 2-12 beds. It also has a four-room, 16-bed bungalow with private baths and verandas, plus 12 *cabinas* for 3-4 people each. Tico fare is cooked over a woodstove and served family style in the book-lined dining room; wash it down by coffee grown on the farm. Rates: $50 pp bunkhouse; $65 bungalow; $80 *cabina,* including all meals, taxes, and guided activities.

Getting There

The turn off to San Luís is immediately east of Hotel Fonda Vela on the road to the Monteverde reserve. Follow this eight km to the Alto San Luís school; turn right. The farm is one kilometer farther. From Monteverde, follow the Lagartos Road. The bus will drop you at the San Luís exit; if you call the lodge in advance, they'll arrange for a taxi to meet the bus. Otherwise, get off in Santa Elena and take a taxi.

MONTEVERDE TO TILARÁN

If traveling to Lake Arenal, you can avoid the long descent to the Pan-Am Highway and the 67-km journey via Cañas to Tilarán by following the rough dirt road west from Santa Elena via Cabeceras and Quebrada Grande (you cut out a lot of mileage, but unless you have a powerful 4WD vehicle you'll probably not save any time; allow a minimum of two hours). The roads are in a terribly muddy state. Worse, there are lots of junctions, and the roads are unsigned. Ask directions at every opportunity. Keep heading west and you're sure to emerge in Tilarán or onto the paved road from Cañas, just below Tilarán. It's beautiful scenery all the way.

Accommodations

Albergue Ecoturístico Monte de los Olivos, tel./fax 283-8305, Spanish only; or Sergio Pastor, tel. 283-5268, fax 283-9116, e-mail: wwfcii@sol.racsa.co.cr, is an ecotourist lodge in the hamlet of Monte los Olivos, near Las Nubes, seven km north of Monteverde. It's run by the local community with the assistance of various international nongovernmental aid organizations. The rustic yet enchanting lodge, which sits on stilts above a lake and is surrounded by forest, boasts four cabins with private baths and hot water plus five cabins in the biolgoical station with shared bath and hot water. There's a restaurant with panoramic views, and trails lead into the forest. A *mirador* offers views of Arenal Volcano. Guided horseback and hiking trips are offered. Rates: $17 s, $24 d, $29 t (40% less for shared bath).

TILARÁN

A road east from Cañas climbs 23 km to Tilarán, a spruce little highland town with a very pretty square and a park with cedars and pines in front of the church. It's the kind of place where after a full day of touring you might rest beneath a tall tree in the park until the tropical odors and the chime of a church bell or the distant braying of a mule lull you to sleep. At this elevation (550 meters), the air is crisp and stirred by breezes working their way over the crest of the Cordillera de Tilarán from Lake Arenal, five km to the northeast. The countryside hereabouts is reminiscent of the rolling hill country of England—the Mendips or Downs. The last weekend in April (and again in mid-June) Tilarán plays host to a rodeo and a livestock show, and the town fills up.

Accommodations

The **Hotel Tilarán**, tel. 695-5043, on the west of the plaza, has 28 simply furnished rooms, some with private baths but no fans. It has a restaurant. Rates: $5 shared bath; $7 private bath. **Hotel Central**, tel. 695-5363, has 12 basic rooms with shared baths, plus eight cabins with private baths. Rates: $5 rooms; $12 cabins. Alternately, try **Cabinas Hotel y Restaurante Mary**, tel. 695-5479, on the south side of the park, with basic rooms and rooms with TV and private baths with warm water. Rates: $8 s, $12 d basic; $20 s, $27 d for TV and private bath.

Cabinas El Sueño, tel. 695-5347, two blocks northwest of the plaza, is one of the best hotels for its price in the country. Twelve rooms, all with private baths with hot water, surround a sunlit second-floor courtyard with a fountain. Herman and Sonia Vargas, the super-friendly owners, provide fruit and toiletry baskets that

include shaving implements. Secure parking. Rates: $9 s, $15 d; $11 s $17 d with TV. Recommended. Downstairs is the hotel's **Restaurant El Parque**, with good seafood dishes.

The **Hotel Guadalupe**, tel. 695-5943, one block south and one east of the plaza, is also modern and attractive, with nine modestly furnished rooms for $10 s, $15 d, $18 t. Some rooms have TV, and there's a TV lounge. **Hotel Naralit**, tel. 695-5393, on the south side of the church, has 26 pleasing rooms with glass-enclosed porches and private baths. It's small but ultraclean and well-run and offers secure parking. Some cabins have cable TV. You'll find a restaurant next door. Rates: $20 s, $28 d with hot water.

Food

Be sure to check out **La Carreta**, tel. 695-6654, fax 695-6593, an Italian restaurant—and local gathering place—with two oxcarts on the front porch, one block east of the church. Here, Billie and Tom Jafek dish up creative sandwiches with homemade bread, pizzas ($2.50-4), and dinners such as baked chicken florentine ($8). They offer a free *refresco*.

Restaurant El Parque, below Cabinas El Sueño, is a good bet. **Mary's Restaurant**, tel. 695-5891, is also recommended and doubles as a tourist information center. Across the street, on the west side of the plaza, is **Bambú Bar/Restaurante Catalá**. **Soda Stefanie** is also reportedly popular; it's 50 meters west of Hotel Grecia. Chef Don Raoul at **Restaurant Catalá** conjures up tasty burgers, roast tenderloin, smoky pork chops, and tender roast chicken with creamy mashed potatoes and yucca.

Information

Tom at **La Carreta** runs a tourist information center. He's extremely friendly and helpful. He also guides tours to see the "Big Tree," a ceiba with a 10-meter base. You can check and send e-mail messages or send faxes. It has a book exchange too.

Lake Arenal Tours, tel. 695-5292, offers sportfishing, boat rental, and water-skiing. **Aventuras Tilarán**, tel./fax 695-5008, rents windsurfers and mountain bikes, and offers mountain biking, windsurfing, fishing trips, and horseback rides.

Services

A **Banco Nacional,** tel. 695-5028, is on the southwest corner of the park. There's also a **Banco de Costa Rica,** tel. 695-5117, and **Cooptilará,** two blocks north of the church, represents **Western Union** and has a 24-hour automatic credit machine for Visa and any cards compatible with the Plus system. There are several pharmacies.

Getting There

Buses depart San José for Tilarán from Calle 14, Avenidas 9/11 (Autotransportes Tilarán, tel. 222-3854), daily at 7:30 a.m., 12:45 p.m., 3:45 p.m., and 6:30 p.m. (four hours via Cañas). The bus continues to Nuevo Arenal. Local buses depart Cañas for Tilarán at 7:30 a.m., 9 a.m., 11 a.m., and 3 p.m. Buses depart Ciudad Quesada (San Carlos) for Tilarán via Fortuna, Tabacón, and Nuevo Arenal daily at 6 a.m. and 3 p.m., tel. 460-0326 (four hours). Return buses depart Tilarán for San José at 7 a.m., 7:45 a.m., 2 p.m., and 5 p.m.; and for Ciudad Quesada at 7 a.m. and 1 p.m. Buses also depart for Puntarenas at 6 a.m. and 1 p.m. The bus station is one block north of the plaza.

Olmec-influenced ax-shaped jade pendant

A bus for Tilarán departs Santa Elena daily at 7 a.m.; returning at 1 p.m. (three hours).

Getting Around

For taxis call **Unidos Tilarán,** tel. 695-5324, or hail one on the west side of the plaza.

LAKE ARENAL

This picture-perfect lake—12,400 hectares—might have been transplanted from the English Lake District, surrounded as it is by mountains kept perpetually emerald-green by winds from the Caribbean that sweep through the gap in the cordillera. The looming mass of Volcán Are-

nal rises over the lake to the east. About 2-3 million years ago, tectonic movements created a depression that filled with a small lagoon. In 1973, the Costa Rican Institute of Electricity (ICE) built a 88-meter-long, 56-meter-tall dam at the eastern end of the valley, raising the level of the lagoon and creating a narrow 32-km-long reservoir. Recent satellite photos have identified several ancient Indian settlements at the bottom of the lake; archaeological studies suggest they may be as much as 2,000 years old.

ICE has installed a tiara of wind turbines atop the ridgecrest along the southwest shore, fed by the howling winds for which Lake Arenal is famous. In the morning the lake can look like a mirror. The calm is short-lived. More normal are nearly constant 30- to 80-kph winds, which whip up whitecaps. November-April, winds up to 100 kph turn the lake into one of the world's top windsurfing spots. It has even been promoted as "a rival to Oregon's Columbia Gorge," though avid windsurfers tell me that that's a bit of a stretch. Water temperatures remain at 18-21° C (65-70° F) year-round. Swells can top one meter. Says local windsurfing aficionado Jean Paul Cazedessus: "None of this, 'Last week it was ripping!' to be heard at Lake Arenal. It's every day, all day. Twenty-five mph is the *average* winter day's wind speed." Adds local surf expert Norman List, "Out here I've seen people get 30 feet of air. Speed is boring. We're out trying to do loops, jumps, jibes, and acrobatics!"

The lake (545 meters above sea level) and volcano are incorporated into the recently created Arenal National Park, a polyglot assemblage encompassing the pristine cloud-forest terrain that extends eastward to Monteverde. The climate shifts eastward and the northeastern shores are backed by thick primary forest. The views from here are fantastic.

The lake is easily reached from Fortuna in the northern lowlands or via the road from

Tilarán. The road swings around the north side of the lake, linking the two towns (don't succumb to the temptation to just go careening along—the next bend may deliver you into an almighty pothole). East of Nuevo Arenal the road is unpaved and notoriously abysmal. Mammoth depressions and potholes. Washboard corrugations. Whole sections washed out by frequent landslides. Though the road had been recently graded, when I drove it last it was already badly eroded in places. (This section of road is under San José's jurisdiction; the road west of Nuevo Arenal is under local jurisdiction. In 1997, local expats grew so fed up with waiting for repairs that they descended on the MOPT office in San José, but ended up paying for and enacting their own road repairs.)

A dirt road winds around the southern rim via Tronadora, east of which it deteriorates rapidly and requires a 4WD. You'll pass only a few homesteads and two tiny hamlets. There are several rivers to ford. (I once drove the "road" at night in a Range Rover during torrential rains but could get no farther than the Río Chiquito, where a bridge was in the process of being washed away.) You can tackle it from the east via the access road to Arenal Volcano National Park.

Lake Coter is a small lake, five km northwest of Nuevo Arenal (signs for Eco-Adventure Lodge direct you along the dirt road). There are watersports but no fishing. There's a small **butterfly farm** at the Eco-Lodge. The road curls around the south shore of Coter, crests the cordillera, and descends through the valley of the Río Quequer to San Rafael de Guatuso, in the northern lowlands. Another dirt road that begins just west of Toad Hall leads over the cordillera to Venado Caverns, where you can crawl around and get muddy in pursuit of stalactites and blind fish.

The area is enjoying a tourism boom, and hotels are springing up like weeds, backed by tours of every description, many based out of Fortuna in the northern lowlands. The only town along the entire perimeter is Nuevo Arenal.

Nuevo Arenal

The small town, on the north-central shore, 32 km northeast of Tilarán, was created in 1973 when the manmade lake flooded the original settlement. There is nothing of tourist interest in town, though fishing trips are offered.

Arenal Botanical Gardens

This marvelous garden, tel. 695-4273, fax 694-4086, e-mail: exoticseeds@hotmail.com, four km east of Nuevo Arenal, blooms on the Continental Divide and harbors 2,200 rare tropical species, including a panoply of Costa Rican plants: anthuriums, bromeliads, ferns, even roses, plus orchids galore, not least all six species of gorguras. There's even an Asian garden with waterfalls. The collection of heliconias and ginger is particularly splendid. Birdlife and butterflies abound. Should you be awed and need to rest and absorb it all, benches plus a fruit and juice bar provide the means. Visitors are limited to 20 per hour. A booklet corresponds to the numbered displays. Trails also lead through the adjacent farm. The owner, Michael LeMay, like any true Englishman, can be seen coddling his roses with solicitude in even the rainiest weather. Open daily 9 a.m.-5 p.m. (closed October). Entrance: $4.

Accommodations

Hotels are listed in clockwise order from Tilarán.

Camping: You can camp at Mirador Los Lagos (see below) for $5.

Shoestring: In Nuevo Arenal try **Cabinas Rodríguez**, tel. 694-4237, with 12 small and basic but clean rooms with wood-paneled walls and ceiling. Room quality varies. There's a laundry. Rates: $5 pp shred bath, $7 private bath. **Cabinas El Río**, tel. 694-4007, has dormitories for $10 pp.

Budget: At Tronadora, **JJ's Bed and Breakfast**, tel. 695-5825, is a charming looking cottage with lake views and gardens. Not reviewed. Nearby, **Cabinas Puerto San Luis**, tel. 695-5797, has four simple cabins by the lakeshore with private bath and hot water, plus a restaurant popular with locals. Rates: $20 s/d.

Cabinas Chico y Meri, tel. 695-5427 or 695-5430, four km west of Nuevo Arenal, has six basic, dingy *cabinas* with private baths and hot water. You'll also find cheap *cabinas* for rent nearby in the hamlet of Guadalajara.

Mirador Los Lagos, Apdo. 182, Tilarán 5710, tel. 694-4271, fax 694-4290, run by a gringo couple, Leslie and Frank Scraggins, is set amid 10 acres—much of it forested—two km west of Nuevo Arenal. It has 11 *cabinas* with private rock-walled baths, and verandas with chairs for enjoying the views. The lofty open-air restaurant with fireplace is popular with locals and serves freshly caught seafood; open 3-8 p.m. There's a *mirador* nearby on a separate hilltop. Biking ($10 per hour) and horseback rides ($8 per hour) are offered, as well as canopy tour in the forest, boat trips on the lake, plus tours to Cote Lagoon, Monteverde, Venado Caves, and Arenal Volcano. One reader claims that money was stolen when placed in the care of the management. Rates: $25 d, $15 extra person. A backpacker special is $10 pp.

La Casona del Lago, tel. 695-5008 or 231-4266, also known as Albergue Tilarán, is affiliated with the youth hostel system and has four rooms, each with four bunks. It's about two km east of Nuevo Arenal. Rates: $15 IYHF members; $25 nonmembers, including breakfast.

East of Nuevo Arenal, the Tico-run **La Alondra,** tel. 284-5575, has a restaurant plus 10 pretty, modern *cabinas* with verandas, private baths with hot water, and lake views. Rates: $30 d, including tax and breakfast.

Inexpensive: Hotel Bahía Azul, Apdo. 2, Tilarán, tel. 695-5750, fax 695-5387, in a sheltered cove at Tronadora, has 19 rooms, all with private baths, roomy showers, and hot water, on sloping landscaped grounds. Basic and somewhat dated rooms are sparsely furnished and have TVs, plus verandas with lake views. A small restaurant overlooks the grounds and a larger one overlooks the lake. You can rent paddleboats, water-skis, and sailboards. Rates: $35 s, $42 d, $50 t.

The hillside **Mystica Lake Lodge,** Apdo. 29, Tilarán, cellular tel. 284-3841, fax 695-5387, run by an Italian couple, Barbara Moglia and Francesco Carullo, has six large, simply furnished rooms and equally spacious bathrooms. Each has desks, open closets, and odd, delightful touches. You can sit on your veranda festooned by an arbor and admire the landscaped grounds cascading to the lake below. Barbara cooks wholesome breakfasts, served in the kitchen, while dinners are served in a cozy, high-ceilinged restaurant complete with a fireplace. Rate: $30 s, $40 d low season; 35 s, $45 d high season, including breakfast.

Xiloe Lodge, Apdo. 35, Tilarán, tel. 259-9806, fax 259-9882, is a family ranch offering very pleasant, rustic ranch-style *cabinas* set amid lawned grounds. Options include spacious three-bedroom *cabinas* with kitchenettes; an older bungalow under a massive shady tree, with kitchenette, terrace, and its own barbecue pit; or two basic two-bedroom *cabinas* sleeping four. Each unit has a private balcony and a private bath with hot water. In addition, a large cabin sleeps six people. There's a small circular swimming pool, plus a river that runs through the property. The **Equus BBQ** is here. Guided horseback rides cost $6 per hour. Rates: $13 three-bedroom *cabina;* $17 bungalow or two-bedroom *cabina;* $42 cabin.

Vista Linda Inn, tel./fax 661-1363, has four pretty, clean, albeit rustic, chalets with lofty wooden ceilings, tile floors, quaint stone private bathrooms with hot water, and stone porches with views through lush ferns. Rates: $29 s, $35 d, $10 extra person.

Rock River Lodge, tel. 222-4547, fax 221-3011, has six romantic Santa Fe-style cabins and nine bungalows with private baths and hot water. A very beautiful open-air restaurant has a magnificent stone fireplace in a Western-style lounge, with hardwood tables and chairs overlooking the lake. A large bar features an open-stove barbecue pit. The lodge rents mountain bikes and a catamaran. Owner Norman List runs the Tico Wind windsurf center. Rates: $45 d, $65 bungalows, $10 extra person.

Villas Alpino, fax 695-5387, one of the best bargains around, has five rustic yet spacious self-contained Swiss-style cabins perched loftily on the hillside above sweeping lawns. Each has abundant hardwood decor, a double bed and bunk with tasteful Guatemalan fabrics, plentiful light, free beer in the fridge, and a veranda for enjoying the views. Each also has a carport. Dutch owner Ernesto de Le Ones operates to high standards. Rates: $35 for up to four people. *Recommended!*

Hotel y Restaurante La Rana de Arenal is a modern, German-owned place with seven rustic cabins and two apartments on landscaped grounds with lake views. All have private baths and hot water. The restaurant leans towards the Teutonic (schnitzel Vienna-style, $7), but also has spaghetti and *típico* dishes. Rates: $25 s, $35 d, including breakfast.

Hotel Alturas del Arenal, Apdo. 166, San José 1007, tel. 694-4039, fax 280-5778, is an upscale, albeit slightly tarnished, place run by a young gringa-Ecuadorian couple who had recently taken over when I called by and were applying some much-needed vigor. It offers 10 small rooms with private baths, plus a restaurant (breakfast only) with terra-cotta tiles and log supports reaching to the roof. The small lounge has a large TV. The lodge overlooks landscaped gardens with a jacuzzi and a freshwater pool fed by natural springs. It offers fishing, boat, and horse trips, plus windsurfing. Rates: $40 d, including breakfast.

Two friendly Great Danes—Max and Minka—welcome guests to the American-run **Chalet Nicholas,** Apdo. 72, Tilarán 5710, tel./fax 694-4041, a splendid three-bedroom Colorado-style guesthouse reached up a bougainvillea-lined driveway two km west of Nuevo Arenal (at road marker Km 48). It exudes charm and all the comforts of home—including private bathrooms festooned with fluffy towels. Two bedrooms are downstairs. A spiral staircase winds up to a larger "semi-private" loft bedroom with cozy sitting room boasting a deck good for birding. All rooms have volcano views, orthopedic mattresses, and intriguing wall-hangings. The inn proffers a TV lounge with video library, a fruit orchard and orchid house, plus hiking and horseback riding ($20, three hours) along trails into an adjacent forest reserve. The organic meals get rave reviews. Americans owners John and Catherine Nicholas top it all with fine hospitality. A splendid bargain. Rates: $49 d, including breakfast; $10 extra person. *Recommended!*

In Nuevo Arenal is the rather soulless, U.S.-run **Hotel Aurora Inn Bed & Breakfast,** tel. 694-4245, fax 694-4262, with seven rooms in the main building, and six cabins facing the lake. The lobby has a satellite TV. Rooms are carpeted and comfortably furnished but homely, even dowdy. It has a petting zoo with monkeys, and a large sundeck with a jacuzzi and a swimming pool with views. A handsome stone-and-timber restaurant hosts occasional dances. Rates: $35 s, $45 d, $55 t, including breakfast.

Moderate: The striking **Hotel Joya Sureña,** tel. 694-4057, fax 694-4059, e-mail: joysur@sol.racsa.co.cr, website www.allgoods.com/joya-surena, one km northeast of Nuevo Arenal (and reached by a skunk of a road), offers 28 handsome rooms in the main lodge, plus rustic *cabinas* on a three-hectare working coffee plantation. Rooms are painted with tropical murals and have telephones, TVs, orthopedic mattresses, and private baths; they vary from standard (two twins or a double) to elegant suites accommodating four adults. Highlights include a restaurant with the roof held aloft by fluted columns, a lounge, a billiards room, and a sauna. Walking paths lead to secluded spots good for meditation. There's a small swimming pool with spacious sundeck and a tennis court, plus boats, horses, and bikes for rent. The Canadian owned complex boasts solar heating and a "micro-biodigester." Rates: $55 s, $65 d standard; $65 s, $75 d deluxe.

The charming **Villa Decary,** Nuevo Arenal 5717, Tilarán, cellular tel. 383-3012, fax 694-4330, is a small country inn on a former fruit and coffee *finca* on three hilly hectares, two km west of the botanical gardens. The contemporary two-story structure glows with light pouring in through French doors and windows. Hardwood furniture gleams. Five large bedrooms each have bright Guatemalan covers, plus a private bath and a balcony with a handy rail that serves as bench and table. There's also a bungalow with kitchenette. Gardens were being planted, and trails offer great birding in the surrounding forest. A deck offers great birding, too, plus views. Howler monkeys come down to the property. I ate breakfast to soothing classical music. A spa is planned. Gay-friendly. Popular with birders. Rates: $49 s, $59 d, $69 casita, including full breakfast. *A bargain!*

La Ceiba Tree Lodge, Apdo. 9, Tilarán, tel./fax 694-4297, e-mail: fingrspm@sol.racsa.co.cr, a small German-run bed and breakfast amid a 16-hectare farm that swathes the hillside about six km east of town and is shaded by a mammoth ceiba tree. It's reached via a very steep, very narrow lane lined with tropical flowers. Four large rooms have plenty of light, plus private baths with hot water. Ursula's oil paintings abound. Go hiking or birding in the private forest reserve, help milk the goats, or simply relax on the veranda beneath the huge ceiba tree and watch the profusion of birds. The place is popular with birders, who head off along nearby trails. You can rent a sailboat. Rates: $30 s, $50 d, including breakfast.

Hotel Tilawa, Apdo. 92, Tilarán 5710, tel. 695-5050, fax 695-5766; in the U.S., tel. (800) 851-8929, inspired by the Palace of Knossos on Crete, is a model of Minoan simplicity carried into the hillsides of Costa Rica. It has 24 rooms and four junior suites with magnificent views over the lake. Thick bulbous columns, walls painted with flowers and dolphins, and ocher pastels play on the Cretan theme. All very atmospheric (but urgently in need of a spruce up when I called by last). The rooms are spacious, simple, and beautiful, with hardwood ceilings, orthopedic mattresses, direct-dial telephones, decor of subdued rough-painted pastels, and bedspreads from Guatemala. Each has two queen-size beds and airy private bathrooms with hot water. Junior suites have kitchenettes, couches, and TVs. A bar and restaurant are shielded from the winds by floor-to-ceiling windows. The Delfin bar offers drinks and snacks beside a swimming pool. The hotel offers car rental, a tennis court, mountain biking ($10 per hour), horseback rides ($10), plus fishing, sailboat tours, and more. It also operates the Tilawa Viento Surf Center. Rates: $51 s; $66 s, $127 d suites. Special packages are offered.

Eco-Lodge, Apdo. 85570-1000, San José, tel. 257-5075, fax 257-7065, is an extremely elegant hardwood-and-brick structure in expansive landscaped grounds on the hills west of Lake Coter. A cozy lounge with deep-cushioned sofas is centered on a large open-hearth fireplace. The lodge has a games room, a lounge bar, and a pleasing restaurant. The 30 rooms with hardwood walls are fairly small and modest, each with double bed and bunk. All share his-and-hers communal baths. A better bet are the four-person duplex cabins atop the hill, with heaps of windows and patios offering great views. The lodge offers guided hiking ($15), horseback ($20) and mountain-bike rides, canoeing ($15), fishing ($50), and watersports, plus tours throughout the region. About 29 km of trails lead through the forest. Most guests arrive in package groups. Rates: $55 d standard; $75 d *cabinas*.

The Swiss-owned **Hotel & Restaurant Los Héroes,** tel./fax 441-4193, is a chalet-style hotel with hints of the Alps at every turn: three Tyrolean lodges replete with gingerbread trim, a Tyrolean chapel, and a Tyrolean restaurant. Twelve nicely appointed rooms feature brass beds. Some have bathtubs and balconies. Upper story rooms are larger. International cuisine is served in the restaurant. Highlights include a pool and jacuzzi, plus stables for horseback rides, and even a boat—*Im-*

possible Dream—for dinner and sunset cruises. Owner Hans Ulrich maintains the place to Swiss standards. Rates: $55 d; $65 d with balcony; $75 d mini-suite, including continental breakfast. Two fully furnished, two-bedroom apartments are available ($115 for up to six people).

Hotel Linda Vista Del Norte, tel. 235-9743, fax 236-6105, e-mail: lindav@vanweb.com; in the U.S., SJO 667, P.O. Box 025240, Miami, FL 33102, enjoys a splendid position with views of both lake and volcano. It's atop a hill on a cattle and horse ranch adjoining a 210-hectare private forest reserve with trails. It has 10 modestly furnished yet attractive cabins with ceiling fans, patios, and large walk-in showers with hot water. One reader thought the rooms were "damp" and the mattresses "uncomfortable." The restaurant also has views (meals cost about $5). There's a laundry. Guided horseback tours are offered to waterfalls ($12; three hours), Volcán Arenal ($20; four hours), and Monteverde ($45 one-way, including lunch; a driver will deliver your car for you to pick up). Rates: $35 s, $51 d, $61 t low season; $47 s, $65 d, $75 t high season, including taxes and breakfast.

The exquisite **Arenal Vista Lodge,** Apdo. 818, San José 1200, tel. 381-1428 or 220-1712, fax 232-3321, two km west at the small community of Pueblo Nuevo, perches on a landscaped terraced hill with a private forest reserve behind. Twenty-five handsome, Swedish-inspired cabins squat on the slopes and feature vast picture windows with window boxes and small balconies with lake views. Each has a private bath with hot water. A dining room and terrace offer panoramic lake and volcano views. Food from the set meal has been called "hohum." There are wide options for activities and touring, plus trails into the forest. You'll need a 4WD to ford two rivers. Rates: $60 s, $70 d.

Expensive: The **Marina Club Hotel,** Apdo. 31, La Fortuna, tel./fax 284-6573, eight km east of Nuevo Arenal, is the most beautiful place for miles. Its stunning setting—grassy meadows sweeping down the hill and grazed by horses— is complemented by bougainvilleas clambering over bamboo rails and 14 luxury *cabinas* with views over the lake (18 more were planned). Each has a mezzanine bedroom with king-size bed, low-lit lamps, and timbered ceiling, with a small lounge below. Radio and CD players are standard (no TVs). Each *cabina* has its own color scheme of tropical pastels. French doors open onto a veranda with Sarchí rockers. Each, too, has its own sheltered carport. Two exquisite, voluminous suites boast polished stone floors with throw rugs, open fireplaces, soaring wooden ceilings, king-size beds, colonial-tiled bathrooms, and kitchenettes with wooden fridge. The former barn is now an open-air bar (shaped like a ship's prow) and restaurant, extremely rustic and decorated with nautical motifs. Peggy serves excellent dinners ($15). The property has a swimming pool, horses, and even its own marina with two catamarans and windsurfers for hire. Waterfowl inhabit the lake below. Rates: $75 d low season; $89 high season, including breakfast and horseback riding; $125 suite.

Arenal Lodge, Apdo. 1195, Escazú 1250, tel. 228-3189, fax 289-6798, e-mail: arenal@sol.racsa. co.cr, website www.centralamerica.com/cr/hotelarlodge.htm; in the U.S., tel. (800) 235-3625, at the extreme east of the lake, is a Spanish colonial-style lodge with an inviting atmosphere. The 29 spacious and attractive rooms—some with volcano view (none with lake view)—include doubles, junior suites, and a full suite, all with private baths and hot showers, and all in wood with wall-to-wall louvered windows. Some dingy rooms (no views) are in an atrium courtyard covered by a tacky plastic skylight. There's a library, a lounge bar with a large stone fireplace, CNN on TV, and a full-size pool table, plus a beautiful restaurant with an all-around window facing toward Arenal and a deck on which to rock and contemplate the view. The lodge specializes in fishing ($250 d per day, with guide); and an evening volcano tour ($30) and a "birding by boat" tour ($25) are available. You reach the lodge via a dauntingly steep, two-km-long road. Rates: $50 s, $55 d no view (overpriced), $81 s, $87 d junior suite, $98 s, $107 d chalet, $118 s, $128 d master suite low season; $62 s, $68 d no view, $101 s, $108 d junior suite, $122 s, $133 d chalet, $147 s, $160 d master suite high season.

Food

Most hotels have restaurants. Check out **Los Heroes** where the French-Swiss menu includes beef bouillon ($1.50), smoked pork cutlet ($4), and fondue ($1.75), washed down with kirsch ($2.50). The charming **Mystica Lake Lodge**

restaurant has a splendid menu: pasta al pomodoro ($4), 12 types of pizzas ($5), and a large Italian wine list. And the **Hotel Tilawa** restaurant has four specials daily ($4-8): beef stroganoff and Hawaiian chicken are typical.

The **Equus Bar,** adjoining the Xiloe Lodge, is a cozy "corral guanacasteco" grill that offers delicious smoked chicken and grilled meats cooked in an open-hearth oven. Very atmospheric. Closed Monday.

The drive along the north shore is worth it merely to arrive at **Toad Hall,** tel./fax 479-9178, where San Francisco transplant Kim West and hubby (a Brit) runs an Aladdin's cave, equal parts deli, cafe, gallery, book shop, and general store. After browsing the superb arts, crafts, and clothing, settle on the outside balcony and admire the view over coffee and divine desserts. You can even buy a Cuban cigar here (Cohibas cost $10 apiece) and smoke your stogie alfresco. Kim serves healthy breakfasts (banana pancakes, granola; $2-3) and California lunches. I enjoyed a grilled ginger sesame chicken salad with macadamia nuts and mango sesame dressing ($5).

On the southeast shore, 100 meters west of the Río Peñas Blancas (requiring a deep breath before fording) atop a muddy road that even my 4WD refused to climb, is the offbeat **Café de Crepe.** A German lady, Mutter Goduma, tel. 382-1288, runs this quaint New Age spot and serves coffee, hot chocolate, crepes (with fruit and alcohol) in a rough-hewn log hut with hammock seats and views. While you nibble, she gives meditative readings ("Ten minutes," she says, "it's not a deep thing!").

Restaurante Chico y Meri, at the northwest corner of the lake, offers inexpensive *típico* meals (lunches average $2) served on a breezy open-air terrace.

In Nuevo Arenal, try **Restaurant Los Arcos,** tel. 695-5266, ext. 196, for Costa Rican fare; **Concha del Mar** for seafood; and the delightful **Tramonti,** tel. 695-5266, ext. 282, for highly praised pizzas baked in a wood-burning oven, and tasty fettucine served on an outdoor patio ($3-5). **Ristorante Italiano,** east of Nuevo Arenal, also serves pizzas and pastas.

Entertainment

The **Full Moon Disco** behind the Xiloe Lodge could be the wildest disco south of Acapulco.

This multitiered open-air hot spot clings to a valleyside, with stone terraces and log-and-thatch eaves. It gets jam-packed with revelers dancing under the moonlight. Even the howler monkeys get in the groove from the branches overhead—true. The place was boycotted for a while by locals because some girls claimed to have been possessed by the Devil here. The issue became a cause célèbre but an exorcist cleared the air, as it were, in late 1997. Saturday only. Entrance is free. Shots—*tragos*—cost 75 cents; beers cost $1.25. Owner Fernando Calderón sometimes has informal **horseraces** on a "country-style track" near the lodge.

Pico's Discotheque used to crank it up at Restaurante Chico y Meri. The place looked forlorn when I last passed by.

Activities
Windsurfing and Watersports: November through January are the best, and June and October the worst months for windsurfing. The **Tilawa Viento Surf Center,** Apdo. 92, Tilarán, tel. 695-5050, fax 695-5766, on the southwest shore, has a rental fleet of ready-rigged boards. The center is on a leeward-access peninsula with side-shore wind, grassy rigging area, and protected cove. Bilingual staff offer complete lesson programs for all levels. They offer a money-back guarantee for beginners. Boards rent for $35-45 half day, $45-55 full day for guests of the Tilawa Hotel ($10 extra for call-ins). The center also rents Hobie-cats ($60 half day, $90 full day) and sailboats ($50 half day, $70 full day), and a large catamaran is available for 20 people for skippered charters ($18 per hour). A small restaurant is planned.

On the western shore is **Tico Wind Surf Center,** fax 695-5387; in the U.S., tel. (503) 386-5524 or (800) 678-2252, fax (503) 387-3300, website www.outworld.compuserve.com/home-pages/ticowind, open Dec.-April 9 a.m.-6 p.m. Rentals are $35 half day, $57 full day including lunch. A week-long package costs $325 including wet suits, harnesses, and choice of board and sail. Private instruction is offered from beginner to advanced ($20 first hour, $15 additional). It also rents mountain bikes ($7-10 per hour, $28-35 daily).

Fishing: The lake is stocked with challenging game fish—*guapote, machaca,* and (for lighter

tackle enthusiasts) *mojarra. Guapote* (rainbow bass indigenous to Central America) is the most fierce fighter among the freshwater fish; a four-kg catch would be a trophy. The *machaca* (Central America's answer to American shad) is a relative of the piranha, whose voracious temperament it apparently shares. They weigh up to three kg and are supposedly very difficult to hook. *Mojarra*—described by angler Chet Young as "Costa Rica's bluegill with teeth!"—are also tricky to hook but are tasty. Most of the hotels hereabouts offer fishing tours; Hotel Tilawa charges $140 for four hours (up to four people). A local resident, **Natanael Murrillo,** tel. 479-9087, also offers fishing trips.

Horseback Rides: Several lodges offer horseback rides. **The Stable,** tel. 694-4092, fax 695-5387, five km west of Nuevo Arenal, rents horses ($30 half-day) on a 200-hectare farm with primary forest.

Tours
Most tour agencies in San José, Fortuna, and towns throughout Guanacaste offer tours of Lake Arenal, often in combination with a visit to Caño Negro or Monteverde. For example, **Agencia Mitur,** Apdo. 91, San José 1150, tel. 255-2031, fax 255-1946, has a two-day/one-night package that includes a cruise on the *Arenal Prince* and overnight on the shores of Lake Arenal (approximately $100). You can also enjoy a sunset cruise aboard the *The Impossible Dream,* tel. 228-9200, which is docked at Los Héroes Hotel; four-hour dinner cruises are offered Tues.-Sun. ($27).

The Hotel Tilawa hosts an **"outdoor skills adventure course"** conducted by Special Forces veterans: wilderness first aid and jungle survival are par for the course ($55 half day, $70 full day). It also has a Spanish language course with credit. The hotel's wide range of tours include one to Tabacón thermal springs by Zodiacs, which whisk you across the lake.

Information
Kim at **Toad Hall,** tel./fax 479-9178, offers an information service. Also try **Stefanie's,** tel. 694-4132, a tourist information center in Nuevo Arenal; a gift store and cafe were being added. Stefanie is German and speaks no English. She arranges tours.

Services

In Nuevo Arenal, there's a branch of the **Banco Nacional,** tel. 695-5266, ext. 122, on the west side of the church, plus a **gas station** as you enter town from Tilarán. You'll find **public telephones** next to Hotel Aurora and another outside Cabinas Rodríguez in Nuevo Arenal.

Getting There and Away

Buses depart San José for Nuevo Arenal via Ciudad Quesada and Fortuna from Calle 16, Avenidas 1/3 (Garaje Barquero, tel. 232-5660), at 6:15 a.m., 8:40 a.m., and 11:30 a.m. Additional buses depart Ciudad Quesada (San Carlos) for Tabacón and Nuevo Arenal daily at 6 a.m. and 3 p.m. and continue on to Tilarán. Buses depart Cañas for Tilarán and Nuevo Arenal at 7:30 a.m., 9 a.m., 11 a.m., and 3 p.m. (50 cents). You can also get to Tilarán direct from San José with Autotransportes Tilarán, tel. 222-3854; they have buses departing from Calle 12, Avenidas 9/11 at 7:30 a.m., 12:45 p.m., 3:45 p.m., and 6:30 p.m. (four hours). An express bus departs Nuevo Arenal for San José via Ciudad Quesada at 2:45 p.m.; additional buses depart for Ciudad Quesada at 8 a.m. and 2 p.m. A bus marked "Guatuso" also departs Arenal at 1:30 p.m. for San Rafael, Caño Negro, and Upala in the northern lowlands.

Schedules change. Check times. I'm often asked about day excursions to Arenal from San Jose. I don't recommend it; it's about three hours each way. Plan on staying overnight.

PARQUE NACIONAL VOLCÁN ARENAL

The 12,016-hectare Arenal Volcano National Park lies within the 204,000-hectare Arenal Conservation Area, protecting eight of Costa Rica's 12 life zones and 16 protected reserves in the region between the Guanacaste and Tilarán mountain ranges, and including Lake Arenal. The park has two volcanoes: Chato, whose collapsed crater contains an emerald lagoon surrounded by forest, and the perfectly conical Arenal. The park is most easily accessed from Fortuna in the northern lowlands.

A joint project involving the Canadian International Development Agency and World Wildlife

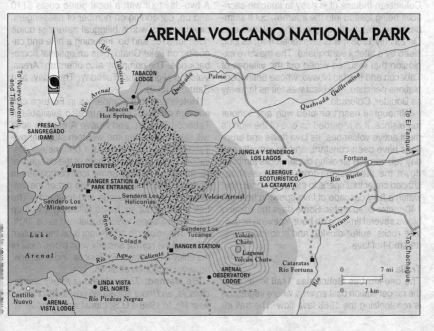

Fund Canada is helping local communities protect buffer zones where the land is under siege by drawing them into ecotourism. Several visitor sites provide toilets and drinking water. And trails and lookout points have been constructed.

The turnoff from the entrance is 3.5 km east of the lake and 2.5 km west of Tabacón. The dirt road leads 1.5 km to the **ranger station,** which sells a small guide ($1). Entrance costs $6. At press time, an **interpretive center** was under construction two km southwest of the ranger station. It will feature a museum with exhibits on vulcanology and local ecology, plus an auditorium for slide shows, a cafe, and souvenir store.

Volcán Arenal

Arenal Volcano (1,633 meters) is a picture-perfect cone. It's also Costa Rica's most active volcano and a must-see on any tourist's itinerary. Note, however, that it is most often covered in clouds and getting to *see* an eruption is a matter of luck (the dawn hours are best, before the clouds roll in; seasonally, you stand a reasonable chance in dry season, and less than favorable odds in rainy season). Arenal was sacred to pre-Columbian Indians (it is easy to imagine sacrifices being tossed into the inferno), but it slumbered peacefully throughout the colonial era. On 29 July 1968 it was awakened from its long sleep by a fateful earthquake. The massive explosion that resulted wiped out the villages of Tabacón and Pueblo Nuevo, whose entire populations perished. The blast was felt as far away as Boulder, Colorado.

Although it hasn't erupted with any serious force since, it is regarded as one of the world's most active volcanoes. Its lava flows and eruptions have been constant, and on virtually any day you can see smoking cinderblocks tumbling down the steep slope from the horseshoe-shaped crater that opens to the west—or at night watch a fiery cascade of lava spewing from the 140-meter-deep crater. Some days the volcano blows several times in an hour, spewing house-size rocks, sulfur dioxide and chloride gases, and red-hot lava.

Trails

The one-km **Las Heliconias Trail** leads from the ranger station past an area where vegetation is recolonizing the 1968 lava flow. The trail intersects the **Look-Out Point Trail,** which leads 1.3 km from the ranger station to a *mirador*—a viewing area—from which you can watch active lava flowing. **Las Coladas Trail** begins at the intersection and leads 2.8 km to a lava flow from 1993 that is still steaming and will take years to cool completely.

The **Los Miradores Trail** begins at the interpretive center and leads southwest 1.2 km to Lake Arenal. It is good for spotting wildlife. Farther east, beyond the Ríos Agua Caliente and La Danta, is the trailhead for **Los Tucanes Trail,** which leads to the southernmost lava flows (one hour).

Hiking too close to the volcano is not advisable. A sign at the base reads: Volcano influence area. Do not exceed established security limits.

Tours and Guided Hikes

Most tour operators in San José and Fortuna offer volcano tours. **Costa Rica Sun Tours,** Apdo. 1195-1250, Escazú, tel. 255-3418, fax 255-4410, e-mail: suntours@sol.racsa.co.cr, specializes in two- and three-day tours to Arenal with nights at the company's Observatory Lodge. A two-day tour with a local guide costs $110 and up, depending on number of passengers; two-day tours with a bilingual naturalist guide goes for $165 and up, including a hike and canoeing on Lake Chato, plus an optional horseback ride. The company also offers an "Arenal Volcano Night Tour" Tuesday, Thursday, and Saturday ($69).

Hotels and tour companies in Fortuna can arrange guides. Guides are also available in Tabacón, Tilarán, and Nuevo Arenal. Guides will take tourists up the western slope above Tabacón to a point at about 1,000 meters' elevation. Signs in Spanish warn of the dangers of climbing any higher. Some tour companies in Fortuna offer hiking trips to the rim of the volcano for the adventurous and foolhardy. The trek takes about six hours following a trail up the eastern slope, which is claimed to be "90% safe." The volcano's active vent is on the western side, and the normal easterly wind blows most of the effluvia westward. Explosions and eruptions, however, occur on all sides.

Be warned: *The volcano is totally unpredictable, and there is a strong possibility of losing your life.* In 1988 a U.S. tourist was killed when hiking to the rim. You also risk the lives of Red Cross personnel who must look for your body. Definitely not recommended!

Accommodations

Arenal Observatory Lodge, Apdo. 321-1007, San José, tel. 257-9489, fax 257-4220, direct tel./fax 695-5033, e-mail: arenalob@sol.racsa. co.cr, is a modern, rustic lodge on a 347-hectare reserve that includes a macadamia farm, with immaculate views over the lake and volcano, which looms menacingly only two km to the north. A deep valley safely separates the lodge from the volcano. The lodge was built in 1987 as an observatory for the Smithsonian Institution and the University of Costa Rica. The dining room and outside terrace have floor-to-ceiling windows facing the volcano's southwest slope, dark with recent lava spills. The rainforests to the southwest join the Monteverde Biological Cloud Forest Preserve and abound with wildlife. Trails lead to the lava fields and to Cerro Chato's lagoon-filled extinct crater. The Lava Trail (a tough climb back to the lodge; don't believe your guide if he/she says it is "easy") offers "howler monkeys, good birding, dangerous lava." The lodge also offers horseback rides ($5 per hour), fishing and boat tours ($25 per hour), 8:30 a.m. lava flow guided walk and Night Lava Tour ($10), and canoeing on Lake Chato (free).

The lodge has 28 rooms of varying standard. Some rooms offer bunks in modern wooden alpine chalets. Nine rooms in the Observatory Block have private baths and hot water (two have volcano views). Fourteen rooms in two new blocks have volcano views. And a converted farmhouse accommodates 10 people. Home-cooked meals are served family style in the dining room. The lodge is closed one week in April and July each year for scientific monitoring. I've received two complaints about "unfriendly" staff and disappointing facilities. Rates: $30-74 s, $35-85 d, $45-84 t, $55-73 quad low season; $35-82 s, $42-94 d, $52-92 t, $62-82 quad high season, depending on rooms.

The lodge is reached by a steep and arduous road from the park ranger station. Four-wheel drive is a must. If you don't have 4WD, you can leave your car at Fortuna and take a local jeep-taxi to the lodge. The lodge provides minibus transfers from San José ($150 one-way, split between passengers).

Camping

Camping is allowed at the western base of the volcano, on the road to Arenal Observatory Lodge, reached by turning hard left at the first Y-fork. There are no facilities. Heed the warning signs. Do not camp any closer to the volcano.

red-eyed tree frog

BOB RACE

CAÑAS TO LIBERIA

The first impression as you continue northwest along Hwy. 1 from Cañas is of Costa Rica at its least welcoming: a vast barren plain, burning hot in dry season, with lone palms rising like tattered umbrellas over the scrubby landscape, flanked to the east by the steep-sided volcanoes of the Cordillera de Guanacaste, from which rivers feed the marshy wetlands of the Tempisque Basin. But the view is not a fair one. Off the main highway, the villages of whitewashed houses are as welcoming as any place in the country. For the traveler interested in history or architecture, there are some intriguing sites. And the area is charged with scenic beauty. Looking at this austere plain, shimmering and phantasmagorical in its infinity, conjures images of the wanderings of the demented Don Quixote across stark La Mancha. And, just as the old knight errant found in that spare landscape, the far northwest of Costa Rica is rich with opportunities for "adventures elbow-deep."

former La Casona de la Pacífica owner Bernard Soto, president of Costa Rica 1885-1890

RÍO COROBICÍ AND VICINITY

Six km north of Cañas, the Pan-Am Highway crosses the Río Corobicí. The 40-km-long river runs down from the Cordillera de Guanacaste to the Gulf of Nicoya and is popular for rafting. It's fed by controlled runoff from Lake Arenal, providing a good rush of water year-round. The trip is a relatively calm run (the river averages a drop of 3.5 meters per kilometer: class II) described as a "nature float." I sampled a trip with Ríos Tropicales. Though it cuts through cattle country and rice paddies, the river is lined with a riparian forest of mahogany, ceiba, and palms. Wildlife gathers by the watercourse—a veritable tropical fantasia. Motmots, herons, crested caracaras, egrets, and tou-

cans are common, as are howler monkeys, caimans, and iguanas basking on the riverbanks. With luck, you might even spot a crocodile. Pools provide excellent swimming (don't worry—the crocs are timid fish-eaters).

The U.S.-run **Safaris Corobicí**, tel. 669-2091, fax 669-1091, e-mail: safaris@sol.racsa.co.cr, website www.nicoya.com, has an office beside Hwy. 1, about 400 meters south of the river. It uses professionally guided oar-boats so you don't need to paddle. Two trips cost $25. It has a three-hour birdwatching float ($43), plus a half-day float including lunch ($60). Trip participants can take a sapling along to plant on behalf of reforestation. The following companies also offer one-day trips ($65 pp) year-round: Costa Rica Expeditions, Ríos Tropicales, Pioneer Raft, and Costaricaraft. See the On the Road chapter, under **Recreation**, for addresses and telephone numbers.

Las Pumas Cat Zoo

Las Pumas is the home and "mini zoo" of Lily Bodmer de Hagnauer, a friendly Swiss-born environmentalist whose passion has been raising big cats: ocelots, a jaguar, cougars, margays, jaguarundis, and "tiger" cats. All six species are housed in large chain-link enclosures. There are also peccaries. Most of the animals were either injured or orphaned and have been reared by Lily. The cougars—which Lily raised from three weeks old (she bottle-fed them using a mixture of chamomile tea and baby formula)—act like giant housecats, purring loudly and licking her face.

Hagnauer works with various government agencies to care for captured or injured animals (many cats are delivered by the Ministry of Natural Resources after being confiscated from illegal hunters). The few animals that are released are radio-tracked by Hagnauer's research assistants. She accepts donations to ease the burden since she receives no official funding (each jaguar costs $1,200 a year to feed). Hagnauer also raises hundreds of Australian budgerigars and rabbits for sale. By selling only nonnative species, she hopes to help change the pet-keeping habits of Ticos.

Hours: daily 8 a.m.-5 p.m. No entrance fee, but donations are requested. The zoo is tucked behind Safari Corobicí. Follow the dirt road 100 meters.

La Pacífica

La Pacífica, Apdo. 8, Cañas 5700, tel. 669-0050 or 669-0266, fax 669-0555, 200 meters north of Las Pumas, is a farm, hotel-restaurant, and Eco-

logical Center on 2,000 hectares, most of it devoted to dairy and beef cattle production, but more than one-third still covered with tropical dry forest. The Ecological Center was founded in 1986. Its objective is to "implement a model of sustained development on an ecological basis," combining agricultural production with forestry, research, education, and ecotourism. The project includes reforestation of prairies and construction of small swamps to attract native wildlife. Its 39 archaeological sites date back as much as 2,000 years; you can visit two of them. La Pacífica publishes a useful *Ecology Guide Book* about the project, including descriptions of the various species to be seen.

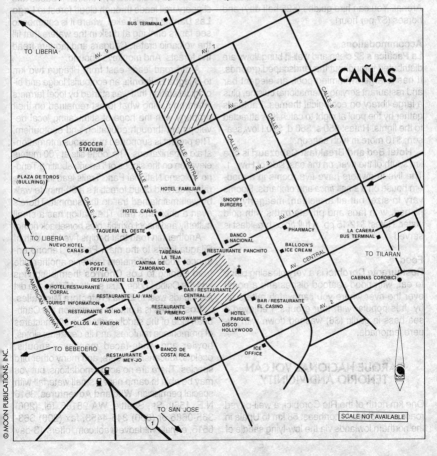

CAÑAS

SCALE NOT AVAILABLE

© MOON PUBLICATIONS, INC.

A trail along the Tenorio River takes you to **La Casona de la Pacífica,** at the northern boundary. The old house was once owned by ex-president Don Bernardo Soto and now functions as a small eco-museum. The Las Garzas and Chocuaco nature-study trails along the Río Corobicí offer a chance to see howler monkeys and some of the property's 225 bird species. The call of the male howlers can scare you silly. I recommend exploring other trails by horseback, of which there are many options for tours. You'll need mosquito repellent. Get a trail map at the office.

Boat trips on the Río Bebedero take guests to Palo Verde National Park. Other options include raft safaris on the Corobicí or bike trips to Lake Arenal. You can hire guides ($25 half day) and horses ($7 per hour).

Accommodations

La Pacífica's 32 clean and well-lit bungalows are distributed throughout the landscaped grounds. It has a large swimming pool, an elegant bar and restaurant serving international cuisine, plus a large library on ecological themes. Fat toads gather by the pool at night to catch flies attracted to the lights. Rates: $50 s, $60 d, $70 t low season; $10 more in high season.

Hotel Bed and Breakfast Capazauri is one km south of the river, on the east side of Hwy. 1. The live-in owners have five rooms in a modern house on a small *finca* and orchards. Rooms vary in size, but all are clean, meagerly furnished, with fans and private baths with cold water. Rates: $12-15 pp. A full *típico* breakfast is served.

Food

Restaurante Corobicí is a very pleasing place to eat, with good seafood dishes and a porch over the river where you can watch rafters go by. It is popular with tour groups. I enjoyed a sea bass in garlic ($6) washed down with superb lemonade.

PARQUE NACIONAL VOLCÁN TENORIO AND VICINITY

One km north of the Río Corobicí, a well-paved road (Hwy. 6) leads northeast 58 km to Upala in the northern lowlands via the low-lying saddle of Tenorio and Miravalles Volcanoes. The road is straight, fast, and currently free of potholes—a splendid, gentle roller-coaster ride that whisks you to the other side before you know it.

The only town is **Bijagua,** a center for cheese-making 38 km north of Cañas, on the northwest flank of Volcán Tenorio, a steep-faced, archetypically conical cone rising to 1,916 meters. The volcano is lushly forested in cloud forest and montane rainforest protected within the recently created Parque Nacional Volcán Tenorio. Local hiking is superb (albeit often hard going on higher slopes), notably one that leads to the Río Celeste, with a waterfall and fumaroles and boiling mud-pools nearby. Another arduous and slippery trail leads through cloud forest to **Lago Las Dantas** (Tapir Lake), where it is common to see tapirs drinking at dusk in the waters that fill the volcanic crater. Cougars and jaguars tread the forests. And monkeys abound.

A dirt road leads east from Bijagua two km to **Bijagua Heliconia,** an ecotourist lodge and biological station that was started by local farmers intent on saving what forest remained on their property with the hope of stimulating local development through education and ecotourism. The project is supported by various international aid organizations. The lodge sits at 700 meters elevation on the slopes of Tenorio abutting Tenorio Volcano National Park. Trails lead into prime rainforest and cloud forest; it's a 90-minute walk by well-maintained trail to the summit. There's even a children's trail. The station has a small butterfly and insect exhibit, plus horseback riding.

Another dirt road that begins five km north of Bijagua leads to the main Parque Tenorio entrance; about 200 meters farther is another side road leading to **Los Chorros** thermal springs and the Ceibo Lodge. Just south of Bijagua, a dirt road leads west to **Zona Protectora Miravalles.**

Los Tigres is a private reserve on the Caribbean side of the saddle protecting 800 hectares of premontane rainforest and its denizens: sloths, howler and white-faced monkeys, agoutis, ocelots, toucans, tanagers, and many other bird species. There are no accommodations, but you may be able to camp near a small waterfall with special permission. **Wildland Adventures,** 3516 N.E. 155th St., Seattle, WA 98155, tel. (206) 365-0686 or (800) 345-4453, fax (206) 363-6615, e-mail: wildadve@aol.com, offers 13-day nature tours that include visits to Los Tigres, La Pacífica, Palo Verde, and Arenal ($1,765).

Accommodations
Bijagua Heliconia Lodge, tel./fax 470-0115; reservations c/o Damaris Chávez, Apdo 516-1002 Paseo de los Estudiantes, San José, tel./fax 283-8305—Spanish only—or Sergio Pastor, tel. 283-5268, fax 283-9116, e-mail: wwfcii@ sol.racsa.co.cr, has six basic but well-kept rooms (two have a double bed and a bunk; four have two bunks) in a simple wooden structure with small bathrooms and hot showers, plus a bar/restaurant serving three meals (breakfasts $2, lunch and dinner $5.25). The biological station has its own cabin with kitchen and propane stove. The setting is splendid, with views of Miravalles volcano and as far north as Lake Nicaragua. A full panoply of hikes and nature excursions is offered. Rates: $12 s, $19 d, $21 t.

A Tico named Andre LeFranc runs **Ceibo Lodge,** Apdo. 4279-1000 San José, a rustic farmstead on the north flank of Tenorio. There's a seven-bed dorm and two double rooms with shared bathrooms (about $30, including all meals). Andre guides hikes and offers horseback riding. It's about eight km from the highway along a rugged dirt road.

Getting There
Buses run between Cañas and Upala several times daily. You can call the lodge from the phone box in Bijagua to request transport to the lodge.

BAGACES

The small, nondescript town of Bagaces is on Hwy. 1, 22 km north of Cañas. Many of the houses are quite ancient, and several adobe-brick houses date back several centuries. Otherwise, even the most diligent search will not turn up anything more interesting than a bust of ex-president General Tomás Guardia on a pedestal in the park honoring the city's most illustrious child.

It is important only as a gateway to Palo Verde National Park and Miravalles volcano. A regional office of **Area de Conservación Tempisque** (ACT), tel. 671-1062, is opposite the junction for Palo Verde, next to the gas station on Hwy. 1. It's open Mon.-Fri. 8 a.m.-4 p.m. ACT comprises

Palo Verde, Barra Honda, and Marino Las Baulas National Parks, plus Lomas Barbudal, and several lesser known reserves. The ACT administrative headquarters, tel. 659-9039, is at Hojancha, in the Nicoya Peninsula, but it has no information for tourists. (The office of Friends of Lomas Barbudal in Bagaces has closed.)

Accommodations and Food
Albergue de Bagaces, next to the gas station on Hwy. 1, has rooms. Rates: $13 s, $17 d. It has a restaurant popular with locals. In town, budget travelers can choose between **Cabinas Miravalles** and **Cabinas Eduardo Vargas,** each with basic rooms with fans and private baths and cold water. Rates: $8.

Eight km north of Bagaces is **Albergue Las Sillas Lodge,** on the Pan-American Highway. Not inspected.

Services
There's a **Banco Nacional,** tel. 671-1049, facing the main square. For the local **police** (Guardia Rural), call 671-1173; for the **Red Cross,** call 671-1186.

Getting There and Away
The bus station is one block north of the main square.

VOLCÁN MIRAVALLES AND VICINITY

A road from central Bagaces climbs steadily north up the western shoulder of Miravalles Volcano (2,028 meters), then descends to the hamlet of San José in the northern lowlands. It is a fabulously scenic drive all the way.

The almost perfectly conical volcano is the highest in the Cordillera de Guanacaste. Some 10,850 hectares of important watershed surrounding the volcano forms the **Miravalles Forest Reserve.** The western slopes are covered with savanna scrubland; the northern and eastern slopes are lush, fed by moist clouds that sweep in from the Caribbean. The southern slopes are cut with deep canyons and licked by ancient lava tongues, and fumaroles can be seen from afar, spouting and hissing like mini Old Faithfuls. The Miravalles forests, which are replete with wildlife (monkeys, cats, coatimundis, tapirs on the higher slopes, and a huge array of bird species) are easily accessed from the road.

If, instead of turning right for Fortuna, you keep going straight, you'll pass through the village of **Guayabo,** 21 km north of Bagaces. It is paved as far as **Guayabal,** seven km north of Guayabo, then gives way to a hellishly potholed road as you descend five km to **Aguas Claras,** where the road divides for Upala (to the right) and the small agricultural community **Colonia Blanca** (to the left), seven km away on the lush, moist north-facing lower slopes of Volcán Santa María.

Las Hornillas

Most of the geothermal activity is concentrated on the southwest flank at Las Hornillas ("Little Ovens"), an area of intense bubbling mudpots and fumaroles expelling foul gases and steam. Here the Costa Rican Institute of Electricity (ICE) harnesses geothermal energy for electric power, with two plants that tap the super-heated vapor deep within the volcano's bowels. You can visit the main **geothermal plant,** about two km north of Fortuna, about 18 km north of Bagaces and four km east of Guayabo.

Signs point the way to a smaller geothermal site three km north of Fortuna, from where you can hike to the Las Hornillas fumaroles (three side roads off the Bagaces-Guayabal road lead to Las Hornillas; all are signed).

Centro Turístico Yökö, tel. 673-0410, fax 673-0770, is a recreation park amid lawns one km west of Las Hornillas, with clean thermal swimming pools and plunge pools, a whirpool spa, plus a bar, a modern restaurant, showers and changing rooms, and fountains. Massage is offered. A gym and *cabinas* are to be added. Entrance: $3.50.

Accommodations and Food

Cabinas Caballos, in Guayabo, rents basic rooms. Rates: $4. Next door is **Restaurant La Amistad,** which offers inexpensive dishes. **Cabinas Las Brisas** has simple cabins one km north of Guayabo at the base of the volcano. **Finca La Reina,** tel. 666-0040, near Fortuna, rents rooms and horses. Reportedly, you can help milk the cows. **Parador Las Nubes,** tel. 671-1011, ext. 280 reservations, tel. 666-1313 information, fax 666-2136, at Guayabal, has rudimentary rooms.

The U.S.-run **Miravalles Volcano Lodge,** four km north of Guayabo, squats amid cattle pasture at the very base of the looming volcano. The lodge has eight spacious, modestly furnished rooms with lofty wooden ceilings, and private baths with hot water. There's a restaurant and lounge with cable TV showing ESPN and other U.S. favorites, plus a rusting Nautilus machine. The modern structure is centered on a garden courtyard; inexplicably, no rooms have volcano views. Trails begin within 50 meters of the lodge and lead into a private 212-hectare reserve at the base of the volcano. The forest includes wetlands fed by thermal waters, sulphur springs, and waterfalls. Monkeys come down to the lodge. Horseback rides are offered. Be prepared for the farm-dog chorus at night, and a wake-up call from blackbirds scuttling berries across the galvanized tin roof. Rates: $21 s, $31 d with fan; $42 s, 52 d with a/c.

The **Santa María Volcano Lodge,** tel. 381-5290 or 235-0642, fax 666-2313 or 272-6236, one km west of Colonia Blanca, is run like a hostel. The basic lodge is a wooden house with rough-hewn furniture and torn leather seats. There are six clean but basic rooms with modern private bathrooms and hot water (two have shared bath). Better are the two small rough-hewn cabins—like something from *Goldilocks and the Three Bears*—with tree trunks for stools, a double bed, a bunk and two single beds, stone-lined bathrooms, and porches looking over the banana and citrus groves. It is part of a cattle *finca. Tepezcuintles* are raised for release into the wild. A rustic bar serves breakfast ($2) and lunch ($3). Horseback rides ($20-30) and hiking tours ($25) to the volcanoes are offered. Rates: $4 pp.

Centro Turístico Yökö is building 40 cabins.

Tours

Miratur, tel. 673-0260, in Guayabo, runs a "geotour" of the thermal plant. It also has ecological packages that feature mountain trail hikes plus a visit to the energy plant and the steaming fumaroles. **CATA Tours,** Apdo. 8, Cañas, tel. 669-1026, fax 669-1995, offers horseback riding tours of Miravalles and Las Hornillas.

Services

There's a **Banco de Costa Rica** in Guayabo. **Bravo Tropical Tours,** next to Restaurant La Amistad, offers tours to Las Hornillas and nearby nature reserves.

PARQUE NACIONAL PALO VERDE

Palo Verde National Park, 28 km south of Bagaces, protects 13,058 hectares of floodplains, marshes, limestone ridges, and seasonal pools in the heart of the driest region of Costa Rica—the Tempisque basin, at the mouth of the Río Tempisque in the Gulf of Nicoya. The tidal river rises and falls up to four meters and is navigable for about 36 km, as far as the confluence with the Río Bolsón. There are 15 different habitats (including several types of swamp and marshland) and a corresponding diversity of fauna. Plump crocodiles wallow on the muddy riverbanks, salivating no doubt at the sight of coatis, white-tailed deer, and other mammals come down to the water to drink. The banks of the Tempisque are also lined with many hundreds of archaeological sites for the curious.

Palo Verde is best known as a birders' paradise. More than 300 bird species have been recorded, not least great curassows and the only permanent colony of scarlet macaws in the dry

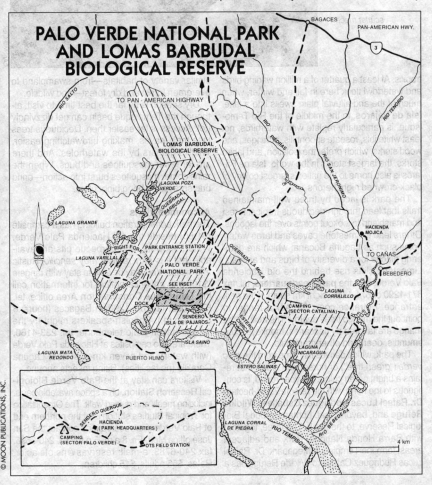

PALO VERDE NATIONAL PARK AND LOMAS BARBUDAL BIOLOGICAL RESERVE

© MOON PUBLICATIONS, INC.

scarlet macaw

JEAN MERCIER

tropics. At least a quarter of a million wading birds and waterfowl flock here in fall and winter, when much of the arid alluvial plain swells into a lake. **Isla de Pájaros,** in the middle of the Río Tempisque, is particularly replete with waterbirds, not least white ibis, roseate spoonbills, anhingas, and wood storks, which prefer the isolation, and jabiru storks, the largest storks in the world. Isla de Pájaros is also home to the nation's largest colony of black-crowned night herons.

The park is laced by three well-maintained trails that lead through deciduous tropical forest and marshland to lookout points over the lagoons. Others lead to limestone caves and large waterholes such as Laguna Bocana, which are gathering places for a diversity of birds and animals. Limestone cliffs rise behind the old Hacienda Palo Verde, now the **park headquarters,** tel./fax 671-1290 or 671-1455, eight km south of the park entrance. Entrance costs $6. Ask a ranger to point out the mango trees nearby. The fruits of the mango are favored by peccaries, monkeys, coatimundis, deer, and other mammals.

The park, which derives its name from the *palo verde* ("green tree") or horsebean shrub that retains a bright green coloration year-round, is contiguous to the north with the remote 7,354-hectare **Dr. Rafael Lucas Rodríguez Caballero Wildlife Refuge** and, beyond that, Lomas Barbudal Biological Reserve, to the north. The three, together with Barra Honda National Park and adjacent areas, form the Tempisque Megapark. Dr. Rafael Lucas Rodríguez Caballero Wildlife Refuge has a

similar variety of habitats—from swampland to evergreen forest and dry forest—and wildlife.

Dry season is by far the best time to visit, although the Tempisque basin can get dizzyingly hot. Access is far easier then. Deciduous trees lose their leaves, making birdwatching easier. Wildlife gathers by the waterholes. And there are far fewer mosquitoes and bugs. When the rains come, mosquitoes burst into action—bring bug spray. And bring binoculars.

Accommodations

The park administration building has a campsite ($1.50) beside the old Hacienda Palo Verde. Water, showers, and barbecue pits are available, but it is *muy rústico, muy sencillo.* Rustic and simple. You may be able to stay with rangers ($10) with advance notice: for information call the **Tempisque Conservation Area** office, tel. 671-1062, fax 671-1290, in Bagaces (hours: 8 a.m.-4 p.m.); Spanish-speakers might try the ranger station radio telephone, tel. 233-4160. There are also campsites at Hacienda Palo Verde (with water), and seven km east near Laguna Coralillo (no facilities). Biting insects abound.

Visitors can stay at the **Palo Verde Biological Research Station,** on a space available basis, including meals and guided walk. The Organization for Tropical Studies station is at the northern end of Palo Verde. For reservations contact the San José office Mon.-Fri. 8 a.m.-5 p.m.: tel. 240-6696, fax 240-6783, e-mail: reservas@ns.ots.ac.cr. Rates: $55 adults, $15 children.

Tours

OTS offers full-day natural history visits, with advance reservations ($17 adults, $11 children). Also, the park rangers will take you out on their boat for $10 pp. Or you can hire boats in Puerto Humo or Bebedero (see **Getting There,** below).

Most tour companies in San José also offer river tours in Palo Verde. **CATA Tours,** tel./fax 669-1203, has trips to Palo Verde, including Isla de Pájaros, plus a "birdwatchers' special" and kayaking on the Río Bebedero. **Transportes Palo Verde,** tel. 669-1091, fax 669-0544, in the Hotel El Corral in Cañas, has a three-hour birdwatcher's tour and a half-day Palo Verde tour. And **El León Viajero,** tel. 233-9398, fax 233-9432, has a guided "Tempisque River Adventure."

Getting There

From Bagaces: The main entrance is 28 km south of Bagaces, along a dirt road that begins opposite the gas station and Tempisque Conservation Area office on Hwy. 1. The route is well-signed; follow the power lines past the turnoff for Lomas Barbudal. No buses. A jeep-taxi from Bagaces costs about $15 one-way.

From Nicoya: In dry season, you can drive from Filadelfia or Santa Cruz to Hacienda El Viejo. The park is four km east from El Viejo, and the Río Tempisque two km farther. Easy to get lost. A local boatman will ferry you upriver to the park dock; the park headquarters is then an hour's walk east along a rough track that is very muddy and swampy in wet season. A bus reportedly operates from Nicoya to Puerto Humo, 27 km north of Nicoya. You can hire a boat and guide to take you to Isla de Pájaros—one km downriver—or three km upriver to the Chamorro dock, the trailhead to park headquarters (it's a two-km walk). Note that boats are not allowed within more than 50 meters of Isla de Pájaros: don't pressure your guide to get closer. Another option is to take the Tempisque ferry to Puerto Moreno, where you can hire a boat to the Chamorro dock.

RESERVA BIOLÓGICA LOMAS BARBUDAL

Lomas Barbudal ("Bearded Hills") is a 2,279-hectare biological reserve fed by protected river systems, some of which flow year-round, among

them the Cabuya, which has sandy-bottomed pools good for swimming. The "beards" at Lomas Barbudal are patches of dry forest that once extended along the entire Pacific coast of Mesoamerica. Dry forest was even more vast than the rainforest, but also more vulnerable to encroaching civilization. For half the year, from November to March, no rain relieves the heat of the Tempisque basin, leaving plants and trees parched and withered. Fires started by local farmers eviscerate the tinder-dry forests, opening holes quickly filled by ecological opportunists such as African jaraguá, an exotic grass brought to Costa Rica in the late 19th century to grow pastures. Jaraguá rebounds quickly from fire and grazing pressures, reaching four-meter-high combustible stands. Rolling, rocky terrain spared Lomas Barbudal from the changes wrought on the rest of Guanacaste Province by plows and cows. Here, the dry forest remains largely intact.

Several endangered tree species thrive here: mahogany, Panamá redwood, gonzalo alves, rosewood, sandbox (popular with scarlet macaws), and the cannonball tree *(balas de cañón).* A relative of the Brazil nut tree, the cannonball tree produces a pungent, nonedible fruit that grows to the size of a bowling ball and dangles from a long stem. Several evergreen tree species also line the banks of the waterways, creating riparian corridors inhabited by species not usually found in dry forests. Look for an educational and amusing field guide, *A White-faced Monkey's Guide to Lomas Barbudal,* published in 1993 by the Friends of Lomas Barbudal. Its thoroughly simian perspective makes for fascinating explanations (of, for example, why monkeys *really* pee on tourists).

Unlike Costa Rica's moist forests, the tropical dry forests undergo a dramatic seasonal transformation. In the midst of drought vibrant yellow and pink flowers synchronistically burst onto bare branches, earning the moniker "big bang reproducers." Myriad bees—at least 250 species—moths, bats, and wasps pollinate the flowers. And moist fruits ripen throughout the dry season, feeding monkeys, squirrels, peccaries, and other mammalian frugivores. Lots of birds live here, including such endangered species as the great curassow, yellow-naped parrot, and king vulture. Lomas Barbudal is also one of the few remaining Pacific coast forests that attracts the colorful scarlet macaw. The macaws are fond of the seeds from the sandbox tree's segmented fruit, whose inner tissue contains a caustic latex strong enough to corrode flesh.

The reserve adjoins Dr. Rafael Lucas Rodríguez Caballero Wildlife Refuge to the south and therefore serves as a vital migratory route. Unfortunately, the corridors of swamp forest linking Palo Verde and Dr. Rafael Lucas Rodríguez Caballero with Lomas Barbudal continue to shrink; local farmers have invested in permits to clear the swamp forest and plant crops, increasing the isolation of both reserves. The **Friends of Lomas Barbudal,** 691 Colusa Ave., Berkeley, CA 94707, tel. (510) 526-4115, raises funds to protect the reserve.

University of California at Berkeley entomologist Gordon Frankie leads an annual "Preserving Biodiversity" tour to Lomas Barbudal. Participants assist with field research. For information, write the University Research Expeditions Program, University of California, Berkeley, CA 94720, tel. (510) 642-6568.

Services

The **park office** and **information center** (Casa de Patrimonio) is on the banks of the Río Cabuyo. Trails span the park from here. Note that it's open on a 10 days on/four days off schedule. Picnic benches sit under shade trees. Camping is permitted ($2.50). No facilities. Entrance: supposedly by donation, but may be $6.

Getting There

The unpaved access road is off Hwy. 1, at the Km 221 marker near Pijijes, about 10 km north of Bagaces. A dirt road—4WD recommended—leads six km through scrubby cattle pastures until you come to a lookout point with views over a valley whose hillsides are clad with dry forest. The road descends steeply from here to the park entrance (you can't drive across the river and into the park, but you can parallel the river for a ways and even, it is said, circumnavigate the reserve; about two-thirds of a kilometer before Casa de Patrimonio is the home of the Rosales family, who reportedly are very helpful). If conditions are particularly muddy you may wish to park at the lookout point and hike to the ranger station rather than face not being able to return via the dauntingly steep ascent from the ranger

station in your car. A jeep-taxi from Bagaces will cost about $25 roundtrip.

LIBERIA

Liberia, 26 km north of Bagaces, is the provincial capital and a social, economic, and transportation hub of Guanacaste. It is called the "White City" because of its houses made of blinding white ignimbrite. There's a rich simplicity, a purity to the surrounding landscape, to the craggy, penurious hills and the cubist houses sheathed in white light like a sort of celestial glow. Many old adobe homes still stand to the south of the landscaped central plaza, with high-ceilinged interiors and kitchens opening onto classical courtyards. Old corner houses have doors—*puertas del sol*—that open onto two sides to catch both morning and afternoon sun. The leafy plaza itself has bright blue benches where you may rest and admire the modern white church and older town hall flying the Guanacastecan flag, the only provincial flag in the country. The plaza fills on Saturday evenings, when locals don their finest clothing to socialize.

Attractions in town are few. The **Museo de Sabanero,** housed in the Casa de Cultura, honors the local cowboy tradition with saddles and other *sabanero* memorabilia. The Casa de Cultura is a pretty colonial-era building that is a perfect example of a structure with doors on each corner: it's three blocks south of the plaza on Calle 1. A statue also honors the *sabaneros* in the central median along Avenida Central at Calle 10. At the far end of Avenida Central, also known as Avenida 25 Julio, is **La Agonía Church,** with a stuccoed adobe exterior and simple adornments within. Behind the church is **Parque Rodolfo Salazar,** surrounded by old cottages. Finally, just one block east of the central plaza, is the old city jail, still in use, with barred windows and towers at each corner.

The **Daniel Oduber International Airport,** tel. 666-0695, is 12 km west of Liberia. It is drawing an increasing number of charter and scheduled flights, bringing vacationers to the resorts of the nearby Nicoya Peninsula.

Día de Guanacaste

The best time to visit is 25 July, when the whole town bursts into life to celebrate Guanacaste's secession from Nicaragua in 1812. Rodeos, a cattle show, bullfights, parades, mariachi and marimba music, firecrackers, and stalls selling local specialty dishes should keep you entertained. A similar passion is stirred each first week of September for the Semana Cultural.

Fiesta Brava

The local chamber of commerce also pushes the Fiesta Brava, tel. 666-0450, held at Hacienda La Cueva, a 3,000-hectare cattle ranch whose adobe house was built in 1824. You're greeted by cowboys in traditional garb performing tricks with their lassoes, and girls—also in traditional dress—serving drinks. As the tour bus continues up to the house, the cowboys

ride alongside, whooping and hollering. Traditional Guanacaste cuisine, beer, and *chicha* (the popular fermented corn drink) are guzzled on the lawn to the accompaniment of marimbas and guitars. A round of explosive firecrackers announces the start of bullfighting in the corral. Cost is $69 pp (less for larger groups). Make your reservations via the tourist information office or any local travel agency.

Accommodations

Shoestring: There are four reasonable choices on Avenida 6. **Hospedaje La Casona,** tel./fax 666-2971, has rooms in a cute rose-pink wooden home. Rates: $5 pp. **Hospedaje Real Chorotega,** tel. 666-0398, is of a similar standard

LIBERIA

TO RINCON DE LA VIEJA (SANTA MARIA)

HOSPITAL

SOCCER STADIUM

CEMETERY

HOTEL DAISYTA

CICLO ROMAR (BICYCLE SHOP)

PUB CASA BLANCA

LITTLE CHURCH OF THE AGONY

TO LA CRUZ

MONPIK

BAKERY

CINE OLIMPIA

PENSION GOLFITO

RESTAURANTE CHANG SAN

RESTAURANTE CANTON

SODAS

PLAZA

POLLO RICO RICO

PENSION MARGARITA

BUS STATION

TAXIS

MERCADO CENTRAL

HOTEL/BAR MEXICO

ICE OFFICE

POLICE

CABINAS EL ENCANTO

PLAZA

BANCO DE COSTA RICA

RESTAURANTE HONG KONG

RIO LIBERIA

POST OFFICE

PLAZA

HOTEL PRIMAVERA

BANCRECEN

HOTEL LIBERIA

CASA DE LAS REVISTAS

RESTAURANTE COPA DE ORO

TO RINCON DE LA VIEJA

HOTEL GUANACASTE

BANCO NACIONAL

AVENIDA CENTRAL

PRONTO PIZZERIA

HOSTAL CIUDAD BLANCA

HOTEL DEL ASERRADERO

SABANERO MONUMENT

TIFFANY'S

TOYOTA RENT-A-CAR

JUAJA RESTAURANT

ICE OFFICE

HOSPEDAJE LAS CASONAS

BANCO POPULAR

CASA DE CULTURA MUSEO DE SABANEROS. TOURIST INFORMATION OFFICE

BANCO DE SAN JOSE

HOTEL LA SIESTA

RESTAURANTE POKOPI

RESTAURANTE/ PIZZERIA DE BEPPE

HOSPEDAJE EL DORADO

HOTEL BOYEROS

HOSTAL CONDEGA

EL CEVICHE DEL REY

HOTEL EL SITIO

TO CANAS

0   250 m

© MOON PUBLICATIONS, INC.

and price, and has a small restaurant. **Hospedaje El Dorado,** tel. 666-1165, has seven simple, well-lit rooms with hardwood floors, fans, small beds, and clean bathrooms (three private) with hot water. Rates: $4 pp.

Pensión Margarita, tel. 666-0468, a white-and-turquoise wooden colonial building at Avenida Central, Calle 5, has 38 very basic rooms with fans and shared bath with cold water. Simple home-cooked meals are served, and there's a TV in the dark lounge. A reader thought it "rundown, with dingy rooms with dirty bathrooms." Rates: $5 pp. You'll also find grim rooms in **Bar México,** opposite, and the ill-named **Cabinas El Encanto** around the corner. The **Pensión Golfito,** tel. 666-0963, 100 meters north of the church, is also a place of last resort.

Budget: Hotel Guanacaste, tel. 666-0085, fax 666-2287, e-mail: htiguana@sol.racsa.co.cr, website www.asstcard.co.cr/guia/homp/htlguana.htm, has 30 simple rooms with fans, some with private baths with cold water (one has a/c). Most are dorms with bunk beds. Some at the back have a lounge, kitchen, and large, communal bathroom. Reportedly, rooms tend to get hot. It is part of the Costa Rican Youth Hostel chain. There's table tennis. A new restaurant and TV lounge are the highlights. It offers its own tours as well as daily transfers to Rincón de la Vieja. Rates: $12 s, $20 d ($29 with a/c), $28 t, $36 quad, $52 six. You can camp for $3.

A recommended favorite is **Hotel Primavera,** tel. 666-0464, fax 666-2271, facing the plaza on Avenida Central. This modern, colonial-style structure has secure parking, plus 30 clean, modestly furnished rooms with small private bathrooms. There's a travel agency on-site. Rates: $15 s, $22 d with fans; $16 s, $29 d with a/c.

Hotel Liberia, tel. 666-0161, in an old building on Calle Central, Avenida 2, has 13 small, very basic but clean rooms with fans and shared bath with cold water. Newer albeit simple rooms have private bath but cold water. It has secure parking, a laundry, and a TV in the pleasant skylit lounge. Rates: $9 s, $15 d, 18 t shared bath; for $11 s, $20 d, $34 t private bath. At Avenida 3, Calle 13 is the **Hotel Daisyta,** tel./fax 666-0197. There's 30 basic rooms with private baths and hot water. Amenities include a small swimming pool, bar and restaurant, secure parking, and laundry. Rates: $12 s, $16 d.

The venerable and popular **Hotel Bramadero,** Apdo. 193, Liberia, tel. 666-0371, fax 666-0203, is a motel-style hotel with 25 simply furnished rooms, 18 with a/c, plus a pool and a large restaurant facing the road. Some rooms may have cold water only. It's popular with Josefinos. Rates: $13 s, $19 d, $23 t, $26 quad with fan; $19 s, $27 d, $32 t, $36 quad with a/c.

You might also consider the **Sinclair Guest House,** tel. 666-2088, in the heart of town. Two km south of town is **Hotel La Ronda,** tel. 666-2799, with large but dour rooms with private baths and fans. Rates: $12 s, $20 d.

Inexpensive: The *posada*-style **Hostal Ciudad Blanca,** Avenida 4 and Calles 1/3, is an atmospheric old wooden house with fleur-de-lys grillwork and colonial tile floors, a charming patio, and 12 modestly decorated—albeit gloomy—rooms with pretty bedspreads. The bar and restaurant is a popular spot. Alas, it's overpriced. Rates: $25 s, $45 d, $55 t. **Hotel La Siesta,** Apdo. 15, Liberia 5000, tel. 666-2118 or 666-0678, fax 666-2532; in San José, tel. 232-2541, on Calle 4 and Avenidas 4/6, has 24 fairly basic rooms with a/c and private bath. It has a pool and a basic restaurant. Rates: $25 s, $40 d.

The Spanish-style **Hotel Boyeros,** Apdo. 85, Liberia 5000, tel. 666-0995, fax 666-2529, has 60 rooms with a/c and private baths with hot water surrounding a large pool and a *palenque* bar in landscaped grounds. All rooms have a private patio or balcony and are modestly yet pleasantly furnished. Next door is a restaurant and bar that can get very noisy on weekends. It's popular with Ticos. Rates: $28 s, $39 d, $44 t.

Hotel del Aserradero is a new motel-style offering on Hwy. 1, 100 meters north of the main junction. It has 16 simply furnished rooms with double beds and a pull-out bed, clean private baths and hot water, and wide verandas with rockers. A restaurant was to be added. Rates: $24 s, $40 d, including continental breakfast.

Moderate: Hotel El Sitio, Apdo. 134-5000, Liberia, tel. 666-1211, fax 666-2059, 100 meters west of Hwy. 1, is a modern motel-type lodging with 52 spacious rooms with private baths; 18 rooms feature a/c. Rooms are modestly furnished and have either a/c or fan, and satellite TV, direct-dial telephones, and security boxes. The hotel has atmospheric Guanacastecan trimmings: red-tiled roofs, local landscape paintings, wagon-wheel chandelier. There's large a swimming pool and sundeck. The El Pinocchio Restaurant serves Italian fare. Rates: $50 s, $65 d, $75 t. Overpriced?

Hotel Las Espuelas, tel. 666-0144 or 293-4544, fax 293-4839; in North America, tel. (305) 858-4567, fax 858-7478, website www.costa-sol.co.cre/espuelas.html, is a modest hotel—now owned by the Costa Sol group—set amid tropical gardens facing Hwy. 1, two km south of Liberia. The 35 spacious rooms and three suites have a/c, telephones, color TVs, and private baths. A country-style, beam-ceilinged restaurant serves expensive seafoods and bread fresh from the oven. The hotel has a pleasant lounge with sofas and lots of potted plants, plus a large pool, hammocks under trees, and a poolside *palenque* bar with nightly folkloric entertainment. A minivan and driver are available for exploring Guanacaste. The hotel also offers tours to nearby attractions. Rates: $50 s, $57 d, $67 t low season; $53 s, $68 d, $78 t high season.

Food
The **Pub Casa Blanca** on Calle 7, Avenidas 1/3, is a surprisingly elegant and chic contemporary bar, restaurant and art gallery. It is closed Sunday (when I called by), but it looks like *the* place to dine.

Also try the breezy patio restaurant at **Hotel Ciudad Blanca,** serving spaghetti and *casados* for $4. **Jauja Restaurante,** Apdo. 17, Liberia 5000, tel. 666-0917, on Avenida Central, Calles 6/8, has tasty Mexican food and wonderful fresh-fruit salads. **Restaurant Pókopí,** tel. 666-1036, opposite Hotel El Sitio, serves varied and inventive continental dishes. Burgers and sandwiches cost $2 or $3, and steaks and seafood dishes less than $10.

Las Tinajas has outdoor tables where you can eat pizzas and deep-fried chicken while watching the activity across the road in the park. Two recommended options for pizza are the atmospheric **Pronto Pizzeria** and **Da Beppe Pizzeria & Ristorante Italiano,** tel. 666-0917. Better yet is **La Casona,** on Calle 1 and Avenida 4. Pizzas here are served in a delightful rustic ambience that includes a wood-fired oven and art gallery.

Plenty of *sodas* serve cheap *típico* dishes; **Pollo Rico Rico** is popular for fried chicken; and there are several Chinese restaurants in town (try **Restaurant Chung San** and **Restaurant Canton** on Avenida 3, one block east of the plaza). **Restaurante El Ceviche Del Rey,** on the south side of town beside Hwy. 1, serves Peruvian seafood.

For ice cream, try **Mönpik,** two blocks north of the park on Calle 2.

Entertainment
The **Disco Kurú,** tel. 666-0769, next to Restaurant Pókopí, pulses on weekends ($3 cover). Restaurant Las Tinajas, on the west side of the plaza, has live music at night. Hotel Las Espuelas hosts folkloric nights.

Information
The helpful and efficient **Liberia Chamber of Commerce Tourist Information Center,** tel. 666-1606, is three blocks south of the plaza in the Casa de Cultura. Hours: Tues.-Sun. 9 a.m.-noon and 1-6 p.m.; Sunday 9 a.m.-1 p.m. It has a 24-hour phone with AT&T USADirect access. It offers packages to Rincón de la Vieja volcano ($135, two days).

You can buy U.S. magazines and newspapers at **Casa de las Revistas,** on Avenida Central and Calles 4/2.

Shopping
Tiffany's, Avenida 2, Calles 4/6, sells quality crafts. Several outlets near the airport sell souvenirs, crafts, hammocks, beachwear, and the like. Also try **Kaltak Handicrafts,** tel./fax 667-0076.

Tours
Swiss Travel and **Transportes Turístico Ciclo Azul** have offices near the airport, as does **Ríos Tropicales/Dos Montañas** offering rafting and hiking.

Services
Banks include Banco Nacional, tel. 666-0996, at Avenida Central, Calles 6/8; Banco de Costa Rica, tel. 666-0148, on Calle Central, Avenida 1; and Banco Popular, at Avenida Central and Calle 12, one block east of Hwy. 1. Banco San José (next to Banco Popular) and BanCrecen, three blocks east at Calle 6, both have **24-hour ATMs.**

There are plenty of **pharmacies. Hospital Dr. Enrique Baltodano Briceño,** tel. 666-0011, is at Avenida 4, Calles Central/2. And **Clinic 25 de Julio**, tel. 666-1881, is a private clinic with 15 specialist doctors; it's open Mon.-Fri. 7 a.m.-10 p.m. and Saturday 8 a.m.-3 p.m.

The **post office** is on Calle 8, Avenida 3, and open 7:30 a.m.-8 p.m. You can make international telephone calls and send faxes from a **communications office** on Calle 8 and Avenidas Central/2. There are **public telephones** in the plaza. The **police station** is on Avenida 1, one block west of the plaza.

Clothes getting grubby? There's a **laundry** in front of the Church of the Agony at Avenida Central, Calle 9.

Getting There

By Bus: Buses depart San José for Liberia daily from Calle 14, Avenidas 1/3 (Pulmitán, tel. 222-1650 or 666-0458), at 7 a.m., 9 a.m., 11:30 a.m., 1 p.m., 3 p.m., 4 p.m., 6 p.m., and 8 p.m. ($3; four hours). Return buses depart Liberia for San José from the new Tralapa bus terminal at Avenida 7 and Calle 12 at 4:30 a.m., 6 a.m., 7:30 a.m., 12:30 p.m., 2 p.m., 4 p.m., 6 p.m., and 8 p.m.

An Empresa Arata bus, tel. 666-0138, departs Puntarenas for Liberia daily at 5:30 p.m. (2.5 hours), returning at 8:30 a.m. Buses from Nicoya and Santa Cruz depart for Liberia hourly, 5 a.m.-8 p.m.

Buses depart from the bus terminal at Avenida 1 and Calle 12 hourly for Filadelfia, Santa Cruz (5:30 a.m.-7:30 p.m.), Nicoya (5 a.m.-7 p.m.); and Playa Coco, Playa Panamá, and other destinations in the Nicoya Peninsula. Local buses also depart regularly for La Cruz and Peñas Blancas via the entrance to Santa Rosa

National Park. The express bus from San José departs Liberia for Peñas Blancas at 5:30 a.m., 8:30 a.m., 11 a.m., 2 p.m., and 6 p.m.

Interbus has a daily shuttle that stops in Liberia en route between San José and Tamarindo.

By Air: SANSA and Travelair have scheduled service between San José and Daniel Oduber International Airport 12 km west of town. Lacsa's Miami-San José flights stops in Liberia on Wednesday and Sunday; the San José-Miami flight stops in Liberia on Tuesday and Saturday. Canada 3000 and American Trans-Air serve Liberia by charter from Canada and New York. The airport has a snack bar, toilets, and public telephones.

Getting Around

By Car: Sol Rent-a-Car, tel. 666-2222, fax 666-2898, e-mail: sol@asstcard.co.cr, has an office next to Hotel Bramadero. In late 1997 it offered daily rates of $27-46, and weekly rates of $147-280 with unlimited mileage. **Ada Rent-a-Car**, tel. 666-2998, has an office near the airport. **Budget Rent-a-Car** also has an office nearby.

There are four **gas stations**—one on each corner—at the junction of Avenida Central and Hwy. 1.

Taxis gather at the northwest corner of the plaza and by the bus station. You can hire one for local touring (around $20 per cab to Santa Rosa National Park; double that to Rincón de la Vieja National Park). You can rent bicycles for $12 daily including helmets and water bottle from **Guanaventura Mountainbike**, tel. 666-2825, 200 meters north of the INS building. It also offers guided bike tours (from $45).

NORTH OF LIBERIA

Settlements diminish north of Liberia, where traffic picks up speed. I don't recall ever seeing a police car between Cañas and the Nicaraguan border, but don't push your luck. Watch for potholes along Hwy. 1, and keep a good distance between you and the massive trucks careening along en route to or from Nicaragua. The scenery is magnificent, with volcanoes—one, two, three—marching in a row to the east, convex, like the volcanoes of childhood vision. Much of the area—the heart of Costa Rica's dry forest ecosystem—is protected in a series of national parks.

PARQUE NACIONAL VOLCÁN RINCÓN DE LA VIEJA

Rincón de la Vieja (1,895 meters), an active volcano in a period of relative calm, is the largest of five volcanoes that make up the Cordillera de Guanacaste. It is composed of nine separate but contiguous volcanic craters, with dormant **Santa María** (1,916 meters) the tallest and most easterly. Its crater harbors a forest-rimmed lake popular with quetzals, linnets, and tapirs. The main crater—**Von Seebach,** sometimes called the Rincón de la Vieja crater—still steams. Icy Lake Los Jilgueros lies between the two craters. The last serious eruption was in 1983. Rincón, however, spewed lava and acid gases on 8 May 1991, causing destructive *lahores* (ash-mud flows). The slopes still bear reminders of the destructive force of the acid cloud that burnt away much of the vegetation on the southeastern slope.

The attractions are protected in the 14,083-hectare Rincón de la Vieja National Park, which extends from 650 to 1,965 meters in elevation on both the Caribbean and Pacific flanks of the *cordillera*. The two sides differ markedly in rainfall and vegetation. The Pacific side has a distinct dry season (if you intend climbing to the craters, Feb.-April is best). The Caribbean side is lush and wet year-round, with as much as 500 cm of rainfall falling annually on higher slopes. The park is known for its profusion of orchid species.

The diverse conditions foster a panoply of wildlife species. More than 300 species of birds include quetzals, toucanets, the elegant trogon, eagles, three-wattled bellbirds, and the curassow. Mammals include cougars, howler, spider, and white-faced monkeys, kinkajous, sloths, tapirs, tayras, and even jaguars.

The lower slopes can be explored along relatively easy trails that begin at the park headquarters. The **Sendero Encantago** leads through cloud forest full of *guaria morada* orchids (the national flower) and links with a 12-km trail that continues to **Las Pailas** ("Caldrons"), 50 hectares of bubbling mud volcanoes, boiling thermal waters, vapor geysers, and the so-called Hornillas ("Ovens") geyser of sulfur dioxide and hydrogen sulfide. The hot bubbling mud has minerals and medicinal properties used in cosmetology. Be careful when walking around: it is possible to step through the crust and scald yourself. This trail continues to the summit.

Between the cloud forest and Las Pailas, a side trail (marked Aguas Thermales) leads to soothing, hot sulfur springs called **Los Azufrales** ("Sulfurs"). The thermal waters (42° C) form small pools where you may bathe and take advantage of their curative properties. Use the cold-water stream nearby for a cooling off after a good soak in the thermal springs. **Las Hornillas** are sulfurous fumaroles on the devastated southern slope of the volcano. Another trail leads to the **Hidden Waterfalls,** four continuous falls (three of which exceed 70 meters) in the Agria Ravine. You'll find a perfect bathing hole at the base of one of the falls.

Hiking to the Summit

The hike is relatively straightforward. You can do the roundtrip from the Las Pailas Ranger Station (also called Las Espuelas) to the summit and back in a day, two days from park headquarters. The lower trail begins at the Santa María Ranger Station, leads past Las Hornillas and the Las Pailas Ranger Station and snakes up the steep, scrubby mountainside through elephant grass and dense groves of twisted, stunted copel clusia, a perfumed tree species common near mountain summits. En route, you cross a bleak expanse of shingly purple lava fossilized

by the blitz of the sun. Trails are marked by
cairns, though it is easy to get lost if the clouds
set in; consider hiring a local guide. The upper
slopes are of loose scree. Be particularly careful
on your descent.

It can be cool up here, but—if it's clear—the
powerful view and the hard, windy silence make
for a profound experience. From on high, you
have a splendid view of the wide Guanacaste
plain shimmering in the heat like a dreamworld
between hallucination and reality, and, beyond,
the mountains of Nicoya glistening like hammered gold from the sunlight slanting in from
the south. On a clear day, you can see Lake
Nicaragua. Magical! You have only the sighing of
the wind for company.

It will probably be cloudy, however, in which
case you may need to camp near the top to ascend to the summit next morning before the
clouds set in (there's a campsite about five km
from Las Pailas; it's about two hours to the summit of Von Seebach from there). The beach of
Linnet Bird Lagoon—a whale-shaped lagoon
filled with very cold water, southeast of the active
volcano—is recommended for camping. Bring
waterproof tent and clothing, plus mosquito and
tick repellent. The grasses harbor ticks and other
biting critters: consider long pants.

Fill up with water at the ranger station before
your uphill hike.

Accommodations
In the park: You can stay in basic *cabinas* at the
ranger stations ($2.50). The two bunk beds
are said to have mildewed mattresses, or you
can sleep on the floor. No bedding or towels.
Bring a sleeping bag and mosquito netting. Make
reservations by calling the park headquarters in
Santa Rosa, tel. 695-5598, or the National Park
radio-communications office in San José, tel.
233-4160. A shady campsite next to an old sug-
arcane-processing plant, 500 meters from the
Santa María ranger station, has a bathroom.
You'll find another campsite on the banks of the
Río Colorado, near the Las Pailas Ranger Station. Camp here if hiking to the summit. Take
water from the creek. Otherwise you may camp
where you like though note that there are lots
of ticks. It can get cold at night; come prepared.
You'll be better off camping in dry season, Jan.-
April being best.

**Outside the Park: Albergue Rincón del Tur-
ista,** in the village of **San Jorge** near the park's
southeastern border, has rustic *cabinas* with
cold water and outhouse bathroom in a forested
valley ($10 pp). You can rent horses and guides.
Make reservations and arrange transportation
through the Casa de Cultura tourist information
office in Liberia, tel. 666-1606. You reach it via a
dirt road that branches off the Liberia-Santa
María road, three km south of the park entrance.

Nearby is **Rinconcito Lodge,** tel. 666-0636 or
666-0267, or beeper tel. 257-8585, ext. 5161,
offering five rudimentary rooms in a cement
blockhouse with shared bathroom with cold
water. Horses and guides are available, and
simple *típico* meals are served ($4-6). The own-
ers—Gerardo and María Inés Badilla—offer
transfers from San José for $40 for up to six
people. Rates: $10 s, $16 d.

Hacienda Lodge Guachipelín, Apdo. 636-
4050, Alajuela, tel. 442-2818 or 284-2049, fax
442-1910, e-mail: hacienda@intnet.co.cr, is a
centenarian working cattle ranch east of Curubandé, 18 km from Hwy. 1 and eight km south
of the Santa María Ranger Station. A rustic hardwood lodge offers 25 small and simple bedrooms plus a "suite" with more elegant decor.
A bunkhouse offers basic accommodations and
is part of the Costa Rican Youth Hostel system
(you can make reservations through the Toruma
Hostel in San José: RECAJ, Apdo. 1355, San
José 1002, tel./fax 224-4085). Tiled communal
bathrooms have cold water. The lodge has a
cozy lounge with deep-cushioned sofas and a
TV, plus verandas with Sarchí rockers. *Típico*
food is served in a dining room overlooking the
corral, where you can watch cattle and horses
being worked. The lodge has more than 1,000
hectares of terrain from dry forest to open savanna, plus a 1,200-hectare tree-reforestation
project. It offers guided horseback rides (and
even gives riding lessons), and has an eight-
day horseback-riding tour around Rincón de la
Vieja. It also has volcano hikes plus a "monkey
trail" tour. The owners had planned to introduce
mountain bikes and open a *mirador* with a bar
facing the ocean; an old coffee-drying trough
was to be turned into a swimming pool; 4WD
vehicles were to be introduced for exploring farther afield; and a bullfight plaza was planned.
However, a reader wrote to say new owners

had dropped these plans. It boasts views of the volcano. Extremely hospitable staff. Highly recommended by some past guests, although one thought it overpriced. Rates: $25 s/d/t ($9 bunkhouse), $45 suite. Horseback tours to Rincón cost $40. A minibus from the Hotel Guanacaste in Liberia costs $7 one-way.

Rincón de la Vieja Mountain Lodge, Apdo. 114, Liberia 5000, tel. 695-5553 or 225-1073, fax 234-1676, e-mail: rincon@sol.racsa.co.cr, five km beyond Hacienda Lodge Guachipelín, on the edge of the park near Las Pailas, is a superb base for exploring the park. The rustic all-hardwood lodge was converted from the family hacienda-home of Alvaro Wiessel (one of the volcano's craters is named Wiessel after Alvaro's German immigrant grandfather). The two-story structure has 27 pleasing though dark bedrooms and private bathrooms with cold water, plus three rustic cabins near the lodge for 6-8 people each with shared bath. There are two small pools in the gardens and, beyond that, forest. The property also includes a roofed corral and a dairy farm, plus a scientific library, an insect and butterfly collection, and a serpentarium. Electricity is generated by a stream. Options for exploring include guided horse tours ($40-50), mountain biking ($16), the canopy tour (see below), and nature tours. The lodge is 500 meters beyond the Río Colorado, which you can safely cross by 4WD. It's 1.5 km to the right from the fork for the park. Meals average $10 for breakfast, $12 dinner. Rates: $40 s, $51 d, $69 t. Three-day packages cost $99, or $190 with a hike and canopy tour; $299 for everything. Students receive discounts.

Canopy Tour

Top Tree Trails, c/o Rincón de la Vieja Mountain Lodge, tel. 695-5553 or 256-8206, fax 695-5553 or 256-7290, e-mail: rincon@sol.racsa.co.cr or AdvntrDive@aol.com, offers trips through the forest canopy using rappelling gear, with pulleys, harnesses, and safety slings. Professional guides are on hand to teach technique. You're at one with the monkeys as you glide between any of 16 treetop canopy platforms elevated up to 170 feet, anchored to the trunks of sturdy trees, and joined by sturdy steel cables. The "trail" lasts four hours ($50). A full-day tour includes horseback riding ($77). A nocturnal trails trip costs $82.

Information

The park headquarters is an old adobe hacienda—**Hacienda Santa María**—about 27 km northeast of Liberia (a sign on Hwy. 1 on the south side of Liberia points the way to the "Sector Santa María"). The 19th-century farmstead was once owned by former U.S. president Lyndon B. Johnson, who sold it to the parks service. It contains an exhibition room and is linked by a six-km trail to the **Las Pailas Ranger Station,** on the southwestern flank of the volcano. Las Pailas is reached via a road from Curubandé. Entrance: $6.

You can rent horses ($2.50 per hour) by calling Cigifredo Marín, the head ranger of the Guanacaste Conservation Area at Santa Rosa National Park, tel. 695-5598.

Tours

Jungle Trails, Apdo. 2413, San José 1002, tel. 255-3486, fax 255-2782, offers a three-day tour from San José, including a horseback ride and a hike to the crater, plus a second horseback ride to the thermal springs at Azufrales.

Most tour companies in San José can arrange tours to Rincón. **Private guides** Rodrigo and Sergio Bonilla escort tours and can provide horses, camping equipment, and more, as needed, tel. 223-0628.

Getting There

The road to the Santa María Ranger Station begins from the Barrio Victoria suburb of Liberia, where Avenida 6 leads east 25 km via Colonia La Libertad (a side road leads to San Jorge, which can also be reached by rough dirt road from Guayabo, north of Bagaces). The road is deeply rutted (and muddy in wet season); 4WD is recommended. Lodges arrange transfers, and the Hotel Guanacaste in Liberia has transfers daily at 7 a.m. and 4 p.m. ($6.25 pp each-way, three people minimum). A taxi from Liberia will cost about $30-40 each way. Park rangers may take you if they're heading to or from town.

The Santa María and Las Pailas ranger stations are linked by trails (see above). However, you can reach Las Pailas from Hwy. 1 via a turnoff about six km north of Liberia: the dirt road leads past the village of Curubandé (10 km) to the gates of Hacienda Guachipelín. The gates are open during daylight hours. Ostensibly you pay a $2.50

fee for the right to use the private road but nobody has been there to collect all the times I've driven it. The dirt road leads three km to Hacienda Guachipelín (the toll fee is reimbursed if you stay here) and, beyond, to Rincón de la Vieja Lodge (no refund) and Las Pailas Ranger Station. A bus departs Liberia for Curubandé at 2 p.m. on Monday, Wednesday, and Friday.

Take your sunglasses, especially if you walk: the roads are blinding white. The rock is ignimbrite, the white volcanic rock used to build the houses of Liberia.

CAÑAS DULCES AND VICINITY

Cañas Dulces, four km east of Hwy. 1 (the turnoff is 11 km north of Liberia), is a village in the midst of cattle country. Nearby is **Las Imágenes Biological Station,** a 1,000-hectare working cattle ranch and biological station with 100 hectares of virgin tropical dry and moist forest and riverine habitat. The station is a former hacienda recently opened to tourists. Horseback trips are offered to Rincón de la Vieja.

Hacienda Buena Vista is a U.S.-run property nestling high on the southwest flank of Rincón de la Vieja, 13 km northeast of Cañas Dulces. The drive is a steeply bone-jarring climb, forcing your car to wheeze uphill in first gear along a winding track as narrow as a toothpick. The lodge offers a variety of guided hikes and horseback trips to Rincón de la Vieja, to local waterfalls, or into the secondary forest surrounding the 1,600-hectare *finca* ($25). It has a **canopy tour,** which uses rappelling equipment on 960 meters of cable slung between trees ($25 for guests; $30 for nonguests). And rodeos and "bullfights" are sometimes hosted in a corral. No meals are available to day visitors. Reservations are advised. You can call for a taxi, tel. 666-0574 or 666-0073, in Quebrada Honda.

Accommodations
Las Imágenes, reservations c/o Hotel Las Espuelas, tel. 666-0144 or 293-4544, fax 293-4839; in North America, tel. 305-858-4567, fax 858-7478, has a rustic cabin with bunks for 20 people, with shared bath. Water is drawn from a well. **Cabinas 2001,** beside Hwy. 1, three km north of the turnoff for Cañas Dulces, has five simple *cabinas* with private bath and hot water for $15 d.

Buena Vista Lodge, Apdo. 373-5000, Liberia, tel. 695-5147, fax 666-2069, on Hacienda Buena Vista, has 45 rooms including dorms, plus three cabins with two double beds and a bunk, and 11 double rooms with private baths with hot water. The rustic and delightful cabins are hewn of stone and rough timbers, with pewter-washed floors and verandas looking down over lush lawns and a lake with waterfowl. A courtyard is bright with blossoms. Locally crafted rockers add to the atmosphere in the rustic restaurant that offers views down the mountain. You can admire the setting while soaking in a natural steam bath ringed by volcanic stone, and there's a bamboo sauna. Rates: $15 pp dorms for six; $20 s, $45 d private room. You can camp for $10. Students receive a 10% discount. Transfers from Cañas Dulces cost $15 roundtrip. *Recommended!*

QUEBRADA GRANDE AND VICINITY

This village, eight km east of Hwy. 1—the turnoff is at **Potrerillos,** 23 km north of Liberia (there's a Guardia Rural checkpoint at the junction)—sits on the lower saddle between Volcán Rincón de la Vieja to the southeast and Volcán Cacao to the northeast. It is surrounded by grasslands ranged by cattle and *haciendas* that welcome visitors.

Cacao Biological Station is 11 km beyond Quebrada Grande, with the road—paved for the first four km—deteriorating gradually. Turn left at the soccer plaza in Quebrada Grande, then right.

A bus operates to Quebrada Grande from Liberia daily at 3 p.m.

Sutton Ostrich Ranch
Sutton Ostrich Ranch, tel. 695-5355, 228-6646, or 331-5068, on the roadside four km east of Potrerillos, claims to be the only commercial ostrich ranch outside of Africa. The hot, dry climate of Guanacaste is perfect for breeding the comical, gawky, long-necked birds. Vivian González and Joe Sutton opened the 160-hectare farm in May 1992 after importing 100 of the blueneck and black ostrich varieties. December to April you might see the magnificent mating dance of the luxuriantly plumed male. If not, you'll probably see him putting on an equally dramatic defensive posture at your approach

along pathways leading to corrals spread amid the rolling, grassy hills. The hatchery contains electronically controlled incubators (young chicks are prone to infection; hence, visitors are asked to shower, change into sterile clothes, and step into an antiseptic dip before entering). Each hen lays 50-100 eggs a year. Each egg weighs 1.5 kg—about the equivalent of 25 chicken eggs—and, when used as food, takes an hour to boil. Adults weigh 90-160 kg, making them the biggest birds in the world. Hope they're in a good mood—their kick delivers a punch of 35 kg per square centimeter. The birds are harvested for meat, hide, and feathers (the meat is high in protein but low in cholesterol and fat).

Guided tours in Spanish are offered on weekdays at 10 a.m., 1 p.m., and 3 p.m. and weekends at 3 p.m. ($3 adults, $1.50 children).

Finca San Antonio
This 2,024-hectare working cattle ranch, northwest of Quebrada Grande, offers horseback trail rides. Scheduled rides are offered every Wednesday and Saturday. You can arrange rides on other days through Hotel Las Espuelas, tel. 666-0144, fax 225-3987. A one-day tour with barbecue lunch includes a visit to Santa Rosa National Park ($65). **Valle Dorado,** Apdo. 340, San José 1002, tel. 220-4250, fax 232-2027, includes a trail ride here on a three-day tour of Guanacaste and Nicoya. **L.A. Tours,** Apdo. 492, San José 1007, tel. 221-4501, fax 224-5828, also has a three-day tour featuring a half day at San Antonio.

Accommodations
Santa Clara Lodge, Apdo. 17-5000, Liberia, tel. 666-4054 or cellular tel. 391-8766, fax 666-4047, e-mail: sclodge@asstcard.co.cr, four km east of Quebrada Grande by rocky road, is a working cattle ranch with a single room, plus two doubles and two triples with shared bath, and a triple with private bath. There's also a double and triple, each with bunk beds. It's part of the Youth Hostel system and well kept. Though rudely furnished, rooms have extremely pretty decor and louvered windows. Home-style meals are served alfresco on a veranda. A *palenque* bar overlooks a small duck pond. A mineral spring feeds a soaking pool, said to be therapeutic. It is surrounded by 118 hectares of savanna and forest. Horseback riding is available ($20-50), as well as a variety of tours,

including to Sutton Ranch, Santa Rosa National Park and Orosí Volcano. Rates: $15 s, $30 d, $35 t with shared bath; $41 d, $45 t, with private bath; $27 d, $32 t with bunk beds. It's a member of Youth Hostels International.

Centro Social La Mata de Caña, in Quebrada Grande, has *cabinas* with shared bath and cold water, and is recommended for stews and other Guanacasteco dishes. The popular bar has a pool table. Rates: $6 pp.

A new hostel named **Albergue Bosque** has reportedly opened on the flanks of Cacao, but I couldn't find it.

PARQUE NACIONAL GUANACASTE

This mammoth park protects more than 84,000 hectares of savanna, dry forest, rainforest, and cloud forests extending east from Hwy. 1 to 1,659 meters atop Volcán Cacao. The park is part of a mosaic of ecologically interdependent parks and reserves—the 110,000-hectare Guanacaste Conservation Area (GCA)—that incorporates Santa Rosa National Park, Rincón de la Vieja National Park, Bolaños Island Wildlife Refuge, the Junquillal Bay National Wildlife Refuge, and the Horizontes Experimental Station, abutting Santa Rosa to the south. The park is contiguous with Santa Rosa National Park and protects the migratory routes of myriad creatures: jaguars, tapirs, sloths, monkeys, three-wattled bellbirds, and other species, many of which move seasonally between the lowlands and the steep slopes of Volcán Cacao and the dramatically conical Volcán Orosí (1,487 meters), whose wind-battered and rain-drenched eastern slopes contrast sharply with the flora and fauna on the dry plains. Orosí long since ceased activity and, interestingly, shows no signs of a crater.

The park includes significant areas of cattle pasture, which are being carefully managed to permit natural reforestation and form an integral part of the migratory mosaic. It is one of the most closely monitored parks scientifically, with three permanent biological stations, all of which offer basic accommodations. The **Pitilla Biological Station** is at 600 meters elevation on the northeast side of Cacao amid the lush, rain-soaked forest. It is reached via a rough dirt road from Santa Cecilia, 28 km east of Hwy. 1 beyond Ha-

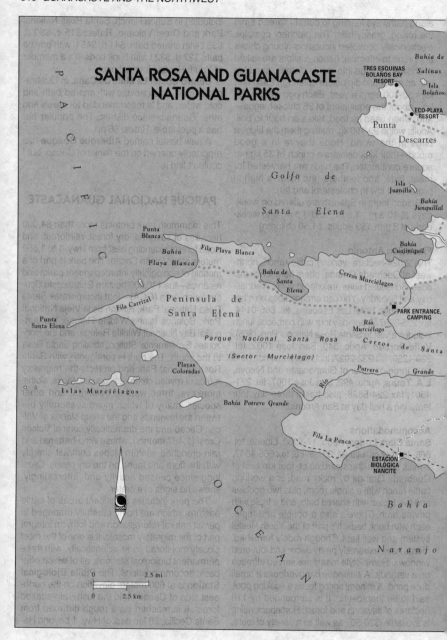

SANTA ROSA AND GUANACASTE NATIONAL PARKS

Bahía de Salinas

Isla Bolaños

TRES ESQUINAS
BOLAÑOS BAY
RESORT

ECO-PLAYA
RESORT

Punta Descartes

PACIFIC

Golfo de Santa Elena

Isla Juanilla

Bahía Junquillal

Punta Blanca

Fila Playa Blanca

Bahía Playa Blanca

Bahía Cuajiniquil

Bahía de Santa Elena

Cerros Murciélagos

Peninsula de Santa Elena

Fila Carrizal

PARK ENTRANCE, CAMPING

Punta Santa Elena

Río Murciélago

Parque Nacional Santa Rosa
(Sector Murciélago)

Cerros de Santa

Playas Coloradas

Islas Murciélagos

Río

Potrero
Grande

Bahía Potrero Grande

Fila La Penca

ESTACIÓN
BIOLÓGICA
NANCITE

Bahía

N

Naranjo

OCEAN

MOON

0   2.5 mi

0   2.5 km

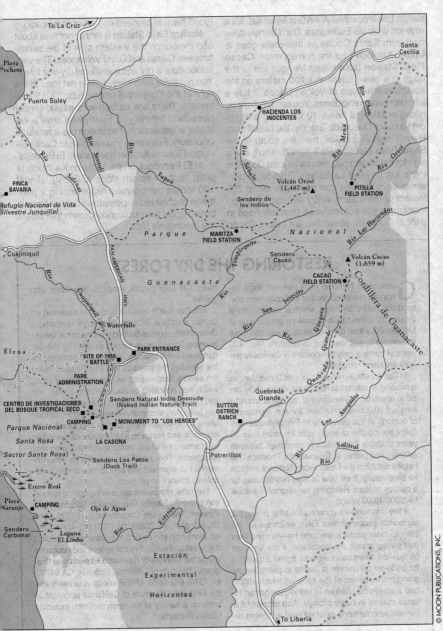

To La Cruz

Playa Pochote

Puerto Soley

FINCA BAVARIA

Refugio Nacional de Vida Silvestre Junquillal

Cuajiniquil

Río Salinas

Río Sentali

Río Sapoá

Santa Cecilia

HACIENDA LOS INOCENTES

Río Sábalo

Río Chiru

Volcán Orosí (1,487 m)

Sendero de los Indios

Río Mena

Río Orosí

PITILLA FIELD STATION

Parque

Guanacaste

PAN-AMERICAN HWY

Elena

Waterfalls

PARK ENTRANCE

SITE OF 1955 BATTLE

PARK ADMINISTRATION

CENTRO DE INVESTIGACIONES DEL BOSQUE TROPICAL SECO

CAMPING

Sendero Natural Indio Desnudo (Naked Indian Nature Trail)

MONUMENT TO "LOS HEROES"

LA CASONA

Parque Nacional Santa Rosa (Sector Santa Rosa)

Sendero Los Patos (Duck Trail)

Estero Real

Playa Naranjo

CAMPING

Sendero Carbonal

Laguna El Limbo

Ojo de Agua

MARITZA FIELD STATION

Río Tempisquito

Río Cuajiniquil

Nacional

Río Las Haciendas

Sendero Cacao

CACAO FIELD STATION

Volcán Cacao (1,659 m)

Cordillera de Guanacaste

Río San Josecito

Río Góngora

Río Grande

Quebrada Grande

Quebrada Grande

Río Los Ahogados

SUTTON OSTRICH RANCH

Potrerillos

Río Salitral

Estación Experimental Horizontes

To Liberia

© MOON PUBLICATIONS, INC.

cienda Los Inocentes. A 4WD is essential. It's a nine-km drive via Esperanza. Don't blithely drive east from Santa Cecilia as that route goes to Upala. Ask locals for the correct route. **Cacao Field Station** (also called Mengo) sits at the edge of a cloud forest at 1,100 meters on the southwestern slope of Volcán Cacao. It has a laboratory and rustic dorms. You can get there by hiking or taking a horse 10 km along a rough dirt trail from Quebrada Grande; the turnoff from Hwy. 1 is at Potrerillos, nine km south of the Santa Rosa National Park turnoff. You'll see a sign for the station 500 meters beyond Dos Ríos (nine km beyond Quebrada Grande). Four-wheel-drive vehicles can make it to within 300 meters of the station in dry season, with permission; in wet season you'll probably need to park at Gongora, about five km before Cacao

(you'll have to proceed on foot or horseback).

Maritza Field Station is farther north, at about 650 meters on the western side of the saddle between Cacao and Orosí Volcanoes. The vegetation here is dry and transitional dry-wet forest. You get there from Hwy. 1 via a dirt road to the right at the Cuajiniquil crossroads. It's 15 kilometers. There are barbed-wire gates: simply close them behind you. Four-wheel drive is essential in wet season. The station has a research laboratory. From here you can hike to Cacao Biological Station. Another trail leads to El Pedregal.

At **El Pedregal,** on the Llano de los Indios (a plain on the western slope of Orosí), almost 100 Indian petroglyphs representing a pantheon of chiseled supernatural beings lie half-buried in the luxurious undergrowth that cloaks the mountain's hide.

RESTORING THE DRY FOREST

G uanacaste National Park includes large expanses of eroded pasture that once were covered with native dry forest, which at the time of the Spaniards' colonization carpeted a greater area of Mesoamerica than did rainforests. It was also more vulnerable to encroaching civilization. After 400 years of burning, only two percent of Central America's dry forest remains.

In Costa Rica, American biologist Daniel Janzen is heading an attempt to restore the vanished dry forest to nearly 60,000 hectares of ranchland around a remnant 10,000-acre nucleus. Janzen, a professor of ecology at the University of Pennsylvania, has spent six months of every year for more than 30 years studying the intricate relationships between animals and plants in Guanacaste Province. He helped establish the Costa Rican National Institute for Biodiversity. It will take at least two decades for a canopy to form. Restoring the original forest will take 500-1,000 years!

A key is to nurture a conservation ethic among the surrounding communities. Fires, which are set initially to clear pasture, become free-running fires that sweep across the landscape. If the fires can be quelled, trees can take root again. Education for grade-school children is viewed as part of the ongoing management of the park; all fourth-, fifth-, and sixth-grade children in the region get an intense course in basic biology. And many of the farmers who formerly ranched land are being re-

trained as park guards, research assistants, and guides.

Another 2,400-hectare project is centered on Lomas Barbudal Biological Reserve in southern Guanacaste. Lomas Barbudal is one of the few remaining Pacific coast forests favored by the endangered scarlet macaw, which has a penchant for the seeds of the sandbox tree (the Spanish found the seed's hard casing perfect for storing sand, which was sprinkled on documents to absorb wet ink; hence its name). Friends of Lomas Barbudal has been very successful in preventing the devastating fires, establishing patrols and forest management, and nurturing a grassroots conservation ethic among the locals, including outreach programs to schools. The group raises funds for environmental management and education and needs volunteers to work on projects.

Two other groups are active in supporting restoration of the dry forests: **Guanacaste National Park Project,** The Nature Conservancy, 1815 N. Lynn St., Arlington, VA 22209, tel. (703) 841-4860. Contributions help secure land to be restored as tropical dry forest and support management and education programs. **University Research Expeditions Program,** University of California, Berkeley, CA 94720, tel. (510) 642-6586. UREP sends volunteers into the field with University of California scientists to work on a variety of research projects, including Lomas Barbudal.

It is one of the least visited and least developed parks in the nation, and facilities are not well developed. The park is administered from the Guanacaste Regional Conservation Area Headquarters at Santa Rosa, tel. 695-5598. Hours: 8 a.m.-4 p.m. Entrance: $6.

Hacienda Los Inocentes Wildlife Conservation and Recreation Center

This 1,000-hectare ranch (once the center for 8,000 head of cattle; the estate once belonged to the Inocentes family, which owned almost one-third of Guanacaste) lies within the park on the lower northern slopes of Volcán Orosí. It now operates as an eco-tourist and biological research center and boasts one of the most stunning settings in Costa Rica, with the great ascendant bulk of Orosí looming ominously to the south, cloud-shrouded and thick with tropical moist forest. The hacienda has a stable of 100 horses and specializes in horseback nature rides ($18 half day with guide, including lunch) to see howler, capuchin, and rare spider monkeys, sloths, anteaters, coatimundis, and white-tailed deer. Birds—especially toucans, oropendolas, and collared aracaris—are prolific. Garrulous parrots and scarlet macaws fly free in the hacienda grounds; a small deer will feed from your hands. And a friendly toucan loves to come down to pick off the dining table. Instead of getting up at dawn to help milk the cows, you can do so now for horseback rides to the very summit of Orosí. There are also hiking trails, and there's a tractor tour ($17). It is on Hwy. 4, about 16 km east of Hwy. 1 (the turnoff is three km south of La Cruz). A taxi from La Cruz costs about $15 one-way.

Accommodations

You can camp at any of the ranger stations ($1.50 per day). The three biological stations provide spartan dormitory accommodations ($15 per day) by contacting the park headquarters in Santa Rosa National Park, tel. 695-5598, which can also arrange transportation. Students and researchers get priority.

Cacao Field Station has a lodge with five rustic dormitories for up to 30 people. It has water, but no towels or electricity. Bring camping gear for cooking. It offers staggering views. **Maritza Field Station** is less rustic and has beds for 32 people, with shared bath, water, electricity, and a dining hall. The **Pitilla Biological Station** has accommodations for 20 people, with electricity, water, CB radio, and basic meals. Even if you've stayed at one of the other stations, Pitilla is worth the visit for its lusher vegetation reflecting Caribbean influences.

Hacienda Los Inocentes, Apdo. 228-3000, Heredia, tel. 679-9190 or 265-5484, fax 265-4385, e-mail: orosina@sol.racsa.co.cr, website www.arweb.com/orosi, is centered on a beautiful vintage lodge—built in 1890 of gleaming teak by the grandfather of Violeta de Chamorro, ex-president of Nicaragua—with 11 modest but pleasant rooms surrounded by a wide veranda with wicker rockers and hammocks for relaxing and savoring the views and sunsets. Two suites have private bathrooms upstairs; the other rooms have private bathrooms downstairs. There are also four cabins down the hill, each with a double and two single beds. The restaurant serves pleasing meals, and there's a small bar. In addition, **Orosí Nature Tours** is based here. Rates: $46 pp low season; $59 high season, including three meals; $28 room only.

PARQUE NACIONAL SANTA ROSA

Santa Rosa was founded in 1972 as the country's first national park. The 49,515-hectare park, which incorporates much of the Santa Elena peninsula, is most famous for Hacienda Santa Rosa—better known as La Casona—the nation's most cherished historic monument. It was here in 1856 that the mercenary army of American adventurer William Walker was defeated by a ragamuffin army of Costa Rican volunteers. The old hacienda-turned-museum alone is well worth the visit. Santa Rosa National Park has other treasures, too.

The park is a mosaic of 10 distinct habitats, including mangrove swamp, savanna, and oak forest, with attract a wide range of animals: more than 250 bird species and 115 mammal species (half of them bats, including two vampire species), among them relatively easily seen mammals such as white-tailed deer, coatimundis, howler, spider, and white-faced monkeys, and anteaters. Jaguars still roam Santa Rosa, as do margays, ocelots, pumas, and jaguarundis; they're all shy and seldom seen. Santa Rosa is a vitally important nesting site for ridleys and other turtle species. In the wet season the land is as green as emeralds, and wildlife disperses. In dry season, however, when the parched scrubby landscapes give an impression of the East African plains, wildlife congregates at watering holes—such as those on the Naked Indian Trail—and is easily seen. Be patient. Sit still for long enough and some interesting creatures are sure to appear. Keep an eye out for snakes.

The park is divided into two sections: the Santa Rosa Sector to the south (the entrance is at Km 269 on Hwy. 1, 37 km north of Liberia) and the Murciélago Sector (the turnoff from Hwy. 1 is 10 km farther north, via Cuajiniquil), separated by a swathe of privately owned land.

Santa Rosa Sector

The Santa Rosa Sector is the more important and accessible of the two sectors. On the right, one km past the entrance gate, a rough dirt road leads to a rusting armored personnel carrier beside a memorial cross commemorating the Battle of 1955, when Somoza, the Nicaraguan strongman, made an ill-fated foray into Costa Rica.

Six km farther on the paved road is **La Casona,** a magnificent colonial homestead with a beautiful setting atop a slight rise overlooking a stone corral where the battle with William Walker was fought. Inside the house are photos, illustrations, carbines, and other military paraphernalia commemorating the battle of 20 March 1856. Battles were also fought here during the 1919 Sapoá Revolution and in 1955. One room

is furnished in period style. Another is a small chapel. Large wooden mortars and pestles are on display, along with decrepit chaps and centenary riding gear. There's also a good nature exhibit. Harmless bats fly in and out. There's a large *guanacaste* tree outside.

Trails are marked in detail on the map sold at the park entrance. The **Naked Indian** loop trail (1.5 km) begins just before the house and leads through dry-forest woodlands with streams and waterfalls and gumbo-limbo trees whose peeling red bark earned them the nickname "naked Indian trees." The **Los Patos** trail, which has several watering holes during dry season, is one of the best trails for spotting mammals. The **Laguna Escondida and Caujiniquil River Trail** (14 km roundtrip) also takes you to a pond that is a magnet for thirsty wildlife. Other good spots for wildlife are **Platanar Lake, Laguna Escondida,** and **La Penca,** reached by trails north from the park administrative area.

The paved road ends just beyond the administration area. From here, an appalling dirt road drops steeply to the **beaches**—Playa Naranjo and Playa Nancite, 13 km from La Casona. It's a good road to break your springs. A 4WD with high ground clearance is essential. Park officials sometimes close the road because they get tired of towing vehicles out. The virtually deserted white-sand beach at **Playa Nancite** is renowned as the site for the annual *arribadas,* the mass nestings of olive ridley turtles which occur only here and at Ostional, farther south. More than 75,000 turtles will gather out to sea

La Casona Historic Museum

BOB RACE

and come ashore over the space of a few days, with the possibility of up to 10,000 reptiles on the beach at any one time in September and October. Although the exact trigger is unknown, *arribadas* seem to coincide with falling barometric pressure in autumn and are apparently associated with a waxing three-quarter moon. You can usually see solitary turtles at other times August through December. Stephen E. Cornelius's illustrated book, *The Sea Turtles of Santa Rosa National Park* (Costa Rica: National Park Foundation, 1986), provides an insight into the life of the ridley turtle. Cornelius initiated studies here in 1972. Today the ongoing research is under the direction of Claudette Mo, of the University of Costa Rica, PRMVS-UNA, Apdo. 1350-3000, Heredia, tel. 237-7039, fax 237-7036, e-mail: clee@irazu.una.ac.cr. Latest data suggests that the turtle population at Nancite is declining. Playa Nancite (about a one-hour hike over a headland from Estero Real, at the end of the dirt road) is a research site. Access is restricted and permits—issued only to scientists and volunteer researchers—are needed; make requests to Programa de Investigación, Area Conservación Guanacaste, Apdo. 169-5000, Liberia, tel. 695-5598.

Very popular and beautiful **Playa Naranjo** is a kilometers-long, pale gray sand beach legendary in surfing lore. Steep, thick, powerful tubular waves and "killer beautiful Witches Rock rising like a sentinel out of the water make this a must stop in the world for top-rated surfers," says surf expert Mark Kelly. The beach is bounded by craggy headlands and frequently visited by monkeys, iguanas, and other wildlife. Crocodiles lurk in the mangrove swamps at the southern end of the beach. At night, planktonic animals light up with a brilliant phospherescence as you walk the drying sand in the wake of high tide. **Witches Rock** is a gigantic crag split in two and jutting up straight from the ocean bottom.

In addition to Playa Naranjo, **Playa Portrero Grande,** north of Nancite, and other beaches on the central Santa Elena peninsula offer some of the best "machine-like" surf in the country, with double overhead waves rolling in one after the other. The makers of *Endless Summer II,* the sequel to the classic surfing movie, caught the Portrero Grande break perfectly. The beaches are inaccessible by road. You can hire a boat at

Jobo or any of the fishing villages in the Golfo Santa Elena to take you to Portrero Grande or Islas Murciélagos ("Bat Islands"), slung in a chain beneath Cabo Santa Elena, the westernmost point of the peninsula. The Bat Islands are a renowned scuba diving site for advanced divers; sharks (bull, tiger, and black-tip) are there in numbers, along with whale sharks and other large pelagics.

Murciélago Sector

The entrance to the Murciélago Sector of Santa Rosa National Park is 15 km west of Hwy. 1, 10 km north of the Santa Rosa Sector park entrance (there's a police checkpoint at the turnoff; have your passport ready for inspection). The road winds downhill to a coastal valley through spectacularly hilly countryside to **Cuajiniquil,** tucked half a kilometer south of the road, which continues northwest to Bahía Junquillal.

You arrive at a Y-fork in Cuajiniquil: the road to Murciélago (eight km) is to the left. There are three rivers to ford en route. You'll pass the old CIA training camp for the Nicaraguan contras on your right. The place—Murciélago Hacienda—was owned by the Nicaraguan dictator Somoza's family before being expropriated in 1979, when the Murciélago Sector was incorporated into Santa Rosa National Park. It's now a training camp for the Costa Rican Rural Guard. Armed guards may stop you for an ID check as you pass. A few hundred meters farther, the road runs alongside the secret airstrip (hidden behind tall grass to your left) that Oliver North had built to supply the contras. The park entrance is 0.5 km beyond the airstrip.

It's another 16 km to **Playa Blanca,** a beautiful horseshoe-shaped white-sand beach—one of the most isolated in the country—about five km wide and enjoyed only by pelicans and frigate birds. The road ends here. Waterfalls are surrounded by ferns and palms in **Cuajiniquil Canyon,** which has its own moist microclimate. The **Poza El General** watering hole attracts waterfowl and other animals year-round and is reached along a rough trail.

Accommodations

Santa Rosa Sector: The **Centro de los Investigaciones Daniel Janzen,** Apdo. 169, Liberia, tel. 695-5598, a science center next to the administrative center near La Casona, accommodates guests on a space available basis. Reservations recommended. Rates: $15 pp; $25 with meals; $5 students.

The Santa Rosa sector has three **campsites**. La Casona campsite is beneath shady *guanacaste* trees, 400 meters west of the administrative center near the hacienda. It has barbecue pits, picnic tables, and bathrooms. It can get muddy here in the wet season. Raccoons abound, so you'll need to be creative to keep your food safe. The shady Argelia campsite at Playa Naranjo has sites with fire pits and picnic tables and benches. There are shared showers, sinks, and outhouse toilets, and water from a well (it is not potable, so boil it or bring bottled water). The campsite at the north end of Playa Nancite is for use by researchers and others with permits. There's a limit of 20 people. Rates: $1.25 pp. The campsite at Estero Real has closed.

Murciélago Sector: You can camp at the ranger station, where there's a bathroom, showers, water, and picnic tables. (There are also cabins for researchers only.) You can also camp at Playa Blanca (no facilities). Rates: $1.25 pp. The raccoons will stop at virtually nothing to get at your food. Do *not* leave food in your tent. Fires are a serious hazard. Take precautions (the Parks Service issues a pamphlet, *Preventing Forest Fires*).

Food

The park administration area has a small *cocina* (kitchen) serving park rangers. Irene, the cook, sells to tourists by reservation only. Meals are served at 6-7 a.m. ($3), noon ($4), and 5-6 p.m. ($3.50).

Information

The park entrance station, tel. 695-5577, at the Santa Rosa Sector sells detailed maps (1:50,000 scale; 75 cents) showing trails and campgrounds. Hours: 7 a.m.-4:30 p.m. Both the natural history museum in La Casona and the GCA **park administration office,** tel./fax 695-5598, can provide additional information. Entrance: $6.

The **Dry Tropical Forest Investigation Center,** located near the park administrative office, undertakes biological research, and features a laboratory, documentation center, and computer center, plus dorm accommodations for 64 people (researchers only). It is not open to visi-

tors, but anyone with a serious interest in dry forest ecology will find the staff and researchers invaluable resources.

Getting There

Buses depart San José for La Cruz and Peñas Blancas from Calle 14, Avenidas 3/5 (Carsol, tel. 224-1968), daily at 5 a.m., 7:45 a.m., 1:30 p.m., and 4:15 p.m., passing the park entrance—35 km north of Liberia—en route to the Nicaraguan border (six hours). Buy your ticket in advance. Buses depart Liberia for Santa Rosa and La Cruz from Avenida 5, Calle 14 at 5:30 a.m., 8:30 a.m., 11 a.m., 2 p.m., and 6 p.m. You'll have to walk or hitchhike from the park entrance (seven km to La Casona and the park headquarters, another 13 km to Playa Naranjo). Hitchhiking is easy.

The bus schedules are posted at the information center at the park entrance and in the natural history room at La Casona. At press time, buses passed the park gate at the following times: La Cruz to San José at 5:45 a.m., 6:10 a.m., 8:25 a.m., 11:25 a.m., 3:25 p.m., and 4:20 p.m.; La Cruz to Liberia at 7:15 a.m., 10:30 a.m., 1:30 p.m., 3:30 p.m., 5:15 p.m., and 6 p.m.; and Liberia to La Cruz at 6 a.m., 9 a.m., 9:30 a.m., 11:30 a.m., 12:30 p.m., 2:30 p.m., 4 p.m., 5 p.m., 6 p.m., 7:30 p.m., and 8:30 p.m.

To Murciélago: Buses depart La Cruz for Cuajiniquil at 5 a.m. and noon, and from Liberia for Cuajiniquil at 6:30 a.m. and 3:30 p.m. (returning at 7 a.m. and 4:45 p.m.). You can catch the Liberia-Cuajiniquil-La Cruz bus from the Santa Rosa entrance at 4 p.m. From Cuajiniquil you may have to walk the eight km to the park entrance (take lots of water).

You can rent a boat from a local fisherman ($25-50 per boatload) to explore the coastline of Murciélago. Try in Cuajiniquil or at the wharf at the end of the road, three km west of the village. The journey can be quite rough in the rainy season because of high winds.

REFUGIO NACIONAL DE VIDA SILVESTRE BAHÍA JUNQUILLAL

The 505-hectare Bahía Junquillal National Wildlife Refuge (formerly Bahía Junquillal Recreation Area), in Bahía Junquillal north of Murciélago, is part of the Guanacaste Conservation Area and is administered from Santa Rosa, tel./fax 695-5598 or 695-5577. The calm bay is backed by tropical dry forest and is a refuge for pelicans, frigate birds, and other seabirds, as well as the olive ridley, hawksbill, green, and leatherback turtles, which come ashore to lay their eggs on the beautiful, two-km-wide, half-moon, gray-sand beach. Not for long, one imagines, as the beach is very popular with Ticos, who descend lock, stock, and barrel to camp on the beach on weekends and holidays. Paths lead along the shore to mangrove swamps.

The recreation area is reached via the road to Cuajiniquil and the Murciélago sector of Santa Rosa National Park. Continue west on the main road past Cuajiniquil for two km, where a deeply rutted dirt road leads north to the recreation area. You can continue around Bahía Junquillal to Brasilia and Puerto Soley, but you'll need a 4WD with high ground clearance in wet season.

The paved road continues past the turnoff for Bahía Junquillal and dead-ends at a wharf where fishing boats berth. It's an idyllically rustic setting. You can watch locals snorkeling for lobster in Bahía Cuajiniquil (separated from Bahía Junquillal by a slender peninsula) using plastic bags and bottles for bouyancy.

There's a ranger station, and an interpretive center is planned. Entrance: $2 foreigners, 75 cents nationals. Rangers offer guided tours.

Accommodations and Food
There's a well-organized camping area under shade trees, with latrines, barbecue pits, tables, and showers. Water is reportedly rationed to one hour daily. Rates: $1.25 pp. Two **camp-sites** are in the hamlet of Brasilito, at the northern end of the beach.

There's a bar—**Coco Loco**—and **Restaurant Cuajiniquil** as you enter Cuajiniquil. Both may have rooms. Inquire by calling the public telephone, 679-9030. The local *pulpería* reportedly has two rooms with shared bath and cold water—**Cabinas Santa Elena**, tel. 679-9112 (leave a message).

About 1.5 km north of the recreation area is **Finca Bavaria**, tel. 238-2119, fax 260-3626, a tiny rustic homestead sitting on stilts atop a breezy hill, surrounded by bougainvillea and shade trees. Herman, the German owner, rents

rooms and permits camping. It's quite funky and has an outhouse at the back. If nobody is there, check with the caretaker, Maritza, who lives in the little shack at the bottom of the hill. Guided hikes, horseback rides, and—supposedly—scuba diving are offered. A 45-minute trail leads to a *mirador* with views over the entire Golfo de Santa Elena. Rates: $6 pp rooms.

LA CRUZ AND VICINITY

La Cruz—gateway to Nicaragua (19 km north)—is Costa Rica's most northerly town, half a km west of Hwy. 1. It is a small town, dramatically situated atop the edge of an escarpment with incredible views over Bahía de Salinas. A good time to visit is May, when it hosts its annual and lively **Fiesta Cívica.**

A turnoff at the police security checkpoint three km south of La Cruz leads east to Upala, in the northern lowlands. Volcán Orosí looms to the south. About 15 km along the road you begin to feel the influence of the moister Caribbean: vegetation and microclimates change dramatically within a few kilometers. East of Hacienda Los Inocentes and the Río Sábalo, dry deciduous forest gives way to evergreen forest cloaked in epiphytes, and flatlands give way to rolling hills covered with citrus plantations. The palette-bright blossoming trees of Guanacaste fade away. In a span of some 10 km you pass into the northern lowlands.

Accommodations
Hotel El Faro, tel. 679-9009, 100 meters west of the gas station on Hwy. 1, has 17 basic rooms with shared bath with cold water. The dingy restaurant downstairs doubles as a disco on weekends. Rate: $5 s, $7 d. A much better bet is **Cabinas Santa Rita,** tel. 679-9062, fax 679-9305, 150 meters south of the plaza; it features 33 rooms. The 13 with shared bath and cold water and fans are clean though basic. Nicer, larger units at the back have a/c, lots of light and roomy private showers. Secure parking. The owner wouldn't give me rates, but expect to pay about $8 for small units with shared bath, $15-25 for larger units.

Hospedaje Pensión La Tica, opposite the bus station, has very basic, tiny but clean rooms with communal bath. Rates: $5. The **Cabinas Maryfel,** tel. 679-9096, nearby, is said to be better.

The best bet by far is **Amalia Inn,** tel./fax 679-9181, 100 meters south of the plaza. This charming place is operated by a friendly Tica, Amalia Bounds, and boasts a fabulous clifftop perch with views over Bahía Salinas and north along the Nicaraguan coast. Its eight rooms are large and cool, with tile floors, leather sofas, and striking paintings by Amalia's late husband, Lester. All have private bathrooms. A pool is handy for cooling off, though the inn's setting is breezy enough. Amalia will make breakfast, and you can prepare picnics in the kitchen. Trails lead down the forested escarpment, and Amalia was planning to add boat trips. Rates: $25-35 low season, including tax; in high season, the tax is added on top of those rates.

The **Iguana Lodge,** tel. 679-9015, fax 679-9054, next door to Amalia, is described as having "a variety of rooms ($50 d, including breakfast), a recreation area for children, and incredible views of Bahía Salinas." Reports are that the old wooden house is "worn around the edges." Apparently it's full of stuffed iguanas. I missed it.

Las Colinas del Norte Ecological Lodge, Apdo. 10493-1000, San José, tel. 679-9132, fax 679-9064, is a cattle *finca* on a hillside about three km north of La Cruz. It has a handsome Colorado-style lodge and 24 simply furnished hardwood bungalows with private baths and hot water under shade trees. The restaurant serves Italian and *típico* dishes prepared in a clay oven (cheeses are homemade on site using milk from the ranch's heifers). There's a TV lounge with leather chairs, plus a large pool, tennis courts, and a disco converted from a cattle pen (a disco that is—or was—a *literal* meat market!). The bar has a resident pianist and singer, Al Moreno. Horseback rides lead through 270 hectares of tropical forest and beachfront plains. A yacht is on hand for cruises, and tours are offered far and wide. Rates: $25 s, $30 d, $35 t.

Food

The simple **Mirador y Restaurante Ehecatl,** tel. 679-9104, sits atop the scarp slope with superb vistas across Bahía Salinas—a great place to enjoy ceviches, shellfish soup ($4), or shrimp, lobster, or octopus dishes; average entrée price

is $15. (Ehecatl is a Chorotega Indian name meaning "God of Wind.") **Bar y Restaurante Thelma,** tel. 679-9150, has reasonably priced *típico* food. Also recommended for cheap *casados* and *gallo pinto* is **Restaurante Dariri,** two blocks south of the main square.

Services

A **Banco Nacional,** tel. 679-9110, is opposite the **gas station** on Hwy. 1 as you enter town. The **police** station, tel. 679-9197, and spiffy new **medical clinic** are here, too.

Getting There

Buses depart San José for La Cruz from Calle 16, Avenidas 3/5 (Carsol, tel. 224-1968), daily at 5 a.m., 7:45 a.m., 1:30 p.m., and 4:15 p.m. The bus continues to the Nicaraguan border at Peñas Blancas. Buy your ticket in advance. Slower buses also operate from Liberia. Buses for San José depart La Cruz at 7:15 a.m., 10:30 a.m., 3:30 p.m., and 6 p.m., though these originate at the Nicaraguan border and are often full by the time they pull into La Cruz. You can buy tickets from the *pulpería,* tel. 679-9108, next to the bus station.

BAHÍA SALINAS

Immediately west of the plaza in La Cruz, a dirt road drops dizzily and dangerously (it's loose scree, making for a slithery descent and tenuous ascent) to the flask-shaped Bahía Salinas, ringed by beaches backed in the center by coastal plains lined with salt pans and mangroves that attract wading birds and crocodiles. The beaches in the center are of beautiful white sand fading to brown-grey along the shore of **Punta Descartes,** separating the bay from Bahía Junquillal to the south. High winds blow almost nonstop Dec.-April (averaging Force 4 about 90% of the time), making this a prime spot for windsurfing (as well as for pelicans and frigate birds, wheeling and sliding magnificently).

The road leads past the hamlet of **Puerto Soley,** where the road splits. The right fork leads to **Jobo,** a little fishing village just inland from Bahía Jobo at the tip of Punta Descartes; and— taking another fork to the left—to **Manzanillo,** where colorful fishing boats and views across the Golfo de Santa Elena make up for the pebbly

Bahía Salinas

beach. The left fork leads to **Brasilito,** on Bahía Junquillal. Turn right in Jobo and then left at a Y-junction for the exquisite beach at **Playa Rajada;** turn right for **Playa Jobo** and **Playa La Coyotera.**

The resort boom that is turning Bahía Culebra, a few miles south, into a mini-Acapulco has begun to spread north to Bahía Salinas. Two resorts had opened at press time on the shore of Punta Descartes, with plans for two golf courses and at least three other major resorts in the works.

Refugio Nacional de Vida Silvestre Isla Bolaños

Bolaños Island is a rugged, oval-shaped rocky crag, 25 hectares in area, about half a kilometer east of Punta Descartes. The island rises dramatically to a height of 81 meters and looks, as Herman Melville described the Galápagos, "much as the world at large might, after a penal conflagration." This pocket of northwest Guanacaste is one of the driest in the country, with less than 150 cm of annual rainfall. It is grown over with drought-resistant shrubs, which feed on the mists and occasional rain. The predominant species are the *paira,* which sheds its leaves during the dry season, and lemon wood, a woody vine that forms dense thickets that serve as nesting sites for island birds.

Bolaños Island is a wildlife refuge protecting one of only four nesting sites in Costa Rica for the brown pelican, and the only known nesting site for the American oystercatcher. As many as 200 frigate birds also nest here during the Jan.-March mating season, predominantly on the southwestern cliffs to take advantage of strong winds that give strong lift to their large wingspans. (Because they have small bodies and tiny feet but very wide wings and extremely long tails, they cannot run to take off but need a high ledge from which to launch themselves into flight.)

Visitors are not allowed to set foot on the island, but you can hire a boat and guide in Puerto Soley or Jobo to take you within 50 meters. Alas, the manager of the Eco-Playa Resort, which faces directly toward the island, told me that the hotel regularly takes guests to the island and seemed surprised when I told him that it was forbidden to land. The resort also had horrifying plans to introduce jet skis!

Accommodations and Food

Las Salinas is a trailer park in pretty grounds right next to the white-sand beach near Puerto Soley. There are bathrooms. RVs and campers are charged $6 pp. Salt ponds behind the site are good for birding; the sheltered bay is superb for swimming. Very peaceful. The simple roadside restaurant serves seafoods and *típico* dishes. There are two basic **campsites** at the hamlet of Brasilito.

The Dutch-owned **Eco-Playa Resort,** Apdo. 87-4003 Alajuela, tel. 289-8920, fax 289-4536, is an attractive modern all-suite complex on Playa La Coyotera, on the western shore of the bay, with lawns leading onto a thin and unappealing

Hacienda Los Inocentes, near La Cruz, with Orosí Volcano in background

beach. Squat, red-tile-roofed bungalows are aligned zig-zag-style in two rows obliquely facing the beach. The large rooms feature open-plan lounges with terra-cotta floors, a/c, ceiling fans, TVs, telephones, kitchenettes, and upscale, motel-style decor. The soaring *palenque* restaurant opens to a crescent-shaped pool and sundeck. A second swimming pool, spa, tennis courts, and a small convention center were be added. The name "Eco-Playa" abuses the concept of ecotourism. For example, managment is considering introducing jet skis, and the nesting sites of Isla Bolaños Wildlife Refuge are only 600 meters away. Rates: $85 studio; $110 junior suite; $145 master suite; $200 luxury suite.

Tres Esquinas Bolaños Bay Resort, tel. 679-9444, fax 697-9654, e-mail: suschrcr@sol.racsa. co.cr, alias the Three Corners Beach Resort, is a carbon-copy of Eco-Playa Resort. It, too, is surrounded by six hectares of lawns backing a slender brown-sand beach and has 72 spacious, red-tile-roofed a/c bungalows (including eight family apartments) with contemporary decor, minibars, TVs, and telephones. The resort is centered on a soaring *palenque* lobby with a thatched restaurant. Facilities include a large irregular shaped pool and children's pool. It's a *very* breezy locale—especially Dec.-April—and operates as a windsurf center. The restaurant serves burgers, pastas, and tuna salads ($4-5). The resort is popular with French and Germans. Iyok Trips and the Bolaños Bay Resort Pro-Center are based here. Rates: from $60 s, $100 d, including

three meals and tax. Several packages are offered, including a two-night weekend package ($118 s, $196 d) and family package for two adults and two children ($270 two nights, $792 weekly). The complex will eventually include **Resort Rancho Mary** (with 32 condos, 50 studios, and 150 hotel rooms plus *two* 18-hole golf courses) to be built on the hills behind the bay.

The **Galbi Club,** adjacent to Eco-Playa, is a super-exclusive private resort for international jet-setters; it was under construction at press time. Another U.S.-owned resort was planned for Puerto Soley. And **Residencial Costa Dorado** is a planned residential resort community slated to go up by 2000.

You can also eat at **La Fonda Restaurante,** a *soda* favored by the salt-pan workers.

Tours and Activities
Iyok Trips at Tres Esquinas, offers mountain biking ($15 per day), horseback riding ($20 two hours; $50 five hours), banana boat rides ($10), waterskiing ($15), snorkeling ($10 two hours), fishing ($100), and trips farther afield.

Bolaños Bay Resort Pro-Center also at Tres Esquinas, is a European-run windsurf center. Boards rent for $15 per hour, $45 daily, $240 per week (wet suits extra). It has a three-day beginner course ($165), special lessons ($100 for 10 hours), and intensive private lessons ($37 hourly).

The first nine holes at **Resort Rancho Mary,** part of Tres Esquinas, should be open by the time you read this, with 36 holes when complete.

Getting There
Buses depart La Cruz daily at 5:30 a.m., 10:30 a.m., and 1 p.m. for Puerto Soley and Jobo. Return buses depart Jobo 90 minutes later. A taxi will cost about $3 one-way to Puerto Soley, $8 to Jobo.

PEÑAS BLANCAS

Peñas Blancas, 19 km north of La Cruz, is the border post for Nicaragua. The entire area is sealed by wire fencing. There's no village. The Costa Rican border post is open 8 a.m.-noon and 1-6 p.m. A minibus operates between the Costa Rican border post and Nicaraguan immigration, four km away. The bus stop—which defines bedlam—is 800 meters north of the Costa Rican post. Note that you cannot drive a rental car across the border.

Be careful driving the Pan-Am Highway, which hereabouts is dangerously potholed and chock-a-block with articulated trucks hurtling along.

Border Crossing
Count on at least an hour for the formalities and be sure to have *all* required documents in order

or you may as well get back on the bus to San José. See **Getting There** in the On the Road chapter for information on this crossing.

Services
The bus terminal building contains the **Oficina de Migración** (immigration office), tel. 679-9025, a **bank** and the **Restaurante Peñas Blancas,** which is well stocked with essentials such as batteries, cookies, and booze. There's a **Costa Rican Tourism Institute** office, ICT, tel. 679-9025, here, too. Change money before crossing into Nicaragua (you get a better exchange rate on the Costa Rican side).

Getting There
Buses depart San José for Peñas Blancas from Calle 14, Avenida 3/5 (Carsol, tel. 224-1968), daily at 5 a.m. 7:45 a.m., 1:30 p.m., and 4:15 p.m. Travel time is six hours. Buy your ticket in advance. Buses depart Liberia for Peñas Blancas from Avenida 5, Calle 14 at 5:30 a.m., 8:30 a.m., 9 a.m., 10 a.m., noon, 2 p.m., 6 p.m., and 8 p.m. ($2; two hours). Buses depart Peñas Blancas at 6 a.m., 7:15 a.m., 9:30 a.m., 10:30 a.m., 12:30 p.m., 2:30 p.m., 3:30 p.m., 5 p.m., and 6 p.m.

BOB RACE

CATHY CARLSON

NICOYA PENINSULA

The Nicoya Peninsula is a broad, hooked protuberance—130 km long and averaging 50 km wide—separated from the Guanacaste plains by the Río Tempisque and Gulf of Nicoya. The region has traditionally been one of the country's least developed. However, more than 70% of Costa Rica's coastal resort infrastructure is in the province and newly cut roads are linking the last pockets of the erstwhile inaccessible Pacific coast. A long dry season, warm waters, and the nation's finest beaches lure visitors seeking the joys of the tropics. Italians are particularly enamored of Nicoya's beaches, and from Tamarindo south they're at the forefront of an explosion of hotels, restaurants, and bars. About half a dozen resort villages line the pacific coast. Each has its own distinct appeal: Coco draws scuba divers and the party crowd; Flamingo sportsfishing folk; Tamarindo surfers and those interested in upscale resorts, with watersports activities; Nosara anyone looking for laid-back escapes on long lonesome beaches; Sámara the offbeat crowd; and Montezuma the even more offbeat crowd. All have wildlife refuges close at hand.

The most developed beaches are concentrated in northern Nicoya. Deluxe resorts are going up in earnest around Bahía de Culebra, with half a dozen golf courses slated (the arrival of golf courses is none too soon, perhaps, for I'm reliably informed that the lack of action has spawned a considerable cocaine trade to keep the many wealthy expat gringos amused).

Otherwise the only true towns are along Hwy. 21, which runs south from Liberia along the eastern plains of Nicoya through the towns of Filadelfia, Santa Cruz, Nicoya, and Carmona.

The Rafael Calderón administration (1990-94), anxious to reap the tourist boom, targeted Nicoya for the kind of resort developments that have swallowed up whole oceanfronts elsewhere in the isthmus of Central America. The center of this frenzy is Bahía de Culebra, where the Gulf of Papagayo Project plans on turning the region into a massive resort complex with several deluxe resorts and residential communities already in place. And the opening of the Daniel Oduber International Airport at Liberia in 1996 has significantly boosted tourist arrivals to the beaches of northern Nicoya; it's just a 20-minute drive to Bahía Culebra and Playa del Coco.

Beaches here come in every hue and every shape, although only a select few compare with those of Cancún, Tahiti, or the Bahamas, and nowhere are the ocean waters the scintillating blue-jade of coral water elsewhere. Budget travelers are well served throughout, though prices are higher than elsewhere in the country, often inordinately so. Reservations are highly recommended for holiday periods.

Away from the coast, Nicoya is mountainous, cut by deep valleys and much denuded for pasture. The region is not blessed with the diversity of natural attractions found elsewhere in the country. But two nature experiences stand out: a visit to the Guanacaste Marine Turtle National Park to see the leatherback turtles laying eggs, and the Ostional National Wildlife Refuge during a mass invasion of olive ridley turtles. These are, for me, singularly the most momentous, guaranteed wildlife encounters in Costa Rica. Curú and Cabo Blanco Wildlife Refuges offer their own nature highlights. And there are sure to be monkeys and other wildlife galore in forests along the shore.

The beaches have been discovered in earnest by surfers, who run thick as pilchard. The offshore waters are beloved of scuba divers and for sportfishing. World-class giants such as 400-kg black marlin, 100-kg sailfish, 30-kg dolphin, and "locomotive-size" tuna swim within easy reach of seasoned anglers off the coast of Nicoya. The Gulf of Papagayo is particularly noteworthy. Flamingo Marina is the major sportfishing center.

Marlin and sailfish are regional specialties at local restaurants. They are particularly delicious when prepared with a marinated base of fresh herbs and olive oil, and seared over an open grill to retain the moist flavor. Ceviche is also favored throughout Nicoya, using the white meat of *corvina* (sea bass) steeped in lemon juice mixed with dill or cilantro and finely cut red peppers.

Several communities publish their own touristic newsletters. Look for *La Revue: North Costa Rica and South Nicaragua Tourist Guide,* tel./fax 670-0168, e-mail: larevue@sol.racsa.co.cr, published in Playa del Coco and focusing on Nicoya's northern beaches.

This is an area where a good wad of cash is advisable, as banks are few and far between. Campers should take all supplies with them.

Climate
It's no coincidence that the majority of Costa Rica's resort hotels are nestled along the shores of the Pacific northwest, where sun is the name of the game. Best time to visit is Dec.-April, when rain is virtually unheard of (average annual rainfall is less than 150 cm in some areas). The rainy season generally arrives in May and lasts until November. September and October are the wettest months. The so-called Papagayo winds—heavy northerlies *(nortes)*—blow strongly January (sometimes earlier) through March. Gusts of 100 kph are not uncommon. Surfers rave about the rainy season (May-Oct.), when swells are consistent and waves—fast and tubular—can be 1.5 meters or more.

History
The peninsula was colonized early by Spaniards, who established the cattle industry that dominates to this day. In pre-Columbian times, the peninsula was the heartland of the culturally advanced Chorotega Indians, who celebrated the Fiesta del Maíz ("Festival of Corn") and worshiped the sun with the public sacrifice of young virgins and ritual cannibalism. As it is today, the town of Nicoya was the regional capital; the Spaniards found well-defined trade routes radiating northward from this small village all the way to Nicaragua.

The people who today inhabit the province are tied to old bloodlines and live and work on the cusp between cultures. In Guaitil, for example, Chorotega women have kept stirred the spark of a nearly dead culture by making pottery in the same fashion their ancestors did one thousand years ago (the battle to maintain traditional influences has also kept kindled the matriarchal hierarchy: women run the businesses and sustain families and village structures). Fortunately, a renaissance of cultural pride is emerging, fostered by tourist interest.

During the colonial era, the area formed part of Guanacaste, a separate province. The province was delivered to Nicaragua in 1787, and to Costa Rica in 1812. After independence, Guanacaste's loyalties were split, with the Nicoyans favoring union with Costa Rica while the rest of Guana-

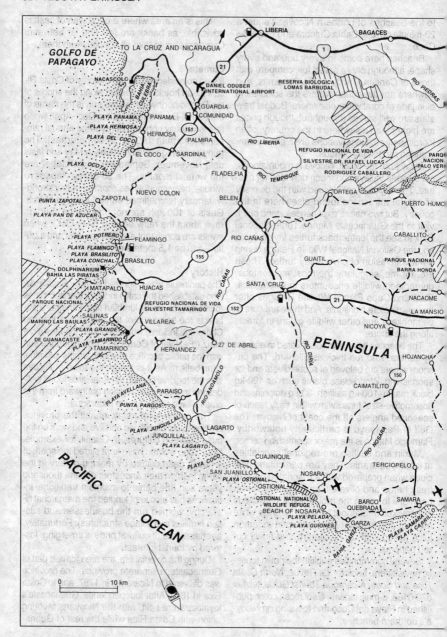

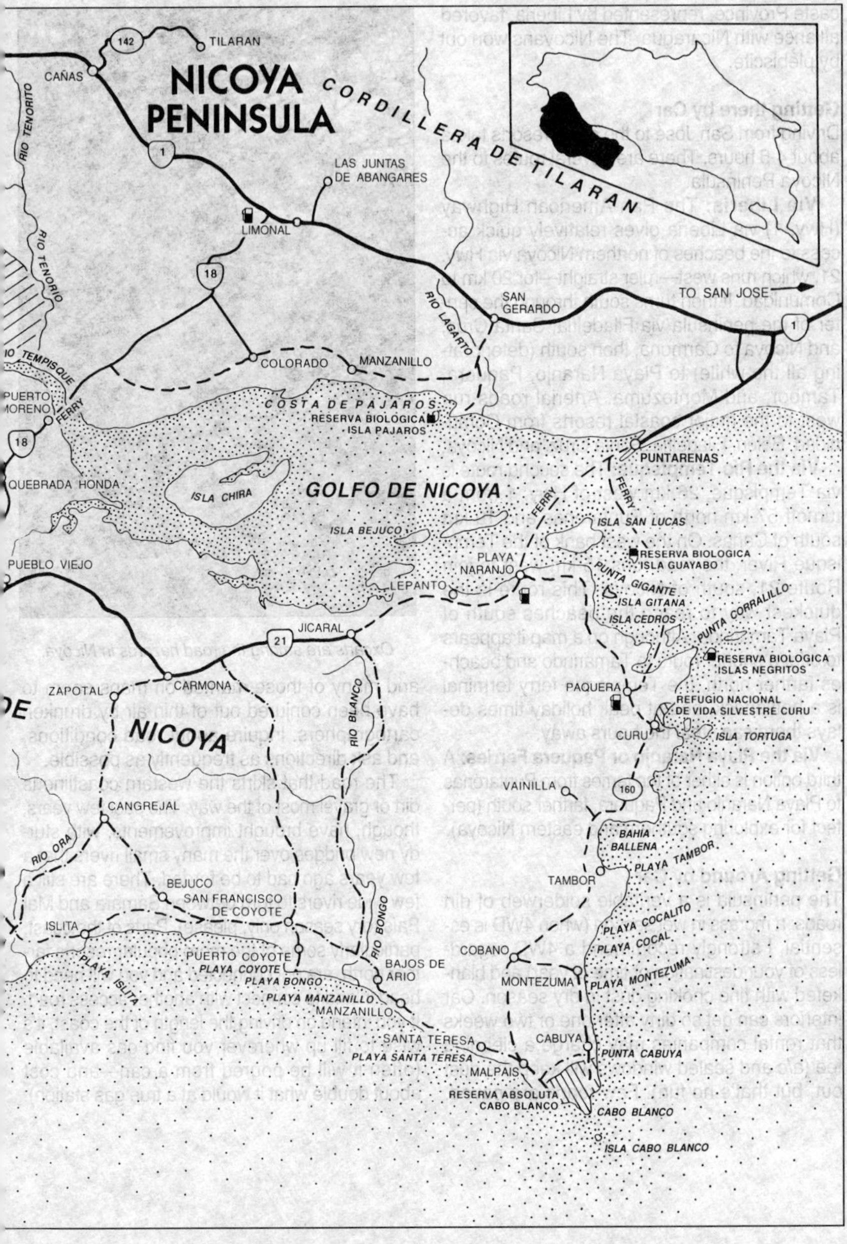

Map of the Nicoya Peninsula showing roads, towns, and geographic features including the Golfo de Nicoya.

Labels appearing on the map:

TILARAN
CAÑAS
142
RIO TENORITO
RIO TENORIO
NICOYA PENINSULA
CORDILLERA DE TILARAN
LAS JUNTAS DE ABANGARES
LIMONAL
1
18
SAN GERARDO
RIO LAGARTO
TO SAN JOSE
IO TEMPISQUE
COLORADO
MANZANILLO
PUERTO MORENO
FERRY
18
COSTA DE PAJAROS
RESERVA BIOLOGICA ISLA PAJAROS
QUEBRADA HONDA
ISLA CHIRA
GOLFO DE NICOYA
PUNTARENAS
FERRY
FERRY
PUEBLO VIEJO
ISLA BEJUCO
PLAYA NARANJO
ISLA SAN LUCAS
RESERVA BIOLOGICA ISLA GUAYABO
LEPANTO
PUNTA GIGANTE
ISLA GITANA
ISLA CEDROS
PUNTA CORRALILLO
JICARAL
21
RESERVA BIOLOGICA ISLAS NEGRITOS
ZAPOTAL
CARMONA
RIO BLANCO
PAQUERA
REFUGIO NACIONAL DE VIDA SILVESTRE CURU
NICOYA
CURU
ISLA TORTUGA
DE
VAINILLA
160
CANGREJAL
RIO ORA
BAHIA BALLENA
PLAYA TAMBOR
BEJUCO
SAN FRANCISCO DE COYOTE
RIO BONGO
TAMBOR
ISLITA
PUERTO COYOTE
PLAYA COYOTE
BAJOS DE ARIO
PLAYA COCALITO
PLAYA COCAL
PLAYA ISLITA
PLAYA BONGO
COBANO
PLAYA MONTEZUMA
PLAYA MANZANILLO
MANZANILLO
MONTEZUMA
SANTA TERESA
CABUYA
PLAYA SANTA TERESA
PUNTA CABUYA
MALPAIS
RESERVA ABSOLUTA CABO BLANCO
CABO BLANCO
ISLA CABO BLANCO

© MOON PUBLICATIONS, INC.

caste Province, represented by Liberia, favored alliance with Nicaragua. The Nicoyans won out by plebiscite.

Getting there by Car
Driving from San José to the coast resorts takes about 4-5 hours. There are several routes to the Nicoya Peninsula.

Via Liberia: The Pan-American Highway (Hwy. 1) via Liberia gives relatively quick access to the beaches of northern Nicoya via Hwy. 21, which runs west—ruler straight—for 20 km to Comunidad. It then turns south through the center of the peninsula via Filadelfia, Santa Cruz, and Nicoya to Carmona, then south (deteriorating all the while) to Playa Naranjo, Paquera, Tambor, and Montezuma. Arterial roads run west to the major coastal resorts from Comunidad, Belén, Filadelfia, Santa Cruz, and Nicoya.

Via the Río Tempisque: The second route is via Tempisque, 26 km west of Hwy. 1 from a turnoff 57 km north of Puntarenas and 19 km south of Cañas. On the west bank of the Tempisque River, the road runs 15 km west to join Route 21, south of Nicoya. This route is the quickest way to reach the beaches south of Playa Tamarindo. Although on a map it appears to offer a shorter route to Tamarindo and beaches farther north, the Tempisque ferry terminal is a bottleneck, and at peak holiday times delays there can steal the hours away.

Via the Playa Naranjo or Paquera Ferries: A third option is either of the ferries from Puntarenas to Playa Naranjo and Paquera, farther south (perfect for exploring southern and eastern Nicoya).

Getting Around by Car
The peninsula is a veritable spiderweb of dirt roads: a morass in wet season (when 4WD is essential; I strongly recommend a 4WD regardless of your destination or time of year) and blanketed with fine choking dust in dry season. Car interiors can get so dirty after one or two weeks that rental companies may charge a cleaning fee (a/c and sealed windows will keep the dust out, but that's no fun). Few roads are paved,

Oxcarts are among the road hazards in Nicoya.

and many of those marked on maps seem to have been conjured out of thin air by drunken cartographers. Inquire about road conditions, and ask directions as frequently as possible.

The road that skirts the western coastline is dirt or gravel most of the way. The past few years, though, have brought improvements, with sturdy new bridges over the many small rivers that a few years ago had to be forded. There are still a few wide rivers to ford between Sámara and Mal País (dry season only, please). Parts of the coast, particularly some of the more popular resorts farther north, are not connected and you will need to head inland to connect with another access road. If you intend on driving the length of the coast, it's wise to fill up wherever you find gas available (often it will be poured from a can—and cost about double what it would at a true gas station).

HIGHWAY 21
(PUERTO MORENO TO FILADELFIA)

The Tempisque ferry berths at **Puerto Moreno,** on the western bank of the Río Tempisque. A paved road leads west 15 km to Hwy. 21; there's a gas station at the junction at Pueblo Viejo. Nicoya, the regional capital, is 15 km north of the junction. Highway 21 runs north past Nicoya via Santa Cruz and Filadelfia to Liberia and the Pan-American Highway (Hwy. 1); and south 54 km to Playa Naranjo and beyond to Paquera, where a dirt road curls southwest to Montezuma and Cabo Blanco. Side roads reach out like fingers to various beach resorts along the coast.

PARQUE NACIONAL BARRA HONDA

This 2,295-hectare park, 13 km west of the Río Tempisque, is distinct in the Costa Rican park system. Barra Honda is known for its limestone caverns dating back some 70 million years (42 have been discovered to date). Remarkably, the caverns have been known to modern man for only two decades, but skeletons, utensils, and ornaments dating back to 300 B.C. have been discovered inside the Nicoya Cave.

The deepest cavern thus far explored is the Santa Ana Cave, which is thought to be at least 240 meters deep (descents have been made to 180 meters). One of its features is the handsome Hall of Pearls, full of stalactites and stalagmites. Another cavern with decorative formations is Terciopelo Cave, named for the eponymous snake found dead at the bottom of the cave during the first exploration, and reached via an exciting 30-meter vertical descent to a sloping plane that leads to the bottom, 63 meters down.

Mushroom Hall is named for the shape of its calcareous formations. The Hall of the Caverns has large Medusa-like formations, including a figure resembling a lion's head. And columns in Hall Number Five, and "The Organ" in Terciopelo, produce musical tones when struck. Beyond the Hall, at a point called the Summit, you can sign your name in a book placed there

by speleologists of the University of Costa Rica. Some of the caverns are frequented by bats, including the Pozo Hediondo ("Fetid Pit") Cave, which is named for the quantity of excrement accumulated by its abundant bat population. Blind salamanders and endemic fish species have also evolved in the caves.

The caves are not easily accessible and are risky for those not duly equipped. Groups will need to call the National Parks office in San José, tel. 233-5284, or the regional headquarters in Bagaces, tel. 671-1062, fax 671-1290, several days in advance for authorization to enter the caves. Descents are allowed during dry season only (although, reportedly, not during Holy Week).

Above ground, the hilly dry forest terrain is a refuge for howler monkeys, deer, macaws, agoutis, peccaries, kinkajous, anteaters, and many bird species, including scarlet macaws. The park tops out at Mount Barra Honda (442 meters), which has intriguing rock formations and provides an excellent view of the Gulf of Nicoya. While here, check out Las Cascadas, strange limestone formations formed by calcareous sedimentation along a riverbed. Hire a guide; the pathways leading throughout the park are convoluted. Two German tourists got lost and died of dehydration in 1993 after setting off for a short hike without a guide.

In March 1997, five percent of the park was destroyed in a devastating fire, so no fooling around with matches. The Barra Honda ranger station, tel./fax 685-5667, has basic trail maps. Entrance: $6.

Accommodations
Proyectos Las Delicias, tel. 685-5580, is a community project to provide employment for the local populace and engage it in conservation. The facility is outside the park entrance. You can camp here; there are also three basic cabins, each with two double beds and showers with cold water. Guide services are offered and meals cooked on a *leña* (woodstove) are provided. Rates: $2 pp campsite; $12 pp cabin.

Hawkview Mountain, tel. 237-8959, is a campsite also offering guided tours; it's beside the main road near the turnoff for Barra Honda.

There's also a campsite close to the Terciopelo Cavern, about 400 meters from the ranger station. It has showers and toilets—grim at last report—plus picnic tables and water. Rates: $1.50 per day.

Guides and Tours

You must be accompanied by a guide, who can be hired from Proyecto Las Delicias. Local guides include Olman Cubillo, Odir Matarrita, and Blas Arias, tel. 685-5406, or Liddier Sánchez, tel. 685-5580. None speak English. They supply ropes and ladders. You can also arrange guides through the Park Service or the Speleology Group of the University of Costa Rica, tel. 225-5555 or 253-7818.

Intertur Agencia de Viajes, Apdo. 2150, San José 1000, tel. 253-7503, fax 324-6308, has a three-day caving tour (on request). Also try **Ríos Tropicales,** tel. 323-6455, and **Turinsa Receptivo,** tel. 221-9185, for spelunking.

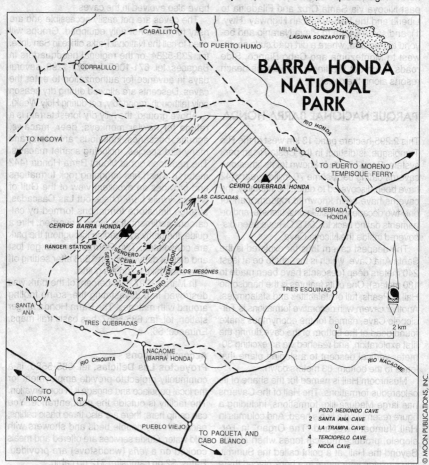

1 POZO HEDIONDO CAVE
2 SANTA ANA CAVE
3 LA TRAMPA CAVE
4 TERCIOPELO CAVE
5 NICOA CAVE

© MOON PUBLICATIONS, INC.

Getting There

The turnoff for the Nacaome (Barra Honda) ranger station is 1.5 km east of Hwy. 21 and 15 km west of the Tempisque ferry. From here, an all-weather gravel road leads four km to Nacaome, from where it climbs steeply in places, all the while deteriorating (4WD recommended); signs point the way to the entrance, about six km farther via Santa Ana. A bus departs Nicoya for Santa Ana and Nacaome daily at noon; you can walk from either to the park entrance. You can also enter the park from the east via a road from Quebrada Honda—tough going and not recommended.

NICOYA AND VICINITY

Nicoya, about 78 km south of Liberia, purports to be Costa Rica's oldest colonial city. The town is named for the Chorotega Indian chief who presented Spanish conquistador and *arriviste* Gil González Dávila with gold. The Indian heritage is still prevalent in the facial features area residents. This town bustles as the agricultural and administrative heart of the region and as a strategic transportation center.

The only site of interest is the **Church of San Blas,** built in the 16th century and aching with pathos and penury. It gleams handsomely now (following a restoration), decorating the town's peaceful plaza. It contains a museum of pre-Columbian silver, bronze, and copper icons, and other objects Two calcified skeletons were found beneath the church during the restoration. Hours: 8 a.m.-noon and 2-6 p.m.; closed Wednesday and Sunday.

If you need to cool off, head to the **public swimming pool** at Piscina Ande, on Calle 1, two blocks south of the plaza.

Twelve km southeast of Nicoya, at La Mansión, a road winds west into the mountains to **Hojancha,** site for the MINAE administrative headquarters, Apdo. 5251, Hojancha, tel. 659-9194 or 659-9039, fax 659-9089, of the Tempisque Conservation Area, two blocks south of the plaza. Coffee is important in these remote hills (a good time to visit is December, during coffee harvest). The region is a fascinating time warp, where working *trapiches* (sugar mills), ox-yokes and hand-painted carts, machetes, and gourd canteens still form part of the daily life of Hojanchan farms.

Monte Alba Forest Reserve

The region around Hojancha has been severely deforested—so much so that the flow of the Río Nosara has decreased 93% since 1970. To face the water crisis, in 1993 the Hojancha community formed a foundation and established the Monte Alba Forest Reserve (now part of the Tempisque Conservation Area), five km south of Hojancha, to buy up remaining forests and pastures where Mother Nature is being permitted to reestablish the watershed, re-creating a habitat for endangered wildlife. At press time, about 155 hectares had been purchased at a cost of $250-500 per hectare. The aim is to buy 1,500 hectares. *Donations are needed* and can be deposited directly into the foundation's account in the Banco Nacional de Costa Rica. The name of the account is Fundación Pro-Reserva Forestal Monte Alto; the account number is 1383486-8.

The foundation works to provide economic alternatives for Hojancheñans, who have relied on raising cattle, lumbering, and coffee. Ecotourism projects are in the works. The U.S. Peace Corps assists in an ecological education program for locals in the 10 communities affected.

Camping is allowed, and there are toilets and showers, and hiking trails. A rustic *cabina* and an interpretive center are under construction.

Festival of La Virgén de Guadalupe

Try to visit Nicoya on 12 December, when villagers carry a dark-skinned image of La Virgén de Guadalupe through the streets accompanied by flutes, drums, and dancers. The festival combines the Catholic celebration of the Virgin of Guadalupe with the traditions of the Chorotega Indian legend of La Yequita ("Little Mare"), a mare that interceded to prevent twin brothers from fighting to the death for the love of an Indian princess.

The religious ceremony is a good excuse for bullfights, explosive fireworks *(bombas),* concerts, and general merriment. Many locals get sozzled on *chicha,* a heady brew made from fermented corn and sugar and drunk from hollow gourds. Ancient Indian music is played, and it is easy to imagine a time when Nicoya was the center of the Chorotega culture.

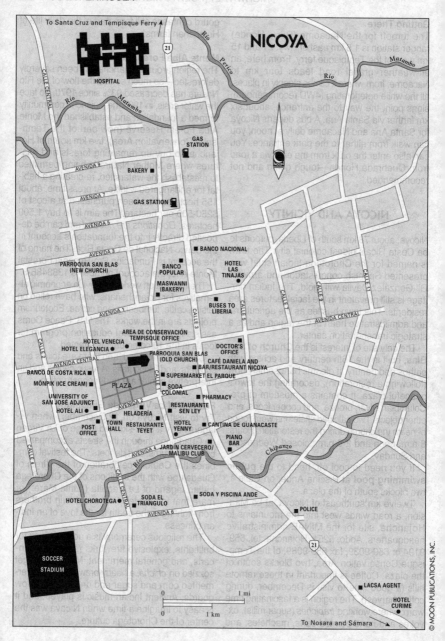

To Santa Cruz and Tempisque Ferry

NICOYA

Río Perico

Río Matambo

Río Matambo

HOSPITAL

CALLE CENTRAL

GAS STATION

MOON

GAS STATION

AVENIDA 9

BAKERY

AVENIDA 7

AVENIDA 5

AVENIDA 3

Banco NACIONAL

PARROQUIA SAN BLAS
(NEW CHURCH)

Banco
POPULAR

MASWANNI
(BAKERY)

HOTEL LAS
TINAJAS

CALLE 13

CALLE 11

CALLE 9

AVENIDA 1

BUSES TO
LIBERIA

AVENIDA CENTRAL

CALLE 7

CALLE 5

AREA DE CONSERVACIÓN
TEMPISQUE Office

HOTEL VENECIA

HOTEL ELEGANCIA

CALLE 3

DOCTOR'S
OFFICE

CALLE 1

PARROQUIA SAN BLAS
(OLD CHURCH)

CAFÉ DANIELA AND
BAR/RESTAURANT NICOYA

BANCO DE COSTA RICA

MÖNPIK (ICE CREAM)

SUPERMARKET EL PARQUE

PLAZA

SODA
COLONIAL

PHARMACY

UNIVERSITY OF
SAN JOSÉ ADJUNCT

HOTEL ALI

AVENIDA 2

HELADERÍA

RESTAURANTE
SEN LEY

POST
OFFICE

TOWN
HALL

RESTAURANTE
TEYET

HOTEL
YENNY

CANTINA DE GUANACASTE

PIANO
BAR

AVENIDA 4

JARDIN CERVECERO/
MALIBU CLUB

Chipanzo

Río

CALLE CENTRAL

HOTEL CHOROTEGA

SODA EL
TRIANGULO

SODA Y PISCINA ANDE

AVENIDA 6

POLICE

SOCCER
STADIUM

21

LACSA AGENT

HOTEL
CURIME

0   1 mi

0   1 km

To Nosara and Sámara

© MOON PUBLICATIONS, INC.

Accommodations
The **Hotel Yenny,** tel. 685-5050, reportedly offers good value. It has 24 rooms with a/c, private baths, and TVs. Rates: $14 s, $18 d. Also try **Cabinas Loma Bonita,** tel. 655-5269, which has 11 rooms with private baths. Rates: $20.

The pleasing **Hotel Las Tinajas,** tel. 685-5081 or 685-5777, has 28 spacious, light, and clean rooms with fans and private baths with cold water. Family rooms can sleep seven people. Rates: $12 s, $17 d, $23 t (students with ID get $5 discount). **Hotel Elegancia,** tel. 685-5159, has six large, well-kept rooms with lots of light plus fans and cold water. Rates: $3.75 pp shared bath; $4 private bath. Next door is the **Hotel Venecia,** tel. 685-5325, with 37 clean but very basic rooms with fans (some with private baths). Rates: $3.50 pp. It has newer, much nicer units in a two-story unit at the back. Rates: $8 s, $12 d, $16 t. Secure parking.

More basic is the **Hotel Alí,** tel. 685-5148, with 10 dingy rooms with smelly bathrooms. It has no sign; it's next to the University de la San José. Rates: $6 d. Perhaps the best budget bet in town is the **Hotel Chorotega,** tel. 685-5245, with 24 spic-and-span rooms with fans and private baths with cold water. Rates: $6 s, $10 d. **Cabinas Nicoya,** tel. 686-6331, 500 meters east of Banco Nacional, also has basic rooms with private baths and TVs.

The nicest place in town—albeit overpriced—is **Hotel Curime,** tel. 685-5238, 400 meters south of town on the road to Playa Sámara. It has 20 a/c *cabinas* and five rooms with private baths with hot water in landscaped grounds. It has a swimming pool and children's pool surrounded by little *ranchitas,* plus a restaurant. Howler monkeys sometimes settle in the trees. Rates (including taxes): $24 s, $33 d, $40 t with fans low season; $33 s, $48 d, $58 t, high season.

In Hojancha, try **Pensión y Cabinas Noemy,** tel. 659-9003, a pretty hostelry on the plaza.

Food
The town's significant Chinese population makes itself felt in the restaurant community. **Restaurante Jade** and the **Restaurante Teyet** are recommended. There are *sodas* on three corners of the plaza. **Restaurante Nicoya** is also recommended; it has a pleasant ambience, as does the open-air **Café Daniela,** tel. 686-6148, which

serves pizzas, fresh-baked breads and cookies, and has *casados* for $2. The **Cantina El Guanacaste** is a working-class bar with fantastic decor: deer hides and antlers on the walls, which are painted with cowboy scenes. The **Cuartel Latino** is also popular with locals.

Services
MINAE, tel. 686-6760, has a regional office facing the church, with wall-charts but no tourist literature. The staff can answer questions concerning parks in the Tempisque Conservation Area. Hours: Mon.-Fri. 8 a.m.-4 p.m.

The town is replete with **banks:** Banco Popular, tel. 685-5167; Banco Nacional, tel. 658-5366, on the road into town from San José; and Banco de Costa Rica, tel. 685-5110, both on the main square. The **post office** is cater-corner to the plaza on Avenida 2, Calle Central; it's open 7:30 a.m.-5:30 p.m.

The **Hospital La Anexión,** tel. 685-5066, is north of town. Dr. Hugo Lopez Rodas has a **medical clinic,** tel. 685-5805. There are several pharmacies on Calles 1 and 3.

The **Lacsa** agent, tel. 686-6840, is 100 meters north of Hotel Curime.

Getting There and Away
Buses depart San José for Nicoya from Calle 14, Avenidas 3/5 (Empresa Alfaro, tel. 222-2750), at 6 a.m., 8 a.m., 10 a.m, noon, 1 p.m., 2:30 p.m., 3 p.m., and 5 p.m. ($5; six hours). Return buses depart Nicoya for San José at 4 a.m., 7:30 a.m., 9 a.m., noon, 2:30 p.m., and 4:55 p.m. Buses also depart for Santa Cruz hourly, 6 a.m.-9 p.m.; for Liberia hourly, 5 a.m.-7 p.m.; for Playa Naranjo at 5:15 a.m. and 1 p.m.; for Sámara and Carillo at 8 a.m., 3 p.m., and 4 p.m.; and for Nosara at 1 p.m. Buses also serve other towns throughout the peninsula from here. The bus terminal is at the southeast corner of town on Calle 5.

Buses run to Hojancha from Nicoya. Empresa Alfaro buses run daily from San José to Hojancha.

PUERTO HUMO

A road leads northeast 27 km from Nicoya via Corralillo to Puerto Humo, due north of Barra Honda on the west bank of the Río Tempisque.

The birding hereabouts is splendid. Puerto Humo is the gateway to Palo Verde National Park, which begins on the other side of the river. Boats can be hired.

A bus leaves Nicoya for Puerto Humo daily at 2 p.m.

Accommodations

The **Hotel Rancho Humo,** Apdo. 322, San José 1007, tel. 255-2463, fax 255-3573, sits on a hill above the river and has 24 a/c rooms and a *palenque*-roofed restaurant serving seafood and *típico* and international dishes. The Rancho Humo Ecotourist Center offers boat tours up the Tempisque and Bebedero Rivers. Rates: $78 s/d; $19 extra person.

At the bottom of the hill is **Albergue Zapanti,** with eight rustic rooms with fans and shared baths. Part of the Rancho Humo complex, it is built as a vivid re-creation of an Indian village and features meals prepared in traditional mud ovens at the restaurant. Rates: $21 s, $38 d, $43 t. At press time I heard a report that Zapanti had closed.

SANTA CRUZ

This small town, 20 km north of Nicoya, is a transportation hub and gateway to Playas Tamarindo and Junquillal, 30 km to the west. The ruin of an old church (toppled by an earthquake in 1950), stands next to its modern replacement with a star-shaped roof, seemingly inspired by the cathedral in Brasilia, Brazil. The gracious plaza boasts a Mayan-style cupola and lampshades with Mayan motifs, and bright bougainvillea whose warm tropical hues match those of the magnificent stained-glass windows in the new church. Directions in the city are normally given from the **Plaza de los Mangos,** a grassy square shaded by mango trees and four blocks east of the church. The two plazas are separated by a quarter of old wooden homes. Alas, a ruinous fire swept through the historic center in March 1993, claiming many fine buildings. I find the town uninspiring except during festivals.

Festivals

Santa Cruz—declared the National Folklore City—is renowned for its traditional music, food, and dance (such as the Punto Guanacasteco), which can be sampled during *fiestas cívicas* each 15 January and 25 July, when the town's cultural heritage blossoms.

Accommodations

The **Hotel Plaza,** tel. 680-0109, facing the Plaza de los Mangos, has an eclectic mix of styles, with basic rooms. Rates: $11 s, $17 d. **Hotel La Pampa,** tel. 680-0586, is a budget alternative, one block east. **Pensión Isabel,** tel. 680-0173, two blocks south of the main plaza, has eight rooms with fans and cold water. Rates: $4 pp.

Hardy budget travelers might try basic and dingy **Pensión Pampera,** five blocks east of the old plaza. Rooms have shared baths. Rates: $4 pp. **Hospedaje Avellanas,** tel. 680-0808, offers rooms in a family home; some shared, others with private baths with cold water. Rates: $5-8. Other basic hotels to consider are **Pensión Anatolia** and the **Hotel Santa Cruz,** next to the Tralapa bus terminal.

The motel-style **Hotel Diriá,** Apdo. 58, Santa Cruz, tel. 680-0080, fax 680-0442, at the junction of Hwy. 21 and the main street into town, is centered on a pool and grounds full of palms. The rooms are undistinguished; bathrooms claim hot water but I could barely squeeze a trickle from the faucet. The El Bambú restaurant overlooks the pool but wasn't serving meals when I stayed there. It also has a video room and live marimba bands. Rates: $20 s, $33 d, $39 t. A better bargain is the motel-style **Hotel La Estancia,** tel. 680-1033, which has 17 pleasing modern units with fans, TVs, and private baths with hot water. Spacious family rooms have four beds. Some rooms are dark. Secure parking. Laundry service. Rates: $15 s, $25 d; $4 extra person.

Outshining all contenders is the **Hotel La Calle de Alcalá,** Apdo. 14-5150, Santa Cruz, tel. 680-0000, fax 680-1633, one block south of Plaza de los Mangos. This Spanish-run hotel boasts a lively contempo decor and pleasing aesthetic. It has 28 a/c rooms with TVs (local), cool white or charcoal-gray tile floors, bamboo furnishings, and pastels. They're set around an attractive amoeba-shaped swimming pool with swim-up *ranchito* bar. Wooden doors are carved with Mayan motifs. Rates: $25 s, $35 d, $43 t, $57 quad, $65 suite.

There are modern, fully furnished apartments, tel. 259-6846, for rent opposite Pensión Isabel.

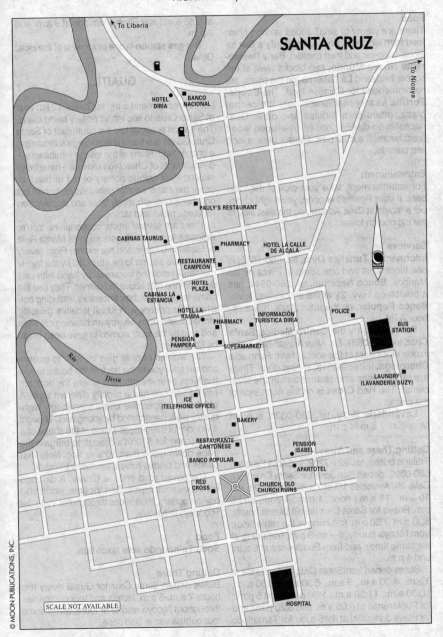

SANTA CRUZ

To Liberia

To Nicoya

HOTEL DIRIA

BANCO NACIONAL

PAULY'S RESTAURANT

CABINAS TAURUS

PHARMACY

HOTEL LA CALLE DE ALCALÁ

RESTAURANTE CAMPEÓN

HOTEL PLAZA

CABINAS LA ESTANCIA

HOTEL LA RAMPA

PHARMACY

INFORMACIÓN TURÍSTICA DIRIÁ

POLICE

BUS STATION

PENSIÓN PAMPERA

SUPERMARKET

Río Diriá

LAUNDRY (LAVANDERÍA SUZY)

ICE (TELEPHONE OFFICE)

BAKERY

RESTAURANTE CANTONESE

PENSIÓN ISABEL

BANCO POPULAR

APARTOTEL

RED CROSS

CHURCH, OLD CHURCH RUINS

HOSPITAL

SCALE NOT AVAILABLE

© MOON PUBLICATIONS, INC.

Food

There are plenty of small *sodas* serving *típico* food from which to choose. Try **Pauly's Bar** for tacos, burgers, and fried chicken. **Bar y Restaurante Nuevo Mundo,** two blocks west of the soccer field, and **La Taberna,** on the plaza, are recommended for Chinese food. The **Coope-Tortilla** factory-restaurant, near the central plaza, offers corn tortillas and other Guanacastecan dishes cooked over open wood fires; hours: 5 a.m.-7 p.m. There's often a long line outside.

Entertainment

For entertainment, take your pick of the local bars. If your Spanish is good, you might check out a movie at **Cine Adelita,** on the east side of the old church tower.

Services

Información Turística Diría, tel. 680-1512, is one block west and one south of Plaza de los Mangos. **Banco Nacional,** tel. 680-0544, has a branch on Hwy. 21 at the entrance to town. **Banco Popular,** on the main plaza, has a 24-hour ATM.

For doctors, try the **Centro Médico Santa Cruz,** tel. 680-0681. Dr. Allan Arayan has a clinic one block east of the soccer field; **Farmacia Chorotega,** tel. 680-0818, is next door. There are other clinics and pharmacies in the town center. The **Red Cross** is on the north side of the plaza.

Lavandería Suzy, tel. 680-0335, is open Mon.-Sat. 7 a.m.-4 p.m.

Getting There and Away

Tralapa buses, tel. 221-7202, in Santa Cruz tel. 680-0392, depart San José for Santa Cruz from Calle 20, Avenidas 1/3 at 7 a.m., 8 a.m., 9 a.m., 10 a.m., 11 a.m., noon, 1 p.m., 4 p.m., and 6 p.m. Buses for Santa Cruz depart Liberia hourly, 5:30 a.m.-7:30 p.m. (returning at the same time); from Nicoya hourly, 6 a.m.-9 p.m. (returning at the same time); and from Puntarenas at 6 a.m. and 4 p.m.

Buses depart fromSanta Cruz for San José at 3 a.m., 4:30 a.m., 5 a.m., 6:30 a.m., 8:30 a.m., 10:30 a.m., 11:30 a.m., 1:30 p.m., and 5 p.m.; for Puntarenas at 6:05 a.m. and 3:20 p.m.; and for Playa Junquillal at 4:45 a.m.; for Tamarindo at 6:45 a.m.; and Playa Flamingo at 9 a.m. and 2 p.m.

The **gas station** is one block west of the Hotel Diría.

GUAITÍL

I highly recommend a trip to Guaitíl, 12 km east of Santa Cruz, to see ethnic pottery being made. The turnoff is about two km southeast of Santa Cruz. Guaitíl is a tranquil little village surrounding a soccer field. Many of the village inhabitants—descendants of Chorotega Indians—have been making their unique pottery of red or black or ocher the same way for generations, turned out on wheels beneath shady trees and displayed on roadside racks and tables.

There are several artists' cooperatives. You're welcome to watch villagers such as Marita Ruíz or Marielos Briseño and her mother Flora (every cooperative seems to be attended by the family matriarch) molding ceramics by hand with clay dug from the hills above the hamlet. They use the same steps as did their ancestors, including polishing the pottery with small jadelike grinding stones taken from nearby archaeological sites and said by the local women to have been made by shamans.

The women happily give lessons to tourists and will take you to the back of the house to see the large open-hearth kilns where the pots are fired. Everyone has a slightly different style. A children's cooperative offers surprisingly high-quality work handcrafted by youngsters. I bought a wonderful three-legged vase in the shape of a *vaca* (cow) for $10 (it's difficult to bargain the price down more than 10% or so). Note that plates and dishes have a tendency to crack.

The paved road ends at Guaitíl. A dirt road continues southeast to **San Vicente,** which also makes pottery, then slices through the Valle del Río Viejo to Nicoya.

Food

Soda Tamarindo sells *típico* fare.

Getting There

Buses depart Santa Cruz for Guaitil every two hours 7 a.m.-5 p.m. Hotels and tour companies throughout Nicoya also offer tours, as do some tour companies in San José.

FILADELFIA AND VICINITY

Filadelfia, 18 km north of Santa Cruz and 31 km southwest of Liberia, is the regional center for northern Nicoya, and the main gateway to Playa Flamingo and Tamarindo via **Belé,** six km south of Filadelfia. For tourists, it's a place to pass through or to stop for a bite to eat en route to the beaches. An annual **fiesta cívica** is held during the first week of January with bullfighting, firecrackers, and general merriment.

Filadelfia is 19 km south of Liberia's Daniel Oduber International Airport. Between them, eight km from the airport, is the hamlet of **Comunidad** and the turnoff for Playa del Coco.

At the village of **Ortega,** about 10 km southeast of Filadelfia, the community has formed Coopeortega, c/o Cooprena, tel./fax 225-1942, e-mail: carnese@sol.racsa.co.cr, a cooperative ecotouristic project. The villagers preserve local sites of indigenous architectural interest, have various projects to revitalize traditional culture, and offer wildlife trips along the Río Tempisque and into Palo Verde National Park.

Accommodations and Food
Cabinas Tita, tel. 688-8073, two blocks north of the town plaza, has seven clean and adequate *cabinas* with fans and private baths (although the one I saw was in need of a good scrubbing) with cold water. Rates: $6.50 pp. Alternately, try **Cabinas Amelia,** tel. 688-8087, one block west of Tita. **Salon Hawaii,** on the west side of the plaza, is a popular *campesino* bar with pool tables.

Comunidad has a couple of basic *cabinas*.

Services
There are two **gas stations** on Hwy. 21, and a **Banco Nacional,** tel. 688-8146, two blocks west of the town square. The **bus station** is one block west of the town plaza; the **Red Cross,** tel. 688-8224, building is also here. There's a **pharmacy,** Farmacía Cristal, tel. 688-8336, and a **police** station (Guardia Rural), tel. 688-8229. For **taxis,** call Taxis Filadelfia, tel. 688-8256.

Getting There
Buses pass through Filadelfia en route between Nicoya, Santa Cruz, and Liberia.

BAHÍA CULEBRA TO PLAYA EL OCOTAL

BAHÍA CULEBRA

Nicoya's most northerly beaches ring the massive horseshoe-shaped Bahía Culebra ("Snake Bay"), enclosed to the north by the Nacascolo Peninsula tipped by Punta Mala and to the south by the headland of Punta Ballena. The huge bay is a natural amphitheater rimmed by scarp cliffs cut with lonesome coves sheltering 17 gray- and white-sand beaches that have been earmarked for major development. There are several small mangrove swamps good for birding, plus the remains of a pre-Columbian Indian settlement on the western shore of the bay at Nacascolo. To the east, the plateau extends for kilometers, flat as a pancake, with volcanoes—Rincón de la Vieja, Miravalles, and Orosí—in the distance, veiled with clouds. Magnificent!

No road as yet encircles the bay (which is so deep that U.S. submarines apparently used it during World War II). The north and south sides are approached separately by a pincer movement. Resorts have been opening thick and fast on the south side, at Playa Panamá, reached via the road from Comunidad to Playa del Coco. Four km west of Sardinal the road divides: the road straight ahead leads to Playa del Coco (three km); a turnoff leads north to Playa Hermosa (three km) and, beyond Punta Ballena, to Playa Panamá. The north shore is reached from two km north of Comunidad, via a road immediately west of the Río Tempisque at Guardia. This road is a fast, sweeping, well-paved, lonesome beauty of a drive that dead-ends after 15 km or so in an arterial network of dirt roads that lead down to a dozen beaches that await the bulldozer's maw.

The **Estación Experimental Forestal Horizontes,** a dry forest reserve incorporated into the Guanacaste Conservation Area, is seven km northeast of the bay; the turnoff also leads to **Playa Cabuyal,** on the north side of the Nacascolo Peninsula.

Playa Panamá and Vicinity

Playa Panamá is a narrow, two-km-wide gray-sand beach in a cove encusped by low, scrub-covered hills—a bay within a bay. The beach is very popular with Ticos who camp among the shady sarno, brazilwood, manchineel, and mesquite trees along the beach. Weekends and holidays get crowded, but midweek you should have the place virtually to yourself.

The road from Playa Hermosa meets the beach at its southern end and dead-ends atop the headland at the northern end at the entrance to Blue Bay Resort, overlooking **Playa Arenilla**. Midway to Playa Arenilla, a turnoff leads inland 0.5 km to the hamlet of **Panamá**, whose inhabitants still live a traditional simple lifestyle. One km south of Playa Panamá, a branch road leads west along a headland to **Playa Buena**, overlooking the mouth of the great flask that is Bahía Culebra.

Gulf of Papagayo Project

In 1993, the Costa Rican Tourism Institute (ICT) began to push roads into the hitherto inaccessible Nacascolo Peninsula. The government also leased 2,000 hectares surrounding the bay as part of the long-troubled Gulf of Papagayo Tourism Project of the ICT, begun in 1974 but left to languish until a few years ago, when development suddenly took off exponentially under the enthusiastic backing of the Rafael Calderón administration. The mini-Cancún that began to emerge was intended to push Costa Rica into the big leagues of resort tourism.

Grupo Papagayo, Apdo. 599-1007, San José, tel. 290-6194, fax 290-6195, a conglomerate of independent companies headed by Mexico's Grupo Situr, planned to build as many as 15,000 hotel rooms on its 911-hectare, 88-km-long coastal concession (almost the entire Nacascolo Peninsula) in a 15-year development. Plans called for more than a dozen major hotels, along with at least two golf courses, a 300-yacht mari-na, an equestrian center and tennis center, time-share condominiums, private villas, and other amenities. The project gathered steam, multiplied, and ground was broken.

The development—and the flagrant environment abuses that quickly became apparent—raised quite a stink. Developers and environmentalists squared off over the project, which featured prominently in the presidential election debate in 1994. An independent review panel created by the victorious Figueres administration expressed particular concern about illegal activities, unlawful exemptions, social problems, and environmental degradation, including sedimentation in the bay caused by poorly managed movement of topsoil. In March 1995 the former tourism minister and 12 other senior ICT officials were even indicted as charges of corruption began to fly.

The Figueres administration created a permanent Environmental Monitoring Plan to oversee the project and declared Bahía Culebra a "coastal marine zone for special management." The Nacascolo Peninsula is an area of archaeological importance with many pre-Columbian sites. When it was discovered that the bulldozers were plowing heedlessly, the government issued an executive decree to declare the peninsula a place of historic importance. To improve its image, the grupo has changed the name of the project to "Ecodesarollo Papagayo," or Papagayo Eco-Development. Then the company ran into financial trouble, bursting the Papagayo bubble. The bulldozers remained idle on the Nacascolo Peninsula when I last visited pending resolution of the legal wrangling that has halted construction, and tall grasses had all but reclaimed the pathways, but word among locals was that construction was to proceed in spring. Around Playa Panamá, it's full steam ahead.

Accommodations

Camping: Until recently Nacascolo's coves were popular with Ticos who found them perfect spots for pitching tents. Unfortunately, signs have recently gone up all over reading Strictly No Admittance. If you ignore these and camp on any of the beaches, be aware that there are no facilities. You *can* camp on Playa Panamá, however. There you'll find showers and toilets. Rates: $3 pp.

wahoo (game fish)

BOB RACE

Budget: Reportedly, a rustic **ecolodge** at Playa Cabuyal, tel. 666-1497, has four rooms with 20 beds, and provides horses and guides.

Expensive: Sula Sula Beach Resort, tel. 670-0000, fax 670-0492, e-mail: sulasula@compuserve.com; in the U.S., SJO-966, P.O. Box 025216, Miami, FL 33102-5216, on Playa Panamá, offers 34 pleasing Thai-style bungalows for up to five people in a forested pasture within a stone-walled enclosure backing the beach. They're spacious and nicely appointed, with a restrained elegance: cool tile floors, lofty beamed ceilings, soft ocher color scheme, subdued hardwood furniture (including bamboo-framed beds), and silent, remote-control a/c. The lofty *rancho* dining room is modestly elegant, with deep wicker seating. A swimming pool (with thatched bar) is set like a jewel amid the parched lawns and tall shade trees populated by howler monkeys. Rates: $75-85 s/d low season; $98-108 s/d high season.

Le Wafou, Apdo. 944, Pavas 1200, tel./fax 231-3463, is half-complete (the project has taken *years*) on a hill overlooking Playa Buena. The hill is uniquely graced by tall organ-pipe cactus—a dramatic setting. It was once slated to feature 50 junior suites, 50 bungalows, plus a casino and discotheque, but plans now seem more modest. A highlight will be architecture on a Chorotega Indian theme: the lodge is dramatic. Tennis courts and watersports, including scuba diving, are planned. Projected rates: $85 s, $95 d rooms; $140 s, $205 d bungalows.

Giardini di Papagayo, tel./fax 670-0476 or tel. 290-6194, fax 290-6195, e-mail: carpag@sol.racsa.co.cr, website www.arweb.com/giardini, is a deluxe Swiss-inspired hotel and condo-villa resort complex that was almost complete at press time. It's superb setting on the headland between Playa Hermosa and Playa Buena offers grand vistas. The theme is a contemporary take on Spanish colonial: lots of red-tile roofs, wrought iron, etc. Plans call for a 100-room hotel and 80 three-bedroom villas. Projected rates: $90-118 s/d hotel; $200-350 villas.

Premium: Costa Blanca del Pacífico is a condotel resort under construction at press time on the tip of Punta Ballena, 400 meters west of Costa Smeralda.

Luxury: An Italian company got the ball rolling hereabouts with the **Costa Smeralda Hotel,**

Apdo. 12177, San José 1000, tel. 672-0070, fax 670-0379, e-mail: smeralda@sol.racsa.co.cr, a beautiful and expansive all-inclusive resort that opened in 1995 at Playa Buena. The airy lobby sets the tone for the contemporary Spanish-colonial resort, with its terra-cotta tile floor and elegant wicker furniture. The 68 beautiful a/c bungalows stairstep grassy lawns, with sweeping views across the bay. Golf carts will whisk you there along winding pathways. Hardwoods and terra-cotta tiles abound. Closet space is plentiful, and good lighting and huge mirrors adorn the bathrooms. Plate-glass walls and doors proffer priceless vistas. Suites have mezzanine bedrooms and king-size beds, plus deep sea-green marble in the bathrooms, which come complete with jacuzzi. The large restaurant is open to breezes and view, as is the large amoeba-shaped pool, set like a jewel on the slopes. There's a tennis court and shops, plus scuba diving and tours. Rates: $115 s, $160 d, $215 t, including breakfast and dinner.

The marvelously situated **Blue Bay Resort,** tel. 233-8566, fax 670-0033, e-mail: costarica@bluebayresorts.com, website www.bluebayresorts.com; in the U.S., tel. (212) 476-9444 or 800-BLUEBAY (800-258-3229), which opened in 1995 as the Malinche Real Jack Tar, is a splendid, sprawling, all-inclusive, five-star property with 96 Spanish-colonial-style duplex bungalows nestled amid bougainvillea, shade trees, and palms on the scarp face overlooking the brown-sand Playa Arenilla, immediately north of Playa Panamá. The *casitas* stairstep the hill and harmoniously blend traditional architecture—red-tile roofs and rough-hewn hardwood accents—with a contemporary feel. All units have marble floors, pine ceilings, a/c, TVs, and direct-dial telephones. Amenities include a casino, three swimming pools, jacuzzi, a sauna, a gym, tennis courts, and workout stations along the pathways, which coil in and out of cleaves on the hillside. A wide range of watersports includes scuba diving. A water-taxi is available to whisk you to any local beach of your choice. Buffet alfresco dining in the casual La Fonda, or "gourmet" Italian cuisine in the a/c Da Vinci Restaurant are your options. A theater and disco are being added. Nightly shows. Rates: $165 s, $240 d, including meals, drinks, and all activities (children $30).

The almost-complete 300-room **Caribbean Village Costa Rica,** an all-inclusive facility owned by Allegro Resorts overlooking Playa Manzanillo on the north side of the bay, fell victim to the moratorium on construction. If and when completed, it will have one-, two- and three-story, a/c villa-style complexes with upscale amenities. The same fate befell the 300-room **Continental Plaza** with three-story, red-tile units that were to spread up the hillsides of Playa Nacascolo. It was almost complete when I visited in April 1995 but now gathers cobwebs due to the legal complications.

Ground has been broken on the **Monte del Barco** resort, tel. 220-0227, fax 231-0223, e-mail: mbarco@ns.goldnet.co.cr, with a marina, golf course, and villas and condos on the east side of the bay, north of Playa Panamá.

Food

Take time to chat with locals at the **Pianguas Bar** or **Soda Kati** in the hamlet of Panamá.

Costa Congrejo is a handsome hacienda-style restaurant at the southern end of Playa Panamá. The place is crafted of gleaming hardwoods and surrounded by bougainvillea, with a pleasing pool and sundeck to boot. Good *típico* dishes.

PLAYA HERMOSA

Playa Hermosa, separated from Playa del Coco to the south by Punta Cacique and Bahía Culebra to the north by Punta Ballena, is a pleasant two-km-wide, curving gray-sand beach in the throes of having been discovered. There are good tide pools at the northern end of the beach. The southern end of the beach (reached by the first turnoff to the left from the main road) is like a piece of rural Mexico: funky tile-roofed shacks, old fishing boats drawn up like beached whales, nets hung out to dry, cockerels scurrying around, pigs lazing beneath the shade trees. It won't last long. Go now.

Accommodations

Playa Hermosa is expensive. Choose your accommodations carefully: many places are vastly overpriced. One place you can't go wrong price-wise is Villas del Sueño.

Camping: You can camp 50 meters from the beach, to the left on the road leading to Playa Hermosa Inn.

Shoestring: The **Ecotour-Lodge,** tel. 672-0488, next to Playa Hermosa Inn, has basic rooms. Rates: $5-10. **Cabina Solyba,** tel. 444-5457, also has basic cabins for the same price.

Budget: Rancho Vallejo, tel. 672-0108, has eight *cabinas* with private baths and cold water. Rates: $17 up to four people. German-owned **Las Casona,** tel. 672-0025, is an old wooden home and offers eight simple rooms with fans, small kitchenettes, and private baths with cold water. Rates: $25 s/d, $27 t/quad.

Iguana Inn, tel. 672-0065, formerly Popeye's & Daddy O's, has 10 airy, well-lit rooms (some with kitchenettes and two bedrooms) in a two-story unit. Also, a dorm-style unit sleeps 10, with a kitchen and spacious, albeit rustic, living area. There's a small pool. The bar has a TV. It looked unkempt when I last called by. The caretaker quoted me $29 s/d rooms, $52 cabins, but expect to pay half that price.

Inexpensive: A gringo named Manny operates **Villa Boni Mar,** tel. 670-0397, fax 228-7640, opposite Huertares, with six pleasing modest units with ceiling fans, refrigerators, and private baths with cold water. One sleeps four and has a kitchen. It has a pool and a barbecue. Rates: $50 and $65 for small units; $75 for the larger unit.

Cabinas/Hotel Playa Hermosa, tel./fax 672-0046, at the southern end of the beach has 22 simple, pink, cement-block *cabinas,* a bit dour but clean and fine if you don't care about aesthetics. An Italian restaurant is in an old home facing the beach. Rates: $25 s, $40 d, $50 t, $60 quad. Nearby, **Cabinas el Cenisero,** tel. 385-7714, has seven modern albeit small, bare-bones cabins with fans and private bath and cold water. Rates: $15 s, $30 d, $40 t/quad.

Hotel El Velero, Apdo. 49, Playa del Coco 5019, tel. 672-0036, fax 672-0016, is an intimate Spanish colonial-style hostelry with 14 modestly appointed rooms. The Canadian-owned hotel has both upstairs and downstairs restaurants open to the breezes, plus a boutique and a small pool surrounded by shady palms. The hotel offers tours, as well as boat trips and scuba diving. Rates: $58 s/d.

Tucked 100 meters behind the southern end of the beach is the splendid Canadian-run **Villas del Sueño,** Interlink 2059, P.O. Box 02-5635, Miami, FL 33102, tel./fax 672-0026, an exquisite

Spanish colonial-style building offering "hotel service with a home ambience." The charming owners offer seven rooms in the main house and eight rooms in two two-story, whitewashed stone buildings surrounding a beautifully and lushly landscaped courtyard with a swimming pool. The rooms boast terra-cotta tiled floors, lofty hardwood ceilings, large picture windows, contemporary artwork, beautiful batik fabrics, bamboo furniture, soft pastels, and private bathrooms with hot water. You can dine alfresco on the best cuisine in town. Rates: $35 s/d low season, $45 high season; $60 peak season standard rooms; $45, $55, and $70 respectively, superior rooms. *A splendid bargain!*

The other sure-fire winner is the new Canadian-owned **Hotel Finisterre**, tel./fax 670-0293, e-mail: finisterra@hotmail.com, website www.electricmall.com/finisterra, atop the breezy headland at the south end of the beach. What views! Finisterre is a handsome contemporary structure painted in soft ochers and cleverly conceived with an open hallway down its center through which the breezes flow. Simple yet tasteful decor includes attractive bamboo furniture. The 10 simply furnished rooms also boast fans, a/c, and wide, screened windows; some have forest (not beach) views. The open-sided restaurant looks over a charming irregular-shaped swimming pool set into a stone terrace atop the ridge. The owners have a boat for picnics ($45 per hour) and sportfishing (from $275 daily for four people). A gift shop was to be added. Rates: $50 s/d, $65 s/d peak season, including continental breakfast.

Moderate: The U.S.-run **Playa Hermosa Inn**, tel./fax 672-0063; in the U.S., tel. 800-GET-2-SJO (800-438-2756), has eight modestly furnished but pleasant rooms and four *cabinas* (plus an a/c apartment) in palm-shaded grounds. All have fans, private baths with hot water, and wide, shady terraces with wicker seats. You'll find a breezy Italian restaurant with rough-hewn hardwood furniture and an aviary, plus white-faced monkeys, on the grounds. Rates: $40 s, $50 d with fan; $50 s, $60 d with a/c, including breakfast; from $95 s, $100 d apartment. Perhaps overpriced.

Villas Huetares, tel. 672-0052, fax 672-0051, is an apartment-style complex of 15 bungalows. They're spacious, with lounges (modestly furnished) and well-stocked kitchens and one bed-

room. The places get hot, though, despite the a/c. And whoever designed the tiny bathroom sink crammed into the corner of a doorway should be made to use it every day as punishment. Still, the whole is pleasant enough, with a pool, sundeck, and small bar. It's popular with Tico families. Rates: $80 daily for 1-6 people; $500 per week. Ridiculously overpriced for one or two people.

Villas del Sueño also rents handsome studio apartments ($75) and villas ($95) of the same style and standard as the hotel itself. *A bargain!*

Villas de Playa is slated to open upscale condo-villas at the roadside, 400 yards from the southern end of the beach.

Expensive: Condovac La Costa, Apdo. 2055, San José, tel. 221-2264, fax 222-5637, e-mail: condovac@sol.racsa.co.cr, commands the hill at the northern end of the beach. The modern and attractive large-scale complex enjoys a marvelous breezy setting with superb ocean views. It offers 101 a/c villas stairstepping down to the beach amid lawns and bougainvillea. Golf carts escort guests up and down the steep hill. Each complex has its own pool and adjacent *palenque* bar. There's a selection of bars and restaurants and a disco. The hotel offers a full complement of tours, sportfishing, and scuba diving (there's a full-service dive shop). Rates: $80 low season; $110 high season (up to four people).

Condovac's former hotel units, adjacent to La Costa, have been sold off and are now run separately by Sol Meliá as the **Sol Playa Hermosa,** tel. 670-0405 or (800) 33-MELIA (800-336-3542), fax 670-0349, e-mail: hermosol@sol.racsa.co.cr; in North America, tel. (800) 572-9934, with 54 deluxe rooms, all with satellite TVs, telephones, two double beds, and oceanview balconies. It also has 47 attractive new villas terraced onto the hillside behind the hotel, 24 with private pools. There's a swimming pool, three restaurants, and a disco, and tours and fishing are offered. Rates: $81 s/d room low season, $110 s/d high season, $10 extra person; $117/135 two- or three-bedroom villa low season, $195/225 high season, $25 extra with private pool.

A massive new property, **El Cacique del Mar,** tel. 293-1212, fax 293-1657, is under construction on Punta Cacique south of Hermosa, complete with golf course. The property has raised the ire of local inhabitants for the wholesale destruction of forests and other ecological transgressions and heavy-handedness.

Food

The best food for miles is served at **Villas del Sueño,** where the daily menu—heavily Italian—may include scalopini parmesan and profiteroles ($5-10). Similarly, the **Hotel Finisterre's** restaurant is open to the public, with creative dishes such as caesar salad ($3.50), and boneless chicken breast in phyllo pastry with orange and ginger sauce ($7).

For more simple dining, head to **Rancho Nando,** tel. 672-0050, a funky bar and *soda* favored by locals. Its eclectic ornamentation includes a decrepit fishing boat turned into tables and chairs, a concrete bartop curved like a wave, an ocelot pelt, a saddle, a stuffed caiman, and other dusty miscellany. Good *casado* and seafood. It has video games.

For breakfast (average $5; portions are large) try Hotel Velero, whose French-Canadian owners take their cuisine seriously. At night, treats in their modestly elegant setting include kebabs and barbecue. Happy hour (2-4 p.m.) features blackberry daiquiris.

Aqua Sport has a pleasing thatched restaurant with crepes, paella, and lobster Provençale on the menu.

Rancho Hermosa and **Bar y Restaurante Ballejos** serve simple meals in an unbeatably simple setting at the southern end of the beach. **El Pescado Loco,** on the frontage road behind Hotel El Velero, is a simple bar serving seafood and *típico* dishes. **Bar Las Lapas,** is a magnificent *palenque* bar and restaurant on stilts at the northern end of the beach—an ideal spot from which to enjoy the sunset.

Condovac hosts the **Chico & Pepe** discotheque.

Tours and Activities

Gaviota Tours, tel. 672-0143, cellular tel. 383-0349, has full-day tours far afield, including to Guaitil ($32), Las Baulas ($55), Palo Verde ($80), and Arenal ($99). It also offers transfers between San José for $140 up to four passengers, $160 up to six.

Aqua Sport, tel. 670-0050, fax 672-0060, offers kayaks ($2 per hour), windsurfers ($10),

aqua bikes ($4.50), canoes ($3), plus banana-boat rides ($20 up to five people), snorkeling ($10), and boat tours ($33 per hour, eight people).

Bill Beard's Diving Safaris, tel./fax 672-0012, e-mail: diving@sol.racsa.co.cr, website www.diving-safaris.com, claims to be the largest land-based dive operator in Costa Rica. It has daily two-tank dive trips (departing at 9 a.m. and 1:30 p.m.; $60) and night dives. It offers beginner and certification courses, plus special trips to Murciélagos or Catalina Islands for more experienced divers ($80-110). It has equipment for 50 divers; rental costs $15 per day for full equipment. Snorkelers can accompany dive boats.

Several locals rent **horses.** And you can rent a Jeep Wagoneer with chauffeur, tel. 672-0065.

Services

Aqua Sport has a **public telephone** and a souvenir shop. There's a well-stocked **general store** next door, and at El Cenisero at the south end of the beach. You can mail letters and cash traveler's checks at Aqua Sports. Dr. Enrique Guillermo Aragon has a **medical clinic,** tel. 670-0119.

Getting There

A bus departs San José for Playa Hermosa from Calle 12, Avenidas 5/7 daily at 3:20 p.m. (five hours). A bus departs Liberia for Playa Hermosa daily at 11:30 a.m. and 7 p.m. (Empresa Esquivel, tel. 666-1249). Both buses continue to Playa Panamá. Buses depart Hermosa for San José at 5 a.m., and for Liberia at 5 a.m. and 4 p.m. Hitchhiking from Coco should be no problem since there are lots of cars. A taxi from Coco will run about $5 one-way; from Liberia about $15.

PLAYA DEL COCO

Playa del Coco, 35 km west of Liberia, is one of the most accessible beach resorts in Guanacaste, and therefore one of the most popular with Ticos. Locals claim that the sun "shines longer and more brightly here than anywhere else in Costa Rica." Maybe, but the place can be crowded during busy weekends and holidays when Josefinos flock. The college crowd—foreign and Tico—likes to think of Coco as its playground, and the plaza is lively at night with youngsters "cruising."

A two-km-wide gray-sand beach (it is often referred to in the plural—Playas del Coco) lines the horseshoe-shaped bay. There's plenty of local color, not least because Coco is still an active fishing village; the touristy area is to the north; the laid-back fishing village is to the south, with fishing boats in the bay making perfect perches for pelicans. A rickety wooden footbridge 100 meters south of the plaza links the two. (The local expat community has initiated beach cleanups to remove trash left by vacationing Ticos, who seem to regard beaches as garbage dumps.)

Coco hosts a five-day *fiesta cívica* in late January, with bullfights, rodeos, folkloric dancing,

female beauty contests, soccer games, and other sources of merriment.

The ocelots, birds, and monkeys that were once common around Coco have been scared away in recent years by dynamiting and wholesale clearcutting by the developers of the Cacique del Mar project. You stand a good chance of seeing such wildlife at **Chaperal,** tel. 284-9011, a 1,000-hectare dry forest reserve-cum-tourist resort one km south of **Sardinal,** eight km east of Coco off the road from Comunidad. It has trails, horseback riding, horse-cart trips, a swimming pool and jacuzzi, and entertainment featuring marimba music.

A rough dirt road two km west of Sardinal leads to Playas Azúcar, Potrero, and Flamingo.

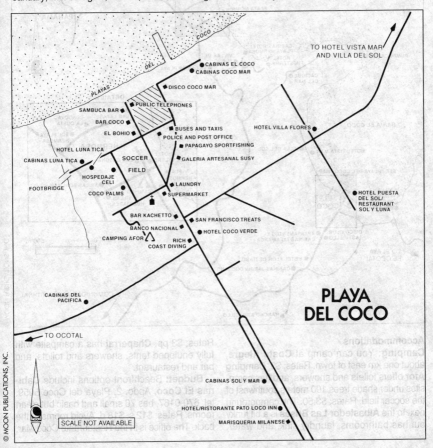

PLAYA DEL COCO

SCALE NOT AVAILABLE

© MOON PUBLICATIONS, INC.

VICINITY OF PLAYA DEL COCO

PLAYA ARENILLA
BLUE BAY RESORT

PLAYA BUENA
COSTA SMERALDA
HOTEL LE WAFOU
PUNTA BALLENA
COSTA BLANCA DEL PACIFICO

BAHIA PANAMA
PLAYA PANAMA
'SULA SULA' BEACH RESORT
COSTA CONGREJO

GIARDINI DE PAPAGAYO
SEE DETAIL

PLAYA HERMOSA

PANAMA

CABINAS/HOTEL PLAYA HERMOSA
HOTEL FINISTERRE
VILLAS DE SUENO
VILLAS DE PLAYA

PUNTA CACIQUE
EL CACIQUE DEL MAR

MOON

DETAIL

BAHIA EL COCO

HOTEL VISTA MAR
VILLA DEL SOL

SEE "PLAYA DEL COCO" MAP

VILLA TROPICAL BED AND BREAKFAST

EL COCO

DISCO CLUB ASTIRELLO
APARTAMENTOS Y CABINAS TALAMANCA

TO PLAYA EL OCOTAL

HOTEL FLOR DE ITABO
CABINAS JARDIN COQUENO

TO COMUNIDAD AND SARDINAL

RANCHO ARMADILLO

BAR LAS LAPAS
CONDOVAC LA COSTA
SOL PLAYA HERMOSA
HERMOSA
HOTEL EL VELERO
LAS CASONA
PLAYA HERMOSA INN
CAMPING
VILLAS HUERTARES
VILLAS BONI MAR

0   500 m

© MOON PUBLICATIONS, INC.

Accommodations

Camping: You can camp at **Costa Alegre**, about one km east of town. Rates: $3. **Camping Afor** offers toilets and showers, and has campsites under shade trees 100 meters southwest of the soccer field. Rates: $3.50. The campground next to the **Albastedor Las Brisas** is a bit funky but has bathrooms, laundry sink, and water.

Rates: $3 pp. **Chaperral** has a campsite with fully equipped tents, showers and toilets, and bar and restaurant.

Budget: Beachfront options include **Cabinas El Coco**, Apdo. 2, Playa del Coco 5059, tel. 670-0167, has 76 small and basic but clean rooms. Rates: $12 s, $18 d. Avoid rooms at the back. The office is in the Restaurante Coco Mar, which has the small, dingy, and overpriced **Cabinas Coco Mar,** tel. 670-0110, next to the disco of the same name. Some rooms are beachfront; the ones at the back are noisier and get no breezes. All have private baths and fans. Rates: $10 pp at the back; $12.50 beachview. The disco is a giant boom box at night. **Hotel Luna Tica,** Apdo. 67, Playa del Coco 5059, tel. 670-0127, fax 670-0459, has 21 rooms with fans and private baths with cold water. The older *cabinas* on the beach are dark and stuffy. Newer rooms in the annex across the street are nicer and the same price. It has rental car service and offers fishing and boating tours. Rates: $12.50 s, $19 d, $25 t. Nearby, facing the soccer field, is **Hospedaje Celi,** tel. 670-0365, with seven dour rooms with cold-water shared bath. Rates: $6 pp.

Villa Tropical Bed and Breakfast, tel. 670-0021, is a funky, offbeat German-run house at the south end of the beach, with six rooms and a shared bath with cold water. Rates: $13 s, $20 d. It's not a bed and breakfast, however; you buy your own food and cook for yourself (or there's a seafood restaurant next door). It's popular with tightfisted Europeans.

One of the better places is **Coco Palms,** tel. 670-0367, fax 670-0117, which has 20 spacious, adequately furnished rooms with fans, and roomy private bathrooms with hot water. There's also a pleasing restaurant and bar. Rates: $20 s, $30 d.

Cabinas Jardín Coqueño, tel. 670-0475, has three basic cabins with fans plus private baths and hot water. Rates: $20 d. Two family apartments have kitchenettes ($33 for five people). Nearby, **Cabinas Sol y Mar,** tel. 670-0587, has six spacious, modern, a/c *cabinas* for eight people with kitchenettes and lounge, plus fans and private baths with cold water. Rates: $15 pp low season; $70 up to eight people high season.

Cabinas Chale, tel. 670-0036, has 25 simply furnished rooms with refrigerators, fans, and private baths with hot water. Six family units have lounges and kitchenettes. There's a large pool, a laundry, and secure parking. Rates: $30 d, $36 t; $55 family units.

Cabinas Las Brisas, tel. 221-3292, does not catch the breezes. Its 13 very basic and simple rooms are sparsely furnished with double and single beds, side tables, and fans, plus spacious private baths with cold water. The owner is not a

particularly friendly soul. Rates: $27. Overpriced.

There are also several options on the approach road east of Coco, about 2-4 km from town. **Villas de Playa Nacascol,** tel. 670-0416 or 257-2993, has comfortable and pleasing a/c *cabinas* with large kitchenettes. It also has a tennis court, pool, and bar. About 800 meters east of the turnoff for Playa Hermosa is the **Costa Alegre,** tel. 670-0218, which is popular with Tico families and can be quite lively on weekends. It has 14 fully furnished apartments with kitchens, beds for five people, plus private baths with cold water. A swimming pool, a volleyball court, and a small soccer field, plus a large open-air restaurant with barbecue grill round out the attractions. A disco under a *palenque* pumps out the music day and night. Rates: $40 per unit.

Inexpensive: The **Hotel Flor de Itabo,** Apdo. 32, Playa del Coco, Guanacaste, tel. 670-0011, fax 670-0003, under German-Italian management, is big on sportfishing. The eight spacious economy rooms have lofty hardwood ceilings, a/c, satellite TVs, and beautiful Guatemalan bedspreads, plus large tiled bathrooms with hot water; five bungalow apartments have kitchens and fans but no a/c. The Da Beppe Italian restaurant is spoken of highly and opens onto a pool in landscaped grounds full of bougainvillea, palms, and birdlife, including parrots and macaws, many of which were rescued from various traumas and arrived with ruffled feathers. (There are caged peccaries, too.) There's also a casino, and the hotel specializes in fishing trips. Its 10-meter sportfishing boat rents for $550 per day (four passengers); an eight-meter boat rents for $450, including lunch and sodas. Rates: $50 s, $55 d economy rooms; $70 four-person apartments; $40 d bungalows.

Hotel Pato Loco Inn, Apdo. 87, Playa del Coco, tel./fax 670-0145, has attractive rooms—three triples, one double, and two fully equipped apartments—with orthopedic mattresses, central a/c, and modest furnishings with hardwood accents. There's an Italian restaurant. Rates: $23 s, $35 d, $45 t. **Hotel Coco Verde,** Apdo. 61, Playa del Coco, tel./fax 670-0494, has 33 spacious rooms with modest decor and silent, remote-control a/c in a modern two-story complex with a lap pool. There's a restaurant with lively decor serving *típico* dishes. Rates: $40 s, $50 d, $60 t, $70 quad.

The nicest place in town—and the best bargain—is **Hotel Puesta del Sol**, Apdo. 43-5019, Playa del Coco, tel./fax 670-0195, an intimate canary-yellow hotel blending soothing simplicity with an Italian aesthetic sensibility. The whitewashed rooms (with tropical pastels in counterpoint) are totally exquisite, with softly contoured "walls" enveloping king-sized beds and melding into wraparound sofas built into the walls (even the sofas have orthopedic mattresses), wrought-iron fittings in the bathrooms, and small patios inset with potted plant-holders. Two suites have balconies, TVs, and refrigerators. A small airy lounge has games and a TV, and there's a garden with a charming lap pool and gym beneath a gazebo. The restaurant is a local favorite. Rates: $40 s, $50 d, $60 t, $85 suites high season ($10 less in low season).

Another of my favorites is **Hotel Vista Mar**, cellular tel. 380-7807, tel./fax 670-0753, a very handsome hacienda-style hotel with eight a/c rooms facing a grassy courtyard with palm-shaded swimming pool and red-tile-roofed bar with wood-fired oven. The lounge—replete with terracotta tile floors, Oriental throw rugs, deep-cushioned sofas—opens to a breezy breakfast terrace with wicker rockers facing onto lawns that lead down to the beach. Room 9 has a voluminous bathroom with step-down shower. Rates: 30 s, $35 d with fans; $50 s, $55 d with a/c.

Hotel Villa Flores, tel./fax 670-0269, is a very handsome Spanish colonial-style hostelry run to high standards. Ceramics abound. It has nine rooms that are, unfortunately, more basic than the public arenas, though with lots of light. A restaurant overlooks lawns with hammocks slung beneath the palms. There's a gym, and an attractive pool with *ranchito* bar. Rates: $35 s, $45 d, $55 t with fans; 45 s, $55 d, $65 t with a/c high season ($10 less in low season).

The **Villa del Sol**, Interlink 2107, P.O. Box 025635, Miami, FL 33102, tel./fax 670-0085, e-mail: villasol@sol.racsa.co.cr, website www.amerisol.com/costarica/lodging/villasol.html, a homey Canadian-run bed and breakfast with an open atrium lounge and a garden fed by rains. Seven rooms have ceiling fans, tile floors, and simple, minimal decor—and vary considerably. Two rooms have private bathrooms and balconies; one has a circular bed and triangular shower. There's a swimming pool and jacuzzi plus barbecue on the sundeck; the place at-

Costa Rica's beauty comes in many forms.

tracts local French-Canadian expats. Lunches (burgers and hot dogs) and French-inspired dinners are sometimes served by the pool. There's secure parking. The delightful owners—Jocelyne and Serge Boucher—also rent upscale villas for $350-1,000 weekly. Rates: $35-45 d high season, including continental breakfast.

Cabinas del Pacífica, tel. 670-0157 or 228-9430, on the road to Ocotal, has 10 simple cabins in shady grounds with a small pool. Each has a kitchen, fans, and private bath with cold water. Rates: $35-90 first day (2-12 people); rates drop for consecutive days.

The German-run **Apartamentos y Cabinas Talamanca,** tel./fax 670-0428, on the road into town, looked nice; there was nobody there to show me around. Several houses are for rent in the village at the southern end of Playa del Coco.

Moderate: Cabaña Tamarindo, tel. 231-3107, opposite Bar Pacífico, has a house for eight people plus two *cabinas* for six people, all with kitchens, fans, refrigerators, and private baths with cold water. Rates: $148 house; $55 *cabinas*.

Apartamentos Casa Lora, cellular tel. 385-1300, has new apartments for 1-7 people. There's a swimming pool and secure parking.

Expensive: The peaceful, reclusive **Rancho Armadillo,** Apdo. 15, Playa del Coco 5019, tel. 670-0108, fax 670-0441; in San José, tel./fax 223-3535, is a winner. This home-away-from-home for erstwhile Texan mariner Jim Procter is a beautiful Spanish-colonial-style hacienda on a 10-hectare hillside *finca* one km from the beach. The four spacious bungalows are each as distinct as a thumbprint. All have fans (two also have a/c; one has a kitchen) and boast magnificent hardwood furniture, wrought-iron balustrades, lofty wooden ceilings, hardwood floors, colorful Guatemalan bedspreads, and rustic touches adding to the plentiful atmosphere. The voluminous bathrooms—adorned with exquisite tilework and stained glass—even have personalized toiletries. Halogen bulbs in the ceiling provide light you can actually read by. The honeymoon suite is huge. There's a rough-hewn *mirador* restaurant—the Wahoo Sportsbar and Grill—beside the swimming pool. The bar has a hammock. There's also a second house for families or groups. Ceramic, stone, and wood miniatures of namesake armadillos pop up all over the house. The place has a parrot and a spider monkey. Want to arrive in style? Take the helicopter. Rates: $65 s, $95 d; $10 extra person, including breakfast; $125 pp all-inclusive (even open bar). *Recommended!*

Food

There's no shortage of places to eat by the plaza. The breezy **Restaurante Coco Mar** offers inexpensive seafood and *típico* dishes and is a good place to check out the action on the beach. An old man sometimes plays mariachi. The **Bar Coco,** on the west side of the plaza, has good seafood dishes, including an excellent mahimahi *al ajillo* (with garlic). Next door is the U.S.-run **El Bohio,** with a menu described as "pancho, wong, and dino's!" (read: Chinese, pizza, burgers, and tacos). **Bar El Roble** has a shady outside dining terrace where you can eat to salsa music from speakers hung in branches. The **Restaurante Las Olas** at Hotel Luna Tica specializes in Cajun-style blackened char-grills.

Bar Kachetto, above the Banco Nacional, serves ceviche, seafoods, lasagne, and fajitas ($5). The decor is tasteful and there's lively music and a veranda from which to watch the world go by.

Pronto Pizzeria, c/o tel. 670-0305, serves inexpensive pizza and Italian dishes alfresco. Hours: 11:30 a.m.-10 p.m., closed Tuesday. Delivery available. **El Pozo** offers Italian fare and has vegetarian dishes. Also try **Ciao; Da Beppe,** in the Hotel Flor de Itabo; **Marisquería Milanese,** serving ceviche and Tico-style seafood in a quaint courtyard ($4-13); and **Ristorante Pato Loco,** serving pastas and lasagne (average $4). The prize for Italian fare goes to **Restaurante Sol y Luna** at Hotel Puesta del Sol; it serves pastas ($5) amid exquisite decor. It also serves cappuccinos and espressos.

Rancho Armadillo welcomes day-guests, but you must consume $12.50 minimum.

San Francisco Treats, tel. 670-0484, bills itself as "a California cafe" and, as you'd expect, serves brownies, fudge pie, banana nut bread, cheesecake, and the like; ex-attorney Michael Salinsky also conjures up rum and walnut cake, killer ice-cream shakes, and brownie sundaes. **Mönpik** has an ice cream stall near the plaza.

Entertainment

Take your pick of bars on the plaza. The **Sambuca Bar** is popular and has a romantic contempo decor. Afterwards, folks gravitate across the plaza to **Disco Coco Mar,** a lively no-frills disco with a Latin beat ($1.50-3 admission, depending on circumstances). It also plays '70s rock. The **Disco Club Astirello** is a slightly more upscale affair. **Bohio Bar & Yacht Club** sometimes has karaoke; the "happy hour" 4-7 p.m. features free *bocas.*

If the discos fail, you can try your hand with Lady Luck at the little casino in Hotel Flor de Itabo.

Tours and Activities

Kovaron Tours, cellular tel. 385-6536, offers four-hour snorkeling trips daily at 9 a.m. from Ocotal aboard a 28-foot pontoon boat ($30, including snack). **Papagayo Sportfishing,** tel. 670-0354, fax 670-0446, offers surfing trips locally ($25) and to Witch's Rock ($175), plus snorkeling and sportfishing ($50-55 per hour, $225-250 half day, $375-450 full day).

Rich Coast Diving, tel./fax 670-0176, e-mail: richcoas@sol.racsa.co.cr, website www.dive-costarica.com; in North America, tel. 800-4-DIV-ING (800-434-8464), has a full-service PADI dive center next to Banco Nacional; it offers instruction (includig PADI certification, $295), snorkeling, and equipment rental as well as dive trips ($45 two tanks local; $110 Islas Murciélagos; $85 Catalina). You can also charter the company's 35-foot trimaran, the *Tahonga* ($40 per hour). **Mario Vargas Expeditions,** tel. 670-0351, offers trips around the bay ($250 half day, $450 full day, per boatload), offshore fishing ($300 half day, $500 full day, per boatload), plus full scuba diving services including PADI certification. **Resort Divers de Costa Rica,** Apdo. 122-5019, Playas del Coco, tel. 670-0421, fax 670-0033, e-mail: beckers@sol.racsa.co.cr, offers diving, sailing, parasailing, and fishing trips and outfits the scuba diving operations of many hotels locally.

Spanish Dancer, tel. 670-0332, is a 36-foot catamaran that sails daily at 10 a.m. from Coco on a five-hour fun cruise ($45 including hotel pickup).

You can rent mountain bikes and fishing gear at **Ciclo Deportes el Coco,** tel. 670-0354, at Disco Coco Mar.

Spanish Language Courses

The **Instituto de Idiomas El Bosque,** tel./fax 670-0021, offers English, Spanish, and German language classes. The Aracari Academy offers summer camps for kids, plus bilingual education.

Shopping

Galería Artesanal Susy sells beachwear, jewelry, and crafts. **AguArtes,** next to Hotel Coco Verde, is the studio of French-Canadian artist Sylvain Royer, who conjures jewelry from gold and "mother of pearl." *Don't buy coral from the hawkers in the town plaza*—this only encourages destruction of the tiny offshore coral reef.

Services

The nearest medical services—include the **Red Cross,** tel. 670-0190, and **clinic,** tel. 670-0192—are in Sardinal, where there's a pharmacy. The **police station** (Guardia Rural), tel. 670-0258, and **post office,** which is open Mon.-Fri. 7:30-11:30 a.m. and 1:30-5 p.m., are next to each

other and face the plaza, where you'll find **public telephones.** There's a coin-op **laundry** at El Bohio.

Genie Travel, tel. 670-0309, fax 670-0382, e-mail: crbyrds@sol.racsa.co.cr, offers tour, air ticketing, and tourist information services.

Getting There and Away

Pulmitán, tel. 222-1650, buses depart San José from Calles 14, Avenidas 1/3 daily at 8 a.m. and 2 p.m. ($3; five hours), returning at the same times. Buses depart Liberia (Arata, tel. 666-0138), for Coco at 5:30 a.m., 8 a.m., 12:30 p.m., 2 p.m., 4:30 p.m., and 6:15 p.m., returning at 5:30 a.m., 7 a.m., 9:15 a.m., 2:30 p.m., 3:15 p.m., and 6 p.m.

PLAYA EL OCOTAL

This secluded gray-sand beach (almost black at its northern end) is three km west of Playa del Coco within the cusp of steep cliffs. It's smaller and more reclusive than Coco, but gets the overflow on busy weekends. The rocky headlands at each end are good for exploring tide pools. Ocotal is a base for sportfishing and scuba diving. At Las Corridas, a dive spot only a kilometer from Ocotal, divers are sure of coming face-to-face with massive jewfish, which make this rock reef their home. Tiny sea horses and hawk fish are among the many species who live among the soft corals. And divers have even seen black marlin cruising gracefully in the area.

Accommodations

Camping is not permitted.

The bay is dominated by **El Ocotal,** Apdo. 1013-1002, San José, tel. 222-4259, fax 223-8483, e-mail: elocotal@sol.racsa.co.cr, website www.centralamerica.com/c/r/hotel/ocotal.htm; in the U.S., SJO 2820, P.O. Box 025216, Miami, FL 33102-5216, a gleaming whitewashed structure that stairsteps up the cliffs at the southern end of the beach. It has 40 attractive rooms, all with a/c, fans, freezers, two queen-size beds each, satellite TVs, direct-dial telephones, and ocean views. The original 12 rooms are in six duplex bungalows stepped into the hillside down to the water's edge; newer rooms with dramatic views open up to the horizon and have their own jacuzzi, sunning area, and pool. The lobby and restaurant sit atop a knoll surrounded by water on three sides, with views along the coast. The landscaped grounds are floodlit at night. There are three small pools, each with a small *ranchito* for shade, plus tennis courts and horseback riding. El Ocotal Diving Safaris operates a fully equipped dive shop. Elegante Rent-a-Car is represented in the reception lobby. El Ocotal also has a fleet of five sportfishing boats. The property had earned a poor reputation in recent years, but word from all quarters is that it has improved markedly under new stewardship. Rates: $58 s, $68 d standard, $95-113 bungalow, $125-143 suite, low season; $70 s, $80 d, $105-123 bungalow, $120-150 suite, high season. Special package rates available.

The much-troubled **Vista Ocotal Beach Hotel,** Apdo. 230, San José 1007, tel. 255-3284, fax 255-3238; in Ocotal, tel. 670-0429, fax 670-0436; in the U.S., tel. (800) 662-1656, 100 meters from the beach, has villas, condo-type studios, and a separate hotel (a casino, health spa, and shops were slated). Each unit includes a fully equipped kitchen, a king-size bed in the master bedroom, two singles in a mezzanine bedroom, and a sofa bed in the tiny lounge. It has sea kayaks, pedal boats, catamarans, and sailboats. Rates: $85 for 1-3 people; $96 for 3-6 people. A "Special Two-Day Offer" is $45 pp (minimum group of four in one villa or suite), including breakfast and half-day fishing.

Los Almendros, tel./fax 670-0442, or tel. 257-0815, fax 223-2817, e-mail: albatros@sol.racsa. co.cr, on the hillside at the north end of the beach, consists of 43 fully furnished, privately owned two-story villas and condominiums (all with ocean view) available as short-term rental units. Each villa features three bedrooms, two baths, kitchen, living and dining area, carport, two bathrooms, and all the luxuries of home. Furnishings are bamboo. A thatched bar (alas, no restaurant) is perched loftily over a pool with huge wooden sundeck and hammocks. Rate: $80 low season; $130 high season.

Hotel Villa Casa Blanca, Apdo. 176, Playa del Coco 5019, tel. 670-0518, tel./fax 670-0448 for reservations, e-mail: vcblanca@sol.racsa.co.cr, sets a standard for Costa Rica's beachside bed and breakfasts. A stay here is like being a guest in a personal home (which it is—and an upscale one, at that). The hotel—a Spanish-style villa on

a hillside about 800 meters from the beach—is surrounded by a lush landscaped garden full of yuccas and bougainvillea. The small swimming pool has a swim-up bar and a sundeck with lounge chairs. Inside, the hotel epitomizes subdued elegance with its intimate and romantic allure: sponge-washed walls, four-poster beds (six rooms), stenciled murals, and massive bathrooms with deep tubs and wall-to-wall mirrors. The 14 rooms include four suites (one with jacuzzi; another with kitchen), each as distinct as a thumbprint. A jacuzzi was to be added in the garden, where there is also a canopied dining veranda and barbecue grill. Canadian-born owners James and Jane Seip have two children and families are welcome. Best yet are the prices—a superb bargain. Rates: $49 s, $59 d; $10 additional person.

The Seips also rent a fantastic Spanish-colonial house atop the hill. It consists of three rental units, including an open-plan, two-bedroom upper apartment decorated with the same supremely tasteful panache as Villa Casa Blanca. Heaps of bright light pours in through wall-to-wall arched windows. And bright Caribbean bedcovers might have been painted by David Hockney. Two thumbs up. And a six-bedroom villa with deep Romanesque pool and exquisite tilework was to be ready for rent by 1999 (rooms will also rent individually).

Bahía Pez Vela, an erstwhile sportfishing resort nestled in its own tiny, secluded cove beyond the headland at the southern end of Ocotal, has been demolished, and construction of a new property seems to be underway.

Food

There're only two places to eat. First is the rustic and offbeat **Father Rooster Restaurant,** serving seafood dishes and Roosterburgers ($2.50) and Roosterfrankfurters ($2). It has a sand volleyball court. Open 11 a.m.-10 p.m. If you're feeling flush, try the cuisine at El Ocotal, which one reader raves about. There's indoor or outdoor dining on a raised deck, below which raccoons hang out awaiting scraps.

Scuba Diving and Sportfishing

El Ocotal Diving Safaris based at El Ocotal, offers a free introductory dive daily. It charges $35 for one-tank dives, $55 two-tanks, offered daily at

9 a.m. Night dives cost $40. Dive trips head to the Catalinas ($70) and Islas Murciélagos ($95), and even a turtle dive at Nancite ($75). Snorkeling

costs $6 full day. It also rents equipment. Coastal sportfishing costs $195 half day, and deep-sea fishing $495 full day (up to six people).

PLAYA AZÚCAR TO TAMARINDO

PLAYA AZÚCAR

The dirt road that begins two km west of Sardinal leads 16 km to the hamlet of Potrero, from where you can follow the coast road north three km to Playa Azúcar (Sugar Beach), a narrow, 400-meter-wide spit of sun-drenched coral-colored sand that just might have you dreaming of retiring here. It is separated from an even more lonesome beach—Playa Danta—by steep cliffs to the north. Several islands—the Catalinas, Chocoyas, and Plata—lie a short boat ride from shore. There's good snorkeling offshore.

You can also reach Playa Azúcar by a *very* rough dirt road (4WD recommended)—known as the "Monkey Trail"—that diverts from the Sardinal-Potrero road and leads past Playa Danta and Playa Zapotal, an as yet undeveloped beauty of a beach and fishing community four km north of Playa Azúcar. (Zapotal has been slated as the site of a proposed 400-hectare tourist project—Project Zapotal—to be styled after a Spanish colonial town, but there's still no sign of it.)

Accommodations

Hotel Sugar Beach, Apdo. 90, Santa Cruz 5051, tel. 654-4242, fax 654-4239, e-mail: sugarb@sol. racsa.co.cr, website www.sugar-beach.com; in the U.S., tel. (800) 958-4735, offers the privacy of a secluded setting amid 10 hectares of lawns and forest. The hotel is perched just high enough to catch the breezes, with bungalows connected by stone pathways and set in a hollow that slopes down to the beach. Shade trees run down to the shore but not in such numbers that they obscure the views. Choose from 16 new rooms in eight handsome Spanish colonial-style duplexes, or 10 older, recently renovated units. The spacious rooms have two queen-size beds, verandas, a/c, fans, and tiled floors, plus hand-carved wooden doors with bird motifs. Decor and furnishings, however, are a bit wanting. Also available are a three-bedroom beach house and an

apartment suite. A large open-air restaurant looks over the beach. A small, amoeba-shaped pool has been added. The place is owned and run by friendly owners Jon Mechem and his wife Soni. Horseback rides ($30) and tours are offered. Monkeys, birds (including an endangered *green* macaw from the Caribbean), and iguanas abound on the grounds. Room rates: $55 s, $83-85 d room, $100 apartment low season; $90 s, $100-138 d room, $225 s/d apartment high season. The beach house rents for $720-1,020 low season; $1,750-2,450 high season.

Getting There and Away

There's no bus service. You can also reach Azúcar by car via Playa Flamingo.

PLAYA POTRERO AND VICINITY

This wide gray-sand beach south of Playa Azúcar (and immediately north of the more attractive Playa Flamingo) is up-and-coming, with several new hotels and *cabinas* concentrated at the northern end. The beach is popular with campers during holidays but is virtually deserted on weekdays. The calm sheltered waters are safe for swimming, and a small islet lies a short swim offshore.

The tiny, rustic and charming hamlet of **Potrero,** one km north of the beach, is built around a soccer field. From its southwest corner, follow the road 50 meters and you'll reach two rustic bars, where you can sup a beer and take in the views south across the bay. A burgeoning community of expats lives south of Potrero village and inland of the beach in wide-spaced houses connected by a gridlike maze of dirt roads.

North of the village, on the road connecting Playa Azúcar, is **Playa Penca,** a beautiful almost-white-sand beach backed by a protected mangrove estuary—that of the Río Salinas—and rare saltwater forest replete with monkeys, coatis, and plentiful birdlife, including parrots, roseate spoonbills, and egrets. About 10 km offshore is **Isla Santa Catalina**, nesting site for bridled terns and other seabirds.

The *Windsong* anchors here every Thursday on its week-long itineraries.

Accommodations

Camping: You can camp along Playa Potrero (no facilities). **Mayra's Camping and Cabins**, tel. 654-4273, has showers and toilets. There's also simple cabins with private bathrooms. Rates: $2 campsites; $12.50 cabins.

Budget: Cabinas Cristina, tel./fax 654-4006, nearby, is of a similar standard with the benefit of a small pool. The simple all-wood *cabinas* are set in shady gardens. Rates: $30 cabins; $55 two-bedroom efficiencies with kitchenettes. **Windsong Cabinas**, tel. 654-4291, on the main road near Supermercado Surfisde, also has attractive and modern *cabinas* with private baths and hot water. Not inspected.

The Italian-run **Cabinas Isolina**, tel. 654-4333, fax 654-4313, one km south of Potrero hamlet, has 10 attractive if simple and some-what dark cabins (two with kitchenettes) with a double and a single bed with beautiful spreads. Rates (low season): $25 d, $30 t; $10 more with kitchenette.

Bahía Esmeralda Hotel and Restaurant, tel. 654-4480, fax 654-4479, is a modern, Italian-run hotel 200 meters on the southern edge of Potrero hamlet. The four simply furnished rooms and a house for six feature red-tile roofs and have all modern conveniences, including closets and lofty hardwood ceilings, double beds and bunks. Italian fare is served in an open-sided restaurant. Horseback tours and bike rental are available, as is a boat for turtle tours and fishing. Rates: $22 s, $29 d rooms; $65-80 for the house, high season.

The **Rancho Costa Azul**, tel. 654-4153, on the north side of the soccer field in the village of Potrero, is a handsome, rustic, red-tile-roofed restaurant with four simple rooms with private bath and cold water. Rates: $20 d.

Cabinas La Penca has budget *cabinas* behind the beach of that name, on the north side of Potrero village.

Inexpensive: The French-run **El Grillo**, tel. 654-4617, has two handsome and roomy cabins in a garden with swimming pool. Each has a private bath and hot water. The restaurant is a local favorite. It's amid the warren inland from the Bahía Potrero Resort; signs point the way from Supermercado Surfside. Rates: $45.

Cielomar Hotel, tel./fax 654-4194, behind a picket fence at Playa Penca, is set amid lawns with lounge chairs shaded by palms. It has 11 a/c rooms, whitewashed, with bright pinks and blues in counterpoint. Each has private bath but only cold water. A little restaurant serves burgers and simple *típico* dishes. It offers sportfishing, snorkeling, diving, and kayaking. Rates: $45 s, $55 d, $65 t, including breakfast.

The best bargain around is **Casa Sunset Bed & Breakfast**, tel. 654-4265, on the hill behind Playa Penca. It's the slightly offbeat home of Martha and John, ably assisted by their half-dozen cats, a parrot, and two Great Danes. Casa Sunset is a true home-away-from-home. Where else are you invited to pull a beer from the ice chest and flop on the couch in front of a giant screen TV? Maybe I got special treatment. Still, it seems there are always friends and neighbors popping in to shoot the breeze, pop a beer, etc. I didn't want to leave. The house sits midway up the hill above a *ranchito* bar that serves *bocas*. Note the fine workmanship of the heavy-duty tables, chairs, and bartop. The same crafts-manship is displayed in the seven simple yet at-tractive cabins cascading down the hill. One has a kitchen. Each has a double (or two singles) and bunk, plus ceiling and floor fans, and large bathrooms with hot water. Verandas have Sarchí rockers. There's a pool and sundeck. Horse-back rides are offered and guests have free use of boogie boards. Rates: $40 d; $10 additional person, including breakfast. Recommended.

Moderate: Bahía Potrero Beach & Fishing Resort, Apdo. 45, Santa Cruz 5051, tel. 654-4183, fax 654-4093, e-mail: villtrop@sol.racsa.co.cr, website www.villtrop.com/bahia set in land-scaped grounds at the north end of Playa Potrero, has 10 older rooms and 16 newer rooms (in-cluding 10 two-bedroom units), all with fans, a/c, refrigerators and private baths with hot water. Standard rooms have two double beds. Deluxe rooms have one queen bed and private patio. The resort has a pleasant restaurant and bar serving pizzas and pastas, plus a small library, a souvenir store, a swimming pool and children's pool, and hammocks under *ranchitas*. Horse-back tours cost $40 per half day. **Flamingo**

Divers has a dive center at the hotel. Rates: $79 d standard; $89 d deluxe, including continental breakfast (15% discount on weekends). It also offers fishing packages. The resort was adding fully self-contained villas—**Villas Tropicales**, Apdo. 249-5051, Santa Cruz, tel. 654-4361, fax 654-4362—for longer stays and time-share (one-bedroom villas from $70).

A large all-inclusive resort called **Club Las Velas Resort** is semi-complete on a pocket-size beach between Playa Penca and Playa Azúcar. The all-inclusive, 300-room village is in a limbo of legal wrangling. Another luxury condo resort—**Jardines de Flamingo**—is underway at the southern end of Playa Potrero.

Food

There are two budget places in Potrero hamlet: **Soda y Restaurante Playa Potrero** and **Bar y Restaurante La Penca.**

El Grillo is recommended for French cuisine. It's closed Monday, and has happy hour Tues.-Fri. 5:30-7 p.m. The most entertaining spot is **Toucan Jungle,** nearby, where Floridians Ron and Nancy run a colorful sports bar with a large-screen TV and toucans in a floor-to-ceiling cage in the middle of the bar. It serves pizzas, burgers, kebabs, and fajitas.

Also recommended are **Stella's Italian** and, nearby, **Harden's Garden Pizzeria Café,** cater-corner to Bahía Potrero Resort.

Tours and Activities

Bo-Mar Tours, tel. 654-4469, in Potrero has horseback rides. **Costa Rica Diving,** tel. 654-4148, is a German-run outfit at the southern end of Playa Potrero. Also see the hotels listed above.

PLAYA FLAMINGO (PLAYA BLANCA)

Playa Flamingo, two km south of Potrero and separated from it by a slender peninsula, is more accurately called Playa Blanca (the name preferred by developers). The two-km-wide scimitar of white sand—one of the most magnificent beaches in Costa Rica—lines the north end of Bahía Flamingo. There are no flamingos. The area is favored by wealthy Ticos and gringos (North Americans now own most of the land

hereabouts), and expensive villas sit atop the headlands north and south of the beach, many with their own little coves as private as one's innermost thoughts.

Playa Flamingo has been called the "Acapulco of Costa Rica." Alas, the moniker has arrived about a decade too early. There's only a smattering of hotels, and little nightlife to speak of. More appropriate is its reputation as home to Costa Rica's largest sportfishing fleet, which anchors in what is supposedly the largest marina between Acapulco and Panamá (the annual **International Sportfishing Tournament** is held here each May and June).

Flamingo is most commonly accessed by road via Filadelfia, Belén, Huacas and Brasilito. It is linked to Potrero by a new bridge over a mangrove estuary that was built at local expense because the MOPT didn't have the funds to repair it after it was washed away in a storm. Local residents and businesses—mostly expats—anted up the $85,000; MOPT supplied the equipment. Two of the biggest hotels—the Aurola Playa Beach and Fantasia—didn't give a dime. Hence, both properties were being boycotted by locals.

Accommodations

Inexpensive: The **Mariner Inn,** tel. 654-4081, is a 12-room Spanish colonial-style hotel down by the marina. Dark hardwoods fill the a/c rooms that feature color TVs, blue-and-white tile work, and terra-cotta tile floors. A suite has a minibar and kitchenette. A pool and sundeck sit next to a moody, elegant bar of dark hardwoods. The restaurant specializes in seafood. Rates: $43 s/d, $60 t/quad, $79 suite low season; $56 s/d, $70 t/quad, $100 suite high season.

Moderate: Flamingo Tower Bed & Breakfast, tel. 654-4109, fax 654-4275, is a contemporary Spanish-colonial home-turned-hotel sitting atop the headland at the southern end of the beach. It's reached by a steep winding road. It has five rooms, each as individual as a thumb-print; rooms have a/c, refrigerators, and private baths. One has a kitchenette. The octagonal tower—there really is one—was built by Harvard University for an astronomer but it's now a suite. You reach the tower by a spiral metal staircase with windows on all sides—favored by honeymooners and would-be honeymooners. South American tapestries, hardwood ceilings, and tiled floors all add charm. Enjoy American breakfasts on a breezy veranda overlooking the beach. The gringo-Tica owners are charming, but during my last visit I sensed that the property was on the verge of becoming run-down. Rates: $50 d, $60 suite low season, including breakfast ($10 more high season). *A bargain!*

Expensive: Villas Flamingo, tel./fax 654-4215, is a complex of 24 very spacious villas at the southern end of the beach. Each sleeps six people and has a large lounge-cum-bedroom and a good-size kitchen. There's a small pool. Daily rates: $100 d, $110 t, $130 quad, $140 for five, $150 for six. Weekly rates: $650 d/t, $700 quad, $750 for five/six. Monthly rates: $1,600 d/t/quad, $1,700 for five/six.

The **Flamingo Marina Hotel,** Apdo. 321-1002, San José, tel./fax 290-1858, e-mail: hotflam@sol.racsa.co.cr; in the U.S., tel. (800) 276-7501, about 300 meters from the beach, has pleasing rooms on the hill, with grand views towards Playa Potrero. All rooms are spacious, with fans, a/c, refrigerators, TVs, and telephones. Sportsman's suites have jacuzzis and bars. A circular swimming pool with poolside *ranchito* bar is inset on a terrace overlooking the bay. The pleasant restaurant, furnished in bright tropical colors, opens onto the pool. There's a tennis court. Fantasy Tours has an office here. Rates: from $18 pp cabin, $58 d standard room, $90 d suite, $100-160 apartment low season; $25 cabin, $78 d standard room, $120 d suite, $140-200 apartment high season (extra at peak season). Special sportfishing, surfing, and golf packages are offered.

Premium: The only place down by the beach is the **Aurola Playa Flamingo,** Apdo. 7082-1000, San José, tel. 654-4010, fax 654-4060, e-mail: aurola@sol.racsa.co.cr, website www.ticonet.co.cr/flamingo.default.htm; for reservations, tel. 233-7233, fax 222-2621, a large-scale complex (formerly the Flamingo Beach Hotel) centered on a voluminous pool with a swim-up bar and expansive sundecks. It has 134 spacious rooms, including eight surfside suites, five ocean-view suites, and 23 luxury two-bedroom apartments. The rooms have a/c, fans, telephones, satellite TVs, and private balconies. Prices in the shaded open-air snack bar and Catalina restaurant are Tokyo-expensive.

There's a souvenir shop, rental car agency, and sportfishing office. Rates: $100 s, $120 d, $225 suite. *Overpriced!*

The same company runs the **Presidential Suites,** on a bluff facing south above the hotel. One- and two-bedroom condominiums feature fully equipped kitchens, living and dining rooms, two bathrooms, color TVs, and telephones. All suites have private balconies overlooking the ocean. I find them overpriced (though I think one reader is overreacting by calling them worse than any motel in the United States). Rates: $150-175 rooms; $250 apartments.

Hotel Fantasías Flamingo, Apdo. 4518, San José, tel. 231-0701 or 222-9847, fax 257-5002, e-mail: flamingo@sol.racsa.co.cr, website www.multicr.com/fantasisas, on the northern headland facing Bahía Potrero, has an inventive contemporary design, with a lounge featuring ceiling-to-floor plate-glass windows the length of one wall offering views of both ocean and bay. Its 42 spacious carpeted rooms have motel-style decor. Ground floor rooms have balconies with direct access to the scalloped pool. Eighteen two-room apartments are planned, as is a casino. Rates: $88 poolside ($77 other) low season; $120 ($110) high season; $15 extra person.

The **Club Talolinga** apartments, next door, were still under construction.

Several of those beautiful hilltop and beachfront villas you admire can be rented. Most come with maids and gardeners, towels, fully equipped kitchens, and laundry service. One delightful option is **Casa Mega,** which has its own tiled spa, three bathrooms, brick patios, two a/c bedrooms, and a tempting ocean view. Contact Megadventures, tel./fax 654-4091, or Fred Schultz or **Sea View Rentals,** Apdo. 77, Santa Cruz, tel. 654-4007, fax 654-4009; in San José, tel. 226-0901. Prices range from $50 a day to $7,500 a month. The office is on the beachfront. Megaventures represents **Casa Tigre,** a new hillside a/c home that rents as a two- or three-bedroom unit for up to six adults (no young children). There's a TV/VCR, maid service, and a large deck with jacuzzi overlooking the beach.

Villas Pacífica, an acclaimed upscale sportfishing and riding center midway between Flamingo and Brasilito, closed, sadly, in 1997 after the owner was indicted for drug trading.

Food

Marie's Restaurant, tel. 654-4136, opposite the entrance to the Aurola Playa Flamingo, offers basic but tasty seafood, plus daily specials and a large selection of sandwiches. The **Bar/Restaurante/Disco Amberes,** tel. 654-4001, up the hill, serves continental and *típico* dishes. **Pizza Ema** serves medium-size pizzas for $5.

Supermercado A&M is a well-stocked general store above the marina. The **Surfside Way Liquor and Grocery Store,** tel. 654-4291, across from the marina on Playa Portrero, specializes in imported and gourmet foodstuffs. The marina office has a product list—you can fax your order in and the store will deliver. Or call, and someone will come pick you up.

Entertainment

Bar/Restaurante/Disco Amberes is the only place to party in town. It has a spacious lounge bar, plus a lively disco with tunes from a DJ booth, and a small casino. The **Hotel Fantasías Flamingo** plans to open a casino. Mariners prefer to booze in the **Mariner Inn,** which features cable TV. **Ecotreks** planned to add pool tables and a bar.

Tours and Activities

Flamingo Bay Pacific Charter, tel. 654-4015, tel./fax 234-0906; in the U.S., 1112 East Las Olas Blvd., Fort Lauderdale, FL 33301, tel. (800) 992-3068 or (305) 765-1993, above the lobby of the Aurola Playa Flamingo, offers sportfishing charters aboard its custom Palm Beach 31 Sportfishermen ($550 half day, $696 full day for four people). **Permit Sportfishing,** tel. 654-4063, e-mail: permit@sol.racsa.co.cr, website www.crica.com/fish/permit.html; in the U.S., tel. (888) 234-7427, above the Mariner Inn, is run by Capt. John LaGrone, the *only* skipper in the world to raise 2,000 billfish in a single year. He fishes the entire Pacific coast according to season using 23- to 47-foot boats. Also try George Cole of **Sol Searcher Charters,** tel./fax 654-4291.

The *Shannon,* a 52-foot cutter, runs day and sunset cruises ($45-95 pp), plus multiday cruises as far afield as Isla Cocos; contact the marina. Excursions are also offered aboard the *Papagayo,* a Hardin 45 Ketch that sails a sunset cruise ($40 with dinner on-board) and can be chartered for customized cruises. Call Capt. Dick Neal or Peter Neal, tel. 654-4063 or 654-4062. You can charter other sailboats and motorboats at the marina and the Chamber of Commerce.

Flamingo Tours, tel. 654-4238, fax 654-4039, offers boat trips into the Tamarindo Wildlife Refuge.

Flamingo Dive Shop, tel./fax 654-4403, e-mail: divecr@sol.racsa.co.cr, website home.t-online.de/home/d.koenig/welcome.html, next to Mariner's Inn, has a range of dive tours ($75 for two tanks) and PADI certification ($350), plus water-skiing ($75 per hour) and 10-day liveaboard dive trips to Cocos Island. **Vic Tours,** c/o Flamingo Dive Shop, offers tours throughout the Pacific northwest.

The **Marina Trading Post,** tel. 654-4156, e-mail: tpostcr@sol.racsa.co.cr, offers tours by minivan throughout the Pacific northwest, including Rincón de la Vieja ($75), Arenal Volcano ($95), and to see turtles at Playa Grande ($35). Ann at the **chamber of commerce,** tel./fax 654-4229, above and behind the Mariner Inn, also acts as a **tourist information center,** does airline ticketing and housing rentals, and arranges trips throughout Nicoya and Guanacaste.

Ecotreks, tel./fax 654-4578 or 228-9826, e-mail: ecotreks@ecotreks.com, on the Potrero side of the bridge, 100 meters east of the marina, offers diving ($65 two tanks), including to the Murciélagos ($125). It also has kayak dives ($40) and snorkeling ($55), plus mountain bike tours ($25) and sailing trips. It rents boogie boards ($2 per hour) and mountain bikes ($5 per hour, $15 half day, $20 full day), and has a 47-foot sportfishing boat for charter.

Costa Rica Riding Adventures, tel. 654-4106, e-mail: crriding@sol.racsa.co.cr, offers horseback trips from Villas Pacífica stables between Flamingo and Brasilito, including a three-day trip to Nosara.

Flamingo Marina

The marina, tel. 654-4203, fax 654-4536, e-mail: marflam@marflam.com, is tucked in the

dolphin (the game fish)

BOB RACE

southern end of Playa Potrero bay. It has dock space for 80 yachts up to 24 meters long (expansion to 200 slips is planned). The fuel dock (with diesel, gasoline, and 120-volt and 220-volt electricity and fresh water) is on the finger pier jutting from the southern breakwater. The marina also has a floating dry dock for maintenance and a 20-ton crane, plus a marine mechanic on duty. Wax-and-wash crews are available. Reportedly, the approach is very shallow. Dockage is $10 per foot for stays of less than three months. A "lease," with first and last months payable in advance at $7 per foot, is offered for longer stays. Moorings inside the breakwater cost $3.50 per foot. Call the **dockmaster** on channels 16, 86 or 87. Office hours: Mon.-Fri. 6:30 a.m.-noon and 1:30-5 p.m., Saturday 7:30-11:30 a.m.

Boats arriving from international waters to the north reportedly must clear customs and immigration at Playa del Coco (Thomas Patrick reports that if you arrange it ahead, the C&I people will come to you in Flamingo). There's a bonding service ($100) if you wish to leave your yacht for extended periods. You'll need four copies of your passport plus the Certificate of Entry (Certificado de Entrada) obtained from immigration in Playa del Coco.

Shopping
Marina Trading Post has a well-stocked humidor selling Cuban cigars. The **Mariner Inn** has a classy souvenir store.

Services
The **Marina Trading Post** acts as a tour information center and reservation agent. Theres's no bank. Restaurante Amberes offers a **money-changing** service. And **Western Union** is represented at Flamingo Marina, which also has **public telephones.** If you need the **Red Cross**, call 680-0522, ext. 168.

Getting There and Away
By Bus: Buses depart San José from Calle 20, Avenida 3 (Tralapa, tel. 221-7202), daily at 8 a.m. and 11 a.m. ($3; six hours). The buses travel via Matapalo and Playa Brasilito and continue to Playa Potrero. Buses depart Santa Cruz for Playas Brasilito, Flamingo, and Potrero (Tralapa, tel. 680-0392) at 6:30 a.m. and 3 p.m. Buses depart Flamingo for San José at 9 a.m. and 2

p.m., and for Santa Cruz at 9 a.m. and 5 p.m. **Interbus** operates a daily shuttle bus to Flamingo from San José.

To get to Flamingo from Playas Coco, Hermosa, or Panamá, take a bus to Comunidad, where you can catch a southbound bus for Santa Cruz or Nicoya; get off at Belén, and catch a bus for Flamingo (buses from San José pass by around 10:30 a.m. and 2:30 p.m.).

By Air: Playa Flamingo is five miles from Tamarindo airstrip. You can charter a private **air-taxi** from San José (about $400 for five people). The **Marina Trading Post** acts as the SANSA agent and can arrange private air transfers. Travelair has an office above the chamber of commerce.

By Car: Economy Rent-a-Car has an office above the chamber of commerce. There's a **gas station** on the road from Brasilito.

PLAYA BRASILITO

Brasilito, two km south of Flamingo and divided from it by a small headland, is undergoing a tourism boom. The hamlet is centered on a soccer field. The light-gray sand melds into the more mesmerizing Playa Conchal to the south (you can negotiate a track to Conchal along the beach by 4WD; be prepared for some deep sand in parts).

The most direct way of reaching Brasilito—and Flamingo—is via Belén (eight km south of Filadelfia), where a road leads west to **Huacas.** From Huacas, a paved road leads four km north to Brasilito past the entrance to the vast, deluxe Meliá Conchal Resort. Meliá's presence, while undoubtedly helping to put Brasilito on the map may not be in the community's long-term interests. Locals were up in arms at press time. The Sol Meliá corporation is a hard-hitting political player and word is that it had twisted elbows in to have Brasilito's delightfully funky beachfront homes and restaurants bulldozed.

Accommodations
Camping: You can camp on the beach, 100 meters south of Hotel Brasilito. **Cabinas Many** allows camping for $2 pp.

Shoestring: A Swiss couple runs **Ojos Azules,** tel./fax 654-4336, 100 meters south of the soccer field, with 14 clean and neatly furnished cabins for up to eight people. Some have hot water. There's a laundry, a small plunge pool, and a *rancho* with hammocks. Fresh home-baked bread accompanies the filling breakfast. Rates: from $5.50 pp.

Budget: Cabinas Conchal, tel. 654-4257, farther south, has nine pretty, ocher-colored Spanish colonial-style cabins with fans and private baths and cold water in a landscaped garden full of bougainvillea. It offers horse and bike rentals. Rates: $17 s/d low season; $22 s/d high season. **Cabinas Nany,** tel. 654-4320, has 12 attractive albeit simple modern *cabinas* with private baths and cold water. Rates: $15 s, 23 d. **Cabinas El Caracol,** tel. 654-4073, a stone's throw away, is of a similar standard and price. It has a children's playground and a small thatched restaurant serving seafood.

Bar/Restaurante La Perla, just outside Brasilito, has three clean, tiled *cabinas* with fans, small kitchens, refrigerators, and private baths with cold water, plus a larger cabin for up to seven. There's a small swimming pool. La Perla is 300 meters from the beach. The owner offers horseback rides, boat tours, and taxi service. The restaurant doubles as a large dance hall and is a popular hangout for expatriate gringos. Miss your "down-home" breakfast? Try here. Rates: $22 s, $29 d, $36 t, $44 quad, including tax; $44 large cabin.

Cabinas Christina, Apdo. 121, Santa Cruz 5051, tel. 654-4006, 200 meters beyond La Perla, has clean, spacious rooms with kitchenettes, double and bunk beds ("hard," by one account), plus rockers on verandas. There's a small pool and a thatched *palenque*. A five-minute walk to the beach. Rates: $25 s, $35 d.

Inexpensive: A German couple, Josef Compes and Manuela Klasen, run **Hotel Brasilito,** tel. 654-4237, 50 meters from both the beach and soccer field. This well-run hotel has a very atmospheric, breezy, bougainvillea-festooned restaurant made of hardwoods, plus 10 simple rooms with fans and private baths with cold water, in a daffodil-yellow wooden home adorned with boxed *veraneras* (flowers). Rates: 24 s, $30 d, $36 t, $42 quad, low season; $30 s, $36 d, $42 t, $48 quad, high season.

Food

Best bet is the Hotel Brasilito's **Las Playas Beach Bar and Biergarten,** serving Teutonic and con-

tinental fare. The pleasant **Marisquería Sea Horse** south of the village specializes in seafoods. The **Pizzeria Il Forno,** tel. 654-4125, is nearby.

Boca de la Iguana is the most intriguing of three basic beachfront eateries selling seafood and *típico* dishes. **Bar y Restaurante Camaron Dorado,** tel. 654-4028, 100 meters north of the soccer field, is a favorite of locals; try the filling specials or Camaron Dorado Salad ($8, for which you get lobster, shrimp, calamari, cheese, and ham heaped in with the greens).

Tours and Activities

Hotel Brasilito operates **Brasilito Excursiones,** tel. 654-4237, fax 654-4247, e-mail: compes@ sol.racsa.co.cr, which offers horseback riding on the beach ($20 one hour) and at **Finca Montejicar,** three km south of Brasilito. It also offers scuba diving ($70 two tanks), sailing ($30 sunset cruise, $75 full-day cruise), sportfishing ($190 half day, $390-750 full day), boogie board and snorkel rental ($2 per hour, $12 per day), and snorkeling trips ($35).

Costa Rica Temptations, tel./fax 654-4585, has an office 100 meters south of the soccer field. It offers tours throughout Nicoya and Guanacaste, including to Santa Rosa ($65), Rincón de la Vieja ($65), and Palo Verde ($80). It also acts as an agent for Nacional Rent-a-Car and SANSA.

Services

There's an **international telephone** and **tourist information center** at Bar y Restaurante Camaron Dorado. A **gas station** is one km north of Brasilito, on the road to Flamingo.

Getting There

Brasilito Excursiones has airport transfers between Brasilito and San José ($25).

PLAYAS CONCHAL AND REAL

Scintillating white-sand Playa Conchal—one of Costa Rica's finest beaches—lies in the cusp of a scalloped bay with proverbially turquoise tropical waters, a rarity in Costa Rica. The beach is composed, uniquely, of zillions of tiny seashells that move with soft rustling sounds as you walk; the waters are of crystalline Caribbean quality perfect for snorkeling. Wading out to Conchal

Point to the north, you'll find larger shells and crustaceans, too, scurrying around. It's illegal to remove shells. Please leave them for future generations to enjoy.

This is one beach you will *not* have to yourself. The land behind and extending the full length of the beach comprises the Meliá Conchal Resort and Golf Club, whose guests spill onto the beach. Fortunately, they are served by watersports concessions available to nonguests, too. You can buy a day pass to the resort ($25; cash only for purchases).

You can walk to Playa Conchal from Playa Brasilito by a sandy path that fringes the shore and can be driven by 4WD, but be aware that the sand is deep. An easier way to get to Conchal by car is from Huacas (four km south of Brasilito), where a wide dirt road leads west three km to the hamlet of **Matapalo**. Here the rough road leading from the northwest corner of the soccer field leads four km to the southern end of Playa Conchal. A side road, 800 meters before the beach, leads west past tumbledown *bohíos* (farmers' and fishermen's shacks) to Playa Real, a stunning little beauty of a beach nestled in a sculpted bay with a tiny tombolo leading to a rocky island. Venerable fishing boats make good resting spots for pelicans. It's the only place in Costa Rica where I can recall exclaiming, "Aah! this is where I want to build my home!"

Dolphinarium

The folks at Bahía los Piratas were due to open a dolphinarium on the east side of the tombolo at Playa Real around press time. The first two bottlenose dolphins arrived from Spain in early 1998. Acrobatic dolphin shows will be featured, and you may even be able to swim with the clever critters. What a treat to slip into the warm waters to be greeted by their endearing smile, as they cavort around you, chattering and giggling.

Accommodations

Hans has three bungalows—**Casa Blanca,** tel./fax 654-4259—on the hill behind stone walls 800 meters from Playa Conchal, at the junction for Playa Real. Each has a sitting room and a kitchen, plus fans and large verandas and large private baths with hot water. They're airy and light. One has a/c and a suite, plus swimming pool. There's also a swimming pool at the simple bar and

restaurant. Hans offers fishing tours. Rates: $25 small; $45 large unit with a/c; $50 with pool.

The **Condor Club Hotel,** Apdo. 102, San José 2300, tel. 654-4050, fax 654-4044, sits atop the hill behind Casa Blanca. The once stunning hotel sat idle for 18 months and has since lost its luster. One reader—the only guest—reported that the staff was "incredibly kind and helpful." When I called by, it was struggling to resurrect itself. The motif is very contemporary. The 41 comfortable and tastefully decorated rooms are set in landscaped grounds and have a/c, fans, cable TVs, telephones, private bathrooms, and king-size beds. There are also two- and three-bedroom houses with kitchens (one-week minimum). The oceanview, open-terrace dining room is topped by a lofty lounge bar. A swimming pool is set on the lofty sundeck terrace. Rates: $29 s, $39 d, $49 t, including continental breakfast.

The **Meliá Conchal Beach & Golf Resort,** Apdo. 232-5150 Santa Cruz, tel. 654-4123, fax 654-4181, e-mail: mconchal@sol.racsa.co.cr; in North America, tel. (800) 336-3542; in the U.K., (tel. 800) 962-720, is a magnificent resort spanning 285 hectares—the largest resort in the country (the PR department also claims it is the "most sophisticated") and one surrounded by rippling fairways. The resort has 308 open-plan junior suites and two master suites in 37 two-story units amid landscaped grounds behind the beach. They are truly beautiful, with exquisite marble bathrooms, mezzanine bedrooms supported by columns, and lounges with soft-cushioned sofas. Each has a satellite TV, a hair dryer, telephone, minibar, safety box, and a/c. The action revolves around a looping amoeba-shaped swimming pool—a setting for noisy aerobics and other classes and games—claimed to be the largest in Central America. It has three restaurants (including the elegant Faisanda Italian restaurant), two bars, a disco (on a hill so as not to disturb sleeping guests), a theater with nightly shows, tennis courts, plus an 18-hole golf course designed by the king of designers, Robert Trent Jones, Jr. There's a pro golf shop, and Swiss Travel, TAM, CATA Tours, and Budget Rent-a-Car have offices here. Hiking, horseback riding, and bicycle tours are other options. Canopied open-air buses whisk you around. The resort caters to children. This is *not* a place to come for peace and quiet, but if you like a canned group experience, this is as good as it gets in Costa Rica. Several readers have written to complain that meals are mediocre and outrageously priced. And the Sol Meliá is accused of throwing its weight around and abusing rather than contributing to the local community. Rates: $154 s/d, $350 master suite low season; $165 s/d, $350 master suite high season; $220 s/d, $450 master suite peak season.

Playa Real is the setting for the Italian-run **Bahía de Los Piratas Resort,** tel. 222-7010 or 221-6410, fax 223-4386, e-mail: inpaca@sol.racsa.co.cr. This complex of 15 Spanish colonial-style condos and villas (40 rooms total of varying sizes) stairsteps the hill amid landscaped grounds with a small swimming pool and thatched bar at the bottom. All have tile floors, lofty hardwood ceilings, a/c and fans, small TVs, CD players, and verandas with splendid coastal views. Horseback riding, scuba diving, and sportfishing are offered.

Food
You can buy a day pass to the **Meliá Conchal** ($25) that permits you to dine and use the facilities. You pay cash for your meals and receive a refund upon departure on any balance due from the $20.

The inexpensive **Restaurante Encanto,** at the southern end of the beach, serves basic Costa Rican cuisine. Hans serves *típico* dishes and *schweinefleisch und apfelstrudel* at the **Casa Blanca,** 800 meters inland from the south end of the beach.

Tours and Activities
Tío Sports, based at Meliá, offers watersports on the beach: kayaks ($10 per hour), windsurfers ($15), catamarans ($45 with skipper), snorkeling ($10 per day), and scuba diving ($72 two tanks). It also rents mountain bikes.

Greens fees at the Meliá Conchal Golf Course cost $80 including cart.

Getting There
The Flamingo-bound buses from San José (10:30 a.m.) and Santa Cruz (3:30 a.m., 5 a.m., 10:30 a.m., and 1:30 p.m.) stop in Matapalo, from where you can walk or catch a taxi. Buses depart Matapalo for Santa Cruz at 5 a.m., 8 a.m., and 4:30 p.m.; and for Santa Rosa and Tamarindo at 12:30 p.m.

PARQUE NACIONAL MARINO LAS BAULAS, PLAYA GRANDE, AND REFUGIO NACIONAL DE VIDA SILVESTRE TAMARINDO

Costa Rican beaches don't come more beautiful than Playa Grande, a seemingly endless curve of coral-white sand with water as blue as the summer sky. Alas, no palms or shade trees grow down by the beach itself. A beach trail to the north leads along the cape through dry forest—good for birdlife—and deposits you at **Playa Ventanas,** a pristine scalloped swath of white sand you will want to claim as your own. You'll find a few tide pools for snorkeling and bathing. Superb surf pumps ashore at high tide—*year-round*. Playa Grande is renowned among surfers for its consistency and good mix of lefts and rights. Surfing expert Mark Kelly rates it as "maybe the best overall spot in the country."

The entire shoreline is protected within the 445-hectare Parque Nacional Marino Las Baulas (Marine Turtle National Park), which protects the prime nesting site of the leatherback turtle on the Pacific coast, including 22,000 hectares out to sea. The beach was incorporated into the national park system in May 1990 after a 15-year battle between developers and conservationists. At issue is the fate of the leatherback turtle—and the amazing fact that humankind stands on the brink of terminating forever a miracle that has played itself out annually at Playa Grande for the past several million years.

The park is the result of efforts of Louis Wilson and Marianel Pastor, owners of Hotel Las Tortugas. In the 1970s, a cookie company was harvesting the turtles' eggs. The beach was subdivided among 30 or so egg poachers, who sold Louis and Marianel "rights" to take tourists on to their sections of sand. Once the tourists left, the *hueveros* would steal the eggs. In the 1980s, Asian fleets began harvesting eggs here. The government agreed to support the couple's conservation efforts only if they could show that the site was economically viable as a tourist destination. Much of the land backing the beach was owned by developers, who had until recently been prevented from constructing homes and hotels. Things have come full circle. The locals have taken over all guiding (each guide is certified through an accredited course), and Las Baulas is now a model for similar experiments worldwide. However, in a typically Costa Rican compromise, developers finally won their battle too: Playa Grande was in the midst of a building boom when I last visited—including the half-complete **Rancho Las Colinas Golf and Country Club** project, which will include 220 residential sites plus an 18-hole golf course (already open at press time)

designed by internationally renowned golf course architect Ron Garl. How this will affect the turtle population is anyone's guess. And the other ecosystems? Locals are complaining that their water pressure has dropped thanks to Las Colinas. The area has water woes in dry season and the course's $1 million irrigation system taps the aquifer that supplies the local area, but still hasn't been able to quench the huge thirst of its 7,000-hectare greens.

THE LEATHERBACK TURTLE

The leatherback turtle (*Dermochelys coriacea*) is the world's largest reptile and a true relic from the age of the dinosaurs. The average adult weighs about 455 kg (1,000 pounds) and is two meters (six feet) in length, though males have been known to attain a staggering 2,000 pounds!

Though it nests on the warm beaches of Costa Rica, the *baula* (as it is locally known) has evolved as a deep-diving cold water critter: its great, near-cylindrical bulk retains body heat in cold waters (it can maintain a body temperature of 18° C in near frigid water). The leatherback travels great distances feeding in the open ocean and often crossing between continents, as far afield as subarctic waters, where its black body helps absorb the sun's warming rays. Like seals, the leatherback has a thick oily layer of fat for insulation. Its preferred food is jellyfish (the leatherback has scissor-like jaws for cutting rubbery prey, and long backward-pointing spines line its throat to prevent squishy prey from escaping), which are most numerous in temperate latitudes.

The females—which reach reproductive age between 15 and 50 years—prefer to nest on steep beaches that have a deepwater approach, thus avoiding long-distance crawls. Nesting occurs during the middle hours of the night—the coolest hours. Leatherback eggs take longer to hatch— 70 days on average—than those of other sea turtles (35-75% of eggs hatch).

Whereas in other turtle species, the bony exterior carapace is formed by flat-

tened, widened ribs that are fused and covered with corneous tissues resembling the human fingernail, the leatherback has an interior skeleton of narrow ribs linked by tiny bony plates all encased by a thick "shell" of leathery, cartilaginous skin. The leatherback's tapered body is also streamlined for hydrodynamic efficiency, with seven longitudinal ridges that act like a boat's keel, and long, powerful flippers for maximum propulsion. Leatherbacks have been shown to dive deeper than 1,300 meters (4,000 feet), where their small lungs, flexible frames, squishy bodies, and other specialist adaptations permit the animal to withstand well over 1,500 pounds of pressure per square inch

Contributions to help save leatherback turtles can be sent marked Programa de Tortugas Marinas to **Fundación de la Universidad de Costa Rica para la Investigación,** University of Costa Rica, San Pedro 2050, Costa Rica, or to Karen and Scott Eckert, Hubbs Sea World Research Institute, 1700 S. Shores Rd., San Diego, CA 92109.

WILDLAND ADVENTURES, INC.

Playa Grande is backed by dry forest. The beach sweeps south to the mouth of the Río Matapalo, which forms a 400-hectare mangrove estuary behind the beach. The ecosystem is protected within Refugio Nacional de Vida Silvestre Tamarindo (Tamarindo National Wildlife Refuge) and features crocodiles, anteaters, and monkeys. Large flocks of waterbirds (and raptors) gather, especially in the midst of dry season. And with hunting by locals a thing of the past, the wildlife population is increasing; deer and even ocelots and other cats are being seen with greater frequency.

Salitral is a hamlet on the main approach road, 600 meters inland from the beach.

Visiting the Turtles of Playa Grande

Turtles call at Playa Grande year-round. The nesting season for the giant leatherback is Oct.-March, when females come ashore every night at high tide. Often, more than 100 turtles might be seen in a single night. (Olive ridley turtles can sometimes also be seen here, as may the smaller green turtles, May-August.) Septemper through November is best for avoiding hordes of tourists.

A visit here is a humbling, reverential experience. One turtle, having patiently withstood the intrusive gawking eyes through her labor, halted and turned to face me as I walked by her side down to the sea. Who knows what sentiment she may have tried to express. Watching her lumbering exertions as the mother-to-be hauled herself back to sea was like saying a final, tearful farewell to a loved one. The experience was so sublime, so profound, that tears welled in my eyes as I typed in my notes the next day.

Each female leatherback will nest as many as 12 times a season, every 10 days or so (usually at night). Most turtles prefer the center of the beach, just above the high-tide mark.

Rangers from the local community roam the beach and lead groups to nesting turtles, guided by other rangers who spot for turtles and call in the location via walkie-talkies. Visitors are no longer allowed to walk the beach after dusk unescorted. Groups cannot exceed 15 people. And no more than 60 people are allowed at any time on the beach at night.

Resist the temptation to follow the example of the many thoughtless visitors who get too close to the turtles, try to touch them, ride their backs, or otherwise display a lack of common sense and respect. Flashlights and camera flashes are *not* permitted. And watch your step. Newborn turtles are difficult to see at night as they scurry down to the sea. Many are inadvertently crushed by tourists' feet.

Marine Park Information

There's a ranger station and information office, tel./fax 653-0470, at Salitral. Hours: daily 8 a.m.-noon and 1-5 p.m.

The Hotel Las Tortugas (see below), by the park entrance, has served as the wildlife center for the marine park, but gradually all functions related to the refuge are being taken over by local community members. Louis Wilson is still the best source of information about anything pertaining to the area.

There are two entrance gates to the beach: one where the road meets the beach by the Hotel Las Tortugas; and the second at the southern end by Villas Baulas. You buy your tickets here: $6. During periods of high demand the waiting time can be two hours before you are permitted onto the beach. The guides police the beach and check for tickets at random. Hiking is allowed on the north side of the estuary and along the beach. Trails are not marked.

El Mundo de la Tortuga

The World of the Turtle museum, tel. 653-0471, fax 653-0491, is 200 meters from the main entrance gate and a *must-visit* before watching the turtles. Self-guided audio tours (20 minutes) are offered in four languages. The displays are splendid and highly educaitonal. Did you know that the brain of a 1,000-pound leatherback weighs only one-quarter ounce? Or that the turtles eat mostly jellyfish? Or that they're found in all of the world's oceans as far north as the Arctic? The museum is open by night and you can sit in the outside patio and await your turn to visit the turtles (the park wardens radio in when the action begins). It has a splendid gift shop. *Fantastic!* Free educational programs are given to locals.

Accommodations

Camping: Camping is not allowed on the beach. You can camp at **Centro Vacacional Playa Grande,** at Salitral. It has showers and toilets. Rates: $2.

Budget: Centro Vacacional Playa Grande, tel./fax 653-0467 or tel. 237-2552, fax 260-3991, has 11 a/c *cabinas* (eight with kitchenettes) with private baths, two bedrooms, kitchens, refrigerators, and fans. They sleep up to six people. There's shade trees on the lawn, plus an outdoor restaurant with tasty and inexpensive seafood dishes. Free laundry service. Rates: $10 s, $20 d, $50 for six. **Cabinas Las Baulas,** behind Centro Vacacional, also has six basic *cabinas* plus camping. Rates: $25 *cabinas,* up to four people.

Inexpensive: Hotel El Bucanero, tel./fax 653-0480, 200 meters south of Las Tortugas, has seven modern rooms with fans and private baths with hot water. It has a breezy upstairs restaurant with beach views and a TV. Rates: $35 d; $40 for the one a/c room. **Hotel Parque de Agua,** next door, is owned by a friendly blonde Russian called Yuri. It's an exquisite little place, blazing white with natural stone terraces featuring little cascades, a small plunge pool, and shady palms. The eight a/c rooms are simple, clean, and well-lit, with orthopedic mattresses and private baths with cold water (hot water was to be added). Yuri has a small gym; there are barbecue sites outside, but Yuri intends to hire a professional chef. Rates: $25 s, $40 d/t.

Rancho Diablo, tel./fax 653-0490; in the U.S., tel. (213) 628-1308 or (888) 299-5748, next door, is a "surf camp" run by a father-and-son duo from Huntington Beach, California. The two-story all-wood, tin-roofed main lodge has thick nautical ropes and bamboo accents, plus eight rooms with private baths and hot water and a dorm with five bunks. There's a boutique, a surf shop, and a satellite TV, table soccer, and pool table for entertainment. Burgers and other simple fare are served. The guys have created a great surf camp and are well-meaning. But the party scene may have gotten out of hand. Locals were disturbed by the loud music and an in-your-face attitude (the brochure shows a snarling pit-bull). I hope this has changed. Rates: $25 pp dorm room; $35 d private room.

Moderate: *The* place to be is **Hotel Las Tortugas,** Apdo. 164, Santa Cruz 5150, tel. 653-0423, fax 653-0458, e-mail: nela@cool.co.cr, website www.cool.co.cr/usr/turtles, a comfortable ecolodge that is much more comfortable than the basic brochure suggests. Rooms have a/c, pewter-colored stone floors, orthopedic mat-

tresses, plus private baths with hot water. The hotel, described as "a mirthful combination of colonial and modern architecture," is bleached-white stucco throughout and has a turtle-shaped swimming pool with sundeck, plus a large jacuzzi. (Since turtles are sensitive to light—newborn turtles are attracted to light; adults can be disoriented by it—there are no ocean views to the south, where the nesting beach is.) The restaurant is a highlight, with sextagonal tables of gleaming hardwood, an outdoor patio, and a marvelous view over the beach through wall-to-wall windows. The food ain't bad either: take your pick of burgers, sandwiches, tenderloin, shrimp, and chicken in wine or garlic sauce. And you *must* try the apple pie with ice cream. "We have a stoked staff and the food is ripping!" says Louis, who recently added a surfer's *soda* selling burgers and beer by the beach. The hotel rents surfboards and two-passenger canoes for trips into the estuary ($30 half day) and also has horseback riding. "We're an ol' Hemingway kind of place," says Louis, who tempts his willing Queensland heelers (Australian cattle dogs) to perform a pantomime for guests. "I ruv roo!" barks June, after Benny sits up and begs her. Rate: $80 d.

The German-run **Hotel y Restaurant Cantarana,** tel. 653-0486, fax 653-0491, facing into the mangrove estuary, two km south of Las Tortugas, is an attractive place with 10 simply furnished a/c rooms around an amoeba-shaped pool in a landscaped garden. Each has tile floors, lofty ceiling, fans, screened windows, and a shady balcony. The elegant restaurant (open to three sides) serves international cuisine, including Teutonic fare. Rates: $45 s, $64 d, including breakfast.

Villa Baula Beach Resort, Apdo. 111-6151, Santa Ana 2000, tel. 653-0493 or 257-7676, fax 653-0459 or 257-1098, e-mail: hotelvb@sol.racsa.co.cr, is a resort with 25 rooms in five thatched hardwood bungalows—a rustic take on African safari huts—raised on stilts within the dry forest immediately behind the beach and in front of the Tamarindo Wildlife Refuge. It's far more humble than the brochure suggests. ¡Muy rústico! Twin rooms have two single beds; double rooms have a double bed. Five bungalows each sleep four people. The Jaguarundi Restaurant and Malinche Bar face onto a swimming pool, plus there are trails for hiking and horseback riding, and mountain bikes, ocean kayaks, and surfboards for rent.

Guided kayak, riding, and hiking tours are offered. Rates: $60 s/d, 64 t, $82 bungalow. All-inclusive packages are available.

Expensive: Half a kilometer north and likewise between beach and estuary is the **Casas Playa Grande/Palm Beach Village,** tel./fax 653-0492, complex, with fully furnished two-bedroom houses for purchase and rent. This little self-contained village of a/c Spanish colonial-style homes has a pool, and maid service is available. Rates: $85 d; $500 weekly.

Rancho Las Colinas Golf and Country Club, SJO 893, P.O. Box 025216, Miami, FL 33102-5216; in Costa Rica, tel. 293-4644, is about four km inland of Playa Grande. The project, which was due for completion in 1999, has turned an erstwhile cattle hacienda into a lush greenspace. Many of the 220 houses and 50 condo units will be available as vacation rentals. The private club will have a limited membership (the price is $10,000). You'll be able to enjoy beach vistas and spectacular sunsets from the lounge, as well as sample the swimming pool, tennis courts, and equestrian facilities. The self-contained resort will include a convenience store, boutiques, and other services, including a beach club.

Linda Vista is a "private hilltop retreat with panoramic views," 400 meters to the right from Centro Vacacional, whose owner also rents hilltop houses—**Casas Kike**—behind the beach. Rates: $140 (for up to 10 people). You'll see other homes for rent by the beach north of Hotel Las Tortugas, including **Villa Pura Vida,** tel. 653-0496, e-mail: juliecrc@silcom.com, a two-bedroom, two-suite, one penthouse unit that rents for $250, or $50 per room.

Louis and Marianel of Hotel Las Tortugas also rent six apartments and four creatively conceived houses, from two beds to 15 people. All have a/c, hot water, and reflective glass windows; some with curved walls, deep-tiled tubs and showers, and one—the three-story "lighthouse"—with a spiral staircase leading up to a 360-degree room with a circular bed. Rates: $150-315.

Tours and Activities
Virtually all the hotels and tour companies in Playa Tamarindo and Flamingo offer turtle-watching tours (about $25), as do major tour operators specializing in Guanacaste: **Rico Tours,** tel. 233-9658, fax 233-9357; **CATA Tours,** tel. 221-5455, fax 221-0200; and **Papagayo Excursions,** tel. 653-0227, fax 653-0254. Most companies also offer the "Jungle Boat Safari," aboard a 20-passenger, environmentally sound pontoon boat that takes you into the mangrove-rich Tamarindo Wildlife Refuge ($20). It's operated by the local community.

Rancho Diablo rents surfboards ($8 half day, $15 full day).

Getting There
By Car: The only road access is via Matapalo, six km east of Playa Grande; turn left at the soccer field in Matapolo.

A **water-taxi** runs between Tamarindo, docking on the estuary near the Hotel Cantaranana. It departs for Tamarindo Mon.-Sat. at 7:30 a.m., then every two hours ($1).

By Bus: The Flamingo-bound buses from San José (10:30 a.m.) and Santa Cruz (10 a.m. and 2 p.m.) stop in Matapalo, where you can walk or catch a taxi.

TAMARINDO

Playa Tamarindo, eight km south of Huacas, is Nicoya's most developed beach resort and is especially popular with North American surfers and chic Italians. It gets very full in high season, when a room in cheaper hotels is often hard to find. The attractive gray-sand beach is about two km wide, and very deep when the tide goes out—perfect for strolling and watching pelicans dive for fish. It's backed by tamarind trees, which give the beach its name. No-see-ums—tiny sand flies that pack a jumbo-size bite—are a problem around dusk. There's a smaller beach south of the main beach, with tide pools and relatively fewer people.

The beach has three surf breaks: a rocky right-point shore break named Henry's Point in front of the Restaurante Zully Mar, a left shore break named Pico Pequeño 100 meters north, and a superb rivermouth break. Local boats will also run surfers to difficult-to-reach surf spots, including **Playa Langosta** (a stunning, undeveloped beautiful white-sand beach two km south of Tamarindo), **Playa Avellana** (10 km south), and **Playa Negra** (12 km south). Langosta is famed

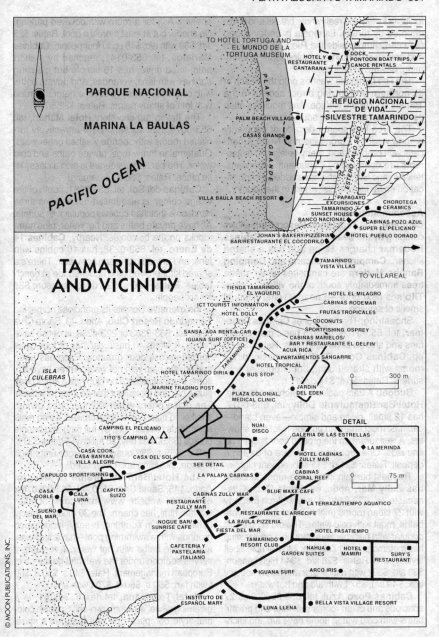

TO HOTEL TORTUGA AND
EL MUNDO DE LA
TORTUGA MUSEUM

PARQUE NACIONAL

MARINA LA BAULAS

PACIFIC OCEAN

HOTEL Y
RESTAURANTE
CANTARANA

DOCK,
PONTOON BOAT TRIPS,
CANOE RENTALS

REFUGIO NACIONAL
DE VIDA
SILVESTRE TAMARINDO

PALM BEACH VILLAGE

CASAS GRANDE

PLAYA GRANDE

ESTERO PALO SECO

VILLA BAULA BEACH RESORT

PAPAGAYO
EXCURSIONES
TAMARINDO
SUNSET HOUSE
BANCO NACIONAL

CHOROTEGA
CERAMICS

CABINAS POZO AZUL
SUPER EL PELICANO
HOTEL PUEBLO DORADO

JOHAN'S BAKERY/PIZZERIA
BAR/RESTAURANTE EL COCODRILO

TAMARINDO
AND VICINITY

TAMARINDO
VISTA VILLAS

TO VILLAREAL

TIENDA TAMARINDO,
EL VAQUERO

HOTEL EL MILAGRO
CABINAS RODEMAR
FRUTAS TROPICALES
COCONUTS
SPORTFISHING OSPREY

ICT TOURIST INFORMATION
HOTEL DOLLY

SANSA, ADA RENT-A-CAR
IGUANA SURF (OFFICE)

ISLA
CULEBRAS

CABINAS MARIELOS/
BAR Y RESTAURANTE EL DELFIN
ACUA RICA
APARTAMENTOS SANGARRE

HOTEL TROPICAL

HOTEL TAMARINDO DIRIA
MARINE TRADING POST

BUS STOP

JARDIN
DEL EDEN

PLAYA TAMARINDO

PLAZA COLONIAL,
MEDICAL CLINIC

0   300 m

DETAIL

CAMPING EL PELICANO
TITO'S CAMPING

NUAI
DISCO

GALERIA DE LAS ESTRELLAS

LA MERINDA

CASA COOK,
CASA BANYAN,
VILLA ALEGRE

CASA DEL SOL

SEE DETAIL

HOTEL CABINAS
ZULLY MAR

CABINAS
CORAL REEF

CAPULOO SPORTFISHING

LA PALAPA CABINAS

BLUE MAXX CAFE

75 m

CASA
DOBLE

CALA
LUNA

CAPITAN SUIZO

CABINAS ZULLY MAR

LA TERRAZA/TIEMPO AQUATICO

RESTAURANTE
ZULLY MAR

RESTAURANTE EL ARRECIFE

SUEÑO
DEL MAR

NOGUE BAR/
SUNRISE CAFE

LA BAULA PIZZERIA
FIESTA DEL MAR

HOTEL PASATIEMPO

CAFETERIA Y
PASTELARIA
ITALIANO

TAMARINDO
RESORT CLUB

NAHUA
GARDEN SUITES

HOTEL
MAMIRI

SURY'S
RESTAURANT

IGUANA SURF

ARCO IRIS

INSTITUTO DE
ESPANOL MARY

LUNA LLENA

BELLA VISTA VILLAGE RESORT

© MOON PUBLICATIONS, INC.

for its rocky left and reefy shore breaks and is frequented by turtles. Langosta is undeveloped (you can camp beside the Río San Francisco) and now used for turtlewatching tours. If swimming, beware of riptides.

The Río Matapalo washes onto the beach at its northern end, giving direct access to the Tamarindo Wildlife Refuge. And monkeys often come to the shore at the southern end.

The area has seen a decade of popularity among wealthy Europeans and North Americans with cash in hand; many hotels and restaurants are operated by Canadians, Americans, Italians, and Swiss, who have added a sophistication so far lacking elsewhere in the country.

Accommodations

Camping: The **Tamarindo Resort Club** allows camping by the beach. Rates: $3 pp. **Cabinas Rodemar** charges $2 pp and has a shared kitchen. **Camping El Pelicano** and **Camping Rancho Madera** are campsites under shade trees immediately south of the village center. **Tito's** is next door—a nearby water channel smells of sewage.

Shoestring: The bare-bones **Cabinas Rodemar,** tel. 653-0109, has 18 basic cabins with fans and shared or private baths. Rates: $6.50 pp. **Cabinas Coral Reef** offers basic, dingy rooms with shared bath, but is popular with surfers. Rates: $8 s, $14 d, $17 t.

Budget: A backpacker's beachfront favorite, **Hotel/Bar/Restaurante Dolly,** tel. 653-0017, has 12 small, clean and simple—even bland—*cabinas;* most share an outside toilet and showers. A restaurant on the ground floor is open on one side. One report says beware of paying a deposit. Rates: $21 d; $15 subsequent nights.

The best bargain in its price range is **Cabinas Zully Mar,** Apdo. 68, Santa Cruz, Guanacaste, tel. 653-0140, a very well-run property with 27 clean rooms (eight with a/c) with private baths, most with cold water. The old wing is still popular with backpackers, though a newer wing has metamorphosed Zully Mar into a simple albeit stylish hotel. Rates: $28 s/d, $34 t high season; $33 s/d, $39 t with refrigerator and safety security box; $49 s/d, $57 t with a/c and hot water.

Cabinas Pozo Azul, tel. 653-0280, has 27 spacious and clean rooms with fans and private baths with cold water; some have a/c and kitch-enettes. Ask for a room with covered parking. No shade, but at least there's a pool. Rates: $23 s/d, $39 with a/c; $48 up to four people. **Cabinas Marielos,** tel. 653-0141, reached by a short palm-lined drive, has 16 simple but pleasing *cabinas* with fans, verandas, and private baths with cold water. They're set in a natural garden with lots of shady palms. Rates: $22.50 pp.

The Italian-run two-story **Hotel Mamiri,** tel. 653-0079, has six simply yet attractively furnished rooms with sponge-washed ocher walls, Guatemalan throw rugs, private baths and cold water. The bar and restaurant is also a classy little place. Rates: $30 d. *A bargain!*

Cabinas del Sol, tel. 653-0081, south of the village center, is also Italian-run and has three handsome thatched *cabinas* popular with surfers. All have private baths and hot water, plus hammocks on the balconies. Nearby, **Cabinas 14 de Enero,** tel. 653-0238, has 10 cabins with fans, and private baths and hot water. There's a shared kitchen; you dine under shade at bench tables. Rates: $20 s, $22 d high season; $35 for six people.

Inexpensive Despite its grandiose name, the **Tamarindo Resort Club,** Apdo. 73, Santa Cruz 5150, tel. 653-0383 or 223-4289, is not so salubrious. It offers 40 basic *cabinas* of four types spread across dour grounds. Each has a fan and private bath with hot water. Three have a/c; some have kitchens. The club has a small pool, plus a bar and restaurant that doubles as a disco. The place offers water-skiing, scuba diving, snorkeling trips, and coastal cruises; it also rents surfboards ($4 half day, $7 full day) and boogie boards ($3.50 half day, $6 full day). Rates: $39 s, $49 d, $55 t, $59 quad, $65 larger units high season, including tax. *Overpriced!*

The **Hotel/Bar/Restaurante El Milagro,** Apdo. 145, Santa Cruz 5150, tel. 653-0050, fax 653-0050, website www.magi.com/crica/hotels/tam.html, has charm. The 30 modern conical cabinas—set in soothing, breezy, landscaped grounds with a swimming pool—have a/c, fans, and private baths with hot water. A restaurant serves seafood under the watchful guidance of European management. Rate: $40 s, $50 d, $60 t with fan; $50 s, $60 d, $70 t with a/c.

Hotel Tropicana, tel./fax 653-0261, is a gleaming white, 43-room, two-unit Spanish colonial-style complex; one unit features a spiral staircase that conjures images of the double-helix staircase of Chateaux Chambord. Within, rooms are pleasant and roomy with heaps of light. The hotel has a swimming pool and restaurant. Rates: $50 d with fan; $60 with a/c.

Another pleasing option is the small **Hotel y Restaurante Pueblo Dorado,** Apdo. 1711, San José 1002, tel. 653-0008, fax 653-0013, or tel./fax 222-5741, a Spanish-style "villa" with 28 rooms featuring a/c and private baths with hot water. The place is simply furnished in a very elegant modern decor of grays, blacks, and whites. A small bar and restaurant overlooks a pool and a tiny landscaped courtyard garden. Mayan-style motifs abound. It has a minibus service to San José ($150 one-way for 12 people). Rates: $40 s, $50 d, $60 t.

Hotel Pasatiempo, tel. 653-0096, has 11 attractive, spacious, well-lit thatched cabins around a pool in pretty grounds full of bougainvillea, bananas and palms. Note the beautiful hand-carved doors. It has a book exchange, pool table, and table soccer, and you can rent snorkeling gear. The Yucca Bar is a good place to sup. Rates: $49 d; $59 with a/c; $10 extra person.

Another exquisite winner is the offbeat **Arco Iris,** tel./fax 653-0330, also Italian run but resembling more a piece of Haight-Ashbury, with wind chimes, New Age music, batiks hanging from the ceiling, and bold color schemes. It has three *cabinas* with private baths and hot water. Each has a striking and endearing decor; the Oriental room has batiks. All have gaily painted exteriors and black or dark-colored floors. It

SPECIAL HOTEL: CAPITÁN SUIZO

It was love at first sight. I was, I suppose, swept away by its tranquility, its beauty. Indeed, the strangely named Capitán Suizo, tel. 653-0075, fax 653-0292, e-mail: capitansuizo@ticonet.co.cr, a member of the Small Distinctive Hotels of Costa Rica, is possibly the *best beach resort in the country.* It was conceived and is operated by a charming Swiss couple who arrived in Costa Rica a few years ago and stumbled under a spell from which they have never escaped. Beach-loving cognoscenti will appreciate the resort's casual sophistication, its thoroughly laid-back, unpretentious exclusivity. Even the local howler monkeys have decided this is the place to be!

Pathways coil sinuously through a botanical rush hour of heliconias, bougainvillea, palms, and shade trees to a wide sundeck and large amoeba-shaped pool: resembling a natural pond, it's rimmed by rocks and lush foliage and faux-beach shelving gently into the water. Here, you may bronze yourself on comfortable lounge chairs superbly contoured with thick foam pads and listen to the rustling of the breeze in the palms until it and the "chirrup" of tree frogs lull you to sleep.

Supremely elegant design and warmly evocative decor blends Tokyo, Tahiti, and Thailand into one. Each spacious bungalow features a mezzanine bedroom with king-size bed set diagonally facing the apex of two huge sliding doors with wall-to-ceiling plate glass. A serene, simple beauty pervades the 22 rooms and eight bungalows with their natural gray-stone floors and deep-red hardwoods

harmoniously balanced by attractive verdigris soft-cushioned sofas and chairs. Halogen lamps inset in the ceiling provide super lighting; soft-lit lanterns provide a more romantic note. And the bungalow bathrooms are the size of some other hotel rooms. A deep tub is set next to the window; outside a cool shower awaits in its own semicircular enclosure. Closets have wicker-mesh to let your clothes breathe.

The bar and restaurant (an open-walled inspiration with soaring pyramid roof) follow the elegant theme, with candlelit dining, hardwood hints that Hepplewhite would be proud of, and tall bar stools with soft hide seats. The German chef, Roland, merges European influences into a tropical setting. The dinner menu changes daily: a set meal of oxtail soup, veal in cheese sauce, rosti, mixed salad, and ice cream costs $12. My corvina in mango sauce ($8) was divine! Check out the terra-cotta tile floor of many colors. Capitán Suizo has its own horse stable ($15 two hours), plus kayaks, boogie boards, and a game room.

Yes, the howler monkeys really do hang out in the trees overhanging the pool! And often a pelican will fly in in mid-afternoon to beg fish from the kitchen. Only one bittersweet thought comes to mind during your stay here: leaving!

Rates (double occupancy): $80 room, $95 with a/c, $115 bungalow low season; $95 room, $110 with a/c, $130 bungalow high season; $110 room, $125 with a/c, $150 bungalow peak season.

serves vegetarian meals, including corn coffee, crepes, fruit salads, and the chappatti "Robin Hood" (homemade Indian bread filled with mushrooms and cheese, $3.50). Tribal Tattoo and massage are available. Rates: $25 d low season; $35 d high season; $10 more with kitchen.

Moderate: Finca Monte Fresco, tel. 653-0241, e-mail: samoniqe@sol.racsa.co.cr, sits atop a hill between Villarreal and Tamarindo, with splendid views over the Wildlife Refuge. This Austrian-run house has four spacious well-lit *cabinas* with tile floors and lofty ceilings, and an apartment, all with private baths and hot water. There's a small kidney-shaped pool and a *ranchito* with hammocks. Breakfast is served on a terrace. Rates: $40 s, $60 d, $80 t, $100 apartment high season.

On the approach road to town, directly opposite the airstrip, is **Hotel La Reserva,** Apdo. 167, Santa Cruz, Guanacaste, tel. 653-0355, fax 287-8725, an impressive Italian-owned property with modestly furnished bungalows with ocher-washed walls and Thai-style (actually Tyrolean, I'm told) roofs. Each has a/c, ceiling fan, telephone, minibar, safety box, plus terra-cotta tile floors and rough plaster white walls. They look down over a pool measuring more than 1,000 square meters and fringed by a wide sundeck. Nearby is Harry's Bar & Cocktail Lounge and an elegant *ranchito* restaurant. Work up a sweat on tennis courts (lit at night) or the sand volleyball court. Rates: $60 d, $85 junior suite, $125 suite low season; $70 d, $95 junior suite, $135 suite high season.

Nahua Garden Suites, tel. 653-0010, has very attractive suites boasting terra-cotta floors, kitchenettes of gleaming white tiles with colonial-tile hints, plus futons, queen-size beds on a mezzanine, and hardwood accents. Lush gardens have a lap pool. In all there are five suites (five more are planned). Rates: from $60 d.

Nearby, looking like a South African kraal, is the **Bella Vista Village Resort,** Apdo. 143, Santa Cruz 5150, tel./fax 653-0036, e-mail: belvista@sol.racsa.co.cr, featuring six hilltop, thatched, four-person bungalows with fully furnished kitchens, living rooms, dining areas and separate loft bedrooms. They're fabulous within—the soaring roofs supported by graceful beams, the fabrics rich, the simple decor highlighted by an individual motif. A pool is set in lush landscaped grounds. The "kraal" commands marvelous views over the treetops to the ocean. Rates: $50 s, $55 d low season; $55 s, $90 d high season.

The Italian-run **Luna Llena,** tel. 653-0082, fax 653-0120, also has conical bungalows around an alluring swimming pool with swim-up bar. Stone pathways runs through the stylish property, whose rooms have tasteful, soothing decor, including terra-cotta floors; a spiral staircase leads to a loft bedroom. All have fans, refrigerators, and private baths with hot water. There's a small restaurant and a laundry. Rates: $55 s, $70 d, including tax and breakfast; $25 extra person.

La Palapa Cabinas, tel. 653-0362, has two cabins with kitchens and private baths and hot water. Also consider **La Casa Sueca,** tel./fax 653-0021, e-mail: viking@sol.racsa.co.cr, a small, cozy Swedish-run hotel with a soothing contemporary colonial look with cool whitewashed walls and soft, appealing decor. They come in three sizes and have private baths and hot water. A path leads to the beach. Rates: $70 d.

Casa Banyan Bed and Breakfast, tel. 653-0072, a beautiful three-story home with a massive fig tree (banyan) out front, was sold just before press time; it was uncertain if it would continue to operate. A stone's throw away is **Casa Cook,** tel./fax 653-0125; in the U.S., tel. (500) 675-0421, fax (500) 677-1781, with two one-bedroom casitas, a pool and patio, and two large bedrooms with private baths in the main house. **Casa Blanca,** tel. 653-0073, nearby, has a large pool. **Casa Doble,** tel. 653-0312, is 400 meters farther south.

Expensive: I love the **Sueño del Mar Bed and Breakfast,** tel. 653-0284, e-mail: suenodem@sol.racsa.co.cr; in the U.S., 4 Mountview Center, Burlington, VT 05401, tel. (802) 658-8041, e-mail: moneyn@aol.com, a truly exquisite Spanish colonial *posada*-style house with rooms cascading down a shaded alcove to a small landscaped garden that opens onto the beach. Each is cool and shaded, with rough-hewn timbers, whitewashed stone walls, terra-cotta tile floors, screened arched windows with shutters, and tasteful fabrics adding to the warm, homey feel. There's a sensuous serenity to the place. It also has a casita for four people. Rates: $75 d, $95 casita low season; $95 d, $160 casita high season.

Californians Barry and Suzie Lawson run **Villa Alegre,** tel. 653-0270, fax 653-0287, e-mail: vialegre@sol.racsa.co.cr, a beachfront bed and breakfast with a private pool set amid landscaped grounds. The main house has four rooms. Two *casitas* each have a living room, bedroom, and small kitchen. Rates include breakfast on the veranda. The rooms are individually decorated with the globe-trotting couple's collection of art, rugs, and miscellany; each room boasts the decor of a particular country, from Mexico to Japan. Rates: $75-80 d, $135 suite, low season; $95-100 d, $175 suite high season. Honeymoon packages—in the Caribbean room with king-size bed, of course—cost $395 (three nights) and $595 (five nights).

Thomas Douglas, owner of Hotel Santo Tomás in San José, rents **Tamarindo Sunset House,** tel. 653-0024 or 255-0448, fax 222-3950, e-mail: hotelst@sol.racsa.co.cr, just east of the Banco Nacional. The two-story, three-bedroom, two-bathroom beachhouse sleeps eight people. It has a CD player, hammocks and barbecue pit on the lawns, and lots of locks. Rates: $135 for up to four people, $165 up to six, $185 for eight.

Expensive: The hillside, all-suite **Tamarindo Vista Villas,** tel. 653-0114, fax 653-0115, e-mail: tamvv@sol.racsa.co.cr, offers oceanview one-bedroom "Tropicale" Suites and three-bedroom Imperial Suites, with spacious verandas and balconies centered on a twin-turreted lounge area. There's an amoeba-shaped pool and sundeck with swim-up bar backed by a waterfall. A jacuzzi was planned. Rates: $75 "Tropicale," $85 "Corona" two-bedroom suite, $115 "Imperial," low season; $95, $115, $195 respectively high season.

Hotel Jardín del Edén, tel. 653-0137, fax 653-0111, on a bluff overlooking Tamarindo, is truly a "garden of Eden." This handsome property comprises five salmon-pink Spanish-style villas with 18 rooms, and two fully equipped apartments owned and managed by a congenial Frenchman, Etienne (who lives on-site) and his Italian partner, Marcello. This place earns laurels for its amorous tenor. Rooms have individual decor. All have satellite TVs, telephones, and spacious terrace-porches offering views out to sea. A stunning, amoeba-shaped pool with swim-up bar and magnificent blue-tiled jacuzzi, a second crescentic pool, and a large sundeck with shady *ranchitos* are surrounded by gar-

dens fit for Adam and Eve. The lush foliage is floodlit at night, creating a colorful quasi-son et lumière. A cool, shady restaurant has heavy-duty hardwood tables inlaid with beautiful Spanish tiles, plus a changing menu that pays special attention to its Mediterranean-inspired seafood dishes. Pop in at breakfast for a fresh croissant from the patisserie. There's an open-air gym, and tours using the hotel's own 29-foot boat. A lamplit pathway leads down to the beach. Six smaller rooms and two suites may be added. Rates: $80 s small; $100 d large; $135 d apartments, including buffet breakfast; $10 children under 10. *Recommended!*

Premium: Down by the shores, **Hotel Tamarindo Diría,** Apdo. 21, Santa Cruz, tel./fax 653-0033 or 290-4340, is a compact hotel with 70 rooms with terra-cotta tile floors, heaps of storage, pleasing if '60s-style furniture, a/c, private bathrooms, hot water, cable TVs, and telephones. Some have a jacuzzi. A very large and airy restaurant with a beautiful hardwood ceiling opens onto an expansive bar, an outside cocktail terrace, and a large swimming pool in shady grounds. There are tennis courts plus a small casino (open 6-11 p.m.), a boutique, and sportfishing and tours. It reminds me of Honolulu resorts a decade ago, despite a recent refurbishment. Rate: $68 s, $84 d low season; $97 s, $112 d high season. *Overpriced!*

Outshining the Diría like a supernova is **Cala Luna Hotel and Villas,** tel. 653-0214, fax 653-0213, e-mail: calaluna@sol.racsa.co.cr, website www.calaluna.com, whose sponge-washed walls in gold-ocher and flame-orange say it all. Exquisitely handsome! Spanish tile and rough-hewn timbers add to the cozy New Mexico-Central American style. The 20 hotel rooms, 16 garden villas, and five master villas surround an amoeba-shaped pool in a small landscaped garden. Each villa, however, has its own pool. Comfort is the keynote: king-size beds are standard, and all villas have TVs and CD players. Tours, horseback rides, and fishing trips are offered. Rates: $130 d; $280 four-person villa; $360 six-person villa. *Recommended!*

Food

Tamarindo is blessed with some of the most creative restaurateurs in the country. **Zully Mar,** on the beachfront, has the best breakfast in town, with fresh-squeezed orange juice, and coconut cream mango and chocolate pies for desserts. You can also buy granola or pancake breakfasts at **Frutas Tropicales,** which also serves rice and octopus ($5), burgers, and a *casado* ($4). The **Nogui Bar/Sunrise Café** is also a popular place for gringo breakfasts. The **Blue Max Café** has good U.S. breakfasts (pancakes cost $2.50) and—listen up you Brits—fish and chips. You can get lattes, espressos and cappuccinos ($1-1.50). For pizza, try **La Baula Pizzeria.**

Fiesta del Mar is an atmospheric restaurant with a lofty Indonesian-style ceiling like something out of a Somerset Maugham novel. It serves steak and seafood dishes and specialty cocktails. **Coconuts** has lost its edge, but still offers candlelit dining and an inventive menu with middling French as well as a hint of Indonesia, especially in its *dorado teriyaki* and *pato á la Thaki.*

Sury's Restaurant (formerly Stella's) offers elegant dining under a pretty *palenque*. It has tempting vegetarian and seafood dishes, and pizzas ($1-6) fired in an earth oven. The **Restaurante El Jardín del Edén,** in the hotel of that name, offers surefire winners: the daily menu has dishes such as jumbo shrimp in whiskey, lobster in lemon sauce, peppered tenderloin, and more, enjoyed in a setting that may well inspire you to check into the hotel. Also check out **La Terraza,** tel. 653-0108, a pizza restaurant with breezy upstairs dining; chef Stefano knows his stuff. So, too, does Roland, the German chef at **Capitán Suizo,** where you should also eat before leaving town. I enjoyed a curried chicken ($6) and tilapia in caper sauce ($10).

El Vaquero Grill serves *típico* fare, plus salads, tenderloin, and a large menu of crepes ($3-9). An Italian winner is **La Meridiana,** tel. 653-0230, serving a fixed dinner of regional cuisines: scaloppines, pennes, and other mouthwatering fare for less than $10. After dessert, take a dip in the pool. Dinner only.

The **Iguana Grill** is an atmospheric spot hewn of logs topped by thatch. It sells smoothies ($2), espressos, mochas, and cappuccinos ($1-1.50).

Johan's Bakery is a shady, open-air cafe overlooking the estuary. Johan, the Belgian owner, conjures real European croissants, chocolate eclairs, pizza, waffles, and bread.

Entertainment

Rancho Cocodrilo is a cool place to hang out for beers and *bocas*. It gets in the groove as a disco, 10:30 p.m.-2:30 a.m. *The* disco of choice is **Disco Naoi** southeast of town, with flashing lights and a/c; it also has live music on Tuesday, a "Fiesta Mexicana" on Friday, and "reggae nite" on Sunday. It shows movies on Monday and Wednesday. **Club Las Olas** is also a popular and tasteful bar.

Shopping

Chorotega Cerámica sells pottery from Guaitil, plus other quality crafts; its 0.5 km east of town. **Galeria de las Estrellas** has an eclectic collection of jewelry. The largest clothing selection is at **Iguana Surf,** which sells beachwear and surf gear.

Fancy a communist stogie? **El Pelicano** supermarket and deli sells Cuban cigars. A number of offbeat foreigners sell jewelry from roadside stalls outside Zully Mar. **Galería Doña Luna,** on the traffic circle, has an eclectic array of arts and crafts. **Tienda Tamarindo** has more conventional souvenirs, plus magazines, swimwear, and the like. Next door is an **artesanía** selling Guaitil pottery, Guatemalan clothing, straw hats, and the like.

Tours and Activities

Papagayo Excursions, Apdo. 162, Santa Cruz, tel. 653-0227, fax 653-0254, e-mail: papagayo@sol.racsa.co.cr, has an office on the right as you enter town. It runs sportfishing trips (half day from $250, full day from $350), windsurfing, water-skiing, scuba diving (from $60 for two guided dives), and nature tours, including a "Jungle Boat Safari" up the Tamarindo Estuary and nocturnal "Turtle Nesting Tours" ($25) that visit Playa Langosta.

Costa Rica Diving, tel. 653-0468, operates scuba trips to the Catalinas, as does **Tiempo Aquatico,** tel./fax 653-0108, below the Terraza Restaurant, which charges $65 for a two-tank dive at the Catalinas. **Agua Rica,** tel./fax 653-0094, has a full range of dive trips ($60 two tanks) and certification courses, and rents snorkel gear for $5 half day, $8 full day. **Captain Gaylord Townsley,** tel. 653-0101, charges $450 half day, $650 full day for sportfishing aboard his 30-foot *Lone Star.*

Tamarindo Sportfishing, Apdo. 188, Santa Cruz, tel./fax 653-0092, has a large variety of modern boats, from a seven-meter Boston Whaler ($250 half day, $350 full day) to a 12-meter Topaz ($500 half day, $800 full day). **Excursiones Tamarindo** has sportfishing and turtle-watching tours. **Santa Rosa Horse Tours,** tel. 653-0044, offers two-hour tours at 7:30 a.m. and 3 p.m. ($20); reservations required. **Casagua Horses,** tel. 380-4664, also has riding at a nearby farm, Finca Casagua.

Tamarindo Rental Tours, tel./fax 653-0078, e-mail: rentals@sol.racsa.co.cr, offers a panoply of tours, including a visit to the Playa Grande turtles ($15) and a Wildlife Refuge boat tour at 8 a.m. and 3:30 p.m. ($12), and tours to Santa Rosa, Arenal, and farther afield ($75-85). There's also mountain bike ($4 half day, $6.50 full day) and boogie board ($3.50 half day, $4.50 full day) rentals.

Iguana Surf Shop, Apdo. 199-5150, Santa Cruz, tel./fax 653-0148, rents surfboards, kayaks, boats, and Hobie Cats. It also has surf tours and kayak trips into the estuary ($25), plus catamaran trips. Sam and Moni operate *Samonique,* tel./fax 653-0241, a 16-meter ketch that sets sail on a sunset cruise ($33), plus half-day ($60) and full-day ($80) cruises.

Spanish Language Courses

The **Instituto de Español Wayra,** tel./fax 653-0359, e-mail: spanish@sol.racsa.co.cr, opposite Iguana Surf, has a three-day Spanish "survival course," week- and month-long programs, plus Latin dance classes.

Services

The **Banco Nacional** is open Mon.-Fri. 8 a.m.-3 p.m.

The **Clínica San Marino,** tel. 666-1793, cellular tel. 284-3359, or c/o the Hotel Tamarindo

Diría for appointments, tel. 653-0031, is in the Plaza Comercial. It has a 24-hour emergency service—beeper tel. 296-5656, English; tel. 296-2626, Spanish).

You'll find **public telephones** outside the Hotel Tamarindo Diría and the Fiesta del Mar.

Babette's Laundry, tel. 653-0231, at Supermercado El Pelicano charges $2 per kilogram. It has hotel pickup. You can buy film and have it developed at **Photo-Flash,** at Cabinas La Palapa.

Getting There and Away

By Air: SANSA and **Travelair** operate scheduled daily service to Tamarindo (see appendix). SANSA also has an excursion flight between La Fortuna and Tamarindo daily ($55 each way). Papagayo Excursions offers private air charters ($380). The SANSA office, tel. 654-4223, is on the main street; Travelair is in the Hotel Pueblo Dorado.

By Bus: Buses depart San José daily from Calle 14, Avenidas 3/5 (Empresa Alfaro, tel. 222-2750), at 3:30 p.m.; and from Calle 20, Avenida 3 (Tralapa, tel. 221-7202), at 4 p.m. Return buses depart Tamarindo from outside the Fiesta del Mar at 5:45 a.m. (Alfaro) and 6:45 a.m (Tralapa). Buy tickets in advance, especially for weekends and holidays. Buses depart Santa Cruz daily at 10:30 a.m. and 3:30 p.m. and return from Tamarindo at 6 a.m. and noon.

Interbus operates a daily shuttle bus between Tamarindo and San José (see appendix).

By Car: There's no **gas station** in town but you can buy gas at inflated prices at a shack on the right as you enter town. Johan's bakery, of all places, has a **rental car** service. **Ada Rent-a-Car,** tel. 653-0001, has an office on the main street. You can rent scooters from **Rent-a-Moto,** tel. 653-0082, at Luna Llena for $20 half day, $40 full day, $110 three days, $210 weekly. **Tienda Tamarindo** also rents scooters.

TAMARINDO TO SÁMARA

From Tamarindo, you must backtrack to Villarreal to continue southward via Hernández (three km south of Villarreal). The coastal road is a lonesome, narrow dirt affair that becomes impassable in sections in the wet season, when you may have better luck approaching Playa Avellana and Lagartillo from the south via Paraíso reached by paved road from Santa Cruz. South of Paraíso, a separate dirt road leads south via Ostional to Nosara.

Nosara, and Sámara, another major beach resort 31 km farther south, can be reached directly by roads from the town of Nicoya.

PLAYA AVELLANA

Playa Avellana, 12 km south of Tamarindo, has been discovered by surfers. This very beautiful coral-colored beach has lots of tide pools and is renowned for its barrel surf. It has left and right breaks. A break named Guanacasteco has been described as a "bitchin' beach break."

You can buy gasoline at Pulpería Juanita in San José de Pinilla, midway between Hernández and Avenllana.

Accommodations and Food

You can camp pretty well anywhere you can pitch a tent or at **Avellanas Surf Camp** ($1.75 pp) or **Gregorio's.**

Cabinas Las Olas, Apdo. 1404-1250, Escazú, tel. 233-4455, fax 222-8685, is an "upscale" surfer's place with 10 bungalows widely spaced amid the dry forest. Each has private bathroom, bidet, and hot water. A raised wooden walkway leads 400 meters across mangroves to the beach. The video-bar and restaurant boast appealing ambience. It has ping-pong, rents kayaks ($8 per hour), and offers mountain bike tours. Rates: $35 s, $40 d low season; $40 s, $50 d high season.

Avellanas Surf Ranch (formerly Freddy's Place) has funky *cabinas* with shared bath and cold water. Rates: $6 pp. **Bar y Restaurante Gregorio's,** a pleasant bar and restaurant under thatch, has three basic *cabinas* 100 meters from the beach with private baths and cold water. Rates: $17 d.

PLAYAS LAGARTILLO AND NEGRA

Playa Lagartillo, beyond Punta Pargos, just south of Playa Avellana, is another white-sand beach with tide pools. Lagartillo is separated by Punta Pargos from Playa Negra, a similarly exquisite beach that has at last been discovered by the surfing crowd. The point break wave is very fast, generally hollow, and stand-up tubes are common. About five km south of Playa Negra, the dirt road cuts inland to the tiny hamlet of **Paraíso,** from where another dirt road leads back to the coast and dead-ends at Playa Junquillal. A self-appointed **tourist information center** can be found on the soccer field in Paraíso, where you turn left for Junquillal. There's a gas station here. **Izarra Boutique,** at the turn for Playa Negra five km north of Paraíso, sells quality batiks.

Accommodations and Food

The **Lagartillo Beach Hotel,** Apdo. 1584, San José 1000, tel. 225-5693, fax 253-0760, atop a hill about 200 meters from the beach, is surprisingly pleasant for being so far off the beaten track. Six pleasant all-wood *cabinas* come with fans, private baths, and hammocks on private verandas. A spacious and atmospheric bar and restaurant overlooks a small swimming pool. The hotel has bicycles and a horse for exploring the adjacent forest. Rate: $35 d, $40 t.

Cofini's Surf Camp, next door, has two cozy two-story wood-and-thatch cabins with kitchens. Rates: $25 d. **Cabinas Los Cocos,** two km farther south, was under construction at press time.

You'll love the three-story, all-hardwood, windowless **Mono Congo Lodge,** Apdo. 177-5150, Santa Cruz, fax 382-6926, a Colorado-style lodge—on a four-hectare farm between Lagartillo and Playa Negra—that has been described as "a mixture of Swiss Family Robinson tree house and Australian outback bed and breakfast." It is run by a transplanted Floridian called Wayne. The main lodge, which is hand constructed of hardwoods, has six simply furnished rooms boasting orthopedic mattresses, mosquito nets, screened windows, and exquisite tilework in the bathrooms (some have stone walls). You can relax in leather lounge chairs and admire the miscellany. A splendid wraparound veranda has hammocks. It's surrounded by fruit trees and dry forest. Horseback riding tours are available ($35-50). There's a restaurant serving homemade breads, vegetarian dishes, and wholesome desserts. There's also a two-bedroom cabin with wet bar, refrigerator, and coffeemaker. Rates: $35 d rooms, $10 extra person; $60 cabin. Packages include a four-day "classic" for $219 s, $333 d.

Pablo's Picasso is legendary among surfers. This rustic hostelry and surfers' gathering spot is run by a Yank called Paul—a John Belushi lookalike with a friendly demeanor. He offers a huge loft with bunks, plus three-person *cabinas* with fans and private baths with cold water, and two a/c *cabinas* with kitchens. You can camp for $4 pp, including toilets and showers. Hammocks are slung beneath the rustic bar where Paul serves "burgers as big as your head," plus pancakes ($3), sandwiches, and pastas. You can enjoy movies on the VCR while sitting in oversized wooden seats that inspire a Goldilocks-in-Papa-Bear's-chair sensation. Rates: $8.50 pp bunks; $10 pp *cabina* with fan; $50 s/d *cabina* with a/c and kitchen.

The Swiss-Spanish, kraal-like **Hotel Playa Negra**, Apdo. 31-5150 Santa Cruz, tel. 382-1301, fax 382-1302; in San José, tel./fax 293-0332, enjoys a breezy locale. Its circular thatched *cabinas* are exquisitely, albeit simply decorated, with sponge-painted walls, sensuous curves and soft pastels—mine had sea-blue floors and ocher walls—Guatemalan print bedspreads, and mosaic-tiled bathrooms. Each has a lofty wooden ceiling and is cross-ventilated through screened, louvered windows to all sides. A French chef conjures tasty food, including a hearty burger which you can enjoy at the huge crook-shaped bar with TV. There's a pool table, and a small swimming pool and lawns. A boutique sells quality batiks. It closes each October. Rates: $40 s, $50 d, $55 t, $60 quad low season; $50 s, $60 d, $70 t, $80 quad high season.

Hotel Restaurant Los Pargos is inland near Los Pargos (the turnoff is 800 meters south of Pablo's Picasso on the Paraíso road). This gaily painted old wooden home has a funky Haight-Ashbury feel. There was only a billy goat there when I called by. **Doug's House,** tel. 653-0441, is a fully furnished apartment for rent by the beach. A large condo complex called **Rancho Playa Negra** is slated for completion by the millennium.

Tamarindo Surf Restaurant, facing the soccer field in Paraíso, serves *típico* dishes.

PLAYA JUNQUILLAL

Playa Junquillal, four km southwest of Paraíso and 29 km west of Santa Cruz, is an attractive four-km-long light-gray-sand beach without shade trees. The beach gets whiter to the north and has extensive rock platforms for roaming tide pools. Beware the high surf and strong riptides; swimming is not recommended. The beachfront road dead-ends to the south at the very wide and deep Río Andumolo, whose mangrove estuary is home to birds and crocodiles. The area has seen lots of new hotels sprout in the past few years. Expect more.

Accommodations and Food
Camping Los Malinches, tel./fax 653-0429, about one km south of Hotel Iguanazul, includes bathrooms and showers and water. It has electrical hookups for RVs. It has hammocks beneath the *malinche* trees, and a small *soda* sells *refrescoes.* Rates: $4 pp; $8 per day RVs. You can also camp along the beach; bring your own water and supplies.

The following are listed north to south.

The **Iguanazul Beach Resort,** Apdo. 130, Santa Cruz 5150, tel./fax 653-0123, e-mail: iguanazul@ticonet.co.cr, website www.ticonet.co.cr/iguanazul/iguanazul.html, enjoys a breezy clifftop setting overlooking the beach, about two km south of Paraíso and two km north of Junquillal. The *cabinas* are set around a pleasant amoeba-shaped pool surrounded by lawns. They're pleasing enough but a bit short on light. The resort has a volleyball court and a small souvenir store. An elegant restaurant and bar open onto the pool. Rates: $50 s, $65 d; $60 s, $75 d with a/c.

The exquisite, ocher-colored **Coco Flotante Restaurant/Hotel,** Apdo. 105-5150, Santa Cruz, tel./fax 653-0427, atop the breezy bluff 200 meters south of Iguanazul, is a small bed and breakfast run by a charming and effusive Italian hostess,

Lidia, who will serve you aperitifs in the *piscina*. "It's very special service, like Relais et Chateaux," she says. The three thatch and red-tile-roofed cottage rooms (one has a king-size bed and kitchen and lounge) have terra-cotta floors and a soft pea-green and ocher color scheme. Very cozy. A piece of Tuscany transplanted. There's a small horizon pool and soft-cushioned wicker chairs beneath shade trees and the thatched veranda. Lidia conjures up Italian cuisine such as lobster ravioli. Rates: $120 pp including one meal of your choice; $150 with all meals. Nonguests may be able to dine here.

A German-Tico couple run **El Castillo Divertido,** tel./fax 653-0428, a crenellated three-story structure with a breezy hillside setting 300 meters inland of the beach. It has seven simply furnished rooms with large, louvered glass windows, private bath (one has hot water; three have ocean view). There's a rooftop sundeck with bar and a small restaurant. Rates: $25 s, $32 d low season; $28 s, $39 d high season.

About 400 meters south is the Swiss-run **Guacamaya Lodge,** tel./fax 653-0431, e-mail: alibern@sol.racsa.co.cr, with six clean, octagonal *cabinas* with private bath, hot water, and hammocks on the porch. The bar-cum-restaurant serving international fare has ocean views. There's a plunge pool and children's pool, and horseback riding ($8 per hour) and diving are offered. Rates: $30 s, $35 d low season; $45 s, $50 d high season, including tax. It also has two smaller rooms with shared bath ($15 d);

plus a house with kitchen for four people ($120 per day).

Hotel Tatanka, tel./fax 653-0426, a stone's throw south, is an Italian inspiration with 10 rooms with ocher-washed walls, fans, simple furnishings, private bath and hot water, and verandas looking onto the lawns. An open-sided pizzeria is elegantly rustic. It rents horses, kayaks, and motorcycles. The **El Lugarcito Bed and Breakfast,** Apdo. 214-5150, Santa Cruz, tel./fax 653-0437, nearby is a two-story home entered through lofty stable-like doors, with stone floors and lofty ceilings and tasteful decor enhanced by traditional pottery. The two simple but pleasant rooms have fans and halogen ceiling lights. Mieke, the Dutch owner, is a PADI-certified instructor; she puts on a weekly barbecue. Her hubbie Maarten leads hikes and offers tours far and wide. Rates: $40 d.

Within shouting distance, 100 meters inland of Playa Junquillal, is the **Hibiscus Hotel,** tel./fax 653-0437, set amid landscaped grounds full of palms and plantains and run by a Costa Rican couple. All have private baths with hot water. The genteel and spotless rooms have hammocks on the terraces. Quality seafood is served in a pretty little dining area. Rates: $35 s, $40 d. **La Puesta del Sol** is an Italian restaurant nearby.

Hotel Playa Junquillal, Apdo. 22, Santa Cruz, Guanacaste, tel./fax 653-0432 or toll free (808) 666-2232, e-mail: hotel@playa-junquillal.com, is an intimate four-room hotel facing the beach. American and Costa Rican fare are served at

Surfing is popular on both coasts.

JOHN ANDERSON

the bar and restaurant adjacent, where locals gather on Saturday nights for the marimba music. Rates: $30d.

In the center of the beach is the German-run **Villa Serena,** Apdo. 17, Santa Cruz 5150, tel./fax 653-0430, which has 10 modern bungalows (one family size). The spacious, light, and airy rooms—all with fans and private baths with hot water—are spread out among palms and surrounded by emerald-green grass and flowery gardens. The villa has a cozy lounge overlooking the beach, a library, and a swimming pool, and a hibiscus-encircled tennis court. Dinners are served on an elevated veranda overlooking the ocean. Rates: $30 s, $35 d low season; $45 s, $50 d high season; $10 extra person.

The German-run **Antumalal Hotel,** Apdo. 17, Santa Cruz 5150, tel./fax 653-0425, 200 meters from the shore near the southern end of the beach, is rather jaded. Expansive landscaped grounds help make amends. The 23 spacious but basically furnished cabins have oodles of light and bright color schemes with birds painted on the walls. The bungalows are spaced well apart, with hammocks on private patios, good for watching the resident parrots and monkeys. Amenities include a large pool with water slide, a beautiful tennis court, a small open-air gym, open-air disco, and two restaurants. The hotel offers horseback riding, fishing, and diving. Rates: $35 s, $40 d, $50 t low season; $75 s, $85 d, $95 t high season.

Tours and Activities

Ron Klein, a friendly and knowledgeable gringo who has lived here for years, hires out as tour guide ($50 daily plus expenses). He offers motorcycle tours ($100 per day), and customizes tours throughout the country. Contact him through Hotel Iguanazul.

Roy Dennison, an amiable Yorkshireman, is planning to open a water-ski and watersports center with an artificial lake and *cabinas* at Florida, five km southeast of Junquillal, by the millennium.

Aguazul Diving, P.O. Box 214-5150, Santa Cruz, tel./fax 653-0436, is based at El Lugarcito. It rents snorkel gear ($15 per day), and offers PADI certification ($360) and a variety of dives.

Getting There and Away

A bus departs San José for Junquillal from Avenida 3, Calle 20 (Tralapa, tel. 221-7202; in Jun-quillal, tel. 680-0392), daily at 2 p.m. ($5; five hours). A bus departs Santa Cruz at 6:30 p.m. Return buses depart for Santa Cruz and San José at 5 a.m.

PLAYA LAGARTO TO OSTIONAL

South of Junquillal, the dirt road leads along a lonesome stretch of coast via the hamlets of Lagarto, Marbella, and San Juanillo to Nosara (35 km south of Junquillal). Goodness knows how many fabulous beaches lie hidden along this route, which for most of the way is out of sight of the shore. There are few hotels. Just forest, cattle pasture, lonesome rustic dwellings, and an occasional ramshackle fishing village.

If driving south from Tamarindo or Santa Cruz, the turnoff—three km east of Paraíso—is easy to miss: a small hand-written sign reads Lagarto. It's directly opposite a thatched *ranchito* called **Pochotes Pamperos** on the north side of the road. The road is okay for ordinary cars in dry season, though 4WD is recommended (essential in wet season). Bridges have been built over most of the little rivers that had to be forded just a few years ago.

Eventually you'll pass a sign for **Matapalo Bar,** a rustic yet welcome *soda* with chickens underfoot. Refresh yourself here with a beer and *casado* and views of the wide crescent beach, **Playa Pitaya.** The surf and tide-pool exploring are good, and turtles come ashore here in winter.

About five km farther south, a turnoff leads to the fishing hamlet of **San Juanillo,** where within the secret cove at the bottom of a very steep, rutted dirt road you'll find fishing boats at anchor down by the tiny white-sand beach.

Accommodations

There are simple *cabinas* just south of **Marbella** for $12.

Treetops, Apdo. 193, Santa Cruz 5150, tel./fax 680-1198, e-mail: jphunter@sol.racsa. co.cr, is a totally reclusive, rustic one-room bed and breakfast tucked above a cove at San Juanillo, with seven hectares of private fruit farm and a freshwater lagoon. This charming place is the home of former race-car driver Jack Hunter and his wife, Karen—delightful hosts who go out of their way to make you feel at home. You're the only guest. There's one simply furnished room with outdoor shower. You're here for the spectacular solitude and setting that includes a horseshoe reef with live coral that's great for snorkeling, and a private beach for an all-over tan. Monkeys cavort in the treetops. You can dine and relax in hammocks on a rustic thatched veranda on stilts. The couple offers turtle safaris to Ostional, plus sportfishing tours; catch your own fish and Karen will prepare a sushi. Jack has been planning a luxury fly-in hotel, but only time will tell. Rates: $60 d, including a real English breakfast. Reservations essential.

REFUGIO NACIONAL DE VIDA SILVESTRE OSTIONAL

The 248-hectare Ostional National Wildlife Refuge begins at Punta India, about two km south of San Juanillo, and extends along 15 km of shoreline to Punta Guiones, eight km south of the village of Nosara. It incorporates the beaches of Playa Ostional, Playa Nosara, and Playa Guiones. The village of **Ostional** is midway along Playa Ostional. The refuge was created to protect one of two vitally important nesting sites in Costa Rica for the *lora,* or olive ridley turtle (the other is Playa Nancite, in Santa Rosa National Park). Ostional was named by the World Conference for the Conservation of Sea Turtles as one of the world's most important sea turtle hatcheries. A significant proportion of the world's Pacific ridley turtle population nests at Ostional, where they head for a narrow sandy strip between Punta División and Ostional estuary, invading the beach en masse for up to one week at a time July-Dec. (peak season is August and September), and singly or in small groups at other times during the year.

Time your arrival correctly and out beyond the breakers you may see a vast flotilla of turtles massed shoulder-to-shoulder, waiting their turn to swarm ashore, dig a hole in the sand, and drop in the seeds for tomorrow's turtles. The legions pour out of the surf in endless waves until they are so densely packed that, in the words of the great turtle expert Archie Carr, "one could have walked a mile without touching the earth—literally. You could have run a whole mile down the beach on the backs of turtles and never have set foot on the sand."

It's a stupendous sight, this *arribada* (arrival). Of the world's eight marine turtle species, only the females of the olive ridley and its Atlantic cousin, Kemp's ridley, stage *arribadas.* Synchronized mass nestings are known to occur at only nine beaches worldwide (in Mexico, Nicaragua, Honduras, Surinam, Orissa in India, and Costa Rica). Playa Ostional is the most important of these.

So tightly packed is the horde that the turtles feverishly clamber over one another in their efforts to find an unoccupied nesting site. As they dig, sweeping their flippers back and forth, the petulant females scatter sand over one another and the air is filled with the slapping of flippers on shells. By the time the *arribada* is over, more than 150,000 turtles may have stormed this prodigal place and 15 million eggs may lie buried in the sand.

Leatherback turtles also come ashore to nest in smaller numbers Oct.-Jan., with *arribadas* most months starting with the last quarter of the moon. In 1997, for the first time, an *arribada* occurred at Playa Nosara, *south* of Ostional.

You can walk virtually the entire length of the beach's 15-km shoreline, which is littered with broken eggshells. Although turtles can handle the very strong currents, humans have a harder time: swimming is not advised. Much of the coastline south of the tiny village of Ostional has been developed and there's not a great deal of wildlife. Howler monkeys, coatimundis, and kinkajous, however, frequent the forest inland from the beach. The small mangrove swamp at the mouth of the Río Nosara is a nesting site for many of the 190 bird species hereabouts. The road parallels the dark-gray-sand beach, although for most of the way you don't have a view of the ocean. There is no shade on the beach.

Wealthy foreigners are buying land surrounding the refuge, with plans to build hotels to profit off the natural spectacle of the turtles. Environmentalists fear that hotels will bring too many people to this sacred refuge, and the lights and human activity will discourage the turtles from nesting. The local community is hostile to tourism development, certainly on the model of Nosara, its southerly neighbor, where foreign land purchases have forced land values out of the reach of local residents. This unwanted de-

RESPITE FOR THE RIDLEY

As the female ridley covers her nest with toeless flat feet and pounds back to the sea without ever looking back, does she know that she was herself hatched at Ostional 20 or more years ago? In those 20 years, the little boys who watched her mother come up to shore and then stole her eggs have grown up. A generation has passed, but the grown men who have not gone to the city to make it big will still take her eggs and sell them to cantinas to be drunk raw so that men might have strength in their loins. At dawn the whole village will descend on the beach. The men of Ostional will feel for the nests with their heels in a sort of two-step fashion. And the women and girls, all nicely dressed and with combs in their hair, will dig deep and remove the eggs and place them in rice sacks ready for shipment to bars.

Though guards were first placed at Ostional in 1979 to protect the endangered ridley, the egg harvest continues. But all is not what it seems. Elsewhere in Costa Rica, harvesting turtle eggs is illegal and usually occurs only in the dead of night. At Ostional it occurs legally and by daylight.

The seeming rape of the ridley—called *lora* locally—is the pith of a bold conservation program that aims to help the turtles by allowing the local community to commercially harvest eggs in a rational manner. "The main goal . . . is to achieve social growth of the community through controlled removal of eggs without compromising the reproduction and conservation of the species," says Claudette Mo, professor of biology at the National University of Costa Rica.

Dramatic declines in ridley populations are evident throughout Central America, and nowhere is the ridley left in peace. During the late 1970s, massive commercial exploitation of ridleys developed in Ecuador, where a significant proportion of Costa Rica's nesting population spends the nonnesting season feeding on macroplankton. Up to 150,000 adult ridleys were being killed to make "shoes for Italian pimps," in the words of Archie Carr. Ecuador banned the practice in 1981, but "resource pirates" from Asia still fish for turtles off Ecuador—routinely violating the latter's territorial rights. Mexico continued the slaughter until 1990. And tens of thousands of ridleys are still caught by shrimp trawlers along the coasts of Central America.

Legislative efforts throughout Central America have attempted to regulate the taking of eggs, but none have been very effective. Costa Rica outlawed the taking of turtle eggs in 1966. But egg poaching is a time-honored tradition. The coming of the first *arribada* to Ostional in 1961 was a bonanza to the people of Ostional. Their village became the major source of turtle eggs in Costa Rica. Coatis, coyotes, raccoons, and other egg-hungry marauders take a heavy toll on the tasty eggs, too. Ridley turtles have thus hit on a formula for outwitting their predators—or at least of surviving despite them: they deposit millions of eggs at a time (in any one season, 30 million eggs might be laid at Ostional). Since the *arribada* follows a strategy that assumes that only a fraction of eggs will incubate successfully, the turtle invasions vary in size and timing year by year. *Arribadas* are unpredictable (which is why ridleys do it—to confuse predators).

Ironically, the most efficient scourge are the turtles themselves! Since Ostional beach is literally covered with thousands of turtles, the eggs laid during the first days of an *arribada* are often dug up by turtles arriving later. Often before they can hatch, a second *arribada* occurs. Again the beach is covered with crawling reptiles. As the newcomers dig, many inadvertently excavate and destroy the eggs laid by their predecessors and the beach becomes strewn with rotting embryos. Even without human interference, only one percent to eight percent of eggs in a given *arribada* will hatch.

In 1972, when the Nancite and Ostional hatcheries were discovered, their destruction was far along. The turtle population seemed to be below the minimum required to maintain the species, and after a decade of study scientists concluded that uncontrolled poaching of eggs would ultimately exterminate the nesting colony. They also reasoned that a *controlled* harvest would actually rejuvenate the turtle population. Such a harvest during the first two nights of an *arribada* would *improve* hatch rates at Ostional by reducing the number of broken eggs and crowded conditions that together create a spawning ground for bacteria and fungi that prevent the development of embryos.

In 1987, the Costa Rican Congress finally approved a management plan that would legalize egg harvesting at Ostional. The statute that universally prohibited egg harvesting was reformed to permit the residents of Ostional to take and sell turtle eggs. The unique legal right to harvest eggs is vested in members of the Asociación Desarrollo Integral de

(continues on next page)

RESPITE FOR THE RIDLEY

(continued)

Ostional (ADIO). The University of Costa Rica, which has maintained a biological research station at Ostional since 1980, is legally responsible for preparing an annual plan and review and for providing the scientific criteria to guide the community toward a sustainable cash-based use of their awe-inspiring natural resource.

A quota is established for each *arribada*. Sometimes, no eggs are harvested; in the dry season (Dec.-May), as many as 35% of eggs may be taken; when the beach is hotter than Hades, the embryos become dehydrated, and the hatching rate falls below one percent. The idea is to save eggs that would be broken anyway, or that otherwise have a low expectation of hatching.

The egg collectors are organized into work groups, each assigned to its own tract of beach. The men mark the nests with a tag. The women follow, extract the eggs, and place them in sacks to be washed in the sea. The eggs are then carted to the village packing center and placed into small plastic bags pre-stamped with the seal of ADIO. By law, eggs may be taken only during the first 36 hours of an *arribada*. After that, the villagers protect the nests from poachers and the hatchlings from ravenous beasts.

The project has seeded a conservationist ethic among community members. When, in 1972, scientists arrived to initiate the first studies, a field assistant was beaten, and the locals punctured the scientists' tires and interfered with their efforts to tag the turtles. Today, the villagers help biologists count and monitor the turtles. Even the mayor of Nicoya was taken to court by ADIO after villagers

caught him with two bags of poached turtle eggs! The Guardia Rural (police) used to confiscate the poachers' eggs and sell them themselves. Now the police, too, are enthusiastic beneficiaries of the program—income from the sale of legally harvested eggs paid for construction of a Guardia Rural office at Ostional.

The eggs are dealt to distributors who who sell on a smaller scale at a contract-fixed price to bakers (which favor turtle eggs over those of hens; turtle eggs give dough greater "lift") and bars, brothels, and street vendors who sell the eggs as *bocas*. The law stipulates that net revenues from the sale of eggs be divided between the community (80%) and the Ministry of Agriculture. ADIO distributes 70% of its share among association members as payment for their labors, and 30% to the Sea Turtle Project and communal projects. ADIO also pays the biologists' salaries. Profits have funded construction of a health center, a house for schoolteachers, the ADIO office, and a Sea Turtle Research Lab.

Scientists claim that the project also has the potential to stop the poaching of eggs on other beaches. It's a matter of economics. Poachers sell green and leatherback eggs for 25 *colones* (15 cents). A report in 1992 found that cheaper eggs from Ostional had captured 94% of the market. Studies also show that the turtle population has stabilized. Recent *arribadas* have included as many as 200,000 turtles. And hatch rates are up to eight percent.

An integrated Management and Development Plan initiated in 1992 aims to stimulate other economic activities so that the community doesn't come to depend exclusively on egg exploitation.

velopment threatens to remove the community's control over its resources. The developers are pushing hard to get permits, but so far Ostional residents have had the courts on their side. The priority is the purchase of the land adjacent to Ostional to establish buffer zones and ensure the protection of the nesting grounds. Only then can the indigenous community be assured that it has taken command of a sustainable egg-harvesting program that meets the challenge of protecting the turtles while addressing the community's needs. Experience elsewhere in

the country suggests, however, that the arrival of foreign landowners may be a good thing: they are usually eco-conscious and at the forefront of conservation efforts. And there's a strong argument that says that the local Tico population's flirtation with conservation is money-driven. They see turtles as a *resource*. Culling live turtles still occurs, and the animals still wash ashore on the beaches with their flippers cut off.

You should check in with the rangers or at the **turtle cooperative** in the village center before exploring the beach.

Accommodations and Food

Cabinas Ostional, 50 meters south of the soccer field, has four clean, pleasing rooms sleeping three people, with fans and private baths. Rates: $6 pp. About 100 meters south is the **Pulpería y Hospedaje Las Guacamayas,** with eight rooms (some with shared bathroom). Rooms are small but clean and have two single beds. Rates: $9 d. **Soda Brisas del Pacífico,** next door, is the eatery of significance. A home on the southwest corner of the soccer field has a **camping** area. Call the National Wildlife Directorate, tel. 233-8112, to see if camping is permitted on the beach, and where.

An American couple, Darin and Kim McBratney, are developing a "Caribbean-style retreat" a few miles south of Ostional and will rent surfboards, motorcycles, and horses; for information contact P.O. Box 2628, Saratoga, CA 95070, tel. (408) 450-9764.

At the north end of Ostional is the Hungarian-owned **Hotel Rancho Brovella,** tel./fax 284-0723, a hilltop retreat with a splendid setting offering views over the forest and ocean. At press time, 10 *cabinas* were open (20 more are planned), wide-spaced amid the valley and hills. Each has fans and a private bath with hot water. There's a breezy terrace with a plunge pool and a sundeck, plus a large U-shaped bar and restaurant. Plans include tennis courts, horseback riding and trails. Rates: $45d with breakfast and choice of lunch or dinner.

The nicest place to eat is **Restaurant Mirador Las Tortugas,** atop a hill at the south end of the village, where you dine at rough-hewn tables carved with turtle motifs under a shady *ranchita.* It sells burgers, spaghetti, seafood, and *casados* ($3-5).

Information

The **ADIO** (Asociación Desarrollo Integral de Ostional) office is beside the road, on the corner of the soccer field. It doesn't have much information, but Geraldo Ordez, the community leader, can assist (his house is first on the right as you enter Ostional from the north), and there's a **Tourism Orientation Place** (closed both times I've visited) run by ADIO, 200 meters south of the soccer field, at the junction of the path to **Laboratorio de Investigación Tortuga Marinos.** The rustic hut houses research volunteers and

scientists: contact the **Douglas Robinson Marine Turtle Research Center,** Apdo. 18-3019, San Pablo de Heredia, tel./fax 260-2658 or tel. 682-0267, e-mail: turtles@gema.com.

The **ranger station,** tel./fax 680-0167, is near the Douglas Robinson station.

There's no cost to go on the beach, nor do you need a guide.

Services

The *pulpería* at the northern end of the soccer field has a **public telephone.**

Tours

CATA Tours, tel. 221-5455, fax 221-0200, offers a "Turtles under the Full Moon" tour June-Nov. ($45), including hotel transfers. So does **Flamingo Tours,** tel. 654-4238, fax 654-4039; in San José, tel. 222-6762.

Getting There and Away

A bus departs Santa Cruz for Ostional daily at noon (three hours, returning at 5 a.m.); it may not run in wet season.

The road south from Ostional has three sturdy bridges over the rivers and merges with the main road south from Nosara about two km south of the village. The old dirt road still fords the Río Nosara just before entering Nosara. It's not as daunting as it looks and was only about half a meter deep when I last crossed it. You can also reach Ostional via a dirt road from Nicoya (35 km east) that leads through Curime, Dulce Nombre, Guastomatal, and Nosara.

NOSARA

The village of **Bocas de Nosara** is five km inland from the coast, five km south of Ostional, on the banks of the Río Nosara. It maintains a simple traditional Tico lifestyle, but otherwise offers little of appeal. The beaches make amends.

A large foreign community lives four km south of the village where much of the land backing Playas Giones and Pelada has been divided into lots and sold for development during the past two decades. Today there are about 200 homes hidden amid the forest in the area known as the **Beach of Nosara.** The roads are an intestinal labyrinth. Like any maze, it's easy to

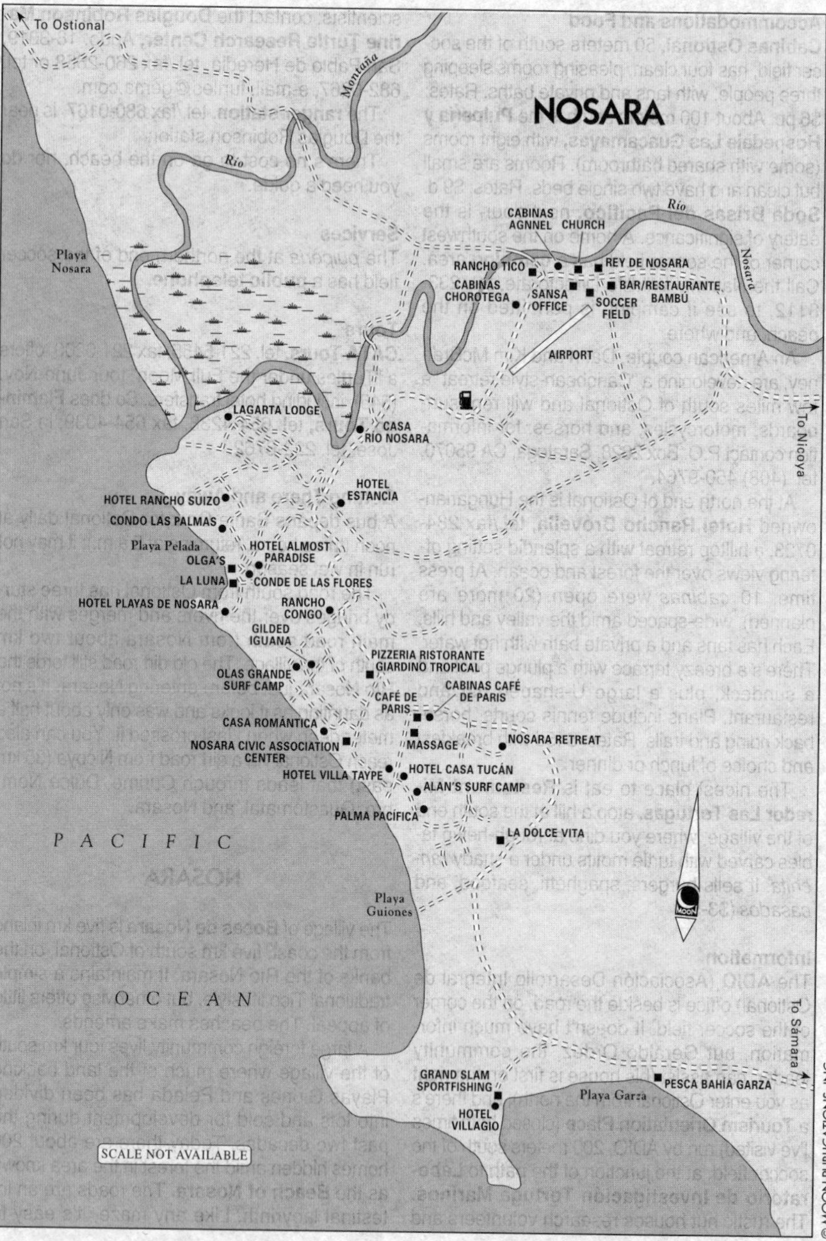

NOSARA

Playa Nosara

Río Montaña

To Ostional

Río

Playa Nosara

Rio

Nosara

CABINAS AGNNEL — CHURCH
RANCHO TICO
CABINAS CHOROTEGA
SANSA OFFICE
REY DE NOSARA
BAR/RESTAURANTE BAMBÚ
SOCCER FIELD
AIRPORT

To Nicoya

LAGARTA LODGE

CASA RÍO NOSARA

HOTEL ESTANCIA

HOTEL RANCHO SUIZO
CONDO LAS PALMAS
Playa Pelada
OLGA'S
LA LUNA
HOTEL PLAYAS DE NOSARA

HOTEL ALMOST PARADISE
CONDE DE LAS FLORES
RANCHO CONGO
GILDED IGUANA
OLAS GRANDE SURF CAMP
CASA ROMÁNTICA
NOSARA CIVIC ASSOCIATION CENTER
HOTEL VILLA TAYPE
PALMA PACÍFICA

PIZZERIA RISTORANTE GIARDINO TROPICAL
CABINAS CAFÉ DE PARIS
CAFÉ DE PARIS
MASSAGE
NOSARA RETREAT
HOTEL CASA TUCÁN
ALAN'S SURF CAMP
LA DOLCE VITA

Playa Guiones

PACIFIC

OCEAN

NOSARA

To Sámara

SCALE NOT AVAILABLE

GRAND SLAM SPORTFISHING
HOTEL VILLAGIO
Playa Garza
PESCA BAHÍA GARZA

© MOON PUBLICATIONS, INC.

enter but getting out is sheer puzzlement, with dirt roads coiling and uncoiling like a snake. Many of the residents are North American retirees, but Germans are well represented. Nosara's land-use policies are a model for others to follow. The Nosara Civic Association, the property owners' organization, maintains trails, shelters, and camping facilities and fosters preservation of natural vegetation cover, as well as sponsoring progressive social endeavors for the villagers of Bocas de Nosara. (It also keeps a tight rein on development—"no surf yobbos," I was told.) The maritime zone fronting the beach is protected by the Forest Service. Hence, wildlife abounds in the sprawling primary forest: coatimundis and howler monkeys are particularly common. About 40 hectares are protected in the private **Reserva Biológica Nosara** along the river, which harbors caimans and crocodiles.

A cool thing to do is to rent canoes ($10) and paddle down the Río Nosara—a birder's nirvana.

Beaches

There are three beaches, all with rocky tide pools where the seawater is heated by the sun. Great for soaking. They are part of the Ostional Wildlife Refuge. Driving vehicles is prohibited.

Playa Nosara extends north from the Punta Nosara and the river estuary to Ostional. It's backed by mangroves. An *arribada* occurred here for the first time in 1997. More are expected.

Playa Guiones, five km south of Nosara village, is a ruler-straight, five-km-long expanse of white sand washed by surf. It's becoming popular with surfers. There's virtually no shade on Playa Guiones, and swimmers need to beware of strong riptides. Tiny **Playa Pelada** is tucked in a cove south of Punta Nosara and is separated from Playa Guiones by Punta Pelada. It has a blowhole at the south and a bat cave at the north end.

Accommodations

Camping: You can camp at Olas Grandes Surf Camp or at Alan's Surf Camp (see below). Rates: $5.

Shoestring: In the village, **Chorotega Cabinas,** tel. 682-0236, is a handsome complex with a restaurant. Rooms have private baths with cold water. It's clean and well run. Rates: $6.50

pp. **Cabinas Agnnel,** nearby, has six basic but well-kept older *cabinas* and nine newer *cabinas* with fans and private baths with cold water. Rates: $6.

Budget : At Playa Guiones, **Rancho Congo** has two large, cool, thatched cabins with tile floors, fans, huge walk-in showers, and breezy verandas. Rates: $25 s/d, $35 t, including breakfast. *A bargain!* A more basic spot is **Olas Grandes Surf Camp,** tel. 682-0080, with five octagonal cabins with shared bath; they vary in size. Its Gringo Grill is a cool place to hang. And it arranges trips to lonesome beach breaks in its 4WD Unimog. Rates: $30 s/d/t. Or try **Alan's Surf Camp,** another mellow spot (this one by the beach) with hammocks in the shady forecourt. It has three simple rooms each with one bunk, and a larger room with a bunk and double bed plus private bathrooms. It does board repair, and has a laundry. Rates: $16 d bunk rooms; $20 d large room.

If all else fails, try **Palmas Pacíficas,** with simple a/c *cabinas* with kitchenettes in shady grounds.

Casa Río Nosara, tel. 682-0117, fax 682-0182, is a German-run rustic charmer on the south bank of the Río Nosara, two km southwest of the village. It has seven Polynesian-style, two-story, wood-and-thatch, A-frame cabins with fans and private baths with cold water. Some are loft rooms with open windows. Canoe tours, horseback rides, sea kayaking, and turtle tours are offered. The place is a menagerie: five dogs, seven horses, a pig, a capuchin monkey, and a zillion cats at last count. Rates: $25 pp, including breakfast served at tables made of sliced logs.

Inexpensive: If setting is foremost in mind, then check out **Lagarta Lodge,** Apdo. 18, Nosara 5233, tel. 682-0035, fax 682-0135, e-mail: lagarta@sol.racsa.co.cr, website www.nosara.com/lagarta; in Switzerland, Doris u. Max Roth, Mutschellenstrasse 60, CH-8038 Zürich, with a setting atop Punta Nosara offering stupendous vistas—north along Ostional—with the estuary below and mountains far off in the distance. Settle in a high seat or Sarchí rocker and relax. The dining table, made from a single piece of hardwood, must be six meters long. Four rooms are in a two-story house (the upper story reached by a spiral staircase) and three are in a smaller unit with whitewashed stone walls. The latter, with one entire wall a screened, glassless window, have mezzanine bedrooms overlooking voluminous open showers and bathrooms. Some have king-size beds. The stone wall and wooden gates of Teutonic proportion hint at the Swiss ownership. The lodge has a swimming pool, and trails leading down to the river and the Reserva Biológica Nosara. One reader has raved about the meals. Rates: $35 s, $40-45 d low season; $50 s, $55-65 d high season, including tax and breakfast.

At Playa Guiones, the **Rancho Suizo Lodge,** Apdo. 14, Bocas de Nosara 5233, tel. 682-0057, fax 682-0055, e-mail: aratur@sol.racsa.co.cr, has 10 thatched *cabinas* with small but pleasant rooms and private baths with hot water. The lush grounds contains hammocks and a small aviary. Trails lead to the beach. It's run by René Spinnier and Ruth Léscher, who have created an agreeable ambience. The thatched bar-cum-restaurant with bamboo furniture serves breakfast and dinner. A jacuzzi was recently added. A notice in the *cabinas* reads No opposite sex visitors (two female German guests reported, "Sex is *verboten!*" I think they jest). Rates: $57 d, including tax, buffet breakfast, and use of boogie boards and mountain bikes.

The German-run **Casa Romántica,** Apdo. 45-5233, Nosara, tel./fax 682-0019, opened in late 1997 with eight rooms in beautiful two-story houses with exquisitely patterned tile floors. The landscaped grounds full of bougainvillea contain an amoeba-shaped pool and a *ranchito* with hammocks, and an outside restaurant serving international fare (from beef stroganoff to spaghetti; dinner only). Upper rooms are cross-ventilated and receive more light. Rates: $45 s/d low season; $45 s, $50 d high season.

The German-run **Hotel Villa Taype,** tel. 682-0188, fax 682-0187, within spitting distance of the beach, offers four small rooms with fans, 12 a/c *cabinas,* and five bungalows with a/c, refrigerator and terrace. All have private baths and hot water. The landscaped grounds boast shade trees, a swimming pool, a tennis court, plus a large bar and restaurant. There's a second restaurant and TV lounge. Rates: $35 s/d with fan; $50 s, $60 d with a/c; $80 bungalow, including breakfast.

Casa Tucán, tel./fax 682-0113, e-mail: casatucan@nosara.com; in the U.S., 1423 Harbor View Dr. #5, Santa Barbara, CA 93103, tel. (805) 962-5505, fax (805) 962-1585, opposite Hotel Villa Taype, is run by Nancy and Richard Moffett. Their home sits amid lawns, with an amoeba-shaped restaurant and airy *ranchito* restaurant (Richard is a graduate of the California Culinary Academy). Four modestly furnished rooms (each for four people, with kitchen and dining table) are in a two-story adjunct. Rates: $30 s, $45 d low season; $40 s, $60 d high season.

Another atmospheric place, a 10-minute walk to the beach, is **Estancia Nosara,** Apdo. 37, Nosara 5257, tel./fax 682-0178, which has beautiful rooms for four people amid tropical gardens. All have minibars, plus private baths with hot water. Some have kitchenettes. The hotel has a small swimming pool, a satellite TV in the *palenque* lounge, and bamboo furnishings in the romantic bar-cum-restaurant, open on all sides. It offers tennis, horseback rides ($7 per hour), and bicycles ($7 per hour), plus a turtle tour ($25), and tours farther afield. *A bargain!* Rates: $25 s , $35 d, $40 t, $45 quad; $30 s, $45 d, $50 t, $55 quad with a/c.

Almost Paradise, Apdo. 15, Nosara 5233, e-mail: almost@nosara.com, is another German-owned property that enjoys a hilltop setting 10 minutes from the beach. Its haphazardly and utterly charming construction is enhanced by creeping vines and flowers bedecking the place. Six rooms are of different sizes, though all have private baths with hot water, plus access to a wide balcony with hammocks and splendid vistas. Original paintings from Haiti and the Dominican Republic adorn the walls. The restaurant, which catches the breezes, serves mostly German and vegetarian fare, plus afternoon tea and cakes. Rates: $35-45 d, including breakfast.

The attractive **Café de Paris,** tel. 682-0087, fax 682-0089, e-mail: cafedeparis@nosara.com, is run by a delightful young French couple who have 10 modestly but appealingly furnished rooms with ceiling fans, screened windows, a slanted wooden ceiling with egress for the heat, and private bath with hot water. The restaurant is beneath a soaring *ranchito.* Facilities include a souvenir store, the splendid cafe, a small lap pool, plus massage. Rates: $39 d small; $59 d large (with kitchenette), including breakfast; $89 for a bungalow. They also have a large dorm room with four beds ($10 pp low season; $15 high season).

The **Gilded Iguana,** tel. 680-0749, also has "budget" apartments for rent. Rates: $35-45.

Moderate: Hotel Playas de Nosara, Apdo. 4, Nosara 5257, tel. 680-0495, squats atop Punta Guiones. Steps lead down to Playa Pelada. What a transformation. When I first came here, in 1986, the hotel was a simple structure with a modest restaurant built over a wooden deck. In 1993, it had metamorphosed into a whitewashed Spanish-colonial-style villa graced by arches and columns. In early 1995 inspirational additions, including a pool, seemed inspired by Gaudi; its walls are awash in surflike waves and a *mirador* resembling a fairy-tale castle. In 1998, it was *still* in Gaudiesque transformation. The 20 rooms—all with fans and private baths with hot water—enjoy a tremendous setting facing south over Playa Guiones and have private verandas. The cabins atop the cliff are recommended; the rooms in the main building don't have cross-ventilation. It's complete with restaurant and swimming pool. Horseback rides are offered. Rates: about $50-65 d, including tax.

Condominiums de las Flores, tel. 680-0696, has modern furnished condos for rent from $60 per night. The rooms are spacious, two-bedroom/two-bath condominium suites with lounges, large kitchens and private balconies fronting onto landscaped gardens with profuse bougainvillea. One of the units—**Chatelle by the Sea,** Apdo. 755, San José 1007, tel. 487-7781, fax 487-7095—rents separately. **Condo Las Palmas** has handsome two-story units amid landscaped grounds behind Playa Guiones.

Many residents also rent their houses (expect to pay about $200 per week). For example, **Monkey Trail,** tel. 227-0088, just a few minutes' walk from Playa Guiones, sleeps four and has watersports equipment and "the jungle as its backyard." Rates: $375 per week. **Turi Nosara Center,** tel. 284-5064, fax 220-1021; in the U.S., SJO 193, P.O. Box 025216, Miami, FL 33102, acts as an agent for home rentals.

Luxury: Nosara Retreat, Centro Comercial El Pueblo #120, San José, tel. 233-8057, fax 255-3351, e-mail: retreat@nosara.com, website www.nosara.com/yogaretreat; in the U.S., tel. (800) 999-6404, in the hills behind Playa Guiones, is the most enriching place around; the

perfect place to relax and recharge. My first visit to Costa Rica was as a participant in a holistic health retreat led by owner Amba Henderson, and on my last visit I enjoyed a stay here with Amba and her husband Don Stapleton, a delightful couple who have imbued the main house—which has five spacious rooms—with exquisite decor: Guaitil pottery, Oriental throw rugs, gleaming and calming whites, glass brick accents, cavernous bathrooms (some with deep tubs for soaking), and French doors opening to wide balconies with sweeping vistas. The focus at this hilltop villa is health and spiritual renewal (its motif—a frog—symbolizes prosperity and abundance). Since 1988 Amba has taught at the renowned Kripalu Center for Yoga and Health in Massachusetts, of which Don was CEO. They offer yoga, meditation, nutrition counseling, fasting and detoxification, Danskinetics, Yogassage (Amba's own technique, combining vigorous massage with Hatha yoga), plus hiking, boogie boarding, and mountain biking. Imagine—sunrise yoga on the beach followed by a hike or horseback ride. The homey placidity is punctuated by the occasional gentle chimes of a gong, indicating that it's time for yoga, perhaps, or another superb meal prepared by Reina, "Queen of the Kitchen." A swimming pool perches on the hillside. The retreat, which is popular with celebrities such as Goldie Hawn, Woody Harrelson, and Robin Williams, offers three-day and week-long courses. Open Nov.-July only. Rates (pp): $250, $300 luxury, shared; $350, $450 luxury, private, including all meals, yoga, and nature walks, etc. There's a two-night minimum. Five-night "Yoga & Wellness Adventure Retreats" (Nov.-July) cost from $825 standard, $975 deluxe.

Food

In the village, take your pick from several *sodas* around the soccer field. **Rancho Suizo Lodge** serves "Ruth's good cooking" at breakfasts and dinners (no lunches).

Olga's, a rustic place fronting Playa Pelada, is recommended for seafood ($5 average). Tucked above the beach 50 meters to the south is **La Luna Bar and Grill** a tremendously atmospheric place with cobblestone floor and bottle-green glass bricks, and a terrace for dining by sunset. It serves ceviche ($2.50), salads, and seafoods ($4-8).

The **Gringo Grill** at Olas Grande Surf Camp is a rustic restaurant favored by surfers. **Alan's Surf Camp** offers a "surfers' breakfast" ($3).

Café de Paris has a restaurant (7 a.m.-11 p.m.) serving burgers, sandwiches, veggie burritos ($3.50), and dinners such as filet en salsa de papaya, lobster in curry sauce ($6-14); plus a bakery with delicious fresh-baked pastries, croissants, and bread (7 a.m.-5 p.m.).

La Lechuza is also popular with expatriate residents; it serves lunches Monday through Sunday. The **Gilded Iguana** is another favorite with locals who gather for bridge games on Saturday; it serves lunches Wednesday through Sunday.

For Italian, check out **Giardino Tropicale** pizzeria, or **La Dolce Vita,** two km south on the road to Sámara; the latter serves such treats as penne fish, and grouper butter lemon ($6-8) in a rustic rough-hewn log-and-thatch restaurant that can get lively in season.

Entertainment

In the village, the most atmospheric bars are **Bambú** and **Disco Bar Tropicana** (the latter serves draft beer). Rancho Suizo Lodge has a disco in the **El Pirata Bar,** and the **Hotel Villa Taype** also hosts a disco some nights.

Tours and Activities

Most hotels offers tours and bicycle rentals. You can rent **surfboards** for $20 per day at Olas Grande Surf Camp. **Discover Diving Tours** is based at Quinta Sirena, in the village. The **Beaches of Nosara Tennis Coub** near Hotel Playas de Nosara charges $5 per hour for public use. Several places rent horses; ask around.

Spanish Language Courses

The **Escuela de Idiomas Rey de Nosara,** tel. 302-8734, 100 meters north of the soccer field, offers Spanish language classes.

Services

Banco Nacional brings a branch office to Nosara each Wednesday 9 a.m.-noon at Super La Paloma, the **supermarket** in Bocas de Nosara, where Santos Zuniga, tel. 680-0857, operates an ambulance for emergency transport to Nicoya. There's also a **Red Cross,** tel. 685-5458, and a **clinic,** which operates Mon.-Thurs. 7 a.m.-4 p.m. and Friday 7 a.m.-noon. The **post office** is at the north end of the runway (Mon.-Fri. 7:30-11:30 a.m. and 1:30-5:30 p.m.).

There's a **laundry** at Escuela de Idiomas, which also acts as a **tourist information center** and has a **telephone service.** Café de Paris also has a laundry; massage is offered as well, and you can rent bikes, surfboards, snorkeling gear, and cars here.

Telephone lines were laid in 1997. The public fax number is 685-5004. Many locals still communicate by CB and VHF radio.

Getting There and Away

By Bus: An Empresa Alfaro, tel. 222-2750, bus departs San José for Nosara from Calle 14, Avenidas 3/5, daily at 6 a.m., returning at 12:45 p.m. from Soda Vannessa, near the Catholic church in Bocas del Nosara. A bus departs Nicoya for Nosara at 1 p.m., returning at 5:45 a.m.

By Air: SANSA and **Travelair** have scheduled service between San José and Nosara (see appendix). However, the airstrip was closed at press time because locals farmers kept pulling down the fence and letting their cattle graze the grass strip. The SANSA office is 50 meters south of the soccer field in the village.

The **Turi Nosara Center,** tel. 232-5626, in San José can arrange private air charters. The airstrip is to the south end of town. SANSA also offers packaged tours, including accommodations at the Hotel Playa Nosara.

By Car: Clemente Matarrita sells gas at his little "Servicentro Nosara" in Bocas de Nosara. José Juárez at Soda Vannessa, tel. 680-0836, has a taxi service.

BAHÍA GARZA

The dirt road from Nosara leads south to Playa Sámara (26 km) via **Playa Rosada** (immediately south of Playa Guiones) and the horseshoe-shaped Bahía Garza, rimmed by a marvelous though slightly pebbly white-sand beach. Beyond Garza the road—4WD recommended—cuts inland from the coast, which remains out of view the rest of the way. About five km south of Sámara, at **Esterones,** the road heads inland uphill to ford the Río Frío, south of which you turn right for Sámara or left for Nicoya via Terciopela (on the main Sámara-Nicoya road).

Accommodations

Hotel el Villagio, Apdo. 860, San José 1007, tel./fax 680-0784, or tel. 233-2476, fax 222-4073, has the bay to itself. Alas, the erstwhile restaurant with a massive two-tier *palenque* roof, and a spiral wooden staircase up to the mezzanine casino has gone, to be replaced by a less dramatic restaurant. Accommodations are in 30 nicely appointed thatched *cabinas* amid landscaped grounds with a 230-square-meter pool with waterfall cascade that reflects the candlelight at night. Two bungalows accommodate up to eight guests each. The beachside **La Tortuga** bar doubles as a dance hall. The hotel has two sportfishing boats ($650 per day) and offers horseback rides ($15 per hour). Rates: $87 s/d with fan; $97 s/d with a/c.

Just south of Garza village is the down-to-earth **Casa Pacífico** with four nice rooms with king-size beds and a rustic beachside bar with tremendous ambience. Rates: $45 d, including gourmet breakfast.

Villas Río Ora has hilltop *cabinas* two km west of Terciopela, 0.5 km east of the turnoff for Garza.

PLAYA SÁMARA AND VICINITY

Playa Sámara, about 15 km south of Garza, is a very popular budget destination for Ticos as well as Germans, surfers, and travelers in search of the offbeat. It is gradually going upscale. The lure is its relative accessibility and extremely attractive horseshoe-shaped bay with a light-gray beach, very deep and about three km long. **Isla Chora** lies offshore to the south. A few palms shade the beach, while manchineel and groundcover plants fringe the shore. Vultures and pelicans provide entertainment.

Sámara can be reached directly from Nicoya by paved road. The village is in the center of the beach. A cattle *finca* divides it from **Cangrejal,** a hamlet at the north end of the beach. They are connected by road, but you can drive along the beach. Cangrejal is separated by a headland from lonesome **Playa Buena Vista,** backed by a lagoon and forest.

Be sure to pay a visit to Jaime Koss's beachside art gallery half a kilometer south of the village. His colorful work combines elements of Picasso, Matisse, and Gauguin. Farther south, the shore is lined with Tico-owned vacation homes.

This is one place where people are still building (apparently with impunity) within the supposedly inviolate 50-meter limit of the shore.

Accommodations

Camping: Camping Mingo has a basic beachside campground on the north side of the village. It's popular with Ticos and unfortunately littered with trash. **Camping Cocos,** tel. 656-0496, has a clean campground on the south side, with bathrooms, water, and sites under shady palms. Rates: $2.50 pp. It abuts **Camping San Martín,** and **Camping Mangoes** is a stone's throw inland. Both charge $2 pp and have basic outside toilets and showers. All sites are on bare dirt grounds. A German-run place called **Flying Crocodile** has camping at Playa Buena Vista.

Shoestring: A favorite among Ticos is the **Hotel/Restaurant Playa Sámara,** tel. 656-0190, a larger, older, and somewhat run-down unit with 54 rooms with fans, telephones, and private baths. Its *soda*-style restaurant is very popular with locals. Be warned: there's a disco downstairs. Rates: $6 pp.

In Cangrejal is the **Hospedaje Tinajitas,** tel. 656-0167, with 10 dark and cramped rooms with bunk beds but no fans. Rates: $4 pp shared bath, $5 private bath. On a similar scale is **Hospedaje Yuri,** tel. 656-0378, which has 12 basic rooms; some have private baths, some share. Rates: $4 pp shared bath, $6 private bath. The owner planned to add a/c and hot water. Next door, the **Hospedaje Katia,** features seven rooms with shared bath and two with private baths. Rates: $4 shared bath, $5 private bath.

Budget: The best bargain is the German-run **Cabinas Belvedere,** tel./fax 656-0213—nine very pretty Swiss-style chalets with attractive bamboo furnishings, mosquito nets, whitewashed walls, fans, and private baths with hot water. Some rooms have king-size beds. A stone-walled, mosaic-tiled jacuzzi sits amid lush gardens. Rates: $30 d, including tax and breakfast. *Recommended!*

The **Hotel Marbella,** tel. 656-0122, fax 656-0121, is compact and has 14 simply furnished

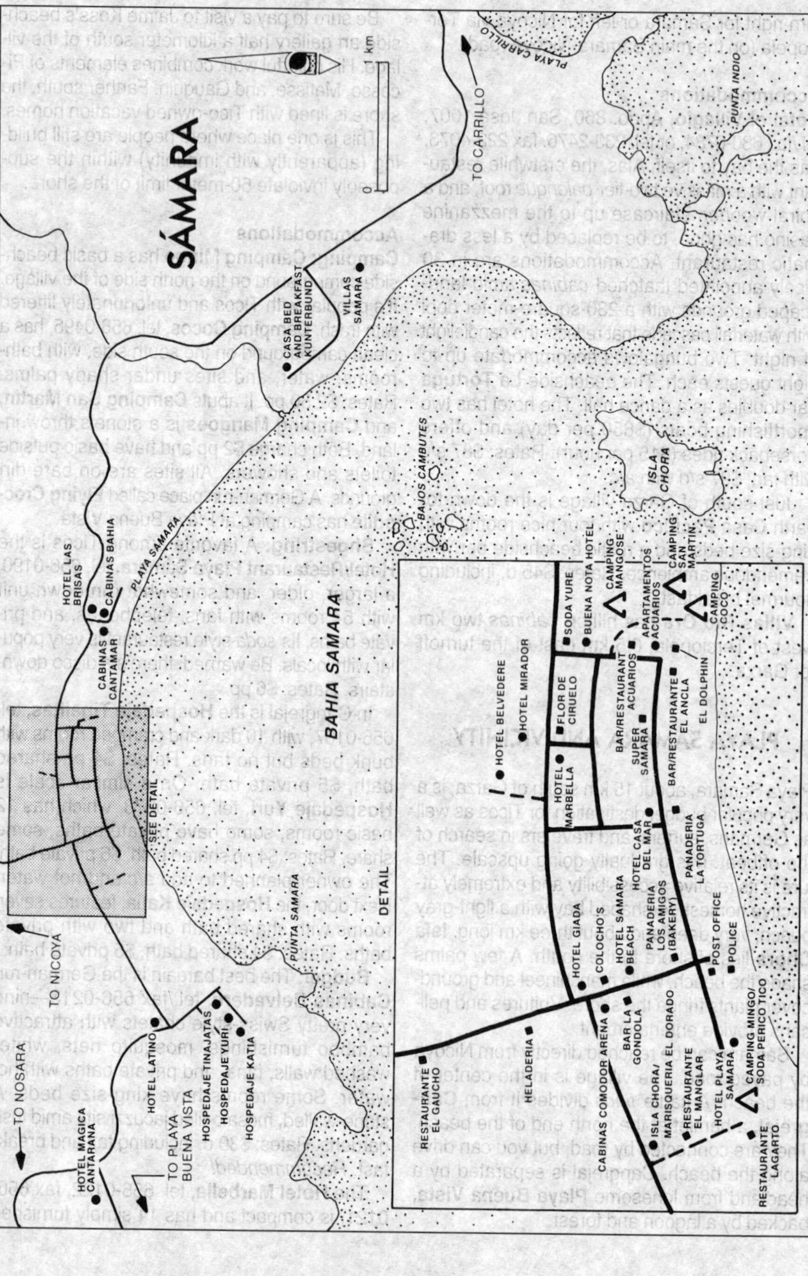

SÁMARA

PLAYA CARRILLO

TO CARRILLO

PUNTA INDIO

ISLA CHORA

BAJOS CAMBUTES

BAHIA SAMARA

PLAYA SAMARA

HOTEL LAS BRISAS

CABINAS BAHIA

CASA BED AND BREAKFAST KÜNTERBUND

VILLAS SAMARA

CABINAS CANTAMAR

SEE DETAIL

PUNTA SAMARA

TO NICOYA

HOTEL MAGICA CANTARANA

TO NOSARA

HOTEL LATINO

HOSPEDAJE TINAJATAS

HOSPEDAJE YURI

HOSPEDAJE KATIA

TO PLAYA BUENA VISTA

DETAIL

SODA YURE

BUENA NOTA HOTEL

HOTEL MIRADOR

CAMPING MANGOSE

APARTAMENTOS ACUARIOS

HOTEL BELVEDERE

FLOR DE CIRUELO

BAR/RESTAURANT SUPER ACUARIOS

CAMPING SAN MARTIN

HOTEL MARBELLA

BAR/RESTAURANTE EL ANCLA

CAMPING COCO

BAR/RESTAURANTE EL DOLPHIN

HOTEL GIADA

COLOCHO'S

HOTEL SAMARA BEACH

HOTEL CASA DEL MAR

PANADERIA LOS AMIGOS (BAKERY)

PANADERIA LA TORTUGA

POST OFFICE

POLICE

RESTAURANTE EL GAUCHO

HELADERIA

CABINAS COMODOR ARENA

BAR LA GONDOLA

ISLA CHORA/ MARISQUERIA EL DORADO

CAMPING MINGO/ SODA PERICO TICO

HOTEL PLAYA SAMARA

RESTAURANTE EL MANGLAR

RESTAURANTE LAGARTO

1 km

© MOON PUBLICATIONS, INC.

rooms and six apartments with whitewashed walls, sea-green decor, fans, and private baths with hot water. They open onto a courtyard with a tiny cooling-off pool. There's a small restaurant. Rates: $25-30 d.

Cabinas Comodor Arena, tel. 656-0320, has 12 clean, simply furnished rooms in a modern two-story unit; each has a fan and private bath with cold water. Upstairs rooms have verandas but catch the nocturnal noises from the disco next door; downstairs, you can almost hear the occupants above breathing. There's a tiny breakfast restaurant. Rates: $21 s/d, $25 t/quad, including tax.

I like the rustic **Cabinas Bahía,** tel. 656-0106, 0.5 km south of the village, with nine simple *cabinas* beside an old wooden beachside home. All have fans and private baths with cold water There's a simple restaurant beneath palms. Rates: 12.50 s, $20 d, $33 up to five people. Even better is **Cabinas Cantamar** next door, with four rooms with private baths and cold water in a two-story wooden home; breezes ease in through the wide windows. One room has an outside bathroom. There's also a *cabina*. The place is run by artist Jaime Koss, who has his studio here and serves banana cakes and coffee to all visitors. Rates: $15-25 rooms; $30 d *cabina. Recommended!*

One km farther is the German-run **Casa Bed and Breakfast Kunterbunt,** a small two-story turquoise house in a garden. There was nobody there when I called by.

Inexpensive: Hotel Latino, tel./fax 656-0043, is awkwardly situated about 400 meters inland betwixt the village and Cangrejal. This attractive modern two-story property has 10 spacious, simply furnished, cross-ventilated rooms with fans, terra-cotta floors, king-size bamboo beds (and a single bed) and private baths with hot water. Breakfast is served on the lawn. A swimming pool was to be added. Rates: $30 s, $40 d, $50 t, including breakfast and tax.

Hotel Casa del Mar, tel. 656-0264, fax 656-0129, run by French-Canadians, is one of several good bargains in town. This relaxing and well-run bed and breakfast has 17 modestly furnished rooms with fans, private baths, hot water, and heaps of light through louvered windows (two rooms have a kitchenette). Attractive decor, good-size beds, and a balcony overlooking the ocean

complete the picture. There's a jacuzzi. Rates: $30 s, $35 d, $45 t low season; $40 s, $50 d, $60 t high season, including breakfast and tax.

The Italian-run **Hotel Mágica Cantarana,** tel. 656-0071, fax 656-0260, e-mail: magica@sol.racsa.co.cr, 400 meters away on the road to Playa Buena Vista, is another modern, two-story complex with six modestly furnished rooms featuring fans, private baths with hot water, and verandas with hammocks. There's a small swimming pool and a shady open-sided restaurant. Upstairs rooms are cross-ventilated by the doors and balconies to the front and rear. Rates: $35 s/d low season; $45 s/d high season. It also has two one-bedroom ($45 low season; $65 high season) and two-bedroom apartments ($85 low season; $115 high season). It has a minibus for tours, and planned to introduce diving.

Hotel Sámara Beach, tel. 656-0218, fax 656-0526, is a two-story, 20-room complex with private baths and hot water. Some have king-size beds and a/c. Rooms are spacious and bright, with private patios. The hotel has a small swimming pool, plus a bar-cum-restaurant under thatch. It offers tours and rents bicycles ($5 per hour). Rates: $58 d; $63 with a/c, including tax.

You'll find plenty of charm and character in **Hotel Giada,** tel. 656-0132, fax 656-0131, with 13 attractive rooms with faux terra-cotta tile floors, ocher/cream decor, bamboo beds (some are king size), and wide balconies. Rates: $29 s, $40 d, $48 t.

The Italian-run **Hotel Buena Nota,** tel. 656-0265, has four clean, simply furnished rooms with king-size beds, fans, verandas, and private baths with hot water. There's also a large unit that accommodates four people. The friendly owner offers scuba diving. A restaurant was to be added. Rates: $20 s, $25 d low season, $30 s, $35 d high season rooms; $45 low season, $60 high season apartment.

Genuinely upscale, **Hotel y Villas Las Brisas del Pacífico,** Apdo. 14, Playa Sámara, tel. 656-0250, fax 656-0076, is located about two km south of Sámara on the road to Playa Carrillo. The German-run hotel has 45 a/c rooms with whitewashed stone walls, and private baths with hot water. Facilities include an open-air restaurant facing the ocean, two swimming pools, a jacuzzi, and a shady lounging area under palms. Separate bungalows sit on a hill, with ocean views and their own pool. The hotel is above. Rates: $50 s/d, $95 t/quad.

Moderate: The striking, gleaming white interpretation of a Spanish parador that commands the hill overlooking Sámara is **Mirador de Sámara,** tel. 656-0044, fax 656-0046. Imagine the panoramic views, especially from the tower containing the open-walled restaurant and bar. Six large apartments each sleep five and have full kitchens. They're clean within, almost clinical, with simple hardwood furnishings and floors. German-owned. Rates: $60 s/d; $10 extra person.

Setting a standard is **Hotel Isla Chora,** tel. 656-0174 or 257-3032, fax 656-0173, e-mail: hechombo@sol.racsa.co.cr, a handsome complex with 10 simple yet elegant rooms and four a/c apartments in two-story units that circle an amoeba-shaped swimming pool amid landscaped grounds. The Italian owners have brought their innate aesthetic appreciation to bear. The rooms have marvelous bamboo beds in Japanese style, showers constructed of natural pebbles, and wide verandas. A restaurant with soaring *palenque* roof serves natural health food, ice cream, and sodas; another serves Italian dishes. The open-air disco is *the* scene in Sámara. Rates: $38 s, $48 d, $53 t, $59 quad low season; $60 s, $70 d, $80 t, $90 quad high season. Apartments cost $83-97 low season and $121-141 high season.

Premium: At the southern end of Playa Sámara, three km south of the village, is **Villas Playa Sámara,** tel. 656-0102 or 256-8282, fax 221-7222, website www.magi.com/crica/hotels/vilsam.html. The upscale "tourist village" has 72 one-, two- and three-bedroom villas with huge interiors, wicker furnishings, large, well-equipped kitchens, spacious bedrooms, and bathrooms with hot water and oodles of light. All have a/c. They're spaced well apart amid expansive grounds. There's a large pool with swim-up bar, jacuzzi, and children's pool, plus a souvenir shop, and a casino. It offers windsurfing, water-skiing, plus volleyball, badminton, and a dive center. You can rent scooters. Rates: $75 s/d room, $95/$145/$195

two-/four-/six-person villa low season; $95 s/d room, $125/$185/$240 two-/four-/six-person villa high season.

Food

For Italian, check out the rustic **Restaurante Al Manglar,** a trattoria behind Hotel Isla Chora, which has a pizzeria and a restaurant serving simple, overpriced breakfasts ($5). My favorite spot is **El Delphin,** an open-air beachfront restaurant run by a charming French family. It's romantically floodlit at night; jazz riffs add their own romantic note. The menu includes salad niçoise ($5.50), T-bone steaks (from $6), pastas, thin-crust pizza, and scrumptious desserts such as banana splits ($2.50). You dine under a quintessentially French striped awning.

The **Bar Acuarios,** behind El Delphin and assembled from driftwood, has lively music and quality seafood dishes such as octopus in garlic ($2-4). The thatched **Restaurante Colocho's** also serves good, reasonably priced seafood. There's even a Chinese restaurant: **Restaurante Flor de Giruelo.**

There's a bakery on the east side of the soccer field, and another 100 meters east opposite Hotel Casa del Mar.

Entertainment

The thatch-roofed **Bar La Gondola,** opposite Hotel Sámara Beach, has darts and a pool table. The **Disco Playa Sámara** is in the hotel of that name. But the *real* disco scene happens at **Hotel Isla Chora** on Thursday, Friday, and Saturday nights. The hotel also has a video bar.

Tours and Activities

Scuba University is based at the Hotel Buena Vista. Dives cost $45 (one tank), $60 (two tanks), and PADI certification courses cost $300. You can rent a boat for touring ($25 per hour), snorkeling ($30), or fishing ($100 half day, $180 full day); guided trips are offered to Isla Chora ($10). **Dolphin Tours,** in the Hotel Giada, offers tours as far afield as Palo Verde, Arenal, and Ostional. **Flying Crocodile**

BOB RACE

offers horseback riding and scenic flights at Playa Buena Vista.

The **Hotel Isla Chora** offers a wide range of tours, including to Cuba.

Services
The Hotel Sámara Beach has a **travel agency** that represents Travelair. The **post office** and **police** (Guardia Rural) are by the beach, cater-corner to the soccer field. There's a **public telephone** at Pulpería Mileth, opposite the post office; and another at Hotel Yuri, in Cangrejal. There's a **supermarket** on the beachfront road.

Getting There and Away
By Bus: Buses depart San José for Sámara from Calles 14, Avenidas 3/5 (Empresa Alfaro,

tel. 222-2750 or 223-8227) daily at noon, returning at 4 a.m. ($5; six hours). Buy tickets well in advance during holidays and weekends. Buses depart Nicoya (three blocks east of the park) for Sámara daily at 8 a.m., 3 p.m., and 4 p.m. (Empresa Rojas, tel. 685-5352), continuing south to Playa Carrillo, and returning at 5:30 a.m. and 6:30 a.m. Schedules may change in wet season. The **bus stop** is behind Cabinas Arenas.

By Air: SANSA and **Travelair** have daily flights (see appendix). The Travelair office is in Hotel Isla Chora. **Air Taxi Sámara,** tel. 232-1355, fax 220-4582, offers private charter service for up to seven passengers in an a/c Cessna 421. The airstrip is at Playa Carrillo, south of Sámara.

SÁMARA SOUTH TO MANZANILLO

The southwest shore of Nicoya Peninsula has been one of the most remote coastal strips in Costa Rica. Sections are still virtually undiscovered, although surfers and hoteliers have begun moving south from Sámara and north from Malpaís, near the southern tip and accessed by road from Cóbano, near Montezuma. The beaches are beautiful and the scenery at times sublime.

South of Carrillo, the dirt road continues a few miles in good condition, then deteriorates to a mere trail in places. In the words of the old spiritual, there are many rivers to cross. The tricky route (there are several unmarked junctions) can thwart even the hardiest 4WD in wet season, or after prolonged rains in dry season. Be prepared to rough it. Don't attempt this section of the coast by ordinary car or at night.

The section just south of Bejuco had been newly widened and leveled by a bulldozer when I last drove by it. If your driving skills are up to it and you don't mind raising a pall of dust, you can put your foot down and run the road in top gear. This isn't recommended for relaxed touring, but for those who thrill to fast driving, it's a helluva lot of fun on the dirt and gravel. The best way to tackle the appalling corrugations is *not* to go slow, which can shake loose your teeth, but to attain a minimum speed—probably around 65 kph—that allows you to ride *atop* the ridges; the speed can vary with the wheelbase of the vehicle.

PLAYA CARRILLO AND VICINITY

South of Sámara, the dirt road continues in reasonably good condition over **Punta Indio** and drops down to coral-colored Playa Carrillo (five km south of Sámara), one of the finest beaches in Costa Rica, fringed with palm trees and encusped by wooded cliffs. An offshore reef protects the bay. The fishing hamlet of Carrillo nestles around the estuary of the Río Sangrado at the southern end of the bay. Hotels and planned residential communities are sprouting along this shore, which has other beaches—Playa Laguna and Playa del Sur—tucked into hidden coves.

Accommodations
The **camping** is superb under palms along the entire length of the beach, and at **Cabinas Mirador,** which has eight basic, dark, and grungy triple rooms with private baths and cold water atop the headland above the village of Puerto Carrillo. Rates: $10.

The following are in order from north to south.

At the north end of the beach is **Inn at Puerto Carrillo,** c/o TAM Travel, Apdo. 1864, San José 1000, tel. 222-2642, fax 221-6465; in the U.S., tel. (800) 848-5874, atop the cliffs of Punta Indio, with views to both Bahía Sámara and Bahía Carrillo. There are 21 *cabinas* with fans, satellite TVs, and private baths with cold water. Rates: $90 d.

Hotel Sunset, tel. 656-0011, is about one km up a dirt road that leads into the hills from the beach. It enjoys a wonderful breezy hilltop setting with spectacular views over the bay. Each tile-floored a/c cabin has two double beds with carved headboards, plus fans and pleasant bathrooms. There's a small swimming pool and wooden deck with *ranchito* bar. Rates: $60 d, including breakfast. The gringo owner also has a fully furnished four-bedroom oceanview house for eight people, including VCR ($100 per night). He also offers sportfishing. The place doesn't seem to get many guests. Another house, **Casa Zerimar,** tel. 244-1191, is for rent below Guanamar.

Another dirt road at the south end of the beach leads uphill, inland, to **Guesthouse Casa Pericos,** tel. 656-0061, a splendid guesthouse run by a young German couple, Tom and Petra, who have three well-lit, cross-ventilated, simply furnished rooms with heaps of large screened windows. Guests can use the kitchen. The downstairs room has a beautiful sea-blue tile floor; two upstairs rooms have A-frame roofs, wooden floors, dorm-style beds (one has three singles; the other has two singles and a bunk), and simple bathroom with cold water. Hammocks are slung on a breezy veranda with views through the trees to the beach. Rates: $12 pp. Tom is a PADI instructor and offers diving and horseback tours.

Guanamar Beach and Sportfishing Resort, Apdo. 7-1880, San José 1000, tel. 656-0054, fax 656-0001, website www.costasol.co.cr/guanamar.html; in the U.S., Costa Sol International, 1717 N. Bayshore Dr., Suite 3333, Miami, FL 33132, tel. (305) 539-1630 or (800) 245-8420, fax (305) 539-1123, on the hillside at the southern end of the bay, is one of Costa Rica's premier sportfishing resorts. Forty cabinas—connected by manicured walkways—cascade down the hillside prettified with bougainvillea. Each has a private patio and satellite TV. The resort has a romantic rough wood-and-thatch restaurant, a small casino, and a small swimming pool. In early 1991, an angler out of Guanamar caught the first Pacific blue marlin ever taken on a fly (the 92-kg marlin was also the largest fish ever caught on a fly). It has a private airstrip, deep sea kayaks, water-skiing, boogie boards, horseback riding, mountain bikes, and jet skis. Rates:

$68 s/d standard, $77 deluxe, $110 suite low season; $94 s/d standard, $102 deluxe, $124 suite high season.

About 200 yards south of Guanamar are several simple *cabinas* along a dirt side road: **Cabinas Noel, El Tucán, tel. 656-0305, and** El Rincón de Manolo, tel. 656-0087. The latter two have restaurants.

Playa Laguna Beach Resort, tel. 231-6205, fax 231-4897, e-mail: plaguna@ciber.co.cr, is a planned residential complex about two km south of Carrillo. The upscale Italian property will have condos, villas, and a hotel. Another expansive tourist complex—**Lomas Alta**—is one km south behind Playa el Sur.

Food

The **Bar y Restaurante El Mirador,** at the top of the headland, serves seafood dishes for about $3, breakfast for $1. Likewise the **Bar Shale** 100 meters along the road to Casa Pericos. **El Yate de Mariscos** opposite Guanamar also serves seafood. Otherwise, you can blow your dollars at the Guanamar's upscale restaurant (the setting is worth it).

The nicest spot is exquisite roadside **Bar y Restaurante Playa Laguna,** tel. 656-0005, part of the Playa Laguna Beach Resort complex. The restaurant was open at press time and serves *típico* and Italian dishes on a shaded wooden deck overlooking a lagoon.

Tours and Activities

Rick Ruhlow, tel./fax 656-0091, e-mail: kingfish@sol.racsa.co.cr, a "displaced California surf bum," is for hire along with his fully equipped nine-meter Palm Beach boat (about $650 per day) for fishing excursions or to ferry surfers to the big waves. Likewise, his pal Tad Cantrell of **CocoRico Verde** offers kayak and surf trips locally and acts as a guide nationwide.

Popos Sea-Kayaking, tel. 656-0086, is 200 yards south of Guanamar. It also rents surfboards.

Getting There

By Bus: A bus departs Nicoya for Playa Carrillo via Sámara Mon.-Fri. at 3 p.m., weekends at 8 a.m. (Transportes Rojas, tel. 685-5352). The schedule may change in wet season. There is no bus service from San José.

By Air: **SANSA** and **Travelair** both operate scheduled service to Playa Carrillo. You can also charter private air-taxis.

PLAYA CAMARONAL TO PUNTA BEJUCO

Playa Camaronal, beyond Punta El Roble about five km south of Playa Carrillo, is a three-km-long gray-sand beach that is a popular nesting site for leatherback and Pacific ridley turtles. You can camp by the mouth of the Río Ora, at the northern end of the beach, but avoid doing so in nesting season. *Loras* (ridley turtles) usually come ashore monthly, during the last quarter of the moon.

A dirt road (newly bulldozed) leads south nine km from Camaronal to **Playa Islita**, a beautiful silvery beach (used by nesting turtles) in a cove squeezed between soaring headlands that will have your 4WD wheezing in first gear. South of the hamlet of **Islita**, in the valley bottom, the road climbs over Punta Barranquilla—the moody **Bar Barranquilla** (made of eclectic marine flotsam; check out the whale vertebrae) perches atop the cliff and offers spectacular vistas—before drop-

ping dizzingly to **Playa Corozalito**, also a nesting site for hawksbill and leatherback turtles. The dirt road cuts inland to the village of **Corazalito** (with an airstrip) and continues parallel to and about two km from the shore. The beach is backed by a large mangrove swamp replete with wildlife, which, given the lack of human intrusion, is relatively easily seen. A mule track climbs inland from Hacienda Barranquilla to the top of **Cerro Potal** (618 meters), from where you can enjoy even grander perspectives of the coast.

At the hamlet of **Quebrada Seca**, two km south of Corazalito, a side road leads to **Playa Bejuco**, a four-km-long white-sand beach with a mangrove swamp at the southern end, within the meniscus of Punta Bejuco. The dirt road continues south from Quebrada Seca four km to **Pueblo Nuevo**, where a road leads inland over the mountains to Carmona and Hwy. 21.

Accommodations

Despite its "end-of-the-road" location, this area has two gems.

About three km south of Carrillo is a true gem: **El Sueño Tropical**, tel. 656-0151, fax 656-0152, which I call the "Three Brothers Inn," as it is run

SPECIAL HOTEL: PUNTA ISLITA

Hotel Hacienda Punta Islita, Apdo. 6054-1000, San José, tel. 231-6122 or 296-5773, fax 231-0715, e-mail: ptaisl@sol.racsa.co.cr, website www.nacion.co.cre/netinc/puntaislita, is a luxurious hotel—a member of Small Luxury Hotels of the World—commanding a hilltop above Playa Islita and embodying the essence of a relaxing invogue retreat. You enter via a lofty *palenque* lobby with a thatched roof held aloft by massive tree trunks and open to three sides, with a sunken bar and a wooden sundeck and two-level, mosaic-tiled horizon swimming pool seemingly suspended in midair and melding into the endless blues of the Pacific.

Everything is deep ochers, softy papayas, and dark greens, enhanced by terra-cotta tile floors and colorful ceramic tilework, and additional intimate touches lent by props from the movie *1492*—log canoes, old barrels, and huge wrought-iron candelabra. A TV lounge and library boasts deep-cushioned sofas. There's a jacuzzi. And the elegant

"1492" restaurant is acclaimed ($9 breakfasts, $19 à la carte lunch, $22 à la carte dinner).

The quaint colony includes 20 hillside *casitas* in Santa Fe style, and four junior suites (each with an outdoor whirlpool spa on an oceanview deck) brushed by the breezes. Each red-tile-roofed, thatch-fringed bungalow is fully and luxuriously equipped with king-size beds (or two queens), spacious bathrooms (complete with hair dryers), ceiling fans and a/c, minibar, TV, and private terrace overlooking the beach. There's also a three-bedroom casita sleeping six people, with its own swimming pool.

A private forest reserve has trails for horseback rides and nature hikes, and a panoply of water sports are available, as is sportfishing ($550 half day, $800 full day), a gym, two tennis courts, and even a golf driving range. You can arrive in style using the ranch's private airstrip (30 minutes from San José; $500 up to four people; $8 airport transfers). And 4WD vehicles can be rented. Rates: $150-175 s/d, $225 suites, $450 casita high season.

by three charming brothers from Verona, Italy. Their hospitality is boundless, blending European savoir faire with marvelously erudite conversations. The tropical motif is everywhere throughout this lushly landcaped setting. There are 12 clean, simple rooms with terra-cotta tiles and king-size bamboo beds. The restaurant (surprisingly elegant with its bright pink table settings, candlelight, and colorful tropical mural) has a commanding presence, with a soaring *palenque* roof commanding a hillock, and the bungalows spread out of sight in a hollow. Vanni, the Italian chef, is gifted; his concoctions include delights such as fusilli, and ravioli de pescado ($5-8). The bar and restaurant has become a popular hangout for local expats; it seems half of Verona has moved here. There's an amoeba-shaped pool and a kids' pool. Howler monkeys abound in the surrounding forest. It's one of the few places from which I've had difficulty tearing myself away, due mainly to the graciousness of the hosts. They have a minibus for tours, and offer river trips on the Río Ora. Rate: $50 d, $55 with a/c high season, including breakfast ($10 less in low season). *Highly recommended!*

Also recommended is the Punta Islita.

Hospedaje Abarrotes, beside the soccer field in Pueblo Nuevo, has basic rooms with shared bath and cold water for $6 pp. The **Bar Los Corrales** is here; it serves simple meals.

Getting There
SANSA and Travelair fly daily from San José (see appendix).

PLAYA SAN MIGUEL TO PUNTA COYOTE

Crossing the Río Bejuco south of Pueblo Nuevo you arrive at the hamlet of **San Miguel,** at the northern end of Playa San Miguel, reached by a side road. The silver-sand beach is a prime turtle-nesting site; there's a ranger station at the southern end of the beach, which is protected as part of the Tempisque Conservation Area. It is backed by cattle pasture and runs south into **Playa Coyote,** a lonesome six-km-long stunner backed by a large mangrove swamp and steep cliffs. The beaches, which are separated by a river estuary, are fantastically wide at low tide.

The wide Río Jabillo pours into the sea at the south end of Playa Coyote, which is reached by a side road that extends two km in each direction along the shore. The surfing is superb and there is good snook fishing and birding in the mangroves at the rivermouths.

The Río Jabillo forces the coast road inland for six km to **San Francisco de Coyote,** where a road leads inland over the mountains to Hwy. 21. The road to Malpaís heads back to the coast. South of San Francisco you must ford the Río Jabillo; the main road leads southwest five km to Punta Coyote but was flooded and impassable when I tried it (if so, take a side road one km south of San Francisco; it leads to a T-junction, where you turn right to continue south for Playa Caletas and Malpaís).

Ticos have vacation homes along Playa San Miguel and appear out of nowhere during national holidays, but you'll have the beaches to yourself at other times of year.

You can buy gasoline at most *pulperías.* Ask around.

Accommodations and Food
The **Blue Pelican** on Playa San Miguel is a rustic bar and restaurant with a TV showing music videos. It permits camping and has five basic rooms with shared bath and hot water in a three-story wooden house on stilts. A large room upstairs sleeps six people; smaller rooms are downstairs. The loft bedroom is cross-ventilated. Beds have mosquito nets, and there's a veranda with hammocks. Rates: $4 per tent in the garden, $6 under the house; $17 s/d/t downstairs room, $42 upstairs room. The bar serves ceviche *bocas* and seafood dishes. You can make reservations c/o **Soda Restaurante El Ranchito,** public tel. 656-0430, nearby.

Hotel Arco de Noe, cellular tel. 382-2603, one km farther south on the main road, is an elegant, modern, Italian-run hacienda-style property with lush landscaped grounds and a large swimming pool lined by mosaic tiles. It has 10 *cabinas* with lofty wooden ceilings, fans, verandas, louvered windows, exquisite fabrics, and private baths with hot water. There's a lounge and restaurant, and an outdoor kitchen for guest use was to be added. You can rent kayaks ($5 per hour) and horses ($5 per hour). Rates: $30 s/d low season; $40 s/d high season, including breakfast.

Soda y Pulpería Rey, beside the soccer field in San Francisco de Coyote, has *cabinas* with private baths and cold water for (up to four people), and rooms with shared bath. It permits camping and has horses for rent ($1.50 per hour). You can make reservations c/o the nearby public telephone, 671-1236. Rates: $2 per tent campsite; $4 pp room with shared bath; $17 *cabinas*.

Bar La Veranera rents basic rooms with cold water at the southern end of Playa Coyote (reached via San Francisco de Coyote). Rates: $4 pp. There were no *cabinas* along Playa Coyote at press time.

PUNTA COYOTE TO MANZANILLO

Playa Caletas is reached by a spur road south of San Francisco de Coyote. This miles-long brown-sand beach has no settlements. Nothing. It's just you and the turtles that come ashore to lay their eggs. Playa Caletas is a great surfing beach. It extends southward into **Playa Bongo, Playa Arío,** and **Playa Manzanillo**—a 12-km-long expanse of sand running ruler-straight and broken only by the estuary of the Río Bongo, inhabited by crocodiles that were recently reintroduced. Marshy shore flats force the coast road inland.

Manzanillo is a small fishing hamlet that is becoming popular with surfers pushing north from Malpaís. You can rent sea kayaks ($10 half day, $20 per day), horses ($5 per hour), plus boogie boards, surfboards, and Hobie Cats at the **Cocos Yacht Club,** a funky place at the north end of the dirt road that extends north from Manzanillo for one km along Playa Arío.

Where the Going Gets Tough

The route to Malpaís is an adventure. Heed my directions carefully.

South of Caletas, keep straight until you reach a major Y-fork by a sugarcane field; turn right and continue one km to **Salon La Perla India,** where a road leads down to Playa Arío. You can drive four km *along the beach* to Playa Manzanillo, where you meet the main road as it comes back to the coast. (*Warning!* Do *not* attempt to drive along Playa Arío except at low tide.) A safe bet is to turn left at Soda La Perla and follow the road inland via the hamlet of **Betel** along the Río Bongo, which you must ford. (*Warning!* The

oblique crossing is shallow until the far—southern—bank, where suddenly your vehicle dips for one breathtaking moment—yes, the hood will go under water—but keep your foot on the gas pedal and you should be across before your next heartbeat; in wet season, the steep bank may be too muddy for purchase.) Soon you reach the 30-meter-wide Río Arío. The shallow crossing is oblique; the egress on the far bank is 50 yards to the left. (*Warning!* Many vehicles have tried to go straight across and have churned up the far bank into what looks like a road; believe me, it is a dead-end grave; if the sudden drop in the river here doesn't get you, the muddy cul-de-sac will). If you arrive at night—as I did—be patient. Wait for a local to arrive and show the way. Turn right in Betel, and you will eventually be deposited by the shore at Manzanillo. *Do not attempt to cross the rivers in wet season.*

South of Manzanillo, the tenuous coast road (a devil in wet season) leads over **Punta Pochote** and alongside **Playa Hermosa** to Playa Santa Teresa and Malpaís. Alternatively, you can opt for a mountain road with a treacherous rocky stretch that deposits you back at the coast on Playa Santa Teresa.

You can also reach Caletas via a rough road from Jicaral, on Hwy. 21. It follows the valley of the Río Bongo, which you cross several times; the road may be impassable in wet season.

Accommodations and Food

At Caletas, **Rancho Loma Clara,** tel. 671-1236, has basic rooms for $5; it serves meals.

In Manzanillo, the **Soda y Atardecer Dorado** has very basic rooms with bed only (and funky outhouse toilets) for $6 pp. The bar (with TV and jukebox) is a lively center for locals. It serves filling meals; try the *filete al ajillo* (garlic fish, $2). Marguerita the parrot will fly to your table to sip your beer.

Cabinas Las Palmeras, Apdo. 58-5361 Cóbano; in Canada, tel. (250) 337-5829, on Playa Manzanillo, is run by Canadians Victoria and Grant, who offer five large, simple, well-lit modern *cabinas* with double beds, verandas with hammocks, and well-kept shared outhouse bathroom and toilet. The upstairs room has a balcony. Rates: $10 s, $15 d. They charge $2 per tent (including use of showers and toilet) for camping on the beach. The duo's rustic **Bar Las**

Palmeras, nearby, is a happening spot for blues music on Saturday nights.

Getting There

Reportedly, a **bus** departs San José daily at 3 p.m. from Calle 12, Avenidas 7/9, and travels via the Puntarenas-Playa Naranjo ferry and Jicaral to Coyote, Bejuco and Islita (arriving around 11 p.m.). Return buses are said to depart Bejuco at 4 a.m., passing San Francisco de Coyote at 5 a.m.

SOUTHEAST NICOYA

HIGHWAY 21
(CARMONA TO PLAYA NARANJO)

South from Pueblo Viejo (16 km west of the Tempisque ferry), Hwy. 21 winds along the southern shore of the Gulf of Nicoya via Jicaral to Playa Naranjo, beyond which it swings south around the Nicoya Peninsula bound for Paquera and Montezuma. When I last drove it, the road was partially paved, with large sections worn to the bone. Jarring! Much of the shore is lined with mangroves but there is little to hold your interest.

Playa Naranjo, 65 km south of Pueblo Viejo, is the terminal for the Puntarenas **ferry.** The opening of a new car ferry service between Puntarenas and Paquera in 1993 led to a drop in traffic through Naranjo. In response, hoteliers are attempting to establish Naranjo on the tourist map. What you'll find here are several unspoilt (yet only marginally appealing) beaches and Islas San Lucas and Gitana for exploring.

There's a **gas station, supermarket,** and **car rental** at the junction for the ferry.

Isla Chira

Isla Chira, Costa Rica's second-largest island, seems to float below the mouth of the Río Tempisque at the north end of the Gulf of Nicoya. Surrounded by mangroves popular with pelicans and frigate birds, it is separated from the Nicoya Peninsula by the one-km-wide Estero Puncha. Despite its size (10 km east to west by six km north to south), Isla Chira is uninhabited except for a few fishermen and farmers, who eke out a meager living, and Gerardo Seas, who oversees the *salinas* (salt pans) on the shores of **Hacienda Encantato.** Gerardo welcomes groups. He gave me a tour of the farm and *salinas* on a flatbed towed by a tractor. Especially noteworthy were the bats in the salt shed. The

salt pans are popular with roseate spoonbills and other wading birds—and, I'm sure, crocodiles. Gerardo's wife, who raises chihuahuas, serves ceviche and cold beers. Gerardo also rents horses.

Local legends about the island include that of La Mona, a woman who turns into a monkey after midnight to haunt drunks and men cheating on their wives.

Local fishermen in Puntarenas, Puerto Moreno, or Puerto Jesús (20 km southeast of Nicoya) may take you to the island. **Blue Sea Cruises,** Apdo. 64, San José 1000, tel. 233-7274, fax 233-5555, includes Chira on a one-day cruise of the Gulf of Nicoya from Puntarenas.

Isla San Lucas

This 615-hectare island, two km off the eastern tip of the Nicoya Peninsula, has been called the Island of Unspeakable Horrors, the Island of Silence, and Devil's Island. From afar, it seems a pleasant palm-fringed place—a place, perhaps, where you might actually *wish* to be washed ashore and languish for a few months or even years in splendid sun-washed isolation. Yet a visit to Isla San Lucas once amounted to an excursion to Hell.

Until a few years ago, this was the site of the most dreaded prison in the Costa Rican penal system, with a legacy dating back 400 years. In the 16th century, the Spanish conquistador Gonzalo Fernandez Oviedo used San Lucas as a concentration camp for local Chara Indians, who were slaughtered on the site of their sacred burial grounds. In the 19th century, Japanese pearl divers reportedly briefly used the island before being ejected by the Costa Rican government, which turned it into a detention center for political prisoners in 1862. In 1991, the government closed the prison.

The island is now a sad, silent place. Should you visit the grim bastion, the ghosts of murderers, miscreants, and maltreated innocents will be your guides. A cobbled pathway leads to the main prison building (the prisoner who built it was promised his freedom once he completed his task; reportedly it took him 20 years). The chapel has become a bat grotto, and only graffiti remains to tell of the horror and hopelessness. Though they are slowly being reclaimed by the jungle, you can still see the underground solitary-confinement cell and other structures. There are still guards here, but today their role is to protect the island's resident wildlife from would-be poachers. The guards will also, though, happily escort you to the diminutive cells where two dozen or more men at a time rotted their lives away. There are no restrictions on visiting.

The Island of the Lonely Men, a biographical account written in 1971 by former prisoner José León Sánchez, tells of the betrayals, the madness, and the perpetual frustrations of attempts to escape this spine-chilling place.

Getting There: You can rent **motorboats** through the Costa Rica Yacht Club in Puntarenas, tel. 661-0784, or Oasis del Pacífico in Playa Naranjo, tel./fax 661-1555. Alan Maquinay offers a tour from Hotel Maquinay, tel. 661-1763, in Playa Naranjo. **Pollux de Golfito,** Apdo. 7-1970, San José 1000, tel. 220-2074 or 231-4055, fax 231-3030, offers a day tour to San Lucas and Playa Escondida from Puntarenas aboard the 16-meter twin-masted sailing yacht *Pollux* ($70, including roundtrip transfers from San José). **Blue Seas,** Apdo. 64, San José 1000, tel. 323-7274, fax 233-5555, offers a cruise around the islands of the Gulf of Nicoya from Puntarenas, including Isla San Lucas, Isla Caballo, and Isla Chira. And **Calypso Cruises,** Apdo. 6941-1000, San José, tel. 256-2727, fax 233-0401, e-mail: calypso@centralamerica.com, or, in the U.S., P.O. Box 025216-819, Miami, FL 33102, tel. (800) 948-3770, visits Isla San Lucas on itineraries aboard the venerable *Calypso* cruise boat; the company also has cruises to **Punta Coral Private Reserve,** where snorkeling, sea kayaking, and other activities are offered.

Accommodations and Food

There are very few hotels between Pueblo Viejo and Playa Naranjo. **Hotel Guamale,** tel. 650-0073; **Pensión San Martín,** tel. 650-0169; and **Cabinas Central** in Jicaral, are basic options.

Bar y Restaurant Gringo Charlie's, four km south of Jicaral, serves *bocas* and simple meals. The roadside sign declares, "Se habla rock 'n' roll," and, sure enough, Gringo Charlie plays old-time favorites. There are many hints at salacious after-dark fancies—the girlie posters festooning the bar, the indecorously clad hostesses who attempt to waylay passing traffic, and the cabins intended to be shared with said hostesses.

El Ancla, tel. 661-3887, just 200 meters from the ferry terminal, has nine brightly decorated a/c rooms fronted by a wide porch with hammocks. The grounds include a kidney-shaped pool and attractive thatched bar and restaurant. Rates: $25 s/d with fan, $29 with a/c. The **Hotel Maquinay,** tel./fax 661-1763, 400 meters north of El Paso, has 10 simple *cabinas* and a swimming pool for $15 s, $8 d. It hosts the lively **Disco La Maquinera** on weekends, for which locals pour in from all around.

Hotel El Paso, Apdo. 232, San José 2120, tel. 661-2610, 600 meters northwest of the ferry, has 14 rooms with fans, queen beds, and private baths with hot water (nine also have a/c and TV). Rooms are simply furnished but clean. Cabinas have kitchenettes. The hotel offers **car rental** and has a swimming pool and a restaurant. A *mirador* overlooks the gulf. Rates: $16 s, $20 s/d with fan, $29 s/d with a/c, $50 large (five-person) *cabinas*.

The **Hotel Oasis del Pacífico,** Apdo. 200-5400, Puntarenas, tel./fax 661-1555; or P.L. Wilhelm 1552, P.O. Box 025216, Miami, FL 33102-5216, has 36 comfortable chalet-type rooms with fans, double beds, and lots of hot water—a rarity in Nicoya. Timeworn toy sailboats and artwork from Bali decorate the large screened restaurant, overseen by Aggie Wilhelm, who serves her native Singaporean dishes—the *corvina al ajillo* (sea bass with garlic) is superb. There's a small library, plus a swimming pool in the landscaped grounds, where horses (available for rides) roam free. Nonguests can use the facilities ($4) while waiting for the ferry—a chance to relax in a hammock or stroll the beach. Yachts can anchor at the 80-meter boat dock. Oasis del Pacífico specializes in sportfishing ($275 full day). It also has sea kayaks ($10 per hour) and offers five-day kayaking tours ($900, including four nights' accommodation). Rate: $30 s, $40 d.

Getting There and Away

The car-and-passenger ferry departs Playa Naranjo for Puntarenas at 5:10 and 8:50 a.m. and 12:50, 5, and 9 p.m. Schedules may change. Buy your ticket from a booth to the left of the gates. Park in line first.Lines get very long—on weekends, get there at least an hour before departure time (even farther ahead of time during holiday periods). Buses meet the ferry for Jicaral, Coyote, Bejuco, Carmona, and Nicoya. Hotel representatives will pick you up with notice. (For more details, see Puntarenas.)

PLAYA NARANJO TO PAQUERA

The coast road turns south from Playa Naranjo and over hill and dale to Paquera (18 km), where the climate begins to grow more humid and the vegetation begins to thicken. This section is very hilly, with tortuous switchbacks, deep potholes, and corrugations and rocks that give a despairingly jolting ride (it improves beyond Paquera). It's all part of the price for marvelous views out over the Gulf of Nicoya—including toward Isla Guayabo, which comes into view about six km south of Playa Naranjo, where the road briefly meets the coast at **Gigante,** at the north end of **Bahía Luminosa** (also called Bahía Gigante), which is lined by Playa Pánama.

Prolific birdlife has earned the area the moniker Costa de Pájaros, the Bird Coast.Diving is good close to shore, where lobsters and giant conches are abundant. Dolphins and whales are often sighted offshore (January is reportedly the best month for whales). The mountainous interior inland of Paquera was recently proclaimed a protected wilderness: the **Zona Protectora Peninsula de Nicoya.**

Isla Gitana

This tiny island in the middle of Bahía Luminosa was once a burial site for local Indians (hence its other name, Isla Muertos—Island of the Dead—by which it is marked on maps), and crosses mark more recent graves (the Indians having adopted Christianity). Tico workers will not stay on the island at night, thanks to superstition. The undergrowth is wild and cacti abound, so appropriate footwear is recommended. The isle, 400 meters offshore from Punta Gigante,

serves up a soupçon of pleasures: a couple of atmospheric if rustic cabins, a palm-thatch beachside restaurant-cum-bar strewn with icons of a mariner's life, plus a scintillating white-sand beach that shelves gently into peacock-blue waters. The place is run almost as a private island resort by residents Carl and Loida Reugg, a lively gringo-Filipina couple, who run the **Fantasy Island Yacht Club.**

There's a large pool for cooling dips and anchorage for yachters, who unwind in a bar that looks as if it washed up from the sea. Eclectic paraphernalia glued and tacked together seems to hold the ramshackle place together. Regulars include a tame monkey (Minkey) and his bosom buddy, Gordo, a coatimundi (the two enjoy a good rough-and-tumble, reports writer Ashley Cavers), a parrot (Rico), an alcoholic raccoon (Rocky), and friendly wild pigs. The Reuggs also offer single- and twin-seat kayaks ($5-6 per hour, $25-35 per day), Hobie Cats ($12 per hour), sailboards ($8 per hour, $40 per day), rowboats ($4 per hour), and a speedboat for trips to Isla Tortugas and Curú Reserve ($50) or any of 15 other tempting isles within view.

The owners charge $20 (up to four people) for transfers from Paquera, $50 from Puntarenas. Or you can call the island to request a boat by VHF Radio 16 from Bahía Luminosa, Bahía Gigante, or the beachside *soda,* where you can hire a boat on the beach. You can also reach it by sea kayak from Bahía Gigante, a 30-minute paddle journey. **Calypso Cruises,** Apdo. 6941-1000, San José, tel. 256-2727, fax 233-0401, e-mail: calypso@centralamerica.com, or, in the U.S., P.O. Box 025216-819, Miami, FL 33102, tel. (800) 948-3770, visits Gitana.

Accommodations

The North American-run **Hotel Bahía el Gigante** (Apdo. 1886, San José, tel./fax 661-2442) has four condos and 12 spacious, modestly decorated rooms with fans and large bathrooms with hot water. Hammocks are strung across verandas and beneath *ranchitos* in the landscaped grounds, which include a swimming pool. *Típico* dishes, seafood, and burgers are served. Trails lead through a small patch of primal forest. The property was to have been turned into a catch-and-release sportfishing lodge, but was looking run-down when I visited in January 1998. It offers horse rentals, plus guided horseback tours to waterfalls ($5 per hour), kayak rentals ($30 half day), and kayak trips to Isla Gigante. Rates: $24 s, $30 d, $35 t rooms, $40-70 condos.

Bahía Luminosa Resort, P.O. Box 210113, Chula Vista, CA 91921-0113, tel. (619) 216-8655 or (800) 365-2342, e-mail: bahia-luminosa@get-awaynow.com, website http://www.getawaynow.com/bahia-luminosa, at Playa Pánama, midway between Paquera and Playa Naranjo, has 14 *cabinas* with private bath plus a secluded two-bedroom house tucked into a forested valley in a cove fronted by the brown-sand beach. They're spacious and modestly furnished, and have fans (and cross-ventilation), a double and two single beds, hammocks on the veranda, and private baths with hot water. A lap pool is set in a concrete sundeck, and there's water-skiing, snorkeling, horseback riding and other activities. The grandly named Nicoya Yacht Club is here; at press time it consisted of a rickety dock, but a new one, with water and electricity, is planned. You'll also find showers, laundry, and supplies. The club has several vessels for charter. The place was a bit dowdy when I called in, but George Perrochet, the new owner, was planning to invest money in landscaping and refurbishment. Day-visitors pay $3. Rates: $60 d, including continental breakfast. A four-day/three-night package is available.

The Reuggs, Apdo. 340, Puntarenas, tel./fax 661-2994 or c/o Rancho Gigante, tel. 661- 2442; in the U.S., 54 Clairvew Ct., San Francisco, CA 94131, tel. 415-281-5906, have two large cement-block *cabinas* with kitchens on Isla Gigante ($40 d, or $45 pp including transfers from Paquera and all meals, or $60 pp with sea kayaking). There are also simple rooms for $10 s, $15 d. You can camp or sleep in a hammock for $5. The place may be *called* Fantasy Island, but be warned that this is *not* Fantasy Island—don't expect luxury.

RESERVAS BIOLÓGICAS ISLAS GUAYABO Y NEGRITOS

These two biological reserves protect nesting sites of the brown booby, frigate bird, pelican, and other seabirds. In winter, 6.8-hectare Guayabo (about three km northeast of Gigante) is

also a nesting site for the peregrine falcon. Negritos (74 hectares), less than one km east of Punta Corallillo (eight km south of Guayabo) comprises two islands separated by a narrow channel. The islands are covered with a scrubby forest of spiny cedar, viscoyol palm, and frangipani. They are off-limits to visitors, but day cruises traveling between Puntarenas and Isla Tortuga pass by both islands.

PAQUERA

This quiet village, 24 km south of Playa Naranjo, is centered at the junction for the **Paquera ferry** to and from Puntarenas. The ferry berth is three km northeast of Paquera, which is landlocked. A dirt track two km east of town on the south side of the ferry road leads to the tip, **Punta Corralillo,** where you have a good view of the Islas Negritos.

Accommodations and Food

You can camp at **Area de Campar,** 0.5 km northeast of town. Otherwise, take your pick of several basic hostelries, such as **Cabinas El Paraiso,** tel. 641-0034, or **Restaurante y Cabinas Ginana,** which has 19 rooms with fans and private baths with cold water for $10 d. **Pensión Bengala,** next to the pool hall in the center of town, has basic rooms with shared baths and fans ($5). **Cabinas Rosita** also has basic rooms ($20 d). A road south from the ferry dock reportedly ends at **Fred's Folly,** tel. 288-2014, with cabins apparently for about $40 d.

Take your pick of several *sodas* in town. The **Restaurant Tres Jotas,** 200 meters before the ferry terminal, serves a great garlic shrimp and fries.

Services

Paquera has a **Banco de Costa Rica,** tel. 661-1444, ext. 190, and a **Banco Nacional,** tel. 661-1444, ext. 101. The **public telephone** is next door to Restaurante Ginana. There's a **gas station** 400 meters northeast of town on the road to the ferry berth.

Getting There and Away

The car-and-passenger ferry departs Paquera for Puntarenas at 6 and 10:30 a.m. and 2:15, 6, and 9:15 p.m. ($1.25 adults, $75 cents children,

$9 cars, $2 motorbikes). A *lancha* (water-taxi) departs Paquera for Puntarenas at 8 a.m. and 12:30 and 5 p.m. Check departures ahead of time. A bus marked "Directo" meets the incoming ferry (for details, see Puntarenas) and travels to Paquera, Tambor, Cóbano, and Montezuma ($3; two hours).

REFUGIO NACIONAL DE VIDA SILVESTRE CURÚ

This private reserve forms part of a 1,214-hectare *hacienda,* two-thirds of which is preserved as primary forest. It is tucked in the fold of Golfo Curú, four km south of Paquera. The 84-hectare reserve includes 4.5 km of coastline with a series of tiny coves and three beautiful white-sand beaches—Playas Curú, Colorada, and Quesera—nestled beneath green slopes. Olive ridley and hawksbill turtles nest on the crystalline beaches. Mangrove swamps extend inland along the Río Curú, backed by forested hills. Birds include motmots, white-fronted amazons, laughing hawks, lineated woodpeckers, and at least 150 other species. Mammals include agoutis; ocelots; margays; pumas; howler, capuchin and endangered spider monkeys; white-tailed deer; sloths; and anteaters. All rather remarkable for so small a place.

Call the owner, Doña Julieta Schutz, tel. 661-2392, for permission to enter, ideally with several days' notice. She has a microwave telephone, and getting through is often difficult. There's no sign for Curú. The gate is normally locked unless you're expected. Doña Julieta will give you instructions to find it. Guided tours are offered (your tip is their pay). Trails are marked.

Accommodations
Basic research huts on the beachfront are sometimes available for overnight stays ($30 per night, meals included). Researchers and students get priority. Showers and toilets are primitive. No camping allowed.

Getting There
The bus between Paquera and Cóbano passes the unmarked gate. Ask the driver to let you off. Several tour companies in Montezuma and nearby hotels offer day tours.

ISLA TORTUGA

This stunningly beautiful, 320-hectare island lies three km offshore of Curú. It's a popular day-trip from Puntarenas, a 14-km, 90-minute journey aboard any of a half-dozen cruise boats. Tortuga is as close to an idyllic tropical isle as you'll find in Costa Rica. The main attraction is a magnificent white-sand beach lined with tall coconut palms. Each of the cruise companies that puts day-trippers ashore gets its own section of the beach. It can get a bit cramped on weekends, when three or four boats might disgorge their passengers at the same time. Still, it makes for a tremendous trip on a sunny day. You can snorkel, swim, play volleyball, hike, or simply snooze in the sun. There are oar and pedal boats and water-bicycles, kayaks, and Spyaks (glass-bottom boats). You can also hike into the forested hills, replete with monkeys and other wildlife that can be viewed on a treetop canopy tour operated by the highly respected Original Canopy Tour (see

Tortuga Island

JOHN ANDERSON

Canopy Tours), which uses professional climbing gear to whiz you along steel cables slung between treetops.

Cruises

Calypso Cruises, Apdo. 6941-1000, San José, tel. 256-2727, fax 233-0401, e-mail: calypso@centralamerica.com, or, in the U.S., P.O. Box 025216-819, Miami, FL 33102, tel. (800) 948-3770, began the trend in 1979 aboard the venerable *Calypso,* which faithfully operated daily until 1994, when it was replaced by a the space-age *Manta Raya,* a catamaran as luxurious as any first-class aircraft lounge, with soft leather seating, full bar, freshwater showers, and even an underwater viewing window. Transfers from San José are provided, with snacks served en route, washed down by *coco locos* (rum, coconut milk, and coconut liqueur, served in a coconut). The $84 fee includes a buffet lunch on the beach. A highlight is Abuelo, Calypso's octogenarian marimba player (the company paid for his eye surgery in 1987; now Abuelo says he's always smiling because he "can see the pretty young passengers in their bikinis").

Though Calypso sets the standard, the following companies also offer similar day cruises to Tortuga: **Bay Island Cruises,** Apdo. 145, San José 1007, tel. 239-4951, fax 329-4404; **Fantasia,** tel. 255-0791; and **Sea Ventures,** tel. 239-4719, fax 239-4666.

TAMBOR AND VICINITY

Tambor, 18 km southwest of Paquera, is a small fishing village fronted by a gray-sand beach in **Bahía Ballena** (Whale Bay), a beautiful deep-pocket bay rimmed by **Playa Tambor** and backed by forested hills. The beach extends north to **Playa Pochote.** The fishing hamlet of **Pochote** is surrounded by mangrove swamps that harbor waterfowl and caimans. Whales are sometimes sighted in the bay (hence the name). Monkeys and other critters hang out by the shore.

About two km northeast of Tambor, a rocky road leads inland four km to the hamlet of **Vainilla** (called Concepción on maps) and **Finca del Sol,** tel./fax 683-0204, a horseback ranch, 1,500-hectare private forest reserve, and teak reforestation project. French expats have settled here.

Accommodations

Camping: In Tambor, **Super Lapa** allows camping on the beach, as does **Albergue y Camping Río Mar,** tel. 683-0025, on the riverbank 0.5 km north of the village ($1.25 pp, including showers and toilets). You can also camp at **Finca del Sol.** There's a campground at the far end of Playa Pochote; it's used by vacationing Ticos and is terribly littered. Take a deep breath before entering the outhouses.

Budget: Cabinas El Bosque has fairly basic accommodations, just before the turnoff into Tambor village. Also try **Zorba's Place,** about three km east of Tambor, which has *cabinas* ($25 d, including breakfast) and a restaurant predictably selling Greek-inspired dishes.

The popular and unpretentious gringo-run **Hotel Dos Lagartos,** Apdo. 5602, San José 1000, tel. 683-0236, on the waterfront in Tambor village, has 17 rooms with shared baths and six with private baths. Rooms are clean and well-lit but small, basically furnished, and have cold water only. There's a bar and restaurant downstairs. Rates: $17 d shared bath, $25 d private bath.

Cabinas y Restaurante Cristina, tel. 683-0028, 100 meters north of Dos Lagartos, has six simply furnished but clean and adequate rooms with fans, large louvered windows, and cold water. Rates: $16 d shared bath, $19 d private bath. **Albergue y Camping Río Mar** has five simple all-wood rooms with fans and shared bath (cold water) for $16 d. It has secure parking and a simple *soda* and offers horseback rides ($5 per hour). Also consider **Cabinas Cabita,** on the north side of town, and **Cabinas Tambor Beach,** under construction in early 1998.

At Pochote, the beachfront **Rest Coqueluche,** tel. 683-0061, has four cabins with fans and private baths with hot water for $200 d weekly including all meals. The setting is exquisite.

Inexpensive: At Vainilla, **La Paillote Hotel y Restaurant,** tel. 683-0190, is a reclusive French-run place with six small, twee *cabinas* amid the dry forest, with bougainvillea spilling over their verandas. They have private baths with hot water. The restaurant serves gourmet French cuisine. Rates: $25 s, $35 d ($40 pp with all meals).

Nearby, the French-run **Finca del Sol,** tel./fax 683-0204, has a rustic cabin for up to six people on the hillside amid trees; it's very simple, with a kitchen and refrigerator and fan ($20 nightly,

$300 monthly). The delightful hosts, Claude Gallisian and Emmanuelle Baudenon, also have two-story *casas*.

Moderate: SIMA, tel. 661-3233 (afternoons), has fully equipped two-bedroom houses four km northeast of Tambor. They rent for $65 daily, including laundry service plus use of bicycles, horses, and snorkeling gear.

Premium: The architecturally dramatic **Tambor Tropical,** tel. 683- 0011, fax 683-0013, e-mail: TamborT@aol.com, website www.lgfx.com/tambor; in the U.S,. Public Affairs Counsel, 867 Liberty St. NE, Salem, OR 97301, tel. (503) 363-7084, fax 371-2471, 100 meters west of Dos Lagartos, is a perfect place to laze in the shade of a swaying palm. Ten handcrafted, two-story hexagonal *cabinas* (one unit upstairs, one unit down) face the beach amid lush landscaped grounds with an exquisite amoeba-shaped swimming pool and jacuzzi. The rooms are graced by voluminous bathrooms with deep-well showers, wrap-around balconies, and fully equipped kitchens with captains' chairs. Everything is handmade of native hardwoods at an on-site workshop (no nails; it's all held together by dowels and joints). Windows are teak, walls are laurel and red oak, with floors and doors of exquisite purpleheart, all of it lacquered to a nautical shine. There's also a boutique, and a restaurant serving simple international cuisine. Fishing, snorkeling, horseback riding, and estuary boat trips are offered. Rates: $125 s/d lower, $150 upper, including breakfast. Overpriced!

The controversial **Hotel Playa Tambor,** tel. 661-1915, fax 661-2069; or Apdo. 458, San José 1150, tel. 220-2034, fax 231-1990; in the U.S., 150 S.E. Second Ave., Suite 806, Miami, FL 33131, tel. (800) 858-0606 or (305) 539-1167, fax 539-1160, was the first megaresort in the nation, a contentious test case that helped shape the future of oceanfront development in Costa Rica. The first phase opened in November 1992 after developers had raised the ire of environmentalists by violating protective laws. Sprawling across a 2,400-hectare site, the all-inclusive planned resort is somewhat similar to Club Med. It has 402 rooms in two three-story blocks, each with terrace or balcony, a/c, refrigerator, cable TV, self-dial phone, and deep bathtub (the resort may eventually contain 1,000 rooms). The grounds are ugly—they were once cattle pasture, which they still resemble—and the private gray-sand beach is unimpressive. The amenities do make some amends. An impressive 350-seat theater has a fully animated stage. Highlights include a massive swimming pool, three poolside restaurants, five bars, a disco, a small open-air gymnasium, a children's playground, a solarium, a large shopping complex, and extensive sports facilities. Nature trails lead into an adjacent reserve featuring a botanical park and a "zoo" with monkeys, squirrels, and tortoises. The resort has its own airstrip and a helicopter landing strip. It may be ideal for gregarious sorts who don't mind endless organized activities. You can buy a day-pass for $50 ($30 children). I was denied permission to enter in January 1998, so I can't say if it has improved. Package rates: $539 pp (double occupancy) for three nights, $969 single; $1,149 d seven nights, $2,069 s; extra night, $149 d, $259 s.

Much more appealing is the **Tango Mar,** Apdo. 2877, San José 1000, tel. 683-0001 or 289-9328, website www.tangomar.com; in the U.S., tel. (800) 648-1136, five km southwest of Tambor. This thoroughly romantic retreat—one of Costa Rica's finest resorts—whisks you 8,000 km to Hawaii, Tahiti, or Fiji. Imagine a beautiful beachfront setting—a long, lonesome strip of coral sand lined with tall palms and a sea as warm as bedtime milk. Add hectares of beautifully tended grounds splashed with bougainvillea and potted hibiscus in blazing yellow and red. Include five Polynesian-style thatched cabañas raised on stilts, tucked neatly amid lush foliage, and a dozen hotel rooms raised over the shore, with large balconies overlooking the sea. Two-, three-, and four-bedroom villas are also available. Free postprandial cigars are offered in the elegant oceanfront restaurant. Although the hotel boasts a large pool, a 10-hole golf course, and water sports, the order of the day is a healthy dose of inactivity poolside or on the stunning beaches, with tide pools nearby for warm-water soaks. The resort also rents 4WD vehicles. Rates: $70 s, $80 d, $90 t, $100 quad oceanfront room, $70-90 s, $80-160 d suites, $180-250 villas (up to four people), low season; $115 s, $125 d, $140 t, $150 quad oceanfront, $115-165 s, $125-175 d suites, $195-275 villas (up to four people), high season, including American breakfast.

Food
Restaurant Cristina proffers good food for those on a budget, as does the small restaurant in Hotel Dos Lagartos. Also check out the restaurant of the **Bahía Ballena Yacht Club,** one-half km southwest of town, where Louisiana's Chef Bob presents Mexican, Creole, and Cajun cuisine ($8 and up). **Pancho's Italian Restaurant** hangs over the water next door.

The Swiss-run **La Perla Tambor,** tel. 683-0152, serves dishes such as spaghetti bolognese and beef stroganoff ($4-8). For a *real* treat, head to **La Paillote Hotel y Restaurant,** tel. 683-0190, for exquisite dishes such as shrimp flambé in whiskey sauce ($13) tuna in pastry ($2.50), and calamari provençal ($5); reservations advised.

Tours and Activities
You can play a round of golf or tennis ($5) at **Tango Mar Golf Club.** Play is free for guests; others pay $25 greens fees per day for unlimited play. A panoply of tours is offered for guests and nonguests—to Tortuga and Curú ($70), sunset birdwatching ($35), sportfishing ($275 half-day up to four people, $500-795 full-day up to six people), and horseback riding to a jungle waterfall ($55). **Finca del Sol** also offers two- to three-hour horseback tours to waterfalls ($15) as well as riding lessons for beginners. Full-day tours go to Montezuma and Malpaís ($45).

The **Bahía Ballena Yacht Club,** at the southwestern end of the bay, has a floating dock with 30 moorings, plus water, gas, and diesel. It also offers scuba diving, windsurfing, sunset cruises, and a **sea-taxi** service, plus Hobie Cat rentals.

Tropic World Diving Station, tel. 661-1915, fax 661-2069, offers diving programs, including PADI certification, out of the Playa Tambor Beach Resort. And **Tropic World Scuba Diving,** tel./fax 683-0024, at Playa Pochote, offers dive trips.

Services
Souvenir Mariana, tel. 683-0043, at the beachfront in town, sells local handicrafts, as does **Tucán Boutique,** with beachwear. **Sol y Arena Travel,** tel. 683-0106, fax 683-0105, is a full-service travel agency next to Tucán. You can rent mountain bikes, buy Fuji film, and receive or send faxes at **Salsa,** a boutique next to Tucán. The Salon/Bar Los Gitanos has a **public telephone.**

Getting There and Away
For bus connections, see Paquera. **SANSA** and **Travelair** offer flights from San José (see appendixes). SANSA, tel. 683-0106, fax 683-0015, has an office by the beach (Mon.-Sat. 8 a.m.-5 p.m.).

Pacific Winds Express, tel. 777-0137, fax 777-1685, offers an express catamaran service—$50—daily between Tambor and Quepos. Call for a schedule.

For a **taxi,** call 683-0073 or 683-0064.

CÓBANO

Cóbano, a small village 25 km southwest of Paquera, is the gateway to Montezuma (five km), Cabo Blanco Absolute Nature Reserve (turn left—south—at the junction in the village center), and Malpaís (continue straight). The dirt road from Cóbano to Montezuma may be muddy, even in the dry season (many of the soils around here are impervious). You drop down a very steep switchback hill into Montezuma (when the road is wet it becomes treacherous; you'll need a 4WD in wet season for this section alone).

Accommodations and Food
The **Hotel y Restaurante Costeña,** tel. 642-0219, at the junction, has nine modest but well-kept rooms, four with private baths, five with shared. Rates: $8 pp with shared bath, $10 with private. **La Vida Natural** has two basic *cabinas* (one sleeps six) on a farm two km east of Cóbano. You can dine here on vegetarian meals or cook for yourself. Rate: $5 pp.

El Santuario de la Luz, tel./fax 642-0047, is an inter-faith religious retreat that offers dorm rooms for $33 including all meals.

Finca los Caballos, Apdo.22, Cóbano, tel./fax 642-0124, e-mail: naturelc@sol.racsa.co.cr, website www.centralamerica.com/cr/hotel/caballos.htm, on a 16-hectare ranch two km south of Cóbano, is the nicest place for miles. This aesthetic beauty (designed in Spanish *hacienda* style) has eight bungalows, simply furnished with sponge-washed ocher walls, orthopedic mattresses, fans, and private bathrooms with hot water, and surrounded by bougainvillea, dry forest, and orchards that attract birds and monkeys. Other than the birdsong, it is an utterly silent and calming spot with views across forested hills to the ocean. Barbara MacGregor, the lively and charming Canadian owner, plays soothing classical music befitting the uplifting setting. Barbara is a champion rider—"I carried my dream of having a dude ranch to Costa Rica"—who competes (and wins) in local rodeos and offers horseback tours, including moonlight trips ($10 per hour). The *finca* has a mosaiclined, fan-shaped horizon swimming pool and small wooden sundeck. The restaurant is open for nonguests (dinner by reservation only). Barbara is also a professionally trained chef whose daily specials might include pasta verde, chicken curry, or prawns with Thai curry ($6-12). Rates: $30 s, $40 d, $50 t low season; $40 s, $50 d, $60 t high-season, including taxes. *Highly recommended!*

Services

There's a **public telephone** at Soda Helena and a **Banco Nacional** in the center of town. The **gas station** is one km east of town.

Transportation

Buses to Montezuma depart Cóbano from outside the Hotel Costeña at 9 a.m. and 6 p.m., and for Paquera at 5:30 a.m. and 2 p.m.

MONTEZUMA

Montezuma is a charming beachside retreat popular with budget-minded travelers seeking an "offbeat" experience. It's favored by backpackers and the counterculture crowd and is blessed with budget accommodations. It also attracts its share of more elderly, monied, cultured folks to whom a vacation means lazing in T-shirts and throwing pretensions to the breeze. Montezuma is also well organized and cleaner than many of Costa Rica's beach villages—especially those popular with Ticos, the world's champion litter-louts, who seem to give Montezuma a wide berth.

Area residents have of late taken less kindly to campers, who had earned a reputation for parading nude on the beach, felling trees for firewood, and leaving garbage and a bitter aftertaste in their wake. Locals thus formed the **Cámara de Turismo en Montezuma** (CATUMA), to organize weekly beach cleanups, educate locals and

tourists on respecting their environment, temper development, and generally work to better the quality of life in the area.

The fantastic beaches east of Montezuma are backed by forest-festooned cliffs from which streams tumble down to the coral-white sands. There are rocks for tide pooling. And you can often see monkeys frolicking in the forests behind the beach. Strong currents are a problem; Playa Grande, about two km northeast of Montezuma, is reportedly the safest. Cool off in the waterfall and swimming hole two km southwest of town, on the road to Cabo Blanco (the trail leads upstream from the Restaurante La Cascada). A new wildlife reserve—**Reserva Absoluta Nicolas Weissenburg**—was created just before press time to protect the shoreline and forested hills to the east of Montezuma.

The town has a small tree-shaded plaza with a large children's playground. It can be noisy late into the night if you're staying in town. This being a laid-back place, business owners are prone to shut up shop on a whim—sometimes for days at a time, or longer. No posted hours. No apologies.

Accommodations

Camping: The community is trying to discourage camping wild on the beach, but you can camp for $3 pp at **Camping El Rincón de los Monos,** 400 meters northeast along the beach. It has showers, toilets, laundry, lockers, and sinks, plus ping-pong and darts, and rents tents, hammocks, boogie boards, etc. **El Pargo Feliz** charges $2 for camping, as does **Pensión Arenas,** west of Montezuma. Don't leave things unattended.

In Montezuma—Budget: The beachfront **Hotel Moctezuma,** tel. 642-0258, fax 642-0058, has 22 spacious and clean rooms with fans; seven have shared baths, 15 have private baths, with cold water. The annex across the road is less appealing. The main unit has a restaurant and bar directly over the beach. A bargain—if you can handle the noise from Chico's Bar. Rates: $8 s, $14 d with shared bath; $14 s, $20 d with private bath, including tax.

Cabinas Mar y Cielo, tel. 642-0036, alias Chico's, has six *cabinas* fronting the beach, all with fans and private baths, from $20 d. The **Capitán Hotel,** tel. 642- 0069, next door, has nine bare-bones rooms behind metal security gates in a rickety old wooden home with hammocks on the upstairs veranda. Three have private bathroom (cold water). Rates: $4 pp low season, $5 high season. It serves Western breakfasts, and its *casados* (fixed-price lunches) are recommended.

A rustic but pleasing option is **Cabinas Tucán,** tel. 642-0284, which has six fairly small cabins of polished hardwoods with fans, screens, and shared baths with cold water. It's raised on stilts: the shaded restaurant downstairs is a popular eatery. Rates: $12.50 s/d.

The **Hotel L'Aurora,** tel./fax 642-0051, is a pleasingly aged, whitewashed house surrounded by lush gardens and run by a German-Tico couple. The nine basic rooms have fans and

private baths with cold water. Upstairs is an airy lounge with bamboo and leather sofas, a small library, and hammocks. Rooms downstairs are dark. Rate: $15 s, $25 d low season, $20 s, $30 d high season, including tax.

The German-run **Cabinas El Pargo Feliz** has modern, clean *cabinas* with fans, queen-size beds, and hammocks on the verandas for $20 s/d. It has a rustic thatched restaurant. The **Montezuma Pacific,** tel. 642-0204, has 10 rooms with a/c, private baths, and hot water. The outside looks like a Bavarian home. Inside, rooms lack atmosphere but are clean and adequate and have small balconies. Rates: $15-25 low season, $25-38 high season.

beach at Montezuma

JOHN ANDERSON

Hotel Liz, tel. 642-0568, has eight simple rooms in an old wooden home with shared bath and cold water for $6 pp. It has a *soda* out front. **Pensión Arenas,** tel. 642-0308, next door, is another two-story wooden house with 15 rooms with shared bath and cold water for $4 pp low season, $6 high season.

The **Cabinas Gitza,** tel. 642-0056, has 12 modestly furnished but appealing rooms and *cabinas* on the slope 100 meters up the hill leading to Cóbano. Each has a fan and private bath with cold water. Rates: $30 d *cabinas,* $35 d hotel rooms upstairs. A swimming pool and restaurant were to be added. **Cabinas Linda Vista,** tel. 642-0274, atop the hill, has six modern brick *cabinas,* each for six people, with fans, kitchens, hammocks on the verandas, and cold water. It has views over the ocean. The owner lives in the house in front of the gate to the *cabinas.* It's a steep climb down and up from the beach. Rate: $15 pp.

Inexpensive: Restaurante El Sano Banano, tel./fax 642-0068, e-mail: elbanano@sol.racsa.co.cr, website www.cfn.org/-timbl/cr/elbanano.htm, has seven bungalows, three rooms, and a three-bedroom apartment behind the beach one km east of the village. All have fans and private baths. Very private—you feel as if you have the beach to yourself. Rates: $53 s/d rooms, $72-83 cabins, $100-160 apartment (up to eight people).

One of the nicest places is **Cabinas Jardín,** tel./fax 642-0074, which offers 10 hillside *cabinas* with fans, hammocks on the veranda, and private

baths with cold water. Each elegant *cabina* is individually styled in hardwoods and shaded by trees in landscaped grounds. Rate: $40 d, $50 oceanview. It also has three *casitas,* for $300 per week.

A newcomer is the three-story **Hotel El Tajalin** with 11 modestly decorated rooms with tile floors, fans and private bath with hot water. Some rooms are dark. There's a cafe on the third floor. Rates: $35 s/d, $40 t, $70 with a/c (up to four people).

West of Montezuma—Budget: Hotel Lucy, tel. 642-0273, has 10 basic rooms with fans, and shared bath with cold water in an old wooden house for $8 pp There's a shady restaurant, and a veranda faces the ocean. In 1993, Lucy's was targeted for razing by local officials eager to be seen enforcing environmental codes (like dozens of hotels along the coast, it's built within 50 meters of the high-tide mark); the community saved it by squaring off against the bulldozers.

Hotel La Cascada, tel./fax 642-0057, has 14 modestly furnished rooms with fans and private baths with cold water for $25 s/d downstairs (dark), $30 s/d upstairs (well-lit) with wraparound balcony. **Cabinas Las Manchas,** tel. 642-0415, nearby, has four attractive, simply furnished wooden cabins with lots of large windows, a kitchen, and private bath and hot water. There's a restaurant and a disco.

Cabinas Las Rocas, tel./fax 642-0393, four km west of Montezuma, has four simply furnished, cross-ventilated rooms with fans and shared bath upstairs in an old wooden home amid large boulders ($20 d). A wide balcony has hammocks and deep sofas. Gisella, the Italian owner, cooks meals ($9 pp) in the small restaurant. She also has a two-story, two-bedroom octagonal cabin with shared kitchen ($30 small downstairs room, $40 upstairs, $50 both).

Inexpensive: One of the more atmospheric places is **Hotel Los Mangos,** tel. 642-0076 or 642-0259, fax 642-0050 or 642-0047, with 10 rooms and 10 thatched *cabinas* made of attractive hardwoods. The small but delightful octagonal bungalows under shade trees have all-around windows, wide porches, both single and double beds, and oodles of hot water. They're set on a marvelously landscaped slope complete with a three-tier waterfall. There's a swimming pool, thatched bar and dining pavilion, and horses for forays into the forest. Greek owner Constantinas Jzavaras runs a great operation. Rates: $20-45 d in older rooms with shared baths, $60 d/t in larger rooms with private baths.

Richard and Ori Stocker will welcome you like family at the **Hotel Amor de Mar,** tel./fax 642-0262, which enjoys a fabulous location on a sheltered headland, with a private tide pool and views along the coast in both directions. The hotel is set in very pleasant landscaped lawns, one km west of Montezuma, with hammocks beneath shady palms. They have 11 rooms (all but two have private baths, some with hot water), all unique but each well-lit, made entirely of hardwoods, and opening onto a large veranda. An abundance of potted plants and beautiful tropical flowers enhance the relaxing atmosphere. Richard and Ori have three boys, and families are welcome here. Richard also asked me to mention the delicious homemade bread. Rates: $30-60 d.

Food
Café Montezuma is a good breakfast spot selling crepes, bagels, omelettes, etc.

Many of the hotels have restaurants. Among the best are Hotel Moctezuma and Cabinas Tucán, for *típico* fare. **El Sano Banano,** tel. 642-0272, is a very popular natural-food restaurant serving garlic breads, pastas, yogurts, a superb vegetarian curry ($6), and ice cream. It also sells filtered water and will prepare lunches to go. It offers a special of the day. You can get tasty pastas and filling *casados* at **Soda Las Gemelas.**

El Chiringuito Restaurant, nearby, has reasonably priced lobster ($12) and fish dishes (about $4). **Restaurant El Parque** is set on the village beach. **Restaurante El Jardín** offers pastas, seafoods, and steaks ($4-10). I enjoyed a paella at **El Chiringuito Trópical,** open 11 a.m.-11 p.m.

West of Montezuma, the **Marisquería La Cascada** offers a streamside setting. **Café La Luna,** nearby, has good breakfasts. The restaurant of the Hotel Amor de Mar is a good bet for breakfasts and lunches (the homemade bread is delicious). And **Bar/Restaurante Las Manchas,** tel. 642-0415, has dining on shady pavilions; seafoods and *casados* cost $4-10. And you owe it to yourself to dine at **Finca los Caballos,** three km north of town (see Cóbano).

Shacks on the beach sell lemonade and *pipas,* freshly opened coconuts.

Entertainment
El Sano Banano shows movies nightly at 7:30 p.m. (free with dinner, or $2.50 minimum order). **Chico's** is a lively place to sup. **Las Machas,** west of town, has a disco and live bands.

Shopping
El Hamaquero offers a good selection of beachwear and batiks. You can shop for a tattoo next door at **Tattoo,** selling permanent souvenirs. Cabinas El Jardín has an upscale boutique and craft store.

Tours and Activities
Robert at **Sacred Ceiba Tours,** tel./fax 642-0047; in Canada, fax 604-871-3365, in El Sano Banano, has horseback rides to nearby waterfalls ($25) and to Playa Hermosa ($45, including transport and dinner). He also rents kayaks and bicycles and offers a birding walk, a tour to Isla Tortuga, plus transport to Cabo Blanco ($5 roundtrip; guides are $20 pp, including car). Claude Gallisian and Emmanuelle Baudenon lead horseback trips at **Finca del Sol** (see Tambor) and offer sailing trips to Isla Tortuga and Curú ($50, including meals) and as far afield as Golfito ($250 for four days) aboard their 23-foot *Marara*. **Ivan's Boat Tours** offers sportfishing plus snorkeling ($35) and trips to Curú ($15). **Aventuras en Montezuma,** tel./fax 642-0050, also has tours to Isla Tortuga ($35) and farther afield and offers horseback rides and

diving. You can also take horseback rides at **Finca los Caballos,** three km north of Montezuma (see Cóbano).

Roger Nuñoz rents horses and offers guided horseback trips to the waterfalls ($20, four hours); ask for him at the Hotel Amor de Mar.

Information
Robert at **Sacred Ceiba Tours** is the best information source. **Librería Topsy** sells maps, guidebooks, and newspapers and has a lending library (Mon.-Fri. 8 a.m.-5 p.m., Saturday 8 a.m.-noon).

Services
Laundry Arco Balenos, next to Café Montezuma, charges $2.50 per kilo (open Mon.-Sat. 8:30 am.-1:30 p.m. and 3-8 p.m.). The Cabinas Jardín office doubles as a **tourist information** office, rents motorcycles ($70 per day) and bicycles ($12 per day), and also represents **Monte Aventuras,** whose tours include kayaking to Cabuya and Río Lajas ($41), speedboat tours to Jacó and Playa Sámara ($26-35 pp), and guided tours to Cabo Blanco ($15).

The **Casa del Mundo,** next to Cabinas Jardín, is a boutique selling hammocks, Guatemalan items, and T-shirts. **Tienda Chico** also sells Guatemalan clothes, sandals, etc., and has a public telephone (tel. 661-2472).

Getting There and Away
A bus for Cóbano and Montezuma ($4) meets the Paquera ferry (take the early ferry if possible, to avoid arriving in Montezuma after dark). Buses to Montezuma depart Cóbano from outside the Hotel Costena at 9 a.m. and 2 and 6 p.m. In wet season, you may need to take a jeep-taxi beyond Cóbano (about $5). The return bus departs Montezuma (dry season) or Cóbano (wet season) at 5:30, 8:15 and 10 a.m. and 2 and 3:45 p.m.

You can hire **water-taxis** in Puntarenas, Quepos, and other points along the central Pacific, as well as at Playas Sámara and Nosara. Check with the information booth opposite the Hotel Moctezuma.

Pacific Winds Express offers an express catamaran service daily between Montezuma, Tambor, and Quepos.

Aventuras en Montezuma is the local representative of Travelair.

Getting Around
Aventuras en Montezuma rents tandems ($20 per day) and small motorcycles ($40 per day).

CABUYA

Cabuya is a tiny hamlet nine km southwest of Montezuma and two km northeast of Cabo Blanco reserve. After years of isolation, Cabuya has been awaked by the traffic to the nature reserve and the spillover from Montezuma. A very rough rock-and-dirt track leads north to Malpaís (seven km; 4WD essential—and even with 4WD passable only in dry season), climbing tenuously over the mountainous cape that forms Cabo Blanco; turn right at Mini-Super Cabuya, where the road to the left leads to the rocky shore. **Isla Cabuya,** about 200 meters offshore, has been used as a cemetery for the village of Cabuya. You can walk out to the island at low tide and see perhaps two dozen graves marked with crude crosses.

Accommodations and Food
Cabinas/Soda Cabo Blanco has small, dingy rooms on the beachfront one km east of Cabuya for about $10. Next door is the nicer **Hotel Cabo Blanco,** tel. 642-0332; in the U.S., tel. (800) 721-4141, with nine rooms with cable TV and orthopedic beds for $25 d with fan, $30 with a/c. You can rent kayaks. Nearby, **Hotel Celaje,** tel./fax 642-0374, has seven simple yet attractive thatched beachfront four-person *cabinas* with private baths and patios with hammocks. It has a nice pool with jacuzzi as well as a tempting *ranchito* restaurant (day-guests can use the pool if they eat). It offers kayak rentals and horseback and sportfishing rides. Rate: $40 d, $50 t, $60 quad.

In Cabuya, **Mini-Super Cabuya,** tel. 642-0350, has four cabins with fans and shared bath with cold water for $4 pp. **Cabinas El Yugo,** tel./fax 642-0303, by the shore, has five cross-ventilated, ocean-facing A-frame hardwood cabins with fans, kitchenettes, loft-bedrooms, and private baths with cold water. Rate: $20 up to four people. **Cabinas David,** next door, is similar (it was for sale in January 1998).

Restaurante y Cabinas El Ancla de Oro, tel. 642-0369, has **camping,** plus three delightful thatched hardwood A-framed cabins on tall stilts (one sleeps five). Mosquito nets are provided. Rate: $4 pp for rooms, $20 d *cabinas*. The restaurant serves tasty treats such as fish curry with coconut milk ($5.50), shrimp curry ($8), and garlic herb bread.

The Villalobosos rent rooms in their house ($6) and have a self-contained thatched *cabina* with kitchen, available by the week or month. You can also rent rooms with Doña Lila, whose thatched house is the last on the left before the park entrance ($10, including meals).

Restaurant El Delfin de la Luna, opposite the Mini-Super, has filling *casados* for $3. **Café Limón Dulce** is a simple cafe and *soda* 400 meters east of the entrance to Cabo Blanco reserve.

Services
There's a **public telephone** and fax in **Mini-Super Cabuya,** which has a large open-air *soda*. You can rent horses from Lolo, who acts as guide. Manolo or Pipo will be happy to take you fishing or even on a boat tour to Isla Tortuga. Alex Villaloboso and his English wife, Fiona (owners of the El Ancla hotel), also rent horses ($20), mountain bikes ($10), and boats.

Getting There and Away
A bus ($1 each way) departs Montezuma for Cabuya at 5:30 and 10 a.m. and 2:30 and 6:30 p.m., returning at 4:45 and 9 a.m. and 1 and 5 p.m. A **jeep-taxi** from Montezuma costs about $25 roundtrip. Many people walk from Montezuma (11 km)—a hot and tiring walk. Hitchhiking is easy. A bridge was being built at press time across the river (previously a tricky fording was required) about one km east of Cabuya.

RESERVA NATURAL ABSOLUTA CABO BLANCO

This jewel of nature at the very tip of the Nicoya Peninsula is where Costa Rica's quest to bank its natural resources for the future began. The 1,172-hectare Cabo Blanco Absolute Wildlife Reserve—the oldest protected area in the country—was created in October 1963 thanks to the tireless efforts of Nils Olof Wessberg, a Swedish immigrant commonly referred to as the father of Costa Rica's national park system (for a discussion of Wessberg's influence, see David

Rains Wallace's excellent book *The Quetzal and the Macaw: The Story of Costa Rica's National Parks*). Olof and his wife, Karen, settled in the area in 1955, when this corner of the Nicoya Peninsula was still covered with a mix of evergreen and deciduous forest—an island in a sea of rapidly falling trees, rising settlements, and cattle ranches. They bought a rocky, mountainous plot of land and spent 10 years developing fruit orchards.

In 1960, when the first patch of cleared land appeared at Cabo Blanco, Olof launched an appeal to save the land. "Only in one spot is there today some of the wildlife that was formerly everywhere in the northwest," Olof wrote. "Here live the puma and the *manigordo* (ocelot), deer, peccary, tepiscuintle, pizote, kinkajou, chulumuco (tayra), kongo (howler monkey), carablanca (capuchin monkey), and miriki (spider monkey). The jaguar and tapir are already extinct. . . . When we settled here six years ago the mountain was always green. Today it has great brown patches, and in March and April it is shrouded in smoke, much of it on fire. . . . Two years more, and the mountain will be dead. Who is going to save it? It can be had at the ridiculously low price of $10 an acre. . . . But it has to be done immediately."

Although several international organizations responded with money, buying the land and protecting the area cost blood, sweat, and tears. Conservation had not yet entered national consciousness. The first warden killed the last 10 spider monkeys for their fat; the third warden felled trees to grow crops. When one of Olof's supporters suggested the need for a national parks service to the Costa Rican government, they responded enthusiastically. "So then," writes Wallace, "they found two students in San José to be the national parks service, one of them 27 years old and one 24. That was Mario Boza and Alvaro Ugalde." Ugalde has been parks service director for most of the past two decades; Boza (who has been denounced as a turncoat for later becoming a developer) is famous for his beautifully written and illustrated book, *The National Parks of Costa Rica*.

Olof Wessberg was murdered in the Osa Peninsula in the summer of 1975 while campaigning to have the region declared a national park. A plaque near the Cabo Blanco ranger station stands in his honor.

The reserve is named after the vertical-walled island at its tip, which owes its name to the accumulation of guano deposited by seabirds, including Costa Rica's largest community of brown boobies (some 500 breeding pairs). Many of the wildlife species that Wessberg gave his life to protect—not least the howler, spider, and capuchin monkeys, tiger cats, agoutis, white-tailed deer, and plentiful snakes—can still be seen. The reserve was originally off-limits to visitors. Today, about one-third is accessible along hiking trails, some steep in parts. **Sendero Sueco** leads uphill and then down onto the totally unspoiled white-sand beaches of Playa Balsita and Playa Cabo Blanco, which are separated by a headland (you can walk around it at low tide). A **coastal trail,** Sendero El Barco, leads west from Playa Balsitas to the western boundary of the park. All have tide pools. Check tide tables with the park rangers before setting off—otherwise you could get stuck. Torrential downpours are common April-December. You cannot take horses in.

A substantial increase in visitation in recent years has spawned efforts to manage the influx and minimize the impact. Certain restrictions may be in effect by the time you read this.

Services
The ranger station, tel./fax 642-0093, sells a trail map and T-shirts. Hours: 8 a.m.-4 p.m. Closed Monday and Tuesday. Entrance: $6. Camping is not allowed, even at the ranger station. There's a parking lot; you walk to the information booth and ranger station.

Getting There and Away
The dirt road deteriorates markedly just before Cabo Blanco and gets very muddy in the wet season. **Aventuras en Montezuma** offers transfers to Cabo Blanco daily at 8 a.m. and 3 p.m. ($6 roundtrip) by reservation. Book early! Collective taxis depart Montezuma for Cabo at 7 and 9 a.m., returning at 3 and 4 p.m. ($5 pp).

MALPAÍS AND PLAYA SANTA TERESA

The shoreline immediately northwest of Cabo Blanco is a lively surfers' paradise in the midst of a tourism boom. Real estate prices are rocketing

as hoteliers move in. (It's easy to understand why local farmers and fisherfolk are selling their land—I was asked if I wanted to buy a plot—for $150,000.) The road from Cóbano hits the shore at the hamlet of **Carmen,** 10 km west of Cóbano. The tiny fishing hamlet of Malpaís is two km south, at the end of the road on the northern border of Cabo Blanco Absolute Wildlife Reserve (at press time, entry to the park was *not* allowed via Malpaís). The beach at the south end of Malpaís is pebbly with rocky outcrops good for tide pooling and has good point breaks for surfers. (The rocky track to and from Cabuya terminates in Malpaís.)

North from Carmen, the dirt road leads alongside Playa Santa Teresa, a seemingly endless beach with coral-colored sand, pumping surf (plenty of beach breaks), and dramatic rocky islets offshore. The community of Santa Teresa straggles along the road but is centered on a soccer field about two km north of Carmen. The road continues to Manzanillo, where the going gets tougher.

Accommodations
The following are in order as they appear south then north of Carmen.

You can camp for free under palms by the **Mambo Café** at Carmen. The cafe charges 50 cents to use toilets and showers. **Frank's Place,** tel. 640-0096, at the road junction, has 12 cabins with private baths for $20, $40 with hot water and kitchen, $45 with a lounge (up to five people).

Malpaís Surf Camp and Resort, tel./fax 642-0047, 200 meters south of the junction, has a panoply of accommodations set in eight hectares of grounds. You can camp for $5 pp, with showers and toilets. A hillside *rancho* has "semi-private" camp beds beneath a tin roof with walls of palm leaves on three sides (the fourth is open to the ocean); $10 pp. There are also *cabinas* for $20 s/d with shared bath with cold water, and stone *casitas* with stone floors, tall louvered screened windows, and beautiful tile bathrooms with hot water for $65 (up to six people). There's an amoeba-shaped swimming pool, and you can rent mountain bikes ($10 per day), horses ($15 per hour), and surfboards ($5 half-day, $10 full-day). A lively bar shows surf videos and has the music cranked up; there's ping-pong, table soccer, and a pool table. It serves American breakfasts (from $3).

Los Carococlos, tel. 640-0016, is a house for rent one km farther south. **Hotel Lauramar,** cellular tel. 382-8876, has 10 basic cross-ventilated *cabinas* with fans and private baths with cold water for $15 low season, $25 high season (up to five people). A little farther is **Cabinas Bosque Mar,** tel. 226-0475, with six modest cabins with private baths and cold water. **Cabinas Marazul,** farther south, is set in its own little cove. It has 10 simple *cabinas* with fans and private baths with cold water ($20 s, $25 d). It permits camping under shade trees for $1.75 pp, including outside showers and toilet. There's a small restaurant with a large menu, plus sea kayaks for rent.

Sunset Reef, Apdo. 100-5361, Cóbano, tel./fax 642-0012, e-mail: sunreef@sol.racsa.co.cr, is built on a rocky headland at the end of the road. It's marvelously reclusive. The 14 spacious, modestly furnished, all-hardwood rooms in a two-story block have two double beds, fans, wide windows, and sky-lit bathrooms. The simple restaurant has an equally simple menu. An exquisite little freeform swimming pool and jacuzzi sit on the cliff face amid beautifully landscaped grounds. Also available are boat tours and diving, plus bicycle and kayak rentals for $10 per day. Rates: $52 s, $65 d low season, $60 s, $75 d high season.

The most appealing place for miles is the **Star Mountain Eco-Resort,** tel./fax 642- 0024, e-mail: info@starmountain.eco.com; in the U.S., tel. (305) 595-0866, fax 595-9732, two km northeast of Malpaís, on the track to Cabuya. This gem is tucked in the hills amid an 80-hectare private forest reserve, with trails. The four charming *cabinas* are simple yet tastefully decorated with soft pastels and hardwood accents, crossventilated with louvered windows, with Sarchí rockers on the veranda ($45 s, $65 d, $10 extra person). A casita bunkhouse sleeps up to nine people ($25 pp). Hammocks are slung between trees, and there's an amoeba-shaped swimming pool. The restaurant is exquisite.

North of Carmen, the delightful **Trópico Látina Lodge,** tel./fax 640- 0062, e-mail: tropico@centralamerica.com, website www.centralamerica.com/cr/hotels/tropico.htm, backs a rocky foreshore with hammocks under shade trees. There's an amoeba-shaped pool and jacuzzi, and a breezy bar and restaurant by the shore. It has six high-ceilinged wooden bungalows amid lawns; each has charcoal tile floors, wide shady verandas with hammocks, a king-size bed and a sofa bed, mosquito nets, fans, and a private bath with hot water. The charming hosts, an English-Tica couple, arrange fishing, horseback rides, and tours. Rates: $60 s/d including tax.

Camping y Cabinas Zenedia is tucked amid shade trees (with hammocks) beside the beach one km north of Trópico Látina. It charges $2.50 pp for camping, including toilets and showers. It also has two A-frame cabins with loft bedrooms and toilets and kitchenettes below, plus a thatched Robinson Crusoe-type cabin ($5 pp). The owners will cook meals ($2.50 breakfast, $3 dinner).

A stone's throw north, Ingo offers eight rooms at **Cabinas Playa Santa Teresa,** built around a massive strangler fig favored by howler monkeys. Two have kitchens; all have two double beds and private baths with cold water. Rates: $15 s/d, $20 t, $25 quad.

Farther north, Jorge Soto has **Cabinas Capitán,** with solidly constructed all-wood cabins with louvered windows for $600 monthly. Nobody was there when I called by, but daily and weekly rentals are offered. He has seakayaks, too. Nearby, Marlena and José Luis Mora have a cabin with kitchen and bathroom for $20 d ($300 monthly).

I missed the **Casa Cecilia,** in Canada, tel. (418) 775-2898, fax 775-9793, run by French-Canadians, with five rooms with private bathrooms and ocean views.

Food

Break Point, opposite Trópico Látina Lodge, sells pastas and pizzas ($3- 8) and *batidos* and natural juices. **Mambo Café** has fresh-baked cinnamon buns, banana bread, breads, and cookies, plus ice-cream. It also sells fruit juices and has an "American" breakfast for $3.50. **Frank's Place** serves *típico* dishes.

Dulce Magía is a simple Italian restaurant 1.5 km south of Carmen; it sells seafoods and pizzas. *Do* check out the marvelous **Star Mountain Bar and Grill,** at Star Mountain Eco-Resort. Grilled meats and fish are prepared in a huge open oven and served at polished log tables in an exquisite open-sided restaurant with sponge-washed ocher walls.

You can buy fresh seafood from local fishermen or even hire a local *panga* to go out and catch your own.

Services
You can buy camping stoves and **gasoline** at a *pulpería* 0.5 km north of the soccer field. The **public telephone,** tel. 640-0026, is at **Pulpería**

El Mango facing the soccer field.

The owner of Cabinas Marazul has a taxi service ($25 to Montezuma, $38 to Paquera), plus a boat for rent.

Getting There
There's a daily bus service between Cóbano and Malpaís.

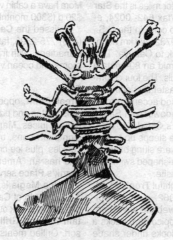

pre-Columbian gold lobster

BOB RACE

CATHY CARLSON

CENTRAL PACIFIC

The central Pacific region—defined as Carara to Punta Mala—is a distinct geographical region, a thin, virtually ruler-straight coastal plain narrowing to the southeast and backed by steep-sided mountains. The coast is lined by long gray-sand beaches renowned for killer surf (i.e., waves surfers love to ride but extremely dangerous swimming conditions for everyone else). Most famous of these is Jacó, once a favorite of Canadian package charter groups, but also famous in surf lore for its offbeat (and limited) appeal.

A string of fabulous, miles-long beaches marches south from Jacó, separated from one another by headlands and mangrove swamps where rivers come down to the coast. Despite their beauty, several beaches remain untrammeled by footprints; on others, surfers have begun to arrive in force. Playa Hermosa (known to locals as "Boom Boom Beach") is the site of an annual international surfing contest. Esterillos Oeste and Esterillos Este are equally popular. Farther south, vast groves of African palms smother the coastal plains.

The best-known—and most beautiful—beaches are the white-sand beaches of Manuel Antonio National Park, just south of the sportfishing town of Quepos. The clear water here makes it a favorite among snorkelers, while bordering the beach is a lush tropical forest home to abundant wildlife. Understandably, Manuel Antonio is beloved of tourists and has dozens of accommodations choices. Carara Biological Reserve and numerous private nature reserves, too, offer a feast of wildlife wonders.

Many such reserves are in the mountains, where there are haciendas-turned-hotels to enjoy, particularly at Escaleras and the southern central Pacific, where Finca Brian y Milena and its neighbor, Bella Vista Lodge, exemplify the best in rustic mountain retreats. And any journey is worth the drive to stay at the finest hotel in the country: Villa Caletas, just south of Carara.

The months of Dec.-April anywhere along the central Pacific coast are particularly busy, when Costa Ricans take their "summer" holidays (the long school break is January and February) and flock to the beaches. Reservations are recom-

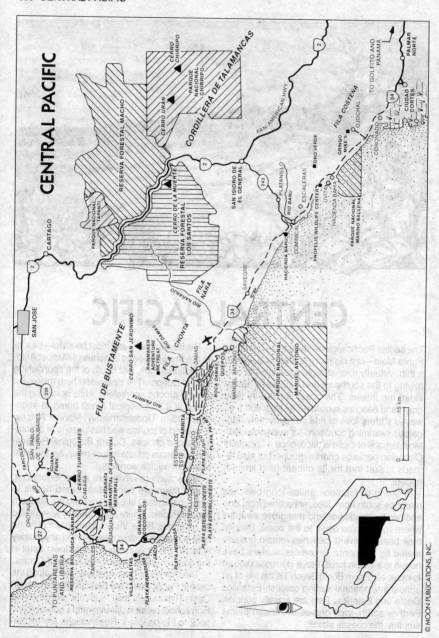

CENTRAL PACIFIC

© MOON PUBLICATIONS, INC.

mended in Manuel Antonio, especially for Christmas, New Year's, and Easter. Consider visiting in the green season (May-Nov.), when many hotels entice with discounts.

A single coast road—Hwy. 34—runs the length of the coast, opening up access to the once hidden beaches and swamps south of Uvita, linking the region with Golfo Dulce and Osa, and linking the Pan-Am Highway (Hwy. 1) that joins San José with Guanacaste and Nicaragua with the Pan-Am Highway (Hwy. 2) that connects San José with the Valle de El General and Panamá. Highway 34 north of Uvita is horribly potholed and so thick with dust in dry season that you need your headlights on. Violence flared in 1993, when local residents barricaded the road to protest its rotten condition. Consequently, a section was paved, and, with luck, the rest will have been by the time you read this. Swimmers should beware of dangerous riptides.

Climate
Carara marks the boundary between the tropical dry zone farther north and the tropical wet to the south. The region grows gradually wetter to the south and has distinct wet and dry seasons: May-Nov. and Dec.-April, respectively. Temperatures average about 30° C (86° F) in dry season, slightly lower in wet season.

NORTHERN CENTRAL PACIFIC

From the central highlands, Hwy. 3 descends from Atenas to Orotina, at the foot of the mountains and the gateway to the central Pacific. The road drops steeply, with hairpin bends, washed-out sections of road, slow-moving trucks holding everyone up, and Costa Ricans overtaking like suicidal maniacs. It's single-lane in each direction. *Drive cautiously!*

You can also take a more southerly, less-trafficked route west from San José through the valley of the Río Turrubares via Santa Ana, Ciudad Colón, and Santiago de Puriscal. The paved road (deteriorated in parts) sidles magnificently downhill to Orotina, where it joins Hwy. 3. (I've driven this route only as far as San Pablo.) A new road linking Santiago de Puriscal with Parrita (just 30 km north of Manuel Antonio) was incomplete at press time.

OROTINA AND VICINITY

Orotina enjoys a strategic location as a transportation hub. The town is hidden 400 meters northwest of Hwy. 3, which six km west of town merges with Hwy. 27 (for Puntarenas) and Hwy. 34 for Jacó and Manuel Antonio. The town is centered on an attractive plaza shaded by palms and has a railway track running down the main street. It has been totally bypassed by tourism, although you can buy traditional ceramic pots and vases from roadside stalls on Hwy. 3 and even visit the workshops of the **Sitapio Handicraft Association** to learn something of the art of pre-Columbian pottery making.

Highway 34 is in good condition as far as Carara, beyond which the paved road is riddled with some of the worst potholes in the country. *Drive slowly.* The holes are big enough to bend a rim.

Iguana Park
This innovative conservation project, on a 285-hectare farm, Apdo. 692, San José 1007, tel. 240-6712, fax 235-2007, on the banks of the Río Turrubares, 14 km southeast of Orotina, is the brainchild of a German-born biologist named Dagmar "Iguana Mama" Werner, who created the **Pro Green Iguana Foundation** in 1985 to research and promote the raising of iguanas by small farmers. Once abundant, the iguana is endangered throughout much of its former range because of deforestation. Dagmar's project—a "pasture in the trees"—is aimed at helping to reverse deforestation and protect the iguana population by raising the dragonlike reptilian livestock for the dining table. The leaf-eating lizard, which can reach two meters in length, has long been considered a tasty treat among Central Americans, who refer to the reptile as tree chicken (an early conquistador declared it "a most remarkable and wholesome food"—indeed, it turns out, since it contains 80% less fat and cholesterol than chicken). If Costa Rica plants more trees—or

As part of an iguana conservation effort, Iguana Park raises the reptiles for food.

preserves what primary forest remains—iguanas will increase, and farmers will have a steady diet of iguana meat. Remarkably, the lizards yield more than 10 times the amount of meat per hectare as cattle. Iguana Mama's farm is home to thousands of iguanas kept in large pens. Already, more than 160,000 have been released to the wild, where only one in 42 eggs they lay survive (the farm successfully incubates 95% of eggs laid in captivity). An airy, rancho-style dining room serves iguana ribs, tail, and breast, and, eventually, iguana sausages and smoked ham. Also planned is a shop where you can buy iguana paraphernalia, including dandy iguana leather shoes. The Iguanosaurus trail leads through the forest. Entrance: $13 adults, $9 children low season; $15 adults, $12 children high season.

A scarlet macaw breeding center has also been initiated in Iguana Park.

Canopy Tour: An intriguing way to get eye-to-eye with the harmless dragons is on a "Canopy Tour," offered daily at 8:15 a.m., 10:30 a.m., and 1:45 p.m. ($69, including transportation from San José). It's a 40-minute hike from the visitor's center. You'll ascend to the treetops and traverse from platform to platform using pulleys on horizontal cables; an expert guide will be there with you to demonstrate the art of "gliding" by harness. Special dawn and dusk departures are offered on request. See **The Original Canopy Tour,** Apdo. 751-2350, San Francisco de Dos Ríos, tel. 257-5149, fax 256-7626, e-mail: canopy@sol.racsa.co.cr.

Accommodations

Palenque Machucha, on Hwy. 3, has *cabinas* and a pleasant riverside restaurant under thatch. Also north of town is the simple **Hotel Yadi.**

In town, **Cabinas Kalin,** tel. 428-8082, one block north and one west of the plaza, is well-run and has a swimming pool and garden.

An upscale option is **Rancho Oropendola,** Apdo. 159, Orotina, tel./fax 428-8600, set in four acres of tropical gardens just outside picturesque San Mateo, on Hwy. 3, a couple of miles north of Orotina. Rustic yet pleasingly decorated cabins have private baths, and a choice of king, queen, or two double beds. Rooms in the main house share a bath; they have a double bed. Choose, too, from either a junior or grand suite. Ranch highlights include a 12-meter swimming pool with sundeck plus a game room, video movies at night, and meals on a dining veranda. Trails wind through the gardens and forest. Rates: $30 rooms; $50 cabins; $60-70 suite, including breakfast.

At Orotina, Hwy. 3 is replete with roadside restaurants and *sodas.* The local seasonal specialty is *toronjas rellenas* (candied grapefruit stuffed with white milk fudge).

WEST OF OROTINA

West of Orotina, the land slopes gently toward the Gulf of Nicoya. Highway 27 leads through savanna land munched by hardy cattle and hits the coast at Mata de Limón, facing the Bahía de Caldera. The bay is shadowed by **Punta Corralillo,** a headland south of which mangrove swamps stretch along the shoreline for 20 km to the mouth of the Río Tárcoles. The coastal flatlands shelter prolific birds and wildlife.

Tivives has a pleasant and peaceful four-km-wide beach backed by 670 hectares of mangrove swamps at the mouth of the Río Jesús María. Crocodiles—toothy and fast—cool off in the mangroves, which here grow to a height of 35 meters. Good birding, too. Howler and white-faced monkeys live here. And jaguarundis and ocelots have even been sighted on the beach. You can reach the northern side of the estuary via a rough, eight-km-long dirt road from Hwy. 27, three km east of Caldera. You can reach the south side from Hwy. 27 from just west of the junction with Hwy. 34.

Two km south of Tivives is **Playa Guacalillo,** site of Proyecto Vacacional Bajamar, centered on the hamlet of Bajamar. The unremarkable gray-sand beach is backed by a lagoon full of wading birds. The beach is most easily reached by a turnoff at **Lagunillas,** on Hwy. 34, five km *south* of Hwy. 27. Here, **Skyline de Costa Rica,** tel. 380-1199, fax 235-3969, offers flights over the mangroves and coast by ultralight plane.

Accommodations and Food

There's just one restaurant/bar but no *cabinas* or hotels in Tivives. It's possible to camp at the southern end of the beach (no facilities).

Hotel Marazul, tel./fax 221-8070, is a resort about 800 meters inland from Playa Guacalillo. It has 10 hotel rooms, plus 10 spacious self-catering units with lots of light (*cabinas* each sleep up to six people). Centerpiece is an Olympic-size pool and a large sundeck fronting a restaurant under thatch set in landscaped grounds. You can rent bikes and horses, or get a game going on the soccer field or tennis and volleyball courts. Rates: $40 d for rooms; $55 for self-catering units.

Hacienda Doña Marta Lodge, Apdo. 23, Santa Bárbara de Heredia 3009, tel. 253-6514, fax 269-9555, in Cascajal de Orotina 16 km west of Orotina, is a charming Arizona-style hacienda on hundreds of acres of cattle pasture. No landscaping here; the hacienda has been very much a working farm with prized Brahmas since the 1930s. The cattle sheds and corral are adjacent to the bedrooms. The six romantic rooms are

as warm as a grandfatherly hug. Highlights include bamboo ceilings and tiled floors, large showers, and lots of rustic, country-style adornments. Two rooms have trompe l'oeil walls, and old hacienda wrought-iron gates and cartwheels as bedsteads. Some rooms have semi-canopied beds. There's a small pool. Horseback riding is offered. It's run by the same folks who operate Finca Rosa Blanca. *Great bargain!* Rates: $50 s, $60 d or $160 d including all meals, farm tour, and horseback riding.

A stone's throw away is **Dundee Ranch,** Apdo. 7812-1000, San José, tel. 428-8776 or 267-7371, fax 428-8096 or 267-7050, e-mail: ticocr@sol.racsa.co.cr, another working mango plantation and cattle *finca* with its own private nature reserve in the Río Machuca canyon. The 11 very appealing red-tiled rooms have fans, TVs, and two double beds, plus tiled bathrooms with showers. A beautiful kidney-shaped pool has a small cascade. A plank walkway leads out into a lake with a viewing platform and a breezy bar from where you can spot the resident crocodile. An elegant screened restaurant with lots of fans and an open grill offers a wide menu. The grounds have lots of old trees festooned with epiphytes. Ana Astorga, the delightful English-speaking manager, is extremely accommodating. Horseback rides are offered, as well as tours through the farm in a canopied "cart" towed by a tractor. *Highly recommended!* Dundee Ranch is well signposted along the highway between Orotina and Puntarenas. Rates: $53 s/d midweek; $63 weekend.

At press time, the $175 million **La Roca Beach Club and Country Resort,** Apdo 10950-1000 San José, tel. 289-4313, fax 289-4247, e-mail: laroca@sol.racsa.co.cr, was under construction on 150 hectares atop the Punta Corralillo headland south of Mata. When complete, the development will have 1,000 condominium apartments, a luxury hotel, a theme Spanish-colonial village complex that includes a four hectare center of shops and restaurants, plus a championship 27-hole golf course and 24 tennis courts, volleyball, basketball and racquetball courts, two swimming pools, a soccer field, and an equestrian center. The course will have nearly a dozen lakes plus signature holes overlooking the ocean. Owners will lease their condo apartments to vacationers.

TÁRCOLES

Twenty-five km south of Orotina, Hwy. 34 crosses the **Río Tárcoles.** The bridge over the river is the easiest place in the country for spotting crocodiles, which bask on the mudbanks below the bridge (don't lean over too far). Crocodiles gather in even greater numbers on the mudbanks of the rivermouth, five km west, where the village of Tárcoles—a down-at-the-heels fishing village strung along a pebbly beach—is deriving new income offering croc-spotting trips (on my last visit, I saw 15 crocs from the riverbank). The estuary is also fantastic for birding: more than 400 species have been identified here. Gulls, terns, and herons congregate on the sandbars. Frigate birds wheel overhead, while cormorants and kingfishers fish in the lagoons. Roseate spoonbills add a splash of color. And scarlet macaws fly overhead on their way to and from roosts in the mangroves that extend 15 km northward.

The turnoff for Tárcoles is three km south of the bridge. The terribly potholed dirt road leads north about two km to a Y-fork. Go right for the river and safari departure point; go left for the beach, which is knee-deep in garbage.

La Catarata
(Manantial de Agua Viva) Waterfall

At the turnoff for Tárcoles from Hwy. 34, another dirt road leads east, climbing steeply to the Manantial de Agua Viva Waterfall. It's not Yosemite, but it's a beaut nonetheless. French-Canadian Daniel Bedard has cut a three-km trail that drops steeply to this spectacular 183-meter-high waterfall on his 70-hectare property. There are *miradors* and benches for wildlife viewing. Best time is rainy season, when the falls are going full tilt. They don't cascade in one great plume but rather tumble down the rockface to natural pools good for swimming. There are scarlet macaw nesting sites. And even a panther has been sighted. The trail is a stiff 45-minute hike. A water bottle and strong shoes are recommended. Entrance: $7; tel. 236-4140 or 661-1787, fax 236-1506. The entrance is on the dirt road, eight km beyond Hotel Villa Lapas. Bedard is building an ecolodge near the top of the falls. Camping is permitted.

You can get there via a bus from Orotina to Bijagual (departs 11:30 a.m.; returns from Bijagual at 5:30 p.m.), a small mountain village a few kilometers beyond the shack that marks the entrance to the waterfall trail. The bus will drop you at the "front gate." You can buy snacks and drinks. Open 8 a.m.-3 p.m.

Accommodations and Food

Budget: Restaurante y Cabinas El Cocodrilo, tel. 428-9009 or 428-8005, on the north side of the bridge of the Río Tarcoles, has seven basic *cabinas* with fans and shared baths with cold water. Rates: $15 s/d. There's a kids' playground, a souvenir store selling Guaitil pottery, and a rustic but atmospheric restaurant serving *típico* dishes (a *casado* costs $2.50). And horses rent for $8 per hour. The office for Jungle Crocodile Safari is also here.

In Tárcoles village, try the very simple **Cabinas El Dorado,** behind Bar El Dorado; **Cabinas y Restaurant la Guaria,** tel. 661-0455; and **Cabinas Villa del Mar,** tel. 661-2478, with basic, grungy rooms for $15 d. **Hotel Carara,** tel. 637-0178, has 25 simple rooms, featuring shared or private bath and fan or a/c. There's a small bar and restaurant, and a small swimming pool, plus ping-pong and a pool table. Rates: $24 pp, including all meals.

At the beach you can camp at the very basic **Cabinas Los Amigos,** or take self-catering units at the well-run, Canadian-owned **Villa Rayos del Sol,** tel. 446-5359 (Rates: $30 d).

Expensive: Hotel Villa Lapas, Apdo. 419-4005 San José, tel. 293-4104, fax 293-4204, is an all-inclusive Allegro Resort on the edge of Carara Reserve on the road to Manatial waterfall. It has 47 clean and comfortable rooms aligned along the river amid lush, beautifully landscaped grounds, with steep forested slopes on the far bank. The a/c rooms have simple yet attractive decor, queen-size beds, terra-cotta floors, fan, and large bathrooms. Facilities include an elegant restaurant/bar with a deck over the river, plus a swimming pool, mini-golf, volleyball, and nature trails that lead into a 280-hectare private reserve of secondary forest bordering Carara. There's plenty of wildlife, including—in the restaurant—a free-flying macaw and toucan, and butterflies flutter about in the netted butterfly garden. A bird walk is offered daily at 6:30 a.m., and a nature walk at 9 a.m. Rates: $85 s, $130 d all-inclusive. Guests can interchange with the Fiesta Caribbean Village in Puntarenas. *Recommended!*

Tarcol Lodge, Apdo. 12071-1000, San José, tel./fax 267-7138, a birder's paradise sitting on the banks of the Río Tárcoles estuary at the north end of the beach. This old, run-down, two-story wooden house has five simple rooms with two shared bathrooms for 10 people. It's owned by the Erbs (of Rancho Naturalista), who run it very badly. Guests see scarlet macaws migrating each dawn and dusk, and you can sit on the veranda and watch hummingbirds, count the crocodiles, and lose count while trying to tally the wading birds. The lodge offers birding and nature tours. It's vastly overpriced. Rates: $84 pp per day for call-ins; $99 pp daily, including all meals and guided nature hikes, transfers, and a visit to Carara (based on minimum six-day stay). Tour guides cost $20 pp.

Crocodile-Spotting Tours
Jungle Crocodile Safari, Apdo. 1542, San Pedro, tel. 224-4167 or 661-0455, fax 225-4852, offers a two-hour croc-spotting river trip aboard a pontoon boat ($30). Departure times vary according to tidal conditions. It has an office in the village, and another on the north side of the bridge on Hwy. 34. You'll even get to see one or more crocodiles the size of a Peterbilt truck lumber out of the river to be hand-fed by Victor Pineda. *Loco!*

In Tárcoles, Mario—the **Crocodile Man**—has a similar tour for $25. He has been highly recommended.

Fantasy Tours, tel. 643-3231, in Jacó, has a three-hour "Jungle Crocodile Safari" ($30, including drinks and snacks). No children under 12. Departure times vary according to high tide.
J.D.'s Watersports, at Punta Leona, also offers jungle river cruises ($79).

RESERVA BIOLÓGICA CARARA

Rainforest exploration doesn't come any easier than at Carara Biological Reserve, 20 km south of Orotina. Carara is unique in that it lies at the apex of the Amazonian and Mesoamerican ecosystems—a climatological zone of transition from the dry of the Pacific north to the very humid

southern coast—and is a meeting place for species from both. The 4,700-hectare reserve borders the Pan-American Highway, so you can literally step from your car and enter the last significant stand of primary forest of its kind on the Pacific coast.

Carara was once part of the huge Finca La Coyola, one of the biggest haciendas in Costa Rica. The Cervantes family protected the area for generations before the land passed to the National Parks Service. The land was expropriated in 1977 as part of an agrarian resettlement program for landless *campesinos;* in April 1979, 4,700 hectares were pared off to form the reserve.

Carara protects evergreen forest of great complexity and density. The diversity of trees is one of the highest in the world. The 10 rarest hardwoods in the country are here, as are some of the rarest and most spectacular animals of tropical America: American crocodiles, great anteaters, ocelots, spider monkeys, and poison-arrow frogs.

Carara is also one of the best birding localities in all Costa Rica. Fiery-billed aracari and toucan are common. Boat-billed herons, with their curious keel-shaped beaks, are common along the watercourses. And toward dusk, scarlet macaws—there are at least 40 breeding pairs—can be seen in flight as they migrate daily from the wet forest interior to the coastal mangrove swamps. The bridge over the Río Tárcoles is a good place to spot them. Crocodiles are there to amuse while you wait for macaws to fly over (The name Carara is the Huetar Indian name for "crocodile." Carara has numerous pre-Columbian archaeological sites dating back at least 2,000 years.)

In an attempt to avoid despoliation, in 1994 the Parks Service introduced a limit of 60 people at any one time on each of the two trails. Be prepared to wait to enter if the reserve is full when you arrive.

If you come across a band of monkeys while hiking, stop. Be patient. It may take 30 minutes for them to pass by, one by one. After a while, other animals may appear in their wake—coatis, peccaries, agoutis—feasting on the fruit dropped by the monkeys. Silence is imperative.

Driest months are March and April. Bring insect repellent.

Information

The Quebrada Bonita Ranger Station (park headquarters) sits beside the coastal highway, three km south of the Río Tárcoles. You'll find picnic tables and restrooms here, plus Las Araceas Nature Trail, a one-km loop. Another short trail—4.5 km long—begins at the highway, two km north of Quebrada Bonita, and follows an old road paralleling the Río Tárcoles. The rest of Carara is off-limits. Entrance: $6. Camping is not allowed, although I've heard a rumor of camping facilities being installed.

Tours and Guides

Most tour operators in San José arrange tours to Carara. **Geotur,** Apdo. 469 Y Griega, San José 1011, tel. 234-1867, fax 253-6338, specializes in Carara.

Even if you want to explore on your own, it pays to have a guide. Of all the guides I've had as my teachers, Rudi Zamora, Apdo. 347, Santa Ana 6150, San José, tel. 282-8538—my guide at Carara—outshone them all. His engaging descriptions are rich in imagery and imagination. He uses marvelous metaphors to explain the complex web of nature, and his theatrical passion will awaken the most docile. You can book him through Costa Rica Expeditions or other tour operators (see appendix).

Getting There

All buses bound between San José or Puntarenas and Jacó and Quepos pass by the reserve. Buses may be full on the weekend.

PLAYA MALO
TO PLAYA HERRADURA

A series of coves and beaches lines the coast south of Tárcoles, beginning with Playa Malo, a scenic bay fringed by a scalloped, 800-meter-wide, white-sand beach. Little fishing boats bob at anchor and are roosts for pelicans. At the south end rises the headland of Punta Leona, smothered with forest protected in a 300-hectare private nature reserve—part of a self-contained resort (what in England is called a "holiday camp") called Punta Leona. The reception gate is roadside, three km south of Punta Malo.

South of Punta Leona the road climbs steeply

before dropping down to Playa Herradura. At the crest of the rise is the entrance to **Villa Caletas,** to my mind the best resort hotel in Costa Rica. You owe it to yourself to pay a visit to sip a cocktail, have lunch, and admire the staggering views.

About seven km from both Tárcoles and Jacó, just south of the Río Caña Blanca, is a turnoff for Playa Herradura. Its pebbly, gray-sand beach is swarmed by Ticos on weekends and holidays. For now—but surely not for long—marine turtles come ashore to lay their eggs July-December. The beach gained attention a few years ago as a film set for the movie *1492,* starring Gerard Depardieu as Columbus. Filming lasted about 10 weeks and pumped an estimated $8 million into the local economy. More than 150 local indigenous people played the parts of native Indians (extras were paid $15 a day; women who appeared topless received $45); another 350 locals were hired for on-site work constructing a cathedral and a replica Indian village. The villagers have organized themselves and now charge a "donation" to pass onto the beach.

Accommodations

Camping: Ticos once poured onto Playa Herradura with their tents, leaving the place looking like a refuse dump. Fortunately, camping on the beach is no longer permitted. **Campamento Playa Herradura,** tel. 221-4491, has a large campground with bathrooms; the entrance is 200 meters before the beach. Rates: $3 pp. The lively **Bar La Puesta del Sol,** midway down the beach, has a large camping area with bathrooms.

Budget: Steve N' Lisa's Paradise Cove, tel./fax 637-0106, on the roadside at Playa Malo, rents four two-story oceanside cabinas—**Villa Lilly**—with kitchens, and **Paradise Cabinas** overlooking Playa Malo. Rates for both: $15 pp. They also have eight cabins in Jacó, and run a souvenir ship, tourist information service, and sportfishing service.

An air-conditioned beachfront home, **Casa del Mar,** tel. 288-2199, is for rent at Playa Agujas, just north of Punta Leona. It's signposted two km off the coast road.

At Herradura, **Cabinas La Turrialberia,** tel. 643-1236, one km from the beach, has handsome rooms for rent in a gate-guarded community. There was no one to show me around. There's a small swimming pool. **Cabinas Herradura,** tel. 643-

3181, has 10 large but basic beachfront *casitas* with kitchenettes, fans, and private baths with cold water. Rates: $12 pp. It offers snorkeling and surfing trips. **Cabinas Romance,** tel. 643-3689, has simple cabins midway between Hwy. 34 and the beach. **Cabañas del Río,** tel. 643-3275, has pleasing little self-catering cabins with verandas and twin bedrooms upstairs, raised on stilts and set back from the beach.

Moderate: Punta Leona, Apdo. 8592, San José 1000, tel. 661-1414 or 231-3131, fax 232-0791, e-mail: puntaleona@sol.racsa.co.cr, is an expansive planned resort behind the bay. An **RV and camping** area is right beside the beach; 73 more expensive apartments, plus Selvamar, a large bungalow complex, are five minutes' walk away. The 108 a/c bungalows and rooms are modern and spacious, with TV and very large showers. Modest cabañas are also an option. A small bar fronts a large kidney-shaped swimming pool and sunning area. The resort also has a small discotheque and a children's video ar-

SPECIAL HOTEL: VILLA CALETAS

Take a steep, 500-meter headland two km south of Punta Leona. Construct a Louisiana-style gingerbread Roman villa and self-contained matching *casitas* overlooking the sea. Surround each with sensuous, tropical greenery: bougainvillea, fuchsia for fragrance, palms, and classical vases with cacti. Then add sublime decor, stunning museum pieces, and an aquarium a zoo would be proud of. The result is Hotel Villa Caletas, Apdo. 12358, San José 1000, tel. 257-3653, fax 222-2059, e-mail: caletas@sol.racsa.co.cr, a glory in stone dreamed up and run by Denis Roy, an effusive Frenchman with an infectious joie de vivre and schoolboy charm, and an exemplary aesthetic vision. The hotel, a member of the Small Distinctive Hotels of Costa Rica, is the *best resort hotel in Costa Rica.*

Centerpiece of this splendid oasis is the sensational, deep-blue horizon pool and huge wooden deck suspended miraculously as if in midair. A whimsical waterfall adds its own fairy-tale note.

Spacious public lounges in black, grays, and whites boast black wicker furniture, hand-painted terra-cotta tilework, tasteful paintings, Renaissance antiques, giant clam shells, and Oriental rugs, with hints of ancient Rome around every corner. You'll think you've entered the Louvre! *Vogue* magazine or *House Beautiful* could not have done better.

Eight huge, high-ceilinged, individually styled bedrooms vibrate with color. Each is done up in warm tropical peaches, papaya, and pinks, with antique-style beds, Japanese-style lampshades, floor to ceiling silk French curtains and bedspreads of Indian provenance, and verandas opening onto stunning ocean vistas. No TVs, but there's state-of-the-art silent a/c. Twenty separate bungalows (including two junior suites and a suite) follow the theme (some are a hefty hike up and down stone-walled pathways zig-zagging through the lush grounds).

A skilled chef and no-expense-spared kitchen guarantee ambitious French cuisine a la Costarricense—*crevettes à l'anis* (shrimps in anise), *noix de marlin au citron* (marlin in lemon), *mousse de maranchaja* (passionfruit mousse)—on a breezy open-air terrace that commands views across the Gulf of Nicoya. Cuisine occasionally reaches sublime heights. The menu changes daily (average $20 lunch/dinner; $9 breakfasts). Nonguests are welcome. A second restaurant serves breakfast and lunch.

The coup de grâce is a Greek amphitheater complete with Corinthian columns set on the cliff-face as a setting for sunset jazz and classical concerts. Sublime! It is pure intoxication itself to gather at sunset, when New Age music is played. One can almost imagine Apollo—the god of light par excellence—stepping onto the stage. It's a perfect stage for Costa Rica's annual International Music Festival, hosted here each July and August.

A 4WD trail leads steeply down to lonesome Playa Caletas. It's a stiff hike, or you can take the twice-daily beach shuttle. Service, hit-and-miss on prior visits, is now exemplary under the tutelage of professional management. A boutique sells fine quality ceramics and jewelry.

It's not for everyone. One English couple I spoke to thought it "OTT . . . Over the top, dear!" But more typically, I overheard one guest say, "We're coming back, and we're bringing friends." Another exclaimed, "You can't help but be happy here; it's so wonderful!"

To experience the contrast between the spectacular and the intimate is a special pleasure. Rates: $116 s/d standard, $163-200 s/d suite, $136 s/d villa low season; $130 s/d standard, $190-230 s/d suite, $160 s/d villa high season.

cade, and full panoply of watersports. It's good for families and is popular with Ticos. You can follow mountain trails into the forest, offering views over the bay. Rates: $107 condominiums; $78 cabañas; $49-98 chalets; $93-122 bungalows.

Premium: The Villa Caletas is a don't-miss. A 1,100-hectare Marriott resort, **Los Sueños Hotel and Golf Club,** Apdo. 662-1007, San José, tel. 290-3311, fax 231-6040, http://www.los-suenos. com, was under construction at press time at Herradura, to be open by 1999.

Food

Steve N' Lisa's Paradise Cove offers breezy patio dining overlooking the beach, and has great burgers, grilled chicken and tuna melt sandwiches ($2), lobster ($12), fettucine ($4), salads, and a whole lot more. It's very popular at sunset. Lisa—an American—oversees the kitchen herself. You'll pass a couple of other attractive *ranchito* restaurants farther south, notably **Fiesta del Mar.**

Villa Caleta has gourmet international nouvelle cuisine ($10 breakfast, $22 lunch, $25 dinner). Breakfast on the mountaintop with New Age music as a backdrop is a sublime way to start the day. A treat!

La Egale, on the road into Herradura, is a modestly elegant Italian restaurant.

Activities

The sleek *Star Chaser* catamaran departs Punta Leona daily for an afternoon-and-sunset cruise ($49 at the boat; $79 including transfers from San José). The vessel is as *pelican* sharp as a cut diamond and as wide as a city block. You fly along with New Age music as a backdrop. The vessel is so stable (perfect for landlubbers) you don't notice the warp-speed pace. It's a superb way to get a tan, feel the breeze in your hair, gain a different perspective of the coast, *and* have fun. Piña coladas, fruits, and snacks are served on board.

J.D.'s Watersports, tel. 356-1028, e-mail: phoyman@aol.com, offers sportfishing, sunset cruises, and diving from Punta Leona. Carlos of **Herradura Bay Charters,** tel. 643-3112 or 643-3181, fax 643-3578, at Cabinas Herradura, is

highly recommended locally for sportfishing trips ($485 half day, $650 full day four people), plus snorkeling and sunset tours ($39), and a full-day trip to Isla Tortuga and Montezuma in Nicoya ($350, four people). **Marinos Charters,** tel. 643-1394, also offers fishing, diving, and surfing.

Getting There and Around

See "Getting There" in the Carara section, above. **Interbus** stops at Punta Leona on its daily shuttle between San José and Manuel Antonio.

Cabinas Herradura has a **water-taxi** service.

JACÓ

Jacó is the closest beach resort to San José and therefore popular with Josefinos as well as backpackers, surfers, and the young offbeat party crowd. It gets packed on holidays and on weekends in dry season. It was the country's first developed beach resort, when it was put on the map by wintering Canadian charter groups (you can still see Canadian flags flying in tribute to the power of the maple-leaf dollar). Jacó faded from the spotlight for a few years but has bounced back with vigor. The town hosts two triathlons annually.

The snowbird scene has been diluted by Ticos (a mix of families and young adults on a fling) and, increasingly, Europeans—especially Italians—bringing a nascent sophistication. It has heaps of hotels, restaurants, and souvenir stores. However, businesses are fluid (between my research trips, about 40% of businesses had disappeared or metamorphosed; I hardly recognized the place). Many places mentioned here are likely to have closed their doors or moved to new locations by the time you read this.

Highway 34 runs parallel to Jacó, which lies 400 meters west of the highway and is linked by four access roads. The main road into town is the second access road, when heading south from Herradura (the turnoff at the crocodile farm is the first turn). The main strip in town runs south two km to the Río Quebrada Seca and the suburb of Garabito.

BOB RACE

Frankly, I've never been enamored of Jacó. The three-km-long beach is not particularly appealing, and swimming is discouraged (signs warn of dangerous rip currents, and the river estuaries at each end of the beach are said to be polluted). Everything lines the single main street, which parallels the beach for its full length. If peace and quiet are your thing, give Jacó a wide berth.

Granja de Cocodrilos

This "Crocodile Park," tel. 643-3745, on Hwy. 34 and the northerly road into Jacó, is a large *zoocriadero* that breeds crocodiles and caimans (plus snakes and freshwater turtles) by the score for release into the wild. Trails lead past marshy lagoons where juveniles thrash about. At the far end are the breeding sheds, where youngsters of different ages clump in great heaps in concrete pools and pipe squeakily for their mamas. You can even hold the teeny ones in your hands. I recommend a guided tour. Biologists from the University of Costa Rica perform research here. Entrance: $4.

Accommodations

Prices in Jacó tend to be higher than elsewhere on the coast. Many hotels are overpriced. Look at standards as much as prices; ask about surfers' discounts, and consider wet ("green") season, when discounts are offered. Reservations are advisable for Christmas, New Year's, and Easter. Accommodations are listed below by price category.

Camping: Cabinas Marriott, at the north end of town, has camping. **Camping Guabito** is 100 meters north of Centro Comercial El Paso, in the center. Alternately, try **Camping El Hicaco,** tel. 643-3004, offering oceanfront camping under shade trees and RV space. It has bathrooms (30 cents). Rates: $2.50 pp campsite, $3.50 RVs. **Camping Madrigal,** tel. 643-3230, at the southern end of the beach, is a large campground with picnic tables beneath shade trees about 100 meters from the beach. It has toilets and showers. It also has a few grubby *cabinas* with private baths and cold water. Rates: $2 campsite; $10 *cabinas.*

Shoestring: At the north end of Jacó is **Cabinas y Restaurante Clarita,** tel. 643-3013, with basic waterfront rooms with fans and private baths

with cold water. Rates: $6 pp. Near Cabinas Sol Palmeras, **Cabinas Cindy** has basic rooms with private baths and cold water. Rates: $10.

Budget: Cabinas Antonio, tel. 643-3043, is a popular bargain for budget travelers, with 13 rooms offering private baths, fans, and hot water. Rates: $14 s, $17 d. It has a laundry. The Italian-run **Hotel Gipsy** nearby has nine a/c rooms in a two-story building; there's a garden with a small lap pool. Each room has a fan, a patio, and private bath with hot water. Rates: $25 s, $30 d year-round, including breakfast ($5 extra person). The basic **Cabinas Manecas** is also here, near the estuary.

Nearby, **Cabinas Emily,** tel. 643-3328, is a good budget beachfront option popular with surfers. Rates: $11 shared bath, $16 with private bath. **Cabinas Carabito,** tel. 643-3321 or 643-3543, has 10 dark, clean, simple rooms with fans, and private baths with cold water. Rates: $19 s, $23 d, $27 t/quad. The **Hotel Lido** is soulless, cramped, basic, and overpriced. Rooms have private baths with cold water, plus kitchenettes (alas, no refrigerators). There's a small pool. Rates: $25. And the **Hotel y Restaurante El Jardín,** tel. 643-3050, has seven rather dark rooms with fans and private baths with hot water. Highlights include a large pool in a small courtyard with palms, and a small restaurant with excellent food and live music. A second floor may be added with ocean views. Rates: $10 s, $12.50 d low season; $21 s, $31 d high season.

In town, **Jacó Jungle Inn,** tel. 643-3193, fax 235-4310, formerly Cabinas La Sirena, has nine rooms in a two-story unit with fans and private baths with cold water. It has a small pool and secure parking. Rates: $25 s, $30 d. **Cabinas Sol Palmeras,** tel. 643-3371, has eight clean, modern rooms with fans, refrigerators, patios and private baths with hot water. Rates: $16 s/d, $23 t low season; $25 s/d, $33 t high season. **Cabinas Mar del Plata,** tel. 643-3580, has simple rooms with private bathrooms and hot water. Rates: $20 s, $25 d.

Cabinas La Cometa, tel. 643-3615, has 12 modern, clean, pleasing rooms. Rates: $20 s, $30 d. The Dutch-run **Restaurant y Cabinas El Flamboyant,** tel. 643-3146, on the main road 200 meters south, has 18 rooms with private baths and fans, plus *apartamentos* with kitchens, fans, and cold water in landscaped grounds.

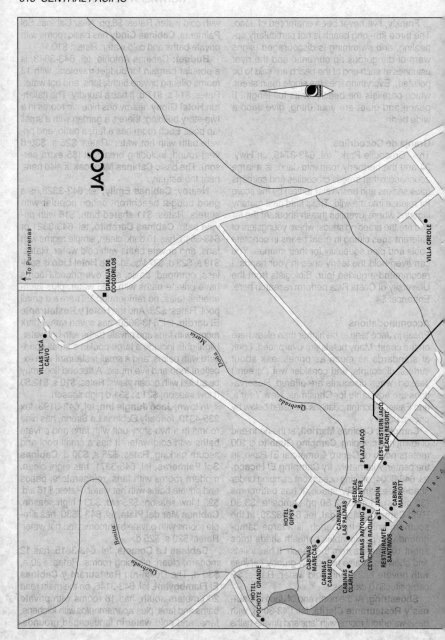

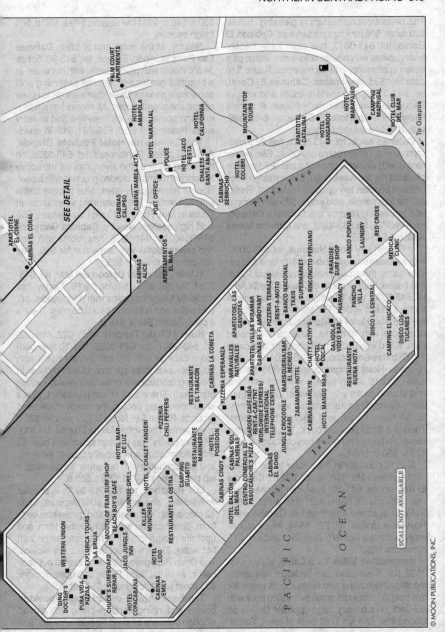

PALM COURT APARTMENTS
HOTEL AMAPOLA
HOTEL NARANJAL
HOTEL CALIFORNIA
HOTEL JACÓ FIESTA
CHALET'S SANTA ANA
MOUNTAIN TOP TOURS
HOTEL COLIBRI
CABINAS SERRUCHO
APARTOTEL CATALINA
HOTEL KANGAROO
HOTEL MARAPAISO
CAMPING MADRIGAL
HOTEL CLUB DEL MAR
To Quepos

POLICE
POST OFFICE
APARTAMENTOS EL MAR
CABINA MAREA ALTA
CABINAS CALIPSO
CABINAS ALICE

APARTOTEL EL CISNE
CABINAS EL CORAL

SEE DETAIL

Playa Jacó

CAMPING LA COMETA
APARTOTEL LAS GAVIOTAS
RESTAURANTE EL TABACÓN
MIRAVALLES NATURALES
PIZZERIA ESPERANZA
APARTOTEL VILLAS MIRAMAR
PIZZERIA TERRAZAS
CABINAS EL FLAMBOYANT
RENT-A-MOTO
BANCO NACIONAL
TAXIS
SUPERMARKET
RINCONCITO PERUANO
BANCO POPULAR
PARADISE SURF SHOP
LAUNDRY
RED CROSS
MEDICAL CLINIC

PIZZERIA CHILI PEPPERS
RESTAURANTE EL FLAMBOYANT
GARDEN CAFÉ/ADA RENT-A-CAR/TNT WORLDWIDE EXPRESS/ INTERNATIONAL TELEPHONE CENTER
MARISQUERIA/BAR EL RECREO
ZABAMARO HOTEL
CHATTY CATHY'S
HOTEL COCAL
CALIGOLA VIDEO BAR
PHARMACY
PANCHO VILLA
DISCO LA CENTRAL

HOTEL MAR DE LUZ
PIZZERIA POSEIDON
RESTAURANTE MARINERO
HOTEL POSEIDON
CABINAS SOL PALMERAS
CENTRO COMERCIAL EL PASO/CALICHE'S PIZZA
CABINAS EL BOHIO
JUNGLE CROCODILE SAFARI
CABINAS MARILYN
HOTEL MANGO MAR
RESTAURANTE BUENA NOTA
CAMPING EL HICACO
DISCO LOS TUCANES

HOTEL Y CHALET TANGERI
CAMPING GUABITO
CABINAS CINDY
HOTEL BALCON DEL MAR

WESTERN UNION
EXPLORICA TOURS
MOUTH OF FEAR SURF SHOP
BEACH BOY'S CAFÉ
SUNRISE GRILL
KILLER MUNCHIES
RESTAURANTE LA OSTRA

DING DOCTOR'S
PURA VIDA PIZZAS
CHUCK'S SURFBOARD REPAIR
LA BRUJA
JACÓ JUNGLE INN
HOTEL LIDO
HOTEL COPACABANA
CABINAS EMILY

Playa Jacó

PACIFIC OCEAN

SCALE NOT AVAILABLE

© MOON PUBLICATIONS, INC.

The beachfront restaurant is pleasing. Rates: $20 room; $38 for four *apartamento*. **Cabinas El Bohio,** tel. 643-3017, has eight funky beachfront *cabinas* with private cold-water baths, plus seven apartments with kitchenettes. Rates: $16 *cabinas;* $35 apartments. **Cabinas El Coral,** tel. 641-3133, 100 meters south and east of Banco Nacional, is similarly priced. A stone's throw east is **Apartotel El Cisne,** tel. 643-3395, with 10 fully equipped rooms.

Cabinas Alice, tel. 643-3061, has 22 motel-style rooms. Older rooms are basic. Five newer rooms with kitchens and hot water are far more pleasant (by the week only). Large mango trees shade a popular, tiny open-air restaurant. Rates: $15 for four people, cold water; $35 with kitchens and hot water. Nearby are **Cabinas Calipso,** tel. 643-3728, fax 643-3208, and **Cabinas Marea Alta,** tel. 643-3554.

In Garabito try **Hotel Naranjal,** tel. 643-3006, with six clean modern *cabinas* with fans and private baths; three have hot water. Rates: $30 d, $45 t/quad. Farther south is **Chalets Santa Ana,** tel. 643-3233, with 10 simple rooms with private baths and hot water. Rates: $25 d. Nearby is the U.S.-run **Hotel California,** a modest, two-story hotel with 10 rooms. Rates: $17 d shared bath; $21 d with kitchen, private bath, and cable TV. **Cabinas Serrucho,** tel. 643-1204, is a nearby option. **Hotel Kangaroo,** tel. 643-3351, farther south, has 10 simply furnished rooms with fans and private baths with hot water. Take an upstairs room; downstairs rooms are very dingy. Some have bunks and shared bathrooms. There's a small pool out back. The owner rents mountain bikes and offers bicycle tours. Rates: $20 s, $30 d, $55 t.

Also to consider in the center is the beachfront **Cabinas Marilyn,** tel. 643-3215; **Cabinas El Recreo,** tel. 643-3012, which has basic *cabinas* with private baths with cold water (rates: $15); and, at the south end of Garabito, the **Hotel Marapaíso,** tel. 221-6544, which reportedly operates a hostel (rates: $9 members, $15 nonmembers).

Inexpensive: Villas Tucá Calvo, tel./fax 643-3532, has five modern two-bedroom villa-apartments with kitchens and living rooms (each for five people) around a small swimming pool with sundeck on a breezy ridge opposite Granja de Cocodrilos, one km northeast of town. Rates: $30 s, $40 d, $50 t low season; $40 s, $50 d, $60 t high season.

Nearby, at the north end of town, **Cabinas Las Palmas,** Apdo. 5, Jacó, tel. 643-3005, has 24 a/c rooms with private baths with hot water, in a beautiful garden with a small swimming pool and secure parking. Older rooms are dark; newer rooms are slightly nicer. All rooms have refrigerators; some have kitchenettes and laundry sinks. Rates: $28-67 d, $35-79 t, $42-91 quad.

The German-run **Hotel Pochote Grande,** Apdo. 42, Jacó, Puntarenas, tel. 643-3236, on the north bank of the river, has 24 attractive beachfront rooms in shaded grounds with a pool. Rooms have kitchenettes, plus private baths with hot water. The restaurant specializes in Teutonic fare. Rates: $40 s/d/t low season; $55 s/d/t high season. Nearby, **Cabinas Gaby,** tel. 643-3080, fax 441-9926, has rooms with fans and private baths with hot water for $40, plus self-catering units for $55.

In town, the **Hotel Balcón del Mar,** tel. 643-3251, fax 283-2283, beside the Río Copey, has modestly furnished rooms with refrigerators, private baths and hot water, plus balconies. There's a pool. Rates: $40 s, $45 d.

Hotel y Chalet Tangerí, Apdo. 622, Alajuela, tel. 643-3001, fax 643-3636, has 10 twin-bedroom *cabinas* with a/c and private baths with hot water, plus three apartments with kitchens in pleasing landscaped grounds (weekly rentals preferred). There's a bar and restaurant, plus a small swimming pool in the neatly manicured grounds. Rates: $45 for up to four people; $85 d apartments. The **Hotel Mar de Luz,** tel./fax 643-3259, opposite, has modest apartment *cabinas* with kitchenettes and security boxes, terraces, and private baths with hot water surrounding a lap pool. Rates: $45 d, $55 t, $65 q.

Los Ranchos, tel./fax 643-3070, is popular with surfers, who receive a 20% discount. It has 12 rooms with kitchenettes and queen-size beds from, larger cabins with kitchenettes from, and upstairs rooms for, all with private baths with hot water. There's a pool, plus laundry service. The Disco Papagayo, next door, cranks out decibels to wake the dead. Rates: $25 upstairs room; $35 room with kitchenette; $50 cabin.

The French/Swiss-owned **Hotel Poseidon** boasts a stunning frontage-piece with carved wooden columns bearing Poseidon motifs, and

Persian throw rugs on the faux-marble floor of the elegant, stone-walled, open-walled restaurant. There's a tiny clover-leaf swimming pool with jacuzzi and swim-up bar. The 15 rooms, albeit large, are an overpriced disappointment—modestly furnished, with soft foam mattresses and see-through curtains. The bathrooms with large mosaic-tiled showers make amends. Upstairs a/c rooms get the light; downstairs (fans only) are a bit dingy. Rates: $35 s, $40 d; $50 s, $55 d with a/c, including breakfast.

The French-owned and rather dowdy **Villas Estrellamar,** Apdo. 33, Playa Jacó, tel. 643-3102 or 643-3453, has 24 a/c *cabinas* with kitchens set in landscaped grounds 50 meters east of the strip. Each has a refrigerator and a stove, plus a double and a single bed. There's a pool and a small bar. Rates: $55 d.

Apartotel Villas Miramar, Apdo. 18, Jacó, tel. 643-3003, fax 643-3617, has 12 pleasing rooms with kitchens, fans, and hot water set in landscaped grounds 50 meters from the beach. Rates: $50 d, $55 t. A stone's throw south is **Apartotel Las Gaviotas,** tel. 643-3092, fax 643-3054, with 12 units featuring patios, kitchenettes, a/c, fans, and private baths with hot water. Rates: $60.

I like **Villa Creole,** tel. 643-3298, fax 643-3882, a French-run place with 10 elegant, well-lit a/c rooms around a large pool with water cascade and a *rancho* restaurant serving French Creole cuisine. Rooms have large closets, fans, refrigerators, kitchenettes, safety deposit boxes, patios, and stone-walled private baths with hot water. A minibus is on hand for tours. Rates: $50 s/d, including tax and breakfast.

The American-run **Zabamaro Hotel,** tel./fax 643-3174, is popular with surfers. Its 20 very clean and modern cabins (10 with fans; 10 with a/c) have hammocks on the patios; some have refrigerators. There's a swimming pool and a small bar and restaurant under thatch. Rates: $30 s, $35 d, $40 t, $45 quad fans; $45 s, $50 d with a/c. The beachside **Hotel Mango Mar,** tel./fax 643-3670, in neoclassical Spanish colonial-style, has two apartments and 12 a/c rooms with kitchenettes. Nice furnishings. It offers a pool with jacuzzi and red-brick sun terrace, plus private parking. Rates: $45 s, $50 d rooms; $75 apartments. Next door, the German-owned **Hotel Cocal,** tel. 643-3067, fax 643-3082; in the U.S., tel. (800) 732-9266, is also very elegant and appealing. The Spanish hacienda-style hotel is popular with charter groups. Arched porticos grace 44 spacious rooms surrounding a courtyard with two pools and a bar. Hot and cold water, private baths, and fans. An upstairs restaurant overlooking the beach serves international cuisine; there's a small casino. No children. Rates: $55 d.

Apartamentos El Mar, tel. 643-3165, fax 272-2280, in Garabito, has 12 well-furnished units built in a C shape around a tiny pool and garden. Clean and spacious rooms have kitchens, plus private baths with hot water. Rates: $33 small unit, $55 large. **Palm Court Apartments,** tel./fax 643-3662, nearby, has fully equipped one-bedroom apartments around a large swimming pool.

Secluded along the beachfront are **Hotel Colibrí,** tel. 643-3419, fax 643-3730, with 12 nice rooms featuring fans and private baths with hot water (rates: $50 d); and **Apartotel Catalina,** tel. 643-3217, fax 643-3544, which has rooms with kitchenettes plus private baths, and either patios or balconies (rates: $55 d). Both have a swimming pool.

Hotel y Restaurante Marapaíso, Apdo. 6699, San José 1000, tel. 221-6544, fax 221-6601, is a pleasant if older and somewhat run-down colonial-style property with a swimming pool and jacuzzi. Rooms are a bit dowdy. Rooms are at the back, away from the beach; they have private baths with cold water. It's popular with Ticos. Rates: $45 s, $55 d.

Moderate: Best Western Jacó Beach Resort, tel. 220-1441, fax 232-3159, e-mail: jaco-hotel@sol.racsa.co.cr; in the U.S., tel. (800) 272-6654; in Canada, tel. (800) 463-6654, at the north end of the drag, offers 130 a/c rooms. Superior rooms have TVs and refrigerators. A TV in the lobby pipes in 24-hour CNN. Amenities include El Muelle restaurant and bar, a discotheque, car rental, a swimming pool, a floodlit tennis court, a volleyball court, plus moped, bicycle, sailboat, sea kayak, and surfboard rentals. Daily transportation to and from the Hotel Irazú in San José. Bargain, but double-check rates. Rates: $80 s/d.

Jacó Princess Villas (same as Best Western), across the road from the Best Western, has 28 deluxe villas for five people. Each has a large bathroom, dining and living rooms, a terrace, and a kitchenette. There's a swimming pool. Rates: $78-99.

Hotel Paradise, tel. 296-2022 or 643-3211 (for the condominiums), fax 296-2023; in the U.S., tel. (305) 861-2501 or (800) 277-6123, fax (305) 864-7487, is a reclusive but rather soulless, self-contained enclave on the main strip. Little *ranchitos* and pools and bars and a jacuzzi are scattered about this huge complex of 153 one-, two- and three-bedroom a/c apartments, with kitchens and satellite TVs. Rates: from $75 d, $89 t, $103 t.

Hotel Copacabana, Apdo. 150, Jacó, tel./fax 643-3131, has 30 poolside standard rooms, each with one double bed and a single bed (it claims "oceanfront" rooms, but only the public facilities face the sea). Beautiful, spacious suites with kitchenettes (some with a/c) sleep five. Hardwoods abound. And lively tropical murals dance on the walls. The hotel boasts a pool with swim-up bar, a restaurant specializing in Italian cuisine, and a sports bar that can remain lively into the wee hours. Weekends, live jazz and rock and roll bands play. Sleep? Are you crazy? The hotel's own "Sunset Booze Cruise" weaves a liquidy course to sea at 3 p.m. Rates: $68 d ($78 with a/c); $108 suite, including breakfast. Perhaps overpriced.

The upscale **Hotel Amapola,** Apdo. 133, Jacó, tel. 643-3337, fax 643-3668, e-mail: amapola@sol.racsa.co.cr, boasts two-story condo-style units, plus a casino and a disco in beautifully landscaped grounds. It has 44 standard rooms, six suites, plus three fully equipped villas—all with a/c, cable TV, security box, modest furnishings, and hot water. Facilities include two swimming pools, a pool bar, and a Jazzcuzzi. Rates: $76 s/d, $86 t, $135 suite, $150 villa.

The **Hotel Jacó Fiesta,** Apdo. 38, Jacó, tel. 643-3147, fax 643-3148; in the U.S. (800) 327-9408, fax (407) 588-8369, is a somewhat sterile upscale resort whose 80 rooms (with a/c and cable TVs) surround a circular pool and tennis court. It's 200 meters from the beach at the mouth of the Río Quebrada Seca. Its hideous facade—a pink and turquoise architectural carbuncle—hides nicely landscaped grounds. It is popular with Canadian charter groups. New owners had taken over at press time. Rates: $70 s, $80 d.

Hotel Club del Mar, Apdo. 107-4023 Jacó, tel./fax 643-3194, nestled beneath the cliffs at the southern end of Jacó, has 10 tasteful cabin-suites with kitchenettes, living rooms, and private sea-view balconies surrounded by pretty landscaped grounds. American owners Philip and Marilyn Edwardes also offer eight rooms with two queen beds. They have a souvenir shop, a small pool and sunning deck, and the breezy Las Sandalias restaurant. You can rent bicycles and boogie boards. Rates: $57 d, $77 with a/c, $108 suite; low season rates (May-Nov.) are 40% less.

Expensive: Hotel Hacienda Lilipoza, Apdo. 15, Jacó 4023, tel. 643-3062, fax 643-3158, was closed during my last research trip but was scheduled to reopen soon. It has 20 hacienda-style units amid expansive landscaped grounds about 600 meters from Hwy. 34, half a kilometer from the beach. Each individually decorated room has two double beds, a/c, and a large TV. Some are done in wicker, some in modern Tudor style. Voluminous bathrooms have twin sinks, reclining bathtubs, and bidets. Some have jacuzzis. Spacious closets. A Swiss chef conjures international dishes at the Banyan Bar Restaurant. Other highlights are a tennis court, and a small swimming pool with a bar and barbecue area screened by tall trees, many festooned with epiphytes. Very tranquil and secluded. Rates: $100-175.

Food

The place for breakfast is **Chatty Cathy's Family Kitchen Cafe,** tel./fax 643-1039, opposite Banco Nacional. Cathy, a portly and loveable Canadian, serves traditional North American breakfasts ($4), granola with fruit and yogurt ($3.50), *gallo pinto,* and kids' breakfasts ($1.50-2). Boy, she sure is chatty. Open Wed.-Sun. 6:30 a.m.-2 p.m. A good alternative is **Sunrise Grill,** tel. 643-3361, also called The Breakfast Place, serving waffles, eggs Benedict ($3.50), omelettes, and more. It's open 7 a.m.-noon. The **Garden Café** is also popular for breakfast (there's a wide-ranging lunch and dinner menu too), but I've heard reports of people being ripped off here; Mark, the gringo owner, is said to bump up the tab and worse (two separate expats used all kind of invectives to describe him). **Restaurante Jacó Mar** also has a bad name.

Seafood? At the north end, **Cevichería Raquel** is a twee little open-air eatery serving ceviche ($1.75), *casados* ($3), and seafood. Nearby, the beachfront **Restaurante Santimos** also has ceviche, *casados*, and seafood, as does **Oceano Pacífico**, by the rivermouth. In town, **Restaurant Emily** follows suit. **Beach Boy's Café** has *casados* for $2, plus burgers, tacos, and similar fare. In the center of town is the budget **Marisqueria El Recreo**, where a seafood platter or jumbo shrimp or lobster costs $9.

For surf-and-turf, try **La Hacienda**, tel. 643-3191, a popular *marisquería* serving steak and lobster; **Restaurant La Ostra**, serving churrasco ($5) and lobster ($13 including soup) on a quaint patio; and **Rinconcito Peruano**, serving paella ($6), *arroz chaufa especial* ($5), *lomito saltido* ($5) and other Peruvian dishes in a shady patio setting.

Cabinas Alice and **Soda Helen** have been recommended for their *típico* food. Helen keeps fickle hours, but "runs the place like one long house party."

For upscale dining, check out the French menu at the elegant restaurant at **Hotel Poseidon**, with dishes such as marlin ceviche ($2), and brocheta wrapped in bacon with veggies ($5). **Creperie La Bretagne** is 50 meters west. Cater-corner to Poseidon, the Italian-run **Pizzeria Esperanza**, tel. 643-3332, is also modestly elegant. It specializes in pastas and pizzas ($4-10) and has espressos, lattes, cappuccinos ($1-2), a wide ice-cream menu, and superb homemade lemonade. **Restaurante Marinero**, opposite, is popular for inexpensive seafoods. **La Bruja**, 100 meters north, is another elegant, thatched, hacienda-style eatery. And **Restaurante Buena Nota** has colorful decor.

Killer Munchies has an eclectic menu: greek salads ($3), burritos ($1.50), and pizzas (from $5). It's open Mon.-Fri. 5-9 p.m. and weekends noon-9 p.m. (closed Tuesday). The rustic **Restaurante El Tabacón** specializes in wood-roasted chicken. **El Bosque**, tel. 643-3009, on the highway south of Jacó, has been recommended for breakfast beneath shady mango trees. It's also popular for its seafood dishes and a local favorite, beef tongue in salsa. For Chinese, try **Restaurante Sen Ly**.

There's no shortage of pizza places. Try **Pura Vida Pizzas, Pizzeria Terrazas**, and **Pizzeria Chili Peppers**, in the center. I enjoyed a tasty quesadilla ($3.50) and burrito ($2.50) at **Caliche's Pizza**, open 11 a.m.-3 p.m. and 5-10 p.m. (closed Wednesday), in Centro Comercial El Paso. **Pancho Villa** is recommended for Mexican fare. A **Pizza Hut** is in Plaza Jacó. Here also is **Flintstone's Burgers**.

You can buy health foods from **Miravalles Naturales** 50 meters south of Centro Comercial El Paso.

Entertainment

Jacó has no shortage of bar action. One of the most romantic bars is the classy **La Bruja**. The moderne **Bar Zarpe** in Plaza Jacó is also lively. The real action happens at **Disco La Central**, tel. 643-3076, on the beach, replete with flashing lights and jet-roar techno music that lures dancers like lemmings on a mission ($3 cover). Jacó is a favored spot for hookers from San José to divest male tourists of their dollars, and this is their favored hangout. Other discos include **Disco Los Tucanes**, and **Disco Papagayo** in the Hotel Jacó Fiesta. You can try your luck in the **casinos** of the Hotel Cocal (open 4 p.m.-3 a.m.), Best Western Jacó Beach, or Amapola (open 7 p.m.-?). There's no cinema.

Eight ball? Check out **El Recreo**, an offbeat pool hall with video games, 50 meters south of and across from Banco Nacional. The more ritzy **Caligola Video Bar** is around the corner near Disco La Central.

The **Tropical Party Bus Tour**, tel. 643-1049, leaves nightly for four hours of boogie-down partying at hot spots at Herradura and Hermosa, departing 8:30 p.m. and depositing you at a disco in Jacó at 9 p.m. ($18).

By day try **Mini-Golf de Jacó**, with 36 holes to keep you amused ($4 adults; $3 children); open Mon.-Fri. 3-10 p.m. and weekends 9 a.m.-4 p.m.

Information

The **Granja de Cocodrilos** has a tourist information center. **CATUJA** (Cámara de Turismo de Jacó), which promotes tourism locally, has an office next to the police station in Garabito.

Tours and Activities

Tour operators come and go like spring blooms. Many are unlicensed and arrive in town to set up only for the Dec.-March season, then disappear. Caveat emptor.

Horseback Rides: You can rent a horse on the beach ($5 per hour), or for trips to the mountains ($20). **Playa Hermosa Horse Tours,** tel. 643-3808, charges $35 for three-hour trips. And **Mountain Top Tours,** tel. 643-1126 or 643-3586, in Garabito, offers beach and mountain rides.

Surfing: As many as a dozen outlets cater to surfers. **Ding Doctor's** and **Chosito del Surf,** to the north end of town, rent and repair boards, as does **Mother of Fear Surf Shop,** with more than 100 boards ($10-20 per day), and **Paradise Surf Shop,** 200 meters farther south. A chap called Chuck offers surfboard repair at, of all places, **Chuck's Surboard Repair,** 50 meters west of La Hacienda. He also offers a surf report, board rentals, and lessons.

Sportfishing: Carlos, of **Herradura Bay Charters** tel. 643-3112 or 643-3181, fax 643-3578, at Cabinas Herradura, is recommended for sportfishing and water-taxis, as is **Victor,** tel./fax 643-3259, at Hotel Mar de Luz.

Excursion Tours: Fantasy Tours, tel. 643-3221 in Jacó, tel. 220-0042 in San José, e-mail: fantasy@sol.racsa.co.cr; in the U.S., tel. (800) 272-6654, in the Best Western Jacó Beach, offers tours to Carara and elsewhere. **CD's Realtors and Tours,** Apdo. 248, Jacó, tel./fax 643-3355, e-mail: cdsreal@sol.racsa.co.cr, has a gamut of offerings—a crocodile and birding safari ($40); horseback tours to Bijagual waterfall ($45); trips to Iguana Park ($30), Palo Verde ($65), Manuel Antonio ($55), Monteverde (two days, $150), and farther afield; plus scuba diving ($90 three hours). **Explorica Tours** also has horseback riding and trips to Isla Tortuga.

Shopping

There are numerous boutiques scattered along the main drag selling batiks, T-shirts, and other tourist souvenirs. **Bali Batik** sells quality clothing from Indonesia. For art, check out **La Heliconia,** a trendy art gallery next to La Piraña restaurant. The "Cuban" cigars sold at the Garden Café are assuredly fakes.

Super Rayo Azul, 50 meters south of Banco Nacional, is the town's largest supermarket.

Services

Banco de Costa Rica has a branch in Plaza Jacó. **Banco Popular,** open Mon.-Fri. 9 a.m.-3 p.m. and Saturday 8:30 am.-noon; and **Banco Nacional,** tel. 643-3072, open Mon.-Fri. 8:30 a.m.-3:45 p.m., both have branches in the town

center. Expect long delays. Banco Popular has a 24-hour ATM for Visa. **Western Union** is opposite La Bruja restaurant.

The **Centro Medico Bolaños,** tel. 643-3616, is at the north end of town. **Farmacia Jacó,** tel. 643-3205, 50 meters south of Banco Nacional, is open 8 a.m.-8 p.m. The **Red Cross,** tel. 643-3090, post is 50 meters south of Banco Popular, with another medical clinic adjacent.

Centro Comerical El Paso contains an **international communications center,** open 7 a.m.-9 p.m., which charges $3 per minute ($2 weekends) for calls to the U.S; a **Fujicolor** store; plus the **post office.** The main post office is opposite the **police station,** 50 meters east of the soccer field in Garabito. You can also send mail more rapidly via **TNT Worldwide Express,** tel. 643-3207, 20 meters south of El Paso.

Banana Bath Lavanderia, tel. 643-3786, can take care of your laundry needs.

Getting There and Away

By Bus: Buses depart San José from Calle 16; Avenidas 1/3, tel. 223-1109, 233-5567, or 643-3074, at 7:30 a.m., 10:30 a.m., and 3:30 p.m. (2.5 hours). Alternatively, buses between San José and Quepos and Manuel Antonio stop at Restaurant El Bosque in Jacó. From Puntarenas, buses to Jacó and Quepos depart from near the train station at 5 a.m. and 2:30 p.m. Return buses depart Jacó for San José at 5 a.m., 11 a.m., and 3 p.m., and for Puntarenas at 6 a.m. and 4 p.m., from the Supermercado in town, and picking up at the north end of town also. Buses are crowded on weekends—get there early.

Interbus stops at Jacó on its daily shuttle between San José and Manuel Antonio.

A microbus operates from the Best Westesrn Irazú in San José to its sister hotel, the Best Western Jacó Beach ($15 one-way). Reservations are advised, tel. 232-4811, but hotel guests get priority.

By Air: Travelair flies daily between San José and Tambor (see appendix). You can charter an air-taxi to the airstrip at the northern end of Jacó.

By Car: Ada Rent-a-Car, tel./fax 643-3207 in Jacó, tel. 233-7733 in San José, and **Elegante Rent-a-Car,** tel. 643-3224, have offices. **Economy Rent-a-Car,** tel./fax 643-3280, has an office in the Best Western.

Getting Around

Rent a scooter, mountain bike, or four-wheel cycle. **Rent-a-Moto,** 50 meters north of Banco Nacional, has scooters, as does **Freyka Rental,** 20 meters south of La Bruja restaurant. You can rent **bicycles** from Rent-a-Bike, next to Restaurante Peruano for $2 per hour, $10 per day; it's $4 per hour for a quadcycle.

For taxis, call **Taxi Jacó,** tel. 643-3009, and **Taxi 30-30,** tel. 643-3030.

PLAYA HERMOSA

Highway 34 south from Jacó crests a steep headland, beyond which Playa Hermosa comes into sight (the view is incredible, but don't get close to the cliff edge); the beach is 10 km long and arrow straight with surf pummeling ashore along its whole length. Playa Hermosa is the setting for an international surfing championship each August and has been put on the holidaymakers' maps in the past few years. A dirt road parallels the beach.

Accommodations and Food

Shoestring: A stone's from Cabinas Arenas is **Ola Bonita,** tel. 643-3990, e-mail: olabonita@usanet.co.cr, with seven fully equipped rooms with private bath and cold water. They're cross-ventilated, have kitchenettes, and walls of whitewashed stone. A pool and cafe were planned. Rates: $10 pp

Budget: Cabinas Rancho Grande, tel. 643-3529, at the north end of the beach, is a three-story Robinson Crusoe-style log and bamboo structure with six basic rooms sharing a single bathroom (smelly when I visited) and kitchen. The top floor has a single A-frame room. There are fans, but no hot water. It's run by Floridians Rhonda and Brian. Perfect for budget-minded surfers.

Nearby is the offbeat **Cabinas Arenas,** tel. 643-3508 or 643-1495, run by a friendly surfer named Tom Ford. The place is beloved by surfers. The six rooms are in a two-story unit, each with refrigerator, fan, stove, and private bath and cold water. Rates: $25 up to five people. Attached is the **Jungle Surf Café,** a *rancho* cafe serving Tex-Mex, "killer omelettes," burgers, and filet mignon. Surf movies play on the TV at the bar.

The older **Cabinas Vista Hermosa,** tel. 643-3422, or 224-3787 in San José, next to Ola Bonita, has 10 simple and spartan rooms (varying in size from 2-8 people) in a rambling home. All have kitchens and private bath with cold water. Some rooms are dingy. Facilities include two small pools. It's favored by Tico families. Rates: $25 d, $42 quad, $67 octet. **Bar y Restaurante Surf** is next door.

Nearby is **Hotel Villas Hermosa,** tel. 643-3373, also very appealing for more modest budgets. Nine spacious, fully furnished, a/c self-catering cabins, each complete with kitchen, one double and two single beds (some have two singles), are set in delightful landscaped grounds with a small pool in the shape of a whale. Rates: $30 s/d, $40 t, $50 quad. For nightlife, there's the **Bar Las Palmereños,** 100 meters north, on the coast road.

Inexpensive: The **Cabinas Las Olas,** tel./fax 643-3687, next to Cabinas Arenas, is a modern three-story structure with six nicely kept rooms with kitchenettes and patios. There are also three cabins, each with two single beds below and a double in the loft. There's a pool and the **Hard Charger's Café** beachside. Rates: $40 d.

Moderate: At the extreme north end of the beach is **Terraza del Pacífico,** Apdo. 168, Jacó, tel. 643-3222, fax 643-3424, or direct tel. 643-3222, fax 643-3424, e-mail: terraza@sol.racsa.co.cr; in the U.S., P.O. Box 31288, Raleigh, NC 27622, tel. (800) 835-1223, a modern, upscale complex. This very appealing contemporary Spanish colonial-style property has a superb location, with cliffs immediately to the north and the vast expanse of beach disappearing into the distance to the south. The 43 rooms, including three suites, have a/c, satellite TVs, telephones, and sofa beds and double beds. A red-tiled causeway leads downhill through pretty landscaped grounds surrounding a beautiful, circular pool with a swim-up bar in the center. You'll also find a casino, and a restaurant and bar that open onto the beach. Sunbathing chairs are provided beneath tiny beach *ranchitas.* Rates: $55 s/d/t low season; $72 high season.

Nearby, the modern **Hotel Fuego del Sol,** tel. 643-2737, fax 643-3637, also known as Hotel David, is a handsome two-story colonial-style structure in landscaped grounds. It has 20 spacious a/c rooms with cool tiles painted in tropical motifs, fans, TVs, minibars, and private baths with hot water, plus an amoeba-shaped pool with swim-up bar, a gym, and a beachfront restaurant. Rates: $60 s, $68 d, $78 t.

The upscale **Club Resort Las Gondolas,** tel. 643-3108, fax 643-3509, was under construction, immediately south of Terraza del Pacífico, with condos and tennis courts; and the beachfront **Beach Club Hermosa,** two km south, was due to open before 2000.

Tours and Activities
Playa Hermosa Stables, tel. 643-3808, has four-hour tours to nearby waterfalls ($35). **Captain Tom's Sportfishing,** tel. 643-3995, offers inshore, offshore, and night fishing using a 26-foot Boston whaler ($300-400 half day, $500-600 full day for four people).

Getting There
Interbus stops at Playa Hermosa on its daily shuttle between San José and Manuel Antonio. A shuttle bus once operated between the Best Western Jacó Beach and the Terraza del Pacífico, at Playa Hermosa, and may still do so.

PLAYAS ESTERILLOS OESTE AND CENTRO

Playa Esterillos Oeste is south of Hermosa, with craggy Punta Judas between them. It's another favorite with surfers and with Ticos on holidays and weekends (the Ticos leave it littered with trash). The seven-km-long beach has tide pools at its northern end, where a sculpture of a mermaid sits atop the rocks. Beware strong currents; you can swim safely in the lee of rocks at the northern end of the beach. Here, when the tide recedes, you can delight in treasures the earth has kept hidden for millions of years: an ancient mosaic of mollusk fossils embedded in the rock strata. Leave them for others to enjoy. The **National Museum,** tel. 257-1433, organizes educational trips to Esterillos Oeste, a good trip for fossil hounds. **Rancho Nuevo,** in Quepos, tel. 777-1503, is a Dutch-run stable nearby.

The sandy beachfront track ends at an estuary, beyond which lies **Esterillos Centro,** accessed by a separate road signed off Hwy. 34.

Accommodations and Food
Lodgings seem to come and go; check before venturing out.

Cabinas Zoricar, tel. 235-2946, on the approach road to the beach, has six small but clean and simple rooms and two larger rooms (for eight people) with full kitchens and dining rooms. All have small private baths and cold water. The **Restaurant Oleaje** is adjacent. Rates: $11 s/d small; $54 large rooms. A side road west of Zoricar leads north to Punta Judas and the **Shake Bar Musical,** a local hangout that serves *típico* dishes (it sits on a rise with views but is otherwise no great shakes). There's a small **campsite** beneath shade trees. En route you'll pass

Oesterillo Oeste

the soulless **Cabinas Sirena,** tel. 779-9194, with 20 meagerly appointed rooms, including three large rooms with kitchens. It's popular with Tico families. Rates: $11 s/d small; $54 large rooms. There are other *cabinas* nearby.

At the beach, options include **Cabinas Don José, Bar y Restaurante Totos,** and **Cabinas, Restaurant y Disco Las Caleteras,** tel. 717-2143, which has a three-room casita with a kitchen and cold-water bath. Rates: $12 s/d; $15 t. It also has a disco complete with flashing lights, a jukebox, and a DJ's booth.

Cabinas Esterillos Oeste, tel./fax 446-5967, one km south, has seven cabins, each with a double bed and bunk plus private bath with cold water. Rates: $10 pp. Following the beachfront road south, you come to the center of the action, with **Camping Oceano,** which also has sportfishing, the **Bar y Restaurant El Barrilito,** and, next door, **Cabinas Las Brisas,** tel. 717-1513, with an open-air restaurant. The latter, writes reader Heinrich Maier, has "double room without fan with extremely run-down disgusting shared bath for $12." It also has rooms with private baths but no fans ("recommended") for $15.

Accommodations at Esterillos Centro is limited to the basic **Cabinas Villarce,** and the French-Canadian-run **La Felicidad Country Inn,** Apdo. 73-6300, Parrita, tel. 779-9003, fax 779-9140, both north of the T-junction at the beach. The latter has nine rooms (some with shared bath) of varying size, with cool tile floors, pleasant bathrooms, and hammocks under *ranchitas.* Three rooms upstairs have wooden floors, kitchenettes with bar counter, and balconies. Two are adapted for travelers with disabilities. The bar and restaurant is popular with locals. There's a small swimming pool. Rates: $15-25 d low season; $20 s, $25 d, $40 d with kitchenette high season.

PLAYAS ESTERILLOS ESTE, BEJUCO, AND PALMA

Playa Esterillos Este, separated by a river from Esterillos Centro, is identical to its northerly siblings: kilometers long, ruler-straight, with gray sand cleansed by high surf. There's a grass airstrip paralleling the beach at its northern end, accessed off Hwy. 34. The southern end of the

beach is known as **Playa Bejuco,** reached via a separate access road.

Farther south, about four km north of Parrita, a dirt road leads west from the coast road—Costanera Sur—and zigzags through African palm plantations until you emerge at Playa Palma (also known as Playa Bandera), separated from Bejuco by yet another rivermouth.

Accommodations and Food
The simple but pleasing **Auberge du Pélican,** Apdo. 47, Parrita 6300, tel. 779-9108, fax 779-9236, is run by French-Canadians. There are eight rooms (two are accessible for wheelchairs) in a two-story house, plus two rooms in a separate casita. Each has ceiling fan, hot water, and safety box. Upper-story rooms have heaps of light and are breezy. Some have shared baths, which are spacious and clean. There are hammocks beneath shady palms, plus a barbecue pit, a small pool, and a shuffleboard court. Three meals daily ($15) are served in a large dining room. Rates: $30 s/d, $40 with private bath.

The **Flor de Esterillos,** no telephone, fax 779-9141, website www.cam.org/-multigr/index.html, 200 meters farther south, has nine chalets, each different but all simply and attractively furnished in twee decor, with terra-cotta tile floors, ceiling fans, small kitchen, patio. There's a small pool and a small thatched restaurant. Occasionally, an ultralight offers 10-minute flightseeing tours ($20). Rates: $65 d; $300 per week.

The University of Costa Rica has basic *cabinas* and a restaurant (open to the public) at Playa Bejuco. Here, too, is **Centro Turístico Bejuco** offering camping, simple cabins, plus bathrooms and a *ranchito* restaurant.

At Playa Palma is the lively **Bar/Restaurant Rancho Bandera.** There are cabins about 200 meters north, including **Cabinas Maldonado,** tel. 286-1116, fax 227-5257, with six cabins with private baths and cold water. Rates: $33 for up to four people, $46 six people, $83 with a/c and large kitchen and lounge, for eight people. The beach road south of Rancho Bandera leads to **Rancho Emel,** a popular bar and restaurant with 10 modest rooms with private baths and hot water (rates: $30 up to four), and, one km farther, the more rustic **Cabinas y Restaurante Concha Mar,** which also has **camping.** Farther south are **Ruta del Sol,** tel. 779-9075, and **Cabinas Alexis.**

PARRITA

This small town, 45 km south of Jacó, is a center for the 1,700-hectare African oil palm ranch established by United Brands Fruit Co. in 1985. Driving Hwy. 34 you'll pass oil-processing plants and plantation villages of gaily painted, two-story stilt houses set around a soccer field.

A road immediately south of Parrita leads to **Playa Palo Seco**, another gray-sand beach (separated from Playa Bandera by a river) that seems to go forever and is backed by the mangrove swamps of the Palo Seco and Damas estuaries.

Hacienda El Tecal, tel. 223-3130, hosts a "forest recreational facility" known as **Bosque y Villas Margarita**, with *cabinas* and camping, a pool, hiking trails, horses, and more. It is 12 km inland via a dirt road about two km north of Parrita.The **Río Parrita** cascades from the Fila Bustamante mountain range, offering class II/III whitewater rafting. **Costa Rica Adventure Tours** offers trips from Quepos (see appendix).

Accommodations and Food
I can't think of a reason to stay in Parrita, but if you do stop here your options include the **Hotel Río Lindo** and **Hotel Nopal,** tel. 779-9216, opposite each other on the main road. The **Pizzeria/Café Yoli,** at the west end of town, has breakfasts and offers tourist information and horseback trips into the mountains.

At Playa Palo Seco, **Complejo Villas Las Flores,** tel. 779-9117, fax 779-9108, is a Canadian-owned apartotel complex with units spread out amid a large field, 150 meters from the beach. Not reviewed. **Cabinas Nidia,** tel. 779-9684, 400 meters south of Beso del Viento, has two-story houses with kitchens for up to 10 people. Rates: $250 weekly.

The best place is **Beso del Viento,** Apdo. 86, Parrita 6300, tel. 779-9674, fax 779-9615; in Canada, tel. (514) 383-7559, fax 383-0971, a handsome Spanish colonial-style home operated as a bed-and-breakfast hotel by an amiable French-Canadian couple, Jean and Huguette. They offer five rooms (one with private bath) and two spacious loft apartments, the latter with kitchens. Rooms share very nice bathrooms with a deep tub/shower and hot

water. A large lounge-cum-dining area boasts a pool table. Artwork abounds. You feel as if you're staying in a friend's home. The pool and wide sundeck with hammocks are good for lazing. Monkeys come down from the forest behind the hotel (you may see them on guided boating trips into the nearby *estero*). An eight-meter sportfishing boat is available for charters and tours to Manuel Antonio and farther afield. Rates: $45 d shared bath; $50 d private bath, including breakfast. Lunch and dinner are offered à la carte.

Apartotel La Isla, Apdo. 472, San José 1007, tel. 222-6561 or 779-9016, fax 233-5384, at the end of Playa Palo Seco, has 18 very spacious twin-bedroom cabins with kitchenettes spread out among lawns, 100 meters from the beach. A large open-air barbecue restaurant has a swimming pool adjacent. It's backed by a river and mangroves. You can rent canoes and horses. Rates: $70 d, $81 t, $93 quad hotel rooms, including tax and breakfast; $52 d, $58 t, $69 quad apartments. *Overpriced!*

Services
Parrita has a **Banco Nacional, Banco de Costa Rica,** and a **gas station.**

RAINMAKER ADVENTURE RETREAT

This 600-hectare private reserve opened in late 1997 on the forested slopes of the Fila Chonta mountains, near the village of Pocares, southeast of Parrita. At its heart—the main draw—is a treetop trail formed by six suspension bridges slung between trees to form a 250-meter aerial walkway (claimed to be the longest treetop tour in the world) through the rainforest canopy. Far below, a wooden boardwalk and other bridges lead you through a canyon that reverberates with the musical notes of rushing water, with cool pools for bathing. (It's a stiff climb up several hundred steps to reach the first platform.)

Other trails lead into the reserve, which forms part of the Quepoa Biological Corridor linking the Chonta range with protected forests of the Río Dota area and the Talamancas, and a vital migratory passage for birds and animals. The reserve climbs through four distinct ecological zones—including cloud forest—up to 1,700 meters elevation. Horseback riding is offered to the Damas Caves, which have stalactites and stalagmites.

Rainmaker, tel. 777-1250, is the brainchild of Jim Damalis, owner of the Si Como No hotel in Manuel Antonio. A restaurant and interpretive center were almost complete at press time. And a campground and cabins will be opened.

Several hotels and tour operators in Quepos and Manuel Antonio offer tour excursions here. For example, **Costa Rica Adventure Travel,** tel./fax 777-0850, e-mail: iguana@sol.racsa.co.cr, has a guided waterfall hiking tour ($45) and a horseback riding tour ($49) twice daily. The turnoff from the Costanera Sur is 10 km east of Parrita, 15 km west of Quepos.

DAMAS ESTUARY

South of Parrita, the waters of the Ríos Palo Seco and Damas form braided channels behind the coast. The estuary is a maze of mangrove swamp, home to crocodiles, monkeys, pumas, coatimundis, and wading and water birds by the thousands. **Isla Damas** lies across the 400-meter-wide estuary and is reached by boat ($1.50 each way) from the dock in **Damas,** one km west of Hwy. 34. You can walk across the island to a beach, or visit the small **zoo** run by Emilda; it has snakes, monkeys, and so on.

At the west end of Isla Damas is a smaller island—**Isla Damita**—popular with excursion trippers from Quepos for its floating restaurant.

Accommodations
At Damas, the **Pueblo Real** resort, tel./fax 777-0536; or Apdo. 1136, San José 2000, tel. 232-2211, fax 232-0587, spreads across 120 hectares on the banks of the river. It features two tennis courts, a free-form swimming pool, a marina, and fully furnished Spanish-style condos with elegant rooms boasting modern furnishings. Rates: $50 s, $65 d per night. A golf course was planned.

Cabinas La Isla, tel. 777-0514, opposite, offers more modest rooms, as does **Cabinas El Tucán,** between Hwy. 34 and the river.

On Isla Dama, **Cabinas Roma** has basic rooms and a restaurant. Or try the simple waterfront **El Bole de Marisco** restaurant. A floating restaurant called **Flotante La Tortuga** leaves from Isla Damita nightly; it serves seafood and "international dishes."

Getting There and Away
Tour operators in Quepos offer guided excursions—typically costing $55 including lunch or dinner. You can also visit Isla Damas by renting a boat with guide ($17 per hour, up to eight passengers) at the waterfront dock. Eduardo Rojas Esquibel is recommended; he operates **Marleni Tours,** tel. 777-0514.

A taxi from Quepos costs about $4.

BOB RACE

QUEPOS AND VICINITY

QUEPOS

Quepos (pop. 11,000) has been catapulted to fame among sportfishers and as the gateway for travelers heading to Manuel Antonio National Park, seven km south. There's little of interest to see in town, except perhaps the dilapidated

fishing village of **Boca Vieja** east of the bridge into town, with rickety plank walkways extending over an unappealing muddy beach called Blue Bay—and the old residential compounds of the Standard Fruit Company, whose clapboard homes are hidden in the hills south of town.

In February 1563, the conquistador Juan Vásquez de Coronado arrived in the region. One

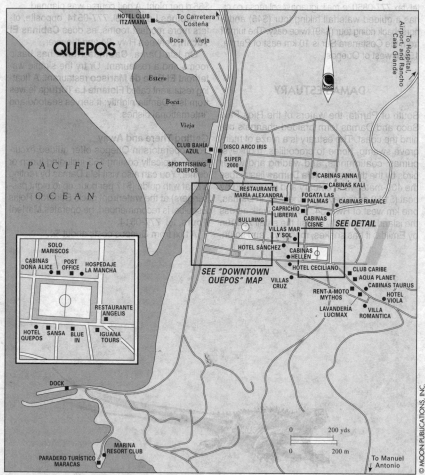

QUEPOS

HOTEL CLUB ITZAMANA

To Carretera Costeña

Boca Vieja

Estero

Boca

Vieja

PACIFIC

OCEAN

CLUB BAHÍA AZUL

DISCO ARCO IRIS

SUPER 2000

SPORTFISHING QUEPOS

To Hospital, Airport, and Rancho Casa Grande

CABINAS ANNA

CABINAS KALI

RESTAURANTE MARÍA ALEXANDRA

FOGATA LAS PALMAS

CABINAS RAMACE

CAPRICHIO LIBRERIA

CABINAS CISNE

BULLRING

VILLAS MAR Y SOL

HOTEL SÁNCHEZ

CABINAS HELLEN

SEE DETAIL

HOTEL CECILIANO

CLUB CARIBE

AQUA PLANET

SEE "DOWNTOWN QUEPOS" MAP

VILLAS CRUZ

CABINAS TAURUS

RENT-A-MOTO MYTHOS

HOTEL VIOLA

LAVANDERÍA LUCIMAX

VILLA ROMANTICA

SOLO MARISCOS

CABINAS DOÑA ALICE

POST OFFICE

HOSPEDAJE LA MANCHA

RESTAURANTE ANGELIS

HOTEL QUEPOS

SANSA

BLUE IN

IGUANA TOURS

DOCK

MARINA RESORT CLUB

PARADERO TURÍSTICO MARACAS

0   200 yds

0   200 m

To Manuel Antonio

© MOON PUBLICATIONS, INC.

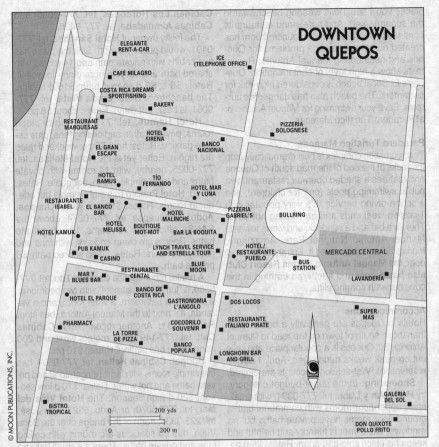

DOWNTOWN QUEPOS

- ELEGANTE RENT-A-CAR
- ICE (TELEPHONE OFFICE)
- CAFÉ MILAGRO
- COSTA RICA DREAMS SPORTFISHING
- BAKERY
- PIZZERIA BOLOGNESE
- RESTAURANT MARQUESAS
- HOTEL SIRENA
- BANCO NACIONAL
- EL GRAN ESCAPE
- HOTEL RAMUS
- TÍO FERNANDO
- HOTEL MAR Y LUNA
- RESTAURANTE ISABEL
- EL BANCO BAR
- HOTEL MALINCHE
- PIZZERIA GABRIEL'S
- BULLRING
- HOTEL MELISSA
- BOUTIQUE MOT-MOT
- BAR LA BOQUITA
- HOTEL KAMUK
- LYNCH TRAVEL SERVICE AND ESTRELLA TOUR
- HOTEL/ RESTAURANTE PUEBLO
- MERCADO CENTRAL
- PUB KAMUK
- CASINO
- RESTAURANTE CENTAL
- BLUE MOON
- BUS STATION
- MAR Y BLUES BAR
- LAVANDERÍA
- HOTEL EL PARQUE
- BANCO DE COSTA RICA
- GASTRONOMIA L'ANGOLO
- DOS LOCOS
- SUPER MAS
- PHARMACY
- COCODRILO SOUVENIR
- RESTAURANTE ITALIANO PIRATE
- LA TORRE DE PIZZA
- BANCO POPULAR
- LONGHORN BAR AND GRILL
- BISTRO TROPICAL
- GALERIA DEL SOL
- DON QUIXOTE POLLO FRITO

0   200 yds

0   200 m

© MOON PUBLICATIONS, INC.

---

of the first missions in Costa Rica was established here in 1570; you can still see the ruins up the **Río Naranjo,** northeast of town and popular today for whitewater rafting. Vásquez found the area populated by Quepoa Indians, a subtribe of the Borucas. In addition to farming, the Quepoa fished and trapped sea turtles. The Spanish soon forced them onto less fertile lands, and it wasn't long before European diseases and musket balls had devastated the indigenous population. Many local inhabitants still bear the facial features of their aboriginal forebears.

Toward the end of the 19th century, agricultural colonies were established in the coastal plains,

followed by banana plantations in the 1930s. Bananas came to dominate the economy, and Quepos rose to prominence as a banana-exporting port. The plantations were blighted by disease in the 1950s, and the bananas were replaced by African palms, which produce oil for the food, cosmetic, and machine-oil industries. The trees stretch in neatly ordered rows for miles north and south of Quepos. The oil is high in cholesterol and now the African-palm industry is in decline, a victim of these health-conscious times.

The town is booming on tourism. The streets were paved in 1997. The locals have adopted a less-is-more dress code (this is one of the few places you'll see Ticas wearing beachwear in the supermarket). And hotels and restaurants continue to improve. But the tourism boom has created numerous sewage problems for Quepos and neighboring Manuel Antonio. Recent tests show a high level of contamination: Quepos's El Cocal beach is considered high-risk for swimmers. The beach also has dangerous currents. Save your swimming for Manuel Antonio or at Paradero Turístico Maracas.

Paradero Turístico Maracas
This recreation complex is built dramatically atop the rocks at the end of the road south of Quepos and features a shaded open-air restaurant, two public swimming pools (one for children), and a scuba-diving service. It's very popular with Ticos on weekends and on sizzling hot days. There's a bar and a sundeck, and views towards Manuel Antonio National Park. Amazingly, tourists haven't discovered it. Entrance: $1. Next door, the **Manuel Antonio Marina Resort Club** also has a pool and sheltered bathing in the cove beneath soaring cliffs.

Accommodations
Hotels in Quepos are generally a better value than those south of town on the road to Manuel Antonio. But Quepos is a popular place and sells out on peak weeks during Dec.-April; I advise reservations. Wet-season discounts are offered.
Shoestring: In the super-budget category, try **Hotel Mar y Luna,** tel. 777-0394, with small, basic upper-floor rooms with communal baths; ground floor rooms have private baths but no windows. The owner is friendly and helpful and keeps his place spic-and-span. Rates: $5-6 pp. More basic is the **Cabinas Doña Alice,** tel. 777-0419, next to the soccer field; and, next door, **Hospedaje La Mancha,** tel. 777-0216, with 10 rooms with shared bath and three *cabinas* with private bath. Rates: $5 pp rooms; $6 pp *cabinas*. **Cabinas Mary,** tel. 777-0128, has eight simple rooms with private bath and cold water. Rates: $6 s, $8.50 d. **Cabinas Anna,** tel. 777-0443, has 23 clean, simply furnished rooms with tile floors, and private bath and cold water. Rates: $6-15 pp; $23 with a/c. There's secure parking.

You'll also find several basic *cabinas* north of the bridge: **Cabinas La Tortuga; Hotel Familiar,** tel. 777-0078, half a kilometer from town;

Cabinas Los Horcones, tel. 777-0090; and **Cabinas Almuedaba,** tel. 777-0426.

The feisty owner of **Hotel Sánchez,** tel. 777-0491, would put anyone off. Still, the place has two cabins with private bath and 14 rooms with shared bath and varying from dingy to well-lit. Rates: $6 s, $8 d shared bath; $15 d cabins. The beachfront **Hotel Linda Vista,** tel. 777-0001, is basic but clean. Rates: about $8 pp.

Hotel Ramus, tel. 777-0245, has clean rooms, private baths, and ceiling fans, plus secure parking. Rates: from $6 pp; weekend rates are higher. Better yet is the **Hotel Melissa,** tel. 777-0025, nearby, with 14 rooms with private baths and fans; simple, clean, adequate. Rates: $9 pp. **Hotel Pueblo** has eight simple but adequate rooms. Rates: $12 s/d. **Hotel Quepos,** Apdo. 79, Quepos, tel. 777-0274, above the SANSA office, has 20 rooms, 13 with private baths. Rooms are clean and airy, with fans and hardwood floors. Rates: $6 pp shared bath, $8 private bath.

A reader recommends **Cabinas Tito,** tel. 777-0589, a "turn-key apartment" with two bedrooms, a kitchen, a bathroom, a washroom, and a veranda. It's next to the Manuel Antonio bus stop. Rates: $13 d. Another recommends **Cabinas Cali,** tel. 777-1491, 200 meters west and 200 north of the bus station. Rates: $10 pp.

Budget: Cabinas Hellen, tel. 777-0504, has five simple rooms with fans, refrigerators, and private baths and hot water. Rates: $10 d low season; $20 d high season. The **Hotel Viña del Mar,** tel. 777-0070; or Apdo. 5527, San José, tel. 223-3334, north of the bridge over the Boca Vieja, has 20 spacious a/c rooms with ceiling fans and private baths. There's a small bar and restaurant overlooking the estuary, plus a boutique. Rates: $15 s, $20 d including breakfast.

Cabinas Ramace, tel. 777-0590, to the north, has three cabins, each with a double and two single beds, fans (one per bed), refrigerator, plus private bath and hot water. Rates: $20 s/d, $30 t; $45 s/d with a/c. Nearby, **Cabinas El Cisne,** tel. 777-1570, also with secure parking, has 12 cabins with fans, private baths, and hot water. Some have a TV and refrigerator, and a/c was planned. Take a room to the left: they're more spacious and appealing than the older rooms on the right. Each has a double and single bed. Rates: $20 s, $25 d, $30 t.

SPECIAL HOTEL: MAKANDA BY THE SEA

Makanda by the Sea, Apdo. 26, Quepos, tel. 777-0442, fax 777-1032, e-mail: makanda@sol.racsa.co.cr, is the class-act in town—a breathtakingly beautiful place blessed by an enviable setting and an aesthetic vision that comes close to perfection. Take, for example, the zigzag shaped pool suspended on the hillside, with a circular jacuzzi inset like a jewel and, to one side, a tiny restaurant—the Sunsport Poolside Bar and Grill—shaded by medieval-style canopies edged by carnal plum-purple curtains shifting slightly in the breeze. The cuisine is much revered hereabouts, so book early.

Three elegant villas and three studios are lined by walkways weaving through a series of Japanese gardens designed into the hillside and enfolded in velveteen jungle. Each is quite different. All, though, are of stunning contemporary conception, with king-size beds, vaulted ceilings, polished hardwoods,

hand-crafted tile enhancing the minimalist decor that melds suave Milan with soothing Kyoto. The timber-beamed bedrooms open directly onto their own wraparound verandas. No doors or windows. Just you and the tropical breezes, with fans and mosquito nets to keep bugs at bay. Even the kitchens are conjured from tropical hardwoods, with simple Japanese statements that are Makanda's calming, universal motif. The "large villa" comprises 1,000-square-foot Villa 1 and three studios (which can be taken together or in part for groups up to eight people). Villa 3 is my favorite.

Makanda is ensconced reclusively 400 meters from the main road, on the side road to Punta Quepos, and proffers miraculous ocean views, an allegorical vision down from Cloud Nine.

Rates: $110 studios, $150 villa low season; $150 studios, $210 villas high season.

Villa Cruz, tel. 777-0271, has four simple yet adequate cabins with fans, refrigerators, private baths and cold water, plus patios; there's also a villa with kitchen and hot water. Rates: $25 s/d/t cabins; $50 d villa; $10 extra person. The oceanfront **Hotel El Parque,** tel. 777-0063, has 12 relatively spacious but simple rooms. Rates: $20 s/d. **Hotel Malinche,** tel. 777-0093, downtown, has 29 well-kept, attractive rooms divided between older (with fans and cold water) and newer wings (with a/c and hot water). Rates: $10 s, $20 d older; $40 s/d newer. The family-run **Hotel Ceciliano,** tel. 777-0192, has 20 light and airy rooms—12 with private baths—with immaculately clean tiled floors, a little garden with caged birds, and a nice patio restaurant. Laundry service. Rates: $15 s/d, $19 t. Also try **Club Caribe,** tel./fax 777-0134, with simple cabins with fans and private bathrooms. Rates: $25 d. It also has villas and private parking.

The following accommodation options are on the southeast outskirts: **Cabinas Primo,** tel. 777-0134, pleasant but basic; **Cabinas Geylor,** tel. 777-0561, 25 meters beyond Primo, with basic rooms with private baths (rates: $20 t); **Cabinas Delicia,** tel. 777-0306; **Cabinas Tauro,** tel. 777-0014, basic but modern and clean; **Cabinas Ipakarahi,** tel. 777-0392; and **Cabinas El Cedros,** tel. 777-0950.

Inexpensive: The **Hotel Kamuk,** Apdo. 18-6350, Quepos, tel. 777-0379, fax 777-0258, is a real class act. It has 28 spacious and elegant, nicely furnished a/c rooms (some with balconies; all with TVs and telephones), all beautifully decorated in light pastels. The Miraolas Bar and Restaurant on the third floor has vistas over El Cocal Beach and serves good international cuisine. There's a small boutique, an amoeba-shaped pool, plus a classy bar and a small casino downstairs. The hotel can organize day tours. Rates: $45 s/d including breakfast.

Hotel Sirena, tel./fax 777-0528, is clean and pleasant, with 14 double rooms with a/c, private baths and hot water. A central sundeck offers a pool. The hotel specializes in horseback trips on Savegre Ranch and also offers rafting and fishing. Rates: $45 s, $55 d, including tax and breakfast.

The aptly named and reclusive **Hotel Villa Romántica,** tel. 777-0037, fax 777-0604, e-mail: villaromantica@hotmail.com, is southeast of town off the road to Manuel Antonio. The two-tiered Mediterranean-style building is set in pretty landscaped grounds. Sixteen simply but nicely appointed rooms have spacious bathrooms, heaps of light, and lots of whites and purples, with murals of bamboo arching to form faux headboards. Balconies and dining terraces (breakfast only) overlook a swimming pool. It offers free e-mail service for guests. *Recommended!* Rates: $35 s, $49 d.

On the road to Manuel Antonio is **Hotel Viola,** tel. 777-0124, with seven very clean rooms with fans and private baths with hot water. Rates: $35 s/d, $40 t, $45 quad.

For self-catering, try **Los Corales Apartotel,** tel./fax 777-0006, which has pleasing modern apartments. Half a block east of Costa Rican Dreams is the **Apartotel El Coral,** tel. 777-0528, fax 777-0044. **Restaurant Nahomi** rents two apartments in the center of Quepos, both with TVs, parking, and full kitchens. Rates: $450 per month apartment for three people; $600 apartment for four. Mrs. Andersson, tel. 222-6756, has a wooden *casita-* style house for rent on the hill south of Quepos.

Moderate: The best place in town is surely **Manuel Antonio Resort Club,** tel. 777-1130, boasting an atmospheric locale beneath soaring cliffs at the end of the road south of the dock, with jade waters for swimming and watersports. There's a small pool and sundeck, plus a bar and restaurant (sushi bar seasonally), and just *one* guest room, with views towards Manuel Antonio National Park. Rates: $70 d.

Self-catering apartments (for five people) are offered for rent in **Pueblo Real,** tel. 777-0845, fax 777-0827. Rates: $70 d. There's a swimming pool.

Lastly, hidden behind walls northeast of town is **Club Hotel Itzamana,** Apdo. 103-6350, Quepos, tel./fax 777-0351, which has modest rooms with private bathrooms. It has a pool.

Expensive: Northeast of town, **Hotel Rancho Casa Grande,** Apdo. 618, Zapote, San José 2010, tel. 777-0330, fax 253-2363, is set in 73 hectares on the road to the Quepos airport, with 14 pleasantly furnished a/c rooms and 10 fully equipped bungalows amid sprawling lawns with winding pathways. Highlights include a kidney-shaped swimming pool, a jacuzzi, horseback riding, nature trails into the surrounding forest, and guided tours. Rates: $80 d, $85-95 bungalow low season; $95 d, $110-125 bungalow high season. It also has sportfishing packages.

Food

Quepos has garnered new sophistication of late, but has excellent budget eating options, too. Food in Quepos runs the international gamut.

The place to start your day is **Café Milagro,** tel. 777-1707, which roasts its coffee fresh, and sells iced coffee, espresso, and cappuccino ($1.75) and a *queppoccino* (chocolate coffee shake, $2), plus a hearty granola and yogurt ($2). Next door, **El Gran Escape Restaurante,** tel. 777-0395, has classy decor and serves seafood, surf-and-turf, tuna melts ($5), enchiladas ($6), burgers, and *típico* meals; upstairs is a sushi bar. **Dos Locos,** tel. 777-1526, also serves Mexican food (my $6 *burrito gigante* was superb). Craving a burger or barbecue? Try **Longhorn Restaurant and Bar,** an almost authentic re-creation of Texas, with barbecue ribs, burgers, and eggs Benedict on the breakfast menu. It serves *bocas* with beers and sells beer for 75 cents during happy hour (5-7 p.m.).

The airy **Restaurante Isabel** on the beach-front "strip" has a comprehensive menu including seafood such as mahimahi with garlic ($3.50) and T-bone steaks ($5). The **Mira Olas Bar and Restaurant,** tel. 777-0379, atop Hotel Kamuk, has an extensive seafood menu (try the octopus in garlic sauce, $4); downstairs, the hotel's open-air patio *soda* serves sandwiches, *refrescos,* and ice creams.

You'll think you're in New York when you pop into **Gastronomia L'Angolo,** a *real* Italian deli. Also for Italian food, try **Pizza Gabriel,** tel. 777-1085, where pizzas cost from $4; and the modestly elegant **Pizzeria Bolognese,** tel. 777-0650, with a large pasta menu, gnocchi, and pizzas ($3-6).

Chinese? Try **Restaurante María Alexander,** tel. 777-0876. There's even a sushi bar, **RoKu,** tel. 777-1130, run by Chef "Shogo" at the Manuel Antonio Marina Club.

Budget eateries include the simple **Soda Mariscos** serving seafood; and the delightfully funky **Fogata Las Palmas,** tel. 777-1841, serving wood-fired oven-roasted chicken on a rustic patio (2-11 p.m.). The **Restaurant La Marquesa** has $1 breakfasts, *casados* for $1.50, and seafood and chicken dishes for $2-3. It's always full of locals.

For ice cream, head to **Escalofrio,** tel. 777-0833, on the road to Manuel Antonio, to gorge on banana splits and shakes at this "Italian ice cream factory."

There's a **bakery** opposite Hotel Sirena. **La Botánica** sells organic farm produce.

Entertainment

Quepos has some of the best bars in Costa Rica. Two sports fans from Texas run the lively, unpretentious **El Banco Bar,** with satellite TV, darts, and live rock bands—a Key West kind of place for aging hippies (open 3 p.m.-1 a.m.; closed Wednesday). **Tío Fernando,** opposite, is a more intimate, romantic bar. The **Pub Kamuk** is for those who like stylish avant-garde decor. It also has live bands and a wide-screen TV. The moody **Mar y Blues,** opposite, is another popular spot that was playing blues music when I called in. The **Bistro Tropical** has soft red lighting and romantic music. The **Gran Escape Bar** in Restaurant Ana is favored by local Ticos. Seeking a piece of American pie? Check out the **Longhorn Saloon,** a down-home bar with satellite TV and Texan decor. There are plenty of bars where you can sup with local Ticos (they have *their* nocturnal hangouts, and the gringos have theirs).

Wanna dance? North of the bridge, **Bahía Azul,** tel. 777-0636, is favored by Ticos and has an open-air disco, with deafening Latin music. Entrance: $2. *The* place to be, however, is **Arco Iris,** on a barge opposite Bahía Azul. It has mirrored walls and flashing lights and costs $2 to enter. It doesn't get in the groove until about 11 p.m. The **Maracas,** tel. 777-0707, fax 777-0706, at the end of the road south of the pier, has disco, with karaoke and dance contests. Wednesday is Ladies' Night. Closed Monday. Entrance: $1.25, or $2 with live band.

Quepos's famous **Carnivale** is back. It's not as debauched as Rio de Janeiro's famous bacchanal, nor as colorful as Trinidad's, but the three-week event (mid-February to early March) offers plenty of salacious fun and cultural entertainment. Also on the salacious side, the **Club Hotel Itzamana** (whose tall, husky Somalian owner was once a man but is now a woman) showcases beautiful exotic dancers—many from Colombia, Dominican Republic, and Puerto Rico—who perform on a mirrored stage beneath thatch. There's a swimming pool and, of course, rooms that rent by the hour. Entrance is free and there's no minimum drink fee, but the club hammers visitors for the drinks ($4 for beer, $7 for hard liquor). And thirsty "hostesses" are on hand to further lighten your wallet.

Alternately, you can try your luck at the Hotel Kamuk's **casino.**

Information

Lynch Tourist Service, Apdo. 97, Quepos, tel. 777-1170, fax 777-1571, e-mail: lyntur@sol.racsa. co.cr, acts as a full-service tourist bureau and information service. **Villas Selva Real Estate,** tel. 777-0495, on the road for Manuel Antonio, also acts as an information bureau, as does the lobby of the Hotel Kamuk.

Planet Quepos, tel. 777-1262, is a free monthly newsletter on the area, with information on tourism happenings, sports, and entertainment. The **Café Milagro** has U.S. newspapers and magazines and operates a tour information service.

sportfishing

JOHN ANDERSON

Compuservicios, tel. 777-1165 or 777-0823, offers computer services; open Mon.-Fri. 1-8 p.m. and Saturday 9 a.m.-5 p.m. **Villa Romántico** charges $5 per connection for e-mail. **Caprichio Librería** is the local bookstore; also try **Librería Luna,** which has a small selection of books and magazines in various languages.

Tours and Activities
Outward Bound, Apdo. 243, Quepos, tel./fax 777-1222 or tel. (800) 676-2018, has an office in Quepos, and offers a wide range of activities from whitewater rafting to conservation service projects.

Rafting and Sea Kayaking: River rafting is becoming popular hereabouts. One of the most important runs is on the **Río Naranjo. Costa Rica Adventure Tours,** tel./fax 777-0850, e-mail: iguana@sol.racsa.co.cr, alias Iguana Tours, offers one-, two-, and three-day sea kayaking trips to the mangrove lagoons of Damas ($55) and Manuel Antonio ($65), plus kayaking and river-rafting trips down the Ríos Naranjo and Parrita (class II/III, $55-70). The company also rents sea kayaks and has a dolphin watch tour, plus trips to Manuel Antonio by inflatable Zodiacs. **Amigos Del Río,** tel./fax 777-0082, offers rafting on the Río Savegre ($70) and Río Naranjo ($55), a trip to Isla Damas ($55), plus sea kayaking ($60).

Horseback Riding, Hiking, and Mountain Biking: Estrella Tours, tel./fax 777-1286, offers off-the-beaten-path guided mountain bike tours ($26-55) and horseback trips ($40-60), plus a full-day hiking trip in nearby mountains ($40), and a crocodile safari ($60). **Unicorn Adventures,** Apdo. 158, Quepos, tel. 777-0489, offers horseback riding tours with a focus on natural history. **Punta Quepos Trail Rides,** tel. 777-0566, also offers half-day guided horseback rides, including lunch on the beach; as does the **Damas Caves Rainforest Tour,** tel. 777-0070.

Scuba Diving and Watersports: Waverunner Safaris, tel. 777-1130, at Manuel Antonio Resort Club, has scuba and rents jet skis. **Aqua Planet Dive Center,** tel. 777-0833, has two dive trips daily ($55 two tanks), plus snorkeling trips ($35) and coastal cruises ($40). **Jungle Coast Jets,** tel. 777-1250, rents jet skis and has guided jet ski tours.

Cruises and Excursion Tours: Eco-Fan, Apdo. 618, Zapote 2010, tel. 777-0330, fax 777-1575, offers some intriguing tours, including one to the Palma Tica Oil Processing Plant, plus horseback riding and nature tours. **Costa Rican Dreams,** tel. 777-0593, fax 777-0592, runs multiday charter trips to Drake Bay and Caño Island, plus half-day coastal sightseeing trips to Manuel Antonio. **Sunset Sails Tours,** tel. 777-1304, has sunset cruises.

Lynch Tourist Service offers a gamut of tours, including trips into the Nara Hills behind Manuel Antonio, with a visit to a fruit farm and lunch plus afternoon cruise through the mangroves of Isla Damas aboard the *Tortuga* cruise boat ($65).

Taximar Tours, tel. 777-1647, offers a two-hour "dolphin watch nature cruise" daily at 9 a.m.($45), plus trips to Isla Caño on Wednesday and Saturday. It also has rafting and scuba diving trips.

Sportfishing: Protected from the heavy winds that restrict fishing on the northern Guanacaste coast for much of the year, the Quepos region offers outstanding sportfishing for marlin and sailfish in the peak season, December through August. The inshore reefs are also home to large populations of snapper, amberjack, wahoo, and tuna. Typical rates are $350 half day, $450 full day.

The following companies are based in Quepos: **Aurora Charters,** Apdo. 393, Quepos, tel./fax 777-1719; **Aventuras Poseidon,** Apdo. 185-6350, Quepos, tel./fax 777-0935, e-mail: cksibush@sol.racsa.co.cr; **Blue Fin Sportfishing,** Apdo. 223-6350, Quepos, tel. 777-1676, fax 777-0674, e-mail: bluefin@sol.racsa.co.cr; **Caribsea,** tel./fax 777-0631, in the U.S. tel. (800) 308-3394; **Costa Rican Dreams,** Apdo. 79, Belén, Heredia 4005, in Quepos tel. 777-0593, fax 777-0592, in San José tel. 239-3387, fax 239-3383; **Jesse Ballet's Sportfishing,** tel./fax 777-0221; **J.P. Sportfishing,** Apdo. 66-1100, Tibás, tel. 777-0757, in San José tel. 257-8503, fax 222-8134, in the U.S., tel. (800) 308-3394; **Pacific Coast Charters,** Apdo. 122-6350 Quepos, tel./fax 777-1382; **Sportfishing "High Tec,"** tel. 777-1172; and **Sportsfishing Quepos,** tel./fax 777-1381, which has an office in a small *ranchito* on stilts over the water in front of the bridge into town.

Surfing: The **Burro Surf Shop** rents and sells surf gear. A fellow called Mauricio "Tule" Jímenez makes surfboards. Another local surfer, Roger "Gafas" Morales, can advise on surfing conditions.

Other: The **Mountain Bike Club** (Cycling Estrella) meets on Sunday at 8 a.m. at the Café Milagro.

Services

Banks: The **Banco Nacional, Banco de Comercio,** and **Banco Popular**—open weekdays 8:30 a.m.-3:30 p.m. and Saturday 8:15-11:30 a.m.—all have branches. The Banco Popular has a 24-hour ATM for Visa and bank cards compatible with the Plus system.

Medical: The **Hospital Dr. Max Teran V,** tel. 777-0020, is three km south of town on the Costanera Sur. There are several pharmacies in town.

Communications: The **post office** is on the north side of the soccer field. The Hotel Melissa has **international telephone** service (Mon.-Sat. $2 per minute to the U.S., weekends $1.60). **Public telephones** face the ocean in front of the park.

Laundry: Casa Tica, tel. 777-0048, next to the bus station, offers same-day laundry service; it's open Mon.-Sat. 8 a.m.-5 p.m. **Lucimax Lavandería,** tel. 777-1721, is 200 meters southeast of the soccer field.

Shopping

Picante Art Gallery is above Iguana Tours, southeast of the soccer field. **Olnwatu** has beautiful batiks. And **L'Aventura,** tel. 777-1019, at Avenida Central and Calle 2, is an upscale store with beautiful leathers, batiks, jewelry, and quality souvenirs. The **T-Shirt Shop,** tel. 777-1110, specializes in sportfishing and ecological designs, while **Mot Mot Boutique** is an outlet for the Fundación Neotropical.

Souvenirs Los Tucanos, next to Cabinas Hellen, has T-shirts, sandals, Guatemalan clothing and artifacts, while **Galería Costa Rica** has print dresses and batiks. **Shock Arte** has a marvelous array of carvings, etc. You'll find several other very good small boutiques opposite the soccer field on the road leading to Manuel Antonio.

You can buy Cuban cigars at the Café Milagro. Look for the imaginative, free-spirited artwork of Baily Bedard, a Canadian artist-in-residence who often sets up easel outside Café Milagro.

Getting There and Away

By Bus: Buses depart San José for Manuel Antonio via Quepos from Calle 16, Avenidas 1/3 (tel. 223-5567, 223-1109 or 777-0318), at 6 a.m., noon, and 6 p.m. (3.5 hours); return buses depart Quepos at 6 a.m., noon, and 5 p.m. Indirect buses (five hours) depart San José at 7 a.m., 10 a.m., 2 p.m., 4 p.m., and 6 p.m., returning at 5 a.m., 8 a.m., 2 p.m., and 4 p.m. Direct buses originate in Manuel Antonio and fill up fast. Buses depart Puntarenas for Quepos daily, tel. 777-0138, at 5 a.m., 11 a.m., and 2 p.m., returning via Jacó at 4:30 a.m., 10:30 a.m., and 2 p.m. Check times ahead. Buses operate from Quepos to Dominical and San Isidro at 5:30 a.m. and 1:30 p.m. Buy your ticket as far in advance as possible. The ticket office is open 7-11 a.m. and 1-5 p.m. daily (Sunday 7 a.m.-2 p.m.).

Interbus stops at Quepos on its daily shuttle between San José and Manuel Antonio.

By Air: SANSA, in Quepos, tel. 777-0161, and **Travelair** have scheduled daily service to Quepos. In Quepos, **Lynch Travel Service,** tel. 777-1170, fax 777-1571, e-mail: lyntur@sol.racsa.co.cr, does air ticketing

By Boat: Taximar, tel./fax 777-1647 or 777-0262; or c/o Lynch Travel Service, tel. 777-1170, has a sea shuttle service between Quepos, Dominical ($20 one-way), Drake Bay ($55 one-way) and Caño Island ($85 roundtrip, including lunch and drinks) four times a week aboard a canopied seven-meter boat that makes a nifty 30 knots. Departs Quepos Tuesday, Thursday, Saturday, and Sunday 7 a.m.-4 p.m.

Pacific Winds Express, tel. 777-0137, fax 777-1685, has a two-hour sea shuttle to Tambor on the Nicoya Peninsula aboard 27-foot SeaCats (powerful and buoyant catamarans that can do 40 knots, cutting commuter time to ribbons), departing Quepos at 7:30 a.m. and 10 a.m. ($50). The owner, Tim Moore (who hangs out at Dos Locos Bar), also runs to Drake Bay.

Getting Around

You can walk everywhere in town. For taxis call **Quepos Taxi,** tel. 777-0277, which charges about $4 to Manuel Antonio. A *colectivo* (shared) taxi to Manuel Antonio costs 40 cents pp; a private taxi costs $2.50 (20% more after 10 p.m.).

Buses depart Quepos for Manuel Antonio at 5:40 a.m. and 7 a.m., then hourly 8 am.-7:30

p.m. and again at 9:30 p.m. (25 cents), returning at 6:10 a.m. and 7:30 a.m., then hourly 8:30 a.m.-8 p.m. and again at 10 p.m.

Elegante Rent-a-Car, tel. 777-0115, has an office next to Café Milagro (but was scheduled to move to an office closer to Manuel Antonio). Only a limited number of cars are available; make reservations in San José.

Rent-a-Moto Mythos, tel. 777-0006, southeast of town, rents bicycles ($16 per day), scooters ($9 per hour, $29 per day), 250cc motorcycles ($35 per day), and four-wheel motorcycles ($19 per hour).

QUEPOS TO MANUEL ANTONIO

Southeast of Quepos, a road climbs sharply over the forested headland of Punta Quepos and snakes, dips, and rises south along a ridgecrest for seven km before dropping down to Manuel Antonio—one of the two most touted destinations in Costa Rica—fringed by **Playa Espadilla,** a two-km-long scimitar of gray sand arcing east to west. There are other beaches tucked into tiny coves reached by dirt trails from the main road; one such leads from Hotel Villa Teca to **Playa La Macha.** There are occasional tantalizing views down to the beaches, but for most of the way the roadside is thickly forested. An army of hotels and restaurants lines the road; some enjoy fabulous ocean views and have become destinations in their own right.

There are lifeguards (*guardavidas*) at Playa Espadilla during high season. Prior to their advent, the ocean claimed 5-10 lives a year. Beware of rip tides when swimming.

The lively little hamlet of Manuel Antonio consists entirely of *cabinas* and restaurants (there's no local community) catering to the hordes of visitors who come to visit Manuel Antonio National Park, 800 meters east. It is still a favorite of budget-oriented travelers and retains its latter-day hippie feel, though the days of unspoiled innocence are long gone and the area has inexorably gone upscale in the past few years.

Jardín Gaia Wildlife Refuge Center

Jardín Gaia, Apdo. 182-6350, Quepos, tel. 777-0535, fax 777-1004, e-mail: wildlife@cariari.ucr.ac.cr, two km south of Quepos, is a wildlife center

that takes in injured and confiscated animals and attempts to rehabilitate them for release back into the wild. MINAE recognizes it as an official rescue center for the Central Pacific. Costa Rican veterinary students study their medicine here, supplementing the work of foreign specialists. All five monkey species are here, plus dozens of bird species, coatimundis, and other mammals. Many of the animals have been severely traumatized, and it is a moving experience to see them being nursed back to emotional health. There's also a walk-through **butterfly farm.** The center sponsors efforts to educate locals in ecosensitivity and assists in introducing programs aimed at improving economic circumstances for local communities.It accepts volunteers willing to work for a couple of weeks to a month or longer ($100 contribution). Donations are desperately needed.

It is *not* open for general visitors but has guided tours at 11 a.m. and 2 p.m. ($5 adults, free for children, 200 *colones* for Costa Ricans). Closed Wednesday.

Accommodations

Manuel Antonio is one of the most expensive areas in Costa Rica—a result of supply and demand. Budget hotels are mostly found down near Manuel Antonio village. More expensive hotels have loftier, breezy perches (some charge for location). Many are vastly overpriced and/or less appealing than their brochures and prices suggest. Most offer off-season discounts. Hill-top hotels may have steep steps; inquire. It can be a tough, hot walk back up the hill from the beach if you don't want to wait for the bus. Check to see if your hotel offers van service to and from the beach.

Hotels in each price category are listed as they appear along the road south from Quepos.

Camping: You can camp near the park entrance under shade trees on lawns at the back of the Hotel Manuel Antonio ($2 pp; showers cost 25 cents); it will supply tents ($6). You'll also find a campsite 100 meters north of Mimo's.

Budget: Cabinas Pedro Miguel, tel. 777-0035, tucked off the road one km south of Quepos, has eight small, basic rooms in a two-story building, with cement floors and cinderblock walls, and fans and private baths with cold water ($8 pp). Four have kitchenettes, are fully furnished, and sleep 4-8 ($30-50). There's a small cooling-off pool in shady grounds. Owners José Astóa and his wife, Nuvia, are on hand and happy to run errands, etc. Rates: $22 d ($4 extra bed).

La Colina, tel. 777-0231, about two km south of Quepos, has six simple rooms in a two-story *ranchito*-style house with black-and-white checkered floors. Rooms are dark but pleasant enough. Six newer rooms are more upscale, with lots of light, plus views from balconies. There's a small two-tier pool with cascade, and a nice *rancho* restaurant. Rates: $25 d including breakfast; newer rooms from $39 are a bargain.

Flor Blanca, tel. 777-1633, fax 777-0032, about three km south, has six large rooms in a two-story hillside house; each has refrigerator, fan, walls painted with tropical murals, plus private bathrooms with hot water. Some rooms are carpeted. There's a simple TV lounge and a small restaurant. Rates: $20 d, $30 with a/c low season; $30 d, $40 with a/c high season, including breakfast.

Cabinas/Restaurante Piscis, tel. 777-0046, about one km north of Manuel Antonio, has six clean and spacious but basic *cabinas* with fans and private baths with hot water. There's a wide patio veranda plus atmospheric restaurant. Rates: $26 d.

Hotel del Mar, tel./fax 777-0543, at the bottom of the hill near the beach, has adequate though relatively small rooms with balconies, fans, and private baths with cold water. It's a great location for the beach, right on the road and without views. Rates: from $25 d.

Cabinas Ramirez, tel. 777-0003, at Playa Espadilla, has 18 rooms with fans and private baths with cold water. Hardy low-budget travelers may love the shady, cool rooms with tiny little patios behind cages. I see them as basic, dingy, cramped, and overpriced. The beach is two minutes' walk away. Rates: $26 d; $4 extra person.

Restaurante/Hotel Vela Bar, Apdo. 13, Quepos, tel. 777-0413, toward the park and 100 meters inland, has nine *cabinas* with fans and private baths, plus a house and an apartment with kitchen. It has a sort of Mediterranean-meets-Switzerland feel, plus a very popular thatched restaurant and bar serving creative seafood dishes and daily specials. Rates: $20 d low season; $28 d high season; $60 for a casita. A stone's throw away is **Albergue Costa Linda,** tel. 777-0304, a hostel with very basic rooms with shared outside toilets and showers, some with private baths. The handsome frontage belies the dour interior, though the restaurant is attractive and serves veggie plates and *típico* specials. Rates: $8 shared bath; $20 private bath.

Hotel Manuel Antonio, tel. 777-1237, 400 meters east near the park entrance, has five clean, well-lit but meagerly furnished rooms upstairs. There's a simple restaurant serving *típico* dishes. Rates: $17 s/d/t.

Inexpensive: The venerable **Hotel Plinio,** Apdo. 71, Quepos, tel. 777-0055, fax 777-0558, near Quepos, has long been a favorite of budget travelers. It has a very tropical ambience: *palenque* roof, hardwoods surrounded by banana groves, and an upstairs open restaurant and bar with hints of a rambling East African treehouse. Some of the 14 rooms have two beds; three have a/c. Rooms are dark but clean and have hot water. There's an attractive swimming pool. A nature trail leads uphill through 10 hectares of primary forest to the highest point around, where a wooden *mirador* proffers a stunning 360-degree vista. I saw several poison-arrow frogs hopping around on the trail. Rates: $50 d, $60 with a/c, $75 two-story suite, $90 three-story suite, including buffet breakfast and tax.

El Mono Azul, Apdo. 297, Quepos, tel. 777-1548, fax 777-1954, e-mail: monoazul@sol.racsa.co.cr, has eight clean and comfortable rooms in handsome condo-style units facing a small and pretty oval pool. Each has one double bed and bunk beds, ceiling fans, and hot shower. Movies are shown free in the highly rated restaurant. Owners New Yorker Jennifer Rice and Spaniard Lilliana Cuore pamper guests (Lilliana offers massage), not least with their pizzas. There's a super-friendly Great Dane. Rates: $25 s, $30 d, $35 t low season; $10 extra high season.

Villa El Oasis, midway between Quepos and Manuel Antonio, has a room and a condo for rent. Rates: $35 room; $55 condo. **Villa La Roca,** tel. 777-1349, nearby, is a whitewashed Mediterranean-style villa run by two Germans. The five units—each different—hold 2-4 people, with terraces overlooking the ocean. Some have kitchenettes. Very pleasing. No telephones. Laundry service. Rates: $35-70 d.

Apartotel El Colibri, Apdo. 94, Quepos, tel. 777-0432, has 10 cozy duplex rooms with kitchenettes, fans, and private baths with hot water. Compact and basic, but light and clean. French doors open onto private terraces with hammocks. A beautiful colonial-tiled cooling-off pool sits amid lush, secluded grounds. Rates: $50 s/d; $10 extra person, including tax.

Villas de la Selva, Apdo. 359, San José 2070, tel./fax 253-4890, has one master bedroom with a double and a single bed, and another room with two bunk beds and a single. A smaller apartment sleeps two people. There's a fully equipped kitchen plus a terrace with ocean view. Rates: $50 s/d; $65 t; $94 d apartment.

Cabinas, Bar y Restaurant Los Almendros, Apdo. 68, Quepos, tel./fax 777-0225, set back from the Playa Espadilla near the park entrance, has 21 modern and clean though sparsely furnished a/c rooms (nine have fans), with private baths with hot water. The hotel has a modestly elegant restaurant and a jacuzzi and offers fishing trips, tours, and horses for rent. Rates: $35 s/d with fan, $45 with a/c, low season; $45 s/d with fan, $55 with a/c, high season.

The well-kept **Cabinas Espadilla,** Apdo. 195, Quepos, tel. 777-0903 or 777-0416, 100 meters inland, has 16 *cabinas* set in attractive grounds; all have refrigerators (eight with kitchenettes), fans, and private baths with cold water. They're basically furnished but spacious; each sleeps up to four people. There are *pilas* (laundry sinks). Rates: from $35 s, $40 d with fan; $45 with a/c.

Sula Bya Ba Villas, tel. 777-0597, fax 777-0279, near Mimo's, appeared to be closed when I visited. It had (has?) 14 rooms with intriguing yet somewhat ascetic decor that blends 1950s utility with a hint of modern Japan. Light pours in through sliding doors at both front and back. There's a tiny open-air restaurant and bar. Rates: about $50.

El Lirio, Apdo. 123, Quepos, tel. 777-0403, has nine pretty rooms with a/c, fans, and private baths with hot water. It features a pool with sundeck plus a tiny *mirador* in lush, secluded grounds. Rates: $55 d, including breakfast and tax.

Divisamar Hotel, Apdo. 82, Quepos 6350, tel. 777-0371, fax 777-0525, is a three-story unit with 12 modestly appealing a/c rooms, 12 junior suites and one master suite around a small kidney-shaped swimming pool in landscaped grounds. The hotel has a whirlpool, plus souvenir shop and an open-air bar and restaurant with a pleas-

ant outside dining terrace (buffet breakfast only). It also has a Rainforest Casino and Cigar Bar. Rates: $50 s/d standard, $60 junior suite.

Moderate: The German-run **Hotel Mirador del Pacífico,** Apdo. 164, Quepos, tel./fax 777-0119, has 20 pretty rooms, with fans and private baths with hot water, lots of light, and private patios and verandas. Rooms are in rough-hewn wood structures raised on stilts amid lush tropical grounds. A plank walkway leads to the swimming pool. A funicular will carry you up the steep hill. Little Polynesian tikis peek from behind tropical plants. It's added three apartments. A reader offered a bad review. Rates: from $40 d low season; $60 high season.

Living it up at the **Hotel California,** Apdo. 159, Quepos, tel. 777-1234, fax 777-1062, is easy. The French-run, three-story, jade-green hotel with the name you'll never forget has 22 rooms with queen-size beds, a/c and fans, cable TVs, piping hot water, kitchenettes, and marvelous views north along the coast from the balconies overlooking a kidney-shaped pool with wooden deck above the forest, with lush plants all around. The rooms are simply, if nicely, furnished, with lots of light, French doors opening onto private verandas, and trompe l'oeil walls representing individual national parks. Choose carefully—some of the paintings are overbearing. I like the Tortuguero Room. The hotel has a cold jacuzzi. It's 200 meters off the road, just beyond Bungalows Las Palmas. Rates vary according to story and view—top story being the most expensive: $45-65 s/d low season; $49-69 high season.

Mimo's Hotel, Apdo. 228, Manuel Antonio 6358, tel./fax 777-0054, is a beautiful Spanish-style villa with spacious and attractive rooms with security box, private verandas, and hammock. Each room has a double bed and futon. There's a small swimming pool. Rates: $60 d; $70 d with a/c and kitchenette.

Villa Teca, Apdo. 180, Quepos 6350, tel. 777-1117, fax 777-1578 or 777-0279, is an exquisite, aesthetically appealing modern property with daffodil-yellow, red-tile-roofed villas scattered throughout the lushly vegetated hillside. There are 40 rooms in 20 a/c bungalows, each with two twin beds (with beautiful tropical floral spreads), terrace, plus private bath with hot water. Other highlights include an attractive pool and sundeck plus thatched restaurant serving

Italian fare, and a free shuttle to and from the beach. Rates: $82 d, including breakfast.

A tremendous spot—highly recommended—is **Hotel Las Tres Banderas**, Apdo. 258-6350, Quepos, tel. 777-1521 or 777-1284, fax 777-1478, e-mail: info@hotel-tres-banderas.com, a handsome two-story Spanish colonial-style property run by super-friendly Polish owner Andrzej ("I'm having fun!") Nowacki. Its 16 a/c rooms come in three types, including three suites abounding in hardwoods and Peruvian wall-hangings. They're roomy and pleasant, with frilly spreads, lots of light, big balconies, and exquisite bathrooms with pretty tiles and deep tubs (suites only). Nowacki is proud of the water pressure in the showers. Suites have minibars and small refrigerators. Meals are prepared at an outside *rosteria* (grill) and served on the patio beside the beautiful lap pool (replete with cascade and mosaic tiles showing the U.S., Polish, and Tican flags—the eponymous three flags—plus a large jacuzzi inset in stone. Try the *bigos*, Polish sauerkraut and meats, and the superb ceviche. Short trails lead through forest to the rear. Rates: from $35 s, $40-45 d, $75 suite, low season; $55 s, $60-65 d, $95 suite, high season. A villa is available for $200 low season, $250 high season.

Hotel Casa Blanca, Apdo. 194, Quepos, tel. 777-0253, has four very bright and pleasing though simply furnished double rooms plus two suites with terraces, fans, and private baths with hot water. Large and well-kept bathrooms. It's very tranquil. Bougainvillea surrounds a small cooling pool. Rates: $60 d, $140 suites.

Villas El Parque, Apdo. 111, Quepos, tel. 777-0096, fax 777-0538, e-mail: vparque@sol.racsaco.cr, has 17 standard rooms, 16 villas (no kitchens), plus 18 suites with kitchen, in colonial style, all with ceiling fans and large balconies with hammocks and views out over the park. Decor includes lively Guatemalan bedspreads. There's a restaurant—the Sukia Bar and Grill—plus a triple-level swimming pool. Monkeys visit the property every afternoon at "monkey hour." Rates: $59 standard, $69 suite, $69-99 suite low season; $73 standard, $84 suite, $95-150 villa high season. It also has sportfishing packages.

El Dorado Mojado, tel. 777-0368, fax 777-1248, has eight attractive modern rooms—some with kitchens—with private baths, hot water, and

a/c. The hotel specializes in fishing. A swimming pool was being added. A larger house has attractive modern units. Rates: $49 d standard, $50 villas low season; $60 d standard, $73 villas high season.

Villas Nicolas, Apdo. 236, Quepos, tel. 777-0481, fax 777-0451, e-mail: nicolas@sol.racsa.co.cr, website www.hotels.co.cr/nicolas, has 12 one- and two-bedroom villa suites (in six types), all with private ocean-view verandas overlooking lush grounds. Upper-story verandas have concrete benches with soft-cushioned sofas. Rooms are large and pleasantly furnished in hardwoods, with fans and private baths with hot water. Smaller bedrooms upstairs have no kitchens. There's a narrow swimming pool and a sundeck. Choose from six types of rooms, including suites. Rates: $39-69 d one bedroom, $112-125 one bedroom low season; $75-90 two bedroom low season, $140-155 two bedroom high season.

Hotel and Villas Mogotes, Apdo. 120, Quepos, tel./fax 777-0582, has two a/c villas with kitchenettes, plus rooms and suites, all with fans, hot water, telephones. Most rooms and all suites have ocean-view balconies. You'll find a pleasing little colonial-tiled bar and restaurant under thatch, plus a small pool on a concrete veranda with wide ocean views. The hotel has its own nature trail. Rates: $60 s, $80 d, $95 t for rooms; $95 s, $110 d, $125 t for villas, including breakfast.

Rustic and intimate **Cabinas La Quinta**, Apdo. 76, Quepos, tel./fax 777-0434, has seven spacious rooms with large private baths with colonial tiles. Triple and quad rooms have a/c and kitchenettes. It nestles in its own grove, with a tiny swimming pool and good vistas. Rates: $45 s, $65 d, $72 t, $80 quad.

Hotel Villa Niña, tel. 777-1628, fax 777-1497, is an attractive, three-story, salmon-pink, thatched structure: part-Mediterranean, part-indigenous. All nine rooms (some with a/c) have a terrace with lounge chairs for enjoying the views over Manuel Antonio. Each, too, has a private bathroom, terra-cotta tiles, coffeemaker, plus double bed and a bunk. There's a pool and restaurant. Rates: $30-75 d low season; $45-90 d high season.

Hotel Arboleda, Apdo. 55, Manuel Antonio, tel. 777-0092, fax 777-0414, has 40 rooms with fans and private baths with hot water. Older units on stilts are dingy and overpriced. More modern units down near the beach are more pleasing, with a/c and wide patios. A breezy open-air restaurant is close enough to the sea that you can hear the waves. You can rent horses, catamarans, and surfboards. Rates: $65 fan, $85 a/c—a little high. It was closed for renovation when I stopped by.

Hotel and Villas Karahé, Apdo. 100, Quepos 6350, tel. 777-0170, fax 777-0152, has 32 modern a/c rooms, including nine *cabinas*. They're large and well-lit but lack ambience. Very nice bathrooms, good views, and beautiful grounds. The rustic restaurant's house specialties include shish kebabs. A private trail leads to the beach, where there's a pool and a snack bar. One reader has written to say that the rooms were dirty; I found them to be clean. The hotel offers sportfishing and boogie board rentals ($5 per day). Rates: $50 hillside with fan, $60 s/d roadside with a/c, $80 beachfront.

I like the **Hotel Verde Mar,** tel. 777-1805, fax 777-1311, e-mail: verdemar@sol.racsa.co.cr; in Canada, tel. (604) 925-4772, behind Playa Espadilla. It's a splendid option with 20 rooms in a two-story structure with balconies supported on rough-hewn logs. Each room is painted in soft pastels and has a queen bed, ceiling fan, and kitchenette; plus eight suites with two queens and a kitchen. Soothing pastels and log timbers add calming notes. There's an amoeba-shaped pool. A raised walkway ("77 steps") leads to the beach. Rates: $55 s/d economy, $65 standard ($75 with a/c), $75 suite; $5 more with credit card.

Hotel Villa Bosque, tel. 777-0463, fax 777-0401, set back from the beach close to the park boundary, is a Spanish-colonial remake with 17 pleasant, atmospheric a/c rooms that each sleep three people; rooms have fans, security boxes, and private baths with hot water, plus verandas/patios with chairs. It has a restaurant serving surf and turf, and a pool on the raised terrace. Potted plants abound. It's nice, but pricey. Rates: $40 s, $50 d low season; $60 s, $70 d ($80 a/c) high season, including tax. Nearby, **Hotel Playa Espadilla,** tel. 777-0903, has 16 large, attractive units with a/c and kitchenettes, and private baths with hot water. Rates: $70 d. There's a small bar and swimming pool.

Expensive: Byblos, Apdo. 112, Quepos, tel. 777-0411, fax 777-0009, is a flamboyantly stylish quasi-Swiss lodge in lush landscaped grounds.

A wonderful amoeba-shaped pool and sundeck are set in a hollow surrounded by jungle. Seven whitewashed stone bungalows are spaced widely apart and have private balconies overlooking banana groves and primary forest. Nine spacious junior suites in the main unit enjoy large triangular bathrooms. Small windows do not take advantage of the lofty position. Rooms have private baths with hot water, refrigerators, TVs, and telephones. Bamboo furniture. A pleasant breezy restaurant serving French cuisine overlooks the grounds. Rates: $84 d (fan), $90 (a/c) bungalow, $98 junior suite.

Hotel La Mariposa, Apdo. 4, Quepos, tel. 777-0355, fax 777-0050, e-mail: htlmariposa@msn.com; in the U.S., tel. (800) 223-6510, has been lauded by travel magazines so many times over the years that it became an institution as the "best hotel" in the country. The hotel—which had begun to rest on its laurels, deteriorated, and has since been taken over by new owners—is dramatically perched on cliffs above the sea and boasts magnificent views over Manuel Antonio through bright bougainvillea. Steps inlaid with hand-painted tiles lead down through hillside gardens to 10 split-level Mediterranean-style cottages, each with its own deck suspended over the steep hillside and a massive skylit bathroom with mosaic tile, murals, and enough flora to stock a greenhouse (but no telephones or, fortunately, TVs). Their setting is splendid, but furnishings remain dowdy despite a vaunted remake (*Condé Nast Traveler* likened the decor to that in the Bates Motel from the movie *Psycho.*). Deluxe rooms have jacuzzi bathtubs. Junior suites have a jacuzzi on the wooden deck. The restaurant—which also has views—serves French-inspired fare. Service is eager but uncertain. Readers have raved, but other than the setting (it *is* an unbeatable location for the price), I remain unsure what the fuss is about. Facilities include a swimming pool and poolside bar, and a gift store. A nature trail leads to the beach. Reservations essential. Rates: $90 d standard, $105 deluxe, $135 villa suite low season; $120 standard, $140 deluxe, $180 villa suite high season.

Arriving at a hostelry rarely sparks the excitement **Hotel Villas Si Como No,** Apdo. 5, Quepos, tel. 777-1250, fax 777-1093, e-mail: sicomono@sol.racsa.co.cr, conjures at first sight, with its flamboyant peaked entrance and open lobby with stained glass windows and a sharp-angled prow-of-a-ship *mirador* terrace. The hotel has 32 spacious suites in split-level luxury villas. All boast terra-cotta floors, tropical prints, king-size beds of rustic teak for a romantic note, and mosquito nets. Two-bath villas have living rooms, master bedrooms, dining rooms, and kitchens; apartments also have kitchens, master bedrooms, and dining rooms; suites have kitchens or wet bars. Halogen reading lamps are inset in the ceiling. Bathrooms have octagonal Tiffany windows of underwater scenes, plus bench seats and glass-brick walls; it's like showering in an aquarium. Tall French doors open to balconies with views. The structures are supported by columns resembling palm trees, with leafy branches for eaves. The rails and fences resemble thick bamboo, as do the trims inside the rooms. Some have said the effect is hokey, like something from a Walt Disney movie (Greek-American owner Jim Damalas, formerly a Hollywood producer, admits to the cartoon influence). The place could also have been designed by Friends of the Earth—there's waste and water recycling, biological marsh sewage systems, low-voltage solar lighting, computer-programmed a/c, and double-pane windows and doors to deflect heat and keep cool air in. Nature plays its part. Si Como No nestles in a valley and benefits from the breezes that flow downhill. The amoeba-shaped pool and sundeck cling to the hillside, with splendid views. The pool features a water slide, cascades, jacuzzi, and swim-up bar. At night it's like a son et lumière—fantastic! The adjoining bar-cum-restaurant is a hip place to sample an assortment of special cocktails and creative Costa Rican dishes. There's also a state-of-the-art movie theater, and a conference center. Nature trails lead through the 14-hectare rainforest across the road. Rates: $50 d room, $72 d suites and apartment room, $124 d villas low season; $75 d room, $95 d suites and apartment room, $165 villas high season.

Hotel Casitas Eclipse, tel./fax 777-0408 or 777-1738; in the U.S., tel. (760) 753-6827, fax 753-2277, e-mail: eclipse@sol.racsa.co.cr, five km south of Quepos, is an exquisite and intimate property, and highly recommended. It offers 25 rooms in nine beautiful, whitewashed Mediterranean-style, two-story, a/c villas set in a hollow around three swimming pools with redbrick sun terraces and bougainvillea cascading over white walls. The effect is marvelous. You can rent the entire villa or one floor only. The spacious rooms have heaps of light and fully equipped kitchens and are brightly decorated with South American covers, etc. French owned. *Marvelous!* Rates: $60 d standard, $75 d suite, $133 casita including breakfast, low season; $91 d standard, $119 d suite, $200 casita high season.

Costa Verde, tel. 777-0584, fax 777-0560 in Quepos; Apdo. 6944, San José, tel. 223-7946, fax 223-9446, e-mail: costaver@sol.racsa.co.cr; in the U.S., SJO 1313, Box 025216, Miami, FL 33102-5216, tel. 800-231-RICA, is a three-story modern unit of 14 studio apartments, 12 two-story villas, and two two-bedroom apartments, with lots of space and heaps of light. Sliding doors backed by screen doors open onto verandas with leather rockers and views over the beach. Some rooms face away from the ocean. Reception is hidden behind a railroad caboose on rails. A restaurant has views over Manuel Antonio. Rates: $40 efficiency apartment, $70 studio, $100 penthouse villa low season; $65 efficiency apartment, $90 studio, $120 penthouse villa high season.

Premium: Hotel and Beach Club El Parador, Apdo. 284, Quepos, tel. 777-1411, fax 777-1437, e-mail: parador@sol.racsa.co.cr, website magi.com/crica/hotels/parador.html, occupies five acres near the tip of Punta Quepos, overlooking Playa Beisanz to the north and Playa Espedilla to the south. El Parador was conceived to be a flashback to the romantic *pousadas* of Spain. You enter through a hall full of Manchegan (from La Mancha, in Spain) decor—a knight in shining armor, antique farm implements, and weaponry. The hub is the main hall-cum-dining room, with hefty oak beams, Spanish tiles, antique wrought-iron chandeliers, balustraded staircase, tapestries, Persian rugs, antiques and historic artifacts, including 17th-century paintings, intricate model ships, and even thick-timbered wooden doors and shuttered windows flown in from ancient Spanish castles. The 25 standard rooms, 20 deluxe rooms, and 15 suites (complete with jacuzzi) are furnished in contemporary (almost Hawaiian) vogue. Most have a king-size or two queen beds, plus minibar, and other concessions to modernity. The Christopher Columbus suite is one of the most sumptuous hotel rooms in the country. Facilities include a huge terrace bar, stone-lined wine-tasting room-cum-casino, a *mirador ranchita* bar-cum-restaurant, mini-golf course, two swimming pools (one a horizon pool with fountain and stone terrace, cascading waterfall and swim-up bar; the other exclusively for the suites), a stage for daily cultural events such as cocktail parties, plus a hair salon and dedicated health spa. El Parador aims squarely at business travelers with a full business center, a banquet room with full audiovisual setup, and a helicopter landing pad. Golf carts are on hand to whisk you around. It has its own horses ($25). It has been called stuffy, but I say not. Rates: $90 standard, $110 deluxe, $150 junior suite low season; $145 standard, $185 deluxe, $265 junior suite high season; $185 standard, $225 deluxe, $305 junior suite peak season.

Luxury: The reclusive and exclusive **Tulemar Bungalows,** Apdo. 225, Manuel Antonio 6350, tel. 777-0580, fax 777-1579, e-mail: tulemar@sol.racsa.co.cr, is the only hotel around claiming its "own exclusive beach," a pink-sand affair reached by a road winding steeply through a 13-hectare private forest reserve. Tulemar's oceanview octagonal a/c bungalows are higher up, surrounded by trees and lawns. All have in-room safes, TVs and VCRs, telephones, fans, hair dryers, kitchenettes, and beautiful interiors highlighted by 180-degree windows, French curtains, and strange, UFO-like bulbous skylights. There's a small horizon swimming pool with a bar suspended over the hill, plus a shop and snack bar. It is adding more bungalows. Guided nature walks are offered. Rates: $119 d, $129 t low season; $180 d high season; $205-235 up to four people.

And don't forget Makanda by the Sea.

House Rentals: Two companies that specialize in house rentals are **Blue Marlin,** tel. 777-0295, and **Manuel Antonio House Rentals,** tel. 777-0560. Also check with **Buena Nota** (see **Information,** below); Anita rents a house near the Hotel La Mariposa, with a stunning view toward Manuel Antonio. **Residencia Alejandria,** tel. 777-0495, is a large house for rent opposite Byblos. A notice board outside the **Restaurante Mar y Sombra** also advertises houses for rent, tel. 777-0003 and 777-0406. Rates begin at about $250 per week. **Villas Residencia el Tucán** has villas for rent and sale. Also try **Bungalows Las Pal-**

mas, tel. 777-0051; in the U.S., c/o Interlink #185, P.O. Box 526770, Miami, FL 33152, which has detached bungalows with complete kitchens with hot water for about $60 d.

Food

The place for breakfast is **Café Milagro** opposite the road to El Parador. Alternately try **El Acuario,** a very atmospheric *ranchito* with rough-hewn furniture. **Costa Linda** has been recommended for its health-food breakfasts.

A sure winner is the **Sunspot Poolside Bar and Grill** at Makanda, a classy spot serving *bocas* such as calamari, and mussels in Chardonnay broth ($7-9), as well as quesadillas, sandwiches, and huge salads for lunch. The huge wine list includes many California reserves. I also recommend a meal at **Tres Banderas** (by reservation only).

El Mono Azul is recommended for its hearty fare, such as vegetarian dishes, a splendid grilled tuna, salads, burgers and fries, home-baked bread, and delicious desserts ($2-10). Open 7 a.m.-10 p.m. They deliver pizza; a large pizza for four costs $12, including a two-liter Coke.

Dulú, tel. 777-1297, atop a hill one km south on Quepos, is run by Juan Carlos Martínez, a BriBri Indian who serves authentic Creole recipes for $5-15 (one reader thought it "the BEST dinner we had in Costa Rica. The avocado appetizer was heavenly and the Mahi Mahi prepared wrapped in banana leaf with vegetables was succulent and flavorful"). It boasts a delightful contemporary aesthetic, is breezy, has views through open arches, and boasts a provocative painting (of an all-male orgy) behind the bar. It also has dancing. **Jardín Gourmet** at Hotel Eclipse serves Mediterranean cuisine such as tagliatelle and salad niçoise (average $5).

For grilled meats and seafoods, try **Fonda Típica. Barba Roja Restaurant,** tel. 777-0331, offers delicious seafood, daily specials, and ocean-view alfresco dining. Great for sunset dining. Good breakfasts include whole-wheat toast. There's an art gallery and a gift shop upstairs. Just down the road is **Karola's Bar and Garden Restaurant,** tel. 777-1557, with a similar setting. Other options include the very atmospheric **Bar y Restaurant Iguanazul,** with terrace dining and ocean view; and the exciting if expensive **Richard's,** tel. 777-0096, serving Tex-

Mex and Spanish seafood dishes and tapas in a dashing setting whose focal point is the triple-tier swimming pool with water cascades. Yes, you can buy a burger, but watch the stuffed jalapeños—they're hotter than Hades. "Monkey Hour" is 4-7 p.m.

Byblos has excellent French dishes. For Italian food at reasonable rates, try **Plinio,** which also has a buffet breakfast for all-comers; or **Italian Club Spaghettería** next to Tuany's Club. Also here is **BBQ Asia,** highly recommended for its Asian seafood and ambience.

Many people rave about the elegant restaurant at **La Mariposa,** which has a large creative menu: *paté de pollo* with green peppercorn, leek and shrimp soup, and breast of chicken in French wine and mustard are typical ($4-12), but in both 1995 and 1997 I found the food okay but undistinguished—but, oh, those views!

Open-air budget restaurants by the beach serve fresh fish and local specialties. **Mar y Sombra,** tel. 777-0003, is the focal point. Here you can sit at palm-shaded tables, talk to the tame macaw, and eat a whole fried fish for under $5. The **Velabar,** tel. 777-0413, 100 meters inland toward the park entrance, is a small ranchita restaurant with elegant place settings and a splendid U-shaped bar with polished hardwood barstools. Typical items include chicken bombay, chicken paprika, and filet fish in mushroom sauce (average $6-8).

Pickles Deli, tel. 777-0048, in the Si Como No Mall is a deli supreme, with baked goods, sandwiches, pastas, health food, and sundaes. It rents coolers ($5) and prepares picnic baskets.

Entertainment
Mar y Sombra doubles as a disco at night. **Tuany's Club,** tel. 777-1645, has a free disco in an elegant home with pool (nightly 8 p.m.-2 a.m.); the Italian owner also hosts aerobics classes.

There's a small unsophisticated casino and cigar bar at the **Hotel Divisamar,** e-mail: casino@sol.racsa.co.cr, open 7 p.m.-2 a.m., and a more sophisticated casino at **El Parador.**

How about a movie in a surround-sound theater? Then head to **Si Como No,** tel. 777-0777, showing top classics nightly at 8:30 p.m., with a little popcorn booth to boot. It offers a two-for-one dinner special in green season for about $10 per couple.

Information
Anita Myketuk runs a tourist-information bureau at **Buena Nota,** tel. 777-1002, fax 777-1946, e-mail: buennote@sol.racsa.co.cr, near Playa Espadilla. It sells maps, books, and international magazines and has a book exchange.

Shopping
Cay Costa Souvenirs, on the beachfront, sells T-shirts, film, postcards, and toiletries. A handful of beach hawkers sell earrings and hash pipes carved in grotesque faces. **Tienda "Si Como No,"** also has souvenirs and clothing. The best stocked place, though, is **Buena Nota,** which sells beachwear, handicrafts, you name it. Several stalls down by the beach offer jewelry for sale. Also check out **Café Milagro,** tel. 777-1707, which sells Cuban cigars.

Tours and Activities
Most hotels in the region can arrange sportfishing, horseback trips, and guided nature hikes.

Marlboro Stables, tel. 777-1108, 200 meters before Playa Espadilla, has rides for $30. **Quepos Trail Rides,** tel. 777-0566, offers guided horseback rides along the beach; follow the trail that begins next to Barba Roja Restaurant. **Equus Stables,** tel. 777-0001, is midway between Quepos and the park.

Iguana Tours, tel./fax 777-0850, alias Costa Rica Adventure Tours, has an office at Si Como No Mall.

You can rent boogie boards ($1.50 per hour; $8 per day) and snorkeling gear ($1.50 per hour; $6 a day) at **Café Mermaid.**

Francisco Delgado of **Toucan Tours and Information Center,** tel. 777-0602, offers everything from whitewater to horseback trips.

Services
There's a **public telephone,** 777-0303, outside Cay Costa Souvenirs, and you can make international calls from the Mar y Sombra. There's a **laundry** opposite Fonda Típica.

Getting There and Away
By Bus: See **Quepos** for bus schedules. Local buses will pick you up (and drop you off) along the road if you flag them down, but note that space sells out early.

Interbus has a daily shuttle between San José and Manuel Antonio.

By Air: See **Quepos,** above. A bus will meet the SANSA plane for the short ride to Manuel Antonio.

By Sea: Temptress Adventure Cruises, tel. 220-1679, fax 220-2103; in the U.S., tel. (305) 643-4040 or (800) 336-8424, fax (305) 643-6438, includes Manuel Antonio National Park on weeklong natural-history cruises aboard the *Temptress Explorer* (see **Natural-History Cruise Tours** for more information). The six-meter catamaran *La Mamá de Tarzán,* tel. 777-1257 or 777-0191, operates half-day trips from Quepos at 9 a.m. and 2 p.m., with drinks and food provided ($35 adults, $20 children).

By Taxi: See **Quepos,** above, for taxi fares.

PARQUE NACIONAL MANUEL ANTONIO

Tiny it may be, but this 682-hectare national park epitomizes everything tourists flock to Costa Rica to see: stunning beaches, a magnificent setting with islands offshore (bird sanctuaries for marine species), lush rainforest laced with a network of welcoming trails, wildlife galore, and all within walking distance of your hotel. You are virtually guaranteed close-up encounters with monkeys, sloths, coatimundis, and scarlet macaws. What a gem!

Despite its diminutive size, Manuel Antonio is one of the country's most popular parks, with as many as 150,000 visitors annually in peak years. A few years ago it became obvious that the deluge of visitors threatened to spoil the very things they had come to see. Park Director José Antonio Salazar believes the park can withstand no more than 300 visitors a day. In recent years, Manuel Antonio has averaged about 1,000 people each day, with significantly more on some peak-season days, when hundreds of people were walking the trails at any one time. The Park Service considered closing the park for a while to let it recover from all those human feet. In early 1994 it began limiting the numbers of visitors to 600 per day (800 on Saturday and Sunday), and the park is now closed on Monday ("to clean up after the throngs of weekend partiers," reckons reader Sally Lourd). If you wish to do your bit to help preserve Manuel Antonio, consider visiting in the "green" or wet season. Litter and pollution are additional problems. Pack out what you pack in.

Nonetheless, the park is too small to sustain a healthy and viable population of certain animals. If the monkeys do not have access to areas outside the park, the population will decline because they cannot breed. Corridors that allow animals access to areas outside the park have been taken up by hotels, so that the park has in recent years become an island. As a result, the titi (squirrel monkey) population is declining.

*Manuel Antonio
National Park*

JEAN MERCIER

Beaches

The park has four lovely beaches, each with its own personality: Espadilla Sur, Manuel Antonio, Escondido, and Playita. The prettiest is Playa Manuel Antonio, a small scimitar of coral-white sand with a small coral reef. It's separated from Playa Espadilla Sur by a *tombolo*—a natural land bridge formed over eons through the accumulation of sand—tipped by **Punta Catedral,** an erstwhile island now linked to the mainland. The hike to the top of Punta Catedral (100 meters) along a steep and sometimes muddy trail takes about an hour from Playa Espadilla Sur (also known as the Second Beach). Espadilla Sur and Manuel Antonio offer tidal pools brimming with minnows and crayfish, plus reasonably good snorkeling, especially during dry season, when the water is generally clear.

At the far right on Playa Manuel Antonio, you can see ancient turtle traps dug out of the rocks by pre-Columbian Quepoa Indians. Female sea turtles would swim over the rocks to the beach on the high tide. The tidal variation at this point is as much as three meters; the turtles would be caught in the carved-out traps on the return journey as the tide level dropped. The Indians also used female-turtle decoys made of balsa to attract male turtles over the rocks. Olive ridley and green turtles still occasionally come ashore at Playa Manuel Antonio.

Beware the **manchineel tree** *(manzanillo),* or "beach apple"—very common along the beaches. It's highly toxic and possesses a sap that irritates the skin. Its tempting applelike fruits are also poisonous. Avoid touching any part of the tree. Also, don't use its wood for fires—the smoke will irritate your lungs. Ask the ranger at the park entrance to show you an example of the tree.

Wildlife Viewing

Between bouts of beaching, you can explore the park's network of wide trails, which lead into a swatch of humid tropical forest. Manuel Antonio's treetop carnival is marvelous, and best experienced by following the **Perezoso Trail,** named after the lovable sloths, which favor the secondary growth along the trail (*perezoso* means "lazy"). You might see marmosets, ocelots, river otters, pacas, and spectacled caimans in more remote riverine areas.

Howler monkeys langorously move from branch to branch, iguanas shimmy up trunks, toucans and scarlet macaws flap by. About 350 squirrel monkeys live in the park, another 500 on its outer boundaries. And capuchin (white-faced) monkeys are also abundant and welcome you at treetop height on the beaches, where they play to the crowd and will steal your sandwich packs given half a chance. Some of them have become aggressive in recent years and attacks on humans have been reported.

Even though *it is illegal to feed the monkeys,* insensitive people still do it. Note that if you're caught, you may—quite rightly—be ejected from the park. Recent studies have found a worrisome increase in heart disease and heart failure among the local monkey population. This is attributed to tourists feeding the monkeys with scraps of food such as cheese sandwiches, peanut butter, potato chips, etc. Unfortunately, the animals are much more prone to rises in cholesterol than humans. Do not leave food lying around.

Hire a guide. a knowledgeable guide can show you many other interesting tree species—among them, the *gaupinol negro,* an endemic species that is in danger of extinction; *cedro maria,* which produces a yellow resin used as a traditional medicine; and *vaco lechoso,* which exudes a thick white latex that also has medicinal properties.

Information

The park **entrance** is at the eastern end of Playa Espadilla, where you wade across the shallow Río Camaronera and pay your park entrance fee ($6). The station sells maps for 40 cents. Little rowboats are on hand at high tide, when you may otherwise be waist-deep. There's a small open-air natural-history **museum** and information center, tel. 777-1302, on Playa Manuel Antonio.

Some maps show a ranger station at Finca Quebrada Azul (reached from the crossroads for London, seven km south of Quepos) and a trail to Playa Playita, which faces Isla Mogote. This trail has been closed for some time. Check with the Park Service. **Camping** is not allowed in the park. There are no accommodations or snack bars. There's secure parking by the creek near the park entrance.

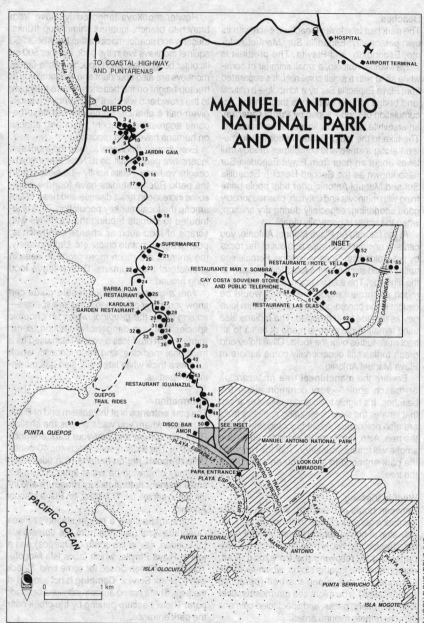

MANUEL ANTONIO
NATIONAL PARK
AND VICINITY

TO COASTAL HIGHWAY
AND PUNTARENAS

QUEPOS

HOSPITAL

AIRPORT TERMINAL

JARDIN GAIA

SUPERMARKET

BARBA ROJA
RESTAURANT

KAROLA'S
GARDEN RESTAURANT

QUEPOS
TRAIL RIDES

PUNTA QUEPOS

RESTAURANT IGUANAZUL

RESTAURANTE / HOTEL VELA

RESTAURANTE MAR Y SOMBRA

CAY COSTA SOUVENIR STORE
AND PUBLIC TELEPHONE

RESTAURANTE LAS OLAS

INSET

RÍO CAMARONERA

DISCO BAR
AMOR

PLAYA ESPADILLA

PARK ENTRANCE
PLAYA ESP

SEE INSET

MANUEL ANTONIO NATIONAL PARK

LOOKOUT
(MIRADOR)

SLOTH TRAIL (SENDERO PEREZOSO)

PLAYA ESCONDIDO

PLAYA PLAYITA

PACIFIC OCEAN

0   1 km

PLAYA ESPADILLA SUR

PLAYA MANUEL
ANTONIO

PUNTA CATEDRAL

ISLA OLOCUITA

PUNTA SERRUCHO

ISLA MOGOTE

© MOON PUBLICATIONS, INC.

MANUEL ANTONIO NATIONAL PARK AND VICINITY

1. Hotel Rancho Casa Grande
2. Restaurante Dulú
3. Hotel Plinio
4. Hotel Mirador del Pacífico
5. Mimo's Hotel
6. Hotel California
7. Cabinas Pedro Miguel
8. El Mono Azul
9. Bahía Hotel
10. Sula Bya Ba Villas
11. Villa Teca
12. Fonda Típica
13. Tuany's Club
14. Italian Club
15. Valle Verde Lodge
16. Hotel Las Tres Banderas
17. La Colina
18. El Lirio
19. Hotel Flor Blanca
20. Super Manuel Antonio
21. Sunset Sails Tours
22. Tulemar
23. Equus Stables
24. Villa Osa
25. Divisamar Hotel
26. Café Milagros
27. Hotel El Dorado Mojado
28. Hotel Casa Blanca
29. Byblos
30. Villas El Parque
31. Villas Nicolas
32. Makanda by the Sea
33. Hotel La Mariposa
34. Hotel Si Como No
35. Villa La Roca
36. Hotel and Villas Mogotes
37. Apartotel El Colibri
38. Hotel Casitas Eclipse
39. Hotel California
40. La Quinta, Hotel Villa Niña
41. Costa Verde
42. Hotel Arboleda
43. Villas de la Selva
44. Hotel and Villas Karahé
45. La Buena Nota
46. Cabinas/Restaurante Piscis
47. Marlboro Stables
48. Hotel El Mar
49. Hotel Verde Mar
50. Cabinas Ramirez
51. Hotel and Beach Club El Parador
52. Cabinas Espadilla Anexo
53. Hotel Villa Bosque
54. Cabinas Espedilla
55. Villa Valentina
56. Albergue Costa Linda
57. Hotel Las Almendros
58. Restaurante Del Mar
59. Sodas
60. Tourcan Tours and Information Center
61. Sodas Lobster
62. Hotel Manuel Antonio

Cautions

Theft is a major problem on the beaches, not least by the monkeys. Don't leave your things unguarded while you swim. I've also heard several reports of stealth burglaries in the hotels. Take whatever precautions you can to protect your goods.

There are **riptides** on Playa Espadilla. Watch your children, as there are no lifeguards.

NARA HILLS AND RÍO NARANJO

South of Quepos, Hwy 34 leads almost ruler-straight to Dominical, 45 km southeast of Quepos. However, potholed and unpaved, it's rough going. The first few miles south of town pass a sea of African palms punctuated by oil-processing plants belching out sickly smoke. A network of dirt roads links various hamlets serving the plantations. One such, 10 km south of Quepos, leads northeast via the community of Londres to the **Fila Nara** mountain range. The area is popular with day-excursions to the waterfalls and nat-

ural pools at **Brisas del Nara,** tel. 777-1889, and **Rancho Los Tucanes,** tel. 777-0290, both on the banks of the Río Naranjo. Both offer horseback rides to the **Los Tucanos** waterfall, a 90-meter cascade near the community of **Quebrada Arroyo.** You'll pass through pepper and vanilla plantations en route to the highland rainforest, full of exotic birds and wildlife.

Westward, the river gathers pace, flowing down from the rainforest-clad mountains and eventually fanning out into an estuary in Manuel Antonio National Park. In high water it offers extremely challenging class II-V whitewater action. At other times the river falls and slows and becomes too low for running. Most rafts put in at **Milo's spice farm** below the unrunnable "Labyrinth" section. Most tour companies require you to hike in for two hours (easy walking).

Accommodations

Mirador del Río, tel. 777-0290, near Londres has four cabins with kitchenette. Rates: $20 pp, including breakfast and dinner. Nearby, **Quinta Tucán,** Apdo. 141, Quepos, tel. 777-1379, also called Arnold's bird sanctuary, has one room for rent by reservation only. You can make day visits.

SAVEGRE AND VICINITY

Twenty five km south of Quepos (20 km north of Dominical), at the hamlet of Savegre, another dirt road inland leads up the valley of the Río Savegre to the community of **El Silencio,** at the base of the mountains. Here, the local farmer's cooperative operates the well-run **Centro Eco-Turístico Comunitario de Silencio.** It's a great spot for lunch and has a butterfly garden, well-marked trails, plus horseback rides ($25, three hours) to nearby waterfalls. Parrots abound. Tours to Playa Matapalo and rafting trips are offered.

The Río Savegre is favored for whitewater trips and washes down to the beautiful and unspoiled **Playa Savegre,** where **Rancho Savegre,** tel./fax 777-0528 or tel. 777-0165, is popular for horseback riding through the riverine lowlands that shelter monkeys, crocodiles, and other rare fauna ($55 full day tour; $40 half day).

Playa Matapalo, five km south of Savegre, is a beautiful gray-sand beach two km east of the coast road via a bone-jarring skunk of a road: the turnoff is in the twee hamlet of **Matapalo.** The beach is a surfer's paradise—it has two rivermouth breaks—and fishing from the beach is virtually guaranteed to deliver a snapper, snook, or other champ species. A large number of expats have settled to live offbeat lifestyles. A dirt road extends north along the beach to **Reserva Ecológico Portalón Refugio de Fauna Silvetre,** a wildlife refuge at the estuary of the Río Savegre. Be cautious when swimming—there are strong rip-tides.

An Italian, Eduardo, at **Finca Tibet,** and a German, Hans, at **Finca Transylvania,** both offer horseback riding on the beach and in the nearby mountains; contact them through the *pulpería* (100 meters south of the soccer field) or local *cabinas.*

South of Matapalo, habitation is sparse and the lonesome road rutted all the way to Hacienda Barú, just north of Dominical. A few kilometers before Barú you cross the Río Hatillo Viejo; you can hike or take horseback rides up the valley to the **Terciopelo Waterfalls,** a three-

tiered cascade tumbling 120 feet into pools good for swimming.

Accommodations and Food

Rainforest Resort & Spa, c/o Costa Rica Adventure Travel, tel. 777-1262, provides accommodations in a thatched tiki hut overlooking the river, amid 400 acres of virgin rainforest containing 300-foot waterfalls. There're hammocks and trails, and hot herbal baths, massages, and mud masks are offered.

Centro Eco-Turístico Silencio, tel. 779-9275, or c/o Cooprena, Apdo. 6939-1000, San José, tel. 259-3401, fax 259-9430, e-mail: cooprena@sol.racsa.co.cr, is a charmer nestled on a breezy hill at the north end of Silencio village, with views down over a sea of palms. The rustic lodge serves meals and has a raised mezzanine. There are six thatch-and-rough-hewn wood cabins (some with bunks) with lofts with two single beds, screened windows to three sides, plus tiled private baths with cold water. Rates: $50 s, $70 d, including breakfast. It's overpriced; expect the prices to fall.

Hungry? Check out the pleasant **Expresso del Pacífico Restaurant** on the roadside in Matapalo (dusty alas; closed Sunday). There are several local *sodas* worth checking out.

At Playa Matapalo, *cabinas* and basic restaurants are spread apart along the beachfront road in the following order northward. Richard and Anna at **Oasis Americana** have a row of tiny, basic cabins with ceiling fans, mosquito nets, and private baths with hot water, set in a garden. Rates: $10-20. Its beach bar serves the "world famous Oasis burger." **Cabinas del Pasito,** tel. 779-9268, has basic *cabinas,* plus a bar and restaurant serving ceviche and *bocas.* **Marisquería Arena Blanca** is a basic eatery serving seafood. The German-run **El Coquito del Pacífico,** c/o Bráun Eco Turismo in San José, tel. 222-4103, fax 222-8849, has six clean and pleasant *cabinas* amid shady palms with hammocks slung beneath. Each has large private bath, hot water, cool tile floors, and fans. There's a small restaurant serving a muesli breakfast with fruit and yogurt ($3), plus *típico* lunches and dinners. A swimming pool was to be added. Rates: $46 d, $56 t, including tax.

Next comes **Terraza del Sol,** which has four simple *cabinas* and bills itself as a "hotel, restaurant, and beach club." Fourth along is the Swiss-run **Restaurant y Cabinas Piedra Blanca** with five handsome cabins raised on stilts amid shade trees, simply furnished with bamboo, mosquito nets, fans, private baths with hot water, and hammocks on the verandas (larger cabin only). A quaint little restaurant offers two dishes daily and there's a *ranchito* bar serving *bocas* by the shore. Rates: $25 s/d (smaller cabins), $35 d (larger). Next door—I missed it—is the **Jungle House** with rooms and apartments, and a TV lounge.

Services

The Oasis Americana has a **tourist information service,** and was planning to add telephone answering and messages, faxes, e-mail, etc. There's a well-stocked *pulpería* next to Expresso del Pacífico in Matapalo, where there's a **public telephone** and **fax service,** tel. 7770-0711. The **post office** is here, too.

Getting There

A bus departs San José daily for Dominical and Uvita at 3 p.m. via Quepos (departing Quepos at 7 p.m.) and passing Matapalo at 8:30 a.m. Another bus departs weekends at 5 a.m. (departing Quepos at 9:15 a.m.) and passes Matapalo at 10:45 a.m. The northbound bus departs Uvita at 4:30 a.m. and Dominical at 6 a.m., passing Matapalo at 6:30 a.m. On weekends, a second bus departs Uvita at 12:30 p.m. and Dominical at 1:15 p.m., passing Matapalo at 2:30 p.m.

Buses depart San Isidro de El General for Dominical and Quepos at 7 a.m. and 1:30 p.m. (departing Dominical one hour later), passing Matapalo at 9 a.m. and 3:15 p.m. Southbound buses from Quepos depart at 5 a.m., 10 a.m., 1:30 p.m., and 4 p.m.

Taxi fares to Matapalo are about $20 from Quepos, $13 from Dominical, and $26 from San Isidro. Locally, "Cookie," tel. 777-1170 or 777-1191, runs an informal taxi.

SOUTHERN CENTRAL PACIFIC

The newly opened stretch of the Costera Sur south of Uvita is bringing new developments to the area and a boom in resorts and other facilities is under way. This forested coast has long beaches with pummeling surf as well as heaps of wildlife. The pencil-thin coastal plain is backed by steep mountains perfect for hiking and horseback trips.

DOMINICAL AND VICINITY

Dominical, 45 km southeast of Quepos, is a tiny, laid-back "resort" favored by surfers, backpackers, and the college-age crowd. The foreign beach-bum crowd mingles here with young Ticos and Ticas. Dress code is distinctly minimal: less is more. Dressing up means putting on a tank top and pair of sandals.

The four-km-long beach is beautiful albeit pebbly, and the warm waters attract whales and dolphins close to shore. Swimming reportedly can be dangerous because of rips, and the Río Barú supposedly empties polluted waters into the sea near the beach north of the village. Locals say the town's name is derived from the

name of a local banana-like fruit. At dusk check out the riverbank, where egrets roost en masse.

Several isolated beaches offer good breaks and points for surfers farther south, as do Barú and Guapil beaches to the north. The reef-protected waters of Ballena Marine National Park, a 30-minute drive south, are perfect for swimming and snorkeling. And if you overdose on the sun, sand and surf, a popular option is to hire a guide and horse for journeys through the forested mountains of Escaleras.

The beach extends south five km from Dominical to **Dominicalito,** a little fishing village in the lee of Punta Dominical, at the southern end of the bay, where there is safe mooring within the protection of the Dominicalito reef. Vultures congregate on the beach, which is prettier and less pebbly than the beach farther north.

The area was once notorious as a marijuana-growing area. "All the *campesinos* were growing it," says one source. It went unchecked for years. But that's history, I'm assured.

Hacienda Barú

Hacienda Barú, Apdo. 215, San Isidro de El General 8000, tel. 787-0003, fax 787-0004, e-mail:

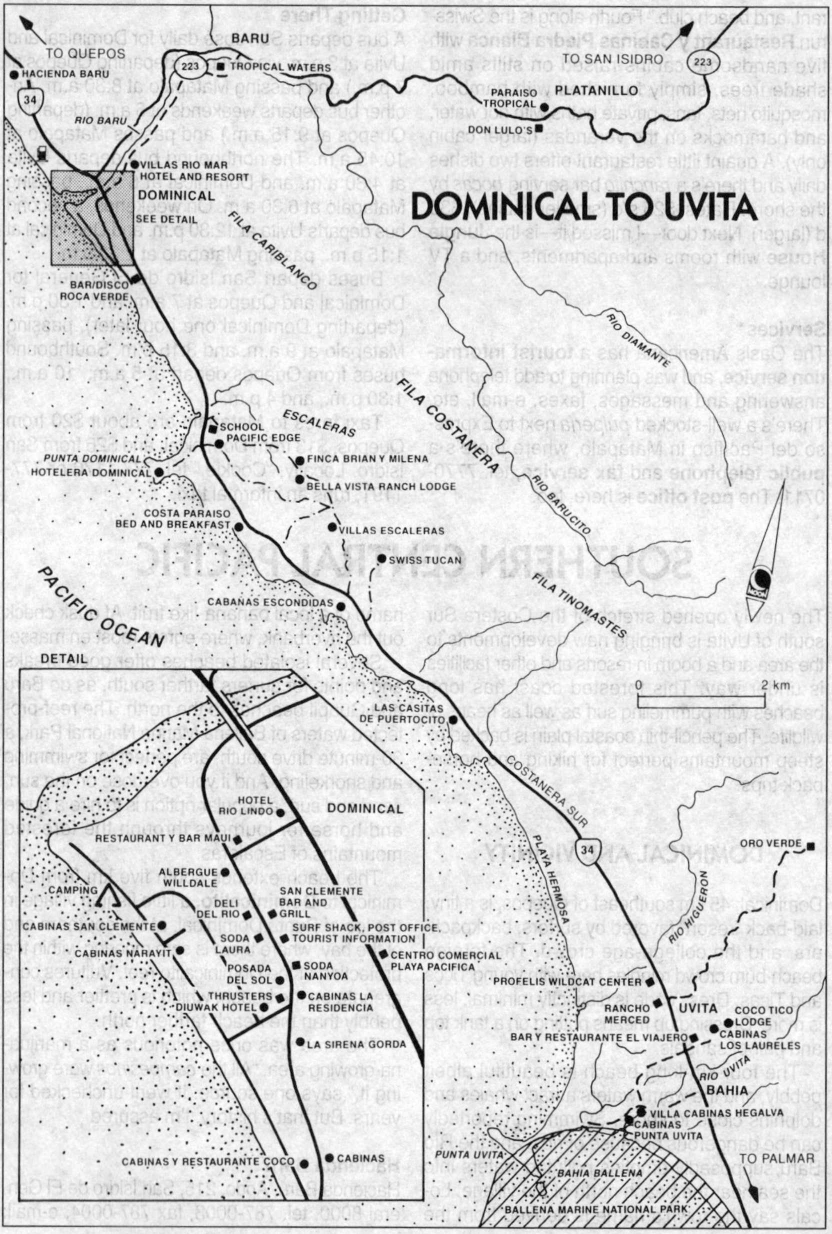

© MOON PUBLICATIONS, INC.

sstroud@sol.racsa.co.cr, website www.cool.co.cr/usr/baru.html; in the U.S., Selva Mar/AAA Express Mail, 1641 N.W. 79th Ave., Miami, FL 33126-1105, one km north of Dominical, is a 330-hectare private preserve—also known as Naturística S.A.—protecting three km of beach, plus mangrove swamp and at least 40 hectares of primary rainforest: a safe haven for anteaters, ocelots, kinkajous, tayras, capuchin monkeys, and jaguarundis. More than 310 bird species have been recorded: roseate spoonbills, magnificent frigate birds, boat-billed herons, kingfishers, currasows, falcons, cormorants, anhingas, and owls, among others. Olive ridley and hawksbill turtles also come ashore to nest at the wide and isolated Playa Barú. Trails and guided birding and nature hikes lead through pasture, fruit orchards, cacao plantations, and forest. Archaeologists are excavating a site on the crest of a hill overlooking the Río Barú north of Dominical. More than a dozen petroglyphs carved onto large rocks are the most obvious remains of what may be an ancient ceremonial and urban site.

There's a canopy observation platform suspended 100 feet up (you're raised by electric hoist), and guided tree-climbing is offered ($40 low season, $45 high season); thus, you can see the beasts eye-to-eye and explore the canopy with a guide ($30 low season, $35 high season), in either a bosun's chair with a winch or using rappelling equipment ($70). You can rent horses (from $15, two hours). A series of guided hikes (from $15) include "A Night in the Jungle" that ends at a fully equipped jungle tent camp ($50 low season, $60 high season). Kayak tours of the mangroves cost $35.

Accommodations

The **Selva Mar Reservation Service,** Apdo. 215-8000, San Isidro de El General, tel. 771-4582, fax 771-1903, e-mail: selvamar@sol.racsa.co.cr, website www.habitat.co.cr/selvamar; in the U.S., AAA Express Mail, 1641 N.W. 79th Ave., Miami, FL 33126, acts as a hotel and tour reservation service for many properties.

Camping: You can camp free of charge under shade trees along the beach. There's camping, too, on the north side of the river at the south end of the beach at Dominicalito.

Budget: Cabinas Coco, tel. 787-0030, has six small, basic but clean beachfront *cabinas*

with fans and shared baths with cold water for $12.50 pp low season, $33 d high season. There's a disco on weekends.

Posada Del Sol, Apdo. 126-8000, San Isidro, fax 787-0024, has four rooms with private bathrooms (hot water, perhaps, by the time you read this). They're pleasant, with plenty of light, fans, patios, plus laundry service. Rates: $15 s, $20 d, $25 t ($5 less low season). An apartment upstairs costs $200 d weekly. Water is drawn from a deep well.

Albergue Willdale, tel. 787-0023, has six small *cabinas* with views over the river estuary. Rooms are clean, screened, and have fans plus private baths with hot water. Rates: $25 s, $30 d. It also rents a spacious house at Escaleras ($100).

Restaurante y Cabinas Roca Verde, tel. 787-0036, is on the beachfront beside a small estuary, one km south of Dominical. You can drive along the beach to reach it. Screened *cabinas* have fans and cold water. A reader reports "austere rooms with shared dingy bathroom and thin walls." The pleasing open-air restaurant is very popular with Ticos and has a great house specialty: grilled fish filled with potato and sour cream, plus salad and garlic bread ($5). The place is lively at night, with dancing and sometimes live music. Rates: $13 s/d shared bath; $25 private bath.

La Residencia has seven small but clean rooms with fans, screens, and shared baths with hot water. Rate: $12.50 d low season; $16 d high season. **Cabinas Narayit,** tel. 787-0033, has 18 clean albeit modest beachside cabins and rooms—some in a two-story unit—with fans, hammocks on patios, and private baths with cold water (eight have hot water). Nice. There's also a nice restaurant. Rates: $12.50 s/d/t without a/c, $17 s/d/t with a/c and hot water low season; $29 s/d/t without a/c, $33 s/d/t with a/c and hot water high season. **La Sirena Gorda,** tel. 787-0262, has three simple roadside *cabinas*.

The owner of **Cabinas Villa Dominical** was so upset that I missed him in my previous research that he didn't want to be included this time.

Inexpensive: Hotel Río Lindo, tel. 787-0028, fax 787-1725, as you enter Dominical, has 10 rooms with fans and very large double shower-bathtubs with hot water. It has a swimming pool and jacuzzi. Upstairs rooms catch the breeze. Rates: $30 s/d, $40 with a/c low season;

$40 s/d, $50 high season. It also rents two houses; one by the beach and one in Escaleras ($60 per night).

DiuWak Hotel, tel./fax 223-0855, has eight simple but tasteful, spacious cabins plus four suites, amid a landscaped garden 50 meters from the beach. Each has a double and single bed, ceiling fan, and charming porch plus private bath with hot water. Four a/c suites have kitchenettes and dining area plus living room, bathroom, and bedroom with bamboo furniture. There's a jacuzzi, restaurant, and souvenir shop. Rates: $41 d, $60 suite.

Cabinas San Clemente, tel. 787-0026, fax 787-0055, offers 15 large airy rooms in a two-story beachfront unit with a bamboo roof, natural stone, and thatched veranda for. All have hardwood floors and shuttered windows and fans. Cheaper hostel-type rooms are above the San Clemente Bar & Grill restaurant. It was looking a bit neglected in January 1998, but Mike, the owner, is a go-getter, so I expect it to be spruced up. Rates: $20 shared bath, $35 d private room.

Hacienda Barú (see above) has a three-bedroom house for rent 400 meters from the beach, with hot water, fans, and kitchen. There are also six two-bedroom cabins in a grassy clearing backed by forest: each has two doubles and one single bed, fans, hot water, refrigerator, and cooking facilities, plus patio. A small restaurant serves Italian and Costa Rican dishes. Camping is allowed. Rates (cabins): $40 low season; $50 d high season; $10 extra person. Meals cost $3-7.

The gas station north of Dominical has a three-bedroom house with kitchenette for rent near the beachfront at Playa Guapil, north of town. Rates: $35 d; $10 additional person. And **Cabinas San Clemente** rents five fully furnished houses (prices vary). Check out the bulletin board at San Clemente Bar & Grill for more houses. There are several houses for rent. They're signed; walk around.

Moderate: Villas Río Mar Hotel & Resort, Apdo. 1350, San Pedro Montes de Oca 2050, tel. 787-0052, fax 787-0054, e-mail: riomar@sol.racsa. co.cr, website www.catalog.com/calypso/cr/hotel/ vriomar.htm, is secluded beside the Río Barú, 800 meters northeast of Dominical, surrounded by forest and landscaped grounds (unkempt when I visited in December 1998). Ten thatch-roofed bungalows house 40 junior suites with comfort-

able king-size beds, louvered windows, bamboo furnishings, lanterns casting warm glows, lacy mosquito-net curtains, and French doors, plus hair dryers, telephones, and steaming hot water. Each has a spacious and elegant veranda with heavy-bamboo-framed sofas and a hammock. Thatch-canopied walkways lead between bungalows, which are spaced well-apart. A restaurant with soaring *palenque* roof features local and international cuisine. The hotel boasts a conference room, plus tennis courts and an attractive pool with swim-up bar and jacuzzi. It provides shuttle service to the beach and has tubes for floats down the Río Barú, and you can rent mountain bikes. Rates: from $60 s, $65 d low season; $70 s, $80 d high season. Overpriced?

Dominicalito Accommodations
Hotelera Dominical, Apdo. 196-8000, San Isidro, tel. 787-0016, e-mail: chdpdsa@sol.racsa.co.cr, alias Cabinas Punta Dominical, sits breezily atop Punta Dominical. It has four rustic but cozy tropical hardwood *cabinas* amid landscaped grounds above the ocean. Each is shaded by trees and has screens, fans, and a private bath with hot water. Cabins sleep seven. A thatched open-air restaurant reportedly has excellent food and marvelous ocean views to left and right. The rocky shoreline is good for tide pools. Rates: $50 s/d, $12 extra person.

Three km south of Dominical is **Costa Paraíso Bed and Breakfast,** Apdo. 578-8000, San Isidro, tel./fax 787-0025, offering two attractive, fully furnished apartments with kitchens, private bathrooms, ceiling fans, and bamboo furniture. It also has a two-room *cabina* with kitchenette, and two bed-and-breakfast rooms in the main house. They're surrounded by lush lawns falling down to the shore. It's reached via a steep trail that leads to a beautiful rocky shore. Rates: $60 d, $350 weekly furnished apartment; $45 d, $260 weekly two-room *cabina;* $35 s, $40 d B&B room.

Food
San Clemente Bar & Grill, formerly Jungle Jim's, is the center of action. Jim Bray no longer runs the place, but fellow Californian Mike McGinnis is doing an equally fine job. The large restaurant and open-air bar serves hearty breakfasts (including a filling "Starving Surfers Special" for $2), plus burgers, Tex-Mex and Cajun (na-

chos, blackened chicken sandwiches for $4), a killer tuna melt (dinner special costs $8). And imagine grilled mahi mahi with honey, rosemary, and orange sauce served with fresh vegetables. Mike—who makes and sells the highly popular "Spicy Mike" hot sauces and chutneys—planned to open **Restaurante Atardecer** by the beach. (But, Mike, ya gotta fix up those toilets!)

Opposite is **Soda Laura,** for granola, fruits, pancakes, and *típico* food ($1-3); try the club sandwich, ceviche, and mushrooms in sauce. **Restaurant Nayarit** has good *casados* for $2-3. Also try **Restaurant y Bar Maui** (serving organic juices, tacos, and a seafood grill), the rustic yet attractive **Soda Nanyoa, Restaurante Coco,** or **Restaurante Roca Verde,** reached via the beach south of Dominical. Don't neglect the restaurant at **Villas Río Mar,** which hosts Sunday brunch.

There's a *panadería* (bakery) and deli opposite San Clemente. **Deli del Río** offers breakfast and fresh breads, muffins, etc., plus deli-style sandwiches, and pizzas; open 7-11 a.m. and 5-10 p.m. At **Ricco's Maui** hosts Ricco and Elena lay on great home-cooked fare and host dances every Friday.

Entertainment

San Clemente Bar & Grill has a pool table, table football, darts, Ping-Pong and a large TV showing videos and sports events. By night everyone gets into the groove on the dance floor beneath a ceiling festooned with broken surfboards. Mike sells Cuban cigars and Guinness ($3.50 per can), and half-price margaritas on "Taco Tuesday." A coupleof margaritas should help you appreciate the mural that took famous artist Rory González five months.

Thrusters is a handsome stone-and-thatch bar with pool tables and music. It serves pizzas and burritos. **Roca Verde,** one km south of Dominical, is the happening disco scene. It's very Latin and very Tico, especially on weekends and holidays, when they flock in from San Isidro.

Enjoying the Surf

San Clemente Surf Shack rents surfboards ($5-15 per day) and boogie boards plus snorkel gear, and sells beachear. **Royal Palm Surf Shop,** tel. 787-0029, is well-stocked with beachwear. It sells boards, but doesn't rent.

Spanish Language Courses

La Escuelita de Dominical, tel. 787-0005, fax 787-0006, e-mail: domini@sol.racsa.co.cr, offers one- to four-week Spanish courses for all levels for $350 per week, including food and housing. You can even earn credit. The tutor is a gringo.

Services

Find the **Dominical Information Center** at San Clemente Bar & Grill, which also serves as a **post office** and has a full-service **laundry** ($1.75 per kg). There's a **public telephone** here (plus a radio telephone), and another outside Cabinas Narayit.

Tropical Waters is a tour information service and tour operator; it's two km east of Dominical on the road to Platanillo.

The **gas station,** about one km north of Dominical, sells maps, film, and fishing supplies. It also rents beach umbrellas and boogie boards. You can rent **bicycles** at Cabinas Narayit.

Playa Pacífica is a **commercial center** 200 meters south of the bridge and the turnoff into the village. It has a supermarket and **Mercado del Mundo** boutique selling upscale crafts, hand-painted ceramics, and more.

Excursions

Pisces Pacific Boat Tours, Apdo. 239, San Isidro de El General 8000, tel. 717-1903 or 221-2053, offers sportfishing trips plus overnight trips to Caño Island and Drake Bay. **Tres Marinos** also offers boat rides as far afield as Caño Island (book through Selva Mar). Torey Lenoch at **White Water Experiences** offers rafting and kayaking trips on the Río Savegre in winter.

Getting There and Away

Buses depart San Isidro for Dominical daily at 7 a.m. and 1:30 p.m. Buses depart Quepos (Transportes Blanco, tel. 771-1384) for Dominical (continuing to San Isidro) daily at 5:30 a.m. and 1:30 p.m. Supposedly a bus originating at Uvita departs Dominical at 7:30 a.m. for San Isidro. Buses to Quepos depart Dominical at 8:30 a.m. and 3 p.m.

Beto's Taxi can be hired by calling CB channel 40, or through San Clemente restaurant.

Taximar, tel. 777-0262; in Quepos 777-1170, offers a water-taxi service between Quepos and Dominical ($20 one-way), Tuesday, Thursday,

Saturday, and Sunday at 7 a.m. (the service continues to Drake Bay and Caño Island).

ESCALERAS

Inland of Dominicalito, a series of dirt roads lead steeply uphill to Escaleras ("Staircases"), a forest-clad mountainous region fantastic for hiking and horseback rides from lodges such as Finca Brian y Milena or Bella Vista Ranch Lodge. Trails lead to waterfalls and the **Poza Azul,** or natural "Blue Lagoon," an azure-colored swimming hole replenished by a cascade. At Bella Vista you can even take a 230-meter **canopy ride** by cable-car through the forest.

Electricity arrived in 1997, and soon there may even be a paved road up the mountain. And houses are beginning to appear illegally (one such, 800 meters west of Finca Brian y Milena, sits over a stream, has been built without permits, and is intended as a bed and breakfast). Things around here get done by bribes: several prominent hoteliers told me about getting "enhancements" approved by monetary donations to local officials.

Most of the land is now owned by foreigners—no bad thing, for they are proving among

SPECIAL HOTEL: FINCA BRIAN Y MILENA

For a totally reclusive, totally rustic escape, head to Finca Brian y Milena, Apdo. 2, San Isidro de El General 8000, fax 771-1903 or 771-3060 (allow at least four weeks for a reply), a 10-hectare *finca* in the hills of Escaleras. The farm is run by Missouri transplant Brian, his Tica wife Milena, and their charming daughter, Emelia. It is intended as a place where guests can find harmony with nature. Reports one reader: "We loved it so much! Their guest cabin was so incredibly ULTIMATE!"

Your home away from home is a cozy and romantic, albeit spartan, cabin with private bath and cold water. It sleeps three; a folding cot on the balcony could accommodate a fourth person. Farther up the mountain is a more basic hut—the "birdhouse." Brian and Milena planned to add an additional shelter for volunteer workers. At night, after Milena's superb Costa Rican-style all-natural meals cooked outside on a wood-fired stove, you can soak by starlight in the streamside rock-walled pool heated by a wood-fired oven.

Brian has developed an economically sustainable fruit farm, cultivating neglected fruit trees that prove productive in wetter areas of Costa Rica. Brian has about 90 species of fruit trees in production, as well as nuts and spices such as ginger and vanilla. He will share his enlightened perspective, enthusiasm, and textbook knowledge on a fascinating tour of the orchard. Most of his fruits are sold and bartered to local fishermen. Key fruits include mangosteen and durian, the most important commercial fruit in Southeast Asia.

There's more! The birding is fantastic (rare chestnut-mandibled toucans and king vultures are com-

mon). As many as 25 species of hummingbirds—including a minuscule, unidentified species—play close by the lodge. Plus Brian will guide you on hikes to waterfalls with superb swimming holes. Overnight trips to Salto Diamante—a multiple waterfall of seven cataracts terminating in a final fall of 137 meters—include an overnight in a cave and meals with *campesino* families. Bring heavy-duty pants and waterproof footwear for hikes.

Brian and Milena are codirectors of ASANA. Brian sees his *finca* as a key to conservation. Alas, in recent years most of the land locally has been bought by foreigners, and Brian's original goal of demonstrating to local farmers how they can benefit ecologically and economically by his example is no longer valid. Now he focuses on educating individuals wishing to reforest their land, and selling them native tree species and seeds.

A 4WD is needed for the steep climb. Or you can arrange to be picked up by horses: simply radio the *finca* from Cabinas San Clemente, Hacienda Barú, or Cabinas del Sol in Dominical (it's often difficult to reach them in midday hours because of interference; early morning and evening are best) and Brian will bring horses and meet you at the turnoff for Escaleras for an additional charge.

Rates: $50 s, $48 pp d, $10 for children under 12. A $2 pp discount applies for each additional day and for each additional person. A day visit is $30 including lunch and farm tour. Discounts are offered for anyone willing to work (and a six-week volunteer program is offered).

the most conscientious of landowners and together have formed ASANA.

ASANA

The Asociación de los Amigos de la Naturaleza de Balúa-Bellena, Barú, y Savegre (ASANA), tel./fax 787-0037, e-mail: selvamar@sol.racsa.co.cr; in the U.S., Selva Mar/AAA Express Mail, 1641 N.W. 79th Ave., Miami, FL 33126-1105, is a nonprofit organization working to create a network of ecological corridors connecting Corcovado National Park with La Amistad International Peace Park via the Pacific coastal mountain range. The project—named **Paso de la Danta** (Tapir Trail)—aims to coordinate community involvement as a prerequisite in creating the 96-km-long pathway of protected forests.

The threat of deforestation faced by the southern Pacific region has been increased since completion of the Costera Sur highway and a subsequent influx of tourism and commercial development. Lands that are not currently held by conscientious owners are being sold and parceled off due to the high price of land and the poor agricultural market. The key is educating local stakeholders on the necessity and long-term benefits of conservation and restoration of natural ecosystems. ASANA urgently needs donations.

Accommodations

Woody Dyer's **Bella Vista Ranch Lodge,** Apdo. 459, San Isidro 8000, tel. 771-1903 or CB Radio Channel 7; in North America, tel. (305) 254-7592, is a rustic Colorado-style ranch—a real piece of the "West"—perched loftily on a plateau high in the Escaleras, with sweeping coastal vistas as far as Nicoya, Osa, and Cerro de la Muerte. The converted farmhouse has four simple but comfortable and quaint rooms with shared bath and solar-heated water. There are also spacious two-bedroom cabins with all-around screened windows, tiled bathrooms, and verandas for admiring the killer views. The lodge has a restaurant and magnificent views from the airy veranda of the mahogany farmhouse, which commands a priceless position. The lodge specializes in horseback tours (typically $35-40, two hours) and can arrange transfers. One reader has raved about this tranquil, environmentally conscious getaway (solar-heated water, septic-tank sewer system, etc.); another tells of the Dyers' "warmth and hospitality." Woody

and his late brother Mike have been cited for their contributions to conservation. The place is beloved of fashion photographers: maybe you saw it featured as a locale for shoots in a 1997 *Playboy* issue or *Sports Illustrated*'s 1995 swimsuit edition. Book through Selva Mar, Apdo. 215-8000, San Isidro de El General, tel. 771-4582, fax 771-1903, e-mail: selvamar@sol.racsa.co.cr. Rates: $25 s, $35 d rooms; $45 d cabins ($5 extra person). *Recommended!*

Another marvelous option is the **Villas Escaleras,** Suite 2277 SJO, P.O. Box 025216, Miami, FL 33102-5216, tel. 771-5247, formerly Escaleras Inn, perched dramatically at 400 meters elevation, one km south of Bella Vista, with staggering views as far south as Osa. It offers three deluxe, vaulted-ceiling bedrooms in the main villa, plus two smaller, albeit equally magnificent villas. All boast an exquisite aesthetic. Decor highlights include purpleheart floors and colorful Guatemalan fabrics, Peruvian wall hangings, and lots of sunlight. The main villa (three-stories, 4,000 square feet, three bedrooms, five bathrooms) has a bar and library, and swimming pool and terrace. Villa 2 has its own small plunge pool and sundeck. The small villa ("guesthouse") is more intimate; guests have access to the pool in the main villa. Tiled bathrooms feature pressurized hot water. The owners donate $1 per room per night to one of three environmental causes of your choice. Rates: $300 daily, $1,800 weekly main villa (up to eight people); $200 daily, $1,200 weekly Villa 2 (up to four people); $125 daily, $750 weekly one-bedroom villa.

More rustic but no less appealing is **Pacific Edge,** Apdo. 531-8000, San Isidro de El General, tel. 771-1903 or 787-0031, reached via its own steep dirt road (4WD recommended) half a kilometer south of the turnoff for Bella Vista. It's simple and secluded, with four cabins stairstepping down the lower mountain slopes at 200 meters elevation, with grand vistas northward. Wooden walkways lead to the rustic yet comfortable cabins, which have all-around screened windows, fans, small refrigerators, and hammocks on their verandas. Each cabin has a "half-kitchenette," but you can hang out in the thatched *ranchito* bar-cum-*cocina*. It's run by an amiable ex-Valley Girl, Susie, and her affable Limey husband, George Atkinson (described in *Condé Nast Traveler,* accurately, as a "merry Londoner

. . .'Appy day!' he keeps croaking like a parrot"). Sound effects, in addition to George's twisted Cockney accent, include the cries of howler monkeys and a zillion squawks, whistles, and chirps of birds. Susie whips up mean cuisine spanning the globe (an Asian influence is prominent) in her thatched bamboo restaurant. These former mariners work with Bella Vista Lodge in arranging hikes and horseback trips, and also offer fishing, sailing, and more. Reservations through Selva Mar. Rates: $35 s, $40 d; $5 extra person; $5 for kitchen use.

Villa Cabeza de Mono is an old mountain home in Spanish colonial style for rent high in the hills. One bedroom has two single beds; another has a double and single. It has a pool, a fully stocked kitchen, maid service, and ocean views. Book through Selva Mar (see above). Rates: $125 daily, $850 weekly. You'll need a 4WD.

And don't miss Finca Brian y Milena.

UVITA AND VICINITY

South of Dominicalito, seemingly endless **Playa Hermosa** extends south to the headland of **Punta Uvita,** a tombolo (a narrow sandbar connecting an island to the mainland), jutting out west of the tiny hamlet of Uvita, 16 km south of Dominical. The Río Uvita, immediately south of the village pours into the sea south of Punta Uvita at **Bahía,** the northern boundary of Ballena Marine National Park. Bahía, one km east of the Costanera Sur and one km south of Uvita, is a popular and lively holiday spot for Ticos, who flock to the river estuary and camp along the beach turning it into a veritable squatter's camp-cum-garbage dump.

Backing the narrow coastal strip are the steep green, green **Fila Tinomastes** mountains—fantastic for hiking and horseback rides that get you close to nature. Spider and howler monkeys are abundant. And crocodiles abound in the lagoons and mangroves around Bahía.

A great place to see both is **Refugio Nacional Mixta de Vida Silvestre Rancho Merced,** tel./fax 771-1903, a private 1,250-hectare biological reserve on a cattle ranch that includes mangrove wetlands by the shore. It offers horseback rides ($15 two hours, $5 extra hours), hiking, and a boating tour to Ballena Marine National Park ($5-55 pp). Coastal mangroves are good for birding and for spotting caimans and maybe even crocodiles. You can even try your hand roping cattle. The reserve incorporates the Profelis Wildcat Center.

Profelis Wildcat Center

This research station—colloquially but incorrectly called a "Cat Farm"—takes in endangered animals (mostly cats) confiscated by government officials. Here, ocelots, jaguars, and other endangered animals are raised or reconditioned for reintroduction to the wild. It is recognized by MINAE as a center for the rehabilitation of wildcats. Most animals are not on public view and human contact is kept to a minimum (and for food they must hunt live animals put in their cages). Quite correctly, I was denied a request for a behind-the-scenes tour. However, you can see ocelots, tayras, margays, spider monkeys, and other mammals that are too domesticated or imprinted on humans to be released into the wild. Some animals have been terribly abused by their Tico owners, such as the ocelot who can't walk because she was kept in a box for 10 years (then there's the margay that had only been fed white rats; when brought to Profelis it wouldn't eat anything else and lost a lot of weight until it decided black rats finally began to look tasty). I even got to hold and stroke Taffa, an imprinted ocelot that almost took my skin off by licking me with her rasp-like tongue. Guided tours can last two hours and are highly educational.

Profelis (400 meters north of Rancho Merced) has no facilities, though a public education center was to be added. It's run by German biologists and volunteers. Donations are *desperately* needed. For information contact Selva Mar, Hacienda Baró, or c/o Carlos de la Rosa, tel. 470-0176, fax 470-0148, e-mail: firema@sol.racsa.co.cr.

Oro Verde

This rustic *finca,* tel./fax 771-3015, is in the mountains, a little north and three km inland of Uvita, in the tiny hamlet of San Josecito de Uvita. Oro Verde is owned by real *campesinos*—the Duartes, a gracious family of three generations including five brothers and their families. The property is set amid jungled mountains at about 600 meters elevation in the valley of the Río Uvita. It boasts 300 hectares of primary forest with trails, and attractions such as remote waterfalls and even a huge pre-Columbian *bola,* or stone sphere. You can watch and even participate in the farming (they raise cattle, grow coffee, beans, rice, etc., and even have a *trapiche,* or traditional sugar press). A five-hour jungle tour costs $20 including lunch. Horseback rides cost $5 pp. The road is steep and rugged: 4WD is recommended (alternately, rent a horse at Rancho Merced; it's about 45 minutes by horse from the road). Oro Verde is signed.

Accommodations
Playa Hermosa and Fila Tinomastes: American-owned **Cabañas Escondidas,** Apdo. 364, San Isidro de El General, tel. 272-2904, fax 771-0735, five km south of Dominical, bills itself as a "Study and Retreat Center" for "those who want to share information and practices of a physical and metaphysical nature." It accepts *all* guests, not just the holistically inclined. It has nine *cabinas* with fans and private baths and hot water plus splendid views over the Pacific from their hillside location. The cabins are spaced apart, from sea level to 125 meters elevation. The landscaped gardens offer tranquility. Massage and tai chi classes are offered ($25 per hour). Guided nature walks and horseback rides are available into the 32-hectare rainforest. Patty Mitchell conjures "exquisite vegetarian cuisine" ($8 per meal; open for breakfast and lunch, dinner by reservation), served in an octagonal *rancho* restaurant. It rents kayaks ($10 per hour). Book through Selva Mar, Apdo. 215-8000, San Isidro de El General, tel. 771-4582, fax 771-1903, e-mail: selvamar@sol.racsa.co.cr. Rates: $25-75 d high season, depending on cabin; $15 less in low season.

The ho-hum **Swiss Tucán,** tel. 297-1965, fax 771-5815, is in the foothills of the Fila Tinomastes, 400 meters south of Escondidas; the dirt road leads two km steeply uphill. It has four red-tile-roofed *cabinas* with private baths and hot water, plus fans, hardwood walls, simple yet attractive bamboo furniture, and views over the coast. There's a swimming pool and shady *mirador* restaurant set in unkempt (very un-Swiss) grounds. Rates: $40 d including breakfast.

Las Casitas de Puertocito, c/o tel. 771-1903, one km south of Escondidas, is a delightful little property—you may recognize it as a backdrop in the movie *A Corner of Paradise*—run by a charming Italian and set amid a lush garden at the head of a valley on the peninsula. Six split-level cabins have a queen-size bed on an open loft, plus a single bed on the ground floor, with bamboo furniture and Guatemalan prints, a bathroom with hot water, and a wide patio complete with tiny kitchenette. A tiny *ranchito* restaurant serves genuine Italian dishes. You can arrange a full array of activities (hiking, horseback rides, snorkeling, fishing, and more). Rates: $35 low season, $39 d midseason, $49 d high season, including breakfast. A four-day "Horseback Adventure" costs $295 pp.

In the mountains, **Oro Verde** has two basic yet comfortable bungalows, each with a kitchen and two bedrooms containing two single beds. There's a cool dip pool. Doña Eida will cook for you ($10 per day). Book through Selva Mar. Rates: $10 pp.

Rancho La Merced has two cabins (one for six people; one for eight) in the foothills on the road to Oro Verde. Each has a kitchen and a private bathroom with cold water only. You can have *típico* meals cooked for you in a small *ranchito* restaurant on the cattle farm east of the road. Rates: $35 d, $10 extra person.

Uvita: The rustic **Cabinas Los Laureles,** tel. 771-1903, 400 meters inland of Uvita and set amid a grove of laurel trees at the foot of the mountains. Four rooms have private bath and cold water. There are also four twin-story, pitched-roofed *cabinas* with timbered beams and private baths, plus parking and porch. A horse-powered *trapiche* extracts sugarcane juice. Congenial owner Victor Pérez offers horseback trips into the mountains ($4 per hour), plus boat rides to Ballena Marine National Park. His wife serves tasty breakfasts at the family table. A swimming pool was to be added. Rates: $15 s, $25 d; $8 extra person. Four rooms with shared bath cost $10 s, $8 each extra person.

Coco Tico Lodge, 100 meters farther up the dirt road, has 12 rustic rooms and six *cabinas* with private bath and cold water next to a twee *soda.* It offers boat trips and horseback rides. Rates: $6.50 pp rooms, $13 d, $20 quad.

Bahía: Villa Cabinas Hegalva, c/o the public telephone, tel. 771-2311, has six *cabinas* with fans and private baths with cold water. The owner permits camping beneath shade trees on trim lawns. There's a rustic bar and restaurant for guests only, plus a volleyball net, and a swimming pool was to be added. Rates: $10 s, $15 d *cabinas;* $12 pp campsite. The more basic **Cabinas Punta Uvita** (c/o Selva Mar), 200 meters farther, has four wood-and-bamboo cabins in an orchard. It also permits camping. Rates: $5 shared bath; $9 s, $15 d private bath.

There are other basic *cabinas* in Bahía village, 600 meters inland from the estuary. Try **Cabinas María Jesús** or **Cabinas Betty.**

Food

At Uvita, try the breezy modern **Bar y Restaurante El Viajero** serving a *casado* of mixed seafood, chicken and rice, and salad ($2.50). You can buy food at the *pulpería* in Uvita. There are several lively bars and *típico* restaurants all in a row near the estuary in Bahía. There's a **pizzeria** 200 meters north of El Chamán.

Tours and Activities

You can arrange boat trips to Isla Ballena and the coral reefs with León Victor González at the *pulpería* in Uvita.

Spanish Language Courses

The **Costa Rica Spanish Institute,** Apdo. 1366-2050, San Pedro, tel./fax 253-2117, e-mail: cosi-cr@sol.racsa.co.cr, offers Spanish language classes at Cabañas Escondidas.

Getting There

Buses depart Dominical for Uvita and Bahía at 8:30 a.m. and 4:30 p.m. (check schedules at San Clemente in Dominical). Buses depart San Isidro from Calle 1, Avenidas 4/6, at 3 p.m. (return buses depart Bahía at 7 a.m.).

There's a full-service gas station at Uvita.

WATCHING AND STUDYING WHALES

August through March, you can count on humpbacks playing up and down the Pacific coast of the Americas. Increasingly, they're showing up off the coast of Costa Rica.

Remarkably little is known about the ecology of whales. Until recently, for example, scientists believed that North Pacific humpbacks limited their breeding to the waters off Japan, Hawaii, and Mexico's Sea of Cortez. New findings, however, suggest that whales may get amorous off the coast of Costa Rica, too. Individual whales are identified by the white markings on the underside of their flukes, and some of the whales sighted off California have been showing up in Costa Rican waters.

To learn more about humpback habits and activities, the Oceanic Society has an ongoing study to identify individual creatures and trace their migrations. The society needs volunteers on weeklong midwinter trips offered through Elderhostel. It's a marvelous opportunity for eyeball-to-eyeball encounters with the gentle giants of the deep.

PARQUE NACIONAL MARINE BALLENA

The Ballena Marine National Park was created in February 1990 to protect the shoreline of Bahía de Coronado and includes the Punta Uvita, several splendid beaches (notably Playa Ballena), plus 4,500 hectares of water surrounding Isla Ballena. The park extends south for 15 km from Uvita to Punta Piñuel, and about 15 km out to sea.

The park harbors within its relatively small area important mangroves and the largest coral reef on the Pacific coast of Cen-

BOB RACE

humpback whale

tral America. A particular curiosity are the green marine iguanas that live on algae in the saltwater pools. They litter the golden-sand beaches like prehistoric jetsam, their bodies angled at 90 degrees to catch the sun's rays most directly. Pretty smart: Once they reach 37° C they pop down to the sea for a bite to eat. Olive ridley and hawksbill turtles come ashore May-Nov. to lay their eggs (September and October are the best months to visit). Common and bottlenosed dolphins frolic offshore. And the bay is the southernmost mating site for the humpback whale, which migrates from Alaska, Baja California, and Hawaii (Dec.-April).

PROTECTING COSTA RICA'S MARINE RESOURCES

In response to ever-increasing threats to the fragile marine habitats of the Pacific coast, the System of Marine Parks and Reserves (SIPAREMA)—a part of the National Parks Service—was formed in 1991 within the Costa Rican Ministry of Natural Resources. The body represents a belated attempt to shield the precious coral reefs and offshore wildlife habitats from a final demise. According to a SIPAREMA publication, "fish, turtle, and sea-faring bird migrations are decreasing in size and frequency [and] calving whales, a common sight not long ago, are abandoning some tropical bays . . . and of greatest concern, sedimentation from coastal development and inland erosion is seriously damaging the coral reefs."

SIPAREMA must design and then execute sophisticated resource-management plans to set catch limits, control tourism, and balance all the competing demands on the marine resources against the needs of the marine fauna itself. It must build park monitoring facilities, hire park rangers, and buy boats and communications equipment.

Donations
SIPAREMA is underfunded and understaffed. Donations (specify Costa Rica Marine Parks Fund) may be made through Fundación de Parques Nacionales, Apdo. 1108, San José 1002, Costa Rica; The Cousteau Society, 930 West 21st St., Norfolk, VA 23517; or The Nature Conservancy, 1815 North Lynn St., Arlington, VA 22209.

Snorkeling is good close to shore during low tides. You can also reach the island at the tip of Punta Uvita at low tide to discover corals, sponges, and sea anemones. There are caves, too, worth exploring. Isla Ballena and the rocks known as Las Tres Hermanas ("The Three Sisters") are havens for frigate birds and boobies as well as pelicans and even ibises. Whales tend to congregate near Las Tres Hermanas.

Despite protection, shrimp fishermen still fish with impunity close to shore (I've seen them) using gill nets that are indiscriminate about the species they trap. As well, erosion and sedimentation resulting from an ill-fated attempt to build a coastal highway in the mid-1980s is claimed to have killed off 60% of the coral reef. Though the government created the park to protect the area, earth movers again began tearing up the rainforest for the Costanera Sur Highway in 1992, creating fears that the massive volumes of disturbed earth may kill the remaining reef.

Information
The ranger station and park headquarters is beside the beach at Hacienda Bahía, three km south of Uvita. There's another ranger station at Playa Piñuela, at the southern end of the park. Nominally the entrance fee is $6, but a fee seems to be charged only rarely.

You can **camp** on the beach. The ranger stations have water.

Getting There
You can hire a **boat** and guide at any of the fishing hamlets between Palmar and the park, or in Dominical or Uvita, to take you to the reef or Isla Ballena (about $30 per hour, $45 two hours). In Uvita, ask for Captain Jenkin Mora Guzmann, or Victor Pérez, of Cabinas Los Laureles.

THE BRUNCA COAST

The lush, once untrammeled section of coastline between Uvita and Cortés is booming. Completion in 1996 of the Costanera Sur Highway—wide and fast and so dusty that everyone drives with headlamps on—has opened the floodgates to one of Costa Rica's erstwhile most inaccessible regions. Its miles-long beaches—notably Playa

Ballena, Playa Piñuela, Playa Ventanas,and Playa Tortuga—have for eons been favored by female marine turtles for nesting and are now finding favor with surfers. The area was virtually unknown to everyone—even Ticos—because the road was so bad. There are sea caves in the cliffs on the south side of Punta Piñuelas that can be entered by kayak; another, accessible by foot, widens to a 100-meter channel.

Playa Tortuga, near the hamlet of **Tortuga Abajo,** sweeps south to the mouth of the Río Terraba and the vast wildlife-rich mangrove swamps of the Delta del Terraba, Costa Rica's largest such habitat. A special attraction—beside viewing wildlife (not least crocodiles)—is mangrove fishing.

The Costanera Sur swings inland at **Punta Mala,** a hamlet (five km south of Tortuga Abajo) at the mouth of the Río Terraba and gateway to the Golfo Dulce and Osa region. One km south of Tortuga Abajo, a road leads inland two km to **Ojochal,** on the slopes of the Fila Costeña. The area has lots of attractions, including La Cascada waterfall, Jardín Tortuga, and Rancho Soluna Indian Art Center. They're all signed at the turnoff.

For some reason, French-Canadians seem to dominate the scene hereabouts. I expect many more hotels and restaurants to open in the next few years.

Accommodations

Two km south of Uvita on the Costanera Sur is **Villas Bejuco,** Apdo. 101, 8000 Pérez Zeledón, tel. 771-0965, fax 771-2003, with six clean, handsome, modern hillside cabins with double and single beds, private baths with cold water (hot water was to be added), and views of both mountain and beach. There's a restaurant, a swimming pool and sundeck, plus horseback riding and boat excursions. Rates: from $45 d, $10 extra person.

Just south of Bejuco, at the entrance to Ballena National Park, is **Hotel El Chamán,** tel. 771-7771, with 11 small, basic cabins and a **campsite** ($5 per tent, with electricity and shared bathrooms) spread out beneath a palm grove behind Playa Ballena. Each cabin has a double bed and bamboo furnishings, plus private bath with hot water (six have private indoor showers; a row of six outside showers

serves the rest). The offbeat place is German-owned and popular with both Germans and Ticos. It has a small pool and a restaurant serving international cuisine. A string of battery-powered lights is strung from trees to light the paths at night. Rates: $21 d shared bath, $29 private bath; $140 for a four-day package including breakfasts, dinners, tours, and all drinks. There's a suite for $42 d. Owner Klaus Gudowius, was planning a theme park in the foothills, Rancho de la Felicidad, with a cliffside 600-square-meter swimming pool from which a 300-meter-long water slide will spiral down through the forested and landscaped hill to another pool. Gudowius plans to install an alpine chairlift to whisk you up the mountainside. A botanical garden is also planned, along with a children's adventure playground.

There's a house for rent 200 meters north of El Chamán.

Pensión Roca Paraiso is an offbeat *albergue* in an old wooden home painted in bright tropical pastels and nestled right up to Playa Ballena—a fantastic, lonesome location facing Isla Ballena in the heart of the national park. It has four simple rooms with a large shared bathroom semi-open to public view (there are screen windows, not walls) and shared kitchen. Windows are screened, and furnishings are bare bones. The owner, Ed Sánchez, lives in a hut nearby. Rates: $25 s, $30 d. The turnoff from the Costanera Sur is just south of a large bridge about eight km south of Uvita.

Cabinas Ana, one km south near the hamlet of Piñuela, has two large two-story, thatched cabins for six people each, with screened windows all around. They're very rustic and sit beneath shady trees. They also nestle up to a large mangrove swamp extending 200 meters to the shore (the mosquitoes eye your arrival greedily; bring repellent) reached via a raised walkway over the oozing mud. Camping is permitted. The French manager, Patrick, makes salads and light meals. Rates: $20 s, $25 d.

Hotel y Restaurant Flamingo is 200 meters south. It has modest, modern *cabinas,* and permits camping by the beach. Again, bring bug spray. **Villas Leonor,** tel. 225-8151, a stone's throw south, has two pretty little thatched *cabinas* with private bath and cold water amid lawns 300 meters inland of the beach. Rates: $15 d.

SPECIAL RESTAURANT: GRINGO MIKE'S

It's hardly a standard recipe for success: I choose the most unlikely, out-of-the-way spot you can find, open an offbeat little pizzeria with concrete chairs and tables in a stone-walled patio beneath the stars, then serve up pizza so fine that the hospital in Cortés sends the ambulance—red lights whirling—to pick up the dinner.

"I'll cook up anything you can dream up," says Mike Terzano, a former chef from Detroit, who makes his pizzas with real Italian gorgonzola in a hand-built brick oven fired by gas or wood (a "regular"-size pizza costs $5-6 and amply serves two people). He also serves pasta and natural juices (75 cents) and all manner of other goodies. Cheesecake. Granny Smith apple pies. Pumpernickel bread. And, yes, even salami and sausage. It's all homemade, conjured by Mike's gentle hands.

Gringo Mike's, tel./fax 433-7864, in Ciudad de Cortes, doesn't appeal only to tourists and expatriates, either. The local campesinos also know a good thing, and pack in every night—though especially on Wednesday for all-you-can-eat pasta.

Mike is one of the most genteel fellas you'll ever meet—an all-around great guy. Get him in the mood and Mike—who was planning a mini-golf course and water slide on the hill out back—might even play his bagpipes for you.

The French-Canadian **Cabinas Piñuela** is attractive. It features four spacious cabinas with terra-cotta tile floors and appealing bamboo furnishings. Fans were to be installed. There are also two meagerly furnished two-story casitas with romantic mezzanine bedrooms (with soaring A-frame ceilings and a four-poster bed) and open-plan lounge and kitchenette, wide-screened windows, and narrow balcony. Each floor can be rented separately. There's no hot water. They're set in landscaped grounds with a plunge pool framed by splashy bougainvillea and a second pool full of turtles and fish. A handsome thatched stone-and-timber restaurant has a fountain. Rates: $35 d, $7 extra person.

Hotel Paraíso del Pacífico, tel. 788-8280, fax 786-6335; in Canada, tel. (514) 662-7555, fax 662-7552, is a modestly elegant French-run hotel on a rise east of the Costanera Sur, two km south of Piñuela and inland of Playa Tortuga. The 12 cabins are spaced along the ridge. It has a pool and sundeck with views of the coast and mountains. The mirador restaurant, predictably, serves French cuisine. Rates: $45 s/d.

The nicest hotel south of Dominical is the delightful Dutch-owned **Villas Gaia,** Apdo. 809, San José, tel./fax 256-9996, e-mail: hvgaia@sol.racsa.co.cr; in the U.S., 1940 N.W. 82nd Ave., Miami, FL 33126, on the Costanera Sur, 200 meters south of Paraíso. The 12 beautiful and colorful wooden cabinas dot the forested hillside: they are uniquely attractive, with muted pastel decor and minimalist furnishings, plus a double and single bed with orthopedic mattresses, and solar hot water. One cabin is equipped for handicapped guests. A pool, sundeck, and handsome bar boast views down over the 400-meter-wide swathe of forest and mangroves between the hotel and Playa Tortuga. The restaurant is blessed with equal ambience. A wide range of boat tours, snorkeling and fishing, hiking, birding, horseback riding, and excursions are offered. Rates: $60 d, $10 extra person. **Villa del Bosque** (not reviewed) is immediately south of Villas Gaia.

Las Ventanas de Osa, P.O. Box 1089, Lake Helen, FL 32744, tel. (904) 228-3356, fax 228-0181, near Tortuga Abajo, is a clifftop nature lodge in a private wildlife refuge—big with birders. The modern lodge is a private club open to members only (lifetime membership costs $500). It is open Dec.-March plus mid-July only (the lodge may open year-round after completion of the Costanera Sur Highway). Six rooms have twin beds and private baths. The lodge has a swimming pool and an open-air dining room with meals prepared by a professional chef. Also nearby are beaches good for swimming, and trails lead through the surrounding forest. Capuchin and howler monkeys are common. More than 380 bird species have been recorded, along with a boat-billed heron rookery. Rates: $900 six-day package including all meals, plus transfers from San José.

At Ojochal, the French-run **Casa Papagayo,** Apdo.16, Pueblo Cortés, fax 788-8210, has 14 rooms in a modest two-story lodge, plus two cabins. Facilities include a bar, restaurant, swimming pool, tennis courts, and horses; boat rides and fishing are also offered. The bar attracts plenty of French-speaking expats. Rates: $20 d ground floor, $41 d upper floor; $51 including breakfast.

The **Auberge El Perezoso** and **Albergue Auberge Inn** (not reviewed) are other options near Ojochal, as is **Rancho Soluna,** with camping and cabins.

Another hotel—**Casa Pura Vida**—should be open just north of Punta Mala by the time you read this.

Food

No journey is too long to dine at **Gringo Mike's Pizza Café** at Ojochal. The Villas Gaia's elegant roadside restaurant serves international, Caribbean, and Latin American fare. You can buy food at a grocery at the turnoff for Ojochal.

Tours and Activities

A gringo named "Kayak-No Last Names Please-Joe" (described as a "holdover from the 70s") runs a "Cave 'n' Wave Tour" ($45 half day) from Cabinas Piñuela, where he rents sea kayaks to experienced kayakers ($10 per hour). He also offers guided tours to Isla Ballena ($10). You can also take horseback rides from Cabinas Piñuela.

Gino—alias "I.O."—has a scuba diving outlet at Villas Gaia. He offers PADI certification plus dive trips to the reefs of Ballena Marine National Park and to Isla Caño from Cabinas Piñuela. Villas Gaia offers a panoply of fishing, snorkeling, and other activities, plus excursions throughout the central and southern Pacific regions.

Captain Dave has snorkeling and fishing excursions by canopied boat ($50 per hour), including to the Delta del Terraba and as far afield as Isla Caño. He also has horseback tours. And "Fred," a French-Canadian and "absolute character," offers a boat trip to his island camp in the Terraba mangroves—a Gilligan's Island called Isla Garza with a pristine nine-km-long beach, an orchard, boardwalks, volleyball and bocci, and hammocks in a coconut grove where seafood barbecue is served. You can contact both men through hotels in the area.

DOMINICAL TO PLATANILLO

A paved road leads east from Dominical to San Isidro, winding up through the valley of the Río Barú into the Fila Costanera mountains, where the climate cools and you may find yourself, within one hour of the hot, humid lowlands, high amid swirling clouds. Break out your camera at **Tinamaste,** 12 km east of Dominical, for the hamlet enjoys a staggering setting atop a plateau with views far and wide.

Cataratas de Nauyaca

Near Platanillo, just north of the village of Barú, signs point the way east to these magnificent waterfalls that tumble 70 meters in two cascades that plunge into deep pools good for swimming. They are surrounded by tropical moist forest full of wildlife accessed by trails. The falls, which are six km east of the road, also go by other names: Don Lulo's and Santo Cristo. You can reach them on horseback from Escaleras or from **Don Lulo's,** tel./fax 771-3187, e-mail: ciprotur@sol.racsa.co.cr, at Platanillo, from where a trail leads via the hamlet of Libano. The guided horseback tour leaves at 8 a.m., returning at 3 p.m.($35, reservations essential). There are bathrooms by the falls, plus pneumatic tires for floats. Don Lulo also has a **mini-zoo** with macaws, toucans, and *tepezcuintles.* Tour companies in Dominical also offer trips to the falls, as do various rustic lodges in Escaleras. **Centro de Amigos,** tel. 771-0444, at San Salvador, east of Libano, offers horseback tours to the waterfalls.

Accommodations

Paraíso Tropical, tel. 771-7353, 100 meters east of Don Lulo's, has four handsome cabins offering mountain vistas. Each has two bedrooms with a double bed and two twin beds, fans, TV, refrigerator, private bath with hot water, and a porch. There's a swimming pool with water slide, and a restaurant. The place is popular with Ticos. It offers horseback rides to Cataratas de Nauyaca. Rates: $48 d low season; $60 d high season, including tax and breakfast.

Camp Santo Cristo across the road has camping, eco-hikes, horseback tours, tree canopy exploration, and river floats.

The **Restaurant La Fiesta,** just west of Tinamaste, has *cabinas,* as does **Restaurant Mirador El Castillo,** in Tinamaste.

BOB RACE

GOLFO DULCE AND PENINSULA DE OSA

Costa Rica's southwesternmost region is a distinct geographic entity, an oblong landmass west of the Fila Costeña, extending into the Pacific and indented in the center by a vast gulf called Golfo Dulce. Curling around the gulf to the north is the mountainous, hook-shaped Peninsula de Osa and, to the south, the pendulous **Peninsula de Burica.** Between them, north and south of the gulf, are two broad fertile plains smothered by banana plantations—the **Valle de Diquis,** to the northwest, separating the region from the central Pacific by a large swamp fed by the Río Grande de Terraba, and the **Valle de Coto Colorado,** extending south to the border with Panamá.

The region boasts many fine attractions and of late has been coming on strong as a tourist destination. Star billing goes to **Corcovado National Park,** which covers much of the Osa Peninsula and is a repository for some of the nation's greatest wildlife treasures. The park is part of the **Corcovado Conservation Area,** encompassing ad-

jacent forest reserves and other protected areas. The waters of the Golfo Dulce are rich in marlin and other game fish, and the area is understandably popular with sportfishers. Three species of dolphin—bottlenose, black spotted, and spinner—are often seen frolicking in the gulf, especially around sunset, following which the gulf waters are charged by photoluminsecent microbes. Surfers flock for the killer waves, particularly around Zancudo and Pavones. And Cocos Island, 300 km offshore, is acclaimed as a world-class dive site.

Protestant evangelists seem to have made stronger headway here than elsewhere in the country judging by the remarkable number of small churches.

A good resource on this region is *The Southern Costa Rica Guide,* by Alex del Sol (Rincón Tourist & Surf Center, Rincón de Osa 8203, Puerto Jiménez; $2), which provides detailed information on the far south.

CLIMATE

This region is climatically distinct. Trade winds from the southeast discharge their rains on the Fila Costeña mountains year-round; be prepared for rain and a lingering wet season. The area receives 4-8 meters of rain annually. Violent thunderstorms move in Oct.-Dec., lashing the region and dumping torrents of rain. They're followed by clear blue skies and brilliant sunshine, which turn the sopping jungle into a steaming sauna. Caño Island (about 30 km offshore) gets struck by lightning more often than any other part of Central America and for that reason was considered sacred by pre-Columbian peoples, who used it as a burial ground.

HISTORY

The area is vitally important as a center of a distinct indigenous culture, for the local peoples, as distinct from their northerly neighbors, had historical links with South America. Alas, despite a plethora of unusual and intriguing phenomena—notably, perfectly spherical granite balls found throughout the Osa region—the archaeological background of the region is less complete than for the rest of the country. The spheres—*bolas*—and occasional small tombs are (along with gold ornaments) the only physical legacy of the indigenous Diquis culture and date back to A.D. 400-1400. The spheres range from a few centimeters to three meters across and weigh as much as 16 tons. They litter the forest floors in no perceptible order, but have been found in groups of as many as 25. No one is certain when they were carved or how, or for what purpose, although it is most probable that they had a religious or ceremonial significance. Erich von Daniken, in his *Chariots of the Gods?*, calls the spheres "projectiles shot from star ships." The most plausible explanation for *how* they were shaped lies in the region's copious rainfall and powerful waterfalls. Hydraulic pressure is the only known force available to pre-Columbian peoples that could have been utilized to grind rocks of such massive size, which were probably "tumbled" like ball bearings at the base of waterfalls.

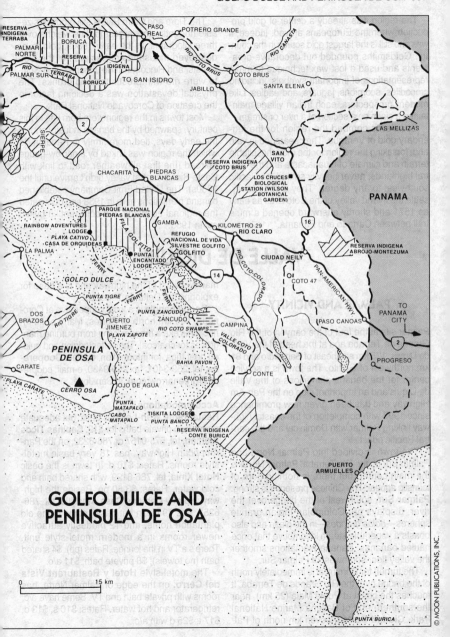

GOLFO DULCE AND PENINSULA DE OSA

0   15 km

© MOON PUBLICATIONS, INC.

The region was already a center of gold production when the Europeans arrived. Indeed, it was and still is the largest gold source in the country. Goldsmiths pounded out decorative ornaments and used a lost wax technique to make representations of important symbols, including crocodiles, scorpions, jaguars, and eagles. Like modern prospectors, each Indian village maintained a claim on a section of a river or stream.

Spaniards combed the region for the legendary gold of Veragua. They searched in vain and, forsaking the region for the more hospitable terrain and climate of Guanacaste and the central highlands, never heavily settled the Pacific southwest to any degree. They did, however, settle the inland valley of the Coto Brus as early as 1571 and shortly afterward opened a mule trail between Cartago and Panamá.

The Tigre and Claro Rivers still produce sizeable nuggets—the largest to date weighs over three kilograms. In the early 1980s, gold fever destroyed thousands of hectares of the Osa forests, and Rincón, Puerto Jiménez, and Golfito were rife with prostitutes and drunks. The physical devastation was a deciding factor in the creation of Corcovado National Park.

Most towns in the region were born late in this century, spawned by the banana industry and, in the early days, tied more firmly to Panamá, to which the region was linked by a narrow-gauge railroad (the first all-weather road to link with Costa Rica's central valley didn't arrive until the 1950s). The United Fruit Company established banana plantations here in 1938 and dominated the regional economy and polity until it pulled out in 1985.

VALLE DE DIQUIS

PALMAR AND VICINITY

Palmar sits at the foot of the canyon of the Río Grande de Terraba and at the head of the Valle de Diquis, 125 km southeast of San Isidro and 81 km northwest of Golfito. The town is a service center for the banana plantations of the Valle de Diquis and an important stop on the Pan-Am Highway and has been given new prominence since 1997 with completion of the coastal highway linking Palmar with Dominical and the central Pacific coast.

The town is divided into Palmar Norte and Palmar Sur by the Río Terraba. **Palmar Norte** is the main center, but there is nothing here of touristic appeal. The Chinese presence is strong. **Palmar Sur,** southwest of the bridge over the river, displays pre-Columbian Indian granite spheres—*bolas grandes*—in the plaza and also boasts a venerable steam locomotive that once hauled bananas. Banana plantations smother the valley floor southwest of Palmar Sur.

The turnoff for Dominical is immediately north of the bridge over the Río Grande de Terraba. It touches the coast at Punta Mala (25 km), near the southern end of Ballena Marine National Park. **Ciudad Cortés,** seven km north of Palmar, lies west of the highway and is a base for exploring the Delta de Terraba.

Coopemangle is a local cooperative at Coronado, five km north of Cortés. Many of its inhabitants eke a meager living from burning mangroves for charcoal. They offer lodging and guided boat trips; for information, contact **Cooperena,** tel. 259-3401, fax 259-9430, e-mail: cooprena@greenarrow.com, in San José.

Accommodations
Restaurante Wah-Lok has basic but adequate rooms with private baths for $12. **Cabinas Ticos Alemán,** tel. 575-0157 or 786-6232, on the Pan-American Highway, has 18 very basic motel-style rooms. Rates: $10 d. In town is the basic **Hotel Xinia,** tel. 786-6129, with shared bath and cold water. Rates: $3.50 pp. Beside the highway, **Hotel y Cabinas Casa Amarilla,** tel. 786-6251, has 19 clean but basic rooms in the old plantation home, and 12 modestly attractive newer rooms in a modern motel-style unit. There's a TV in the lounge. Rates (pp): $4 shared bath (no towels); $8 private bath; $11 a/c.

The motel-style **Hotel y Restaurant Vista del Cerro,** on the edge of Palmar Norte, has rooms with private bath and TV. Some have a/c, refrigerator and hot water. Rates: $10 s, $13 d, $17 t; $25 d with a/c.

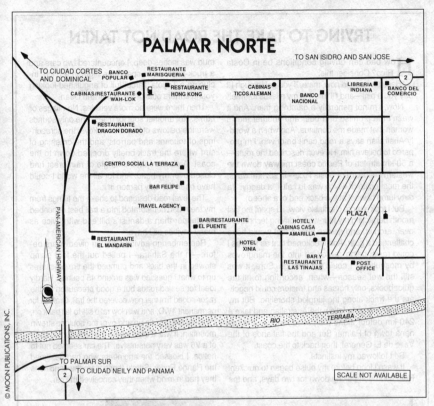

The preferred spot is **Hacienda Doña Victoria,** tel. 786-7123, fax 786-6269, a fruit farm replete with rainforest, about two km from the highway, just south of the airport. It offers fully equipped two-story, four-bedroom casas, each sleeping up to 10 people and each with a lounge, two bathrooms with hot water, a kitchen, and patio with hammocks. Screens keep the bugs out but let in the breezes. There's a restaurant and bar plus laundry, and tours are offered. Rates: $25 s, $45 d, $60 t, $70 quad, including breakfast and one-hour horseback riding. A full house rents for $120.

Food
No hope of gourmet fare here, I'm afraid. Three Chinese restaurants—**Restaurante Dragon Dorado** and **Restaurante Wah-Lok,** immediately north of the bridge, and **Restaurante Hong Kong** 100 meters east—all serve ho-hum meals. There are several basic restaurants serving *típico* fare, including the clean **Soda El Puente. Restaurant Vista al Cerro** specializes in barbecue dishes, served in a patio; open 6 a.m.-10 p.m. The restaurant at **Casa Amarilla** is open 6 a.m.-midnight.

Services
There's a stationery shop—**Librería Indiana**—on Hwy. 2 on the northeast edge of town. There's a gas station immediately north of the bridge. The **Banco Nacional** is off the Pan-Am Highway. Hidanuel Lopez Valerín, tel. 786-6065, represents **Travelair** and also operates **Chino Taxi** service and travel agency, in Palmar Sur. The **police station** (Guardia Rural) is on the south side of the park.

TRYING TO TAKE THE ROAD NOT TAKEN

How bad can driving conditions be in Costa Rica? Consider this.

"Best turn around now, mate. If you get through I'll buy you a pint—and I'll throw in my missus for free!"

Now, I'm not generally a gambling man. And it wasn't the promise of a beer and another man's woman that made me continue. And when a worldly Australian says a road can't be driven, I'm prepared to believe him. He even described the route—a 50-km stretch of Pacific coast midway down the western seaboard of Costa Rica—in several ways, the most polite of which was to call it "a daggy!" (a dirty lump of wool at the back end of a sheep).

But I took a more charitable view. I'd spent the last month perfecting my four-wheel-driving techniques over, around, and across terrain that would have challenged a goat. And I reckoned that as long as I could resist being carried off into the mangroves by mosquitoes, I could get through. Sure, it was still the wet season—when, according to all the guidebooks, only horses and tractors could negotiate the track along the jungled shoreline. But my alternative was to follow the Australian and take a 240-km detour along the paved road via the banana town of Palmar Sur and the flatlands of the Valle de El General, then back to the coast.

So I followed my instincts.

It wasn't long before my pulse began to quicken. Rain had been pelting down for two days, and the mud was inches deep. I encountered two cars and a truck destined to spend the night in a ditch, including a Toyota Tercel full of anguished-looking young surfers outskating Torvill and Dean.

Then there were no more vehicles. No villages or farms. Not another soul for miles. The only sounds were the bellows of howler monkeys, the screechings of toucans and parrots, and the crashing of surf where the track briefly dropped down to the coast. A claustrophobic tangle of rainforest had closed over my head. And for all the world I could have been the only person in it.

The level road designed to shake the fillings from my teeth had deteriorated into a trail best described as steeper than a dentist's bill and with twice as many cavities as I have.

Remembering advice I'd been given years before—in the Sahara—I pulled out the foot pump stowed in the back and bumped the tire pressures up to what I guessed was around 45 pounds. Hardly ideal for sealed roads but a good precaution on the razor-edged flint that now covered the trail. Grateful for permanent 4WD, and with low ratio still to fall back on, I walked the vehicle up and over the boulder-strewn mountain. It was a case where the argument in favor of a V6 was very persuasive. The car seemed not to notice. I blessed the engineers who had designed the Range Rover. Surely these were the conditions they had in mind when they conceived the car.

negotiating the
Fila Costanera

I inched along the map through more mud. More clifflike hills. More boulders. A small landslide. A fallen tree to manhandle out of the way. More bruising rain. More raging streams to ford. And mile after mile of really wild country that had been barely explored.

"Aaawright! I'm through!" I chimed, looking down into a canyon that seemed to descend into the Stone Ages, but which I knew would disgorge me onto the surfaced road, which began at the coast near Uvita.

Instead, the gorge descended into a morass of fathoms-deep, vacuumlike mud. My stomach tightened sickeningly as my vehicle sank until the doors wouldn't open. Yikes! There really was an actual Shit Creek, and this was it.

I climbed out of the window, sank up to my knees, and began dripping sweat like a faucet. Somewhere beyond the forest canopy the sun heliographed the heavens and sank from view. Blackness descended. The rainforest was suddenly silent. Then the night noises began.

I curled up in the back of the Range Rover and listened to my stomach rumble. Why hadn't I stocked up on food? When dawn came, rain was drumming down from a sky as dark as Costa Rican coffee. I groaned miserably as the mosquitoes pressed up against the windows and eyed me greedily.

Fortunately, even atheists have their angels of mercy. Mine was a giant earth-mover that miraculously appeared around noon and plucked me from my muddy grave. The giant "Cat" was one of several tearing up the rainforests for the long-awaited Costanera Sur Highway, a four-year project that when completed, in 1997, provided a final link in communications along the Pacific coast. I retraced my tracks and—tail between my legs—arced around the Fila Costanera mountain range to Dominical.

"Told ya ya'd nivver git through, ya great dill," the Aussie said, as we swigged beer together at a bar called Jungle Jim's.

"You remind me of something Paul Theroux once wrote," I replied, "about how when things were at their most desperate and uncomfortable, he always found himself in the company of Australians, a reminder that he'd touched bottom."

Getting There and Away

By Air: SANSA and **Travelair** have scheduled service to Palmar Sur; see charts, **SANSA Schedule** and **Travelair Schedule**.

By Bus: Buses depart San José for Palmar from Avenida 18, Calles 2/4 (Tracopa, tel. 221-4214), at 5 a.m., 6:30 a.m., 8:30 a.m., 10 a.m., 2:30 p.m., and 6 p.m. Buses leave from Supermercado Térraba for Sierpe five times daily (50 cents).

SIERPE

Sierpe, 15 km due south of Palmar, is a funky little village on the banks of the Río Sierpe, trapped forlornly between banana plantations and swamp. If driving north along the Pan-Am Highway, you can bypass Palmar: turn west 400 meters south of the Río Culebra and follow a dirt road eight km through cattle pasture and forest until you reach Eco-Manglares Lodge, where a suspension bridge (*narrow* vehicles only) over the Río Estero Azul deposits you two km northeast of Sierpe.

Sierpe serves as the "port" from which boats travel downriver to Drake Bay but is also a worthy spot from which to explore the Delta de Terraba.

Delta de Terraba

This vast network of mangrove swamps, west of Sierpe, is fed by the waters of the Ríos Terraba (to the north) and Sierpe (to the south), which near the sea form an intricate lacework of channels and tidal *esteros* punctuated by islets anchored by *manglares* (mangroves). The delta, which extends along 40 km of shoreline, is a home to crocodiles, caimans, and myriad wading and water birds. Fabulous!

You can hire dugouts for guided tours from Sierpe, Palmar, or Cortés ($125 full day, up to six people). In Sierpe, boats leave from the dock beside the Las Vegas bar. The Hotel Pargo and other lodges also offer excursions and activities, including nighttime crocodile safaris.

Accommodations and Food

Cabinas Las Gaviota de Osa has six new *cabinas* with fans and private bath (four with hot water). Rates: $7 s, $12 d. **Cabinas Estero Azul,** tel. 233-2578, fax 222-0297, two km north of town, has basic *cabinas* with fans and refrigerators. It offers sportfishing and boat tours. Rates: $30 d.

In town, the two-story, motel-style **Hotel Pargo,** tel. 786-6092, fax 232-9578, 50 meters from the dock, has nicely furnished rooms with a/c, ceiling fans, double and single beds, and private baths with hot water. A veranda and *ranchito* restaurant overlook the river. Rates: $15 s/d with fan; $20 s/d with a/c; $60 d, $75 t with all meals. An apartment is also available. The owners offer boat excursions, including croc spotting. The **Hotel Margarita** has basic rooms with shared bath. Rates: $8.

The secluded **Eco-Manglares Lodge,** tel. 773-3192 or 788-8111; in San José, tel. 296-1362, on the banks of the Río Estero Azul (accessed by a narrow suspension bridge), two km northeast of Sierpe, has rustic, all-wood, thatched *cabinas* set on stilts amid lawns and fruit trees. Each has rough-hewn bed-frame, Sarchí rockers, large screened windows, private bath with hot water shower, plus a patio. There's an old farmhouse where *bolas* (Indian stone spheres) are displayed, trails into the surrounding forest, and a dock from where boat excursions depart. There's even Italian food in the midst of mangroves—at the lodge's **Pizzeria Piccola Osa,** with a wide menu boasting salads and American fare alongside pizzas and pastas. Tours are offered. Rates: $35 pp with breakfast; $45 with all meals.

About 500 meters south is the more rustic **Estero Azul Lodge,** tel. 788-8111 or fax 788-8251, also replete with orchards and tropical foliage attracting monkeys and other wildlife. The large, all-wood *cabinas* each sleep four people and are modestly yet nicely furnished, with ceiling fans, cross-ventilation, private baths with hot water, and fully screened porches. There's a laundry. The simple restaurant specializes in seafood and has a bar-lounge overlooking the river. The lodge offers river trips, sportfishing, diving at Caño Island, plus nocturnal crocodile spotting trips. New owners planned to upgrade and add five cabins and a self-catering bungalow. Rates: $65 pp, including all meals and drinks (even beers).

The best place for miles—a real charmer—is the Italian-run **Veragua River Lodge,** tel. 788-8111 message; or c/o Costa Rica Top Tours, tel. 296-3896, fax 231-7089, an old two-story, thatched riverside house that Benedicto has turned into a splendid *albergue.* Inside is like a piece of Sienna transplanted, simply yet tastefully furnished with sponge-washed walls, old wicker and antiques, aging sofas, and Oriental throw rugs on the terra-cotta floors, with hardwood floors and ceilings in counterpoint. There's a pool table in the parlor. The upper floor has a library-lounge. There are three rooms in the house, four cabins in the garden, and a bungalow by the beach. Those in the house share a Victorian-style bathroom with clawfoot tub, louvered windows, and a rocker. One of the rooms is in the loft, with dormer windows and a honeymoon feel. Cabins are more simple yet still romantic; some have iron-frame beds. Guests share the kitchen and outside rotisserie oven in a stone courtyard. Benedicto offers tours to the swamps and as far afield as Corcovado. The lodge, on the east bank of the Río Estero Azul, is reached by a rickety wooden walkway over the mangroves, then a canoe ride across the river. (Be careful—the young kids who paddled me across almost tipped over.) Rates: $70 d with breakfast, $100 with all meals and tour; the beach house costs $100 for up to five people.

The Italian-run **Mapache Lodge,** tel. 788-8111 or fax 786-6358, e-mail: mapache@greenarrow.com, website www.greenarrow.com/travel/mapache.htm, amid landscaped grounds in the midst of mangroves and rainforest at Boca Taboga, eight km upriver from Sierpe, is a homey place centered on the ranch-style main lodge, which features a huge deck, dining room, and TV lounge and library. Owners Guilio and Guiseppina offer two large rooms in the lodge, each with private bath. Three rustic rooms in a separate lodge ("Casita Tica") have shared baths and toilets; and there are three large tents raised on decks, with twin camp-beds. Italian and continental dishes get rave reviews. There's a small swimming pool and sundeck. It can be accessed solely by boat—a marvelous journey. Monkeys, birds (more than 400 species locally), crocodiles, caimans, and other wildlife abound. Excursions are offered, including horseback riding and kayaking. Rates (pp, including all meals): $75 in the lodge; $55 in Casita Tica; $45 tents. Special packages are offered.

Río Sierpe Lodge, Apdo. 85-8150, Palmar Norte, cellular tel. 284-5595 or 257-7010, fax 786-6291, e-mail: escapes@sol.racsa.co.cr, 25 km downriver from Sierpe near the rivermouth, specializes in fishing and diving excursions (the lodge provides dive tanks, weights, boat transport, and guides) using a 14-meter three-decked yacht and seven-meter airboat. Guides and equipment are provided. The 11 rooms are rustic but large and were remodeled in 1997. Each has a private bathroom. There's a large dining and recreational area with a library. The lodge also has trails into the nearby rainforests, and offers hiking, horseback trips, mangrove kayaking, and a range of excursions, including to nearby islands, plus overnight camping trips, and even a four-day trip to the Panamanian cloud forest ($225). Rates: $65 pp, including meals and transfers from Palmar. A range of diving, fishing and other packages are offered, including a five-night/six-day mangrove kayaking program for $1,055.

Getting There and Away
Buses and taxis (about $12) operate from Palmar Norte.

BAHÍA DRAKE AND VICINITY

Drake Bay (pronounced "DRA-cay" locally), a large sweeping bay on northwest Osa, extends southward below the mouth of the Río Sierpe, which provides the main access. A small village—**Agujitas**—lies at the southern end of the two-km-wide crescent bay, which is good for forays into Marenco Biological Reserve (eight km) and Corcovado National Park (13 km south), or to Caño Island, which dominates the view out to sea. The indigenous heritage is strong: the village is famous as one of only two places in Central America that make reverse-appliqué stitched *molas* (the other place is the San Blas islands in Panamá, where the work is far more ornate), featuring simplistic designs and motifs of birds, animals, and fruit in bright colors. Otherwise, it has changed little since the day in March 1579 when Sir Francis Drake sailed past Caño Island and anchored the *Golden Hind* in the tranquil bay that now bears his name.

The village is "landlocked," and accessible by 4WD during dry season only. Supposedly it's the last village in Costa Rica without road access and electricity (the public cellular telephone is solar powered). Take time to visit the local

school (three grades attend in the morning; another three in the afternoon); open to the public Mon.-Thurs. 4-6 p.m.

The beach is mediocre, but there are good tide pools and the wilderness surrounding Drake Bay is replete with wildlife, including scarlet macaws, toucans, and tanagers. Humpbacks and other whale species pass by close to shore. You'll find good snorkeling at the southern end of the bay, where a coastal trail leads through small coffee, cacao, and guava plots to the mouth of the **Río Agujitas,** good for swimming and jungle exploration by canoe. You can follow a trail up the river canyon, which you cross by a suspension bridge, to **Playa Cocalito** (immediately south), **Playa Caletas** (four km), and a paternoster of golden sand beaches farther south, ending at **Playa Josecito** on the edge of Corcovado National Park. Josecito offers good snorkeling. The ocean here is the warmest I've ever experienced. There's a **Blue Morphis Butterfly Farm** (part of Corcovado Lodge Tent Camp) at Playa Caletas.

Marenco
This 500-hectare nature reserve, formerly Marenco Biological Station, sits above Playa Caletas. The reserve forms a buffer zone for Corcovado National Park and is home to all four monkey species and other wildlife species common to Corcovado. The area's 400-plus bird species include the scarlet macaw, great curassow, toucan, and several species of brightly colored tanagers, not least the endemic black-cheeked anttanager. Watch for whales out at sea.

The wilderness lodge serves as a center for scientific research and welcomes ecotourists, too. Resident biologists lead nature hikes ($35; one reader complains that the guides aren't up to snuff) along the rocky shore to the Río Claro, where a refreshing deep freshwater pool behind the beach is perfect for a swim, and to Corcovado National Park. A self-guided tour booklet is available, as are horses. September and October are the rainiest months. Many tour operators feature packages to Marenco.

Accommodations
Camping: You can camp on the lawn behind the beach at **Rancho Corcovado,** in the village of Agujitas. Rates: $6.

Budget: Albergue Jinetes de Osa, tel. 273-3116 or 253-6909, at the southern edge of Agujitas, offers eight basic rooms, each sleeping three people, four each with shared and private baths with cold water. Private bathrooms were being built in every room. A very rustic but attractive open-air bar serves Costa Rican cuisine as well as great burgers and hot dogs. You can rent horses here ($20 up to four hours) and arrange guides plus stays with local *campesinos.* When I visited, new owners were upgrading it and turning it into a dive resort. Rates: $35 pp, including breakfast and dinner.

Casa Mirador, tel. 227-6914, atop a hill at the southern end of the bay, has simple but pleasing rooms, with private baths and cold water. Meals included. Rates: about $15. A gringa, Cecilia Steller, runs the basic **Cabinas Cecilia,** Apdo. 84, Palmar Norte, tel. 717-2436 or 717-3336, otherwise known as Cabinas Sir Francis Drake, at the east end of the beach. Twelve bunks in two rooms have shared bath with cold water, plus there are four double rooms. Cecilia rents horses ($25 full day), offers hiking trips, and can arrange a cruise to Caño Island. Rates: $25 per day, including three meals; $20 for dorm.

Inexpensive: Rancho Corcovado, c/o the *pulpería,* tel. 788-8111, has two sets of basic wooden *cabinas,* by the shore and atop a ridge— all with private bathrooms with showers, plus electricity at night. The restaurant serves tasty local fare, and excursions with English-speaking guides are offered. Rates: $35 pp, including meals.

The environmentally sound **Cocalito Lodge,** Apdo. 63, Palmar Norte, tel./fax 786-6335, operated by siblings Marna and Mike Berry, is the southerly neighbor to La Paloma Lodge and sits between forest and beach amid orchid-filled gardens. The node is the rustic lodge, a model ecological project on the edge of a 14-hectare property (most of the meals prepared here, for example, are made of organically homegrown products). Simple but clean and handsomely appointed cabins—reached at night along torch-lit paths—have private tiled baths with cold water, and electricity supplied by a stream-driven generator and solar panels. Monkeys, toucans, and other critters call in to sneak fruit from the trees, while local inhabitants pop in to eat, sup, and chat in the popular restaurant/bar on the bottom floor of the lodge, which boasts a large li-

brary. Hikes, horseback rides, and scuba diving packages are available. Rates: $39 s, $50 d low season; $50 s, $65 d high season, including tasty multicourse meals.

Marna and Mike Berry also operate a rainforest lodge near Los Planes, on the border of Corcovado National Park, in the Ganada mountains east of Drake Bay. The lodge is part of a sustainable agriculture project featuring a reforestation project and medicinal herb garden. It has five cabins.

Moderate: Drake Bay Wilderness Camp, Apdo 98-8150, Palmar Norte, Osa, tel./fax 771-2436, beeper 223-3333, radio tel. 220-2121, e-mail: emichaud@drakebay.com, on the south side of the Río Agujitas rivermouth, has pleasant two- and four-person thatched *cabinas* with ceiling fans and solar-heated hot showers. Some cabins have oceanview patios; double-occupancy cabins have private baths and ceiling fans. Roomy tents with electricity and comfortable folding beds are provided for campers. American-Tico food is served in a rustic dining room. There's an open-air bar and clubhouse slung with hammocks. The camp specializes in diving expeditions to Caño Island ($90, one-day, including two tanks). Fins and masks can be rented, plus horseback riding ($30), whale-watching trips, rainforests trips, and tours to a local butterfly farm, Corcovado National Park, and Caño Island. Rates: $648 pp d, three-days/three nights including all meals and scuba diving plus domestic airfare and transfers; $48 pp daily for tents. Transfers from San José cost $160, including charter flight, Palmar-Sierpe taxi transfer, and Sierpe-Drake Bay boat transfer. The camp is popular with squirrel monkeys.

A Swiss-Tico couple runs **Cabinas Las Caletas,** cellular tel. 381-4052, fax 786-6291, a small, rustic place perched on a steep ridge above Playa Caletas, about a one-hour hike south of Drake Bay. The thatched lodge has a lounge, dining room, and library, plus a deck with hammocks. Take your pick of shared rooms in the main house, or one of the all-wood private cabins with your own bath and deck. Electricity is supplied by solar panels. The property is surrounded by forests, fruit trees, and landscaped gardens. Excursions are offered, and there's laundry service. Rates (pp): $35 shared, $50 cabins, including all meals. Launch transfers cost $35 pp.

At Playa San Josecito, a Tico named Pincho Amaya—a renowned sportfisherman—and his gringa wife, Jenny, run **Poor Man's Paradise,** fax 786-6358; in the U.S., 12430 Nixon Rd., Minocqua, WI 54548, tel. (715) 588-3950, which is open Dec.-May. They have two rooms, plus 12 tent-cabins with shared baths. You can also camp at a bare site. Electricity shuts off at 9 p.m. Pincho will take you sportfishing for $185 half day—a steal. Rates: $45 pp room; $35 pp tent-cabin, including all meals (prepared by Pincho's mom); $5 pp campsite (plus $6 per meal).

Nearby, a home called **Quillotro,** c/o tel. 223-7961, fax 257-7668, has two bedrooms—each with queen-size beds—and kitchen and shared bathroom, plus two cabins with private bath, and two walk-in tents with double bed and shared bath. Meals are offered in a lounge-cum-dining room. Excursions are offered. Rates: $45 s, $65 d tents; $75 s, $115 d cabins; $115 s, $165 d room, including all meals.

Expensive: A serene option is **La Paloma Lodge,** Adpo. 97-4005, San Antonio del Belén, tel./fax 239-0954, radio tel. 239-2801; in the U.S., P.O. Box 025216, Miami, FL 33102, tel. (305) 785-2260, fax 785-2372. The lodge, built by Mike and Sue Kalmbach from Ohio, perches atop a cliff overlooking Playa Cocalito and offers a superb view of Caño Island. Five spacious thatched ranchos—simply furnished with hammocks on the balcony—and five more attractively furnished comfortable cabins perched on stilts have ceiling fans, orthopedic mattresses, private baths with solar hot water, and balconies overlooking the landscaped grounds and ocean and jungle. Number Three has the best views. The thatched clubhouse is a perfect spot for dining and relaxing. There's a small and handsome swimming pool with bar. Scarlet macaws nest nearby. Meals are family style. Hikes and horseback rides ($20) are accompanied by a resident guide and naturalist. La Paloma has three boats fully outfitted for trips to Caño Island, sportfishing ($325 half day, $600 full day), and light-tackle fishing ($150 half day, $275 full day). It's a steep hike from the suspension bridge. Rates: $70 s, $55 pp d. Four- and five-day packages with air transfers are available.

Corcovado Adventures Tent Camp, tel. 223-2770, fax 257-4201; in Quepos, c/o Hotel Dorado Mojado, tel. 777-0368, fax 777-1248,

lies within the forest on a 14-hectare property beside Playa Caletas; don't mistake this with Costa Rica Expeditions' more salubrious tent camp at Carate. Two-person tents are pitched on wooden platforms, protected by thatched tarps, and are big enough to stand up in. Each has a closet, wooden beds made up with cotton sheets, plus two armchairs for quiet meditation. Washrooms have showers and toilets, and hearty meals are served in a rancho-style dining room. A trail leads into the jungle, though monkeys, macaws, toucans, and other forest creatures, come into camp to feast in the almond and water-apple trees. Owner Larry Hustler also offers guided hikes and horseback rides ($45) to Corcovado National Park. You can also rent sea kayaks ($10 per hour). There's a butterfly garden too. Hustler arranges boat transfers via Sierpe from Palmar. Rates: $399 d (low season; two nights), including all meals, transfers, and guided tour to Caño Island and Corcovado; $60 pp high season, including meals.

Marenco Beachfront and Resort Lodge, Apdo. 4025-1000, San José, tel. 221-1594, fax 255-1346, e-mail: marenco@sol.racsa.co.cr, website www.crdirect.com/corcovado; in the U.S., tel. (800) 278-6223, features a hilltop lodge set in beautiful gardens, and accommodates up to 40 people in rustic thatched bamboo-and-wood cabins, each with four bunks, a private bath, and a terrace offering panoramic ocean views. Meals are served family style in a large, folksy dining hall overlooking a rocky shore. Book well in advance. Rates: $85 s, $110 d; $65 pp bungalow, including three meals; packages cost $405 two nights, $548 three nights, $643 four nights low season; $444 two nights, $612 three nights, $725 four nights high season, including air transportation and all meals.

Luxury: The gringo-run **Aguila de Osa Inn,** Apdo. 10486, San José 1000, tel. 296-2190, fax 232-7722, e-mail: aguilacr@sol.racsa.co.cr, Web site: www.centralamerica.com/cr/hotels/ aguila.htm; in the U.S,. Interlink #898, P.O. Box 025635, Miami, FL 33102, is on the north bank, at the mouth of the Río Agujitas. The 14 double rooms have private baths, fans, and ocean views and are set in a landscaped garden at the head of the canyon. The warm decor includes bamboo beds, hardwood floors, and tropical furnishings. The focal point is the circular open-air restaurant with high-pitched *palenque* thatched roof and beautiful hardwood floors. A veranda offers good ocean views. Meals include treats such as sashimi with ginger and horseradish sauce. The inn offers scuba diving trips to Caño Island, and there are Garrett 31s for sportfishing. A nice touch is the free wine offered with dinner. Rates: $145 s, $220 d, $242-270 suites, including three meals (no credit cards). Roundtrip transfers from Sierpe cost $45 pp. Special diving and sportfishing packages are offered. *Surely overpriced?*

Abutting the north side of the park is **Casa Corcovado Jungle Lodge,** Apdo. 1482-1250, Escazú, tel. 256-3181, fax 256-7409, e-mail: corcovdo@sol.racsa.co.cr, website www.centralamerica.com/cr/hotel/corcovad.htm, run by Chicago expat Steven Lill, who has conjured a wonderful hilltop resort from a defunct cacao plantation. There are seven thatched, conical *cabinas* with hardwood four-poster beds, ceiling fans, and twin-level ceilings for open circulation, including two "honeymoon" units with mosquito nets and huge showers with hot water. The rooms have ceramic tile floors and are enlivened by sponge-washed walls in blue pastels. Dining is family style; there's also a lounge and library, plus a *mirador* bar. Trails lace the 120-hectare property and lead to a waterfall with beach chairs suspended over the water. A swimming pool, a "saloon," and a canopy tour were to be added. It has two 19-foot speedboats with Bimini tops, plus a Zodiac, and a 26-canopied boat for transfers from Sierpe. Guided hikes, sea kayaking, scuba diving, and other tours are offered. Once ashore, a tractor-pulled jitney takes you up to the lodge. Multiday packages begin at $322 two nights, $392 three nights low season; $357 two nights, $435 three nights high season.

At press time, **Esperanza Fishing Lodge** was due to open a few kilometers north of Drake Bay. Owner Dennis McDermid has two 10-meter Dawsons.

Entertainment
The hotels have bars. For local color, check out the local *pulperías* by night. There's a basic disco at the **Bar Mar y Sombra** with dances twice weekly, plus billiards, and a veranda offering views.

Services
In Agujitas, the well-stocked *pulpería* has the only public telephone, 771-2336. There's a clinic with a nurse; a doctor visits every two months.

Water Sports
Canadian Ben Miltner runs river and coastal sea kayaking trips out of Drake Bay Wilderness Camp (Dec.-April).

Angling Adventures, tel./fax 717-2436; in San José, tel. 233-8090, fax 222-2238; in the U.S., tel. (708) 931-1608, fax 931-1719, offers fishing charters. It's operated by husband-and-wife team Skip and Elizabeth Foulk.

Kapper Dau, once "king of the Santa Cruz, California line-up," offers a charter **surfing** service aboard a custom-designed seven-meter cabin cruiser built for surfing and overnighting. Half-day trips go to Caño Island ($125) or to Violin and Rincón breaks ($80); overnight trips including two days' surfing cost $600 d. Contact the Drake Bay Wilderness Camp, tel. 717-2436.

All the lodges can arrange scuba diving, snorkeling, sportfishing, horseback rides, and jungle hikes into Corcovado National Park or Caño Island. Scuba divers must bring their own buoyancy compensators and regulators.

Getting There and Away
By Road: A lonesome mountain road—graded for the first time in 1997—runs from Rincón, on the eastern shore of the Osa Peninsula, via Rancho Quemado (there's bus service from Rincón) and over the Fila Ganado to Drake Bay; at press time the road reached to within 2.5 km of Drake Bay, with the remainder a rough dirt track. (Speculation is that logging interests lobbied for the road to be built into the heart of the forest, but not all the way.)

By Boat: Boats travel downriver to Drake Bay from Sierpe. The trip takes two hours down the jungle-draped Río Sierpe (about $15). Watch for crocodiles and caimans in the mangroves. At the river's mouth, boats make a run past the surf (ensure you have an experienced local guide, as dugouts and other light craft have been known to capsize at the rivermouth; larger vessels are fine). On the 20-minute journey across Drake Bay to the mouth of the Río Agujitas you sometimes pass whales and dolphins. Lodges arrange transportation for guests.

Taximar, tel. 777-1170 or 771-1903, offers a water-taxi service from Quepos ($55) via Dominical ($35), continuing to Playa Caletas and Caño Island. The 22-seat boat will reportedly do a speedy 30 knots. **Pacific Winds Express,** tel. 777-0137, fax 777-1685, whisks you from Quepos to Drake Bay in two hours aboard Sea-Cats capable of doing 40 knots ($50 one-way).

The *Temptress Explorer* includes Drake Bay on a six-day nature cruise from Puntarenas to national parks and wildlife refuges on the Pacific coast. The day ends with folkloric dancing by the local schoolchildren dressed in traditional costume on board. See special topic, **Natural-History Cruise Tours.**

By Air: You can charter a small plane direct to Drake Bay; there's a landing strip near La Palom, but until the road is completed the surface journey can only be finished by taking a boat to Drake Bay.

PENINSULA DE OSA

This massive, mountainous, horsehead-shaped peninsula wraps around the western Golfo Dulce. Its bulk and erstwhile inaccessibility protect vast rainforests, much of them preserved as Corcovado National Park.

A single road that runs along the east coast alone provides access via Puerto Jiménez (the only town of significance) to Cabo Matapalo (the southeastern naze of Osa), and then curls west to dead-end midway along the southern coast at Carate, on the border with Corcovado. The western side of the peninsula is accessed solely by sea and has only one hamlet of any significance: Agujitas, in Drake Bay. Nonetheless, this shore has several nature lodges and private rainforest reserves bordering Corcovado, which offers some of the finest wildlife viewing in Costa Rica. There are some marvelous beaches. Surfing is top-notch. And there are some valuable experiences to be had with local indigenous communities, including ex-gold miners who will lead you on gold-mining forays.

Gold Mining

Pre-Columbian Indians sifted gold from the streams of the Osa millennia ago. But it wasn't until the 1980s that gold fever struck. After gold panners—*oreros*—found some major nuggets, prospectors poured into the region. The Banco Central established an office in Puerto Jiménez just to buy gold. At the boom's heyday, at least 3,000 miners were entrenched in Corcovado National Park. Because of the devastation they wrought—dynamiting riverbeds, polluting rivers, and felling trees—the Park Service and Civil Guard ousted the miners in 1986. The *oreros* were promised indemnity for their lost income, but it went unpaid for over a year. In a dramatic protest, they camped out in the parks of San José until the government came up with the money. Most *oreros* have turned to other ventures—not least ecotourism—but it is not unusual to bump into a lucky (or luckless) *orero* celebrating (or commiserating) over a beer in a bar.

PAN-AM HIGHWAY TO LOS PATOS (PARQUE NACIONAL CORCOVADO)

The turnoff from the Pan-Am Highway (Hwy. 2) is at **Chacarita,** about 32 km southeast of Palmar and 26 km northwest of Río Claro (the turnoff for Golfito). There's a gas station at the junction.

The road to Puerto Jiménez is in excellent condition as far as **Rincón,** 42 km south of Chacarita. Rincón is where you get your first sense of the cathedral-like immensity of the rainforests of the Osa Peninsula. The **El Mirador,** 21 km south of Chacarita, is a pleasing hilltop *soda* with splendid views of the gulf and Diquís Valley. The magnificent coastal vistas are spoiled only by the patches torn up by loggers, exposing soil as red as bright lipstick. At press time, the paved road ended at the coast at Rincón. It's dirt thereafter, and dusty.

At **La Palma,** a hamlet 11 km south of Rincón, turn left for Puerto Jiménez. To the right, the gravel and mud road leads 12 km up the **Valle del Río Rincón** to the **Estación Los Patos** ranger station, easternmost entry point to Corcovado National Park. It's a great hike through virgin jungle from here to the Sirena ranger station on the coast (but you'll want to get going at sunup).

Osa Peninsula

En route to Los Patos, you'll pass the **Reserva Indígena Guyamí,** with a primary rainforest reserve; the Indian community sells handicrafts. Two km south of La Palma a dirt road leads to **Playa Blanca,** a gray-sand beach where boats can be hired.

CoopeUnioro, tel. 225-8966, fax 735-5073; or c/o Cooprena, Apdo. 6939-1000, San José, tel. 259-3401, fax 259-9430, e-mail: cooprena@sol. racsa.co.cr, is a local cooperative of ex-gold miners who voluntarily gave up gold mining and now experiment with development of responsible tourism and sustainable uses of natural resources. The cooperative, on a hillside about four km before Los Patos, has a meeting room for workshops and seminars. It offers guided tours, and horses can be rented.

Accommodations and Food

In La Palma, **Cabinas El Tucáno,** tel. 775-0522 or 775-0033, has six small cabins with private baths (cold water) and fans. Rates: $4 s, $7 d. There's a tiny restaurant. Next door is **Soda Centro Social** with a small *soda* and, **Centro Turística Playa Blanca,** boasting *cabinas* and an open-air restaurant (specializing in seafood) next to the beach. You can also camp ($2); there's access to showers and bathrooms. There's dancing here some nights.

Outside the Guyamí reserve, one km from Los Patos, is **Cabinas Corcovado,** tel. 775-0433 (message only), fax 775-0033, which has basic rooms, private baths and cold water, plus a platform where you may sling a hammock.

The lodge and cabins sit on a hill, surrounded by fruit trees. There's also a restaurant. There are two small rooms with shared bath upstairs, where campers can tether their tarps or tents on the deck. Four private rooms with private bath are downstairs. The owner, ex-miner Luis Angulo, is a trained guide ($8 hourly) who offers camping trips; horses can also be rented ($6 hourly). His wife prepares *típico* meals. Rates: $5 per tent, $5 pp shared bath, $6 pp private bath. Meals cost $10 daily.

About 10 km farther, beyond the Los Patos trailhead, is the rustic **Cerro de Oro Lodge** run by CoopeUnioro. Rooms with hardwood floors have shared baths with cold water, and solar electricity. There are also three houses available. The cooks conjure tasty meals from local produce, including wild plants, nuts, and herbs, served in a rancho-style dining room. The lodge offers guided hikes and horseback trips to Corcovado. Rates: $35 s, $50 d, $45 t, including breakfast.

Restaurante Sabores del Golfo, at the turnoff for Playa Blanca outside La Palma, has meals with a view enjoyed from the open patio; open 6 a.m.-9 p.m. daily. Alex del Sol recommends the bread pudding.

Services

You should call in on Alex de Sol at the **Rincón Tourist & Surf Center,** an information service 700 meters north of the school in Rincón. Alex is author of a dandy little booklet, *The Southern Costa Rica Guide* ($2). He rents sea kayaks and offers massages.

In La Palma, a self-proclaimed **tourist information center** and guide service operates beside El Tucáno, where you can hire a knowledgeable, Spanish-speaking guide ($10 per day). Luis Flores of **Visión Verde**, tel. 735-5062, offers guided hikes, kayaking, boating, and gold-panning trips. You can rent boats at Centro Turística Playa Blanca, next to Cabinas El Tucáno.

Getting There and Away
Buses operate four times daily between La Palma and Puerto Jiménez. The earliest departs Puerto Jiménez at 5:30 a.m. You must hike or hitch the 12-km dirt-and-mud road to the park entrance at Los Patos. The last bus from La Palma to Puerto Jiménez is at 2 p.m.

DOS BRAZOS DE RÍO TIGRE

About 25 km southeast of La Palma, four km before Puerto Jiménez, a turnoff to the right fol-

THE DEPREDATIONS OF MAN AGAINST NATURE

The Osa region has had a tormented history in recent decades at the hands of gold miners, hunters, and loggers (half of the land that now forms Corcovado National Park, for example, was obtained in a land trade from the Osa Productos Forestales logging company). The forest is so precious that loggers have routinely bypassed the law, which was written by the Forestry Chamber—which happens to represent logging interests (logging companies, for example, were given control of the approval process for MINAE's timber harvest plans). And the opening of a road linking Rincón with Bahía Drake has resulted in a cutting frenzy within the forest reserves (it is claimed that the road was put in against the wishes of local inhabitants following lobbying by the loggers).

In November 1997, a special commission found serious violations by loggers and "technical errors" by ministry officials in favor of logging interests. That month a 90-day moratorium *(veda)* on logging in Osa was issued following a grassroots campaign by local residents. Still the logging continued (I passed several logging trucks when I drove through last). The loggers are accused of being a *mafiosa* who pay locals to allow illegal logging on their land, while people who speak out against them often end up being intimidated into silence or even killed. Even the Indians of Guaymi reservation succumbed to the profit interest and sold out to loggers. Fortunately, the environmental ministry is to be split into two distinct units, separating officials who grant permits from those who oversee industry compliance (at press time, several officials were under investigation for corruption).

Meanwhile, the United Fruit Co. is accused of formerly hiring professional poachers to systematically hunt out native animal and bird species that might adversely affect their food crops. Although those days are over, hunting continues under the nose—and

even in collusion with—park staff. *Oreros* occasionally show up in Puerto Jiménez with ocelot skins and other poached animals for sale. And the system of issuing wildlife permits is routinely abused by people who obtain a permit for "rescuing" a specific animal, then use the permit to trade other animals. It's a lucrative trade. Local expats claim that some of the money finds its way to park rangers who routinely turn a blind eye (one conscientious ranger was fired for reporting his superiors after catching them eating endangered *tepezcuintles*). In any event, the rangers are not equipped to fight fire with fire. "They're ticket-sellers!" says a prominent expat.

The turtle population continues to be devastated by the local populace, who poach the nests simply because there is nobody to stop them. Poison is being used to harvest fish from coastal breeding lagoons such as Peje Perro and Peje Perrito. And scarlet macaw nests are routinely poached (and tapirs and jaguars hunted). All because there is no effective system in place to pursue violators.

In 1997, concerned citizens formed a Forest and Wildlife Protection Project, now formalized as the **Fundación Cecropia,** to support existing local environmental action groups working to prevent further destruction. The most important of these is **COVIRENA,** tel. 283-4746, fax 283-5148, a branch of the park service recently created in an attempt to combat logging and poaching. The moving force behind efforts is the local expat community, led by Jeff Lantz of Iguana Lodge and John Lewis of Lapa Ríos. To resolve the politically charged issue, there's even talk of privatizing Corcovado. Stay tuned.

For a history of the problem, including violence associated with creation of Corcovado National Park, see David Rains Wallace's *The Quetzal and the Macaw: The Story of Costa Rica's National Parks.*

lows the Río Tigre 14 km west to Dos Brazos, the old center of gold mining, at the easternmost entrance to Corcovado National Park. When the gold petered out, the miners found themselves without a livelihood and turned to ecotourism rather than abandon their riverside homes. In 1990 they formed the **Asociación de Productores Villa Nueva**, tel. 775-1422, fax 735-5045, to organize tours and provide lodging. You can see them still panning for *oro* in the soupy rivers and in the old tunnels, and you may even want try your hand at it. But be careful—gold fever is contagious. The association members will even take you 270 meters deep into their mining tunnels ($20).

Dos Brazos is one km from the border of Corcovado National Park. Guided trips to the park ($20) are offered daily at 7 a.m., returning around 3 p.m. Buses service Dos Brazos from Puerto Jiménez.

La Llanta Picante
The name means "the spicy tire," referring (I guess) to the mountain bike trips offered at this ecotourism lodge in the midst of a 100-acre farm—**Finca Tiñeque**, Apdo. 49-8203, Puerto Jiménez, tel./fax 735-5414; in the U.S., La Llanta Picante, 137 N. Sunset Ave., Freeport, IL 61032, tel./fax (815) 235-9307—enshrouded by beach and forest on Playa Ñesque at the mouth of the Río Tigre, four km north of Puerto Jiménez. The five nature-loving folks who run it offer customized mountain bike touring throughout Osa. Horseback rides, kayak trips, and guides hikes are offered.

Accommodations and Food
The **El Tigre Lodge**, tel. 775-1422, fax 735-5045, or c/o Aeroviajes, Apdo. 12742, San José 1000, tel. 233-6108, fax 233-6293, also called Ecological Corcovado Guest House, is an "ecotourist shelter" with six rooms of varying sizes (the largest sleeps six people) with hardwood ceilings, bamboo furnishings, and private baths, plus electricity in the evening. A large open restaurant serves Costa Rican dishes and looks out over the river. Handcrafted highlights include the fretwork on the wooden balustrade and murals painted on the bedroom walls. The lodge is run by the Asociación de Productores Villa Nueva. Gold panning and Corcovado excursions are offered, as

are horseback rides to the park. Rates: $12 s, $18 d. Aeroviajes also offers weeklong tour packages from $775. Turn right at the bridge as you enter Dos Brazos; the lodge is one-quarter mile up the valley, surrounded by forest.

Finca Tiñeque has *cabinas.*

PUERTO JIMÉNEZ

This small, laid-back town is the gateway to Corcovado National Park. It's popular with the younger backpacking crowd and surfers and has attracted a considerable population of gringos and Europeans, who make a living offering tours such as sea kayaking in search of crocodiles. An Ecotourism Chamber oversees tourism development. Locals have colorful tales to tell of gambling and general debauchery during the gold-boom days in the 1980s, when the town briefly flourished, prostitutes charged by the ounce, and miners bought bottles of whiskey just to throw at the walls. The good old bad old days are over, though La Taberna still owns a brothel license (but was not utilizing it at press time) and Zorro, the amiable local drunk, has never been seen sober (a charitable trust was in the offing at press time to keep him in funds).

A narrow mangrove estuary lies immediately to the northeast of town (supposedly there are crocodiles and caimans), with a pleasant brown-sand beach lined by a newly paved sidewalk and popular with locals on weekends. To the south stretches a string of beautiful white-sand beaches, including some with good surfing at Playas América, Backwater, Pan Dulce, and Carbonera. **Playa Platanares** is a gorgeous miles-long swathe of white sand about three km east of town. A reef lies offshore in jade-colored waters, the forest behind the beach abounds with monkeys and other wildlife, and the views across the gulf are fantastic. The **Río Platanares** feeds a large mangrove swamp behind the beach, where you stand a superb chance of seeing caimans, white-faced monkeys, freshwater turtles, rays, and lots of birdlife; scarlet macaws can be seen and heard squawking in the treetops and flying overhead. The two beachfront lodges are reached by a deep-sand track (4WD essential).

A CHIP MILL FOR OSA

The Osa Peninsula is slated to get Central America's largest woodchip mill, courtesy of Ston Forestal, a Costa Rican subsidiary of the paper giant Stone Container Corporation of Chicago. The mill will export more than one million tons of chipped wood each year to the U.S. and Asia for paper pulp.

Instead of clearing primary forest (now protected in the peninsula under a moratorium on logging), the company plans to grow and harvest a nonnative tree species called gmelina. The ecology of the Osa Peninsula, nonetheless, will be threatened.

The chip mill will operate 24 hours a day, causing excessive pollution and dramatically increasing truck traffic. Seeds dispersed from Stone's 30 million trees may well displace native species, changing the local ecosystem. Also, opponents argue, the fruit of the gmelina will attract birds and mammals from nearby habitats, creating abnormal migration patterns with unknown consequences to the ecosystem. And the marinelife of the Golfo Dulce may be seriously threatened.

The gulf is an anoxic (lacking oxygen) body because of its limited water circulation. The weak dispersion makes the gulf especially susceptible to a buildup of chemical pollution and sediment runoff from the chip mill project. Coastal estuaries, mangroves, and coral reefs could well be destroyed, and the offshore waters that are breeding grounds for whales, dolphins, and many species of fish may be irretrievably altered.

A coalition of environmental, indigenous, and community organizations called the **Puerto Jiménez Comité de Pro-Defensa de Recursos Natural** is working to have the Golfo Dulce region named a national aquatic park. In 1994, the group's efforts forced Ston Forestal to agree to relocate the mill farther away from Golfito.

Accommodations

Camping: You can camp on breezy oceanfront lawns at the Puerto Jiménez Yacht Club, northeast of town.

In Town: Cabinas Iguana Iguana, tel. 735-5158, at the entrance to town, has seven basic but comfortable rooms with fans plus private baths and cold water. Three more cabins share a bath. There's a lively little bar and restaurant, plus a

swimming pool. More cabinas were in the works. Rates: $6 s, $9 d rooms low season; $4 pp cabins.

North of the soccer field is **Cabinas Brisas del Mar,** tel. 735-5028, fax 735-5012. It has nine older, basic rooms with fans and private baths with cold water, but views over the gulf; and five newer rooms with hot water. Rates: $8 pp basic rooms, $15 pp newer rooms. **Cabinas Marcelina,** tel. 735-5007, fax 735-5045, 200 meters south of the soccer field, has basic rooms with private baths and fans. It can arrange fishing trips, horseback rides, and even gold-panning expeditions. Rates: $6 pp.

Cabinas Carolina in the heart of town, is associated with the popular restaurant. They're spacious and have private baths. Rates: $6 pp. **Pensión Quintero,** tel. 735-5087, an old wooden home one block west of Oro Verde, is a bargain at $4 pp, though its 12 rooms are bare bones, without fans, and with cold-water shared baths. (A sign on the door reads, We are Catholic. Protestants not welcome—but let's assume they're referring to evangelists.)

The best place in town is **Cabinas Oro Verde,** tel. 735-5241 or 383-3615, e-mail: oroverde@sol.racsa.co.cr, a two-story building run by the local doctor and his charming wife. It has clean, simple but adequate rooms with lots of light. Some are large. The bakery and restaurant downstairs are recommended. Tours are offered. Rates: $20 s, $25 d/t, $30 quad.

Hotel Las Manglares, Apdo. 255-8203, Puerto Jiménez, tel. 735-5002, near the airstrip, has 10 modestly appointed rooms surrounded by mangroves, where crabs scurry about. The rooms have private baths with showers and cold water. The new owner was planning to remodel and raise his prices. Rates: $25 s, $30 d, $40 t. There's secure parking and a laundry.

On the beachfront, try the modern **Cabinas Agua Luna** with clean a/c rooms with large windows, TVs, and private baths with hot water (ask next door in the restaurant). Nearby, **Doña Leta's Bungalows,** Apdo. 91, Puerto Jiménez, tel. 735-5180, e-mail: letabell@sol.racsa.co.cr, on the oceanfront northeast of the airstrip, has modestly furnished, octagonal wood-and-thatch cabins with ceiling fans, kitchenettes, plus private baths and hot water. There's beach volleyball, and a restaurant and bar. Tours to Corcovado are offered. Rates: $35 d.

Carlos Dominick, a well-known local environmentalist, offers basic bunks and shared baths with cold water but no fans at **Dormitorio Cockadoodledoo,** fax 735-5073, near the Texaco station. Rates: $1 plus one-hour's labor in his reforestation nursery, Vivero y Jardines Joyosa. South of town, 400 yards past the gas station en route to Cabo Matapalo, is **Cabinas Eylin,** tel. 735-5011, with three rooms attached to the home of "Gato" William. The spacious front rooms sleep four people each and are handsomely appointed, with cathedral ceilings, hardwood furniture, TVs, lounge chairs, and tiled floors and bath. A smaller room for two is to the rear. Rates: $15 per room large front rooms, $10 per room smaller rooms.

If all else fails, or you're flat broke, $3 will get you a box with a bed at the **Hotel Valentín.** Another last resort is **Cabinas Thompson,** two blocks west of the soccer field, offering five very basic rooms with fans and private cold-water baths. Rates: $5 pp.

Playa Platanares: I recommend the beachfront **Iguana Lodge,** Apdo.8, Puerto Jiménez, tel./fax 735-5205, which boasts a breezy setting and a grand aesthetic. The *casa grande* (lodge), which is named for the "iggies" hanging out in nearby trees, has a Gaudiesque feel to the decor. Upstairs, held aloft by stripped treetrunks, is a thatched *mirador* restaurant with ocean views and hammocks on the wide veranda (tasty

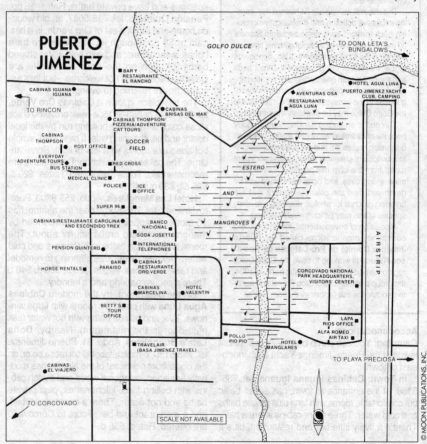

PUERTO JIMÉNEZ

GOLFO DULCE

TO DOÑA LETA'S BUNGALOWS

BAR Y RESTAURANTE EL RANCHO

HOTEL AGUA LUNA

PUERTO JIMENEZ YACHT CLUB, CAMPING

CABINAS IGUANA IGUANA

TO RINCON

AVENTURAS OSA

RESTAURANTE AGUA LUNA

CABINAS BRISAS DEL MAR

CABINAS THOMPSON/ PIZZERIA/ADVENTURE CAT TOURS

CABINAS THOMPSON

POST OFFICE

EVERYDAY ADVENTURE TOURS

BUS STATION

SOCCER FIELD

RED CROSS

MEDICAL CLINIC

POLICE

ICE OFFICE

ESTERO

AND

SUPER 96

CABINAS/RESTAURANTE CAROLINA AND ESCONDIDO TREX

BANCO NACIONAL

SODA JOSETTE

INTERNATIONAL TELEPHONES

MANGROVES

PENSION QUINTERO

BAR PARAISO

CABINAS/ RESTAURANTE ORO VERDE

HORSE RENTALS

AIRSTRIP

CABINAS MARCELINA

HOTEL VALENTIN

CORCOVADO NATIONAL PARK HEADQUARTERS, VISITORS' CENTER

BETTY'S TOUR OFFICE

TRAVELAIR (BASA JIMENEZ TRAVEL)

LAPA RIOS OFFICE

ALFA ROMEO AIR TAXI

POLLO PIO PIO

HOTEL MANGLARES

CABINAS EL VIAJERO

TO PLAYA PRECIOSA

TO CORCOVADO

SCALE NOT AVAILABLE

© MOON PUBLICATIONS, INC.

seafood meals are served). There were two hardwood cabins at press time, with eight more planned. They're raised on stilts, with louvered windows to all sides. Shared showers and bathrooms are in the grounds, but private bathrooms were to be added, along with five tent-cabins. Iguana Lodge bills itself as a "sportfishing and nature lodge" and is backed by profuse wilderness with the beach and ocean forward. Fishing trips are aboard a 35-foot Bertram. It's run by two friendly Californians: Jeff and "Stig." Rates: $45 pp *cabinas;* $10 pp tent-cabins, including meals.

The German-run **Preci-Osa Cabinas,** tel. 735-5062, fax 735-5043, shares the idyllic locale. There's a rustic lodge where meals are served, plus cylindrical, simply yet tastefully furnished *cabinas* with conical thatched roofs resembling African *rondavels.* Each sleeps three people and has ceiling fans, mosquito nets over the beds, and private bathrooms with gravity-fed showers. Water is drawn from a well; a small generator provides electricity at night (bring flashlights). Trails lead into the forest and mangroves at back. Rates: $50 per *cabina.*

Food

There's no good breakfast spot, although most *sodas* serve *típico* breakfasts. **Restaurante Carolina,** tel./fax 735-5073, is popular with local expats for its large menu, including *típico* dishes and chicken cordon bleu and fettucine alfredo. It's open 7 a.m.-10 p.m.

The restaurant **Agua Luna,** on the northeast side of town, catches the breezes and has good seafood dishes; try the *pescado al ajillo* (fish with garlic) for about $3. **Restaurant Caribeño,** next door, is run by Kenny from Belize. He serves curried goat and fish ($6) and a barbecue plate with beans ($4).

On Tuesday, head to **Iguana Lodge** for its all-you-can-eat spaghetti ($6), or on Thursday for its "taco nite" and *kung pao* chicken. The rustic *mirador* restaurant is closed to the public on other nights.

Pollo Frito Opi is a tiny open-air diner next to the soccer field. There's a **bakery** opposite the ICE building. You can also buy grilled meat on a stick from roadside stalls at night—but be warned that local expats swear it's *ratton* (yes, rat), which also sells in the *carnicería* (butcher shop) for 75 cents a kilogram.

Entertainment

The favored spot at press time was **Bar y Restaurant El Rancho,** tel. 735-5120, fax 735-5073, run by a sad Dutch fellow who seems to have rubbed all the locals the wrong way. Still, he runs a good show. The open-air bar, with bamboo roof, has dart boards and occasionally a *discomovil* (mobile disco) which sets up its oversized speakers on the open-air patio and sends the air reverberating for miles. It serves good music and *bocas.* And hidden behind the wooden door next to the toilet (you'll never guess it) is a fixed disco with a DJ booth and red leather walls. (admission $1—a bargain for a sauna, which is what it feels like; dress lightly). Happy hour is 5-6 p.m.

Giving El Rancho a run for its money is **Cuatro Ventas,** on Playa Platanares. Back in town, there are plenty of funky bars where you can sup with local menfolk.

There's a **softball** game every Sunday at 9 a.m. on the soccer field: Ticos versus gringos (and honorary gringos).

Tourist Information

Escondido Trex, Apdo. 9, Puerto Jiménez, tel./fax 735-5210, e-mail: osatrex@sol.racsa.co.cr, in the Restaurante Carolina, is a great resource. Matt is really knowledgeable and helpful. You can send and receive e-mail messages ($5 per outgoing). **Souvenir Corcovado,** tel./fax 735-5005, also acts as an information office and booking agent for hotels, plane tickets, and local transportation.

There's a government-sponsored tourist information bureau opposite Super 96 on the main street, but they reputedly give bad information. It arranges everything from horseback rides to flights.

The **Corcovado National Park Headquarters,** tel. 735-5036, fax 735-5276, is beside the airstrip and open Mon.-Fri. 7:30 a.m.-noon and 1-5 p.m. It has a tourist information office (closed Sunday). You must register here if you plan on visiting Corcovado. **Fundación Neotrópica,** tel. 735-5116, has an office here.

Tours and Activities

Escondido Trex Apdo. 9, Puerto Jiménez, tel./fax 735-5210, e-mail: osatrex@sol.racsa.co.cr, offers half-day sea kayaking trips through the mangrove "swamps" of the Río Platanares ($35); full-day paddling on the Golfo Dulce ($65); rapelling down waterfalls and hiking in Corcovado ($35-75); gold-mining trips to Dos Brazos ($35); a sunset dolphin watch ($35); plus fishing and snorkeling and multiday excursions locally and farther afield. It also offers mountain biking and nature treks, and rents out camping gear.

Olivier—alias "Frenchie"—operates **Adventure Cat Tours** (the office is beside the soccer field). **Everyday Adventures,** Apdo. 15, Puerto Jiménez, tel./fax 735-5138, has kayak trips into the Río Coto mangroves ($35), open-ocean kayaking ($45 half day, $65 full day), a rainforest hike ($45), and a rainforest canopy exploration ($65 full day) that includes climbing *inside* a giant strangler fig. And "Alex", Apdo. 31, Puerto Jiménez, tel. 735-5148, leads three-day trips into Corcovado for $75 including meals.

George at the Puerto Jiménez Yacht Club (the name is a bit of a joke), tel./fax 735-5051, offers dolphin watching, kayak trips, plus a sunset cruise daily at 5 p.m. ($10 pp). He also rents bicycles. Kenny of **Sportfishing y Aventuras Osa,** tel./fax 735-5546, rents a fishing boat for $350 half day, $600 full day (up to six people).

Local guide **Taboga Loaciga,** tel. 735-5092, or marine radio channel 12, also offers fishing and boat trips, plus water-taxi service to virtually any point you wish. Expect to pay $150 for three people for a day's fishing. And Windfried Zigan offers charters aboard *Pacific Child,* a 12-meter trimaran based at Doña Leta's Bungalows.

Finca Franceschis, tel. 735-5007, fax 735-5045; or at the Souvenir Corcovado shop, tel./fax 735-5005, is a family-owned farm and private wildlife refuge offering horseback tours along the winding Río Platanares past mangroves and through primary rainforest to Playa Platanares, where you can canter along the deserted beach or relax at a shady rancho with hammocks. Tours include lunch and the services of an English-speaking guide.

Services

There's a **Banco Central de Costa Rica** and a **Banco Nacional,** tel. 735-5020, which will happily buy any gold you may find in the Osa. The *pulpería* will also change traveler's checks and money.

Isabel at Bosque Jiménez, tel. 735-5062, on the main street is the **Travelair** representative.

Getting There and Away

By Bus: Transportes Blanco, tel. 771-2550, buses depart San José for Puerto Jiménez from Calle 12, Avenidas 7/9 daily at 6 a.m. and noon (eight hours; $7); and from San Isidro de El General at 5:30 a.m. and noon (five hours; $4.50). Buses depart Ciudad Neily for Puerto Jiménez at 7 a.m. and 2 p.m. ($2.50); and from Golfito for Puerto Jiménez from the municipal dock daily at 11 a.m.

The bus station in Puerto Jiménez is one block west of Super 96 (the ticket office is open Mon.-Sat. 7-11 a.m. and 1-5 p.m., Sunday 8 a.m.-noon; buy your tickets in advance). Buses depart for San Isidro and San José at 5 a.m. and 11 a.m.; and to Ciudad Neily at 5:30 a.m. and 2 p.m.

By Air: SANSA and Travelair both have scheduled daily flights; see appendix. **Aeronaves de Costa Rica,** tel. 575-0278 or 232-1413; in Golfito, tel. 775-0278, offers daily flights between Golfito and Puerto Jiménez, with a 10-kg luggage limit. You can charter flights from Golfito (about $40). **Alfa Romeo Aero Taxi,** tel. 735-5178 or 775-1515, has an office at the airstrip.

By Ferry: A ferry runs daily from the Muelle Bananero in Golfito at 11:30 a.m., and returns at 6 a.m. (tel. 775-0472; $2.50; 90-minute journey). The ferries hold 30 people, but no vehicles. Private **water-taxis,** tel. 775-0712 or 775-0357, charge $20-33 for points around the Golfo Dulce.

By Taxi: Taxis from Golfito charge about $80. Oscar Blanco offers taxi service.

PUERTO JIMÉNEZ TO CARATE

The southeast shores of Osa are lined with hidden beaches—**Playa Tamales, Playa Sombrero**—in the lee of craggy headlands, notably **Cabo Matapalo** at the southeast tip of the peninsula about 18 km south of Puerto Jiménez. The area is popular with the long-board surf set. The waters offer a variety of wave types, all left breaks. According to local surf expert Mark Kelly, deep water close to shore and a southerly swell can generate powerful six-foot waves, usually in late July through August.

The Matapalo region has been discovered by foreigners in recent years, and many have settled, bringing a new dynamic to attempts to preserve the forests and wildlife. New accommodations are springing up all along the coast, which is backed by steep, forested hills, with cattle *fincas* on the lowland valley bottoms.

The road south to Carate and Corcovado National Park takes about two hours under good conditions. Just as the Río Reventazón is no place for birchbark canoes, the road between Puerto Jiménez and Carate is no place for a Ford Escort or Honda Civic. It gets gradually narrower and bumpier and muddier. There are a few streams to ford, though the more egregious now have bridges, thanks to the U.S. Army Corps of Engineers.

Carate, 43 km from Puerto Jiménez, consists of an airstrip and a *pulpería* where you can grab an ice-cold Coke or *refresco*. Linger long enough and an *orero* might appear bearing gold and tall tales. If you intend to stay at Corcovado Lodge Tent Camp (see below), the *pulpería* will radio the camp to send a guide with a horse; it's a 30-minute ride along a magnificent, kilometers-long black-sand beach. You have to leave your vehicle at the *pulpería*. Alternately, you can camp on the beach in front of the *pulpería*, which has bathrooms, showers, and water faucet.

The La Leona Ranger Station, at the entrance to Corcovado National Park, is about two km along the beach.

Canopy Expedition
The Corcovado Lodge Tent Camp (see below) has a private forest reserve abutting Parque Nacional Corcovado; at this reserve you can fulfill your dream of making out like a monkey or a harpy eagle. Owner Michael Kaye has fulfilled his childhood dream of building a fabulous tree house—this one 30 meters aloft, midway up a 60-meter tall *ajo* in an "arboreal pasture" that attracts myriad monkeys and birds. Once harnessed into a secure bosun's chair, you are whisked to a platform at the height of an eight-story building, where you can study life in the forest canopy. Scarlet macaws often fly in to pluck seeds and fruits just a few feet from the platform railing. Monkeys swing in to do the same, occasionally taking breaks to demonstrate their urinary skills—with you as target. Your $69 is well spent.

Accommodations
Camping: Camping Bosque Mar, about eight km south of Puerto Jiménez, has camping amid

landscaped grounds 200 meters from the beach.

Fabulous is the word for **Corcovado Lodge Tent Camp,** a civilized "safari-style" tent camp fronted by palms immediately behind the beach and 1.5 km west of Carate, flush against the border of Corcovado National Park—the perfect base for exploring the park. It's operated by Costa Rica Expeditions, Apdo. 6941-1000, San José, tel. 257-0766, fax 257-1665, e-mail: crexped@sol.racsa.co.cr. Livingstone never had it so good. The beachfront facility has 20 roomy and comfortable walk-in tents that are raised on pedestals at the base of the hill. Guests sleep on sturdy bamboo cots raised well off the floor. Ablutions are in two shared bathhouses (cold water only). Electricity is supplied by a small generator and is limited to certain hours in the dining area and bathhouse. Bring flashlights. Family-style meals are eaten in a screened *palenque* restaurant. An atmospheric bar has a large veranda on tall stilts. Quite rustic, but it's a marvelous experience being lulled to sleep by the sound of surf and good-night wishes from the bullfrogs and Pacific screech owl. A 10-meter inflatable pontoon vessel, *Guacamaya*, designed to navigate through the crashing Pacific surf, is available for reaching Corcovado National Park. Enhancements were planned. Rates: $58 s, $96 d including breakfast and dinner; $77 s, $144 d with all meals. Multiday packages offer discounts. *Recommended!*

Those with loftier pretensions can try **canopy platform camping,** sleeping in a tent suspended 30 meters in the air courtesy of Corcovado Lodge Tent Camp ($125); see **Canopy Expedition,** above.

Budget: The **Carate Jungle Camp** is a very basic place set back from the beach in a banana grove near Carate. It has bare-bones rooms in a two-story rough-hewn structure, with soft sponge mattresses, screened windows, and mosquito nets. The basic shared showers and toilets are outside, where there's the most fantastic giant strangler fig you'll ever see. Rates: $30, including all meals.

Tierra de Milagros, Lista de Correos, Puerto Jiménez, Peninsula de Osa, tel. 233-0233, fax 735-5073; in the U.S., P.O. Box 35203, Siesta Key, FL 34242, tel. (813) 349-2168, or "The Land of Miracles," is a "counterculture" earth-worship kind of place (yoga, moon rituals, etc.) at

Playa Sombrero, about 15 km south of Puerto Jiménez. It specializes in holistic retreats and attracts an eclectic crowd. Basically, you're sharing the peace-and-harmony lifestyle of founders Nicky and Edie. Stone pathways lead to eight thatched *ranchitos* dispersed throughout the lush five-hectare fantasia with organic garden. They're simply furnished, Robinson Crusoe affairs featuring charming rough-hewn beds with mosquito nets, screened windows, and a loft bedroom. The bamboo-walled, shared bathrooms and showers are in the garden (privacy is not part of the plan). No electricity. Center of things is a soaring circular *rancho* where guests laze in hammocks and adopt a kind of back-to-the-Amazon lifestyle. Musical instruments are strewn around. Meals are served here: mostly vegetarian, with plenty of fish and fruits. A separate studio is used for yoga, and there's a yoga deck by the seashore where you may birth your baby (you won't be the first). Trails lead 50 meters to the beach where a little cascade tumbles over a man-made rock dam, and there are horses for use. "Volunteers" participate in the reforestation work. Edie and Nicky encourage groups interested in art, yoga, tai chi, holistic medicine, and the like. Look for a wooden gate with bull's horns, on the left (50 meters south of unmarked green gates). Rates: about $30 per night, including all meals. If a 1970s Marin County lifesetyle is your thing, then this place is for you.

Inexpensive: Playa Tamales de Osa, fax 735-5332, one km north of Camping Bosque Mar, midway between Puerto Jiménez and Cabo Matapalo, is a French-owned "guesthouse" in handsome Polynesian style set amid lawns bursting with bougainvillea bowers which lead down to the splendid beach, where locals can be seen fishing knee-deep with nets. At press time it had two simple four-person cabins with soaring thatched roofs (a remake intends to imbue a classier French aesthetic), plus four smaller bedrooms. Four more upscale bedrooms were planned along with a swimming pool and "classy" restaurant near the beach, and "budget" accommodations for surfers ($35-45 including all meals). It's popular with European skiers and surfers but the owner, the welcoming and delightfully erudite Jean-Françoise (a former professional restaurateur) does not take in all-comers; he is selective about his clientele. He is

adding boats for trips to Pavones and elsewhere. He promises it will be a "simple pleasure palace."

Enchanta la Vida, tel. 735-5062, fax 735-5043, near Matapalo, comprises three-story wooden lodges, fringed by wide verandas with hammocks and rockers with views over both ocean and jungle. It requires a two-day minimum stay. Not reviewed.

Moderate: The **Look Out Inn,** tel. 735-5205, recently opened on the hillside one km east of Carate. Terry and Wendy, from New Mexico, are live-in owners of this newly constructed three-story house with three, tall-ceilinged, tastefully decorated bedrooms on the first floor. Decor combines American Southwest and Costa Rican features: sponge-washed walls merging with bamboo furnishings and tropical hardwood accents, not least bedframes made from tree trunks. A lounge has a small library, plus a TV/VCR and a collection of 200 movies. A spiral staircase opens onto a *mirador* with natural driftwood rails, hammocks, and a telescope to assist in admiring fabulous vistas along the coast to Corcovado. Monkeys, however, come down to the forested property, which extends uphill to the ridge; and macaws screech by like jet fighters. Solar electricity heats the water delivered in large showers. A swimming pool and deck were planned for the garden below. Rates: $75 including all meals (organic and homegrown, plus fresh-smoked meats and cheeses) and drinks (including Terry's homemade wine), plus use of kayaks, canoes, mountain bikes, and boogie boards.

Premium: Hacienda Bahía Esmeralda, tel. 775-0131, cellular tel. 381-8521, fax 735-5045, is the splendid home-cum-hostelry of ex-musician Brett Harter of the rock group Route 66. Eighteen km south of Puerto Jiménez, near Matapalo, it commands a hillside amid 37 hectares of rainforest overlooking the southernmost part of the Golfo Dulce. The inn has three bedrooms plus three luxury cottages, each with two queen-size beds with orthopedic mattresses, and private bathroom. The eclectic menu spans the world: from Indian and Chinese to Mexican and French cuisine. Swim in the pool fed by a local creek (at night you can follow the lanterns for a moon-lit dip). You can hike, or rent horses, for nature trips along forest trails, and a splendid beach awaits just a five-minute walk away. Harter was adding *cabinas*. Rates: $103 pp low season;

$117 high season, including tax, transfers, gourmet meals, beers, and horse rental.

Luxury: The much-heralded **Lapa Ríos,** Apdo. 100, Puerto Jiménez, tel. 735-5130, fax 735-5179, e-mail: laparios@sol.racsa.co.cr, website www.centralamerica.com/cr/hotel/laparios. htm; in the U.S., P.O. Box 025216, SJO 706, Miami, FL 33102-5216, overlooking Cabo Matapalo, is an exquisite resort—an "anteroom for heaven"—that enjoys a great location atop a ridge overlooking the ocean. It has a small amoeba-shaped swimming pool with sundeck, and a poolside bar that catches the breezes. Fourteen romantic bungalows—reached by wooden walkways—are luxuriously appointed, each with two queen-size beds, gleaming hardwood floors, screened glassless windows, a patio garden complete with outdoor shower (you also have a tiled indoor shower), and louvered French doors opening to a private terrace. The thatched *palenque* lodge has a soaring roof and a twisting spiral staircase to an all-around walkway *mirador* (lookout platform), with a restaurant below. *Lapas* (macaws) and monkeys abound on the property, which is backed by a 400-hectare private reserve. Walks in the rainforest are complemented by a tree-planting program in the 100-hectare Volunteer Rainforest. Guided tours ($20-45) include kayaking, horseback rides, and hikes by day and night, plus a full-day Corcovado tour with air transfers to/from Sirena ($550-600). You can also visit Carbonera School, funded by the owners, John and Karen Lewis, who are active environmentalists and wizards of self-promotion (they have a reputation in Costa Rica for self-aggrandizement but, hey, they've built a success story), thanks to which their resort attracts the rich and famous. Marvelous—but overpriced? Rates: $178 s, $241 d, $345 t, $448 quad low season; $201 s, $276 d, $396 t, $512 quad high season, including taxes and all meals.

Bosque del Cabo, tel./fax 735-5206, voice mail 381-4847, e-mail: boscabo@sol.racsa.co.cr, one km west atop the 180-meter cliff of Cabo Matapalo, is another winner. The resort is part of a private, 140-hectare forest reserve. Walkways lined by poinsettias lead through expansive lawns and landscaped grounds to seven pretty, thatched, clifftop *cabinas* with superb ocean views over Playa Matapalo. There are lanterns, but no electricity. Screened open-air showers have their own little gardens. Verandas have hammocks. Three splendid deluxe cabins offer the nicest ambience for miles: each has terracotta floors, king-size bed with mosquito net, subdued yet chic decor, and lofty rough-hewn stable doors that open to a wraparound veranda with sublime ocean vistas. Then there's the **Casa Blanca,** a sublime home away from home perfect for honeymoon couples. This exquisitely decorated villa has an open-plan kitchen, bedroom with bamboo-framed king-size bed (a second bedroom has two double beds), CD player, and a wraparound veranda with hammocks and rockers. Lanterns light the place at night. There's a "cooling-off" pool fed by spring waters and a sundeck for tanning. Meals are eaten family style under a *palenque*, which has a small raised bar. Scarlet macaws nest on the property, as do howler monkeys. You can enjoy hikes and horseback rides ($20 all day, including lunch) to waterfalls, a jacuzzi-like tide pool, and prime wildlife-viewing areas. The walk to the beach is a stiff 150-meter clamber. Owner Phil Spear provides 4WD taxi pickup from Puerto Jiménez. Rates: $105 s, $168 d, $207 t, $236 quad standard, $115 s, $188 d, $237 t deluxe low season; $119 s, $188 d, $237 t, $276 quad standard, $129 s, $208 d, $267 t deluxe high season. The house costs $750 per week low season; $850 high season.

Food
The **Buena Esperanza** is a pleasant little European cafe on the roadside midway between Camping Bosque Mar and Tierra de Milagros.

Getting There
A *colectivo* taxi runs to Matapalo ($3) and Carate ($7) from Puerto Jiménez daily at 6 a.m.; it leaves from Mini Mercado El Tigre, tel. 735-5075. You can rent a jeep-taxi (about $50 per carload). You can also try hitching to Carate; most people will stop and give you a lift.

Water-taxis are available to make the run to Playas Tamales and Sombrero.

PARQUE NACIONAL CORCOVADO

Corcovado—the Amazon of Costa Rica—is the largest stronghold of primary forest on a Pacific coastline that has been all but destroyed from

Mexico to South America. Its 41,788 hectares (excluding Piedras Blancas) encompass eight habitats, from mangrove swamp and jolillo palm grove to montane forest. The park protects more than 400 species of birds (20 are endemic), 116 of amphibians and reptiles, and 139 of mammals—representing 10% of the mammals in the Americas—on only 0.000101777% of the landmass. Its healthy population of scarlet macaws (about 1,200 birds) is the largest concentration in Central America. You can expect to see large flocks of macaws in flight or feeding on almond trees by the shoreline.

A shower of vegetation and dead wood usually calls attention to a tamandua, or banded anteater, feeding in the canopy. Corcovado is a good place to spot the red-eyed tree frog (listen for his single-note mating "cluck"), the glass frog with its transparent skin, and enamel-bright poison-arrow frogs. And you can watch fishing bats doing just that over rivers at night. You can even try your own hand for snook inside the mouths of the coastal rivers on incoming tides. They strike plugs all year and during the fall become very aggressive.

Corcovado is also one of only two places in the country that harbor squirrel monkeys (the other is Manuel Antonio). It's one of the last stands in the world for the harpy eagle, although it hasn't been seen here in the last several years and may now be extinct in Costa Rica. As recently as the 1970s, tapirs were so numerous around Lago Corcovado that squatters were killing them just for fun. Four species of sea turtles—green, Pacific ridley, hawksbill, and leatherback—nest on the park's beaches. And the park supports a healthy population of big cats and crocodiles, which like to hang around the periphery of the Corcovado Lagoon. Jaguar paw prints are commonly seen in the mud trails, and the cats are often sighted.

The Osa Peninsula bears the brunt of torrential rains from April to December. It receives up to 400 cm per year. The driest months, Jan.-April, are the best times to visit.

Information

The park **administrative office** is in Puerto Jiménez.

The park has three entry points: **La Leona,** on the southeast corner near Carate; **Los Patos,** on the northern perimeter; and **San Pedrillo,** at the northwest corner, 18 km south of Drake Bay. You can hike or fly into the park headquarters at **Sirena,** a large research station set back from the beach, midway between La Leona and San Pedrillo (it has an airstrip). There's also a remote ranger station at **Los Planes,** on the north-

waterfall, Corcovado

ern border midway between San Pedrillo and Los Patos. All are linked by trails. Entrance: $6.

Hiking Trails

Several short trails (2-6 hours) make for rewarding half- or full-day hikes. Each has its own points of interest. Longer trails grant excellent opportunities for an in-depth backpacking experience in the rainforest. You'll come across occasional shelters in addition to the ranger stations. Allow about three days to hike from one end of the park to the other. It can be hot and sweaty. Horseflies and mosquitoes can be a pain in the butt. And spiderwebs span the trails, which are in places badly eroded, poorly maintained, and poorly marked. I strongly recommend buying the Instituto Geográfico 1:50,000 scale maps if you plan on serious hiking.

From La Leona: It's 15 km to Sirena following the beach for most of the way. Beyond Salsipuedes Point, the trail cuts inland through the rainforest—good for spotting monkeys and coatimundis. Don't try this at high or waning tide: you must cross some rocky points that are cut off by high tide. Don't trust exclusively to the ranger's statements: consult a tide table before you arrive. Allow up to eight hours. The hike from La Leona to the Magrigal waterfall is particularly recommended, but few local guides will take you.

From Sirena: A trail leads northeast to Los Patos via Corcovado Lagoon. Another trail—only possible at low tide (not least because sharks, mostly hammerheads, like to come up the rivermouths in the hours immediately before and after high tide)—leads to the San Pedrillo Ranger Station (23 km), where there are showers, beds, and water, and seats placed strategically under shady palms for sunset viewing. There are three rivers to wade. The trick is to reach the Río Sirena and slightly shallower Ríos Llorona before the water is thigh-deep. Here, watch for the crocodiles upstream. Don't let me put you off; dozens of hikers follow the trail each week, and the wary crocodiles give humans a wide berth. Halfway, the trail winds steeply into the rainforest and is often slippery—good shoe tread is essential. The last three kilometers are along the beach. The full-day hike takes you past La Llorona, a 30-meter high waterfall that cascades onto the beach. From San Pedrillo, you can continue another 10 km to Drake Bay and Marenco Beachfront and Resort Lodge.

Tapirs are said to come down to the beach around sunrise but you must remain silent at all times, as the animals are timid and may never return once scared away. Treat these magnificent creatures with respect or don't go in the first place.

From Los Patos: From Los Patos, the trail south climbs steeply for six km before flattening out for the final 14 km to the Sirena Research Station. The trail is well marked but narrow, overgrown in parts, and has several river crossings where it is easy to lose the trail on the other side. You must wade. Be especially careful in rainy season, when you may find yourself hip-deep. There are three small shelters en route. A side trail will take you to Corcovado Lagoon. Allow up to eight hours. Another trail reportedly leads from Los Patos to Los Planes.

Precautions: There are trails for lengthy hikes, some of which require you to wade rivers or skip around craggy shorelines. Beware of riptides: swim only where rangers advise it may be safe. Sharks reportedly cruise the inshore waters, though they're are no recorded incidents of unprovoked attacks here. And crocodiles inhabit the estuaries of the Río Claro and Río Sirena; if crossing either river, do so as far upriver as possible.

Corovado also has a large population of peccaries, a massive-necked razorbacked hog that grows to the size of a large hound These myopic, sharp-toothed animals are excitable and very aggressive, and attacks by groups of a dozen or more peccaries sometimes occur when the animals feel threatened. If attacked, climb a tree. Don't try to frighten them away—that's a sure way to get gored. One guide told me of being surrounded by them in a clearing for 20 minutes. The dominant male bluff-charged him a few times. He stood stock-still. Eventually the peccaries got bored and disappeared.

Accommodations

Basic rooms with foam mattresses (but no linens) are available at Sirena; reservations are essential. Rates: about $1.50. Other ranger stations may be able to squeeze you into one of their basic rooms. Meals are available at each station by prior arrangement ($4.50 breakfast, $6 lunch and dinner). Contact the National Park headquarters in San José, tel. 192, or the Corcovado park headquarters in Puerto Jiménez as far ahead as possible.

Camping is allowed at ranger stations (50 cents). Rangers can radio ahead to the various stations within the park and book you in for dinner and a tent spot. No-see-ums (pesky microscopic flies you'll not forget in a hurry) infest the beaches and come out to find you at dusk. Take a watertight tent, a mosquito net, and plenty of insect repellent. You can rent tents and stoves in Puerto Jiménez from Escondido Trex, Mini Mercado El Tigre, tel. 735-5075, and Cabinas Iguana Iguana ($7 per day).

Tours and Activities

See "Tours And Activities," in the Puerto Viejo section. Most tour operators in San José also offer or can arrange tours. **Costa Rica Expeditions,** Apdo. 6941-1000, San José, tel. 257-0766, fax 257-1665, e-mail: crexped@sol.racsa.co.cr, is recommended for guided hiking trips and horseback rides. **Ecole Travel,** Calle 7, Avenidas Central/1, San José, tel. 223-2240, fax 223-4128, e-mail: ecolecr@sol.racsa.co.cr, has a three-day/two-night trip for $145.

Getting There and Away

By Air: You can charter an air-taxi to fly you to Sirena or Carate. **SAETA,** tel. 232-1474, flies from San José ($400 per planeload). **Aeronaves de Costa Rica,** tel. 575-0278, offers charter flights from Golfito ($110 per planeload). I've heard it has a reputation for stranding passengers. Air charters may not operate in "wet" season, from May to December.

By Boat: Boats from Marenco and Drake Bay will take you to either San Pedrillo or Sirena.

GOLFITO AND VALLE DE COTO COLORADO

The Golfo Dulce region fringes the huge bay of the same name encompassed by the Osa Peninsula to the west and the Fila Costeña mountains to the north and, to the east, flatlands planted with banana trees stretching to the border with Panamá. Dangling "below" these flatlands is the virtually uninhabited Peninsula de Burica, the southernmost tip of Costa Rica. The region is centered on the town of Golfito, which lies on the north shore of the gulf. The bay is rimmed by swamplands, lonesome beaches (several with nature and/or fishing lodges at which to rest your head), and remote tracts of rainforest accessible only by boat.

RÍO CLARO

Río Claro, about 15 km west of Ciudad Neily and 64 km southeast of Palmar, is a major junction at the turnoff for Golfito from Hwy. 2. Its about 23 km to Golfito. Río Claro has a plethora of restaurants and *sodas,* plus a gas station and taxi service. You can hire local guides at La Casona (see below) to take you to mountain caves boasting stalagmites and stalactites.

Accommodations and Food

Hotel Conechan, on Calle Mopt, three blocks north of the intersection, has 38 spacious, clean rooms secluded from the noise of highway traffic. There are ceiling fans and private baths with cold water (some have hot water), and varying numbers of beds. Secure parking. Rates: $4 per room.

La Casona, tel. 789-9125, one km west of the junction for Golfito, has *cabinas* and a superb seafood restaurant. It's a lively spot, with music thrumming on the sound system. There's a wood-grill barbecue on weekends. Try the ceviche. Open 11 a.m.-11 p.m.

You'll find pizzas and other tasty Italian fare served at **Soda Chirripó,** at the junction. It also serves sandwiches, burgers, and tacos, which you should wash down with deliciously sweet *agua dulce* (sugar cane juice) or hot chocolate.

GOLFITO AND VICINITY

Golfito, the most important town in the Pacific southwest, is for travelers who love adventures in forlorn ports. Its setting is pleasing, but the

Golfito

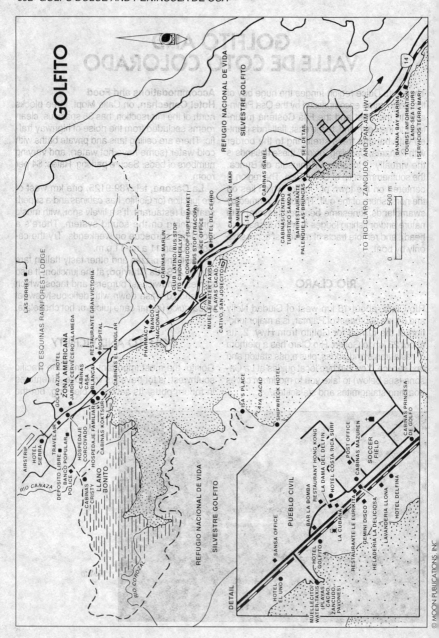

GOLFITO

GOLFITO AND
VALLE DE GOTO COLORADO

REFUGIO NACIONAL DE VIDA
SILVESTRE GOLFITO

SEE DETAIL

500 m

0

TO RIO CLARO, ZANCUDO, AND PAN-AM HWY.

BANANA BAY MARINA
TOURIST INFORMATION
LAND-SEA TOURS
(SERVICIOS TERRA MAR)

14

CABINAS ISABEL

CABINAS SOL Y MAR

MINERVA

BAR RESTAURANTE
PALENQUE LAS BRUNCAS

CABINAS CENTRO
TURISTICO SAMOA

HOTEL DEL CERRO

ICE OFFICE

CONSUCOOP (SUPERMARKET)

14

CABINAS MARLIN

CLUB LATINO / BUS STOP
(TO CIUDAD NEILLY)

BUS STOP (TRACOPA)

MUELLE / WATER TAXIS
(PLAYAS CACAO,
CATIVO, SAN JOSECITO)

BANCO
NACIONAL

PHARMACY

HOSPITAL

RESTAURANTE GRAN VICTORIA

CABINAS EL MANGLAR

LAS TORRES

GOLFO AZUL HOTEL

TRAVELAIR

JARDÍN CERVECERO ALAMEDA

ZONA AMERICANA

CABINAS
CASA
BLANCA

CABINAS KOOTSUR

HOSPEDAJE FAMILIAR

HOSPEDAJE
CORCOVADO

DEPÓSITO LIBRE

BANCO POPULAR

POLICE

CABINAS
CRISTY

LLANO
BONITO

HOTEL
SIERRA

AIRSTRIP

RIO CANAZA

TO ESQUINAS RAINFOREST LODGE

REFUGIO NACIONAL DE VIDA
SILVESTRE GOLFITO

RIO COROZAL

ISA'S PLACE

PLAYA CACAO

SHIPWRECK HOTEL

DETAIL

PUEBLO CIVIL

SANSA OFFICE

BAR LA BOMBA

RESTAURANT HONG KONG

LA DAMA DEL DELFIN

HOTEL COSTA RICA SURF

LA CUBANA

RESTAURANTE LE EURIKITA

GEMINI DISCO

HELADERÍA LA DELICIOSA

LAVANDERÍA LLONA

POST OFFICE

CABINAS MAZUREN

SOCCER
FIELD

CABINAS PRINCESA
DE GOLFO

HOTEL DELFINA

HOTEL
GOLFITO

MUELLE / ICE
WATER TAXIS
(PLAYAS
CACAO,
ZANCUDO,
PAJONES)

HOTEL
EL UNO

© MOON PUBLICATIONS, INC.

town itself is a disappointment unless you like funky, semi-down-at-the-heels places that you may recognize from the movie *Chico Mendes*, the true story of the Brazilian rubber-trapper murdered for his efforts to protect the rainforest. Character it has. Charm, it has not. Use it as a jumping-off point for the Osa Peninsula and Corcovado National Park, and the surf spots of Zancudo and Pavones.

The town was born in 1938, when the United Fruit Company moved its headquarters here after shutting down operations on the Caribbean coast. By 1955, over 90% of the nation's banana exports were shipped from Golfito. Back then both sailors and prostitutes struck it rich, especially when World War II came along and Allied sailors came ashore. "Men in fatigues had parties with our women for $100 a night," says Louis Vinicio Elizondo Arguello, the municipal administrator. "After a while the women wouldn't go out with Costa Rican men." The United Fruit Company closed its doors and pulled out of Golfito in 1985 after a series of crippling labor strikes. Today Golfito attracts its fair share of tropical vagabonds, broken-hearted misfits, and roughneck military-type expatriates, many of them on the lam from the law (be cautious with whom you interact; one German named Rolf is notoriously untrustworthy). There are still plenty of prostitutes around to part them from their money. All add color to the place.

The town sprawls for several kilometers along a single road on the estuary of the Río Golfito, which opens onto the Golfo Dulce. Forested mountains form a backdrop a few hundred meters inland. There are two distinct parts of town. First entered, to the southeast, is the **Pueblo Civil**, the run-down working-class section full of tumbledown housing (many hanging on stilts over the water) and cheap bars. The Pueblo Civil extends northwest to the compact town center—a lively quarter of cheap bar life and colorful local action. About two km farther is the **Muelle de Golfito,** the banana-loading dock (also called Muelle Bananero) at the southern end of the **Zona Americana,** a more tranquil and orderly quarter where the administrative staff of United Fruit used to live. The architectural style of the Zona is distinct—it reminds me of a scene from the British Raj, with brightly painted, two-story wooden houses raised on

stilts to catch the breezes and set in manicured gardens shaded by tall trees hung with epiphytes and lianas. Here, too is the **Depósito Libre,** a duty-free shopping compound (enclosed by high walls) that lures Ticos in droves on weekends, when the town's dozens of cheap *cabinas* fill up.

The town is popular as a sportfishing center. The bay is not recommended for swimming. Take a water-taxi to a nearby beach, such as Playa Cacao, a popular relaxation spot for locals about 10 km north of town (the road curls around; Cacao, which actually faces Golfito across the bay, is two km on water as the crow flies, and can be reached by water-taxi for $1).

Cruise ships are slowly beginning to arrive. *Norwegian Dynasty* and *Windsong* are regular visitors.

Refugio Nacional de Vida Silvestre Golfito
This 1,309-hectare Golfito National Wildlife Refuge, created to protect the city's watershed, is formed of primary rainforest covering the steep chain of low mountains behind the harbor and extending around the bay to the north. Abundant year-round rains feed the insatiable jungle. Trails lead through the reserve. With patience, you might spot an anteater, an agouti, a margay, a raccoon, or a jaguarundi. All four species of Costa Rican monkeys live in the refuge, as do scarlet macaws. **Land-Sea Tours** (see below) arranges guided hiking, including a lunch at Playa Cacao.

Getting There: There are several routes. A sign across from the Plaza Deportes soccer field in the Pueblo Civil about two km south of the town center points the way along a dirt road that leads about five km uphill to Las Torres radio station and along the ridgecrest within the reserve. Alternately, you can also take a steep trail from Restaurante Samoa. The road that parallels the airstrip leads past the Hotel Sierra and, deteriorating the while, deposits you three km farther at a sign for "Senderos Naturales" (nature trails). Lastly, you can take the dirt road beyond the Depósito Libre that leads through the reserve to Esquinas.

Playa Cacao
The vision of Golfito improves dramatically from across the bay at Playa Cacao, an idyllically

breezy and offbeat spot literally at the end of the road, five km southwest of Golfito. Popeye might have felt at home here. I love the place. Funky charm was never funkier or more charming. There's a brown-sand beach, some delightful offbeat spots to rest your head, and you get to have Golfito at hand when (and if) you want it. The road from Golfito winds around the shore, with great views towards Golfito, and spills steeply down to the shingly beach, lined with bougainvillea.

About 200 meters to the east is a beached 19-meter-long trawler, virtually derelict and looking like a set for a Popeye movie. John Wayne anchored here in 1966 and left his signature in the guestbook.

Depósito Libre

Golfito was declared a duty-free port in 1990—an attempt to offset the economic decline that followed United Fruit's strategic retreat. The duty-free zone—Depósito Libre—is restricted to a massive shopping compound north of the Zona Americana and is administered by the Instituto Mixto de Ayuda Social (Joint Institute of Social Assistance), tel. 775-0889, or IMAS, whose rational is to eradicate poverty throughout Costa Rica. Rows of 52 shops are overflowing with luxury goods, electronics, and household appliances. Shoppers must arrive in Golfito 24 hours before they can shop. You must get a "shopping card" (*boleto*) from the Centro de Computo, opposite store number one in the complex (open Tues.-Sun. 8 a.m.-4:30 p.m.). Ticos are allowed to buy about $500 worth of goods each six months (anything over is charged regular duty), but locals sell their *boletos* for about $25. Avoid early mornings. You'll need to present your computer printout shopping card plus your passport each time you make a purchase. Keep the sales receipts. Supposedly, you must leave Golfito 24 hours after shopping. If you think you can snap up superb bargains, forget it. This isn't Hong Kong. Yes, foreigners can buy as much as they can carry, but you can do just as well back home (there *is* a nominal tax). If you pay cash, you can negotiate discounts on sticker prices. There are porters and local shipping companies on-site.

Bus excursions from San José cost about $15 roundtrip, plus overnight stay.

Accommodations

The town is awash in budget—and often grim—accommodations, but Golfito gets very busy on weekends and holidays. Plan a weekday visit.

Shoestring: East of Golfito and Pueblo Civil, the North American-run **Hotel Costa Rica Surf**, Apdo. 7, Golfito 8201, tel./fax 775-0034, on Calle Civil, has 29 dark rooms, plus a restaurant and bar. The hotel is favored by the surfing and budget crowd. Rooms vary: some have bunks; others have private baths and kitchenettes. There's a laundry. The American Legion meets here the first Tuesday of each month. Rates: $6 shared bath; $14 private bath and a/c. Monthly rentals cost $300.

Cabinas Isabel, tel. 775-1775, 800 meters north of central Pueblo Civil, has 14 clean but simple rooms (some are dingy) with fans, plus private bath and cold water. Rates: $5.50 pp. Near the Hotel Delfina, **Cabinas Mazuren,** tel. 775-0058, has basic box-like rooms. Rates: $4 pp ($5 with private bath). **Hotel El Uno,** tel. 775-0061, nearby, is also very basic and lacks windows—about what you could expect considering the cost. Rates: $3.

In the Zona Americana, **Hotel Golfito,** Apdo. 80, Golfito, tel. 775-0047, at the south end of the Muelle Bananero dock, has 14 very basic rooms with private cold-water baths and fans. Rates: $10 pp.

Near the Hotel del Cerro, a series of budget *cabinas,* including **Cabinas Marlin,** tel. 775-0191, **Cabinas Adelia, Cabinas Princesa del Golfo,** tel. 255-0442, and **Cabinas Wilson,** tel. 775-0795, all have basic rooms in the $5 category.

Cabinas Koktsur, tel. 775-1191, near the Depósito Libre, has eight simple, clean rooms in a well-kept old wooden home in a garden on the waterfront. Each has a fan plus a private bath with cold water. The hostess is very friendly. Rates: $12.50 s/d. **Cabinas El Manglar,** next door, is of a similar price and standard, as is **Hospedaje Corcovado,** 200 meters north.

Cabinas Casa Blanca, tel. 775-0124, 400 meters south of the Depósito Libre, has pleasing *cabinas* with fans, screens, and private baths with cold water in a house below the owner's home. Rates: $10 s/d. Opposite, in another home, is **Hospedaje Familiar,** tel. 775-0217, with a/c rooms, shared baths, and kitchen access. If you love ornamentals, you'll like this place. Rates: $10 pp. Also here is **Jardín Cervecero Alameda,** tel. 775-0126, 75 meters east of the duty-free zone, featuring cabins with private baths and hot water plus fans.

There are several cheap *cabinas* about 200 meters west of the Depósito Libre, on the road to Playa Cacao. Try **Cabinas Cristy,** an attractive modern two-story home painted pink and white. The three *very* budget *pensiones*—**Familiar, Minerva,** and **Cabinas Villa Mar**—that sit next to each other in a block midway between the north and south sections are for the truly desperate.

At Playa Cacao, the most unusual hotel for kilometers around is the aptly named **Shipwreck Hotel**—to be considered only by those with an appetite for hardy adventure. A one-legged sailor, Thomas Clairmont (alias Captain Tom), turned his wreck into a "hotel" when he washed ashore in 1954 after his boat capsized. Alas, Tom died in 1993 and the infamous bar where Tom told his tales is no longer operating. Tom's wife, Rocío, tel. 383-6093, still rents rooms onboard, but it's as dour as you'll find in the country. There's electricity, but no hot water or fans. You share the toilet in Captain Tom's house, nearby. Tom and Rocío's daughter, Lulu, will cook for you ($2). Rates: $4 pp. You can also **camp** in the front yard.

Budget: Cabinas Mar y Luna, tel. 775-0192, fax 775-0149, has eight spacious *cabinas* with a double and single beds, and large private bath and hot water. They're simple, but clean and adequate. It sits over the water and has a reputable restaurant. Rates: $19 s/d/t.

Hotel Delfina, tel. 775-0043, 400 meters south of the dock in the center of town, has 12 rooms: some with ocean views, most with shared bath. Rates: $5 pp shared bath (some without windows), $10 private bath, $22 with a/c.

The **La Purruja Lodge,** tel. 775-1054, four km east of Golfito, is a great bargain. It has five attractive modern *cabinas* with lots of windows, and is set amid landscaped lawns on a hill overlooking a forested valley. Swiss owner Walter Rosenberg offers hiking tours to Corcovado. Rates: $15 s, $20 d, $25 t. Breakfasts cost $2.50, dinner $3.50, and barbecue $6. There's a **camping** area ($4 per tent).

Hotel del Cerro, tel. 775-0006, fax 775-0551, opposite the old United Fruit dock (Muelle Ba-

nanaero), has 20 spotlessly clean albeit basic rooms with private baths, hot water, fans, and large single beds. There's an open-air restaurant upstairs, plus free laundry. The owner crams in more beds and bunks for the weekend shoppers. There's a TV in the upstairs lounge and art on display. The Chinese owner offers boat tours to a private island where you can see birdlife and caimans in the mangrove swamps. Rates (upstairs): $10-25 pp with private bath. It also has $5 "backpacker" rooms with shared baths.

The best bargain is the **Hotel Sierra,** Apdo. 5304, San José 1000, tel. 233-9693, fax 233-9715; or Apdo. 37, Golfito, tel. 775-0666, fax 775-0087, between the airport and the duty-free zone, with 72 well-lit, modestly furnished a/c rooms with jade-tile floors, TVs, private baths, telephones, and room service. There's a pool with wet bar, a children's pool, plus a restaurant, a bar, and a disco. The hotel was closed for 18 months and reopened in 1997, but receives few visitors midweek. Rates: $27 s/d, $31 t, $35 quad.

Nearby, the modern **Golfo Azul Hotel,** formerly the Hotel Costa Sur, tel. 775-0801, fax 775-1849, has 20 pleasing, spic-and-span, a/c rooms with lofty ceilings, fans, and private baths with hot water. There's a small restaurant downstairs in the old home, which also has four basic rooms without a/c. Rates: $18 s, $15 d with fans only; $22 s, $27 d with a/c.

A stone's throw away is **Jardín Cervecero Alamedas,** tel. 775-0126, a modern two-story structure with six large, well-lit *cabinas* with lofty ceilings, hardwood floors, fans, and private baths with cold water. Each has a double, a single, and a bunk bed. The restaurant is adjacent in an old home. Rates: $17 s, $21 d, $23 t, $27 quad.

Inexpensive: In Pueblo Civil, **Hotel y Restaurante el Gran Ceibo,** tel. 775-0403, at the far east end of Golfito, has 27 rooms in modern two-story and one-story units. Rooms vary but all have cool tile floors and handsome bathrooms. Ten rooms have a/c and hot water. There's a pleasant open-air restaurant, plus a swimming pool and kids' pool. Rates: $25 s/d with fan; $35 s/d with a/c.

Las Gaviotas, alias the Yacht Club, Apdo. 12, Golfito 8201, tel. 775-0062, fax 775-0544, 100 meters east of Gran Ceibo, has 21 modest and slightly dowdy *cabinas* with private porches and spacious tiled bathrooms with large showers.

The outdoor restaurant overlooks the gulf and serves excellent seafood plus expensive breakfasts. There's a pool, a sundeck, and a souvenir shop, plus scarlet macaws in the garden. Yachts anchor at the basic wharf. Rates: $42 s/d, $48 t; $52 with a/c and kitchenette. *Overpriced!*

Centro Turístico Samoa del Sur, tel. 775-0233, on the waterfront, has *cabinas* with fans, TVs, and private baths with hot water. There's a restaurant and disco here at night. The owners rent bicycles and boats. Rates: $28 s, $37 d.

Moderate: At Playa Cacao, **Isa's Place** (formerly Rancho-Not-So-Neato), Apdo. 201, Golfito, tel. 385-9622, fax 775-0373, is an eccentric charmer with six African-style thatch-roofed, tile-floored cottages, each with two beds, fan, refrigerator, and private bathroom with hot water. Three have kitchens. A master suite was being added, as was a restaurant that promises exquisite cuisine (Isabel, who is Austrian, is a master chef). Also being added when I called in was a small, rambling clover-leaf swimming pool fed by a multitiered cascade falling from a jacuzzi set in the hillside. Isa's offers horseback rides and deep-sea fishing (there are two boats and it has its own dock). You can rent canoes. There's a laundry. If there's nobody there, ask for Sheila or Isabel at the log cabin on the left where the road meets the beach. Rates: $50 low season; $65 d high season ($75 with breakfast). There's also a fantastic octagonal open-plan apartment—**Casa Grande**—of rough-hewn logs and stone centered on an octagonal kitchenette; it has a loft bedroom with queen-size bed, plus two double beds downstairs (rate: $110 d).

Food
La Dama del Delfín, tel. 775-0235, fax 775-0042, opposite Hotel Costa Surf, is a meeting spot for expats eager to start their day with omelettes, pancakes, and other hearty breakfasts cooked by owner Judy Goll, who whips up burgers and fries, peanut butter sandwiches, and killer strawberry margaritas (among other things).

El Balcón, above the Hotel Costa Rica Surf, is advertised by a windsurf sail hanging outside. You can nibble buffalo wings and other appetizers, and medicinal teas are served. The restaurant in the **Hotel del Cerro** is said to serve acclaimed ceviche.

The **Restaurante la Eurekita,** on the main road, opens at 6 a.m. and is popular for its *refrescos* and bay vistas. It has a wide international menu. The **Heladería La Deliciosa,** serving ice cream, is adjacent; it serves sundaes, banana splits, and other yummy favorites.

A popular spot is the **Restaurante Mar y Luna,** acclaimed for its fresh seafood served in copious portions, with tropical decor to boot. It's open Tues.-Sun. 7 a.m.-10 p.m. Alternatively, try the thatch-roofed **Samoa,** which offers a wide choice, from burgers ($2) and pizzas to paella and seafood. The portions are filling, and my *corvina al ajillo* (garlic sea bass; $5) was splendid. The thatched **Palenque Las Bruncas,** 100 meters south of Samoa, also specializes in seafood.

There are a few Chinese restaurants. Try **Restaurant Gran Victoria,** tel. 775-1729, in an aged wooden home near Muelle Bananero; or, in Pueblo Civil, **Restaurante Hong Kong,** or the venerable **Restaurante Uno.**

The American-run **Rio de Janeiro Restaurant,** tel. 775-0509, cooks burgers, barbecued ribs, and steaks ($2-12). Also popular with locals is **Pequeño Restaurant,** tel. 775-0220. **Restaurante Siete Mares, Jardín Cervecero Alameda,** and **Bar Mariscos del Sur Restaurante** serve good seafood.

Other personal favorites include **La Cubana** and **Café Coconut.**

Entertainment
There's a **public swimming pool** in the Zona Americana ($1.25), popular with locals on weekends.

Samoa has a dart board, table soccer, and a pool table, plus music at the bar. An old jukebox plays outdated tunes at the lively **El Balcón,** but there's also a library of 1,000 cassettes—from classical to rock—for the tape deck, and live music each Wednesday and Saturday. The **Bar La Bomba** upstairs in the Hotel Costa Rica Surf, is another lively bar. There's a Latin dance club downstairs on Sunday nights (75 cents).

Discos include the **Palenque** and **Club Latino.** The aforementioned **El Balcón** is a popular watering hole, as is the **Marea Baja Discotheque,** tel. 775-0139. The latest addition is the **Gemini Disco,** tel. 775-0681, with its own seafood restaurant.

Land-Sea Tours (see below) has a rustic little lounge with a book exchange, dart board, and CD player.

Information and Tourist Services

Your first resource should be **Land-Sea Tours,** Servicios Terra-Sur, Apdo. 113, Golfito, tel./fax 775-1614, e-mail: landsea@sol.racsa.co.cr, run by Katie Duncan, a friendly and helpful gringa who knows the local scene like the back of her hand. Land-Sea is a one-stop, full-service tourist center. It acts as an airline, tour, and hotel reservation center. Katie offers secretarial services. You can send and receive faxes ($2), and make international calls. There's storage and a yachters service. She rents Suzuki Samurai jeeps ($50 per day) and surfboards ($25 per day). And Katie offers tours ($35), including to the Golfito Wildlife Refuge, the Río Coto swamps, and horseback riding in the jungle with **Tres Amigos Horseback Tours.**

La Dama del Delfin also has a tourist information and real estate center, plus souvenirs; like Katie, Judy Goll has checkers and dominoes at hand. Also try **Golfito Centro,** tel. 775-0449, next to the Hotel Costa Rica Surf. Rodolfo Hernandez, tel. 775-0230, will act as local guide; Land-Sea Tours can recommend other guides.

A 45-foot sailing vessel—the *Anastasia*—offers **cruises of Golfo Dulce** including a visit to Casa de Orquídeas ($150 pp per day).

Services

There's a **laundry** service (Lavandería Elona) downtown, and at Land-Sea Tours ($1.50 per kg).

Golfito has an **immigration office,** tel. 775-0487. The **police** (Guardia Rural) post is in front of the Depósito Libre. There are branches of **Banco Nacional,** tel. 775-0323, in the Depósito Libre and on the main road. You can make withdrawals with your Visa and MasterCard at both banks. The **Banco de Costa Rica** at the Depósito Libre has an international ATM machine.

Eager for a good paperback? Two places— the all-purpose El Balcón, above Hotel Costa Rica Surf, and Land-Sea Tours—both have **book exchanges.**

Sportfishing and Other Activities

Many sportfishing vessels are berthed here. Prime season for sailfish is Dec.-May; for marlin, June-Sept.; and for snook, May-September. Private skippers are listed around town. They come and go with the seasons, however, so check with Katie at Land-Sea Tours (see above), next to the **Banana Bay Marina,** tel. 775-0838, VHF 16/11, formerly Eagle's Roost Marina. **Leomar Sportfishing and Diving,** Apdo. 14, Golfito, tel. 775-0230, fax 775-0373, offers sportfishing aboard a seven-meter Aquasport. **Golfito Sailfish Rancho,** tel. 235-7766; in the U.S., P.O. Box 290190, San Antonio, TX 78280, fax (512) 377-0454, specializes in sportfishing packages.

Yak-Yak Kayaks, tel./fax 775-1179, at Hotel Las Gaviotas, has sea kayak rentals for $8/10 per hour and $45/65 per day, single-/twin-seat kayaks. It also offers guided trips.

Getting There and Away

By Air: SANSA and **Travelair** operate scheduled flights to Golfito (see appendix). **Aeronaves,** tel. 775-0278; in San José, tel. 232-1413, **Aero Costa Sol,** tel. 775-0607; in San José, tel. 441-1444, and other air charter companies have offices at the south end of the airstrip.

By Bus: Direct buses depart San José (Tracopa, tel. 775-0365 or 221-4214), from Avenida 18, Calles 2/4 daily at 7 a.m., 11 a.m., and 3 p.m. (eight hours, $5); an indirect bus leaves at 6:30 a.m. The Zona Sur bus to Ciudad Neily and Paso Canoas will drop you at Río Claro, where you can catch an hourly bus from Ciudad Neily to Golfito.

Tracopa buses depart Golfito for San José at 7:30 a.m., 11:30 a.m., 12:30 p.m., and 4 p.m. (Sunday at 7:30 a.m. and 11:30 a.m. only). Buses depart for Ciudad Neily hourly from Club Latino; buses to Zancudo depart the Muellecito (the little dock immediately north of the gas station in the center of Golfito) at 1:30 p.m.; and for Puerto Jiménez from the Muelle at 11 a.m.

By Boat: Golfito is a popular port-of-call for yachters. Immigration and the **port captain,** tel. 775-0487 (open Mon.-Fri. 7-11 a.m. and 12:30-4 p.m.), are beside the old Muelle Bananero dock. Most yachties berth at the Banana Bay Marina, tel. 775-0838 (50 cents per foot nightly, plus electricity).

Association ABOCOP, tel. 775-0712, opposite the ICE, operates **water-taxis** to Playa Cacao, Punta Encanto, Zancudo, and Puerto Jiménez from the waterfront facing Muelle Bananero. Other water-taxis operate a regular schedule to Playa Cacao (about $3), Playa Zancudo (about $8), and other beaches from the dock just south of Banco Costa Rica. Many locals also offer boat services to Zancudo and Playa Cacao; try **Rodolfo**, tel. 775-0348, or the **Burbujas de Amor**, tel. 775-0472.

For ferry services, refer to the **Getting There and Away** section in Puerto Jiménez, above.

Getting Around

Buses run between the two ends of town. *Colectivos* also cruise up and down and will run you anywhere in town for 75 cents, picking up and dropping off passengers along the way.

PIEDRAS BLANCAS~ "RAINFOREST OF THE AUSTRIANS"

In 1991, a tract of the Esquinas Forest north of Golfito and centered on the village of **La Gamba** was named Piedras Blancas and incorporated (as the Esquinas Sector) into Corcovado National Park. It has been a troubled park, as land within its bounds is still in private ownership, and logging permits issued before 1991 apparently remain valid. That year, Michael Schnitzler, a classical violist, founded the Regenwald der Österreicher ("Rainforest of the Austrians") to raise funds to buy land in the Esquinas Forest. By 1993, 1,200 hectares had been purchased and donated to the nation.

Local farmers in La Gamba decided to turn to ecotourism as an alternative source of income. In turn, in 1993 the Austrian government decided to underwrite the local population's efforts to save the forest, and "Rainforest of the Austrians" was appointed to oversee and direct the project. A cooperative was formed to provide income for 25 families whose members are employed at Esquinas Rainforest Lodge and on fruit farms and a botanical garden. In time, the cooperative will become owner of the lodge. Plans are to create a "megapark" linking Esquinas to Corcovado National Park and Golfito National Wildlife Refuge. Trails are being opened up through the forest. A guide ($15) is strongly recommended.

The "Rainforest of the Austrians" also operates **La Gamba Biological Station** in conjunction with the University of Vienna through a grant of the Austrian government. The station, on land adjoining the Esquinas Rainforest Lodge, is open to any student or biologist wishing to study there.

Punta Encantado, Playa San Josecito, and Playa Cativo

Playa San Josecito, about 10 km northwest and a 25-minute boat ride from Golfito, is a wide, lonesome, shingly brown-sand beach, popular for day-trips from town. The shoreline forms part of the Esquinas Sector of Corcovado National Park and is good for nature hikes, with monkeys, sloths, and prolific birdlife. The jungle sweeps right down to the shore, as it does at Playa Cativo, 10 km farther northwest. Dolphins swim thick as sardines close to shore.

Casa de Orquídeas, Apdo. 69, Golfito, tel. 775-0353 (leave a message), is a private botanical garden at the northwest end of Playa San Josecito. This labor of love culminates the 20-odd-year efforts of Ron and Trudy MacAllister, who lead fascinating and illuminating tours (school groups are encouraged). Masses of ornamental plants attract zillions of birds. There's a trail through the jungle. Two-hour guided tours are offered Sun.-Thurs. at 8:15 a.m. ($5 entrance, with guided tour). Zancudo Boat Tours, tel./fax 776-0012, e-mail: loscocos@zancudo.com, runs tours to the garden; otherwise take a water-taxi from Golfito or any of the local lodges.

Accommodations

Esquinas: At **La Gamba Biological Station**, Regenwald der Österreicher, Sternwartestrasse 58, A-1180 Vienna, Austria, tel. (431) 470-4297, fax 470-4295, accommodates eight people in a small, self-contained farmhouse. Rates: $6 pp.

Esquinas Rainforest Lodge, tel. 775-0131, fax 775-0631; in San José, tel. 227-7924, fax 226-3957, next to a burbling stream amid landscaped grounds, is a stone's throw from the entrance to Piedras Blancas. It's built of natural stone and tiles to minimize use of tropical hardwoods. Five cabins sit atop a hill and are connected by a covered walkway to the main lodge. Each of the 10 rooms has rattan furniture and bright tropical colors, plus private bath, fan, tiled floors, and a shady veranda with easy chairs and hammocks. The main building features an open-walled lounge offering views of the forest. Highlights include a bar, gift shop, library, and

splendid thatched dining room plus naturally fil-
tered swimming pool. Trails lead through the
cacao and bananas groves and botanical gardens (which attract toucans, parrots, and other
exotic birds), and beyond into the rainforest. No
more than 25 people at a time are allowed, to
minimize impact on wildlife. Excursions include
half-day tours of the coast, Río Coto mangroves,
and Playa Cacao and a full-day rainforest hike.
Three- to 10-day packages are offered in combination with nearby lodges. The lodge is six km
from the Pan-Am Highway turnoff at Km 37 in
Villa Briceño (4WD not required). Alternately,
you can hike in from Golfito. Rates: $95 s, $130
d, $135 t, including three meals and taxes. Mul-
tiday packages offer discounts.

**Punta Encantado: Punta Encantado/En-
chanted Point,** tel. 735-5062 or 789-9713, fax
735-5043; in the U.S., P.O. Box 481, Chautauqua,
NY 14722, is a comfortable yet casual log-and-
bamboo lodge with matching rattan furniture
tucked into the jungled shoreline. There's six
rooms with private baths and ceiling fans. Somerset Maugham would have felt at home. Family-
style meals and beach barbecues keep you fed.
You'll find a *ranchito* bar down on the beach,
which has a small coral reef offshore. It offers
scuba, snorkeling, and sportfishing. The week
after full moon, the phosphorescent bay is a
spawning ground for *aguja* (needlefish). The only
way to get here is by water-taxi. Not inspected.
Rates: $95 s, $65 d pp, including all meals and
transfer from Golfito (three-day package only).

Golfito Sailfish Rancho, tel. 235-7766; in
the U.S., P.O. Box 290190, San Antonio, TX
78280, fax (512) 377-0454, the sportfishing lodge
run by lively Texan Ginny Cotner 15 minutes by
boat from Golfito, closed down in 1996 but may
be open again.

Playa San Josecito: The Swiss-run **Golfo
Dulce Lodge,** Apdo. 137-8201, Golfito, tel./fax
775-0373, surrounded by 275 hectares of privately owned primary and secondary forest
(much of it incorporated into Piedras Blancas
park), has five handsome wooden bungalows
plus a brick cabin with bamboo furnishings, large
veranda with hammocks, and tiled bathrooms.
There's a small swimming pool and a *rancho*-
style restaurant and bar. Sea kayaking, horseback riding, hikes, and excursions are offered.
Electricity is supplied by a Pelton wheel; water is

recycled; and sewage is treated in septic tanks.
Rates: $115 s, $170 d, $215 t low season; $130
s, $200 d, $255 t high season, including boat
transfers, all meals, and taxes. Multiday packages offer discounts.

Casa de Orquídeas, Apdo. 69, Golfito, tel.
775-0353 (leave a message), has a lone two-
room cabin for four people, with kitchenette, private bathroom, and solar electricity ($125 d five
nights; $150 weekly, including transfers); bring
your own food.

Nearby is **Dolphin Quest,** Apdo. 141, Golfito,
tel. 775-1481 (leave a message for Raymond) or
775-1742, fax 775-0363; in the U.S., P.O. Box
107, Duncan Mills, CA 95430, a unique, rustic,
back-to-basics getaway for folks whose idea of a
good time is swimming with dolphins and hanging out with the alternative-lifestyle set. The
wooden nature lodge, on a beach surrounded by
700 acres of forested mountainside 13 km north
of Golfito, is run "in harmony with nature" by
Amy Khoo and Raymond Klchko, who operate
New Age scientific studies (telepathic communication, herb garden, etc.) on dolphins. They
offer scuba, snorkeling, kayaking (free to guests),
and horseback rides. Plans included a hot tub
and swimming pool. Spanish lessons, massages,
and acupuncture are offered. Trails lead into the
forest. The lodge is accessible only by boat and
you *must* call ahead to arrange transportation.
Lodging includes five ranchos, three cozy *casitas,* four rooms, and a dormitory for 15. Rates
(including all meals): $35 dorm; $50s, $80 d
cabin; $25 camping. Reductions for work-share
and groups. Children 7-14 free.

Playa Cativo: Rainbow Adventures Lodge,
Apdo. 63, Golfito, tel. 775-0220; in the U.S.—
and recommended by the owner for faster
replies—5875 N.W. Kaiser Rd., Portland, OR
97229, tel. (503) 690-7750, fax 690-7735, is on a
private nature reserve at Playa Cativo, 20 km
northwest of Golfito (much of the property lies
within Corcovado National Park). The sturdily
handsome three-story lodge—run by a Virginian,
John Lovell—is constructed of hardwoods and
set in a lush, landscaped garden. Antiques and
beautiful rugs adorn the walls, and vases are full
of fresh-cut flowers. Three double rooms with private baths open onto ocean-view verandas.
There's a penthouse suite on the third level, plus
exquisite, handcrafted *cabinas* (with two bed-

rooms and private bathrooms) on the grounds. Solar heating provides warm water. There's also an open-air dining terrace. The lodge offers free use of snorkeling gear, boats for hire ($35 per hour with guide and fishing equipment), and guided tours to Corcovado ($4 pp), which begin virtually on the back doorstep. No road access; instead, it's a 45-minute boat journey. Be warned: There's no dock at the lodge and you may need to hike in over sandy tidal flats after jumping into thigh-deep water (you may wish to take into account any physical infirmity). You can request a video of the lodge and region. Rates: $100-150 s, $150-180 d, including all meals and transportation from Golfito (you're picked up from the boat dock near Las Gaviotas in Golfito). Children under four free. Yachts anchor for free.

Rainbow Adventures also recently built the **Buena Vista Beach & Jungle Lodge** on a private sandy beach about 800 meters away (inquiries and reservations as above). I haven't yet visited. The following is provided by owner Michael Medill: "The open-air main house has the lounge and dining area. Nearby are two two-story buildings each with four double rooms with private baths. All are constructed of hardwoods and have spectacular jungle and ocean views. The grounds are lush, with the jungle at your doorstep. Solar-heated water." But one reader has written to complain about "small rooms without views, no mirrors (like shaving while camping) and unscreened windows in the bathrooms; and they ran out of food!" The rates are the same as Rainbow Adventures Lodge.

Cabinas Caña Blanca, Apdo. 34, Golfito; David Corella; c/o fax 775-0373, offers two handsome cabins on the next cove north of Cativo. Each cabin has a stove and refrigerator (don't forget to bring your own food). Rates: $70 d, or three-day packages for $179 d (cook for yourself) or $399 d including all meals, transfers, river tour, and fishing.

PLAYA ZANCUDO

Playa Zancudo, strung below the estuary of the Río Coto Colorado, is one of my favorite spots, exuding a South Seas feel. Absolutely ultimate! The ruler-straight gray-sand beach (littered with coconuts) stretches about six km along a slender spit backed by the eerie mangroves of the Coto Swamps. The fishing is good in the fresh water (there are several docks on the estuary side) and in the surf at the wide rivermouth. The beach is splendid for swimming, windsurfing and, when the waves are up, surfing. (Avoid it at dusk, and during the full moon, when the no-see-ums are voracious.)

The tiny hamlet of Zancudo (which, remarkably, has a Patagonia clothing outlet) is at the north end of the spit, reached along a sandy rollercoaster of a track along which a few dozen North American and European residents have chosen to live a laid-back life beneath the palms (as one gringo told me, "It's a party town—most of the gringos are out of their heads"). There are some interesting characters here, including a willowy German named Monika Hara and her hubbie, "Chino" Bob, a Japanese-American from California, who accept donations for the local school. Zancudo is also popular with locals from Golfito on weekends, when it can get quite crowded.

On my recent research trip, there were hardly any visitors—thanks to a U.S. State Department travel advisory issued ostensibly to help tourists avoid the risk of getting in the middle of land disputes in the area but actually intended as a bit of political arm-twisting.

Zancudo is only 10 km from Golfito as the crow flies, but driving there is another thing. The village is 44 km from the Pan-Am Highway.

Río Coto Swamps
This swampy estuary (also known as El Atrocha) is fed by the waters of the Río Coto Colorado and is a great place for a waterbound nature trip into La Etrocha and other mangrove-lined river channels. You'll pass it by water-taxi en route between Golfito and Zancudo. Waterfowl are plentiful. And with luck you may see crocodiles and caimans basking on the riverbanks, motionless as logs, as well as monkeys and river otters. One night a fully grown caiman (or was it a juvenile crocodile?) crossed my path as I was driving from Zancudo to Pavones.

Sue and Andrew Robertson offer trips through **Zancudo Boat Tours** at Cabinas Los Cocos, tel./fax 776-0012, e-mail: loscocos@zancudo.com. Captain Franz (c/o Land-Sea Tours, in Golfito) offers a four-hour "Crocodile Trip" for $35 pp. And guide Joseph Rousseau offers trips from Golfito.

Accommodations

The following are in order along the road south to north.

Residencias Arco Iris, tel. 776-0069, is a home for rent. **Los Cocodrilos Surfeadores,** tel. 776-0052, formerly Cabinas La Vista, is a laid-back place popular with surfers. It has three simple *cabinas* in varnished hardwoods on stilts over the beach; each has a large, well-lit private bathroom, ceiling fans, and hammocks. There's also a house with six rooms. The restaurant is a local hangout. Trails lead through surrounding jungle and mangroves. Rates: $30 s/d/t *cabinas;* $10 pp rooms.

Cabinas Luna Linda, one km north, has very handsome wood-and-thatch cabins, but was for sale in January 1998.

The node of local action is **Cabinas Sol y Mar,** Apdo. 87, Golfito, tel. 776-0014, fax 776-0015, e-mail: solymar@zancudo.com, website www.zancudo.com, amid landscaped grounds, 1.5 km north of Los Cocodrilos. It boasts a pleasant casual ambience. The four simple *cabinas* (two are geodesic domes) and larger rooms are tastefully furnished with canvas sofas, Guatemalan bedspreads, ceiling fans, and private skylit bathrooms with hot water and pebble-and-tile floors. *Nice!* There's volleyball and other games, plus a small restaurant housing a bar popular with locals. It's run by Californians, Rick and Lori, who also sell batikwear. Rates: $28 s, $36 d for *cabinas* (third person free), $40 for "honeymoon" suites. The couple also has a three-story oceanfront cottage for four people ($550 monthly).

Casa Tranquilidad Bed & Breakfast, tel. 776-0151, fax 776-0153, e-mail: aerolanc@sol.racsa.co.cr, is a self-sufficient cabin with kitchen for $200 per week.

Cabinas Los Cocos, tel./fax 776-0012, e-mail: loscocos@zancudo.com, about 600 meters north of Sol y Mar, has attractive, self-catering, oceanfront units tucked amid landscaped grounds with walkways lined with shells. One is a thatched, hardwood unit with a double bed downstairs and another in the loft; two others are venerable, refurbished banana company properties shipped from Palmar. Each has a kitchenette, mosquito nets, both inside and outside showers, and a veranda with hammocks. Rates: from $30 per night, $175 per week, $600 month (30% less in green season). The place is run by a delightful couple: Susan (a gringa) and Andrew (a Brit) Robertson.

Restaurant Suzy, 600 meters north, is a simple Tico-run place with modern *cabinas.*

Another half a kilometer brings you to the hamlet, where **Cabinas Froilan,** tel. 776-0102, opposite the *abastecedor* (grocery), has 24 basic cubicle-style *cabina* rooms with fans and private bath and cold water. Rates: $8 s, $15 d. Mauricio at **Cabinas Los Ranchitos,** tel./fax 776-0073, has two large two-story thatched cabins, each with four beds and private bathroom with tiled showers. Rates: $24 (up to four people). One has hot water. **El Coquito** has basic rooms with private baths and cold water. Rates: $8 pp. Things can get very noisy when the music is cranked up in the thatched bar. **Cabinas Las Palmeras,** tel. 776-0134, opposite Estero Mar, opened in late 1997 with five handsome new thatched *cabinas* with a/c and fans, private baths with hot water, and black tile floors. Rates: $33 d, 450 t/quad. A swimming pool was to be added.

Roy's Zancudo Lodge, Apdo. 41, Golfito, tel. 776-0008, fax 776-0011; in the U.S., 8406 Lopez Dr., Tampa, FL 33615, tel. (800) 515-7697, fax (813) 889-9189, 400 meters north of Estero Mar, is a sportfishing lodge with 10 screened *cabinas* set around lawns with palms and a small swimming pool. The two-tone green cabins each have beautiful hardwood floors, simple furnishings, private baths (no hot water), fans, and veranda. Larger units have a lounge and attractive fabrics. There's also a restaurant. The lodge—which closes each October—uses 22- to 25-foot center console boats Owner Roy Ventura arranges boat cruises and will ferry you by boat from Golfito. Rates: $75 pp. Three-day packages cost $1,655 s, $1,355 pp d; five-day packages cost $2,435 s, $1,935 pp d, including one night in San José, roundtrip airfare from San José to Golfito and boat transfer to Zancudo, plus meals, drinks, and accommodations at the lodge. Additional fishing days cost $375 s, $325 pp d.

Río Mar, tel. 775-0350, half a kilometer farther north near the tip of Zancudo, has basic cabins with private baths and fans. Rates: $17 d, $25 quad.

Somewhere near the village (I missed it) is the Tico-run **Restaurante y Cabinas Tranquilo,** tel. 776-0131, fax 776-0143, reportedly offering four rustic rooms of handsome hardwoods above the restaurant, with a double and single bed, and hammocks on the veranda. Two larger rooms are in a separate building. All share bathrooms and showers downstairs. There's a laundry. Rates: $6 s, $8 d, $10 t. Another option is **Cabinas Zancudo,** tel. 773-3027, with simple yet adequate *cabinas* facing the beach. Rates: $20 d. Also try **Hotel Pitier,** tel. 773-3027, which has basic but clean cabins ($7).

Lastly, Ecopavones—contact through **Cooprena,** Apdo. 6939-1000, San José, tel. 259-3401, fax 259-9430, e-mail: cooprena@sol.racsa. co.cr.—runs the **Eco-Agro Touristic Lodge** at Playa Langostino, two km from Zancudo. The main lodge has four rooms. There are also four rustic cabins (each with two rooms for three people each) and a restaurant, plus forest trails. There's no electricity. Rates: $35 s, $50 d, $45 t, including breakfast.

Food and Entertainment
For breakfast, head to **Cabinas Sol y Mar,** where the breakfast menu includes real omelettes, French toast, home fries, and homebaked breads and muffins, and a real espresso machine. Nightly specials include Mexican on Friday. Japanese dishes are served.

Macondo, tel. 776-0157, serves superb pizzas (Monday and Friday), homemade pasta, seafood, desserts, and more in a beautiful two-story restaurant with open decks. It's worth the drive. Open noon-3 p.m. and 5:30-9:30 p.m. Likewise, Alberto at **Los Cocodrilos Surfeadores** cooks up killer pasta and other Italian fare in the breezy upstairs restaurant overlooking the beach. The menu also includes seafood and *Tico* fare, served in generous portions, and there's a bar with VCR and tape cassette deck, plus musical instruments for impromptu jam sessions.

Sol y Mar serves American breakfasts, burgers, and "Western-style" food with an Italian and California twist. The nightly special when I visited was tuna with capers, rice, choyote squash and green beans with roasted pepper sauce ($6). Yummm! The bar is a local meeting spot. A volleyball game is hosted Saturday, horseshoes on Sunday.

For quality *típico* meals, head to **Restaurante Tranquilo,** where Doña María serves seafood and meat dishes accompanied by tasty homemade bread. **Restaurante y Bar Los Ranchitos** offers ceviche, lobster, and *típico* dishes, and has barbecue on Friday; *bocas* are served with beers. **Restaurante Rancho El Coquito,** next door, serves good local fare fresh to order and in huge portions. Both spots, and **Estero Mar,** 200 meters north, host occasional dances favored by locals. Expats and surfers gravitate to **Hans' Jungle Club** (La Jungla), at the south end of Zancudo, playing progressive dance music on weekends. Happening!

The two *pulperías* sell a modicum of fresh produce and groceries. Every Tuesday, a chap called Willy comes into town with produce.

Tours and Activities
Captain Steve Lino's **Golfito Sportfishing,** tel. 288-5083 or 775-0268, fax 775-0373, has a nine-meter sportfishing boat for charter ($350 a day for two people, including lunch and drinks). **Big Al's Sportfishing,** tel. 776-0016, e-mail: bigals@zancudo.com, charges $275 d a day; his office is near Macondo. **El Pez Volador,** tel. 282-7437, fax 282-7241; in the U.S., tel. (800) 308-3394, is a fully equipped 28-foot center console sportfishing boat used for fishing packages, with accommodations at a two-bedroom house with kitchen, and full-time cook and housekeeper.

Zancudo Boat Tours, tel./fax 776-0012, e-mail: loscocos@zancudo.com, rents surfboards, paddleboats, and snorkeling equipment. Susan and Andrew also offer nature trips up the Río Coto as well as to the Casa de Orquídeas botanical gardens and to snorkeling spots (from $15 d, per hour). Surfers can reshape their boards at Cocodrilo Surfeadores. **Golfo Dulce Realty,** tel. 775-0105, has an "express boat service," snorkeling, and snorkel gear rentals.

BOB RACE

You can rent **mountain bikes** from Wally Hastings ($10 a day, $50 a week).

Services

There are **public telephones** at Estero Mar, tel. 775-0056, and outside Restaurante Froilan.

Getting There and Away

By Car: The paved road to Zancudo begins about eight km south of the Pan-Am Highway, midway along the road to Golfito; turn right at El Rodeo Salon, in Únion. An aging two-car ferry will transport you across the Río Coto, 18 km beyond El Rodeo; the ferry operates daily 5 a.m.-9 p.m. ($1 per car, 20 cents pedestrians). The wiry locals—often bare-chested—who operate the motor look as if they were born in the reeds of the river edge with the crocodiles; someday soon a bridge may put the ferry men out of work. On the south bank, the intermittently paved road runs five km to a Y-junction (La Cruce) at Pueblo Nuevo; turn right for Zancudo and Pavones and continue about 10 km to a T-junction at Conte. Turn right here: Zancudo (18 km) and Pavones (22 km) are signed. The road divides two km along; take the right-hand fork for Zancudo and the left for Pavones.

You can buy **gasoline** in Zancudo at Abastacedor Froilan and Cabinas Río Mar.

By Bus: A bus departs from outside La Bomba Bar at the municipal dock in Golfito for Zancudo daily at 2 p.m. Another departs Ciudad Neily for Zancudo at 1:30 p.m.

By Boat: A water-taxi departs Golfito's public dock for Zancudo daily at 6 a.m. and noon, returning from Zancudo one hour later ($2). **Zancudo Boat Tours** also offers service ($8). Another local boatman, **Fernando Sandé**, tel. 783-4090, reportedly goes to Zancudo in the midafternoon Monday, Wednesday, Friday, and Saturday. You can also hire a private boat at the dock (about $15). Casa Tranquilidad has an "air-boat" water-taxi.

Getting Around

You can walk everywhere, but Zancudo is stretched out over several kilometers. Rent a bike from Los Cocos or Macondo, or take a ride with Mike Cansini (c/o Sol y Mar)—described affectionately by his pals as "fucked up"—in his VW beetle, a piece of "rolling sculpture."

PAVONES TO PUNTA BANCO

From Conte, a bumpy potholed road clambers over the hills south of Zancudo and drops to Punta Pilón and Pavones, a legend in the surfing world for possessing the longest wave in the world—more than a kilometer on a good day. The waves are at their best, apparently, during rainy season, when surfers flock for the legendary very-fast-and-very-hollow tubular left. Best surfing months—April through October—are also the rainiest. Riptides are common and swimmers should pay attention to the tides: swim only on an *incoming* tide.

The fishing village of Pavones, which is backed by hills clad in rainforest, is no more than a string of houses and *cabinas* (multiplying in numbers year by year), a restaurant, and a *pulpería* next to the soccer field. There are no phones. Surfboards are available for rent. And the fishing for tarpon and snook is good right from shore.

South from Pavones, the dirt road crosses the Río Claro and follows the dramatically rocky coast about five km to the tiny beach community of Punta Banco, at the easternmost naze of Golfo Dulce. Punta Banco boasts a *pulpería* and cantina, plus a church, school and soccer field. A waterfall and swimming hole next to Rancho El Borica provides cooling dips if you tire of the sea. About two km south of Punta Banco you reach the end of the road. From here, the Peninsula de Burica sweeps southeast 50 km to Punta Burica along a lonesome stretch of coast called **La Estrechura.** Estrechura lies within the **Reserva Indígena Guyamí,** protecting the jungle-covered mountainous lands of the Guaymi Indians.

The region recently went through a period of land disputes that have resulted in the area getting negative press. *Tourists are not affected,* and when I passed through the place was as calm as could be, despite the simmering tensions.

Tiskita Lodge

Farm. Nature lodge. Exotic-fruit station. Biological reserve. Seaside retreat. **Tiskita Lodge,** Costa Rica Sun Tours, Apdo. 1195, Escazú 1250, tel. 255-3418, fax 255-4410; also see **Accommodations,** below) is all these and more. Situated at 400 meters atop Punta Banco, one

PAVONES AND COSTA RICA'S UGLY LAND DISPUTES

Pavones' problems date back to the 1980s, when the United Fruit Co. pulled out of the region, and wealthy gringos—including FBI fugitive Robert Vesco—bought up large tracts of coastal property. In 1988, one of the landowners—Danny Fowlie—was convicted of drug trafficking and ended up in the slammer. His attorney parceled off the land and sold it—to himself and other gringos. The government, however, issued an expropriate decree for Fowlie's lands (although the authroities have yet to enact the decree). Squatters—*precaristas*—also rushed in to claim it. A violent showdown between those who had bought parcels and squatters ended in a fatality in 1992.

Tensions continued to simmer and exploded again in November 1997, when a 79-year-old U.S. cattle breeder and a squatter shot each other to death. The uneducated *campesinos*, it is claimed, are being manipulated by left-wing agitators and crooked land speculators who have arranged for gangs of *precaristas* to intimidate legal owners and invade their farmland to gain title. (Under Costa Rican law, a settler who remains on a piece of land for three months gains right of usufruct; after a year, he is nearly impossible to evict. Eventually, the squatter can legally claim the land.) Several gringo landowners have had their homes burned down after evicting squatters. The vote-conscious government has been hesitant to enforce the law, while the local police have proved too timid to act against the *precaristas*.

Meanwhile, Fowlie claims that his lawyer had no right to sell his land and promises to claim his land back once released from prison. Clearly this sad situation is heading for an ugly denouement.

Ecopavones is a local cooperative dedicated to assisting local farmers who have had to struggle for their land. Food and lodging is available, as are guided hikes, to help integrate the families into ecotourism. For more information, contact **Cooprena**, Apdo. 6939-1000, San José, tel. 259-3401, fax 259-9430, e-mail: cooprena@sol.racsa.co.cr.

---

km north of the village, Tiskita—the Guaymi name for "fish eagle"—garners gentle sea breezes and proffers sweeping panoramas of the Pacific and the Osa Peninsula. The rustic old farmhouse that serves as the lodge is surrounded by 150 hectares of privately owned virgin rainforest, with pools for swimming and a Minotaur's maze of extensive trails, perfect for nature lovers; one leads to the beach (most follow the ridges, in old Indian fashion). Sixteen stops along the rainforest trail describe the vegetation and ecology of the region. A booklet helps birders identify scarlet-rumped and blue-gray tanagers, toucans, laughing hawks, blue parrots, macaws, and others; a similar one describes Tiskita tide pools for beachcombers. One trail leads sharply uphill to a series of cascades and pools. Guided birding hikes are offered by request.

Owner Peter Aspinall's pride and joy is his tropical-fruit farm, which contains the most extensive collection of tropical fruits in Costa Rica, a kind of botanical garden redolent with odors and birdcalls. Peter plans on setting up a pulp mill to sell pulp for juices. Peter, who was raised as a child locally and farmsteaded the property in the 1970s and has reforested vast acres of former pasture, is also actively involved in plans to release scarlet macaws locally, as well as being instrumental in the Tiskita Foundation Sea Turtle Restoration Project.

Tiskita Foundation
Sea Turtle Restoration Project

Endangered ridley turtles (plus hawksbill and green turtles in lesser numbers) come to lay their eggs along these shores, predominantly Aug.-December. The locals have long considered them a resource to be harvested for eggs and meat, and the majority of female turtles have had their nests poached.

In 1996, the Earth Island Institute began a program to educate the local community and instill a conservation ethic. It initiated a program to collect and hatch turtle eggs. Locals are now paid with groceries to bring in turtle eggs in good condition. Eggs are placed in a nursery to be incubated and the hatchlings then released directly into the ocean, dramatically increasing their chance of survival. Poaching of nests has been reduced from 100% of nests in 1995 to 19% in 1998, when the hatcheries achieved a 76% hatching rate for translocated eggs. Three hatcheries were in operation in January 1998. Local Guaymi Indian chief, Rafael Bejarano, has expressed a desire to extend the project south to protect the turtle population of Estrechura.

Fundación Tiskita operates a small arts and crafts store (open Tuesday, Friday, and Sunday 3-5 p.m.) in Punta Banco. Profits go to local artisans and the foundation's conservation and reforestation projects, as well as efforts to save the turtles.

Accommodations and Food

Pavones: Two cheap options include **Esquina del Mar**, a *soda* with basic rooms above the bar ($10 d); and **Pavón Tico,** another cantina with four basic rooms. If they're full try Doña María Jiménez, who has a couple of *cabinas* for about $5 pp. **Hotel Maureen** is set amid lush grounds and has six small albeit high-ceilinged, hardwood rooms in a two-story unit (each sleeps four people); they share four bathrooms. Rates: $8 pp. It has a restaurant serving *típico* dishes; open 6 a.m.-10 p.m.

About two km south of the Río Claro is **Casa Impact,** tel. 775-0637; in the U.S., tel. (407) 683-1429, tucked amid lush rainforest and fruit trees on the hill above the hamlet, 200 yards from the beach. This surfers' paradise has two bare-bones rooms in the octagonal lodge, each with two double bunk beds and shared bath with hot showers. A separate, large, spartan octagonal cabin has floor-to-ceiling screens instead of exterior walls, plus its own kitchen and private bath. There's a lounge with TV/VCR, and a large sky-lit dining area (Ted's food is highly recommended) with a beautiful hardwood table shaped like a grand piano. There's a large deck with hammocks—the deck is good for birding (the birds flock to the fruit trees). Rates: $10 pp lodge room; $35 d cabin, $10 extra person, including two meals and all fruit drinks.

Rancho La Ponderosa, tel. 775-0131, fax 775-0631; in the U.S., tel. (407) 783-7184, about 400 meters south, offers simple wooden, two-story cabins with private baths in lush gardens. There's a basic dining room and lounge with bar

and TV. Rates: $35, including three meals. **Soda/Restaurant La Piña** is 400 meters north. Nearby is **Cabinas Mira Olas,** Apdo. 32, Golfito, radio tel. 775-0120; VHF channel 74, which has two *cabinas* with private baths and warm water (one with kitchenette). Rates: $10-15 s, $15-20 d. Also close Rancho La Ponderosa, **Bahía Pavones Surf Lodge** squats atop a huge rock with a wooden deck overhanging the beach. Here, rooms in the main building are basic and small; separate *cabinas* are larger and have their own porches and private baths. Meals are provided. Make reservations at the Tsunami Surf Shop, tel. 222-2224, fax 222-2271, in San José. Rates: about $18 s, $28 d, including breakfast.

Pavones has gone upscale with the opening of **Casa Siempre Domingo Bed and Breakfast,** tel./fax 775-0631, a deluxe, breeze-brushed Colorado-style lodge nestled on the hillside 400 meters inland, 1.5 km south of the Río Claro (the turnoff is just north of Casa Impact). Owned and run by East Coasters Greg and Heidi, this beautiful lodge is set amid hibiscus-tinged lawns surrounded by 15 acres of jungle-clad slopes— with access to the rainforest along trails. A mammoth cathedral ceiling soars over the lounge and dining room done up in evocative tropical style, with plentiful bamboo and jungly prints. The four rooms have two doubles or a double and single, ceramic tile floors, plus walk-in closets. The restaurant serves hearty fare and home-baked breads and desserts (bring your own booze). There's a laundry. And you'll enjoy dramatic ocean vistas from the sprawling deck. Rates: $90 s, $120 d, $180 t, including all meals ($30 kids under 10).

Punta Banco: Patrizio Baltadano rents seven rooms in a pension by the school at the entrance to the village. Rates: $12.50 per room. The Vargas family offers three rustic *cabinas* with electricity, fans, and outside bathroom at **Rancho El Borica,** at the very end of the road. Rates: $9 pp. One is a two-story house, another is conical, with a thatched roof. Meals are served in a thatched cantina popular with locals (breakfast costs a whopping $1, twice that for lunch or dinner). There's a waterfall 100 meters away in the grounds.

Casa Punta Banco, tel. 775-0006, fax 775-0087; in the U.S., Continental Associates, 202 W. Fifth Ave., Royal Oak, MI 48067, tel. (313) 545-

8900, fax (313) 545-0536, is a six-bedroom house with fully equipped kitchen, hot water, washer/dryer, and its own generator and caretaker. Rates: $700 d, $50 each additional person, per week. There's another oceanfront house—**Surfwind**—for rent half a kilometer south of the village.

Tiskita Lodge (see above) is centered on a charming old farmhouse that serves as lounge and dining room. There are 14 rooms in seven rustic, sparsely furnished but huge and comfortable cabins (made of purpleheart) that can accommodate up to 28 people in a combination of double, twin, and bunk beds (one even has a resident iguana). Each cabin is screened and has a wide veranda plus an exquisite bathroom with a stone-lined and shower. Some *baños* are outside. Yes, ablutions beneath the stars. Hot water was to be added. Bedding and towels are provided. A water-powered Pelton wheel and solar panels provide electricity. All meals—"Costa Rican country-style"—are included and served family style. (Meals are served at set times; don't be late.) Packed lunches are provided for hikers. The lodge sells straw hats and other crafts made by local Guaymi Indians. And a delightful little swimming pool has been added. Peter can arrange trips to the adjacent reserve. Rates per person: $93 s, $67 d, $58 t, including all meals plus guided "fruit walk" and "rainforest walk."

Activities

You can rent surfboards at Casa Impact, which arranges surfing tours, horseback riding, and fishing trips, as do Greg and Heidi at Casa Siempre Domingo, who offer trips to the Guaymí Indian reserve. You can hire a boat at Rancho El Borica for fishing trips or to reach Matapalo, on the Osa Peninsula ($70 for four people). Patrizio Baltanado rents horses for $20 a day. Alexis of Hotel Maureen rents a 15-foot boat for fishing trips; $30 d for three hours.

Getting There and Away

By Bus: A bus departs Golfito for Pavones and Punta Banco at 2 p.m., returning at 5 p.m.

By Car: See **Zancudo**, above, for a description of the route. Note that the coast road that leads south from Pavones ends at the mouth of the Río Claro, one km south of the village. To cross it and continue to Punta Banco, back-up and turn inland at Escuela Las Gemelas, then right at Super Mares; you'll cross a bridge, then drop back down to the coast. Tiskita is one km farther south. A 4WD taxi will cost you about $50 from Golfito.

A coast road from Zancudo to Pavones was being touted. Meanwhile, you can drive by 4WD between Zancudo and Pavones along the beach—*but only at low tide*. Don't attempt this without trustworthy local advice, otherwise the sea will take your car.

By Air: A private airstrip allows direct access to Tiskita by chartered plane (55 minutes from San José).

By Boat: Water-taxis from Golfito cost about $65 one-way. Walter Jiménez in Pavones reportedly has a water-taxi service (about $35 to Zancudo).

CIUDAD NEILY

Ciudad Neily squats at the base of the Fila Costeña mountains, beside the Pan-Am Highway, 18 km northwest of Panamá and 15 km east of Río Claro and the turnoff for Golfito. The town, which lies on the west bank of the Río Corredores, is surrounded by banana plantations and functions as the node for plantation operations. There is nothing to hold your interest here, though you are likely to see Indian women in colorful traditional dress, usually sitting on the sidewalk with their children, begging for a meager living.

agouti

BOB RACE

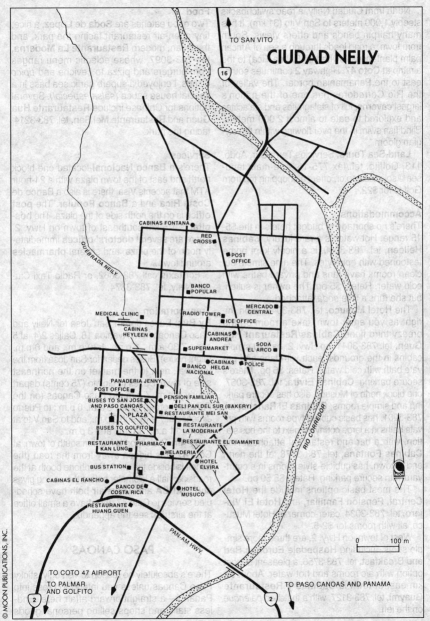

CIUDAD NEILY

TO SAN VITO

TO SAN VITO

QUEBRADA NEILY

RÍO CORREDOR

CABINAS FONTANA

RED CROSS

POST OFFICE

BANCO POPULAR

MEDICAL CLINIC

MERCADO CENTRAL

RADIO TOWER

ICE OFFICE

CABINAS HEYLEEN

CABINAS ANDREA

SODA EL ARCO

SUPERMARKET

CABINAS HELGA

POLICE

BANCO NACIONAL

PANADERIA JENNY

POST OFFICE

PENSION FAMILIAR

BUSES TO SAN JOSE AND PASO CANOAS

DELI PAN DEL SUR (BAKERY)

RESTAURANTE MEI SAN

PLAZA

RESTAURANTE LA MODERNA

BUSES TO GOLFITO

RESTAURANTE KAN LUNG

PHARMACY

RESTAURANTE EL DIAMANTE

HELADERIA

BUS STATION

HOTEL ELVIRA

CABINAS EL RANCHO

BANCO DE COSTA RICA

HOTEL MUSUCO

RESTAURANTE HUANG GUEN

PAN-AM HWY.

0   100 m

TO COTO 47 AIRPORT

TO PALMAR AND GOLFITO

TO PASO CANOAS AND PANAMA

© MOON PUBLICATIONS, INC.

North from Ciudad Neily, a road switchbacks steeply 1,000 meters to San Vito (31 km). It has many hairpin bends and offers views. South from town, a road leads through a sea of African palm plantations (owned by Palma Tica) to the airstrip at **Coto 47.** Highway 2 continues southeast to the Panamanian border. The valley of the Río Corredores has one of the nation's largest **caverns,** full of stalagmites and stalactites and explored to date to almost 2,000 meters. Blind fish swim in the river flowing within the stygian gloom.

Land-Sea Tours, Servicios Terra-Sur, Apdo. 113, Golfito, tel./fax 775-1614, e-mail: land-sea@sol.racsa.co.cr, offers a shopping trip from Golfito for $22.

Accommodations

There's no shortage of budget hotels in the $5-15 range. Hot water is a rare luxury. **Cabinas Heileen,** tel. 783-3080, is a nicely kept home festooned with epiphytes. The nine simple but clean rooms have fans and private baths with cold water. Rates: $5 pp. The owner is sullen, but she runs a little *soda,* attached.

The **Hotel Musuco,** tel. 783-3048, is on the right as you enter town; take a room on the breezy third floor. **Cabinas/Restaurant Hua Guen,** tel. 783-3041, on Hwy. 2, has 20 simple cabins in the grounds, each with fans and private bath with cold water. Rates: $6 pp. There's secure parking. **Cabinas Elvira,** tel. 782-3057, one block north of Musuco, also has secure parking and simple rooms. **Cabinas El Rancho,** tel. 783-3201, has basic cubicle-type rooms with private baths in a large courtyard next to the bus station, with a bar and restaurant attached. And **Cabinas Fontana,** tel. 783-3078, at the north end of town, has cubicle-style rooms in a courtyard with secure parking. Rates: $5.50 pp.

The most basic options include the **Hotel Central, Pensión Familiar,** and **Hotel El Viajero,** tel. 783-3034, cater-corner to Hotel Musuco, all with rooms for $2-5.

West of town, on Hwy. 2, are three more simple spots, including **Hospedaje Eurotica Bed and Breakfast,** tel. 783-3756, a pleasant budget option with a/c rooms and hot water. About six km east of town is **Cabinas y Restaurante Guaymi,** tel. 783-3127, with a thatched *palenque* on the left.

Food

Two good eateries are **Soda de López,** a nice, tiny open-air restaurant facing the park, and the clean, modern **Restaurante La Moderna,** tel. 783-3097, whose eclectic menu ranges from burgers and pizza to ceviche and *típico* dishes; I enjoyed a superb garlic sea bass in a special house sauce *(salsa especial).* Several options for Chinese include **Restaurante Hua Guen** and **Restaurante Mei San,** tel. 783-3214, facing the park.

Services

There's a **Banco Nacional** located one block north and east of the town plaza with a 24-hour ATM that accepts Visa, there is also a **Banco de Costa Rica** and a **Banco Popular.** The **post office** is on the north side of the plaza. The **hospital** is 1.5 km southeast of town on Hwy. 2. There are several **doctors' offices** immediately north of the plaza, and several **pharmacies** around town.

For **taxis** call 783-3862, or Radio Taxi Ciudad Neily, tel. 783-3374.

Transportation

By Bus: Buses depart San José for Neily and Paso Canoas from Avenida 18, Calles 2/4, at 5 a.m., 7:30 a.m., 1 p.m., 4:30 p.m., and 6 p.m. (eight hours). Buses depart for San José from the terminal, next to the market on the northeast side of town. Buses to Golfito (75 cents) depart hourly 6 a.m.-7 p.m.; to Paso Canoas (on the Panamá border) hourly 6 a.m.-6 p.m.; to Puerto Jiménez at 7 a.m. and 2 p.m.; and to San Vito at 6 a.m., 11 a.m., 1 p.m., and 3 p.m.

By Air: The airport is four km south of town, at Coto 47; it is hidden away from the road (the turnoff is beside the public telephone booth at the roadside, half a kilometer before the paving gives out). **SANSA** and **Travelair** both have scheduled service to Coto 47 (they have a small office at the airstrip); see the appendix.

PASO CANOAS

There's absolutely no reason to visit ugly, stinky Paso Canoas unless you intend to cross into Panamá—a straightforward affair here. Endless stalls and shops selling personal goods are strung out along the road paralleling the border. The place is popular with Ticos, who pour in to buy the duty-free goods. Avoid Easter week and the months before Christmas, when Paso Canoas is a zoo.

Note: There's a police and Customs checkpoint on the Pan-Am Highway for all vehicles leaving town. You have to show an affidavit from the Customs office 100 meters east, adjacent to the Tracopa bus terminal. Even if you don't cross into Panamá, you must get a clearance from Customs before leaving town. It can be a long wait. Fortunately there's a separate, clearly marked booth for foreigners. If you're visiting town for curiosity's sake, park on the west side of the police station to avoid paperwork hassles when exiting.

Accommodations

There's plenty of choice, though all have only cold water unless noted. Hotels fill up on weekends. One of the best is the modern, motel-style **Cabinas Alpina,** tel. 732-2018, offering rooms away from the bustle with tiled floors, TVs, and private baths. It also has secure parking and a laundry. Rates: $4 pp for basic rooms; $14 s/d, $22 t for nicer a/c rooms upstairs. Even nicer is the modern **Hotel Real Victoria,** tel. 732-2586, one block east, with 33 modest but adequate rooms with fans, TVs, and private baths. Some rooms have a/c. Rates: $5 pp.

Nearby, **Cabinas Interamericano** is also acceptable, offering basic rooms with private bath. The upper-story rooms catch the breezes. There's a restaurant downstairs. Rates: about $10.

PASO CANOAS

SCALE NOT AVAILABLE

MEDICAL CLINIC
TRACOPA BUS TERMINAL
CUSTOMS CHECKPOINT
POLICE
CUSTOMS INSPECTION
CABINAS LUIS
CABINAS KARLA
CABINAS LOS ARCOS
RESTAURANTE BRUNCA
PHARMACY
SODAS
TO CIUDAD NEILY AND SAN JOSÉ
GUARDIA RURAL
BORDER CHECKPOINT
BUSES FOR CIUDAD NEILY
TAXIS
POST OFFICE
PANAMANIAN BUS TERMINAL
PAN - AMERICAN HIGHWAY
TO PANAMA CITY
INTERAMERICANO CABINAS
HOTEL DEL SOL
HOTEL PALACE SUR
HOTEL MIAMI
BAR LA TERMINAL
HOTEL HILDA
BAR/DISCOTEQUE MALIBU
PENSION FAMILIAR
CABINAS ALPINA
CABINAS JIMENEZ
HOTEL EL PASO
HOTEL REAL VICTORIA
BAR/RESTAURANTE KOKI'S
CABINAS CUEVAS
ANEXO CABINAS JIMENEZ
COSTA RICA
PANAMA
RIO CHIRIQUI VIEJO

© MOON PUBLICATIONS, INC.

Cabinas Los Arcos, tel. 732-2256, 400 meters north of the border checkpoint, has eight very basic cabins with private baths. Rates: $6.50 pp. Next door, **Cabinas Karla,** tel./fax 732-2234, is much nicer, with nine cleaner, newer cabins in a garden courtyard. All have private bath; some have TVs. Rates: $4-8.

Hardy budget travelers might also try the very basic **Cabinas El Hogar,** tel. 732-2301; **Cabinas Evelyn,** tel. 732-2229; **Cabinas Velise,** tel. 732-2302; **Cabinas Luis; Anexo Cabinas Jiménez,** tel. 732-2258; **Hotel Azteca,** tel. 732-2217; and **Hotel el Descanso,** tel. 732-2261.

There are two places on Hwy. 2 midway between Ciudad Neily and Paso Canoas: the modest **Hotel Camino Real** and **Cabinas/Centro Turístico El Retiro,** about 1.5 km farther south. You can **camp** at Camino Real.

Services

The **immigration** office, tel. 732-2150, is next to the bus terminal. Get there early; the interminable line moves at a snail's pace. You're advised to get rid of *colones* before crossing into Panamá (there are plenty of moneychangers).

Taxis wait at the triangle in front of the border crossing. A taxi from Ciudad Neily will cost about $10. There's a **pharmacy,** Farmacía Paso Canoas, tel. 732-2293. The **police** station, tel. 732-2106, is on the south side of the triangle.

Getting There and Away

Tracopa, tel. 221-4214, buses depart San José for Paso Canoas from Avenida 18, Calles 2/4, daily at 5 a.m., 7:30 a.m., 1 p.m., 4:30 p.m., and 6 p.m. (eight hours). Tracopa buses leave Paso Canoas for San José at 4 a.m., 7:30 a.m., 9:30 a.m., and 2:45 p.m. (eight hours; approximately $6.50). **TICA,** tel. 221-8954, buses depart San José from Avenida 4, Calles 9/11 at 10 p.m. Buses also run frequently from Ciudad Neily to the border (about 25 cents). Weekend buses to and from Paso Canoas fill up early; reservations are recommended. Local buses depart for Neily every hour. Taxis to/from Neily cost $10.

See chart, **Buses From San José** for bus service to Panamá. There's a **gas station** just west of town. The SANSA office is in Cabinas Interamericano.

COCOS AND CAÑO ISLANDS

ISLA COCOS

The only true oceanic island off Central America, Cocos Island—500 km southwest of Costa Rica—is a 52-square-km mountainous chunk of land that rises to 634 meters at Iglesias Peak. Declared a UNESCO World Heritage Site in 1997, the island is the northernmost and oldest of a chain of volcanoes, mostly submarine, stretching south along the Cocos Ridge to the equator, where several come to the surface as the Galápagos Islands. These islands were formed by a hot spot, which pushes up volcanic material from beneath the earth's crust. The hot spot remains stationary while the sea floor moves across it. Over time, a volcano is transported away from the hot spot and a new volcano arises in the same place.

Cliffs reach higher than 100 meters around almost the entire island and dramatic waterfalls cascade onto the beach, fed by 800 cm of rain a

year. The island was discovered in 1526 by Juan Cabezas and first appeared on a map in 1542. Prisoners lived here in watery solitude in the late 1800s, and occasional settlers have tried to eke a living. Today it is inhabited only by national park guards who patrol the park equipped with small Zodiacs. The only safe anchorage for entry is at Chatham Bay, on the northeast corner, where scores of rocks are etched with the names and dates of ships dating back to the 17th century. Even Jacques Cousteau has left his indelible mark: a substantial and beautiful engraving made in 1987.

There are no native mammals. The surrounding waters, however, are home to four unique species of marine mollusks. One endemic plant is christened Franklin Roosevelt, after the U.S. president who made several visits to the island. The island has one butterfly and two lizard species to call its own. And three species of birds are endemic: the Cocos Island finch, Cocos Island cuckoo, and Ridgeway or

Cocos flycatcher (the Cocos Island finch is a subspecies of the famous Galápagos finches, which inspired Darwin's revolutionary theory of evolution). Three species of boobies—red-footed, masked, and brown—live here, too. Cocos is also a popular spot for frigate birds (archrivals of boobies) to roost and mate. The white tern, which may hover above your head, is the *espíritu santu,* or Holy Spirit bird. Feral pigs introduced in the 18th century by passing sailors today number about 5,000 and have caused substantial erosion. The island's isolation attracts poachers seeking black coral, seashells, and lobster, and fishermen who violate the no-fishing zone to net sharks for fins, which are treasured in the Orient. Access to the island is restricted.

In 1997, the Costa Rican and French governments were negotiating a plan to create a trust fund by which the debt Costa Rica has with France would be exchanged for environmental projects on Cocos Island.

Treasure

Cocos' forested hills supposedly harbor gold doubloons. More than 500 expeditions have sought in vain to find the Lima Booty—gold and silver ingots that mysteriously disappeared while en route to Spain under the care of Captain James Thompson. The pirate William Davies supposedly hid his treasure here in 1684, as did Portuguese buccaneer Benito "Bloody Sword" Bonito in 1889. The government has placed a "virtual moratorium" on treasure hunts, although the Ministry of Natural Resources sanctioned a hunt in January 1992 by North American computer company owner John Hodges—for a rights fee of $100,000. Christopher Weston's book, *Cocos Island—Old Pirate's Haven* (San José: Imprenta y Litografia Trejos, 1990), tells the tale.

Diving

The island is one of the world's best diving spots, famous for its massive schools of white-tipped and hammerhead sharks and eerie manta rays, which haunt these waters at deeper depths. Pilot whales, whale sharks, and even sailfish are also abundant. Cocos is for experienced divers only: drop-offs are deep, currents are continually changing, and beginning divers may freak at the huge shark populations (in fact, converging ocean currents stir up such a wealth of nutrients that the sharks have a surfeit of fish to feed on, and taking a chunk out of divers is probably the last thing on their minds). Snorkelers swimming closer to the surface can revel in moray eels and colorful reef fish.

Information

For information on visiting, contact the National Parks Service, tel. 257-0922. There are no accommodations, and camping is not allowed.

Getting There and Away

The only way to get to Cocos is by sea. Most people arrive aboard a dedicated dive vessel.

A twin-masted motor-sailing yacht, the *Pollux,* offers a 10-day diving package ($2,285), plus an eight-day nondiving excursion ($1,429) to Cocos. The vessel sleeps six people and is available for charter. Contact **Pollux de Golfito,** Apdo. 7-1970, San José 1000, tel. 661-1224, fax 661-2061. **Ocean Voyages,** 1709 Bridgeway, Sausalito, CA 94965, tel. (415) 332-4681, offers chartered yacht cruises to Cocos.

RESERVA BIOLÓGICA ISLA CAÑO

Caño Island is 17 km off the western tip of the Osa Peninsula. It is of interest primarily for its inshore coral reefs and its importance as a pre-Columbian cemetery. Many tombs and artifacts—pestles, corn-grinding tables, and granite spheres *(bolas)*—are gathering moss in the rainforest undergrowth.

The 300-hectare island is ringed with secluded white-sand beaches that attract olive ridley turtles. Among its residents are boa constrictors (the only poisonous snakes here are sea snakes), giant frogs, a variety of hummingbirds, and three mammal species: a marsupial, the paca (which was introduced), and a bat. Surprisingly, only 13 terrestrial bird species are found here. Snorkelers can see brilliant tropical fish and moray eels among the coral beds. Offshore waters teem with common and bottle-nosed dolphins, and sperm, pilot, and humpback whales, which migrate from Alaska.

THE EERIE PROCESSION OF THE SOLDIER CRABS

If you think you see the beach moving, it's not the heat waves nor last night's excess of *guaro* messing with your mind. Daily, whole columns of seashells—little whelks and conchs of green and blue and russet—come marching down from the roots of the mangroves onto the sand. Scavengers only an inch long, soldier crabs are born and grow up without protective shells. For self-preservation they move—"lock, stock and abdomen," says one writer—into empty seashells they find cast up on the beach. Although they grow, their seashell houses do not; thus whole battalions of crabs continually seek newer and larger quarters. When threatened, a soldier crab pulls back into its shell, totally blocking the entrance with one big claw.

In 1973 Caño was leased to a Spanish developer with plans to build a megaresort. The island, however, was heroically saved by an outburst of popular displeasure. Although now administered as part of Corcovado National Park, uncontrolled sportfishing and poaching of coral goes virtually unchecked because of underfunding and understaffing.

A wide and well-maintained trail leads steeply uphill from the ranger station and provides an excellent entrée into a rainforest environment.

Pre-Columbian tombs are scattered along the trail. Entrance: $6.

Volunteers

Arborea Project Foundation, Apdo. 65-8150, Palmar Norte, tel. 786-6565, fax 786-6358, recruits volunteers to work for one, two, or three weeks alongside park rangers. You'll help maintain trails, archaeological sites, etc. You pay $30 a day, plus your own transportation costs to Costa Rica and Osa.

Accommodations

It is normally forbidden to sleep overnight. You may be able to camp near the ranger station on the beach, but don't count on it. No facilities.

Getting There and Away

You can hire a boat from Drake Bay. Alternately, the park rangers might squeeze you into their boat from San Pedrillo or Sirena, in Corcovado National Park.

Several tour operators in San José and Golfito, as well as nearby lodges, offer trips.

Temptress Adventure Cruises sometimes includes the island on its natural-history cruises; see chart, **Natural-History Cruise Tours** in the appendix. **Pollux de Golfito,** Apdo. 7-1970, San José 1000, tel. 661-1224, fax 661-2061, operates a four-day trip to Caño Island aboard the twin-masted motor-sailing yacht *Pollux* ($561); you can also charter the boat ($1,500 per night).

CATHY CARLSON

SOUTH-CENTRAL COSTA RICA

The southern central highlands and Valle de El General are the Cinderella of Costa Rican tourism. A larger proportion of the region is protected as national park or forest reserve than in any other part of the country. Much remains inaccessible and unexplored—no bad thing, for huge regions such as Chirripó National Park and La Amistad International Peace Park harbor healthy and incredibly diverse populations of Central American flora and fauna.

The region is also home to the nation's largest concentration of indigenous people—especially Guaymis and Borucas, concentrated in remoter mountain regions. Like native people worldwide, they are caught in a vicious cycle of poverty. But, says Gail Hewson Gómez, associate director of the Wilson Botanical Gardens, "These people are not at all preoccupied by the fact that they are poor. In fact [they] are extravagantly rich in spirit and cheerfulness." Around Ciudad Neily and the highlands to the west, you'll see Indian women walking barefoot, their small frames laden with babies or bulging bags.

The region is divided into highland and lowland, dominated to the east by the overwhelming bulk of the **Talamanca massif,** sometimes called the Blue Mountains because of the haze that often smothers them. Slanting southeast and paralleling the Talamancas to the west is a range of mountains called the **Fila Costeña.** Between the two mountain ranges lies a huge valley (a tectonic depression), about 100 km long by 30 km wide, called the **Valle de El General** to the north, **Valle de Coto Brus** to the south. The valley is a center of agriculture, with pineapples predominant covering the flatlands of the Río General, and coffee smothering the slopes of Coto Brus. The valley is drained by numerous rivers that merge to form the Río Grande de Terraba, which slices through the Fila Costeña and meanders through a vast swampland to reach the sea.

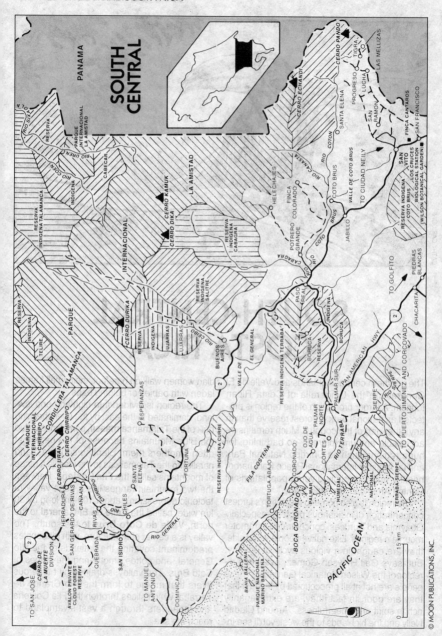

© MOON PUBLICATIONS, INC.

The region is linked to San José by the Pan-American Highway (Hwy. 2), which runs south from Cartago, climbs over the Cordillera de Talamanca forming the Continental Divide and descends to San Isidro in the Valle de El General. South of Buenos Aires, the Pan-Am exits the valley via the gorge of the Río Grande de Terraba, linking it with the Golfo Dulce region. Another road transcends the Fila Costeña and links San Isidro de El General with Dominical on the central Pacific coast.

It wasn't until the mid-1950s that a paved road was cut across the mountain ridge known as Cerro de la Muerte to link the Valle de El General and the Pacific southwest with San José and the Meseta Central. Before then, communications were by mule, plane, or sea, and many mountain folk eked a meager living as *carboneros*—charcoal burners—using majestic local oaks, as told in "The Carbonero," by Carlos Salazar Herera in *Costa Rica: A Traveller's Literary Companion.* The *carboneros,* who forever blackened by soot staggered to San José with their loads, still exist today.

The **Brunca Regional Union of Tourism Chambers** (Unión Brunca de Cámaras de Turismo), Apdo. 258, Pérez Zeledón, tel. 771-6096, fax 771-2003, e-mail: ciprotur@sol.racsa.co.cr, also known as CIPROTOR, provides information and works to promote the conservation and protection of the natural and cultural heritage by encouraging small-scale ecotourism as an alternative option of local income and a resource for sustainable development. **Selva Mar,** tel. 771-4582, fax 771-1903, e-mail: selvamar@sol.racsa.co.cr, website www.habitat.co.cr/selvamar, acts as a reservation service for lodging and tours in the Brunca region, centered on San Isidro.

Climate

The regional climate varies with the topography. The Valle de El General sits in a rain shadow (the saturated clouds moving in from the Pacific dump most of their rain on the western slopes of the Fila Costeña). Nonetheless, the mountain slopes receive considerable rainfall, increasingly so to the south, where the slopes are clad in montane rainforest.

The area took a beating in July 1996 when Hurricane Cesár roared in off the Pacific, causing huge flooding and landslides and washing out whole sections of roads in the Valle de El General and Coto Brus. Such an event is a once-in-a-blue-moon occurrence.

VALLE DE EL GENERAL

CERRO DE LA MUERTE TO SAN ISIDRO

From the 3,491-meter summit of Cerro de la Muerte, about 100 km south of San José, the Pan-Am Highway drops steeply to San Isidro, at 709 meters, in the Valle de El General. (Avoid this road at night!) The route is often fog-bound and there are many large trucks—some without lights. There are frequent landslides, fathoms-deep potholes, and too many accidents for your own safety. Take extreme care. Your reward, once you drop below the cloud level, will be a fabulous vista, with the whole Valle de El General spread out before you.

If the sun is shining, you may see a statue of Christ balancing precariously on the cliff face above the highway two km north of **San Rafael** (Km 104). A small, traditional *trapiche* (ox-driven

sugar mill) is still in operation immediately below at a roadside *soda* called **El Trapiche de Nayo.**

Much of the forest flanking the highway is protected as the **Los Santos Forest Reserve,** accessed by a dirt road from the Km 107 turnoff, at División.

Avalon Private Reserve

This 150-hectare private reserve, Apdo 846, San Isidro de El General, tel. 380-2107 or tel./fax 771-7226, at 2,800 meters elevation, high atop a ridge of the Talamancas known as the Fila Zapotales, is named for the mythical kingdom of Arthurian legend where a priestess magically lifts the mists on the far side of the holy lake. Appropriately, the lodge sits in the midst of a magical cloud forest realm, surrounded by 375 acres of primal forest, with spectacular views down over the Valle de El General—best enjoyed while soaking in the wood-fired hot tub.

Time your soak for 8 p.m., when the clouds religiously part. On a really clear day you can see as far as Osa. *Muy tranquilo.*

Birding is superb (with similar flora and fauna to Monteverde), including lots of quetzals (the owners are planting *aguacatillo* trees on which the birds feed), three-wattled bellbirds, the collared trogon, and toucanets. An expert birding guide costs $60 per day, but a two-hour "Cloudforest Birding" hike costs $3 pp. Hikes include a tough three-hour river walk ($6), and a five-hour slog to waterfalls ($8) with lunch in a Tico farmstead. You can even help milk the cows at a mountaintop farm, reached by a tough trail. Gwenavyer—the horse—and her equine pals will take you on rides ($5 per hour). And there's trout fishing nearby. A friendly gringo, Scott Miller, owns the place (he lives in San Isidro), which is ably run by Robert, the friendly Tico-gringo manager. Day use costs $3 pp. Simple yet tasty meals are cooked on a wood-fired stove and served family style. For entertainment, there's a radio, Adultrivia, and Nimue, the pet goat.

The turnoff is signed at Km 107, at División. It's a three km drive along a deeply rutted dirt road (4WD recommended). You can take a bus from Coca-Cola to San Isidro de El General; get off at División, where you can get a taxi at the *pulpería* (ask for Arturo).

Centro Biológico Las Quebradas

The 2,400-hectare Las Quebradas Biological Center research station and nature reserve, Apdo. 95, 8000 Pérez Zeledín, tel./fax 771-4131, was established to protect the cloud-shrouded watershed of San Isidro. It is in the upper basin of a ravine on the southern flanks of the Cerro de la Muerte. The forest is a vibrant world full of bromeliads, ferns, orchids, giant trees, and profuse bird and animal life. It's open to ecotourists who, with luck, might see quetzals while hiking to waterfalls. The Foundation for the Development of Las Quebradas Biological Centre (FUDEBIOL) has installed trails and camping and picnic sites, plus a souvenir store. Open Tues.-Fri. 8 a.m.-2 p.m., and weekends 8 a.m.-3 p.m.

A bus from San Isidro goes to the hamlet of Quebradas, from where its a 2.5 km hike to the station. There are no signs—grrrr!—and it's a harpy to get to along a steep muddy track that your sedan may refuse to ascend. You have to

walk for about 30 minutes after parking to reach the reserve.

Accommodations and Food

Five km below the summit at Villa Mills is **Hotel/Restaurant Las Georginas,** popular with buses, which unload their passengers for meals. It has basic rooms (rates: $5). Locally grown apples and other produce are sold by the roadside.

Avalon Private Reserve, Apdo 846, San Isidro de El General, tel. 380-2107 or tel./fax 771-7226, e-mail: smiller@sol.racsa.co.cr, has three rustic cabins with private baths. There are also some rooms with shared bath. All have portable heaters, plenty of thick woolen blankets, hot water, electricity, and astounding views best enjoyed from a wood-fired hot tub. Rates: $9-17 pp in bunks with shared bath; $22 private room with shared bath; $35-45 private room with private bath. A week-long package is $99 including meals. And volunteers can enjoy a workstay for $39 weekly. Green-season discounts. You can **camp** for $6 pp. Home-cooked meals cost $3-7. Highly recommended!

At Km 119 is **Mirador Vista del Valle,** tel. 284-4685, fax 771-2003, a restaurant named for its stunning view. Birding and fishing are offered. **Mirador la Torre,** tel. 771-6462, fax 771-2003, is a mountainside restaurant and bar at Km 130, five km north of San Isidro de El General. It has a Latin dance night on Thursday and mariachi on Saturday. Open Tues.-Sun. 11 a.m.-11 p.m.

SAN ISIDRO DE EL GENERAL

San Isidro, regional capital of the Valle de El General, is an important transportation center and agricultural market town that is the gateway to Chirripó National Park and Dominical. San Isidro is also a base for rafting trips on the Ríos Chirripó and General, and has attracted a large population of expats. The town is laid out in a grid centered on a **plaza** at Calle Central and Avenida 0, one block west of Hwy. 2, with the grid aligned obliquely at 45 degrees to the highway.

There is little to see in town. The small **Southern Regional Museum,** Calle 2 and Avenida 1, tells the story of the local indigenous peoples. It's open Mon.-Fri. 9 a.m.-noon and 1-5 p.m. Attesting to San Isidro's lack of classical lineage (the town was founded in 1897, though most of it is post-WW II) is the concrete carbuncle—ahem, I mean **cathedral**—on the east side of the plaza, looking like a massive Nazi fortification transplanted from Normandy. In a cultural mood? Nearby, next to Café el Teatro, there's a cultural complex, including a museum, art gallery, and theater, plus artisans' workshops.

Walter Fonseca has an **orchid garden** south of town, with more than 800 species from around the world, plus hybrids, and rare native species. The Hotel del Sur offers tours.

Civic Festivals
The town comes alive late January and early February for its **Fiestas Cívicas,** when agricultural fairs, bullfights, and general festivities occur. The best time to visit, however, is 15 May, for the **Día del Boyero** ("Day of the Oxcart Driver"), featuring a colorful oxcart parade.

Accommodations
Shoestring: There are several options for super-budget travelers. Most are grim. The run-down **Hotel Lala,** tel. 771-0291, has 25 rooms with

SAN ISIDRO

fans and cold water. Rates: $3 pp, shared bath; $7 d private bath. The **Hotel El Jardín,** tel. 771-0349, is also basic, with 38 prison-like rooms with shared bath and cold water, plus a restaurant with a wide-screen TV. Rates: $3.50 pp. The ho-hum **Hotel Jerusalem,** tel. 771-3219, has 13 rooms with shared bath and cold water. Rates: $3 pp. **Hotel Balboa,** tel. 771-0606, is also basic—30 rooms with cold water. Rates: $5 s/d shared bath; $10 private bath. **Cabinas El Prado,** tel. 771-0578, and **Cabinas Río Mar,** tel. 771-2333, are both in the $4-8 pp range.

Hotel Amaneli, tel. 771-0352, on Hwy. 2, is a condo-style hotel with 40 rooms featuring fans, private baths, and hot water. Rooms facing the highway are noisy. Rates: $9 pp.

Budget: Better options include the **Hotel/Restaurante El Chirripó,** tel. 771-0529, fax 771-0410, on the southwest side of the square, is the best place, offering 41 rooms with *real* hot water, plus a pleasing outdoor restaurant. Rates: $5 s, $9 d shared bath; $8 s, $14 d, $21 t private bath. The **Hotel Iguazú,** tel. 771-2571, has 21 modest rooms—a reader reports "cockroaches"—with private and shared hot-water baths. Rates: $12 s, $19 d. The **Hotel El Valle,** tel. 771-0246, has 18 well-lit rooms with fans, balconies, and hot water. Rates: $6 pp shared bath; $9 s, $15.50 d private bath and TV.

Hotel Astoria, tel. 771-0914, facing the square, has 54 gloomy rooms without windows and with cold water. Modern rooms towards the back are more spacious and nicer. There's a laundry. Rates: $9 pp older rooms; $15 s/d/t modern rooms; $17 s/d/t modern rooms with fans and hot water.

Outside town, María Morales, the friendly owner of the eatery **Rincón de Papa,** tel. 771-2042, has a bamboo *cabina* with one room up and one down, plus hot water and natural ventilation.

Inexpensive: The **Hotel del Sur,** Apdo. 4-8000, Pérez Zeledín, San Isidro, tel. 771-3033 or 234-8871, fax 771-0527, e-mail: ciprotur@sol.racsa.co.cr, six km south of San Isidro, is the best hotel nearby and popular with businessfolk. The 27 a/c rooms are spacious and clean, albeit still dowdy despite a recent facelift. It also has 20 newly renovated suites plus 10 self-sufficient *cabinas* with separate living and dining room. A large restaurant (the cuisine is dull) and bar opens onto a heavily chlorinated swimming pool and landscaped grounds with volleyball and tennis courts. You can rent horses and mountain bikes. There's a small spa and a small casino. Rates: $25 s, $30 d standard; $35 s, $40 d superior; $45 s, $50 d with a/c; $75 suite.

About 200 meters north of the Hotel del Sur is the **Apartotel El Tecal,** tel. 771-0664.

Food

The **Restaurant Chirripó,** facing the plaza, is popular with Ticos and expat gringos and is recommended for an early breakfast. **Restaurant La Piccolina,** tel. 771-8692, is a pizzeria two blocks west of the bus terminal. **Restaurante/Pizzeria El Tenedor,** tel. 771-0881, has also been recommended for pizzas and has a balcony overlooking the park, next to Hotel Iguazú. For Chinese, try **Restaurant Hong Kong,** facing the park. **Marisquería y Bar Marea Baja,** tel. 771-0681, is recommended for seafood.

You can buy fresh fruit and vegetables at the public market. Outside town, **Rincón de Papa,** tel. 771-2042, is an elegant eatery with bamboo furniture and tasty *típico* dishes served beneath a large open-air *palenque* beside the Río Paja, southeast of San Isidro, two km from Hwy. 2 (ask for directions).

Entertainment

The last "in spot" was **Video Bar Río Sur,** near the market, and **Disco Prado,** both favored by local young adults. Rumor has it there's a **roller-skate disco.** A reader recommends **Bar Mexicana,** on Hwy. 2 north of town, for single males seeking companionship.

Spanish Language Courses

SEPA, Spanish Language and Environmental Protection Center, Apdo. 352-8000, San Isidro, tel. 771-4582, fax 771-8841; in the U.S., c/o AAA Express Mail, 1641 N.W. 79th Ave., Miami, FL 33126, has Spanish courses lasting from one week to several weeks, starting every Monday year-round. Groups are limited to four people.

Tours and Activities

Brunca Tours, tel./fax 771-2150, on Hwy. 2 about two km south of San Isidro, offers guided tours and excursions from one to eight days throughout the Pacific southwest, including hiking up Chirripó plus one- to three-day whitewater rafting on the Río General.

Tourist Information

CIPROTUR, tel. 771-6096, fax 771-2003, e-mail: ciprotur@sol.racsa.co.cr, the regional promotion board, has a tourist information office on Calle 4, Avenida 0/1. **Selva Mar,** tel. 771-4582, fax 771-1903, e-mail: selvamar@sol.racsa.co.cr, website www.habitat.co.cr/selvamar, offers a complete tourist information and reservation service for the Brunca region. Alternately, try Cámara de Comercio, tel. 771-2525—the Chamber of Commerce—on Calle 4, Avenidas 1/3, which also has an information desk.

You can get information on Chirripó National Park or La Amistad International Peace Park at the regional **parks service office,** tel. 771-3155, fax 771-4836, on Calle 2, Avenidas 4/6; open Mon.-Fri. 8 a.m.-noon and 1-4 p.m.

Services

Conexiones Internacionales, tel./fax 771-3015, next to the Restaurant Chirripó, has an international telephone service and claims to cash traveler's checks. A reader refutes this and recommends **Bazar Xiomaro** (look for the SANSA sign out front) next to Banco del Comercio.

The **Banco Nacional** is two blocks northeast of the plaza. The **Banco Popular,** next to Restaurant Chirripó, on the west side of the plaza, has a 24-hour ATM, as do **Creditalianza,** next door; **Banco de San José,** one block south on Avenida 4; and **BanCrecen,** two blocks west of the plaza on Avenida 2. BanCrecen also represents **Western Union,** and is open Mon.-Fri. 9 a.m.-9 p.m. and Saturday 9 a.m.-2 p.m. BanCrecen accepts Visa and MasterCard; all others accept Visa only.

The **Centro Médico San Isidro,** tel. 771-4467, is one block south of the plaza, on Avenida 4 between Calles Central/1. There are several **pharmacies** downtown, where you'll also see **doctors'** offices and clinical laboratories.

Fujicolor, tel. 771-4563, has an outlet selling film on Avenida 1, Calles 2/4. You can have film processed here. There's a **library** (hours: Mon.-Fri. 7 a.m.-noon and 1:30-5:30 p.m.) above the museum on Calle 2, Avenida 1.

Getting There and Away

By Bus: Musoc, tel. 222-2422; in San Isidro, tel. 771-0414, operates express buses from San José (Calle 16, Avenidas 1/3) at 5:30 a.m. 7:30

a.m., 10:30 a.m., 11:30 a.m., 1:30 p.m., 2:30 p.m., 4:30 p.m., and 5 p.m. Return buses depart San Isidro at 5 a.m., 5:30 a.m., 7:30 a.m., 8:30 a.m., 10:30 a.m., 11:30 a.m., 1:30 p.m., and 4:30 p.m. Tuasa, tel. 222-9763 or 771-0419, has buses departing San José from opposite the Musoc terminal at 6:30 a.m., 8:30 a.m., 9:30 a.m., 12:30 p.m., and 3:30 p.m., returning at 6:30 a.m., 9:30 a.m., 12:30 p.m., 2:30 p.m., and 3:30 p.m. The Musoc and Tuasa terminals in San Isidro are next to each other on Hwy. 2 at the junction of Calle 2.

The regional bus station in San Isidro is at Calle Central and Avenidas 4/6. Transportes Blanco, tel. 771-2550 or 771-1384, operates buses from Quepos via Dominical at 5 a.m. and 1:30 p.m., returning from San Isidro at 7 a.m. and 1:30 p.m.; and from Uvita via Dominical at 7 a.m. and 3 p.m., returning at 6 a.m. and 3 p.m. You can also catch Tracopa buses to Buenos Aires, Ciudad Neily, David in Panamá, Golfito, Palmar, Puerto Jiménez, and San Vito. Buses depart for San Gerardo at 2 p.m.; Quebrada at 9:15 a.m., 11:15 a.m., 12:15 p.m., 3:15 p.m., and 5:15 p.m.; for Palmares at 9:30 a.m., noon, and 4:30 p.m.; and Buenos Aires at 5:15 a.m., 7:30 a.m., 10 a.m., 12:15 p.m., 3 p.m., and 5 p.m.

Buses fill up fast—buy tickets in advance, especially on weekends and holidays.

By Car: There are several **gas stations** on the the Pan-Am Highway. **National Car Rental,** tel. 771-4336 or 771-1037, has an office on Calle 1, two blocks south of the plaza; open daily 8 a.m.-6 p.m.

SAN ISIDRO TO DOMINICAL

West from San Isidro de El General, the road to Dominical climbs up and over the Fila Costeña and beyond **Alfombra,** 16 km west of San Isidro, drops down to Platanillo and the central Pacific coast. It's a dramatically scenic drive. **Sibu Recreation Farm,** tel. 771-6096, fax 771-2003, in Caño Blanco, three km north of Alfombra, is an ecotourist facility offering hiking and horseback tours to waterfalls. There are cabins and a restaurant.

Fruit orchards abound, and the heavily-potholed mountain road is lined with fruit stalls.

VALLE DEL RÍO CHIRRIPÓ

The valley of the Río Chirripó cuts deeply into the Talamancas northeast of San Isidro, fed by waters cascading down from Cerro Chirripó (3,819 meters), Costa Rica's highest mountain. The river is favored for kayaking and whitewater rafting and for trout fishing, while the warm valley microclimate is kind to fruit trees: orchards of peaches and apples cover the lower slopes.

The drive offers spectacular scenery and great birding, which can be appreciated at **Parque Ecológico Quebrada Bonita,** c/o Hector Fallas, tel. 771-0008 or 771-6096, two km northeast of town. This small (two hectares) reforestation project is run by the local municipality. Trails follow the river (I saw a motmot within one minute of entering the forest). **Centro Turística La Pradera,** tel. 771-0819 or 240-5665, two km farther, also has trails into a forest and through beautifully landscaped grounds offering views over the valley of the Río General and towards Chirripó. There's a rustic restaurant and bar, plus horse rentals, and a children's playground. Hours: daily 11 a.m.-11 p.m.

The paved road continues via **Rivas,** a pleasing little village six km east of San Isidro. It's famous for the "Rock of the Indian," a giant rock carved with pre-Columbian Indian motifs. This, and a 150-year-old *trapiche,* or sugar mill, are part of **Rancho La Botija,** tel. 382-3052 or 771-1401, fax 771-2003, a coffee and fruit *finca* with trails, a cafe, a swimming pool with changing rooms and security boxes, plus horse rentals, a game room, and children's playground amid lawns. Open Tues.-Sun. 7 a.m.-5 p.m. Day visits cost $2.50 ($1.50 children).

Passing through **Canáan,** 18 km northeast of San Isidro, you arrive at a Y fork where the Río Blanco flows into the Río Chirripó. A dirt road to the left follows the Río Blanco upstream three km to the hamlet of **Herradura** and thence, growing steeper and more tenuous, to the tinier hamlet of **Río Blanco** from where you can hike to Cerro Chirripó and Cerro Urán. En route to Herradura you'll pass the entrance to **Aguas Termales,** hot springs reached by a 20-minute climb up a steep path that begins opposite **Parqueo Las Rosas** (with secure parking for $1.50).

The road to the right at the Y fork crosses the Río Blanco and leads uphill 600 meters to San Gerardo de Rivas.

San Gerardo de Rivas

This quaint village, on the southwest flank of Chirripó at 1,300 meters, is the gateway to Chirripó National Park. The setting is temptingly alpine. The air is crisp. The scent of pines and the burbling of rushing streams fills the air. Mountain flanks rise sheer from the valleys. And the locale is perfect for hiking and birding. Quetzals nest hereabouts.

Every February a **marathon** is held from San Gerardo to the peak of Chirripó and back to San Gerardo. Francisco Elizonda, owner of the Cabinas del Descanso, has won the marathon's trophy several times (the walls of his restaurant are covered with trophies and certificates from various marathon races). His best time? Up and down in four hours.

The **ranger station** for Chirripó National Park is on the south side of the Río Blanco, 600 meters below San Gerardo.

Museo el Pelicano

Check *this* out! This small museum on a coffee *finca* between Canáan and San Gerardo displays the eclectic and unique works of local artist Rafael Elizondo Basulta, crafted from stones and natural timbers. The items on exhibit include a five-meter snake hewn from a branch. My favorite is a half-scale motorbike made from 1,000 twigs and other pieces of wood. Many of Rafael's stone sculptures are displayed in the beautifully landscaped garden. With luck you may be invited into his charming house to see the tree trunks hewn magically into a storage cupboard and even a wooden fridge.

Whitewater Rafting

The Río Chirripó and the larger Río General, which it feeds, are popular for rafting, with enormous volume of water creating class III and IV rapids with gigantic waves. **Costaricaraft** offers three-day ($305) and four-day ($410) rafting trips on the Ríos General and Chirripó, August through December. **Costa Rica Expeditions** and **Pioneer Raft** offer three- to five-day trips on the Chirripó (from $305), June through December. See the On The Road chapter, under **Recreation,** for addresses and telephone numbers.

Locally, call **Selva Mar Reservation Service,** tel. 771-4582, fax 771-1903, or **Brunca Tours,** tel./fax 771-2150, which offers rafting trips, plus hiking and excursions as far afield as Chirripó and Caño Island.

Accommodations and Food

Below San Gerardo: Midway between San Isidro and San Gerardo is **Talari Auberge de Montagne,** Apdo. 517, San Isidro 8000, tel./fax 771-0341, a small resort nestled over the Río Chirripó on an eight-hectare property partially reforested with secondary forest good for birding. There are tables and chairs under shade trees. The setting is remarkably like that of the foothills of the California Sierras in the U.S. Much of the balance is made up of orchards. It's very calming. The eight rooms—adequate but soulless—have private baths and hot water; four have minibars and terraces proffering grand vistas. There's a swimming pool and a little restaurant where Pilar, the Dutch owner, plays jazz on the piano. Horseback rides cost $5 per hour, and you can take full-day trips to San Gerardo ($25). Rates: $30 s, $42 d low season; $35 s, $48 d high season.

Rancho la Botija, tel. 382-3052 or 771-1401, fax 771-2003, has three simple yet beautiful little cabins with wooden walls and bamboo ceilings and oddles of romantic charm, plus private bathrooms with hot water. Modern *cabinas* were to be added. Rates: $52 s/d, including breakfast. There's a garden with a handsome swimming pool, and the rustic and charming Café Trapiche is attached. Tours are offered.

The **Chirripó Lodge,** Albergue de Montaña Río Chirripó, c/o CIPROTUR, tel. 771-6096 or 771-4582, fax 771-2003 or 771-1903, one km above Canáan, enjoys an exquisite setting in a ravine beneath huge granite boulders. Eight rustic wooden cabins hang over the river. They're cross-ventilated and each has a double and single bed, balcony, and simple bathroom with hot water. The main lodge is a rough-hewn log structure with soaring *palenque* roof and open walls with views towards the mountains. Lively dances are hosted. Trails lead down to a natural pool by the river. Horses can be rented ($3.50 per hour), and tours are offered to Cerro Polón thermal springs and mountaintops. Rates: $45 s/d low season; $60 s/d high season, including tax and breakfast.

Albergue Montaña El Pelicano, Apdo. 942-8000, San Gerardo de Rivas, Peres Zeledon, tel. 771-1866, nearby, is another splendid option on the mountainside coffee *finca* of Rafael Elizondo. Focal point is a large alpine-style wooden lodge with 10 rooms upstairs sharing four spic-and-span toilets and tiled showers with hot water. The simple hostel-type rooms are sky-lit and bare bones, but have tasteful fabrics. Walls do not reach the ceiling, so no nocturnal antics please. Trails lead into the forest. There are views down the valley. And the place is full of intriguing art hewn from driftwood. Rates: $10 s, $19 d.

San Gerardo: Cabinas y Soda Marín, public tel. 771-0433, next to the ranger station below San Gerardo, has eight simple but clean cabins with shared bath and hot water. Rates: $4 pp. It has a basic restaurant and *pulpería* (general store) where you can buy food for the hike up Chirripó. **Bar/Restaurant El Bosque,** 100 meters uphill, has four clean but small bare-bones cabins, each with two bunks and shared bath with cold water. Rates: $2 pp.

Cabinas del Descanso, tel. 771-1866, 200 meters uphill from the ranger station, has 10 newer, more spacious and relatively salubrious *cabinas* with double beds and private baths with hot water; plus three tiny dorms with bunks and shared baths with cold water. There's a rustic yet charming restaurant serving filling *típico* meals. The Elizondo family welcomes you warmly. Don Francisco leads treks, including birding trips, and offers trout fishing. Rates: $21 s/d/t *cabinas;* $4 pp dorms.

A stone's throw north is **Cabinas Elimar,** with simple rooms in a house. It offers private baths with cold water, plus a pleasant restaurant with a small swimming pool. The live-in owners are said to be noisy. Rates: $20 pp. *Overpriced!*

Farther up the road on the hillside near the church is **Cabinas y Soda Chirripó,** which has three rooms with shared baths and hot water, plus a restaurant. Rates: about $3. For something different, try **Roca Dura** ("Hard Rock"), a rambling wooden house favored by trekkers. It has nine simple rooms, some built onto the rock face with granite boulders for the walls and ceiling. Some have bunks. The rustic wooden bar/restaurant serves pizzas and *típico* dishes and looks down over the river. The owners were remodeling at press time. They offer guided horseback rides ($21). Rates: $4 pp; $3.50 pp rooms with bunks.

Finca las Cascadas, tel./fax 771-1037, is a pretty Hansel-and-Gretel-type house for rent, with three rooms, hot water, and a fully equipped kitchen.

Herradura: Cabinas Villas is a three-room bare-bones wooden cabin with double-bed bunks on the west bank of the river. It has a basic kitchen with three-ring burner, but the owner's daughter will cook for you; check at the *pulpería*, public tel. 771-1199, on the east side of the river. Rates: $4 pp. The **Pensión Quetzal Dorado,** tel. 771-0433, ext. 109, is an hour-long hike away in Río Blanco. It has a dorm that sleeps 45, plus shared toilets. You can rent horses here. Rates: $3 pp; $10 pp including meals.

Services
You can hire **horses** for $24 a day.

Getting There and Away
Buses depart San Isidro for San Gerardo de Rivas at 5 a.m. and 2 p.m., returning at 7 a.m. and 4 p.m. A 10:30 a.m. bus from San José (Calle 16, Avenidas 1/3; $1 each way) to San Isidro will get you there in time for the 2 p.m. bus. There's another San Gerardo nearby, so be sure to specify San Gerardo *de Rivas.*

If driving, the turnoff for Rivas and San Gerardo is opposite the **Pollo Brasilita,** one km south of San Isidro. A 4WD taxi from San Isidro will cost $22.

PARQUE NACIONAL CHIRRIPÓ

Chirripó National Park protects 50,150 hectares of high-elevation terrain surrounding Cerro Chirripó (3,819 meters), Central America's highest peak. The park is contiguous with La Amistad International Peace Park to the south; together they form the Amistad-Talamanca Regional Conservation Unit. Much of the area remains terra incognito—a boon for flora and fauna, which thrive here relatively unmolested by humans. One remote section of the park is called Savannah of the Lions, after its large population of pumas. Tapirs and jaguars are both common, though rarely seen. And the mountain forests protect several hundred bird species.

Cloud forest, above 2,500 meters, covers almost half the park, which features three distinct life zones; the park is topped off by subalpine rainy *páramo,* marked by contorted dwarf trees and marshy grasses that dry out on the Pacific slopes Jan.-May (presenting perfect conditions for raging fires fanned by high winds). Much of this area still bears the scars of a huge fire that raged across 2,000 hectares in April 1992, causing such devastation that the park was closed for four months. The region is still trying to recover from this and even worse fires in 1976 and 1985.

Cerro Chirripó was held sacred by pre-Columbian Indians. Tribal leaders and shamans performed rituals atop the lofty shrine; lesser mortals who ventured up Chirripó were killed. Magnetic fields are said to swing wildly at the top, particularly near Los Crestones, huge boulders thought to have been the most sacred of Indian sites.

Just as Hillary climbed Everest "because it was there," so Chirripó lures the intrepid who seek the satisfaction of reaching the summit (the first recorded climb was made by a priest, Father Agustín Blessing, in 1904). Many Ticos choose to hike the mountain during the week preceding Easter, when the weather is usually dry. Avoid holidays, when the huts may be full. The hike is no Sunday picnic but requires no technical expertise. The trails are well-marked, and basic mountain huts are close to the summit. You must stay overnight in San Gerardo de Rivas, from where you begin your hike early the next day.

Excessive wear and tear on the trails led the National Parks Service to begin phasing in new regulations in 1993. Only 60 visitors are allowed within the park at any one time (you may be told there's a waiting list; experienced hikers recommend showing up anyway as there are usually lots of no-shows). And nobody is allowed to hike without a guide. The park service is pushing the less-known Herradura Trail (minimum three days/two nights), via Paso de los Indios, with the first night atop Cerro Urán.In January 1998 the park was closed while a new *albergue* was being constructed. It was scheduled to reopen by summer 1998. Check for current regulations.

Entrance: $6, plus $2 for each night's use of mountain huts.

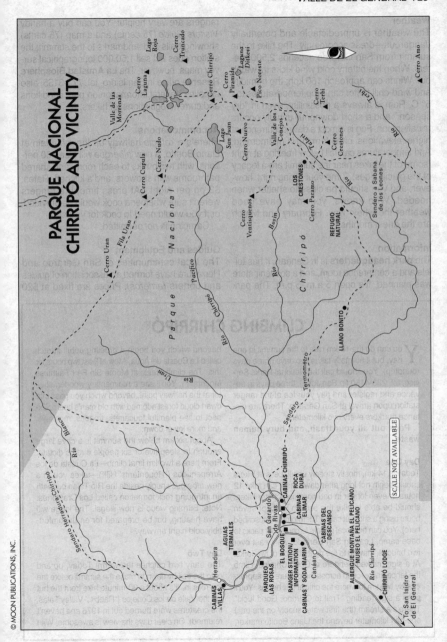

SCALE NOT AVAILABLE

© MOON PUBLICATIONS, INC.

Weather

The weather is unpredictable and potentially dangerous—dress accordingly. The hike to the summit from San Gerardo ascends 2,500 meters. When the bitterly cold wind kicks in, watch out. Winds can approach 160 kph: the humidity and wind-chill factor can drop temperatures to - 5° C. Rain is always a possibility, even in "dry season," and a short downpour usually occurs midafternoon. Fog is almost a daily occurrence at higher elevations, often forming in midmorning. And temperatures can fall below freezing at night (some of the lakes near the summit are a legacy of the glacial ages). Time your hiking right, however, and you should be close to shelter when needed. Who knows, you may have good weather the whole way. February and March are the driest months.

Information

The **park headquarters** is in Canáan. It has toilets and a conference room, and a souvenir store was planned. It's open 5 a.m.-5 p.m. The park rangers are very helpful. You can buy a handy *Visitors Guide* (75 cents) and a map (75 cents) showing trails and landmarks to the summit; the station does not sell 1:50,000 topographical survey maps, however. The **La Amistad Biosphere Reserve** office in San Isidro, tel. 771-3155, also supplies general information on park conditions and current regulations for hikers.

Accommodations

There's a *refugio* halfway up the mountain at Llano Bonito. A new *albergue* will sleep 60 persons, with two bunks to each room, and shared bathrooms with showers, and a kitchen. Rates: $2 pp per night. (At press time, the rangers weren't sure whether a cook would be provided, or if you would need to cook for yourself.)

Camping is *not* permitted.

Guides and Equipment

The local communities of San Gerardo and Herradura have formed an association of guides and porters *(arrieros)*. Prices are fixed at $20

CLIMBING CHIRRIPÓ

You can do the 16-km hike to the summit in one day, but it normally takes two days (three days roundtrip). You should call the National Parks Service, tel. 233-4160 (in San José), three days in advance and register and pay your fee at the ranger station upon arrival at San Gerardo. There are distance markers every two kilometers.

Pack out all your trash, and bury human waste.

Day One

Today is 14 km, mostly steeply uphill. Less fit hikers should begin not long after dawn, as it can take 12 hours or even longer in bad conditions (fitter hikers should be able to hike this section in six or seven hours using a shortcut called Thermometer, described here). You can hire local porters to carry your packs to base camp. Leaving San Gerardo, walk east over two bridges, staying to the right at each of two forks. At a sign marked Sendero al Cerro Chirripó, climb the fence and ascend across the pasture for approximately two km to where the official trail begins. You'll pass a sign reading "Trail to Chirripó. Good luck!" There's a stream (the first water supply on the trail) one-half kilometer beyond the Llano Bonito marker,

beyond which you begin a grueling uphill stretch called La Cuesta del Agua. Allow at least two hours for this. The climb crests at Monte Sin Fé ("Faithless Mountain"). You'll see a rudimentary wooden shelter at the halfway point, beyond which you pass into dwarf cloud forest adorned with old man's beard. Expect to see plentiful toucanets, trogons, monkeys, and more lower down.

About six km below the summit is a cave large enough to sleep five or six people if rains dictate. From here a two-km final climb—La Cuesta de los Arrepentidos ("Repentants' Hill")—takes you to a new *albergue* snugly beside the Río Talari beneath an intriguing rock formation called Los Crestones. Note: Burning wood is now illegal. The lodge will have heating, but be prepared for an uncomfortably cold night anyway.

Day Two

The early bird catches the worm! Today, up and onto the trail by dawn to make the summit before the fog rolls in. It's about a 90-minute hike from the hut via the Valle de los Conejos ("Rabbits' Valley;" alas, the creatures were burned out in 1976 and haven't returned). On clear days the view is awesome! With

per day, with a 35-pound limit per porter. Hire one, thereby contributing to the community and lightening your load. The porters are selected democratically from a rotating list. If you want to attempt the Herradura Trail, check with Sigifredo at the *pulpería,* tel. 771-1199, in Herradura.

You can rent stoves, gas canisters, sleeping bags, and more at **Roca Dura** and other *pulperías* in San Gerardo. Check with the rangers for the latest restrictions on using stoves. A good investment is the *Visitor's Guide,* which covers all the bases for hiking.

quetzal birds

BOB RACE

RESERVA BIOLÓGICA LOS CUSINGOS

This neotropical bird sanctuary, 15 km southeast of San Isidro, is run by Dr. Alexander Skutch (author of *Birds of Costa Rica*) who uses the 142-hectare property along the western bank of the Río Peñas Blancas as an open-air laboratory to study birds. The reserve is surrounded by primary forest, home to more than 300 bird species.

It's on the lower slopes of Chirripó, near the small community of Santa Elena. You get there via General Viejo (five km east of San Isidro from the San Gerardo de Rivas road, then south for Peñas Blanca) or from the Hwy. 2 via Peñas Blancas (then north for General Viejo). Turn east for Quizarra-Santa Elena. After three km go straight at the crossroads for Santa Elena. At the cemetery,

luck, you'll be able to see both the Pacific and the Caribbean. Take time, too, if you can stand the cold, for a dip in Lago San Juan (if it's sunny, you'll quickly dry off and warm up on the rocks). You'll pass waterfalls en route to the top, giving you an understanding of why the Talamancan Indians called it Chirripó—"Place of Enchanted Waters."

You can head back to San Gerardo the same day, or contemplate a roundtrip hike to Cerro Ventisqueros, the second-highest mountain in Costa Rica: the trail begins below the Valle de los Conejos. You can spend your second night at another hut in the Valle de las Morenas, on the northern side of Chirripó (reportedly you need to obtain the key from the ranger in San Gerardo). With a local guide, you could also follow the Camino de los Indios, a trail that passes over Cerro Urán and the far northern Talamancas. Do not try to follow this or any other trails without an experienced guide!

Maps
The ranger station sells a map showing the trail and highlights. For forays off the main trail, you might want to back this up with 1:50,000-scale topographical maps (sections 3444 II San Isidro and 3544 III Durika; if you plan on hiking to nearby peaks, you may also need sections 3544 IV Fila

Norte and 3444 I Cuerici) available from the Instituto Geográfico Nacional in San José.

What to Bring
• Warm clothes—preferably layered clothing for varying temperatures and humidity. A polypropylene jacket remains warm when wet.
• Raingear. A poncho is best.
• Good hiking boots. The path is wet and slippery.
• Warm sleeping bag—good to 0° C.
• Flashlight with spare batteries.
• A compass and map.
• Water (one liter minimum). You will lose body fluids. Avoid dehydration at all costs. There is no water supply for the first half of the hike.
• Food, including snacks. Dried bananas and peanuts are good energy boosters; bananas have potassium (good for guarding against cramps).
• Bag for litter/garbage. Take only photographs, leave only footprints.
• Wind/sun protection.

Tours
Brunca Tours, tel./fax 771-2150, in San Isidro, offers a five-day trip to Chirripó. **Camino Travel,** tel. 234-2530, fax 225-6143, has a three-day trekking program departing San José each Tuesday ($315).

go downhill for Los Cusingos. Hotel del Sur, in San Isidro, offers tours ($25 including lunch).

BUENOS AIRES AND VICINITY

About 40 km south of San Isidro the air becomes redolent of sweet-smelling pineapples, the economic mainstay of the Valle de El General which is centered on **Buenos Aires**, a small agricultural town in the midst of an endless sea-green sea of spiky *piñas,* near the base of the Talamanca mountains. The nondescript town, 63 km south of San Isidro de El General, is three km northeast of Hwy. 2 (there are *sodas* and a Texaco gas station at the junction). It makes a good base for exploring La Amistad International Peace Park, but there is no other reason to stop here (while in town, check out the attractive mural on the coffin-shaped church in the plaza).

Reportedly, it's possible to take a tour of the Pindeco pineapple-processing plant, tel. 730-2053. **Tropical Rainbow Tours,** Apdo. 774, San José 1000, tel. 233-8228, fax 255-4636, includes a tour of the plantation as part of a two-day tour to La Amistad ($175).

Southeast from Buenos Aires, the Pan-Am Highway follows the Río General 25 km to its confluence with the Río Coto Brus at Paso Real. The area is a center for several indigenous tribes, and there are several indigenous reserves in the nearby mountains. At the gas station at **Brujo,** 10 km southeast of Buenos Aires, are turnoffs leading north to the **Reserva Indígena Cabagra,** and to the south for **Reserva Indígena Boruca.** Several of the Indian communities have museums—*museos comunitarios indígenas*—where you can learn something about local culture. A dirt road also leads 10 km north from Buenos Aires to Reserva Biológica Durika.

Reserva Biológica Durika

This private reserve on the western flank of Cerro Durika (3,280 meters), 20 km northeast of Buenos Aires is inside La Amistad. It is a two-hour uphill journey from Buenos Aires to a trailhead that leads steeply through cloud forest to the hamlet of Ujarrás, within the **Reserva Indígena Ujarrás/Durika.** It is a good access point for hikes into La Amistad International Peace Park. Though the slopes are severely denud-

---

FIESTA DE LOS DIABLITOS

Every year on 30 December a conch shell sounds at midnight across the dark hills of the Fila Sinancra. Men disguised as devils burst from the hills into Boruca and go from house to house, performing skits and receiving rewards of *tamales* and *chicha,* the traditional corn liquor. This is the Fiesta de los Diablitos. Drums and flutes play while villagers dress in burlap sacks and traditional balsa-wood masks, energizing a pantheon of chiseled supernatural beings. Another dresses as a bull. Plied with *chicha,* the man becomes the animal and the animal the man, just as in the Roman Catholic tradition the sacrament becomes the body of the Lord. The *diablitos* chase, prod, and taunt the bull. Three days of celebrations and performances end with the symbolic killing of the bull, which is then reduced to ashes on a pyre. The festival reenacts the battles between Indian forebears and Spanish conquistadors with a dramatic new twist: the Indians win.

---

ed, the forests provide excellent opportunities for spotting quetzals, trogons, toucans, and monkeys. And animals not seen for many years, such as pumas and jaguars, have been spotted recently, suggesting that community efforts at reforestation may be paying off.

Those efforts have been fostered by **Finca Anael,** Asociación Durika, Apdo. 9, Buenos Aires, tel. 730-0082, fax 730-0003, e-mail: durikas@ gema.com, website http://www.gema.com/durikas, or c/o Annie McCormick, tel. 240-2320, fax 223-0341, a self-sufficient agricultural community near Ujarrás that works on behalf of harmony and conservation. Its 20 or so members—mostly Ticos, but with some foreigners—operate this 50-hectare farm on land contiguous with the Durika Reserve. It's an oasis of greenery amid the bare mountains (project members hope to buy surrounding forest). The community was founded by a group of city folks who wanted to escape the rat race for a stress-free, more peaceful existence. The community welcomes ecotourists. A guide is assigned to you. Besides the opportunity to milk the goats, feed the goats, make yogurt and cheese, try your hand at carpentry, and learn—and even participate in—organic farming, you can attend classes in martial arts, meditation, and art. Guided hikes include one to a waterfall, another to Indian villages, and a third, a five-day camping trip to the summit of Cerro Durika.

Finca Anael is a tough trek in, but the dirt road may have reached the *finca* itself by the time you read this.

Accommodations and Food

In the center of Buenos Aires, the **Cabinas Kanajaka** has four modern albeit simple little *cabinas*. Rates: about $8 pp. **Cabinas Violeta,** next to the fire station, has 20 simple cabins in a courtyard. Rates: $6 s, $9 d. **Cabinas la Redonda Familiares** also offers cheap accommodations. **Cabinas Mary** and **Cabinas El Buen Amigos** are next to each other, about one km southwest of Buenos Aires; take the right turn at the Y fork when approaching from Hwy. 2. Both have clean *cabinas* with fans and private baths (rates: $5) and shared baths and cold water. Cabinas Mary has a small restaurant. There's a *pulpería* next door.

Finca Anael, Apdo. 9, Buenos Aires, tel. 730-0082, fax 730-0003, has three simple, candlelit cabins with fantastic views (one has two beds and a private bathroom; the others each have four beds and share a bathroom). Rates: $30-35, including all meals, which are vegetarian (don't fail to try the *chicha,* a heady home brew of fermented corn and sugar), plus transfers.

In Buenos Aires, **Restaurant Ling Cheng** is an Italian restaurant—just kidding! The **Panadería Santa Marta** is opposite. **La Restaurante la Flor de Sabana,** tel. 730-0256, serves tasty *típico* dishes.

Services

There's a **Banco Nacional** on the north corner of the plaza and a **Banco de Costa Rica** one block northwest. The **police,** Guardia Rural, tel. 117 or 730-0103, is one block east of the Banco Nacional. There are three **pharmacies** in town, and a **Red Cross,** tel. 730-0078, when entering town.

Getting There and Away

The Zona Sur bus to Ciudad Neily and Panamá departs San José from Avenida 18, Calle 4, tel. 221-4214, and will drop you at Buenos Aires if you ask. See **Getting There and Away** under San Isidro de El General, above, for bus schedules from San Isidro.

VALLE DEL RÍO GRANDE DE TERRABA

Paso Real, where both road and river turn southwest and descend to Palmar and Golfo Dulce region through a ravine in the Fila Costeña mountains. About five km south of Paso Real is the Indian village of **Rey Curré,** looking much like most small hamlets in the country but also with a strong hint of an indigenous heritage. There's a crafts cooperative next to the school where you can buy carved gourds and other Indian crafts.

About 10 km south of Paso Real, a dirt road leads uphill to **Boruca,** a slow-paced hamlet set in a verdant valley in the heart of the reserve.

Reserva Indígena Boruca

This reserve, in the Fila Sinancra west of the canyon, is accessed by dirt tracks that lead to a series of Indian villages and tiny *fincas* scattered throughout the mountains. A visit here offers a very different perspective on traditional life. Here, you can watch delicate female fingers weaving tablecloths, purses, and belts on traditional hand looms, while men carve balsa-wood masks. Gourds *(jícaras)* are made, too, carved with intricate pastoral scenes. A compelling eco-museum (Spanish only) honors the local culture. The Indians sell beautiful carved masks and hand-weavings not available in San Jose. A proposed dam project threatens much of their land.

Accommodations

There are no hotels in Boruca, but it is possible to stay with families by prior arrangement through **Tur-Casa,** tel. 225-1239. Alternately, ask at the village *pulpería.*

Getting There and Away

A bus departs Buenos Aires for Boruca, supposedly at 1:30 p.m. (two hours). Alternatively, the Zona Sur bus from San José will drop you off at either the trailhead, two km south of Brujo (13 km south of Buenos Aires), or at the dirt road south of Rey Curré.

SPECIAL HOTEL: VISTA DEL VALLE

Vista del Valle, Apdo. 185-4003, Alajuela, tel./fax 451-1165 and 450-0800, e-mail: mibrejo@sol .racsa.co.cr, website www.vistadelvalle.com, formerly Posada Las Palomas, is a serene "bed and breakfast" on a working citrus and coffee *finca* on the edge of the Río Grande Canyon Preserve. The main lodge—a piece of Marin transplanted—is a Frank Lloyd Wright-style architectural marvel in wood: all cantilevers and mezzanines and hanging stairs and wall-to-ceiling plate-glass windows through which the sunlight pours, flooding Vista del Valle with light.

Vista del Valle is named for its sublime setting on a hillside overlooking a river chasm with glorious views over and across the central valley. Lush lawns fall away to meld into tall bamboo forest. Trails lead steeply down to the river. There's a tantalizing beautiful pool and jacuzzi—big enough for a Democratic convention—fed by a water cascade suspended over 12 acres of botanical gardens giddy with bougainvillea. The silence is overwhelming.

Two guestrooms with private bathrooms are in the main building. Four reclusive cottages (including the two-bedroom Mango Manor) reached by stone trails have their own kitchens. All rooms and cottages boast luxurious hints of Japan in the tasteful yet minimalist decor and furnishings—polished hardwood floors, and four-poster beds with mosquito nets adding a romantic note—that epitomize the terms "harmonic simplicity" and "splendid aesthetic." Each has a private balcony and wraparound veranda. Some rooms have hammocks. And all have lofty cathedral ceilings and lavish Oriental-style bathrooms with granite tilework.

The amiable owners—Californians Johanna and Michael Bresnan—were planning to add 10 more cabins, plus a two-bedroom, hexagonal executive suite-cottage suspended over the gorge.

Facilities include mountain bikes and a two-horse stable (lessons and trail rides are offered). An upstairs lounge has a huge stone hearth. Fresh-brewed coffee and fresh-squeezed orange juice are delivered to your room in the morning or served, as are recherché nouvelle lunches and dinners prepared by a professionally trained chef, on an outdoor veranda with a glass atrium ceiling. An outdoor kitchen was to be added to the sundeck.

Room rates: $65-85, including breakfast; dinner $10.

There are turnoffs—one at two km and one at 400 meters east of the toll booth on the Pan-Am Highway. The hotel—which is less than a 30-minute drive from the airport—is well-signed from there.

*ax-shaped
jade pendant*

BOB RACE

VALLE DE COTO BRUS

This large valley—running northwest-southeast—is drained by the Río Coto Brus and its tributaries, which flow northwest to meet the Río General at Paso Real, where the rivers turn south as the Río Terraba. Coffee is the principal crop in the valley, with dark-green bushes flanking the steep slopes of the lower Talamancas to the north and, to the south, the various ridges that make up the Fila Costeña. The summits of Cerro Kamuk (3,549 meters) and Cerro Fabrega (3,336 meters) loom massively overhead. Though coffee production only arrived in Coto Brus in 1949, today the town is the nation's largest coffee-producing region.

The regional capital is San Vito, on a ridgetop at the head of the valley.

PASO REAL TO SAN VITO

The Río Terraba is spanned by a bridge one km south of Paso Real. From here, Hwy. 237 leads to San Vito. Highway 237 follows the valley floor for 10 km then climbs onto the **Fila Guacimo,** forming the southern flank of the Valle de Coto Brus; the road then follows the ridge to San Vito. It's one of the most scenic drives in the country, with magnificent views across the valley toward the bulk of the Talamancas.

Three km southeast of the bridge, a dirt road leads north five km to Potrero Grande and La Amistad International Peace Park. The **Estación Tres Colinas** ranger station is 28 km from here, at Helechales.

Another rough dirt road at Guácimo, 20 km southeast of the Terraba River, leads 21 km to **Altamira** and the **Estación Altamira** ranger station (5.5 km; see **Parque Internacional La Amistad,** below). Neither the road nor Altamira are marked on most road maps. The Altamira station has a small museum and lecture room, a camping area with toilets and showers, drinking water, a covered picnic area (you'll need to bring stoves and gas containers), and a *mirador* for admiring the views. Trails lead into primary forest. The **Sendero Valle del Silencio** is a six-hour, 20 km hike into the cloud forest and is good for spotting quetzals (there's a basic campsite). The **Sendero Alatmira-Sabanas Esperanzas** reaches above the tree line at 1,800 meters and passes an Indian cemetery marked by tumuli. Pizotes, monkeys, *tepezcuintles,* and quetzals are often seen. The three-km-long **Sendero Gigantes del Bosque** is good for experiencing the wildlife of montane rainforest. TRACOPA buses between Buenos Aires and San Vito will drop you at Las Tables, where you can take a jeep-taxi to Altamira. Call tel. 771-3297, fax 771-5116 for reservations.

Accommodations

Monte Amou Lodge, tel./fax 229-3618; in San José, tel. 265-6149, cellular tel. 380-4253, near Helachales, 12 km east of Potrero Grande, lies at the foot of Mt. Fallas, at an elevation of 1,000 meters in a transition zone between humid tropical forest and tropical cloud forest on the edge of La Amistad. Stupendous views. Trails penetrate the park. The lodge and *cabinas* have thatched roofs, with locally handmade furniture. The lodge has four guest suites, each with three beds, a desk, and private shower (hot water at night only, when the generator is turned on). There's a cozy lounge, and family-style dinners are served in a large dining room. Bring warm clothing. Tucan Ecological Tours offers guided nature tours to La Amistad International Park using Monte Amou as a base. Manuel and Anna Vargas, the owners, are warm and sociable. Perfect for birders. Four-day package rates per person: $484 s, $424 d, $404 t, including transport from San José, three meals daily, plus guided tours.

SAN VITO AND VICINITY

San Vito is a pleasant and hilly mountain town that nestles on the east-facing flank of the Fila Costeña, overlooking the Valle de Coto Brus, at 990 meters above sea level. The town was founded by Italian immigrants in the early 1850s. There's no main plaza, but there's a tiny park at the top of the hill as you enter town from Buenos Aires or as you descend into town on the

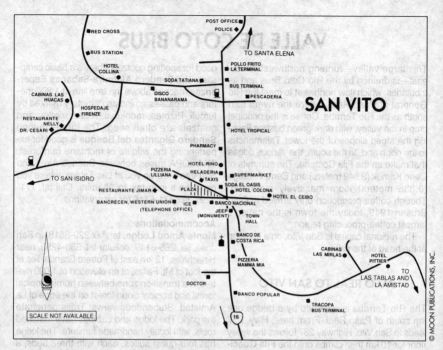

© MOON PUBLICATIONS, INC.

road from Ciudad Neily; note the patinated life-size statue of two children under an umbrella dedicated to "La Fraternidad Italo-Costarricense." The strangest edifice is the rusting hulk of a WWII jeep on a pedestal opposite the town hall.

Parque Ecológico, downhill 200 meters to the east, is a re-creation of a tropical rainforest complete with rushing river.

Wetlands of San Joaquín/Cañada Wetlands Project
The Association for the Protection of Natural Resources of Coto Brus (APRENABRUS) works to preserve and stabilize a species-rich fresh-water wetland—a habitat now rare in Costa Rica—three km east of San Vito. In addition to fish, reptiles, and insects that live only in aquatic environments, the area attracts more than 100 species of birds. The goal is to make the wetlands more accessible. Facilities will include parking areas, observation platforms, benches, and trails. If you're interested in contributing or visiting, contact the Wilson Botanical Gardens at

Apdo. 73, San Vito de Java, Coto Brus, tel. 773-4004, fax 773-3665.

Finca Cántaros
This six-hectare reserve surrounding a one-hectare lake, at Linda Vista, three km southeast of San Vito, is owned by Gail Hewson de Gómez, deputy-director of Las Cruces Biological Station. It's centered on a beautifully restored farmhouse converted into a fine art and crafts gallery, with a children's library and education center attached. The focus is on teaching respect for local ecology and culture. Trails lead to the lake—**Laguna Julia**—which attracts grebes, gallinules, herons, and cormorants who come to feed on the fish and frogs. The gallery sells exquisite ceramics, jewelry, Ecuadorian blankets, and hand-painted wooden statues. Open Tues.-Sun. 8 a.m.-4 p.m.; entrance $1.

Accommodations
Cabinas Las Mirlas, tel. 773-3714, on the road to Cañas Gordas, has pretty landscaped grounds

overlooking a valley, plus eight basic cabins with cold water but no fans. Rates: $5.50 pp. **Hospedaje Firenze,** tel. 773-3741, on the west side of town, has six rooms with private baths and hot water but no fans. It is small but pleasing. Rates: $5 pp. **Hotel Colona,** tel. 773-4543, has 25 very basic rooms with hot water but no fans. Rates: $4 pp. **Hotel Collina,** tel. 773-3173, has six pleasant rooms with private baths, hot water, and fans, plus a lively bar and open-air restaurant upstairs. Rates: $6 pp. The new **Hotel Rino,** tel. 773-3071, is ample simple but adequate rooms with cable TV, plus private baths and hot water. Rates: $6.50 pp.

Hotel Tropical, tel. 754-2473, has 16 rooms with cold water and fans, but there's a disco downstairs and it's said that rooms are used by the hour. Rates: $2.50 pp. **Hotel Pittier,** tel. 773-3027, has 12 rooms with hot water but no fans. It was terribly run-down when I called by. The office is hidden around the corner. Rates: $4 s, $7 d. Also try **Cabinas Las Huacas,** tel. 773-3115, with 13 modest but pleasant rooms with private baths and hot water in a dour compound on the west side of town. There's a popular bar with TV, and a disco on weekends. Rates: $6 s, $10 d without TV; $7.50 s, $12 d with TV.

The nicest place in town is **Hotel El Ceibo,** tel. 773-3025, behind the Municipalidad. It has 38 modern rooms with private baths and hot water, a large restaurant, a lounge with TV, plus a small bar. Each room has one double and a single bed. Rooms at the back face Parque Ecológico. Rates: $15 s, $24 d, including breakfast.

There are also modest cabinas—**Mirador Cabinas**—three km northeast of San Vito, at Lourdes, en route to La Amistad.

Food
San Vito's Italian heritage shines. **Pizzería Mamma Mía** has a large menu of Italian dishes, from lasagne and ravioli to gnocchi, *orechiette a la Mamma Mía,* and *cotolette a la bolognesa,* all under $4. The **Hotel El Ceibo** restaurant serves cannelloni, lemon scallopini, and fresh tuna spaghetti. **Pízzería Lilliana** is recommended for Italian fare; I had a tasty pizza (from $3) served on the patio. Also consider the upstairs restaurant of the **Hotel Collina,** which serves Italian and Chinese.

Pescadaría Río Mar serves ceviche and seafood. The **Restaurant Jimar,** tel. 773-4050, is a nice modern cafe-style eatery serving burgers and *casados* ($2.50) and *batidos* ($1).

There are several other cheap *sodas* selling Tico fare.

Entertainment
Nightlife centers on the bar of the **Hotel Collina, Bar Hermanos Ureña,** and the **Disco Bananarama,** next to the gas station. **Centro Turístico Las Huacas** has live bands and dancing on weekends. You can shoot eight ball with locals at the **Sala de Billares,** upstairs opposite the main bus station.

Services
The **hospital** is two km south of town, on the road to Ciudad Neily. **Dr. Pablo Ortíz, tel. 773-3407, is bilingual.** Dr. Stefano Cesari, tel. 773-3206, only speaks Spanish, but is recommended; hours are 10 a.m.-noon and 2-6 p.m. There's a **pharmacy,** tel. 773-3076, on the main street. **Banco Nacional** and **Banco de Costa Rica** have branches on the main street; **BanCrecen,** tel. 773-4400, has an ATM and represents **Western Union.** It's open Mon.-Fri. 9 a.m.-9 p.m. The **post office** and **police station** adjoin each other, 200 meters up the hill north of the main bus station.

Getting There and Away
By Bus: Tracopa, tel. 221-4214 and 773-3410, buses depart Avenida 18, Calles 2/4, at 2:45 p.m.; indirect buses depart at 6:15 a.m., 8:15 a.m., and 11:30 a.m. and travel via Paso Real and the Wilson Botanical Gardens. Empresa Alfaro buses depart for San Vito from San José on Avenida 5, Calle 14. Buy tickets in advance.

There are three bus terminal in San Vito. Tracopa's direct buses depart San Vito for San José at 5 a.m. and 3 p.m.; indirect buses depart at 7:30 a.m., 10 a.m., and 3 p.m. Buses from San Isidro depart at 5:30 a.m. and 2 p.m., returning at 6 a.m. and 1 p.m. Buses from Ciudad Neily depart at 6 a.m., 11 a.m., 1 p.m., and 3 p.m. Autotransportes Cepul buses depart Terminal Cepul for Ciudad Neily at 5:30 a.m., 7 a.m., 9 a.m., 11 a.m., and 2 p.m. ($1.50); and to Las Mellizas at 9:30 a.m., 2 p.m., and 5 p.m. Autotransportes Blanco Quiros buses depart from Terminal Cepul to Las Tablas at 10:30 a.m. and 3 p.m. Additional buses to these destinations depart from Terminal San Vito.

By Air: You can charter an **air-taxi** direct to San Vito.

CAMP TRES

Feel like saving the earth? Then call in on Frances Lynn Carpenter's *finca,* Camp Tres, fax 734-0267, where the ecology professor and wannabe Johnny Appleseed from the University of California at Irvine, is raising a rainforest from previously depleted, steep-sided cattle pastures at 3,300 feet. She needs volunteers for her tropical tree farm that she hopes will demonstrate to local farmers the viability of reaping a cash crop from hardwoods in this desperately deforested quarter of land (she plants native trees that thrive on hardship and depleted soil aided, of course, by nutritious mulching and TLC).

University Research Expeditions Program, University of California, Berkeley, CA 94720, tel. (510) 642-6586, sends volunteers into the field to assist Dr. Carpenter in her scientific studies and ecological efforts; two-week programs cost $1,495.

LAS CRUCES BIOLOGICAL STATION

This biological research station, six km south of San Vito, is much more than its name suggests and well worth the drive south in itself. The center, in the midst of a 236-hectare forest reserve, is run by the Organization of Tropical Studies and acts as a center for research and scientific training by staff and students of the 50 or so universities that make up OTS, as well as for public education (there's a research library and laboratory, plus lecture room with audiovisual equipment). New plants are propagated for horticulture, and species threatened with habitat loss and extinction are maintained for future reforestation efforts. The forest reserve is one of the few intact forest remnants in the area, since all other adjacent lands have been clearcut for agriculture.

The reserve is in midelevation tropical rainforest along a ridge of the Fila Za-

pote. During the wet season, heavy fog and afternoon clouds spill over the ridge, nourishing a rich epiphytic flora of orchids, bromeliads, ferns, and aeroids. The forest is a vital habitat for pacas, anteaters, opossums, kinkajous, porcupines, armadillos, sloths, tayras, monkeys, deer, small cats, and more than 35 species of bats. Birdwatching at Las Cruces is especially rewarding: more than 330 species have been recorded.

Maintaining the reserve—proclaimed part of La Amistad Biosphere Reserve—is the cornerstone of a larger effort to save the watershed of the Río Java. It would be devastating to the garden and forest reserve if the adjacent forest were cut. Not only would the carrying capacity of the Las Cruces forest diminish with regard to species, but the opening of edges would increase exposure to wind and sun, further affecting species that rely on moist, dark areas. Inevitably, many larger species would die off. You may send donations (earmarked for the Las Cruces Land Purchase) to OTS, Duke University, P.O. Box 90630, Durham, NC 27708-0630, tel. (919) 684-5774, fax 684-5661; or OTS, Apdo. 73-8257, San Vito, tel./fax 773-3278, e-mail: lcruces@ns.ots.ac.cr. Visitation only accounts for about 30% of funds required to support the station, which seeks donors, or "amigos." You can subscribe to the *Amigos Newsletter* published by Gail Hewson de Gómez, associate station director (e-mail: ghewson@ns.ots.ac.cr).

A gift store sells T-shirts, the beautiful OTS calendar souvenirs, and a wide array of booklets on ecology.

Wilson Botanical Gardens

A spectacular highlight of the Las Cruces station is the 10 hectares of cultivated gardens established in 1963 by Robert and Catherine Wilson, former owners of Fantastic Gardens in Miami. The garden—a must see—was inspired, in part,

ocelot

BOB RACE

by the famous Brazilian gardener Roberto Burle-Marx, a friend of Wilson's, who designed much of the garden following his vision of parterres as a palette. Wilson and his wife are buried in a humble grave on the grounds. There's a picnic area and benches to sit on and absorb the beauty. Approximately 10 km of well-maintained, gently sloping trails (and many more in the forest reserve) meander through the Fern Grove, Orchid Grotto, the largest palm collection in the world (with about 700 of the world's 2,600 or so species), agave and lily beds, and heliconia groves containing more than 7,000 plant species. Oh, and the birding is top-notch.

The garden is a repository for the Begonia Society and Heliconia Society, and also has many cacti species that are already extinct in their native habitats. There are also greenhouses with large collections of anthuriums, ferns (a specialty of Luis Diego Gómez, the Las Cruces director), elkhorns, and more. The garden is desperately short of gardeners (there were only *four* at press time)—again, your financial support would be appreciated.

Dry season is mid-December through mid-April (afternoon showers are not unknown). The rainiest period is Sept.-November. Annual rainfall is a whopping 380 cm, but the gardens will enliven your spirit in even the rainiest weather.

Reservations are not required for day visits. Hours: 8 a.m.-4 p.m., closed Monday. Entrance: $5 half day; $8 full day (children $4); $16 with lunch. Students receive discounts.

Accommodations

A devastating fire in November 1994 destroyed most of the complex. An even more impressive biological station has arisen Phoenix-like from the ashes thanks mostly to generous donations. Consequently, there are 12 spacious, modestly elegant twin rooms in stylish, contemporary vogue with vast picture windows opening to prow-shaped verandas with views. Hardwoods abound. There are bedroom lights you can actually read by. Dining is family style on a wide veranda, or inside when its cold and rainy. There's a laundry ($4). Rates: $69 s, $114 d low season; $85 s, $140 d high season, including all meals.

Reservations should be made c/o OTS, Apdo. 676, San Pedro 2050, tel. 240-6696, fax 240-6783, e-mail: reservas@ns.ots.ac.cr (or contact Wilson Botanical Gardens, Apdo. 73, San Vito de Java, Coto Brus, tel. 773-4004, fax 773-3665).

Las Cruces will accept drop-by overnighters on a space-available basis. It's advisable to reserve. Special discount rates apply for researchers and students with accredited projects. Researchers can also rent cars ($40 daily).

If the station is full and you're not fussy about standards, try **Cabinas La Cascada,** 800 meters north of the gardens, with basic cabins providing cold water only. Rates: $6.

Getting There

Local buses stop at the gardens and operate from San Vito at 7 a.m., 11 a.m., 1:30 p.m., and 4 p.m.; and from the garden gate to San Vito at 6:30 a.m., 7:30 a.m., 1:45 p.m., and 4 p.m. Buses depart Ciudad Neily for the gardens at 7 a.m. and 1 p.m. A **taxi** from San Vito costs about $3; from Golfito expect to pay about $40.

PARQUE INTERNACIONAL LA AMISTAD

The 193,929-hectare International Friendship Park is shared with neighboring Panamá. Together with the adjacent Chirripó National Park, the Hitoy-Cerere Biological Reserve, Las Tablas and Barbilla Protective Zones, Las Cruces Biological Station, and a handful of Indian reservations, it forms the 600,000-hectare Amistad Biosphere Reserve, a UNESCO World Heritage Site also known as the Amistad-Talamanca Regional Conservation Unit—the largest biological reserve in the Central American isthmus.

The park transcends the Cordillera Talamanca ranges, rising from 150 meters above sea level on the Caribbean side to 3,819 meters atop Cerro Chirripó. The Talamancas are made up of separate mountain chains with only a limited history of volcanic activity; none of the mountains is considered a volcano. La Amistad's eight life zones form habitats for flora and fauna representing at least 60% of the nation's various species, including no fewer than 450 bird species (not least the country's largest population of resplendent quetzals and 49 endemic species), as well as the country's largest density of tapirs, jaguars, harpy eagles, ocelots, and many other endangered species. The park protects such important watersheds as the Ríos Térraba, Estrella, and Sixaola, whose valleys harbor the largest stands of tropical rainforests and moist forests in the isthmus. Cloud forests extend to 2,800 meters, with alpine *páramo* vegetation in the upper reaches.

The indigenous heritage is particularly strong here, and this is one of the few areas in Costa Rica where you are likely to see Indians dressed in traditional, brightly colored ethnic clothing.

Trails and Access

Much of this massive park remains unexplored. It has no facilities, and those few trails that exist are unmarked and often barely discernible. Unless you're an experienced trekker, don't even think about hiking into the park without a guide. Weather is extremely fickle. And you are most likely too many kilometers from human contact in case of an emergency.

The park has four official access points (entrance is $6). **Park headquarters** is at Progreso, about 30 km northeast of San Vito, and reached via the road through Sabalito, Unión, and Río Negro (at Sabalito, six km northeast of San Vito, turn left at the gas station, and left again at Centro Social El Nicoyano, at La Trucha; 4WD required). From here, trails lead to the Las Tablas Ranger Station (camping, but no facilities); it's about 10 km to the station. (Note that the Estación Mellizas is now closed.)

You can also enter via **Estación La Escuadra** ranger station, 14 km northeast from Agua Caliente, reached by a dirt road from Santa Elena, in the Cotón valley, about 20 km north of San Vito.

The **Estación Tres Colinas** ranger station at Helechales is about 12 km northeast of Potrero Grande and is signed as 28 km to Helechales; 4WD required. There are no facilities at Helechales. The **Estación La Amistad** ranger station is 26.5 km northeast of Guácimo and 18 km southeast of Río Terraba.

Another trail from Ujarrás, 10 km northeast of Buenos Aires, crosses the Talamancas via Cerro Abolado and the valley of the Río Taparí, ending in the Hitoy-Cerere Biological Reserve on the Caribbean side (you can catch a bus to Sixaola and thence to Puerto Limón from Shiroles). It is a very strenuous, 54-km, five- or six-day hike. *Do not attempt this hike without an in-*

digenous guide. Register in advance at the CONAI (Indigenous Affairs) office at Ujarrás. The San José CONAI office, tel. 221-5496, can provide updated information on restrictions and protocol.

Accommodations

There are no accommodations in the park. The Swiss-style **La Amistad Lodge** (formerly Las Mellizas Lodge), Apdo. 774-1000, San José, tel. 290-2251 or 220-2331, fax 232-1913, is on a 1,215-hectare farm within Las Tablas Protective Zone, a private wildlife reserve adjoining La Amistad near the Panamanian border. It is built of multihued *cristóbal,* a beautiful hardwood that lends the A-frame structure a warm glow. The three-story lodge has seven simple yet adequate rooms with large, tiled bathrooms. The lodge boasts a stone fireplace, lathe-turned balustrades, a third-floor balcony, and a restaurant where meals are served family style (there's also a patio with stone oven for barbecues). There are also three *cabinas* which have verandas complete with rocking chairs. The husband-and-wife managers Carmen and Roy Arroyo are friendly. You'll need a sturdy 4WD to get there in the wet season. Horseback rides and guided hiking are offered along 60 km of trails graded according to difficulty and ranging from 1,200 meters to 1,800 meters above sea level. A 24-room lodge, similar in appearance, was under construction (the original lodge will revert to family use by the owner). Rates: $65 pp, including meals. To get there, continue straight at Centro Social El Nicoyano at La Trucha; there are no signs until you reach the orange-and-white police station at Mellizas (La Amistad Lodge is 3.5 km to the left along a bumpy skunk of a road).

La Amistad Lodge also has two high-mountain camps: one (at 1,600 meters) with a dining room and bathroom but no electricity; the other at 1,800 meters with very basic facilities. They are recommended for anyone serious about spotting quetzals, pumas, and other rare wildlife. Rates: $65 including meals.

La Amistad Lodge is utilized on tour packages offered by Universal Tropical Nature Tours, Costa Rica Expeditions, Tropical Rainbow Tours, and Rico Tours. See the appendix for more information on these companies.

Five km south of Tigra is **Finca Las Tablas,** La Lucha, Sabalito, Coto Brus 8257, where the Sandí family offers **camping** and meals. The fruit farm and forest have a healthy population of quetzals. Horseback and hiking tours are offered.

Information

Contact the **Amistad Bisophere Reserve Office,** tel. 771-3155, fax 771-4836, in San Isidro, or the toll-free National Parks Service information line, tel. 192, in San José.

Getting There and Away

Buses depart San Vito for Cotón at 3 p.m., for Progreso and Las Mellizas at 9:30 a.m. and 2 p.m., for Las Tablas at 10:30 a.m. and 3 p.m., and for Santa Elena at 10 a.m. and 4 p.m. Buses depart Buenos Aires for Potrero Grande at 6:30 a.m. and noon. **Jeep-taxis** will run you there in dry season from Buenos Aires or San Vito (about $50 roundtrip).

Horizontes (see appendix) has tours to La Amistad.

BOB RACE

APPENDIXES
INTERBUS SCHEDULE

For further information, you can reach Interbus directly at tel. 283- 5573, fax 283-7655, e-mail: vsftrip@sol.racsa.co.cr.

ARENAL ROUTE

DEPART	HOTEL	TIME
San José	Various hotels	8:00 a.m. (depart)
Los Angeles	Villa Blanca	10:30 a.m.
San Lorenzo	Valle Escondido	11:00 a.m.
La Fortuna	Various hotels	12:30 p.m. (arrive)
La Fortuna		13:30 (depart)
Muelle	Tilajari	2:30 p.m.
Florencia	La Garza	2:45 p.m.
San Carlos	El Tucano	3:00 p.m.
San Lorenzo	Valle Escondido	4:30 p.m.
Los Angeles	Villa Blanca	5:15 p.m.
San José	Various hotels	7:30 p.m. (arrive)

PACIFIC ROUTE

DEPART	HOTEL	TIME
San José	Various hotels	8:00 a.m.
Punta Leona		10:30 a.m.
Jacó	Various hotels	11:10 a.m.
Playa Hermosa	Tierra Pacifico	11:30 a.m.
Quepos	Various hotels	12:30 p.m.
Manuel Antonio	Various hotels	12:45 p.m. (arrive); 1:30 p.m. (depart)
Quepos	Various hotels	1:45 p.m.
Playa Hermosa	Tierra Pacifico	2:45 p.m.
Jacó	Various hotels	3:15 p.m.
Punta Leona		3:45 p.m.
San José	Various hotels	6:30 p.m. (arrive)

CARIBBEAN ROUTE

San José	Various hotels	8:00 a.m.
Puerto Limón	Various hotels	11:00 a.m.

CARIBBEAN ROUTE

DEPART	HOTEL	TIME
Cahuita	Various hotels	12:00 p.m.
Puerto Viejo	Various hotels	12:30 p.m. (arrive); 1:00 p.m. (depart)
Cahuita	Various hotels	1:30 p.m.
Puerto Limón	Various hotels	2:30 p.m.
San José	Various hotels	5:30 p.m.

GUANACASTE ROUTE

San José	Various hotels	8:00 a.m.
Cañas	Rincón Corobicí	11:00 a.m.
Liberia	Hotel Las Espuelas	11:30 a.m.
Flamingo	Various hotels	12:30 p.m.
Tamarindo	Various hotels	1:15 p.m. (arrive); 2:00 p.m. (depart)
Flamingo	Various hotels	3:15 p.m.
Liberia	El Sitio	4:15 p.m.
Cañas	Rincón Corobicí	4:45 p.m.
San José	Various hotels	7:30 p.m.

BUS FARES FROM SAN JOSÉ TO:

DESTINATION	FARE
Cahuita	$30
Cañas	$27
Ciudad Quesada	$20
Flamingo	$35
Florencia	$29
Jacó	$19
La Fortuna	$29
Liberia	$29
Manuel Antonio	$29
Muelle	$29
Playa Hermosa	$22
Puerto Limón	$25
Punta Leona	$19
Puerto Viejo	$35
Quepos	$29
Tamarindo	$35

SANSA SCHEDULE

FROM/TO	DEPARTURE	DURATION
San José/Barra del Colorado	6 a.m.	35 min.
Barra del Colorado/San José	6:45 a.m.	55 min.
San José/Ciudad Neilly (Coto 47)	9:45 a.m.	70 min.
Palmar Sur/San José	11:05 a.m.	55 min.
San José/Fortuna	1:05 p.m.	25 min.
Fortuna/San José	3:10 p.m.	25 min.
San José/Golfito	6 a.m., 2:40 p.m.	55 min.
Golfito/San José	7:05 a.m., 3:45 p.m.	60 min.
San José/Liberia	11:45 a.m.	52 min.
Liberia/San José	12:50 p.m.	52 min.
San José/Palmar Sur	9:30 a.m.	45 min.
Palmar Sur/San José	10:30 a.m.	45 min.
San José/Puerto Jiménez	(Tues., Wed., Sat., Sun.)9:45 a.m.	50 min.
Puerto Jiménez/Ciudad Neilly	10:45 a.m.	10 min.
Ciudad Neilly/San José	11:05 a.m.	55 min.
San José/Puerto Jiménez	12:20 p.m.	50 min.
Puerto Jiménez/San José	1:25 p.m.	50 min.
San José/Punta Islita	7:32 a.m.	38 min.
Punta Islita/Nosara	8:20 a.m.	34 min.
Nosara/San José	8:57 a.m.	48 min.
San José/Quepos	8:10, 8:25 a.m., 1:25 p.m., and 4 p.m. (also 9:45 a.m. Mon., Wed., and Friday)	25 min.
Quepos/San José	8:50 a.m., 9:05 a.m., 2 p.m., and 4:40 p.m. (also 12:30 p.m. Mon.,Wed., and Friday)	25 min.
San José/Sámara	7:32 am.	60 min.
Sámara/San José	8:42 a.m.	63 min.
San José/Tamarindo	5:15 a.m., 11:45 a.m., and 3 p.m. (9:45 a.m. Tues., Thurs., Sat., Sun).	50 min.
Tamarindo/San José	6:20 a.m., 12:50 p.m., and 4:05 p.m. (10:50 a.m. Tues., Thurs., Sat., Sun)	50 min.

TRAVELAIR FARES

FARES (ONE-WAY/ROUNDTRIP)

San José to Carrillo	$80/131
San José to Golfito	$81/138
San José to Jacó	$37/73
San José to Liberia	$88/146
San José to Palmar Sur	$78/$127
San José to Puerto Jiménez	$87/146
San José to Punta Islita	$80/131
San José to Quepos	$48/7
San José to Tamarindo	$88/146
San José to Tambor	$66/105
San José to Tortuguero	$45/90

NORTH AMERICAN TOUR COMPANIES

The following are leading tour operators with Costa Rica programs. Additional companies are listed under activity headings in the section on **Recreation**, this chapter, and in regional chapters. Many other companies offer group and independent package tours; see your travel agent.

COSTA RICA SPECIALISTS

Central American Travel Exchange, 968 Lincoln St., Denver, CO, 80202, tel. (303) 860-0874 or (800) 711-5055, fax (303) 860-0864, e-mail: cate@travelexchange.com, website www.travelexchange.com. A wholesaler specializing in adventure travel and customized tours.

Costa Rica Connection, 975 Osos St., San Luis Obispo, CA 93401, tel. (805) 54-8823 or (800) 345-7422, fax (805) 543-3626, e-mail: tours@crconnect.com, website www.crconnect.com. Custom travel planning, with more than 10 years as a leader in ecotourism to Costa Rica. A wide range of package tours emphasizing natural history.

Costa Rica Experts, 3166 N. Lincoln Ave. #424, Chicago, IL 60657, tel. (312) 935-1009 or (800) 827-9046, fax (312) 935-9252, e-mail: crexpert@ris.net, website www.crexpert.com. One of the most respected and longest established Costa Rica specialists, with a wide range of special interest programs and full independent travel arrangement services.

Costa Rica Travel Exchange, 123 David St., New Orleans, LA 70119, tel. (504) 482-2800 or (800) 256-0124, fax (504) 488-6114, e-mail: CostaTravel@aol.com. Offers a gamut of special interest travel options as wholesaler and tour operator, plus car rentals, hotels, etc.

Costa Rican Vacation Getaways, 18123 E. Lakeshore, Bigfoot, MT 59911, tel. (406) 982-3307 or (800) 982-7679, fax (406) 952-3337, e-mail: vacget@pti.net, website www.montana.com/vacation. Specializes in wholesale travel, car rentals, tours, and beachfront villas.

Irazú Travel and Tours, 2500 Wilshire Blvd., Suite 105, Los Angeles, CA 90057, tel. (213) 569-9691, fax 569-1087. Small company with tour packages to Costa Rica and Guatemala.

Pacific Sunspots Tours, 201-196 West 3rd Ave., Vancouver, BC, Canada V5Y 1E9, tel. (604) 606-1750, fax 606-1751. Specializes in customized travel to Latin America, with intimate knowledge of Costa Rica and special interest activities.

Preferred Adventures, One W. Water St., Suite 300, St. Paul, MN 55107, tel. (612) 222-8131 or (800) 840-8687, fax (612) 222-4221, e-mail: paltours@aol.com. Specializes in adventure and natural history expeditions, and customized trip planning to Costa Rica., with multiday tours throughout the country.

Rico Tours, 130809 Research Blvd., Suite 606, Austin, TX 78750, tel. (512) 331-0918, fax 331-8765, e-mail: lac@amtvl.com. Specializes in Costa Rica, with emphasis on nature and horseback riding.

Tico Travel, 151 E. Commercial Blvd., Ft. Lauderdale, FL 33334, tel. (800) 246-2822, fax (305) 493-8466, e-mail: tico@gate.net, website www.ticotravel.com. Offers package tours and customized itineraries, especially surfing, fishing, and discount airfares.

Tropical Escapes, 4850 W. Panther Creek Dr., The Woodlands, TX 77381, tel. (281) 367-3990, fax 298-7322. Specializes in Costa Rica, Belize, and Guatemala, especially for honeymooners.

Wildland Adventures, 3516 N.E. 155th St., Seattle, WA 98155, tel. (206) 365-0686 or (800) 345-4453, fax (206) 363-6615, e-mail: wildadve@aol.com, website www.wildlands.com. A leader in offering in-depth natural history and cultural exploration in Costa Rica, with almost 100 scheduled trips annually. Also custom itineraries and family tours. Winner of a *Condé Nast Traveler* 1995 Ecotourism Award.

NATURE

Cheeseman's Ecology Safaris, 20800 Kittredge Rd., Saratoga, CA 95070, tel. (408) 741-5330 or (800) 527-5330, fax (408) 741-0358, e-mail: cheesemans@aol.com, website www.cheesemans.com.

Ecoadventures, 960 N. San Antonio Rd., Suite 201, Los Altos, CA 94022, tel. (415) 917-1856, fax 917-1857, e-mail: eco4adven@aol.com. Wholesaler specializing in group and customized independent travel, with focus on ecology and culture.

Eco-Travel Services, 5699 Miles Ave., Oakland, CA 94618, tel. (510) 655-4054, fax 655-4566, e-mail: ecotravel@wonderlink.com. Small travel agency specializing in retail and wholesale packages to Central America.

Field Guides, P.O. Box 160723, Austin, TX 78716-0723, tel. (512) 327-4953 or (800) 728-4953, e-mail: fgileader@aol.com, website www.fieldguides.com. Birding!

Geostar, 4754 Old Redwood Hwy., Suite 650A, Santa Rosa, CA 95403, tel. (707) 579-2420 or (800) 624-6633, e-mail: mansellw@crl.com. Offers seven- and 10-day trips specializing in birding, botany, and natural history.

Holbrook Travel, 3540 N.W. 13th St., Gainesville, FL 32609, tel. (352) 377-7111 or (800) 858-0999, fax (352) 371-3710, e-mail: travel@holbrooktravel.com, website www.holbrooktravel.com. Specializes in birding and natural history trips; introduced gay and lesbian tours in 1997.

International Expeditions, One Environs Park, Helena, AL 35080, tel. (205) 428-1700 or (800) 633-4734, fax (205) 428-1714, e-mail: intlexp@aol.com, website www.infomedia.net/intexp. A world leader in nature travel, with several Costa Rica packages.

Natural Habitat Adventures, 2945 Center Green Ct., Boulder, CO 80301, tel. (303) 449-3711 or (800) 543-8917, fax (303) 449-3712, e-mail: nathab@worldnet.att.net. Top-end natural history and family programs, including wildlife and photo workshops.

Nature Tours, 3629 Laurel St., New Orleans, LA 70115, tel. (504) 895-0092, fax 895-0970. Specializes in Central America.

Osprey Tours, P.O. Box 832, W. Tisbury, MA 02575-0823, tel./fax (508) 645-9049, e-mail: soosprey@aol.com. Specializes in natural history tours, with emphasis on birding, including packages for individuals and educational institutions.

Quest Nature Tours, 36 Finch Ave. W, Toronto, Ont., Canada M2N 2G9, tel. (416) 221-3000 or (800) 387-1483, fax (416) 221-5730, e-mail: travel@worldwidequest.com.

Wilderness Travel, 1102 Ninth St., Berkeley, CA 94710, tel. (510) 558-2488 or (800) 368-2794, fax (510) 558-2489, e-mail: info@wildernesstravel.com, website www.wilderenesstravel.com. World-class adventure travel operator with a Costa Rica natural history program. Small groups.

SPECIAL INTEREST ACTIVITIES

Adventure Center, 1311 63rd St., Emeryville, CA 94608, tel. (510) 654-1879 or (800) 227-8747, fax (510) 654-4200, e-mail: crh@adventure-center.com, website www.adventure-center.com. Has monthly departures of a 10-day "Costa Rica Explorer" multi-activity tour visiting Monteverde, Arenal, and Tortuguero ($1,498-1,698); plus a 15-day "Rainforest Adventure" ($1,495-1,670) offered by U.K.-based Explore Worldwide.

American Wilderness Experience, 2820-A Wilderness Place, Boulder, CO 80301-5454, tel. (303) 444-2622 or (800) 444-0099, fax (303) 444-3999, e-mail: awedave@aol.com. Offers canoeing, hiking, and horseback riding in Costa Rica.

Backroads, 801 Cedar St., Berkeley, CA 94710-1800, tel. (510) 527-1555 or (800) 462-2848, fax (510) 527-1444, e-mail: goactive@backroads.com, website www.backroads.com. North America's leading active-vacation company, with walking, bicycling, and multi-activity group tours in Costa Rica.

Go Diving, 5610 Rowland Rd., Suite 100, Minnetonka, MN 55343, tel. (800) 328-5285, fax (612) 931-0209, website www.godiving.com. Offers diving packages to Costa Rica.

Mariah Wilderness Expeditions, P.O. Box 248, Pt. Richmond, CA 94807, tel. (510) 233-2303, fax 233-0956, e-mail: rafting@mariahwe.com. Whitewater and multi-activity programs with a specialist focus on Costa Rica. Gay-friendly. Family and women-only trips. Independent travel planning.

Mountain Travel-Sobek, 6420 Fairmount Ave., El Cerrito, CA 94530, tel. (510) 527-8100 or (800) 227-2384, fax (510) 525-7710, e-mail: info@MT-Sobek.com, website www.mtsobek.com. High-end adventure travel specialist with rafting and hiking programs focusing on natural history.

Overseas Adventure Travel, 625 Mt. Auburn St., Cambridge, MA 02138, tel. (800) 221-0814. Another highly respected adventure tour operator with a multi-activity Costa Rica tour focusing on cultural interaction and natural history.

Pancho Villa Moto-Tours 685 Persimmon Hill, Bulverde, TX 78163, tel. (830) 438-7744 or (800) 233-0564, fax (830) 438-7745, e-mail: 102502.631@compuserve.com, website www.panchovilla.com. One of North America's most respected motorcycle touring companies, specializing in Latin America and Costa Rica.

Pioneer Raft, P.O. Box 22063, Carmel, CA 93922, tel. (408) 648-8800 or (800) 288-2107, fax (408) 648-8300, e-mail: Lynn_D@ix.netcom.com. Specializes in whitewater rafting in Costa Rica, plus other tours and tour planning.

Serendipity Adventures, P.O. Box 2325, Ann Arbor, MI 48106, tel. (313) 995-0111 or (800) 635-2325, fax (313) 426-5026. Specializes in active vacations, from ballooning—its specialty—to windsurfing.

Triple Dare: The Multi-Adventure Company, 450 E. Strawberry Dr. #53, Mill Valley, CA 94941, tel. (415) 381-1920, fax (415) 383-0878. As its name suggests, tours for the gung-ho traveler.

Tropical Adventures, 111 Second N., Seattle, WA 98109, tel. (206) 441-3483 or (800) 247-3483, fax (206) 441-5431, e-mail: dive@divetropical.com, website www.divetropical.com. A pre-eminent tour operator specializing in scuba diving, with a strong focus on Costa Rica.

Worldwide Adventures, 599 Sherwood Ave., Suite 101, Satellite Beach, FL 32937, tel. (407) 773-4878, fax 773-4216, e-mail: surfer@surfingadventures.com. Specializes in customized surfing and special-interest activity trips, including 4WD adventures.

Myths & Mountains, 251 Cheswold Lane, Haverford, PA 19041, tel. (610) 896-7780, fax 896-9897. Offers tours focusing on indigenous culture and traditional healing practices.

OTHER COMPANIES

Abercrombie & Kent, 1520 Kensington Rd., Oak Brook, IL 60521, tel. (708) 954-2944 or (800) 323-7308, fax (708) 954-3324. Deluxe tours of a general nature.

Adventure Vacations, 10612 Beaver Dam Rd., Hunt Valley, MD 21030-2205, tel. (800) 638-9040, fax (410) 584-2771. Range of packages including hotel vouchers, fly-drive adventures, and generic itineraries.

Calypso Island Tours, 3901 Grand Ave., Suite 304, Oakland, CA 94610, tel. (510) 653-3570.

Center for Global Education, 2211 Riverside Ave., Minneapolis, MN 55454, tel. (612) 330-1159 or (800) 299-8889, e-mail: globaled@augsburg.edu. Offers study abroad programs in Central America focusing on gender issues, sustainable development, environment, and societal change.

Elderhostel, 75 Federal St., Boston, MA 02110, tel. (617) 426-8056. Educational trips for seniors over 55, with strong natural history focus.

Festival Tours, 737 W. Oakridge Rd., Orlando, FL 32809, tel. (407) 850-0680, fax 240-1480.

Island Flight Vacations, 6033 W. Century Blvd. #807, Los Angeles, CA 90045, tel. (310) 410-0558 or (800) 426-4570, fax (310) 410-0830. Charter package groups from the West Coast.

Ladatco Tours, 2220 Coral Way, Miami, FL 33145, tel. (305) 854-8422, fax 285-0504. One of North America's largets wholesale tour operators to Central and South America offering group package tours.

Latin American Escapes, P.O. Box 9359-421, Walnut Creek, CA 94598, tel. (510) 935-5241, fax 945-0154, e-mail: laescapes@aol.com. Customized group tours and independent travel.

Latin American Travel, 329 Clematis St., West Palm Beach, FL 33401, tel. (561) 832-8101, fax 655-9259. Wholesaler specializing in Costa Rica and Central America.

Lifestyles Exploration, 101 Federal St., Suite 1900, Boston, MA 02110, tel. (617) 342-7359, fax 342-7080, e-mail: khr007@msn.com.

Lost World Adventures, 220 Second Ave., Decatur, GA 30030, tel. (404) 373-5820, fax 377-1902, e-mail: lwa@lostworldadventures.com. Offers soft adventures and natural history programs throughout Latin America.

Ocean Connection, 211 E. Parkwood #106, Friendswood, TX 77546, tel. (281) 996-7800, fax 996-1556, e-mail: adventure@oceanconnection.com. Specializes in ecotourism, diving, and resorts.

Smithsonian Odyssey Tours, 222 Berkeley St., Boston, MA 02116, tel. (800) 258-5885. Natural history study tours.

Southern Horizons Travel, 5315 Laurel Canyon Blvd. #210, Valley Village, CA 91607, tel. (818) 980-7011, fax 980-6987, e-mail: tripman@delphi.com. More than 100 package options, including for independent travel.

Tourlite International, 551 Fifth Ave., Suite 1001, New York, NY 10176, tel. (212) 599-2727 or (800) 272-7600, fax (212) 370-0913.

Tourtech International, 17780 Fitch, Suite 180, Irvine, CA 92664, tel. (714) 476-1912, fax 476-2210. Wholesale tour operator specializing in Central America.

COSTA RICAN TOUR COMPANIES

The following are leading tour operators in Costa Rica. Additional companies are listed under activity headings in the section on **Recreation**, this chapter, and in regional chapters. The Costa Rican Tourism Institute (ICT) publishes a catalog listing all registered tour operators and specialties.

THE BIG LEAGUE

Calypso Cruises, Apdo. 6941-1000, San José, tel. 256-2727, fax 233-0401, e-mail: calypso@centralamerica.com, website www.calypsotours.com; in the U.S., P.O. Box 025216-819, Miami, FL 33102, tel. (800) 948-3770. Originated the Isla Tortuga cruise in 1975, now offered aboard the sophisticated 70-foot *Manta Ray* catamaran (including nighttime star-gazing trips), plus cruises to a private island aboard the venerable *Calypso.*

Camino Travel, Apdo. 1049-2050, San Pedro, tel. 234-2530, fax 225-6143, e-mail: caminotr@sol.racsa.co.cr. A full-service travel agency and tour operator with a "one-stop travel shop" at Calle 1, Avenidas Central/1 in central San José, tel. 257-0107, fax 257-0234. Specializes in customized itineraries for individuals, including hiking. Helena Chavarría Saxe speaks fluent English and German and fair Italian.

Costa Rica Expeditions, Apdo. 6941-1000, San José, tel. 257-0766, fax 257-1665, e-mail: crexped@sol.racsa.co.cr, website www.crexped.co.cr or www.expeditions.co.cr. Pioneers in natural history and adventure travel in Costa Rica, and one of the finest companies. Specializes in natural history trips, whitewater rating, special interest activities, and customized tours. It has a complete range of tour packages to destinations throughout the country, including from its acclaimed Monteverde Lodge, Tortuga Lodge, and Corcovado Tent Camp. Also car rentals, guide recruitment, etc. It has received several Ecotourism Awards from *Condé Nast Traveler.* Top notch guides. *Highly recommedned!*

Costa Rica Sun Tours, Apdo. 1195-1250, Escazú, tel. 255-3418, fax 255-4410, e-mail: suntours@sol.racsa.co.cr. A highly respected, family-run business with customized planning services and a wide range of tours to destinations throughout Costa Rica, with an emphasis on ecotourism. Also special interest activities such as mountain biking, etc. Affiliated with Tiskita Lodge (see **Golfo Dulce and Osa Peninsula** chapter) and Arenal Observatory Lodge (see **Guanacaste** chapter).

Costa Sol International, Apdo. 8-4390-1000 Cariari, San José, tel. 293-2151, fax 293-2155; in the U.S., tel. (800) 245-8420, fax (305) 858-7478, website www.costasol.co.cr. Owns and operates two deluxe hotels, a fleet of sportfishing boats, a fishing and nature lodge, air-taxi service, and a whitewater rafting company. It has been beset by difficulties in recent years and has been divesting assets.

Costa Rica Temptations, Apdo. 1199-1200, San José, tel. 220-4437, fax 220-2792, e-mail: crtinfo@sol.racsa.co.cr. A full range of tour and package options, including half- and full-day excursions, special hotel rates, customized itinerary planning, car rentals, etc. Recommended.

Horizontes Nature Tours, Apdo. 1780-1002, San José, tel. 222-2022, fax 255-4513, e-mail: horizont@sol.racsa.co.cr, website www.horizontes.com. One of the most respected tour operators specializing in natural history programs, as well as customized programs. A panoply of quality-operated tours and excursions, plus car rental, hotel reservations, etc. Recommended.

Ríos Tropicales, Apdo. 472-1200, San José, tel. 233-6455, fax 255-4354, e-mail: info@riostro.com, website www/riostro.com. A premier rafting and kayaking company that also offers hiking and mountain biking, rock-climbing, and other adventure activities.

Swiss Travel, Apdo. 7-1970-1000, San José, tel. 282-4898, fax 282-4890. One of the largest inbound ground handlers, representing most with half-day to multiday packages throughout the country and for every interest.

TAM Travel, Apdo. 1864-1000, San José, e-mail: info@tamtravel.com. Another major inbound handler that specializes in one-day packages and customized itineraries. Has branch offices in select hotels nationwide.

Tikal Tour Operators, Apdo. 6398-1000, San José, tel. 223-2811, fax 223-1916, e-mail: advtikal@sol.racsa.co.cr. Wide range of one- and multiday package tours and specialist programs including ecotours and trips to Cuba! It also has three-day "Costa Rican Lifestyle" packages that immerse you in local culture.

SPECIALIST COMPANIES

Agencia Mitur, Apdo. 91-1150, San José, tel. 255-2262, fax 255-1946, e-mail: mitour@sol.racsa.co.cr. Specializes in Tortuguero, featured in package tours that also visit other areas.

Aguas Bravas, Apdo. 1504-2100, San José, tel. 292-2072, fax 229-4837, website www.hway.com/arenas/abravas. Offers rafting, kayaking, mountain biking, and horseback trips in the Northern Lowlands.

Arenas Tours, tel. 221-6839, fax 257-7735, e-mail: larenas@sol.racsa.co.cr.

Aventuras Arenal, Apdo. 13-4417, San Carlos, tel. 479-9133, fax 479-9295, e-mail: adarenal@ns.goldnet.co.cr. Specialist in tours of the northern lowlands.

Conexiones Uni, Apdo. 583-1150, San José, tel. 231-3637, fax 231-5221, e-mail: conexion@sol.racsa.co.cr. A boutique operator specializing in nature and adventure trips for groups and individuals.

Coast to Coast Adventures, Apdo. 2135-1002, San José, tel./fax 225-6055, e-mail: ctocsjo@sol.racsa.co.cr, website www.ticonet.co.cr/CtoCadventures.html. Specializes in rafting, mountain hiking, and sea kayaking.

J.D.'s Watersports. tel. 257-3857, fax 256-6391, e-mail: jdwater@sol.racsa.co.cr; in the U.S., tel. (970) 356-1028, fax 352-6324, e-mail: phoyman@aol.com. Specialist in sportfishing, scuba diving, and jungle river and sunset cruises.

Motorcycles Costa Rica, Villas de la Colina, Atenas, tel./fax 446-5015; in the U.S., P.O. Box 56, Redwood, VA 24146, tel. 489-9181, fax (540) 228-6557.

The Original Canopy Tour, Apdo. 751-2350, San Francisco de Dos Ríos, tel. 257-5149, fax 256-7626, e-mail: canopy@sol.racsa.co.cr, website www.canopytour.co.cr. Pioneered rainforest canopy tours using interconnected platforms and pullies. Five locations throughout Costa Rica. Not to be confused with similar companies its success has spawned.

Papagayo Excursiones, Apdo. 162, Santa Cruz, tel. 653-0227, fax 653-0254, e-mail: papagayo@sol.racsa.co.cr. Specialist in tours of Guanacaste and Nicoya, including horseback trips, turtle-watching, jungle cruises, and sportfishing.

Sky Tours, Apdo. 1442-1250, Escazú, tel. 383-3673, fax 228-9912, e-mail: skytours@sol.racsa.co.cr. Offers a series of flightseeing tours spanning the country, from 90 minutes to four days.

OTHER COMPANIES

Aeroviajes, Apdo. 12742-1000, San José, tel. 233-6108, fax 233-6293, e-mail: aero@arweb.com, website www.arweb.com/crpages/tours/aero/aero.htm. Full complement of half- and full-day tours nationwide, plus special interest packages including fly-drive.

Aventuras del Sol, Apdo. 78-1007, San José, tel. 257-1138 or 257-1345. Mix-and-match package tours and fly-drive packages.

Conexiones: The Adventure Connection to Costa Rica, Apdo. 583-1150, San José, tel. 231-3637, fax 231-5221, e-mail: conexion@sol.racsa.co.cr; in the U.S., SJO-210, P.O. Box 025216, Miami, FL 33102.

Destination Costa Rica, in the U.S., SJO-2059, P.O. Box 025216, Miami, FL33102-2059. Wide range of one- and multiday tour packages and specialist activities.

Eko-Alternativo Tours, Apdo. 1287, San José 1002, tel. 221-6476, fax 223-7601. Calls itself a "National Park Specialist," and has a series of tours to national parks and reserves.

Expediciones Tropicales, Apdo. 6793-1000, San José, tel. 257-4171, fax 257-4124, e-mail: expetrop@sol.racsa.co.cr, website www.costaricainfo.com.

Explore Costa Rica, Pavas, San José 1200, tel. 220-2121, fax 232-3321, e-mail: explore@sol. racsa.co.cr. Specializes in tours for seniors and students, as well as offering a wide range of ecotour and other packages.

Fantasy Tours, Apdo. 962-1000, San José, tel. 220-2127, fax 220-2393, e-mail: fantasy@sol. racsa.co.cr.

Fiesta Tours International, Adp. 146-1005, San José, tel. 233-8167, fax 222-2707. A wide range of escorted nature tours and other special-interest programs.

Kapi Tours, Apdo. 566-1200, San José, tel./fax 231-7071, e-mail: kapijm@hotmail.com, website www.zurqui.com/crinfocus/kapi/kapi.html.

Marbella Travel and Tours, Apdo. 333-2400, San José, tel. 259-0055, fax 259-0065, e-mail: marbella@sol.racsa.co.cr. Full range of one- and multiday packages, including customized tours, epecially Lake Arenal and northern lowlands.

María Alexander Tours, Apdo. 3756-1000, San José, tel. 228-9072, fax 289-5192, e-mail: matour@sol.racsa.co.cr.

Travelexellence, Apdo. 12468-1000, San José, tel. 258-1046, fax 258-0795, e-mail: tvlexcel@sol. racsa.co.cr. Offers health and cosmetic surgery programs, plus nature and cultural trips.

NATURAL-HISTORY CRUISE TOURS

Natural-history cruise touring is becoming increasingly popular, with new vessels participating every year. The experience is similar, though vessels vary in size and standard. Normally you'll cruise at night so that each morning when you awake, you're already anchored in a new location. You spend a large part of each day exploring ashore, with landings through the surf aboard inflatable rubber dinghies. Options for land excursions usually include a natural-history tour guided by a professional biologist and perhaps a recreational-cultural excursion (this sometimes means a more relaxed natural-history tour, or perhaps beach hiking) followed by water sports. The comforts and amenities make all the difference after a day of hiking. Highly recommended!

Temptress Adventure Cruises

Temptress Adventure Cruises, Apdo. 1198, San José 1200, tel. 220-1679, fax 220-2103; in the U.S., 351 N.W. LeJeune Rd., Suite 6, Miami, FL 33126, tel. (305) 643-4040 or (800) 336-8424, fax (305) 643-6438, e-mail: temptress@worldnet.

att.net, website www.TemptressCruises.com, in La Sabana Centro Comercial on the north side of Sabana Park, operates the *Temptress Explorer,* a 56-meter semi-luxury eco-cruise ship offering natural-history cruises to national parks along the Pacific coast. The ship operates out of Puntarenas year-round. The cruise offers a condensed and comfortable means of reaching a broad combination of remote, prime wilderness sites.

Itineraries vary throughout the year, with three-, four-, and seven-night trips offered. Highlights include Curú National Wildlife Refuge, Corcovado National Park, Drake Bay, Manuel Antonio, Caño Island, and Carara Biological Reserve. Rates start at $895 for the three-day cruise, and $1,695 for the week-long cruise.

Temptress Explorer comfortably accommodates up to 99 passengers in spacious ro cabins with double or single beds. Her crew is all Costa Rican, mostly bilingual. All cabins are outside, with large windows and private showers/baths. The ship is outfitted with sportfishing boats and scuba diving equipment for dives led by certified divemasters (there's a Resort Course program for noncertified folks). The top deck has a large sundeck and a bar where the crew and passengers mingle at night to dance beneath the stars. The vessel even has a film-developing lab on board. And the cuisine is excellent.

This is casual button-down cruising without the formality of most other cruise ships: pack your tux and you'd be with the boys in the band (if there was one). The company offers a "Family Adventure Package" that includes special activities for children. One-way air transfers from San José are available.

A sister ship, the 63-passenger *Temptress Voyager*, sails week-long cruises in both Panamá and Belize/Guatemala. And the company has also chartered the *Spirit of Endeavor,* which follows similar routes as the Voyager (from $995 and $2,195 for three- and seven-night cruises).

Windstar Cruises
In December 1997, Windstar Cruises, 300 Elliott Ave. W., Seattle, WA 98119, tel. (206) 298-3057 or (800) 258-7245, fax (206) 286-3229, website www.windstarcruises.com, repositioned its spectacular, 148-passenger, luxury motorsail vessel, the *Wind Song,* which now sails seven-day itineraries weekly, Nov.-April, down the Pacific Coast departing Puerto Caldera. Calls include Playa Flamingo, Quepos, Cano Island, Drake Bay, and Isla Coiba in Panamá. The itinerary and focus on natural history resembles that of Temptress Adventure Cruises. An onboard naturalist gives slide presentations, and there are guided rainforest excursions, plus op-

tions such as sea kayaking, snorkeling, and diving. This is sophisticated sailing.

The fares range $2,197-2,876, with low-cost air add-ons from U.S. and Canadian gateways.

Other Cruises
Clipper Cruises, 7711 Bonhomme Ave., St. Louis, MO 63105, tel. (314) 727-2929 or (800) 325-0010, fax (314) 727-6576, e-mail: SmallShip@aol.com, features Costa Rica cruises aboard the 78-meter-long *Yorktown Clipper,* which carries 138 passengers and a team of naturalists. It follows a similar routine as the *Temptress,* with an eight-day itinerary called "Costa Rica's National Parks, The Darien Jungle and the Panamá Canal" (from $2,150).

Special Expeditions, tel. (800) 762-0003 or (212) 765-7740, offers three itineraries combining Costa Rica and Panamá aboard the 80-passenger *Polaris,* including a one-week "Journey on the Wild Side" (from $2,750 in 1997) featuring Curú, Marenco, and Poás, as well as a Panamá Canal transit and calls in Panamá (departures in December, January, and March). A 13-day cruise—"From the Panamá Canal to the Maya Coast"—takes in Tortuguero, plus Belize (from $5,520). Pre- and post-tours of Costa Rica are available.

Tauck Tours, tel. (800) 282-7626 or (203) 226-6911, offers a nine-day package of Costa Rica and Panamá aboard chartered vessels, with a focus on nature. For 1997-98, the company used a super-sleek 60-passenger sailing yacht, the *Le Ponant,* for 10-day Costa Rica and Panamá cruises ($3,875).

RESOURCES

PRINT

General

Chalfont, Frank. *Medical Systems of Costa Rica.* San José, Costa Rica: 1993. A heavily anecdotal review of Costa Rica's medical services.

Costa Rica at a Glance. San José: Market Date, 1990. Handy mini-compendium of statistical data.

Hall, Carolyn. *Costa Rica: A Geographical Interpretation in Historical Perspective.* Boulder, CO: Westview Press, 1985.

Jones, Julie. *Between Continents, Between Seas: Pre-Columbian Art of Costa Rica.* Detroit: Detroit Institute of the Arts, 1981.

Mayfield, Michael W., and Rafael E. Gallo. *The Rivers of Costa Rica: A Canoeing, Kayaking, and Rafting Guide.* Birmingham, AL: Menasha Ridge Press, 1988.

Moser, Don, ed. *Central American Jungles.* Amsterdam: Time-Life Books, 1975.

Ras, Barbara, ed. *Costa Rica: A Traveler's Literary Companion.* San Francisco: Whereabouts Press, 1994. Twenty-six stories by Costa Rican writers that reflect the ethos of the country.

Trejos, Alonso, ed. *Illustrated Geography of Costa Rica.* San José: Trejos Editores, 1991. Coffee-table format. Lots of colorful photography belies matter-of-fact text covering everything from government structure and social aspects to industrial production.

Nature and Wildlife

Alvarado, Guillermo. *Costa Rica: Land of Volcanoes.* Cartago: Editorial Tecnológia de Costa Rica, 1993. A detailed guide to the volcanoes, with science for the layman and a practical bent for the traveler.

Boza, Mario, and A. Bonilla. *The National Parks of Costa Rica.* Madrid: INCAFO, 1981. Available in both hardbound coffee-table and less bulky softbound versions. Lots of superb photos. Highly readable, too.

Carr, Archie F. *The Windward Road.* Gainesville: University of Florida Press, 1955. A sympathetic book about the sea turtles of Central America.

Caulfield, Catherine. *In the Rainforest.* Chicago: University of Chicago Press, 1986.

Cornelius, Stephen E. *The Sea Turtles of Santa Rosa National Park.* San José: Fundación de Parques Nacionales, 1986.

DeVries, Philip J. *The Butterflies of Costa Rica and their Natural History.* Princeton, NJ: Princeton University Press, 1987. A well-illustrated and thorough lepidopterist's guide.

Dressler, Robert L. *Field Guide to the Orchids of Costa Rica and Panama.* Ithaca, NY: Comstock Publishing, 1993.

Emmons, Louise H. *Neotropical Rainforest Mammals—A Field Guide.* Chicago: University of Chicago Press, 1990. A thorough yet compact book detailing mammal species throughout the neotropics.

Forsyth, Adrian, and Ken Miyata. *Journey Through a Tropical Jungle.* Toronto: Greey de Pencier Books, 1988. An educational children's book that provides a lighthearted introduction to rainforest ecology.

Forsyth, Adrian, and Ken Miyata. *Tropical Nature.* New York: Scribner's & Sons, 1984. A readable, lighthearted insight into tropical ecosystems.

Herrera, Wilberth. *Costa Rica Nature Atlas-Guidebook.* San José: Editorial Incafo, 1992. A very useful and readable guide to parks, reserves, and other sites of interest. Text is supported by stunning photos and detailed maps showing roads and gas stations.

Janzen, Daniel, ed. *Costa Rican Natural History.* Chicago: University of Chicago Press, 1983. The bible for scientific insight into individual species of flora and fauna. Weighty, large format. 174 contributors.

Kricher, John C. *A Neotropical Companion: An Introduction to the Animals, Plants, and Ecosystems of the New World Tropics.* Princeton, NJ: Princeton University Press, 1989.

Lellinger, David B. *Fern and Fern-Allies of Costa Rica, Panamá, and the Choco.* Washington, D.C.: American Fern Society, 1989. A scientific tome for botanists and fernophiles.

Mitchell, Andrew W. *The Enchanted Canopy.* New York: Macmillan, 1986.

Mitchell, Sam. *Pura Vida: The Waterfalls and Hot Springs of Costa Rica.* Beaverton, OR: Catarata Press, 1993. Not reviewed.

Perry, Donald. *Life above the Jungle Floor.* New York: Simon & Schuster, 1986. A fascinating account of life in the forest canopy, relating Perry's scientific studies at Rara Avis.

Schmitz, Anthony. *Costa Rica Mammal Flip Chart.* San José: Educación Ambiental, 1994. Marvelous, handy, bound "flip chart" identifies more than 40 mammals, with pictures, vital statistics, and habitat maps for each.

Skutch, Alexander. *A Naturalist in Costa Rica.* Gainesville: University of Florida Press, 1971.

Stiles, F. Gary, and Alexander Skutch. *A Guide to the Birds of Costa Rica.* Ithaca, NY: Cornell University Press, 1989. A superbly illustrated compendium for serious birders.

Wallace, David R. *The Quetzal and the Macaw: The Story of Costa Rica's National Parks.* San Francisco: Sierra Club Books, 1992. An entertaining history of the formation of Costa Rica's national park system.

Young, Allan. *Field Guide to the Natural History of Costa Rica.* San José: Trejos Hermanos, 1983.

Politics and Social Structure

Ameringer, Charles D. *Democracy in Costa Rica.* New York: Praeger, 1982.

Ameringer, Charles D. *Don Pepe: A Political Biography of José Figueres of Costa Rica.* Mexico City: University of Mexico Press, 1978.

Barry, Tom. *Costa Rica: A Country Guide.* Albuquerque, NM: The Inter-Hemisphere Resource Center, 1989.

Bell, John P. *Crisis in Costa Rica: The 1948 Revolution.* Austin, TX: University of Texas Press, 1971.

Biesanz, Richard, et al. *The Costa Ricans.* Englewood Cliffs, NJ: Prentice-Hall, 1987 (updated).

Edelman, Marc, and Joanne Kenen, eds. *The Costa Rican Reader.* New York: Grove Weidenfeld, 1988. An excellent compendium of extracts on politics, history, economics, the contras, etc.

Palmer, Pauline. *What Happen: A Folk History of Costa Rica's Talamanca Coast.* San José: Ecodesarollos, 1977.

Travel Guides

Baker, Bill. *Essential Road Guide for Costa Rica.* San José, Costa Rica: B. Baker, 1992. A handy reference for self-drive exploring, especially strong on San José. The regional route charts are difficult to follow unless you have a navigator along.

Bell, Vern. *Vern Bell's Walking Tour of Downtown San José.* San José: Bell's Home Hospitality, 1994. A concise, entertaining pocket-size aid to exploring the capital city.

Beresky, Andrew, ed. *Fodor's Central America.* 2nd ed. New York: Fodor's, 1994. Good for travelers not seeking a detailed guide.

Berkeley Guide: Central America on the Loose. New York: Fodor's, 1993. Excellent, concise compendium for those on a shoestring. Very hip, very thorough, very well organized. Money to blow? Forget it.

Blake, Beatrice, and Anne Becher. *The New Key to Costa Rica.* 12th ed. Berkeley: Ulysses Press, 1993. Solid, well-structured travel guide packed with information.

Box, Ben, ed. *Mexico and Central American Handbook.* New York: Prentice Hall, 1994. A bulky yet concise bible for those traveling throughout the isthmus. Written for British travelers. Amazing volume of information, if not always easy to find.

Bradt, Hilary, et al. *Backpacking in Mexico and Central America.* 3rd ed. Boston: Bradt Publications, 1992.

Castner, James L. *Rainforests—A Guide to Research and Tourist Facilities at Selected Tropical Forest Sites in Central and South America.* Gainesville: Fekine Press, 1990. Information on 39 sites throughout Central America for travelers intent on visiting rainforest preserves.

Drive the Pan-American Highway. Miami: Interlink, 1991. A do-it-yourself guidebook offering practical advice and tips on paperwork, routes, etc., for those driving to Costa Rica.

Franke, Joseph. *Costa Rica's National Parks and Preserves: A Visitor's Guide.* Seattle: The Mountaineers, 1993. Excellent guide specifically for those heading into protected zones. Detailed maps and trail routes of most parks and reserves, plus bare-bones information on preparing for your trip. No hotel or restaurant reviews.

Glassman, Paul. *Costa Rica.* 5th ed. Champlain, NY: Passport Press, 1994. A very good general guide, much improved over previous editions. Well organized, sound information. No photos.

Haber, Harvey. *Insight Guide to Costa Rica.* Hong Kong: APA Publications, 1992. Stunningly colorful photography and maps. A pleasurable read with in-depth coverage of the history, geography, and social aspects of Costa Rica. Armchair reading to accompany a more practical "how-to" guide.

Hatchwell, Emily, and Simon Calder. *Travellers Central America Survival Kit.* England: Vacation Work, 1991. A budget traveler's guide written in a literary vein. Solid.

Instituto Costarricense de Turismo. *Costa Rica: Tourist Orientation Guide.* San José, 1993. Concise "guidebook" with hotel, tour operator listings, and more, arranged like the *Yellow Pages.*

Instituto Costarricense de Turismo. *Real Guide of Costa Rica.* San José, 1992. A few useful maps and listings. Otherwise, forget it.

Itiel, Joseph. *Pura Vida! A Travel Guide to Gay & Lesbian Costa Rica.* San Francisco: Orchid House, 1993. An uninhibited anecdotal account of an experienced gay traveler's time in Costa Rica, including practicalities on accommodations, nightlife, and more.

Keller, Nancy, Tom Brosnahan, and Rob Rachowiecki. *Central America on a Shoestring.* Berkeley: Lonely Planet, 1992. Good resource for budget travelers exploring the isthmus. Lots of practical advice and maps.

Lougheed, Vivien. *Central America by Chickenbus: A Travel Guide.* Quesnel, B.C.: Repository Press, 1988. For those roughing it overland.

Norton, Natascha, and Mark Whatmore. *Central America.* London: Cadogan Guides, 1993. Handy for those planning to explore the isthmus. Lacks regional details and the jolly literary style of other Cadogan guides.

Ocampo, Tobia Meza, and Rodolfo Mesa Peralta. *Discover Costa Rica: A Historical Cultural Guide.* San José: Universal, 1992. Homegrown perspectives on history, politics, etc. Pocket-size. Unfortunately, also pocket-size on practical advice.

Panet, J.P. *Latin America on Bicycle*. Champlain, NY: Passport Press, 1987. Anecdotal account of cycling through Latin America, including a chapter on Costa Rica.

Pariser, Harry S. *The Adventure Guide to Costa Rica*. 2nd ed. Edison, NJ: Hunter Publishing, 1994. A thorough, well-presented guidebook with solid coverage on history, the economy, politics, etc., plus comprehensive practical details. Color photos.

Price, Carolyn, ed. *Fodor's Costa Rica, Belize, Guatemala.* New York: Fodor's Travel Publications, 1993. Well-organized and concise guidebook. A boon to the traveler wanting easy reference, though treatment is light. Minimal hotel and restaurant reviews and off-the-beaten-track information.

Pritchard, Audrey, and Raymond Pritchard. *Drive the Pan-Am Highway to Mexico and Central America.* Heredia, Costa Rica: Costa Rica Books, 1992. Handy preparatory text with hints on packing, customs, and more.

Rachowiecki, Rob. *Costa Rica—A Travel Survival Kit.* 2nd ed. Berkeley: Lonely Planet, 1994. Well-written, comprehensive, and well-structured coverage of what to see, where to stay, and how to get there. Substantially larger than the first edition. Detailed maps.

Red Guide to Costa Rica: National Map Guide. San José: Guias de Costa Rica, 1991. City and regional maps in one book; recommended for self-drive exploration.

Reisefuhrer, Peter Meyer. *Costa Rica: Reisehandbuch fur das Naturparadies Zurischen.* Frankfurt, 1993. A thorough, handy, compact guide for German travelers.

Samson, Karl. *Frommer's Costa Rica & Belize on $35 a Day.* 4th ed. New York: Frommer Books, 1997. Concise and well-structured guide to the major destinations. Selective, and not strong on off-the-beaten-track travel. Good for the grand tour of Central America.

Searby, Ellen. *The Costa Rica Traveler.* 3rd ed. Occidental, CA: Windham Bay Press, 1991. Venerable but not very detailed guide. Black-and-white photos.

Sheck, Ree S. *Costa Rica: A Natural Destination.* 3rd ed. Santa Fe, NM: John Muir Publications, 1994. Good guide to the national parks and reserves, substantially more detailed than prior editions.

Sienko, Walter. *Latin America by Bike: A Complete Touring Guide.* Seattle, WA: The Mountaineers, 1993. Splendidly organized practical guidebook to cycling in the Americas, including a chapter on Costa Rica.

Tattersall Ryan, Judy. *Simple Pleasures: A Guide to the Bed and Breakfasts and Special Hotels of Costa Rica.* San José, 1993. No photos or illustrations, but good descriptions of select hostelries. Order by writing to Apdo. 2055, San José 1002, or faxing 222-4336.

Tico Times. *Exploring Costa Rica: The Tico Times Guide.* San José: Tico Times, 1993. Excellent little compendium replete with information. A no-nonsense directory with feature articles, too.

Tucker, Alan, ed. *Costa Rica: The Berlitz Traveler's Guide.* New York: Berlitz Publishing, 1994. Handy, pocket-size guidebook in lively, upbeat style.

Verlag, Heller. *Costa Rica: Kreul Und Quer Durch.* Munich: 1993. Good pocket-size guidebook (in German).

Wood, Margo. *Charlie's Charts of Costa Rica.* Surrey, B.C.: Charlie's Charts, 1991. One-of-a-kind guide for sailboaters, with bays and moorings described and charted.

Living in Costa Rica

Howard, Chris. *The Golden Door to Retirement and Living in Costa Rica.* 6th ed. San José: C.R. Books, 1994. Another splendid comprehensive guide to making the break. Leaves no stone unturned. Also highly useful information for travelers passing through.

Howells, John. *Choose Costa Rica: A Guide to Wintering or Retirement.* San Rafael, CA: Gateway Books, 1992. Well-written book that answers most questions asked by those thinking of settling in Costa Rica.

The Official Guide to Living, Visiting, Investing in Costa Rica. San José: Lawrence International Publishing.

United States Mission Association. *Living in Costa Rica.* San José, 1989. Comprehensive listings of services not covered by other books. Aimed at those already settled in Costa Rica.

English-Language Newsletters and Newspapers

Adventures in Costa Rica. Monthly newsletter with "no punches pulled" and "no axes to grind." Strongly oriented to would-be residents. Starflame Publications, P.O. Box 508, Jackson, CA 95642. ($36.95 annual subscription)

Costa Rica Adventure and Business. Full-color quarterly magazine on tourism and investment. Publications & Communications, Inc., 12416 Haymeadow Dr., Austin, TX 78750. ($19.95)

Costa Rica Report. Covers topics of interest to travelers and residents. Apdo. 6283, San José. ($42 annual subscription)

Costa Rican Outlook. An upbeat newsletter with insightful background stories and handy tidbits for travelers. Highly recommended. Subscribers receive an identification card for discounts on restaurants, tours, car rental, etc., in Costa Rica. Away From It All Press, P.O. Box 5573, Chula Vista, CA 91912, tel./fax (619) 421-6002 or (800) 365-2342. ($19 annual subscription with money-back guarantee)

Costa Rica Today. Excellent full-color newspaper geared to the foreign traveler. Widely available in hotels and other lodgings. P.O. Box 025216, Miami, FL 35102. ($59.95 annual subscription)

The Tico Times. Superb weekly newspaper covering all aspects of Costa Rican life. Includes comprehensive listings of events. P.O. Box 145450, Coral Gables, FL 33114. ($40 annual subscription)

Other

Americans Abroad is a newly updated U.S. government booklet that discusses many aspects of international travel, from visa and passport requirements to health and safety concerns. Ask for booklet #599W. Consumer Information Center, P.O. Box 100, Pueblo, CO 81002.

VIDEOS

Adventures in Costa Rica. Away From It All Press, P.O. Box 5573, Chula Vista, CA 91912-5573, tel. 800-365-2342. Features 15 thrilling adventures, from hikes and horseback rides to bungee jumping and sportfishing. (55 minutes; $25.50 including shipping.)

Costa Rica: Making the Most of Your Trip. Marshall Productions, P.O. Box 534, Carlsbad, NM 88221. (90 minutes; $35 including shipping)

Costa Rica: The Key. Videorama, Apdo. 6709, San José 1000, tel. 221-8110, fax 221-0540. (31 minutes)

Costa Rica: The Land and Its People; Costa Rica: Sun, Water and Fun; Costa Rica: The National Parks. Producciones La Mestiza, Apdo. 3011, San José 1000, tel. 253-8071, fax 253-5911. (25 minutes)

Costa Rica Today. Cota International, P.O. Box 5042, New York, NY 10185. Includes information for potential residents. Widely available at hotels. (60 minutes; $30)

Costa Rica Video. Megaview Productions, 255 N. El Cieto, Suite 155, Palm Springs, CA 92262. (34 minutes; $25 including shipping)

This is Costa Rica. Swiss Travel Service, Apdo. 7-1970, San José 1000. (35 minutes; $25)

The Video for Costa Rica. The Young and New Tone of Costa Rica, Apdo. 6709, San José 1000. (60 minutes; $30)

WEB SITES

(Note: All sites below are preceded by http://)

Information on Moon Publications and the Author
Moon Travel Handbooks: www.moon.com
Christopher P. Baker: www.moon.com/authors/bakerbio.html

Generic Sources
The highest-level domain about Costa Rica on the Internet is www.cr, which covers every possible topic. Lower-level domains specific to Costa Rica include:
www.centralamerica.com
www.crica.com
www.greenarrow.com
www.ticonet.com
www.tuanis.com
www.yellowweb.com

Airlines
American Airlines: www.amrcorp.com
Continental Airlines: www.flycontinental.com
Pitts Aviation: www.greenarrow.com/travel/skytours.htm
Travelair: www.centralamerica.com/cr/tran/travlair.htm
United Airlines: www.ual.com

Car Rental Companies
Ada Rent-a-Car: www.iCR.co.cr/ada
Dollar Rent-a-Car: www.centralamerica.com/cr/tran/dollar.htm
Prego Rent-a-Car: www.pregorentacar.com/

Information Sources
British Foreign Office's Travel Advice: www.fco.gov.uk
CIA *World Factbook:* www.odci.gov/cia/publications/pubs/html
CIPROTUR: www.ecotourism.co.cr
Costa Rica Books: www.mastertek.com/crbooks
Costa Rican Outlook: www.webspace-designs/costarica.html

Instituto Costarricense de Turismo (ICT): www.tourism-costarica.com or www.cr/turismo.html
La Nación: www.nacion.co.cr
Specialty Travel Index: www.spectrav.com
Surf Reports: www.centralamerica.com/cr/surf
Tico Times: www.ticotimes.com
U.S. Center for Disease Control and Prevention (travelers' site): www.cdc.gov/travel/travel.html
U.S. State Dept. Travel Advisories: www.stolaf.edu.network/travel-advisories.html

Language Schools
Academia de Idiomas Escazú: www.crspanish.com
Centro Linguístico Conversa: www.centralamerica.com/cr/ school/conversa.htm
Centro Panamericano de Idiomas: www.westnet.com/costarica/cpi.html
Forester Instituto Nacional: www.cool.co.cr/forester
ILISA: www.langlink.com
Insituto de Lenguaje Pura Vida: www.arweb.com/puravida

Conservation Organizations
Amigos de las Aves: www.greenarrow.com/nature/macaws.htm
Arborea Project: www.greenarrow.com/travel/arbor.htm
Caribbean Conservation Corp: www.cccturtle.org
Earthwatch: www.earthwatch.org
Fundación Ríos Tropicales: www.riostro.com
Global Services Corps: www.earthisland.org/ei/gsc/gschome.html
Jardín Gaia: skynet.ul.ie/~gwh/jg/index.html
Monteverde Conservation League: www.monteverde.or.cr
Nature Conservancy: www.tnc.org
Organization of Tropical Studies: www.ots.ac.cr

Travel Organizations
Adventure Travel Society: www.adventuretravel.com/ats
American Society of Travel Agents: www.ASTAnet.com
Hostelling International: gnn.com/gnn/bus/ayh/
International Gay Travel Association: www.rainbow-mall.com/igta
South American Explorers Club: www.samexplo.org

Miscellaneous

Biesanz Woodworks: www.biesanz.com

Bosque de Paz Rain/Cloud Forest Reserve:
www.expreso.co.cr/bosque

Café Britt: www.cafebritt.com

Centro de Educación Creativa: www.sewa-
nee.edu.cbrockett/cec/cec

Costa Rican Marathon Reservation Center:
www.novanet.co.cr/toptours/

Club Elite: www.he.co.cr

COOPRENA: www.greenarrow.com/nature/
cooprena.htm

KitCom: yellowweb.co.cr/kitcom.html

Marina Flamingo: www.marflam.com

Marina Trading Post: www.cool.co.cr/usr/marina

Monteverde Cloud Forest Preserve: www.cct.or.cr

Outward Bound: www.centralamerica.com/cr/
crrobs

LIVING IN COSTA RICA

Peter Dickinson, author of *Travel and Retirement Edens Abroad* (American Association of Retired Persons, $16.95), considers the quality of life in Costa Rica among the highest in the hemisphere. "It's probably one of the easiest places in the world for Americans to settle," he says. More than 30,000 U.S. citizens share Dickinson's sentiments and have settled here for genteel retirement, the carefree lifestyle, or to escape wrecked marriages or other crises.

For years, the Costa Rican government has wooed North American retirees with tax and customs incentives. To become a *pensionado,* or government-approved retiree, you must have a steady source of foreign income exceeding $600 a month and live in Costa Rica at least four months out of the year. Until April 1992, foreign income was exempt from Costa Rican income tax, there was no tax on interest from bank deposits, funds could be transferred in and out of the country without restriction, and you could import personal effects worth up to $7,000 and an automobile valued at up to $16,000 without paying duty on any of it.

In 1992, things changed. Pressured by the International Monetary Fund, the Costa Rican legislature eliminated many of the *pensionado* tax breaks as part of a deficit-reduction austerity package. The *pensionado* program remains in place, but foreign retirees now have to pay the same duties on imported cars and household goods as Costa Ricans.

Pensionados cannot hold salaried jobs in Costa Rica, but they are encouraged to start businesses. In all, *pensionados* contribute some $150 million annually to the local economy. Whatever you choose to do in Costa Rica, the first $70,000 of your local earnings are exempt from U.S. income tax. After five years, you are eligible for Costa Rican citizenship. Benefits include access to the low-cost medical care by paying $50 a year into the Costa Rican social-security system.

If you wish to buy a vacation home, consider the Pacific coast, where land costs $1,000-20,000 an acre, depending on location. That will get you a verdant slope within walking distance of a pristine white beach. The price of a three-bedroom beach house ranges $40,000-150,000. In Escazú, one of San José's most desirable outskirts neighborhoods, a four-bedroom Spanish-style stucco house with swimming pool, sauna, two-car garage, and a stunning view of the Escazú Mountains goes for as little as $100,000. Dealing with the bureaucracy can be maddening. But a good lawyer can do your paperwork for about $2,000.

Resources

For more information, contact the **Association of Residents of Costa Rica,** Apdo. 232-1007, Centro Colón, San José, tel. 233-8068, fax 233-1152, e-mail: arcrsacc@sol.racsa.co.cr, in Casa Canada at Calle 40 and Avenidas 4. This private, nonprofit organization serves the interests of all types of foreign residents as well as those considering living in Costa Rica. It acts as an advocacy forum and provides a panoply of services to members, including AAA-type road service and legal and insurance services, as well as hosting social events and providing publications of interest. It can help prepare the way for your move. ARCR recommends several extended visits as a tourist prior to settling in Costa Rica. A provisional membership ($60) entitles you to the same information and services as full members, which includes a subscription to its newsletter, *La Voz.* The association charges $500 to process your *pensionado* application.

The Departamento de Jubilados/Instituto Costarricense de Turismo, Apdo. 777, San José 1000, located on the ground floor of the ICT Building, Calle 5, Avenida 4, can also help.

The best of several books geared to would-be retirees is Christopher Howard's *The Golden Door to Retirement and Living in Costa Rica,* Costa Rica Books, Suite 1 SJO 981, P.O. Box 025216, Miami, FL 33102-5216, tel. 232-5613, e-mail: crbooks@sol.racsa.co.cr, Web site http:/www.mastertrek.com/crbooks; in the U.S.A., P.O. Box 1512, Thousand Oaks, CA 91358, tel. (800) 365-2342, fax (619) 421-6002; $17.95 including shipping. The company also sells a wide range of books and videos on real estate, legal and medical issues, and retirement living in Costa Rica and Central America. *Choose Costa Rica: A Guide to Wintering or Retirement,* by John Howells (Gateway Books, 1992), is another good resource. Another is *Paradise Properties: Costa Rican Real Estate and Investment,* Apdo. 779, Escazú 1250, tel./fax 223-0331; in the U.S., SJO-1769, P.O. Box 025216, Miami, FL 33102-5216, a monthly magazine that lists properties for sale and provides feature articles and news of interest to retirees and investors.

The **Costa Rican-American Chamber of Commerce,** Apdo. 4946, San José 1000, tel. 233-2133, fax 223-2349, publishes *The Guide to Investing & Doing Business in Costa Rica* ($30, including shipping).

You can order a video called *Retire in Costa Rica* ($25 plus $3 shipping) from *Costa Rican Outlook,* P.O. Box 210113, Chula Vista, CA 91912-0113, tel./fax (619) 421-6002, or tel. (800) 365-2342, e-mail: sagcm@electriciti.com, a newsletter that includes features written by and for folks living or planning to live in Costa Rica.

Study Tours
Chris Howard leads fact-finding trips to Costa Rica for would-be retirees. The tours, called "Live or Retire in Paradise," are offered through **Overseas Retirement Network,** 950 Surrey Dr., Edwardsville, IL 62025, tel. (888) 535-5289, fax (618) 659-0283, e-mail: orn@il.net.

SPANISH PHRASEBOOK

PRONUNCIATION GUIDE

Consonants

c   as c in cat, before a, o, or u; like s before e or i
d   as d in dog, except between vowels, then like th in that
g   before e or i, like the ch in Scottish loch; elsewhere like g in get
h   always silent
j   like the English h in hotel, but stronger
ll   like the y in yellow
ñ   like the ni in onion
r   always pronounced as strong r
rr   trilled r
v   similar to the b in boy (not as English v)
y   similar to English, but with a slight j sound. When y stands alone it is
     pronounced like the e in me.
z   like s in same
b, f, k, l, m, n, p, q, s, t, w, x as in English

Vowels

a   as in father, but shorter
e   as in hen
i   as in machine
o   as in phone
u   usually as in rule; when it follows a q the u is silent; when it follows an h or g
     its pronounced like w, except when it comes between g and e or i, when it's also
     silent

NUMBERS

0	cero	11	once	40	cuarenta
1	uno (masculine)	12	doce	50	cincuenta
1	una (feminine)	13	trece	60	sesenta
2	dos	14	catorce	70	setenta
3	tres	15	quince	80	ochenta
4	cuatro	16	diez y seis	90	noventa
5	cinco	17	diez y siete	100	cien
6	seis	18	diez y ocho	101	ciento y uno
7	siete	19	diez y nueve	200	doscientos
8	ocho	20	veinte	1,000	mil
9	nueve	21	viente y uno	10,000	diez mil
10	diez	30	treinta		

DAYS OF THE WEEK

Sunday — *domingo*	Thursday — *jueves*
Monday — *lunes*	Friday — *viernes*
Tuesday — *martes*	Saturday — *sábado*
Wednesday — *miércoles*	

TIME

What time is it? — *¿Qué hora es?*	tomorrow, morning
one o'clock — *la una*	— *mañana, la mañana*
two o'clock — *las dos*	yesterday — *ayer*
at two o'clock — *a las dos*	day — *día*
ten past three — *las tres y diez*	week — *semana*
six a.m. — *las seis de mañana*	month — *mes*
six p.m. — *las seis de tarde*	year — *año*
today — *hoy*	last night — *anoche*

USEFUL WORDS AND PHRASES

Hello. — *Hola.*	see you later; literally, "until later"
Good morning. — *Buenos días.*	— *hasta luego*
Good afternoon. — *Buenas tardes.*	more — *más*
Good evening. — *Buenas noches.*	less — *menos*
How are you? — *¿Cómo está?*	better — *mejor*
Fine. — *Muy bien.*	much — *mucho*
And you? — *¿Y usted?*	a little — *un poco*
So-so. — *Más ó menos.*	large — *grande*
Thank you. — *Gracias.*	small — *pequeño*
Thank you very much. — *Muchas gracias.*	quick — *rápido*
You're very kind. — *Muy amable.*	slowly — *despacio*
You're welcome; literally, "It's nothing."	bad — *malo*
— *De nada.*	difficult — *difícil*
yes — *sí*	easy — *fácil*
no — *no*	He/She/It is gone; as in "She left," "He's
I don't know. — *Yo no sé.*	gone" — *Ya se fue.*
it's fine; okay — *está bien*	I don't speak Spanish well.
good; okay — *bueno*	— *No hablo bien español.*
please — *por favor*	I don't understand. — *No entiendo.*
Pleased to meet you. — *Mucho gusto.*	How do you say . . . in Spanish?
excuse me (physical) — *perdóneme*	— *¿Cómo se dice . . . en español?*
excuse me (speech) — *discúlpeme*	Do you understand English?
I'm sorry. — *Lo siento.*	— *¿Entiende el inglés?*
goodbye — *adiós*	Is English spoken here? (Does anyone
	here speak English?)
	— *¿Se habla inglés aquí?*

TERMS OF ADDRESS

I — *yo*
you (formal) — *usted*
you (familiar) — *tú*
he/him — *él*
she/her — *ella*
we/us — *nosotros*
you (plural) — *vos*
they/them (all males or mixed gender)
    — *ellos*
they/them (all females) — *ellas*

Mr., sir — *señor*
Mrs., madam — *señora*
Miss, young lady — *señorita*
wife — *esposa*
husband — *marido* or *esposo*
friend — *amigo* (male), *amiga* (female)
sweetheart — *novio* (male), *novia* (female)
son, daughter — *hijo, hija*
brother, sister — *hermano, hermana*
father, mother — *padre, madre*

GETTING AROUND

Where is . . . ? — *¿Dónde está . . . ?*
How far is it to . . .?
    — *¿A cuánto queda . . . ?*
from . . . to . . . — *de . . . a . . .*
highway — *la carretera*
road — *el camino*
street — *la calle*
block — *la cuadra*
kilometer — *kilómetro*

mile (commonly used near the
    U.S. border) — *milla*
north — *el norte*
south — *el sur*
west — *el oeste*
east — *el este*
straight ahead — *al derecho* or *adelante*
to the right — *a la derecha*
to the left — *a la izquierda*

ACCOMMODATIONS

Can I (we) see a room?
    — *¿Puedo (podemos) ver un cuarto?*
What is the rate? — *¿Cuál es el precio?*
a single room — *un cuarto sencillo*
a double room — *un cuarto doble*
key — *llave*
bathroom — *lavabo* or *baño*
hot water — *agua caliente*

cold water — *agua fría*
towel — *toalla*
soap — *jabón*
toilet paper — *papel higiénico*
air conditioning — *aire acondicionado*
fan — *ventilador*
blanket — *frazada* or *manta*

PUBLIC TRANSPORT

bus stop — *la parada del autobús*
main bus terminal
    — *terminal de buses*
railway station
    — *la estación de ferrocarril*
airport — *el aeropuerto*
ferry terminal
    — *la terminal del transbordador*

I want a ticket to . . .
    — *Quiero un boleto a . . .*
I want to get off at . . .
    — *Quiero bajar en . . .*
Here, please. — *Aquí, por favor.*
Where is this bus going?
    — *¿Adónde va este autobús?*
roundtrip — *ida y vuelta*
What do I owe? — *¿Cuánto le debo?*

DRIVING

Full, please (at gasoline station).
— *Lleno, por favor.*
My car is broken down.
— *Se me ha descompuesto el carro.*
I need a tow. — *Necesito un remolque.*
Is there a garage nearby?
— *¿Hay un garage cerca?*
Is the road passable with this car (truck)?
— *¿Puedo pasar con este carro (esta troca)?*

With four-wheel drive?
— *¿Con doble tracción?*
It's not passable — *No hay paso.*
traffic light — *el semáfora*
traffic sign — *el señal*
gasoline (petrol) — *gasolina*
gasoline station — *gasolinera*
oil — *aceite*
water — *agua*
flat tire — *llanta desinflada*
tire repair shop — *llantera*

AUTO PARTS

fan belt — *banda de ventilador*
battery — *batería*
fuel (water) pump —
  bomba de gasolina (agua)
spark plug — *bujía*
carburetor — *carburador*
distributor — *distribuidor*
axle — *eje*
clutch — *embrague*

gasket — *empaque, junta*
filter — *filtro*
brakes — *frenos*
tire — *llanta*
hose — *manguera*
starter — *marcha, arranque*
radiator — *radiador*
voltage regulator — *regulado de voltaje*

MAKING PURCHASES

I need . . . — *Necesito . . .*
I want . . . — *Deseo . . .* or *Quiero . . .*
I would like . . . (more polite)
— *Quisiera . . .*
How much does it cost? — *¿Cuánto cuesta?*
What's the exchange rate?
— *¿Cuál es el tipo de cambio?*

Can I see . . . ? — *¿Puedo ver . . . ?*
this one — *ésta/ésto*
expensive — *caro*
cheap — *barato*
cheaper — *más barato*
too much — *demasiado*

HEALTH

Help me please. — *Ayúdeme por favor.*
I am ill. — *Estoy enfermo.*
pain — *dolor*
fever — *fiebre*
stomache ache — *dolor de estómago*
vomiting — *vomitar*
diarrhea — *diarrea*

drugstore — *farmacia*
medicine — *medicina, remedio*
pill, tablet — *pastilla*
birth control pills — *pastillas anticonceptivas*
condoms — *preservativos*

FOOD

menu — *lista, menú*
glass — *vaso*
fork — *tenedor*
knife — *cuchillo*
spoon — *cuchara, cucharita*
napkin — *servilleta*
soft drink — *refresco*
coffee, cream — *café, crema*
tea — *té*
sugar — *azúcar*
purified water — *agua purificado*
bottled carbonated water — *agua mineral*
bottled uncarbonated water — *agua sin gas*
beer — *cerveza*
wine — *vino*
milk — *leche*
juice — *jugo*
eggs — *huevos*
bread — *pan*

watermelon — *sandía*
banana — *plátano*
apple — *manzana*
orange — *naranja*
meat (without) — *carne (sin)*
beef — *carne de res*
chicken — *pollo*
fish — *pescado*
shellfish — *mariscos*
fried — *a la plancha*
roasted — *asado*
barbecue, barbecued — *al carbón*
breakfast — *desayuno*
lunch — *almuerzo*
dinner (often eaten in late afternoon)
  — *comida*
dinner, or a late night snack — *cena*
the check — *la cuenta*

INDEX

BIRDS/BIRDWATCHING

CONSERVATION AREAS AND NATIONAL PARKS

SPECIAL HOTELS

Casa Turire: 343
Capitán Suizo: 563
Finca Brian y Milena: 656
Finca Rosa Blanca: 311
Grano de Oro: 226
Makanda by the Sea: 633
Punta Islita: 587
Villa Caletas: 615
Vista del Valle: 728
Xandari: 289

ABOUT THE AUTHOR

Christopher P. Baker was born and raised in Yorkshire, England. He received a B.A. (Honours) in Geography at University College, University of London, during which he participated in two Sahara expeditions and an exchange program at Krakow University, Poland. Later, he earned a master's degree in Latin American Studies from Liverpool University and another, in Education, from the Institute of Education, University of London. He began his writing career in 1978 as Contributing Editor on Latin America for *Land & Liberty*, a London-based political journal. In 1980, he received a Scripps-Howard Foundation Scholarship in Journalism to attend the University of California, Berkeley. Since 1983 he has made his living as a professional travel and natural-sciences writer. His byline has appeared in publications as diverse as *Newsweek, National Wildlife, Islands, Elle,* the *Christian Science Monitor, The Los Angeles Times,* and *Writer's Digest.* He has also written for such outlets as the BBC and The Discovery Channel. For seven years, Baker was president of British Pride Tours, which he founded. He has escorted group tours to New Zealand, Hong Kong, Korea, England, and Cuba. He appears frequently on radio and television talk shows and as a guest lecturer aboard cruise ships throughout the Caribbean and farther afield. His other books include *Jamaica: Travel Survival Kit, Bahamas* and *Turks & Caicos, Trav'Bug Guide to California, Passport Illustrated Guide to Jamaica,* the best-selling *Cuba Handbook,* and *Mi Moto Fidel: Motorcycling Through Castro's Cuba.* He has also contributed chapters to *Frommer's America on Wheels: California & Nevada, I Should Have Stayed Home, Writer's Digest Beginner's Guide to Getting Published,* and Time-Life's *Nature Company Guides: World Travel Guide to International Ecojourneys.* Baker is a member of the Society of American Travel Writers and has been honored with several awards for outstanding writing, including—four times—the prestigious Lowell Thomas Travel Journalism Award and the 1995 Benjamin Franklin Award for Best Travel Guide for the *Costa Rica Handbook.* He lives in California.

www.moon.com

Enjoy our travel information center on the World Wide Web (WWW), loaded with interactive exhibits designed especially for the Internet.

ATTRACTIONS ON MOON'S WEB SITE INCLUDE:

ATLAS
Our award-winning, comprehensive travel guides cover destinations throughout North America and Hawaii, Latin America and the Caribbean, and Asia and the Pacific.

PRACTICAL NOMAD
Extensive excerpts, a unique set of travel links coordinated with the book, and a regular Q & A column by author and Internet travel consultant Edward Hasbrouck.

TRAVEL MATTERS
Our on-line travel zine, featuring articles; author correspondence; a travel library including health information, reading lists, and cultural cues; and our new contest, **Destination X,** offering a chance to win a trip to the mystery destination of your choice.

ROAD TRIP USA
Our best-selling book, ever; don't miss this award-winning Web guide to off-the-interstate itineraries.

Come visit us at: **www.moon.com**

MOON TRAVEL HANDBOOKS

LOSE YOURSELF IN THE EXPERIENCE, NOT THE CROWD

For 25 years, Moon Travel Handbooks have been the guidebooks of choice for adventurous travelers. Our award-winning Handbook series provides focused, comprehensive coverage of distinct destinations all over the world. Each Handbook is like an entire bookcase of cultural insight and introductory information in one portable volume. Our goal at Moon is to give travelers all the background and practical information they'll need for an extraordinary travel experience.

The following pages include a complete list of Handbooks, covering North America and Hawaii, Mexico, Latin America and the Caribbean, and Asia and the Pacific. To purchase Moon Travel Handbooks, check your local bookstore or order by phone: (800) 345-5473 M-F 8 am.-5 p.m. PST or outside the U.S. phone: (530) 345-5473.

"An in-depth dunk into the land, the people and their history, arts, and politics."
—*Student Travels*

"I consider these books to be superior to Lonely Planet. When Moon produces a book it is more humorous, incisive, and off-beat."
—*Toronto Sun*

"Outdoor enthusiasts gravitate to the well-written Moon Travel Handbooks. In addition to politically correct historic and cultural features, the series focuses on flora, fauna and outdoor recreation. Maps and meticulous directions also are a trademark of Moon guides."
—*Houston Chronicle*

"Moon [Travel Handbooks] . . . bring a healthy respect to the places they investigate. Best of all, they provide a host of odd nuggets that give a place texture and prod the wary traveler from the beaten path. The finest are written with such care and insight they deserve listing as literature."
—*American Geographical Society*

"Moon Travel Handbooks offer in-depth historical essays and useful maps, enhanced by a sense of humor and a neat, compact format."
—*Swing*

"Perfect for the more adventurous, these are long on history, sightseeing and nitty-gritty information and very price-specific."
—*Columbus Dispatch*

"Moon guides manage to be comprehensive and countercultural at the same time . . . Handbooks are packed with maps, photographs, drawings, and sidebars that constitute a college-level introduction to each country's history, culture, people, and crafts."
—*National Geographic Traveler*

"Few travel guides do a better job helping travelers create their own itineraries than the Moon Travel Handbook series. The authors have a knack for homing in on the essentials."
—*Colorado Springs Gazette Telegraph*

MEXICO

"These books will delight the armchair traveler, aid the undecided person in selecting a destination, and guide the seasoned road warrior looking for lesser-known hideaways."

—*Mexican Meanderings* Newsletter

"From tourist traps to off-the-beaten track hideaways, these guides offer consistent, accurate details without pretension."

—*Foreign Service Journal*

Archaeological Mexico	**$19.95**
Andrew Coe	420 pages, 27 maps
Baja Handbook	**$16.95**
Joe Cummings	540 pages, 46 maps
Cabo Handbook	**$14.95**
Joe Cummings	270 pages, 17 maps
Cancún Handbook	**$14.95**
Chicki Mallan	240 pages, 25 maps
Colonial Mexico	**$18.95**
Chicki Mallan	400 pages, 38 maps
Mexico Handbook	**$21.95**
Joe Cummings and Chicki Mallan	1,200 pages, 201 maps
Northern Mexico Handbook	**$17.95**
Joe Cummings	610 pages, 69 maps
Pacific Mexico Handbook	**$17.95**
Bruce Whipperman	580 pages, 68 maps
Puerto Vallarta Handbook	**$14.95**
Bruce Whipperman	330 pages, 36 maps
Yucatán Handbook	**$16.95**
Chicki Mallan	400 pages, 52 maps

LATIN AMERICA AND THE CARIBBEAN

"Solidly packed with practical information and full of significant cultural asides that will enlighten you on the whys and wherefores of things you might easily see but not easily grasp."

—*Boston Globe*

Belize Handbook	**$15.95**
Chicki Mallan and Patti Lange	390 pages, 45 maps
Caribbean Vacations	**$18.95**
Karl Luntta	910 pages, 64 maps
Costa Rica Handbook	**$19.95**
Christopher P. Baker	780 pages, 73 maps
Cuba Handbook	**$19.95**
Christopher P. Baker	740 pages, 70 maps
Dominican Republic Handbook	**$15.95**
Gaylord Dold	420 pages, 24 maps
Ecuador Handbook	**$16.95**
Julian Smith	450 pages, 43 maps
Honduras Handbook	**$15.95**
Chris Humphrey	330 pages, 40 maps
Jamaica Handbook	**$15.95**
Karl Luntta	330 pages, 17 maps
Virgin Islands Handbook	**$13.95**
Karl Luntta	220 pages, 19 maps

NORTH AMERICA AND HAWAII

"These domestic guides convey the same sense of exoticism that their foreign counterparts do, making home-country travel seem like far-flung adventure."

—*Sierra Magazine*

Alaska-Yukon Handbook	**$17.95**
Deke Castleman and Don Pitcher	530 pages, 92 maps
Alberta and the Northwest Territories Handbook	**$17.95**
Andrew Hempstead and Nadina Purdon	530 pages, 72 maps,
Arizona Traveler's Handbook	**$17.95**
Bill Weir and Robert Blake	512 pages, 54 maps
Atlantic Canada Handbook	**$17.95**
Nan Drosdick and Mark Morris	460 pages, 61 maps
Big Island of Hawaii Handbook	**$15.95**
J.D. Bisignani	390 pages, 23 maps

Boston Handbook		**$13.95**
Jeff Perk	200 pages, 20 maps	
British Columbia Handbook		**$16.95**
Jane King and Andrew Hempstead	430 pages, 69 maps	
Colorado Handbook		**$18.95**
Stephen Metzger	480 pages, 59 maps	
Georgia Handbook		**$17.95**
Kap Stann	370 pages, 50 maps	
Hawaii Handbook		**$19.95**
J.D. Bisignani	1,030 pages, 90 maps	
Honolulu-Waikiki Handbook		**$14.95**
J.D. Bisignani	400 pages, 20 maps	
Idaho Handbook		**$18.95**
Don Root	610 pages, 42 maps	
Kauai Handbook		**$15.95**
J.D. Bisignani	320 pages, 23 maps	
Maine Handbook		**$18.95**
Kathleen M. Brandes	660 pages, 27 maps	
Massachusetts Handbook		**$18.95**
Jeff Perk	600 pages, 23 maps	
Maui Handbook		**$15.95**
J.D. Bisignani	420 pages, 35 maps	
Michigan Handbook		**$15.95**
Tina Lassen	300 pages, 30 maps	
Montana Handbook		**$17.95**
Judy Jewell and W.C. McRae	480 pages, 52 maps	
Nevada Handbook		**$18.95**
Deke Castleman	530 pages, 40 maps	
New Hampshire Handbook		**$18.95**
Steve Lantos	500 pages, 18 maps	
New Mexico Handbook		**$15.95**
Stephen Metzger	360 pages, 47 maps	
New York Handbook		**$19.95**
Christiane Bird	780 pages, 95 maps	
New York City Handbook		**$13.95**
Christiane Bird	300 pages, 20 maps	
North Carolina Handbook		**$14.95**
Rob Hirtz and Jenny Daughtry Hirtz	275 pages, 25 maps	
Northern California Handbook		**$19.95**
Kim Weir	800 pages, 50 maps	
Oregon Handbook		**$17.95**
Stuart Warren and Ted Long Ishikawa	588 pages, 34 maps	
Pennsylvania Handbook		**$18.95**
Joanne Miller	448 pages, 40 maps	

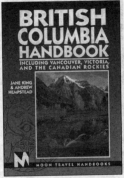

Road Trip USA	$22.50
Jamie Jensen	800 pages, 165 maps
Santa Fe-Taos Handbook	$13.95
Stephen Metzger	160 pages, 13 maps
Southern California Handbook	$19.95
Kim Weir	720 pages, 26 maps
Tennessee Handbook	$17.95
Jeff Bradley	530 pages, 44 maps
Texas Handbook	$18.95
Joe Cummings	690 pages, 70 maps
Utah Handbook	$17.95
Bill Weir and W.C. McRae	490 pages, 40 maps
Virginia Handbook	$15.95
Julian Smith	340 pages, 30 maps
Washington Handbook	$19.95
Don Pitcher	870 pages, 113 maps
Wisconsin Handbook	$18.95
Thomas Huhti	590 pages, 69 maps
Wyoming Handbook	$17.95
Don Pitcher	610 pages, 80 maps

ASIA AND THE PACIFIC

"Scores of maps, detailed practical info down to business hours of small-town libraries. You can't beat the Asian titles for sheer heft. (The) series is sort of an American Lonely Planet, with better writing but fewer titles. (The) individual voice of researchers comes through."

—*Travel & Leisure*

Australia Handbook	$21.95
Marael Johnson, Andrew Hempstead, and Nadina Purdon	940 pages, 141 maps
Bali Handbook	$19.95
Bill Dalton	750 pages, 54 maps
Bangkok Handbook	$13.95
Michael Buckley	244 pages, 30 maps
Fiji Islands Handbook	$14.95
David Stanley	300 pages, 38 maps
Hong Kong Handbook	$16.95
Kerry Moran	378 pages, 49 maps
Indonesia Handbook	$25.00
Bill Dalton	1,380 pages, 249 maps

Micronesia Handbook Neil M. Levy	$14.95 340 pages, 70 maps	
Nepal Handbook Kerry Moran	$18.95 490 pages, 51 maps	
New Zealand Handbook Jane King	$19.95 620 pages, 81 maps	
Outback Australia Handbook Marael Johnson	$18.95 450 pages, 57 maps	
Philippines Handbook Peter Harper and Laurie Fullerton	$17.95 670 pages, 116 maps	
Singapore Handbook Carl Parkes	$15.95 350 pages, 29 maps	
South Korea Handbook Robert Nilsen	$19.95 820 pages, 141 maps	
South Pacific Handbook David Stanley	$22.95 920 pages, 147 maps	
Southeast Asia Handbook Carl Parkes	$21.95 1,080 pages, 204 maps	
Tahiti-Polynesia Handbook David Stanley	$15.95 380 pages, 35 maps	
Thailand Handbook Carl Parkes	$19.95 860 pages, 142 maps	
Vietnam, Cambodia & Laos Handbook Michael Buckley	$18.95 760 pages, 116 maps	

OTHER GREAT TITLES FROM MOON

"For hardy wanderers, few guides come more highly recommended than the Handbooks. They include good maps, steer clear of fluff and flackery, and offer plenty of money-saving tips. They also give you the kind of information that visitors to strange lands—on any budget—need to survive."

—*US News & World Report*

Moon Handbook Carl Koppeschaar	$10.00 141 pages, 8 maps	
The Practical Nomad: How to Travel Around the World Edward Hasbrouck	$17.95 575 pages	
Staying Healthy in Asia, Africa, and Latin America Dirk Schroeder	$11.95 230 pages, 4 maps	

MOONBELTS

Looking for comfort and a way to keep your most important articles safe while traveling? These were our own concerns and that is why we created the Moonbelt. Made of heavy-duty Cordura nylon, the Moonbelt offers maximum protection for your money and important papers. Designed for all-weather comfort, this pouch slips under your shirt or waistband, rendering it virtually undetectable and inaccessible to pickpockets. It features a one-inch high-test quick-release buckle so there's no fumbling for the strap or repeated adjustments. This handy buckle opens and closes with a touch, but won't come undone until you want it to. Moonbelts accommodate traveler's checks, passport, cash, photos, etc. Measures 5 x 9 inches and fits waists up to 48".

Available in black only. **US$8.95**
Sales tax (7.25%) for California residents
$1.50 for 1st Class shipping & handling.

To order, call (800) 345-5473
outside the US (530) 345-5473 or fax (530) 345-6751

Make checks or money orders payable to:
MOON TRAVEL HANDBOOKS
PO Box 3040, Chico, CA 95927-3040 U.S.A.
We accept Visa, MasterCard, or Discover.

MOON TRAVEL HANDBOOKS

ROAD TRIP USA

Cross-Country Adventures on America's Two-Lane Highways

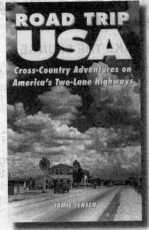

ROAD TRIP USA
Cross-Country Adventures on America's Two-Lane Highways

JAMIE JENSEN

$22.50   800 pages

"For those who feel an adrenaline rush everytime they hear the words 'road trip,' and who understand that getting there is at least half the fun, this is quite simply the best book of its type ever published."
—*Conde Nast Traveler* web site

"Just might be the perfect book about hitting the summoning highway . . . It's impossible not to find something enticing in *Road Trip USA* to add to your next cycling expedition. An encyclopedia of roadside wonders."
—**Harley Davidson** *Enthusiast*

"For budding myth collectors, I can't think of a better textbook."
—*Los Angeles Times*

"A terrific guide for those who'd rather swat mosquitoes than take the interstate."
—**Colorado Springs** *Gazette Telegraph*

"Jensen is well-versed in travel, has an enjoyable yet informative style and will guide you along each mile. Don't leave home without it!"
—*Mobilia*

"Zany inspiration for a road Gypsie in search of off-the-beaten-path adventure."
—*The Toronto Globe and Mail*

"A historic journey into the heart and soul of America."
—*Route 66 Magazine*

"Jamie Jensen and the 12 intrepid contributors to *Road Trip USA* have been everywhere and seen everything compiling this exhaustive, delightful, destination-anywhere guide to American road-tripping."
—*Citybooks*, **Washington D.C.**

"Not only a fantastic guide . . . a great companion!"
—*The Herald*, **Columbia S.C.**

THE PRACTICAL NOMAD

✈ TAKE THE PLUNGE

"The greatest barriers to long-term travel by Americans are the disempowered feelings that leave them afraid to ask for the time off. Just do it."

✈ TAKE NOTHING FOR GRANTED

"Even 'What time is it?' is a highly politicized question in some areas, and the answer may depend on your informant's ethnicity and political allegiance as well as the proximity of the secret police."

✈ TAKE THIS BOOK

"Full of hard-won road wisdom."
—San Francisco Examiner

THE PRACTICAL NOMAD
HOW TO TRAVEL AROUND THE WORLD

EDWARD HASBROUCK

$17.95   576 pages

With experience helping thousands of his globetrotting clients plan their trips around the world, travel industry insider Edward Hasbrouck provides the secrets that can save readers money and valuable travel time.
An indispensable complement to destination-specific travel guides, *The Practical Nomad* includes:

    airfare strategies

    ticket discounts

    long-term travel considerations

    travel documents

    border crossings

    entry requirements

    government offices

    travel publications

    Internet information resources

WHERE TO BUY MOON TRAVEL HANDBOOKS

BOOKSTORES AND LIBRARIES: Moon Travel Handbooks are distributed worldwide. Please contact our sales manager for a list of wholesalers and distributors in your area.

TRAVELERS: We would like to have Moon Travel Handbooks available throughout the world. Please ask your bookstore to write or call us for ordering information. If your bookstore will not order our guides for you, please contact us for a free catalog.

> Moon Travel Handbooks
> P.O. Box 3040
> Chico, CA 95927-3040 U.S.A.
> tel.: (800) 345-5473, outside the U.S. (530) 345-5473
> fax: (530) 345-6751
> e-mail: travel@moon.com

IMPORTANT ORDERING INFORMATION

PRICES: All prices are subject to change. We always ship the most current edition. We will let you know if there is a price increase on the book you order.

SHIPPING AND HANDLING OPTIONS: Domestic UPS or USPS first class (allow 10 working days for delivery): $4.50 for the first item, $1.00 for each additional item.

Moonbelt shipping is $1.50 for one, 50 cents for each additional belt.

UPS 2nd Day Air or Printed Airmail requires a special quote.

International Surface Bookrate 8-12 weeks delivery: $4.00 for the first item, $1.00 for each additional item. Note: We cannot guarantee international surface bookrate shipping. We recommend sending international orders via air mail, which requires a special quote.

FOREIGN ORDERS: Orders that originate outside the U.S.A. must be paid for with an international money order, a check in U.S. currency drawn on a major U.S. bank based in the U.S.A., or Visa, MasterCard, or Discover.

TELEPHONE ORDERS: We accept Visa, MasterCard, or Discover payments. Call in your order: (800) 345-5473, 8 a.m.-5 p.m. Pacific standard time. Outside the U.S. the number is (530) 345-5473.

INTERNET ORDERS: Visit our site at: www.moon.com

ORDER FORM

Prices are subject to change without notice. Be sure to call (800) 345-5473,
or (530) 345-5473 from outside the U.S. 8 a.m.–5 p.m. PST for current prices and editions.
(See important ordering information on preceding page.)

Name: _____ Date: _____

Street: _____

City: _____ Daytime Phone: _____

State or Country: _____ Zip Code: _____

QUANTITY	TITLE	PRICE
		Taxable Total _____
	Sales Tax (7.25%) for California Residents	_____
	Shipping & Handling	_____
	TOTAL	_____

Ship: ☐ UPS (no P.O. Boxes) ☐ 1st class ☐ International surface mail

Ship to: ☐ address above ☐ other _____

Make checks payable to: **MOON TRAVEL HANDBOOKS**, P.O. Box 3040, Chico, CA 95927-3040
U.S.A. We accept Visa, MasterCard, or Discover. **To Order**: Call in your Visa, MasterCard, or Discover number,
or send a written order with your Visa, MasterCard, or Discover number and expiration date clearly written.

Card Number: ☐ **Visa** ☐ **MasterCard** ☐ **Discover**

☐ ☐ ☐ ☐ ☐ ☐ ☐ ☐ ☐ ☐ ☐ ☐ ☐ ☐ ☐ ☐

Exact Name on Card: _____

Expiration date: _____

Signature: _____

U.S.~METRIC CONVERSION

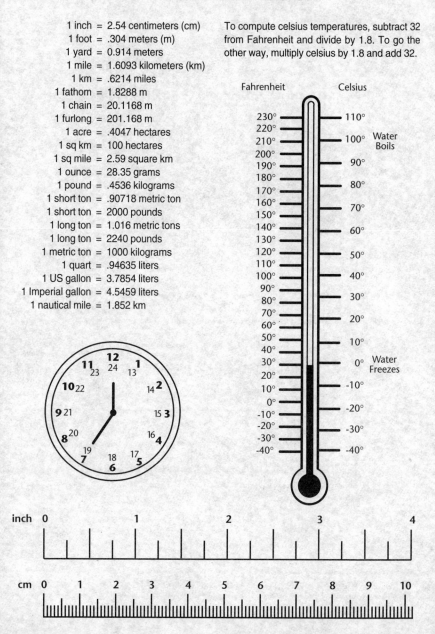

1 inch = 2.54 centimeters (cm)
1 foot = .304 meters (m)
1 yard = 0.914 meters
1 mile = 1.6093 kilometers (km)
1 km = .6214 miles
1 fathom = 1.8288 m
1 chain = 20.1168 m
1 furlong = 201.168 m
1 acre = .4047 hectares
1 sq km = 100 hectares
1 sq mile = 2.59 square km
1 ounce = 28.35 grams
1 pound = .4536 kilograms
1 short ton = .90718 metric ton
1 short ton = 2000 pounds
1 long ton = 1.016 metric tons
1 long ton = 2240 pounds
1 metric ton = 1000 kilograms
1 quart = .94635 liters
1 US gallon = 3.7854 liters
1 Imperial gallon = 4.5459 liters
1 nautical mile = 1.852 km

To compute celsius temperatures, subtract 32 from Fahrenheit and divide by 1.8. To go the other way, multiply celsius by 1.8 and add 32.

GREEN TORTOISE ADVENTURE TRAVEL

BAJA BEACH DAZE

ENJOY OUR 18 YEARS OF EXPERIENCE OFF THE BEATEN PATH IN BAJA
TRAVEL ABOARD A LEGENDARY GREEN TORTOISE SLEEPER COACH
WE OFFER 9 OR 14 DAY TOURS NOVEMBER THRU APRIL—FROM $25 A DAY

GREEN TORTOISE ADVENTURE TRAVEL
494 BROADWAY, SAN FRANCISCO CA. 94113
USA & CANADA: 800-TORTOISE
S.F. BAY AREA & WORLDWIDE: 415-956-7500
www.greentortoise.com

STUDENT TRAVEL

Because education & adventure are not mutually exclusive.

With our staff of experienced travelers, a global network of offices, great prices, ticket flexibility and a ton of travel services, we know firsthand what it takes to put together a mind-blowing trip...

...just don't be surprised if you learn something while you're having the time of your life.

STA TRAVEL
We've been there.

800-777-0112
OR CONTACT YOUR NEAREST STA TRAVEL OFFICE

AUSTIN	CAMBRIDGE	MADISON	ORLANDO	SEATTLE
BATON ROUGE	CHICAGO	MIAMI	PHILADELPHIA	TAMPA
BERKELEY	GAINESVILLE	MINNEAPOLIS	SAN FRANCISCO	WASHINGTON DC
BOSTON	LOS ANGELES	NEW YORK	SANTA MONICA	WESTWOOD

BOOK YOUR TICKET ONLINE: WWW.STA-TRAVEL.COM